The Qur'an:
an Encyclopedia

The Qur'an is the source of inspiration for one of the world's major religions, followed today by over a billion people. It plays a central role in Islam and ever since it appeared over fourteen centuries ago has been the subject of intense debate. Some of this has been carried out by Muslims and some by those hostile or indifferent to Islam, producing a very wide range of views.

Authored by 43 international experts, the objective of *The Qur'an: An Encyclopedia* is to present this diversity of thought, approach and school in order to give a strong appreciation of the range of response that the text has provoked throughout its history. It provides students and researchers with a powerful one-volume resource covering all aspects of the text and its reception.

Islam and the Qur'an are much in the news today and there is a public debate going on in which things are said about the Qur'an without much knowledge or understanding of the book.

Every effort has been made to help the reader use the encyclopedia as an investigative tool in Qur'anic studies. The volume assumes no previous knowledge of the Qur'an, Islam or Arabic. Technical terms are explained in the text itself and the style of each entry is designed to be as self-contained as possible. Entries are cross-referenced and many include a brief bibliography. At the end of the work there is a substantial annotated bibliography providing a detailed guide to the most significant books, journals and articles in Qur'anic studies. Three comprehensive indexes are included.

The readership will include those seeking basic information on the Qur'an; in addition, the substantial number of longer entries means that it will also be used by specialists.

Oliver Leaman is Professor, Department of Philosophy, University of Kentucky, USA.

The Qur'an:
an Encyclopedia

Edited by

Oliver Leaman

LONDON AND NEW YORK

First published 2006
by Routledge
2 Park Square, Milton Park, Abingdon, Oxon, OX14 4RN

Simultaneously published in the USA and Canada
By Routledge
270 Madison Avenue, New York, NY 10016, USA

Routledge is an imprint of the Taylor and Francis Group

© 2006 Routledge

Typeset in Times New Roman and Optima by Taylor & Francis Books
Printed and bound in Great Britain by TJ International Ltd, Padstow, Cornwall

British Library Cataloguing in Publication Data
A catalogue record for this book is available from the British Library

Library of Congress Cataloging in Publication Data
A catalog record for this book has been requested

ISBN10: 0-415-32639-7
ISBN13: 9-78-0-415-32639-1

Taylor & Francis Group is the Academic Division of T&F Informa plc.

وَالسَّلَامُ عَلَى مَن اتَّبَعَ الْهُدَى

Peace to all who follow guidance (20.47)

Contents

Introduction

I have for a long time felt that it would be very helpful for there to be a reference work on the Qur'an which is not enormous in size and written only for the specialist, and yet which is more substantial than some of the very short introductory works on the topic. It is the aim of this book to bridge that gap between the highly scholarly and technical text and the rather skimpy elementary books. Even a cursory glimpse at the contents will reveal that we have not eschewed scholarship. Many of the entries are substantial and deal at some length with the intricacies of the subject matter. Others are brief and explain relevant terms and ideas in a concise manner. This is not a dictionary of the Qur'an and no attempt has been made to explain every term that appears in the Book. Some terms have been selected for discussion because they are so crucial to understanding the Book, and others which are less central have been included for discussion because they are interesting. We also wanted to give readers a taste of the style of dictionaries and glossaries of the Qur'an so that they could usefully use these and know what to expect.

Contributors to this volume come from a wide variety of backgrounds. Some are Muslims, some are not, and some have no religious beliefs whatsoever. They are united in being interested in the Qur'an. The authors come from all doctrinal backgrounds and readers should expect to find a wide variety of views in this book. We do not in any way attempt to present the last word on any of the topics raised, quite the reverse. The editor has included accounts that often go against each other in order to illustrate to readers the contested nature of interpretation that exists in the subject area. What this volume represents is very much interpretation and commentary, *tafsir* in Arabic, an attempt at understanding the text of the Qur'an.

This is a collection of entries on the Qur'an, not Islam, but it is of course difficult to separate the two. There is a good deal of discussion of Islam, and not all of it relates apparently closely to the Qur'an, but readers will find that it does pertain to the Book in a more subtle way. This is the problem of commentary; one never knows how much extraneous material one is allowed to bring in to help interpret the text. Readers will find that this very topic was much discussed by commentators on the Qur'an, and the different views on what might be introduced, and what should be excluded, help define the different theological and religious schools in Islam.

It is always difficult thinking of what to put in and what to leave out of a work of this kind, and we certainly have not put in everything that is relevant to the topic of the Qur'an, its commentators and those issues which are related to it. On the other hand, we have tried to present a reasonably comprehensive guide to some of the most important concepts and figures in the Book, together with its commentators. Many important commentators and thinkers have not been discussed here, and not all the concepts of the Qur'an have their own entry; it is not our aim to produce a complete guide to everything relevant. We have tried, however, to include the most important concepts and figures, and those thinkers who are representative of different schools of thought in the interpretation of the Qur'an.

How to Use this Encyclopedia

Authors have used whichever translations they prefer, or have translated themselves. References to the Qur'an are given thus: *sura.aya*. So 2.24 refers to chapter or *sura* 2 and verse or *aya* 24. References to the Bible are given as chapter: verse. References to the *hadith* literature generally just give the italicized name of the collection in which it is to be found, so *Bukhari* indicates the traditional saying is in the collection put together by al-Bukhari. References are not given to specific books of *hadith*, they are so varied in nature and now widely available on the web that this is not necessary. Detailed bibliographic information is provided in the specific chapter at the end of the book that deals with bibliography.

Arabic terms are transliterated without the use of macrons and diacritics. Place names have generally been given their familiar spellings, and some Arabic terms have not been transliterated entirely uniformly if there is a fairly well-known different version of it (e.g. *basmala*, Allah, etc.). Similarly, the final hamza has not always been reproduced in the volume. We have selected the version of the term that is most easily recognized.

Square brackets in a quotation indicate supplementary material not in the original quotation, while round brackets mean the equivalent expression in a different language. On the whole, the honorifics that tend to be applied by Muslims to God, the Prophet and other significant figures in Islam such as 'peace on him' have been omitted, not out of disrespect but because this is an academic and not a religious work. Similarly, the practice of capitalizing the attributes of God has been restricted, although not done away with altogether. Dates have been given sometimes using both Hijri and Gregorian dates, thus: AH/CE.

Entries include cross-references to other entries. Where these are obvious, we have left it up to the reader to follow them as he or she wishes. For example, in the entry on Mary, there are of course references to Jesus, and readers who want to read more on Jesus should go to that entry. We did not feel the need to identify Jesus as a cross-reference in the entry on Mary. At the end of each entry we have indicated entries that are relevant and where this may not always be obvious to the reader. For example, the entry on 'oaths' has 'see also: fig' at the end, to indicate that there is relevant material in the entry on the fig.

Some entries deal with the same issues as other entries, so a degree of repetition is inevitable in a work of this nature. Since readers are unlikely to read each entry, it is important that the entries should each be as self-contained as is feasible. Readers should note that different authors produce different arguments and analyses, and these have all been included to reveal something of the variety of views that exists in Qur'an commentary.

There are many dummy references that consist only of a term and point the reader to the relevant entry. For example, 'Abraham' is in the appropriate alphabetical position and directs readers to 'Ibrahim', where the entry actually is to be found.

Some references to books are placed after the relevant entry, but most are in the bibliographic chapter to be found at the end of the book. This has been annotated and the references selected for their relevance to the entries and also for their bibliographical usefulness. Many of them have substantial reference material of their own, so the reader will find that it is not difficult to work out which supplementary texts would be worth reading. Many entries do not have references following them since they deal with concepts and terms that appear in the Qur'an and these are dealt with in the various dictionaries and glossaries on the Qur'an, plus the commentaries. Of particular value for the ethical concepts in the Qur'an that are briefly dealt with in this book is T. Izutsu (*Ethico-Religious Concepts in the Quran*, Montreal: McGill-Queens University Press, 2002), which is a mine of useful information on the links between the moral vocabulary of the Qur'an. The various glossaries and dictionaries of the Qur'an are helpful in dealing with specific terms.

The following reference works all have useful things to say on each topic, and they have in general not been cited in the references, since they could have been cited on every occasion:

Reference works

Brockelmann (1943–49) *Geschichte der arabischen Litteratur*, Leiden: E.J. Brill.
Encyclopedia of Islam
Encyclopedia Iranica

Abbreviations

BSOAS	*Bulletin of the School of Asian and African Studies*
EI	*Encyclopedia of Islam*
EQ	*Encyclopedia of the Qur'an*
HIP	*History of Islamic Philosophy*, Nasr and Leaman (eds)
JAL	*Journal of Arabic Literature*
JAOS	*Journal of the American Oriental Society*
MIDEO	*Mélanges de l'Institut Dominicain d'Etudes Orientales*
ZDMG	*Zeitschrift der Deutschen Morgenländischen Gesellschaft*

Editorial Board

Contributors

Hussein Abdul-Raof
University of Leeds, UK

Asma Afsaruddin
University of Notre Dame, USA

Ahmet Albayrak
Karadeniz Technical University, Turkey

Kecia Ali
Brandeis University, USA

M. Shamsher Ali
University of Dacca, Bangladesh

Redha Ameur
University of Melbourne, Australia

Rifat Atay
Harran University, Turkey

Rafik Berjak
Edmonton Public School Board and Center for Islam and Science, Canada

James A. Beverley
Tyndale Seminary, Canada

Massimo Campanini
State University Milan, Italy

Abdin Chande
Sidwell Friends School, USA

Peter Cotterell
London School of Theology, UK

Bahar Davary
University of San Diego, USA

Adnan Demircan
Harran University, Turkey

Yanis Eshots
University of Latvia, Latvia

Afnan H. Fatani
King Abdul Aziz University, Saudi Arabia

Adam Gacek
McGill University, Canada

Bilal Gökkır
Süleyman Demirel University, Turkey

Necmettin Gökkır
Istanbul University, Turkey

H. Chad Hillier
Wycliffe College, University of Toronto, Canada

A.H. Johns
Australian National University, Australia

Nevad Kahteran
University of Sarajevo, Bosnia-Herzegovina

Kiki Kennedy-Day
Rutgers University, USA

Marianna Klar
School of Oriental and African Studies, London, UK

Arzina R. Lalani
Institute of Ismaili Studies, London, UK

Oliver Leaman
University of Kentucky, USA

Richard McGregor
Vanderbilt University, USA

Yasien Mohamed
University of the Western Cape, South Africa

CONTRIBUTORS

Irfan A. Omar
Marquette University, USA

Abdul Ghafoor Raheem
*King Khaled Islamic College of Victoria,
Australia*

Ameur Redha
University of Melbourne, Australia

Peter G. Riddell
London School of Theology, UK

Andrew Rippin
University of Victoria, Canada

Neal Robinson
Catholic University, Louvain, Belgium

Abdullah Saeed
University of Melbourne, Australia

Harun Sahin
Harran University, Turkey

Zeki Saritoprak
John Carroll University, USA

William E. Shepard
University of Canterbury, New Zealand

Tamara Sonn
College of William and Mary, USA

Ibrahim Sumer
Harran University, Turkey

Colin Turner
University of Durham, UK

Brannon Wheeler
United States Naval Academy, USA

Stefan Wild
University of Bonn, Germany

Alphabetical List of Entries

ALPHABETICAL LIST OF ENTRIES

ALPHABETICAL LIST OF ENTRIES

ALPHABETICAL LIST OF ENTRIES

ALPHABETICAL LIST OF ENTRIES

ALPHABETICAL LIST OF ENTRIES

A

AARON
see: **Harun**

ʿABD AL-RAʾUF AL-SINGKILI
see: **al-Singkili, ʿAbd al-Raʾuf**

ʿABDU, MUHAMMAD
Muhammad ʿAbdu was born in 1849 in lower Egypt and received a traditional religious education at home, in Tanta and finally at al-Azhar in Cairo, very much the headquarters of Sunni legal expertise. In his early years of higher education he was attracted to mysticism, but contact with al-Afghani changed his direction radically, and he took on a much more public and political role, regarding Sufism as too individual and too private an activity for modern times. His nationalism led to his expulsion from Egypt in 1882, after which he worked in Beirut for some years until his return in 1889. The year of his expulsion he joined al-Afghani in Paris from where they published the influential journal *al-ʿUrwa al-wuthqa* (Strong Grasp), which advocated resistance to imperialism and the defence of Islamic unity. He became a judge and then returned to education, where he could continue his reforming mission. Like al-Tahtawi, another modernizer, he often served in administrative roles in order to try to reform Egyptian institutions, and in particular the Arabic language, the education of girls and the whole legal and educational structure of the state, thus combining a theoretical interest in reform with a practical commitment to change.

As with so many of the modernizers, ʿAbdu's chief problem was finding a path between *taqlid* (blind obedience) to tradition and abandoning Islam for a Western form of modernity. This conflict runs throughout his writings. He argued that there are plenty of indications in the Qurʾan itself of the means of adapting Islam to modern circumstances – indeed, the Book itself insists on it – and

1

so a reliance on the past way of doing things is not acceptable. The Qur'an was sent to the world in order to assist its inhabitants, and it is full of invitations that it be rationally interrogated and interpreted. This suggests that it should enable us to adapt to changing circumstances. This does not apply to every aspect of the Book – some things may not be challenged or even doubted – but to rely on a traditional interpretation of every aspect of Islam is a failure to accept the plausibility of the Book's relevance to changing needs and circumstances.

Further reading

'Abdu, Muhammad (1966) *The Theology of Unity* (*Risalat al-tawhid*), trans. I. Masa'ad and K. Cragg, London: George Allen & Unwin.

—— (1972) *A'mal al-kamila* (Complete works), ed. M. 'Imara, Beirut: Mu'assat al-'arabiyya li al-dirasat wa'l nashr.

Hourani, A. (1982) *Arabic Thought in the Liberal Age 1798–1939*, Cambridge: Cambridge University Press.

Keddie, N. (ed.) (1972) *Scholars, Saints and Sufis*, Berkeley, CA: University of California Press.

—— (1983) *An Islamic Response to Imperialism: Political and religious writings of Sayyid Jamal al-Din 'al-Afghani'*, Berkeley, CA: University of California Press.

Kedourie, E. (1966) *Afghani and Abduh: An essay on religious unbelief and political activism in modern Islam*, London: Frank Cass.

Kurzman, C. (2002) *Modernist Islam: A source book*, New York: Oxford University Press.

*See also: **Nahda; taqlid***

OLIVER LEAMAN

ABLUTION

The purpose of *wudu'* or ablution is referred to in 5.6: 'O you who believe, when you observe the contact prayers (*salat*) you shall wash your faces, wash your arms to the elbows, wipe your heads and wash your feet to the ankles.'

There are then four steps to ablution and these involve washing the face, the arms up to the elbows, wiping the head and washing the feet to the ankles.

By contrast with this very clear command in the Qur'an, the majority of Muslims carry out their ablutions in a different way. They follow the *sunna*, the way in which the Prophet carried out his ablution, as it has been reported. To the four steps prescribed in the Qur'an they added washing the hands to the wrists, the mouth, the nose (in particular the nostrils), the ears, and the neck. The reasoning for this is not only based on the *sunna* but also the desirability of cleanliness, especially before prayer. Yet it must be said that there is no evidence that the reason behind ablution is cleanliness. Rather, it is a formulation of God's will. Were cleanliness to be the issue, the requirement might be to clean other more important parts of the body. To back up this view there is the case of dry ablution, which is to be carried out when water is unavailable: 'if you are ill or travelling, or you had urinary or faecal-related excretion, or physically contacted women, and you cannot find water, you shall observe *tayammum* (dry ablution), by touching clean dry soil, then wiping your faces and hands with it' (4.43); this does not seem to have much to do with hygiene.

The word *tahara* (purification) does not necessarily mean physical cleanliness: 'The angels said, "O Mary, God has chosen you and *tahharik* (purified you). He has chosen you from all women"' (3.42) and 'Take from their money a charity to *tuttaherahum* (purify them) and sanctify them' (9.103). In the case of Mary, surely it is not physical purity that is at issue; this might even go towards challenging the Qur'anic doctrine that Mary was chaste. The other passage clearly does not refer to physical cleanliness. 'God does not wish to *yotahir qulubahum* (purify their hearts). They have incurred humiliation in this world, and in the Hereafter, they will suffer a terrible retribution' (5.41). It seems clear that what is at issue here is spiritual, not physical, purity, and one aspect of this is presumably following God's original command.

On the other hand, there is an emphasis on the significance of cleanliness and purity in both body and clothing: 'And thy Lord do magnify, And thy garments do purify, And uncleanness do shun' (74.3–5). 'Attend to your adornment at every time of prayer' (7.31). In the *aya* 'Surely God loves those who turn to Him again and again, and He loves those who purify themselves' (2.222), the reference could be to physical or spiritual purity, or both. However, the *hadith* literature giving details of the practice of the Prophet is enormously detailed, and includes instructions for using a toothbrush or stick, where and how to go about one's natural functions, the etiquette of bathing, combining modesty with cleanliness, and so on. The implication is that it is important to follow this practice even where explicit religious issues are not in question, since following the *sunna* of the Prophet is invariably desirable and earns merit.

See also: **purify;** *tayammum*

OLIVER LEAMAN

ABRAHAM
see: **Ibrahim**

ABRAHAM'S WIFE
see: **Ibrahim's wife**

ABROGATION

Some Qur'anic verses or passages are regarded by Muslim exegetical tradition as cancelled wholly or in part by an abrogating Qur'anic passage. In these cases abrogation usually means not only repeal but also substitution of a new wording or ruling for an outdated one. In line with Islamic dogma, the agent of abrogation and substitution is always God, never the Prophet. In the Qur'anic text itself the concept is more opaque; it was widely considered to mean the internal, intra-Qur'anic abrogation of Qur'anic verses and passages, but was also taken to refer to the abrogation of pre-Qur'anic, i.e. Jewish and Christian revelations by Qur'anic verses. Only later scholars such as al-Shafi'i (d. 204/820) discussed whether a Prophetic tradition (*hadith*) could abrogate a Qur'anic verse, or vice versa.

The Qur'an nowhere specifies which Qur'anic verses are abrogated by which other verses or which passages from Jewish or Christian scriptures are superseded by which Qur'anic verses. Therefore, there was never any agreement among exegetes on these matters. Most of the discussions about abrogation in the Qur'an concern legal issues. Thus, abrogation became not only an important concept of Qur'anic exegesis but also one of Islamic law. Knowing which verses were abrogating and which were abrogated was as necessary a condition for the competent exegetical scholar and jurist as was the ability to distinguish between Meccan and Medinan verses.

The abrogating verse is called in Muslim tradition *nasikh*, the abrogated passage *mansukh*, and abrogation *naskh*. Only the verb *nasakh*, however, occurs twice in the Qur'an. In 2.106 the divine speaker addresses the Prophet: 'And for whatever verse We abrogate or cast into oblivion, We bring a better or the like of it.' In 22.52–53 it is said: 'We sent not ever any messenger or prophet before thee, but the Satan casts into his fancy, when he was fancying; but God annuls what Satan casts, then God confirms His signs – surely God is All-knowing, All-wise – that He may make what Satan casts a trial for those in whose heart is sickness, and those whose hearts are hard.' 2.106 states that revealed verses may have been forgotten and other verses revealed in their place. Muslim exegesis did not agree on whether this referred to internal abrogation or whether it referred to the abrogation of pre-Islamic scripture by Qur'anic verses. If 2.106 is taken to mean intra-Qur'anic abrogation – and only then – it has important consequences for the history of the Qur'anic canon. 22.52 seemingly only concerns pre-Islamic prophets. But Muslim exegetical tradition explains that at least in one instance the Prophet Muhammad claimed that one of his pronouncements was divinely revealed and later disclaimed it as a result of satanic temptation (Satanic Verses). The text had later been set right by divine intervention, i.e. by a second revelation. The fact that the Prophet could 'forget' part of revelation is also mentioned in 87.6–7: 'We shall make thee recite, to forget not save what God wills; surely He knows what is spoken aloud and what is hidden.' Also in this case, Muslim commentators were in doubt whether the verse referred to the Prophet's forgetting Qur'anic verses or to the Prophet's 'forgetting' passages from Jewish or Christian scripture which contradicted Qur'anic verses. In both cases the Prophet's forgetfulness was explained as being divinely guided.

In *sura* 16.101 the divine speaker says 'And when We exchange a verse in the place of another verse – and God knows very well what He is sending down – they say, "Thou art a mere forger".' This is another verse which might be taken to prove that an 'exchange' of verses did occur in the pre-canonical period, but again it is not clear whether the exchange mentioned in this verse refers to an internal change or to a difference between the Qur'an and earlier scripture. God reserves the right to remove from revelation what He wants: 'God blots out, and He establishes whatsoever He will. And with him is the Mother of the Book' (13.39). At any rate, according to Muslim tradition this phenomenon caused polemics between the Prophet and his contemporaries, because some accused the Prophet of fabricating revelation. To these attacks, the Qur'an answered that the Prophet did not have the right to change anything. In 10.15 God orders the Prophet with regard to revelation: 'Say: "It is not for me to alter it of my own accord. I follow nothing, except what is revealed to me."' In 17.86 the divine speaker tells the Prophet: 'If We willed, We could take away that which We have revealed to thee, then thou wouldst find none thereover to guard thee against Us, excepting by some mercy of thy Lord', – thus stressing the absolute sovereignty of God even to annul all that was revealed to the Prophet.

The ambiguity of the term 'abrogation' in the Qur'an mirrors the ambiguity of other self-referential key-terms such as 'book' (kitab), 'Qur'an' and others in which the difference between Islamic and pre-Islamic revelation is often blurred or at least not easily discernible. The self-view of the Qur'anic text changed during the process of its revelation and its historical development. Here, as in other cases, it seems often difficult, if not impossible, to achieve a complete and clear understanding of what a particular verse 'really means'.

The numerous Muslim treatises on abrogation usually deal only with internal abrogation and list hundreds of cases. Not infrequently one verse was taken to abrogate several verses. In legal matters, jurists and exegetes followed a chronological principle: only a Qur'anic verse revealed at a later time could abrogate an earlier one. A Medinan verse could therefore abrogate a Meccan one, but not vice versa. The so-called 'sword verse' (9.5), a harsh verse regarding the treatment of Jews and Christians which had been revealed in Medina, said: 'Then, when the sacred months are drawn away, slay the idolators wherever you find them, and take them, and confine them and lie in wait for them at every place or ambush.' It was taken by some commentators to abrogate as many as 114 more conciliatory verses, among them the Meccan 109.6, 'To you your religion and to me my religion.' Then 9.5, in its turn, was considered by some to be partly abrogated by the verse immediately following (9.6): 'But if they repent, and perform the prayer, and pay the alms, then let them go their way.' Similarly, 2.180, 'Prescribed for you, when any of you is visited by death, and he leaves behind some goods, is to make testament in favour of his parents and kinsmen honourably – an obligation on the godfearing', was declared by some as abrogated. The abrogating verse was the long 'verse of inheritance' (4.11) which lays down exact shares of distribution between the heirs and thus makes a testament superfluous.

Jurists who were the principal participants in these discussions developed complicated and often mutually irreconcilable theories on the issue of internal abrogation. An abrogated verse could be omitted from the text and disappear without leaving a trace, the abrogated passage and the abrogating passage could both be found in the Qur'an (the normal case), and a verse could be 'withdrawn' from the text while its legal content remained valid. An example of this last rather bizarre possibility was a verse that was said to have enjoined the punishment of stoning for certain kinds of adultery. This verse is not to be found in any extant version of the Qur'an but some adherents of this punishment claimed to be sure that for some time there had been a Qur'anic verse to support it. In their view, God had withdrawn this verse – but the ruling continued.

Abrogation served to explain and justify real or imagined internal contradictions in the Qur'anic text and strengthened the explanation of verses and *suras* by linking verses to traditions relating specific historical circumstances. In many cases, abrogation reflected the radical difference between the position of the Prophet and his community in Mecca before the *Hijra*, on the one hand, and in Medina after the *Hijra*, on the other. In other cases, the discussion of abrogated verses was merely a battlefield of exegetical ingenuity. Great commentators viewed an exaggerated use of abrogation-theory with distrust. Al-Tabari (d. 310/923) only admitted abrogation when the outward sense of a verse (*zahir*) could not be upheld without recourse to this principle (Goldziher, *Richtungen* 89, fn. 4). A slightly different case was that the 'Uthmanic canonical form of the Qur'an was taken to have 'abrogated' all other competing versions.

The concepts of abrogation, exchange and forgetting of a verse oscillate between the intra-Qur'anic harmonization of contradictory verses revealed at different times and the explanation of scriptural differences between Qur'anic verses and rulings, on the one hand, and pre-Islamic Christian and Jewish revelation, on the other. The concept of abrogation also led to numerous theological and exegetical disputes. How could the concept of scripture as the eternal and perfect word of the omniscient God be reconciled with abrogation, change and withdrawal? How could the Prophet 'forget' or 'be made to forget' a revealed verse (22.52)? Today the concept of abrogation is sometimes invoked by modernists in order to adapt the Qur'anic text to the exigencies of modernity.

A far-reaching and unusual theory of abrogation was developed by the Sudanese scholar Mahmud Muhammad Taha (executed in 1985). He tried to show that the Qur'an contained two messages: the Meccan one, which was the original and universal message for all humankind, and the Medinan one, which temporarily superseded the Meccan message and adapted it to the demands and limitations of the early Muslim community in Medina. According to Taha, in the fourteenth/twentieth century the time had come to return to the original Meccan message; the secondary Medinan compromises could be abandoned. This radical exegesis was based partly on a variant reading of 2.106. Practically, it meant the abandonment of traditional Islamic law. This was strongly resisted by most Muslim scholars and resulted in Taha's execution as an apostate.

Some modern commentators, such as the Syrian Mohamad Shahrour (b. 1938), break with a long learned tradition and dismiss the concept of internal abrogation within the Qur'an altogether. According to him and others, only Islamic revelation as a whole should be described as 'abrogating' the revelations of Judaism and Christianity. The Ahmadiyya Movement and many Sunni commentators, especially from the Indian subcontinent, preceded him in this. When so many Qur'anic verses could be considered abrogated, the authority of scripture itself seemed endangered. Non-Muslim scholarship is almost as divided about the origin and essence of the abrogation-issue as is traditional Muslim scholarship. Burton (1977) sees in it the proof that in contrast to the traditional Muslim foundation story there was no final redaction of the Qur'anic consonantal text (*mushaf*) by the third caliph 'Uthman (d. 35/655). Burton's far-reaching conclusion of his discussion of abrogation is that the Qur'anic text we have today in our hands is the *mushaf* of the Prophet Muhammad.

References and further reading

Burton, J. (1977) *The Collection of the Qur'an*, Cambridge: Cambridge University Press.
—— (1985a) 'The Exegesis of Q. 2:106', *Bulletin of the School of Oriental and African Studies* 48: 452–69.
—— (1985b) 'The Interpretation of Q. 87:6–7', *Der Islam* 62, 1: 5–19.
—— (2001) 'Abrogation', in *EQ*, Vol. 1, 11–19.
Christmann, A. (2003) '"The Form is Permanent, But The Content Moves": The Qur'anic text and its interpretation(s) in Mohamad Shahrour's *al-Kitab wa-l-Qur'an*', *Welt des Islams* 33, 2: 143–72.
Coulson, N.J. (1964) *A History of Islamic Law*, Edinburgh: Edinburgh University Press, 56–9.
Goldziher, I. (1970) *Die Richtungen der Islamischen Koranauslegung*, Leiden: Brill.
Madigan, D.A. (2001) *The Qur'an's Self-image: Writing and authority in Islam's scripture*, Princeton, NJ: Princeton University Press.
Taha, M.M. (1987), *The Second Message of Islam*, trans. and ed. 'Abd Allah Ahmad Na'im, Syracuse, NY: Syracuse University Press.

See also: **asbab al-nuzul; canon; kitab; Mother of the Book; self-referentiality**

STEFAN WILD

ABU BAKR

Abu Bakr b. Abi Quhafa, was from the clan of Taym, part of the powerful tribe of Quraysh. Born around 572 CE in Mecca (he was roughly three years younger than Muhammad), Abu Bakr was a wealthy merchant before his conversion to Islam and was renowned as a *nassab*, that is, as a master genealogist of the Arab tribes. In the course of his life he had four wives and six children. He became Muhammad's father-in-law when his youngest daughter 'A'isha was wed to the Prophet.

Abu Bakr is praised in Sunni sources for his early conversion to Islam (the sources variously report that he was the first male ever or the first adult male to do so) and for his unquestioning loyalty to the Prophet and the cause of Islam. This loyalty is best exemplified by his sojourning in a cave with Muhammad during their journey to Medina while being stalked by hostile Meccans, an event referred to in Qur'an 9.40 and known as *ayat al-Ghar* ('Verse of the Cave'). Abu Bakr is said to have spent 40,000 dirhams (or dinars) before the emigration to Medina in 1/622 in various acts of charity, especially in the manumission of slaves persecuted by the Meccans. He is most commonly called *al-Siddiq* ('the truthful'), a sobriquet earned on account of his having believed the Prophet when the latter related the account of the *isra'Atiq*, referencing Abu Bakr's status as 'freed [from hellfire]'. After the *Hijra*, Abu Bakr served as a counsellor to Muhammad and took part in all the major expeditions led by the Prophet.

After Muhammad's death in 632, Abu Bakr was selected as the first of the four Rightly-Guided caliphs at the portico (Saqifa) of the Banu Sa'ida in Medina after being opposed in particular by the Medinan Ansar. His impressive service to the early community, which included his appointment as the leader of the pilgrimage in the ninth year of the *Hijra* and his designation as the prayer-leader

during the Prophet's last illness, won over many of his opponents, according to Sunni sources. In Shi'i sources, however, Abu Bakr continues to be regularly vilified as the man who usurped 'Ali's 'right' to assume the caliphate after the Prophet's death.

Abu Bakr ruled only two years, dying in 634. His major accomplishment for which he is forever glorified in Sunni sources is the preservation of the unity of the Muslim polity by decisively putting down the uprising of some of the Arab tribes against the Medinan government in what has come to be known as the *ridda* ('apostasy') wars.

Further reading

Afsaruddin, A. (2002) *Excellence and Precedence: Medieval Islamic discourse on legitimate leadership*, Leiden: E.J. Brill.

Madelung, W. (1997) *Succession to Muhammad: A study of the early caliphate*, Cambridge: Cambridge University Press.

al-Tabari (1990) *The Crisis of the Early Caliphate*, trans. R. Humphreys, Albany, NY: SUNY Press.

See also: **fitna; ridda and the case for decriminalization of apostasy**

ASMA AFSARUDDIN

ABU HANIFA, NUMAN B. SABIT

Numan b. Sabit b. Zuta b. Mah, known as Imam al-A'zam (the most Excellent Imam) was born in Kufa in 80/699 and died in Baghdad on Shaban 150/September 767. He was the founder of one of the four mainstream legal schools in Islam, which bears his name.

Abu Hanifa's family was probably of Persian or Turkish origin. His grandfather Zuta, a silk manufacturer, is said to have come to Kufa from Kabul during the reign of the caliph 'Ali. Abu Hanifa's interest in Islamic sciences started from an early age. Abu Hanifa first memorized the Qur'an, then studied *qira'at* with Imam Asim b. Bahdala, one of the mainstream *qira'at imams*. Abu Hanifa joined theological debates in Kufa and Basra, the two intellectual centres of the region, where a number of theological groups, such as the Jahmiyya, Qadariyya and the Mu'tazila were active. Abu Hanifa's main theological views are that reason is an important source of human knowledge in comprehending the existence of God. He allowed the use of reason or personal opinion (*ra'y*) and analogy (*qiyas*) in legal reasoning. For this reason he was severely criticized by his traditionalist opponents. He argued that God's names and attributes are eternal. The nature of God's attributes, such as his face and hand, cannot be known. For him, faith consists of knowledge, acceptance and outward expression. Although the sinner is liable to punishment, he or she remains a believer. According to him, human actions are created by God but willed and performed by us. His theological views were further developed by Abu Mansur al-Maturidi. Because of his opinion on faith, Abu Hanifa was labelled by some classical theologians such as Abu al-Hasan al-Ash'ari and some traditionalists such as al-Bukhari as a member of the Murji'a, the sect who refused to rule out any Muslims as unbelievers, leaving that decision to be taken by God.

Abu Hanifa did much more work on *fiqh* (jurisprudence) than on theology, although the theology comes very much into the legal discussions. He attended the lectures of Hammad b. Abi Sulayman (d. 120/738), who was a prominent religious *faqih* of Kufa, for eighteen years. When his teacher died, Abu Hanifa took over his post and started teaching *fiqh*. His teacher had himself learned *fiqh* from Ibrahim al-Nakha'i,

Abu 'Amr Sha'bi, Masruk b. Ajda, Qadi Shurayh, 'Abdullah b. Masud, the caliph 'Ali and the caliph 'Umar. This chain (*silsila*) is important and establishes his good grasp of some of the ideas of the best thinkers on law at his time.

Abu Hanifa produced a number of works, some of which are extant. In his *al-Fiqh al-akbar* (The Great Book of Jurisprudence), he summarized the theological views of Sunni orthodoxy. His *al-Fiqh al-absat* (General Jurisprudence) and *al-'Alim wa'l muta'allim* (The Scholar and the Educated) dealt with theological issues. *Al-Wasiyya* (A Written Will) deals with theology. *Musnad Abu Hanifa* was a collection of traditions which were reported by his disciples. Although is a prominent founder of the Hanafite school of law, Abu Hanifa did not himself actually compose any works on Islamic law. His legal views were reported by Muhammad al-Shaybani, and it is these that have had a major impact on Islamic law.

Further reading

Abu Hanifa (2001a) *al-'Alim wa'l muta'allim* (The Scholar and the Educated), ed. M. Zahid al-Kawthari, Cairo: al-Maktaba al-azhariyya li al-turath.
—— (2001b) *al-Fiqh al-akbar* (The Great Book of Jurisprudence), ed. M. Zahid al-Kawthari, Cairo: al-Maktaba al-azhariyya li al-turath.
—— (2001c) *al-Fiqh al-absat* (General Jurisprudence), ed. M. Zahid al-Kawthari, Cairo: al-Maktaba al-azhariyya li al-turath.
—— (2001d) *al-Wasiyya* (A Written Will), ed. M. Zahid al-Kawthari, Cairo: al-Maktaba al-azhariyya li al-turath.
Watt, W. Montgomery (1998) *The Formative Period of Islamic Thought*, Oxford: One-World.
Wensinck A.J. (1932) *The Muslim Creed: Its genesis and historical development*, Cambridge: Cambridge University Press.

See also: **tafsir in early Islam**

OLIVER LEAMAN

ABU LAHAB

'Abd al-'Uzza b. 'Abd al-Muttalib, who sported the nickname Abu Lahab ('Father of Flame') reportedly on account of his good looks, was Muhammad's uncle and staunch opponent during the early years of the Prophetic mission in Mecca. Upon the death of Abu Talib, the head of the clan of Hashim, the leadership went to Abu Lahab, who, instead of offering his nephew support, contrived to harangue and oppress him at every turn; indeed, Abu Lahab's stubborn opposition was one of the reasons Muhammad decided to migrate to Medina. He is one of the few non-Prophetic personalities to be mentioned by name in the Qur'an, with the dubious honour of having a whole *sura* (111) revealed with reference to him.

COLIN TURNER

ABU LAHAB'S SIGNIFICANCE

During the time of the Prophet Muhammad, the authenticity and credibility of Islam, the Qur'an and the Prophet himself were often questioned. When Abu Lahab was still well and alive, according to what we are told, a short *sura* of the Qur'an was revealed to the Prophet. The chapter (*sura* 111) said that Abu Lahab would die in a state of unbelief and so would go to hell for not believing in the One God. We are told: 'The power of Abu Lahab will perish, and he will perish. His wealth and gains will not exempt him. He will be plunged in flaming fire, And his wife, the wood-carrier, will have upon her neck a palm-fibre rope.'

Abu Lahab lived for many years after this prophecy was revealed and this means that he could have harmed the early years of Islam and the Prophet's mission by pretending to convert and

thus confounding the prophecy. The *sura* named al-Lahab may have been revealed in the period when the Quraysh had boycotted the Prophet together with the people of his clan and besieged them. Abi Talib and Abu Lahab were the only people to join the enemies against their own relatives.

This was a major decision, given the importance of tribal relationships in the area at the time. Abu Lahab was the Prophet's uncle, or so it is said, and public condemnation of the uncle by the nephew would not be proper until the older man had behaved so disgracefully as to invite public rebuke. If the *sura* had been revealed before this, people would have regarded it as impolite that the nephew should be so critical of his uncle. Of course, it was safe for God to reveal the *sura* later since he knew that Abu Lahab was not going to convert, or even pretend to convert; it thus plays the role of a warning message.

This is the only place in the Qur'an where a person from among the enemies of Islam has been condemned by name, yet there were plenty of others who were just as hostile to Islam as Abu Lahab. The question is: why was he so deserving of being attacked by name? To understand, it is necessary to understand Arabian society of that time and the role that Abu Lahab played within it. In those times clan loyalty was revered and was indeed essential to survival, given the vagaries of life within a hostile environment and with many competing tribes and individuals. When the Prophet started preaching, the Quraysh often opposed him but the Bani Hashim and the Bani al-Muttalib not only did not oppose him but continued to support him openly, although most of them had not yet accepted Islam nor the veracity of the Prophet's message. The exception here was Abu Lahab, son of 'Abd al-Muttalib, and the uncle of the Prophet.

In Arabia an uncle represented the father, his brother, especially when the nephew was fatherless. The uncle was expected to look upon his nephew as one of his own children. Yet Abu Lahab could not even preserve the social niceties of the time, so great was his emnity towards Islam. Traditionists have related from Ibn 'Abbas the tradition that when the Prophet was commanded to present the message of Islam openly and instructed in the Qur'an to warn first of all his nearest relations of the punishment of God, he ascended Mount Safa one morning and called out aloud: '*Ya sabaha*' ('O disaster of the morning!'). This alarm in Arabia was raised by the person who noticed early at dawn an enemy tribe advancing against his tribe. When the Prophet made this call, the people asked who had made it. They were told that it was Muhammad, and the people of all the clans of the Quraysh rushed out to defend themselves. The Prophet then addressed each clan by name and said: 'If I were to tell you that behind the hill there was an enemy host ready to fall upon you, would you believe?' The people responded with one voice, saying that they never had so far heard a lie from him. The Prophet said: 'Then I warn you that you are heading for disaster.' But before anyone else could speak, Abu Lahab said: 'May you perish!' This extraordinary hostility to his own nephew at such a crucial stage in the Prophet's mission is marked by the naming of a *sura* after Abu Lahab (111).

See also: **Arab**

OLIVER LEAMAN

ABU'L HUDAYL AL-'ALLAF
see: **al-'Allaf, Abu'l Hudayl**

'AD

The people of 'Ad are mentioned twenty-four times in the Qur'an, most commonly in connection with the prophet Hud (see, e.g., 7.65–72; 11.50–60; 26.123–140; 41.15–16; 46.21–25). They are also included in lists of the most notorious of those people who rejected their prophet and sinned against God (e.g. 9.70; 14.9; 22.42; 38.12; 40.31; 50.13; 65.38).

According to the Qur'an, the 'Ad were destroyed by a violent wind after a long period of drought imposed upon them by God for rejecting the calls of their prophet Hud (see 51.41–42; 53.50–52; 54.18–21; 69.6–8).

Muslim exegetes state that the 'Ad are descendants of Uz b. Aram b. Shem b. Noah. The 'Ad are grouped with the Thamud, Jurhum, Tasm, Amin, Midian, Amalek, Abil, Jasi, Qahtan and Banu Yaqtan as the 'Original Arabs' (*al-'arab al-'ariba*) as opposed to the 'Arabicized Arabs' (*al-'arab al-musta'riba*) descended from Ishmael.

In the exegesis of 7.69, it is said that the people of 'Ad were giants, being 60–100 cubits tall, and had great strength. The 'artifices' mentioned in 26.129 are interpreted as references to great castles of gold and silver and artificial water containers constructed by the 'Ad. The 'Iram dhat al-'Imad' of 89.6–14 is taken by Muslim exegetes to be a reference to the great city of 'Ad, which is described in fantastic terms and said to be located somewhere near the Hadhramawt in Yemen.

Further reading

Clapp, Nicholas (1998) *The Road to Ubar: Finding the Atlantis of the Sands*, New York: Houghton Mifflin.

Hamblin, W.J. (1983) 'Pre-Islamic Arabian Prophets', in S.J. Palmer (ed.) *Mormons and Muslims: Spiritual foundations and modern manifestations*, Provo, UT: Brigham Young University Press, 85–104.

Serjeant, R.B. (1954) 'Hud and other Pre-Islamic Prophets of Hadramawt', *Le Muséon* 6: 121–79.

BRANNON WHEELER

ADAM

The first man and prophet, mentioned by name twenty-five times in the Qur'an. 33.7 refers to Adam along with Noah, Abraham, Moses and Jesus as prophets from whom God took a covenant. Muslim exegetes also mention a saying of the Prophet Muhammad that Adam was one of four 'Syrian' prophets including Seth, Idris and Noah. This same saying also mentions a number of 'scriptures' (*suhuf*) which were revealed to Adam, perhaps a reference to the 'first scriptures' of 87.18.

The creation of Adam

The Qur'an and Muslim exegesis narrate how God created Adam in opposition to the advice of his angels. According to the exegesis of 2.30–33, God taught Adam the names by which people know things in the world and this knowledge was superior to that of the angels. In 15.26 God says that he created human beings from dried clay and stinking slime. Muslim exegetes explain that the name 'Adam' is derived from the fact that God took the clay with which he made Adam from the 'skin' (*adam*) of the earth, and that the different colours of clay used account for the different skin colours of later people.

The Qur'an does not refer specifically to the creation of Eve, nor does it mention her by name, but Muslim exegetes relate that she was created from one of the ribs of Adam. The Arabic name for Eve (Hawa') is said to be derived from the word meaning life (*haya*) since Eve is the mother of all humanity.

The Garden of Eden

A number of passages in the Qur'an tell of the expulsion of Iblis (see, e.g., 7.11–18; 15.26–44; 17.61–65; 18.50–51; 38.67–88) from Eden and his subsequent temptation of Adam and Eve. In these verses Iblis refuses to follow God's command that he bow down to Adam and is thus transformed into Satan.

The test of Adam and Eve is described in 2.34–39 and 20.115–126. Unlike the biblical account of Eden, the Qur'an mentions only one special tree in Eden, the Tree of Immortality, from which Adam and Eve were prohibited. According to 20.120–121, Satan told Adam to eat from the forbidden tree, and when both Adam and Eve ate from the tree their private parts were revealed to them.

Muslim exegetes report that Adam was cast out of Eden to India or Sri Lanka, Eve to Jeddah and the serpent, in which Satan hid when he entered Eden, to Isfahan. It is also reported that Adam was so tall that he could stand on the highest mountain in Sri Lanka and see into heaven, so God reduced him in height to 60 cubits (about 30 metres). After complaining to God about missing the sights and sounds of Eden, Adam is sent on the first pilgrimage to Mecca. Some exegetes claim that the first *Ka'ba* was a tent erected by Adam, and others report that God sent down a special jewelled *Ka'ba* from heaven that was later raised during the Flood in the time of Noah.

Muslim exegetes explain that Adam was punished by having to grow his own food, and Eve was punished with menstruation and difficult childbirth. The origins of civilization are also closely associated with the fall of Adam and Eve to earth. Tools and the technology necessary for the growing of food, making of clothing and shelter, language, law, religion and sexual reproduction are among the arts of civilization revealed to Adam and Eve by the archangel Gabriel according to Muslim exegesis.

Adam's repentance

2.37 makes reference to Adam's asking God's forgiveness and permission to return to the Garden of Eden. According to Muslim exegesis, Adam and Eve both did penance on earth for forty years after their fall, standing in water up to their necks and abstaining from sex. God's promise to Adam that he could return to Eden is taken to be the basis for the revelation of religion, specifically the rituals instituted by the prophets (e.g. prayer, fasting, almsgiving, pilgrimage), by which Adam and Eve's descendants would be allowed into Eden after the Day of Judgement.

Several verses also refer to a covenant made between God and the descendants of Adam before their birth (e.g. 7.172; 30.30; 33.7; 53.56). Muslim exegetes explain that all humanity was taken from Adam's back or loins and caused to acknowledge the existence of God. Other reports state that God took all humanity from Adam and divided them into those destined for paradise and those destined for hell.

Adam's death

Muslim tradition states that Adam volunteered forty years of his own life to be added to the life of his descendant David. According to some reports, Adam was shown his descendants before their birth and noticed that David's lifespan was shorter than the others, so he took forty years and added it to the sixty years already allotted to David. This shortened the allotted 1,000-year lifespan of Adam to 960 years, although some exegetes claim that Adam lived the full 1,000 years.

Although Seth is not mentioned by name in the Qur'an, it is reported by Muslim exegetes that the prophet Seth, the son of Adam and Eve, was responsible for preparing Adam's body for burial, and that he was taught how to do this by the angels. It is also said that Adam did not die until he saw the birth of four generations of his offspring, some 1,400 people.

According to Muslim tradition, the tomb of Adam is located in a cave, called the 'Cave of Treasure', on Mount Abu Qubays near Mecca. Some exegetes report that the bodies of Adam and Eve were taken on the Ark with Noah and reburied in Jerusalem after the Flood, or that Adam's body was dismembered and buried in different locations, including Hebron.

Further reading

Abdel-Haleem, M. (1997) 'Adam and Eve in the Qur'an and the Bible', *Islamic Quarterly* 41: 255–69.

Beck, E. (1976) 'Iblis und Mensch, Satan und Adam: Der Werdegang einer koranische Erzählung', *Le Muséon* 89: 195–244.

Kister, M.J. (1993) 'Adam: A Study of Some Legends in Tafsir and Hadith literature', *Israel Oriental Studies* 13: 113–74.

Schöck, C. (1993) *Adam im Islam: ein Beitrag zur Ideengeschichte der Sunna*, Islamkundliche Untersuchungen 168, Berlin: K. Schwarz.

Zwemer, S.M. (1937) 'The Worship of Adam by Angels', *Muslim World* 27: 115–27.

BRANNON WHEELER

'ADHAB
see: **punishment**

'ADL

A word meaning justice, the meaning of justice in the Qur'an is linked to the concepts of balance and just measure both in the action of God and humanity. Two verses are particularly important here: 5.8 for the foundation of justice in juridical action; and 4.58–59 for the political dimension of the issue of justice.

'Adl is the common name with which we translate the concept of justice and it is found fourteen times in the Qur'an. In some accounts, 'adl is also one of the beautiful names of God, because it means the action of God as a just ruler and judge, but it is not attributed to God explicitly in the Qur'an as such, and this explains the disagreement among theologians regarding the name's attribution (Gimaret, 1988: 69ff.). The Holy Book always uses 'adl, but never 'adala, which is another common term used to express justice and of which there are several declensions of the verb 'adala, 'to act with fairness' or 'to be equal'. These terms are generally linked with the concepts of equivalence, balance and just measure: obviously the just measure involves equivalence. For instance, twice in the sura al-An'am, 'adl and the verbal form ya'diluna point to different kinds of equivalence: giving God equals among the creatures, that is to say, polytheism (6.1); or trying to ransom sins for a just price on the Day of the Last Judgement (6.70). These are actions regarding men and their destiny, but 'adl is also an aspect and a presupposition of God's action. In 82.7 (a chapter revealed early in the first Meccan period), God is said to be creator, modeller and fashioner of man: God 'adala man, namely, God gives him the right measure and balance in shape and form. In 16.90 God commands justice and commands by justice (ya'muru b'adl) at the same time. He acts justly and fairly and, at the same time, he commands men to act accordingly. The verse can support the Mu'tazilite view that God acts best for all creatures. In 6.115 the Word of God is established by truth (sidq) and justice ('adl): the decree of God is inspired by justice and the

firmness of his decision implies that there is no change and modification in this decree. The rationality of the world is grounded both in justice and truth (haqq).

Verse 5.8 is important: 'Ye who believe, stand in front of God as witnesses of equity (qist) and your hatred for other men does not allow you to turn away to act justly (ta'dilu). Act justly (a'dilu), because this is the thing nearer to piety.' Here we find the term 'adl connected with qist, another key term to express justice. Qist is the balance of equity, and the Qur'an resorts to the metaphor of balance to indicate justice. For instance, in 57.25 balance (mizan) is revealed by the Book (kitab) in order to observe equity (qist) on behalf of humanity. The idea of equilibrium employs the principle of 'adl, and it happens either from a juridical or from a moral point of view. From a juridical point of view, it is necessary to judge (hakama) in compliance with the right measure (qist) (5.42) and to judge among men with justice ('adl) (4.58; see below).

The Holy Book does not stress explicitly the concept of judgement (hukm) and its links with justice ('adl) in legal trials. However, men possessing the attribute of justice ('adl) must judge (yahkumu) in legal quarrels regarding cattle, in order that a man, who killed intentionally an animal in a state of ritual consecration, brings to the Ka'ba an 'equivalent' from his flock or fasts in an 'equivalent' way ('adl) (5.95). In legal vocabulary, 'adl means the integrity and probity of a witness who must be just to practise his function in the courts, or the honesty of a judge. Integrity of the witness is hinted at also by qist in 4.135, where men are warned to act justly even though parents and relatives are involved. From a moral point of view, the great theologian al-Ghazali (1058–1111) emphasized that 'the meaning of justice (*'adl*) is to put all things in their right place' (al-Ghazali, 1970: 104–5). Justice is the straightening (*ta'dil*) of the heart obtained when the body follows the just rule (*qanun al-'adl*). There is a close relation between the lower world (*mulk*) and the upper world (*malakut*), so that we cannot be pure inside if we are not pure outside. Al-Ghazali interpreted correctly the Qur'anic aim to balance inner and outward dimensions, so that – it is said in 4.135 – we must not follow our passions lest we should swerve from justice.

Justice is the presupposition of the so-called verse of the powerful rulers (*ayat al-Umara'*): 'God commands you to give back the trusts to their rightful owners, and if you judge (*hakamtum*) among the people, to judge with justice (*'adl*) .... Believers, obey God and obey the Messenger and those who have authority among you, and if you disagree about anything, refer it to God and the Messenger if you are true believers' (4.58–59). This is one of the very few 'political' verses of the Qur'an, and it states the norms for rulers and for the ruled. The Hanbalite theologian Ibn Taymiyya (1263–1328) took this as his base when setting up the *siyasa shar'iyya* (politics in accordance with the religious law). He wrote that in the first part of the verse the rulers are referred to, and their duty is to act justly and to enforce justice among their subjects. In the second part of the verse, the ruled are mentioned since their duty is to obey the rulers until such time as they turn aside from the way of God; obedience is not a duty to evil rulers (Ibn Taymiyya, 1939: 2). The ruler must have moral integrity (*'adl*) to practise his office; and just rulers (like the first four *rashidun* caliphs) agree with God and the Prophet in preferring justice (*'adl*) and in choosing truth (*haqq*): this is how al-Zamakhshari glosses the verse dealing with the powerful rulers in his commentary (al-Zamakhshari, n.d., Vol. I: 275).

References and further reading

al-Ghazali (1970) *Kitab al-arba'in fi usul al-din* (Book of the Forty Principles of Religion), Cairo: Maktaba al-Jindi.

Gimaret, D. (1988) *Les noms divins en Islam* (The Divine Names in Islam), Paris: Cerf.

Ibn Taymiyya (1939) *Le traité de droit publique de Ibn Taymiyyah* (The Treatise of Public Right), ed. H. Laoust, Damascus: Institut Français de Damas.

al-Zamakhshari (n.d.) *al-Kashshaf 'an haqa'iq al-tanzil* (Discovering the Truths of Revelation), Beirut: Dar al-ma'rifa.

See also: **Ash'arites and Mu'tazilites; *hukm*; Ibn Taymiyya**

MASSIMO CAMPANINI

ADULTERY
see: zina

'AHD | 'AHADA

The word *'ahd* is mentioned forty-six times in thirty-six verses of seventeen chapters in the Qur'an. It means to make a promise (2.124, 177; 9.75, 111; 23.8; 70.32), making an agreement (19.78, 87), making a covenant (2.177), swearing (16.91, 95; 17.34), commending (2.125; 20.115).

Another term synonymous with *'ahd* is *mithaq*, which is mentioned twenty-three times in nine chapters. In verses of the Qur'an, both terms were used together with the same meaning (2.27; 13.20, 25).

It is usually accepted that there are two types of covenant in the Qur'an. The first is the implied primordial covenant, which is supposed to have taken place before the universe came into existence when God asked the souls 'Am I not your Lord?', they said, 'Yea! We do testify' (7.172). Even though neither *'ahd* nor *mithaq* is mentioned in this verse, owing to the context, this has always been considered as the first covenant. The background for this understanding might be the verses referring to the general covenant made with the children of Adam (Banu Adam) (36.60). The second and more general type of covenant was made with different communities through the prophets, starting with Adam and ending with Muhammad. More specifically, the Qur'an mentions covenants made with the children of Adam (36.60–61), Adam, Abraham and Ishmael, the Children of Israel (Banu Israel), Moses and lastly Muhammad and his followers (7.102; 3.183).

It is well known that the subject of covenant with Adam was not to eat from the forbidden fruit (20.115–124). God tested Abraham and his son Ishmael and when they succeeded, he promised to make them leaders of the people and in return asked them to keep his house (the Holy Ka'ba) clean (2.124–125). The covenants made with Banu Israel and the People of the Book (ahl al-kitab) have a significant place in the Qur'an. Allah asked the Children of Israel to believe in the Qur'an and to accept that it is a holy book sent by Allah, like the Torah, and that Muhammad was the messenger of Allah. They were also asked to 'be steadfast in prayer, practise regular charity', not to cover 'truth with falsehood', to 'enjoin right conduct' while 'not forgetting to practise it themselves' and to 'be patient and guard themselves against a day when one shall not avail another nor shall intercession be accepted' (2.40–48). Nevertheless, the Qur'an also reports that whenever the Children of Israel made a promise to Allah, one group among them always broke their promise (7.102–103). They acted as though they had never read the book of Allah (2.100–101; 3.183–184).

The subjects of the covenant made with Moses are various. During his stay in Egypt, Allah asked Moses to make an agreement with Pharaoh, who would let the Children of Israel exit from Egypt, provided that God removes plagues from the Egyptians. However, whenever God kept his promise by removing the penalty, they broke their promise. Then, more plagues were sent on them: wholesale death, locusts, lice, frogs and blood, successively. Eventually Pharoah and his people were drowned in the sea as punishment for failing to fulfil their promise (7.133–136; 43.46–56).

Covenant is also used in the Qur'an vis-à-vis Muhammad and his followers on several issues. Among them are Muhammad's asking his followers to swear allegiance to him by placing hand on hand to fight with the enemy (48.10), not to retreat when confronted with the enemy (33.15, 22–23), to keep one's promise on all occasions whether it is made with Allah, or the Prophet or among each other, even with the unbelievers (16.91, 95; 9.75–76; 70.32; 23.8; 17.34; 6.152).

Lastly, it should be noted that the Qur'an employs covenant in the context of life after death also. Two examples illustrate this well. One is the declaration that only those who were promised by Allah shall have the power of intercession on Judgement Day (Maryam 19.87). The other example forms the bedrock of religious conviction. According to that, Allah made a covenant in the Torah, the Gospel and the Qur'an that he would reward the believers who fight in his Cause with the Garden of Paradise. 9.111 reads: 'Allah has purchased from the believers their persons and their goods; for their [return] is the Garden [of Paradise]. They fight in his cause, and slay and are slain. A promise binding on him in truth, through the Torah, the Gospel, and the Qur'an. And who is more faithful to his covenant than Allah?

Then rejoice in the bargain which ye have concluded. That is the achievement supreme.'

See also: **covenant;** *mithaq*

IBRAHIM SUMER

AHL AL-BAYT

References to the Family of the House occur in the Qur'an in interesting contexts. When Sara was told that she is going to give birth to two prophets, she laughed and remarked on how strange it was at her advanced age for such a thing to occur. 'But the angels said: "Do You wonder at Allah's decree? The grace of Allah and His blessings be upon you, O People of the House! He is indeed worthy of all praise full of all glory!"' (11.73). At 33.33 there is a reference to the purity and the excellence of the *ahl al-bayt* of Prophet Muhammad, and this has led some commentators to extend the term to the wives of the Prophet. But Sara was only addressed as a member of the *ahl al-bayt* after she was told of her imminent motherhood of a prophet, so perhaps the title is dependent not on marriage but on offspring. 'And We ordained that he refuse to seek any foster mother before so she said: "Shall I point out to you a household who will take care of him for you, and will be kind to him?" So We restored him to his mother that she might be comforted and not grieve, and that she might know that the promise of Allah is true. But most of them know not' (28.12–13). The mother of Moses is classed as a member of the *ahl al-bayt,* not for being the wife of 'Imran, but for being the mother of Moses. Marriage cannot confer the title since the wives of Noah and Lot were not considered *ahl al-bayt* despite the significance of their spouses. They shared the fate of the rest of community at that time.

Noah actually tried to get God to class his son as a member of the Family of the House but to no avail: 'And Noah cried unto his Lord and said: "My Lord! Verily my son is of my family; and verily Your promise is true, and You are the most just of the judges." He [God] said: "O Noah! Verily he is not of your family. In fact, he does not behave as a righteous person; therefore do not ask what you have no knowledge about; I truly advise you not to behave like an ignorant person"' (11.45–46). Noah argued for his son, and the reply was that he was not worthy to be his son. Noah had three other sons who were believers and who with their wives entered the Ark and were saved and Kanan was Noah's son by his other wife, who was a disbeliever and who perished along with her son. Merit is a criterion of membership. *Ahl al-bayt* are only the individuals among the Prophet's descendants who also had close affinity in character and spiritual attainment with Prophet.

The term *ahl* signifies the members of a household of a man, including his fellow tribesmen, kin, relatives, wife (or wives), children, and all those who share a family background, religion, housing, city and country with him. *Bayt* refers to habitation and dwelling, including tents and buildings. The *ahl al-bayt* of any person refers to his family members and all those who live in his house. The term *ahl al-bayt* (People of the House) is used twice in the Qur'an: 'the mercy of Allah and his blessing are on you, O people of the house' (11.73). This verse refers to the people of the House of Ibrahim. 'Allah only desires to keep away uncleanness from you, O people of the House! And to purify you [with] a [thorough] purifying' (33.33). This verse may refer to the members of the household of the Prophet. The Shi'i consider the *ahl al-bayt* to include exclusively

Muhammad, 'Ali, Fatima, Hasan and Husayn. They do not consider the Prophet's other offspring, wives, sons of paternal uncles and dwellers in his house as the Messenger's *ahl al-bayt*. They base their argument on the genuine and authentic traditions narrated by the companions of the Prophet recorded in the Sunni and Shi'i sources. However, there are, as is often the case, a wide variety of different rulings on this issue. Different religious groups in the Islamic world tend to value different personalities as they appear in the Qur'an and so membership of the *ahl al-bayt* varies from one group to another.

See also: **al-Qadi al-Nu'man; punishment and original sin; Shi'a;** *zahir*

OLIVER LEAMAN

AHL AL-DHIKR

It says in the Qur'an: 'Ask the *ahl al-dhikr* (those who know) if you do not know' (16.43; see also 21.7). Who are the *ahl al-dhikr*? This verse instructs the Muslims to refer to the people who know in all things which perplex them so that they may discern the path to the truth, because God, having taught them, has nominated them for that particular purpose. Their knowledge is deeply rooted and they know how to interpret the Qur'an. This verse could have been revealed to introduce the family of the (Prophet's) house, the *ahl al-bayt*. They are the Prophet Muhammad, 'Ali, Fatima, Hasan and Husayn, and possibly their successors. There are traditions accepted within the Shi'i school to that effect. The meaning of the *aya* suggests to some that the *ahl al-dhikr* refers to the people of the book, i.e. Jews and Christians. But the Qur'an has mentioned in a number of verses that they altered the Word of God (*tahrif*) and they wrote their religious books themselves, claim-

ing that it was from God. It also refers to their lies and turning the truth upside down. Given this state of affairs, it is unlikely that the Qur'an instructed the Muslims to refer to them on issues about which the Muslims themselves are confused.

Al-Bukhari has reported in his *Sahih* collection of traditions in 'The Book of Testimony' under the heading 'The *ahl al-shirk* (polytheists) are not to be asked' (Vol. 3: 163): 'The Prophet said: "Do not believe the people of the book and do not consider them as liars but say: 'We believe in God and what was revealed.'"' This means we should not refer questions to them, rather, we should abandon and ignore them because the command not to believe them or to consider them as liars would remove the point of asking them, i.e., awaiting the right reply. Al-Bukhari has reported in his *Sahih* in 'The Book of Unity' (Vol. 8: 208) that Ibn 'Abbas said: 'O Muslims! How come you ask the people of the scriptures, although your book which was revealed to his Prophet has the most recent information from Allah and you recite it, a book which has not been distorted? Allah has revealed to you that the people of the scriptures have changed with their own hands what was revealed to them and they have said: "This is from Allah" in order to get some worldly benefit thereby.' Ibn 'Abbas added: 'Isn't the knowledge revealed to you sufficient to prevent you from asking them? By Allah, I have never seen any one of them asking [Muslims] about what has been revealed to you.'

Among the People of the Book, the Christians claim that Jesus is God while the Jews will not accept him even as a prophet. Both of them criticize Islam and the Prophet and call him a liar. Bearing this in mind, it is highly unlikely that God would command us to ask them if we accept that the *ahl al-dhikr* from the apparent meaning of the verse refers to the People of the Book, i.e. the Jews and Christians. More plausible is that God granted knowledge of the Book on those spiritual and intellectual leaders whom he has chosen so that people can refer to them in trying to understand those points of the Qur'an that are less clear than others. From a Shi'i point of view, the experts here are the *imams*. God wished the people to submit to this elite group, and so he chose them and taught them the knowledge of the book. As a result the leadership of the community was improved and the affairs of the people organized efficiently. Whether this interpretation of the verse is satisfactory or not, it is certainly true that the idea that the Jews and Christians would be asked to decide on difficult issues in a religious book not their own seems highly improbable. There is also a plausible Sunni interpretation in terms of the *ahl al-dhikr* being the leading '*ulama*' (scholars) and legal authorities (*fuqaha*'), or any other group in which they placed confidence in religious matters.

See also: **ahl al-bayt**; **ahl al-kitab**

OLIVER LEAMAN

AHL AL-KITAB

There are varying attitudes in the Qur'an to those called the People of the Book, who are sometimes regarded in a friendly way as allies and at other times with rather more suspicion and hostility. During the Meccan period, the believers were few, disorganized, and in danger. Revelations dealt with the existence and identity of the One God, the signs of his existence, and the coming of the Last Judgement. Believers in Islam were in the process of learning the nature of piety and virtue, forming their characters accordingly and recognizing these

virtues in others, perhaps especially those recipients of earlier books such as the Jews and Christians. In the Medinan period, the community was organized and cohesive but was, at first, impoverished and threatened politically and militarily. Still, revelations continued to praise the virtuous Jews and Christians: 'Not all of them are alike: of the People of the Book are a portion that stand [for the right]; they rehearse the signs of God all night long, and they prostrate themselves in adoration. They believe in God and the Last Day; they are involved in what is right and forbid what is wrong; and they hasten to carry out good works: they are in the ranks of the righteous. Of the good that they do, nothing will be rejected of them; for God knows well those that do right' (3.113–115).

But in other places the text is far harsher about the People of the Book, especially the Jews. In an interesting passage Muslims are told to 'Say to the People of the Book and the Gentiles "Do you also surrender yourselves to God?" If they surrender (*aslama*) they are rightly guided' (3.20). This could mean they need to carry out their normal religious obligations according to the rites of their own faiths, and the Qur'an is particularly favourably inclined to the Jews observing the Sabbath, for example. On the other hand, it could mean they are rightly guided only if they actually become Muslims. Yet we are told that all the creatures in heaven and earth have submitted to him, using the same word, and presumably this does not mean that they have all become Muslims.

The Sabeans are referred to as People of the Book in 2.62 and 5.69, so it is not exclusively a category reserved for Jews and Christians. At 22.17 everyone is divided up into three groups: those who believe in the Qur'an; the Jews, Christians, Sabeans and Magians; and the polytheists. As a sort of middle category, the People of the Book are not promised salvation unless they behave well and have faith in God. Some verses are critical of them in these respects, and link them more with the polytheists. Thus we are told that the Christians often claim that Jesus is a divine being, committing the sin of *shirk* or associating partners with God, while the Jews often do not obey their own Torah, even the falsified version that they say is the Word of God. A particular complaint against them is that they may seek to mislead Muslims, and the latter are instructed to be careful of them in this respect. In any case Muslims are called the best people and the People of the Book are mainly evildoers thoroughly set in their ways (3.110). Further on in this *sura* we are told that only those People of the Book who accept all the divine revelations, including those of the Prophet himself, deserve an eventual reward (3.198–199).

In 5.51 Muslims are instructed not to be friends with Jews or Christians, and 3.118 advises Muslims to only have fellow Muslims as friends. There are also references to the need to fight non-Muslims, and sometimes the People of the Book are put into the same category here as the polytheists. Perhaps this is a reflection of the growing disappointment at the obduracy of the Jews in particular as the Prophet's mission continued and the groups whom he earlier hoped to convert proved less welcoming than he had expected. Perhaps the change of direction of the *qibla* reflected this change of attitude, since praying initially in the direction of Jerusalem might be regarded as a gesture designed to win the allegiance of the Jews. Clearly they would not be attracted by the idea of praying in the direction of Mecca. The Jews tend to be regarded with more hostility than the Christians, perhaps because as a political group in Arabia they were a more present danger; the Christians were generally more distant in the foreign empire of Byzantium and not an immediate obstacle. 'You will find that the most implacable of men in their hostility to the faithful are the Jews and the pagans, and that the nearest in affection to them are those who say "we are Christians"' (5.82), and the *sura* continues with accounts of Christians appreciating the truth of the Qur'an.

Further reading

Geiger, A. (1970) *Judaism and Islam*, ed. M. Perlmann, New York: Ktav.
Ridgeon, L. (2000) *Islamic Interpretations of Christianity*, New York: St Martin's Press.

*See also: **hanif**; **Judaism**; **kitab**; **Qur'anic Studies**; **wali***

OLIVER LEAMAN

AHL AL-SUNNA
*see: **sunna***

AHMAD
*see: **Injil**; **Muhammad***

AHMAD B. HANBAL
Abu 'Abdullah Ahmad b. Muhammad b. Hanbal al-Shaybani al-Marwazi was born in Baghdad in 164/780 and died in the same city on 12 Rabi al-Awwal 241/ 31 July 855. He was the founder of one of the four Sunni legal schools in Islam.

Ahmad b. Hanbal belonged to an Arab family known as Banu Shayban. His family moved from Marw to Baghdad. His genealogy stretches back to one of the grandfathers of the Prophet, Nizar. His own grandfather, Hanbal b. Hilal, was a governor of Sarakhs during the reign of the Umayyads, who supported the 'Abbasid revolution and then served in the 'Abbasid army.

Ahmad b. Hanbal was initially educated in Baghdad where he memorized the Qur'an and then studied Arabic grammar, Islamic law (*fiqh*) and prophetic tradition (*hadith*). He continued his education with eminent teachers such as Hushaym b. Bashir, 'Abd al-Rahman b. Mahdi, Sufyan b. 'Uyayna, Yahya b. Sa'id al-Kattan and Imam Shafi'i. He learned Islamic law (*fiqh*) and Islamic legal methodology (*usul al-fiqh*) from Shafi'i. Ahmad b. Hanbal taught a number of students such as the famous traditionalists al-Bukhari, Muslim, Tirmidhi and Nasa'i.

Under the influence of Mu'tazilite scholars, the 'Abbasid caliph al-Ma'mun (813–833) had pressured Ibn Hanbal into accepting the Mu'tazilite dogma of the createdness of the Qur'an. Ibn Hanbal refused to accept this principle, which he considered to be contrary to orthodox belief. Because of his refusal, he was persecuted and imprisoned. The caliph al-Mu'tasim (r. 833–842) adopted the same policy and Ibn Hanbal remained in prison where he was severely tortured. Fortunately for him, al-Mutawakkil (r. 847–861) took control and re-established a more orthodox approach, and as a result Ibn Hanbal was able to continue his teaching activity.

Ibn Hanbal was one of the leading defenders of the Salafi position. His main theological views can be summarized as follows: one must believe in God as described in the Qur'an. For him, the nature of God's attributes cannot be known rationally. We cannot understand how we can ascribe attributes to God rationally. In this respect, he rejects negative theology (*tanzih*) and anthropomorphism (*tashbih*). For Ibn Hanbal, the attributes and the names of God are eternal. Considering the issue of human action he adopted a middle approach between the doctrine of the Mu'tazila

and the Jabriyya. On his view the Qur'an is the eternal speech of God and it is uncreated. He bitterly criticized the Mu'tazilite dogma of the createdness of the Qur'an. For him, faith consists of acceptance by heart, outward expression and action. Although the sinner is liable to punishment, he or she remains a believer. Faith can increase through virtuous behaviour and decrease with the opposite. His theological views were developed and defended by scholars of later generations such as Abu Sa'id al-Darimi, Ibn Abi Ya'la, Ibn Taymiyya and Ibn al-Qayyim.

A number of works were attributed to Ibn Hanbal. Among them only the *Musnad*, which is a collection of around 30,000 traditions, was written by him. Other works were collected and written by his son 'Abdullah b. Ahmad b. Hanbal and by his other students upon his death. Ibn Hanbal gave traditions (*hadith*) a key role in Islamic law and theology. His legal approach was centred on revealed texts, i.e. the Qur'an and the traditions and on the sayings of the Companions. He opposed using personal opinion (*ra'y*) and analogical reasoning (*qiyas*) in his legal theory. On the methodological level, he took a literal approach to the text of the Qur'an and the traditions.

Further reading

Bell, J.N. (1979) *Love Theory in Later Hanbalite Islam*, Albany, NY: SUNY Press.

Ibn Hanbal (1985) *Kitab al-sunna* (Book of Tradition), ed. Muhammad Said Basyuni, Beirut: Dar al-kutub al-'ilmiyya.

—— (1987) *Kitab al-'ilal wa ma'arifat al-rijal* (Book of the Deficiencies and the Knowledge of Narrators' Biographies), ed. Talat Koçyiğit and Ismail Cerrahoğlu, Istanbul: al-Maktaba al-islamiyya.

—— (n.d.) *al-Rad 'ala al-jahmiyya wa'l-zanadiqa* (The Refutation of the Jahmites and the Heretics), ed. 'Abdurrahman Umayra, Riyadh: Adwa al-shari'a.

See also: **al-Ash'ari;** *tafsir* – **Salafi views**
OLIVER LEAMAN

AHQAF

Ahqaf is the plural of *hiqf*, meaning a long and curved body of sand. *Al-Ahqaf* is the name of long tracts of sand in the region of Esh–Shihr, the country of the 'Ad.

Al Ahqaf is the title of the Meccan *sura* 46 in the Qur'an. It was revealed to Prophet Muhammad during his struggle with the polytheist Quraysh. The Qur'an tells the story of the tribe of 'Ad who fought their prophet Hud as the Meccans fought him. It reports that because of their vehement rejection of him, the people of 'Ad were totally destroyed by the command of Allah, but their dwellings remain as a warning.

See also: 'Ad

RAFIK BERJAK

'A'ISHA

'A'isha was the third wife of the Prophet, and the only virgin he married. His first and only wife for twenty-four years was Khadija bint al-Khuwaylid, who was about nineteen years older than him. He married Khadija when she was 40 and he was 21 and stayed married only to her until her death. Just after Khadija's death, when he was around 46 years old, the Prophet married his second wife, Sawda bint Abi Zam'a. It was after this second marriage that the Prophet became betrothed to 'A'isha. She was the daughter of Abu Bakr, one of the Prophet's closest friends and devoted followers. Abu Bakr was one of the earliest converts to Islam and hoped to solidify the deep love that existed between himself and the Prophet by uniting their families in marriage.

The betrothal of Abu Bakr's daughter 'A'isha took place in the eleventh year of Muhammad's Prophethood, which was about a year after he had married Sawda bint Zam'a and before he made his *hijra* (migration) to Medina. There are four *ahadith* in the *Sahih* of al-Bukhari and three *ahadith* in *Sahih Muslim* that clearly state that 'A'isha was 'nine years old' at the time that her marriage was consummated by the Prophet. These *ahadith* are very much the same and they read as follows: 'A'isha narrated that the Prophet was betrothed (*zawaj*) to her when she was six years old and he consummated (*nika*) his marriage when she was nine years old, and then she remained with him for nine years (*Bukhari*, Vol. 7, Bk 62, No. 64). Of the four *ahadith* in *Bukhari*, two were narrated by 'A'isha herself (7, 64 and 7, 65), one by Abu Hisham (5, 236) and one via 'Ursa (7, 88). All three of the *ahadith* in *Muslim* have 'A'isha as a narrator. Additionally, all of the *ahadith* in both books agree that the marriage betrothal contract took place when 'A'isha was 'six years old', but was not consummated until she was 'nine years old'. Additionally, a *hadith* with the same text (*matn*) is reported in *Sunan Abu Dawud*. This evidence is very strong from an Islamic point of view. So there is really no room for debate about 'A'isha's age, although some have argued that in fact she was a lot older when she married. But until someone proves that in the Arabic language the words meaning 'nine years old' mean something other than 'nine years old', then we need to accept that she was 'nine years old'. Nonetheless, some continue to argue that she was really a lot older when the marriage was consummated.

From the accounts we have, the marriage with 'A'isha was consummated in Shawwal, seven months after the Prophet's *hijra* from Mecca to Medina. At the time of his marriage to 'A'isha, the Prophet was over 50 years old. It should be noted that the Prophet's marriage to

'A'isha was apparently a very happy one for both parties, as the *hadith* literature attests. 'A'isha was his favourite wife and the only virgin that he ever married.

After migrating to Medina, Muhammad married numerous other wives, eventually totalling fifteen in his lifetime. Each of these marriages was done either for political reasons, to strengthen the ties of kinship or to help a woman in need. Quite a few of the wives were widows, older women or had been abandoned and thus were in need of a home and protection. Additionally, it should be mentioned that the same collection of Muslim *hadith* literature that tells us that 'A'isha was only nine years old at the time of the marriage tells us that the marriage was divinely ordained: "A'isha is reported to have said that "The Messenger of God said (to me): 'You have been shown to me twice in (my) dreams. A man was carrying you in a silken cloth and said to me, "This is your wife." I uncovered it; and behold, it was you."' He continued: 'I said to myself, "If this dream is from God, He will cause it to come true"' (*Bukhari*, Vol. 7, Bk 62, No. 15). The Prophet also told her Jibril came to him and showed him a picture of her on a piece of green silk and said, 'She is your wife in this world and in the next world.'

Just before her wedding, 'A'isha related that shortly before she was to leave her parents' house, she slipped out into the courtyard to play with a friend. The stories that were produced by 'A'isha are worth repeating in that they give a good indication of the light and easy style of her prose, which must have played an important role in presenting a less serious side to Islam. 'I was playing on a seesaw and my long streaming hair became dishevelled', she said. 'They came and took me from my play and made

me ready.' They dressed her in a wedding dress made from fine, red striped cloth from Bahrain and then her mother took her to the newly built house where some women of the Ansar were waiting outside the door. They greeted her with the words, 'For good and for happiness, may all be well.' Then, in the presence of the smiling Prophet a bowl of milk was brought. The Prophet drank from it himself and then offered it to 'A'isha. She modestly declined it, but he insisted she drink as well and then offered the bowl to her sister Asma' who was sitting beside her. The others who were present also drank from it, and that was all there was to the simple and solemn occasion of their wedding.

Her marriage to the Prophet did not change 'A'isha's playful ways, and her young friends continued to regularly come to visit her in her own room. 'I would be playing with my dolls', she once said, 'with the girls who were my friends, and the Prophet would come in and they would slip out of the house and he would go out after them and bring them back, for he was pleased for my sake to have them there.' Sometimes he would say, 'Stay, where you are', before they had time to leave, and would also join in their games. 'One day', 'A'isha said, 'the Prophet came in when I was playing with my dolls and said, '''A'isha, whatever game is this?'' "It is Solomon's horses," I replied, and he laughed.' On another occasion, during the days of the Eid al-Adha, two young girls were with 'A'isha in her room, singing a song about a famous battle and beating a tambourine. 'The Messenger of Allah came in', said 'A'isha, 'and lay down with his face turned away. Then Abu Bakr came, and scolded me, saying, "What is this musical instrument of Shaytan doing in the house of the Messenger of Allah?" The Messenger of Allah turned towards him and said, "Leave them alone, for these are the days of the Eid."' This report was used subsequently as religious authority for music, albeit of a limited kind.

After a while, 'A'isha asked the girls to leave, and the Prophet asked 'A'isha whether she would like to watch the Abyssinians who were giving a fighting display with their weapons in the mosque and she said yes. 'By Allah', said 'A'isha, 'I remember the Messenger of Allah standing at the door of my room, screening me with his cloak, so that I could see the sport of the Abyssinians as they played with their spears in the mosque of the Messenger of Allah. He kept standing for my sake until I had enough and then I went back in, so you can well imagine how a young girl enjoyed watching this display.'

'A'isha seems to have been an intelligent and observant young girl with a very good memory. Her reports do a great deal to lighten the narratives describing the Prophet's life, and her contribution to the image of the Prophet is significant. 'A'isha spent the next nine years of her life with the Prophet and she is usually held to have remembered all that she saw and heard with considerable accuracy. Whereas Khadija was already a mature woman when she married the Prophet, 'A'isha was a lively young girl who still had much to learn, and she was very quick to do so; nor was she afraid to talk back in order to find out the truth or make it known to others. Whenever she beat someone else in argument, it is said that the Prophet would smile and say, 'She is the daughter of Abu Bakr!' Musa ibn Talha once said, 'I have not seen anyone more eloquent than 'A'isha.' 'A'isha became so profound in her comments that one of her contemporaries used to say that if the knowledge of 'A'isha were placed on one side of the scales and that of all other women on the other, 'A'isha's side would outweigh the other. Abu Musa once said, 'Whenever a report appeared doubtful to us, the Companions of the Prophet, and we asked 'A'isha about it, we always learned something from her about it.'

When she first came to live in the Prophet's household as a young girl, we are told that a strong and lasting friendship grew up between her and the Prophet's second wife Sawda, and Sawda took care of her along with the rest of the household. When 'A'isha grew up, Sawda, who was by then an old woman, gave up her share of the Prophet's time in favour of 'A'isha and was content to manage his household and be *umm al-mu'minin* ('The Mother of the Believers), a title of respect that was given to all of the wives of the Prophet. Their special status is reflected in that the Qur'an clearly states that no man could marry any of them after they had been married to the Prophet, for: 'The Prophet is closer to the believers than their ownselves, and his wives are as their mothers' (33.6). Also, we read:

> O you wives of the Prophet, if any of you is openly indecent, the punishment for her will be doubled – and that is easy for Allah. And whoever of you submits to Allah and His Messenger and does right, We shall give her a reward twice over and We have prepared a generous provision for her. O you wives of the Prophet, you are not like any other women. If you are fearful of Allah, then do not be soft in your speech, lest someone whose heart is sick is attracted to you, but speak words that are wise. And stay quietly in your houses, do not make a dazzling display like that of the earlier time of ignorance, and establish prayer and give money to charity and obey Allah and His Messenger. Surely Allah wishes to remove impurity far from you, O People of the

House, and to purify you completely. (33.30–33)

It was because of the Prophet Muhammad's unique station with God that his wives and his Companions were expected by Allah to behave with such respect towards the Prophet that his wives could not possibly marry anyone else after having been married to him: 'When you ask his wives for something, ask them from behind a screen. That is purer for your hearts and for their hearts. It is not for you to cause injury to the Messenger of Allah, or ever marry his wives after him. To do that would be something dreadful in the sight of Allah' (33.53).

It is not difficult to grasp the role that 'A'isha played in softening the image of the Prophet and linking him more closely to the lifestyles of his followers. During the nine years that 'A'isha was married to the Prophet she witnessed many of the significant events that shaped the destiny of the first Muslim community of Medina, and she presented a view of them which was both highly personal and compelling. It was during the course of their marriage that the direction of the qibla was changed from Jerusalem to Mecca, thereby more clearly distinguishing the Muslims from the Jews and the Christians, and it was when they were married that she must have listened to many of the Jews and the Christians and the idol worshippers who came to argue with the Prophet in the hope that they could find a plausible excuse to justify their rejection of him, which is certainly how 'A'isha represented them. It was also during the course of their marriage that drinking alcohol was finally forbidden, that it was made clear what food was halal and what food was haram, that many thought it became necessary for women to wear the hijab in public and when

praying, that the guidance as to how to fast was revealed, that paying zakat (alms) became obligatory for all Muslims, and that all the rites of the hajj were established and regularized.

In fact, every aspect of life, from birth to death and everything that happens in between, was illuminated by the way in which the Prophet behaved – and it was this way of behaviour, the sunna, that 'A'isha helped to preserve and protect, not only by embodying it herself but also by teaching it to others. 'A'isha was once asked to describe the Prophet and she replied that he was 'the Qur'an walking', meaning that his behaviour was the Qur'an translated into action. She did all that she could to do likewise. Thus she not only knew and embodied the sunna, but also she memorized the Qur'an by heart and understood it. It was during the course of their marriage that, among other things, the battles of Badr, and Uhud, and al-Khandaq (the Ditch) were fought. These were the three major battles against the Quraysh, that shifted the balance of power out of the hands of the kafirun (unbelievers) and into the hands of the Muslims. Although she was still very young, 'A'isha participated in them all, bringing water for the Muslims and helping to look after the wounded. She certainly seems to have been loath to stay at home passive.

It was when they were married that the Jews are said to have plotted and tried to kill the Prophet on more than one occasion, without success, and were punished for this. First, Jewish tribes such as the Banu Qayunqa and the Banu Nadhir were expelled from Medina; and then the Banu Qurayza – who, we are told, had broken their agreement with the Muslims during the battle of al-Khandaq and conspired to destroy them – were subjected to the punishment that was decided by the man whom they themselves had chosen to judge their actions, Sa'id ibn Mu'adh. In accordance with the commands contained in their own book, the Torah (although it is not clear where in the Torah this law is to be found), all the men were killed – with the exception of four who accepted Islam; all the women and children were taken as slaves. It was after this event that another tribe, the Banu al-Mustaliq began to prepare to fight the Muslims, and accordingly the Prophet led an army against them. This campaign led to an interesting controversy that arose in relation to the conduct of 'A'isha.

Often when the Prophet went to war, he took one of his wives with him. He did not choose anyone in particular, but simply drew lots and took the wife whose name came out. When he went to fight the Banu al-Mustaliq, the lot fell to 'A'isha. 'A'isha, who was then 13 years old, was small, slim and graceful, so that it was difficult for the men who carried her litter to know for certain whether or not she was actually inside it when they lifted it up, or so it has been said. On the way back to Medina, after the Banu al-Mustaliq had been subdued, the Muslim army stopped for a rest, but then the Prophet unexpectedly ordered the army to continue the march back. Unknown to everyone else, 'A'isha had stepped out of her litter for a few minutes and had left the camp, seeking some privacy. On her way back she had noticed that her onyx necklace was missing and so she retraced her steps to try and find it. When at last she found it and returned to the camp, it was to find that everyone had gone. The men who had been carrying her litter had thought she was still in it and had picked it up, strapped it to the camel and marched on. 'A'isha, who trusted completely in Allah, sat down and waited, hoping that someone would notice her absence and come back for her. Fortunately she did not have long to wait, for a young Muslim man named Safwan, who had fallen behind the army after taking a rest, reached the camp during the night and found her lying fast asleep.

Safwan immediately recognized her, because he had seen her in the early days before God was interpreted as having instructed women to wear the *hijab*. '*Inna lillahi wa inna ilayhi raji'un*! (Surely we come from Allah and surely to Him we return!)', he is said to have exclaimed in surprise, waking 'A'isha up with the loudness of his voice. He did not say anything else, and 'A'isha put back on the scarf that had fallen off her head while she was asleep. Safwan made his camel kneel down close to her so that she could climb up on to it, then, leading the camel by hand, he set off on foot after the army, hoping that they would soon catch up with it, which they eventually did later the next morning, since the army had halted for a rest during the hottest part of the day. Unfortunately, some slanderers who had seen Safwan and 'A'isha arrive alone together began to gossip and spread lies about them. Eventually the story reached the Prophet himself, and by then the whole community was talking about what might or might now have happened between the two young Muslims. Naturally the faithful were certain that nothing bad had happened, but the *munafiqun* (hypocrites) thought otherwise and were happy to make insinuations as to the honour of the wife of Muhammad.

When Safwan was confronted with the allegations that had been made, he replied, 'Glory be to Allah! By Allah, I have never removed the veil of any woman!', and 'A'isha also proclaimed her innocence by apparently quoting the verse 'Patience is beautiful, and Allah is my protection against what you describe'

(12.18). Just after she finished speaking, the Prophet received a direct revelation of some more *ayas* of the Qur'an, and when it was over, he smiled and said, 'Do not worry, 'A'isha, for Allah has revealed proof of your innocence.' Then the Prophet went to the mosque and recited what had just been sent down. He denounced slanderers (24.11–19) and the implication is that the stories about his wife were lies and false accusations. This account gives an excellent description of the complex ways in which the Qur'an, the *hadith* and historical events of the time are taken to play against each other. It also builds up a rich picture of the *sunna* of the Prophet, his activities and manner, which was to become such a potent source of material appropriate for emulation by future generations of Muslims.

See also: **backbiting; dreams; Judaism; music**

OLIVER LEAMAN

AKHAR

Akhar means another, the other, or a thing or a person other than the former or the first. This word appears in the Qur'an thirty-eight times. It appears in the singular and indefinite form, and without the definite article *al-* eleven times. It appears with *al-* in the singular form three times. *Akhar*, by itself, was mainly used in the description of the process of polytheism and the association of a partner with God. So this process as a broad issue has been described in the Qur'an in general terms as in 'Those who adopt, with Allah, another god' (15.96). Also, the Qur'an uses *akhar* in the position of forbidding the attribution of an associate to God: 'So call not on any other god with Allah, or thou wilt be among those under the Penalty' (26.213). In these verses *akhar* is used as an adjective referring to an alleged god with Allah. And the Qur'an warned those polytheists about claiming there is another god with Allah (*ilah akhar*). The Qur'an describes another universal topic – the creation of the human being. After the mention of the stages of human creation from a drop of water to a complete body with flesh and blood, the Qur'an says 'then We developed out of it another creature' (23.14). Once again, the word *akhar,* describing the new nature of the living person, appears without the definite article.

Al-akhar (the other) was used twice in the *sura* of Yusuf in verses 36, '... Said the other: "I see myself" (in a dream) ...' and in 41, '... as for the other, he will hang from the cross ...'. *Al-akhar*, in these examples, describes a specific person, in this case Yusuf's prison companions.

Akhir

Akhir (last one; later) is mentioned in the Qur'an twenty-eight times. The Qur'an describes God as the First and the Last. The Prophet praised God by saying, 'You are the first one and there is nothing before You, and You are the last and there is nothing after You.' The Muslim theologians described Allah as the first with no beginning, and the last without an end. However, this term *akhir* is mentioned in the Qur'an at length referring to the Day of Judgement (*al-yawm al-akhir*). This extensive use of the term indicates the importance of the belief in the Day of Judgement in Islam. The Day of Judgement is called The Last Day because there is no day after it. The term *al-yawm* (the daytime) was so called in Arabic in relation to the night that follows it. The Last Day is also referred to as The Barren Day because it will no longer bear a new night. The Muslims are addressed in the Qur'an as those who believe in Allah and the Day of Judgement. There has always been a strong connection between believing in God and the Day of Judgement in the Qur'an. The word *akhir* has a crucial use in the Qur'an pertaining to a fundamental pillar of faith. On that day Allah will exchange this familiar universe pertaining to his earthly temporary life with the unseen, permanent, everlasting world. The destiny of every soul will begin with the resurrection when Allah raises all the dead from their graves and makes them alive again to face his trial.

Al-akhira

Al-akhira (hereafter; Last Abode; next life) is mentioned in the Qur'an 116 times. It appears in almost every chapter. It is one of the most important terms in the Qur'an because it represents the foundation on which the Islamic faith was built. The faith of a Muslim is tested by belief in the hereafter. One cannot be genuinely Muslim until one believes in the unseen and still to be experienced next life. The Qur'anic message is intended for the entire universe, yet it will only be a guide for those '... who believe in the Revelation sent to you (Muhammad), and sent before you, and in their hearts they have the assurance of the hereafter' (2.4).

The hereafter has been vividly depicted in the Qur'an. It is the true life that every soul should strive to reach safely. It begins with the Day of Judgement and continues perpetually. All creatures will be divided into two major groups: the righteous believers will be welcomed to *janna* (paradise) while the disbelievers and evildoers will be sentenced to reside in *jahannam* (hellfire). So the hereafter is a life of happiness and joy for those who believed in Allah, his angels, books and his messengers, and those who did good deeds in their lives, while the disbelievers will be severely punished.

Al-akhira is very valuable. All the prophets conducted their lives and practised their religious rituals and taught their followers to pursue the hereafter. This earthly life is too short and worthless, and it is no more than a passage to real life in the hereafter. Islam insists that this temporary life is a testing period for every soul and the hereafter is the prize to be won or lost.

See also: **eschatology; heaven; hell; yawm; zuhd**

RAFIK BERJAK

'ALAQ

The linguistic definition of *'alaq* (singular *'alaqa*) is 'leech', 'medicinal leech', '(coagulated) blood', 'blood clot', or 'the early stage of the embryo'. The name of the ninety-sixth *sura* in the Qur'an is the *surat al-'Alaq*. In classical commentaries the word *'alaq* is taken to be blood and identified with *al-dam al-jamid* (mud-like blood), in accordance with the science of the time. Now the interpretation of the word has changed and the latest meaning that is given to it is 'the early stage of the embryo'.

According to Sikandar Hussain (1980), verses 1–5 of this *sura* (al-'Alaq) are the first of the Qur'an and mention the origin of humanity from *'alaq*, relating it to reading, learning and writing. He suggests that *'alaqa* is the third stage of embryogenesis as described by the Qur'an (23.14). The embryologist Keith Moore (1986) claims in his essay that the Qur'an brings to light aspects of embryology that are only now being understood, and there are several passages in which the developmental order shows the pattern of human development from the beginning (viz. 39.6; 23.13; 23.14; 32.9; and 22.5).

Bucaille (1979) also rejects the classical translation of *'alaq* as 'blood clot', and 'adhesion'. He says that 'something which clings' is the translation of the word *'alaq*, by which he meant 'egg'. He claims that it is the original meaning of the word. A meaning derived from it – 'blood clot' – often figures in translation; it is a mistake against which one should guard: humanity has never passed through the stage of being a 'blood clot'.

References and further reading

Asad, M. (1984) *The Message of the Qur'an* (Translation and Explanation of the Qur'an), trans. M. Asad, Gibraltar: Dar al-andalus.

Bucaille, M. (1979) *The Bible the Qur'an and Science*, trans. A. Pannell, Indianapolis: American Trust Publications.

Hussain, S. (1980) 'The Clot (al-'Alaq)', *Islamic Quarterly* 24: 107–10.

al-Mawdudi, Syed Abul A'la (1973–1988) *The Meaning of the Qur'an*, trans. 'Abdul 'Aziz Kamal, Delhi and Lahore: Islamic Publications.

Moore, K. (1986) 'A Scientist's Interpretation of References to Embryology in the Qur'an', *Journal of the Islamic Medical Association* 18, Jan.–June. 15–16.

HARUN SAHIN

See also: **Creation**

ALCOHOL
see: **intoxication**

'ALI IBN ABI TALIB

'Ali's name is inextricably linked with the Qur'an, but despite much that has been written on him, his pride of place with regard to his unique, profound knowledge of the Qur'an is yet to be explored. He was not only one of the finest reciters of the Qur'an, he was also, as sources reveal, exceptionally skilful and adept with regards to its contents. His extraordinary knowledge of the Qur'an as well as his influence on later generations is well documented in the earliest surviving sources – Shi'i, Sunni and Sufi. Traditions are replete with examples of his wisdom and deep understanding of the Book as well as his distinction and judiciousness in passing legal judgments based on his knowledge of the Qur'an. These have come down to us in the form of *qadaya*, or legal decisions that he gave during the Prophet's lifetime as well as during the reigns of the early caliphs including his own caliphate. The title al-Dayyan meaning 'the Judge' is usually reserved for God but according to the *Lisan al-'Arab* people applied it to 'Ali b. Abi Talib as the sage of the community.

Among the many companions of the Prophet who claim a special place in the general exegeses of the Qur'an, a few names stand out including those of 'Abd Allah ibn 'Abbas, 'Abd Allah ibn Mas'ud, 'Ubayy ibn Ka'b and 'Ali ibn Abi Talib. Early reports by al-Dhahabi suggest that Ibn 'Abbas credited all his interpretation of the Qur'an to 'Ali while Ibn Mas'ud reports that 'Ali possessed both the outer and the inner Qur'an. This statement is significant when we take into consideration that 'Ali referred to himself as *natiq al-Qur'an* at Siffin when the opponents tried to hurriedly end the conflict by raising leaves of the Qur'an on spearheads.

'Ali's crucial role in history is acknowledged by all Muslims. He is held as a great champion of Islam in its early struggle to survive, and as one of the Rightly Guided caliphs who features as the fountainhead of esoteric knowledge. 'Ali figures at the head of most of the initiatory chains (*silsilas*) of Sufi orders and he is also credited with laying down the first rules of Arabic grammar. The Shi'a, however, see in 'Ali a unique spiritual function alongside that of the Prophet that gave him pre-eminence and endowed him with the right to the leadership or Imamate. The Prophet Muhammad's affection and regard for

'Ali were evident to all. They had the same grandfather, being first cousins, and besides that 'Ali later married Fatima, the Prophet's daughter. In addition, Ibn Ishaq notes that the youthful 'Ali had been brought up in Muhammad's care, and was the first male to believe in him and accept the message of Islam. Muhammad himself had been brought up in the household of 'Ali's father, Abu Talib, who at the time was the chief of the Banu Hashim clan of the Quraysh. He died in 40/661.

References in the Qur'an

The close kin (*ahl al-bayt*) of the Prophet enjoyed an exclusive status during his lifetime, recognized by the Qur'an. 'Ali had a special rapport with the Prophet which did not remain unnoticed within the community. 'Ali was, as is known, singled out by the Prophet for many important tasks that involved many far-reaching decisions, either preceded or followed by Qur'anic injunctions. When aged only 13, 'Ali responded to the Prophet's earliest request for help when the injunction was revealed: 'And warn thy clan, thy nearest of kin' (26.214). The task of communicating the *sura al-Bara'a* to the people of Mecca, following a Qur'anic revelation was eventually given to 'Ali. In the episode of *mubahala* (mutual cursing) connected with the Qur'anic verse 3.61, revealed when the Christian delegation from Najran visited the Prophet in the year 10/631–2, the Prophet decided to take his family – 'Ali, Fatima, Hasan and Husayn. The Qur'an provides numerous instances where the family (*ahl al-bayt, aal, ahl, dhurriya, qurba* and *itrat*) are given more honour and privileges than other believers. The narratives in the Qur'an regarding the preceding prophets and their descendants are also quite explicit about their status, rank and unique position. In Shi'i literature, 'Ali and the *imams* in the Qur'an are therefore these descendants of the Prophet referred to also as the signs of God, the way, the straight path, the light of God, the inheritors of the Book, the people of knowledge, the holders of authority and other such designations.

'Ali and the exegeses of the Qur'an – *tafsir* and *ta'wil*

'Ali has a distinct place in the genesis of the Qur'anic exegesis. His profound and extraordinary knowledge of the Qur'an is well attested in early and medieval sources, although not evidently so in modern scholarship. Muhammad envisaged that 'Ali would have to fight for the *ta'wil* – interpretation of the Qur'an – just as he fought for its *tanzil* (the revelation). Early traditional literature such as the *Sahih al-Bukhari* record that 'Ali b. Abi Talib possessed both the inner and the outer aspects of the Qur'an. His exceptional wisdom and influence are attested to in various historical, exegetical, biographical, traditional, mystical, poetical and legal works. Traditions such as "Ali is with the Qur'an and the Qur'an is with 'Ali' and 'I am the city of knowledge and 'Ali is its gate' are indications of his exclusive erudition regarding the Book of God. Sunni and Shi'i commentators concur that the Qur'anic verse 2.269 on wisdom refers to 'Ali who was graced with this unique gift. Tradition maintains that wisdom is divided into ten parts, nine of which were with 'Ali while the remaining is disseminated among other people.

In esoteric Islam the revelations of the Qur'an are regarded as symbolic expressions in human language of inner spiritual realities. It thus contains more profound depth and understanding than what is apparent, and this deep, inner meaning is extracted through *ta'wil* – causing something to return to its origin. In Abu Ya'qub al-Sijistani's *Kitab al-Iftikhar*, for instance, Muhammad is the *natiq* (proclaimer) receiving the revelation (*tanzil*) and giving the *shari'a*, while 'Ali as his associate (*wasi*) explains the inner meaning (*batin*) through the science of *ta'wil*. He is therefore the master of *ta'wil* and *haqa'iq*, explaining the true meaning of the Qur'an and the inner truths of religion.

'Ali is also portrayed as one of the four wellsprings: namely, intellect (*'aql*), soul (*nafs*), proclaimer (*natiq*) and executor (*wasi*). The other term used for 'Ali is *asas* (founder or foundation), as he not only founded the historical line of the Imamate but also his successors' knowledge of the divine mysteries derived from him. The inner and the outer aspects are not independent but interdependent and complementary to each other; they are intertwined like the body and the soul according to the *Shawahid wa'l-bayan* of Ja'far b. Mansur al-Yaman. Neither can be functional without the other, just as a body without the soul is unfit for life and the soul's existence is impossible to prove without the body. Al-Sijistani explains this succinctly in his *Kitab al-Maqalid,* referring to the *tanzil* as the raw material and the *ta'wil* as the manufactured goods. The function of the *ta'wil* comes after the *tanzil* just as a craftsman is unable to operate without raw materials.

'Ali's role as an Imam was also accomplished through the *ta'wil* of the Qur'an by unfolding layers of meanings within the verses for those capable of understanding. The knowledge that he imparted to some specific individuals, including Salman al-Farisi and Kumayl b. Ziyad, was special, allowing them to comprehend the Qur'an experientially. His unique gift and miraculous ability lay in enabling people to understand

and emulate Muhammad's inexplicable spiritual phenomenon. Many recognize this pre-eminent role of his as the supreme *wali* whose love for God – losing oneself in the essence of God – is epitomized in the tradition 'he who knows his self, knows his Lord'. When 'Ali referred to his intimate disciples as his Shi'a – his followers during the lifetime of the Prophet – as attested in early historical sources such as the *Kitab al-zina* of Abu Hatim al-Razi, it is in the sense of initiating them into their own inner reality.

'Ali and the compilation of the Qur'an

Scholars are unanimous regarding the fact that 'Ali possessed his own transcript of the text of the Qur'an that he had collected himself, and his version, although not available, is therefore the first compilation ever of the Qur'an. This is recorded in numerous traditions reported in both Sunni and Shi'i sources. The unique aspect about this version was that it had been collected in the order it was sent and Companions such as Ibn Sirin, among others, have regretted the loss of this text. Evidence of this is to be found in sources such as Ibn Sa'd's *Tabaqat*, al-Baladhuri's *Ansab* and al-Suyuti's *Itqan*. Frequently, 'Ali is known to have reminded people to 'ask me before you lose me ... there is not a single verse of which I do not know whether it was sent down at night or during the day, or whether it was revealed on a plain or in a mountain'.

Alongside this is the belief that the versions compiled by 'Ali and those by 'Abd Allah b. Mas'ud, 'Ubayy b. Ka'b and others were not the same as those collected by Zayd b. Thabit's group. It is true that it was some time before this version later became the official one under 'Uthman. This is well attested in the early historical, biographical and exegetical sources but it was not until the early nineteenth century that modern scholarship first raised these issues, with Garcin de Tassy publishing in 1842 the additional chapter of the two lights. This received a critical review from Mirza Kazem Beg, who doubted the first of the two chapters. Saint Clair Tisdall (1913) accepted its possible authenticity and also discovered the *sura al-Walaya*, in which 'Ali's name is explicitly mentioned. The explicit mention of 'Ali's name is found also in *Kitab al-Qira'a* by Abu 'Abd Allah al-Sayyari (ninth century), which, however, does not include the *sura al-Walaya* (see Amir-Moezzi, 1994). Schwally considers the appearance of this *sura* late, although outlines several *suras* that were abbreviated. Examples of this include *sura al-Nur, sura al-Hijr* and *sura al-Ahzab* (Nöldeke and Schwally, 1909).

The basic premise in early Shi'i Ithna'ashari literature is that certain changes in the order of verses and *suras* did take place and that there are variant readings, *tabdil*, exchange of words such as *umma* to *a'imma*, rearrangement of words and deletion of words such as *fi 'Ali, Al-Muhammad, fi walayat 'Ali* in the extant text. A list of variant readings and additions found in early Shi'i Ithna'ashari literature is described by Meir M. Bar-Asher, who outlines the clear distinction between scholars of the Buwayhid period (334/945–447/1055) who display a tolerant attitude exemplified by al-Tusi and al-Tibrisi, and the early exegetes such as Furat al-Kufi, al-Qummi and al-'Ayyashi who had concerns with the existing text. Generally, Shi'i Ismai'ili works highlighting the *ta'wil* remain silent on aspects of change, substitution or alteration. But in Ibn al-Haytham's *Kitab al-Munazarat*, there is a record of not only numerous verses revealed in relation to

'Ali and his Imamate but also specific mention of the words *'aliyyan, 'aliyyun* and *'alayya* in the extant text, referring actually to 'Ali according to grammatical rules. Examples of these are: 'In the mother of the Book which is with Us, he is 'Ali, full of wisdom' (43.4); 'We appointed for them 'Ali as a voice of truth' (19.50); and 'This is the straight path of 'Ali' (15.41).

Additional research on early manuscripts of the Qur'an in San'a by G.R. Puin (1996) proposes that even more varied arrangements of the Qur'an existed besides those of Ibn Mas'ud and 'Ubayy b. Ka'b. Evidence of this in their respective *Mushafs* as well as in the Sana'ni manuscripts would, however, invalidate the assertion that all *suras* were put in their definitive form during Muhammad's lifetime. It would seem fair to suggest that the compilation of the Qur'an took place after the Prophet's death and that 'Ali was the first to do so from the version that he himself had collected over the years that he had known the Prophet intimately. 'Ali's version, although regrettably not available, did become dispersed through his family's teachings, especially those of al-Baqir and al-Sadiq, both of whom were well-known authorities on the Qur'an.

Further reading

Amir-Moezzi, M.A. (1994) *The Divine Guide in Early Shi'ism*, trans. David Streight, Albany, NY: SUNY Press.

Ayoub, M.M. (1988) 'The Speaking Qur'an and the Silent Qur'an: A study of the principles and development of Imami Tafsir', in A. Rippin (ed.) *Approaches to the History of the Interpretation of the Qur'an*, Oxford: Clarendon Press, 177–98.

al-Dhahabi, M. Husayn (2000) *al-Tafsir wa'l mufassirun,* 2nd edn, 2 vols, Beirut: Dar al-yusuf.

Garcin de Tassy, A. (1842) 'Chapitre inconnu du Coran', *Journal Asiatique* 13, May.

Ibn Sa'd (1957–60) *Tabaqat al-Kubra*, Beirut: Dar Sadir, Vol. 2.

Jeffery, A. (1937) *Materials for the History of the Text of the Qur'an*, Leiden: E.J. Brill.

Kohlberg, E. (1972) 'Some Notes on the Imamite Attitude to the Qur'an', in S.M. Stern *et al.* (eds) *Islamic Philosophy and the Classical Tradition: Essays presented to Richard Walzer*, Oxford: Bruno Cassirer, 209–24.

Lalani, A. (2000) *Early Shi'i Thought: The teachings of Imam Muhammad al-Baqir*, London: I.B. Tauris.

—— (2003) 'Judgment', in *EQ*, Vol. 3, 64–8.

Lawson, B.T. (1991) 'Note for the Study of the Shi'i Qur'an', *JJournal of Semitic Studies* 36: 279–95.

Madelung, W. (1997) *The Succession to Muhammad: A study of the early caliphate*, Cambridge: Cambridge University Press.

Meir, M. (1993) 'Variant Readings and Additions of the Imami-Shi'a to the Qur'an', *Israel Oriental Studies*, 13: 39–74.

—— (1999) *Scripture and Exegesis in Early Imami Shiism*, Jerusalem: Magnes Press.

Momen, M. (1985) *An Introduction to Shi'i Islam*, New Haven, CT: Yale University Press.

Nöldeke, T. and Schwally, F. (1909) *Geschichte des Qorans: Über den Ursprung des Qorans*, Leipzig: Dietrich'sche Verlagsbuchhandlung.

Poonawala, I. (1988) 'Isma'ili ta'wil of the Qur'an', in A. Rippin (ed.) *Approaches to the History of the Interpretation of the Qur'an*, Oxford: Clarendon Press, 199–222.

Puin, G. (1996) 'Observations on Early Qur'an Manuscripts in San'a', in Stefan Wild (ed.) *The Qur'an as Text*, Leiden: E.J. Brill.

al-Qadi al-Nu'man (1951–61) *Da'a'im al-Islam*, Cairo: Dar al-ma'arif; English trans., *The Pillars of Islam*, Vol. 1, trans. Asaf A.A. Fyzee, 2002; rev. I.K. Poonawala, New Delhi: Oxford University Press.

al-Qummi, 'Ali b. Ibrahim (1968) *Tafsir al-Qummi*, ed. Tayyib al-Musawi al-Jaza'iri, Beirut: Matba't al-Najaf.

al-Razi, Abu Hatim (1972) *Kitab al-zina* (Excerpts), in 'Abd Allah al-Samarra'i (ed.) *al-Ghuluww wa al-firaq al-ghaliyya fi al-hadarat al-Islamiyya*, Baghdad: Dar al-hurriya.

Saint Clair Tisdall (1913) 'Shi'ah Additions to the Koran', *Muslim World*, 3, July, 3.

al-Tabari, Abu Ja'far Muhammad b. Jarir (1954) *Jami' al-bayan 'an ta'wil ay al-Qur'an*, Cairo: Mustafa al-Babi al-Halabi and sons.

al-Walid, Ali b. Muhammad (1967) *Taj al-'aqa'id wa ma'dan al-fawa'id*, ed. Aref Tamer, Beirut: Dar al-machreq.

al-Yaman, Ja'far b. Mansur (1984) *Kitab al-Kashf*, Beirut: Dar al-andalus.

al-Ya'qubi (1960) *Ta'rikh*, Beirut: Dar Sadir, Vols 1 and 2.

See also: **caliph; Shi'a**

ARZINA R. LALANI

AL-'ALLAF, ABU'L HUDAYL

Abu'l Hudayl Muhammad b. al-Hudayl b. Abd Allah al-'Allaf al-Basri was born in Basra around 135/752 and died in Samarra around 235/850. He was a significant thinker in early Islam and a founder of the Basran branch of the Mu'tazilite school of thought.

Probably of Persian descent, Abu'l Hudayl spent a great part of his life at Basra, where he studied with Uthman b. Khalid al-Tawil, Bishr b. Sa'id and Abu 'Uthman Zafarani, all students of Wasil b. Ata. From an early age, Abu'l Hudayl joined scholarly debates and also studied philosophy through the Arabic translations which were available to him. Later when he moved to Baghdad, Abu'l Hudayl was admitted to the court circle during the time of Harun Rashid and al-Ma'mun, and there he met with a number of scholars and had lively discussions with them. He spent the last years of his life in Samarra where he died at the grand age of a hundred years.

Abu'l Hudayl, together with Wasil b. 'Ata and Amr b. 'Ubayd, was an important figure in the formation of the Mu'tazilite school of thought. He taught a number of students, among whom were Nazzam, Shahham, Thumama b. Ashras, Ja'far b. Harb. Abu'l Hudayl was also a prolific writer; he wrote a number of works related to different theological issues and polemical works against different religious and philosophical groups. None of his works is extant, hence the only way to determine his views is to look at the works of figures such as al-Ash'ari, al-Baghdadi, al-Shahrastani, Khayyat and 'Abd al-Jabbar.

For Abu'l Hudayl, apart from the senses, reason and true reports are the sources of human knowledge. Any religious report can be accepted only if it is reported by at least one of the candidates for paradise, in other words, by a true believer. The world consists of atoms. Bodies are agglomerates of atoms held together through the accidents of composition, juxtaposition, contiguity and conjunction. There are basic accidents inherent in every single atom, such as movement or rest, contiguity or isolation, and being. Some of the accidents may endure over a succession of moments, some of them are instantaneous. Since atoms are finite and hence created, the world is also finite and created.

Abu'l Hudayl defines man as this visible body that eats and drinks. Although he uses the terms soul (*nafs*), spirit (*ruh*) and life, their relation to the body is not clear. Our power of acting is the permanent accident that characterizes us as fundamentally moral. Only voluntary actions belong to us. Will presupposes knowledge, which is either innate or acquired. Abu'l Hudayl considers sense perception, natural knowledge of God, perception of good and evil and that good may be pursued and evil avoided as all innate. Hence, every human being has an innate knowledge of God's existence. Although he affirms in God a number of attributes, he does not consider God's essence different from his attributes. God created humanity for their wellbeing. Hence, although he is able, God's doing evil to them is inconceivable.

Again, God always does what is most salutary for mankind.

Abu'l Hudayl considers the Qur'an as the greatest miracle. For him there will always be some saints in the world, protected from committing any sin. There will be reward and punishment in the life to come. However, since the world has a beginning and an end, at a certain moment all movement in heaven and hell will cease and will be converted into a state of eternal consummation.

Further reading

Frank, R. (1966) *The Metaphysics of Created Being According to Abu'l Hudayl al-'Allaf*, Istanbul: Nederlands Historich Archaeologish Institute in Het Nabije Oosten.
—— (1969) 'The Divine Attributes According to Abu'l Hudayl al-'Allaf', *Le Muséon* 82, 3–4: 451–506.

OLIVER LEAMAN

ALLAH

The concept of God in the Qur'an

All Muslims across the world believe that there is only one God, who has created 'the heavens, the earth and what is between'. The expression of this faith takes place in the first part of the *shahada*, or the statement of faith: 'there is no deity but God and Muhammad is His Messenger'. The statement is repeated by Muslims in their five daily prayers, in the call for prayer and in their daily lives. To believe in one God constitutes the central issue in Islam. The Qur'an presents the Arabic name of God as Allah. Unlike the ancient Greek god Zeus, or the Hindu god Vishnu, Allah, who has ninety-nine beautiful names, is the same God of Christianity and Judaism.

Etymology

According to Muslim theologians, the name Allah can be defined as 'The proper name of the One who is necessarily existent in himself and deserves all praises'. Indicating the oneness of God, the word has no plural form and no one can be named with it except God. Creatures can be related to it as *'abd* or servant, such as 'Abd-Allah or the servant of God. The root of the name is *al-ilah*, meaning 'the God'. The word *ilah* (pl. *'aliha*) in Arabic is used as a generic term for deities. In order to ease the usage, Arabs frequently contract the words based on certain grammatical rules. Therefore, the two words, *al* and *ilah*, were contracted into one and became Allah. The name 'Allah' is referred to in the Qur'an 2,697 times.

Despite their polytheistic traditions, Arabs before Islam were also familiar with the name Allah as the name of the Supreme Being in heaven, which is evident in the Prophet's father's name, 'Abdullah, the servant of Allah. The Qur'an refers to their familiarity with Allah in the following verse: 'If you ask them who has created the heavens and the earth, they will say Allah'. Accordingly, the Holy Book speaks of false gods of Meccans, who were considered mediators between human beings and Allah. The Holy Book ridicules them for worshipping powerless stones and wood.

Although scholars link the name Allah with El or Elohim, terms for God in Hebrew, most Muslim theologians and linguists believe that the origin of the name is Arabic. Regardless of the origin of the name, Muslims believe that Allah is the same God as that of Christianity and Judaism. It is he who sent the Torah to Moses and the Gospel to Jesus. He is the true God of all creation.

Existence of God

Scholastic Muslim theologians have developed many arguments to prove the existence of God. Two of them are well known in Islamic theology: *huduth* (creation) and *imkan* (contingency) arguments. The first argument proves that the universe existed and cannot come into being without the One who originates it. Therefore it cannot be created by itself. Unlike the Aristotelian argument, which operates on the principle of causality, in this argument the world is not eternal. The Qur'an uses the *huduth* argument in various verses without referring to the term itself. Therefore, the world is originated and needs an originator. In other words, whatever exists must have a sufficient cause for its existence. The latter argument is based on the view that what exists is divided into two categories. The first category is one whose existence is necessary in itself. The other category is one whose existence depends on others. The goal of this argument is to prove that there is only one thing that necessarily exists. It argues that the world's creation is contingent (*mumkin*), and a contingent thing cannot be created by another contingent thing. Otherwise it would lead to an infinite series of contingent causes. Consequently, it needs the One who is necessarily existent in himself. All other causes found in the universe are contingent, thus there must be an uncaused cause or the Cause of Causes (*musabbib al-asbab*) to create them.

Through a sustained examination of the Qur'anic verses, one finds a variety of arguments to prove the existence of God. Besides the above-mentioned two arguments, the argument from universal consent and teleological argument are among those arguments found in the Qur'an under various names. The wonderful design of the universe, which is the basis of the teleological argument, is frequently referred to as a point of contemplation in the Qur'an. This marvellous and interrelated system of order cannot have been brought about by chance. As thinkers such as Nursi point out, whoever created the eye of the mosquito is the same person who created the solar system. That is because they are interrelated; the eyes of a mosquito are designed in accordance with the level of the sunlight. 'It is He who has created seven heavens in harmony. You cannot see any fault in the Beneficent One's creation; then look again: Can you see any flaw?' (67.3)

The Holy Book invites human beings to contemplate the ways of God. The Qur'an calls it 'signs' or *ayat*. Various verses condemn those who do not use their minds and reason to understand the signs of God in the universe and in their own creation. The Qur'an encourages people to appreciate God's signs, since they are intelligent creatures. The verse says: 'We have sent down upon you signs, clear indications, and none denies their truth save the transgressors' (2.99). The word 'sign' is repeated many times in the Qur'an. Everything in the heavens and the earth gives news of God, and they are signs of God. Everything that happens tells us something about God. Therefore, in the heavens, in the natural world, in historical events, and inside us, are signs of God. 'We [God] have appointed the night and the day as two signs' (17.12). 'A sign for them is the dead earth which we brought to life, and from which we brought forth grain that they eat' (36.33). 'And of His signs is the creation of the heavens and earth, and the variety of your tongues and colours' (30.22). 'Of His signs are the ships that run on the sea like landmarks' (42.32). 'In the earth are signs for those having certainty, and in yourselves' (51.20–21). In short, everything is a sign because all things are God's creatures. Referring to the verse 'For people who think intelligently there are signs in the creation of the heavens and earth and in the alteration of night and day' (3.190), the Prophet of Islam says, 'Woe to those who read this and do not contemplate'. The Qur'anic text provides another significant reference to the signs of God:

> Your God is one God: There is no God but He. He is the most Merciful, the Most Compassionate. For a people who think intelligently, there are signs in the creation of the heavens and earth, in the alteration of night and day, in ships which voyage on the seas to benefit people, in the waters God sends down from heaven giving life to the earth after it was dead, in the populating of the earth with every kind of living creature, in the hither and thither of winds and clouds harnessed to His purposes between sky and land. (2.163–4).

Muslim theologians such as Abu Mansur al-Maturidi (d. 944 CE), Sayf al-Din al-'Amidi (d. 1233 CE), Nasr al-Din al-Tusi (d. 1274 CE), Adud al-Din al-'Iji (d. 1355 CE) refer to the Qur'anic verses relating to the creation of heavens and earth as well as the creation of human beings in their arguments designed to prove the existence of God. The Qur'an contains many verses that refer to the amazing design and order in all creation. Abu Hanifa (d. 767 CE), founder of the Hanafi school of Islamic law, offers the parable of a ship in the ocean. Such a ship needs to have a captain who will guide it in the right direction.

The Qur'an also refers to aesthetic arguments on various occasions. On the creation of heavens and earth the Book says that God has ornamented (*zayanna*) the sky for you with stars (67.5), and that He has made your water pure (*ma'in*) (67.30). Furthermore it eloquently refers to the beautiful creation of the human being and rebukes the heedless: 'man! What has seduced you from your gracious Lord? He who created you, and fashioned you, who proportioned you suitably, and in the form He wished He contrived you' (82.6–8). 'Surely We have created human beings in the best fashion' (95.4). The Qur'an emphatically refers to God's attribute of creation (*al-khaliq*): 'Have they not beheld the heaven above them, how We established and adorned it in its unbroken reach? The earth We stretched out, setting there on the mighty hills, where We made every kind of joyous thing to grow; a vision and a reminder for every penitent servant' (50.6–8). With reference to the creation of the human being, the Qur'an repeats again the beauty of its form. 'He created the heavens and the earth with the real, formed you and made your form beautiful, and to Him is your return' (64.3).

The nature of God

Muslim theologians believe that the first thing to learn is knowledge about God. Al-Razi (d. 1209) says that the knowledge which is compulsory for every Muslim is the knowledge of God. There have been many attempts to elaborate on God's essence. It is often assumed that the question of God's nature has occupied the minds of early Muslims, and as such the Prophet forbade them from thinking about it. 'Think about God's bounties, but do not think about God's essence (*dhat*). Otherwise, you will vanish.' God's essence (*dhat*) cannot be understood by the limited human capacity. A famous statement with regard to the nature of God has dominated Islamic theology for centuries: 'Whatever comes to your mind about His nature, God is different than that'. He is unique, is unlike all creation, and

nothing is like Him' (see 42.11). He is immeasurably distinct from every creature. According to the teachings of Islam, we, as human beings, are distant from God while he is closer to us than our jugular vein. A contemporary Islamic thinker, Bediuzzaman Said Nursi (d. 1960), elaborates on this by employing the parable of the sun and its light. We are distant from the sun, but it is close to us through its heat, light and reflections, as the whole sun can be reflected in the eyes of an individual. Consequently, human beings are unable to comprehend the essence of God, but they are able to manifest his attributes and his names, and to conceive these manifestations in themselves as well as in other creatures. The concept of the creation of humans in God's image has no reference in the Qur'an; however, the *hadith* refers to the notion of his image. The Prophet says, 'God has created humans in the image of *al-rahman*.' According to some theologians, the Prophet indicates that a human being constitutes the most reflective mirror of *al-Rahman's* name, as far as the manifestation of God's names is concerned.

Yet the subtle question of the knowability of God remains. First of all, we cannot understand God's nature, but can comprehend and attain the knowledge of him according to our level through reflection on God's names. For instance, one of God's beautiful names is *al-'alim* ('the Most Knowledgeable'). Intuitively, humans know that their knowledge is limited, but at the same time they are fully aware of the concept of knowledge and the meaning of being knowledgeable about certain objects. This limited knowledge becomes a measure for human beings to imagine, although in a limited way, the unlimited knowledge of God. His essence is beyond knowledge, we know in a limited way, through his attributes. All his attributes are absolute, because nothing can be compared to him. Even the Prophet Muhammad, the most knowledgeable man about God in Islam, in one of his invocations confesses his limitation: 'Lord, we have not known you as you deserve.' The only one who knows God's essence is God himself. Accordingly, prophets, saints and the righteous know God, yet they know him through his attributes and names, not his essence. And even this knowledge is not an easy task. Sufis, the mystics of Islam, believe that over seventy veils remain as obstacles in the way of attaining knowledge of God. To remove each veil requires an enormous amount of spiritual effort. One might try to reach God through removing all these veils. Paradoxically, the Prophet narrates a statement from God (*hadith qudsi*) in which he says: 'The heavens and the earth cannot encompass Me, but I dwell in the heart of My believers.' Students of the mystical path in Islam have made attempts to experience the knowledge of God. They developed a three-stage pattern: belief in God (*iman billah*); knowledge of God (*ma'rifatullah*); and love of God (*muhabetullah*). The highest of these stages seems to be love of God.

According to the Qur'an, God has revealed himself through his messengers in general and through Muhammad, the seal of the prophets, in particular. Muhammad received divine revelation from God over a period of twenty-three years, and the total of this revelation constitutes the Holy Book of Islam, the Qur'an. Muhammad's first experience of the divine presence and heavenly revelation represent a remarkable event in the history of Islam. In this very first experience, the archangel Gabriel (Jibril) becomes visible to Muhammad and reveals several short verses in which God describes himself as the One who has created humans (*khalaq al-insan*)

and has taught them (*'allama*) what they knew not. The active particle of both verbs has been repeatedly stated in the Qur'an among God's most beautiful names. Therefore, two points can be derived from these early verses. The first point is the concept of *tawhid*, the oneness of God: 'Your God is one God' (41.6). The opposite of *tawhid* is *shirk*, that is to claim a partnership with God, or to worship someone along with God: 'Worship God, and do not associate any others with Him' (4.36). Another verse says, 'Do not associate others with God. To associate others is a mighty wrong' (31.13). The central message of the Qur'an is the avoidance of associating others with God: 'God forgives not that any others should be associated with him, but less than that He forgives to whomsoever He will' (4.48). The Qur'an, by emphasizing the concept of *tawhid*, ultimately challenges the main religious traditions of the time, in particular the Meccan idol worshippers who had been housing 360 idols in the Holy Shrine, the *Ka'ba*, for centuries. The Qur'an also challenges the Christian Trinity as well as the claim of attributing a son to God. 'And the Jews say: Ezra is the son of Allah and the Christians say: the Messiah is the son of Allah. That is their saying with their mouths. They imitate the saying of those who disbelieved of old' (9.30). One of the short chapters of the Qur'an, which is considered one-third of the Holy Book in value as far as recitation is concerned, puts this challenge very eloquently: 'He is God, One, and God, the Everlasting Refuge, who has not begotten, and has not been begotten, and equal to Him is not any one' (112.1–4). He is exalted from being physically involved in any act of creation. His command for creation is 'Be! And it is' (2.117). Nothing can be seen as too hard to him; for him there is no difference between the creation of a fly and an elephant.

One of the most controversial issues in relation to the divine nature is the question of God's visibility (*ru'yatullah*). The Qur'anic verse says: 'The eyes cannot see him, but He can see eyes' (6.103). The majority of Muslim theologians accept that God can be seen, but not through our naked eyes. When a Companion asks the Prophet 'Have you seen your Lord?', the Prophet replies, 'Yes, with my heart.' Islamic scholars refer to the Qur'anic verses related to the story of Moses when he asks God to show himself to him. If it was impossible, a prominent messenger of God such as Moses would not ask such a question as this would imply ignorance about his Lord. Consequently, according to the Qur'an, God did not reject his request and asks him to look at the mountain. One of the Qur'anic verses represents a significant reference for the view of the majority, which suggests that on the Day of Judgement some of us will look joyfully at our Lord (75.22–23). Indeed, in the body of *hadith* one can find references to divine visibility in the afterlife when the Prophet says, 'You will see your Lord on the Day of Judgement, as you see the moon.'

Attributes and names of God

The Qur'an uses various names related to God. All chapters of the Qur'an with one exception, start with one of the most known phrases in the Islamic tradition: 'In the name of God the Most Compassionate (*al-Rahman*), the Most Merciful (*al-Rahim*)'. The term used in the Qur'an for name is '*i-s-m* (pl. '*asma'*) and the Qur'an employs both singular and plural forms of the word in various verses. For God's attributes, Muslim theologians use the term *sifa* (pl. *sifat*). This term is not used in the Holy Book,

yet as a topic it comprises a great component of the Qur'an. Before examining the names of God, it is significant to give some examples of his attributes, which are divided into two groups. The first group are those related to God's essence:

1. *wujud* (Existence). This attribute designates that God is necessarily existent in himself (*Wajib al-Wujud*). In other words, God's existence is not preceded by non-existence. All other creatures are *hadith* or created in time. To come into the realm of existence, they need someone whose existence is necessary in himself.
2. *qidam* (Divine Eternity). God is eternal, and has no beginning and no end.
3. *baqa* (Divine Permanence). Everything in the universe eventually will vanish except God.
4. *mukhalafa li'l-hawadith* (Divine Dissimilarity to Created Things). Nothing is like God. He is different to everything that one can imagine.
5. *qiyam bi nafsih* (Divine Self Subsistence). In order to continue his existence, God does not need support from anyone or anywhere.

The second group of attributes are those related to God's actions:

1. *qudra* (Divine Power). God has power over everything; nothing can be out of his control or his power.
2. *irada* (Divine Will). Nothing can happen without God's will. His divine will encompasses everything in the universe. He has given human beings a limited will so they become responsible for their actions.
3. *'ilm* (Divine Knowledge). God is omniscient. He has infinite knowledge of all things both actual and

possible. A leaf cannot fall down without his knowledge.

4. *hayat* (Divine Life). God has an infinitely perfect life which is the source of all lives in the universe. Every living creature takes its life from the divine life.

5. *kalam* (Divine Speech). Allah speaks to his messengers from behind a veil. The divine scriptures such as the Torah, the Psalms, the Gospels and the Qur'an are his speeches at the level of humans. If they were at his level no one would be able to hear it. Muslim theologians refer to the story of Moses. On the Mount of Sinai he endured to hear only a few words of God's speech and then fainted. When Moses asked God if this was the way of his speech, God said, 'Moses, I have the power of all languages.' All speeches on the face of the earth are reflections of this divine speech.

6. *sam* (Divine Hearing). God hears everything from the lowest to the highest sounds. Theologians state that he hears the sound of the feet of an ant moving around in the darkness of the night. He hears the cry of all his servants, the supplications of all his righteous people, the prayer of all his creatures. 'Call on Me; I shall answer you' (40.60).

7. *basar* (Divine Sight). Nothing can be hidden from God's sight. He sees everything in the universe every moment. All eyes of creatures are the reflections of this divine attribute. Only the one who sees everything perfectly can give sight to God's creatures. The Qur'an refers to all these attributes virtually in every page. It would not be an exaggeration to state that one quarter of the Qur'an is about God.

In reference to God's names, the Qur'an employs the term *al-'asma' al-husna* (the Most Beautiful Names), which is referred to four times in the Qur'an on various occasions. 'Say Muhammad! Call upon God or call upon the Merciful (*al-Rahman*); whichsoever you call upon, to Him belongs the names, Most Beautiful' (17.110). The Qur'an portrays about fifteen names of God together in the following verses:

> He is Allah, than whom there is no other God, the Knower of the invisible and the visible. He is the Beneficent, the Merciful. He is Allah, than whom there is no other God, the Sovereign Lord, the Holy One, Peace, the Keeper of Faith, the Guardian, the Majestic, the Compeller, and the Superb. Glorified be Allah from all that they ascribe as partner (unto Him). He is Allah, the Creator, the Shaper out of naught, the Fashioner. To Him belong the most beautiful names. All that is in the heavens and the earth glorifies Him, and He is the Mighty, the Wise'. (59.22–24)

The Qur'an does not present any reference to the number of God's beautiful names. Traditionally Muslim theologians speak of the ninety-nine names of God. The number can increase to 313, if the names related to God's actions are included. The number ninety-nine derives, in fact, from a tradition narrated by Abu Hurayra in which the Prophet says: 'There are ninety-nine names of God. Whosoever memorizes and accepts these names will enter paradise.' In another version of the same *hadith* all names are listed. Scholars of Islamic theology have come to a consensus that the above-mentioned tradition is not meant to limit the number of God's names, but to give an idea of his many names. In fact, there are some names, such as *al-nasir* (the Helper), *al-mawla* (the Friend) and *al-ghalib* (the

Defeater) cited in the Qur'an, but not found in the list provided by the afore-mentioned *hadith*. Furthermore, if one calculates the names mentioned in the two versions of the *hadith*, the number will rise to 124. The Prophet himself supplicates God with his known and his unknown names as well: 'I pray to You by the names that you have pre-served for Yourself in the realm of the unseen.'

Muslim theologians have developed various categories of divine names. One might go on to elaborate on each cate-gorization. Bekir Topaloğlu, a promi-nent theologian in modern Turkey, provides a comprehensive categorization. According to his categorization, the divine names are divided into four groups: those related to God's essence, to the Universe, to the natural world, and to the human being.

1. The names such as Allah, *al-haqq* (the True), *al-awwal* (the First), *al-akhir* (the Last), *al-baqi* (the Per-manent), *al-warith* (the Inheritor), *al-samad* (the Refuge of All) con-stitute examples of the first group of this category. All of these names define God's essence, to make the unknowable, knowable and understandable by our mind.

2. The following names represent examples of the second group: *al-khaliq* (the Creator), *al-bari* (the Originator), *al-mubdi* (the Starter), *al-muʿid* (the Resurrector), *al-muhyi* (the Giver of Life) and *al-mumit* (the Giver of Death).

3. The names such as *malik al-mulk* (the Owner of the Kingdom), *al-malik* (the Owner), *al-qayyum* (the Sustainer), *al-wali* (the Ruler), *al-muhaymin* (the Sovereign) and *al-hafiz* (the Guardian) comprise examples of the third group of this categorization.

4. The names related to human beings seem to be many. The following names represent some of those which involve the examples of the fourth group: *al-ʿadl* (Justice), *al-hakam* (the Keeper of Balance), *al-fattah* (the Opener), *al-afuww* (the Forgiver of Mistakes), *al-ghafur* (the Forgiver of Sins), *al-tawwab* (the One who Accepts Repen-tance), *al-halim* (the Kind), *al-mujib* (the One who Answers all Calls), *al-hasib* (the One who Reckons the Deeds of his Servants), *al-wahhab* (the One who Gives) and *al-wadud* (the Lover and Beloved).

The names of God represented in the Islamic teaching are for the practical purposes of human understanding. There are some names restricted to God, which cannot be used for any other being, for example Allah and *al-Rah-man*. However, we relate some attributes such as living, knowing, desiring, power, hearing and seeing to humans as well as to God, albeit with an evident differ-ence. Human attributes are transient and a pale reflection of reality, while God's attributes are eternal.

Further reading

al-Ghazali, Abu Hamid (1995) *The Ninety-Nine Beautiful Names of God*, trans. and ed. David Burrell and Nazih Daher, Cambridge: The Islamic Texts Society.

Cragg, Kenneth (1998) *Readings in the Qurʾan*, London: Collins Religious Pub-lishing, 86–112.

Gorden, Christian Van (2003) *No God but God: A path to Muslim-Christian dialogue on God's nature*, New York: Orbis Books.

McAuliffe, J.D. (1990) 'Fakhr al-Din al-Razi on God as al-Khaliq', in D. Burrell and B. McGinn (eds) *God and Creation: An ecumenical symposium*, Notre Dame,

IN: University of Notre Dame Press, 276–96.

See also: **ninety-nine names of God; al-Rahman**

ZEKI SARITOPRAK

AMARA / AMR
see: ulu'l-amr

ANGEL
see: **malak**

ANNE
see: **Mary's mother**

ANTICHRIST
see: **Dajjal**

'AQIDA

'Aqida (pl. aqa'id) is a technical term used for the Muslim creed. The earliest and simplest 'aqida (creed) of Islam appears in the shahada formula and it is generally believed that most of the later creedal formulas are expansions of it. The shahada is as follows:

> I witness that there is no god but Allah and that Muhammad is the messenger of Allah.

The shahada is frequently used liturgically as 'a confession of faith'. In practice, when anyone is converted to Islam, he or she is required to pronounce the shahada formula, and it is also required of every Muslim that it shall be pronounced at least once in a lifetime and also confessed by heart. It occurs in the adhan, which is an invitation to a Muslim to prayer five times a day. It is also regularly uttered by Muslims in the course of daily praying as it arises in every prayer as a recitation in tahiyyat (in prayers).

In terms of articles of faith, shahada contains two basic articles, namely: unity of God (deity) and the prophecy of Muhammad (prophecy). These two fundamental articles of faith presented in the shahada have always been stressed in the Qur'an, and as a creedal formula. The shahada has been declared in a hadith from al-Bukhari to be the first of the 'five Pillars of Islam': 'Islam has been built on five (pillars); testifying that there is no god but Allah and that Muhammad is the messenger of Allah.'

As another creedal formula amantu exists only in the Maturidi school of Islam. The term literally means 'I believed'. It arises first in Imam 'Azam's al-Fiqh al-Akbar, then in Hakim es-Samarkandi's al-Sawad al-A'zam and Abu'l-Layth Samarkandi's Bayanu 'Aqidati'l-usul. The formula takes its name amantu from the first word of the formula and the word is used in the Qur'an in the same meaning and context and in hadith (Tirmidhi, Fitan: 63).

However, the etymological analysis of the Christian Credo and Muslim amantu leads to an interesting comparison between the Christian and Muslim traditions. This resemblance between the Christian credo and amantu formulation depends on the fact that both formulas start with 'I believe(d)' = Credo = amantu. It is likely that the amantu formula has come to Islamic literature as a contribution from Samarkand 'ulama and from a broader Maturidi central Asian contribution which later spread with their migration to Asia Minor and India. Socio-religious and political motivations behind the formulation are well worth considering here also. As happened in Christian creedal formulations, the Muslim polemical and religious interaction with surrounding religions and faiths is very likely the origin of the amantu formula. It must be noted that this is just after the time of the Islamization of Central Asia. It is highly likely that the formula was introduced to protect Muslim believers from being attacked as unbelievers. It must have functioned as a declaration of faith expected to lead to security.

In the *amantu* formula, six articles of faith are declared:

1. God;
2. angels;
3. books;
4. messengers;
5. life after death;
6. destiny.

As a creedal formula, *amantu* survived until modern times and is still in use. In most Turkish mosques today, for example, the *imam* recites the formula every Friday night with the congregation. Also, every child who receives an Islamic education and learns the Qur'an and basic Islamic teachings is taught to recite this formula and also expected to memorize it, and so is capable of reciting it by heart. This applies also in countries such as India, Pakistan, Afghanistan and other Central Asian Muslim countries where the Muslim population largely follows the Maturidi/ Hanafi school of Islam.

There are numerous treatises entitled *'aqida* belonging to various scholars, schools and sects. These *'aqida*s are not official formulations of the doctrinal beliefs of the main body of believers, but merely statements of the tenets of a particular theologian or school, often set out for the purpose of 'defining the position of an individual, school or sect on some disputed point'. Hence there have even been cases of disputed legal and political problems in relation to these creeds, such as that of the Imamate. It is interesting to note that the content of *'aqida*s is influenced not only by theological discussions among Muslims but also by philosophical, political and even legal discussions, to the extent that some philosophical terms were introduced into theologians' creeds – terms such as substance (*madda*) and accident (*jawhar*). Similarly, there are certain political-legal preferences in the religious dogma. In this context, it is an interesting fact that Imam 'Azam's book *al-Fiqh al-Akbar* claims (by definition or by virtue of its actual title) to be *fiqh* (jurisprudence). This offers a clue about the mind of people who did not precisely distinguish *'aqida* from practice, with the result that it was absolutely acceptable to discuss legal and political matters in *'aqida* treatises.

The earlier instances of *'aqida*s are brief but some of the later ones are very lengthy so that it is difficult to draw a firm line between the creed (*'aqida*) and the theological (*kalam*) treatises. In Sunni tradition Najm al-din 'Umar al-Nasafi (d. 537/1142–1143), commentaries written by Sa'd al-Din al-Taftazani (d.791–792/1389–1390), al-Tahawi (d. 321/933), al-Samarkandi (d. 342/953–954) and Imam al-Haramayn (d. 478/ 1085–1086) are renowned for their *'aqida*s. It is also noteworthy that in Arabic, Persian and Turkish a number of poetical creeds were written such as Usi's *Amali*, Laknawi's *Jawharatu't-Tawhid* and Hizir Beg's *Kasidatu'n-Nuniyya*.

Further reading

Goldziher, Ignaz (1981) *Introduction to Islamic Theology and Law*, trans. Andras Hamari and Ruth Hamari, Princeton, NJ: Princeton University Press.
Watt (1994) *Islamic Creeds: – A Selection*, Edinburgh: Edinburgh University Press.
Wensinck, A (1965) *The Muslim Creed: Its genesis and historical development*, London: Frank Cass & Co.

See also: **aya**

BILAL GÖKKIR

ARAB /ARABIA

Arabia as an entity during the period of the *jahiliyya* (period of ignorance) just prior to the start of Islam was very much a marginal area in the region. In contrast with the rest of the Middle East, it was largely pastoral as opposed to agricultural, and had no very large cities and fixed population centres. The Arabian peninsula was certainly not isolated; it was frequented by traders and also people passing through to get to other places. In particular, its position between the Byzantine and Sassanian empires made it of frequent interest to these competing powers. It was not only trade that became important, but undoubtedly preachers from the neighbouring monotheistic faiths sought followers among the largely pagan Arabs, at the same time as the Arabs themselves learned from their neighbours about the very different lifestyles of people in the major centres of civilization.

Within the Arab world clashes and less severe conflicts often took place between the different clans and family groups that traversed the area looking for pasture and habitable resting places, perhaps an inevitable aspect of nomadic and pastoral life. The solidarity of these clans was an important survival mechanism in a region where both the climate and the people could be hostile. The groupings were patriarchal and familial links within them were significant sources of prestige and wealth. But not all the peninsula was pastoral in nature; two important regions – Yemen in the south and the Nabatean kingdom in the north-west – were more settled, and they tried to exercise influence over the wilder parts of the area. One of the interesting features of this situation was that the kingdoms and empires that surrounded Arabia were always fragile and their influence transitory. For one

thing the Nabateans and their centres at Petra and Palmyra were destroyed by the Romans and incorporated into the Roman Empire, while Yemen seems to have lost control of much of the trade that used to travel through its territory. The Sassanians in the east did not show much interest in the region and it is not difficult to understand their lack of enthusiasm. There were hardly significant assets to be gained from mastery of a difficult terrain with fractitious inhabitants, as it was presented in the literature of the time.

Mecca

Mecca was traditionally a place of pilgrimage and also a place where disputes were settled and where a community that spent its time largely on the move could gather together with other families and clans and settle whatever differences they had, and make whatever deals they were interested in, albeit usually temporary, within an environment that fostered conditions appropriate to a truce. The Arabs were enthusiastic about their language but even this proved to be more a source of conflict than harmony, since they met at Mecca to compete poetically. The local worship at Mecca was of idols, and there were also significant Jewish and Christian tribes and communities there, and doubtless other representative religions also. The Quraysh was the tribe in control of Mecca, its rites and rules, and so acquired a strong influence, insofar as any group had influence at all over the region as a whole.

The historical role of Mecca is a controversial topic. For a long time it was accepted that Mecca was an ancient city that had been on the route of important caravan traffic across the Hijaz. Research by Patricia Crone (1987) quite brilliantly suggests this is not the case at

43

all, or at least that there is no evidence that this is the case. Whatever the truth of the matter, there can be little doubt about the status of Mecca at the time of the Prophet and the message of Islam. The relative decline of the surrounding empires had created a power vacuum in the region, and Mecca and its rulers, the Quraysh, became important in establishing a place and a structure for society to regulate its disputes, celebrate its achievements and carry out its religious duties. These latter were largely in the form of worshipping local and highly personalized deities, and Mecca had long been associated with such rituals.

The pastoral lifestyle of most of the transient clans and tribes probably did not produce much in the way of surplus wealth, and we know from accounts of tribal life that a good deal of expense was involved merely in protecting each community from hostile competitors, or common thieves and marauders. What wealth was created, however, would naturally find its outlet in Mecca, where goods would be stored for the eventual arrival of Arab groups with the resources in money or barter for exchange to take place. While rudimentary jewellery and clothes would be produced in the region, more sophisticated products were available as imports from more settled regions on the periphery. Grain, dates and weapons in particular were bought, and in return the migratory Arabs could offer some livestock, in particular camels, and the funds they had acquired through working with caravans, breeding and selling camels, and providing protection for travellers across the desert and wild places of Arabia. Since cash is highly portable, it was probably an important part of the purchasing power of the Arabs and played a large part in making Mecca such an important marketing centre.

The city is located on the sandy, narrow valley of the Wadi Ibrahim and is surrounded by hills ranging in height from 200 to 500 ft. The 3,000-ft Jabal Khandama is located nearby.

Although Mecca is often represented in Islamic iconography, it is not an important political or economic site in Saudi Arabia, its status being largely limited to its religious role. Mecca is defined by its physical difficulties. It is in a barren region and can produce no food of its own. This led to an early dependence on imports, initially from Egypt, and on water from the Zamzam well outside the city and elsewhere. Water has been a continual problem, and many large projects have been carried out to solve this problem, all usually failures. Even when adequate supplies were established, the local bedouin often interfered with the supply for financial reasons. During the *hajj* water often became a crucial issue, and sometimes was sold to the *hajjis* at exorbitant rates. The Meccans provided food, drink and accommodation to the pilgrims, they provided animals to be sacrificed, barbers to shave them and all the facilities that were required for the visitors to perform the necessary rites in accordance with Islamic law. It is hardly surprising that in the Islamic world the Meccans are sometimes regarded as having as their main motive fleecing the pilgrims, and there is a long tradition of their purchasing goods and services for eventual resale to the pilgrims at a substantial profit. On the other hand, it has to be said that they have a short period of only a few weeks a year to earn what is in effect their annual income, so they do need to be shrewd in their treatment of the visitors. It has become something of a theme of many *hajjis* that they are shocked by the rapacity of the Meccans, who are after all their co-religionists and who are fortunate to live permanently in the holy city.

The origin of the city

Mecca is a very ancient city, and its origins are surrounded by historical controversy. It lies in a sort of corridor between two ranges of hills, and has been prone to flooding when the infrequent rain falls. According to many historians, its position was initially favourable for trade, a good deal of traffic going north to Syria as did merchandise for the Red Sea port of Jeddah, Iraq in the north-east and Yemen in the south. There is taken to be evidence that Mecca attracted much of the trade passing through Syria and the Mediterranean, and between South Arabia and the Indian Ocean, especially when there was conflict between the Persians and the Byzantines in the pre-Islamic period, and there often were such conflicts.

The climate is extremely dry, with very occasional but heavy rain (hence the floods) and the area is incapable of any significant agriculture. The wells were very important for the city's water supply, and one of the roles of the early political groups in the area was to oversee and safeguard those supplies. The lack of physical resources in Mecca was compensated for by an apparent sophistication of the city as a service centre, a role that continues up to this day. In particular, Mecca was a commercial force in the region, both financing and investing in enterprises along the trade routes through the town. This standard view has recently been challenged by historians, who point to the absence of any solid evidence to support such a view of the city (Crone, 1987).

Of great significance is the fact that the Prophet Muhammad was born in Mecca in about 570 CE. The Qur'an is scathing about the merchant culture of Mecca, and calls on its inhabitants to embrace the One God and abandon their overwhelming materialism. Their polytheism was linked to their desire for wealth, since they made money out of the visitors who came to worship the gods then based in the main shrine, the *Ka'ba*. Initially the message fell on stony ground, and Muhammad left for Yathrib (Medina) in 622, a far more sympathetic environment for him, and over the next few years there was continual struggle between the Muslim forces of Medina and the Meccan authorities. In the end the Muslims overcame the Meccans, and the *Ka'ba*, the central religious shrine in Mecca, was cleansed of its association with idols, eventually becoming the *qibla* or direction of prayer for Muslims. Of particular importance was the area around the *Ka'ba*, which was soon surrounded by a mosque, the *masjid al-haram*, thus formalizing the territory as holy space.

Over the next few centuries Mecca frequently suffered invasion and destruction by different religious and tribal groups. The pilgrimage was often disrupted or rendered impossible, and the Meccans sometimes flirted with a degree of independence under the Sharif (literally 'noble' and linked with being a descendant of the Prophet) clan, which came to a head in the twentieth century when the Ottoman Empire was embroiled in World War I and could not defend the Holy Places properly. But another local ruler, from the family of Sa'ud who came from the Nejd to the east of the Mecca and Medina region, overcame the Hussayns of the Sharif clan and brought Mecca and Medina under Sa'udi authority. They brought a Wahhabi orientation to the city, and this has had a long-lasting effect on its cultural and physical life. The previously high status of the Sharifs has now disappeared, with business people, *mutawwifun* (guides) and religious teachers (*'ulama*) becoming the dominant force in town.

The *Ka'ba*

The *Ka'ba* is said to have been built by God for Adam, and to be modelled on the divine residence itself. Abraham is taken to have rebuilt it after its destruction during the Flood, and today it is considerably larger than it was originally, when it was said to be made up of loose stones and not that much taller than an average human being. It is made of black meteoric stone and is covered with a large cloth, and is quite simply decorated with writing and embroidery. The *Ka'ba* today stands in the midst of an open courtyard, the *masjid al-haram,* or 'sanctuary'. It is a cubical flat-roofed building, 50 ft in height, from a narrow marble base on mortared bases of a local blue-grey stone. The entire *Ka'ba* structure is draped with a black silk covering, called a *kiswa,* upon which passages from the Qur'an are embroidered in gold. Opposite the northwestern wall of the *Ka'ba* is an area of special sanctity called the *Hijr,* which Muslim tradition identifies as the burial place of Hagar and Ishmael. In Muhammad's time, the *Hijr* was a place used for discussion, prayer and, significantly, for sleep and visions. The *Ka'ba,* the Zamzam well, the *Hijr* and the hills of Safa and Marwa are now all enclosed in a vast structure called the *haram al-sharif* or 'Noble Sanctuary'. Ringed by seven towering minarets and sixty-four gates, this truly monumental building has 160,000 yards of floor space and is capable of holding more than 1.2 million pilgrims at the same time.

The *hajj*

In Islam the *hajj* pilgrimage is a fundamental obligation to be performed at least once by all male and female adults whose health and finances permit. The pilgrimage takes place each year between the 8th and 13th days of Dhu al-Hijja, the 12th month of the Islamic lunar calendar. When the pilgrim is about seven miles from Mecca, he or she enters the state of holiness and purity known as *ihram* and dons special garments consisting of two white seamless sheets that are wrapped around the body. Entering the great Mosque in Mecca, the pilgrim first walks seven times around the *ka'ba* shrine in a counterclockwise direction; this ritual is called turning, or *tawaf.*

Next, entering the shrine, the pilgrim kisses the sacred stone. The stone is mounted in a silver frame in the wall, 4 ft above the ground, in the south-east corner. It is of an oval shape about 12 inches in diameter and is composed of seven small stones (possibly basalt) of different sizes and shapes joined together with cement. During the next few days the pilgrim walks a ritualized route to other sacred places in the Mecca vicinity (Mina, Muzdalifah, Arafat, the Mount of Mercy and Mount Namira) and returns to the *Ka'ba* on the final day. Once a believer has made the pilgrimage to Mecca they may add the title *al-hajji* to their name. Pilgrims use a variety of signs to indicate they have made the *hajj,* including painting pictures of the *Ka'ba* upon the walls of their homes, and there is a good deal of iconography involving the *Ka'ba* and the mosque surrounding it in Muslim homes.

Mecca's physical structure

The history of Mecca has been tempestuous. The different factions in the Islamic world fought each other for control of Mecca, often in Mecca itself, and the city and its population have suffered at the hands of the invaders. On the other hand, Mecca was generally a long way away from the main centres of power and authority, and so perhaps was not as affected by political and military upheaval as the other important cities such as Damascus, Cairo and Baghdad. Muslim politicians would often seek influence in Mecca by financing supporters within the city, as a means of religious legitimation of their policies in general, a policy which not unnaturally greatly increased the wealth of the leading families. Since the different political groupings would each have their own representatives, a good deal of wealth circulated.

At some stage around the tenth century walls were constructed around the city, and lasted for a few centuries. The city is said to have been around 40 acres in 661, 350 acres in 1924 and is well over 2,000 acres today. The intimate nature of the old city has certainly become seriously diminished, and serious attention to other buildings such as the houses of Khadija, the Prophet's first wife, or his Companions, is discouraged and certainly not made a focal point. There has also been a certain amount of destruction of ancient buildings associated with those close to the Prophet. This marks an attempt to discourage visits to them by Muslims such as the Shi'ites who may regard them as holy sites, something which goes very much against the Wahhabi interpretation of such places as merely buildings and inappropriate places for worship for monotheists. In response, in recent years there has been something of a local campaign to safeguard and preserve ancient buildings.

Economic life

Mecca, and indeed the Hejaz as a whole, was declared open only to Muslims ever since the caliphate of 'Umar (634–44 CE). Jeddah was and is open to non-Muslims,

and was an important commercial centre, but the exclusion from Mecca did presumably leave the commerce in the hands of the local Muslims. On the other hand, it also limited the scope of Mecca to diversify outside its sacred role, since any large commercial undertaking might involve those of other faiths. This was a significant issue even before globalization. As a sacred city Mecca suffered several serious problems. The religious endowments (*waqf*) on which the colleges and mosques relied for their regular running expenses frequently collapsed due to the distance of the city from the centres of power, and hence the facility with which such funding could be curtailed. In any case, *waqf* finance is always rather uncertain, relying as it does on using the income produced by one enterprise to finance another, and the records suggest that although often considerable funds were officially directed to Mecca, far less seems to have actually arrived. The expenditure was often on prestige projects, those with religious relevance, and so did not add to the ability of Mecca to generate income by itself. The distance between donor and beneficiary also meant that there was little control as to how the money was spent, and the returns in Mecca itself were often feeble.

The physical position of the city resulted in frequent floods, and the flimsy construction of the original buildings did not survive such regular periods of destruction. The religious significance of the city meant that it was often attacked by those seeking to impose their views on the Islamic world, and the pilgrimage trains to and from the city were far from secure. Finally, the various rulers of the city have sought to copy the Prophet in restoring what they took to be the appropriate rituals. In Islamic tradition, Abraham initially set up the *Ka'ba* to worship God but it was subsequently used by polytheists to worship false gods. Meanwhile Muhammad instituted pilgrimages, the *hajj*, which only takes place once a year, and the minor *'umra,* which can take place at any time, to replace pagan pilgrimages. Subsequent rulers have all altered the city physically in order to make it fit in better with their conception of its sacred role. Few were as radical as the Qarmatians, who in 929 massacred many of the inhabitants and removed the *Ka'ba* stone to Bahrain.

Throughout all the changes in policy, however, there do not appear to have been any radical changes to the *Ka'ba* itself, which is now much as it was when the Prophet's tribe, the Quraysh, constructed the building in 605. On the other hand, the buildings around the *Ka'ba* have been continually altered, and often have simply fallen down. Different rulers put up palaces near the shrine and financed religious institutions as ways of projecting their authority. Changes in regime would frequently lead to change in the buildings and what went on in them, and the new projects must have injected considerable funds into the city. They also must have put a lot of strain on communications, since virtually all building materials had to be imported over difficult and lengthy distances. Again, one can only assume that this boosted the local economy, renewing the nature of Mecca as a dynamic service centre well able to absorb and benefit from large-scale public and private works.

Mecca in modern times

The great oil wealth has radically changed the city in the period since World War II. The mosque at the centre of the city itself has been greatly enlarged. One of the major influences of the Saudi regime on Mecca has been on the secondary sites, those associated with the life of the Prophet Muhammad, rather than the *Ka'ba* itself. From pre-Islamic times there had apparently been many holy sites in the vicinity of Mecca, and the Prophet's tribe, the Quraysh, had control over some of these and the provision of water. One of their motivations for hostility to Muhammad was their fear of losing this valuable monopoly, since they thought that the pilgrimage trade might be destroyed by the new religion of Islam. As it turns out, the pilgrimages were only strengthened by Islam, and the various groups and families who controlled different parts of the holy city and its environs benefited greatly over the centuries, although of course the groups who actually enjoyed this power also changed over time. The secondary sites were particular popular with Muslims, who stayed on in Mecca after either the *hajj* or *'umra* pilgrimage, captivated as they were by the holiness of the environment. There have been less of these kinds of inhabitants recently due to the Saudi hostility to the secondary sites and their increased policing of those visiting the country on pilgrimage visas.

As the guardians of the two holy cities, Mecca and Medina, the Saudis have a difficult task in facilitating the safe arrival and departure of so many pilgrims over such a comparatively brief period. In recent decades the majority of pilgrims have arrived by air, further changing the nature of the *hajj* from its previous status as an activity that was physically strenuous even prior to arrival in the city. Although the *hajj* brings in considerable funds, it also requires considerable expenditure, yet the changing of money, the provision of animals for sacrifice and just the incursion of up to 2 million people from every corner of the Islamic world have an effect on Mecca which is difficult to quantify.

Undoubtedly much of the city lives for the *hajj*, surviving through the rest of the year on the income which it earns in this relatively brief period. Some of the facilities, such as hospitals, lie idle for most of the year, only really being used during the *hajj*.

Many plazas have been constructed near the central mosque, roads built and widened, and a lot of attention has been paid to parking and other forms of transport, such as tunnels for pedestrians between the different areas which are part of the *hajj* itinerary. The buildings have often been demolished and rebuilt on a grander scale, inevitably with a certain loss of charm, and the widespread introduction of electricity has made the city yet one more modern site.

There is a considerable foreign presence in the exclusively Muslim city due to the large number of educational institutions that have been set up and which flourish there. For believers this would obviously be an excellent place to study and live, and many of the residents come from the variety of Islamic communities that exist all over the world. This multicultural domestic influx gives the city a cosmopolitan atmosphere all year round, not only during the pilgrimages.

There have until recently been no elections in Saudi Arabia, and the city government was appointed centrally. However, at the time of writing (2005), the first election of a local nature has taken place, albeit limited to a male electorate.

References and further reading

Crone, P. (1987) *Meccan Trade and the Rise of Islam*, Princeton, NJ: Princeton University Press.

Peters, F.E. (1986) *Jerusalem and Mecca: The typology of the holy city in the Near East*, New York: New York University Press.

—— (1994) *The Hajj: The Muslim pilgrimage to Mecca and the holy places*, Princeton, NJ: Princeton University Press.

OLIVER LEAMAN

ARABIC LANGUAGE

Arabic belongs to the South West Semitic languages, but is sometimes also described as an offshoot of the group of Central Semitic languages. 'Arabs' as inhabitants of the Arabian peninsula are already mentioned in Assyrian sources, but we know little about their language (or languages?). Epigraphic South Arabian and its modern dialects belong to a different cluster of Semitic languages. To differentiate South Arabian from Arabic, the latter is sometimes called 'North-Arabic', as is the language of some pre-Islamic inscriptions. One of the oldest documents of this Arabic proper is a funeral inscription in five lines, found in Namara (120 km south east of Damascus), in honour of the 'king of the Arabs Imra'al-qays' (dated 328 CE), written in Nabatean (i.e. in Aramaic) letters. It is generally assumed that part of what was centuries later codified as pre-Islamic bedouin poetry goes back to the sixth or possibly even the fifth century CE. The most important event for Arabic and its linguistic history, however, was the advent of the Qur'an in the first third of the seventh century CE.

Our knowledge of what came to be known as Classical Arabic (*al-lugha al-'arabiyya al-fusha*) rests: (1) on the Qur'an as a recited and codified text; (2) on what was transmitted orally as pre-Islamic poetry, proverbial sayings and stories of bedouin intertribal warfare; and (3) on what the Arab grammarians and lexicographers in the second/eighth and third/ninth centuries said they picked up as linguistic information from bedouins on the Arab peninsula. These three strands were interwoven and systematically described by Arab scholars in Basra and Kufa to form the corpus of Arabic grammatical and lexicographical works that enshrine Classical Arabic. The linguistic data available seem to show that this Arabic was 'a supra-tribal unity, a language that served as a binding factor for all those who lived in the Arabian peninsula' (Versteegh, 2001: 37). Scholars are mainly divided on two interlinked questions: (1) was the Arabic as codified by Arabic scholarship identical with everyday spoken Arabic at the time or was there a poetic *koinē* which differed markedly from the spoken language?; and (2) does the language and/or the orthography of the Qur'an reflect the variant of Arabic spoken in Mecca or in the larger region of Hijaz?

Arabic and the Qur'an

The Qur'an is the first Arabic document which mentions the Arabic language as such (*lisanun 'arabiyyun*, 16.103). It stresses repeatedly that it was revealed in Arabic. 43.2–3 states: 'By the clear book, behold, We have made it an Arabic Qur'an, haply you [pl.] will understand.' The text which was revealed to the Prophet was 'made easy', because it was in Arabic: 'Now We have made it [the Qur'an] easy by thy tongue that thou mayest bear good tidings thereby to the godfearing, and warn a stubborn people' (19.97). The fact that this revelation was in Arabic was for the Qur'an the major difference between Muslim revelation and all previous revelation: 'We have sent no messenger save with the tongue of his people that he might make all clear to them' (14.4). Enemies of the Prophet accused him of taking over revealed material from others: 'And We know very well that they say: "Only a mortal is teaching him (i.e. the Prophet)." But the speech of him at whom they hint is barbarous (*a'jami*);

and this is speech Arabic, manifest (*'arabiyyun mubin*)' (16.103). It follows that the Qur'anic revelation was at first directed at speakers of Arabic only. Not all speakers of Arabic were Muslims at that time, but all Muslims at the time of the Qur'anic revelation were speakers of Arabic.

The Qur'an was for Arab grammarians, lexicographers and scholars of rhetoric the paradigmatic example of Arabic; its form and content were considered 'inimitable'. Islamic dogma saw in the Qur'an divine speech. Qur'anic Arabic was held to surpass not only all other utterings in Arabic but all that could be expressed in all other human languages. The Qur'an could only be recited in Arabic, it could not be translated; translations were and are considered a kind of commentary. Ritual prayer (*salat*) had to be performed in Arabic. Because of the Qur'an, al-Shafi'i (d. 204/820) claimed that Arabic was the most perfect of all languages, which nobody but a prophet could master completely. Thus the Qur'an became an immensely powerful linguistic matrix. However, there were and are numerous features of Qur'anic language and style that were never taken up as productive models in Classical Arabic.

Arabic was also the language of the words of the Prophet Muhammad, collected in *hadith*. It was the language of the sermon (*khutba*), and became the language of religious discourse and jurisdiction. Under the Umayyad 'Abdalmalik (r. 65/685–86/705) Arabic superseded Greek as the language of administration. Under the influence of Islam in the conquered territories Arabic became the language of political power. It also became the language of a flourishing literature in prose and poetry.

Development of Arabic in the shadow of the Qur'an and diglossia

The main motive behind the codification of the Arabic language by lexicographers and grammarians was to defend the pure Arabic language against linguistic corruption and to teach non-Arab-speakers correct Arabic. Standardising, codifying, developing orthographic and orthoepic symbols were based on the absolute necessity to preserve the correct form and pronunciation of the Qur'an. The Qur'an, but with it also Classical Arabic as a whole, had to be protected against influences of Arabic dialects and against the influences of languages of subjected peoples in the new Arabo-Islamic empire, for example, Persian, Aramaic, Coptic or Greek. Soon urban forms of spoken Arabic were felt to be more open to 'corruption' than the language of bedouin tribes. The rift between the language of the city-dwellers and Arab nomadic or semi-nomadic tribes was to make a lasting imprint on the history of Arabic dialects. To this day these are often subdivided into urban, rural and tribal dialects. For large parts of the Near and Middle East, Classical Arabic became a religious and cultural *lingua franca*. It became the scholarly medium of Muslims all over the world. Arabic deeply influenced other languages spoken and written by Muslims. In the case of Persian, Ottoman Turkish, Pashto, Urdu and Haussa even the Arabic writing system was adopted. The Islamic vocabulary which has penetrated most languages spoken by Muslims to some degree is Arabic. It starts with religious formulas used in the ritual prayer and does not end with Muslim proper names.

The model of Classical Arabic was so powerful mainly because it was inspired by the Qur'an. In morphology and syntax the rules had been laid down once and forever by Arab grammarians. Strict linguistic norms assured linguistic unity over time and space, but on the other hand they blocked development and flexibility. This led in the course of centuries to a diglossia which is until today one of the most important features of the linguistic space of Arabic.

Diglossia in Arabic has often been described as a split between a written formal language which is also used for speech on formal occasions, on the one hand, and informal language, which is not written, on the other. The formal language is Classical Arabic; the spoken language is one of numerous different Arabic dialects. While we can be sure that such a situation characterized the choice of any speaker or writer of Arabic from 'Abbasid times onwards at least, modern research has shown for the linguistic situation of modern Arab speakers that the term 'diglossia', which implies the existence of two different layers of language, is too simplistic. In reality, today one has to distinguish at least five socio-linguistic levels of Modern Arabic: the classical heritage; contemporary classical; the colloquial of the cultured; the colloquial of the enlightened; and the colloquial of the illiterate. Real speech moves inside this continuum, involves frequent code switching and moves freely between these registers. We can assume that this situation prevailed in Arabic in premodern times also.

The language of Classical Arabic was and is a language of the highest cultural prestige, but nobody speaks it as his or her mother tongue. It has to be acquired. The language spoken at home and in the market was and is one of the Arabic dialects; such a dialect is the first language of each Arab. As the means of informal communication it carries no prestige whatsoever. The gulf separating the formal and the informal mode of expression became historically wider and wider until the formal and the informal levels became mutually almost or totally incomprehensible. At the same time the differences between the Arabic dialects which were spread over a wide geographic area developed centrifugally even further. A speaker of a Moroccan dialect today cannot make himself understood to the speaker of an Iraqi dialect. They can communicate only if both have learned Classical Arabic. Whether modern means of communication, which are dominated by Modern Standard Arabic, will influence this pattern remains to be seen.

Middle Arabic

While the situation of diglossia accompanied Classical Arabic almost from the beginning, not all written communication in Arabic conformed to the norms of Classical Arabic grammar and lexicography as developed by Arab philology. As can be already seen from the earliest Arabic papyri from the middle of the seventh century, written Arabic could deviate in some or many aspects from these rules. In personal correspondence, in non-religious and non-literary writing, in works concerning geography or medicine, mathematics or botany, Arab philologists distinguished a 'low style' from an 'elevated style' – the latter showing vernacular or otherwise incorrect, i.e. 'faulty', forms, words and syntax. It seems that Jews and Christian were often more tolerant in this respect than Muslim scholars. 'Christian Arabic' and 'Jewish Arabic' were special cases of a sub-standard Classical Arabic. Their distance from Classical Arabic grew when Arabic was written in non-Arabic letters; many Jews, for instance, wrote Arabic in Hebrew letters.

The term 'Middle Arabic' was coined by Western scholarship to designate this genre of written Arabic which would not or could not comply completely with the norms of Classical Arabic. 'Middle Arabic' does not mean a linguistic stage in a chronology between 'Old Arabic' and 'Modern Arabic', but an intended or unintended breach between a normative, often almost unattainable ideal of written formal Classical Arabic, on the one hand, and a lower, 'incorrect' style characterized by interference of the spoken informal language, on the other. Usually Middle Arabic is the consequence of inadequate mastering of or deliberate neglect of norms of Classical Arabic. This Middle Arabic is also characterized by pseudo-correct forms, which as such do not belong to either one of the two levels.

Factors of change in Classical Arabic

The normative pressure of Classical Arabic was lightest in the vocabulary. In areas outside the strictly legal and religious field, scholarly Arabic from the second/eighth century onwards underwent a massive influx of foreign words, loanwords and loan translations. Greek medicine, alchemy, botany, geography, astronomy, philosophy and other sciences were introduced into Arabic culture, Classical Greek and Hellenistic works were translated into Arabic. The centre of this activity was Baghdad in the third/ninth century. The translators, usually Syriac-speaking Christians, translated from Greek into Syriac and from Syriac into Arabic and were encouraged by the Muslim rulers in the 'Abbasid court. Aristotle and Plato, Galen and Hippocrates became part of Arabic culture.

Toward the end of the fourth/tenth century Arabic had to compete with other languages in the disintegrating Islamic empire. Under the Seljuks, Arabic as a language of court and diplomacy was gradually superseded by New-Persian, and with the fall of Granada (897/1492) Arabic ceased to be used in the Iberian peninsula. The Ottoman conquest of wide areas of the Near East (and Eastern Europe) in the fifteenth and sixteenth centuries included most regions in which Arabic was spoken. Ottoman Turkish was established as the language of administration and the language of the court. Arabic was still spoken widely and Classical Arabic did not disappear. But it receded, and lost much of its prestige as a culturally dominant language. For Muslims it never lost its strictly religious importance.

Renaissance of Arabic

In the second half of the nineteenth century and under the onslaught of European colonialism, most Arabic-speaking intellectuals inside and outside the Ottoman Empire saw Arabic language and literature, Arabic culture and Arabic political life in a stage of deplorable decline and decadence. The counter-movement to overcome this decadence was called 'renaissance' (*Nahda*). A very important element in this project was linguistic reform. The new 'modern' Arabic language was supposed to become a medium of natural sciences and political progress. At the same time it was also to be developed to compete with European literatures, poetry, prose and drama. The pioneers of the *Nahda*, therefore, encouraged and supported the translation of European books, technical and scientific, political and literary, into Arabic – mainly from French and English. This was the second systematic movement of translation into Arabic

and became even more momentous than its predecessor in 'Abbassid times.

The project was concerned with creating a new technical and scientific vocabulary, with introducing new literary genres such as drama and the novel, and with adopting new means of communication such as newspapers and journals. In all these areas the *Nahda* was successful. While the ideal of one Arabic written language was strenuously kept up, the Qur'anic model as such faded. Many Arab Christians were active in the *Nahda* movement. They were often as much pro-Arab as anti-Ottoman and played a leading role in the development of Arab nationalism. Arabic was at that time often seen less as the language of the Qur'an, but rather as the language of all Arabs regardless of their creed. Classical Arabic became the only common bond for the emerging Arab national states. The linguistic unity of Classical Arabic turned into a symbol of Arab cultural and political unity (Pan-Arabism). Many discussions dealt with the question of whether a foreign word should be taken over and possibly be Arabicized or whether a purely Arabic word or root should be given a new or extended meaning. Right up until today Arab academies propose lists of Arabic words recommended as translations for specialized English or French terms.

The discussion of how much linguistic and cultural reform was necessary and admissible led towards the end of the twentieth century to the widely debated question of how modernity (*'asriyya*) and authenticity (*asala*) could be reconciled. While morphologically and syntactically the modern form of Classical Arabic, which is called Modern Standard Arabic (*al-lugha al-'arabiyya al-mu'asira*), has much in common with Classical Arabic, both vocabulary and idiomatic use have changed drastically. Arabic is today the official language of Algeria, Bahrain, Djibouti, Egypt, Iraq, Jordan, Kuwait, Lebanon, Libya, Mauritania, Morocco, Oman, Qatar, Saudi Arabia, Somalia, Sudan, Syria, Tunisia, the United Arab Emirates and Yemen, and in the territories administered by the Palestinian Authority. Arabic became in 1973 one of the official languages of the United Nations.

Arabic dialects

In the period of Arab conquests after the Prophet's death (11/632) many newly conquered regions were Arabicized. Arabicization in some cases preceded Islamization, and in many cases was faster than Islamization. In Iraq and in Egypt, for example, after the Muslim conquest, numerous Jews and Christians did not convert to Islam but took over Arabic as their language. While Classical Arabic became the one language of formal discourse, the spoken language was not unified but was split instead into different regional vernaculars. The main factors that contributed to the development of a new type of colloquial Arabic ('New Arabic') were: (1) the variants of Arabic spoken by the conquering Arab tribes; and (2) the different sorts of diglossia that developed in different situations of linguistic interference with a variety of languages. There is no agreement among Arabists about exactly how this situation developed. Are all modern dialects to be traced back to one kind of spoken Arabic? It is generally admitted that long periods of diglossia between Arabic, on the one hand, and Berber, Coptic, Aramaic, Persian, etc., on the other, must have played a role. It seems probable also that the highly prestigious Classical Arabic always influenced in

some way the different vernaculars. In the present time (2003), an Arabic dialect is spoken by an estimated 170 million Arabs.

Some important differences between most of the Arabic dialects of today and Classical Arabic are:

1. *phonological*: the absence of the glottal stop (except as a reflex of classical /q/); merger of the classical phonemes *d* and *ḍ*; disappearance of final short vowels and shortening of final long vowels.
2. *morphological*: disappearance of the dual in verbs and pronouns; disappearance of the internal passive of the type *fuʿila*; disappearance of the verb-pattern *faʿula*; disappearance of the nominal case-endings; levelling of the three verbal imperfect moods; replacement of the inflected relative pronoun with an uninflected form.
3. *syntactical*: the classical genitive is replaced by a construction with a possessive marker; the verbal system developed aspectual or temporal markers for the prefix conjugation.

References and further reading

Edzard, L. (1998) *Language as a Medium of Legal Norms: Implications of the use of Arabic as a language of the United Nations*, Berlin: Dincker & Humblot.

Jastrow, O. (1984) 'Ein islamischer Sprachraum? Islamische Idiome in den Sprachen muslimischer Völker', in W. Ende and U. Steinbach (eds) *Der Islam in der Gegenwart*, Munich: C.H. Beck, 582–9.

Jenssen, H. (2001) 'Arabic Language', in *EQ*, Vol. 1, 127–35.

Versteegh, K. (2001) *The Arabic Language*, Edinburgh: Edinburgh University Press.

STEFAN WILD

ARGUMENTS AND THE QUR'AN

Many different kinds of argument are found in the Qur'an, as in all religious texts. One of the interesting features of the book is that it often refers to arguments and reasonings that are to be taken to indicate the truth of the book. There is frequent observation in the Book that the verses of the chapters, the *suras*, are called *ayat*, and an *aya* (sing.) is a sign. The verses are called signs because they are taken to be indications of the truth of the book, by contrast, say, with verses of the Torah that are on occasion historical accounts or family genealogy, or a poetic invocation of the greatness of God. Of course, these verses also may be regarded as parts of an argument, but they do seem to be more distantly related to argumentation than much of the Qur'an that constantly calls on its readers and hearers to reflect, ponder and consider what they are hearing or reading.

Critics of the Qur'an have taken seriously its claim to constitute itself the proofs of its veracity, and have tried to pull these proofs to pieces. One very strong claim that the Book makes is that it is itself miraculous in structure. This claim is actually very complex and could mean a host of different things, but one interpretation that Muslims sometimes adopt is that if we examine the text then we will have to conclude, if we are fair-minded, that it could only have come about miraculously. This is a plausible account of the miraculousness claim, especially as many converts to Islam become Muslim after hearing the Book recited or after coming across it in some other way. They hear the Book, or read it perhaps in a non-Arabic version, and it strikes them as true. It has this effect on them because it appears to them that the language is peerless and could come

only from God, or perhaps they are impressed with the arguments in the Book. Many Muslims, it has to be said, are perplexed at people who have access to the Book, who seem not to be obviously evil or stupid, and yet who fail to embrace Islam. Visitors to Islamic countries will find themselves taken to mosques or invited to listen to the words of the *adhan*, the call to prayer, and then see that their hosts are a bit confused as to why they do not become Muslims. Whereas Judaism is strongly linked with ethnicity, and Christianity with a leap of faith, Islam has successfully grown by contrast with these religions by stressing its rationality and evidentiality. It is hardly surprising then that Muslims are sometimes surprised that individuals who appear to be rational, and quite good-hearted nonetheless do not accept that the Book is more than just one book among many others, with many positive qualities no doubt but its very existence is hardly a compelling argument in the competition for adherents.

Where the argument on the inimitable style of the Book gets going is in its opposition to the thesis that the Qur'an is a confused and confusing text. There is a line of approach to the Book that counters the miraculousness claim with the suggestion that, on the contrary, the text is replete with errors. This is linked with the thesis, unacceptable to many Muslims, that there is no final version of the Qur'an that represents the teaching committed to the Prophet, and so it has changed and developed over time before a final version was generally, although not universally, agreed upon. The other general claim is that the text of the Qur'an is not especially well constructed, and that if we examine it impartially we will not be impressed with it, since there is little impressive about much of it. The defenders of this thesis use evidence in just the same way as do their opponents.

Many people read the text and are unimpressed with it, even though they do their best to approach it in a sympathetic and interested manner.

This form of attack against the Book has produced a particular kind of response that is very interesting. What this response does is appeal to the structure of Arabic grammar to point to the careful and logical structure of the very *suras* that are criticized from a stylistic point of view. This is appropriate; after all if a text is criticized as muddled and confused, then showing that it is semantically coherent and logically structured goes a long way towards defeating the sceptic.

So the way to resolve the conflict is presumably to examine a particular *sura* or *aya*, look at how it is criticized from a stylistic point of view, and then examine the defence. We should be able to assess the arguments for and against the style and come to some conclusion about what the most reasonable view is. Defenders of the Qur'an tend to vouch for the perfection and coherence of the style; those uncommitted to it interpret particular *suras* otherwise, or even perhaps the whole text. There is then a dialogue very much of the deaf, with one side proclaiming the style to be wonderful and the other side criticizing it, with it being very unclear what, if anything, would settle the issue. Muslims may regard critics of the texts as stubborn orientalists, intent on finding a non-transcendental explanation for the text. In that way the latter seek to defeat Islam by attacking its main source of written authority. The critics often see the defenders of the text as uncritical and unscholarly in their approach. They are so blinded by faith and advocacy of their spiritual cause that they cannot understand the text objectively and scientifically. Qur'anic Studies, they will say, are a long way behind Biblical

Studies in this respect, since Biblical Studies has for many centuries taken seriously the idea that there are infelicities in the text. Some Biblical scholars identify what they regard as significant problems in the text of the Bible without seeing this as a challenge to their faith, and are annoyed when Qur'anic scholars fail to follow their approach. The Islamic response is that, in contrast with the Bible, the Qur'an is the direct Word of God as transmitted to the Prophet only works if one believes it, and even if one believes it, there is still scope to wonder whether the text available now is the correct text. It is worth pointing out also that many Jews believe that the Pentateuch was received directly from God, that Moses was the direct recipient and that the Israelites were the indirect recipients.

The attacks on the text take a variety of forms, but the most interesting are based on the accusation that the Qur'an is not very successful from a literary perspective. Verbose, confused, disorganized, these are all labels applied by those hostile to the style of the text. The Qur'an is certainly very different from either Bible. For one thing it is not that interested in history, unlike the Jewish and Christian bibles. Defenders of the style of the text try to show that the style is in fact excellent. They point out that in a typical *sura* there is a clear theme, a topic that the *sura* is about. The theme is shown to have consequences for human beings, and so we should learn from it. The content of the *sura* will often consist of rhyming or assonant verses, and these involve grammatical or stylistic development of rhyming or assonant phrases. There is certainly repetition, but the different series of verses work together, so there is a theme in the *sura* that is unified by this variety of different phrases all built around a common idea. The structure, the tone and the content, then, all work together to expand a particular concept, endowing the whole with an underlying unity and coherence.

Word order

Let us take as an example word order. The Qur'an may appear to have a word order that is haphazard. Often particular phrases will be repeated with slight differences, and it is far from clear why. Defenders of the text find a rationale for the word order and for seeing order in what is apparently arbitrary. For example, we have two very similar sentences at 2.62:

Those who believed and those who were Jews or Christians or Sabeans,

and at 6.59 and 22.17 we find:

Those who believed and those who were Jews or Sabeans or Christians.

What is the point of the variation? It could be the context. At 2.62 the emphasis is on the People of the Book, the Jews and the Christians, so they are linked and the Sabeans come afterwards. But in the other passages the emphasis is on history, and since the Sabeans came before the Christians in time, they come before them in the sentence. There is a good way of deciding how plausible this sort of argument is, and that depends on how far we can find similar arguments for an alternative word order. For example, if the Sabeans comes at the end of the phrase at 2.62 because the context is a discussion of polytheism and they are polytheists unlike the other two religions, why do Jews come first in the phrase? Is this because they are less polytheist than Christians, who are themselves less polytheist than the Sabeans? But both Jews and Christians

are People of the Book, and if anything the Qur'an tends to be more critical of the Jews than the Christians. It is difficult to see significance in word order when disjunctives are in operation, since logically 'a or b or c' could just as easily be expressed as 'c or b or a'.

Take the familiar expression '*al-'aziz al-hakim*' (the Excellent, the Wise). This occurs forty-seven times in the text and always in this order. It is sometimes argued that the order is significant since there is no point in having wisdom if you do not have the power to use that wisdom, and the excellence that is referred to here is linked with power. Then there is the phrase '*sami'a basir*', used to describe God, the All-Hearing, the All-Seeing, which occurs twenty-six times, in that precise order. One reason for the order is that hearing is regarded in Islam as more significant than sight. For instance, at 20.46 God says 'I hear and see everything', clearly prioritizing hearing, and at 16.78 'He gave you hearing, sight'. On the other hand, the order is reversed when God compares the blind and the deaf, the seeing and the hearing (11.24). But for complete consistency there is no reason for this order not being reversed to cohere with the other formulations of this phrase. On the other hand, it does make for a more attractive text if there is occasional variation of familiar phrases. There is certainly a point to repetition, but occasional variation does emphasize the repetition and produce a more lively text.

While we are dealing with sound, let us look at the phrase '*al-jinn wa'l-insan*' (the *jinn* and humanity), that occurs in that order at 6.130; 7.38, 179; 27.17; 41.25, 29; 46.18; 51.56; 55.33. Both words end with an alveolar nasal sound, and clearly the combination of these two endings produces a pleasant aural tone. Of course the tone is just as pleasant if the words are reversed, as they are at

6.112; 17.88; and 72.5. Yet in the latter cases the *jinn* are taken to refer only to unbelieving beings, and so come after human beings. In the former cases the *jinn* refers both to unbelieving beings and to angels, and so come before human beings. It is worth pointing out that this explanation appears to place angels above human beings, a strange occurrence given that God orders the angels to bow to Adam. A more plausible explanation for the variation is that occasional variation in some phrases produces a more interesting sound quality in the text, and we must never forget that the Qur'an is meant to be heard – reading it lags well behind in terms of impact. As we have seen, hearing is stressed in Islam over sight, and the sound of the recited text is highly significant in the effect that it produces in the listener. Obviously that effect is itself to a degree a function of the lexical meanings of the text, but these may resonate against the sounds of the words and phrases themselves and help the listener concentrate on particular phrases by observing slight variations in them.

Is the Qur'an a code?

Let us examine the logic of this kind of hermeneutic strategy. There is a long tradition in religious thought to see the main text of the faith as a code. Often this is presented as the text having two main messages, one for everyone and one for a limited group of people. This is not a doctrine in any way disparaging to the understanding of the majority of the believing community, it is simply that they are happy with the apparent meaning of the text, as they should be since that meaning is clear, true and divinely inspired. They find within the book a guide to their lives, a system of rules of behaviour and a discussion of the doctrines that they are to accept,

and they are perfectly satisfied with what they find.

Another group of believers accepts everything that the main body of believers accepts, at least nominally, but think that the words of the text contain within them hidden meanings. For example, a word in the text may need to be linked with a different word because it has the same numerical value as that word, while reading the text itself would never reveal the point of that comparison. This only works for languages whose letters have numerical equivalences, of course, but even languages without such equivalences may be studied numerically, in the sense that one can link every tenth letter, or fiftieth letter, or every twentieth chapter, and so on. The notion of the text being a code is important here. A code gives us the rules for transforming one sort of text into something else, into what it really means.

It will be said that this account of religion fails to capture something that the code idea does capture – the mystery involved in religion. There certainly is a notion of mystery in many religions, but this can be overdone. Many religious believers treat their faith as just another aspect of their lives, like their nationality or the place in which they live; it is not something that they have spent agonized days, weeks or months pondering over. One of the aspects of religion that many Muslim theologians stress is its naturalness, and the clarity of the Qur'an as a text is something it reminds us of quite often (44.58; 54.17, 21, 32, 40).

The naturalness of belief

The idea that religious belief is natural tends to support the ideas of the Qur'an as a code. The Sufis often compare natural objects with the letters of the Qur'an, and just as an education in

Arabic can lead a reader to understand the text, so seeing the world in the right sort of way can help us understand what it really means. When Adam is in the Garden of Eden, God teaches him the names of things, implying that the natural world is something to be understood by us. Without knowing how to put the various individual items of the world together in the right way, one cannot understand their meaning, since like the letters in a word, their individual meaning is very much part of their potential combination in something larger.

Religions often want to go in two directions at once. They want to emphasize their accessibility and to assert that anyone can understand the main propositions and principles of the faith. This is equivalent to saying that the religion is natural and acceptance of it just as smooth and fitting. On the other hand, they want to point to levels of understanding that require special training or thought, and that are not available to every believer. This tension is often misinterpreted as a battle between faith and reason, but of course it is something else entirely. It is not in fact a battle at all, but a way of seeing the same thing in two different yet compatible ways, to express it in Averroist language. The philosopher Ibn Rushd (Averroes, 1126–1198) argued that religion and philosophy were two different ways of coming to the same conclusion.

There has been a long discussion in Islam about the significance of *taqlid* or imitation. Who should be followed or imitated when it comes to religious practice and doctrine? Clearly any religion requires interpretation, and there are some people who are skilled in interpretation. They are the people to follow when it comes to seeking an understanding of what the religion means or requires us to do. In any area we follow the expert, since if we knew what to do, we would not need to ask an expert in the first place. But two issues arise here. One is familiar to people who need work to be done on their houses, and that is how to recognize precisely who is an expert. The other is the inadvisability of blindly following the expert. There is merit in working things out for oneself, and these are not solely based on the personal satisfaction of doing so (although this is indeed very pleasing). The Qur'an is full of injunctions to its hearers and readers to consider, think, reason, and that is because Muslims are supposed to use their rational faculties to work out what the text means and indeed what everything means, insofar as they can.

Taqlid can be appropriate in that there are people who can help us understand a text and its contemporary relevance while we are unable to grasp this, given our lack of knowledge of the whole book and other appropriate sources of information. It is rational to follow such authorities, but this is not blind obedience. This is submitting oneself to the authority of another when one has good grounds for so doing. Those good grounds are established rationally.

This brings out a problem in the notion of religious government. Who better can govern the state than those who are in tune with higher metaphysical realities? This point was made as early as Plato, and he makes a direct comparison between learning a skill and political ability. But even those who are broadly in favour of such a strategy often advise caution. To take a fairly recent case, Ayatollah Taleqani and Murtaza Mutahhari in Iran discussed the necessity for collective leadership to meet the very complex problems of modernity. Ayatollah Khomeini commented that the religious leadership in contemporary society needs to reflect the complexity of that society if it is really going to establish a religious state. What is this complexity? It is not the complexity of new problems arising due to the changing structure of society and the problems it brings with it. These can be dealt with entirely successfully using traditional legal techniques. Rather, the idea that religious and legal theses should be the ruling principles of the state itself in every particular does call for radical steps in interpretation, since it is often not clear how to use religious law to resolve modern problems. That they can be so used is not problematic, but precisely how to use them may be. Hence the advisability of a number of legal authorities conferring and discussing the appropriate way forwards rather than just one outstanding authority prescribing the way that things will be.

Another point made by Mutahhari is that religious belief is natural, in his view, while atheism is unnatural. The Qur'an itself considers the idea that the world is merely a material place, and rejects it. Belief is natural because it is so obviously part of a worthwhile lifestyle, according to Mutaharri, and rejecting belief as a valuable set of ideas is akin to rejecting health as a desirable state to enjoy. So there is something clear and evident in the legal judgements of the religious leader; they key into basic human needs and interests, albeit not necessarily present human desires. Again, we may talk about a logic there, in that the realm of law follows a reasoning process that fits in with human beings, and by this is not necessarily meant a legal school that employs the principle of *istihsan* or human welfare in coming to its conclusions. Even legal theories that do not apply such a principle will see themselves and the law itself as fitting in with the world and its creatures, since that very law was established by the creator of that world and

everything in it, and one would be right to expect that everything would cohere with what is in the best interests of creation.

The Qur'an is full of arguments, and many of them have at their basis the idea that God, the ultimate creator, knows the nature of everything in the world, and especially his human creatures, and that he has brought about a type of creation that is very much in the interests of his creation. As one might expect, the Creator then establishes rules that he expects people to obey if they are to get the best out of the world. The text constantly provides reasons for believing what it asserts, and these reasons owe their plausibility to the idea that God wishes to communicate with his creation. He does this through messengers, and although God has the best interests of his creation in mind, his creatures often reject what he has to say. This is not because of any doctrine of original sin, but because God has made everyone differently and so is not surprised at the differences in their responses to him. He could have made everyone the same, and thus avoided this sort of diversity of opinion (11.118; 10.19; 16.93) but he chose not to do so.

Does the text really argue for the existence of God? Not very seriously; this is taken to be an obvious fact, based on the facts of life, and nature, like the verses of the Qur'an, is full of 'signs (*ayat*) for people who understand' (2.164). There is quite a bit of argument about why we should believe in the existence of one God as opposed to many gods, and why associating partners with God, *shirk*, is to be rejected totally. There are also plenty of arguments for the fact of resurrection, a basic doctrine given the importance of rejecting materialism and the idea that our deaths are followed by nothing more than the collapse and decay of our bodies. There is sometimes the suggestion that the opponents of Islam in their hearts know it is right ('and they rejected [our signs] while their souls were convinced of them' (27.14)). There are also many arguments for the prophethood of the Prophet himself, and much of this clearly replicates the sort of to and fro of debate that took place in Mecca and Medina when Islam was becoming established in the face of fierce opposition.

A whole variety of argument types are employed here. The Peripatetic philosophers, *falasifa* like Ibn Rushd and his predecessors such as al-Farabi used the *Organon* of Aristotle as an example of how such arguments may vary in form and in particular in the universality of their conclusion. So we have a hierarchy of argumentative strength, with demonstration at the summit, where we operate with true premises and use them to arrive at valid and entirely general conclusions. Then comes dialectic, where the premises we use are those supplied by the side with which we are debating, and so we have no reason to think they are true. After this a number of other argument types follow, rhetoric and poetry, for example, where the point is to change people's mind by the use of imagination and appeals to the emotions, and where the validity of the conclusion may be quite limited, limited to a particular audience within a particular context. This does not mean that there is anything wrong with the argument – it is a perfectly acceptable argument of its type– but not up to the rigour of demonstration, nor even dialectic. The Qur'an advises Muslims to speak with others in a 'beautiful preaching' (16.125; 29.46) and this refers to stimulating an audience by stressing what it would be interested in and avoiding the more technical and less obviously attractive aspects of the religion.

The Qur'an is full of arguments that appeal to our understanding of what is in our interests and how we should live our lives. These are indeed arguments, but we should bear in mind the warnings of the *falasifa* who acknowledged that they were only as strong as their premises are true. If it is not the case that Tony the Tiger really knows what I should eat for breakfast in the morning, then my being persuaded by him may be based on a degree of rationality, but ultimately it is based on something that is not true, his incorrect claims about a particular series of facts about diet, health, taste, and so on.

This makes it look like the logic of the Qur'an is weak, if it can be likened to using figurative language to try to persuade an audience of the truth. We do not normally regard that sort of communication as particularly impressive. Yet it is worth bearing in mind how much that is important in our lives is decided through reasoning that on the face of it is far from demonstrative in the Aristotelian sense. So while the reasons we give for action may explain the action in the sense of showing that it was carried out for certain purposes and within a particular context, it does not explain it in the sense of showing that it had to happen. The *falasifa* were quite clear on this, and in their analysis of different sorts of writing and speech they sharply distinguished between different levels of logical strength in the variety of language forms that are available to us, and they argued that each type of argument form was appropriate to different kinds of human activity.

The use of reasons

The fact that reasons may explain but not determine subsequent actions was not properly grasped by al-Ghazali, advocate though he was of the use of logic in theology and of its incorporation as a natural part of Islamic thought. Al-Ghazali criticized thinkers such as Miskawayh for believing that God had reasons to establish certain rituals which link up with human nature. Miskawayh suggests that many of the rites of Islam have the aim of strengthening the links between believers, so that religion uses social norms to encourage and increase religious observance. Al-Ghazali is horrified by this suggestion, arguing that God institutes rules just because he wants to; there is no necessity for him to bow to our social instincts, nor even to employ them. Where al-Ghazali goes awry here is thinking that because God may have had reasons for what he did, those reasons would make his actions inevitable. He would be forced by the reasons to act in a particular way. The Mu'tazilites did in fact argue in this way that God has to follow certain principles of morality in his behaviour; he has to have justice in mind when he acts. Al-Ghazali rejected that theory, arguing plausibly that it is an error to think that God must have a particular purpose in mind when he does something. But he went too far in suggesting that God could have nothing in mind when he does something; that all he wants to do in telling us how to act is to demonstrate his power and the necessity on our part to obey him. Having reasons for action only constrains us if they inevitably result in particular actions, but this is not the case for God and it is not the case for us.

One might think that the case for God would be different here than it is for us. After all, our action is always rather haphazard; we lack a firm understanding often of the situation we are in or how we ought to act. We are finite creatures with a partial view of the world and ourselves. None of this is true of God, who is perfect, infinite and understands everything. Yet for him also reasons do not determine. There are many things he can do and might wish to do, given the same set of facts. This comes out in a very nice story by al-Juwayni designed to show the shallowness of the Mu'tazilite theory. The tale involves three people who die. One is evil and goes to hell; one is going to become evil, so God kills him and as a child he goes to the *barzakh*, so avoiding hell; while another who has lived well goes to heaven. The child complains that he missed the opportunity of going to heaven by dying early, although God informs him that had he lived he would have been evil and gone to hell. The sinner in hell complains that God should have killed him while a child so that at least he would have avoided hell and earned the *barzakh*. Al-Juwayni quite rightly took this example to show that the idea that there is just one concept of justice, that expounded by the Mu'tazilites, and that this represents the general principle according to which God has to operate, is vacuous. God could decide to intervene directly in our lives to prevent us from developing in the ways in which we otherwise would do, but he also might not. That is true of us also; we can often intervene to help or hinder others, and we sometimes do and sometimes do not. There are reasons for what we do, but those reasons do not determine the action.

When the angels are told by God to bow down to Adam, and they complain saying that Adam and his descendants will wreck the earth if they gain power over it, the angels have a point. But God replies that he understands this and will send human beings a guide. The notion of a guide is important here: a guide guides, indicates the right direction and the appropriate sources of information for determining the right direction. The guide does not force people to obey him nor even to accept him. The guide brings a message, but messages get distorted and twisted, or are just honestly misunderstood. God provides general advice and instructions to his creation, but within that context there is a great deal of freedom for believers to make their own decisions and take their own risks. The reasons they accept as significant in controlling their actions do not point to a set of clear and distinct propositions, since if they did, there would be no variety of understandings of religion, or even of Islam. Since the Qur'an tells us sometimes to respect diversity in humanity and forbids us from compelling religious allegiance, the idea that reasons are not followed inevitably by particular actions and beliefs is presumably well taken.

Reasons and the logic of the Qur'an

There are two worrying aspects of this rather relaxed atmosphere towards the role of reasons in explaining our actions and beliefs. One is that it looks like the Qur'an is not using the gold standard of argument – i.e. demonstrative argument – as its main argument form. On the contrary, it is using a whole variety of what from a logical point of view has to be called weaker forms of argument. The other problem follows from this. The putative link between reasons and action is the only basis upon which we can talk about Qur'anic *logic* in the first place. If this link starts to look very weak, or even non-existent, then the description of the Book as containing a logic will have to be reconsidered. The first objection can be resolved if we point out that different audiences and different situations call for different sorts of argument. One of the ways in which *tafsir* or commentary often operates is to discuss the particular situation in which a *sura* was revealed. So if it occurred at a certain time and place, perhaps in Medina after a particular event, then we can understand what the text was designed to do. The audience of the time would have had certain experiences of the religion and its followers at that point, and so they would be addressed in a certain way. Although commentators argue about the precise dating of the *suras*, it does seem broadly clear which are Meccan and which are Medinan, and which a mixture, and what the order of revelation is. We could also here refer to the famous Aristotelian principle that degrees of exactitude are never themselves exact. Precision is relative to the situation in which we find ourselves. Someone in the street who asks me the time should be happy with the report of my wristwatch. She is not asking me to discover what an atomic clock says the time is.

The other objection looks stronger, and it suggests that the whole concept of a Qur'anic logic falls down because the link between the argument for the statements in the text and our logical need to accept the conclusions of those arguments is quite weak. Some hearers and readers will accept them, and some will not. Although the Qur'an sometimes suggests that people will wilfully deny the truth ('and they rejected [our signs] while their souls were convinced of them (27.14)'), this does not seem to be a very sensible policy, since the penalties for such behaviour are pretty severe. We have already seen that reasons for belief are not the same as the premises in a syllogism that compel acceptance of a conclusion if one is to be rational. Then how can we refer to the reasoning itself as logical? The answer here is that the logic of the argument lies in the production of reasons that make a particular conclusion plausible, albeit perhaps not compelling.

For al-Farabi, the prophet is someone of sterling moral character chosen by God to transmit a message. From a philosophical point of view he is someone of sterling moral character whose mind is in line with the active intellect and so who knows how to persuade an audience of a particular point of view. The philosopher and the believer both see the same thing, the Prophet, but analyse what they see differently; nonetheless both judgements are true. It would even be wrong to see one of the judgements as primarily intellectual and abstract and the other as 'popular', since the sort of language that surrounds religious description is hardly simple and perspicuous. Often theology is more complex than philosophy, and the views of the ordinary believer are more complicated than those of the thinker who can organize his or her thought into clear and distinct categories. This was very much the point of the *falasifa*, the Islamic philosophers in the Peripatetic tradition, namely, that each way of talking was valid.

There is clearly a Qur'anic logic in the sense of many arguments in the text, very different kinds of argument that are designed to meet particular objections and establish basic points. Whether the style is really unique is an aesthetic claim that is rather dangerous, since it is of the nature of such claims that they may be challenged by those with opposite reactions. It is worth adding here that of course for Islam the Qur'an itself is not the only significant source of information: the *sunna* or practice of the Prophet, the Traditions (sayings attributed to the Prophet and those close to him – *ahadith*) and other authorities, depending upon one's school of thought, are also crucial. But it is only the Qur'an that has been claimed as inimitable, and as the main repository of detailed arguments both for and against

particular propositions. We can talk of such a logic if by that we mean different kinds of arguments that are designed to help us see the world in a particular way. Since many people are Muslims and become Muslims after examining the Qur'an, presumably those arguments are effective in helping their audience see the world in the appropriate way.

But can we say that the text contains a logic that is unique in its strength or persuasiveness? If by strength, we mean logical rigour, then the answer is certainly no. If by persuasiveness, we mean actual success in persuading people that this looks more plausible, it would also require some proof that it was the logic of the text that did the persuading, rather than something else like marrying someone or wishing to annoy someone else. This is always a problem in religion, of course, that of working out what it is that motivates a believer, and it would surely be wrong to insist that the argument was *never* experienced as persuasive. On the other hand, it would also be wrong to insist that claims to have been persuaded by the text are always accurate, since we often do not really understand why we adopt a particular propositional attitude.

One aspect of the Qur'an that is very important and that has hardly been mentioned so far is its beauty. This is often taken to be a decisive proof of its divine status, since the challenge (*tahaddi*) is made to produce anything as beautiful. A difficulty with this argument is based on the difficulty of any argument that has as its main factor an aesthetic attitude. As we know all too well, what one person calls beautiful, another person may find very different, so it seems a rather slim foundation for an important claim about the divine origin of the text. Even if we see aesthetic judgment as being based on logic, as the *falasifa* certainly did, we are still left with a rather vague proposition as a conclusion, either dealing with the eliciting of an emotion or the sharing of an attitude. Here again we can talk about a Qur'anic logic in the sense of a reasoning process in which reasons and argument have an important but not compelling role. The Qur'an does indeed display an unusual commitment to argument and logic in its self-explanation.

Further reading

Abdul-Raof, H. (2000) 'The Linguistic Architecture of the Qur'an', *Journal of Qur'anic Studies* 2, 2: 37–51.

al-Baqillani, Abu Bakr Muhammad (1994) *I'jaz al-Qur'an*, Beirut: Dar Ihya' al-'Ulum.

Benmakhlouf, A. (2004) 'Assent and Truth in the Medieval Arab: Philosophical Tradition', in *Keywords: Truth*, ed. D. Posel. New York: Other Press, pp. 53–84.

Cragg, K. (1994) *The Event of the Qur'an*, 2nd edn, Oxford: OneWorld.

Gwynne, R. (2004) *Logic, Rhetoric, and Legal Reasoning in the Qur'an: God's arguments*, New York: RoutledgeCurzon.

Izutsu, T (1966) *Ethico-Religious Concepts in the Qur'an*, Montreal: McGill University Press.

—— (1980) *God and Man in the Koran: Semantics of the Koranic Weltanschauung*. Tokyo: The Keio Institute of Cultural and Linguistic Studies.

Jomier, J. (1997) *The Great Themes of the Qur'an*, London: SCM Press.

al-Juwayni (1950) *Kitab al-irshad ila qawati al-adilla fi usul al-i'tiqad*, ed. M. Musa and A. 'Abd al-Hamid, Cairo.

Leaman, O. (1990) *Averroes and his Philosophy*, London: RoutledgeCurzon.

—— (2001) *Introduction to Classical Islamic Philosophy*, Cambridge: Cambridge University Press.

—— (2004) *Islamic Aesthetics: An introduction*, Edinburgh, Edinburgh University Press, esp. 141–64.

Marshall, D. (1999) *God, Muhammad and the Unbelievers: A Qur'anic study*, London: RoutledgeCurzon.

McAuliffe, J.D. (ed.) (2001) 'Debate and Disputation', in *EQ*, Vol. 1, 511–14.

Mutahhari, M. (1985) *Fundamentals of Islamic Thought*, trans. R. Campbell, Berkeley: Mizan.

Nasr, S. and Leaman, O. (eds) (1996) *History of Islamic Philosophy*, London: Routledge.

Peters, F.E. (ed.) (1999) *The Arabs and Arabia on the Eve of Islam*, Brookfield: Ashgate.

al-Qurtubi, Abu 'Abd Allah Muhammad (1997) *al-Jami' li Ahkam al-Qur'an*, Beirut: Dar al-kitab al-'arabi, Vols 1–20.

Radscheit, M. (1997) 'Word of God or Prophetic Speech? Reflections on the Qur'anic *qul*-statements', in L. Edzard and C. Szyska (eds) *Encounters of Words and Texts: Intercultural studies in honor of Stefan Wild on the occasion of his 60th Birthday, March 2, 1997, presented by his pupils in Bonn*, Hildesheim: Georg Olms, 33–42.

Rahman, F. (1980) *Major Themes of the Qur'an*, Minneapolis: Bibliotheca Islamica.

Robinson, N. (1996) *Discovering the Qur'an: A contemporary approach to a veiled text*, London: SCM Press.

Urvoy, M. (2002) 'De quelques procédés de persuasion dans le Coran', *Arabica* 49: 456–76.

Waardenburg, J. (1980) 'Faith and Reason in the Argumentation of the Qur'an', *Perennitas: Studi in Onore di Angelo Brelich*, Rome: Edizioni dell'Ateneo, 619–33.

Welch, A. (1980) 'Allah and Other Supernatural Beings: The emergence of the Qur'anic doctrine of *tawhid*', *Journal of the American Academy of Religion* 47: 733–758.

—— (2000) 'Formulaic Features of the Punishment-Stories', in I.J. Boullata (ed.) *Literary Structures of Religious Meaning in the Qur'an*, London: RoutledgeCurzon, 77–116.

al-Zamakhshari, Abu al-Qasim (1995) *al-Kashshaf*, Beirut: Dar al-kutub al-'ilmiyya, Vols 1–4.

Zebiri. K. (2003) 'Towards a Rhetorical Criticism of the Qur'an', *Journal of Qur'anic Studies* 5: 95–120.

—— (2005) 'Polemic and Polemical Language', in *EQ*, Vol. 4.

—— (forthcoming) 'Argumentation in the Qur'an', in A. Rippin (ed.) *Blackwell Companion to the Qur'an*, Oxford: Blackwell.

See also: **inimitability; language and the Qur'an; philosophy and the Qur'an; self-referentiality**

OLIVER LEAMAN

ARKOUN, MOHAMMED

Mohammed Arkoun (b. 1928) is an internationally acclaimed Franco-Algerian historian and philosopher who spent most of his working life in Paris where he held the post of Emeritus Professor at the Sorbonne. He has persistently sought to recover the breadth and diversity of classical Arab thought and to rethink Islam and Islamic studies in the light of the social sciences and modern philosophy. His principal contribution specifically to the study of the Qur'an comprises seven articles written between 1970 and 1980 which were republished as *Lectures du Coran* (Readings of the Qur'an) in 1982. The book also included an introduction in which Arkoun assessed the current state of Qur'anic Studies and indicated avenues for future research. He returned to this theme almost twenty years later in an equally thought-provoking essay on 'Contemporary Critical Practices and the Qur'an'.

A bio-bibliographical sketch

Mohammed Arkoun is at the time of writing (2004) Emeritus Professor of the History of Islamic Thought at the Sorbonne, Senior Research Fellow and member of the Board of Governors of The Institute of Ismaili Studies in London, and Editor of the journal *Arabica*. He was born in Algeria in 1928. Although his mother tongue is Berber, he studied Arabic at the University of Algiers and then moved to France where he gained the coveted *agrégation* in Arabic language and literature in 1956. Apart from brief periods in Strasbourg

(1956–59) and Lyons (1969–72), and sabbaticals in the USA, the Netherlands and Germany, he spent most of his academic career in Paris. On retiring in 1992, he took up a one-year fellowship at the Institute of Advanced Studies in Princeton. He was decorated as an Officer of the French Légion d'honneur in 1996. He was also awarded the Georgio Levi Della Vida Award for his lifelong contribution to the field of Islamic Studies in 2002 and the Ibn Rushd Prize for Freedom of Thought in 2003.

Arkoun usually writes in French, although many of his works have been translated into Arabic and a few have appeared in English. We cannot here offer an exhaustive account of his wide-ranging scholarly output but in this and the next section we will attempt to situate his contribution to Qur'anic Studies in relation to his other research interests. In his doctoral thesis, which was published in 1970, he wrote on the tenth-century philosopher Miskawayh, arguing that he was the product of an incipient Arab humanism that fostered the pursuit of knowledge in the interests of society, unhampered by a priori theological considerations. The same might be said of Arkoun himself, although in his case it would be more accurate to speak of him as the product of an incipient Franco-Arab humanism.

In 1975 he published *La Pensée Arabe* (Arab thought), an analytical sketch that covers the whole 1,400-year history of Islam. The first chapter focuses on the event of the Qur'an. There are brief sections on 'Revelation', 'The Qur'an' and 'Exegesis' in *Rethinking Islam* (1989; English translation, 1994), and the first two chapters of *The Unthought in Contemporary Islamic Thought* (2002) set the parameters for a comparative approach to the study of revelation in Judaism, Christianity and Islam. However, Arkoun's principal contribution specifically to Qur'anic Studies is in seven articles that were re-issued in a single volume in 1982 as *Lectures du Coran* (Readings of the Qur'an). An English rendering of the chapter headings is given below. The dates of the articles are indicated in brackets.

1. How to Read the Qur'an (1970)
2. The Problem of the Divine Authenticity of the Qur'an (1977)
3. A Reading of the al-Fatiha (1974)
4. A Reading of *sura* 18 (1980)
5. Can We Speak of Marvels in the Qur'an? (1974)
6. Introduction to the Study of the Connections between Islam and Politics (1979)
7. The Hajj in Islamic Thought (1977).

The book has a valuable introductory essay which is now available in English as 'Introduction: An assessment of and perspective on the study of the Qur'an'. Arkoun returned to this theme almost twenty years later in an equally thought-provoking article on 'Contemporary Critical Practices and the Qur'an', which was commissioned for the first volume of *The Encyclopaedia of the Qur'an*.

Arkoun's critical philosophy and epistemology

Lectures du Coran is not the only collection of articles that Arkoun had contributed to academic journals in the course of the 1960s and 1970s. It was preceded in 1973 by *Essais sur la pensée islamique* (Essays on Islamic thought) and followed in 1984 by *Pour une critique de la raison islamique* (For a critique of Islamic reason). The three volumes constitute a trilogy insofar as they are all concerned with the method or grounds of knowledge in Islamic studies as practised in the Arab-Muslim cultural system and in its non-Muslim Western counterpart. Arkoun's researches on the Qur'an are thus part of a larger long-term project and cannot be understood in isolation.

The title of the third volume gives some indication of the aim and scope of the project as a whole. Like the eighteenth-century philosopher Immanuel Kant, author of the seminal *Critique of Pure Reason*, Arkoun seeks to 'critique' or come to grips with the limitations of our mental capacities by showing that we are constrained to perceive and think about the world in certain ways. However, whereas Kant attributed the constraints on our perceptions and thoughts to the innate structures of the human mind which he assumed were more or less identical in all societies and all ages, Arkoun rejects the notion of a 'pure' transcendent reason and maintains that consciousness has a history that should be studied in its own right. He argues that for an author who lives at a given time and place, and belongs to a specific linguistic community, some things are 'thinkable', insofar as it is possible to think and express them with the help of the available mental equipment, whereas others are 'unthinkable', because of the cognitive limits of the social-cultural system, or simply remain 'unthought', because the author has internalized the constraints imposed by the dominant ideology.

Arkoun's views on the history of consciousness and the relationship between power and knowledge were influenced by the writings of his near contemporary Michel Foucault (d. 1984), who occupied the chair in the History of Systems of Thought at the Collège de France. Foucault coined the term 'episteme' to denote the mass of assumptions that we tend to take for granted, the invisible boundaries of our thought. He held that the historical succession of epistemes is arbitrary; there is no necessary connection between them. Consequently we should not assume that concepts and ideas can be easily and accurately understood and translated through the ages. Our impression that history is a linear progression and that there are continuities between successive worldviews is an illusion created by the dominant discourses that have triumphed over other forms of knowledge and projected their own origins into the past. What people take as truth in a given historical situation is thus produced by the operations of power. Taking his cue from Foucault, Arkoun has exposed the ideological dimensions of the principal Islamic epistemes. He has also begun the task of thinking the 'unthought' in the field of Qur'anic Studies.

The Qur'an in the Arab–Muslim cultural system

Arkoun identifies the years 632 CE and 936 CE as major turning points when the borders between the thinkable, the unthinkable and the unthought shifted decisively. The first date is that of the Prophet's death, which brought the twenty-three year period of revelation to a close. The second is that of the reform instigated by Abu Bakr ibn Mujahid, which ended the rivalries between scholars of Qur'an recitation by proscribing the variant readings attributed to the Prophet's companions 'Ubayy, Ibn Mas'ud and 'Ali b. Abi Talib, some of which differed considerably from the 'Uthmanic text. This event marked the final step in the protracted process of collecting the revelations and fixing them in writing. It also inaugurated 'the time of orthodoxy', which extends from 936 CE to the present and is dominated by a vision of Islam as a complete all-embracing system established by the Prophet on the basis of the Qur'an. Those who share this vision revere the Qur'an in its entirety as the Word of God and hold that it has been transmitted reliably from generation to generation by an unbroken succession of impeccable guarantors who have likewise handed down its authoritative interpretation. Sunnis and Shi'ites differ over the routes of transmission, the ethico-religious status of the transmitters and the details of the interpretation, but not over the divine origin of the revelations and the manner in which they were preserved. They are thus bound by the same basic episteme.

When investigating the secondary literature on the Qur'an produced by orthodox scholars, Arkoun has focused primarily on the Sunni classics. Apart from the major commentaries, which will be mentioned later, the single most important work is the 1,500-page *Itqan fi 'ulum al-Qur'an* (Quest for certainty in the Qur'anic sciences) compiled by the mediaeval Egyptian scholar al-Suyuti (d. 1505). This scholastic encyclopedist reproduced the information that had accumulated over the previous 900 years, arranging it under eighty headings or 'categories' of knowledge. Arkoun makes a number of observations about the subjects that al-Suyuti covers and how he deals with them. He notes for instance the extensive treatment of prosody and textual units (thirteen categories), which he attributes to their relevance to the memorization and recitation of the Qur'an. He also notes that because rhetoric and logico-semantic analysis are needed for deducing the requirements of the *shari'a*, al-Suyuti allots far more space to them (twenty-three categories) than he does to syntax and vocabulary (six categories). As regards chronology and the modes of revelation (sixteen categories), here too the relevance of the information for establishing Islamic law is paramount. Hence, instead of offering his readers historically based discussions of these topics, al-Suyuti merely gives them brief summaries of the 'orthodox' position. Arkoun concludes that the *Itqan* and other books of this genre do not yield many genuine insights concerning the Qur'an. Their aim is to furnish Muslims with indispensable practical information and nourish their belief in the divine basis of the Law, the supernatural character of the revelation, and the utterly reliable conditions under which it was transmitted and reproduced.

Arkoun is equally sceptical about the contribution of the classical commentaries to our understanding the Qur'an. In the course of Chapter 4 of his *Lectures*, where he focuses on *sura* 18, he discusses the 30-volume commentary of al-Tabari (d. 923), which became the basis for almost all subsequent exegesis. Because it comprises a wealth of reports, each supported by one or more chains of guarantors tracing it back to a named Companion, Successor or other early authority, this commentary is often viewed as the work of an objective compiler who made an exhaustive collection of the available traditions. Arkoun insists, however, that al-Tabari selected and arranged his material in view of his political and religious convictions, seeking to legitimize the 'Abbasids and disqualify the Umayyads and political Shi'ism. That is why he attempted to harmonize variant readings, gave a clear paraphrase of the verses and tackled controversial points with calculated prudence. Arkoun also draws attention to the importance that al-Tabari and his fellow commentators attached to real or imaginary episodes in the life of the Prophet which allegedly constituted the spatio-temporal framework for the revelation of individual verses, longer

sections or, in some cases, whole *suras*. These framing narratives, as he calls them, assure the Qur'anic datum a concrete historical basis that is absent from folk tales and works of fiction. In the process, however, they tend to make the highly allusive symbolic text appear excessively banal because they transcribe it into a realist commentary.

Napoleon Bonaparte's expedition to Egypt in 1798–1801 brought the Arab world face to face with modernity. However, although Arkoun recognizes that extensive contact with Europeans over the past two centuries has altered the conditions in which Arab Muslims engage in thinking, he denies that it has led to a radically new episteme in the Arab-Muslim cultural system. On the contrary, he laments that Muslim scholars remain imprisoned in the same dogmatic enclosure and have not contributed to the contemporary debate on revelation, truth and history. Modern Qur'an scholarship is inferior to classical: the textbooks on Qur'anic Studies used in traditional Islamic institutions are little more than digests of the *Itqan* of al-Suyuti, and the great classical commentaries continue to function as orthodox corpora of interpretation. The reasons for this state of affairs are complex. They include the relative neglect of the humanities and social sciences in Arab universities, and the continued ideological importance of Islam both to the governing elites and their political opponents. In addition, Arkoun suggests that the framing narratives in the classical commentaries receive from the Qur'anic discourse a special value that places them above all profane narratives: they are 'contaminated by transcendence', which explains why believers remain attached to classical exegesis and distrust modern intellectualist analyses.

Orientalist and social-science approaches to Qur'anic Studies

Arkoun's attitude to orientalist scholarship is ambivalent. He acknowledges that during the colonial period advocates of the historical-critical method performed a valuable task by opening up fields of enquiry considered taboo by most Muslims. These included textual criticism and the chronological ranking of the *suras*, both of which are of vital importance to the historian. However, he laments that European Qur'an specialists have tended to restrict themselves to the philological restoration of the text and the historical reconstruction of simple facts, and have largely neglected methodological issues and questions of an epistemological nature. Similarly, those concerned with the history of exegesis have usually focused on the works of 'orthodox' writers and concentrated on translating them or summarizing them for the benefit of non-Arabists. What is needed, and what Arkoun urges, is a full-scale rethinking and revitalization of the discipline in light of the social sciences.

It is relatively easy to grasp what this might entail as regards the history of interpretation. Instead of majoring in the key works of scholars who are considered orthodox or who stand out because of their intellectual stature, researchers would seek to situate exegesis within the history of Islamic consciousness of a given society by drawing on every scrap of available evidence concerning people's beliefs and practices. They would not neglect writers who belonged to marginalized groups or run-of-the-mill orthodox scholars. On the contrary, the works of such individuals are invaluable for charting shifts in the boundaries between the thinkable, the unthinkable and the unthought.

Arkoun's approach to the Qur'an itself is more difficult to summarize. He considers that the collection of the revelations and the production of a closed written corpus paved the way for successive generations of Muslim rulers to monopolize the sacred text. They did this, and still do, by patronizing religious scholars willing to legitimize their claim to power by linking it with the Qur'an's transcendent authority. Therefore, while recognizing that our knowledge of the period of the Prophet will inevitably remain incomplete, we should strive to recapture the spirit of the revelations as a living Word that enunciates what is ultimately significant, rather than as a closed corpus of Scripture standardized by the state and expounded by accredited interpreters in accordance with the ideology of their political masters. Arkoun has issued lists of programmatic statements concerning how this is to be done but in many instances the details remain to be fleshed out. In broad terms what he proposes is an exhaustive analysis of sixth- and seventh-century Middle Eastern culture followed by an equally exhaustive investigation of how the Qur'an transforms the religious consciousness of those who listen to it receptively. Both entail using the methods of cultural anthropology, political science, religious psychology, structural linguistics and semiotics. In the first chapter of his *Lectures*, for example, he outlines the symbolic universe or 'mythical structure' of the Qur'an and analyses several of the semantic fields of Qur'anic Arabic.

Although some Muslims view Arkoun with suspicion, scholars of all hues who are committed to the cognitive project of understanding religious phenomena cannot fail to find his writings stimulating. Despite his lifelong quest for a universal perspective on Islam, his approach nevertheless appears unmistakably

French. There is also an unresolved tension in his work. At times he writes as a self-confident modernist who is convinced that the secularization of knowledge has led to genuine progress and that the social sciences have at long last furnished the keys for unlocking many of the mysteries of the Qur'an and the history of its interpretation. At others, he seems more attracted to a postmodernist relativism.

Further reading

Arkoun, M. (1975) *La Pensée Arabe*, Paris: Presses Universitaires de France.
—— (1982) *Lectures du Coran*, Paris: G.-P. Maisonneuve et Larose.
—— (2001a) 'Contemporary Critical Practices and the Qur'an', in *EQ*, Vol. 1, 412–31.
—— (2001b) 'Introduction: An assessment of and perspective on the study of the Qur'an', in A. Rippin, *The Qur'an: Style and contents*, Aldershot: Ashgate; translation of Arkoun 1982, V–XXXIII.
—— (2002a) 'Islam', in *EQ*, Vol. 2, 565–71.
—— (2002b) *The Unthought in Contemporary Islamic Thought*, London: al-Saqi.

NEAL ROBINSON

ʿARSH

see: **heaven; miraculousness of the Qur'an**

ART AND THE QUR'AN

There are four strong arguments in the Qur'an against art.

First, art through its emotional impact can easily overcome our rationality. The Qur'an emphasizes the significance of using reason, calmly considering the evidence, pondering over what one is told, and this is very different from the sort of impact that art may have on us. Its miraculousness lies in the way in which it combines orality, writing, sound and subsequent behaviour. Yet this emphasis on balance is negated by anything that directly affects our senses in a way likely to unbalance them.

Then there is the issue of how far we should act on the basis of what we experience. The Qur'an accepts that much of its message goes against experience and relies on a deeper understanding of that experience. For example, the materialists say plausibly that there is no evidence of life after death, but we are supposed to consider the words of the text and work out that such a future life is likely given the nature of God and his creation. Yet art encourages us to take what we see and hear as real, since it encourages us to regard visual and auditory representations as important and appropriate objects of admiration. King Solomon is referred to several times in the Qur'an as having made things; he got the *jinn* to make things for him, and some of these things seem to have had an aesthetic purpose (34.12; 34.13). In order to test the Queen of Sheba, he built a *sarh* covered with glass (27.45), and from the description of it this seems to have been a screen built into the floor in such a way as to resemble water. The queen was supposed to think it was water, different from what it really is, and it succeeded in its purpose, since she was fooled by it. So it could hardly be argued that there is a basic Qur'anic prohibition on using human imagination and skill to construct illusory images. The wisest of men delighted in his ability to commission art, and there is no criticism of him in the text for having done so. On the other hand, the point of this exercise was to reveal to the queen that the level of experiential knowledge upon which she had up to that point relied was unsatisfactory. It was precisely because she was fooled by the visual that she was encouraged to look beyond the visual at what lies deeper. She did this, and so art had a useful religious purpose.

There is a good deal of evidence that the Prophet was critical of idolatry, and the *hadith* literature refer to this quite often. Of course, the Qur'an itself is particularly critical of idolatry. What is the relevance of this to art, and in particular representative art? There is a famous *hadith* comparing owning pictures to having a dog in the house, both of which are said to prevent the visits of angels. It is not clear what the criticism of pictures, means however. It might mean that he advocates simplicity in interior design, and indeed simplicity in general. Contact with dogs does bring about ritual impurity, but it is difficult to put contact with pictures in the same category unless we link pictures with idolatry. The Prophet may well have had in mind the use of pictures by Christians and others for religious purposes, including as that did an image of their deity and those close to the deity. The local beliefs of those living in Arabia, including the belief in many gods, were often represented in terms of images, and the Qur'anic *sura al-Ikhlas* (Purity of Faith) criticizes the ideas that God could have had a creator and that there are other gods like him. So a general ban on images and representative art might be justified on Qur'anic grounds.

On the other hand, there is no shortage of anthropomorphic language in the Qur'an, and there was a long debate on how this language is to be understood. There is no intent to represent God in a picture, but there were many pictures of major religious characters, the prophets and even the Prophet himself, pictures of paradise and other significant religious ideas. Representations of the Prophet often show him with a veil over his face, especially prevalent in the image of his flight on Buraq from Mecca to Jerusalem and back again, and when leading his army. In some paintings of the miraculous journey the Prophet's face is visible on the first stage of the journey, and veiled on the return. The implication is that during this journey he was transformed in such a way as to make his appearance no longer of significance. On the other hand, there are pictures that show the Prophet's face quite clearly. It might be argued that just as the language of the Qur'an itself is frequently representational, painting and sculpture can share in this mode. Why should the Prophet not be represented in a picture? He was after all a human being, and to suggest that he is too holy to be represented visually suggests that he shares in God's divine status, which is directly in opposition to the central principles of Islam. There is no doubt according to the Qur'an that he is a man and only a man, albeit an unusually perfect sort of person.

One of the most determined enemies of *shirk* or idolatry are the neo-Hanbali thinkers, and in particular Ibn 'Abd al-Wahhab, the spiritual source of the recent governments in Saudi Arabia. He argues that there is a close connection between *shirk* and *kufr* (unbelief). Al-Wahhab sees the Christians and Jews, although People of the Book, as essentially unbelievers, pointing out that the Prophet did make a clear distinction between them and Muslims. One of his targets was Sufism. Sufism portrays itself as representing the inner and hidden side of Islam, whereby followers on the path (*tariqat*) to God require the guidance of a *shaykh* or *pir*. One of the main symbols in Sufism is wine, as a symbol of intoxication, but not the physical intoxication that results from drinking real wine. Loving God is like being drunk; one's ordinary senses are in disarray and it is as though one has been transported from the ordinary world to the divine realm. Wine represents the means to move from one world to the next and the spiritual guide is the cupbearer, the one who presents us with the wine. Music and poetry are important methods for inculcating the right spirit in the seeker after truth.

Sufism and art

There is also a lot of emphasis in the Qur'an on being in the right place and having the appropriate atmosphere. Quite often groups of Sufis would meet in private homes or tea houses, at saints' tombs or in gardens, and those hostile to such gatherings often claim that they are characterized by drunkenness, drugs and perhaps the illicit meeting of men and women. More importantly, perhaps, is that such gatherings always have the potential for being subversive, for opposing the rules of official Islam and for allowing interpretations of religion that can go in any direction. After all, under the influence of poetry and music, one may acquire all sorts of emotional ideas that have no relevance at all to Islam. Poetry and music affect our emotions and may overturn reason and religious bounds, and lead us to accept a version of how we should act or what we should believe that is at variance with Islam.

Calligraphy

Some have suggested that calligraphy is the essential Islamic art. Reading calligraphy can be difficult, requiring preparation and application, and the consequent pleasure of the achievement is a reflection of our success in understanding God more profoundly, moving in his direction and developing a conception of the deity. The project of endlessly constructing a concept of God through calligraphy is because the appearance of Arabic writing itself is of something without an end, where the letters are linked with many shapes and keep on moving across the page and the manuscript. We acquire in this way experience of dealing with continuity and infinity, and since these are aspects of the deity, this helps us conceive of him. Similar remarks are often made about the arabesque, the unbroken wavering and curling line that, initially at least, is derived from the intricate patterns made by the vine tendril. This is sometimes said to mimic the idea of eternal movement and the existence of a variety of forms, both of which can serve as ideas of the eternal God. The fact that the central motif is a plant – the vine – serves as an indication of the holiness of everyday creation, of the natural, and of the fact that God has provided us with such objects so that we may enjoy looking at them and learn from them if we think about them.

Geometry

It is often argued that geometric forms come closest to presenting an abstract concept of God, as their shapes suggest the unlimited nature of God and because one is presented with symbols that need to be explored and considered for what is behind them before one can really grasp them. Perhaps the reliance of Islamic art upon ornamentation brings out the fact that for Muslims there is no contrast between the temporal and the spiritual, that all acceptable art has a religious meaning and is designed to help us reflect on the deity. Some have suggested that there can be no secular art for Muslims because everything for Muslims is holy: 'An essential difference between Islam and Christianity is that the former does not divide life into the temporal and the spiritual' (Piotrovsky and Vrieze, 1999: 26).

Muslims may see calligraphy as providing a reminder of the eternal power of God, because it has a shape and continuity that seems to be endless. At the same time they may accept that not everyone needs to see it in this way. It could be argued in opposition to this and similar views that there are different levels of meaning in images and not everyone needs to follow the meaning all the way down to its most basic level. So, if someone takes a drink out of a glass flask that has a religious inscription on it and does not reflect on the Light Verse from the Qur'an while doing so, that person is not necessarily at fault. How is writing an indication of the endless, or the arabesque and geometric patterning a symbol of the infinite? Writing does come to an end, as does the arabesque and geometric designs, and the fact that they could all be extended does not mean they are endless. For one thing, unless space is infinite, whatever goes on in that space will have to come to an end at some point. Many have commented on what is taken to be a *horror vacui* in Islamic ornamentation, a dislike of the empty, and this accounts for the ways in which space is filled up so comprehensively in Islamic art. Yet space cannot be filled up entirely, for if it was there would be no ornamentation. In arabesques the line is unbroken, but that does not mean it goes on forever. The line finishes somewhere and then the design is complete, not an excellent depiction of the infinite – or one that is no more excellent than anything else.

The meaning of ornamentation

Geometric patterns are often said to be empty of content, and so to stimulate the mind to think of a deity existing without companions. But it could also get the mind to think of all sorts of things. How are geometric shapes infinite? There is nothing infinite about a square or a triangle; on the contrary, such a specific shape is precisely finite,

with recognizable and visible limits that define it. That is not to suggest that in Islamic art these forms of ornamentation are not used effectively to produce beautiful designs, and consequently objects, but whether they are really supposed to produce particular ideas in us, their viewers, is questionable. There is no reason to think that we have to see geometrical design as having any religious meaning whatsoever.

One of the characteristic features of the sort of geometrical illustration that is so common in Islamic art is its balance. The shapes and their quantity that are produced seem to be just the right number. Too many shapes would have produced a fragmented effect, and too few would have made us concentrate on particular areas of space too much. In some designs the use of a grid provides a tight formal structure that gives the impression of being endlessly and infinitely repeatable. Larger areas cohere by colour and shape rather than by subject matter, since the whole notion of subject matter does not make sense in this sort of design. Repetition within a specific section, or rephrasing of a section within the whole, produces a subtle rhythmic and harmonious pattern of sameness and difference, and this is vital if the work is to escape from both tedious monotony and a gradual loss of aesthetic identity. The work itself defies an obvious interpretation; it sometimes seems to exude a sensual exuberance and sometimes to be imbued with pathos. Sometimes it looks as though the flow of time has been arrested, and sometimes as though it has not been constrained at all, because the patterning is so excessive that it makes the attempt to restrict it, or render it coherent, futile. Any attempt at decoding or categorizing the combination of shapes is questionable, and perhaps that is the point of the intricate patterning, an attempt to overwhelm the viewer with its intricate nature. But a result of this is that it is difficult to see how any particular religious meaning can be given to the ornamentation.

This brings us to another difficulty with the religious interpretation of ornamentation. It insists on a single reading or meaning as acceptable for a huge variety of aesthetic material. The entire genre of calligraphy, and of the arabesque, not to mention geometric design, is said to have just one meaning, a meaning that refers to God. But if everything in the universe reminds us of God, then so does art. This would work for any form of art and also for anything that is not art. There is nothing then specifically about Islamic art that reminds us of God, yet the claim is that Islamic art is specifically devised to carry out that purpose. It is too narrow because we have to find something in these artistic styles that makes us think of God, and unless everything makes us think of God, we cannot easily find anything that performs the task. Despite the claims of those who write on this topic, there is nothing infinite about writing or geometric and arabesque design. There is, then, no obvious route from these designs to thinking about an endless and infinite being. They could stimulate us into thinking about God, but they also could stimulate us to think of anything at all. Perhaps the main problem here is the idea that signs are natural, that they only point in one direction and have one meaning.

Music

Music became an important issue in Islamic thought right from the start of Islam. The Prophet made several references to it in his conversations with others, and quite soon a controversy arose as to the role, if any, of music within the religion. Before we examine some details of that controversy, let us look at the main theories of music that arose within Islamic philosophy.

There are two main theories of music: on one side are al-Farabi and Ibn Sina, and on the other the Brethren of Purity (Ikhwan, al-safa') and al-Kindi. It is worth examining this conflict because it is very revealing of similar conflicts that lie at the heart of Islamic aesthetics itself. Ibn Sina and al-Farabi did not take the Neoplatonic line on music, unlike al-Kindi and the Ikhwan. For the latter, music is linked with arithmetical and celestial facts, in a very Pythagorean sort of way, so that music has an affinity to something real and objective, from which it derives its power. For the Ikhwan music is a mirror of the music of the spheres, and represents a route of spiritual advancement to that higher realm of existence. For al-Kindi, more prosaically, music as a system of harmony connects with physical and emotional balance, and can be used therapeutically in that way. But this is also to suggest that music is linked with something that is really there in the external world, and which can be assessed in terms of accuracy or otherwise.

By contrast, both al-Farabi and Ibn Sina treat music as independent of anything else, in terms of sound itself and the ways in which the organization of that sound can produce pleasure in the hearer. What is important about music is the way in which it can lead to our enjoyment of sound – and that is all. The contrast between these two views cannot be exaggerated. For al-Kindi and the Ikhwan, what is important about music is what it reflects; for al-Farabi and Ibn Sina, what is important about music is what it does for us.

Al-Farabi is actually a very significant musical theorist, not to mention composer, and there is music said to be by him still played today in the Middle East.

What is even more interesting is that he is largely responsible for what is known as the Arabian tone system, which divides the octave into twenty-four equivalent intervals. This is still the basis of traditional Arabian music, while a slightly different system based on the Pythagorean analysis of music produced the Turkish and Persian tone systems. From the number of books written on music in the first few centuries of Islam we can tell that this was an area of great theoretical interest, and much music was obviously played. The Pythagorean theory became the reasoning behind Sufi music, which sees itself as doing far more than simply producing pleasure in its listeners. The notes and movements in Sufi dance and music are designed to replicate the basis of reality and to worship God by using our body in ways that are not customarily parts of prayer. Our concern here is not with issues of musicology but with those of aesthetics, and it is worth looking at some of the issues arising within the Islamic world that are related to music.

Following the line established by al-Farabi, Arabic music places a lot of stress on *tarab*, or the enjoyment one derives from listening to music. There is a saying '*al-fann ihsas*' ('art is feeling'). One of the words in Arabic for music – *sama'* – means both listening and hearing, presenting music as a holistic experience and placing it within a spiritual category. The Tarab player must play the neutral Arab intervals properly and accurately and feel their musical effect, in particular by responding to the cadential formulae at the end of each melodic phrase, especially in modal improvisations. He must have *ihsas* or feeling, i.e. correct intonation, rhythmic accuracy, good judgement about modal progressions and tonal emphases. These are assumed to be more than merely technical skills. He also should have an intuitive ability to find the right delicate musical balance between renditions that are too static and too repetitive to be emotionally engaging, and those that are too excessive and wild to generate and maintain a true sense of musical achievement. The Tarab culture attributes creativity to the interactive circle of communication between the performer and the audience. In ideal circumstances there should be a dynamic nexus between a talented performer who is ecstatically transformed and a similarly talented and emotionally transformed audience. For this there must by ambience (*jaww*). It often takes a long time to start the performance because the artist is trying to establish the right sort of ambience. This is both a matter of his trying to get himself into the right state of mind, but also of the audience trying to do the same thing, and the performer trying to help the audience achieve this. This synchronization process may come about, but it may not, and may have to be simulated or just abandoned. Music can be seen as an essentially spiritual activity, although not necessarily directly religious.

One of the greatest singers of Arabic music of all time was Umm Khulthum (1903–75), and she exemplifies many of the structural aspects of Arabic music. When Umm Khulthum came to learn a piece, she would first leave it to her qanun player to approve it and then work with the composer on adapting it to her particular approach. She would memorize it and work with the orchestra on it, and then change it all the time to make it fit better with her feelings and voice. When she sang it in public, she again changed it in line with the reactions of her public. One of the unusual features of Arabic music is that the reaction of the audience is important. The singer and musicians know what they are going to sing and play, but they have scope to vary it, and the parameters of that variation lie to a degree in the reaction of the audience. It has to be the right kind of audience, an audience who genuinely understands the music and responds in an intelligent and sensitive way. One should not necessarily think here of a small group of connoisseurs listening to music in refined surroundings. The audience can be an enormous number of people, as often occurred in the concerts of Umm Khulthum, for instance; she would give them the opportunity to respond to the music and on the basis of that response she would vary not what she sang but how she sang, to a degree at least. Actually, in the case of Umm Khulthum this response was often rather phony, since she was so famous and held in such awe by her audience that she had a tendency to manipulate them into producing the response which fitted how she wanted to sing anyway. This is not an essentially critical comment, it was not, after all, her fault that she had such a justifiably high reputation, and nor was it her fault that as a result she was obliged to sing to very large audiences. There was sometimes criticism of her style as heavy. Such criticisms are unfortunate, since her public performances had to be ponderous to an extent in order for her to be heard. But this is an issue that will be taken up again.

The reactions of the audience are often very noisy, sometimes too noisy. They can interfere with the music itself, and they can sometimes be a performance in themselves, a self-indulgent and uncreative performance. To a degree the audience reacts as it has seen Sufis react, and this is often in a rather wild and free way. Yet in many of the leading writings on the topic, the Sufis stressed the significance of remaining quiet and contemplative when listening to music, and if the music and dance throws one into ecstasy, then obviously we might act wildly, but when that stage is over we should be quiet and still, both physically and mentally. As al-Ghazali puts it, in the *Ihya 'ulum al-din* (Vol. 2: on Sama'), it is often the quietest person who achieves the highest degree of ecstasy (*wajd*). Sufi thinkers often point out that silence is an effective means of relating to God. In some old customs in the Middle East, when a marriage proposal was made, if the answer was silence then this signified acceptance, and a silent acceptance of the presence of God might be thought far more sincere than many loud declarations of faith. Music consists after all of connected silences, and the periods of silence both before, during and after music may form a very potent space for contemplation. That is perhaps one of the criticisms that can be made of the Tarab culture; it does not give much scope for silence and the reflection it can encourage.

Some forms of music, recitation and song are clearly religious in nature. For example, the call to prayer (*adhan*) can be a very beautiful sound and is not purely functional, or at least it does not have to be. The *adhan* is characterized by contrast, providing an individual musical profile to teach repetition of a phrase as well as to different phrases. During the first appearance of a phrase the melodic line generally comes out short and simple, with a limited tonal range, but the repetition may be extended, becoming far more complex and with a tonal range extending over an octave. On special occasions there may be two *mu'adhdhinin* in operation (*mu'adhdhinayn*) to produce an antiphonal *adhan* of considerable charm and complexity. In the main Umayyad mosque in Damascus every tower has a *mu'adhdhan* reciting the *adhan* in a slightly different way, producing an extraordinary impression. It might be argued that the point of the *adhan* is merely to call people to prayer, and that an over-elaboration is to turn into an aesthetic event what should be basic and simple. On the other hand, it is worth pointing out that even the minarets themselves from which the *adhan* is produced are nowadays entirely redundant, given the existence of microphones, and yet they are still used. They are used because they are beautiful, and their beauty is surely intended to be an encouragement to prayer, as is the musicality of the caller to prayer himself.

Similarly the *imam* or leader of prayers will often be respected because of the way in which he pronounces the language of prayer and of Arabic, and the recitation of the Qur'an itself (*tajwid*) is rightly often called a science. There are a variety of styles, each popular in particular areas of the Islamic world, which makes the competitions for excellence in this skill difficult to judge when they are international. Some audiences will find a simpler form of expression more compelling, while others favour something more florid. At the competitions, frequently very interesting arguments emerge, with some suggesting that the point of reciting the Qur'an is to produce in the simplest and purest manner possible the words themselves, which are after all taken to be the actual words of God. This approach to recitation argues that the words are so radiant themselves with beauty that all one has to do to produce a beautiful rendition of the text is to say it clearly. Some of the leading reciters deny that they have any musical ability or training at all, and claim that the beauty of their expression comes directly from God. Certainly the idea that the verses are sung would be entirely rejected. The rules about how to read the Book are said to have been laid down since the time of the Prophet himself. They regulate pronunciation,

intonation and breaks, but within those rules there is considerable scope for development, extending even into what sounds like a *maqam* or musical performance, There is nonetheless a great deal less freedom of expression that is involved with secular music. One is limited by the text itself and the necessity to stop at particular places, although it is possible to start at various places, and before coming to the end of the whole *sura*. In all cases the stress is on each consonant and vowel, so that each word is pronounced clearly and with regard to the syntactic structure of the sentence in which it occurs.

The other school, and there are many variations between these two extremes, supports the idea that since the words are so beautiful, they have to be pronounced in an especially beautiful way. This follows the principle behind the transformation of the written Qur'an into a very beautiful object through calligraphy and painting, something which we have seen is so important in Islamic culture. The argument could have been that since the text is already so beautiful it does not need further beautification, as it were. Yet much effort went into the celebration of the text in art, and we can understand why. We can also think of equally strong arguments against any decoration of the text at all, returning us to the prolonged arguments that took place in Arabic literature between those who advocated simplicity and naturalness, and those who see literature as essentially artificial anyway, and so as ripe for the application of elaborate exaggeration.

Reciting the Book

There is little instruction in the Qur'an itself as to how the Qur'an ought to be recited, although the very name of the book, which means 'recitation', suggests that this is a question which needs answering. We are told at 72.4 to *rattil il-Qur'ana tartilan* ('repeat the recitation in a collected distinct way'). This has been the principle used in Qur'anic recitation, which is produced at a steady rate, is calm, rhythmic but not melodic, and has the emphasis throughout upon the clarity and distinctness of the diction. The significance of not rushing is that the reader and the listeners can then concentrate on the meaning of each individual word and phrase, as is surely appropriate for such a text. *Tajwid* or the techniques of recitation is then to a degree assessed in terms of a clear criterion, that of how accessible the recitation is to those intent on concentrating on the words.

The place where many comments on recitation can be found is the *ahadith*, but since this is a text which is now written, not much of the information is of direct value to this topic. Clearly the Prophet appreciated the beauty of recitation when performed by some talented individuals, but on the other hand he was critical of those who used the melodies from love poetry and extravagant singing. Clarity is always important, but there are several ways of being clear: seven, in fact, following a tradition which mentions seven ways of reading (*al-qira'at al-sab'*). Skilled readers will often be expected to know more than one style. It is difficult to over-emphasize the significance of the oral nature of the Qur'an, and the consequent significance of how it is pronounced. Reciting the text is more than just reproducing the words, because it is done to evoke an emotional as well as an intellectual response. The *hafiz*, or memorizer of the Qur'an, is more than someone who simply remembers how the text goes and can reproduce it at will. For the superstitious the words themselves have a *baraka* which is only increased by their oral delivery. Putting

that aside, the oral reading or recitation of the text in a sense reproduces what God did originally when he transmitted the message to the Prophet, and so the reciter is imitating God, insofar as one can.

Recitation and music

Although the recitation of the Qur'an is not supposed to be musical, it often does incorporate musical principles. It is not difficult to identify different styles when listening to a variety of reciters. In particular, there are large differences in the speed of recitation. But the differences are not only in speed. Some recitation can be emotional and display considerable virtuosity, and such reciters are often criticized for making a performance out of something that is too serious for such a form of expression. It is the task of the *muqri'* to produce a correct recitation, not necessarily one that draws the attention to the reciter rather than the recitation. This is perhaps the greatest problem with the incorporation of too much musicality into recitation; it treats the text as just a means to produce aesthetic beauty, whereas the attention should be on the text itself, not on how it is recited. Similar reasoning leads to problems in incorporating Qur'anic passages in secular and political songs.

In 1999 the Lebanese singer Marcel Khalife was tried for offending Islam. His alleged crime was to have used a short *aya* or verse from the *sura Yusuf* in the Qur'an in a song. In fact, the song was a poem by the Palestinian poet Mahmud Darwish which incorporated the line 'I saw eleven stars and the sun and the moon. I saw them kneeling in prayer before me'. Darwish was comparing the suffering of Yusuf at his brothers' hands with the suffering of the Palestinians at the hands of the Israelis. Khalife turned this into a song in an attempt to support the Palestinian movement. In his defence he claimed that only the Qur'an could really provide the inspiration for human creativity, at least for Muslims. But the complaint was not that he had used the quotation inappropriately, nor that there was anything objectionable about the song as a whole. The complaint was that he had used a part of the Qur'an in a secular context, that he had actually sung it and set it to music as part of a melody. The argument was that this was far beneath the dignity appropriate to anything which comes from the Qur'an and should be punished.

The confrontation offers an interesting perspective on the role of music in the Qur'an. Some would argue that a beautiful text is appropriately complemented by beautiful music, while others would suggest that to use music to illustrate a text implies that it needs supplementing in some way. For the Qur'an this implication is a direct attack on its nature as a religious authority, and so setting it to music is forbidden.

This may seem a narrow and repellent view. After all, if someone with a genuine love of God in his heart seeks to use his skill at music to portray that love, and wishes to use the central book of his religion with that music in some way, what more appropriate religious activity could one find? In the case of Marcel Khalife, he actually claimed that the Qur'an inspired him to write the song, and this seems an honourable motive, from a religious point of view. We can understand why the Prophet may not have wished the Qur'an to be recited in the sorts of tunes that the People of the Book used, since it was important to distinguish Islam from the two older religions, but today that differentiation has been well established, and there seems no good reason to exclude the Qur'an from use in artistic expression. In fact,

the calligraphy that exists for the text is often very beautiful, and sometimes one gets the impression that the style operates in opposition to its readability. It might at least be said that in many of the most beautiful Qur'ans that clarity of expression is not the most significant issue, but the beauty of the script is. If it is acceptable to use writing to illustrate the beauty of the words, why it is not similarly acceptable to use musical notation?

It is not clear why there should be a distinction between writing and music here, but the whole discussion reveals an interesting view of art itself, as having largely the function of concealing and confusing. That is perhaps why the Qur'an often insists that it is not poetry, although at the same time it demands that we regard it as miraculous in its perfection, and part of that perfection is its aesthetic quality. We can see why there might be an injunction not to produce anything like it, because such an attempt would imply that one thought one could, and that would suggest that one did not think it was unique and miraculous. But that does not show why one should not use art, or in this case music, to bring out the essence of the text in ways which make them easily transmittable to the widest possible public.

Umm Khulthum

Umm Khulthum was a most extraordinary musical figure of the twentieth century, someone whose skill and virtuosity place her in the very first rank of singers in the world. A lot of emphasis is placed in accounts of her on the influence of her father, a religious figure, and her participation in the recitation of the Qur'an, but we should not take this too seriously. This is an attempt to put her femininity and the sensual nature of much of her music within an acceptable cultural context. The fact that she was born in an obscure village to an equally obscure family is sufficient to establish her *baladi* credentials, and the stories that she had to dress up as a boy to perform initially are quite probably true, given the dubious status of female singers at that time. A contemporary 'Ud player and singer of great skill, Farid al-Atrash, suggested that only he and Umm Khulthum knew how to enunciate Arabic properly since only they among major performers of the time had received a training in *tajwid*. Again, we should not necessarily accept this at face value. He is symbolically linking what it is that they do with Islam itself, when, as he knew, there was and continues to be significant religious disquiet about secular music, and indeed about music in general in the Islamic world.

References and further reading

Art of Islam (1999) *Heavenly Art, Earthly Art*, ed. M. Piotrovsky and J. Vrieze, London: Lund Humphries.

See also: baraka; **Bilqis; calligraphy and the Qur'an;** *hafiz*; **music; noise;** *tajwid*
OLIVER LEAMAN

ASBAB AL-NUZUL

Meaning 'circumstances' or 'occasions of revelation' the term refers to information describing the historical contexts in which Qur'anic verses were delivered. Generally transmitted in verbal reports (*ahadith*; sing.: *hadith*) codified in the second and third centuries of Islam, they are consulted by scholars of Qur'anic interpretation (*tafsir*) to determine the legal and moral impact of verses. The Qur'an is considered the literal Word of God, providing guidance for humanity (*hudan li'l-nas*) for all time. However, it was revealed over a period of some

twenty-two years, during which time conditions changed significantly. The circumstances in which verses were delivered help explain whether they should be considered descriptions of current conditions, general principles, prescriptions for specific circumstances, prescriptions for all circumstances, ideals to be achieved, etc.

See also: **Qur'anic Studies**
TAMARA SONN

ASBAT

The 'tribes' mentioned five times in the Qur'an (2.136; 2.140; 3.84; 4.163; 7.160). Muslim exegetes usually interpret the term to be a reference to the 'tribes' of the Israelites, based on 7.160, in which God states that he divided the Israelites into twelve tribes (*asbat*). The other references in the Qur'an include Asbat in a list of Israelite prophets including Abraham, Ishmael, Isaac and Jacob (which appear before), and Moses and Jesus (coming afterwards). The eponymous ancestors of the tribes appear in the Joseph story (*sura* 12) but are not identified by name in the Qur'an. Muslim exegetes provide the same names as the biblical account but sometimes assign the births to different mothers. In this context, the Arabic term *asbat* is said to signify a 'twisted tree' with many branches, just as the tribes of the sons of Jacob were plentiful. Muslim travellers and geographers describe the shrines and tombs of the *asbat* as being places of pilgrimage for Muslims as well as Jews and Christians. Some exegetes claim that Asbat is the name of a particular prophet, for example, Wahb b. Munabbih argues that Asbat is another name given in the Qur'an to Elisha.

Further reading

Lemaire, A. (1978) 'Les Bene Jacob: Essai d'interprétation historique d'une tradition patriarchale', *Revue biblique* 85: 321–7.

MacDonald, J. (1956) 'Joseph in the Qur'an and Muslim Commentary', *Muslim World* 10: 113–31, 207–24.

BRANNON WHEELER

AL-ASH'ARI

Abu'l Hasan Ali b. Isma'il al-Ash'ari was born in Basra around 260/873 and died in Baghdad in 324/935. He was the founder of one of the main theological schools within Islam which bears his name, the Ash'ariyya or Ash'arites.

He was a descendant of Abu Musa al-Ash'ari, a well-known companion of the Prophet. When his mother married Abu 'Ali al-Jubba'i, a well-known Mu'tazilite theologian and head of the school at Basra, Ash'ari was raised by Jubba'i, who introduced him to Mu'tazilite theology, which initially he enthusiastically adopted. He subsequently left the Mu'tazilite school and joined the 'People of Tradition', as they described themselves (*ahl al-sunna*) and accepted the line of the *salaf* (ancestors) represented by such figures as Ahmad b. Hanbal and other scholars of the prophetic traditions.

There are several reasons suggested for this conversion. According to one report, the Prophet appeared to him several times during the month of Ramadan and commanded him to follow the prophetic traditions and defend the doctrines related in the traditions, thus abandoning Mu'tazilite hermeneutics that were based more on *'aql* than on *naql*. According to other stories, his discussion with al-Jubba'i about the fate of three brothers, of whom one died as a pious man, the other as a wicked man and the last as a child, is the reason for his abandonment of the Mu'tazila. In this story the one who dies young complains that he missed out on the chance of heaven since he did not live long enough to merit heaven, and he is told that had he lived longer he would have become evil and deserved hell. So his early death and future in the *barzakh* were beneficial to him. This leads the man in hell to complain that had he only died earlier, he too would have avoided hell, and this sort of comparison of different fates is taken to provide a critique of the Mu'tazilite doctrine that we can grasp the principles of justice which determine our paths through this and the next world. After his conversion, al-Ash'ari went to Baghdad, where he spent the rest of his life, playing a lively part in debates both within Islam and with other faith groups.

Although he opposed the rationalism of the Mu'tazila, replacing it with the fideism of Ahmad b. Hanbal, he then tried to support his beliefs with rational arguments. The Qur'an, which is God's eternal speech, is uncreated. Attributes of action such as creating and sustaining are not eternal, otherwise the eternity of the world must be accepted, which is impossible. The nature of God's face, of his hand or of his sitting on the throne cannot be known. He does not offer an interpretation of these expressions, but thinks that they cannot be taken literally, for God is not a corporeal being. God will be seen in the world to come, but since he is not corporeal, the exact nature of this vision cannot be known. Human actions are willed and created by God through a power created in us before each act. As a result of this power, the human being is responsible for his or her actions. Actions are good or bad not in themselves but because of the will of God. There does not have to be a kind and just purpose behind these actions, for nothing can necessitate God's acting in any way.

Al-Ash'ari adopts the atomism of the Mu'tazilite school. Atoms can come together and produce bodies only through the will and power of God. As a result of God's grace, he can choose any human being as a prophet. Miracles are the most important indication of the truthfulness of a prophet. Eschatological issues can only be known through revelation, and their reality cannot be rejected rationally. Faith consists of acceptance and does not include outward expression. This means that a sinner is liable to punishment, but he or she remains a believer. Human beings do not receive rewards as a result of good action but because of the grace of God.

His *Maqalat al-islamiyyin* (Accounts of the Muslims) is his chief work. In this, he provides an objective account of the views of the different Muslim sects, non-Muslim sects and of the philosophers. It was probably written during his Mu'tazilite period and then slightly modified. This work became a model for similar works produced afterwards. It symbolizes his break with the Mu'tazilites, in that he incorporated a good deal of their conceptual machinery and in particular the commitment to rationality and argument, while rejecting their particular conclusions. In the *al-Luma'* (The Lights), he discusses such theological issues as God's attributes, determination (*qadar*) and other dogmatic issues. In the *al-Ibana an usul al-diyana* (The Elucidation of the principles of religion), he again discusses theological issues. In the *Risala fi istihsan al-hawd fi 'ilm al-kalam* (Treatise on the advisibility of discussing the science of the Kalam), he defends the use of *kalam* and its rational methods. In the *Risala ila ahl al-saghr* (Treatise to the people of Saghr), he gives a list of basic principles that he argues were accepted by the *salaf* (the original Muslims).

Further reading

al-Ash'ari (1953a) *al-Luma'* (The Lights), ed. and trans. R. McCarthy, *The Theology of al-Ash'ari*, Beirut: Imprimerie Catholique.
—— (1953b) *Risala fi istihsan al-hawd fi 'ilm al-kalam*, ed. and English trans. R. McCarthy, *The Theology of al-Ash'ari*, Beirut: Imprimerie Catholique.
—— (1963) *Maqalat al-islamiyyin* (Accounts of the Muslims), ed. H. Ritter, Wiesbaden: Franz Steiner.
—— (1987a) *al-Ibana an usul al-diyana*, ed. F. H. Mahmud, Cairo.
—— (1987b) *Risala ila ahl al-saghr* (*Usul ahl al-sunna wa'l jama'a*), ed. M.S. al-Jalyand, Cairo: Kulliyya dar al-'ulum.
Leaman, O. (1999) *Brief Introduction to Islamic Philosophy*, Oxford: Polity Press.
Watt, W. Montgomery (1998) *The Formative Period of Islamic Thought*, Oxford: One-World.

See also: **Ash'arites and Mu'tazilites; kalam**

OLIVER LEAMAN

ASH'ARITES AND MU'TAZILITES

Two of the most significant theological schools in the study of the Qur'an are the Mu'tazilites and the Ash'arites, and it is fitting to treat them together since so much of their respective doctrine was established in opposition to the other. The Mu'tazilites or Mu'tazila derive their names from the expression 'those who withdraw themselves' and originated with Wasil ibn 'Ata' in the second/eighth century in Basra. It had in the next century a brief period of great success when it became the official doctrine of the caliphate in Baghdad. One of its doctrines was that the Qur'an is the created Word of God and civil servants had to state this in public until 238/848 when al-Mutawakkil reversed the edict of al-Ma'mun. The Mu'tazilites carried on, however, and lasted for a few more centuries, surviving in the Shi'i world, especially in Persia, although they became largely irrelevant in the Sunni world.

Al-Ash'ari (d. 324/935) was a pupil of Abu 'Ali al-Jubba'i (d. 303/915), the head of the Basran Mu'tazilite School. He came to reject the teaching of the Mu'tazilites, however, and became their chief opponent, his followers being named after him. Some of the most significant Islamic thinkers came to adopt Ash'arism, including al-Ghazali and Fakhr al-Din al-Razi. The differences between the two schools on a range of issues is not great; they were in agreement on the atomic nature of the world and also in giving a high status to human reason in working out how to understand that world. Between them they formulated the idea of an Islamic theology, a discussion of the basic concepts of Islam as an acceptable and appropriate activity for Muslims.

The distinctive doctrine of the Mu'tazilites is based on a number of principles. They emphasize the unity of God to such an extent that they deny that the descriptions of him as having hands (38.75), eyes (54.14) and a face (55.27) should be taken literally. The idea of God sitting on a throne (20.5) should not be understood as his having a body. While the Ash'arites agree that God does not have a body, they did not want to rule out seeing him, nor did they want to say that these terms are used allegorically. We should just accept that God has these qualities in a way we do not grasp (*bi la kayfa*). But the Mu'tazilites rejected the idea that one can apply attributes to God at all as though they were separate from him, for this is to import plurality into the divine unity. For God these qualities are merely expressions of his essence, and indistinguishable from it.

The desire to emphasize divine unity led to problems in describing the Qur'an. The Mu'tazilites argued that it could not be part of God since there is no plurality in God, and so it must be separate from him, a created thing created initially in the Preserved Tablet (85.22). By contrast, the Ash'arites held that the Qur'an must be eternal, since it represents God's speech, and that speech is eternal.

Another locus of argument was based on the notion of divine justice. For the Mu'tazilites God had to be just, he had to act in accordance with the moral law, and so reward the good and punish the evil at least in the next world. This view is based on the idea of free will, and God cannot dominate our moral vocabulary if we are to be free to act. It seems to follow that God has to act in our best interests if he is to be just. Al-Ash'ari famously is said to have asked al-Jubba'i about the likely fate of three dead brothers: a believer, an unbeliever and one who died as a child. Al-Jubba'i answered that the first would be rewarded, the second punished and the third neither rewarded nor punished; instead he would be sent to the *barzakh*. Would it not have been better for God to have allowed the child to live longer so that he also might be rewarded with paradise? The Mu'tazilite response is that God knew that had the child lived he would have become an unbeliever and so ended up with the worst fate of hell. Al-Ash'ari is supposed to have refuted his teacher by asking him why in that case God did not make the second brother die as a child in order to save him from hellfire. What this is taken to show is that God does not have to accede to general principles of justice, and alleging that he does results in all manner of implausible positions. Justice ends up meaning what God wants us to do, and the only source of guidance is revelation. We are not free to decide how to act; we can acquire the action from God and think of it as our own but we should not think that we can act without any connection with God. God is in charge of our actions and of our way of seeing those actions, and we are entirely dependent on him for everything.

It is often said that the Ash'arites resemble the forces of religious orthodoxy and the Mu'tazilites the philosophical radicals, but this is far from the truth. Both groups shared several beliefs and especially the belief in the significance of argument and rationality. This led the Ash'arites to be opposed by those in the Islamic world who saw them as rationalists intent on providing an over-intellectual account of faith.

Further reading

Leaman, O. (1999) *Brief Introduction to Islamic Philosophy*, Oxford: Polity Press.
van Ess, J. (1991–97) *Theologie und Gesellschaft im 2. und 3. Jahrhundert Hidschra: Eine Geschichte des religiösen Denkens im frühen Islam*, Berlin and New York: Walter de Gruyter, Vols i–vi.

See also: **Abu'l Hudayl; al-Ash'ari; Qadi 'Abd al-Jabbar;** *ta'til*

OLIVER LEAMAN

'ASIYYA

Pharoah's wife, known as 'Asiyya or 'Asya in Muslim tradition, was a woman of virtue and faith, whose actions were instrumental in fulfilling God's plans for the prophet Moses. After Moses was rescued, by a member of Pharoah's household, from the river where, under divine inspiration, Moses' mother had set him afloat, 'Asiyya convinced Pharoah not to slay the infant, arguing that he might be useful or that they could adopt him as a son (28.9). She was kind to Moses as he grew and rejected her husband's evil deeds. According to numerous exegetes, she was martyred for her opposition to Pharoah. 'Asiyya's

rejection of Pharoah's oppression and her sincere appeals to God made her 'an example for those who believe', an honour that she shared with Mary, mother of Jesus (66.11–12). Modern interpreters use 'Asiyya's example to stress a woman's individual moral accountability before God.

Along with Mary, the Prophet's wife Khadija, and his daughter Fatima, 'Asiyya is one of four perfect women. In paradise, according to Tradition, she will be one of Muhammad's consorts, along with the Virgin Mary and his earthly wives.

KECIA ALI

AYA

In the Qur'an, the word *aya* (pl. *ayat*) has four interrelated meanings: 'sign', 'token', 'miracle', or 'verse of the Qur'an'. The original meaning in pre-Islamic poetry, like the related Hebrew *oth* and Aramaic *atha*, is 'sign', in the sense of token of God's power and will. It occurs in the Qur'an around 480 times, most frequently premodified by the definite article *al-* or postmodified by the words 'God' (*ayat Allah*), 'the Merciful' (*ayat al-Rahman*), 'the Qur'an' (*ayat al-Qu'ran*), 'the Book' (*ayat al-kitab*), or collocated with the adjective *bayyinat* meaning 'clear' or 'manifest' (*ayatin bayyinat*). As such, the word *aya* points simultaneously to both God and the verses of the Qur'an within which his signs are conveyed. Although it does occur as a free morpheme, i.e. without modifications, such as in the schematic ending 'Indeed, in this there is a sign' (*in fi thalika l-aya/ayat*), it is most often attached to possessive pronouns pertaining to God or to the Qur'an, such as 'His signs' (*ayatahu/ayatihi/ayatuhu*), 'My signs' (*ayati*), 'Our signs' (*ayatina/ayatuna*). The various contextual meanings

85

of the word *aya* are discussed in more detail below.

Technical definition

It is important to note that the word *aya* in the sense of 'verse of the Qur'an' has technical signification in the Qur'an since it is used to refer to the Qur'anic unit of revelation. Muslim scholars provide us with the following technical definition: a term referring to the smallest division of the Qur'an, separate from preceding or following material, and included within the larger unit of the *sura* (chapter). The boundaries of an *aya* are marked by breaks or separation-markers called *fawasil* (sing. *fassila*), which are an integral part of an *aya* since they function as important punctuation marks without which disruptions of meaning might occur. It is important to note that these *fawasil* were there from the very first moment of revelation, i.e. from the first five verses revealed to the Prophet on Mount Hira (96.1–5):

1. Read in the name of your Lord who has created
2. He has created man from a clot
3. Read and thy Lord is the Most-generous
4. Who has taught by the pen
5. He has taught man that which he knew not

to the last five verses (2.278–282) revealed just nine days before his demise. Contrary to popular opinion among Western commentators (cf. Paret, 1965: 411), these separation markers were present in the earliest manuscripts of the Qur'an, for example, in the famous slanted script fragments discovered in Yemen, where they are clearly represented by four small dots or small superimposed lines drawn in the same ink as the text. However, within individual *ayas,* these pauses or breaks are left unmarked; hence the variation in verse numbering and verse divisions in some modern editions of the Qur'an. In some Indian editions, for example, 6.73 of the 'Uthmanic codex (which is followed closely by the Egyptian Concordance *Fath al-rahman*) is divided into two verses. It is perhaps significant that the earliest group of *suras* revealed in Mecca were also called *al-mufassal,* which translates as the sectioned *suras* or those which contain many *fawasil*. In essence, these *fawasil* are iconically indicative of the fragmented and piecemeal, *aya*-by-*aya*, manner of revelation of the Qur'an. The *ayas* of the Qur'an were revealed to the Prophet Muhammad in fragmented form over a period of twenty-three years (roughly from 610 to 632 CE) either individually or in successive combinations of threes and fives, for example, or in their entirety, as with *sura* 6 which comprises 165 verses.

This complex fragmentation is many times referred to in the Qur'an and is meant to be viewed as a miracle in its own right: 'And (by) those dividers that divide (*fa al-fariqati farqa*) and those that deliver the revelation' (77.4–5). Reliable Tradition has it that the Prophet was instructed by the archangel Gabriel to place each individual *aya* in its predetermined slot within the *suras*. At the time of inspiration, or shortly afterwards, each *aya* was recited by Muhammad to his followers, then memorized and committed to writing in fragment form by appointed scribes (twenty-nine in the Medinan era with the most well-known being Zayd Bin Thabit) upon leather or palm-leaf scrolls. Western commentators of the Qur'an have now accepted the conclusions put forward by scholars that *ayas* from different dates were put together to form the present *suras*, that written documents were involved, and that this fragmented compilation was carried out under Muhammad's supervision. However, it is important to note that this fragmentation does not mean that the arrangement of the *ayas* is disjointed or 'chaotic' as many Western scholars have suggested. On the contrary, the close connection between *ayas* is obvious to any speaker of Arabic, basically because of the striking density of conjunctions such as 'and' (*wa*), 'or' (*aw*), 'so' (*fa*), and 'then' (*thum*); in addition to the sheer number of substitute and co-referential pro-forms, i.e. items in a sentence that substitute for or replace other items, such as pronouns (which substitute for noun phrases), demonstratives (that, those, these), adverbs of time, place and process (then, here, there, so, thus), synonyms, repetitions and syntactic ellipsis. This aspect of the Qur'an as a cohesive and well-structured text is mentioned many times in the Qur'an itself: 'And thus do We explain in various ways (*nusarif*) the verses (*ayat*) so that they may say: "You have studied" and that We may make it clear to people who have knowledge' (6.105). Undoubtedly, the most explicit references to the fragmented-cohesive manner of compilation can be found in 17.106: 'A Qur'an which we have divided-into-parts (*faraqnahu*) so that you might recite it to people, gradually. And we have sent it down in stages.' Muslim scholars often cite a passage in the Bible (Isaiah 28: 10–11) which they contend foreshadows this piecemeal and verse-by-verse manner of revelation: 'For precept must be upon precept, precept upon precept; line upon line, line upon line; here a little, and there a little. For with stammering lips and another tongue will he speak to his people.'

Contextual meanings

In the Qur'an, the word *aya* is used in four interrelated senses which can be categorized as follows:

1. Tokens or remarkable events indicating the will of God: for example 3.41: 'He [Zakariah] said: "O my Lord. Make me an *aya* (sign)." Said (the angel): "Your *aya* (sign) is that you shall not speak unto men for three days except by gestures".'

2. Natural signs of God's creation (i.e. miracles): for example 2.73: 'Thus God brings the dead to life and shows you his *ayat* (miracles) so that you may understand.' Other miracles referred to in the Qur'an include the creation of the heavens and the earth, the formation of mountains, the striking of lightning, the descent of rain, the movement of wind and the sailing of ships, and the diversity of languages and skin colour. Also included among natural signs are the devastating destruction of sinful towns and communities (i.e. Noah, 'Ad, Thamud and Lot) in punishment for their refusal to believe in God's messengers and prophets. These verses have been technically termed sign-verses by Western scholars and classified according to their schematic openings and closings. The majority of *ayas*, for example, start with the schematic sentence – 'And of his signs X' – and end with – 'Surely in that are signs for those who X'.

3. Verbal signs of God, i.e. the verbatim words or 'verses' of God as revealed in the Qur'an: for example, 11.1: '*a/l/m/* A book whose *ayat* (verses) have been made decisive and then explained from One who is All-wise, All-informed';

12.1–2: 'These are the *ayat* (verses) of the clear Book/Verily, We have sent it down as an Arabic Qur'an so that you may understand.'

4. Verbal signs of God as revealed in other scriptures: for example, 19.58: 'These were the prophets upon whom God bestowed his blessing from the offspring of Adam, and of those whom we carried with Noah, and from the offspring of Abraham and Israel and from among those whom We guided and chose. When the *ayat* (verses) of the Most-Gracious were recited to them, they fell down prostrating themselves and weeping.' Another more explicit example occurs in 3.3–4: 'And He sent down the Torah and the Gospels/before as guidance for the people and he sent down the *furqan*. Indeed those who disbelieve in the *ayat* (verses) of God, for them there is severe torment.' This juxtaposition of Qur'anic verses and the verses of the Torah is further accentuated by the fact that both the Qur'an and the Torah (*Tawrat*) are explicitly referred to as *al-furqan* – 'the criterion', i.e. that which differentiates right from wrong (see, e.g. 2.53). In addition, there are various references in the Qur'an to the presence of actual word-for-word quotations from the Torah, as in 6.152 which begins with the words: 'Say: Come I will recite what your Lord has prohibited you from'.

It is perhaps noteworthy that the distinction between verbal and natural signs is quite often blurred or neutralized in the Qur'an. For example in 17.101, 'And Indeed we gave Moses nine manifest signs (*ayatin bayaninatin*)', the context is made neutral and hence the word *aya* can refer simultaneously to

both the verses (commandments) given to Moses as well as to the miracles. What seems to augment this convergence of the verbal and the physical is the fact that both types of signs are frequently collocated with the same adjective, namely *bayinat* (*ayatin bayinat*). In some instances the word *ayat* is deleted and substituted by the definite form *al-bayyinat* (the clear-ones), as in 3.184: 'Then if they reject, so were Messengers rejected before you who came with *al-bayyinat*.' This again blurs the distinction between the verbal and the physical because *al-bayyinat* can simultaneously apply to both. Further evidence of this deliberate convergence of signs is their repetitive co-occurrence with the same verbs, namely *sarrafa* ('to diversify or move in various directions') and *dabbara* ('to arrange or plan'). For example, there appears to be no apparent difference between God's directing of the winds and clouds (natural *ayas*) and his diversification of verses; both activities are expressed by the same verbal root *s/r/f*: 'the directing (*tasrif*) of the winds and the clouds controlled between the heaven and the earth are signs for a people who use reason' (2.164); 'And thus we have writ it down as an Arabic Qur'an and we have diversified (*sarafna*) therein the warnings that perhaps they will fear God or it may cause them remembrance' (20.113). The same can be said of the verb *dabbara*. In 13.2, for example, it is used to refer to God's arrangement of all affairs: 'He arranges all affairs (*yudabir al-amr*); he details the *ayat* that you may of the meeting with your Lord be certain.' But the root verb *d/b/r* is also used to refer to man's attempt to discern God's divine arrangement of the Qur'an: 'Then do they not *yatadabarun* (ponder-the-arrangement-of) the Qur'an. If it had been from other than God, they would have found within many discrepancies' (4.82).

Aya numbering

The total number of *ayas* in the Qur'an has been the subject of debate among Muslim scholars. According to al-Suyuti in his famous encyclopedia of the Qur'anic sciences, the unanimous agreement among Muslim scholars is that the number of *ayas* in the Qur'an is 6,000; anything beyond this number is disputed depending upon whether the following are regarded as separate *ayas*: the *basmala* or idiomatic opening phrase – *bism illah al-rahman al-rahim* ('In the name of God the Most-merciful, the Compassionate') found in all *suras* except *sura* 9; the *fawatih* or abbreviated letters found at the beginning of some chapters (e.g. *a.l.m.* and *a.l.r.*); and controversial pauses or breaks within some *ayas* such as mentioned above.

All 6,000 *ayas* are divided among the 114 *suras* of the Qur'an, which range in length from 3 to 286 *ayas*. Authentic traditions suggest that the *suras* were known not only by their titles but also by the number of *ayas* they contained. For example, *sura* 46 (*al-Ahqaf*) was referred to as the 'thirtieth of the *h.m.* collection' (i.e. it begins with the abbreviated letters *h.m.* and has a total of 30 *ayas*). The *ayas* themselves, however, were never numbered by the Prophet, although their sequential order was known and often singled out by him. For example, the last ten *ayas* of *sura al-Kahf* ('The Companions of the Cave'), and the last two *ayas* of *sura* 2 (*al-Baqara*), were deemed to be especially blessed. The *ayas* were normally referred to by their names rather than their numbers, e.g. *aya al-Kursi* (the Throne Verse) and *aya al-Nur* (the Light Verse). Most of these names were established during the Prophet's lifetime and

usually indicated the subject matter or key word used in the *aya*.

Aya length

The length of each *aya* varies, ranging from one word, phrase or clause to a number of coordinated sentences. The longest *aya* in the Qur'an, commonly referred to as *aya al-dayn* ('the debt *aya*' – 2.282) is a whole paragraph long and consists of eleven sentences coordinated by *wa* ('and') and *fa* ('then'), and calculated to be 128 'words' and 540 'letters' long. The shortest is *aya* 64 in *sura* 55 which consists only of one adjective in the dual form, *madhamatan* or 'dark-green'. As is apparent from the above examples, not all *ayas* are end-stopped or independent sentences; many are run-on verses that are syntactically joined to the following or preceding *ayas*. For example, in the above-mentioned adjectival *aya,* the word *madhamatan* is a postmodifier of the noun *jannatan* ('two-gardens'), which is mentioned in the proceeding *aya*. In many *suras* one finds sentences that spread out across ten or more *ayas*. For example, in 25.63–74 a series of seven *ayas* comprising complex relative clauses beginning with the words 'and those who ...' (*wa aladhina*) are syntactically fronted to the beginning of the sentence whereas the *aya* containing the matrix clause (*aya* 75) is postponed until the very end of the sentence.

Major classifications

According to al-Suyuti in his encyclopedic work, *al-Itqan fi 'ulum al-Qur'an*, there are twenty-five different classifications of *ayas*. One of the more common of these, listed in all major editions of the Qur'an, is the Meccan/Medinan classification, based primarily on whether the *ayas* were revealed before or after the Prophet's emigration (*hijra*) to Medina. In general, many of the *ayas* placed at the end of the Qur'an are from the Meccan era, whereas those in the long *suras* placed at the beginning of the Qur'an belong to the Medinan era. Attempts have also been made to identify the stylistic features of Meccan and Medinan *ayas*. For example, all *ayas* that begin with the word *kala* ('nay') or that include a *sajda* (prostration) are designated Meccan. Other classifications include specific times of revelation (i.e. whether revealed at night or during the day, in winter or summer); occasions or reasons of revelation (*asbab al-nuzul*); the first to be revealed and the last to be revealed (i.e. chronology of revelation); the *muhkam* and *mutashabih* (see below); those revealed whole (such as *suras* 6 and 77) and those revealed fragmented (most of the Qur'an); those revealed to other prophets and those revealed only to the Prophet Muhammad; the abrogator and the abrogated (*nasikh* and *mansukh*).

Thematic and stylistic classifications have also been identified by many modern commentators and include categories such as sign-*ayas* (see below), say-*ayas* (i.e. *ayas* that begin with the imperative verb *qul*) and *ayas* containing parables, sacred history of the prophets, oaths, dialogue, supplications, dietary prohibitions and prostrations. Perhaps one of the most interesting categorizations is that pertaining to *ayas* 'revealed to other Prophets' and those revealed 'only to the Prophet Muhammad'. Examples of the former type include ten verses of *sura* 6 (from *aya* 151–160) and all the *ayas* of *sura* 87 in which there is a specific reference to the correspondences between the Abrahamic/Mosaic scriptures and the verses of the Qur'an: 'Indeed, this is in the former scriptures/ The scriptures of Abraham and Moses'. Al-Suyuti lists a number of verses said

to have been revealed only to the Prophet, among them the famous 'Throne Verse' (*aya al-Kursi*, 2.256) and the last two verses of *sura* 2. It is perhaps interesting to note the stylistic resemblances between the Throne Verse and Psalm 121:4; in both, for example, reference is made to how God shall 'neither slumber nor sleep'. There are a number of traditions that record the Prophet's allusions to the similarities between some of the verses he had been given and the verses of the Torah and the Gospels. This is particularly illustrated in a famous *hadith* recorded by Wathila b. al-Asqa (quoted in al-Tabari: 44) in which the Prophet names the four basic divisions of the Qur'an and classifies them in terms of their relationship to other scriptures:

> The Prophet, may God bless him and grant him peace, said: 'I was given *alsab' altul* (the seven long (*suras*)) in place of the Torah, and I was given *al-mi'un* (the hundreds) in place of the Psalms, and I was given *al-mathani* (the duplicated) in place of the Gospels, and I was privileged with *al-mufassal* (the sectioned).

Indeed, the striking similarities between the Qur'an and the Gospels have brought about a number of contrastive studies by Western scholars. For example, the opening *sura* of the Qur'an (*al-Fatiha*) has been compared with the Lord's Prayer, and the whole of *sura* 55 (*al-Rahman*) to Psalm 136. It has even been suggested that the whole of *sura* 55 was a direct imitation or duplication of the Psalm (for a thorough examination of Western views about this *sura*, see Abdel Haleem, 2001: 158, 183). This allegation is of course anachronistic given the fact that there had never existed an Arabic version of the Psalms for the Prophet to imitate, just as there never was an Arabic Bible. It is noteworthy that this accusation of forgery is not a modern-day development brought about by extensive scrutiny. In fact, a thousand years before, the Prophet's own pagan contemporaries in Mecca had concluded that the powerful verses he was reciting must have been dictated to him, word-for-word, by some Jewish or Christian informants. In several *ayas* of the Qur'an this error is explicitly referred to and refuted: 'And indeed We know that they say: Only a mortal teaches him. The tongue of him they hint at is foreign, and this is clear Arabic language' (16.103). It is important to remember at this stage that the Qur'an was never meant to be received as a new religion but simply as a confirmation of revelations that went before it: 'This Qur'an is not such as can be produced by other than God; rather it is a confirmation of [revelation] that went before it, and a fuller explanation of the book – wherein there is no doubt – from the lord of the worlds' (10.37).

Content and subject matter

The verses of the Qur'an introduce hundreds of different types of issues. As the Qur'an itself tells us, the *ayas* provide details about almost everything: 'We have neglected nothing in the Book' (6.38); 'We have sent down upon you the Book, an explanation of all things' (16.89). According to recent quantitative studies, the larger part of the Qur'an deals with beliefs; this is followed by morals, rituals, and lastly legal provisions. Of the 6,200 verses of the Qur'an, it is calculated that one hundred deal with ritual practices, seventy with personal affairs, seventy with civil laws, thirty with penal laws and twenty with judicial matters and testimony. Many of the *ayas* are direct answers to questions asked of the Prophet by his followers or opponents, or even direct complaints to the Prophet, such as *sura* 58 ('The Dis-

puter') which starts with the *aya*: 'Indeed God has heard the statement of she who argues with you concerning her husband and complains to God; and God hears your dialogue; God is indeed All-Hearing and All-Seeing.' Some *ayas* are also comments on the numerous historical events and circumstances that arose during the twenty-three years of Muhammad's prophetic ministry, albeit devoid of all references to dates, or names, or other indications as to exactly when these events occurred. They remain throughout distant and far removed from the personal life of the Prophet himself. His joys and his moments of grief and suffering, such as the death of his children or friends, or the loss of his wife and uncle, are never recorded. The *ayas* speak to Muhammad but he is never allowed to explain his own thoughts. It is always God who dictates, relates and warns. It is perhaps important to note that the Arabic term *Allah* is not a proper name like Zeus or Mars; it is simply the Arabic way of saying God and corresponds closely to Aramaic *Alaha* and Hebrew *Eloha* (pl. *Elohim*). In general, the *ayas* contain little that is local and much that is cosmic. As one Western scholar has pointed out, the Qur'an does not furnish any usable details that would help in the description of the climate or weather of its country, while it goes into ecstasies over the stars, the mountains, the clouds and other phenomena whose marvels it points out. There is no attempt to trace Muhammad's own genealogy or that of his Quraysh tribe to Abraham and Ishmael; instead we are given a general account of the genealogy of God's messengers beginning with Adam and ending with Muhammad. In general, only the prophets are ever mentioned by name in the *ayas*; general and more universal statements such as 'those who' and 'he who' are used instead, although there are two exceptions, namely the mention of Muhammad's fiercest opponent Abu Lahab in 111.1 and the name of his freed slave and scribe Zayd in 33.37.

Structure and parallelism

Perhaps the most striking structural feature of the Qur'an is the prevalence of symmetrically parallel verses that seem to explicate and complete each other; in more modern terms, what is striking is its intertextuality. Muslim exegetes often mobilize this parallelism to explicate a difficult word or concept by juxtaposing parallel *ayas*, an exegetical method referred to as *tafsir al-Qur'an bi-al-Qur'an* (interpreting the Qur'an by the Qur'an) or as *al-Qur'an yufassir ba'duhu ba'da* (the segments of the Qur'an explicate each other). Western scholars have labelled this type of functional parallelism, now a distinctive feature of Arabic prose style, as 'synthetic parallelism'. To locate these binary *ayas* one merely searches the text for repetitive material or structural similarities between two *ayas*. Take, for example, the opening segment of *aya* 118 in *sura* 16 – *al-Nahl*):

> And unto those who are Jews, We have forbidden such things as We have mentioned to you. The ambiguous phrase 'such things' can only be explained when juxtaposed with *aya* 146 in *sura* 6 where we are given a listing of prohibited dietary items:

> And unto those who are Jews, We have forbidden every [animal] with undivided hoof, and we have forbidden them the fat of ox and the sheep except what adheres to their hinds or their entrails.

Another oft-quoted example is the elucidation of 2.37:

> Then learnt Adam from his Lord's words, and his Lord accepted his repentance; Indeed, He is the one who accepts repentance, the Most Merciful

by 7.23, where we are given the verbatim words of repentance that God taught Adam:

> Our Lord! We [Adam and Eve] have wronged ourselves. If Thou forgive us not, and bestow not upon us Thy mercy, we shall certainly be among the losers.

It must be noted that this binary method of juxtaposing counterparts was often used by the Prophet himself when elucidating to his followers the meaning of difficult *ayas*. For example, one tradition records how he juxtaposed 6.82 to 31.13. The statement in the former

> Those who believe and do not mix their belief with injustice (*zulm*)

appeared confusing and ambiguous (*mubham*) to the Prophet's followers, for how could one mix true belief and injustice, or how could one be a true believer and yet be unjust? This ambiguity was explained by reference to the Sage Luqman's advice to his son in 31.13:

> O my son: Do not worship idols along with God. Indeed, worshiping idols along with God is a great injustice (*zulm*).

The Prophet thus explained that *zulm* here simply meant polytheism or worshipping idols along with God. Another oft-quoted example is 40.32:

> O my people. I fear for you the Day of Mutual Calling (*tanad*)

which can only properly be explained with reference to 7.44:

And the dwellers of Paradise will call out to the dwellers of Hell: We have indeed found true what our Lord had promised us; have you also found true what your Lord promised? They shall say: 'Yes'.

Here the juxtaposition reveals that the 'Day of Mutual Calling' is in fact the Day of Judgement, not at the moment of reckoning but a time after when every man has been placed either in Heaven or Hell.

A more modern way of describing this exegetical method used by the Prophet is to say that meaning is elucidated through the use of anaphoric or cataphoric reference, i.e. material mentioned earlier or later in the text. Perhaps the phrase that best describes this structure is the oft-quoted and controversial phrase *mutashabihan mathani* in 39.23 (also 15.87): 'God has sent down the best of discourse, a book *mutashabihan* and *mathani*'. These two terms have puzzled Muslim and Western scholars alike and have given rise to several theories. *Mathani*, for example, was interpreted as referring to the whole of the Qur'an, the seven verses of the opening *fatiha*, the seven long chapters, or the so-called seven prominent punishment-stories. Although most Muslim scholars now accept the view that the phrase refers to the 'repetitive' and 'consistent' structure of the Holy Book, it is significant to note that within the Arabic language-system the words have different, albeit related, meanings. *Mutashabihun* derives from the consonantal root *sh/b/h* and means to 'be similar to' or 'to resemble'; and *mathani* is derived from the adjective *mathna* which means 'double', by twos, or in pairs, i.e. a numerical meaning equivalent to the Latin '*binus*' (see Lane, 1955–56). In light of the above definition, it is thus plausible to interpret this phrase as referring not to any specific *sura* or collection of *suras* or narratives but rather to the binary principle of parallelism inherent in the text, i.e. it gives us a clue as to the whole method of reading the Qur'an.

Muhkamat and *mutashabihat*

Muhkamat and *mutashabihat* present a major and problematic dichotomy used in the classification of *ayas* first mentioned in *aya* 7 of *sura* 3, a long chapter of the Medina period entitled 'The Family of 'Imran' which owes it name to the mention of the Virgin Mary, Christ, Zachariah and John. Various definitions of these two contrastive terms have been offered by scholars, among the more common being clear/decisive for *muhkamat* and similar/allegorical/ambiguous for *mutashabihat*.

The *muhkamat/mutashabihat* dichotomy was widely debated by medieval Arab scholars such as al-Tabari, al-Razi, al-Zamakshari and al-Suyuti. Individual treatises were also written on the subject by prominent theologians, the first being by the famed Qur'an reciter 'Ali ibn Hamza al-Kisa'i entitled 'Mutashbihat al-Qur'an (second century of the Hijra; manuscript Paris 665/4); others include al-Karamani's *Al-burhan fi mutashabih al-Qur'an* and al-Razi's *Dura al-tanzil fi al-mutashabih*. It has presented commentators with two main questions: one concerns the meaning of the terms *muhkamat* and *mutashabihat*; the other touches on identifying these *ayas* in the Qur'an. The literature of exegesis is full of a great variety of definitions of these terms. In most cases they are found in the commentaries to 3.7 where the two terms are first contrasted. However, it is important to note from the outset that the word *mutashabihat* was not perceived by early Muslim commentators of the Qur'an as a controversial term. As is evident from the works of Kisa'i and al-Karamani, the word simply meant 'resemblances' and was correlated with 'repetition'. Obviously the controversy around the two words only occurred at a much later date. Here is the *aya* in its entirety:

It is He who has sent down to you the Book. In it are verses that are *muhkamat*. They are the foundation of the Book (*umm al-kitab*); and others that are *muta-shabihat*. As for those in whose hearts there is perversity, they follow those that are similar/allegorical/ambiguous (*ma tashabah minhu*), seeking discord, and seeking to interpret it, but none knows its interpretation save God. And those who are firmly grounded in knowledge say: 'We believe in it; all of it is from our Lord. And none will grasp the message except those who possess an understanding mind.'

Punctuation of the verse

Even more problematic than the lexical meaning of *muhkamat* and *mutashabihat* is the punctuation of the text. Since the original text provides no indication of where stops and pauses occur within individual *ayas*, it was thus possible to read the latter part of this verse in two different ways. The controversy centres around whether the *and* functions as a coordinator or as a transition. If it is perceived to be coordinated to the previous noun phrase then the verse reads: 'Only God and those grounded in knowledge know its interpretation. [They] say . . .' If, on the other hand, it is perceived to be a transition, then it signals the beginning of a new sentence and the verse reads: 'Only God knows its interpretation. And those grounded in knowledge say . . .'. The theological implications of the first reading are obvious; that certain scholars can know the interpretations of difficult *ayas* and

thus hold the secrets of the Qur'an. This interpretation is viewed as invalid by the majority of Muslim scholars, who cite the fact that within the verse there is an explicit criticism of those who strive to interpret the *mutashabihat*, reference to them as those whose hearts are 'deviant' and an explicit praise of those who refer all knowledge to God and refuse to become preoccupied with minute resemblances between the verses of the Qur'an or to rationalize on matters of faith.

Preferred interpretations of the verse

Two traditions or occasions of revelation (*asbab al-nuzul*) recorded by al-Tabari going back to al-Rabi' are often quoted to explicate this *aya* and to ultimately define for us the meanings of the contrastive pair *muhkamat/muta-shabihat*. The first tradition suggests that the *mutashabihat* are the abbreviated letters $a/l/m/$ which begin the *sura*. Although Western scholars have viewed this interpretation as being too simplistic, one must not lose sight of fact that these letters were the object of much controversy especially among the hypocrites and Jews of Medina. According to this tradition, the verse was revealed in response to a particular incident in which a group of Medinans, led by Yasir and Huyaiy b. Akhtab, tell the Prophet that the letters $a/l/m/$ referred to their numerical values and that they were meant to indicate the duration of his authority. Thus they counted the A (*alif*) as 1, the L. (*lam*) as 30 and the M. (*mim*) as 40, making 71 years. 'Will you enter a religion of a prophet whose duration of authority is only seventy-one years?', they asked the people of Medina. However, once they realized that there were other letters ($a/l/m/s/$ totalling 160 years, $a/l/r/$ totalling 231 years, *a/l/m/r/* 271 years, etc), they become confused as to how much time Muhammad was given and wonder whether or not these letters should all be added up to make a total of 734 years. The tradition explicitly mentions the verb *tashabah* used in the *aya* in question: 'His affair confuses us (*tashabah 'alayna*).' Obviously, this tradition gives us more definite contexts and implies that the *mutashabihat* are not just the abbreviated letters but all resemblances among *suras* that are deliberately twisted and distorted out of their true contexts. The word *ta'wil* in the later half of the *aya* could consequently mean misinterpretations or the imposition of a literal interpretation upon something which is essentially of a more spiritual nature.

The second tradition also suggests that the *mutashabihat* are similarities or resemblances between verses, but this time the similarity is not an internal one between various verses of Qur'an but rather resemblances between verses of the Qur'an and of the Gospels. According to this tradition, the expression 'those who follow the *mutashabihat*' is an allusion to the Christian delegates from Najran, who disputed with the Prophet concerning the question of Christ being a messenger and servant (*'abd*) of God rather than his 'Son' (mentioned in verses 59–63 of the same *sura* and occurring in the tenth year of the Hijra). The delegates insisted on accepting only the verses of the Qur'an that referred to Christ being 'the Word and Spirit of God' and refused to believe in any verses concerning Christ. The tradition explicitly mentions the Prophet as saying: 'There is no son but resembles his father (*yashba aba*)'. *Aya* 59, which likens Christ to Adam, both of whom were created out of dust, is said to be a direct response to the question put forth by the delegates concerning who Christ 'resembles'.

General interpretations

There are two other verses in the Qur'an that mention these two divisions separately, namely *sura* 11.1 and *sura* 39.23. According to 11.1 ('A book whose verses have been made decisive and then explained in detail' – *kitabun uhkimat ayatuhu thuma fussilat*) all the verses of the Qur'an are characterized as *muhkamat* while 39.23 ('A book consistent and repetitive' – *kitaban mutashabihan mathani*) implies that all the verses of the Qur'an are *mutashabihat*. To resolve the issue, commentators usually deal with all three verses together, saying that there is general *muhkam/mutashabih* and a particular *muhkam/mutashabih*. The first has to do with verses 11.1 and 39.23 in which the *muhkam* and *mutashabih* are taken to mean 'perfected/decisive' and 'consistent' respectively. The second has to do with verse 3.7 and all the various interpretations of *muhkamat/mutashabihat* that this generates. Obviously, it is clear from all three examples that these binary terms are not meant to be regarded as opposites but rather as complementary terms. It is perhaps significant that the opposite of the word *mutashabih* is *ghayr mutashabih* and not *muhkam*; this is quite explicitly referred and reiterated in 6.114 and 6.99. It must also be noted that although the *muhkamat* are presented as fundamental and as the essence of the book (*umm al-kitab*), that does not mean that the *mutashabihat* should in any way be considered less important. An alternative interpretation is to view them as a having a part–whole relationship where the *muhkamat* are the source *ayas* that are capable of generating all the *mutashabihat*. The notion of similarity encapsulated in the word *mutashabihat* would seem to strengthen this idea that they are somehow derived from the *muhkamat*, hence their stated similarity or resemblance. In addition, the use of the phrase *umm al-kitab* (the source or origin of the book) would seem to further reinforce the notion of the *muhkamat* as the primordial source, akin to the *al-lawh al-mahfuz* (Preserved Tablet), out of which all *ayas* in the Qur'an and other scriptures are derived. It is also significant to note that, according to 11.1, the revelation of the Qur'an is a two-stage process, as suggested by the conjunction *thumma* which denotes a sequence in time. (Although some commentators have preferred to view *thumma* here as a coordinating conjunction, it is more commonly used and generally understood in the language to mean sequence.) The first stage involves the establishing of fundamental principles and commandments; the second stage involves generating a multitude of *ayas* detailing and explicating these principles and injunctions. There thus appears to be two categories: one fixed for all time, reserved for fundamental discourse, and another for those that reiterate, expound and comment. There is no question of the two terms being opposites. And because it is never made explicit what the *mutashabihat* are supposed to 'resemble', the word can designate either the subdivision of the Qur'an into similar-looking *ayas* or the subdivision of the *muhkamat* into *ayas* that resemble it but are yet different from it. The implication of this two-stage process is that the *muhkamat* and the *mutashbihat* cannot be considered separately; they must be viewed in combination as components in a system of interdependent verses in which, on the one hand, the verses that are *mutashbihat* are the counterparts of the *muhkamat* verses, and on the other hand, they themselves are in turn the counterparts of each other.

Contextual meanings of *mutashabihat*

In addition to the two occurrences, *mutashibihat* and *tashabah*, in 3.7, the root form *sh/b/h* occurs in ten other instances in the Qur'an. In eight of these, the meaning is clearly that of similarity, resemblances and sameness between two objects (cf. 2.25, 70, 118; 4.157; 6.99, 141; 13.16; 39.23). In six instances, it is used in its adjectival form *mutashabih/mushtabih*, as in *sura* 6 where the word appears four times and denotes how the fruits of heaven, specifically pomegranates and olives, are similar (*mutashabihan/mushtabihan*) and yet dissimilar (*ghayr mutashabihin*). In all these examples, the word has positive connotations derived mainly from the positiveness of the items being compared, i.e. olives, pomegranates. It is only when it is used as a verb, i.e. in derivatives such as *shubbih*, *tashabahat*, *tashabah*, that negative connotations of prevarication, distortion and false or pretended confusion set in. In 4.157, for example, the verb *shubbih* is used to indicate that it was not Christ who was killed and crucified but that it 'appeared to be so' to some people (*shubbih laham*). In 13.16, the polytheists are ridiculed for seeming to be confused between what God has created and what their idols have allegedly created. Perhaps the more famous and oft-quoted example of false resemblances is 2.70, where the Israelites three times ask Moses to pray God to identify for them which heifer they were supposed to slaughter in expiation for a murder (compare Deut. 21: 1–19). The verb *tashaba* ('to become similar') is here used by the Israelites: 'Pray thy Lord to show us what she [the heifer] is to be: for the heifers have become similar to us (*tashaba 'alayna*).' It is made clear here by the repetitive form of questions that the confusion of the Israelites is not accidental, i.e. due to genuine resemblances between heifers, but more of a deliberate or contrived confusion which arises from the very nature of their deviant hearts. It is perhaps for this reason that Palmer in his translation (see Palmer, 1880) renders the term *tashabah* as 'confusingly similar'. In the final analysis, as all these examples illustrate, the notion of similarity or resemblance is an essential component of the word *mutashabih*, which cannot be eliminated without ultimately distorting the very essence of the word. Contrary to the views of some Western lexicographers (for example, Lane, 1955–56) who maintain that anything which is confused can be called *mutashabih* or *mushtabih*, the verb *tashabah* does not mean being confused for any other reason beside resemblances.

English equivalents of *mutashabihat*

Because the meaning of *muhkam* is so clear-cut, there has not been much controversy over the topic. The word *muhkamat* derives from the root *h/k/m/* which means to decide between two things. As a verbal noun it denotes judgments, decisions. When collocated with speech, the meaning is to perfect by making the words more decisive, precise and clear-cut. Ahmad von Denffer (1983: 79) in his *Introduction to the sciences of the Qur'an*, p. 99 al-'Uzza Abu Muslim al-Isfahani, defines the *muhkamat* as verses that 'decide between legal matters as well as between truth and falsehood by giving clear definitions'. The word occurs in numerous other places in the Qur'an with the explicit meaning of being decisive or perfected – it refers to anything made or rendered

firm, stable, strong or solid. The meaning of *mutashbihat*, on the other hand, has aroused countless speculations and a wide variety of translations, ranging from similar and allegorical to ambiguous and confusing. In his (1952) translation, Pickthall renders the terms as 'clear revelations' and 'allegorical' respectively, which is in accordance with the exposition of the two prominent Muslim commentators al-Baydawi and al-Zamakhshari. Sale, in his (1900) interpretation of this *aya*, points out the judicial aspect of these terms and, following Pickthall, renders the *muhkamat* as 'clear to be understood' and the *mutashabihat* as 'parabolical'. It is perhaps significant that the word *tashbih* is also the technical word for simile and metaphor in Arabic, a fact that accentuates the appropriateness of the English translation 'allegorical/metaphorical'. Both Bell and Arberry, on the other hand, render the term *muhkamat* as 'clearly formulated verses' and *mutashbihat* as 'ambiguous'. In general, Muslim scholars tend to interpret the term *mutashbihat* as either similar or allegorical, but never as ambiguous. Western scholars, on the other hand, following the lead of Bell and Arberry, prefer the word 'ambiguous'. The basic problem with the use of the word 'ambiguous' as an English equivalent is that it negates the presence of correspondences and emphasizes difference, multiplicity and imprecision of thought. This is far from the core meaning of the Arabic root *sh/b/h* which emphasizes sameness and similitude. Even more important is the fact that *mutashabih* is a neutral term that can be used to refer to both positive and negative resemblances, depending on the items being compared, whereas in ambiguity there are only negatives without positives. What further increases this semantic non-equivalence of ambiguity is the fact that the one-to-one equivalent of ambiguous is *mubham*; it is never *mutashabih*. The use of the term ambiguous has therefore been rejected by many Muslim scholars who see it as a biased misinterpretation of the Arabic original since it is linguistically evident, even a priori, that *mutashabihat* can never in the final analysis be said to denote multiplicity.

At first glance, therefore, *mutashabihat* would seem to constitute the very reverse of ambiguity. It comes then somewhat as a surprise to see the extent to which this less orthodox interpretation has come to be assimilated to *mutashabih/mutashabihat* in the recently published *Encyclopedia of the Qur'an*, where the Arabic term can only be accessed through a seven-page entry entitled 'ambiguous' and devoted almost entirely to the active participle *mutashabih* or *mutashabihat* interpreted as such. Although reference is made to the sense of similarity, it is stated that the reading *mutashabihat*, meaning ambiguous, is a common way to treat the term and has 'wider implications' since it bears upon some of the most prominent Qur'anic issues. Even more striking is the fact that the familiar variant 'allegorical' is never even mentioned, although it has been used by three prominent translators of the Qur'an, namely, Pickthall, Ali and Asad.

Types of contrasts

Six basic types of contrasts are offered by medieval Muslim commentators. They can be summarized as follows:

1. The *muhkamat* are *ayas* whose meanings are capable of being known or grasped by people. In contrast, the *mutashabihat* are *ayas* whose meanings are known only to God. The examples given of *mutashabihat* are the Day of Resurrection, conditions in the After-

world, rewards and punishments in the Afterworld, the appearance of Gog and Magog, the rising of the sun from the West, and in general anything that pertains to *'ilm al-ghayb* ('knowledge of the Unseen' as summarized in 31.34). Two of the more controversial of these *mutashabihat* are the abbreviated letters and God's attributes (*sifat Allah*), i.e. his face, his hand, his throne. Since any interpretation of the above would be absurd or a matter of conjecture, Muslim commentators and exegetes were strongly opposed to any kind of interpretation of the *mutashabihat*. In a sense, this definition not only imposes a restriction on esoteric or symbolic interpretations of words, it also bans the attempt to rationalize basic articles of faith.

2. The *muhkamat* are *ayas* that can have only one distinct meaning. In contrast, the *mutashabihat* are *ayas* whose lexical and syntactic structures allow more than one meaning. Injunctions, commands, prohibitions, all are viewed as *muhkam* items. The *mutashabihat* are subdivided into two kinds: (a) verbal (*lafz*) – such as difficult words or difficult syntax involving ellipsis, fronting or embedding; and (b) semantic (*ma'na*) – such as those verses that need to be explicated by extra-linguistic knowledge of the occasion of revelation or contemporary customs of pre-Islamic times. One explicit example often cited is 43.17: 'And when one of them is given glad tidings of that which he attributes to the Most-Merciful, his face turns dark and grief-stricken', which can only be explicated by reference to 16.58: "And when one of them is given glad tidings of [the birth of] a

female, his face turns dark and grief-stricken'. What is needed to explicate the text is historical knowledge that the three pagan idols or goddesses of Mecca, al-Lat, al-'Uzza, and Manat, were believed to be the daughters of God.

3. The *muhkamat* are *ayas* that are decisive and clear in and by themselves (i.e. self-explanatory) and hence are independent since they do not need additional explanations. In contrast, the *mutashabihat* are *ayas* that are dependent or interdependent and need illustration by means of reference to other *ayas* or other sources of interpretation. This definition also implies that the *mutashabihat* have to be examined or checked against the *muhkamat*. According to al-Razi, the *muhkam* are 'the source from which everything stems' (*al-asl minhu yakunu al-shay*) – hence the dependency of the *mutashabihat* on the *muhkamat* as a basis of interpretation. One of the examples given is 17.17: 'And when we decide to destroy a city, we command the opulent ones thereof: and they transgress therein; and thus the word is justified. Then do we destroy it a complete destruction.' The outward meaning of the verse is that the opulent are commanded to transgress while the *muhkam* on the same subject, found in 7.27, strictly forbids transgression and rebukes those who suggest that they were simply following God's commandments: 'And when they commit an evil deed, they say: We found our fathers doing it, and God commanded it upon us. Say: Nay, God never commands transgression. Do you say of God what you know not.'

4. The *muhkamat* are *ayas* whose meanings cannot be distorted or perverted (*tahrif*). In contrast, the *mutashabihat* are liable to be distorted or to be given a false interpretation (*ta'wil*) by people with malicious intentions. This view is expounded by al-Tabari and Ibn Kathir who support their arguments by the fact that the verse in question identifies those who follow the *mutashabihat* with those whose hearts are full of deviance (*zaygh*) and bent on schism (*fitna*). The list of *mutashabihat* cited by Abu Muslim Al-Isfahani and quoted by al-Razi all pertain to how people with deviant hearts try to impose a certain interpretation depending on their particular ideologies, thus perverting the true meanings of the text. One example of such distortions occurs in the interpretation of 27.4: 'Verily, those who believe not in the Hereafter, We have adorned for them their works, and they shall wander blindly on.' According to Abu Muslim, this *aya* has been misinterpreted to mean that God has adorned or made seeming the act of wandering blindly or being astray, although it clearly contradicts with 49.7 where it is made clear that God has made faith beloved and seemly to man: 'God has made faith beloved to you; and He has adored it in your hearts, and has made disbelief, wickedness, and rebellion hateful to you.' The deliberate attempt to misconstrue the words of God by not juxtaposing the *mutashabihat* and the *muhkamat* is offered as an example of those who follow the *mutashabihat*. What seems to strengthen this argument are the various allusions in *sura* 2 to the

lexical distortions and derisive punning practiced by the hypocrites and Jews of Medina who were bent on distorting every single verse revealed by the Prophet and twisting them out of context (see especially 4.46). One well-known historical example is how they used to distort the traditional Arabic greeting – "Peace be upon you' when encountering the Prophet. Instead of saying *salam* ('peace' in Arabic), they used to mumble it in such as a way as to make it indistinguishable from a word with a similar sound meaning 'death' in Hebrew. In a sense, then, this classification implies that the *mutashabihat* are not ambiguous in and of themselves but are portrayed as such by those hostile to the whole of the Qur'an, both the *muhkam* and the *mutashabih*.

5. The *muhkamat* are *ayas* that are accurate and free of contradiction. The *mutashabihat*, on the other hand, are *ayas* that are similar or bear resemblances either to each other or to the *muhkamat*, or to verses of other scriptures. This definition is advocated by al-Tabari, who states that the *mutashabihat* are verses, the words of which resemble one another when repeated in other Qur'anic chapters. Consequently, repetition is presented as one of the characteristic features of the *mutashabihat*. Other commentators see the resemblances in more figurative terms, e.g. as a resemblance in beauty and eloquence, or rightness and truth. Undoubtedly, this represents the most classical explanation of the word *mutashabihat*, first expounded by al-Kisa'i in his book on the *mutashabihat* of the Qur'an, where the word is clearly taken in its literal sense of 'resemblances' and 'repetitions'. This second-century Hijra treatise, described by John Wansbrough (1977: 212) as a 'distributional analysis of Qur'anic diction', is ordered by the number of occurrences of a given phrase – once, twice, three to ten times, fifteen times and twenty times; it also deals with unique phraseologies. A similar listing of material can be found in al-Zarkashi's more systematic treatise, *al-Burhan fi 'ulum al-Qur'an*, which covers unique expressions and expressions that occur from two to twenty-three times. Evidently, this genre of enumeration provides evidence that the *mutashabihat* were originally regarded as being similar or repetitive verses of the Qur'an.

6. The *muhkamat* are *ayas* of injunctions and commandments, i.e. those that deal with what is allowed (*halal*) and what is prohibited (*haram*), that define punishments (*hudud*) and obligatory duties (*fara'id*) and dogma ('*aqida*), i.e. *ayas* that are decisive as regards Islamic law. In contrast, the *mutashabihat* are *ayas* that deal with God's attributes and divine epithets mentioned in the Qur'an, the abbreviated letters, parables, oaths and metaphors. It is significant to note that there exists a series of early texts which contain the term *al-mushtabihat* or *al-mutashabihat* in their title and which treat the *mutashabihat* of the Qur'an as equivalent to metaphorical expressions (see the description of the Paris manuscript in *Islamica*, Vol. 1: 241; see also Brockelmann, Vol. 1: 416). A related definition describes the *muhkamat* as those *ayas* that contain

ordinances and injunctions which can never be abrogated by any later ordinance, and the *mutashbihat* as those *ayas* that can be abrogated. The examples most often cited of *muhkamat* are 6.152 and 17.24 as well as all the *ayas* that begin with 'say' (*qul*) or 'command them'. Obviously, this definition has implications for jurisprudence and is more of a judicial classification than a theological one.

Ayat al-sajda

The *sajda* is an *aya* of the Qur'an containing the root verb *s/j/d/* (to prostrate), in which voluntary prostration is offered by anyone who recites it or hears it, in adoration of God and as an expression of deep faith and humility. According to scholars, *sajda*s occur only in the early Meccan *ayas* which can be found embedded in many of the later *suras* of Medina. Tradition has it that the Prophet Muhammad consistently prostrated during the recitation of these *ayas*, even while performing his ritual prayers (*salat*), in which case he would stop at the end of the *aya*, prostrate himself, recite a number of supplications, and then rise to continue his prayers. In all, there are fourteen *ayas* of prostration agreed upon by all Muslim scholars, with one extra *aya* advocated by al-Shafi'i citing a reliable Tradition. These *ayas* are scattered in fourteen different *suras* of the Qur'an, with no specific order of occurrence being followed: 7.206; 13.15; 16.50; 17.107; 19.58; 22.18; 25.60; 27.26; 32.5; 38.24; 41.38; 53.62; 84.21; 96.19. The extra *sajda* suggested by al-Shafi'i occurs in *sura* 17 (*al-hajj*), *aya* 77, which thus inadvertently highlights *sura al-Hajj* as being the only chapter of the Qur'an that contains two *sajda*s.

There seems to be no specific Tradition recording the reasons why these particulars *ayas* containing a form of the verb *s/j/d/* were singled out by the Prophet. Although the root verb *s/j/d/* is integral to the *sajda*, it is not the case that all occurrences of the verb signal a prostration; in fact, the verb occurs over sixty times in the Qur'an. What we do know from Tradition is that according to the Prophet, the closest one can be to God is during moments of prostration, and hence he urged the faithful to prostrate long and to offer heartfelt supplications, especially after midnight in the small hours of the morning. The most preferred supplication during prostration is the one recited by the Prophet himself during the five obligatory prayers: 'I prostrate my face to the One who has created it and fashioned it and cleft its hearing and its vision. Blessed is God, the best of Creators' (*Sajada wajhiya lilladhi khalaqahu wa sawwarahu, wa shaqqa sam'ahu wa basarahu, tabarak Allahu ahsan al-khaliqin*). All Arabic editions of the Qur'an clearly demarcate *sajda*s, usually by placing a line above the root verb *s/j/d/* and some form of icon before the verse-number so as to clearly signal the end of the *sajda*. It is significant to note that there is also a whole *sura* devoted to the notion of prostration (*sura* 32, *al-Sajda*) which takes its name from *aya* 15 in which the adjectival form *sujadan* occurs: 'Those who believe in our *ayat* are those who, when reminded of them fall down prostrate (*sujadan*) and glorify the praises of their Lord, and they are not proud.'

Perhaps the most famous of prostration-*ayas* is the one that occurs at the end of *sura* 53 (*al-Najm*), because this is the first *aya* in which the Prophet offered a prostration. The occasion of its revelation is well known. According to Tradition, the Prophet recited the *sura* beside the *Ka'ba* in front of a group of

Meccan chieftains who had assembled there. Although the words of the *sura* contained much mockery of the polytheists of Mecca and a strong condemnation of their three main idols, al-Lat, al-'Uzza and Manat, yet when the Prophet recited the *sajda*, which clearly called for the polytheists to prostrate themselves – 'So prostate (*fa-asjudu*) to God and worship Him' – the whole assembly spontaneously and involuntarily prostrated themselves with one accord on the ground and worshipped. Once the chieftains realized what they had done, they quickly made up the allegation that the Prophet had actually praised their idols rather than demeaned them and accused him of suppressing his supposed words of praise.

Although this was the first *sajda* revealed to the Prophet, one must not confuse it with the first *sajda* to appear in the Qur'an in its present arrangement, namely the last *aya* of *sura* 7 (*al-A'raf*): 'Surely, those who are with your Lord (i.e. the angels) are never too proud to worship Him, and they glorify Him and to Him they prostate (*yasjudun*).' Nor must we confuse it with the *sajda* that appears at the end of the famous *sura* 96 (*al-'Alaq*), which is credited to be the first complete *sura*: 'Nay! Do not obey him [Abu Jahl]. But fall prostrate (*asjud*) and draw near [to God].'

It would appear then that although there seems to be no systematic order of occurrence, these *sajda*s are somehow meant to mark important landmarks of the Qur'an, such as the first *sura* to be revealed or the first in which the *sajda* occurs. Thematically, they seem to enumerate all things that worship God, the Creator; the list is cosmic and includes not only the angels and the prophets, but everything in the heavens and on earth: 'See you not that unto God doth prostrate (*yasjudu*) whatever is in the heaven and whatever is on the earth, and the sun and the moon and the stars, and the mountains and the trees and all creatures and many of the people' (22.18). This is again reiterated in 13.15, but this time even their very shadows seem to worship the Lord: 'And unto God doth prostrate (*yasjuda*) whatever is in the heavens and the earth, willingly or unwillingly, and so do their shadows in the mornings and in the afternoons'. Quite striking in this *sajda* is the reference not only to how all non-human things must ultimately obey God, but also to the fact that even their very shadows prostrate in worship. The time reference to the mornings and afternoons would seem to suggest that the movement of shadows in relation to the sun is itself a form of continuous prostration and prayer. It is perhaps significant to note that before the ordaining of obligatory prayers, it was customary to pray twice, once in the mornings and once at nightfall. This imagery of shadows in prostration to God is again reiterated in 16.48–49, but this time it is explicitly spelled out: 'Have they not observed the things that God has created; how their shadows incline to the right and to the left, prostrating (*sujjadan*) unto God in a most humble manner/And to God prostrate (*yasjudu*) all that is in the heavens and all that is in the earth, of living creatures and the angels and they are not proud.' There is also explicit reference to the fact that people of all religions since the time of Adam were required to prostrate in worship: 'Those are the Prophets whom God bestowed His grace upon from among the offspring of Adam, and from those We carried with Noah, and from the offspring of Abraham and Israel, and from among those whom We guided and chose. When the verses of the Most Gracious were recited to them, they fell down prostrate (*sujjadan*) and weeping' (19.58). Certain prophets are also singled out, most notably David, who, according to Tradition, was continually praised by the Prophet Muhammad as being the most passionate of the prophets in prayers and exultation. In 38.24 there is a recounting of the Old Testament story of David and Uriah (II Samuel 11:4–5), bar the biblical allegation that David committed adultery with Uriah's wife. The *sajda* occurs at the point where two angels are sent to bring home to him his sin: 'And David guessed that We had tried him and he sought forgiveness of his Lord, and he fell down in prostration and repented'.

References and further reading

Abdel Haleem, M. (2001) *Understanding The Qur'an: Themes and styles*, London and New York: I.B. Tauris.

Abu-Hamdiyyah, M. (2000) *The Qur'an: An introduction*, London: Routledge.

al-Alalam'i, Z. (2002) *Dirasat fi 'ulum al-Qur'an al-Karim*, Riyadh, n.p.

Ali, A.Y. (1991) *The Meaning of the Holy Qur'an*, Baltimore, MD: Amana Corporation.

Arberry, A. (1964) *The Koran Interpreted*, Oxford: Oxford University Press.

Asad, M. (1980) *The Message of the Qur'an*, Gibraltar: Dar al-andalus.

Bell, R. (1970) Introduction to the Qur'an, Edinburgh: Edinburgh University Press.

Denffer, A. von (1983) '*Ulum al-Qur'an: An introduction to the sciences of the Qur'an*, London: The Islamic Foundation.

Draz, M.A. (2000) *Introduction to the Qur'an*, London and New York: I.B. Tauris.

Gruendler, B. (2001) 'Arabic Script', in *EQ*, Vol. 1, 135–44.

al-Hilali, M.T. and Khan, M. (1993) *Interpretations of the Meanings of the Noble Qur'an in the English Language*, Riyadh: Maktaba Dar-as-salam.

Ibn Kathir (n.d.) *Abu l-fida' Isma'il, Tafsir al-Qur'an al-'azim*, Cairo.

Jeffery, A. (1965) 'Aya', in *EI*, Vol. I, 773–4.

Kinberg, L. (1999) '*Muhkamat* and *Mutashabihat*: Implications of a Koranic pair of terms in medieval exegesis', in A. Rippin (ed.) *The Qur'an: Formative inter-pretation*, Aldershot: Ashgate/Variorum, 283–313.

—— (2001) 'Ambiguous', in *EQ*, 70–9.

al-Kisa'i, Ali b. Hamza (1994) *Kitab Mutashabih al-Qur'an*, ed. Sabih al-Tamimi, Tripoli, n.p.

Lane, E.W. (1955–56) *Arabic English Lexicon*, New York: Frederick Ungar Publishing Co.

Mayer, T. (2002) 'Review Article: The Qur'an and its interpretive tradition by Andrew Rippin', *Journal of Qur'anic Studies* IV, 2: 91–104.

Palmer, E.H. (1880) *The Koran*, Oxford: Clarendon Press.

Paret, R. (1965) 'al-Kur'an', in *EI*, Vol. V, 400–17.

Pickthall, Marmaduke M. (1952) *The Meaning of the Glorious Koran: An Explanatory Translation*, London: George Allen & Unwin.

al-Qatan, M. (1998) *Mabahith fi 'ulum al-Qur'an*, Beirut: al-Resalah Publishers.

Rahbar, D. (1960) *God of Justice: A study in the ethical doctrine of the Qur'an*, Leiden: E.J. Brill.

Rippin, A. (2001) 'Lexicographical Texts and the Qur'an', in *The Qur'an and its Interpretive Tradition*, Burlington: Ashgate, Vol. XX, 158–73.

Sale, G. (1900) *The Koran*, London and New York: Frederick Warne and Co. Ltd.

al-Suyuti, J.A. (2003) *al-Itqan fi 'ulum al-Qur'an*, ed. F. Zamarli, Beirut: Dar al-kitab al-'arabi.

al-Tabari, (1954) *Jami' al-Bayan fi tafsir al-Qur'an*, Cairo.

Wansbrough, J. (1977) *Qur'anic Studies: Sources and methods of scriptural inter-pretation*, Oxford: Oxford University Press.

al-Zamakhshari (1947) *al-Kashshaf*, Beirut, n.p.

See also: '*aqida*; *fitna*; **Mother of the Book; Preserved Tablet;** *ta'til*

AFNAN H. FATANI

AYATULLAH AL-UZMA SAYYID ABUL-QASIM AL-KHO'I

see: **al-Kho'i, Ayatullah al-Uzma Sayyid Abul-Qasim**

AYYUB

The prophet Job is mentioned by name in the Qur'an four times. Job's descent from Abraham is indicated in 6.84 where he is listed along with David, Solomon, Joseph, Moses and Aaron. Some Muslim genealogists state that Job was Roman or an Israelite living among the Romans, being a descendant of Esau who is considered to be the forefather of all the Roman people. There is disagreement among Muslim exegetes concerning the time when Job lived, some saying that he was a grandson of Lot and others saying that he lived after the time of Solomon.

21.83–84 and 38.41–44 relate the story of Job, stating that he was afflicted with 'distress' and then restored by God after calling out to him in prayer. Muslim exegetes add that Job was a rich man with a large family but all of this was taken away from him, including his health. Job remained steadfast through his affliction although all of the people around him abandoned and loathed him because of it. It is reported that the Prophet Muhammad stated that Job was the most afflicted of all the prophets, and because all people are tried according to the strength of their religion, this means that Job was the most steadfast of all the prophets. Muslim exegetes say that the trial of Job lasted anywhere from three to eighteen years, and they acknowledge that the Bible contains many stories about the details of this trial.

Of Job's sickness, Muslim exegetes claim that it afflicted all of his body except for his heart and his tongue, with which he continued to praise God. Others claim that his sickness was smallpox, and that his body became only bones and sinews.

Muslim exegetes also relate stories about Job's family. According to some,

Job's wife remained faithful to her husband, serving other people for wages and selling her hair in order to provide Job with sustenance. Some exegetes claim that it was the sight of his wife's cut hair that finally made Job call out to God for help (21.73). Job is also said to have had brothers who came and debated with Job about the cause of his distress.

38.42–44 refers to God's alleviation of Job's affliction with cold water and to the restoration of his family. Medieval Muslim illustrations of the story of Job often feature Job bathing in the spring of water provided by God. Muslim exegetes add that God clothed Job with clothing from heaven, caused locusts of gold to rain down upon him and allowed him to live for another seventy years in the land of Rome.

Some exegetes maintain that Job passed the mantle of prophethood to one or more of his sons, one of which is usually identified as the prophet Dhu al-Kifl who is also mentioned in the Qur'an. A *hadith* report states that on the Day of Judgement, Job will intercede on behalf of people who suffered persecution. Numerous tombs attributed to Job exist throughout the Middle East, India and Central Asia.

Further reading

Bowman, J. (1963) 'Banu Israil in the Qur'an', *Islamic Studies* 2: 447–55.

Cohen, G.D. (1991) 'Esau as a Symbol in Early Medieval Thought', *Studies in the Variety of Rabbinic Cultures*: 243–69.

Heller, B. (1928) 'Récits et personnages bibliques dans la légende mahometane', *Revue des études juives* 85: 113–36.

BRANNON WHEELER

'AZIZ

'*Aziz* signifies mighty, potent or strong. In the Qur'an '*aziz* is one of the names of God. It signifies 'the Mighty who overcomes everything' or 'He who resists or withstands so that nothing ever overcomes Him'. It also means 'the incomparable, or unparalleled'.

It usually comes at the end of the *sura*, as a closing phrase expressing and indeed summarizing the total power, strength and glory of God. Its presence at the end signifies that in the end everything belongs to God alone; he possesses the final authority, and the ultimate power. Everything is dependent on God, and all return to him at the end. All his servants are created by him, and he brings them back on the Day of Judgement and determines their ultimate fate.

'Aziz generally ends a description of struggle between the prophets of God and their enemies. The word is used to emphasize the claim that God is victorious and that he grants victory to his prophets and their followers against the unbelievers. The Qur'an describes the unbelievers as plotters and their deception as so powerful that it almost shakes the mountains. God responds to their evil and apparent strength, and the powerful nature of their means of deception, by saying 'never think that God would fail his apostles in His promise, for God is exalted in power the Lord of Retribution' (58.21).

'Aziz is also used to indicate support for the Prophet Muhammad. During his struggle against the idolaters, and while he was in a state of sadness and distress because of their evil actions, God gave him strength and support, indicating that he was on the right path and would eventually succeed.

'The Mighty Book' (*al-'Aziz*), is a title often given to the Qur'an. It suggests both that the text is powerful and that its creator is strong and capable of following up its words with actions.

RAFIK BERJAK

AZRA'IL

Of the four recognised archangels in Islam, the Qur'an names only two: Jibra'il (Gabriel), the angel of revelation; and Mika'il (Michael), the angel of rain and fertility. It is left to Prophetic Tradition (*hadith*) to name the other two: Israfil, the angel who will blow the trumpet to announce the Resurrection at the end of time; and Azra'il, the angel who separates the soul from the body at death. Known also as *malak al-mawt* (32.11) or the angel of death, Azra'il is traditionally depicted as being of cosmic size: he has 4,000 wings and a body formed by as many eyes and tongues as there are living human beings, and he stands with one foot in the seventh heaven, the other on the razor-sharp bridge that divides paradise and hell.

COLIN TURNER

B

BACKBITING

Backbiting, slander or calumny is criticizing or mocking others in their absence. Normally the intention of backbiting is to put someone down by commenting on a negative characteristic of that person. Backbiting is one of the social illnesses that the Qur'an strongly denounces: '... nor speak ill of each other behind their backs. Would any of you like to eat the flesh of his dead brother? Nay, ye would abhor it. But fear Allah: for Allah is Oft-Returning, Most-Merciful' (49.12). This verse clearly declares the rejection by revelation of backbiting.

To understand the nature of backbiting we need to consult the Tradition of the Prophet Muhammad about this phenomenon. He had many sayings that have been reported on this issue, denouncing this behaviour and discouraging the Muslims from getting involved in it. When he was asked about backbiting, he explained that mentioning a fault of an absent person is considered backbiting. Falsely attributing a fault to an absent person is considered defamation. The Prophet discouraged Muslims from backbiting along with other illicit actions: 'Do not envy, abominate, or shun each other, nor should you backbite each other.'

There are different ways of backbiting. Speaking of someone's fault or mocking a certain person with a gesture are the obvious ways. Backbiting could also comprise writing derogatory statements, thus insulting a person is another method of backbiting. Listening to someone who is slandering another person and supporting that action by smiling or expressing agreement in any form is considered another way of backbiting. Slandering people with physical disabilities, poor manners or discriminating against them because of their race, skin colour or place of origin are considered different kinds of backbiting. The Qur'an gives a very graphic image to backbiters. Slander is portrayed as a human beast or a cannibal creature that feeds on the flesh of his brother's corpse. This image is so vivid that it brings home hard the unpleasant aspect of this ugly inhuman action: God created humans with a pure nature that enjoys the beauty of its humanity, nature and the universe, and simultaneously abhors the images of blood, death and the corpse. The use of this image in the Qur'an has very strong significance for many reasons. First, people are disgusted by cannibalism. Second, people do not feel comfortable coming into direct contact with a dead body. Third, according to Islam the dead human body should be respected and treated with dignity. Islamic tradition honours the dead by washing the corpse, shrouding it with clean, white winding sheets and giving it a speedy burial. The pure, righteous believers and God-fearing Muslims with pure conscience will naturally be disturbed by the image of cannibalism and will therefore avoid becoming involved in backbiting. This sickening image of eating a dead body gives the human imagination an unlimited space to stretch and try to grasp the ugly image of such an action. If someone would hate to eat the rotten and wormy flesh of a dead human body, then one should control one's mouth and refrain from backbiting.

The backbiter may have strong feelings of hatred, jealousy or envy towards another person, which gives the former the motivation to insult the latter behind his or her back. But when the Qur'an drew this image of cannibalism as similar to backbiting, it created a deterrent.

This revelation did not come down to the Prophet simply for theoretical preaching, but as something to be reinforced in this life. Islam creates in the Muslim's conscience the fear of God and of his punishment and also the hope of his reward on the Day of Judgement as a process that obliges the Muslim to abide by the orders and commands of God. After all, the main objective of the revelation is to establish the representation of God on earth. Its aim is to build an exemplary society and the ideal individual, based on the principle that Muslim society as a whole is one integral structure and the individual is its building block. In order to establish a strong and healthy nation in which individuals form its overall shape, each individual as a basic unit needs to be healthy and strong. In order to achieve this strong, just and healthy nation, Islam introduces to its followers a very strict scheme of discipline, which has been very powerful and influential in enforcing a firm code of behaviour. This system of discipline speaks to the conscience of the Muslim; it speaks to the heart and the mind at the same time. For this reason Islam was able to guide its followers to obey its rules and code of conduct, as this will apparently result in the founding of the ideal nation that can truly represent God's will on earth and implement his law. Following this disciplinary programme, backbiting is considered a major sin and violation that believers should avoid, as a vicious disease that threatens the unity and the healthy ties that hold the nation together. Islam is deeply concerned about social justice and fairness because God is fair and he hates unfairness. His orders are aligned with this principle. He clearly prohibited such actions that may do someone injustice, stating: 'O my servants, I declared that injustice is prohibited upon myself, so you do not do injustice on each other.' Backbiting is a form of injustice and as such is prohibited.

See also: '**A'isha; character; miraculousness of the Qur'an; rumour**

RAFIK BERJAK

BADR

More correctly, Badr Hunayn, a small town to the south-west of Medina, and at the junction of the old caravan route from Mecca to Syria. At the time of Muhammad it was a small market centre, situated in a plain, encircled by steep hills and sand dunes. It was the site of the first great battle between Muhammad and the pagan Meccans in the middle of Ramadan 2/March 624. The battle of Badr was a huge psychological victory for the nascent Muslim community, with 300 of the devout of Medina overcoming 1,000 well-equipped Qurayshis, of whom over seventy were slain, including their leader, Abu Jahl. There are various references to the battle in the Qur'an, although it is to the *hadith* and the *sira* (historical stories) that one must turn for details.

COLIN TURNER

AL-BAGHAWI

Al-Husayn b. Mas'ud b. Muhammad al-'Allama Abu Muhammad al-Farra' al-Baghawi was born in Bagh, or Baghshur, near Herat. Arab sources often identify him by the nickname al-Farra'. He was known for temperance and piety, renouncing sumptuous foods and surviving on bread and olive oil. He died an octogenarian in Marw al-Rudh some time between 510/1117 and 516/1122.

Al-Suyuti describes him as a Shafi'ite authority on exegesis, traditions and jurisprudence. Al-Baghawi's works include *Masabih al-sunna* (Lights of the way of the Prophet) and *Sharh al-sunna* (Making the Prophets' way known), both studies of the traditions; *al-Tahdhib* (The Expurgation), a study of jurisprudence; and *Ma'alim al-tanzil* (The signposts of the Revelation), a commentary on the Qur'an. All his writing draws on narrative in illustrating doctrine

and interpreting scripture. In this he followed the model of al-Tha'labi (d. 427/1035).

In *Masabih al-sunna*, al-Baghawi presents traditions in a set order and hierarchy, according to authority, namely: reliable, good, unusual and weak traditions. In the introduction, al-Baghawi states his aim as to address topics on which the Qur'an is silent. He omits the chains of authority for the traditions cited, but names the Companion through whom each of the *hadith* could be traced.

The extant version of *Ma'alim al-tanzil* represents three stages of composition. First, al-Baghawi drew on al-Tha'labi's commentary for the core of his own work. He then added supplementary material from other sources, identified in the introduction. Finally, the work underwent an editing process at the hand of Taj al-Din Abu Nasri 'Abd al-Wahhab b. Muhammad al-Husayni (d. 875/1471).

Al-Baghawi undertakes a verse-by-verse treatment of the Qur'anic text. Debates from earlier commentators are reported, often without an indication of al-Baghawi's preferred interpretation. As stated, he avoids lengthy chains of authority, resulting in a relatively fluid prose style that helps the reader focus on the text and its stories, rather than on philological minutiae. *Ma'alim al-tanzil* also includes information on variant readings of the Qur'anic text, with occasional discussion of grammatical detail.

Al-Baghawi draws the narratives for his commentary from Jewish, Christian and Islamic materials, although non-Islamic sources are not identified. Examples are the account of David and Bathsheba from Jewish tradition presented in *sura Sad*, and the lengthy account of the Seven Sleepers of Ephesus from Christian tradition presented in *sura al-Kahf*. The length of the stories often seems out of proportion to the small theological point being made in individual Qur'anic verses.

Ma'alim al-tanzil has an ambiguous reputation. Ibn Taymiyya (d. 728/1328) wrote that al-Baghawi had safeguarded his commentary from inferior traditions and heretical opinions. However, some later scholars criticized it for the inclusion of weak traditions and stories derived from Jewish and Christian sources.

Further reading

al-Baghawi, al-Husayn b. Mas'ud b. Muhammad al-'Allama Abu Muhammad al-Farra' (1407/1987) *Ma'alim al-tanzil*, 2nd edn, Beirut: Dar al-ma'rifa.

al-Dhahabi, Muhammad Husayn (1405/1985) *al-Tafsir wa al-Mufassirun* (Exegesis and the Commentators), 3rd edn, 3 vols, Cairo: Wahba.

Riddell, P.G. (1997) 'The Transmission of Narrative Based Exegesis in Islam: al-Baghawi's use of stories in his commentary on the Qur'an, and a Malay descendant', in P.G. Riddell and Tony Street (eds) *Islam: Essays on Scripture, Thought and Society*, Leiden: E.J. Brill, 57–80.

al-Suyuti, Jalal al-Din (1976) *Tabaqat al-Mufassirin* (The generations of commentators), Cairo: Wahba.

See also **Isra'iliyyat**; *tafsir* – **Salafi views**
PETER G. RIDDELL

BAQA

Baqa is the root of a verb meaning 'remained, continued, lasted' and was or became 'perpetual'. The noun is verbal and signifies a thing's remaining, continuing, lasting, or enduring in its first state, for a period determined by the will of God. In the Qur'an this term indicates the eternity of Allah Almighty: 'And Allah is better and more lasting' (20.73). It also signifies the everlasting face of God: 'And the Face of your Lord Full of Majesty and Honour will remain forever' (55.27). *Baqa* describes the hereafter, and *dar al-baqa* is the abode of everlasting existence.

RAFIK BERJAK

BARAKA

The expression *at-tabarruk* means to seek blessings (*baraka*) in something. It is derived from *al-baraka*, which means, or is often translated as, 'blessing', 'honoured' and 'respected'. *Al-baraka* is measured in terms of *ziyada* (increase). Hence someone who performs *tabarruk* is seeking an increase or growth in something that is regarded as positive, such as property, wealth, health, children and so on: 'And We have placed mountains on top of it and we have placed blessings (*baraka*) there' (41.10), where the reference is to the earth, and the ways in which God has created it in such a way as to make life easy for his creatures. 'And then We made to inherit those who were weak and oppressed the eastern and western parts of the earth, in which We had placed blessing (*baraka*)' (7.137), where the Jews are given land and allowed to defeat the apparent might of Pharaoh. Yet these blessings are dependent upon the behaviour of the recipients: 'We would have opened blessings (*barakat*) for them from the heavens and the earth had they only behaved well, but they did not so they suffered the ultimate fate of disobedience and evil' (7.96). We read: 'And We blessed him and Ishaq, and from their offspring are those who do right and those who wrong themselves' (37.113). Also: 'O Nuh, come down from the ship with peace from Us and blessings on you and the people who are with you' (11.48). It is clear that the blessing which pertains to Abraham, Isaac and Noah does not extend to everyone in the Ark or to the families of the messengers, since some will no doubt act in dubious ways and so not merit blessing.

Baraka can be found frequently as a descriptive term: 'But when you enter the houses, greet one another with the greeting from Allah (*as-salamu alaykum*), blessed and good' (2.61); 'And this is a Blessed Reminder which We have sent down. Will you then deny it?' (2.50). We are encouraged to greet each other by repeating God's greeting, which is itself a reflection of the blessings he applies to his creation. When one reflects upon the Qur'an one finds that it indicates that *baraka* is from God, and that perhaps it should be thought of as coming only from God:

Blessed be Allah, Lord of the worlds. (7.54)

Blessed be He in whose hand is the dominion. (67.1)

Blessed be He who sent down the criterion upon His slave. (25.1)

Blessed be He who has placed in the heaven big stars. (25.61)

So blessed be Allah, the best of all creators. (23.14)

Blessed be the Name of your Lord, the owner of majesty and honour. (55.78)

The word *tabaraka* occurs in the Qur'an only in reference to God. This suggests that all *baraka* belongs to God, that it all originates from him and that he gives *baraka* to various things in his creation. For example, rain is blessed because an increase in agriculture and life in general is obtained by it and there is considerable growth on account of it: 'And We sent down blessed rain from the sky and produced from it gardens and grain that are reaped' (50.9). There are other examples similar to these in which there is a type of *baraka* from which one obtains benefit, goodness, growth and increase. However, it is not always the case that everything which comes from the heavens and earth always brings *baraka*. This is dependent upon other things, which, if found, provide *baraka*, and which, if not found, mean *baraka* will end. There is not absolute *baraka* and things do not on their own or in and of themselves produce *baraka*. The rain might come down, but if it is not followed up by some sunshine, and if the soil is not right, and if there is too much rain, then the crops will not flourish. By contrast, some things always exhibit *baraka*. 'Glorified and exalted is He who took His slave [Muhammad] for a journey by night from *masjid al-haram* to *masjid al-aqsa*, the neighbourhood of which we have blessed' (17.1). We also read: 'Verily the first House [of worship] appointed for mankind was that at Bakka [Mecca], full of blessing and guidance for the world [men and *jinn*]' (3.96).

Blessing applies to whatever God has sent down by way of guidance and revelation: 'And this is a blessed book which We have sent down' (6.155); and 'This is a Book which we have sent down to you, full of blessings, that they may ponder over its verses' (38.29; see also 21.50). The Qur'an itself is often seen as a blessed reminder and reflection upon its verses as a blessed action. Following the Qur'an and the *sunna* (the way of the Prophet) is blessed. By extension, all the Islamic sciences are blessed. So the reciter of the Qur'an, the lawyer who deals with religious issues, the *muhaddith* (transmitter of Traditions), all perform actions that are blessed. The specific type of *baraka* in the places of worship such as *masjid al-haram* and *masjid al-aqsa* is generally regarded as not to be found in the physical parts of the *masjid*, such as the walls, the floor or the ceiling. These are blessed places only insofar as they are sites appropriate for the growth in a person's *iman* (belief) and general state of morality. As a result of this, it is sometimes said that the reward for prayer in a *masjid* is much more than elsewhere, and the more significant the *masjid*, the greater the reward.

The messengers and prophets also have *baraka* attached to them, as a result of their righteous action. Anyone who follows them will increase his or her reward for the very reason that the right person was followed and emulated. The *baraka* in the Book and the *sunna* is of two types. First, there is a *baraka* stemming from the *dhat* (physical essence) and whatever remains of it from some outstanding individuals. This is true of the prophets and the messengers, although some argue that no one else is included among them. This view excludes even the best of the Companions of God's Messenger, such as Abu Bakr, 'Umar, 'Uthman and 'Ali. No one can obtain the *baraka* of the prophets, except someone who follows their teaching of *tawhid* and who is guided by their actions and who obeys their commands and prohibitions. However, following this line, the Companions should in fact be eligible.

With this type of *baraka* of physical essence presence alone is irrelevant: the presence of the Messenger (Muhammad) did not benefit those Companions who disobeyed his command in the battle of Uhud (3.152). This *baraka* is often thought of as ending with the death of the Messenger, except in terms of what remains of the physical essence, e.g. hair. However, the certainty that something remains today, and the truthfulness of that, has diminished with the passing of time. Many can make a claim to physical essence, so anyone making

the claim has to provide an *isnad* (chain of transmission), to prove that something really is from the Messenger.

The *baraka* of righteous action and following the Messenger is available to everyone whose action follows the *sunna* of the Prophet. Every Muslim has *baraka* to the same extent that he or she follows the commands and prohibitions of God. Hence the *hadith* in al-Bukhari: 'Certainly there is within this tree a *baraka* like the *baraka* of the Muslim' (referring here to the date-palm). Therefore, every Muslim has *baraka* to the extent that he or she follows the Book and the *sunna*. Similarly, the righteous servants of God have the *baraka* of righteous action; the scholar of the *sunna* has the *baraka* of knowledge; the *hafiz* of the Book of Allah who guards its commandments has the *baraka* that results from that, and so on. The greatest *baraka* goes to those who are the most rigorous in following the Book and to the *sunna*, those who adhere to all the obligatory duties and who refrain from the prohibited actions.

As for seeking *baraka* from the places the Messenger went, such as a place in which he stopped and rested or a place in which he prayed or where he placed his foot or his hand etc., the issue arises whether the *baraka* of the physical essence rubbed off onto these places so they possessed *baraka* by derivation and so that *tabarruk* can occur through them. Some argue that none of the *sahaba* (Companions) sought this while Muhammad was alive or after his death. In that case, wherever the Messenger went or stopped it is not acceptable to seek *tabarruk* through these places or through what is still there, as this is a glorification of such things and places which it is not permissible for us to glorify. Following such a practice leads to *shirk*, something forbidden by 'Umar according to Ma'rur bin Suway al-Asadi, who said: 'I went along with 'Umar [from Mecca to Medina]. When we arose in the morning, 'Umar saw people going in a certain direction. He said, "Where are they going?" and they said, "They are going to a mosque in which the Prophet prayed." 'Umar said, "In fact the earlier prophets were destroyed because of the veneration of the places where the prophets prayed. People used to follow the tracks of their prophets and turned them into places of worship."' It is worth adding here that the Prophet said of 'Umar: 'Allah has placed the truth upon the heart and tongue of 'Umar.'

As a result of these arguments the *salaf* (traditional predecessors) opposed seeking *tabarruk* from places. We are told that 'Umar alone followed the tracks of the Prophet and would pray where he prayed, and so on. He was the only Companion that did this. Perhaps Ibn 'Umar did not seek *tabarruk* from these places, perhaps he was trying simply to imitate the Prophet. After all he could not hold them to contain *baraka* in their physical essence; the *tabarruk* did not come from these places but from the *baraka* of imitation and faithfulness. None of the other Companions made this a habitual practice and they did not agree with 'Umar in this. Even his own father opposed the practice, and hence his statement has greater precedence over Ibn 'Umar's actions, opinion or view. To give an example, 'Umar, when he kissed the black stone, said, 'You are only a stone and I only kiss you because I saw the Messenger kiss you.' This shows the understanding of 'Umar, and with this we can accept that the action of his son Ibn 'Umar was only an attempt to imitate the Messenger in action, not to seek *tabarruk* from those places the Messenger had travelled to or touched. This is the theological position accepted by many Sunni thinkers, but

popular practice often takes a different direction.

We have seen that the *baraka* of physical essence is only feasible if we can find some authentic text that shows God has granted *baraka* on something, such as is true in the case of the Prophets and Messengers. As far as righteous people are concerned then, the *baraka* that they may acquire is the *baraka* of righteous action. Some examples of the *baraka* of the actions of the righteous are that they call people to good behaviour, make supplications for them and that they bring about benefit to creation because they behave benevolently towards them with pure and good intentions. So all of this brings about *baraka* for people in general. Among the effects of this *baraka* of action is what good it is that God brings about on account of them and what harm he pushes away. 'And Your Lord would never destroy a township wrongfully, whilst its inhabitants are righteous' (11.117). But we should not try to make *tabarruk* through them, such as seeking to kiss their hands thinking that they contain physical *baraka* or by touching them and so on, for all of this is forbidden for anyone besides the prophets. Performing this type of *tabarruk* with someone besides the Prophet could be seen as a type of *fitna* (dissension), since it leads to arrogance and pride, or even *shirk* (idolatry),since it might be regarded as associating God with partners

Tabarruk is basically acting in accordance with the Book and the *sunna* and this is the type of *baraka* that remains extant today. As for *baraka* through the remnants of the messenger (i.e. hair etc.), then whoever claims to be in possession of any artefact needs an *isnad* (source) to prove that it is indeed such an artefact, since this is an arena in which *shirk* can quite easily be committed. However, the certainty of proving such a sin has diminished over time. Nevertheless, the *salaf* (traditionalists) sometimes affirm the existence of this type of *tabarruk*, and also that the prophets and messengers have the *baraka* of physical essence, and that with respect to the final messenger, Muhammad, the Companions could make *tabarruk* through their physical essence. One confronts frequent caveats from *sira* (history) books that, while admitting *tabarruk* with the Prophet's personal effects, tend to add that this is unique to him.

What is the proof for limiting *tabarruk* to the Prophet? Al-Nawawi said in his commentary on the *hadith* of Asma' bint Abi Bakr: 'She said: "Here is the cloak (*jubba*) of Allah's Messenger," and she brought out to me ['Abd Allah, her *mawla*] that cloak made of Persian cloth with a hem of [silk] brocade, and its sleeves bordered with brocade, and said: "This was Allah's Messenger's cloak with 'A'isha until she died, then I got possession of it. The Apostle of Allah, upon him be peace, used to wear it, and we washed it for the sick so that they could seek cure thereby."' Muslim relates this in the first chapter of the book of clothing. Al-Nawawi comments in *Sharh Sahih Muslim* (Bk 37, Chap. 2, verse 10): 'In this *hadith* is a proof that it is recommended to seek blessings through the relics of the righteous and their clothes (*wa-fi hadha al-hadith dalil 'ala istihbab al-tabarruk bi-athar al-salihin wa-thiyabihim*)'. Even if we say 'it is limited to him' then it could be argued that his *umma* (community) is indeed still connected to him and his *baraka* is not gone but continues in the *umma*. The *tabarruk* through anything other than the Prophet could be regarded in reality as being through him, just as the *baraka* through him is really from God. Those who insist in their denial of *tabarruk* perhaps should let others continue to seek blessings while they themselves live their lives without the possibility of this sort of *tabarruk*.

The *hadith* (adduced by Ibn 'Abd al-Wahhab) – 'No-one's help is sought but Allah's' –is quite clear in the view that it is only God who can succour us, not objects touched by a human being, however elevated these may be. Yet even Muhammad ibn 'Abd al-Wahhab concedes in *Majmu'at al-Tawhid* (232): 'We do not deny nor reject the invocation of help from a creature insofar as the creature can help, as Allah Most High said in the story of Musa – upon him peace: "And his countryman sought his help (*istaghathahu*) against his enemy"' (28.15); also 'A'isha's *hadith*: 'anyone who says the Prophet (peace be on him) knew the *ghayb* (unseen) is mistaken'. We certainly know any and all *ghayb* that God teaches us, as in the verses: '[He is] the knower of the unseen, and He reveals to none His *ghayb* except to every messenger whom he has chosen, and then He makes a guard to go before him and a guard behind him' (72.26–27). The implication is that claiming there is *baraka* in something physical is to claim access to *al-ghayb*, and this is highly questionable from a religious point of view. On the other hand, the *ghayb* that is made accessible to believers through the Qur'an, the *sunna* and ethical action is full of *baraka*. Ibn 'Abd al-Wahhab is pointing out that there are occasions when other people can help us, and we can then ask for their help without denying that the ultimate source of help is God. He argued that there is no point in seeking *baraka* in an object or a place, however strong its connection with the Prophet, because that sort of *baraka* can only be found in God, and glorifying particular locations would be viewed as an especially serious form of *shirk*.

References and further reading

Ibn ʿAbd al-Wahhab, M. (n.d.) *Kitab al-tawhid*, Riyadh: Majmuʿat al-tuhaf.

al-Nawawi (1966) *Sharh Sahih Muslim*, 3rd edn, Beirut: Dar al-maʿrifa.

See also: **art and the Qurʾan; death; haram**

OLIVER LEAMAN

BARZAKH

The existence of an intermediate realm and subsequently of separate destinations for the virtuous and the wicked is called a *barzakh*. A limit or boundary separating two things, or a barrier, obstacle, partition – *barzakh* in Arabic – is enjoyed by the virtuous because they are already suspicious of the material delights of the mortal realm and are quite happy to exchange that form of existence for something more spiritual, which is found in the *barzakh*, where they await resurrection with some confidence in their eventual reward. By contrast, the evil suffer in the knowledge both of their future torments and also due to the absence of their material wants in the intermediate realm, where everything is spiritual. 'The intermediate realm extends from now until the time of resurrection' (23.100), we are told. 'Do not imagine those who have been killed in God's path to be dead; rather they are alive and receive sustenance in the presence of their lord' (3.69). Their spirits are alive and waiting for the day of resurrection.

'God has bought the properties and souls of the believers in exchange for paradise. They are to strive in the path of God, destroying the enemies of religion or themselves being killed. This is a firm promise of God, binding upon Him, contained in the Torah, the Gospels and the Qurʾan, and who is more faithful to his promises than God? O believers, rejoice in this transaction, for it truly guarantees great happiness' (9.11). By contrast, 'Hellfire has already encompassed the unbelievers' (9.9). 'Those who obey the commands of God and His Messenger shall be resurrected together with, and enjoy the company of, those upon whom God has bestowed His kindness and favour in full measure: the prophets, the sincere devotees, the martyrs and the righteous. What noble and precious companions they are!' (4.4).

Further reading

al-Ghazali, A. (1995) *The Remembrance of Death and the Afterlife (Book 40 of The Revival of Religious Sciences)*, trans. T.J. Winter, Cambridge: The Islamic Texts Society.

See also: **death**

OLIVER LEAMAN

BASHAR

Bashar means mankind or human being and applies to both men and women. It is used in the singular: 'I am only a man like you' (19.110). It is also used in the dual form but the Qurʾan uses the regular dual form *bashrin* as well: 'Shall we believe in two human beings like ourselves' (23.47). The same term, *bashar*, signifies the plural (human beings): 'A warning to mankind' (74.36). The Qurʾan uses *bashar* to distinguish humankind from other beings: 'No man is this! This is none other than a noble angel!' (12.1).

Bashar is also the plural of *bashara*, which signifies the outer skin of the human body. The Prophet said: 'I did not send my delegates to you so they hit your skin.' Hence there is a relationship between the two words. Some linguists claim that the human being was called *bashar* because his skin is bare of hair and wool. Also, Adam was called *Abu al-bashar*, the father of mankind.

Bashir is a person who delivers good news to someone else. In the Qur'an Muhammad is described as a *bashir* (a bearer of good news) to those who believe in God and do good deeds. The Prophet brings them the good news which includes the satisfaction of God and his great reward to them in this life and hereafter: 'Verily, We have sent you with the truth, a bearer of glad tidings and a warner' (35.24). Although *bashir* commonly signifies the bearer of good news, it could also mean the opposite, i.e. the bearer of bad news: 'Then announce to them a painful torment' (3.1).

RAFIK BERJAK

BASMALA

An acronymic abbreviation taken from the first two words of the formula *bi-smi llahi l-rahmani l-rahim* (In the name of God, the Merciful (and) the Compassionate), this invocation precedes each *sura* in the Qur'an except *sura* 9. It has become the most widely used Islamic expression of piety all over the Islamic world and throughout the ages. It is used to start a meal, to set out on a journey and on countless other occasions of importance. Documents, books, letters and formal oral communications are even today often preceded by the *basmala*. In the Qur'an, Solomon's letter to the Queen of Sheba is introduced by the *basmala* (27.30). At the same time, the *basmala* is the most widely used element of Islamic calligraphy and ornament. It is also used as a magical tool and symbol.

To start an act 'in the name of God is in Islam, as in Judaism and Christianity, a powerful appeal to God's protection, grace and mercy. To invoke God's name and to know how to address him

ensures privileged access to divine intervention. The two parallel attributes *rahman* and *rahim* are derived from the same root and are associated with *rahma* (mercy). They are usually interpreted by Muslim exegesis as related attributes or divine names carrying subtle differences of meaning, e.g. that *rahman* is an exclusively divine epithet, whereas *rahim* can be attributed to God and man.

Another possibility, one normally neglected by classical Muslim scholarship, is to take *al-rahman* historically as the name of a pre-Islamic god, which yields a translation similar to: 'In the name of God, the compassionate *Rahman*'. *Al-Rahman* was the name of a pre-Islamic, possibly henotheistic deity in Central and Southern Arabia and is frequently used in the Qur'an as a synonym for Allah, especially in the *suras* of the second Meccan period. Musaylima, a contemporary of Muhammed who was denounced by Muslim sources as a 'false prophet', called the divine source of his inspiration *al-Rahman*. The competition among different gods in the pre-Islamic pantheon is attested to in a tradition which reports that the pagan Meccans refused to begin a written armistice treaty with the Prophet with the *basmala* because in this formula *al-Rahman* was mentioned. Instead they insisted on *bi-smika allahumma,* or 'in thy name, Allah', to which the Prophet is reported to have agreed. Part of the original message of the *basmala* for the contemporaries of the Islamic revelations may therefore well have been that al-Rahman was not different from Allah but the same as Allah, who was revealing the Qur'an to Muhammed. This message was spelled out in 17.110: 'Say: "Call upon God, or call upon the Merciful (*al-Rahman*); whichsoever you call upon, to Him belong the Names Most Beautiful."' Today and for a very long time, however, the general Muslim understanding of the formula is and has been to take *al-rahman* and *al-rahim* as two closely connected attributes or bywords for God which became in due course two of the 'most beautiful names of God' (*al-'asma'* and *al-husna*).

The *basmala* is for the Muslim community as well as for classical Muslim scholarship part of the revealed and canonical Qur'anic text. There are, however, several indications that this was not always the case. Hanafis and Shi'is do not recite the *basmala* audibly at ritual prayers. Furthermore, the *basmala* is never counted as a separate verse except in *sura* 1. Even in the case of *sura* 1, only the Kufan tradition did so, while the majority of the canonical reading traditions did not. The fact that the Kufan tradition of separating and numbering verses has in modern times become the dominant style is largely the result of the success of the Azhar-sponsored printing of the Qur'an in Cairo (1924; and many later editions), not of an inherent superiority of the Kufan reading tradition. In all other *suras*, the *basmala* is considered part of the first verse in recitation, or a separate line in writing or printing. In the oldest extant manuscripts of the Qur'an in Yemen the *basmala* is always integrated into the *sura*-text and not separated from it. Numerous early readers of the Qur'an in Medina, Basra and Syria regarded the *basmala* as nothing more than a pious human formula of blessing that should precede any Muslim act of importance, and of course the recitation of any part of the Qur'an. This custom may well go back to the time of the Prophet. Such a recitation did not, and does not, necessarily coincide with the beginning of a *sura*. Graphically the *basmala* was seen as a device to separate the *suras* in a codex from each other. The question of whether the *basmala* was or was not part of

revelation was also posed regarding the text of *sura* 1 (*al-Fatiha*). The *Fatiha* should have seven verses and its verses are counted as seven by all authorities because 15.87 – 'We have given thee seven of the oft repeated, and the mighty Qur'an' – was usually seen as an allusion to *al-Fatiha*. But only Kufa and Mecca counted the *basmala* in *al-Fatiha* as verse 1, whereas the readers of Basra, Damascus and Medina did not count the *basmala* as a separate verse but achieved the number of seven verses by subdividing other verses in this *sura*.

Why the *basmala* is missing in *sura* 9 is unclear. Muslim exegetes explain that the subject matter of *sura* 9, which announces God's wrath and punishment of idolators, made an allusion to God's mercy inappropriate. Whatever the case, some Muslim scholars regarded *sura* 8 and *sura* 9 as a unit precisely because the *basmala* between them was missing.

Further reading

Spitaler, A. (1935) *Die Verzählung des Koran nach islamischer Überlieferung*, Munich: Bavarian Academy of Science.

See also: **canon; al-jahr bi al-basmala; ninety-nine names of God; al-Rahman; repentance**

STEFAN WILD

AL-BAYDAWI

'Abd Allah ibn 'Umar ibn Muhammad ibn 'Ali Abu al-Khayr Nasir al-Din al-Baydawi was a prolific writer, but his greatest legacy lies in his Qur'anic commentary, which has served as a standard text in Islamic educational institutions around the Muslim world for many centuries.

Al-Baydawi spent most of his life in Persia, the land of his birth. He lived in troubled times and experienced the Mongol invasions which swept through

Persia and destroyed the last remnants of the 'Abbasid caliphate in Baghdad in 1258. He rose to scholarly prominence, being appointed as chief *qadi* (judge) in the city of Shiraz. There is little other biographical information available on al-Baydawi that is reliable. Even his date of death is a matter of debate. Ibn Kathir and al-Suyuti reported it as occurring in Tabriz in 685/1286. Ibn al-Subki identifies the date as 691/1292. Some scholars date it even later.

The clearest window into al-Baydawi's life is presented through his works, which covered diverse scholarly disciplines. He wrote a history of the world up to his time in Persian, entitled *Nizam al-tawarikh* (The system of historical records). He wrote on law, including *al-Ghaya al-quswa* (The most extreme transgression) and a book of jurisprudence entitled *Minhaj al-wusul ila haqiqa al-usul* (Method for attaining knowledge of jurisprudence). He also wrote on scholastic theology and on grammar, including a commentary on *al-Kafiya*, the important grammatical study by Ibn al-Hajib (d. 646/1249).

Al-Baydawi is best known for his commentary on the Qur'an, entitled *Anwar al-tanzil wa asrar al-ta'wil* (The lights of revelation and the secrets of interpretation). In drawing up this commentary, al-Baydawi set out to compile a digest of certain earlier scholarly works. The core of his commentary is drawn from al-Zamakhshari's *al-Kashshaf 'an haqa'iq ghawamid al-tanzil wa-'uyun al-aqawil fi wujuh al-ta'wil* (The unveiler of the real meanings of the hidden matters of what was sent down and the choicest statements about the various aspects of its interpretation). Al-Baydawi also drew on Fakhr al-Din al-Razi's famous commentary as well as various other sources.

In selecting his core from al-Zamakhshari, al-Baydawi was taking a calcu-lated risk. Al-Zamakhshari's work, although widely used, has had its reputation smeared down the centuries by the author's Mu'tazilite leanings. In order to avoid falling into the same trap, al-Baydawi carefully selected those sections from al-Zamakhshari's work which were in harmony with orthodoxy as perceived during his time. For example, in commenting on 18.9, where al-Zamakhshari emphasises a Muslim's freedom of choice, al-Baydawi stresses that the verse does not mean that the believer is solely responsible for his own acts. The wish of the believer is not independent of God's overall sovereign will. Moreover, al-Baydawi does not restrict himself to merely copying al-Zamakhshari verbatim. On occasions he adds exegetical comment where al-Zamakhshari has remained silent.

Al-Baydawi employs a technique of phrase-by-phrase exegesis. The exegetical content reflects the author's diverse literary activities. He presents a range of Tradition materials, usually under the heading *Asbab al-nuzul* (Circumstances of the revelation). For these materials he makes particular reference to al-Baghawi's *Masabih al-sunna* (Lights of the way of the Prophet). Al-Baydawi also includes extensive linguistic detail, including information on the variant readings. For this he draws primarily on the seven canonical readers identified by Ibn Mujahid, plus Ya'qub of Basra. Al-Baydawi's commentary also addresses legal issues, in a way that reflects his Shafi'i position.

His style is varied, at times using narrative for exposition, at other times engaging in philosophical speculation. Generally al-Baydawi's discussion is derivative, reflecting opinions and interpretations of his predecessors. Moreover, he does not always bother to identify the sources of his varying accounts. However, this is not necessarily a criticism in itself, as a common feature of commentary writing by the classical writers was the selection of an earlier commentary as a core, rather than setting out to produce an entirely original commentary. Moreover, al-Baydawi's achievement lay in condensing a vast body of information drawn from diverse sources into a relatively short commentary.

This work has enjoyed a solid reputation among Sunni theologians since its composition. A mark of its success lies in the number of commentaries which have been written upon *Anwar al-tanzil wa asrar al-ta'wil*. Brockelmann (1898) lists eighty-three such works, with the most prominent being the multi-volume commentary by Shihab al-Din al-Khafaji (d. Egypt 1069/1659) and the gloss by Muhammad b. Muslim a-Din Mustafa al-Kuhi (d. 951/1544), which also includes lengthy quotations from the commentary by Fakhr al-Din al-Razi.

Al-Baydawi's commentary has proven popular in regions of the non-Arab Muslim world, such as in the Indo-Pakistan region and Muslim Southeast Asia. It served as an important source for 'Abd al-Ra'uf al-Singkili's Malay commentary upon the whole Qur'an, *Tarjuman al-mustafid* (The interpreter of that which gives benefit), written around 1085/1675. It has served as a core text in Muslim seminaries in Pakistan's Northwest Frontier Province, Malaysia, Indonesia and other locations, providing an excellent introduction to the science of Qur'anic exegesis.

Nevertheless, al-Baydawi has attracted some criticism for the brevity of his writings, and for some inaccuracy, with some scholars accusing him of allowing some Mu'tazilite views held by al-Zamakhshari to filter through into *Anwar al-tanzil wa asrar al-ta'wil*.

References and further reading

Al-Baydawi's commentary has been published many times since the initial published version edited by H.O. Fleischer (1846–48). The work has not yet been translated in its entirety into English, but partial translations have been undertaken by Margoliouth (*sura* 3, 1894), Bishop and Kaddal (*sura* 12, 1957) and Beeston (*sura* 12, 1963).

al-Baydawi, "Abd Allah ibn 'Umar (1996) *Tafsir al-baydawi al-musamma anwar al-tanzil wa asrar al-ta'wil*, 5 vols, Beirut: Dar al-fikr.

Beeston, A.F.L. (1963) *Baidawi's Commentary on Surah 12 of the Qur'an*, Oxford: Clarendon Press.

Bishop, E.F.F. and Kaddal. M. (1957) *The Light of Inspiration and Secret of Interpretation: Being a translation of the Chapter of Joseph (Surat Yusuf) with the commentary of Nasir Id-Din al-Baidawi*, Glasgow: Jackson.

Brockelmann, C. (1898) *Geschichte der arabischen Litteratur*, Leiden: E.J. Brill.

al-Dawudi, Shams al-Din Muhammad b. Ahmad. (n.d.) *Tabaqat al-mufassirin* (The Generations of Commentators), 2 vols, Beirut: Dar al-kutub al-'ilmiyya.

al-Dhahabi, Muhammad Husayn (1405/1985) *al-Tafsir wa al-mufassirun* (Exegesis and the Commentators), 3rd edn, 3 vols, Cairo: Wahba.

Gätje, H. (1997) *The Qur'an and its Exegesis*, Oxford: OneWorld.

Johns, A.H. (1999) 'Exegesis as an Expression of Islamic Humanism: Approaches, concerns and insights of al-Baydawi', *Hamdard Islamicus* XXII, 4: 37–58.

Margoliouth, D.S. (1894) *Chrestomathia Baidawiana: The Commentary of el-Baidawi on Sura III translated and explained for the use of students of Arabic*, London: Luzac.

See also: **asbab al-nuzul; tafsir in early Islam**

PETER G. RIDDELL

BAYYANA | ABAN

Bayyana is the root of a verb and is in the past tense. It means to clarify one's ideas and thoughts and applies to both thought and speech. It signifies the ability to explain and argue or articulate thoughts clearly and strongly. *Bayyana* applies to making a theory or an idea apparent to the mind, distinct and clear from other things or ideas. *Bayyana* also signifies the power of expression, cognition in spoken or written language. In the Qur'an the term is used frequently to refer to God's eloquent articulation of his revelation: 'We have made plain to you the verses so you understand' (3.118). Allah told the Prophet Muhammad that: 'We have also sent down unto you the reminder that you may explain clearly to mankind what is sent down to them and that they may give thought.'

Aban means spoken clearly, directly or with eloquence. *Aban* and *bayyana* are very close in meaning, although *aban* means separated or cut off. This highlights the clarity of the speech of the Qur'an and its clear and eloquent text. This notion was established in the Holy Book as an argument in support of the *i'jaz* of the Qur'an in reference to the miracle of the Qur'an itself. This is based on the Qur'anic claim that its *suras* are revealed by God and no one else will be able to create similar text or *suras*.

RAFIK BERJAK

BEAUTY

The aesthetically pleasing does not play a significant role in the Qur'anic text. A statement such as 'God is beautiful and loves beauty' is not Qur'anic but a saying ascribed to the Prophet. The word 'beauty' (*jamal*) occurs only once in the Qur'an (16.5–6). The context of this admonition to mankind is the divine creation of nature and the word 'beauty' refers to cattle and its uses. The word *jamil*, usually translated as 'beautiful', means in the Qur'an 'laudable, morally right'. But this does not mean that the

Qur'an does not have a strong aesthetic dimension.

The Qur'an has this to say about its own effect: 'If We (God) had sent down this Qur'an upon a mountain, thou (Muhammad) wouldst have seen it humbled, split asunder out of the fear of God' (59.21). That comes out even more forcefully in the following description of human reactions towards the Qur'an: 'God has sent down the fairest discourse as a book, consistent and repetitive, whereat shiver the skins of those who fear their Lord; then their skins and their hearts soften to the remembrance of God' (39.23). The meaning of the words 'the fairest discourse' (*ahsan al-hadith*) could include the aesthetic, but also includes the good and morally uplifting. The same is true for the expression 'the fairest of stories' (*ahsan al-qasas* 12.3), with which the Qur'an introduces the long narrative about Joseph and his brothers. The effect of the recitation of the 'fairest discourse' is described as overwhelming and terrifying. It is in general primarily associated with the Qur'anic verses describing the catastrophes preceding the Day of Judgement and depicting hell. The inimitability of the Qur'an, as far as it was connected to aesthetics, lay thus more in its overwhelming and frightening power than in its sweetness.

On the other hand, a recitation (reading) of the Qur'an performed by a trained Qur'an reader could and can have an effect on the Muslim listener, which exceeds the effect that a Bach Passion may have on a Protestant listener. It is, therefore, undeniable that the Qur'an evoked and evokes a deeply emotional experience, troubling and pleasing at the same time, wherever the Qur'an is recited. In this sense it has an enormous aesthetic potential. There are many reports that Muslims, especially Sufis, died under the impact of Qur'anic recitation. They were called 'those killed by the Qur'an'. On a different level, a calligraphic rendering of the Qur'anic text can be a source of the greatest aesthetic gratification. As sculpture and painting in a religious context were frowned upon by many Muslims through the ages, much of the religious-artistic creative energy of Muslim culture went into the highly developed art of calligraphy, and in the first place into the calligraphy of the Qur'an. As a mural inscription in a mosque or as a precious page of a manuscript Qur'anic calligraphy was and is the artistic form of the revealed Word of God.

Further reading

Gwynne, R.W. (2001) 'Beauty', in *EQ*, Vol. 1, 212–13.
Kermani, N. (1999) *Gott ist schön: Das ästhetische Erleben des Koran*, Munich: Beck.
Ory, S. (2001) 'Calligraphy', in *EQ*, Vol. 1, 277–86.

See also: **art and the Qur'an;** *sama'*; *tajwid*

STEFAN WILD

BECCA / BAKKA

Becca is the name of the valley in which Mecca is situated, in Arabic where the initial letter of Makka (Mecca) is replaced to make the word Bakka. It is said to stem from the word *tabakka*, which means people crowded together or lacking water. *Baka* is to cry or lament, and this is appropriate since the valley is one in which harsh conditions prevail, its status as a valley leading to flooding when rain does eventually come. The first house of God was built there (3.96), an impressive assertion of belief in the One God in a difficult environment.

A different interpretation links it with Psalm 84: 6, where the same place name

is also associated with crying, but this is near Jerusalem. This could hardly be the place suggested in the Qur'anic verse, however, so it has been suggested that the notion of Bakka as a place comes from a misreading of the Arabic letters to arrive at *bibakkata* (at Bakka in rather clumsy Arabic) as opposed to *tayyakahu* (he fenced in), on the grounds that a sacred place would be distinguished from the rest of the area by a fence or boundary (Luxenberg, 2000: 302).

References and further reading

Luxenberg, C. (2000) *Die Syro-aramäische Lesart des Koran: Ein Beitrag zur Entschlüsselung der Koransprache*, Berlin: Das Arabische Buch.

See also: **Arab**

OLIVER LEAMAN

BILQIS

Bilqis appears in the *sura al-Naml* (27.15–44). Here the Queen of Sheba, Bilqis (although she is not given this name in the Qur'an), calls upon King Sulayman (Solomon) in a visit that is replete with symbolism. She represents the pagan world visiting the world of a prophet and eminently wise authority. The queen enters the palace and comes across a floor which is made of a reflective material and thus looks like water. She is so convinced it is water that she lifts her skirt, offending against social convention, and then the king tells her that it is only a *sarh*, an area paved with glass. She immediately admits her error and accepts the king's religion.

There are lots of stories built around this incident, some of which say that the purpose of the *sarh* was to prove to the king that the queen really did not have hairy ankles! Clearly a central theme of the story is the overcoming of the power and wisdom of the world of *jahiliyya* (ignorance; pre-Islamic) by Islam and belief in the One God. In just the same way that the queen was taken in by the appearance of water when there was no water, she was unable initially to see the truth of the One God who is the master of everything. She concluded perhaps that since Sulayman had the correct view of the world around us on an empirical level, he might well also have the correct view about what is behind the world. In the story the queen mistakes glass for water, and why should she not, given that they resemble each other, at least when constructed cleverly, as *jinn* tend to do. This is also not the only time that the queen discovered that what she had taken to be one thing was in fact something else. Her reasoning presumably was that since she sometimes seemed to confuse what appeared to be the case with what really was the case, her religious ideas might similarly be linked not with what is real but with what is only apparently real. This is a good characterization of idolatry from a monotheistic point of view. Physical objects look much more plausible as deities than does an invisible being, because the former, unlike the latter, can at least be seen. The problem is, however, that what they look like, i.e. strong, powerful, effective, is only an appearance with no basis in reality. Like the glass floor which resembles water, it is merely a resemblance. In fact, the floor is dry; in fact, the gods are powerless. This is not the only surprising experience the queen undergoes. An *ifrit* or learned man brings Sulayman Bilqis' throne, and this is one of the tricks played on her, to see whether she recognizes it.

A number of things had happened, and indeed her journey to see the king had in itself the flavour of spiritual quest. Sheba is often seen as being a particularly sublime realm, and Suhrawardi refers obliquely to the Qur'anic passage in his *Hikmat al-Ishraq*. He talks of a hoopoe bringing greetings, the arrival at the Valley of the Ants (the *sura* in which the story is positioned is called 'the Ant'), being told to shake our skirt and then to 'kill your woman'! The hoopoe is a wise bird, who brings a message of revelation, which explains how a mystical journey may start. The Valley of the Ants represents the carnal or physical realm, and shaking skirts and killing the woman means repressing our physicality in order to extend our spirituality. This is the real problem, which as Suhrawardi often argued, Ibn Sina had raised but not settled, namely, how to move from this realm of generation and corruption to the highest level of spiritual knowledge. In his *Hayy ibn Yaqzan* Ibn Sina was taken to have correctly identified the problem but he did not provide a solution, a gap that Suhrawardi was only too ready to fill. This gap is actually a live issue in the controversy over Ibn Sina's 'Eastern philosophy', where he is sometimes taken to have contrasted the limited scope of *mashsha'i* (Peripatetic) thought with the expansive nature of the mystical. One reason for Ibn Sina's hesitancy, Suhrawardi suggests, is that the former did not appreciate the constitutive power of imagination, in the sense of the imaginal realm (*al-'alam al-khayali*). For the *mashsha'i* (peripatetic) thinker, the important faculties of thought are the active intellect and the acquired intellect, the latter representing the highest form of reasoning that we can attain when our thought is perfected as far as it can be. Imagination itself operates predominantly at a much lower level of knowledge, and although it can function to a degree in syllogisms and logical reasoning, on the whole, it is most closely related to our sensuality and so should be treated with a degree of suspicion.

For Suhrawardi, imagination is far more significant, not when it is linked with the world of Platonic ideas (*muthul al-Aflatuni*) but when it is extended by the suspended ideas (*muthul al-mu'allaqa*). These are ideals, and as such they play a role in leading us intellectually to a higher level of knowledge than we could otherwise attain. If Ibn Sina is correct, then aesthetics has to be limited to a peripheral role in our spiritual lives. If Suhrawardi is right, then aesthetics is crucially important, and is far from merely an aspect of decoration. Aesthetics represents a direct route to the truth, and without it the scope for spiritual growth is bound to be restricted.

We are moving here towards an appreciation of the role of architecture in representing a religious attitude. The architecture designed by Muslims often is intended to bring about the sort of imaginative leap that Bilqis took. The thing worth noticing about the *sarh* is that it must have been very beautiful – the skilful fusing together of pieces of glass or some similar reflective material must have been a staggering sight. This is what we should notice about the story; not that Bilqis was fooled, but that she was fooled as a result of the beauty of the work. She quite naturally felt that whoever could create such a thing was worthy of her attention, and the *jinn* who created it were instructed by the king. One assumes that much Islamic architecture and design had this purpose; to impress, to captivate, to entrance. This is after all a familiar feature of sacred art. Bilqis was impressed by what she saw and as a result made a decision about her life and her religion.

What comes to mind at the end of this extended discussion of a Qur'anic passage is how significant a role in the text art plays. Although we are often erroneously told how antagonistic Islam is to representative art, here we have the great King Sulayman, a man of extraordinary wisdom, engaging the services of *jinn* and others to construct beautiful objects. If there is something un-Islamic about art, why was the king so intent on producing it? We also find in the story an important pagan embracing Islam because of her confrontation finally with a superb aesthetic object, the imaginary lake inside the palace. There is no hint that the creativity of the king's servants or the *sarh* are in any way objectionable; on the contrary, they are entirely praiseworthy, and if they were not, then Sulayman would hardly have used them.

Bilqis exercises her right to make a leap of faith, to embrace Islam because a Muslim has impressed her. In fact, we know that this is a potent source of conversion both in the past and in the present, and it is part of the methodology of *jidal bilati hiya ahsan* as recommended in the Qur'an (16.125).

One of the features of Bilqis worth noting is her equanimity throughout. When she receives a message from Sulayman inviting her to embrace Islam, a message which could be taken to be threatening, her advisors tell her that they have sufficient forces to deal with an interloper and invader. She responds by pointing out that invasions tend to cause great harm even if they are overcome (27.34). When her gift to the king is rejected and sent back, she comes to visit him, but she is not insulted at his behaviour and does not respond to it as the ruler of a great territory confronting a potential foe. She realizes, according to the text, that what she is called on to do is to change her beliefs in such a way as to acquire understanding of how the world really works, how the One God operates. This is knowledge that the king to a degree already possesses, and she wants to have it also. Her stepping on the *sarh*, that symbol of something that is other than it appears to be, is the final straw that encourages her to adopt the new faith,

The Sufis have a saying that *al-majazu qantaratul haqiqa* – the apparent is a bridge to the truth. Sufism does not regard the ordinary world as illusive or imaginary, on the contrary there is nothing unreal about this world. But it should not be taken as the only form of reality that exists, because this world is only an indication of the nature of another and deeper level of reality. In his commentary on Jami's poem about Yusuf and Zulaykha, Pendlebury (Jami 1980: 4) points out that one definition of idolatry is confusing the relative with the absolute, and this is something which Zulaykha does throughout the story. Not only does she worship idols, but she is obsessed with Yusuf, and not with him as a person but with him as a physical being. She acts as though that (relative) factor about him was absolutely the most important, as though his material beauty did not hide a much more significant spiritual form of beauty. Once she learns that physical beauty is only an idol, and she manages to shatter it, her physical beauty is restored to her and she finally attains the objective of her whole life, to live harmoniously with Yusuf. In his commentary Pendlebury suggests that this is a case of her abandoning the self, of arriving at the truth and finally attaining peace.

How we interpret symbols is important. The Queen of Sheba was confused by the *sarh*, the glass floor in the palace, and she decided that her error was an indication of a much wider error, and so she determined to abandon idolatry and accept the king's religion.

Zulaykha also abandons idolatry in the end, recognizing that the mistake she made earlier, of confusing physical with spiritual beauty, had made her life chaotic and meaningless. Like the Queen of Sheba she came to realize that her view of the world was only partial, and she exchanged it for what she took to be a more comprehensive and accurate view. What these stories share is an interpretation of a symbol, a recognition that some feature of the world which both women took to be real is in fact only a symbol of something which is genuinely real. But they also share the idea that discovering the real is a long and difficult process, requiring many different stages and trials. We need to bear this in mind, for without sophistication in linking the symbolic with the real we are likely to carry out the process in far too ham-fisted a manner. When Zulaykha hears of Yusuf's death in Jami's poem she is distraught, collapsing, tearing her cheeks and hair, and eventually pulling out her eyes and throwing them on the ground! She has not really managed to abandon her passionate nature, and there is no tranquillity in her response to tragedy, despite Yusuf's hope that tranquillity would give her strength to bear his loss. She dies with her nose in the earth, just above Yusuf's body, and Jami reflects how lucky the lover is who dies in the aroma of union with the loved one, a bold statement given that shortly before this point Jibril (Gabriel) had given Yusuf an apple from the garden of paradise so that he died with the smell of the celestial perfume in his nostrils. As a symbol of passion finally brought to book, as it were, Zulaykha here is not an entirely satisfactory character from a religious point of view, and even in the Qur'an her readiness to act without thinking contrasts her with the calm and collected Queen of Sheba.

In his *Mathnawi* Rumi tells us of a competition between the Chinese and the Greeks over the most beautiful screen that could be painted (Vol. I: 3465–85). The Chinese take over the side of a room and go to work on it, using the king's 'hundred colours' and working steadily. The Greeks concealed what they did, although they seemed to be polishing away at an equal rate as the Chinese were painting. When the Chinese were finished, they displayed an extraordinarily beautiful painting, but the Greeks produced a burnished mirror, which then magnified the beauty of the Chinese painting. They were said to have won, and they won because they stuck to essentials. Colour is linked by Rumi to the clouds; it conceals and confuses, while colourlessness is related to the moon, and we are told that whatever illumination arrives in the clouds comes originally from the moon and higher celestial bodies. So colour is a physical property of which we should remain cautious; what is significant is our ability to get in touch with what is higher than us, with what is real, and it is this that the Greeks manage to do. On the other hand, when we examine the story more closely it is not so clear that this is what happens. They manage to reproduce the Chinese picture and make it even more radiant than it is originally. Anyone who has ever seen Persian miniatures will appreciate the Persian ability to incorporate an enormous amount of light into their pictures, even on what are after all the pages of books. But what the Greeks do is to make what the Chinese do a bit brighter, that is all, and if Rumi is a bit critical of the colours that the Chinese use, then he should be even more critical of the Greeks, since they make the colours brighter.

On the other hand, the meaning of the story might be something very different. It may not be critical of colour at all, but rather of the idea that we can do anything significant artistically. The Chinese thought they could, and what they accomplished was impressive, but not as impressive as the impact of nothing more than light and reflection on their work. The Greeks could be seen as modest, only working to increase the ability of light to illuminate what already exists, while the Chinese presumptuously seek to outdo the glories of nature. Of course, it is ironic that an attack on art should appear in a very skilfully organized poem, but then so many attacks on art do in fact use art to make their point. In one version of the story the Greeks are said to have won the competition, and their reward is a pile of money which is given to the Chinese artists. All the Greeks get is the reflection of the money!

The story of Yusuf and Zulaykha is presented time and time again pictorially, and with its heady mixture of passion, desire, violence and ultimate redemption and death, it is clearly the stuff of soap opera and spiritual instruction. Quite a few of the illustrations are very humorous, and we should not assume that simply because this is a religious story it has to be treated with great solemnity throughout. By contrast, the pictures of Bilqis at the court of Sulayman are invariably serious and reflect the calmness of the main characters' personalities and their corresponding actions. It might be thought that their calmness makes them very appropriate Muslims, and the conversion of Bilqis is hardly surprising given her predisposition to assess situations in a cool and collected manner (according to the Qur'an). A comparison of Bilqis and Zulaykha is useful in drawing out the complexity of the Qur'an's treatment of the links between appearance and reality.

In *sura* 34 we are told that, after Sulayman's death, the *jinn* are hard at work under his apparent gaze until a small creature eats away at the wood of his staff and he eventually collapses to the ground. Then the *jinn* know they have been working for nothing, since Sulayman was not looking at them at all. The insect knew this, while the much more advanced *jinn* did not. Bilqis realized that there was something significant behind what was in front of her, the *sarh*, and the contrast between the unseen and the seen led her to convert to Islam, because she took the contrast to indicate her inability to understand the world by herself, without the help of the One God.

References and further reading

Gonzalez, V. (2001) *Beauty and Islam*, London: I.B. Tauris, in association with the Institute of Ismaili Studies, London and New York: St. Martin's Press, 28–33.
Jami (1980) *Yusuf and Zulaikha: An allegorical romance*, ed. and trans. D. Pendlebury, London: Octagon Press, 171.
Lassner, J. (1993) *Demonizing the Queen of Sheba: Boundaries of gender and culture in postbiblical Judaism and medieval Islam*, Chicago: University of Chicago Press.
Leaman, O. (1999) *Brief Introduction to Islamic Philosophy*, Oxford: Blackwell.
—— (2004) *Islamic Aesthetics: An introduction*, Edinburgh: Edinburgh University Press.
Rumi (1982) *The Mathnawi of Jalaluddin Rumi*, trans. R. Nicholson, London: Luzac.
al-Suhrawardi (1982) *The Mystical and Visionary Treatise of Suhrawardi*, trans. W. Thackston, London: Octagon.

See also: **art and the Qur'an; beauty; Zulaykha**

OLIVER LEAMAN

BOOK
see: kitab

BURHAN | BAYNA | SULTAN

Burhan

Burhan means the firmest, strongest and most valid evidence or proof. In the Qur'an, *burhan* refers to proofs for the arguments of Allah strengthening the position of his prophets and his righteous servants. It also provides proofs to defeat the arguments of Satan and the disbelievers: 'O mankind! Verily there has come to you a convincing proof from your Lord' (4.174). Allah addresses all mankind in that he has sent to them a clear proof through the Prophet, Muhammad, and that proof is the Qur'an, which will guide them on the straight path of Islam.

Burhan signifies a warning sign as when Yusuf was tempted by the wife of the ruler of Egypt. He was protected from falling into the sin of adultery by his Lord's *burhan*: 'And with passion did she desire him, and he would have desired her, but he saw the evidence of his Lord' (12.24).

Burhan implies divine authority. This term in the Qur'an has a special particularity and presence indicating the ultimate authority of God over his kingdom; 'If anyone invokes, beside Allah, any other god, he has no authority' (23.117).

The Qur'an dismisses the claims of those who fabricate stories about the existence of other gods besides Allah as false since they are not supported by any genuine evidence. The Qur'an challenges them to present their *burhan*, their proof of truth.

Burhan appears in the Qur'an eight times only, although it is a powerful supporting tool to assure that the Word of Allah is well argued. It is also a confrontational device, however, which decisively dismisses the allegations of disbelievers and refutes them. Using *burhan*, the Qur'an authenticates and legitimizes proof and evidence. Whatever was revealed by the revelation or was in accordance with it is considered authentic and legitimate.

Bayna

Bayna means clear or manifested evidence, proof or an argument, perceived either intellectually or by the senses. It also signifies being distinct from others and being apparent, to be clearly and plainly perceived. The key meaning that *bayna* possesses and contributes to the Qur'anic text is clarity.

Bayna signifies the lucidity of the divine revelation to the world. It explains that God is one and that he sent the prophets to the world with his clear and plain revelation. God makes his message clear and perceptible so that every soul receives and identifies with it simply and clearly and without any ambiguity, consequently everyone who follows the right path leads to the satisfaction of Allah and thus the perpetual happiness of mankind. For this reason Allah sent all his messengers with clear signs.

The Qur'an was revealed through the Prophet Muhammad as providing a means to guide and judge between right and wrong. The stress on clarity in the Qur'an is very significant because those people who receive a clear message cannot have any excuse to disbelieve in it or any reason to fight it. Whoever opts to take such a path will have to bear the consequences.

Al-bayna also refers to the original revelation sent to the People of the Book, i.e. the Jews and the Christians: 'Ask the children of Israel how many clear signs We have sent to them' (2.211).

Sultan

Sultan means strength, might, force or power. It signifies the possession or exercise of superior power, dominion or of authority.

Sultan occurs thirty-three times in the Qur'an. Most commonly this term signifies proof or evidence to support the prophets' positions and arguments: 'And we sent Moses with our signs and clear evidence' (11. 96). It also means an agreement, a plea or an allegation.

Sultan refers to ultimate and absolute authority. It is also a title of the ruler who possesses and exercises absolute authority, power and dominion. The *sura al-Hijr* contains a dialogue between Allah and Iblis (Satan), demonstrating Satan's intention to dominate and control mankind. Allah makes it clear that Satan will not have any *sultan* or authority over those who are true believers in God: 'For over My servants no authority shall thou have, except those who put themselves in the wrong' (16.99–100).

In the story of the people of 'Ad and their prophet Hud there was a constant argument. 'Why dispute over names and imaginary Gods, the invention of your minds?', Hud argued, and proclaimed: 'You are disputing me over names which you have devised and your fathers without authority from God' (7.71).

In the *sura al-Haqa*, during the transitional moment of death the person who had possessed authority during his life will see it slip away and he will say: 'The power has perished from me' (69. 29). The *aya* describes the intense agony when the soul loses power over itself while it tries to realize itself in new conditions but cannot.

Under the code of a life for a life, the heir of the slain was given the right or the authority to demand the life of the killer: 'And if anyone is slain unjustly, we have given his heir authority to demand punishment' (17. 33). *Burhan, bayna* and *sultan* are different terms and each one of them has its unique significance, yet they have a related role in the Qur'an. They establish the authenticity and the legitimacy of the proofs, evidences and arguments of the divine revelation as the ultimate true and the final option that mankind should embrace for the salvation of their souls and for eternal happiness.

RAFIK BERJAK

C

CAIN AND ABEL
see: **murder; sacrifice**

CALENDAR

The Qur'an does not initiate a calendar, although it includes comments upon several calendrical elements. It informs believers that God has specified twelve months (9.36) but, beyond that, assumes the pre-Islamic lunar calendar. It does, however, refocus certain elements of that calendar within an overall context that stresses divine manifestations in nature as signs for humanity. God is described as the one who brings daybreak, who has made the night for rest, and the sun and moon for keeping time (6.96). The Qur'an explains that God made the moon and established its stages so that people could count the years and regulate time (10.5). The new moon is specifically described as a means of regulating time for human beings (2.189; also: 14.33; 16.12; 31.29; 35.13; 36.39; 39.5).

The Qur'an mentions two months by name. Ramadan (the month of 'scorching heat') is identified as the month 'in which the Qur'an was revealed as guidance for humanity' and one during which believers should fast as a sign of worship (2.185). The month of pilgrimage is described as 'well known' (referred to in this instance in the plural: *ma'lumat*) and 'sacred' (*haram*) (2.197, 194; 5.97). This is a reference to the fact that the practice of making pilgrimage to the *Ka'ba* in Mecca during specified months was already established by the time of Prophet Muhammad. The Qur'an then proceeds to discuss regulations concerning conduct of the pilgrimage itself and the prohibition of fighting during the month(s) of pilgrimage. It specifically prohibits the pre-Islamic practice of postponing the month of pilgrimage in order to avoid the prohibition against fighting (9.37).

The point from which the pre-Islamic Arabian calendar begins is unclear. Frequently, significant events were used as reference points. One of the several terms used by the Qur'an for the word 'year' is *hijjaj* which, derived from the term for pilgrimage, could indicate that a year simply is measured from one pilgrimage to the next, since the month of pilgrimage is the final month of both the pre-Islamic and the Islamic calendars. Significant events also served as reference points for measuring years. The year of Prophet Muhammad's birth is identified as 'the Year of the Elephant', when Mecca was attacked by invaders accompanied by an elephant. The event was already auspicious; according to the Qur'an, God saved the Meccans from this overwhelming force by sending a swarm of birds that pelted the invaders with clay stones and drove them away (105.1–6).

The fact that it is the year of Prophet Muhammad's birth made the Year of the Elephant even more important and the early Muslim community appears to have continued using the Year of the Elephant as a calendrical reference point. Caliph 'Umar (d. 644 CE) changed that practice, identifying the Prophet's pilgrimage from Mecca to Medina (622) as the beginning of the Islamic calendar. Since then the Islamic calendar is known as the Hijri (or Hegirian) calendar.

The Islamic calendar retains the twelve months of the pre-Islamic calendar, and the principle of beginning each month with the physical sighting of the new moon. Days therefore are assumed to run from sunset to sunset, and each month is 29–30 days long. In cases in which cloud cover makes physical sighting of the new moon impossible, the new month is assumed to begin after the thirtieth day of the previous month.

Although the calendar is lunar, the names of some of the months reflect a system of recognizing the seasons. The first month is called 'sacred' (Muharram), and the second called 'empty' (Safar). But the third and fourth months are called the first and second months of spring (Rabi' al-Awwal and Rabi' al-Thani), and the fifth and sixth months are called the first and second months of drought (Jumada al-Ula and Jumada al-Thaniyya). The seventh month is called the month of 'awe' (Rajab), and the eighth is the month of 'separation' or 'division' (Sha'ban). But the ninth and tenth months return to season-specific references: As noted, Ramadan is the month of 'scorching heat'; Shawwal is the month of hunting. The year draws to a close with the month of 'rest' (Qa'da) and concludes with the month of pilgrimage (Dhu al-Hijja). The names of the months in the Islamic calendar therefore reflect diverse pre-Islamic influences, as well as modifications to existing patterns initiated by the Qur'an.

Friday is designated as the day of congregational prayer by the Qur'an (62.9), but it is not specified as a day of rest. Believers are told to cease their business when called to collective prayer on that day and, after the prayer is finished, to 'disperse in the land and seek God's grace'. Saturday retains the designation of Sabbath day (Yawm al-Sabt), presumably a day of rest. The Qur'an repeatedly criticizes those who do not keep the Sabbath (2.65; 4.154) although it does not specify regulations for doing this. The rest of the days of the week are simply identified by number, counting Sunday as the first day. As with the identification of months, then, the identification of specific days in the Qur'an reflects both pre-Islamic and uniquely Islamic elements.

In the modern era, the essential elements of the calendar as described in the Qur'an have been maintained with only a few exceptions. Most countries accept regularization of the beginnings of months based on astronomical calculations. Only in the case of the beginning of the month of fasting, Ramadan, is the tradition of sighting the new moon retained. Several holidays have also been added to the calendar based on Qur'anic events, including commemoration of the 'Night Journey' (Laylat al-Mi'raj, celebrated on 27 Rajab), Prophet Muhammad's miraculous ascent from Mecca through Jerusalem to heaven; Laylat al-Qadr (the 'Night of Power' when the Qur'an is believed to have been sent to the Prophet Muhammad), celebrated 27 Ramadan; 'Id (Eid) al-Fitr ('Feast of Breaking the Fast'), celebrated at the end of Ramadan; and the Feast of the Sacrifice ('Id al-Adhha, celebrated 10 Dhu al-Hijja), commemorating Abraham's willingness to sacrifice his son on the command of God.

TAMARA SONN

CALIPH, CALIPHATE

Khalafa means to succeed, be the agent of or substitute for someone. *Istakhlafa* is to appoint as successor, while *khalifa* is chief, successor and, at 2.30, is used to describe the children of Adam, i.e. everyone. The word in its various forms is used 127 times in the Qur'an. The issue of who is the rightful caliph proved to be the cause of the first major schism in the Islamic world, with the Shi'i supporting 'Ali and the family of the Prophet, and the Sunni adopting a different criterion for selecting the caliph.

OLIVER LEAMAN

CALLIGRAPHY AND THE QUR'AN

Arabic belongs to the group of Semitic alphabetical scripts in which mainly the consonants are represented in writing, while the markings of vowels (by diacritics) is optional. The North Semitic alphabet, which developed around 1700 BCE in Palestine and Syria consisted of twenty-two consonant letters. The North Arabic script, which eventually prevailed and became the Arabic script of the Qur'an, is linked most directly to the Nabatean script, which itself was derived from the Aramaic script. Arabic script still shares with Aramaic many features. The Arabic alphabet contains eighteen letter shapes, and by adding one, two or three dots to letters with similar phonetic characteristics a total of twenty-eight letters is obtained. These contain three long vowels, with diacritics added to indicate short vowels.

With the spread of Islam, the Arabic alphabet was adapted by several non-Arab nations for writing their own languages. In Iran Arabic letters were used to write Farsi or Persian, with the addition of four letters to represent those phonetics that did not exist in Arabic, namely: p, ch, zh and g. The Ottoman Turks used the Arabic alphabet until 1929 and added yet another letter. This alphabet was also used to write other Turkic languages and dialects, such as Kazakh and Uzbek. Several other languages used the Arabic alphabet at one time or another, including Urdu, Malay, Swahili, Hausa, Berber and Hebrew.

The Arabic alphabet developed rapidly after the rise of Islam in the seventh century into a beautiful and complex form of art. The main two families of calligraphic styles were the dry styles, called generally the Kufic, and the soft cursive styles, which include Naskhi, Thuluth, Nastaliq and others.

Early calligraphic developments

The North Arabic script, which was influenced by the Nabatean script, was established in north-eastern Arabia and developed by the fifth century among the Arabian tribes who inhabited Hirah and Anbar. It spread to the Hijaz in western Arabia and its use was popularized among the Quraysh, the tribe of the Prophet Muhammad, by Harb ibn Umayya. Although early Arabic sources mention several calligraphic styles in reference to the cities in which they were used, they are generally classified into two broad categories: the 'dry styles', the early predecessors of Kufic; and the 'moist styles', the early predecessors of the more cursive scripts.

The reform of Arabic script

With the growing number of non-Arab Muslims, there was a greater need for developing and disseminating the reading and learning of Arabic, the language of the Qur'an. Since several letters of the Arabic alphabet share the same shapes, and since vowels are not clearly indicated, something was needed to avoid confusion, thus a system of *naqt* or *i'jam* (letter-pointing), and *tashkil* (vowel indication) was developed in order to make clear how to pronounce a word and how to write it.

Abu'l Aswad al-Du'ali (d. 688) was the legendary founder of Arabic grammar and is credited with inventing the system of placing large coloured dots to indicate the *tashkil*, which makes some of the early Qur'ans so delightful to look at. It was used with the Kufic scripts, but proved to be somewhat cumbersome for use with smaller scripts, or in ordinary writing, as it was so time-consuming to produce.

The Umayyad governor al-Hajjaj ibn Yusuf al-Thaqafi enforced a uniform system to distinguish letters by using dots, which he asked two of al-Du'ali's students to codify.

Al Khalil ibn Ahmad al-Farahidi (d. 786) devised a *tashkil* system to replace that of Abu al-Aswad. His system has been universally used since the early eleventh century, and includes six diacritical marks:

fatha	(a)
damma	(u)
kasra	(i)
sukun	(vowel-less)
shadda	(double consonant)
madda	(vowel prolongation; applied to the *alif*)

Development of cursive scripts

Cursive scripts coexisted with Kufic and date back to before Islam, but because in the early stages of their development they lacked discipline and elegance, they were usually used for secular purposes only. Under the Umayyads and 'Abbasids, court requirements for correspondence and record-keeping resulted in many developments to the cursive scripts, and several styles were devised to fulfil these needs. Abu 'Ali Muhammad ibn Muqla (d. 940), along with his brother, became accomplished calligraphers in Baghdad. Ibn Muqla became vizir to three 'Abbasid caliphs and is credited with developing the first script to obey strict proportional rules. His system utilized the dot as a measuring unit for line proportions and a circle with a diameter equals the *alif*'s height as a basic standard for letter proportionality.

Ibn Muqla's system became a powerful conceptual vehicle in the development and standardization of the script, and his calligraphic work elevated a particular previous cursive style into a place of prominence and made it the standard way of writing the Qur'an. The presence of Arabic calligraphy is significant in all cultures in which the

Qur'anic text is significant. Whether displayed on a building or on the face of a coin, calligraphy serves as a reminder of the Holy Book. There is plenty of evidence that the Arabs had before Islam recorded stories in graffiti on rocks in the desert, and there were also writings on palm leaves and camel bones. With the Qur'an Arabic became the language in which the Qur'an was revealed to the Prophet Muhammad early in the seventh century; it was the script in which it was subsequently written down and thus acquired a huge significance for religious reasons. It also meant it was considered a defining feature of Islamic art.

The strong association between writing and God is mentioned several times in the Qur'an. It was God who gave writing to man: 'He who taught by the pen taught man that which he knew not' (96.4–5); 'And if all the trees on earth were pens and the ocean were ink with seven oceans behind it to add to its supply, yet the words of Allah would not be exhausted in the writing' (31.27).

The person writing the words of God is naturally expected to use the most beautiful form of script possible, for the most beautiful form of text. This led to precise rules being established at different times about the shapes of letters and their relation to each other, the relative proportions of the various strokes, rules which are still followed by traditional calligraphers today, although there are now more inventive artists in the field also. Calligraphers are upon occasion encouraged to experiment, and outdo each other in creating even more beautiful styles. Numbers were also significant in combination with letters. Letters had a numerical value, so in the design of amulets, for example, the appearance of a word and its numerical value could all have relevance. *Yawm*, the Arabic word for 'day', appears 365 times in the Qur'an while *shahr*, the word for 'month', appears 12 times.

Cubes such as the *Ka'ba* (which means cube), and cube shapes such as the area of the dot, are vital to Islamic design. The additions to the basic letter forms actually distinguish between different letters, and it is often claimed that they all have particular significance quite apart from their actual meaning. The dot – considered to be the initiation of any line and subsequent drawing – is important in Islam because it is contained in the letter *ba*. *Ba* begins the word *B'ismi*, which, in turn, begins the phrase *B'ismi lahi Rahman ir-Rahim* – the first verse in *al-Fatiha*, the opening chapter of the Qur'an. This is a particularly important phrase as it is used by Muslims to ask for God's blessing and is found at the start of almost every *sura* of the Qur'an. On the other hand, the dot also distinguishes other letters from each other, and they can all be linked to an important Qur'anic phrase, so it is perhaps invidious to emphasize one use of the dot over others.

In India the Hindus never bothered much with the art of writing. Their art is often said to be one of the plane, with a concentration on structures that work by constructing physical shapes which work against and with each other. By contrast, Islamic art is an art of the line; Islamic artisans can produce simple horizontal, vertical and curved lines in a thousand varieties, rhythmically flowing like a river, or intricately formed in a geometrical pattern. The earliest monuments in India such as Quwat-ul-Islam Mosque and Qutub Minar at Delhi contain Qur'anic inscriptions finely carved on red sandstone. Calligraphic inscriptions are generally found on Islamic monuments such as mosques, *madrasa*s, tombs, palaces and public buildings. Much calligraphy is actually in the Persian script, the official court language, but many inscriptions are in Arabic.

Two facts were primarily responsible for the development of this art under Islam. According to Islamic tradition, words of the Qur'an are divine both in form and content and so the words of the Qur'an are sacred symbols of Islam, particularly when used by contrast with the icons or figurative images of other religions, whose use was totally prohibited in Islam. Thus the only possibility throughout the Islamic world is that mosques and other religious buildings are decorated with verses from the Qur'an.

It is worth pointing out that the Arabic and Persian scripts, with their liquid and almost lifelike letters and numerous dots, make them an inherently ornamental script. The regularity of a calligraphic line is based on three coordinates: the *alif*, dot and circle. The interplay of these three shapes along different angles, planes and shapes, keeping in mind the geometric rules, establishes the aesthetic look of this script and invokes a feeling of movement and rhythm.

Yet, when we examine monumental inscriptional art we find that the calligraphic inscriptions provide important information about the cultural, political, social, economic and religious history of the period. The inscriptions are generally dedicatory in nature, recording the date of construction of the building or the event or the political and social status of the builders and their names, and often some combination of these details. These kinds of inscription usually praise the patron and builder of the building and also provide valuable information about the local history of area, and some contain poetic verses. But in most cases the inscription represents religion in the form of verses from the Qur'an.

Types of calligraphy

There are various types of calligraphic styles, and as the script became more and more used, it was itself the site of much development in style.

Kufic is the primitive form of the Arabic writing and it was in this style that the Word of God – 'The Holy Qur'an' – was first written. The name is derived from the Iraqi city Kufa, where it was used in the seventh century CE. Before the twelfth century almost all Islamic architectural calligraphy was executed in Kufic script. The script itself is angular, its lines are parallel and they cut at right angles without any mixture of rounded contours, so it is perfect for architecture. It is in the form of geometric designs, and both calligraphy and geometric designs can assume a spare and beautiful artistic form, while the geometric designs so formed came to acquire a status based both on their content and form. The combination of square and angular lines, and compact, bold, circular forms, where the vertical strokes were short and the horizontal strokes long, produces a powerful effect. As Kufic reached perfection in the second half of the eighth century, it superseded other earlier attempts of development of Arabic calligraphy and became the only script used for copying the Qur'an for the next 300 years.

When the cursive styles were becoming popular and refined in the tenth century, Kufic responded by trying to adapt to the new fashion in calligraphy. It overemphasized many qualities of the cursive scripts in a geometrical style called 'Eastern Kufic', where slender vertical strokes and oblique strokes animated the more rigid early Kufic. This style was mainly a book calligraphy rather than an architectural calligraphy style, but was very popular on ceramics.

On architectural monuments, serifs were added to simple early Kufic beginning in the eighth century, and leaf-like vegetal ornaments appear as early as 866 at the ends of vertical strokes. These ornaments were later added to round strokes, and Foliate Kufic became the most popular style for architectural inscriptions from the tenth century onwards.

In the eleventh century the letters themselves started to be modified and used as ornaments, and new geometric elements started to appear in the form of plaiting, knotting and braiding. The exaggerated use of such ornaments created complex compositions, which were difficult to decipher at times. During the thirteenth and fourteenth centuries, Square Kufic developed out of the use of calligraphy in buildings. Its simple forms contrast with the trend to develop more complex calligraphic compositions. It was the only calligraphic style used to cover entire buildings, a practice unique to Islamic architecture.

The cursive script dates back at least to the first decades of the Muslim era. The early examples, however, lacked elegance and discipline and were used mainly for secular and practical, rather than aesthetic, purposes. In a slow but continuous process, older styles were perfected while new styles were invented to meet the demands of different occasions. Naskh, which means 'copying', was developed in the tenth century and refined into a fine art form in Turkey in the sixteenth century. Since then it has been generally accepted for writing the Qur'an. Naskh is legible and clear and was adapted as the preferred style for typesetting and printing. It is a small script, the lines of which are thin and the letter shapes round. Use of Kufic declined when Naskh developed. The script merges neatly with traditional arabesque decoration. It is characterized by an apparent irregularity in shape of its letters and its highly expressionistic movement.

Thuluth is a more impressive, stately calligraphic style which was often used for titles or epigrams rather than lengthy texts. Its forms evolved over the centuries, and many variations are found on architectural monuments, as well as on glass, metalwork, textiles and wood. Mamluk Thuluth of the fourteenth century was heavy and large, while the Ottomans preferred the simpler, more refined version still practiced today. Thuluth is really a modified version of Naskh. Thuluth means a third, and the ratio between the curves of the letters and the straight line is one-third compared to Naskh. It is used most widely in Islamic monuments from the fourteenth century onwards. Thuluth is extremely regular in appearance and its letters are always well proportioned and uniform in thickness. It embodies the fluidity of Naskhi while maintaining some of the regularity of Kufic.

The term *taliq* means 'suspension' and nicely describes the tendency of each word to drop down from its preceding one. At the close of the same century, a famous calligrapher, Mir 'Ali of Tabriz, evolved Nastaliq, which, according to its name, is a combination of Naskhi and Taliq. Like Taliq, this is a fluid and elegant script, and both were popularly used for copying Persian literary works. It is part of the Naskhi group, with an emphasis on the strength of the strokes and regular linking of letters.

From the sixteenth century onwards, at the time of Mughals, when Persian was the official court language in India, Nastaliq really became established. A rounded script, the letters of which end in more circular curves, most of the monuments of the Mughal period use this style.

Riqa, the simpler style of everyday writing, is very economical and easy to write. It is popular for writing both Turkish and Arabic. It has verticals without any serifs and deep, curved horizontals. It slants to the right in contrast to all the other styles which slant to the left.

The Diwani script is a cursive style of Arabic calligraphy developed during the reign of the early Ottoman Turks (sixteenth/seventeenth centuries). It reached its height of popularity under Suleyman I the Magnificent (1520–66). As decorative as it was communicative, Diwani was distinguished by the complexity of the line within the letter and the close juxtaposition of the letters within the word.

A variation of the Diwani, the Diwani al-jali, is characterized by its abundance of diacritical and ornamental marks. Distinctive scripts were developed in particular regions. In Spain the Maghribi ('Western') script evolved and became the standard script for Qur'ans in North Africa. Derived ultimately from Kufic, it is characterized by the exaggerated extension of horizontal elements and of the final open curves below the middle register.

Both Persia and Turkey made important contributions to calligraphy. In these countries the Arabic script was adopted for the vernacular. Peculiar to Turkish calligraphy is the Tugra (*tughra*), a modified form of Nakshi. A kind of royal cipher based on the names and titles of the reigning sultan and worked into a very intricate and beautiful design, a distinctive Tugra was created for each sultan and affixed to imperial decrees by a skilled calligrapher, the *neshani*.

There has always existed in the Islamic world a keen appreciation of fine handwriting, and from the sixteenth century it became a practice to assemble in albums specimens of penmanship. Many of those assembled in Turkey, Persia and India are preserved in museums and libraries. Calligraphy, too, has given rise to a considerable literature, for example, manuals for professional scribes employed in chancelleries.

OLIVER LEAMAN

see also: **art and the Qur'an; letters and the Qur'an**

CAMEL

Of all the animals mentioned in the scriptures – dogs, horses, donkeys, birds, locusts, etc. – God picked the camel as the one we should reflect upon. Of course, it was a very important animal in Arab culture. In 88.17 we find: 'Why do they not reflect on the camels and how they are created?' The camel's creation is often regarded as a bit of a miracle. The camel is not always seen as a beautiful animal. But it is absolutely perfect for what it needs to do and where it needs to survive. This could be seen as a gift from God. Without camels, no one could travel in the deserts, so huge sections of the world would have been not just difficult to live in, but completely uninhabitable.

All of the camel is practical for its survival and for its service to humanity. A camel's feet, although hoofed, have large pads that spread out in the soft sand to keep the animal from sinking in. The camel's face is designed as protection from the ubiquitous problems of the sun and sand. The thick eyebrows, heavy eyelids and thick lashes all keep out sand, and there is a third eyelid that can close in heavy storms. The nostrils have muscles that can be closed against blowing sand. The ears have thick hair inside as well as outside to prevent dirt and sand from getting down inside and possibly causing infection. A camel's hump is a lump of fat that is used as a source of energy when food is scarce. The hump may actually shrink when no food is available but the camel can live off it for many days. As food is scarce in the desert the camel must be able to eat anything so the lining of the mouth is very tough, allowing the animal to bite and chew thorny cactus plants without harming its mouth. Finally, the camel has a low metabolic rate, meaning energy is used slowly.

It is remarkable how the camel deals with heat and lack of water. Its body temperature may start the day at 94ºC and hit 105ºC in the heat of the afternoon. In terms of reducing body heat, sweating is a more efficient cooling system than panting (as in dogs) because less precious fluid is lost, and the camel is one of the few animals that can sweat, More, it does not begin to do so until its body temperature nears the top of its range. No other creature can process water in the same way as a camel. It does not lose water from blood, only from tissue. Thus the blood stays properly thin enough to circulate and remove body heat. The camel will only drink when needed and only replace what is lost, and it can do so quickly. It may not drink at all in winter.

Camels are truly remarkable animals. When we reflect on their creation, as God instructs us to do, we cannot help but be impressed at the ways God made them fit perfectly into their environment.

See also: **colours; natural world and the Qur'an**

OLIVER LEAMAN

CANON

The Qur'anic canon is the form of the Qur'an as recited and written in which it became religiously binding for the Muslim community. This canonical corpus is closed; nothing can be added to it or taken from it. It is also fixed in the sense that nothing in the Qur'an can be changed or modified.

While there is no Arabic term corresponding exactly to the term 'canon' or 'canonization', the concept is closely linked to the notions of revelation (*wahy, tanzil, inzal*) and is of paramount importance for the understanding of the nature of the Qur'an. It is also at present one of the most contested issues and represents an area in which non-Muslim and Muslim scholarship often clash.

There have been two basic attempts to reconstruct the history of the canonization of the Qur'an:

1. The reliance on a critical reading of extra-Qur'anic Muslim traditions on the genesis of the canonical text. These traditions are either traditions ascribed to the Prophet or his contemporaries, or other early historical reports. These sources tell us how the Qur'an was 'collected'. While full of details, they are also full of contradictions and apparent manipulations. The most widely accepted strand of traditions says that the process of canonization ended under the third caliph, 'Uthman Ibn 'Affan (r. 23/644–35/655), who collected and promulgated the so-called 'Uthmanic codex (*al-mushaf al-'Uthmani*). All copies of the Qur'an which showed differences were then destroyed. According to this tradition the end of the canonization process could be set at about twenty years after the Prophet's death. This is the version favoured by many non-Muslim as well as Muslim scholars.

2. A reading which dismisses the early Muslim narratives altogether and is based on a close reading of the Qur'anic text. This approach distinguishes different scriptural and literary genres with the text and postulates on the basis of this a much longer historical process and consequently a much later date of canonization. According to this view, the Muslim community agreed on a text: the 'Uthmanic codex as a final, fixed text only a century or even two to three centuries after 'Uthman reigned. This revisionist version is upheld by Wansbrough (1977) and many of his students.

Whatever the history and correct dating, the 'Uthmanic codex is the one and only version of the Qur'anic text that the Muslim community has come to accept as the revealed basis of oral and written tradition.

We must distinguish here between canonization of a written text and canonization of an oral recital tradition. Until the third/ninth to the fourth/tenth century a written Qur'anic passage or a complete codex looked like any other piece of Arabic writing, i.e. an ambiguous consonantical 'skeleton' (rasm) without signs for vowels. This writing system allowed for a considerable number of homographs which could be open to two or more interpretations. Basically an early codex of the Qur'an was not much more than a mnemotechnical device to support recitation. The oral tradition of how to recite this text – the 'reading' (qira'a) – was of equal or possibly of greater importance than the ability to interpret the defective and polyvalent graphemes. As this rudimentary 'Uthmanic text could be read and recited in many different ways, and as there were numerous different recital traditions, the necessity arose to put a stop to the production of more and more divergent readings. The vast majority of the Muslim community accepted with Ibn Mujahid (d. 324/936), and under pressure from the 'Abbasid rulers, a limit of seven readings of the 'Uthmanic text, which were ascribed to Qur'an readers and their different local traditions of the second/eighth century. All of these seven readings were declared equally 'canonical'; in the language of the time Muslim scholars explained that God had revealed the Qur'an in seven different but equally authoritative forms. Later the circle of readings was widened, so that ten and then even fourteen equally legitimate readings were accepted. Other readings compatible with the 'Uthmanic codex were also collected and preserved but were considered extra-canonical (shadhdha, literally: 'aberrant, deviant'). The variants in these canonical readings affected vocalization, diacritical dots in orthography, variants in the consonantic rasm and the division of verses and therefore the number of verses (ayat). This is a somewhat simplified version of a history that was in its details certainly far more complex.

In its generally accepted form, the 'Uthmanic text comprises all 114 suras in the established order known to us – roughly following the length of the suras. The basmala marks the beginning of all suras except sura 9. The single letters or groups of single letters (al-huruf al-muqatta'a) which introduce 29 suras and whose meaning has never been cleared up are part of the canonical text. The names of the suras, however, are not considered to be part of the revealed text, and neither are the observations on the number of verses, the description of a sura as Meccan or Medinan or remarks on the relative chronology of the sura part of the canonical text.

Muslim tradition has preserved reports of some important and far-reaching textual differences in pre-'Uthmanic versions: in Shi'ite circles there were rumours that the 'Uthmanic codex had suppressed passages that confirmed 'Ali Ibn Abi Talib's claim to the immediate sucessorship to the Prophet, a view maintained by some Shi'ite scholars until the nineteenth century; in the codex of 'Abdallah ibn Mas'ud *sura* 1 and *suras* 113 and 114 were missing; meanwhile the codex of 'Ubayy ibn Ka'b showed two additional *suras*. There are numerous differences in readings, some important, mostly marginal, and the exact relationship between the early Qur'anic fragments found in Sana'a/Yemen and the 'Uthmanic codex has still to be determined: a '*sura* of the Two Lights' (*surat al-Nurayn*) has been proven a Shi'ite forgery of the sixteenth century.

Whereas the Muslim community in the fourth/tenth century had *de facto* accepted the 'Uthmanic text as the canonically binding form, some Muslim scholars still upheld in theory that other versions should be also considered of divine origin. The vast majority of scholars, however, considered all pre-'Uthmanic texts 'abrogated'. One of the last Muslim Qur'an readers who tried to go back to pre- or extra-'Uthmanic tradition was Ibn Shanabudh (d. 328/940), a contemporary of Ibn Mujahid, who was later forced to revoke. At the beginning of the twenty-first century, there remain only two versions in use in the Muslim world, both going back to the 'seven readings':

1. the reading Warsh (d. 197/812), in the tradition of Nafi' ibn 'Abdal-rahman (d. *c*.169/785), used mainly in North and West Africa;
2. the reading Hafs (d. 180/769), in the tradition of 'Asim ibn Bahdala

(died 128/745); this reading is practically universal and has become an unofficial standard version since the prestigious Azhar University in Cairo sanctioned the Cairo 1924 printing and many later editions.

Over the course of more than a thousand years the written text has become more and more *the* canonical text and the orally recited text has lost much of its previous canonical equality. With the authorized printing of the Qur'an, the preponderance of the written word over the recited word seems to have been strengthened.

The canonicity of the Qur'an is in principle pluralistic, but this pluralism is regulated. The cluster of canonical readings as a recited and a written multiplicity centred around the 'Uthmanic codex is at the heart of the canonicity of the Qur'anic text as it stands now. The text itself shows traces of discussions about canonicity, for example, in the case of abrogation. However, during the process of canonization the canonical text lost almost all its history and all of its context; the mechanical device to arrange the *suras* roughly according to length is in itself proof of this. We have no information as to why this structure was chosen. The canonical unity '*sura*' is in itself complex. covering short splinter-like fragments (e.g. *sura* 108), compositions with a distinct and elaborate compositional and liturgical structure (many of the Meccan *suras*) as well as cut-and-paste, unstructured agglomerations, especially in the case of some of the long Medinan *suras* (e.g. *sura* 2). Muslim exegetical tradition also mentions numerous Medinan insertions into Meccan *suras*, as well as Meccan insertions into Medinan *suras*. Efforts to re-contextualize and rehistorize the text are an extremely difficult undertaking. In any case, the history of the reception of the holy text, the commentaries known to us, the liturgy, as far as it is connected to the Qur'an and to Islamic culture in general, depend solely on the readings of the 'Uthmanic codex.

References and further reading

Motzki, H. (2001) 'The Collection of the Qur'an: A reconsideration of Western views in light of recent methodological developments', *Der Islam* 78: 1–34.
Neuwirth, A. (2002) 'Form and Structure of the Qur'an', in *EQ*, Vol. 2, 245–65.
Wansbrough, J. (1977) *Qur'anic Studies: Sources and methods of scriptural interpretation*, Oxford: Oxford University Press.

See also: **abrogation;** *aya;* **Meccan and Medinan** *suras* **and the Qur'an; revelation;** *sura*

STEFAN WILD

CHARACTER

Character refers more to the inward condition of the human soul, and should therefore be distinguished from personality, which refers more to the outward qualities of human behaviour. Character is also different from morality, which pertains to rules of moral conduct. Character pertains rather to the innate motivation and virtues of the soul and is a guide to moral conduct.

Character may be defined as the sum of all the intellectual and moral qualities that distinguish one person from another. A good character blends good qualities in a person. A man's character pertains to his soul, not to his possessions; to what he is, and not to what he owns. A healthy soul depends on moral living; on being kind, truthful and just, not on material possessions. However, possessions do have a role to play in the nurturing of character, but they are not fundamental to it.

Just as a muscle grows stronger with exercise, character grows strong with practice. Our ability to tell the truth, to behave honestly or to conduct ourselves graciously towards others is a power that grows with use, and the good act becomes easier to us each time we do it. This is the principle of habituation expounded by Aristotle and the Islamic philosophers who followed him. Habit is the basic method of making the cardinal virtues of wisdom, justice, courage and temperance intrinsic to the human soul. When we express them in action habitually, they will become natural to us, and hence become part of our character. A man is not generous because he is charitable, but because the quality of generosity is intrinsic to his soul. It is so imprinted in his soul that he is unable to act in any other way than to be generous. Stinginess has become repugnant to his nature; but it has become so on account of his practice of generosity.

Similarly, all other virtues can become natural to a person by practice. Thus, moral character is an art to be acquired by practice and individual experience. The Qur'an refers to the Prophet Muhammad as the 'good example' (*ustawatan hasana*), and so Muslims are required to emulate Muhammad's moral and religious example. By dwelling on his example, and on the ideal of the perfect man who unites all virtues and excellences, we are inspired to become better than we are; by patient continuance in doing good we are slowly transformed into the image of our hope.

There are abundant references in the Qur'an to virtues, but these have not received the attention of the jurists, who were more concerned with the outward rules of religious behaviour.

The Muslim philosophers and Sufis turned to these verses of the Qur'an to build up a theory of cultivating character. They were partly conditioned by the philosophical thought of the time, especially the psychology of the soul and its three faculties, which in their balance produce the three cardinal virtues of the soul. Al-Ghazali is an example of a religious philosopher who made the Platonic division of soul the foundation for his theory of virtue. However, he went beyond al-Isfahani and Miskawayh by adding to his theory a Sufi method of purifying the soul of vices, called by Ibn Rushd 'the ethics of the soul'. Important issues are the purification of character, the capacity to change it and examples of different kinds of characters. In particular, al-Isfahani supported his description of the virtues by extensive quotations taken from the Qur'an, and so his account is especially significant.

Purification of the soul

According to Miskawayh, the balance of the three faculties of the soul produces the four cardinal virtues of wisdom, courage, temperance and justice. This constitutes the purification of the soul, whereby it is liberated from matter and dominated by the faculty of reason. This is the key to moral character (Daiber, 1996: 852). Al-Isfahani holds the same view, and stresses that purification implies the control, not the obliteration, of desires. Furthermore, he defines the relationship between moral character and the Qur'anic law. The revealed law provides the foundation for the nurturing of character. Chastity and charity are part of prescribed worship ('ibada), but outwardly they do not imply character; it is only if they become internalized within the soul that one can say they constitute character. Previously we used charity as an example, but let us now take the example of chastity and modesty.

The Qur'an provides a certain code of dress for women in order to promote

modesty. However, it is possible for women to wear the *hijab* and still act in a manner that is immodest. This is because modesty is not ingrained within the soul, and the outward forms of it are not expressions of the inner quality of modesty. The inner qualities of the soul are internalized states based on voluntary actions. Since they are voluntary actions, they fall into the category of supererogatory acts of worship. It is in this area of worship that man is brought near to God, and where he can arrive at the level of vicegerency (*khilafa*) and sainthood (*wilaya*). The esoteric dimensions of the revealed law bring to our attention these kinds of voluntary practices. These supererogatory virtues and devotions are left up to the individual to pursue and they cannot be enforced by the Islamic state.

Al-Ghazali and al-Isfahani gave more attention to this esoteric ethics, which for them was the key to character, and character was in turn the key to sainthood (*wilaya*) and vicegerency (*khilafa*) (al-Isfahani, 1987: 94). Vicegerency is the 'The imitation of God in accordance with man's ability to rule by the application of the noble qualities of the Law'. The application of these qualities leads to paradise and proximity to God (al-Isfahani, 1987: 59). Al-Isfahani identifies the purification of the soul with the Qur'anic concept of *khilafa* and quotes two Qur'anic verses (2.30 and 6.165) to support his view that vicegerency surpasses servitude to God ('*ubudiyya*), bringing man to the level of the righteous (*siddiqin*) and the martyrs (*shuhada*'). These people are happy both in this world and the next.

Change of character

Moral philosophers of the eleventh century debated about whether character is something innate or acquired. Al-Isfahani held that it has both dimensions. The innate dimension is universal and unalterable, and it is to be identified with *fitra* (humanity's archetypal nature). The acquired aspect is to be identified with the *nafs* (self), which is dynamic and changing. The Qur'an mentions three levels: the Commanding Self; the Self-accusing Self; and the Tranquil Self. The lowest level is that of the commanding or animal self, but this can change and be transmuted to the two higher levels of the self. Purification therefore implies the change of the soul (also *nafs*) which is dynamic because of its dual tendencies of good and evil. The Qur'an refers to the good and evil that have been instilled in the human soul. Man can choose between them and can nurture the one in such a way so that it can predominate over the other.

Miskawayh acknowledges both the nature and nurture dimensions of character, stating:

> Character is a state of the soul which causes it to perform its actions without thought and deliberation. This state is of two kinds. One kind is natural and originates in the temperament, as in the man whom the least thing moves to anger or who is aroused for the least cause ... The other kind is that which is acquired by habit and self-training. It may have its beginning in deliberation and thought, but then it becomes by gradual and continued practice, an aptitude and trait of character. (Zurayk, 1968: 29)

Thus, character is the internal state of the soul, while moral action is its external manifestation. Here is a clear distinction between character and morality. Character is related to the virtues of the soul, and morality is related to the external conduct of a person. Morality could express social conformity or legal norms, but when internalized expresses character. For example, obligatory

charity is a legal act, but voluntary charity is a moral act. There is no compulsion in a morally free act; it is a spontaneous act of the soul. Genuinely good acts come from character, and so praise for these acts should be directed at character, and not merely at the actions. We have already stated that true generosity is a mark of the soul, not necessarily of the generous action.

For al-Isfahani, character is an innate disposition (*hay'a*) of the soul, but it can also be expressed in outward action. A virtue is both innate and acquired, and it is through action that it can be acquired (al-Isfahani, 1987: 113). Character, which makes up the sum of virtues, can therefore be nurtured with practice. Reason should dominate the lower soul. This is the key to its purification and happiness. By reflecting on the soul, man can perfect his character and attain happiness in this world. Thus, happiness is related to moral character, and moral character depends on the soul's purification and perfection.

Al-Isfahani identifies three broad Qur'anic characters. The pious (*salihin*) worship God; the martyrs (*shuhada'*) do good and curb their passions; and the veracious (*siddiqin*) are satisfied with God's decree, both inwardly and outwardly (al-Isfahani, 1987: 158). We will now discuss some examples of more specific character types.

The Truthful Character

Truthfulness (*sidq*) and lying are expressed in human speech as questions, commands or supplications, but we are concerned here with how they affect our character. Truth must correspond with reality, otherwise it is false (*kidhb*). A true statement could, however, be false, if for example an unbeliever says 'Muhammad is the Messenger of God'. The unbeliever is speaking the truth from an Islamic perspective, but because the statement is not said with conviction, it is false. The Qur'an makes reference to such persons: 'When the hypocrites come to you, they say: "We bear witness that you are indeed Allah's Apostle." Allah knows that you are indeed His Apostle and Allah bears witness that the hypocrites are liars' (63.1).

Truthfulness is the source of praiseworthy acts, prophecy and piety (*taqwa*), and it validates the revealed Law as God states: 'O you who believe, fear Allah and side with the truthful' (9.119). Lying is opposed to piety; it makes a human being worse than the beast: 'Or do you suppose that most of them hear or understand? Indeed, they are merely as cattle; no, even more wayward' (25.44).

Many theologians (*mutakallimun*) believe that truthfulness and falsehood are by nature good and bad, and many sages (*hukama*) and Sufis (*mutasawwifa*) say that they are good and bad only according to their outcome. Lying is harmful; but there are some exceptions. When Abraham was asked who broke the idols, he said: 'This big idol'; he lied in order to tell the people that the idols are useless. And while truth can be found in gossip and backbiting, this is a harmful truth. Truth can also be distorted and based on suspicion (al-Isfahani, 1987: 270–6). The Qur'an warns: 'O believers, avoid much suspicion; for some suspicion is a sin' (49.12).

The Proud Character

Humility (*tawadu'*) is to accept one's lot, even if one deserves a better condition. Kings, nobles and scholars who accept less, but deserve more, are humble and benevolent. They forfeit their rights, which is not an act of servility as suggested in the Qur'an (65.43; 20.108).

Pride (*kibr*) comes from feeling superior about one's position and power. The learned and the pious find it difficult to curb their pride. A proud person deems himself greater than his worth, and shows it by boasting. Pride is a prerogative of God, not of man. Pride proceeds from conceit, conceit proceeds from ignorance, and ignorance strips man of his humanity. A proud person is not open to truth. Thus, God states: 'Is not there in hell a resting place for the arrogant?' (39.60). The proud person thinks of his high status, but the humble person thinks of his low origin, no matter what his status. God also states: 'So let man consider what he was created from. He was created from flowing water; emanating from what lies between the loins and the breast-bones' (86.5). Pride without a just cause (*bi-ghayri haqq*) is blameworthy. God speaks of 'those who behave arrogantly in the earth without a rightful cause' (7.146) (al-Isfahani, 1987: 301–3).

The Irascible Character

The irascible character is the one who is inclined to become angry quickly. Anger is an emotion that is contained in the irascible faculty of the soul. We do not wish to debate about whether anger is innate or acquired, but we need to mention that it is part of human nature and that it has both a positive and negative role. It is not something to be obliterated, but should be controlled within the limits of reason and the revealed Law.

The angry character can become temporarily insane because of a desire for revenge, jealousy or pride. Anger is destructive when it blocks the natural heat of the heart. It is caused by conceit, boasting, quarrelling, obstinacy, joking, confusion, injustice, mockery, rivalry, envy and the desire for vengeance. Al-Isfahani compares man's anger to the igniting of fire. Some people are like grass: quick to burn and slow to be put out; others are like leaves, slow to burn and slow to be put out. Differences are also relative to one's nature: those with a hot and dry temperament have a fiery temper, while those with a cold and humid temperament possess a mild temper. Differences in temper depend on custom: some people are quiet and calm, described as gentle and modest; others are noisy and thoughtless, becoming furious over small things such as a dog who barks at a person because it doesn't know them. Young boys, women and the old are prone to become angry quickly; it is their anger which is most easily aroused (al-Isfahani, 1987: 345–6).

It is a virtue to control one's anger, and the Qur'an commends those who do so and classifies such people as beneficent: 'Those who curb their anger and those who pardon their fellow-men. Allah loves the beneficent!' (3.134). The Prophet said to some people who were lifting a stone: 'Shall I inform you of the strongest among you? It is the one who has controlled his anger.' Thinking and waiting, rather than reacting impulsively, help to control anger. It is easy to react to one's subordinate, but it is better to be calm (al-Isfahani, 1987: 345–6).

The Forbearing and Forgiving Character

The treatment for anger is forbearance (al-hilm) and pardon ('afwu) and to avoid being too hasty in blame and condemnation.

Forbearance means self-restraint in times of anger; it is 'to manage the soul and temper when it is aroused to anger'. This management is done by restraining one's hands from violence, the tongue from indecency, the ears from eavesdropping and the eyes from excessive gazes (al-Isfahani, 1987: 342–4).

Forgiveness is to pardon someone for a mistake or an offence, but if this transgresses the law of the state, it is up to the ruler to pardon the person. If the person has to be punished, then it should not be out of anger. Delay in punishment will abate the anger. When Alexander the Great forgave a criminal, a man said: 'If I were you, I would have killed him.' So Alexander said: 'So since I am not you and you are not me, I will not kill him.' To forgive is better than revenge; the former will lead to good, the latter to regret (al-Isfahani, 1987: 342–3).

The Patient Character

Patience is mentioned in the Qur'an ninety times, in various contexts. Examples include: as a condition of prosperity (3.200); as a prerequisite for leadership (32.24); to earn God's companionship (8.46); as a condition for God's help (3.125); as a standard of courage (42.43); and as a condition of God's love (3.146). According to Ibn Qayyim al-Jawziyya (d. 1350), a person with moral character is patient in all difficulties and devoted to God no matter what the hardship (al-Jawziyya, 1998: 24–5).

For al-Isfahani, there are two kinds of patience: physical patience, which is to endure difficulty such as carrying a heavy stone; and spiritual patience, which is to endure calamity, avoid luxury and respect secrecy (al-Isfahani, 1987: 326).

The Virtuous Character

If a virtuous character dies, he is relieved of the world, but if a vicious character dies, the world is relieved of him. The virtuous are content with God's bounties, detached from the world, fearless of death and ready for the hereafter. The vicious do not take care of their souls and fear death: 'And he who is blind in this world will be blind in the Hereafter, and will stray even more from the right way' (17.72) (al-Isfahani, 1987: 337f.).

References and further reading

Daiber, H. (1996) 'Political Philosophy', *HIP*: 841–85.
Donaldson, M.D. (1953) *Studies in Muslim Ethics*, London: SPCK.
—— (1997) *The Qur'an: A modern English version*, London: Garnet.
al-Isfahani, R. (1987) *al-Dhari'a ila makarim al-shari'a*, Cairo: Dar al-wafa'.
al-Jawziyya, Ibn Qayyim (1998) *Patience and Gratitude: An abridged translation of 'Uddat as-sabirin wa dhakirat ash-sha-kirin*, trans. Nasiruddin al-Khattab, London: Taha Publishers.
Zurayk, Constantine (1968) *The Refinement of Character*, Beirut: The American University of Beirut.

See also: fitra; forgiveness; haqq; humility; nafs; taqwa

YASIEN MOHAMED

CHRISTIANITY

There are a number of objections in the Qur'an to the main doctrines of Christianity, or what are taken to be these doctrines.

Jesus as God

First is the belief that God had a partner in his generation of Jesus: 'To Him is due the primal origin of the heavens and the earth: How can He have a son when He has no consort? He created all things, and He has full knowledge of all things' (6.101). Also we are told: 'And Exalted is the majesty of our Lord: He has taken neither a wife nor a son' (72.3). This implies that Christians believe that God had a physical relationship with Mary, something that the New Testament text does not say. There

are verses in the Qur'an that state, or at least strongly imply, that Christians worship Jesus and Mary in addition to God: 'In blasphemy indeed are those that say that Allah is Christ the son of Mary. Say: "Who then has the least power against Allah, if His will were to destroy Christ the son of Mary, his mother, and all that is on the earth?" For to Allah belongs the dominion of the heavens and the earth, and all that is in between. He creates what He wishes. For Allah has power over all things' (5.17). 'Christ the son of Mary was no more than a messenger, many were the messengers that passed away before him. His mother was a woman of truth. They had both to eat their food. See how Allah makes His signs clear to them [people]; yet see in what ways they turn away from the truth!' (5.75).

Here we have the implication that Jesus and Mary are treated by Christians as divine. This is not the case; but they are simply human beings who eat and have no more power than anyone else. Jesus is presented as denying any special authority or power by contrast with the total authority of the deity: when Allah says, 'O Jesus, the son of Mary! Did you say to men, "Worship me and my mother as gods in derogation of Allah?"' Jesus says: 'Glory to You! Never could I say what I had no right. Had I said such a thing, you would indeed have known it. You know what is in my heart, I do not know what is in yours. For you know completely everything that is hidden' (5.116).

The Trinity

The concept of the Trinity (5.73) is seen as being very problematic, especially if it means that there are three kinds of deity, or that God needs others to help him carry out his purposes. The idea that God is Jesus (5.17) is also highly objectionable, although again whether this really is a Christian mainstream doctrine is dubious. While Christian thinking about God puts Jesus centre-stage in order to see the invisible God, the Qur'an pushes Jesus to the sidelines with God's other prophets in order that God's glorious unity not be obscured or confused. The Qur'an offers a spectrum of opinions of Christianity, from the friendly – 'nearest among them in love to the believers will you find those who say, "We are Christians"' (5.82); 'those who believe ... and the ... Christians any who believe in Allah and the Last Day and work righteousness on them shall be no fear, nor shall they grieve' (2.62; 5.69) – to the more hostile – 'O People of the Book, commit no excesses ... say not "three"' (4.171).

The Qur'an also portrays Christians as fellow believers in Allah who will receive an eschatological reward (2.62; 5.69). Alongside this is a verse describing them as people having 'a portion of the Book' who are 'invited to the [entire] Book of Allah to settle their dispute', that is, to repent of their incomplete lives and come to the fulfillment that is Islam (3.23). 'Come to common terms', 3.64 exhorts, 'as between us and you', terms of theological surrender, recognition that the Muslims worship Allah rightly and are not guilty of *shirk* as are the Christians. Some Christians and Jews do exactly this (3.199), so that 'not all of them are alike: of the People of the Book are a portion that stand [for the right]', having already embraced Islam (3.113–114). It is not clear, however, whether they are accepted as monotheists and broadly on the right path while remaining Christians or whether they have to take the step of actual conversion to receive the ultimate reward of heaven.

The punishment of Christians

Contrasted with these converts are 'those who reject Faith' and who 'will be Companions of the Fire, dwelling therein (forever)' (3.116). And elsewhere, those that, given 'a portion of the Book ... traffic in error, and wish that you should lose the right path' (4.44). Christians and Jews, then, are subject to a range of critiques. These have yielded an even greater range of interpretations: convergence-minded texts relying on 5.82 on the one hand and bitter anti-Christian polemics relying on the most critical passages. There is a theme that respects Christians as long as they eventually repudiate their mistaken beliefs and revert to the true Islam, which is after all seen as the original faith upheld by Christians before the Gospels were falsified and erroneous beliefs arose over the nature of Jesus.

The Qur'an predicts that those Christians who ignore its warnings are subject to apocalyptic divine judgement on the Day of Judgement (4.47–49, 172; 5.73). There is scope for God's mercy, but also the necessity of God's desire that 'the truthful will profit from their truth' (5.119). The Qur'an's objection to Christian practice is Christianity's *shirk*, its worship of Jesus, Mary and the saints 'in derogation of Allah' (5.116). There is no justification in believing in the Trinity (5.72), for Jesus never would have condoned such a concept (5.116), viewing it as 'joining other gods with [Allah]' (4.116) or saying 'Allah is one of three in a Trinity' (5.73). Such practices inevitably confuse Christians and distract them away from the worship of the One True God. The best description of this Qur'anic material is polemic: it is ostensibly directed against Christians, but its audience is surely Muslim, for Christians would see its account of the Trinity as inaccurate.

Many read the Qur'an not as a criticism of orthodox (i.e. truly Trinitarian and incarnational) Christian theology but of Monophysite and Nestorian Christian theologies that may have predominated in Arabian society in and around the Arabian peninsula. The Qur'an's critique of Christian theology and practice does not ring true of many varieties of Christianity. Qur'anic appeals to Jesus' true humanity, that he and Mary 'had both to eat their [daily] food' (5.75) and that his similitude 'before Allah is that of Adam; He created him from dust, then said to him: "Be", and he was' (3.59) are effective only against schools that deny Jesus' true humanity. Many Christians, like Muslims, would decry those 'joining other gods with [Allah]' (4.116). Saying that 'Allah is one of three in a Trinity' (5.73) is more ambiguous. Christians might well argue that worship of Jesus is not worship of someone besides God but worship of God himself. The Three in One doctrine does seem to be very different from the concept of *tawhid*: 'For Allah is One God: Glory be to Him: [Far exalted is He] above having a son. To him belong all things in the heavens and on earth. God is sufficient as a disposer of affairs' (4.171). Christians argue that an emphasis on unity occurs also in the Jewish and Christian bibles, so they would reject the accuracy of this particular version of what the Trinity doctrine means.

Further reading

Goddard, H. (1996) *Muslim Perceptions of Christianity*, London: Grey Seal.

Robinson, N. (1991) *Christ in Islam and Christianity: The representation of Jesus in the Qur'an and the classical Muslim commentaries*, London: Macmillan.

Waardenburg, J. (1999) *Muslim Perceptions of Other Religions*, New York: Oxford University Press.

See also: 'Isa; John of Damascus; *tawhid*

OLIVER LEAMAN

COLOURS

Six basic or primary colours are present in the Qur'an: white, black, red, green, yellow and blue. Except for blue, all colours refer to natural phenomena and are explicitly used to call attention to the multi-coloured world created by God. In addition to their descriptive sense, some colour words, such as black, white and blue, are also used metaphorically to suggest a psychological or emotional state of being. It is perhaps interesting to note that these six words are psychological primary colours, and indeed they are used as such in the text; white denotes happiness or bliss (3.107), black denotes both gloom (39.60) and anger (16.58), and blue denotes a spectrum of sensations ranging from emotional terror and fear, to physical sensations of cold and suffocation (20.102). In terms of distribution, the most frequently used colour is white (eleven times), followed by green (eight times), black (seven times), yellow (five times), red (once) and blue (once). In addition to these basic colour terms, there are also eight references to the word 'colour' (*lawn*), most often collocated with the adjective 'diverse', i.e. 'diverse colours' (16.69, *mukhtalifun alwanu-hu*). The use of this adjective, especially in connection with multicoloured natural entities such as mountain rocks, fruits, plants and animals, suggests that the range of the red, green and yellow is likely to be much wider than the assumed norm. Red, for example, will probably include not just the most typical example of the colour represented by the term but all the dark reds, browns, purples and oranges.

Surprisingly enough, although the Arabic language-system during the time of the Prophet Muhammad possessed a large range of colour terms, only these six primary colours are used in the

Qur'an, suggesting perhaps that colour categorization in the Qur'an is not arbitrary or random and that there is some kind of sequential relationship between these colour-terms. It might also suggest that the selection of colour-terms is not based on the cultural needs of the community or how familiar they are in the environment but basically upon the physical features of the colours themselves. Red (*humr*) (35.27) and blue (*zurqan*) (20.102), for example, occur only once in the corpus, although they clearly designate familiar entities such as the 'sky' and 'sea' for blue, and 'fire' and 'blood' for red. If we look at the frequency of occurrence of all six terms, we will find, strangely enough, an ordered ranking system that corresponds closely with modern theories of universal colour distribution.

Before proceeding further, it seems best to provide a brief outline of the classical theory of colour developed by Berlin and Kay (1969). On the basis of investigation into ninety-eight languages, Berlin and Kay claim that there is a universal inventory of only eleven colour categories from which all languages derive eleven or fewer basic colour terms. English has eleven – white, black, red, green, yellow, blue, brown, purple, pink, orange and grey. Berlin and Kay also claim that there is a partial ordering of these categories, so that it can be predicted that, if a language has a certain colour term, it will have certain other ones (cf. Palmer 1981: 72–5). The rule is as follows:

$$\begin{vmatrix} white \\ \\ black \end{vmatrix} < [red] < \begin{vmatrix} green \\ \\ yellow \end{vmatrix} [green]$$

$$< [blue] < \begin{vmatrix} purple \\ pink \\ orange \\ grey \end{vmatrix} [brown] <$$

The sign < means that, following the above example, in any language a term appearing on the right will include within its spectrum all the terms to the left. Thus, if it has 'green', it will include 'red', and, if it has 'brown', it will include blue. Some of the terms are not ordered, but are grouped together. All languages have 'black,' and 'white', but some languages have 'green' without 'yellow' and others have 'yellow' without 'green'. The last four colour terms usually occur together, although some do not have them all. The rule gives us a possible set of only twenty-two language types. As examples, we are told that some languages of the New Guinea Highland group are Type 1, with only 'black' and 'white', while Plains Tamil (India) is Type 6, with 'white', 'black', 'red', 'green', 'yellow' and 'blue'. It is also suggested that we may set up evolutionary stages of language, according to the number of colour terms, and that there is some evidence that children acquire terms in the same order.

If we apply Berlin and Kay's classification, we will find the language-system of the Qur'an to be a Type 6, with white, black, red, green, yellow and blue. However, it is significant to note that some colours are not lexicalized even though their referent is quite explicitly pointed out. For example, in 39.21 reference is made to how the bees are inspired by God to 'eat' from all fruits and thence out of their bellies will come forth a 'drink of different colours wherein is healing for man'. It is evident here that the reference is to honey and that the different colours refer to a colour range that extends from light yellow to dark brown. It seems highly unlikely that Arabic did not possess a term for this range of colour. Consequently, one can assume, if we were to adopt Berlin and Kay's theory, that had the Qur'an lexicalized 'brown' it would have by necessity also lexicalized all or some of the terms on the right side of the example, namely, purple, pink, orange and grey.

If we use the frequency of occurrence as criteria for ranking, all six colours will be found to be set up approximately in the same order as has been suggested by the researchers. The variation occurs in the first category, where it appears that white and green rather than white and black are the two most frequently occurring colour-terms. However, this analysis might be adjusted if we were to rank the colours in terms of their frequency of co-occurrence, i.e. by the number of times they appear in combination. Here we will find that white, red and yellow are the only three colours that occur concomitantly in one verse: 'Have you not seen how God sends down water from the sky, and therewith We bring fruits of diverse colours? And among the mountains are streaks white and red, of diverse colours, and pitchy black. And likewise men, and beasts and cattle, diverse are their colours' (35.27). Here it is evident that white and red point to a range of colours and that they refer not only to the diverse colours of mountain rocks but 'likewise' to the three basic skin colourings of mankind. It would appear then that these three colours are the most universal of all types. And even though red occurs only once, it is used in a generic or universal context and this gives it ascendancy, thus correlating with Berlin and Kay's ranking order.

It is also significant to note that the colour red is also inherent in the word *warda* (55.37), which means 'red rose' or 'red flower': 'Then when the heaven is rent asunder and it becomes like a greasy rose.' (In recent times, scholars have noted the interesting fact that when small stars erupt in space they turn into a rose-like greasy shape.) The second most important combination is the white–black pattern found in three different locations (twice in 3.106 and once in 2.186). This combination is significant since it refers both to the physical properties of the two colours (i.e. the white thread and the black thread separating daybreak and night) as well as the psychological primary colours of white (bliss and happiness) evident on the 'faces' of those in paradise, as opposed to black (gloom and dismay) on the 'faces' of those in Hell: 'On the Day [of Resurrection] when some faces are whitened and some faces blackened; as for those whose faces are blackened: Did you disbelieve after you accepted faith? Then taste the torment of your disbelief. And as for those whose faces are whitened, they shall be in God's mercy, therein dwelling forever.' According to Asad (1980: 714), the phrase *iswadda wajhuhu* (lit. 'his face became black') is used idiomatically to describe a face expressive of grief or ignominy, just as its opposite, *ibyadda wajhuhu*, describes a countenance expressive of happiness. It is also important to note also that black and white occur separately and most often in the same context of bliss and gloom. One exception, apart from the triadic combination white–red–black, is the repetitive references (five occurrences) to Moses' 'white hand' (e.g. 20.22) which, along with his staff, is described as a miraculous sign of God's power. Equally interesting is the 'white wine' (37.46) served in the Garden of Bliss as reward for the faithful: 'Round them will be passed a cup of pure wine (*ma'in*) White, delicious to the drinkers.'

The colour green (*khudran*) ranks high in terms of frequency of occurrence; it is in fact the second in line after white. One can therefore postulate an inherent white–green grouping of colours. Semantically, these two colours seem to share one aspect, namely that they seem to be the primary colours of paradise. The dwellers of heaven are not only repetitively described as having 'white' faces full of comfort and peace but also as being adorned in 'green': 'For them there will be Gardens of Eden, underneath which rivers flow, and they shall be robed in green (*khudran*) garments of silk and brocade, therein reclining upon couches. O how excellent a reward! And O how fair a resting-place' (18. 31). In addition, although all vegetation is referred to as green, a special and rare term is used to refer to the luscious foliage of paradise – *madhamatan* (55.64). Notice that this word is doubly marked since it is not only a rare or archaic term, used only once in the Qur'an, but it is also in the dual case (ending in *–an*) and credited to be the shortest verse (*aya*) in the Qur'an.

Yellow is many times used to denote the withering process of plants, with an explicit reference to the fact that plants of all colours must by necessity turn to yellow: 'Then He brings forth crops (*zar'an*) of diverse colours, then they wither, and you see them turning yellow (*musfarran*), then he makes them dry and shrivelled' (39.21). However, in addition to death and decay, yellow is also used to denote more positive senses of brightness and beauty. This is evident in a famous and oft-quoted passage (2.69), referring to the heifer of 'bright yellow colour' (*safra faqi'un lawniha*) that Moses had ordered the Israelites to slay in expiation of a murder. Here the use of the amplifying adjective 'bright' (*faqi'un*) not only heightens the colour in terms of luminosity and saturation, but also succeeds in stripping away the element of negativity attached to the word. This is further augmented by the use of the qualifying expression, 'pleasing to the beholders' (*tasurru al-nadhirin*). One other occurrence of the term *sufrun* is especially interesting since it has been

the subject of much debate (cf. Rippin, 2001b: 106–13). In 77.30–33, a reference is made to the thick sparks of hellfire lashing out at the disbelievers: 'Depart you to a shade of three-columns neither shady nor of use against the flames. Verily it [Hell] throws sparks that look like forts as if they were yellow (*sufrun*) ropes [or camels].' The controversy centres around the word *jimalatun,* translated as either 'ropes' or 'camels'. Obviously the basis of comparison between the gigantic flames and the ropes/camels is the thickness of each. Camels are proverbial in Semitic languages and indeed in the Qur'an as in the Bible there is a reference to the proverbial expression 'until the camel (*al-jamalu*) passes through the eye of the needle' (7.40). However, one must note that these two words, although they share the same trilateral consonant *j/m/ l/* are not equivalent; it is not *jamal* but *jimala* which according to Ibn 'Abbas means 'bundled ropes' or 'fortified ropes' used in ships. This seems to be the more plausible explanation, as certainly the image of flames resembling 'yellow camels' does not coincide with the diametrical accuracy of the images used in the Qur'an. Geometrically speaking, camels cannot be made to lash out like soaring flames of fire. Camels, like elephants, are basically thick and big. They are usually measured in terms of their width, not their height. Ropes, on the other hand, are an iconic image of length; they are definitely capable of conveying the quick whipping movements of the flames, both diametrically and in terms of linear movements in time. A final reference must be made to what has erroneously been described as 'yellow wind' (Rippin, 2001b: 363) or 'sandstorm' in 30.51. Western commentators often fail to comprehend the syntactic processes of substitution and deletion operative in the Qur'an. In actual fact, the term *musfarran* here is not a postmodifier of 'wind' but of the ellipted term 'crop' (*zar'an*), which is readily recoverable from 39.21, mentioned above. The complete or undeleted version of the verse thus reads: 'And if we send a wind and they see it [their crop] turning yellow (*musfarran*), behold, they then would become disbelievers.' The pronoun is here used as a proform substituting for the deleted term *zar'an*. It is perhaps significant to note that many of these proforms and deletions can be found in explanatory translations of the Qur'an such as that by al-Hilali and Khan, where they are inserted as in-text parentheses.

The colour blue (*zurqan*) in 20.102 has been a subject of much debate, especially among translators who seem perplexed as to how to render the term: 'The day when the Trumpet is blown; that Day, We shall gather the criminals blue (*zurqan*) Murmuring among themselves: "You have tarried only ten [days]".' According to al-Qurtubi, the blue here refers to the utmost 'thirst' of the criminals which thereby makes their body turn blue. However, this plausible explanation and the specific reference to the colour blue have been ignored by most translators. Pickthall (1930), for example, translates the term *zarqan* as 'white-eyed (with terror)', obviously preferring to negate the 'blue', and even translating it in terms of its near opposite 'white' while emphasizing the psychological sense-component of the term in parenthesis. Arberry (1964), on the other hand, translates this as 'with eyes staring', totally obscuring any reference to colour while inserting the association with eyes; *zurqan* is made equivalent to a certain posture of the eyes rather than a specific eye-colour, although there does not seem to be any kind of direct or indirect association between staring and the notion of blue. Ali (1991) translates

the term as 'blear-eyed (with terror)', adding in a footnote that it denotes eyes afflicted with dimness and blindness and hence metaphorically bleary or tearful with terror. Although many translators connect it with blindness, it must be noted that the colour most often collocated with blindness in Arabic is not blue but white. Hence the reference in 12.84 to Jacob's eyes turning white and blind in grief over the loss of his son Joseph: 'And he turned away from them and said: "Alas my grief for Joseph". And his eyes turned white with the grief he was suppressing'. In 12.96 it is made even more explicit that his whitened eyes is a reference to his blindness: 'Then when the bearer of glad tidings arrived, he cast it [the shirt] over his face and he regained his sight (*fa-artada basiran*).' What is certain is that the context in which the colour blue occurs is a neutral context, i.e. there is no way of ascertaining whether blue is an aspect of the eyes (blue-eyed), of skin colour or of psychological colouring.

It seems important to mention this fact because a number of Western scholars have viewed this term as a reference to latent hostility against 'sinful blue-eyed' people in the Qur'an (cf. Rippin, 2001b: 363). As we can see, in the text itself there is no mention whatsoever of eyes, and certainly the 'criminals' in hell are not in any way designated as blue-eyed or fair of skin. Contrary to Rippin's argument, blue is not commonly associated with eyes any more than are black or brown. We should not read things into the fact that blue occurs in negative contexts in the Qur'an, nor should we see it as an indication of the cultural relevance of the colour blue in the Arabic language-system. Although it is indeed 'one of the essential colours of nature', as Rippin states, the truth is that all the colours of the spectrum are integral to nature, including black. It is quite common in all cultures, for example, to refer to the blackness of hell. Should this be taken as a racist statement against black people? All colours have a psychological sense-component and in all probability these components will be the same in all languages. In the case of *zarqan*, what is being designated is not so much a psychological state as a physical one, i.e. the criminals are visibly blue in colour, whether it is their lips or tongues or bodies, and this is symptomatic of their physical predicament.

The racist suggestion that in the Qur'an blue refers to the blue-eyed people in hell is just as implausible as the suggestion that green refers to the green-eyed people in heaven, or black to black people in general. Indeed, the bluish tint is often associated with diseases characterized by hyperaemia, haemorrhages, and swelling and sloughing of the tongue and mouth. To turn blue in the face or lips is also often suggestive of suffocation and a painful inability to breathe. On a more literal level, it could also be taken to denote a sort of congenital defect of the heart since blue is often a medical symptom of the mingling of venous and arterial blood. It is perhaps significant that turning blue in the face is a common expression denoting extreme exasperation, and this description also holds true in Arabic. Although the exact psychological connotations of the colour are deliberately left obscure in the verse, what seems to support a psychological reading of the colour is the fact that the adjacent verses concentrate on the extreme fear, confusion and exasperation of the 'criminals' as they await the judgement of God.

References and further reading

Ali, A.Y. (1991) *The Meaning of the Holy Qur'an*, Baltimore, MD: Amana Corporation.

Arberry, A. (trans.) (1964) *The Koran Interpreted*, London: Oxford University Press.

Asad, M. (trans.) (1980) *The Message of the Qur'an*, Gibraltar: Dar al-andalus.

Berlin, B. and Kay, P. (1969) *Basic Colour Terms: Their universality and evolution*, Berkeley and Los Angeles: University of California Press.

al-Hilali, M. and Khan, M.M. (trans.) (1993) *Interpretations of the Noble Qur'an in the English Language*, Riyadh: Maktaba Dar-as-salam.

Mir, M. (1987) *Dictionary of Qur'anic Terms and Concepts*: New York: Garland.

—— (1989) *Verbal Idioms of the Qur'an*, Ann Arbor, MI.

Palmer, F.R. (1976) *Semantics*, Cambridge: Cambridge University Press.

Pickthall, Marmaduke M. (trans.) (1930) *The Meaning of the Glorious Koran: An Explanatory Translation*, London: George Allen & Unwin.

Rippin, A. (2001a) 'Colours', in *EQ*, Vol. 1.

—— (2001b) *The Qur'an and its Interpretive Tradition*, Aldershot: Ashgate, 361–5.

al-Tabari (1992) *Tafsir*, 12 vols, Beirut.

See also: **camel; heaven; hell; natural world and the Qur'an**

AFNAN H. FATANI

COMPANION
see: sahiba

COMPANIONS OF THE CAVE

The Companions are young believers who found refuge from persecution in a cave. According to the Qur'an (18.9–22), when the boys asked God for mercy they were put into a sleep-like condition for some years, the exact number serving as a test of prophetic knowledge. Tradition explains that Muhammad's persecutors sought advice from rabbis regarding ways to test his knowledge. They were instructed to ask how long the Companions of the Cave had slept. Muhammad responded that he would answer the next day, but after several days it was revealed to him that only God knows the answer and that people should not say they will do something the next day without adding 'if God wills'. The story, often associated with the Christian tradition of the Seven Sleepers of Ephesus, is interpreted as a sign of Muhammad's sincerity and humility.

TAMARA SONN

CONVERSION

The term conversion stands for a total change, a change in belief, conviction or state. In general, conversion denotes 'turn around', 'transformation', 'to bring over or persuade to a particular view' and 'to change from one state to another'. In psychology and sociology, this term is used to refer to 'a change in conviction' in the social and aesthetic fields. Religious conversion, however, is defined as the process of renouncing one's own religious standing or affiliation for the sake of another religious ideal; a process which encompasses 'spiritual evolution and development', including the change of direction of one's religious beliefs and attitudes. One who changes his religion is called a convert. However, when applied to a non-Muslim who identifies himself with Islam, the term *ihtida* is used rather than conversion, and the person who commits *ihtida* is called *muhtedi*. The term *ihtida* denotes entrance to Islam whereas conversion is used in a wider sense to refer to entrance to any religion.

The Qur'anic approach

The term conversion finds two different references in the Qur'an. The first is the word *huda* (the guide), which stems from the same root as the word *hidayet* (righteous guidance, or guidance) and which means showing someone the right path and guiding him thereupon. Although the word 'guidance' (*hidayet*) is not mentioned in the Qur'an, *huda* is repeated eighty-five times. In Islamic culture the term 'guidance' is used to refer to the transition from an insincere, superficial religious lifestyle to an entirely religious path. The second reference is the word *ihtida*, which means to arrive at righteous guidance, identifying oneself with the right; this is repeated sixty times. According to the Qur'an, *ihtida* is the process by which a non-Muslim, pagan or atheist accepts Islam and re-establishes his life according to its teachings; a process of purification and subjection to the will of the guide. By extension, we can term an act of *hidayet* as a 'return to the religion'; and an act of *ihtida* as a 'change of religion'.

The Qur'an also contains other terminology associated with *ihtida*. *Dahale* (entrance) is one of these: 'And thou seest mankind entering the religion of Allah in troops' (110.2). Another is the word *gayyara*, which means 'change': 'Lo! Allah changeth not the condition of a folk until they [first] change that which is in their hearts' (13.11).

The Qur'anic perspective points to *wahy* (revelation) as the key factor underlying one's guidance. In a sense, the mind is a lamp and the revelation is a path, whereby the necessity required by the revelation and the path to it can be distinguished from each other. The Qur'an has disapproved of all endeavours that consider human mind and knowledge sufficient and thus lead to backsliding and turning away from divine revelation, that prefer a stance in materialistic knowledge to the flow of divine wisdom, and that seek to value the apparent stability of nature over a more subtle investigation.

The Qur'an argues that guidance is bestowed only by Allah, the only source of guidance: 'He who Allah leadeth, he indeed is led aright, while he whom Allah sendeth astray they indeed are losers' (7.178). 'Then Allah sendeth whom He will astray, and guideth aright whom He will. He is the Mighty, the Wise' (Ibrahim 14.4) (see also 2.120; 10.35; 17.97; 18.17). However, Allah does not force people to accept righteous guidance; rather, he expects individuals to make their own preferences through their free will (*irada*). 'Lo! We have shown him the way, whether he be grateful or disbelieving' (76.3) (see also 28.56; 47.17). Heading the list of factors conducive to one's guidance stand free will and determination. With the term *tawba* (repentance) defined in *suras* 5 and 11 of *at-Tawba* (the Chapter of Repentance), the process of guidance begins: 'But if they repent and establish worship and pay the poor due, then are they your brethren in religion' (9.11). People are invited to divine guidance by means of prophets: 'And thus have We inspired in thee [Muhammad] a Spirit of Our Command. Thou knewest not what the Scripture was, nor what the Faith. But We have made it a light whereby We guide whom We will of Our bondmen. And lo! Thou verily dost guide unto a right path' (42.52); 'Go thou unto Pharaoh Lo! He hath rebelled' (79.17). Prophets represent the ideal: 'each of them We guided ... Each one [of them] was the righteous ... Each one of them did We prefer above [Our] creatures; and We chose them and guided them unto a straight path; Those are they whom Allah guideth' (6.84–90). The ultimate situation of people in the afterworld depends on their reaction to the guidance sent. The opposite of guidance in the Holy Qur'an is *dalalet* (error), which means being led astray.

As the unique factor underlying the relation of one's guidance to Allah is divine revelation, one who does not accept the prophets and denies the principle of the Holy Message will have rejected an obligatory guidance by Allah, which means denying Allah himself. At this point there is no difference between the total rejection of all of the prophets or any single one of them, since the flow-line of the guidance of all the prophets relies upon the same truth. A single ray cannot be deconstructed then multiplied; on the contrary, the rejection of a single ray among many rays equals a total rejection of all rays.

As the Qur'an points out, the guidance bestowed upon people by Allah assumes three distinct forms:

1. *Inborn guidance*: 'And inspired it [with conscience of] what is wrong for it and [what is] right for it' (91.8). Everything has been equipped with a guidance appropriate to its inborn disposition. Reflection and being cognizant of the unknown can only be a fact that embraces inborn disposition, that does not change with eras and cities changing, and that is apparent in its essence. In that sense, *ihtida* is not the acceptance of a new religion, rather, it is a return to the old religion as the Qur'an clarifies that one is born with the dispositional religion, which is Islam. By extension, one who commits *ihtida* remembers his/her religion and returns to it. The agreement expressed in the Qur'an between Allah and people during their creation and some *ahadith* of the Prophet emphasize this very fact (*Bukhari*; *Muslim*). That is why a majority of Western converts to Islam prefer to use the term 'revert' rather than 'convert' for those who change religion.

2. *Conscious guidance*: As a conscious being, humanity needs more than dispositional guidance. Allah,

through bestowing upon man a mind to think, has made it possible for him to reflect both on himself and the outer world, thus arriving at certain conclusions as to his place and duty in the world: 'We shall show them our portents on the horizons and within themselves until it will be manifest unto them that it is the Truth' (41.53).

3. *Divine guidance*: Allah has endowed mankind through revelation with a guidance that, if followed, makes it impossible to err. The Law of Moses and the Gospel of Jesus count as sources of guidance: 'He hath revealed unto thee [Muhammad] the Scripture with truth, confirming that which was [revealed] before it and even as He revealed the Torah and the Gospel' (3.3). It is also clarified that the Qur'an provides the straightest of guidance: 'Lo! This Qur'an guideth unto that which is the straightest, and giveth tidings unto the believers who do good works that theirs will be a great reward' (17.9).

The only condition for *ihtida*, according to the Holy Qur'an, is to recite the words of the *shahada*: 'I bear witness that there is no god but Allah and that Muhammad, peace be upon him, is His servant and His Messenger.' This needs not be carried out by any ceremony or in the presence of a religious authority or institution. Yet it has come to be a tradition to recite the words of the *shahada* in the presence of at least two persons. The guided (*muhtedi*) is first expected to have a total ritual ablution (*ghusl*) and to learn the basics of the religion afterwards. He need not change his name unless it has an anti-Islamic association. It is advisable for the male convert to be circumcised.

The concept of conversion discussed in the Holy Qur'an indicates that guidance is up to Allah in order to ensure the general welfare of individuals and society, in this world and in the hereafter, and that secular solutions fall short of success in paving the way for widespread, permanent and comprehensive guidance. Besides this, it is suggested that individuals can guide themselves aright or lead themselves astray through their own free will, whereupon they will encounter divine support (*tawfiq*) or punishment according to their orientation.

The verses in the Qur'an assure us that one who believes in Allah will never live through an existential vacuum, and that each instant of life will scatter holy meanings from the truth to embrace the person.

Further reading

Brinner, W.M. (1995) 'Conversion', *The Oxford Encyclopedia of the Modern Islamic World*, Oxford: Oxford University Press, Vol. 1, 318–21.

Dudley, W.J. (1992) 'Conversion in Islam', in H. Newton Malony and S. Southard (eds) *Handbook of Religious Conversion*, Alabama, GA: Religious Education Press, 22–40.

Guénon, R. (1999) *The Crisis of the Modern World*, trans. M. Pallis and R. Nicholson, Lahore: Suhail Academy.

Kim, H.C. (2003) *Din Değiştirmenin Entelektüel Arka Planı* (The Intellectual Background of Conversion), Istanbul: Kaynak Publications.

Köse, A. (1996) *Conversion to Islam, A Study of Native British Converts,* London: Kegan Paul International.

Levtzion, N. (ed.) (1979) *Conversion to Islam*, London: Holmes & Meier.

Lofland, J. and Skonovd, N. (1981) 'Conversion Motifs', *Journal for the Scientific Study of Religion* 4: 373–85.

Mir, M. (1987) *Dictionary of Qur'anic Terms and Concepts*, New York and London: Garland Publishing Inc.

Nortbourne, L. (1999) *Religion in the Modern World*, Lahore: Suhail Academy.

Pickthall, M.M. (1981) *The Meaning of the Glorious Qur'an*, Beirut: Dar al-kitab al-lubnani.

Rambo, L.R. (1987) 'Conversion', in Mircea Eliade (ed.) *The Encyclopedia of Religion*, New York: Macmillan Publishing Company, Vol. 4: 73–9.

—— (1996) 'Conversion', in Alan Richardson and John Bowden (eds) *A New Dictionary of Christian Theology*, London: SCM Press, 123–4.

Smalley, S.S. (1996) 'Conversion', in S. Ferguson and D. Wright (eds) *New Dictionary of Theology*, Leicester: Inter-Varsity Press.

Smith, H. (1999) *Forgotten Truth, The Primordial Tradition*, Lahore: Suhail Academy.

Strachan, J. (1981) 'Conversion', in James Hastings (ed.) *Encyclopaedia of Religion and Ethics*, Edinburgh: T. & T. Clark, Vol. 4, 104–10.

See also: **ridda and the case for decriminalization of apostasy**

AHMET ALBAYRAK

COVENANT

The idea of a covenant is used in different ways in the Qur'an to describe various relationships and agreements. In many verses we read about God's ancient covenant with humanity, that in return for God's protection, help and guidance, we need to abide by his rules and accept his advice. 'And when We made a covenant with the children of Israel: You shall not serve any but Allah and [you shall do] good to your parents, and to the near of kin and to the orphans and the needy, and you shall speak to men in virtuous ways and keep up prayer and pay the poor-rate. Then you turned back except a few of you and you must turn aside' (2.83). We read: 'It is not piety, that you turn your faces to the East and to the West. True piety is this: to believe in God, and the Last Day ... to give of one's substance ... and to ransom the slave, to perform prayer, to pay alms. And they who fulfil their covenant ... and endure with fortitude' (2.177). There is also: '... but He causes not to stray, except those who forsake [the path], those who break Allah's covenant after it is ratified, and who sunder what Allah has ordered to be joined, and do mischief on earth: These cause loss to themselves' (2.27).

Part of this covenant is to accept God's messengers: 'Certainly We made a covenant with the children of Israel and We sent to them apostles; whenever there came to them an apostle with what their souls did not desire, some they called liars and some they killed' (5.70). Not surprisingly God is not impressed with this behaviour: 'O children of Adam! When messengers come to you from among you, who convey my verses, then those who take heed and amend will have neither fear nor regret' (7.35). A theme is often that the covenant with the Jews is broadened into a covenant with all mankind, especially after the Jews did not behave as they ought in terms of their original agreement with God. Obeying God is vital if there is a covenant. This covenant is established through allegiance to the Messenger, and through obedience to the teachings he brings: 'Surely those who swear allegiance to you do but swear allegiance to Allah; the hand of Allah is above their hands. Therefore whoever breaks [his faith], he breaks it only to the injury of his own soul, and whoever fulfils what he has covenanted with Allah, He will grant him a mighty reward' (48.10).

God has also made a covenant with his prophets: 'And call to mind when We took from the Prophets their covenant, and from you [Muhammad], and from Noah and Abraham, and Moses and Jesus, son of Mary, and We indeed took from them a solemn covenant' (33.7). This covenant with the prophets is explained in this verse: 'And when

Allah made a covenant through the prophets ... an apostle comes to you verifying that which is with you, you must believe in him, and you must aid him. He said: "Do you affirm and accept My compact in this?" They said: "We do affirm." He said: "Then bear witness, and I shall bear witness too. Whoever therefore turns back after this, these it is that are the transgressors'" (3.81–82). But the covenant only goes so far: 'And when his Lord tried Abraham with certain words, he fulfilled them. He said, "Surely I will make you a leader (*imam*) of men." Abraham, said, "And of my offspring?" "My covenant does not include the unjust", said He' (2.124).

See also: 'ahd; ahl al-bayt; 'ishq; mithaq

OLIVER LEAMAN

CREATION

There are two views of creation: the emanationist view represented by the Ikhwan al-Safa', and the creationist view, represented by al-Raghib al-Isfahani (d. 1060). The Qur'an is a point of departure for both these perspectives, although the emanationist view developed with the influence of the doctrine of Neoplatonic emanation. The Qur'an provides two main principles for cosmology: the principle of *tawhid*, which is that God is the One Creator of the heavens and the earth; and the high status that God accords to man in the cosmos (Jachimowicz, 1975: 143–5).

The idea of a creator of the universe was not alien to the pre-Islamic Arabs, but it had little influence on their notion of human destiny. However, the Qur'an, which recognizes that God is the source of all things in creation, changed their view of God's relation to human destiny. God is the creator of man and man is his creature. Note the potential impact of the following verse: 'That is Allah,

your Lord; there is no god but He, Creator of all things' (6.102). The Qur'an reminds us in many places that God is the creator of everything; including the heavens and earth (51.47–48), the mountains and the rivers (13.3) and all kinds of animals (24.45) (Izutsu, 1980: 1).

Creation (*khalq*) comes from the verb *khalaqa* (to create). This verb is used in the Qur'an with prepositions to indicate that beings are created out of concrete substances such as water, clay or fire; or, to indicate the mode of being out of which things are created, such as: 'We created man out of the fairest stature' (95.4). The verb is also used to express the act of creation in general. God is the first agent of natural phenomena, but this does not mean that the natural phenomena do not have their own power. Similarly, God represents the first pattern of things, and yet the world does not exclude things deriving their form from other lower forms. So it does not exclude, for example, the creation of man being made of clay (15.28–29). This verse suggests the superiority of man over creation because he has a divine spirit within him, which brings him into closer affinity to God than any other created being.

The creation *ex nihilo* is explicit in only a few verses such as the words addressed to Zacharias (19.9): 'I created you beforehand when you were nothing'. The most popular verse quoted by the exponents of the creationist theory is: 'When God decrees a thing he only has to say to it, Be! and it is' (2.117; 3.47; 19.35; 16.40; 36.82; 40.68). God is therefore the absolute commander of the universe, and because of this mastery he is able to say: 'Come hither, voluntarily or involuntarily' (41.11). The whole of creation, except for man, obeys God by an automatic volition. Hence, the Qur'an refers to the universe as Muslim because it surrenders itself to God (3.81) and glorifies him (57.1; 59.1; 61.1).

Qur'anic commentators in general state precisely that the universe was created *ex nihilo* and that the act of creation is the prerogative of God alone. Hence creation is associated with divine lordship. For many theologians creation does not only imply bringing into existence, but also the sustaining of existence, which is also a quality of God, who alone provides sustenance. However, the Qur'an also hints at the unfolding of the universe: 'Did the disbelievers not see that the heavens and the earth were one undifferentiated mass and then we unfolded them?' (21.30). The entire process of creation is said to have taken 'six days' (7.54; 10.3; 11.7; 25.59), after which God established himself on the throne (7.54; 10.3). From his throne God governs the affairs of the world; he sends commands through angels and the spirit, and they come back to him with reports (22.5; 70.4; 34.2; 57.4).

The Qur'an makes frequent use of natural phenomena, not as an end in itself, but as a means to remind man of God's power and majesty. They are signs that depict God's mercy and reminders for man to be grateful to God. 'Nature's magnitude and utility of man, as well as the stability and regularity of natural phenomena, are stressed. If you sow seeds and nurture the saplings, you can expect to reap the harvest; otherwise not … The working of natural causes is inevitable and undeniable' (Rahman, 1980: 66).

It is possible to speak of a creation *ex nihilo* which is primordial and universal, then of succeeding creations which, during various stages of their development, give life to particular beings. The Qur'an actually refers to the first beginning of creation: 'As we originated the primordial creation, so We will repeat it' (21.104; 10.4, 34). This refers to the visible world in its entirety and to the second creation in the hereafter. Zamakhshari, followed by Jalalayn, explains that the primordial creation is the fact of giving existence to the world by making it emerge from a void. This world will come to an end (10. 44), but the second creation, which is the life to come, has no end. Man will abide in it eternally.

Generally, philosophers used the term 'creation' in a sense of *ab aeterno*. Proclus formulated this concept, which was revived by Ibn Sina and al-Farabi, refuted by al-Ghazali (in the *Ihya'*) and defended by Ibn Rushd. According to Ibn Sina, the prime innovator is an intellectual substance which is innovated in the true sense of the word, and from it (this intermediary), God creates another intellectual substance. Here we have the theory of emanation (*fayd*) of the intellect, which is derived from al-Farabi, and the idea that all things of this world are but mere manifestations of God.

The emanationist view

Philosophical arguments in opposition to the creation *ex nihilo* doctrine are either Aristotelian or Neoplatonic, and the Neoplatonic doctrine of creation as exemplified by the Ikhwan al-Safa' is particularly interesting. Plotinus (d. 270) developed a Neoplatonic cosmology, relating God to man in a way that was meaningful to later Islamic philosophers. It contained three elements: Aristotle's astronomy and metaphysics; the aspiration of the material towards the non-material; and mystical experience. The universe originates from an absolute transcendent One, and from it emanates the Universal Intellect, and from the latter emanates the Universal Soul. The human soul is akin to the Universal Soul, and man must purify it in order to apprehend the intelligibles and to return to God. This is how we honour and worship

God. Islamic philosophers and Sufis have adapted the Neoplatonic cosmology.

The Ikhwan al-Safa' adopted the Neoplatonic system of emanation, which is based on four entities: the One; the Spirit; the Soul; and the material world. Man stands at the top of the terrestrial realm. Below are the minerals that yield to plants, which in turn support animals, until man as a microcosm is produced, containing both the spiritual and physical dimensions of the cosmos. When the human soul is liberated from materiality, it is able to return to God, the creator of both it and the cosmos (Nasr, 1964: 44f.)

God is detached from the creation, but through his immanence, he can bridge the gap with creation. When man transcends his material nature, he is able to come close to God and overcome the separation between him and God. The creation begins with the Creator, descends through the multiple states of Being and ends with the terrestrial creatures whose final link is man. It follows this sequence: Creator, Intellect, Soul, Matter, Nature, Body, the Sphere, the Elements, and the Beings of this world (Nasr, 1964: 51f.). God first created the Universal Intellect; from it emerged the Universal Soul (*al-nafs al-kulliya*), and from the latter, Matter emerged. Man is the last in the 'Chain of Being' (Nasr, 1964: 52).

The creationist view

Although al-Isfahani was influenced by the Ikhwan in certain respects, his view of the creation is more in keeping with the literal, traditional understanding of the Qur'an. Al-Isfahani conceived of God as a personal being, and not one who is detached from the creation and connected to it only by a series of intermediaries. For al-Isfahani, God is transcendent. It was God who created the universe out of nothing. He did, however, use the natural elements of clay and fire to create

beings and their functions (Mohamed, 2000; al-Isfahani, 1988: 105).

There is the higher, celestial, part of creation, and the lower, terrestrial part. The celestial, starting with the Universal Intellect, was created first. The rest of creation, including humans, animals and plants, followed later. Adam went through seven grades: he was created first from dust (3.5); then from clay (6.2) (a combination of dust and water); then from mud moulded into shape (which is clay altered slightly by air); then from sticky clay (suggesting the clay's readiness to receive form); then from sounding clay (indicating dryness and the emission of sound); and finally from mud moulded into shape (indicating a kind of pottery made with fire from which emerged man's satanic power). Thus God said: 'He created man from hard clay, like bricks. And He created the *jinn* from tongues of fire' (55.14, 15). God then perfected man by blowing his own spirit into him: 'When your Lord said to the angels: "I am going to create a mortal out of clay, when I have fashioned him and breathed into him of My Spirit, fall prostrate before him"' (38. 71–72). Here we note the perfection of Adam through the Divine Spirit, and also through knowledge of the names (2.31) (al-Isfahani, 1988: 73).

Like Adam, man too has been created in seven stages: 'We have created man from an extract of clay; then We placed him as a sperm in a secure place; then we created out of the sperm a clot; then made from the clot a lump of flesh, then made the lump of flesh into bones, and then covered the bones with flesh; then fashioned him into another creation' (23.12–14). The expression 'another creation' suggests that God has created a special being with the faculties of intellect, thought and speech (al-Isfahani, 1988: 74).

Thus, by a process of seven stages before birth, the material and spiritual elements of a human being are shaped. Although the order of creation is Neoplatonic, each aspect of creation was a direct result of God's creative power, and not a result of certain intermediaries. The Ikhwan adopted the Neoplatonic scheme of creation, and al-Isfahani, although fascinated by the emanationist theory, adopted instead the traditional view of creation *ex nihilo*.

To conclude, the Qur'an is clear about the creation of man out of nothing, but the philosophers found it too simplistic to adopt the doctrine of creation *ex nihilo*. So the Neoplatonic Muslim scholars Islamized the doctrine of emanation to introduce an alternative explanation for creation. Al-Isfahani adopted two main elements of emanationist creation: first, the concept of man as a microcosm of the universe, and second, the sequence of creation, whereby man was created last after the minerals, plants and animals. However, Al-Isfahani viewed the cosmos as having been created by a personal God who is transcendent.

Whether it is the creationist view as conceived by al-Isfahani or the emanationist view as conceived by the Ikhwan, they both share the belief that man is a microcosm of the universe. Man and nature are therefore intimately connected. Thus, both al-Isfahani and the Ikhwan share cosmological views that encourage human respect for nature.

References and further reading

Farukh, O. (1963) 'Ikhwan al-Safa', in M.M. Sharif (ed.) *History of Muslim Philosophy*, Wiesbaden: Otto Harrassowitz.

al-Isfahani, R. (1988) *Tafsil al-nash'atayn wa tahsil al-sa'adatayn*, ed. A. Najjar, Beirut.

Izutsu, T. (1980) *God and Man in the Koran*, Tokyo: Ayer Co.

Jachimowicz, E. (1975) 'Islamic Cosmology', in C. Blacker and M. Loewe (eds) *Ancient Cosmologies*, London: George Allen & Unwin, 143–77.

Leaman, O. (2002) *An Introduction to Classical Islamic Philosophy*, Cambridge: Cambridge University Press.

Mohamed, Y. (2000) 'The Cosmology of Ikhwan al-Safa' and Miskawayh and Isfahani', *Islamic Studies* 39, 4: 657–79.

—— (2001)'The Classical Islamic Concept of Man as a "Small World"', *AFKAR Journal of 'Aqidah and Islamic Thought* 2: 87–106.

—— (2004) *The Path to Virtue*, Kuala Lumpur: ISTAC.

Nasr, S.H. (1964) *Islamic Cosmological Doctrines*, Cambridge: Thames & Hudson.

Rahman, F. (1980) *Major Themes of the Qur'an*, Minneapolis: Bibliotheca Islamica.

See also: **'alaq; natural world and the Qur'an; science and the Qur'an**

YASIEN MOHAMED

CYBERSPACE AND THE QUR'AN

Entering the word 'Qur'an' in an Internet search engine will quickly reveal the extent of the presence of the Qur'an in cyberspace. The text is readily accessible both in Arabic and in many other languages (with numerous different translated versions frequently available in any given language); it is available for downloading and it can be searched in straightforward manner (i.e. word-by-word) and in more complex ways (with Boolean algebra, for example). The recited Qur'an may be found at a number of sites with many different voices and styles represented. Manuscripts, ancient and contemporary, are displayed as textual witnesses, as illustrations of Islamic art and as museum items of heritage. Discussions of the Qur'an abound, as do classical works of commentary (*tafsir* becoming increasingly available in the original Arabic and, in a few cases, in translation).

The ever-changing content of the World Wide Web creates difficulties in providing stable referencing to available resources. Established meta-sites such as Alan Godlas' 'Resources for studying

Islam' (available at: http://www.uga.edu/islam/), are probably the best places to start a search for Qur'anic material. Highlighting a few sites in this article, however, does provide some sense of the types of material currently available. The Arabic text of the Qur'an is available for download in fully vowelled text format at www.al-kawthar.com/kotob/Qur'an.zip. A UNICODE version can be found at http://www.sacred-texts.com/isl/uq/index.htm. Certain limitations with regard to these texts must be recognized; even the UNICODE format does not allow for a full representation of all the subtleties of the Arabic text as it was printed in what has become the 'standard edition' (Cairo, 1923; and in its second edition of 1956). The text is also available for direct consultation on the web in a variety of graphic formats, partially to overcome the above-mentioned limitations which are imposed by the readily available synthetic typefaces (although even this is not always fully successful); the implication of the employment of these graphic formats is that users are limited in the ways in which they may use the text in other computer applications. Useful sites that bring together the text (in graphic form), translations and recitations are the Egyptian http://Qur'an.al-islam.com/ and the American http://www.islamicity.com/mosque/Qur'an/. A number of classical and modern commentaries in Arabic are available in fully searchable form at http://www.altafsir.org/Home.asp.

Currently, there are significant limits to searching the Arabic text of the Qur'an as it is found on the web. Searching by Arabic root is possible at http://www.altafsir.com/Qur'anSearch.asp and these results allow for successful 'cut-and-paste' operations from one's web browser into other applications. Far more sophisticated but presently only available in an idiosyncratic transliterated form of

Arabic is the morphologically tagged version of the text developed at the University of Haifa (available at http://cl.haifa.ac.il/projects/Qur'an/). This text and application allow for searching the Qur'an for specific grammatical parts of speech and other grammatical phenomena and display the power and unique abilities of computerized versions of texts which may well be commonplace in the future.

It has already become a cliché among scholars to remark on the impact this move of the Qur'an into its new cyber-existence is having upon Muslims in general and, potentially, upon Islam itself. At the current time, because the process is still underway, no definitive study of the phenomenon is truly possible although a few specific aspects may be highlighted to illustrate future avenues of investigation.

The impact of the cyber Qur'an upon access to knowledge and all the resulting changes which may come about because of shifting social, political and intellectual power structures have already become apparent at least in legal fields, where the invocation of the Qur'an does, of course, play a central role. The notion of a '*fatwa* on-line' means that the influence of a jurist can extend far beyond the geographically bound areas previously experienced by Muslims in their search for answers to day-to-day questions that arise in a life lived in an Islam-conscious fashion. Further, the theoretical accessibility of the web to anyone (restricted primarily by economic resources) has resulted in a shifting composition of those who provide legal opinions on subjects. The anonymity of the web means that anyone may assert his (or her, for gender, too, is hidden) qualifications as a *mufti* and the appropriate citation of sources is no longer limited to those who have undergone a traditional education in the religious sciences or even those who have access to a physical library of books. While it must be admitted that authority is frequently still being asserted through the invocation of sources from the past and that this very fact signifies a substantial level of learning (the classical works of law or Qur'anic commentary are not easier to understand simply because they are available on the web), it is clear that the composition of the scholarly classes among Muslims is being altered.

An effect upon the recitation of the Qur'an may also be observed. The process of putting recitations on record and then cassette has been going on for almost a century and the controversies which this practice initially engendered appear to have subsided fully. It is thus the internationalization of certain recitations that is primarily being enhanced by their presence on the web. However, a development which might be anticipated may be conceived in relation to the readings (qira'at), the web possessing the potential both to make variant traditions within recitation more widely known, with the resultant increased realization of the diversity of tradition in Islam, and a greater certainty of the survival of the various traditions of reading and recitation by facilitating their distribution through the Internet.

Some observers have commented upon the increasing sense of the commodification of the Qur'an under the impact of technology. On the web one now finds the Qur'an 'alongside' (in a digital sense) the less refined aspects of human behaviour. This might be argued to be true of a library as well, but the uncontrolled nature of the cyber context does change its dimensions. With the Qur'an available to anyone, for free, open to whatever changes it might be subjected to with very little effort – and with an awareness of that context being felt by Muslims themselves – the sanctity of the text and the emotions which that evokes are being subjected to subtle but substantial change. The impact on the status of the Qur'an through its manifestation in an electronic form is still being absorbed by Muslims, with questions regarding the need for purity in interacting with a digital Qur'an and the problem of the impermanence of the image of the text when it displays on a screen being grappled with by those whose frame of reference remains the memorized and recited text. Online fatwas often try to address such questions. For example, among the rulings provided at Islamicity.com, special attention is paid to whether or not one must be in a ritually pure state when reading the Qur'an on the Internet (or, for that matter, from a CD); the answer provided is that it is not required – because this is not the same as a tangible, physical text – but that it is desirable to maintain purity while interacting with the text regardless of the form in which it is presented. Encountering the recited Qur'an by hearing it play as a background track at a website also raises questions; this practice of web design was determined objectionable because those encountering the recited Qur'an in such a context would not necessarily pay appropriate attention to the recitation given that the purpose of their visit to the website would presumably be to another end.

There is no doubt as well that academic research into the Qur'an and its place in Muslim society will be altered and, potentially, enhanced by the emergence of the cyber Qur'an. For example, the previously mentioned website, altafsir.com, sponsored by Al al-Bayt Foundation for Islamic Thought in Jordan (a foundation established in 1980 by the late King Hussein), currently includes the Arabic text for thirty-six books of exegesis, including sixteen Sunni and four Sufi texts, plus ulum al-tafsir texts specializing in variant readings, grammar, law, abrogation and occasion of revelation. All are indexed by verse of the Qur'an making access ready and easy. Scholars around the world no longer need such an extensive library of these reference works on their shelves.

The most significant aspect of the electronic versions of these texts is that they are fully searchable electronically. Given that it is not always predictable where a Qur'anic word or idea may be treated within a work of exegesis, having a full text which is searchable for individual words suggests a major transformation in investigative methods on every level. It is here that we witness in this use of technology what has already been recognized as fundamental transformation in global terms but it still needs to be remarked upon within this context: a wholesale change in access to knowledge that alters fundamental aspects of exegetical procedure, well beyond issues related to scholarly investigations. One of the presuppositions of the entire method of classical Muslim exegesis is the cumulative nature of the enterprise and how the person involved within the process needs to be immersed not just in the Qur'an itself but in the world of *tafsir* literature, in grammar, in lexicography, and so forth. The authority of one's pronouncements on meaning is intimately tied to one's ability to be able to cite cross-references, authorities, information, rules and opinion. Such abilities demand training, dedication, intelligence and acumen. This is what electronic access and searchability truly transform.

Now, of course, because the material is available electronically, and because one does not have to have all the material memorized, does not make the products of exegetical work easier to understand, or immediately accessible in an intellectual manner, or even appealing to many people. But it does have the potential to result in a radical transformation of the notion of exegesis, one comparable to,

and perhaps even a continuation of, the tendency which commenced with Ibn Kathir in the eight/fourteenth century and which aimed to make exegesis authoritative on an entirely different basis than it has been, previously. Authority would reside not in grammar, but in the words of the Prophet. The contemporary instant access to a vast quantity of material may result in an increased tendency to distil information into monovalent readings of the Qur'anic text, relying on the accessibility of the resources lying behind those readings to preserve the diversity. On the other hand, the net result may well be an increased emphasis on the diversity of Muslim opinion about the meaning of the Qur'an through studies that bring together all the many sources which are now so much more easily accessible. Such transformations in attitude are taking place in the Muslim world but the final outcome is far from clear.

As is well known, the World Wide Web is also an extremely active venue for modern polemics. Sites such as 'Islamic Awareness' and 'Answering Islam' abound with tracts on the Qur'an from the Muslim and Christian perspectives respectively. These are resources to which the unwary are drawn and to which the convinced contribute. The very sophistication of such sites is both their appeal and their danger, in their glossing over of critical questions while asserting the veracity of what they claim on the authority of established academic scholarship. The web has also fostered intra-Muslim polemic, with Iranian websites being very active in providing Ithna Ashari Imami interpretations of the Qur'an and Saudi sites promoting a conservative Salafi view. The group know as 'The Submitters', based in the USA and following notions promulgated by Rashad Khalifa in relation to the Qur'an (especially the role of the number 19), have garnered much greater attention as a result of their presence on the web than would otherwise have been the case. The Internet can thus be a place for the creation of a community of like minds and at the same time a place for the aggravation of contemporary contention, strife and disagreement.

Further reading

Bunt, G. (2003) *Islam in the Digital Age: E-jihad, online fatwas and cyber Islamic environments*, London: Pluto Press.

Dror, J., Shaharabani, D., Talmon, R. and Wintner, S. (forthcoming) 'Morphological Analysis of the Qur'an', *Literary and Linguistic Computing* 19; preprint available online at http://cs.haifa.ac.il/shuly/publications/Qur'an.pdf.

Rippin, A. (1999–2000) 'The Study of Tafsir in the 21st century: E-texts and their scholarly use', *MELA Notes: The Journal of the Middle East Librarians Association* 69–70: 1–13; available online at http://www.lib.umich.edu/area/Near.East/MELANotes6970/tafsir.html.

ANDREW RIPPIN

D

DAʿA

Daʿa is the root of a verb meaning to call up, ask for, invoke or pray. *Daʿa* also means to invite. In the Qur'an, *daʿa* often means to spread the revelation or supplicate. In the Qur'an are many commendations for the prophets and the believers to make *duʿa* or supplication to God, 'Invoke your Lord with humility and in secret. He likes not the aggressors' (7.55); and in another verse describing the attributes of Allah: 'And all the most beautiful names belong to God, so call on Him by them' (7.180).

The Qur'an describes the *daʿwa* or the call of disbelievers as a call to hell and the way of the Prophet as a call to salvation.

RAFIK BERJAK

DAJJAL

A prominent figure in Islamic eschatology is the Dajjal, the Anti-christ who is going to appear at the end of time and sow confusion among the ranks of the believers. It certainly is true that a lot of the language about the Mahdi and Jesus, and their collaboration against the Dajjal, seems to suggest that this is more along the lines of a miraculous intervention by God than anything else. On the other hand, it is an interesting fact that the Dajjal does not himself figure in the Qur'an, and one might ask the question why. He is much referred to in the *hadith* literature, and here we learn that he has one eye, is very powerful, Jewish, will not successfully invade Mecca and Medina since they are guarded by angels, and that his campaign will initially be very successful, leading many to believe that he has right on his side.

The Dajjal is perhaps referred to in the *aya*: 'The day that certain of the signs of your Lord occur, no good will it do to anyone to believe in them then, if it was not believed before and if righteousness was not earned through faith' (6.158). The participation of Jesus is hinted at in: 'They said, "We killed Christ Jesus the son of Mary, the Apostle of

164

Allah," but they did not kill him or crucify him, but it was made to appear to them like that, and those who argue about it are full of doubts, with no knowledge, but only conjecture, for they certainly did not kill him. No, God raised him up to himself; and God is exalted in power, wise. The People of the Book must believe in him before his death, and on the Day of Judgement he will witness against them' (4.157–159).

The expression 'before his death' (*qabla mawtihi*) refers to Jesus; i.e. he will descend and the People of the Book who differed concerning him will believe in him. The Christians claimed that he was divine, while the Jews tried to kill him and claimed he was the result of an adulterous relationship. When Jesus descends before the Day of Judgement, he will correct all these differences and lies. The Dajjal is not directly mentioned in the Qur'an, perhaps because he is only a human being and is therefore beneath contempt. However, Pharaoh and his false claims 'I am your Lord, Most High' (79.24) and 'O Chiefs! No god do I know for you but myself' (28.38) are quoted in the Qur'an, and he is hardly someone to be admired. The important difference is that Pharoah and his misdeeds are in the past, while the Dajjal is in the future, and God is confident that true Muslims will have learned enough from the past and from their faith not to be misled by the Dajjal.

The interesting feature of the Dajjal account is that the various *ahadith* are written in such a way as to make acceptance of the Dajjal in a positive light by the *umma* (community) very plausible. The Dajjal is successful, he revives the dead, he is very powerful, he leads a huge army, and so his claim to be the representative of the divine has some strength to it. Rather like the evidence of the world around us, because we are material beings we can expect from our experience that when we die we just disintegrate physically and that is the end of us. Rather like the apparent crucifixion of Jesus, the evidence suggests to someone who does not know otherwise that Jesus was killed. But why is the implication that if one believed this, then came to change one's belief when Jesus eventually appeared in the company of the Mahdi, one would not earn merit for such a change of mind? It is because whatever the evidence of Jesus' death, perhaps one should have concluded that God would never allow one of his prophets to die in that way, despite the apparent evidence, and so that apparent evidence should have been disregarded. Similarly, with regard to belief in the afterlife, if we came to such a belief only when we experience it, then we have rejected all the teachings of the prophets and the Qur'an. Again, with the arrival of the Dajjal, he provides evidence of his divine role and some superficial success in his mission, and yet it is incumbent on the Muslim to see the evidence in a different way, as a test. He knows this first because of the warnings about the Dajjal in the *ahadith*, but more importantly because what the Dajjal does is clearly against Islam. The arrival of Jesus to fight on the side of the Mahdi and indeed to pray with the Mahdi clinches the argument. Note here that it is up to the individual believer to adopt the appropriate intellectual and moral strategy; this is not something that miraculously descends from heaven. To be sure, he has the support of the Qur'an and the other Islamic texts and authorities, but it is for the believer to make his own decisions on how he understands those texts and how he is prepared to live.

Further reading

Leaman, O. (2004) 'Imam Mahdi, Materialism and the End of Time', in *Imam Mahdi,*

Justice and Globalization, London: Institute of Islamic Studies, 203–17.

See also: **ahl al-kitab**; **eschatology**; '**Isa**

OLIVER LEAMAN

DAR

Dar and its different forms are used in the Qur'an fifty-five times. *Dara* is a root verb that signifies to go round, revolve or circulate. *Dar* is a noun meaning a large house, especially one with a court. *Dar* can be a mansion or a house comprising several sets of apartments and a court or it can mean any sort of house. The plural form, *deyar*, means homes, but it also means homeland. In Arabic literature, the word occurs frequently, particularly in pre-Islamic poetry. The ancient Arabs, especially the Bedouins, lived as tribes, scattered over the vast desert of Arabia. Their continuous search for water and pasture forced on them a nomadic lifestyle and they had to keep on moving from place to place. The youth of different tribes who lived near each other would have romantic relationships but the continuous movement of the tribes would severely disturb those relationships. The moving tribe carries with it their young boys and girls, who may have fallen in love with another youth from the other tribe. The lovers would pass by the *deyar al-mahbub* (the homes of the beloved ones) and with tears they brought back the bright memories of the beautiful past. *Al-atlal* (the ruins of the abandoned homes of the bygone tribes) gives an atmosphere of melancholy in Arabic literature. It became a popular nostalgic theme in the pre-Islamic *qasida*, the poem. It was an established tradition in classical Arabic poetry to begin the poem with a longing – *muqed-dima talalliya* or Introduction of the Homes' Ruins.

The pre-Islamic poet Imru al-Qays began his popular *mu'alaqa* or poem by saying to his two friends when they approached his lover's abandoned home: 'stop, you two, so we can cry for the memory of a lover and a home'.

Dar in the Qur'an has many different uses. The earth is also called a *dar*. *Dar al-fana* or the abode of the finite signifies this earthly life. Since this life on earth is going to end in destruction, it is the abode of extinction. By contrast, the world after death and resurrection is *dar al-baqa* or the abode of everlastingness.

In the Qur'an the hereafter is also described as *dar al-qarar*, meaning the abode of settlement or stability or stable home: 'O my people! Truly, this life of the world is nothing but a quick passing enjoyment, and verily the Hereafter that is the home that will remain forever' (40.39).

The hereafter is also called *al-dar al-akhira*. It is the eternal home for both believers and disbelievers. The disbelievers will be forced to dwell in hellfire: 'That is the recompense of the enemies of Allah; the Fire. Therein will be for them the eternal home' (41.28). However, for the believers or righteous people the hereafter is *dar al-salam*, the abode of peace, or the freedom from evil: 'For them will be the home of peace with their Lord. And He will be their protector because of what they used to do' (6.127). The dwellers of paradise will enjoy everlasting happy life. 'Who, out of His Grace, has lodged us in home that will last forever, where toil will touch us not nor weariness will touch us' (35.35).

Dar al-Islam is the country or countries governed by Muslims, i.e. those countries in which the constitution is based on Islamic law and applied by an Islamic government. The opposite of *dar al-Islam* is the Abode of War or *dar al-harb*. *Dar al-harb* means the country of war and refers to the country or countries of the unbelievers or the polytheists with whom the Muslims have conflicts. The *shari'a* (Islamic law) has established different sets of laws and codes that apply to Muslims and non-Muslims in either state.

Dar al-hijra (Hegira) signifies the place of emigration and is applied to Medina, the city of the Prophet. The Prophet Muhammad was born and raised in Mecca. He lived in his hometown for fifty-three years. He spent the last thirteen years calling on its citizens to believe in his message and to switch from polytheism to Islam. The Meccans saw the new religion as a threat to their political privileges and economic benefits. They fiercely and vehemently rejected the call of the Prophet and they fought him for all that period. He was afterwards ordered by Allah to emigrate and he left secretly for Yathrib, which was renamed after his arrival 'the Medina of the *rasul'*, meaning the City of the Messenger. Medina became *dar al-hijra* or the abode of migration. Those who wanted to embrace Islam were obliged to immigrate to Medina and meet the Prophet and announce their acceptance of Islam. After the triumph of Islam in Arabia and the opening of Mecca by the Prophet the status of *dar al-hijra* was eradicated. During his stay in Medina, the Prophet was permitted by God to fight the pagans of Mecca due to their aggressive persecution of him and his followers: 'Those who have been expelled from their homes unjustly only because they said: Our Lord is Allah' (22.40). Furthermore the Qur'an has mentioned that Allah made a covenant with the Children of Israel with the comment: 'Shed not the blood of your [people], nor turn out your own people from their dwellings' (2.84).

Dayyar means inhabitant. When Noah was rejected by his community he asked God to annihilate all the disbelievers: 'O my Lord! Do not leave of the unbelievers, a single inhabitant' (71.26).

RAFIK BERJAK

DARAJA

Daraja means degree or rank, referring to one being taking precedence over another. God has the highest degree, but otherwise this is a word with relative rather than absolute indication of position. So *daraja* refers to relative status in implicit comparisons with others, named or unnamed. It requires a second entity with which the first is compared, whether this is a select group of believers being compared to each other, to believers, to non-believers or to God. The Qur'an refers to God bestowing a higher rank to some than others, even among the messengers. God's favor is bestowed as he wills. In other usages the emphasis is upon certain believers receiving higher ranks (pl. *darajat*) as a result of their actions. Although the commentators attempted to pin down specific degrees, only the Prophet's wives were promised a specific increase that would double the rewards. From the way the verses are cast, the degree appears to have more meaning to God than to humans, or to put it another way, God knows what *daraja* means while humans have only an incomplete idea.

Darajat appears in the Qur'an twice in the verbal form and four times in the singular and fourteen times in the plural as a noun, according to 'Abd al-Baqi's concordance. Although the plural form, 'degrees', is the most commonly used form, the most noted usage is at 2.228: 'Men have a degree over women'. *Daraja* appears in both Meccan and Medinan *suras* in the plural form and in the singular only in Medinan *suras*.

In the tenth form (*istadaraja*) it appears twice as the future tense, *sanastadrijuhum*, with the attached pronominal object 'them', meaning 'we will lead them gradually (or step by step) into ruin' (7.182 and 68.44). Both these occurrences are Meccan. With the exception of 2.228, the degrees (*darajat*) refer to God having status over humans or humans being given ranks by God, or humans ranking themselves by their actions.

The degree or rank frequently refers to a higher reward to be given in heaven. Although the rank is stated to be higher (4.96; 3.163), the amount of increase is not given. Thus the degree of superiority is not specified in the way that the Prophet's wives are promised double reward and punishment (33.30–31).

The most frequently discussed verse containing the word *daraja* is verse 228 of 'The Cow', sometimes known as the 'Degree Verse'. It is frequently translated as, 'Men have a degree over women'. This remark comes at the end of a verse discussing the waiting period of divorced wives, during which time they discover whether or not they are pregnant. What the degree is and which women men have it above is widely disputed. The 'Degree Verse', the 'Beating Verse' (4.34), the 'Polygyny Verse' (4.3) and the unequal validity of men's and women's witnessing (2.282) outline the main areas that feminist interpreters of the Qur'an consider problematic. Modern commentators, such as Sayyid Qutb, have ignored the 'Degree Verse' altogether in their discussions of the role of the sexes, preferring to discuss appropriate gender roles in other places. Although modern commentary generally limits the degree of superiority to financial considerations with regard to wives, other commentators have considered it a sweeping affirmation of the status of men over women in the public sphere, particularly combined with the *hadith* that no enterprise will succeed where women lead.

In his commentary on 2.228, Ibn al-'Arabi first states that men and women are equal in respect to their humanity. He says the degree men have over women is accidental, not essential. He combines this verse with the idea of women's intrinsic earthly inferiority, based on Eve's creation from Adam's rib. In his remarks the second created being is lower in creation because it is second and therefore women are lower in intellect than men. However, the rib creation story is not Qur'anic; it is found in Islam in the *hadith*.

Another idea commonly found in the verses alongside *darajat* is that those who struggle and fight to advance God's way (*sabil*) will be given higher ranks (*darajat*) than those who sit idly at home (4.96). According to al-Tabari, some of the commentators say the degree is a doubling of the believers' reward (al-Tabari, 1954–57, on 5.232). Others specifically give one degree for each: accepting Islam; going on the *hijra* (flight); participating in *jihad*; and killing in the *jihad*. In this usage *jihad* must be the war to spread Islam. Additionally, God gives higher degrees as he wills: for example, in the story of Joseph and his brothers (12.76), Joseph is an example of a favoured servant whose status God raises. According to al-Tabari, the degree may refer to raising one over others, in this world; it is a degree of knowledge (al-Tabari, 1954–57, on 13.26). God favours some over others. In the hereafter there will be different ranks. Parallel to the idea that God gives ranks as he wills, there is the idea that humans are responsible for their own outcomes, as they will receive ranks based on their deeds (6.132; 46.19). There is also the promise that whoever does good actions will be rewarded in the hereafter with high ranks (20.75). This leads to the question of which takes precedence – God giving ranks to whom he will (predestination and God's power) or the responsibility of believers for their own actions (free will and God's justice). Thus the *darajat* verses give leverage to arguments for both predestination and free will.

Rafi'u al-darajati, sublime of ranks, is used as a description for God (40.15). One of the interesting points of *daraja* is that it is a word implying comparison, whether stated or not. The previously mentioned epithet for God implies humans are below God and God is above everything. In fact a commentator on another verse (6.132) adds that such ranks apply to *jinn* as well as humans (Qurtubi, 1980–, on 7.87).

In conclusion, the 'Degree Verse' can be interpreted as a factual statement of life in Muhammad's day. That is, men must support women during their waiting period, as women had no means of financial support; men have a degree over them in terms of being able to provide for themselves.

References and further reading

Ibn al-'Arabi (1989) *Rahman min al-rahman: fi tafsir wa-isharat al-Qur'an*, 4 vols, Damascus: Mahmud Mahmud al-Ghurab.
Qurtubi, Muhammad Ahmad (1980) *al-Jamili-ahkam al-Qur'an*, 20 vols, Beirut: Dar al-kutub al-'arabi.
Stowasser, Barbara (1994) *Women in the Qur'an: Traditions, and Interpretation*, New York: Oxford University Press.
al-Tabari (1954–57) *Jamial-bayan 'an ta'wil ay al-Qur'an*, 2nd edn, 30 vols in 12, Misr: Mustafa al-babi al-halabi.

See also: 'Isa; money; *nisa*

KIKI KENNEDY-DAY

DAVID

see: Dawud / Da'ud

DAWUD / DA'UD

Prophet and second king of the Israelites, mentioned by name sixteen times in the Qur'an. According to 2.251, it was David who killed the giant Goliath (Jalut) and received kingship and prophethood from God. Muslim exegetes add considerable detail to the accounts of David's life in the Qur'an, most of it in agreement with the account found in the Bible and in Jewish and Christian tradition.

The Qur'an and Muslim exegetes attribute to David a number of wonders and special abilities. 21.80 and 34.10–11 refer to David's special abilities with the making of armour. It is said that David was the first person to make chain mail and that God made the iron soft for David so that he could work it without tools or heating it. 21.79 and 38.17 state that God made the mountains subservient to David, that they sang praises along with the birds. The musical abilities of David are also stressed in Muslim tradition: Muslim tradition relates that when David sang, animals would gather around and listen to him so mesmerized that they would die of thirst and hunger (see 38.19). Some claim that his voice was unique, and that he was able to recite the whole Qur'an in the time it took to saddle his horse.

David is said to have had great piety. The 'strength' given to him by God (see 38.17) is interpreted to be a reference to the strength of David's adherence to God and religion. Muslim exegetes report that David used to stand vigil all night and fast every other day. A saying of the Prophet Muhammad states that the prayer most beloved to God is that of David.

As a king, David is said to have had a large number of wives, one of whom is identified by Muslim exegetes as Uriah, the mother of Solomon. According to some exegetes, David had a hundred wives, but his son Solomon had even more. Like Solomon, David is attributed with great judgment. 38.21–26 relates a case that David judged with wisdom, and exegetes relate that God gave David a special chain in Jerusalem by which people could tell the veracity of a person's claims against another.

According to 17.55, God revealed the Psalms (Zubur) to David. 4.163 also states that God gave the Psalms to David but a variant reading has 'Qur'an' instead of 'Psalms' and the identity of the two books is discussed by some Qur'anic Studies scholars.

The death of David is not mentioned in the Qur'an but his funeral is described in elaborate terms by Muslim exegetes. It is said that his funeral was attended by many thousands of people who were shaded from the sun by flocks of birds summoned by Solomon.

Further reading

Jensen, P. (1922) 'Das Leben Muhammeds und die David-Sage', *Der Islam* 12: 84–97.

Johns, A.H. (1989) 'David and Bathsheba: A case study in the exegesis of Qur'anic story-telling', in C. Poché (ed.) David and the Ambiguity of the Mizmar according to Arab Sources, Melanges de l'institut dominicain des etudes orientales, 19: 225–66.

Lindsay, J.E. (1995) "Ali ibn 'Asakir as a Preserver of Qisas al-Anbiya': The Case of David b. Jesse', in *Studie Islamica*. 82.2: 45–82.

See also: **Jerusalem**

BRANNON WHEELER

DAY

see: **yawm**

DEATH

The Qur'an is insistent throughout that death is not the absolute end of human beings. This was one of the initial issues between the Prophet and the Meccans, many of whom were materialists and did not believe in any sort of life after death. The Qur'an often suggests that the purpose of our existence is the worship of God: 'And I [Allah] created the *jinn* and men so that they should worship Me [alone]' (51.56). This world is a testing ground to determine whether we will end up in paradise or hell. It is to our advantage to have our eventual end in mind at all times. After all, death occurs to everyone: 'Every soul will taste death' (3.185). Most people do not think about it, however: 'Certainly, they see it as distant, but We see it as near' (70.6–7). 'He who has created death and life, that He may test you, which of you is best in deed' (67.21). The *hadith* literature is replete with comparisons of this world with the next one, and the claim is that we should not regard this world as very significant since in the long run we are going to be either in paradise or hell for the rest of time.

'O you who believe! What is the matter with you, that when you are asked to march forth in the cause of Allah you cling heavily to the earth? Are you pleased with the life of this world rather than the Hereafter?' (9.38). 'But truly the home of the Hereafter is the actual life, if only they knew' (29.64). We have reminder upon reminder, about how nations before us were destroyed and a common sickness which they were plagued with was 'love of this world'. Regarding the Jews, who claim to be the best of all people and inheritors of the Promised Land, God says: 'And verily you will find them the greediest of mankind and [even greedier] than those who do not believe in resurrection [i.e. the idolaters]. Every one of them wishes that he could be given a life of a thousand years. But the grant of such life will not save him even a little from [due] punishment. And Allah sees everything that they do' (2.96). The Book recommends: 'And die not except in a state of Islam' (3.102), and 'of those that do not die during their sleep. He retains those souls for which He has ordained death, whereas He releases the rest for an appointed term' (39.42). Those who are evil are told: 'Deliver up your souls. This day you will be awarded a degrading punishment' (6.93). Here it is stated that death is painful for the disbelievers. Although they are ordered to surrender their souls to the angels, they are unwilling; therefore, the soul must be forced out as it does not wish to meet its punishment.

According to a *hadith*: the angel of death says: 'O you foul soul, come out to the anger and wrath of your Lord.' The soul inside the disbeliever's body is overcome by terrible fear and does not want to deliver itself up, whereupon the angel of death violently pulls it out. Umm Salama reported that Allah's messenger came across Abu Salama's corpse, whose eyes were wide open, and the Prophet closed his eyelids and then said, 'When the *ruh* (spirit) is taken out, the eyesight follows it' (*Muslim; Ahmad*). The Angel of Death comes to the [dying] believer, sits at his head and says, 'O you good soul, come out and receive your Lord's forgiveness and pleasure.' Then the soul flows out effortlessly just as water flows from the mouth of a waterskin. Abu Hurayra narrated that the messenger of God said: 'When the soul of a believer comes out [of its body], two angels receive it and rise with it towards the heavens, whereupon the inhabitants of the heavens say, "'A good soul has come from the earth. Allah has blessed you and the body which you used to occupy"' (*Muslim*).

The soul

What happens to the soul upon death? This introduces two important concepts:

those of the *nafs* and the *ruh*. The majority of Muslim theologians often make no distinction between the *ruh* and the *nafs*, holding that the terms *nafs* and *ruh* are interchangeable. However, the term *nafs* is usually applied when the soul is inside the body, and the word *ruh* is used when the soul is apart from the body. However, each one has clearly distinct and restricted applications in certain contexts. *Nafs* may represent self as in 24.61, or revelation as in 42.52, or Jibril as in 26.192–193, or in an even more restricted sense the spirit of faith as in 58.22. Some *hadith* suggest that both are the same: Umm Salama reported, as we have seen, that the messenger of Allah said: 'When the *ruh* is taken out, the eyesight follows it.' Abu Hurayra reported that the messenger of Allah said: 'Do you not see that when a person dies his gaze is fixed intently; that occurs when his eyesight follows his *nafs* [as it comes out]' (*Muslim*; Qurtubi's *al-Tadhkira*).

Hardships and agonies

'And the agony of death comes, in truth; that is what you wished to avoid' (50.19). In this verse the phrase *sakrat al-mawt* is used to indicate the swoon of death. This verse implies that every dying person must experience some pain and torment. Here is 'A'isha speaking in connection with the Prophet's approach to death: 'Allah's messenger had a small vessel of water placed before him. He began to dip his hands in the water, wiping his face with them. He said: "There is none worthy of worship except Allah. Indeed death brings with it agonies!" Then he raised his hand up and kept repeating, "In the most exalted company" until his soul was taken and his hand fell limp' (*Bukhari*). 'A'isha is also reported as saying that upon his death the Prophet said: 'O Allah help me to overcome the agonies of death.'

Repentance at the last minute might well not succeed in saving the individual: 'Their faith was of no use to them once they saw Our doom' (40.85); 'Forgiveness is not for those who continue to do evil deeds up until death comes to one of them [and] he says, "Truly, I repent now!"' (4.18). Allah says, 'Every soul shall have a taste of death, and only on the Day of Judgement shall you be paid your full recompense. Only those who are saved far from the Fire, and admitted to the Garden will have succeeded. For the life of this world is but goods and chattels of deception' (3.185). 'O you who believe! Revere Allah, and let every person look to what he has sent forth for the morrow; and revere Allah. Allah is well aware of what you do. And be not like those who forgot [disobeyed] Allah, and He caused them to forget themselves. Those are the disobedient. The dwellers of the Fire and the dwellers of Paradise are not the same. It is the dwellers of Paradise who will be successful' (59.18–20). He also tells us that we do not know the hour of our own deaths, or in what land we will die. But through his unending mercy toward us, he has given us ways to prepare for the inevitable now, because once we have passed from this life to the next, there is no coming back to do the things we should have done. For God says: 'Until death comes to one of them, he says, "My Lord, send me back. Perhaps I may do good in that which I have left behind." No, it is but a word that he speaks, and behind them is a *barzakh* until the day when they are raised up' (23.99–100).

God has given us ways to protect ourselves from the punishment of the grave. One of these ways is by fighting in the cause of Allah. It is reported that a man asked the Prophet, 'O Messenger of Allah, why are all the believers tested in the graves except a martyr?' God replied: 'The flashing of swords over his head was a sufficient test for him.' There are many ways apart from martyrdom to earn a reward in the next life. These include reciting *surat al-Mulk* (*sura* 67), because the Prophet referred to it as 'the protector from the torment of the grave'. He also said, 'When a human being dies, all of his deeds are terminated except for three types: an ongoing *sadaqa* (good action), a knowledge of Islam from which others benefit, and a righteous child who makes *du'a* (bears witness) for him' (*Muslim*). Another way to earn a continuing reward is by reviving a lost *sunna* (practice) of the Prophet, who said: 'He who initiates in Islam a good way gets his reward for it, as well as rewards similar to those who follow him into it, without reducing any of their rewards' (*Muslim*). This suggests that Muslims who have already begun their journey, or who are about to enter into the next life, can be assisted through prayer for the deceased, fulfilling the deceased's vows, payment of the deceased's debts and subsequent good actions.

The living and the dead

This idea of a continuing connection between the living and the dead has been much discussed in the literature. Some argue that the dead in their graves have the ability to hear a visitor's greeting, his supplication, talk, etc. Such a concept is difficult to accept, for it has no proof from clear texts of the *shari'a*. In fact, it is in open contradiction to several texts of the Qur'an and the authentic traditions of the Prophet which deny the possibility of the dead possessing this faculty.

There are two unequivocal texts from the Qur'an that deny the possibility of the dead in their graves possessing the faculty of hearing. God states: 'Verily you cannot make the dead hear and you cannot make the deaf hear the call when they turn their backs and retreat' (27.80). And also: 'The living and the dead are not alike. Allah makes whoever he wishes hear, but you cannot make those in the graves hear' (35.22). In the first verse God addresses his messenger, Muhammad, reminding him that he cannot make the disbelievers hear the invitation to Islam, for they are like the dead, who do not hear either. In the second verse God points to the difference between the living and the dead – they are not all alike. He further clarifies to his prophet that he cannot make the rejectors of faith hear the message (for they are dead in heart and in spirit) any more than he can make those in the graves hear what is spoken to them. Just as the Qur'an denies the possibility of the deceased possessing the faculty of hearing, there are a number of texts in the *sunna* that arrive at the same conclusion.

One such *hadith* comes through Ibn Mas'ud, who reported that the Prophet said: 'Allah has angels who travel about the earth; they [do and will] convey to me the peace greeting from my *umma*' (*Abu Dawud*). This *hadith* clarifies that the Prophet does not hear the greetings of peace from Muslims when they pronounce it upon him, for if he could hear it directly, there would be no need of angels to convey it to him. Therefore, it follows that the Prophet cannot hear other forms of conversation directed to him either; and it stands even more to reason that the deceased, being at a less elevated level than the Prophet, also cannot hear the *salam* (greeting of peace) or any other form of speech. Thus, and contrary to popular belief, because the Messenger cannot directly hear either one's invocation of blessings or one's *salam* addressed to him, such greetings

may be conveyed to him from anywhere, regardless of the distance or proximity of the greeter to the Prophet's grave. This is an argument against venerating particular sites and seeking blessing (*baraka*) there. The erroneous belief that the Prophet hears these greetings directly disregards the previous *hadith*, which specifies that the greetings are conveyed to him by the angels, and is based on a dubious tradition. It has been narrated that the Prophet said: 'Whoever asks blessings for me at my grave, I hear him, and whoever asks blessings upon me from afar, it is conveyed to me.' Actually, even if this *hadith* is authentic, it still suggests that place is of no significance, because it implies that any appeal is available to the Prophet, not just those made at his grave.

Do the dead hear?

In order to throw doubt upon suggestions which claim that the deceased in the grave possess the faculty of hearing, it is necessary to analyse them and discover the means by which such ideas are dependent upon weak and forged traditions or due to erroneous interpretations of various texts. They could also be survivals of long-established folk beliefs. There are a number of authentic narrations relating the Prophet's address to the corpses of the *mushrikin* (polytheists) of the Quraysh who were slain by the Muslims in the battle of Badr and then thrown into a dried well. The following two examples suffice for the purpose of the present discussion. Abu Talha reported:

On the day of the Battle of Badr, Allah's Prophet ordered that the bodies of twenty-four leaders of the Quraysh be thrown into one of the foul, abandoned wells of Badr. On the third day after the battle the Prophet called for his mount and saddled it. Then he set out, so his companions followed him. They said amongst themselves, 'He must be going to something important.' When the Prophet arrived at the well he stood at its edge and began addressing those in it by calling upon them by their names, 'O so and so, son of so and so; and you, so and so, son of so and so! Would it not have been easier to have obeyed Allah and His Messenger? We have found that which our Lord promised us to be true. Did you find what your Lord promised you to be true?' Thereupon 'Umar said, 'O Messenger of Allah, what are you saying to these bodies without souls?! Do they hear? For Allah, the Majestic and Mighty, says, "Verily, you cannot make the dead hear."' (27.80)

The Prophet answered:

By Him in whose hand lies the soul of Muhammad, you did not hear better than them and what I just said.

Qatada added:

Allah brought them back to life [momentarily] in order to make them hear as a means of scorn and belittlement and [so that they would feel] regret and remorse. (*Bukhari; Muslim*)

In another narration of this incident there is a slight variation in the wording of the text:

Ibn 'Umar related: 'The Prophet stood at the edge of a well at Badr and said, 'Did you find the promise of your Lord to be true?' Then he added, 'Verily at this moment they hear what I am saying.'

Later on, this was mentioned to 'A'isha, whereupon she commented, 'What the Prophet meant was, "Now they know that what I used to tell them is the truth."' Then she recited, 'Verily you cannot make the dead hear' (27.80) up to the end of the chapter (*Bukhari*). Some often under-stand the texts of these two *ahadith* as proof for the contention that the dead can hear. However, the following interpretation goes against such a claim. This miraculous circumstance in which the corpses of the slain Quraysh were made to hear the Prophet's address to them is a special case – an exception to the general rule that the dead *do not* hear. By a miracle, God made them hear the Prophet, but only for the moment he spoke to them. This is clearly proven by the second narration itself, for their hearing was said to start at the moment when the Prophet called out to them in criticism. He said: 'At this moment they hear what I am saying.' Furthermore, in the first narration the Prophet does not deny 'Umar's sound understanding of the verse's general ruling that the dead do not hear. Rather, the Prophet merely clarifies for 'Umar that what occurred at Badr was a divine miracle and, therefore, an exception to the general ruling of the verse.

Another text often quoted by those who believe that the dead can hear is the following tradition: Anas bin Malik reported that Allah's Messenger said: 'After the deceased is placed in his grave and his companions turn to leave, he hears the shuffling of their feet as they walk away. Then there comes to him the two angels' (*Bukhari; Muslim*). This text is not valid evidence for the general claim that the dead can hear; rather, this tradition only specifies another exception to the general rule. In this case, the deceased hears the shuffling feet of those who attended his funeral as they walk away. This is a momentary possession of the faculty of hearing that is terminated at the point at which the two questioning angels come to him.

Intercession for the dead and visiting graveyards

It is fairly clear that the deceased generally are not held to have the faculty of hearing, for they are beyond the barrier (*barzakh*) which separates our world from theirs. This proves the gross error in the thinking of those who attempt to carry on 'conversations' with the dead, or worse, petition them for certain things. Petitioning the dead is *shirk* (idolatry), and this is sometimes denounced as the greatest of all sins. Anyone who dies enters the dimension called the *barzakh* wherein his deeds come to an end. He is unable to do anything for the living, although the results of his deeds may affect the living and continue to earn reward or punishment for himself. Abu Hurayra's report of Allah's Messenger states: 'When a man dies, his [good] deeds come to an end, except three types: charity of continuing benefit, knowledge beneficial to people and a righteous offspring who prays for him' (*Muslim*). The recitation of the Qur'an in graveyards is not allowed as neither the Prophet nor his companions were known to do it. In particular we should note that the Prophet's wife, 'A'isha, asked him what to say when visiting graveyards and he told her to give *salama* (greetings of peace) and a prayer, but he did not tell her to recite *al-Fatiha* or any other chapter from the Qur'an. The text of the *du'a* is as follows: 'Peace be upon the Believers and Muslims among the inhabitants of these dwellings. May Allah have mercy on those who have gone ahead of us, and those following us. And we shall – if God wishes it – be joining you.' Abu Hurayra also reported that the Prophet said: 'Do not make your houses graveyards, for verily Satan flees from the house in which *sura al-Baqara* is read' (*Muslim*).

This narration and others like it imply that the Qur'an is not to be read in graveyards. Qur'anic recitation is encouraged in the house, and making it like a graveyard, in which no recitation should take place, is forbidden. As for the recitation of *sura Ya sin*, there is no narration concerning graveyards and the narration about its recitation over the dying is inauthentic. Most of the scholars hold it permissible for women to visit graves. This is based on the following *hadith* from 'A'isha: 'What should I say to them, O Messenger of Allah when visiting graves?' 'Abdallah ibn Abi Mulayka is also reported to have said, 'Once 'A'isha returned after visiting the graveyard. I asked, "O Mother of the Believers, where have you been?" She said: "I went out to visit the grave of my brother 'Abd ar-Rahman." I asked her: "Didn't the Messenger of Allah prohibit visiting graves?" She said, "Yes, he did forbid visiting graves during the early days, but later on he ordered us to visit them."' (This is reported by al-Hakim and al-Bayhaqi, who also remarked that this *hadith* was narrated only by Bistam bin Muslim al-Basri; al-Dhahabi, however, said that it was a sound *hadith*). Anas reported: 'The Prophet saw a woman crying by the grave of her son, and said to her, "Fear Allah, and be patient." She replied, "What do you care about my tragedy?" When he went away, someone told her, "Indeed, that was the Messenger of Allah." The woman felt extremely sorry and she immediately went to the Prophet's house, where she did not find any guards. She called out: "O Messenger of Allah! I did not recognize you." The Prophet said, "It is certainly the case that patience is needed at the time of the first loss"' (*Bukhari*; *Muslim*). This supports the argument in favour of the permissibility of women visiting graves, for the Prophet saw her at the grave and did not show his disapproval of it.

While it is permissible, this is not recommended, because of the great sin of weeping at the grave. The purpose of visiting graves is to remember the hereafter, which is something that both men and women need. Men are by no means more in need of this reminder than women. Some scholars disliked women visiting graves as they are less patient and too emotional. The Prophet said: 'May Allah curse the women who are frequent visitors of the graves' (Ahmad; Ibn Maja; Tirmidhi, all of whom said that it is a sound *hadith*). Al-Qurtubi said: 'The curse mentioned in this *hadith* applies only to those women who visit graves frequently. The reason for this curse lies perhaps in the fact that it involves infringement of the rights of the husband, and leads to adornment and exhibition of their beauty to strangers, and shouting, yelling, and other similar things.' It may be said that, 'If no such harm is feared from women visiting graves, then there is no valid reason for preventing them from visiting graves, for indeed remembrance of death is something that both men and women equally need.' Commenting on al-Qurtubi's view, al-Shawkani said, 'This statement may form the basis for reconciling apparently contradictory *hadith*. A wife is allowed to mourn for her husband for four months and ten days.' Zainab bint Abi states: that upon news of the death of Abu Sufyan, Umm Habiba on the third day, asked for a yellow perfume and scented her cheeks and forearms, saying: 'No doubt, I would not have been in need of this, had I not heard the Prophet saying: "It is not legal for a woman who believes in Allah and the Last Day to mourn for more than three days for any dead person except her husband, for whom she should mourn for four months and ten days"' (*Bukhari*).

Crying at graves

Crying for extended periods of times, and/or crying where the voice is very loud, is called *haram*. The Prophet said: 'The deceased who is wailed over is tortured for that wailing' (*Bukhari*). The Prophet said: 'He who slaps the cheeks, tears the clothes and follows the traditions of the *jahiliyya* is not from us' (*Bukhari*). Islam always tends to stress the importance of being moderate, taking the middle position, and excessive demonstrations of grief do not accord with this. In any case, they imply that there is something at fault in what happened, as though God would not have acted in the way in which he wished to, or ought to have acted, and this is not the sort of attitude that is appropriate for a believer.

We are told that the Prophet shed tears but did not cry out in a loud voice: 'We went with Allah's Apostle to the blacksmith Abu Sayf, and he was the husband of the wet-nurse of Ibrahim (the son of the Prophet). Allah's Apostle took Ibrahim and kissed him and smelled him and later we entered Abu Sayf's house and at that time Ibrahim was on his last breath, and the eyes of Allah's Apostle started shedding tears. 'Abd ur Rahman bin 'Auf said: "O Allah's Apostle, even you are weeping!"' The Prophet then said: '"O Ibn 'Auf, this is mercy." Then he wept more and said, "The eyes are shedding tears and the heart is grieved, and we will not say anything except what pleases our Lord, O Ibrahim! Indeed we are grieved by the separation"' (*Bukhari*).

Talking of the dead

There is a suggestion that it represents punishment for the deceased when you speak ill of them at the time of the funeral. This does not mean that the deceased person hears you speaking ill or well of them. As Abu al-Aswad narrated:

> I came to Medina when an epidemic had broken out. While I was sitting with 'Umar bin al-Khattab a funeral procession passed by and the people praised the deceased. 'Umar said: 'His fate has been decided accordingly.' And another funeral procession passed by and the people praised the deceased. 'Umar said: 'His fate has been decided accordingly.' A third (funeral procession) passed by and the people spoke badly of the deceased. He said: 'His fate has been decided accordingly.' I [Abu al-Aswad] asked, 'O chief of the believers! What has been decided?' He replied, 'I said the same as the Prophet had said, that is: if four persons testify the piety of a Muslim, Allah will grant him Paradise.' We asked, 'If three persons testify his piety?' He [the Prophet] replied, 'Even three.' Then we asked, 'If two?' He replied, 'Even two.' We did not ask him regarding one witness.' (*Bukhari*)

Narrated Anas bin Malik:

> A funeral procession passed and the people praised the deceased. The Prophet said, 'His fate has been decided accordingly.' Then another funeral procession passed and the people spoke badly of the deceased. The Prophet said, 'His fate has been decided accordingly.' 'Umar bin al-Khattab asked [Allah's Apostle] 'What has been decided?' He replied, 'You praised him, so Paradise has been granted to him; and you spoke badly of him, so Hell has been given to him. You people are Allah's witnesses on earth'. (*Bukhari*)

The implication is that one has to be very careful about talking of the dead.

Abu Hurayra said: 'Make your funerals speedy, for it is only good that you are advancing him towards, or evil that you are taking off your necks' (*Muwatta*).

Euthanasia and suicide

Euthanasia is a practice accepted by certain sections of the medical profession. It means to bring about a mercifully easy and painless death for persons suffering from a painful and, what seems to be, an incurable disease. 'Voluntary' euthanasia is when the affected person requests to be killed painlessly. If the person is not in a position to decide for himself or herself (maybe because they are brain dead), it is the doctors or the person's relatives who must decide, and this is called 'compulsory' euthanasia. Islam does not consider euthanasia as a 'merciful release' but rather as murder (in the case of compulsory euthanasia) or suicide (in the case of voluntary euthanasia). It may be acceptable to a person who does not believe in God; to this person life is not sacred. But for a believer it is hardly thinkable to contemplate such a thing. The *shari'a* bans suicide (viz. voluntary euthanasia): 'And do not be cast into ruin by your own hands' (2.195); 'O ye who believe ... Neither kill (or destroy) yourselves: for really Allah has been to you most merciful!' (4.29). The *shari'a* also bans murder (viz. compulsory euthanasia) 'Do not take life – which Allah has made sacred – except for just cause' (17.33). Life is God's gift; it is not given by man. Therefore, man has no right to terminate it, except on strictly legal grounds on the course of justice.

God is compassionate and merciful. To think that suffering is to no purpose is to question his wisdom and forget his compassion. No disaster occurs except by God's permission: 'And whoever believes in Allah He guides his heart.

And Allah is knower of all things' (64.11). Only Allah knows the reasons for our sufferings, and they will be revealed to us in due course. Muslims should remember that life is a test from him. Euthanasia is like cheating by trying to speed up this test. Faith in God, patience and endurance, and the knowledge that God sees all suffering, bring a person much nearer to him when in a bad state. What he suffers is a purification of his soul and body and is a test of his faith in God. Muhammad said that a Muslim soldier who committed suicide because he was dying a painful death on the battlefield would not be admitted to heaven.

The Prophet also said: 'None of you should wish to die because harm befalls him. If he is so determined, let him say "Oh God! Let me live as long as life is good for me, and let me die if death is good for me."' It is for God to decide when someone should die, it is not up to us to pre-empt his decision. Also, euthanasia takes away the affected person's chances of recovery. And, in the case of compulsory euthanasia, it does not give him any choice. The loneliness of people in modern society, the total isolation of the individual, the apathy and coldness of those who are around us and the abandonment of individuals by relatives and friends, are the real enemies of the human soul, which is left on its own to suffer. It is understood that God alone is the giver of life, and it is he who takes it away. In this regard, God says in the Qur'an in *sura al-Mu'min* (The Believer): 'It is He who gives life and death; and when He decides upon an affair, He says to it, "Be", and it is' (40.68). While life and death are from God, we have to remember that they are to take place with the permission of God alone. All issues of life and death are decided by God. It is stated in the Qur'an: 'Nor can a soul die except by

God's leave, the term being fixed as by writing. If any do desire a reward in this life, We shall give it to him, and if any do desire a reward in the hereafter, We shall give it to him. And swiftly shall We reward those that [serve us with] gratitude' (3.145). It should be stated here that God makes us die daily at night during sleeping. He makes most of us wake up from our temporary death to praise him and to worship him.

The Qur'an states in *sura al-Zumar* (The Crowds) the following:'It is God that takes souls at death; and those that die not during their sleep; those on whom He has passed the decree of death, He keeps back but the rest He sends [to their bodies] for a term appointed. There are in this signs for those who reflect' (39.42). The life of a Muslim on this earth is a short one, but his deeds and actions are eternal if he knows how to channel them in the right direction. As far as the lifespan of a Muslim is concerned, and as narrated by Abu Hurayra, Muhammad said: 'The lifespan of my followers are between sixty and seventy.' This represented the Prophet's view of a normal lifespan.

Further reading

Bowker, J. (1993) *The Meanings of Death*, Cambridge: Cambridge University Press.

al-Ghazali, A. (1995) *The Remembrance of Death and the Afterlife (Book 40 of The Revival of Religious Sciences)*, trans. T.J. Winter, Cambridge: The Islamic Texts Society.

Howarth, G. and Leaman, O. (eds) (2000) *Encyclopedia of Death and Dying*, London: Routledge.

Rosenthal, Franz (1946) 'On Suicide in Islam', *JAOS* 66: 239–59.

Umri, J. (1987): 'Suicide or Termination of Life', *Islamic Comparative Law Quarterly* 7: 136–44.

See also: barzakh; jihad; noise; repentance; salat; zuhd

OLIVER LEAMAN

DEVIL

After God created Adam, the devil (originally an angel or *jinn*) refuses to obey God's order, which enjoins the angels to bow or to prostrate before the first man. God curses and banishes the devil but grants him respite until the Day of Judgement and allows him to lead astray all who are not true servants of God. The devil's first evil deed is to incite Adam and his wife to disobey God's command not to eat from the forbidden tree. Throughout history the devil is, and will be, active to counter God's divine plans concerning the well-being of mankind in this world and in the afterlife.

The devil is known under two designations in the Qur'an: Iblis, used always as a proper name, and *al-shaytan* ('the satan'), originally a generic designation but with the definite article used as a proper name as well. The generic *shaytan* (pl. *shayatin*) takes up a pre-Islamic notion of a superhuman entity not unlike the *jinn*, which may govern the words and deeds of humans as did the pagan demons and deities. An Arab poet was seen as possessed by a *jinn* or a *shaytan*. This is probably alluded to when the Qur'an insists on its divine origin and says of itself: 'Not by the satans has it been brought down' (26.210). In 6.112 it is asserted that God created 'satans' for all his prophets: 'We have appointed to every prophet an enemy – satans of men and *jinn*', which implies that metaphorically men can also be called 'satans'. A certain ambiguity between *shaytan* and *al-shaytan* prevails in the Qur'anic text. The name Iblis is usually seen as derived from the Greek *diabolos*, the name of the devil in Christian scripture, and is thus etymologically related to the word 'devil'. *Shaytan* is most probably derived from the Hebrew *shatan* (Satan). Arab-Muslim philologists suggest different etymologies. They

derive Iblis from an Arabic root, meaning 'to render hopeless', and find also an Arabic etymology for *shaytan*. (*Al-*)*Shaytan* in its different forms occurs more frequently in the Qur'an than Iblis.

Iblis, the rebel

The Qur'an describes the devil's revolt against God in four versions of a dramatic dialogue between God and Iblis (7.12–19; 15.31–40; 17.61–65; 38.71–85). The shortest of these versions is 17.61–65:

> And when We said to the angels, 'Bow yourselves to Adam'; so they bowed themselves, save Iblis. He said: 'Shall I bow myself unto one Thou hast created of clay?' He said: 'What thinkest Thou? This whom Thou hast honoured above me – if Thou deferrest me to the Day of Resurrection I shall assuredly master his seed, save a few.' Said He: 'Depart! Those of them that follow thee – surely Gehenna shall be your recompense, an ample recompense! And startle whomsoever of them thou canst with thy voice; and rally against them thy horsemen and thy foot, and share with them in their wealth and their children and promise them!'

Here as in many other instances the text creates the pessimistic impression that those who follow the devil will be in the majority.

In all four versions of the dialogically enacted revolt of the devil against God the devil's name is Iblis. When, however, the devil tempts Adam and his wife to disobey God's command not to eat from the Tree of Immortality (20.120), the devil's name changes to *al-shaytan* (2.36). It seems that the devil in the role of the proud, disobedient rebel against God's command, who refuses to bow before Adam, was originally called Iblis, whereas the devil as a tempter of Adam and mankind is called *al-shaytan*. Later, both names tend to blend, but *al-shaytan* is never a designation of the diabolical rebel in the aftermath of Adam's creation. Outside of this particular context, however, a *shaytan* may be called rebellious (*Marid* 22.3).

The Qur'anic story of Iblis' refusal to bow before Adam and his subsequent fall agrees in many details with Christian apocryphal writings and Lucifer's fall. One of these details is that Iblis refuses to bow before Adam by saying to God: 'I am better than he [i.e. Adam]. Thou createdst me of fire, and him Thou createdst of clay' (38.76). Some Qur'anic passages seem to suggest that Iblis before his fall was an angel, others that he was a *jinn*. In 18.50 he is both. The question of whether Iblis was originally an angel or a *jinn* was discussed at length but inconclusively by Muslim exegetes. It is, however, only in mystical and modern writings that Iblis is seen as a heroic or even tragic figure: by refusing to prostrate himself before a created being he is depicted as the only true monotheist.

Satan, the tempter

The devil as *al-shaytan* is in the Qur'an the opponent of God, and he plays the counterweight to the divine guidance for mankind. Abraham warns his father not to serve Satan (19.44), and God is said to address the sinners on the Day of Judgement as follows: 'Made I not a covenant with you, Children of Adam, that you should not serve Satan?' (36.60). The devil describes his own role in one version of his dialogue with God in some detail by saying: 'Now, for Thy perverting me, I shall surely sit in ambush for them [i.e. mankind] on Thy straight path; then I shall come on them from before them and from behind them, from their right hands and from their left hands; Thou wilt not find most of them thankful' (7.16–17).

Satan's first victims are Adam and his wife. God had made a covenant with Adam by saying that Adam and his wife could dwell in the paradisaical garden (*janna*) and that they could eat freely of it but not of a particular tree (2.35; 7.19). 'Then Satan whispered to them, to reveal to them that which was hidden from them of their shameful parts. He said, "Your Lord has only prohibited you from this tree lest you become angels, or lest you become immortals." And he swore to them, "Truly, I am for you a sincere adviser." So he led them on by delusion, and when they tasted the tree their shameful parts revealed to them' (7.20–22; a parallel with significant variations in 20.121, both passages echoing Genesis 3). Adam's fall, however, is not conceived of as a transmittable original sin, causing the sinfulness of mankind in general.

Satan's pernicious cunning is everywhere and his deceit spares nobody: he often 'whispers evil' (7.20) to mankind; he leads astray (4.60) – an action, which in the Qur'an is usually ascribed to God (e.g. 13.27); he causes hatred and emnity (5.91); he succeeds in inducing prophets to forget momentarily the ways of the Lord (12.42); and he even tries to interfere with revelation by tempting the prophets to insert into revelation what was not revealed (22. 52). He causes not only intercommunal strife among Muslims (*fitna*; 22.52) but is in general the enemy of mankind (17.53). On the Day of Judgement humanity will be divided into Satan's party (*hizb al-shaytan*; 58.19), who will be punished by damnation, and God's party (*hizb allah*; 58.22), who will enter paradise.

In the first curse that God pronounces upon the devil ('Then go thou forth hence; thou art accursed. Upon thee shall rest the curse, till the Day of Doom';

15.34) the devil is called *rajim*, meaning both 'accursed' and 'stoned'. The ritual stoning of a construction, which most pilgrims identify with the devil, is an important part of Muslim pilgrimage. The idea of stoning the devil may have its origin in 67.5: 'And We adorned the lower heaven with lamps, and made them things to stone Satans', in which God seems to throw stars at the devils.

The obligatory formula to be pronounced before each recitation of the Qur'an and consequently before each ritual prayer is: 'I take refuge with God from the accursed Satan'. This honours the Qur'anic injunction: 'When thou recitest the Qur'an, seek refuge in God from the accursed Satan' (16.98). The formula bans the fear that the devil may disturb or otherwise intervene in the recitation of the holy text. Today the formula is mostly explained as a safeguard against omissions or other mistakes in recitation.

Neither in his role as Iblis nor in his role as *al-shaytan* is the devil the master of hell. After the Day of Judgement the devil and his hosts are thrown into hell (26.94–95) just as are the human sinners.

Further reading

Awn, P.J. (1983) *Satan's Tragedy and Redemption. Iblis in Sufi psychology*, Leiden: E.J. Brill.
Rippin, A. (2001a) 'Devil', in *EQ*, Vol. 1: 524–7.
—— (2001b) 'Shaytan', in *EI*, 406–9.
Wensinck, A.J. and Gardet L. (2001) 'Iblis', in *EI*, Vol. VI, 668–9.

See also: **eschatology;** *fitna*; **revelation**

STEFAN WILD

DHAQA / ADHAQA

Dhaqa is the root of a verb meaning tasted. It signifies the tasting of food by the tongue. It also means to try or to know the taste of a food. Originally *dhaqa* signified the process of sampling a little portion of food; however, it also could mean to eat. One would say 'I did not taste any food today' meaning 'I did not eat anything.'

In the Qur'an *dhaqa* not only means to taste food; it also signifies the perceiving by all other senses in addition to tasting by the tongue. In most cases taste in the Qur'an is related to punishment: 'Taste ye the punishment of the blazing fire' (8.50). The taste of punishment is also eternal and is down to what wrongdoers did (earned) in their worldly life: 'Taste you the everlasting torment, Are you recompensed save what you used to earn?' (10.52).

Death itself, according to the Qur'an, is tasted by every soul: 'Everyone shall taste death' (3.185). Prophet Muhammad referred to love-making between husband and wife as tasting each other's sweetness.

Adhaqa is the transitive form (to taste), meaning to make someone taste. It is composed of *dhaqa* preceded by the transitive *alif* (A). It signifies making someone taste food through the normal sense, i.e. by the tongue. It also signifies to make someone try or discover something. In the Qur'an the term is used to convey the meaning of making someone taste in both good and bad situations. For example, God makes people taste his mercy: 'And when We let mankind taste mercy after some adversity has afflicted them' (10.21). In another verse mercy has been granted by God for people to taste: 'But when He gives them taste of His mercy' (30.33). On the other hand, God also makes people taste torment. In the Qur'an God mentions *adhaqa* often to describe the imposing of punishment on the wrongdoers: 'So, Allah made them taste extreme hunger and fear' (16.112).

RAFIK BERJAK

DHU AL-KIFL

Mentioned by name in the Qur'an two times (21.85; 38.48), many Muslim exegetes identify Dhu al-Kifl as a prophet, the son of Job. Others claim that Dhu al-Kifl is to be identified as the prophet Elijah or Zechariah (see 3.37). Many exegetes associate the prophet Ezekiel with 2.243 because of its mention of the resurrection of bones, as in the biblical account of Ezekiel's vision of the bones. Others state that Dhu al-Kifl was the prophet Elisha, his successor, or a righteous person whom Elisha imitated in his pious actions. The Qur'an itself only states that, along with Ishmael and Idris, Dhu al-Kifl was steadfast and upright (21.85), and, along with Ishmael and Elisha, he was chosen (38.48). According to a saying of the Prophet Muhammad, Dhu al-Kifl was an Israelite who became righteous after recognizing the sinful ways of the other Israelites. Those who identify Dhu al-Kifl with a son of Job state that his real name was Bishr, but that he was called Dhu al-Kifl because he told the people of Rome about the 'guarantee' (*kafil*) that God had given to them. Others relate that Dhu al-Kifl was sent to the people of Damascus. It is reported that Dhu al-Kifl lived and died in Syria but there is no extant tomb attributed to him there.

Further reading

Heller, B. (1928) 'Récits et personnages bibliques dans la légende mahometane', *Revue des études juives* 85: 113–36.

BRANNON WHEELER

DHU AL-QARNAYN

The story of Dhu al-Qarnayn appears in 18.82–102. These verses describe the journeys of Dhu al-Qarnayn to a series of locations and peoples (18.85–88, 89–91, 92–93). Muslim exegetes describe the encounters in fantastic terms, detailing the unusual features of the people and the places visited. Verses 94–99 describe Dhu al-Qarnayn's building of a barrier between two mountains to hold back the hordes of Gog and Magog until the end of time. Verses 100–102 describe events related to the end of time and the preparation of hell for the unbelievers. According to many exegetes, the passage was revealed to the Prophet Muhammad in Mecca when a group of Jews from Medina came to test him concerning his knowledge of the name and the story. Muslim tradition holds that Dhu al-Qarnayn was one of only four kings who ruled over the entire world.

Muslim tradition identifies Dhu al-Qarnayn with various historical and mythical figures. Some exegetes report that Dhu al-Qarnayn was an angel or a prophet. Others identify him with different kings from pre-Islamic South Arabia or with a Greek man from Egypt named Marzban b. Mardaba. Some historians and exegetes claim that there were two different people called Dhu al-Qarnayn, one living in the time of Abraham, the other living about 300 years before Jesus. In Muslim historical accounts, Dhu al-Qarnayn appears at the well of Beersheba and at the *Ka'ba* in the presence of Abraham.

The most popular identification of Dhu al-Qarnayn is with Alexander the Great, and many exegetes relate 18.83–102 and the verses preceding (18.60–82) with episodes from the Alexander Romance literature. Later Persian and Ethiopian recensions of the Alexander Romance refer to Alexander with the epithet Dhu al-Qarnayn, and include the prophetic figure Khidr as accompanying Alexander on his journeys.

The name Dhu al-Qarnayn is interpreted by Muslim exegetes as referring to the two horns (*qarnayn*) or other features resembling horns that Dhu al-Qarnayn had on his head. Muslim exegetes also make mention of the horns as symbolizing his kingship over Rome and Persia, perhaps an allusion to the vision of the horns in Daniel 8. In one account Dhu al-Qarnayn's name is said to refer to the fact that he was hit on his head (*qarn*) two times by his people who rejected his worship of God. Others say that the name refers to Dhu al-Qarnayn's journey to the two ends of the earth where the rim (*qarn*) of the sun rises and sets.

All of these explanations are also applied to the identification of Dhu al-Qarnayn with Moses, who is also said to have had horns appear on his head when he descended from Mount Sinai (see Exodus 34: 29). 18.60–82 narrates how Moses travelled to the ends of the earth in search of the water of life. Some exegetes repeat the account of Wahb b. Munabbih that Dhu al-Qarnayn visited Jerusalem where he met a prophet named Khidr-Moses.

Further reading

Friedländer, I. (1913) *Die Chadirlegende und der Alexanderroman*, Leipzig: J.C. Hinrichs.
Lidzbarski, M. (1892) 'Wer is Chadhir?', *Zeitschrift für Assyriologie* 7: 104–6.
Wheeler, B. (1998) 'Moses or Alexander? Q 18:60–65 in Early Islamic Exegesis', *Journal of Near Eastern Studies* 57: 191–215.
—— (2003) 'The Prophet Muhammad Dhu al-Qarnayn: His journey to the cities at the ends of the earth', *Byzantinorossica* 2: 179–219.

BRANNON WHEELER

DIVORCE

Islam gives the husband the right to *talaq* (to divorce) his wife. Moreover, Islam also grants the wife the right to dissolve the marriage. If a husband dissolves the marriage by divorcing his wife, he cannot retrieve any of the marriage gifts he has given her. The Qur'an explicitly prohibits divorcing husbands from taking back their marriage gifts no matter how expensive or valuable these gifts might be: 'But if you decide to take one wife in place of another, even if you had given the latter a whole treasure for dower, take not the least bit of it back. Would you take it by slander and a manifest wrong?' (4.20). In the case of the wife choosing to end the marriage, she may return the marriage gifts to her husband. A reason for this is that it is compensation for the husband who wishes to keep his wife while she chooses to leave him. The Qur'an has instructed Muslim men not to take back any of the gifts they have given to their wives except in the case of the wife choosing to dissolve the marriage, and then it seems to be permissible for him to accept the gifts, albeit not compulsory: 'It is not lawful for you [men] to take back any of your gifts except when both parties fear that they would be unable to keep the limits ordained by Allah. There is no blame on either of them if she gives something for her freedom. These are the limits ordained by Allah so do not transgress them' (2.229).

The *hadith* and Qur'anic literature are very supportive of marriage and critical of divorce. Just disliking a spouse is no reason for divorce – 'Live with them [your wives] on a footing of kindness and equity. If you dislike them it may be that you dislike something in which Allah has placed a great deal of good' (4.19). But, 'As to those women on whose part you fear disloyalty and ill-conduct, [1] Admonish them, [2] refuse to share their beds, [3] beat them; but if they return to obedience' seek not against them means of annoyance, for Allah is most high, great. [4] If you fear a break between them, appoint two arbiters, one from his family and the other from hers. If they wish for peace,

Allah will cause their reconciliation' (4.34–35). The *hadith* literature is usually quite clear that the Prophet emphasizes gentleness and harmony in marital relations, but the sanction of force is always present and has to be acknowledged.

Sura 65 is entitled *al-Talaq* (the Divorce) and adds details to the earlier discussion of the topic in *sura al-Baqara*. There is a waiting period ('*iddat*) in divorce: 'Divorce may be pronounced twice; then the wife may either be kept back in fairness or allowed to separate in fairness' (2.229) 'And the divorced women [after the pronouncement of the divorce] must wait for three monthly courses ... and their husbands are fully entitled to take them back [as their wives] during this waiting period, if they desire reconciliation' (2.228). 'Then, if the husband divorces his wife [for the third time], she shall not remain lawful for him after this divorce, unless she marries another husband ...' (2.230). 'When you marry believing women, and then divorce them before you have touched them, they do not have to fulfill a waiting period, the completion of which you may demand of them' (33. 49). 'And if those of you who die, leave wives behind, the women should abstain [from marriage] for four months and ten days' (2.234). The rules prescribed in these verses were as follows: a man can declare three times that he is divorcing his wife, with the first two times setting the stage for the last declaration upon which the divorce is final. Until the last declaration they are still married, but once he has uttered the divorce formula for the third time, they are not. They can then only marry by remarrying, after she has married someone else and either herself been divorced again or become a widow.

Triple, instantaneous, verbal *talaq* is often regarded as repugnant to the spirit of Islam. It has been called by Islamic feminists *talaq-e-bid'at*, which means '*talaq* of the wrong innovation'. The clear instruction in the Qur'an can be found at 2.226, which instructs that *talaq* must be pronounced twice (in two months) and then (a woman) must either be retained in honour or released in kindness. Further, it says that it is not lawful that you take from women anything which you have given them. The commandment is clear. *Talaq* has to be pronounced twice with an intervening period in which to rethink, reconsider and reconcile. Here, the important instruction is to take time, and, once again, take more time, during which period there should be interlocutors from both sides to try to mediate the conflict. After the second *talaq*, there is still an intervening period, during which time the husband has to think about the two choices available to him; either to reconcile with his wife in an honourable way or to pronounce the third (irrevocable) *talaq* with kindness and allow her to go. At the end of the third interval, he must exercise this choice. But then follows the absolute command. If he decides to let her go, he must do so 'without taking from the woman anything you have given her'. The spirit of the Qur'an towards the process of divorce and the divorced woman, as reflected in this command to the man, is imbued with sensitivity towards gender.

The same command is repeated in *aya* 241 of the same *sura* as a reminder to Muslims that in matters of *talaq* (as in other matters) women must be treated with utmost kindness. The Qur'an is replete with passages outlining the proper and egalitarian treatment of women. Muslims are commanded never to create impediments if a divorced woman wishes to contract another marriage. If a Muslim wants to exchange one wife for another he is commanded not to take anything from her, even if he has given her a pile of gold (4.20). In the same *sura*, Muslims are commanded to return the wife's *mehr* (dowry) with good grace, unless she decides to defer it of her own free will.

Talaq is permissible in the Qur'an only if there is a complete breakdown of marriage. Parting of ways must be graceful, and utmost care is taken to inflict no suffering on the woman. The common practice of impulsively uttering *talaq* thrice all at once, or writing *talaq* three times on a postcard, or getting a *qadi* to write it down, is often criticized as against the spirit and letter of the Qur'an. Just as the man is permitted *talaq*, so also is the woman permitted to take *khula*. In this matter, as in all others, women and men have equal rights in Islam. In *sura al-Baqara* (2.228) women are said to have the same rights over men as men have over women. In 2.229 a woman is permitted to end a difficult married life by taking *khula* (initiating divorce), although she has to go through the *qadi*, unlike the man who does not have to fulfil this condition. This condition was stipulated, once again, to protect the woman because of the possibility of a patriarchal backlash. If the woman for good reasons takes *khula*, and if she forfeits part of her *mehr* of her own free will, it is permissible. Yet many women are obliged to act as though a virtuous wife has to forfeit her *mehr* altogether. But the clear instruction in Islam is that even if a wife takes divorce, she is entitled to *mehr*, although she may of her own free will give up part of it as a bargain for her freedom. The intervention of a *qadi* is then desirable in protecting her rights to control what is rightfully hers in the case of a divorce that she initiates.

See also: **marriage**

OLIVER LEAMAN

DREAMS

Several terms are utilized in the Qur'an with the commonly interpreted sense of 'dream': *ru'ya* and related items (cf. 12.4–5, 36, 41, 43, 100; 17.60; 37.105; 48.27), *hulm* (cf. 12.44; 21.5; 52.32), *manam*, 'sleep' (cf. 8.43; 30.23; 39.42; 37.102), *hadith*, literally 'account' or 'narrative' (cf. 12.6, 21, 101) and *bushra*, 'good tidings' (cf. 10.64). Ten of these references occur in the context of the Joseph story (12.4–6, 21, 36, 41, 43–44, 100, 101), two fall within the tale of Abraham (37.102, 105), and the remainder are taken by some to deal with dreams in general (e.g. 10.64; 39.42) or with incidents that took place during the life of Muhammad (cf. 8.43; 17.60; 21.5; 48.27). Within the framework of expanding on these verses, the commentators tell us that the dreams of prophets may represent revelations and that they must be true, that the interpretations of these dreams may or may not come from God, and that interpretations given by prophets must be fulfilled. For some, dreams can serve as a tool whereby God influences events. Commentators also touch on limited aspects of the well-established Islamic science of dream interpretation. The role played by God and the angels in arranging our dreams is alluded to, as are the mechanics of dreaming and the fact that Muhammad received inspiration through his dreams for six months prior to the advent of Qur'anic revelations. Dreams are thus heralded as the last remaining avenue to divine inspiration; dreams can also, however, arise from personal circumstances, or be sent by Iblis.

Within the Joseph story, 12.4–5 refers to Joseph's dream (*ra'aytu*; *ru'ya*) of the eleven stars, the sun and the moon, all bowing before him, and of his father's advice to him to conceal this from his brothers, while 12.100 tells us that Joseph later considered this dream (*ruʾya*) to have been fulfilled. The commentators make mention of a previous dream with twelve staffs, which occurred when Joseph was seven years old (Thaʿlabi, Tabarsi, Razi). Regarding the Qurʾanic dream, there is some debate over whether the moon should be taken to represent Joseph's mother or his aunt (Tabari, Zamakhshari, Tabarsi, Razi, Qurtubi, Naysaburi), with some arguing that, on the grounds that the dreams of prophets must be true, the moon is Joseph's aunt, as Joseph's mother was (some say) dead by the time the dream was fulfilled (Razi); Razi points out that, as the dreaming Joseph was not yet a prophet, this need not be taken into consideration. Both Tabari and Tabarsi state at this point that the dreams of prophets are, or contain, revelations.

Zamakhshari details Jacob's interpretation of his son's dream (an indication of God's bestowal of wisdom and prophethood), as does Baydawi (that God had chosen him for his message and would raise him above his brothers), and Ibn ʿArabi (a sign of Joseph's prestige, nobility, and higher rank); Qurtubi comments on how this is clear proof of Jacob's ability to interpret dreams; Shawkani simply tells us that Jacob understood its meaning. Thaʿlabi and Shawkani state that Jacob feared his other sons would likewise understand the dream; Tabarsi also implies that the brothers would have been able to read the meaning behind Joseph's dream, but singles out Joseph as the best dream interpreter of his age. That God gifted Joseph with the ability to interpret dreams is implicit in 12.6 (cf. Tabari, Thaʿlabi, Zamakhshari, Tabarsi, Razi, Baydawi, Naysaburi, Shawkani), 21 (cf. Tabari, Qurtubi, Baydawi, Shawkani) and 101 (cf. Thaʿlabi, Tabarsi, Baydawi and Shawkani), all of whom state that God taught him *taʾwil al-ahadith*.

12.36 and 12.41 describe the dreams (*ara*) of Joseph's fellow-prisoners and their interpretation (*taʾwil*): the dream of pressing grapes indicates the return of that prisoner to serving his master, the dream of birds and bread the other prisoner's death. Tabari, Qummi, Tabarsi, Qurtubi and Shawkani tell us that Joseph had previously informed his fellow-prisoners of his ability to interpret dreams; Baydawi and Naysaburi merely that he was in the habit of interpreting dreams for them. Tabarsi and Razi state that Joseph's readings of the prisoners' dreams were not based on a science of dream-interpretation; many commentators mention Joseph's knowledge of the unknown in this context. There is some discussion of whether or not the reported dreams were in fact fabricated (Tabari, Qummi, Tabarsi, Qurtubi, Baydawi, Shawkani) or switched (Naysaburi), with Tabari and Qurtubi in particular focusing on their fulfilment according to Joseph's interpretation regardless of their veracity; Qurtubi also makes mention of the *hadith* describing punishment for such mendacious behaviour on the Day of Judgement. The commentators tend to restrict their interpretation of the dreams to the Qurʾanic explanation of their meaning, Ibn ʿArabi, however, adds such detail as the dream of grapes representing the strength of the dreamer's secret wish to squeeze the wine of passion from the vine of the heart's knowledge, and the dream of birds indicating the dreamer's urge to satisfy the desires of his mental faculties.

12.43–44 describe the fact that Pharaoh dreamt of seven fat and seven thin cows, seven green and seven withered ears of corn and the failure of his counsellors to make sense of this dream (*adghathu ahlam*; *taʾwiliʾl-ahlam*). The commentators expound upon the dream (Tabari, Thaʿlabi; Zamakhshari; Tabarsi; Razi Qurtubi; Bagdowi; Naysaburi, Shawkani) and state that God sent it to Pharaoh in order to bring about Joseph's release from prison (Razi, Qurtubi); in some accounts God informs Joseph in advance of the dream's correct interpretation (Qurtubi); in others he prevents Pharaoh's counsellors from understanding it (Naysaburi). Tabarsi states that Joseph's interpretation reflects not the dream *per se* but his God-given knowledge of the unknown, and, in an alternative account, that Joseph's ability to translate the dream's meaning belies the counsellors' declaration that these were 'muddled dreams'. Tha'labi and Shawkani describe 'muddled dreams' as those disturbed by, for instance, herbs or hashish.

The Joseph story provides an opportunity for the commentators to discuss the religious aspects of dreams in general. Qurtubi, for instance, deals at length with the role dreaming plays in prophethood; he also suggests that the pious will have truer dreams than other believers, and Muslims in general will have a greater proportion of true dreams than non-Muslims, and he describes an angel whose task it is to suggest images into the mind of the dreamer. In the context of 12.36, Razi explains how God created the soul such that it could separate from the body during sleep and move to a higher plane; Tabarsi states that dreams, just like prophecy, inform us about future events. Another point of interest concerns the realization of dreams: God has arranged it so that bad dreams are promptly fulfilled, while good dreams occur well in advance of their actualization, in order to limit anxiety and augment pleasant anticipation (Razi, Naysaburi). Indeed, Malik recommends that the interpreter dissemble or remain silent when faced with an apparently ominous dream (Qurtubi). Ibn 'Arabi refers the reader back to his discussion of dreams with reference to 11.74. There he describes true

dreams and prophecy as differing from one another only in whether the receiver is asleep or awake. He gives Muhammad's dream in 48.27 as an example of a true dream, which requires no interpretation, and explains how the Prophet received six months of true dreams as a prelude to his waking revelations; Ibn 'Arabi also discusses the spiritual aspects of one's openness to dreams.

Regarding Abraham, meanwhile, 37.102 informs us that Abraham told his son that he saw himself sacrificing the latter in a dream (*manam*), and in 37.105 Abraham is told that God now considered this dream (*ru'ya*) to have been fulfilled. Tabari, Zamakhshari, Razi and Naysaburi all explain that Abraham had promised to sacrifice his son the moment his birth was announced, and in the dream is told to fulfil his promise. In another account (Tha'labi, Zamakhshari, Razi, Qurtubi, Baydawi, Naysaburi), after Abraham hears a voice in his dream telling him of God's command, he spends the whole day deliberating whether the dream came from God or Iblis. When the dream is repeated the following night, the prophet realises that it comes from God; nonetheless, the dream comes a third time. Both Baydawi and Naysaburi state that Abraham could either have seen himself sacrificing his son, or seen what he interpreted as this sacrifice. Tabari, Tabarsi and Shawkani tell us that prophets' dreams are true and always acted upon; a further account states that the dreams of prophets are tantamount to revelation (Tabari; Zamakhshari; Tabarsi; Razi; Naysaburi; Shawkani), and Razi discusses the implications of this, arguing that if this were the case, Abraham would not have asked his son's opinion, nor deliberated for a day. Razi concludes that Abraham's dream was followed by a clear revelation, and it is this that was taken by the prophet as decisive.

Zamakhshari raises the issue of why God sent his command to the sleeping Abraham, and suggests that the bestowal of revelations during both waking and sleeping hours is a further confirmation of sincerity. Qurtubi likewise explains that prophets receive revelations when asleep and when awake; their hearts in fact never sleep. Razi, meanwhile, discusses the legality of commandments issued during sleep: he adduces 48.27 and 12.4 as indications that the dreams of prophets are realised by God, and sees the dreamt-of sacrifice both as a gentle introduction to the real situation and as a further indication of the sincerity of father and son. He concludes by stating that the dreams of prophets can be fulfilled (cf. Muhammad), contradicted (thus Abraham), or interpreted allegorically (cf. Joseph). Tabarsi in contrast divides the dreams of prophets into only two types: the straightforward (e.g. Muhammad's dream that he would enter the Sacred Mosque), and those that require interpretation (e.g. Joseph's dream of the sun, moon and stars, and Abraham's dream, as above).

Three of Muhammad's dreams are referred to in the Qur'an. 8.43 refers to a dream (*manam*) in which the Prophet was shown the enemy combatants in the battle of Badr to be few. The commentators focus again on the matter of whether a prophet's dream can in fact be deliberately untrue or misleading in this way: one response is that God does as He wishes (Razi); another is that Muhammad was shown only part of the enemy army (Tabarsi; Razi); Tha'labi meanwhile explains that God also made the enemy army appear small during the battle itself, thus verifying the dream. Tabarsi gives the explanation that the correct interpretation of a dream can in fact be the polar opposite of its *prima facie* reading and, moreover, the whole

meaning of a dream is not transparent to mankind. He goes on to divide dreams into four types: those from God, those from Satan, those that arise from the four humours, and those that emanate from thoughts, with only the first of these, dreams that come from God, being open to interpretation. 17.60 describes a vision (*ru'ya*) shown to the Prophet by God. This is interpreted as, *inter alia*, referring to a dream in which Muhammad saw people ascending his pulpit (Tabari), the Banu Marwan (Qurtubi; Shawkani) or the Banu Ummaya (Qummi, Qurtubi, Baydawi) leaping on it like apes, simply apes on the pulpit (Qummi; Tabarsi), or the downfall of the disbelievers of the Quraysh (Zamakhshari; Razi; Shawkani), or to the fact that Muhammad first received revelation via dreams (Naysaburi). 48.27 describes God's fulfilment of Muhammad's vision (*ru'ya*), possibly indicating a dream (Tabari, Tabarsi, Razi, Qurtubi, Naysaburi), that the believers would be able to perform pilgrimage to Mecca without fear. Razi states again here that a true prophet sees no falsehood in his dreams. Moreover, 21.5 alludes to the accusations of the disbelievers that the Qur'an is merely Muhammad's muddled dreams (*adghathu ahlam*), which Tabari, Tha'labi and Qurtubi expand to mean nightmares as well as mixed up or lying dreams, and Shawkani explains as lying or uninterpretable dreams.

As for dreams in general, the good tidings (*bushra*) described to the believers in 10.64 are explained by most commentators as representing pleasant dreams, and it is with reference to this verse that Razi cites the *hadith* that a good *ru'ya* comes from God, and a *hulm* from Iblis, and mentions invocations against the latter; Naysaburi specifies that, prior to receiving the Qur'an, Muhammad had revelatory dreams for the first six months of his term of prophecy (cf. Bukhari for an example of such a dream); Tha'labi gives the *hadith* that prophecy will, after the death of Muhammad, be replaced by pleasant dreams (bad dreams should not be recounted), and divides dreams into those sent by God, those that arise from man himself, and those inspired by Iblis. This verse was traditionally taken by Muslim oneirocrits as justification for an interest in dream interpretation (cf. Ibn Sirin). The commentators also mention dreams with reference to 39.42 and its discussion of God's seizing of souls during death and sleep. Qurtubi, for instance, takes this opportunity to explain that true dreams are those visions experienced while the soul is separated from the body during sleep; nightmares and lying dreams occur once the soul has returned to the body, but before it has again taken firm root.

References and further reading

al-Baydawi (1988) *Anwar al-tanzil wa asrar al-ta'wil*, Beirut: Dar al-kutub al-'ilmiyya.

al-Bukhari (1979) 'Kitab al-Ta'bir', *Sahih*; Istanbul: al-Maktaba al-islami.

Fahd, T. (1987) *La Divination Arabe: Études religieuses, sociologiques et folkloriques sur le milieu natif de l'Islam,* Paris: Sindbad, 247–367.

Ibn al-'Arabi (1978) *Tafsir al-Qur'an al-karim*, Beirut: Dar al-andalus.

Ibn Sirin (1996) *Tafsir al-ahlam al-kabir,* Beirut: Dar al-fikr.

Kinberg, L. (1993) 'Literal Dreams and Prophetic Hadith in Classical Islam: A comparison of two ways of legitimation', *Der Islam* 70: 279–300.

—— (1994) *Morality in the Guise of Dreams: Ibn Abi Dunya's Kitab al-Manam (A Critical Edition with Introduction)*, Leiden: E.J. Brill.

Kister, M. (1974) 'The Interpretation of Dreams: An unknown manuscript of Ibn Qutayba's '*Ibarat al-ru'ya*', *IOS* 4: 67–103.

Lamoreaux, J. (2002) *The Early Muslim Tradition of Dream Interpretation,* Albany, NY: SUNY Press.

al-Naysaburi (n.d.) *Tafsir Ghara'ib al-Qur'an wa ragha'ib al-furqan*, Beirut: Dar al-kutub al-'ilmiyya.

Oberhelman, S. (1997) 'Hierarchies of Gender, Ideology, and Power in Ancient and Medieval Greek and Arabic Dream Literature', in J. Wright and E. Rowson (eds) *Homoeroticism in Classical Arabic Literature*, New York: Columbia University Press, 55–93.

Qummi (1404/1983/4) *Tafsir al-Qummi*, Qum: Mu'assasat Dar al-kitab li'l tiba'a wal'l nashr.

Qurtubi (2000) *al-Jami' li-ahkam al-Qur'an*, Beirut: Dar al-kutub al-'ilmiyya.

al-Razi, Fakhr al-Din (2000), *Mafatih al-ghayb*; Beirut: Dar al-kutub al-'ilmiyya.

Shawkani (n.d.) *Fath al-qadir*, Beirut: Dar al-kutub al-'ilmiyya.

al-Tabari (1999) *Jami' al-bayan fi tafsir al-Qur'an*, Beirut: Dar al-kutub al-'ilmiyya.

Tabarsi (1936) *Jawami' al-jami' fi tafsir al-Qur'an al-karim*, Saida: Matba'at al-'urfan.

Tha'labi (n.d.) *al-Kashf wa'l-bayan*, Beirut: Dar ihya al-turath al-'arabi.

von Grünebaum, L. and Cillois, R. (eds) (1966) *The Dream and Human Societies*, Berkeley, CA: University of California Press.

al-Zamakhshari (n.d.) *al-Kashshaf 'an haqa'iq al-tanzil wa 'uyun al-aqawil fi wujuh al-ta'wil*, Beirut: Dar al-ma'arifa.

See also: **prophecy**

MARIANNA KLAR

E

EDUCATION AND THE QUR'AN

God says in the Qur'an that if all the trees on the planet became pens and all its oceans became ink, the words of Allah (and the meanings contained in them) would not be exhausted (31.27; 18.109). That means there is no end to knowledge. Allah enjoins on every one of us (those who call themselves Muslims) to use our reason, intellect and up-to-date human knowledge to directly try to understand and explore the meanings of his revelations (see especially verse 25.73). We will never be able to exhaust the meanings of God's words but we are asked, nevertheless, to keep striving continuously. We read: '*afala uta-dabbarun al-Qur'an*? (Do they not consider the Qur'an?)' (4.82). *Tadabbur* means highly concentrated and innovative critical thinking like the way scientists think when challenged to find something new or when we embark upon solving a difficult problem. The Qur'an is constantly making demands upon our intelligence in reading and grasping it, and so it is hardly surprising that the implication of the Book is that education is a significant activity for Muslims.

There can be no incompatibility between Islam and science because for many centuries the main centre of scientific investigation was precisely the Islamic world. So the Qur'an does not restrict education as far as the natural sciences go, although it might well be interpreted as arguing that there are certain scientific activities which Muslims should not pursue. But what about traditional Islamic education, especially in the Qur'an? Does this incline the student to avoid study of the wider and secular curriculum? It is certainly true that in many countries in the Islamic world the *madrasa* system acts in an uneasy relationship with state schools. These religious schools and colleges often offer free accommodation, free books, rigid discipline and a suspicious

190

attitude to any subject or curriculum that is largely secular.

It must be stated from the start, however, that there is no good reason why the secular system of education and the religious schools need to regard themselves as in opposition to each other. In some countries the religious school does incorporate a full curriculum of the normal subjects in addition to the religious ones, to no apparent detriment of the students' development in either. Thus, the opposition of the two school systems to each other probably has more to do with local political disputes and rivalries than it has to do with a basic clash between religion and the secular world.

The Qur'an does stress the significance of our relationship with God and the importance of orienting ourselves with respect to the afterlife. However, it is also a very realistic text, with lots of advice on issues such as money, trade, economic exchange, personal manners, and so on, and it can hardly be claimed that the Qur'an advocates not involving oneself in the everyday practical affairs of the world. Secular subjects are then highly appropriate for the Muslim student, just as they are for everyone else.

What is mainly at issue in the religious schools is not the curriculum but the pedagogy. The curriculum is based on the Qur'an, and students may be encouraged to learn to recite it by heart and then to interpret it, studying perhaps some of the leading commentators and legal thinkers and what they had to say about different parts of the Book. Particular issues will be selected and their solutions in the Qur'an discussed, with the variety of ways of interpreting such solutions often analysed and grouped together in certain ways. As well as the Qur'an, the *hadith*, the *sunna* of the Prophet and his history will all be studied, together with the language of Arabic which for most Muslims is a thoroughly foreign tongue. Even for Arabs, the type of Arabic used in the Qur'an is not necessarily familiar and the grammar of the Book is often studied in *madrasa*s. There is no reason to think that this sort of religious curriculum is in any way antagonistic to general education; it is merely an intellectual exercise carried out on a religious subject matter, and so forms part of a useful educational training.

It might be said that such a benign view of Qur'anic schools is misleading as it ignores the particular style of teaching that goes on there. The Qur'an is often learnt by rote, and the status of the teacher is elevated since he is passing on religious truths, not subjects that may be acquired or rejected at will by the student. So the pedagogy is based on the view that knowledge is acquired rather than discovered, that the student's mind is passive and receptive rather than active and creative, and that the general attitude is one where all knowledge is seen as unchangeable and books need to be memorized, not questioned. A dichotomy is thus set up between Islamic and modern education. The former has an otherworldly orientation, aims at socialization into Islam, uses curricula largely unchanged since medieval times and treats knowledge as something to be revealed and acquired because of a divine command. The questioning of what is taught is not welcomed, the teaching style is authoritarian, education is mainly undifferentiated and memorization is important. By contrast, modern education has an orientation towards the modern world, and aims at the development of the individual pupil. Curricula change to reflect changes in the subject matter, and knowledge is acquired through empirical or deductive methods and treated as a problem-solving tool. Teachers welcome student participation and questions, and the emphasis is on internalizing the main aspects of the subject, not memorizing them. Modern education can be very specialized, with very clear boundaries between disciplines.

It has been argued by Hoodbhoy (1991) that the two styles of education are in conflict with each other because they differ not only in subject matter but also in style. Students who go through the *madrasa* system and then enter the state system find it difficult to adjust because they have to play by an entirely different set of rules. They are not used to thinking independently, to taking risks with what they learn or to being inquisitive. So even if they do enter the modern education system, they are unlikely to thrive; their mindset is too enmeshed in an entirely different process of education. As Talbani (1996: 77–8) puts it when referring to Islamic society: 'originality, innovation, and change were never upheld as intrinsic values. The ideal of Islamic culture was not mechanical evolutionary progress, but the permanent immutable transcendental divinely revealed moral, theological, spiritual values of the Kur'an and Sunna.' It is certainly true that the use of constant repetition, which trains the power of recall, reflect an Islamic tradition of recitation and of seeing knowledge as external and as something to be revealed.

On the other hand, this view of the clash between the two pedagogies might be regarded as exaggerated. After all, how much of the so-called modern curriculum is really taught in accordance with the principles of modern education? There is a good deal of rote learning here also, and many students do not feel that they can question or challenge their teachers. Even at the level of tertiary education many students in the modern system of education are passive and concentrate on taking notes and repeating what they hear in the lecture hall. In addition, how much of the religious curriculum is really as traditional as the stereotype suggests? There is always going to be some mechanical learning when a new language is at issue, and students may also be encouraged to learn to recite the Qur'an as a propadeutic to understanding it, but these things do not in themselves orient the student away from independent thought. There is no evidence that children brought up within the confines of traditional religious education are any less innovative or active than children brought up within the modern system. We are familiar with the phenomenon of the religious thinker who is at the same time highly skilled outside the religious environment, and presumably his or her religious training does not impede adopting a distinct methodology when working on non-religious subjects.

Rather than wonder whether people can switch from one type of thinking to another, we might ask whether these two pedagogies are really so distinct. The *madrasa*s that allow commentary and different views on the Qur'an to be explored surely err more on the modern side of pedagogy, as their students will be spending a lot of their time arguing, debating, sifting evidence, challenging the views of those set above them, and so on. Religion does not consist of the mere repetition of religious material, but rather often also in an attempt at understanding it and working with it to apply religion to contemporary issues. This is just as true for Islam as for any other religion, and we need to remind ourselves of the subversive nature of the Qur'an itself. When the Holy Book was revealed, it challenged the prevailing views and what up to that point had defined authority. The Qur'an argues that individuals should not do what their fathers had done just because this was accepted practice; instead it advocates thinking, reasoning and arguing until the truth is revealed. It is difficult to argue, then, that Qur'anic education is in itself opposed to modern principles of teaching and learning. This is not to ignore the fact that in many places Qur'anic education follows a traditional model which does stand in the way of modern education. However, when this occurs perhaps it is simply the case of adopting too much respect for tradition, something that the Book itself constantly counsels against.

References and further reading

Hoodbhoy, P. (1991) *Islam and Science: Religious orthodoxy and the battle for rationality*, Karachi: Zed Books.
Leaman, O. (2003) 'The Search for Tradition: Islamic art and science in the thought of Seyyed Hossein Nasr', in M. Faghfoory (ed.), *Beacon of Knowledge*, Louisville: Fons Vitae, 305–15.
Talbani, A. (1996) 'Pedagogy, Power and Discourse: Transformation of Islamic education', *Comparative Education Review* 40, 1: 66–82.

See also: **Arabic language;** *hafiz*; **language and the Qur'an;** *Nahda*; **Nursi, Said;** *qalam*; *taqlid*

OLIVER LEAMAN

ELIJAH

Elijah (Ilyas) is a prophet in the Qur'an. In the Bible he is often identified with Elijah or Elias. With the death of Sulayman, his kingdom fell apart. This allowed the influence of Satan to become widespread among the people of Israel. The religious people were mocked and the ruler of Samaria killed a large number of learned people. When the evil reached its apex, during the reign of King Ahab of Israel, God sent Ilyas to reform mankind. He tried his best to save the people from polytheism and forbade them to worship the Tyrian Baal. He advised the people to ward off

evil and to worship the One God. However, his efforts bore no fruit. Then he suddenly appeared before the king and foretold that a severe drought and famine would overtake the kingdom. Ilyas added that the Tyrian Baal would be powerless to avert such an event.

The people paid no heed to his warnings and did not mend their ways. The prophecy of Ilyas turned out to be true; the kingdom experienced famine and its people began to starve. After three years Ilyas prayed to God to show mercy to the famine-stricken people. They acknowledged the authority of God and felt regret. Soon afterwards rain ended the drought and God lifted his curses. After this Ilyas was directed by God to call upon al-Yasa to be his successor. Ilyas did this and then disappeared mysteriously. Qur'anic references can be found at 6.85; 37.123; and 37.130.

OLIVER LEAMAN

ELISHA

Known in Arabic as al-Yasa', Elisha is a prophet who is mentioned by name two times in the Qur'an (6.86; 38.48), along with a list of other prophets including Ishmael, Jonah, Lot and Dhu al-Kifl. Many exegetes also identify Elisha with the name 'Asbat', also mentioned in the Qur'an in a list of prophets. Various genealogies are given to Elisha but it is commonly asserted that he was the son of the paternal uncle of the prophet Elijah, and exegetes state that Elisha went with Elijah to Baalbek, Mount Qasyun, and was with Elijah when he was raised up into heaven (see 37.123–132). Wahb b. Munabbih relates that when Elijah was raised into heaven he was clothed with feathers and fire, making him part-human and part-angel, and that Elijah passed on his prophetic mantle to Elisha. The close relationship between Elijah and Elisha parallels the biblical account (1 Kings 19: 19–2; Kings 13: 20) in which Elisha repeats and improves upon the miracles of Elijah. Unlike the chronology of the biblical account where he is placed approximately 150 years after David, Muslim exegesis puts Elisha immediately before Samuel and the first kings of Israel.

Further reading

Bronner, L. (1990) *The Stories of Elijah and Elisha as Polemics against Baal Worship*, Pretoria Oriental Studies 6, Leiden: E.J. Brill.

Coote, R.B. (ed.) (1992) *Elijah and Elisha in Socioliterary Perspective*, Atlanta, GA: Scholars Press.

Renteria, T.H. (1992) 'The Elijah/Elisha Stories: The socio-cultural analysis of prophets and people in ninth century BCE Israel', in R.B. Coote (ed.) *Elijah and Elisha in Socio-cultural Perspective*, Atlanta, GA: Scholars Press, 75–126.

BRANNON WHEELER

ENOCH

see: **Idris**

ESCHATOLOGY

The concept of the hereafter in the Islamic tradition

The Qur'anic term for eschatology is *al-akhira* (the afterlife) or *ahwal al-akhira* (situations related to the afterlife) as represented in the manuals of Islamic theology. The Qur'an clearly states that *al-akhira* (the afterlife) is better for you than *al-'ula* (the world). Belief in the afterlife constitutes one of the six articles of faith in Islam. The Qur'an teaches that the life of this world as well as the life of every individual will come to an end. For human beings, the life after death starts as soon as they die. The existence of the afterlife is necessary.

God's beautiful names require such an existence. Only God knows the time of the universal death of the world. The Prophet mentions some warnings: the signs of the Hour indicate the closeness of the final Day of Judgement.

Al-akhira

The subject of the afterlife constitutes one of the three branches of Islamic theology. One quarter of the Qur'an is dedicated to its existence and details. As one of the articles of faith, all Muslims have to believe in it. The Qur'an also uses the term *al-yawm al-akhir* or the Final Day to describe the life to come. Muslim theologians employ the term *ahwal al-akhira* to designate those things related to the hereafter, such as the existence of the afterlife, the time of its occurrence, the signs of its nearness, death and resurrection, the reckoning, the reward and punishment in the afterlife and the final abodes.

The Qur'an uses the term *al-akhira* or the Day of Judgement in opposition to *al-'ula* or this world. The word is used in the Qur'an with its masculine form *al-akhir* and the feminine *al-akhira* over 100 times. The Holy Book employs some other terms for the afterlife such as *qiyama* (resurrection), *al-sa'a* (the Hour), *al-naba' al-'azim* (the Great News) and *al-yawm al-din* (the Day of Judgement).

According to the teachings of the Qur'an, this life is transient; the real life is the life to come. Life on earth is believed to be a gift from God and has to be spent properly, following God's way. The Prophet uses the parable of a farm, saying: 'this worldly life is the farm of the afterlife', that is, one would sow the seeds to harvest in the hereafter. The Prophet's duty is to warn people about this inevitable and imminent event. The Holy Book speaks of various stages of the afterlife. Based on some

Qur'anic references and the body of *hadith*, one can arguably conclude the following scenario as far as the afterlife is concerned.

God will bring the order of this world to an end through a mighty earthquake. The celestial bodies will clash into one another. The planet earth, the home of human beings, will be destroyed. As a result, every living creature will die. As a gift from God, the people of faith will die naturally before this extremely horrific event. The people of disbelief will see the event, then die. After a certain period of time the archangel Seraphiel, one of the four archangels in Islam, will blow into a trumpet. As a result, all people will be resurrected both bodily and spiritually. God is the Judge on this day of resurrection. He will ask people about their deeds in their worldly life. To show God's utmost justice scales will measure the bad and the good deeds of people. If good deeds outweigh bad deeds, the person will be among the people of paradise; if the reverse is the case, the person will be among the people of hell. The measurement is not based on quantity but on the quality of deeds. Therefore, sincerity, honesty, seeking the pleasure of God while doing good deeds, play a vital role in the measurement process. Subsequently, both groups will stay in their final abode forever.

Existence of the afterlife

It would not be an exaggeration to claim that one of the most striking aspects of the Qur'anic revelation to Meccan society, the first addressee of the Qur'an, was its emphasis on the hereafter. One can see this in the Prophet's debate with Meccan idol worshippers, as outlined in some Qur'anic verses dealing with the existence of the afterlife. The Qur'an narrates the story of a prominent figure in Mecca who comes to the Prophet and challenges him by saying, 'Who can resurrect these rotten bones?' God asks Muhammad to reply that the One who created them first will resurrect them (36.79). For God, it is not difficult to bring about the afterlife, since he creates examples of resurrection every spring: 'Now, look at results of Allah's mercy, how He resurrects the earth [in the spring] after it is dead [in winter]. The One [who] makes this, surely will resurrect the dead in the same way. With Him every thing is possible' (30.50); 'You were dead and He resurrected you. He will make you dead again and resurrect you again. All of you will return to Him' (2.28).

Muslim theologians have different approaches in arguing for the existence of the afterlife. Although Ibn Sina (d. 1037 CE) says that the concept of resurrection and afterlife cannot be understood by reason, a number of theologians have attempted to prove the existence of the afterlife. Fakhr al-Din al-Razi (d. 1210 CE) in his monumental work on the interpretation of the Qur'an says that the existence of the afterlife can be proven through both textual and rational arguments. Through reason one can conclude that the human body is not eternal, but transient, and the world in which we live suggests that the existence of the afterlife is possible. Al-Razi refers to the Qur'anic references for his textual arguments.

Some recent theologians such as Said Nursi (d. 1960 CE) also argue that the concept of the afterlife can be demonstrated through reason. In *The Treatise of Resurrection,* he refers to various names of God and through each he argues for the existence and necessity of the afterlife. For instance, one of the names referred to in the treatise is *al-'Adl* (the Just). According to his argument one can evidently see a supreme balance, justice and order in this universe as well as a quick response to the needs of every creature. Logically, it would not be possible for such a dominant justice that responds to the need of the smallest creatures to ignore the paramount need of humanity for eternal life. Although physically human beings are small creatures, yet their duties, their mental capacity of construction and destruction, are virtually unlimited. Accordingly, there must be a supreme court to reward and punish the good and bad deeds of such an important and intelligent creature. It is evident that this world is not a place wherein the application of justice among humans is thoroughly practiced. As a matter of fact, the reverse seems to be applicable. The oppressed dies still oppressed while the oppressor dies as an oppressor, without any fulfilment of justice. The manifest balance and order in the universe demonstrates that there must be a place where the oppressed receives some reward and the oppressor receives punishment. Therefore, the existence of the afterlife, which includes *janna* and *jahannam* (paradise and hell), is inevitable.

With regards to the existence of the afterlife, references have been made to some other names of God, for example, *al-Jawad* (the Most Generous) whose reflections are seen in the innumerable bounties bestowed upon creatures in the world. Through an infinite generosity, God made the face of the earth an exhibition for his beautiful creatures, the moon and the sun as two lamps for their benefit. He has filled the face of the earth with a variety of delicious foods, and made the fruitful trees full of food for us. Such generosity evidently necessitates the existence of eternal guests to show them the everlasting sources of these temporary bounties.

Referring to a group of materialists who deny the existence of the afterlife,
the Holy Book says: 'It is God who gives life and death. He will gather you on the Day of Judgement about which there is no doubt' (45.26). The statement of 'no doubt' seems to be emphasized twice on the same page. To bring the afterlife is the promise of God, who is powerful over everything and who never breaks his promise. Referring to God's power with regard to the resurrection of all human beings, the verse indicates that the creation and resurrection of all human beings are as easy as the resurrection of one human being (31.28). In fact, the verse refers to God's command 'Be!' Since creation and resurrection take place as a result of God's command, the proliferation in numbers of objects does not make any difference. Qur'anic logic in arguing for the existence of an afterlife seems to be based on the necessity of the afterlife and the power of God. It is based on the idea that there is no reason why the most powerful being in existence would not create an afterlife and resurrect all human beings.

Death

Human experience of death, an inevitable part of human destiny, constitutes the first stage of the hereafter. Accordingly, death is believed to be a door to the realm of the afterlife, which according to Islamic tradition starts with the grave. The Qur'an teaches that everyone with no exception will taste death. The Prophet describes the life of the grave as the first station of the afterlife. Islamic teaching depicts life as a test and death as the end of the test. Therefore, when death comes, the chances to return to this worldly life are exhausted. Muslims call the life of the grave *barzakh*, a term that corresponds to the period one spends in the grave until the time of the final Hour. The Qur'an refers to death as a gift from God, because if there were no death, then life, especially that of the sick and old, would be miserable and even unbearable.

Every soul eventually tastes death. The Prophet, using allegorical language, says that people are asleep, that they wake up when they die; that is to say that with death real life starts and the eye sees the reality of everything. God has appointed a time for both types of death, yet no one knows the exact time with certainty. When the time comes, there will be no delay, not even for a second. Therefore, the Qur'an asks people to be prepared for the next life. In the *sura al-Hashr* (the Resurrection) the Holy Book of Islam asks people not to forget their meeting with God: 'O believers! Be respectful to your Lord. Every soul should look at what it has prepared for tomorrow ... Do not be like those who have forgotten Allah' (59.18–19)

The second event is the death of the world, in other words, the end of human civilization. Muslim theologians consider our planet to be like a living creature, appointed to serve humans and other creatures for a certain period of time. Since it lives, consequently it will die. One can hardly imagine the horrendous death of such a sizeable creature. Through a quick examination of the Qur'an, one can find many *suras* named after this great event of the final Hour. It is an event through which God will bring human civilization to an end and create a new world where another dimension of life takes place. Thirteen Qur'anic *suras* are directly related to the afterlife and its preparations:

sura 22 (*al-Sa'a* or the Hour, the same chapter has been named also *al-Hajj* or the Pilgrimage);
sura 44 (*al-Dukhan* or Smoke);
sura 45 (*al-Jasiya* or the Kneeling);
sura 56 (*al-Waqi'a* or the Imminent Occurrence);

sura 59 (*al-Hashr* or Gathering);
sura 69 (*al-Haqqa* or the Reality);
sura 75 (*al-Qiyama* or the Resurrection);
sura 78 (*al-Naba'* or the Great News);
sura 81 (*al-Takwir* or the Darkened Sun);
sura 82 (*al-Infitar* or the Shattering);
sura 84 (*al-Inshiqaq* or the Sundering);
sura 88 (*al-Ghashiya* or the Overwhelming Event);
sura 101 (*al-Qari'a* or the Imminent Hour Striking).

Some of the above-mentioned *suras* indicate the closeness of the event and warn people to be prepared for the imminent day. For instance, the first verses of the *sura* 22, which deal with the mighty earthquake and the situations of people on that day, represent this style of divine address:

O People! Be respectful to your Lord. The earthquake of the Hour is a mighty thing. It is a day when you see a horrified nursing mother throw her baby away, every pregnant being drops her fetus, and you will see the people drunk. In fact they are not drunk, but the chastisement of God is severe. (22.1–2)

One of the most descriptive *suras* of the Qur'an on the afterlife is *sura* 78, the Great News. In the beginning emphasis is placed on the bounties and the power of Allah. For instance, it is God who has made the earth as a cradle for human beings, the mountains as supports to protect the balance of the earth, he has created humans male and female, has made the night a time for resting and the day a time for living. Towards the end of the chapter a comparison between the transgressors (*al-taghin*) and the righteous (*al-muttaqin*) takes place. The first will receive a great chastisement; the latter will receive a great reward.

The Day of Judgement

After the death of the world, God will resurrect all people. As indicated above the resurrection of one person and of all humanity are the same before the power of God. The Holy Book of Islam, the body of *hadith* and the works of Muslim theologians have focused on the details of this day. In his depiction of the gathering for the Day of Judgement, the Prophet speaks of an extremely high temperature as a result of which many will almost be drowned in their sweat. People will desperately ask for intercession by the prophets (Abraham, Moses, Jesus and Muhammad). Due to their ablution before the five daily prayers in worldly life, the Prophet will easily recognize the members of his community. On this day, divine justice will be completely fulfilled. The Qur'an speaks of a book (*kitab*) in which there would be a record of every action, bad and good. Therefore, people would not be able to deny their deeds done in this worldly life.

The Holy Book divides people on this terrible day into two groups; those who receive their book through their right hands are the people of paradise. They will find what the Lord has prepared for them from his eternal treasures. The second group comprises those who receive their book through their left hands; they will be taken to the eternal abode of punishment that is Hell. The Prophet gives hope to some in this group, indicating that anyone who has faith, even as small as a seed of mustard, will not stay in hell forever. Instead, after finishing the period of punishment they will be taken to paradise. To illustrate the life of paradise, various Qur'anic verses provide details of pleasures that God will give to this group of people. The pleasures of this world compared to the pleasures of paradise seem to be nothing but a shadow of the real pleasures. The highest pleasure in paradise is to see God (*ru'yatulla*). Describing the life of paradise in a comparative way, a recent Muslim theologian states that a thousand years of happiness in this worldly life cannot be compared to an hour of the life of paradise; similarly a thousand years of the life of paradise cannot be compared to an hour of seeing the beauty of God. According to the teachings of Islam, these two places are the final destinations of the human being.

The Signs of the Hour

Yet the question of *when* remains. According to the Qur'an, the knowledge of the time of the final Hour belongs only to God. It can be any time and will be as fast as the twinkling of an eye (*lamh al-basar*). The Prophet lists a number of events that will take place before the coming of the final Hour and Muslim theologians have developed special sections in their books on the *'alamat al-sa'a* (the Signs of the Hour). The body of *hadith* and Islamic theology contain a rich literature on the details of the events that signal the Hour. Although there are Qur'anic verses which hint at such signs, Muslim scholars consider the body of *hadith* as the main reference point in the Islamic tradition. Based on the sayings of the Prophet, they have categorized the events before the Hour into two groups. The first group of events are called *small signs* and relate to the decrease of spirituality and the spread of all kinds of corruption on the earth. The *hadith* speaks of the decrease of knowledge, the spread of adultery and fornication in public places, etc.

The second group of events, called the *major signs* of the Hour, comprises ten signs according to the *hadith* of Huzayfa bin Asid, a prominent companion of the Prophet. The Prophet points out that before the coming of the Hour, the following signs will emerge to signal its imminence:

1. the emergence of the Anti-Christ (*al-Dajjal*);
2. the spread of smoke (*al-dukhan*);
3. the emergence of a beast (*dabbat al-ardh*);
4. the rise of the sun from the west (*tulu' al-shams min al-maghrib*);
5. the descent of Jesus (*nuzul 'Isa*);
6. the emergence of Gog and Magog (*Ya'juj wa Ma'juj*);
7. the disappearance of three lands in the East, the West and the Arabian peninsula;
8. the emergence of a fire from the south to gather people in the place of the final gathering (*al-hashr*).

It should be noted that the list provided in this *hadith* does not imply that these signs will occur consecutively. Five of them signal that the time of the Hour is extremely close: the emergence of Anti-Christ, the descent of Jesus, the emergence of a beast, the emergence of Gog and Magog, and finally the rise of the sun from the west. Muslim theologians argue that when the final sign, the rise of the sun from the west, occurs, God will not accept repentance any more, because the time of the Hour has already arrived.

Some theologians think this language should not be interpreted literally, while others insist on the literal truth of every word in the Qur'an and the *hadith*. A third group is more balanced with respect to the Signs of the Hour. They accept the authenticity of the sayings of the Prophet on this subject, although they also accept the existence of some fabricated *hadith* on this matter. This group asserts that the words of the Prophet should not be taken literally, otherwise it would lead to confusion. The use of allegorical language constitutes a great part of the Prophet's sayings; accordingly, the Prophet's mention of these events should also be understood metaphorically. For instance, when the Prophet speaks of the descent of Jesus, one should understand that it is the strength of spirituality, which is symbolized by Jesus, that is meant. One should not expect a man descending from the sky physically. Such a literalist idea would not match God's actions in the world of nature. Furthermore, according to these scholars of Islamic tradition, Jesus will descend in the form of an angel, and angels can ascend and descend at any time without our knowledge and even without being visible.

The majority of Muslims believe in the Signs of the Hour, without questioning the exact way of their occurrence. They affirm that since the Prophet has stated this on many occasions, it will happen.

Further reading

Cragg, K. (1998) *Readings in the Qur'an*, London: Collins Religious Publishing.

Nursi, Bediuzzaman Said (1990) *Resurrection and the Hereafter*, trans. Hamid Algar, Istanbul: Sözler Neşriyat.

al-Razi, Fakhr al-Din (1990) *al-Tafsir al-kabir, aw, mafatih al-ghayb*, Beirut: Dar al-kutub al-'ilmiya.

Saritoprak, Z. (2003) 'The Legend of al-Dajjal (Antichrist): The personification of evil in the Islamic tradition', *The Muslim World* 93, 2: 291–307.

Smith, J. and Haddad, Y. (1981) *The Islamic Understanding of Death and Resurrection*, Albany, NY: SUNY Press.

See also: '*adl*; *akhira*; **arguments and the Qur'an**; **Dajjal**; **repentance**; *shafa'a*; *zuhd*

ZEKI SARITOPRAK

EZRA

see: 'Uzayr

F

FADA'IL AL-QUR'AN

The *fada'il al-Qur'an* (excellences of the Qur'an) traditions found in common in the so-called canonical and non-canonical *hadith* compilations deal largely with the memorization of the Qur'an, its compilation and recording, its best reciters, and the excellences of certain chapters and verses. Five of the six authoritative Sunni *hadith* collections have a separate chapter or section on the excellences of the Qur'an.

Discrete works on *fada'il al-Qur'an* began to emerge in the third/ninth century. The jurist Muhammed b. Idris al-Shafi'i (d. 204/819) is said to have been the first to compose such an independent treatise: called *Manafi' al-Qur'an* (lit. benefits of the Qur'an), it appears not to be extant. Shi'i authorities attribute an earlier work with an identical title to Ja'far al-Sadiq (d. 148/763), part of which is still supposedly extant. The titles *Manafi' al-Qur'an* and, less frequently, *Thawab al-Qur'an* (merit[s] of the Qur'an) are alternative titles for collections of *fada'il al-Qur'an* traditions.

The third/ninth and fourth/tenth centuries were the *floruit* for treatises on excellences of the Qur'an. From the third/ninth century we have Abu 'Ubayd al-Qasim b. Sallam al-Baghdadi's (d. 224/837) *Fada'il al-Qur'an*, which is still extant and the oldest work now available in published form. From later centuries we have the *fada'il al-Qur'an* of the well-known exegete 'Ali b. Muhammad al-Wahidi (d. 468/1075) and of another well-known commentator, Abu'l-Fida' Isma'il Ibn Kathir (d. 774/1371).

The *fada'il al-Qur'an* literature provides valuable insights into, for example, the position of Qur'an reciters in early Islamic society, early attitudes towards writing conventions in the *mushafs*, modes of recitation, the probity of accepting wages for teaching the Qur'an, and the authority of oral versus written transmission of the Qur'anic text.

Further reading

Afsaruddin, A. (2002) 'The Excellences of the Qur'an: Textual sacrality and the organization of early Islamic society', *JAOS*, 122: 1–24.

—— (2002) 'In Praise of the Word of God: Reflections of early religious and social concerns in the *fada'il al-Qur'an* genre', *Journal of Qur'anic Studies* 4: 28–48.

al-An'ani, 'Abd al-Razzaq (1971) *al-Musannaf*, ed. H. al-A'zami, Beirut: al-Maktabi al-islami.

Denny, F. (1980) 'The Adab of Qur'an Recitation: Text and context', in A.H. Johns and S. Jafri (eds) *International Congress for the Study of the Qur'an*, I, Canberra: Australian National University.

al-Nasa'i (1980) *Fada'il al-Qur'an*, ed. F. Hamada, Casablanca: Dar al-thaqafa.

ASMA AFSARUDDIN

FADL

Fadl means excessiveness. As a technical term, it is used to express acts of kindness, bounty (*lutf*) and grace (*ihsan*) performed willingly for no particular reason and with no expectation of return. *Fadl* finds its roots in deep knowledge and comprehension ('*irfan*), which coexist with ethics and faith, and is a form of wisdom expected of the learned ('*alim*). This phrase is also used to express the bounty and the benevolence of Allah: '... and Allah is the Lord of grace abounding' (57.21, 29), 'Grace is [entirely] in His Hand, to bestow it on whomsoever He wills' (57.29). Hell is from Allah's justice and Paradise is from Allah's bounty. Allah's *fadl* for his beloved servants is bountiful sustenance in this world, and Paradise in the hereafter. The infinitive and the derivatives of the phrase *fadl* occur 104 times in the Qur'an, and they are used with three meanings. First, the term is used to mean 'high merit': 'But the chiefs of the Unbelievers among his people said: "We see [in] you nothing but a man like ourselves ... Nor do we see in you [all] any merit above us: in fact we think you are liars!"' (11.27). Second, it is used to mean 'virtue', which expresses goodness and high moral character as attributes of people: 'To forgo is nearer to piety. And do not forget kindness among yourselves. For Allah sees well all that you do' (2.237). Third, the phrase *fadl* is generally used in other verses of the Qur'an as an attribute of Allah as in 'the grace of Allah' and 'the bounty of Allah'.

The number of such verses exceed eighty: 'Such is the grace of Allah which He giveth unto whom He will. Allah is All Embracing, All Knowing' (5.54), 'Were it not for the grace and mercy of Allah on you, in this world and the Hereafter, a grievous penalty would have seized you in that you rushed glibly into this affair' (24.14); see also 62.10, 73.20, and so on. The concept of *fadl* is also used in the Qur'an to describe the graces of Allah as bestowed on the people of Islam in particular (49.7–8; 57.29). There is also the phrase *fadilet*, which is derived from *fadl* to mean 'virtue' and 'kindness'. *Fadilet* is an advanced level of *fadl*, and it expresses the degree of adherence to the religious codes and ethics. *Fadilet* is the advanced and mature stage of the good manners and attributes a person possesses at birth. Each faculty of *fadilet* is a state of moderation (*itidal*). *Fadilet* is the phrase used for the spiritual abilities that determine the ongoing and unchanging capabilities of a person towards doing good and abstaining from evil. In Islamic culture, the formation of a systematic theory of virtue coincides with the development of philosophical culture.

Further reading

Abdulbaqi, M.F. (1986) *al-Mu'cemu'l-Mufehres li-Elfazi'l-Qur'an*, Istanbul: Cagri Publishing House.

Firuzabadi, T. (1991) *al-Qamusu'l-Muhit*, Beirut: Dar al-ihya'it-turasi'l-'arabiyye.

Ibn Manzur, M.M. (1995) *Lisan'ul-'Arab*, Beirut: Dar al-ihya'it-turasi'l-'arabiyye.

al-Isfahani, R. (1992) *al-Mufredatu Elfazi'l-Qur'an*, Damascus: Dar al-qalem.

Pickthall, M.M. (1981) *The Meaning of the Glorious Qur'an*, Beirut: Dar al-kitab al-lubnani.

al-Razi, F. (1985) *Imam Razi's 'Ilm al-akhlaq, Kitab al-Nafs Wa'l-Ruh Wa Sharh Quwahuma*, trans. M. Saghir Hasan Ma'sumi, Islamabad: The Islamic Research Institute.

Sami, Sh. (1996) *Qamus-ı Turki*, Istanbul: Cagri Publishing House.

See also: **lutf**

AHMET ALBAYRAK

FAKHR AL-DIN AL-RAZI
see: **al-Razi, Fakhr al-Din**

FASAQA

Fasaqa is a term in the past tense and it means a thing that came about from another thing in a bad or corrupt manner; the Arabs would say '*Fasaqat al-rutub*' (the fresh, ripe date came forth from its skin). In the Qur'an, this term signifies that someone departed or quit the way of truth, indicating disobedience to God or neglect of his commands. *Fasiq* is a noun and refers to a transgressor or sinful person who, although acknowledging the authority of religious law and undertaking to observe what it ordains, has nonetheless fallen short in its observance. That person has chosen to disobey the law and would have probably gone even further and fought it. Satan was the first creature to disobey God and the Qur'an says that he *fasaqa* (disobeyed God): 'And remember when we said to the angels "Prostrate yourselves unto Adam." So they prostrated themselves except Iblis (Satan). He was one of the Jinn; he disobeyed the command of his Lord' (18.50).

Not only those who committed themselves to abide by the law and then abandoned it are *fasiqin* (transgressors): those who do not believe in the oneness of God and the message of Muhammad are also described by *fasaqa*. 'Thus is the word of your Lord justified against those who rebel [disobey Allah] that they will not believe in the oneness of Allah and in Muhammad as the Messenger of Allah' (10.33).

The Qur'an indicates that those who commit *fisq* (transgression) are mostly the corrupt elite within a certain society. There has always been this connection between luxurious life and transgression. In most cases the Qur'an describes the corrupt rich as disobedient and aggressors. This upper class is the weakest link in society; with their evil actions, they could cause the destruction of the entire society: 'And when we decide to destroy a town we first send a definite order to obey Allah to those among them who lead a life of luxury. Then they transgress therein and thus the word of torment is justified against it' (17.16). The people who committed *fisq* are threatened by the Qur'an with a severe and everlasting torment in the fires of Hell: 'And as for those who are *fasiqin*, their abode will be the Fire, every time they wish to get away from there, they will be put back there and it will be said to them "'taste the torment of the fire which you used to deny'" (32.20).

RAFIK BERJAK

FASTING

Fasting or *sawm* is regarded in the Qur'an as very important. It helps us control our physical urges and trains us to obey the Word of God. A major fast runs from the sighting of the new moon that begins the month of Ramadan to the end of the lunar month: 'Oh you who believe, fasting is prescribed for you as it was prescribed for those before you, so that you may learn self-restraint' (2.183). The ninth Islamic month is called Ramadan and fasting is prescribed in that month. By *fajr* (dawn) the fasting starts, until the time dusk falls; every dusk *iftar* occurs when the fast finishes, and right at the end is the Eid al-Fitr. Fasting brings our life into a state of submission and surrender to the law of the creator. In the Qur'an, fasting is mentioned twelve more times and clearly plays an important role in helping human beings align themselves with virtue and reject evil. Patience is a key Qur'anic virtue and restraining our natural desires is an excellent way of inculcating virtue in our characters.

See also: **Ramadan; *sabr; salat***

OLIVER LEAMAN

FATE

The concept of fate or divine predestination is discussed as *qadar*. The term *qadar* (measuring out, divine determination) is used synonymously with *qudra* (ability, power); it appears in ten verses that form the basis of the doctrine of predestination, divine destiny or fate. Divine destiny also implies God's power and knowledge, which are referred to in the Qur'an in many places (2.256; 6.9; 54.49; 15.21).

Various Islamic thinkers have dealt with the problem of freedom (*huriyya*), choice (*ikhtiyar*) and free will (*irada*). The jurists are more concerned with the rights and liberty that are the outcome of conformity to the divine law (*shari'a*); Sufis seek inner freedom through liberation from man's bondage to the lower self; philosophers generally assert the reality of human free will from the

standpoint of al-Farabi's (d. 970) political philosophy; and the theologians (*mutakallimun*) are mainly concerned with the relationship between the divine will and human will, and how the former limits the latter (Nasr, 1981: 18–23).

One of the issues that theologians discussed was whether God predetermines human activity or whether human beings are free to act. This is not just a theoretical question of a particular group or historical period, but has puzzled man throughout the ages. Today, the debate between nature and nurture among social scientists is but a continuation of the earlier theological debates.

Fate is implied in the verse: 'He created everything and meted out for it a measure' (48.21). The operative word is *taqdir*, which literally means to fix for a thing a certain measure or quantity. It has several implications. The first is that God has endowed every being with certain qualities or potentialities that are peculiar to it: a particular plant has a specific shape, smell and size. The second is that God has appointed for all his creatures a certain place, time and environment: one man is different from another because of his colour, race and cultural background. Third, there is death, which is an unalterable part of human life and has a specific time. The Qur'an states: 'No soul can ever die except by Allah's leave and at a time appointed.' (3.145)

The question that is posed is whether these fates have a bearing on man's destination in the hereafter. Most scholars say it does not. Man has a limited free will, and how he uses it determines his destiny on the Day of Judgement. However, divine decree implies God's omniscience, and if God has foreknowledge of future human actions, then how could man be held responsible for his actions? Theologians and philosophers had to grapple with this question, and came up with different answers.

Theological views

In this section, the views of the early predestinarians (Jabarites) and libertarians (Qadarites/Mu'tazilites), as well as the Ash'arites who attempted to reconcile these two extreme positions, will be disussed (Watt, 1973: 82–9).

The early Muslim community had no time or inclination to indulge in the theological controversy surrounding divine determinism and human free will, which emerged as a later issue. By the end of the seventh century, two views emerged: first, the predestinarian view that was held by the fatalists (Jabarites) who were inspired by Qur'anic verses that stressed the absolute power of God over all human actions; and, second, the libertarians (Qadarites) who were inspired by verses that accentuated the will of man and his responsibility. This division continued within Islamic theology (*kalam*) between those who retained the original predestinarian or fatalistic view and those who retained the original libertarian view, with the Mu'tazilites here succeeding the Qadarites (Wolfson, 1976: 734). I shall now briefly explain the positions held by these two conflicting schools.

The fatalistic view

Jahm ibn Safwan was among the first to formulate a doctrine of human action, some time before the middle of the eighth century. His doctrine of compulsion emphasized the sovereignty of God, and appealed to the fatalistic scholars. Jahm ibn Safwan maintained that there is no difference between things that happen in the world in general and the actions of human beings; they are all continuously and directly created by God. Man's actions are like the manifestations of natural phenomena, with the difference that man possesses power (*quwwa*), will (*irada*) and choice (*ikhtiyar*). These are human qualities that, in any case, are created by God in man, which therefore makes man compelled (*majbur*) to obey God's will in his actions, leaving him without will and choice in matters even of religious obligation. The fatalists adhered to this view, basing their arguments on verses of the Qur'an that imply God's absolute power. Verses such as: 'To Him belongs the dominion of the heavens and the earth. He brings to life and causes to die, and He has power over everything' (57.2) and 'Say: "Nothing will befall us except what Allah has decreed for us"' (9.51).

As a reaction to fatalism, Ma'bad al-Juhani (49/669) and his followers, who were the first to discuss *qadar* (predestination) at Basra, rejected it. They were the Qadarites, associated with their leader Hasan al-Basri (110/728), who held that moral action implies freedom, and that guidance comes from God and error from man.

The libertarian view

The libertarians (Qadarites) made a distinction between the acts of nature and human actions. The former are from God, and the latter from man. Their main support for the idea of free will is that divine justice required it. Some believed that God endowed man with it at birth; others held that God gives it to man before each act. The assertion of free will gives rise to the problem of God's foreknowledge and power. The majority of the libertarians held that God has no power over that with which he endowed man. Man's power is not determined by God's power. God delegates this free will to man; a power that possesses a free action of God (Wolfson,

1976: 615–19). This view conflicts with the fatalists, who regard God's power as absolute.

Another view is that human actions are created by God, but acquired by man. Two Mu'tazilites, Dirar and Najjar, held this view. The former held that God gave man the power to act freely from birth, while the latter held that God creates both man's power and his act of acquiring that power. The fatalists identified with these views. The Ash'arites adopted Najjar's view (Wolfson, 1976: 736–7).

On divine foreknowledge, some libertarians believed that it nullifies man's free will and responsibility. However, the Qur'an points to God's foreknowledge: 'He knows all things' (57.3); 'He is fully cognizant of what ye do' (63.11); 'Allah surely has the knowledge of the Hour and He sends down the rain. He knows what is in the wombs, whereas no soul knows what it shall earn tomorrow; nor does any living soul know in what land it shall die. Allah is all-knowing, well-informed' (31.34). The libertarians denied God's knowledge of any future events, saying that 'one cannot properly be a knower, unless an object of knowledge is already existent'. Furthermore, divine foreknowledge makes nonsense of free choice. Some libertarians, instead of denying foreknowledge, only denied its causative function; that is, they argued that it does not cause the generation of the thing. This resolved for them the contradiction between God's foreknowledge and man's free will (Wolfson, 1976: 661–2).

The middle-of-the-road view

The middle view reconciles the fatalistic and libertarian views. It is associated with Sunni theology, and represented by the Ash'arite and Maturidite schools.

The Ash'arite school, founded by Abu'l-Hasan al-Ash'ari (d. 324/935), reacted against the Mu'tazilite denial that human acts were created by God. Al-Ash'ari held that man's acquisition is created by God, but is due to a power in man. God has absolute power but, contrary to the fatalists, man has a free will. There is also no limitation to God's foreknowledge. To harmonize divine power with human power, they introduced the doctrine of *kasb* (acquisition), holding that acquisition is a 'power' created in man by God at the very moment of the act. This created power is essential for voluntary action. Thus man acquires the act which God alone can bring into existence. Man's appropriation of the act created by God gives him a free will. This free will renders him responsible for his actions.

The Ash'arites denied causality within nature. God does not have arbitrary power. God has power over all action, but does not command evil action. However, his will is contained in the Preserved Tablet and, in this sense, all actions, good and evil, come from his will, even before the creation of the world. God is the author of moral law. He creates evil without being evil, just as he can create motion without moving. There is no disparity between God permitting evil and forbidding it. His permission is not equal to his approval or command. Thus evil does not reflect on God's moral nature (Legenhausen, 1988: 259).

The Ash'arite solution to the determinism/freedom problem appeals today to the majority of Sunni Muslims who adhere to the belief of the *ahli sunni wa'l jama't* (traditionalists). The fatalists denied human free will, which makes nonsense of responsibility: if we are compelled to act, the foundation of ethics is destroyed and exhortation, prohibition, reward and punishment make no sense.

Human will can diverge from the divine will when it goes against God's will, and this constitutes sin. Though the actual movement of will can diverge from God's will, the outcome cannot diverge from it, for it is the fulfilment of God's will for man. But as to the mode of willing, human will cannot be expected to conform to God's will as he wills things eternally and infinitely, and humans cannot.

The philosophical view

In classical Islamic philosophy God's knowledge of future particulars posed a problem, as it implies that man does not have the freedom to choose; yet, if we assume the absence of this divine knowledge of particulars, it implies that God is not omniscient. The Qur'anic perspective is clear about God's knowledge of particulars when it states: 'There does not escape Him the weight of an atom in the heavens and in the earth' (34.62). So God has knowledge of particulars, even of those that change. However, this poses a further problem for the philosophers in the sense that the divine intellect will 'mirror the great diversity and mutability of empirical events', which is foreign to the notion of a perfect and transcendent God. Ibn Sina tried to resolve this problem by suggesting that God has a universal knowledge of particulars: God knows the abstract principles behind the particular events, but not their details. Al-Ghazali regarded this explanation as heresy, because it conflicts with the teaching of the Qur'an about the omniscience of God. Ibn Rushd had a problem with al-Ghazali's insistence that God has a particular knowledge of the particulars. He argued that this implies a change in God's knowledge, but God is not affected by external events in the way we are. Ibn Rushd also had a problem with Ibn Sina's explanation of divine knowledge of particulars, this time because it implies God only has knowledge of things in their potentiality and not in their state of actuality (Leaman, 1998: 71–81). Ibn Rushd believed this undermines God's knowledge, which is superior to ours. He argues that, on the contrary, 'it is through knowing his essence that God knows the existents, since his essence is the cause of their existence' (Leaman, 1998: 79).

The Sufi view

The Sufi thinkers attribute all human actions, good and evil, to God, and they cite clear verses from the Qur'an to prove that no action is possible without the power of God. They emphasize that God is described as the real agent in human action in such verses as: 'It is not you who have killed them, but it is Allah who has killed them' (8.17); 'You do not will unless Allah wills' (76.30). However, this view should not be confused with the view of the fatalists who deny man his free will. The Sufis acknowledge human volition, but at the same time acknowledge that the real agent is God. A good representative of this view is Amir 'Abd al-Kader, who states: 'He who knows [that God alone acts] with a knowledge based on spiritual experience and on direct vision, and not upon imagination and conjecture, knows that the creatures are nothing other than the receptacles of the acts, the words and the intentions which God creates in them and over which they have no power even though, on the other hand, God calls them, imposes obligations on them, or gives them orders' (Chodkiewicz, 1995: 147–53).

References and further reading

Chodkiewicz, M. (1995) *The Spiritual Writings of Amir 'Abd al-Kader*, Albany, NY: SUNY Press.

Fakhry, M. (1991) *Ethical Theories in Islam*, Leiden: E.J. Brill.

Leaman, O. (1998) *Averroes and his Philosophy*, Richmond, Surrey: Curzon Press.

Legenhausen, G. (1988) 'Notes Towards an Ash'arite Theodicy', *Religious Studies* 24, 2: 259–61.

Mohamed, Y. (2004) *The Path to Virtue*, Kuala Lumpur: ISTAC.

Nasr, S.H. (1981) *Islamic Life and Thought*, London: George Allen & Unwin.

Rosenthal, F. (1960) *The Muslim Concept of Freedom*, Leiden: E.J. Brill.

Watt, M. (1973) *Formative Period of Islamic Thought*, Edinburgh: Edinburgh University Press.

Wolfson, A. (1976) *The Philosophy of the Kalam*, London: Harvard University Press.

See also: **Ash'arites and Mu'tazilites; kalam; qada'; tafsir in early Islam**

YASIEN MOHAMED

FEAR

see: taqa

FEAR GOD (TO)

see: ittaqa

FEASTING

There are two major Islamic feasts: 'Id or Eid al-Adha (the Feast of Sacrifice) and Eid al-Fitr (the Festival of Fast-breaking). The term Eid signifies feast or festival. They were both established by the Prophet Muhammad. He said, 'For every people there is a feast, and this is our feast (*Eid*).' When the Prophet arrived at al-Medina, he found its people celebrating two feasts. The Prophet announced that 'Almighty Allah has given you something better than those feasts, Eid-al-Fitr and Eid-al-Adha'.

Eid al-Fitr signifies the end of fasting for Ramadan. Ramadan, the ninth month of the Islamic lunar calendar, is the holy month of fasting, and fasting (*sawm*) is the third pillar of Islam: 'Fasting is prescribed for you' (2.183). Muslims observe this month by abstaining from satisfying bodily appetites from dawn to sunset. Ramadan is a time for Qur'anic recitation, self-purification and charitable acts. This is the month in which the Qur'an was revealed to Prophet Muhammad, providing 'Guidance for mankind' (2.185).

Eid al-Adha, or the Feast of Sacrifice, concludes the rituals of *hajj* (pilgrimage) to Mecca. It celebrates Abraham's resolve to sacrifice his son, Ishmael, as a sign of his submission to Allah: 'O my son! I have seen a dream in which I am offering you in sacrifice to Allah' (37.102). Abraham was about to sacrifice his son when he was stopped by a revelation from Allah: 'And we ransomed him with a great sacrifice [a ram]' (37.107). Muslims sacrifice an animal for Eid al-Adha and donate most of the meat to the poor.

See also: **calendar; fasting; qurban; sacrifice**

RAFIK BERJAK

FIG

The ninety-fifth *sura* is *sura tin*. It says:

In the Name of Allah, the Beneficent, the Merciful
By the fig and the olive,
And [Mount] Tur of Sinin,
And this city of security [Mecca]
We have indeed created man in the best of moulds,
Then we render him the lowest of the low,
Save those who believe and do righteous deeds, for them is a reward unending.

What then makes you reject there-
after the Last Judgement?
Is not Allah the most just of judges?

The oaths at the beginning of this *sura* are very interesting. They are: 'By the fig and the olive', followed by 'And [Mount] Tur of Sinin' and finally 'And this city of security [Mecca]'. *Tin* means 'fig' and *zaytun* means 'olive', the fruit that provides a useful oil. Are the oaths to these two well-known fruits or perhaps to something else? There is, as one would expect, a good deal of discussion among the commentators as to the exact meaning.

Some take the oaths at face value and say they mean those same two fruits that, after all, contain nutritional properties. Others believe that they refer to the two mountains on which the cities of Damascus and Jerusalem are located, since these two sacred cities are the lands where many great prophets have appeared. These two oaths would then fit in with the third and fourth oaths, which refer to other sacred lands. Some have also said that these two mountains are called *tin* and *zaytun* because fig trees are cultivated on one and olives on the other.

Again, some believe that *tin* refers to the time of Adam, when he and Eve clothed themselves with the leaves of the fig tree, whereas *zaytun* refers to the last stage of the deluge at the time of Noah, when he sent a pigeon out to search for land after the flood and it came back with a small branch from an olive tree, by which Noah understood that the flood was over and dry land had appeared (hence the olive branch is a symbol of peace and security).

Furthermore, some think that the term *tin* refers to Noah's mosque, which was built on Mount Judi of the Ararat range, and that *zaytun* refers to Jerusalem. There is a tradition from the

Prophet which says that God selected four cities and referred to *tin* as Medina, *zaytun* as Jerusalem, *tur-i-sinin* as Kufa and *al-balad-il-amin* (the city of security) as Mecca. The purpose of using the term *tur-i-sinin* is, according to some commentators, for its similarity to *tur-i-sina* (the Mount of Sinai), where olive trees are found, and which was visited by Moses, of course.

The word *tin* (fig) is mentioned only in this *sura*, its sole mention in the whole Qur'an, while the word *zaytun* (olive) appears six times. Even if we think these two oaths about figs and olives are just about figs and olives, they are still meaningful oaths, because these are both highly desirable foods and it is entirely appropriate to swear on something of that nature.

The *sura* continues: 'We have indeed created man in the best of moulds.' The term *taqwim* means to form something into an appropriate shape – that is, in due proportion. God has created us proportionately in all respects, from both physical and spiritual points of view.

After all, he says 'We have honoured the sons of Adam' (17.70), about whose creation he says: 'So blessed be God, the best to create!' (23.14). But, if the same 'man', with all his privileges, deviates from the path of truth and justice, he will fall very far. Hence, in the next verse, it says: 'Then we render him the lowest of the low'. If we use our abilities correctly and follow divine law, we may reach the noble destiny intended for us. But if we rebel against God, and use the talents and faculties he has given us to go awry, we will fall even lower than the beasts and become 'the lowest of the low'.

In the phrase 'Save those who believe and do righteous deeds, for them is a reward unending', the term *mamnun* is based on *man* which, here, means 'broken off' or 'deficiency'. Hence the term *qayru mamnun* is translated as 'an uninterrupted reward without any deficiency'. Some have interpreted the sentence, 'Then we rendered him the lowest of the low' in the sense of 'weakness and feebleness of mind due to old age', but this does not fit with the contrast made with the next *aya*. This addresses the individual who is uninterested in the signs and evidences of the resurrection, and asks 'What then makes you reject thereafter the Last Judgement?' What we know about ourselves and indeed the whole universe suggests that nothing physical lasts, and so the fleeting life of this world cannot be the final goal of the creation or of this complex and well-organized universe. These transitory events must be a prolegomenon to a more perfect and complete world; as the Qur'an points out, 'the first form of creation' warns you of that: 'And you certainly know already the first form of creation: Why then do you not celebrate His praises?' (56.62). Every year, plants and nature as a whole become renewed and remind us of the cycle of death and rebirth. Each of the stages of the developing cycle of a plant is like a new resurrection and a new life, making us more aware of the eventual Judgement Day.

It is clear that it is humanity that is being addressed here. The possibility that the target is the Prophet himself, with the meaning of 'having the evidences of the resurrection, who or what is able to contradict you' seems improbable. Also, it seems likely that the meaning of *din* here is not 'religion' (its usual meaning) but 'Judgement Day', and the following *aya* supports this view: 'Is not Allah the most just of judges?' So, if we take the word *din* as 'religion', this verse means: 'Are Allah's laws and decrees not wisest of all?' or 'God's creation of man is full of knowledge and wisdom'.

This would work, but a more plausible interpretation links the word to the Day of Judgement. It ties in nicely with the previous theme of punishment and redemption, and also with the use of oaths, often a rather threatening or warning use of language.

See also: **natural world and the Qur'an; oaths**

OLIVER LEAMAN

FITNA

Fitna (trial and discord) means that matters become confused, mistakes increase, and minds and intellects begin to waver. This ever-present danger is often taken to suggest that there is a need for a body or person or some type of institution to resolve doubts or problems that can end up as *fitna*, perhaps an *imam* or a group of legal scholars:

> When there comes to them some matter related to public welfare of security or fear, they make it known by the people. If only they had referred it back to the Messenger, or to those in authority amongst them, then the proper people would have investigated and reviewed the matter from them. Were it not for the grace and mercy of Allah upon you, you would have indeed followed Shaytan – except a few of you. (4.83)

This suggests that one should be careful about spreading dangerous news, but if it is unavoidable it needs to be resolved by those capable of resolving it.

Some matters can be easily resolved, those dealing perhaps with questions of ritual or religious performance. But if the issue involves detailed matters, or matters connected to *ijtihad* (the science of extracting rulings from the revelation), then the general body of Muslims cannot enter into it, nor is it for them to order or prohibit: 'Ask the people of knowledge if you do not know' (21.37). There are many *ahadith* pointing to the importance of relying on the authority of the community and its experts, and not dissenting from an opinion properly arrived at.

The Qur'an discusses the reasons for trials and tribulations afflicting people and how God will lift these trials and tribulations from his servants. Some examples are: 'That is because Allah will never change a grace which He has bestowed on a people until they change what is in themselves' (8.53); 'Whatever misfortune befalls you, it is because of what your hands earned. He pardons much' (42.30); 'Evil has appeared on land and sea because of what the hands of men have earned [by oppression and evil deeds], that He may make them taste a part of that which they have done, in order that they may return' (30.41); and 'Allah puts forward the example of a town [Mecca] that dwelt secure and well-content, its provisions coming to it in abundance from every place, but [its people] denied the favours of Allah. So Allah made it taste extreme hunger and fear because of that [i.e. denying the Prophet] which they used to do' (16.112).

God does not afflict a nation with trials except because of their disobedience to him and opposition to his commands. In particular, in modern times detachment from and disregard for *tawhid*, and the spread of the manifestations and practices of *shirk* in many of the Islamic countries that suffer trials and tribulations are seen as the inevitable result of the failures to behave appropriately. So these trials and tribulations will not be removed except by returning to the *tawhid* of Allah and ruling by his *shari'a*, both in oneself and society as a whole.

The Qur'an discusses the behaviour of the *mushrikin* (idolaters) and the fact that they tended to call on God only when they were suffering trials, tribulations and difficulties. However, when they were safe from that which had befallen them, they returned to *shirk* and so stopped appealing to God for his help: 'When they embark on a ship, they invoke Allah, making their faith pure for him only, but when He brings them safely to land, behold, they give a share of their worship to others' (29.65). Equally, when misfortune befalls many Muslims, they call on authorities other than God. They practice *shirk*, in opposition to the instructions of God and the speech of his messengers.

A frequently cited example is the defeat of the Muslims at the battle of Uhud, due to the opposition of some of their archers to the leader. Furthermore, the Muslims were surprised at the defeat, so God points out to them: 'Say: "It is from yourselves"' (3.165). In the battle of Hunayn, some Muslims said: 'We shall not be defeated by this small number'. However, they were defeated and God pointed out: 'On the day of Hunayn when you rejoiced at your great number, ... it availed you nothing' (9.25). The point is that success is held to lie in no hands except those of God, and when the community experiences dissension and lack of unity it is especially weak and unlikely to prosper. If individual Muslims do not respect the principles of Islam then *fitna* is liable to prevail.

See also: **ahl al-dhikr**; **persecution**; **suffering**; *tawhid*

OLIVER LEAMAN

FITRA

Fitra (primordial nature, humanity's archetypal nature) derives from the Arabic triliteral root *ftr*, which means to have a natural disposition or inclination for something, to aspire to or have a propensity for something; or that something is innate or native to a person. However, the term is generally used to designate inner nature, moral constitution and suitability. *Fitra*, as the primordial nature of the human individual, designed for perfection, is the genuine Islamic concept of human nature formulated from Islamic sources. It designates the primordial nature of creation itself, and the place of the human race within creation. The Qur'an says:

> So set thou thy face truly to the religion being upright, the nature in which Allah has made mankind: no change [there is] in the work [wrought] by Allah: that is the true Religion: but most among mankind know not. (30.30)

The term itself appears another fourteen times with the same meaning, in other forms of the verb. Furthermore, it is one of the central terms for an enquiry into the receptiveness to be discerned within the Islamic philosophical tradition from the perspective of the perennial philosophy itself. The linguistic and religious meaning of *fitra* is the immutable natural predisposition to the good, innate in every human being from birth, or even from the pre-existent state in which, as Islamic doctrine teaches, the human soul enters into a covenant with God (*al-Mithaq*, by allusion to the Qur'anic *aya* from *sura al-A'raf*; 7.172).

In fact, the Qur'an refers in general to Islam as *din al-fitra*, which indicates that human beings are inclined by their inner nature to submit to the Will of God; that it is inherent in human nature to aspire to the supreme good, to perfection, to both outward and inner purification. *Fitra* is thus a kind of paradigm of the Islamic outlook on life, a state of equilibrium and harmony between the Creator and the created. Through the meaning of this metaphysical principle, we come to an understanding of our position as human beings in the cosmos and of our inherent nature and ultimate destiny. In the light of these observations, it can be seen that every other implication of *fitra* is rooted in this metaphysical primary design, for what is in question here is the metaphysical correspondence between we human beings and the cosmos. Outwardly, we are a microcosm; inwardly, however, we reflect the reality that is the source of the cosmos itself. To be sure, this is attained in the conscious awareness of a superior force, of the divine nature, a force that is real, not utopian or idyllic.

It is this that is meant by the Islamic belief that every child is born in a natural, inherent state of humankind that is *fitra*. According to a well-known *hadith* found in almost every authentic collection of *ahadith*, every child possesses an intuitive awareness of living in *fitra* – *kullu mawludin yuladu 'al al-fitra* (every newborn child is born according to this true nature) or, as another two traditions have it, *man yuladu yuladu 'al al-fitra* (whoever is born is born according to this true nature) and *ma min mawludin illa yuladu 'ala al-fitra* (every newborn child is born in accordance with this true nature). It should be noted here that the pronouns used in *hadith* traditions are those that designate universality and generality, and are so used to embrace every individual without exception, whether in the positive or the negative sense. The tradition goes on to say it is the child's parents – or, by extrapolation, its cultural and social environment – that make a newborn child into a Christian, a Jew or a fire-worshipper. What is crucial is to perceive that these and other factors modify the primordial design, which is the result of reshaping the original divine imprint with which every child is born and which is instilled into the child from its very origins – a remaking, in short, of the true nature that constitutes the essence of the child's human condition.

Fitra is thus an important concept in relation to human nature considered from an Islamic perspective. What is more, in denoting this primordial state of the human individual, our natural position and disposition, *fitra* offers an optimistic view of the individual character of human nature rooted in this concept. Islam postulates the natural state of the human individual as positive, as the true state – a state of submission and obedience to God. Each individual is thus called, from the perspective of this primordial nature, personally to perform the 'priestly' task, since there is no separate category of priesthood in Islam – another difference between the Christian and the Islamic outlook. What is more, as *din al-fitra*, Islam does away with the distinction between the religious and the secular, the sacred and the profane, by making the human being a natural being who is the most immediate symbol of the spiritual world in nature and who is in direct collusion with that world.

Furthermore, the reality of *fitra* implies the reality of the soul that is predisposed to know and submit to the Divine Will, which indicates that the knowledge of *fitra* can be attained through a reunification of the soul or self (*nafs*) with the human spirit (*ruh*). This designates the state attained when the inner being of the human individual is in complete harmony with his *fitra*, and the state achieved when the principle of *tawhid* manifests itself in utter submission to God, given that the monotheist perspective of Islam is in fact rooted in the metaphysical principle of *tawhid* in which every aspect of life is within the power of God. This, of course, is the reason for there being nothing that is of profane nature, for everything has its origins in the world of divine creativity. Even the Prophet of Islam himself brought no new truth, for he came to institute the true, primordial tradition (*al-din al-hanif*), the tradition that is Islam in its original essence and Islam in its final form. What is more, in the Qur'anic *aya* quoted above (30.30), God equates the term *fitra* with the term *hanif*, which denotes the praxis of pristine monotheism as practised by Ibrahim (Abraham), and which is in fact the common denominator of the Judaeo-Christian-Islamic tradition. The Islamic ideal is thus to achieve this balance and harmony between *fitra* and *nafs*, since the inner human nature is an immutable given, and the spiritual essence of the human being – *fitra* – is absolute, but the soul – *nafs* – is changeable in nature and exists in a dynamic relationship with the phenomenal reality.

The current radical difference in the way the nature of human reality is imagined and represented, as between the Islamic perspective, on the one hand, and the majority of modern schools of thought, on the other, derives in fact from that overwhelming difference in their understanding of the nature of reality. In the Islamic view, this is the reason for the refusal to accept as valid the truncated vision of reality that typifies the modern, Western worldview, the origins of which lie in the post-medieval rationalism and empiricism that became the prevailing models of thought in Europe – models that, what is more, form the background even to most religious studies, particularly in present-day academic circles. The spiritual dimension of *fitra* is of crucial significance, and it is that very aspect of human nature which is disregarded within the Western definition of human nature – a definition requiring that the biological and physical dimension be the sole relevant variable of this outlook.

Further reading

Yasien, M. (1996) *Fitrah: The Islamic concept of human nature*, London: Taha Publishers.

*See also: **hadnif**; **nafs**; **ruh***

NEVAD KAHTERAN

FOOD

'O you people, eat of what is on earth lawful and good, and do not follow the footsteps of Satan, for he is to you an avowed enemy' (12.168). This immediately suggests that the issue of food is an important one from a religious point of view: 'O you who believe, eat of the good things that We have provided for you, and be grateful to God, if it is him you worship' (12.172). The world has been provided by God with a variety of tasty things to eat, and we need to acknowledge the source of the food when we eat it.

> He has only forbidden you carrion, blood, the flesh of swine and that on which any other name has been invoked besides that of God. But if one is forced by necessity, without wilful disobedience or transgressing due limits, then is he guiltless. For God is very forgiving and most merciful. (12.173)

By contrast with other religions, such as Judaism, the rules of acceptable food are simple, and in circumstances of necessity may be relaxed even further. This reflects the merciful nature of God. The underlying message about food is that the Qur'an allows food that is good in itself, and forbids things that are harmful (5.4–5; 7.157). In the case of the Jews, they were punished by having more severe restrictions placed on their diet (3.93; 4.160–161; 6.146), but some of the restrictions about food are similar. The name of God needs to be said over

the animal as it is slaughtered and Muslims can eat the food of the People of the Book. The suggestion that the strenuous nature of the laws of *kashrut* is a means of punishing the Jews for their obduracy is interesting, and the Qur'an does argue that the rules of food to be followed by Muslims, in contrast to those for Jews, are simple, clear and rational.

*See also: **halal**; **haram***

OLIVER LEAMAN

FORGIVENESS

One of the many Qur'anic-Arabic equivalents of the term 'forgiveness' is the word *'afw*, repeated about forty times, along with a host of other terms. The word *'afa*, a cognate of *'afw*, is used seven times to imply God's forgiveness for those who have preferred this world to the hereafter, God forgiving the Prophet, and a general statement on the benefit of forgiveness over revenge: 'whosoever forgives and seeks reconcilement shall be recompensed by God' (42.40).

In its Qur'anic usage, the word *'afw* is generally applicable to forgiveness for wrongdoing either to oneself or to others. From the perspective of the Qur'an, committing an injustice against others includes doing wrong to oneself. The distinction between *haq-Allah*, rights of God, and *haq-an-nas*, rights of people, is significant within Islamic law and culture. It is easier to receive forgiveness for a sin against oneself than a sin against others, for the latter requires the forgiveness of the victim as well as God's forgiveness. In one instance the term *'afw* within the Qur'an is translated as superfluous: 'And they ask thee what they ought to spend. Say that which is *'afwa* (superfluous)' (2.219). Based on this usage, which suggests a donation of what exceeds one's needs in material wealth to the poor, *'afw* (to forgive) means in the spiritual sense to give not in wealth but in spirit to those in need.

In verses 35–38 of chapter 42 of the Qur'an, and across numerous other references, restraining one's anger and offering forgiveness when one has the power to take revenge supersedes prayer and almsgiving. In addition to the countless references to forgiveness throughout the Qur'an, there are numerous examples of the practice of it in the life of the Prophet, who is celebrated within the tradition as *al-insan al-kamil* (the perfect human). The Qur'an describes the Prophet with characteristics of magnanimity and nobility. It goes on to say that his gentleness, lightheartedness and kindness are the characteristics that attract people to him and therefore he should 'pardon them and ask pardon, for them, and take counsel with them' (3.159). To emulate the Prophet is a mission not only for his family and his Companions, but also for the common Muslim believers. There are several references within the *hadith* literature suggesting that disputes must be reconciled before the time of prayer. The time limit on seeking reconciliation is rather short. A specific *hadith* suggests that if one gets into a dispute with someone after the afternoon prayer, they must make peace and embrace each other by the time of the early evening prayer. Prayer is a pillar of Islam, and forgiveness and reconciliation of conflicts its prerequisite, thus to forgive and to seek forgiveness must be an essential Muslim practice.

Forgiveness is overcoming the sense of resentment towards those who have committed a moral injury. It is not a denial of moral injury, nor does it refute the sense of resentment it may have created. The act of forgiveness, as well as the recommendation to forgive, does recognize both, but suggests going beyond

them. Forgiveness is therefore distinguishable from justification and excuse. In other words, an imperative to forgive does not deny wrongdoing, nor does it take away the responsibility of the wrongdoer, yet it involves a change of heart toward the wrongdoer, without necessarily excluding the retribution due.

Nevertheless, it is a virtue, for it implies a commitment to reconciliation and mercy. However, there is a distinction between forgiveness and mercy. While mercy has a direct bearing on the action taken, forgiveness need not. That is to say that forgiveness involves a change of heart that may advocate that the wrongdoer receives punishment or be considered accountable for redressing the wrong.

Most references to forgiveness in the Qur'an are in regard to people begging forgiveness of God or God encouraging people to ask for forgiveness of God and of one another. Persian poetry, especially the collections of Rumi, Hafiz and Sa'adi, is kindred to the Qur'an, in that it often offers interpretations of the sacred text. Sa'adi, the seventh-century Persian poet, gives an interpretation of forgiveness in his *Bustan*, with the story of a drunkard who takes refuge in a mosque asking to be forgiven. As a pretext for his request for forgiveness, the drunken man quotes the Qur'anic story of Joseph and his brothers:

> *Joseph, who so much affliction saw and bondage –*
> *When his rule ran and his rank rose high,*
> *Did he not forgive the sins of Jacob's house?*
> *For their evil doings he placed them not in chains.*

The drunkard of Sa'adi's story draws on a case of human/prophetic forgiveness in order to argue for God's forgiveness for himself. If it is appropriate for a human to forgive, how much more fitting is it for God to forgive? In this case God is being modelled after humans; in most other cases, human action is modelled after God's. *'Afuw* (most forgiving) is among the names of God, and humans most seek to adorn themselves with the attributes of God.

There are two basic categories of forgiveness in the Qur'an: God's forgiveness for humanity, and forgiveness of fellow humans for each other – that is, forgiveness as a human option. A category found neither in the Qur'an nor anywhere in the Islamic texts is human forgiveness of God. For forgiveness follows a wrongdoing or a shortcoming and, in Islamic theology and ethics, God does not commit wrong and has no association with evil. Evil is merely the lack of good.

The first case of God's forgiveness in history, according to the Qur'an and the Abrahamic traditions, concerns the creation story. The story of creation points out one of the main theological distinctions between Christianity and Islam, as well as some similarities. Adam and Eve eating of the forbidden fruit and God's forgiveness of them is one case in which the retribution (i.e. the exile from the Garden of Eden) stood in place. Islam views the fault of Adam as a mistake for which repentance was sought and forgiveness was offered. The Qur'anic account emphasizes forgiveness in a way that no pre-committed sin remains for descendants of Adam. Adam is not only forgiven but is also appointed vicegerent of God on earth. No sin is inherited, yet the propensity to repent and to ask forgiveness is. Adam and Eve are positive examples for all of humanity and not the contrary.

The Qur'an counsels the Prophet with the following words: 'Forgive them therefore and ask forgiveness for them, and take counsel with them in the affair' (3.159). God did just this in the affair of Adam and Eve when, on repenting, they were forgiven and Adam was appointed as a prophet and an example to humanity. Human action is to be modelled after God's action. According to the Qur'an, forgetfulness is what leads to sin. In fact, forgetfulness is one of the Qur'anic characteristics in describing humanity. Yet that is not the only human trait. The story of *alast* in the Qur'an describes some other human characteristics, all of which are also divine characteristics.

The story of *alast* goes on to say that after the creation, when God asked the angels to prostrate themselves before Adam (here representing all of humanity), the angels objected and said they would not bow down to anyone other than God, certainly not to Adam who was created from *adama* (mud). God's counter-argument was 'I know something that you do not know' and pointed out that Adam knows the *'asma'* (the names) of which the angels had no knowledge. The implications of the knowledge of the names, be it the names of God and/or of the creatures is ambiguous, but what most commentators seem to agree is that this quality, knowing of the names, is tantamount to, on the one hand, bearing the potential of attaining the highest merit and, on the other, of transgression. In other words, humanity has the potential to elevate itself to the highest of the high or to decline to the lowest of the low. Thus it is also human to be adorned with the qualities of God (*ta'ayyun be 'asma' Allah*). 'Assume the character traits of God' is a saying most repeated throughout the writings of the Sufis and is paralleled by a notable verse from the Qur'an: '[we take our] colour from God, and whose colour is better than God's?' (2.138). To ascribe to oneself the attributes of God, among them generosity, forbearance, clemency, mercy and forgiveness, is to stride on the path of perfection. For the believer, the first step on the path is Islam or submission to the will of God. Yet the greater step is the leap of faith (*iman*), which cannot be achieved without acquiring some of God's attributes. Forgiveness is one of the many attributes of God and therefore worthy to be sought after; it is also a characteristic of the Prophet to be emulated. This is an undertaking, the value of which lies in the fact that it is not mandatory but rather it is striven for without having been obligated.

Forgiveness is a change of heart through which mercy replaces resentment or rage, in a case where it is morally justifiable to resent. Forgiving is a virtue, as is asking for forgiveness. Yet this virtue, like most others, is conditional; that is to say, a change of heart that brings about forgiveness, if accompanied with a sense of pride and self-aggrandizement, has little or no value. One of the ethical sayings of 'Ali Ibn Abu-Talib, the first Shi'a *imam* and the fourth caliph, is: 'The sin that displeases you is better in the sight of God than the virtue which makes you proud.'

Forgiveness is indeed a virtue from the point of view of the Qur'an. Nevertheless, it is not associated with servility and lack of self-respect. It must come from the heart, especially if healing is to be expected. The woman saint of Basra, Rabi'a al-Adawiyya, one of the most eminent figures of Islamic mysticism who is known to have initiated a new phase in Sufism (that of *mahabba*, love), considers forgiveness effective only when accompanied by a change of heart and not as a matter of gain or loss. According to Rabi'a, 'seeking forgiveness with the tongue is the sin of lying'.

Within Islamic theology it is the balance between God's wrath and mercy that has been the focal point of such discussions. That God's mercy takes precedence over God's wrath is often agreed on by theologians and Sufis alike. Ibn al-'Arabi, the twelfth-century Spanish philosopher, states that everyone will end up with mercy, simply because God is the root of all diversity of beliefs within the cosmos. Wrath, in his opinion, enters the picture only at the second level of sensory existence.

Even in strictly legal matters, leniency marks Islamic teachings. Repentance is highly encouraged throughout the Qur'an, and the promise of forgiveness is strongly stated. Making amends for major penal offences, even apostasy, has been considered within the *shari'a*. Conflict resolution and the settling of mutual differences are considered more important than prayers and fasting. The Prophet is quoted as having said that the best deeds before God are to pardon a person who has wronged you, to show affection for relatives who have broken ties with you, and to act generously towards a person who has deprived you of something important. In the Qur'an, God describes himself as always 'forgiving to those who turn back [to him]' (*a-inna-hu kana li-'l-awwabina ghafura*; 17.25).

Further reading

Abdel Haleem, M. (1999) *Understanding the Qur'an: Themes and styles*, New York: I.B. Tauris.

'Ali Ibn Abu Talib (1985) *Nahjul balagha* (Peak of Eloquence), New York: Tahrike Tarsile Qur'an.

Bawa Muhaiyaddeen, M.R. (1987) *Islam and World Peace: Explanations of a Sufi*, Philadelphia, PA: The Fellowship Press.

Esack, F. (1999) *On Being a Muslim: Finding a religious path in the world today*, Oxford: OneWorld.

Renard, J. (1998) *Windows on the House of Islam: Muslim sources on spirituality and religious life*, Berkeley, CA: University of California Press.

See also: **ghafara; repentance**

BAHAR DAVARY

G

GABRIEL

see: **Jibril**

GARDEN

see: **Paradise**

GENEROUS

see: *karim*

GHABA

Ghaba is the root of a word that means to be absent. The present tense is *yaghib*, to be away, distant, remote or beyond reach. The noun *ghayb* signifies the unseen, invisible or unapparent; it signifies anything unperceivable or beyond the range of perception physically by the senses, or mentally by the intellect. *'Alama al-ghayb* therefore is the unseen world or the invisible world. The Qur'an was revealed to the Prophet to tell the people in this life about the hereafter, which is the unseen world.

The Prophet's job was to make people aware of elements of the unseen such as the resurrection after death, the Day of Judgement and everlasting abodes such as Paradise and Hell. This was not an easy task: he had to convince the people to believe in an invisible and yet-to-be-experienced future.

In the *sura al-Baqara*, the Qur'an was introduced as the book 'whereof there is no doubt, a guidance to the believers who are pious and who believe in the *ghayb* (the unseen world)' (2.3). This term is of great importance in the Qur'an because of the vast significance of what it refers to: belief in Allah, angels, holy books, Allah's Messengers, the Day of Resurrection and *al-qadar* (divine necessity). It also includes what Allah and his Messenger told people about matters in the past, present and future.

See also: ***al-ghayb***

RAFIK BERJAK

217

GHADIR KHUMM

This is the name of a pond or pool (*ghadir*) in a place called Khumm, between Mecca and Medina. The place acquired its fame from an incident associated with Muhammad's last year, when he was returning from the Farewell Pilgrimage on 18 Dhu 'l-Hijja, 10/16 March, 632. Some sources mention that the Prophet stopped there in the company of 'Ali and other prominent Companions and uttered the following: 'Of whomever I am the *mawla* (patron/ friend), 'Ali is his *mawla* too.' A variant report uses the word *wali* instead of *mawla*. Shi'i sources are practically unanimous in understanding this *hadith* as confirming 'Ali's status as Muhammad's first successor as the leader of the polity, construing *mawla* as referring to 'master' or 'patron'. Those Sunni sources that record this event point rather to the polysemy of the lexeme *mawla* (and, by extension, of *wali* as well), whose meanings range from 'master' to 'friend' to 'client', thereby casting doubt on the *hadith*'s value as unambiguous proof-text attesting to 'Ali's designation as the caliph. Significantly, some major Sunni authorities and chroniclers such as Ibn Hisham and Ibn Sa'd do not refer to this event; among the compilers of major Sunni *hadith* works, al-Tirmidhi and Ibn Hanbal record it, but al-Bukhari and Muslim do not. Some Sunni sources have also questioned the 'occasion of occurrence' (*sabab al-wurud*) of this *hadith*, saying that the Prophet made this statement on a different occasion to express his support for 'Ali in response to a complaint against the latter by either the Companion Zayd b. al-Haritha or Burayda al-Aslami, rather than at the time of the Farewell Pilgrimage.

In the Buwayhid period, the Shi'i feast ('Id) of Ghadir Khumm was instituted in Iraq by Mu'izz al-Dawla Ahmad b. Buya in 352/964 and, under the Fatimids, by al-Mu'izz in Egypt in 362/973.

See also: **Shi'a;** *wali*

ASMA AFSARUDDIN

GHAFARA | GHAFFAR | GHAFUR | GHAFIR | MAGHFIRA

The Arabic term *ghufran* means clemency or forgiveness. The propensity to forgive is one that is highly praised within both Islamic law and practice. The Qur'an and the *hadith* literature are filled with statements encouraging forgiveness, yet the academic study of Islam has given the topic little or no attention, with markedly few references to forgiveness within the introductory and reference sources available in English. This does not negate the fact that offering forgiveness to fellow humans and seeking forgiveness from both humans and God are fundamental imperatives within Islamic culture and the Islamic textual tradition.

The verb form of the term is used over a hundred times throughout the Qur'an, often referring to God's act of forgiveness. The three adjectives *ghaffar/ghafur/ghafir* are names of God, and all mean the same thing: one who forgives, the Clement. The only difference in the meaning of the three words is the intensity of the act of exoneration. The Qur'an describes God by many names and attributes, often referred to as the ninety-nine names of God. Among the most repeated names, appearing 101 times, are *al-Ghaffar* (ever forgiving), *al-Ghafur* (most forgiving), *al-Ghafir* (forgiver). There are multiple other names that bear God's attribute of forgiveness: *al-'Afuw* (ever indulgent; 8 times), *al-Tawab* (relenting; 11 times), *al-Wahhab* (generous; 3 times), *al-Halim* (clement; 15 times), *al-Karim* (generous; 27 times), *al-Wadud* (loving; twice), *ar-Rahim* (most merciful; 95 times, with an additional 114 times at the beginning of each *sura*, with only 2 exceptions), *ar-Rahman* (compassionate; 57 times, plus 114 times at the beginning of each *sura*, with 2 exceptions), *as-Salam* (peace; 33 times) and *al-Latif* (gentle; 6 times). Many of the verses end with a message reminding the reader or listener of the merit of mercy, kindness and forgiveness, and that God is indeed merciful and compassionate.

Islamic theology divides the attributes of God in two categories: the attributes of essence (*dhat*), such as *hay* (alive) and *'alim* (all knowing), or the attributes of action (*fi'l*). The attributes of essence have always been with God and the opposite of them cannot apply: namely, God has always been alive and death does not apply to God's essence. However, God's attributes of action, which became necessary only after creation, can be qualified by their opposites: for example, God is *'affuw* (forgiver) and also *al-muntaghim* (avenger). The complexity of the matter ensues from the prevailing use of the contradictory attributes of God. The God of the Qur'an is *arham ar-rahemin* (the compassionate of compassionates) and *khayr-ul ghaferin* (the best of forgivers) but also *dhul-intigham* (avenger), *jabbar* (forceful), *muntaghim* (avenger), *ghahhar* (subduer) and *sari'ul-'ighab* (quick in retribution). If forgiveness is an attribute of God, by the same token so are retaliation and vengefulness. To add to the complexity of the matter, in some cases forgiveness for one group seems to require vengeance and retribution against others. These seemingly contradictory attributes provide the space for justice.

Those who repay an injury in kind and then are wronged again shall be helped by God. God is merciful and forgiving (22.60), but those who have committed an injustice will face God's reprisal, which is in accordance with God's mercy and forgiveness: mercy for the victims is retaliation against the oppressor. The Qur'an implies that one who has been oppressed has the right to speak to the oppressor using unkind words: God does not love harsh words, except when uttered by one who is truly wronged. God hears all and knows all: whether you do a good deed openly or keep it secret – whether or not you forgive an injustice – God is forgiving and all-powerful (4.148–149).

A common observation made when comparing Islam to Christianity is that Christianity is the religion of love, whereas Islam is above all the religion of justice. Is the God of the Qur'an a loving God (*wadud*) or a vengeful God (*al-montaghem, jabbar*)? How do these two attributes come together, and are they compatible with the attribute of justice – for the God of Qur'an is also called *'adil* (the Just)? The emphasis on love within the Islamic sapiential tradition is such that all of creation is considered to rely on love. As for justice, the references to the words *'idala, 'adl, qist* (justice) and *mizan* (scale) permeate the Qur'an. The Arabic term *'adl* means 'to bring about balance', 'to put something in its right place'. The relation and balance between divine love and mercy and God's wrath presents a quandary for Muslim theologians, just as it does for Christian theology. On the one hand, God is utterly incomparable and distanced from the cosmos but, on the other, God is closer to humans than their jugular veins. The names of majesty and severity (*Jalal*), as well as the names of beauty and gentleness (*Jamal*), are comparable to Rudolph Otto's *mysterium tremendum* and *mysterium fascinans*. Just as the two aspects of awe and intimacy have to function together, so the attributes of love and wrath cannot be asserted, one in the absence of the other. If justice is to be realized, the equilibrium between the two must be maintained, within both the microcosm and the macrocosm. Even in strictly legal matters, leniency marks Islamic teachings. Repentance is highly encouraged throughout the Qur'an, and the promise of forgiveness is strongly stated. Making amends for major penal offences, even apostasy, has been considered within the *shari'a*. Conflict resolution and the settling of mutual differences are considered more important than prayers and fasting. *Ghufran* (forgiveness) is more compatible with the essence of the Qur'an than an 'eye for an eye' approach that follows the letter of the law. The strictness of the letter of the law and the leniency of its practice are to be viewed as a means of maintaining the moral order while denying opportunities to injustice.

Further reading

Abdel Haleem, M. (2001) *Understanding the Qur'an: Themes and style*, New York: I.B. Tauris.

Ayoub, M. (1998) 'The Numinous in the Qur'an: An assessment of Rudolf Otto's view of Islam', *Muslim World* 88, 3–4: 256–67.

Rahman, F. (1980) *Major Themes of the Qur'an*, Minneapolis: Bibliotheca Islamica.

Rosen, L. (2000) *The Justice of Islam*, Oxford: Oxford University Press.

See also: '*adl*; **forgiveness**

BAHAR DAVARY

AL-GHAYB

Literally, *al-ghayb* means absence. In the Qur'an, the concept of *ghayb* refers to the hidden reality from which all creation is screened. It pertains to that domain of transcendent sense and reason that defies human understanding and cannot be subjected to abstract rational speculations. To believe in *ghayb*, to be awed by it and to be conscious of it, represents man's primary response to religion, without which there is no Islam. Those who wish to attain faith only after they have had a concrete sight of the unseen are ridiculed, with their demands seen as the very antithesis of the Qur'anic vision of faith: 'And remember ye said: "O Moses! We shall never believe in thee until we see Allah face to face (*jahratan*) [with our own eyes]"' (2.55). In his commentary on verses 2–3 of chapter 2 ('those who are awed by God's reality, and believe in the unseen'), al-Tabari (d. 310/923) views belief in the unseen as akin to belief in the fundamentals of faith (al-Tabari, 1418/1997, Vol. 1: 133–4). Drawing on a number of traditional positions, he concludes that the unseen pertains to the resurrection, the Day of Judgement, heaven and hell, the angels, past prophets and their scriptures, 'all of which are hidden from the believers (*fe hadha kulluhu ghayb*)'.

Often in the Qur'an *al-ghayb* is mentioned as if to awake in human beings consciousness of their limited knowledge and also of another dimension of reality known to God alone: 'To Him belongs the keys of the unseen; none knows them but He' (6.59) and 'With Him are the secrets of the heavens and the earth ... nor does He share His Command with any person whatsoever' (18.26). While verses like these unequivocally state that knowledge of the *ghayb* is exclusive to God, others suggest that prophets have been privy at least to some of this knowledge. In one instance, the angel Gabriel reveals to Muhammad 'that it is some of the tidings of the unseen (*tilka min anba' al-ghayb*) that we reveal to you (*nuhiha ilayk*)' (3.44). Despite his status, the Qur'an insists that what Muhammad knows of the unseen is only limited, in keeping with his human condition, and that he knows it only by God's leave: 'I tell you not that with me are the treasures of Allah, nor do I know what is hidden (*al-ghayb*), nor do I claim to be an angel. Nor yet do I say, of those whom your eyes do despise, that Allah will not grant them [all] that is good: Allah knoweth best what is in their souls: I should, if I did, indeed be a wrongdoer' (11.31). Primarily, the *ghayb* disclosed to the Prophet embraces hidden knowledge about past events, previous prophets, and the fate of past nations and civilisations, or events of an eschatological nature such as those surrounding the apocalypse, the resurrection and its aftermath, none of which either the Prophet Muhammad or the addressees of the scriptures would have had knowledge of prior to the revelation. Hence, according to some accounts, *ghayb* refers to the revelation itself (al-Tabari, 1418/1997, Vol. 1: 134); indeed, one reads in the Qur'an: 'And thus have We inspired in thee [Muhammad] a Spirit of Our command. Thou knewest not what the Scripture was, nor the Faith' (42.52).

Relying on the last verse of *sura Luqman* (31.34), Muslim scholars identified five hidden realities, known as *al-ghaybiyyat al-khams*, to highlight aspects of the hidden knowledge of God that human beings could never attain. These are knowledge of the hour of the apocalypse, knowledge of the advent of rainfall, knowledge of an infant child's condition and destiny while still in its mother's womb, knowledge of the fate of every single individual, and knowledge of an individual's place and time of death.

Another major aspect of the concept of *ghayb* in the Qur'an pertains to God in his hidden (*al-batin*) aspect, in his transcendental absence or as *Deus absconditus*. In the Qur'an, this dimension of the Godhead is often referred to by the third person he (*hu* or *hua*), the pronoun of absence in grammar. In this sense *ghayb* pertains to God in his supreme concealment, without attributes to qualify him ('Naught is like him'; 42.11); to the Supreme beyond, about whom Jesus says: 'Thou knowest what is in my heart, though I know not what is in Thine' (5.116); and to God without relation to his creation: '... He begets not, and neither is He begotten' (112.3). Whatever metaphors or analogies man may produce to articulate this ultimate reality, however much intellectual acumen or however many mystical insights he may have to envisage it, at this level and from this aspect God simply defies human understanding. Commenting on the prophetic tradition, which describes God as being concealed and separated by 70,000 veils of darkness and light, al-Ghazali (d. 1111) noted that even the most advanced on the path of the Sufis – those who had shed all veils of darkness, as it were – still remained veiled from this reality, albeit by veils of pure light (al-Ghazali, 1981: 41–2). Sufis like Ibn al-ʿArabi called this station of absolute transcendence the station of abysmal 'Dark Mist' (*ʿama*), as a way of illustrating its sheer impenetrability to any understanding or approximation.

Despite its emphasis on the *via remotionis* of the Godhead, the Qur'an does not preclude the dimension of immanence from its vision of God: transcendence and immanence are not mutually exclusive in the Qur'an, although scholars of *kalam* and Sufis have generally tended to put the accent on one at the expense of the other. Beside his hidden or inward aspect, God also has an outward aspect in accordance with his name *al-Zahir* or Self-revealing. Sufis often refer to the sacred revelation (*hadith qudsi*) 'I was a hidden treasure and I loved to be known, so I created the creation that I might be known' to highlight God's disposition towards self-revealing. At this secondary stage, he is *Deus revelatus* who, while being transcendent, is qualified through attributes and names, and is inclined towards his creation. Believers at this level are urged to turn to him in supplication: 'call me and I will respond to you' (40.60). They address him as 'Thou', and are reminded of his mysterious presence: 'Whithersoever ye turn, there is the face of God' (2.115). The Qur'an beckons humanity to contemplate nature and most notably their own selves, for these contain signs (*ayat*) that make evident his transcendence and bring near his exalted presence. Human intellect (*'aql*), according to the Qur'anic vision, is a spiritual non-material substance that resides in the heart and is the seat of intuition and gnosis (*ma'rifa*). Its cognitive operations are not confined to the sensible reality and knowledge of the world of phenomena, but may, through worship and spiritual discipline (*mujahada*), embrace the transcendental reality and thus attain to knowledge of aspects of the noumenal world. This knowledge of God and of his existence is not reached through rational demonstration but through what the Sufis call taste (*dhawq*), witnessing (*mushahada*) or intuitional insight (*kashf*).

References and further reading

al-Attas, Syed Muhammad Naquib (1995) *Prolegomena to the Metaphysics of Islam*, Kuala Lumpur: ISTAC.
'Ayyahi (1981) *Tafsir al-Qur'an al-Karim*, attr. Ibn al-'Arabi, 2 vols, Beirut.
Chittick, W. (1998) *The Self-Disclosure of God*, New York, Albany: State University of New York Press.
al-Ghazali (1981) *Al-Ghazali's Mishkat al-anwar (The Niche of Lights)*, trans. and intro. by W.H.T. Gairdner, New Delhi.
al-Tabari (1418/1997) *Tafsir al-Tabari*, 30 vols, Beirut.

Vahiduddin, S. (1986) *Islam in India*, ed. C.W. Troll, 4 vols, Delhi: Vikas.

See also: **death; *dhaqa*; *zahir***

REDHA AMEUR

GHULUWW

The word means exaggeration and, in general, extremism. It may be considered to be the very antithesis of the Qur'anic assertion (2.143) that Muslims should constitute a 'middle/moderate nation' (*umma wasatan*). This verse and related *ahadith* led to moderation being eulogized in ethical and humanistic literature as one of the quintessential traits of a Muslim, with a corresponding disapproval of excess in any action, including in the performance of obligatory and general pious duties. Historically, however, the term *ghuluww* has mainly been used to characterize the activities of some early Shi'i factions, called the *ghulat* (sing. *ghali*), many of whose doctrines were later declared to be heterodox and 'extreme' from the viewpoint of classical Shi'ism by the fourth/tenth century. These doctrines included the notion of *raj'a*, which asserted that righteous Muslims would return to earth after their death, along with the Hidden Imam; the principle of reincarnation (*al-tanasukh*) and transmigration of the soul (*al-maskh*); and belief in the Imam's possession of a kind of 'prophetic authority' (*nubuwwa*), albeit inferior to that of Muhammad, and of a spark of divine light inherited from Adam. The earliest *ghali* is reckoned to be 'Abd Allah b. Sab'a, who is said to have denied 'Ali's death and who believed that the latter would return to earth. Other well-known *ghulat* are al-Mughira b. Sa'id, Abu Mansur al-'Iji and the Kaysaniyya, who were the loyalist supporters of Muhammad b. al-Hanafiyya, 'Ali's son through a wife other than Fatima. Some early *ghuluww* positions were retained *mutatis mutandis* as part of mainstream Shi'i thought; thus *raj'a* becomes transformed into the concept of occultation (*al-ghayba*) of the Imam and his reappearance at the end of time, and the notion of the possession of prophetic authority facilitated the imputation of impeccability, sinlessness and privileged knowledge to the *imams*.

Further reading

Modarressi, H. (1993) *Crisis and Consolidation in the Formative Period of Shi'ite Islam: Abu Ja'far ibn Qiba al-Razi and his contribution to Imamite Shi'ite thought*, Princeton, NJ: Princeton University Press.
ASMA AFSARUDDIN

GHUSL
see: **ablution**

GOG AND MAGOG
see: **Ya'juj wa Ma'juj**

GOLIATH
see: **Jalut**

GOOD
see: khayr

GOSPEL
see: Injil

GRACE

The word 'grace' refers to God's favour and mercy, it also refers to man's generosity and benevolence. We deal with both meanings below. God's grace is expressed in *al-Rahman*, which implies that he has granted the creation favours

(*ni'ma*), irrespective of whether they believe in him or not, but he has granted special favours to those servants who have submitted to him with sincerity and love.

The ninety-nine attributes of God mentioned in the Qur'an are repeated daily by Muslims, which means they make a deep impression on their consciousness. Among the frequent attributes mentioned are: *al-Rahman* (the Merciful; 170 times), *al-Rahim* (the Compassionate; 227 times), *al-Ghaffar* and *al-Ghafur* (the Forgiving; 97 times) and *al-Latif* (the Kind; 7 times). Thus God is not only just, but also merciful.

> He is God, other than whom there is no god. He knows the unseen and the seen. He is the Merciful, the Compassionate ... To Him belong the most beautiful names. Whatever is in the heavens and on earth glorifies Him and He is the exalted in Might, the Wise. (59.23–4)

It is interesting that the Qur'an does not refer to God's love as much as it refers to his mercy. God's grace and mercy include the whole of creation, even the worst of sinners (7.156; 30.33; 30.36; 30.46; 40.7; 42.28). But when God speaks of love, it is pointing to a special relationship, wilfully entered into by God and man, a relationship that the Qur'an says most of humanity will reject (17.89; 25.50; 27.73).

The special favour of God

Man's nature is such that he must live a life that is self-conscious, and not one that is blissful in its abstraction from the social reality in which he finds himself. Human grace comes to us from other people. We have all experienced some kinds of grace from our mother, father, nurse or teacher. Later in life we experience the grace of friends, the grace of moral men and women, and the grace of a spiritual mentor. There is the grace we experience from religious institutions, a grace that has helped even the most timid individuals, and then there is the grace that comes from our ideals, from our faith. Such grace comes either from a transcendental supreme being or from a personality that is the embodiment of grace.

Although God's grace shines through all mankind and he bestows his favours on all people, including sinners, his love is reserved only for those among the saints and prophets who surrender themselves totally to him. These are the ones who will experience a special bond of love with God. Since this category belongs only to the spiritually elite, we should not be surprised that the term 'love' (al-wadud) is used so little in the Qur'an. God's love is available to all, but not all people will enter into this relationship of love.

We sometimes turn to saintly personalities for grace or favours. Many saints have become the recipients of divine grace because they have denied their own individuality, as in the case of al-Hallaj who acknowledged God as the only reality and even saw the divine within himself. Authentic spiritual masters become the instrument of divine grace, and guide their disciples to a level of consciousness that even transcends the self, preparing them also to become recipients of divine grace. The disciple in turn becomes a master, and an instrument of God's grace.

Divine grace is the source of all good, even of our ultimate destiny in the hereafter. In Christianity, salvation is wholly dependent on divine grace because our corrupted nature cannot do anything to save us: we have a perverted will that, if corrected, could direct us towards good, yet salvation depends wholly on God's grace. In Islam, man is born good (fitra) and so he does not need a saviour to deliver him from innate evil; he does, however, require faith and must do good deeds to gain his salvation. This does not undermine divine grace, but it does allow for greater freedom and moral responsibility.

Shaykh 'Abdul Qadir al-Jilani felt that he was the recipient of divine grace, and that he was granted a special talent to judge character. In the *Utterances* (*Malfuzat*), he states: 'I know your best from your worst as a result of God's preparing me and by His grace.' He warns those who are proud on account of divine grace bestowed on them, whether it be wealth, noble descent or whatever.

Human response to God's favour

God in the Qur'an is ethical: he responds to his servants with justice and goodness. His justice is not merely mechanical, following certain laws, but is balanced with mercy. Man is answerable for his free actions on the Day of Judgement, but, if he is remorseful for his sins and turns to God in repentance, God will be gracious towards him.

There are some sixty-nine verses in the Qur'an that refer to God's favours, including the following: 'For Allah is He who gives all sustenance' (51.58), 'There is no moving creature on earth but its sustenance depends on Allah' (11.6) and 'If you are grateful, I will add [more favours] unto you' (14.7). These verses affirm that God wants man to enjoy his bounty, and also to acknowledge him as the source of this bounty.

We have already indicated that grace implies divine favours (ni'ma) being granted to God's creatures, and we observe these favours in the form of ayat (signs) that reflect God's grace. Besides ni'ma, the Qur'an also uses fadl (bounty), rahma (mercy) and maghfira (forgiveness) to express divine grace. Man is expected to ponder over these signs and, if he is perceptive, he will know the real source of these signs and respond with gratitude to God. As for the ungrateful ones, God considers them to be guilty of *kufr* (unbelief): 'Verily man is ungrateful to his lord' (100.6; 43.14–15). Thus man responds to God's grace in the form of either gratitude or ingratitude: the believer is grateful and the unbeliever ungrateful (Izutsu, 1987: 230–3).

Sin is carried out through free will, but although the unrepentant person faces divine punishment, the repentant sinner is redeemed by God's grace. All people, whether they are sinful or sinless, have to display gratitude to God for his grace. The man of piety also cannot afford to be proud of his own good deeds, but must be humble and grateful before God, who is the real power behind all actions. The good that man does also depends on God's grace, and so the good man should always be repentant and pray for paradise.

Human grace

The divine attributes *al-Rahman* and *al-Rahim* may be translated, respectively, as the Beneficent and the Merciful. The former includes believers and non-believers, and signifies the conferring of God's favours on his creation. The latter (*al-Rahim*) is more specific to believers, and may not include the general meaning of divine beneficence (*al-Rahman*) (Lane, 1984). Its application to believers is contained in the verse: 'They are graceful [and compassionate] towards each other.'

The grace of kindness is greater than justice. Where justice means that one must demand one's due according to the law, grace requires one to forgo this right and give to another person more than his due. We noted above that God's beneficence is universal and he bestows his blessings to all people, irrespective of their beliefs, through natural phenomena. Furthermore, God is merciful to the believers who are recipients of his special favours, especially the Friends of God (*awliya'*).

Human beings act with grace by sharing their bounty, but grace is not only understood as sharing, it has another dimension. The possessor of grace is also benevolent. He does not take what is due to him: that is, he forgoes his right.

Al-Raghib al-Isfahani (d. 1060) uses the term *fadl* or *tafaddul* (benevolence) and compares it with justice (*'adl*). Justice is a legal quality because it implies the implementation of the law, but benevolence is a spiritual quality because it implies a voluntary action of the soul. Benevolence does not constitute justice because benevolence implies excess, whereas justice implies equality. Yet one cannot have benevolence without justice, for it is benevolence that moves a person to justice, not merely as an act of deference to the law, but as a condition of a balanced soul, an upright character. Isfahani regards benevolence as nobler than justice because it transcends the law, the judgement of the courts. A benevolent person will not turn to the court for justice, but will act from the dictates of his soul. The court has to implement legal justice, but the individual can forgive and forgo his rights (Isfahani, 1987: 355). This is not a defiance of justice, but a free act of the soul. A man who seeks justice for a wrong done to him is a restless soul until he achieves his purpose, but, if he acts with a benevolent, forgiving spirit, he will overcome his restlessness and his soul will be in a state of quiet repose. One way of developing a benevolent temperament is by being fully alive to the fact that no man is perfect, that we have all wronged someone in our lives. So instead of being judgemental and seeking vengeance, we should act with grace and forgiveness.

Isfahani supports justice fully when he cites these verses: 'But if you judge, judge between them justly' (5.42) and 'God commands you to deliver back what you have been entrusted with to their owners and, if you judge between people, to judge justly' (4.58). But he also supports benevolence and human grace when he cites this verse: 'To forgo it is more righteous. And do not forget to be bountiful to each other. Allah sees what you do' (2.237). Furthermore, he says, friendship is founded on grace (*fadl*), not on justice; grace leads to intimacy and justice to separation. God elevates those who act with grace: 'To those who do the good is the best reward and more' (10.26) (Isfahani, 1987: 356).

References and further reading

Isfahani, R. (1987) *al-Dhari'a ila makarim al-shari'a*, Cairo: Dar al-wafa'.

Izutsu, T. (1987) *God and Man in the Koran*, Salem: Ayer Company Publishers.

Lane, E. W. (1984) *Arabic-English Lexicon*, 1–2, Cambridge: The Islamic Texts Society.

Mohamed, Y. (1996) *Fitrah: The Islamic concept of human nature*, London: Taha Publishers.

—— (2004) *The Path to Virtue*, Kuala Lumpur: ISTAC.

See also: **fadl; lutf; ni'ma**

YASIEN MOHAMED

H

HABB / HABBA

Habb (grain, corn) and *habba* (a seed, seed grain) appear in the Qur'an eleven times altogether (the former is used on six occasions, the latter on five). The related verb *ahabba* (to produce grain), which does not appear in the text, is derived from the same root *h/b/* as *habba* (to love) and is sometimes used with the same meaning.

In the Qur'an, *habb/habba* is treated as an important symbol of creation and resurrection, and as an *aya* (sign) of Allah's mercy, care, generosity, all-encompassing awareness and scrupulous justice.

Habb / habba as a proof of creation and resurrection

Habb/habba is a symbol that carries a number of Allah's messages, the most important of which is the message of creation and resurrection. In four verses (6.95, 99; 36.33; 78.15) Allah's action

towards the *habb* is described by the verb *akhraja* (to bring forth, to cause to come out). Prior to the exertion of Allah's influence, the properties of the *habb* are hidden and not manifest: before the *ikhraj* (bringing forth) has taken place, the *habb* is unknown and virtually non-existent.

In 6.95 Allah describes himself as *faliq al-habb wa'l nawa yukhrij al-hayy min al-mit wa yukhrij al-mit min al-hayy* (splitter of the grain and the date-stone, [who] brings forth the alive from the dead, and brings forth the dead from the alive). The *habb* (as well as the *nawa*, date-stone) is characterized as being simultaneously alive and dead, i.e. as something that is situated on the border between life and death and apparently endowed with properties of both. To make the properties of life prevail, a 'splitter', who causes the hidden life to break the dead shell, is needed. The *aya* of resurrection, strictly speaking, is the splitting and sprouting of the *habb*, not the seed grain *per se*, because it is unable

227

to leave its dormant state without an external agent (something that brings it into its next stage).

The eschatological content of the symbol of *habb* appealed to esoteric commentators on the Qur'an such as Sadr al-din al-Shirazi (Mulla Sadra) (d. 1050/1640), who interpreted it predominantly from the position of his doctrine of *al-haraka al-jawhariyya* (substantial motion) (see Shirazi, 1986, 7: 83–4). The eschatological symbolism of the *habb* was also important to the Sufis, who treated it as an *aya* describing the mystic's spiritual awakening.

Care and mercy

On each of the six occasions that the *habb* appears in the Qur'anic text (significantly, it is always mentioned together with other vegetables and fruit: dates, grapes, olives, pomegranates, basil), it also delivers the message of Allah's care for human beings and his mercy towards them. As one of the essential items of human food, it is indispensable for our survival. Since human existence directly depends on the accessibility of food, its availability in sufficient quantities is a powerful sign of Allah's care and mercy. For their part, human beings are supposed to be grateful to their carer and merciful provider: they should thank him whenever they partake of any of his bounty and not be a *kafir* (ungrateful concealer) of the truth, pretending to be unaware of Allah as their only provider.

Mithqal habba (the weight of a seed): perceptiveness and justice

Another important message the symbol of the *habb/habba* conveys is that of Allah's perceptiveness, experience and scrupulous justice. The *habba* (seed grain) is the smallest entity perceptible to a naked eye. In terms of weight, the Qur'an twice (21.47; 31.16) mentions *mithqal habba min khardal* (the weight of a mustard seed) – the smallest unit of weight measurable by traditional, non-high-tech scales.

31.16 (which is outwardly a *nasiha* (admonishment) given by Luqman to his son, but is essentially Allah's own pledge) contains an unspecified promise to bring out the *mithqal habba* of every property hidden inside a rock and in heaven and earth. *Mithqal habba* is used there to indicate the subtlety of Allah's perception and completeness of his experience: full possession of these qualities allows him to describe himself as *latif* (perceptive) and *khabir* (experienced).

In 21.47, which deals with the events of the *qiyama* (rising/resurrection), *mithqal habba min khardal* is used to give an idea of the precision of the *mizan al-qist* (scales of justice), on which people's deeds and intentions will be weighed. This precision eliminates any possibility of injustice.

The excellent precision of the *mizan al-qist*, which is able to weigh the *mithqal habba*, points to the scrupulous justice Allah will bring to bear on every human soul during the trial of the Last Day. Simultaneously, it implies that such precision and justice may be not present in this world: it is Allah's practice to postpone the exertion of full justice for a certain time, in order to give the wrongdoers a chance to repent.

Habba (grain seed) and *sunbula* (ear): generosity of Allah's reward

A *habba* (grain), when it falls to the earth, produces an ear of corn that contains dozens of grains. Similarly, the tiniest amount of bounty spent for the sake of Allah is recompensated by him with a reward that exceeds the amount spent many times.

The issue is discussed in the verse 2.261, which is part of the address to the faithful, in particular the well-off ones, encouraging them to support materially the war against the unbelievers. Here a *habba* that produces seven ears, each of which has a hundred grains, is directly called a *mathal* (similitude) of those who spend their substance in the way of Allah.

It can be concluded that while Allah's justice is fully exerted on the unbelievers and wrongdoers, his treatment of the believers and the *muhsinin* (those who do what is beautiful) exceeds the limits of justice proper and can best be described as generosity. Thus *habba* is used in the Qur'an as the symbol of both justice and generosity, each of which is brought to bear on a particular group of human beings.

References and further reading

Murata, S. and Chittick, W.C. (1994) *The Wisdom of Islam*, New York: Paragon House: 80–4.
Shirazi, S. (1986) *Tafsir al-Qur'an al-karim*, (Commentary on the Revered Qur'an) Qum: Entesharate bidar, 7: 83–4.

See also: *'adl*; *aya*; eschatology; *'ishq*; *lutf*; wealth

YANIS ESHOTS

HABL ALLAH

Habl is a noun meaning rope, link or leash. It also signifies strength or unity. *Habl Allah*, or 'the rope of Allah', signifies connection with God. The Qur'an itself is the rope of Allah, as are the unity of the Muslims and also the following of Allah's commands. The following *aya* illustrates this meaning: 'And hold, all of you together, to the rope of Allah, and be not divided among yourselves' (3.103). *Hablu Allah* signifies his covenant. The Qur'an describes the People of the Book as being humiliated except

when they are under covenant of protection by Allah.

RAFIK BERJAK

HADID

Hadid, a noun derived from the root *h/d/d/*, means iron in Arabic. It is the title of *sura* 57 of the Qur'an, which was delivered during the period between the battle of Uhud and the Truce of Hudaybiya between the fourth and fifth year after the Hijra. It takes its name from a sentence in verse 25: 'We sent down iron' (*Wa anzalna' l-hadida*). *Hadid* (iron) stands for strength, power, discipline and the sanctions of law; it was also one of the sources of political and economic power, and therefore it is a means of testing man's attitude towards divine law and order. Elsewhere the *sura* encourages Muslims to make monetary sacrifices, and points out that Islam does not merely consist in verbal affirmation and some outward practices, but its essence and spirit are sincerity towards God and his religion.

NECMETTIN GÖKKIR

HADITH

A very important source of Islamic law, not to say interpretation of the Qur'an, comes from the traditional sayings of the Prophet and those close to him. These have been collected and are called *hadith*. Many collections of traditions (*ahadith*, sing. *hadith*) had been made during the third century/ninth century, but six works became recognized as authoritative in Sunni Islam, especially the *Sahih al-Bukhari* and the *Sahih Muslim*. The adjective *Sahih* actually means accredited: the other four are also highly esteemed, but it is allowed by the Muslims that some of the *hadith* in them are suspect and may not be genuine. *Al-Bukhari, Muslim* and the other texts are much quoted and have become highly regarded, considered second only to the Qur'an itself as sources of authority for the laws and customs of Islam. The *al-kutub al-sitta* ('the six books') comprise the canonical *hadith* literature and, as such, form the main sources for traditional law. The *Muwatta* of Imam Malik is not really a collection of *ahadith* in the sense of the legal traditions for its own sake, but includes them specifically as a guide to law, and so is a useful source also. Some Muslim authorities include it instead of the *Sunan* of Ibn Maja among the six canonical collections.

Malik did not share the approach of Shafi'i towards the *sunna*. He declared that the only true *sunna* was found in the *hadith* and not in the *ijma'* (consensus) of Muslim scholars, however unanimous it might be, when it could not produce relevant traditions to support it. For Malik the value of the tradition literature is not so much in supplying a grounding for the laws of Islam but more in illustrating the application of those laws. For Shafi'i each tradition was the basis for a legal decision and the resolution of a problem. For Malik the *hadith* were there to bring out the relevance of a legal principle, not establish it by virtue of the *hadith* itself. His *Muwatta* is one of the earliest collections of traditions, most of which were approved by al-Bukhari and Muslim, so his work is significant in *hadith*.

The collection of Abu 'Abdulla Muhammad ibn Isma'il al-Bukhari is the most highly regarded work of *hadith* literature. Bukhari's compilation includes all known traditions of Muhammad's life considered to be authentic. There are 7,275 *ahadith*, some rather similar to others, which he says he refined out of 600,000 sayings that were *prima facie hadith*. He classifies the *hadith* in terms of the different schools of law, usefully showing how the different schools tend to prioritize different *hadith*.

Muslim ibn al-Hajjaj also was loath to enter into the legal debate personally, but collected the *hadith* that would be useful to others involved in the law. The latter would then have available to them a range of authentic sayings that could help guide them in their legal work. The legal emphasis and objective of these works nevertheless resulted in each one being considered one of the *Musannaf*, the collections in which the traditions were grouped under specific topical headings (as opposed to the *Musnad* works, which concentrated on grouping them under their *isnad*s going back to their earliest transmitters). Muslim records most of the *hadith* found in Bukhari's collection but, whereas the latter placed parallel versions of the same tradition under various headings relating to various points of law, Muslim put them all together under their own topical headings. The former made the traditions fit his subject-titles, the latter made his subject-headings fit the subject-matter of the traditions. The main difference is the absence of the paragraph headings characteristic of Bukhari. Muslim's work is arranged according to *fiqh* (jurisprudential categories), but he does not follow his plan scrupulously: thus while Bukhari often arranges the same tradition with a different *isnad* under different paragraphs when it is suitable to support more than one point of law and custom, Muslim places the parallel versions together. While Bukhari's compilation is considered the more reliable of the two, Muslim's arrangement of his material has been recognized as superior, and rightly so. While Bukhari made the traditions in his collection testify to his own schedule of various points of law, Muslim left them to speak for themselves.

The *sunan* works of Abu Dawud and others

The remaining four works are called *sunan* (the word has the meaning 'path' or 'way') because they concentrate on the example of Muhammad's actions and decrees insofar as these provide the ultimate foundation of all Islamic law. The work recognized as the best of these collections is the *sunan* of Abu Dawud, which contains many of the *hadith* in the two *Sahihs* but also includes traditions not found there. He likewise was a scrupulous collector and, although some of his traditions are regarded as weak and suspect, he was aware of the problem and was careful to distinguish between sound and weak *hadith* in his text. Abu Dawud did his best to deal faithfully with the material at his disposal. Unlike al-Bukhari and Muslim, he includes material that is not very reliable, or even considered actually unsound, but he does not fail to draw attention to it.

Two collections very similar to Abu Dawud's are the *sunan* works of al-Tirmidhi and al-Nasa'i. The former is called a *Jami'* (collection) because it covers not only legal traditions but also, like Bukhari and Muslim, historical and other *hadith* as well. Nevertheless Tirmidhi confined himself to traditions on which the principles of Islamic law had already been based and did not venture to record such as might lead to new interpretations. His collection is therefore primarily a reference work as well.

The *sunan* of al-Nasa'i is very comprehensive. Unlike Tirmidhi he did not limit himself to recording individual *hadith* as a resource work for issues concerning the jurists of his day but sought to catalogue all the variant editions of each *hadith* known to him, just as Muslim had done before him. His work accordingly has a place of its own in the heritage of the tradition literature.

Al-Nasa'i's main object was only to establish the texts of traditions and the differences between their various versions – almost all of which he quotes at length, instead of only referring to them as Abu Dawud and al-Tirmidhi had done.

The last work, the *sunan* of Ibn Maja, is regarded as the weakest of all the six major works of *hadith* literature and some traditionists prefer the *sunan* of al-Darimi to it. Nonetheless, although a great many authorities have openly declared some of the traditions found in this collection to be forged, it has established itself among the approved works. The other scholars, such as Abu Dawud and Tirmidhi, also recorded weak *ahadith,* but they mostly noted them in their books, whereas Ibn Maja, even when he recorded a false *hadith,* went on to use it.

Further reading

Burton, J. (1994). *An Introduction to the Hadith*, Edinburgh: Edinburgh University Press.

Cook, M. (1981) *Early Muslim Dogma*, New York: Cambridge University Press.

Rippin, A. (1990) *Muslims: Their religious beliefs and practices*, Vol. 1, *The Formative Period*, London: Routledge.

Siddiqi, M. (1993) *Hadith Literature: Its origin, development and special features*, Cambridge: The Islamic Texts Society.

Wensinck, A. (1927) *A Handbook of Early Muhammadan Tradition*, Leiden: E.J. Brill.

See also: **al-Shafi'i**

OLIVER LEAMAN

HAFIZ | TAHFIZ | HIFZ | MUHAFFIZ

Hafiz means 'one who remembers', 'guardian, custodian', and is one of the names of God. It comes from the Arabic triliteral root *hafiza*, meaning to protect, to guard, to preserve in memory, to remember. The word is used to designate a person who knows the Qur'an by heart, for such a person preserves it in his memory. *Tahfiz* is the process of learning or the method of memorizing the Qur'an; *Hifz* is knowing and keeping the Qur'an not only in the head but also, as the English phrase so aptly has it, by heart, and acting according to its explicit commandments, as well as constantly repeating it while understanding the meaning of the Arabic in which it was revealed. *Muhaffiz* is the candidate's mentor during the process of learning *hifz*, in which the student/candidate repeats the passages he has mastered or learned by heart, sitting in the traditional manner on the floor knee-to-knee with the teacher. This, indeed, is typical of all Eastern models and methods of transmission of knowledge from teacher to pupil, part of the chain of transmission reaching right back to the founder, in this instance the Prophet Muhammad himself.

But what place does learning the Qur'anic text by heart have in the modern age, the age of mass media and the vast computer industry, when everything is stored on disks, video and audio tape? What is the point of *hifz* in the age of the computer? In this era of splintered, fragmented audio-visual culture, of the meretricious glitter and impersonal sound of the digitized media image of the global village – on which fortune ostensibly smiles – it must seem obvious that the formal approach to the Qur'an cannot bear fruit. This is the attitude of those who, when they look at the Qur'an, see only the form of the Arabic *hurufat*, not the spiritual value of the universal, eternal Qur'anic message; for the *hafiz* is not merely the guardian of the Qur'anic text, but also the implementer of its universal, inclusivist message. Such a *hafiz* will not be seduced by the multitudinous ramifications of the audio-visual culture, which offer not true reality but a virtual image of the

reality of this world. What is more, the *hafiz* of today must perceive that learning the Qur'an by heart (*hifz al-Qur'an*) is not just a matter of preserving all the Words of God that sundered the Heavens for the last time to be sent down as a message to all of humankind, but also that to learn them is to be focused on conscious practice, on living one's life according to the Qur'an. Consequently, the dilemma of whether or not to learn *hifz* is a false dilemma.

Since *hifz* entails one's incessant physical involvement, the *hafiz* has a huge advantage over a person who has merely saved the Qur'anic verses to a computer hard disk. Seen in this light, it is wholly understandable that the presence of the Qur'an in the form of learning and applying *hifz*, the universal Qur'anic message, in one's day-to-day life, bears with it the lasting stamp of God's benevolence and mercy on the person who is the guardian of the Qur'an – the *hafiz*. The daily learning and repetition of the Qur'anic *ayas* are intended as a mind-building exercise, and in a sense entails turning one's back on the modern way of life, which is led at breakneck speed and where tradition and traditional values are forgotten. It is precisely in this that there lies the deeper spiritual significance and role of learning *hifz* in our day.

In giving a brief historical overview of this, it is essential to note that the Prophet Muhammad himself was the first *hafiz*, followed by his closest *ashabs*: the first four khalifas, *hazreti* Hafsa, *hazreti* Ummi Salama and many others. They did not merely learn the Qur'an by heart, however; they lived it in their daily lives – they were the living Qur'an. *Hifz* is not a race to see who can learn the most pages in the shortest time, nor is it just a matter of storing the Qur'anic text in its entirety within the memory paths of our brains. What *hafiz* are most concerned about is that their life and conduct conform to the Qur'anic *ayas* that they hold in their memory and their hearts.

Furthermore, in Islamic literature, to denote a person who recites the Qur'an in its different *qira'at* skilfully, beautifully, fluently and, which is particularly important, correctly according to *tajwid*, one says that such a person is *qurra' hafiz*, meaning an expert in Qur'anic recitation, in which seven (or ten) *mutawatir qira'at* are recognized (*qira'at*, sing. *qira'a*, are the different linguistic, lexical, phonetic, morphological and syntactical forms permitted when reciting the Qur'an). The origin of these refinements lies in the fact that the linguistic system of the Qur'an incorporates the most familiar Arabic dialects and vernacular forms in use at the time of the Revelation. What is more, *qira'at* may be seen as the pieces of a single mosaic, each fitting perfectly into the supernatural text of the Qur'anic expression. Then again, *mutawatir qira'at* may be recited both during and independently of *salat* (prayers), while others that are not of this degree may be used only for the purposes of *tafsir* (commentary).

There are, of course, various methods of learning *hifz*; however, the author of this entry, himself a *hafiz*, recommends learning by the circular or cyclic method (this means that one learns the last page of each *juz'*, followed by the penultimate and so on to the end of each *juz'* in turn, so that after twenty cycles one has completed learning *hifz*), in conformity with the rules of *tajwid*. This method of learning is dynamic in nature and does away with a degree of monotony in the actual process of learning. Of course, when the pages that have already been learned are repeated, which must be done without fail every day, they are repeated in their normal order. Another

piece of advice to anyone who has embarked on, or intends to begin, this painstaking and demanding process of learning is that they use only a single *mushaf* (compilation), both when learning and when repeating.

Then again, it is vital that a candidate who wishes to earn the honourable title of *hafiz al-Qur'an* finds himself a good *muhaffiz*, a mentor who will listen to his recitation and encourage him during the learning process; for both the *muhaffiz* and his pupil must make their way along a hard and uncertain path. The *muhaffiz* listens to his pupil, corrects any *tajwid* or textual errors, gives him advice and instruction, helps him and encourages him to persist and to hold out to the end, which is particularly important at moments of crisis and when the pupil begins to tire. On the other hand, the pupil will comport himself with due respect and show proper esteem for his teacher, and will be regular and disciplined in attending the sessions at which the set passages he has learned are to be heard. Thus the role of the mentor or *muhaffiz* is undoubtedly of great importance. Of course, a candidate may set out alone on that long and unpredictable path, but there is a great likelihood of his straying off it and not knowing how to return. There is something similar in the ancient Indian tradition of pandits learning one, two, three or even four collections of the Vedas by heart over a period of ten or more years.

Finally, repeating the Qur'an and constantly being in its presence are the very essence of *hifz*. It is not that hard to learn the entire Qur'an; the difficulty lies in retaining it, in learning it by heart in the full sense of the phrase. In the charming metaphorical expression of the author's own *muhaffiz*: 'I recommend, noble brother, that you recite [repeat from memory] at least one *juz'* a day, for the Qur'an is like a bird – if you let it go, it loses no time in flying out of your hand.' The only guarantee of high-quality, stable *hifz* is intensive repetition of the Qur'an. This is particularly important in the actual process of learning *hifz*. Every Muslim who wishes to learn *hifz*, which is truly a hard and painstaking process, should begin with the firm resolve that he will persist to the last so as to attain this noble goal he has set himself, rejecting any thought of material advantage or profit from it. Without this firm resolve (*niyyat*), there can be no persistence or disciplined will, no valid timetable – and this, too, is essential and must be drawn up.

See also: **education and the Qur'an;** *tajwid*

NEVAD KAHTERAN

HAJAR

It is worth noting that the *Encyclopedia of Islam* has no entry entitled Hajar or Hagar. She was the mother of the biblical Ishmael, Abraham's first-born son. If you look up the entry on Ishmael, you find one cryptic sentence towards the end of the single-page entry, which alludes to the expulsion of Hajar and her child described in commentaries on the Qur'an and 'stories of the prophets' (*qisas al-anbiya*), in accordance with the Jewish tradition (Genesis 21). Nowhere is it mentioned that Hajar was Abraham's second wife and that she was the mother of his son. In fact, Ishmael himself is never identified in the entry as even being related to Abraham. What is even more startling is the further claim that the Qur'an never establishes a direct link between Abraham and Ishmael, and that it must therefore be assumed that originally the Prophet Muhammad was not well informed about the family relationship between them. This total effacement of Hajar and Ishmael in

comprehensive reference works like the *Encyclopedia of Islam* is, to say the least, unscholarly. However, it is understandable given the degree of vilification that Hajar has suffered at the hands of Western scholarship. The entry 'Hagar' in *Webster's New Collegiate Dictionary* is representative of how fossilized this disparagement of Hajar has become in the English-speaking world: 'a concubine of Abraham driven into the desert with her son Ishmael because of Sarah's jealousy according to the account in Genesis'. The entry in *The American Heritage College Dictionary* (*AHC*) provides the following: 'In the Bible, the Egyptian servant of Abraham's wife, Sarah, and the mother of Ishmael'. The entry under 'Ishmael' reads: 'In the Bible, the son of Abraham and Hagar who was cast out after the birth of Isaac'.

To remedy this sorry recasting of facts, one has only to cite a number of statements from the Bible. First, in Genesis 16: 11 (KJV), Ishmael is never despised in the eyes of God or in the eyes of his father; in fact, he is named by God himself: 'And the Angel of the Lord said unto her [Hagar], Behold thou art with child, and shalt bear a son, and shalt call his name Ishmael, because the Lord hath heard thy affliction' (Ishmael or Isma'il is derived from the triconsonantal root *s/m/'/* meaning 'to hear'). Ishmael is referred to as the 'son' and 'seed' of Abraham (Genesis 21: 13). In addition, Hagar is never presented as a 'concubine' but rather as Abraham's 'legal' wife: '...and [Sarah] gave her [Hagar] to her husband Abram to be his wife' (Genesis 16: 3). Abraham is stricken with grief over their so-called expulsion and pleads with the Lord to revoke the command: 'Oh that Ishmael might live in thy sight!' (Genesis 17: 18). God hears his pleas and reveals to him Ishmael's far-reaching destiny: 'As for

Ishmael, I have heard you; behold, I will bless him and make him fruitful and multiply him exceedingly; he shall be the father of twelve princes, and I will make him a great nation' (Genesis 17: 20).

It is thus evident that, contrary to popular opinion in the West, Abraham was not succumbing to some kind of vindictiveness on the part of Sarah when he left his wife and child in the desolate desert, but merely fulfilling God's divine will. When, later on, after their banishment, Hajar and her son were close to dying of thirst in the wilderness, they were saved by the angel who showed Hajar the spring (called Zamzam in Mecca). One concluding fact needs to be asserted before ending this brief attempt to provide a more accurate account of the biblical Hajar. One of the major distortions that occurred is the claim that Hajar and her child were cast out 'after the birth of Isaac', as the above *AHC* entry stipulates. In actual fact, they were resettled in the valley of Becca or Mecca almost thirteen years before the birth of Isaac. It is clear from Genesis 21: 17–18 that Ishmael is only a child, a 'crying' infant, when he and his mother are left in the barren desert: 'And God heard the voice of the lad where he is. Arise, lift up the lad, and hold him in thine hand; for I will make him a great nation.' The image is of a mother 'lifting up' a crying infant in her 'hand'; it is certainly not an image of a 16-year-old lad (if Isaac was two years old when Hajar was said to have been banished, then Ishmael was 16: according to Genesis 21.5, Abraham was 86 years old when Hagar bore Ishmael and a hundred years old when Isaac was born). This is made even more explicit in Genesis 21.14–21, where we see Abraham giving Hajar bread and a bottle of water, 'putting it on her shoulder', and helping her carry the child. Once in the desert, she 'casts the child under one of the shrubs'. The basic implication of all this is that Hajar is not meant to be seen as a lowly servant, despised and hated by her husband and by God. In fact, if one reads without the bias, one finds that even in the Bible she is portrayed as a woman of faith and strength, who was sent away against her husband's will. It is also clear that she and her child, as Frieling states (1978: 28), were involved in the 'far-reaching plans of divine providence'. Whether she was a bondwoman or not, or whether she was Abraham's first or second wife, is quite irrelevant. Abraham himself married two other wives after the death of Sarah. Isaac, Jacob and Moses all had several wives. David and Solomon had hundreds of wives. The fact is that for thousands of years, the common custom was to keep several wives and even to marry their servants – as in the case of Jacob, who married two women and two of their maids.

Having first exposed the vilification of Hajar, perhaps one can now go on to discuss Hajar as she appears in the Qur'an and in Islamic Tradition. Like so many other significant people in the Qur'an, Hajar is never mentioned by name in the text. We never see her talking to Abraham or hear her communications with the Angel of God as we do in the Bible. However, we feel and live her predicament indirectly through the eyes of Abraham. His prayer to God as he walks back from the desert sums up her situation and reveals the extent of the anguish that Abraham must have felt on leaving his wife and his only infant in the desert. Here are two verses from Abraham's famous and oft-quoted prayer for his small family: 'Our Lord, I have settled (*askantu*) some of my offspring in a valley with no cultivation by Your Sacred House; Our Lord, so that they may establish regular Prayer, so make the hearts of some people yearn towards them, and provide them with fruits and produce so that they may be thankful. Our Lord, truly, You know what we conceal and what we reveal: For nothing is hidden from God, whether on earth or in heaven' (14.37–38).

As is evident from Abraham's prayer, this was a 'resettlement' and not an expulsion. Notice that the location, though desolate and unfertile, was obviously once a settled community as suggested by the reference to the Sacred House. This is in keeping with Islamic Tradition, which traces the history of the Sacred House or *Ka'ba* to Adam and Eve, who established the first settled community (see 3.96).

There are other indirect references to Hajar in the Qur'an, the most significant being 2.158 where the sacred rites of the *hajj* are mentioned, in particular those connected with the twin mountains, al-Safa and al-Marwa. According to tradition, when Hajar was left by herself in the valley, she went back and forth seven times between the hills of al-Safa and al-Marwa, frantically in search of water for her crying infant. The angel Gabriel then appeared and, by striking the ground next to the infant, caused the well of Zamzam to be formed. When Abraham was later commanded by God to rebuild the *Ka'ba* on its earlier foundations, the sacred rite of *al-sa'y* was also established, which was basically a re-enactment of Hajar's movement back and forth between al-Safa and al-Marwa.

As to Hajar's origins, the following information is provided by Tradition and *Qisas al-anbiya* (Stories of the Prophets). According to al-Rabghuzi, the famous Turkish collector of prophetic stories, Hajar was the daughter of the King of Maghreb, a descendant of the Prophet Salih (i.e. the ancient community of Thamud). When her father was killed by the Egyptian Pharaoh Dhu l-'arsh, she was captured and taken away

as a slave. Later, because of her royal blood, she was made the mistress of all the female slaves and given access to all of Pharaoh's wealth and possessions. We are told that Dhu l-'arsh later converted to Abraham's religion and readily granted Sarah's request to have Hagar. Since Sarah was incapable of bearing children, she bestowed Hajar on her husband as recompense. It is said that Hajar was not her original name but that she received her name because of Sarah's words to Abraham: 'Here is your recompense', or *Ha ajruka* in Arabic. In time, her name became Hajar. The significant thing about the above account, which is also corroborated by medieval Arab sources, is that Hajar was neither Egyptian nor a lowly maid, but an Arab of royal blood and a descendant of an Arabic prophet. In a way, this makes her vilification in the Judaeo-Christian tradition much more difficult for Muslim scholars to accept.

References and further reading

Azami, R. (trans.) *Ibn Kathir: Stories of the Prophets*, Riyadh: Darussalam.

Frieling, R. (1978) *Christianity and Islam*, Edinburgh: Floris Books.

al-Rabghuzi (1995) *The Stories of the Prophets: Qisas al-Anbiya: An Eastern Turkish version*, Vol. 2, trans. H.E. Boeschoten, J. O'Kane and M. Vandamme, Leiden: E.J. Brill.

al-Tabari, M.H. (1989) *The History of al-Tabari: General introduction and From the Creation to the Flood*, Vol. 1, Albany, NY: SUNY Press.

See also: **Arab**

AFNAN H. FATANI

HAJJ

The pilgrimage to the *Ka'ba* in Mecca was an ancient ritual – in the *jahiliyya* (pre-Islamic period), the aim of the visit was to worship the local gods. There are two pilgrimages: the greater one, the *hajj* itself, which every Muslim is supposed to undertake at least once if at all possible, and the *'umra*, the minor pilgrimage. The *hajj* can only take place in the sacred months. The rituals and institutions involved are partially mentioned in the Qur'an (2.189, 196–203; 3.97; 5.1–2, 95–96; 9.3; 22.30) and the event itself was established by Ibrahim (2.125; 22.26–29), although it was corrupted by idolaters later on. The rituals are described in some detail, including donning the *ihram* (5.1, 95–96), the simple clothing symbolizing entering a holy state; not shaving the head; being polite, virtuous and pacific; and not hunting. Among positive actions are circumambulating the *Ka'ba*, praying at particular places, visiting the hills of Safa, Marwa and Arafat, listening to a sermon and, finally, sacrificing an animal. The other ceremonies that have developed are kissing the Black Stone in the *Ka'ba*, throwing stones at a pillar representing evil, moving swiftly between Safa and Marwa, and visiting Arafat. Different sects of Islam have slightly different rituals connected to the *hajj*, but the basic ceremonies are agreed on and fixed.

See also: **Arab;** *salat*

OLIVER LEAMAN

HAKIM | HIKMA

A term used in the Qur'an to signify wisdom, but which later acquired a range of technical meanings relating to religious, gnostic or esoteric philosophy and philosophers (*hakim*, pl. *hukama'*). It should be noted that the concept of wisdom in Arabic-Islamic philosophy, and indeed in the Asian philosophical traditions as a whole, is not wholly congruent with the term 'philosophy' in the Western tradition. The very concept of *hikma* is now seen as the authentic Islamic

response to the confusion generated by profane philosophies, and this analysis is necessary if one is to avoid any theoretical errors with regard to this concept. A further reason is to save anyone studying the term from thinking that it has to do with some kind of philosophy lacking self-realization. In its most basic of exoteric connotations, then, *hikma* is the accumulated experience of the human race, transmitted from generation to generation as an oral or written tradition.

This view is certainly contrary to the destructive discontinuities that can be seen in the development of the Western sciences and social theory, and goes beyond the notion of *falsafa*, or Greek-inspired knowledge. As a result, it was already possible in the late tenth century for the heritage of this kind of wisdom in the growing, pluralist Islamic culture to be summed up and appraised by the Persian philosopher and mystic Miskawayh in his anthological work *al-Hikma al-khalida* (The Eternal Wisdom), which retained its influence right through to the modern era as a source of inspiration for those Muslim intellectuals with a predilection for 'freedom of thought' and a pluralist outlook on human culture. Abu Hamid al-Ghazali had already written his debate on (or repudiation of) philosophy and philosophers when he wrote of wisdom: 'And wisdom is what God Almighty, All-powerful, extols in these words: "He granteth wisdom to whom He pleaseth; and he to whom wisdom is granted receiveth indeed a benefit overflowing"' (2.269).

Linguists often make the very interesting observation that the word for wisdom is of the feminine gender in Arabic, Hebrew, Aramaic and Syriac. The etymological and semantic relationship between *hikma* and *hukm* (regulation, ordinance, legal judgement or verdict) has a parallel in the noun pair *al-hakim* (wise man, sage) and *al-hakim* or *hakam* (judge), both of which number among the most beautiful names of God. Further, the word *hikma* itself appears twenty times in the Qur'an, and there is a mass of evidence in support of the belief that *hikma* is the actual denotation of the Qur'an (see, for example, the Qur'anic *ayas* 10.1; 31.1–2; 36.1–2; 43.3–4; 44.1–4). Equally, the marked difference between *hikma* and *tanzil* (revelation) lies in their relation to pure human knowledge. Revelation teaches humankind what it did not know (96.5), while wisdom teaches us what humankind has always known.

Traditional wisdom, or what the Qur'an calls *al-hikma,* lies at the heart of every authentic tradition, and is to be found in every tradition that has retained the dimension of wisdom to this day. This true wisdom can play a significant part in equipping modern man to rediscover the full teachings of the nature of God as Reality, and Islam is capable of contributing in this sense to attaining this goal, not only because of the nature zof the Qur'anic revelation, but also because it has to this day preserved inviolate its tradition of wisdom. This is consistent with Islamic doctrine itself (see, in particular, the following Qur'anic *ayas*: 2.136; 3.84). What is more, this doctrine is not characteristic only of Islam, but is at the heart of every sacred tradition.

Sophia and *sapientia, hokmah* and *hikmah, shes-rab* and *prajna* (in Sanskrit) are but different names for the wisdom that is of divine nature, and that is apostrophized as the eternal wisdom. This is certainly not only because it is laid down in the revealed scriptures of the Revelation and the inspired or God-given words and deeds of the entire Prophetic Tradition, and still less because its graphic representation and more or less profuse literary form remained enduringly impressed on the face of Mount Sinai, or because its power – in the form of light or fire – penetrated the immaculate womb of the Virgin of Jerusalem and there implanted the seed of the revelatory divine Spirit, nor yet because its pure light shone in all its fullness on the head and the heart of the extraordinary young Man of Mecca, finally to come to rest on the parchment of the inscribed Book (*Kitab marqum* – the Qur'an). It is eternal primarily because it comes from the mouth of the eternal divine Spirit, as the living force of the divine Life and the eternal, inexhaustible force of the Will that makes all things visible and invisible new and unrepeatable at every moment. Then again, it is eternal divine wisdom (*al-Hikma al-Ilahiyya* or *al-ladunniyya*) because its supernatural nature rests on immutable metaphysical or metacosmic principles that are none other than the suprapersonal or transcendent regard of God, which traditional Semitic spirituality in its entirety apostrophizes as the Absolute, the Truth, the Good, Beauty, Justice, Mercy and Bliss.

As a result, its concordance with previous religious traditions is a pronounced feature of this eternal wisdom (the Arabic term *al-hikma al-khalida,* or the *sanatana dharma* of the Hindus), a concept that has played a continued and major role in Islam, whether as an exoteric model for cultural and religious pluralism or as the esoteric treasury of the mystics. The Holy Spirit or Breath of God, however, blows gently through every tradition, for how else is one to understand the passage in the Gospel according to St John that reads: 'The wind bloweth where it listeth, and thou hearest the sound thereof, but canst not tell whence it cometh, and wither it goeth: so is every one that is born of the Spirit' (John 3: 8).

Finally, *hikma* is not merely mental conceptual knowledge, given that knowledge is inseparably linked with deed and practice. Nor is it mere pragmatism and utilitarian action for gain, although the practical side of life derives from the Truth itself. The meaning of the term lies in this, that if one merely knows but does not comport oneself in a manner consistent with that knowledge, or merely conducts oneself without a knowledge of the fundamental principles of true knowledge, one cannot be a *hakim* in the meaning of the term defined above. The overwhelmingly significant fact, at a time when the theory that Islamic philosophy ostensibly had only a mediating role is still popular among scholars and academics, is that the term *hikma* indicates a broader context of conceptual issues within Islam than that denoted by the term *falsafa*, an Arabic neologism designating the Greek philosophical tradition within Islam. The wholly unjustified restriction of the role and significance of the Islamic philosophical tradition, the reductive view that it was no more than a vehicle for the transmission of ancient Greek philosophy to Europe, fades into oblivion and is revealed as inconsistent when one accords the concept deeper consideration. It is here that there lies the advantage of regarding the Islamic philosophical tradition as *hikma*, for by using this Qur'anic term one avoids ever-present stereotypes about the tradition.

By way of final observation, it is worth noting that the concept is moulded and synthesized in various ways, based on centuries of reflection by various Islamic thinkers (*hukama'*) who have striven to reconcile faith, philosophy and the foundations of faith on the one hand with, on the other, the knowledge derived from the heart or inner purification. For instance, in Mulla Sadra Shirazi's synthesis it is called 'metaphilosophy' (*al-hikma al-muta'aliya*), and philosophers of this particular type are called 'theosophers' (*al-hakim al-*

muta'allih), in the non-sectarian meaning of the term.

See also: **philosophy and the Qur'an**
NEVAD KAHTERAN

HALAL / *AHALLA*

The root *ha-lam-lam* in Arabic is polysemous, with meanings related to 'untie' and 'alight' being found in dictionaries and employed in the Qur'an, alongside the major meaning of the root in its sense of 'permit'. It is in this latter sense that the word has its most important usage and on which this entry will focus. The dichotomy between permitted (*halal, ahalla*) and forbidden (*haram, harrama*) permeates the Qur'an and provides one element of the foundations of Islamic ethics. With this word the ethical aspects of the worldview of the Qur'an come into play, providing insights into the understanding of the relationship between the sacred and the profane, of God's will for human existence, and of the moral categories by which people will be judged eligible or not to spend the hereafter in paradise.

The word *halal* is employed in a manner that suggests a level of somewhat greater complexity than the simple permitted/forbidden dichotomy might suggest, although *haram* finds a greater degree of diversity in its usage than does *halal*. Among the senses of *halal* are the opposites of both senses of the word *haram*: *halal* can mean 'profane' (in opposition to the sense of *haram* as 'sanctify') as well as 'permit' (as opposed to *haram*'s 'forbid'). As with *haram* in the sense of 'sanctify', *halal* can suggest a special relationship with God that marks its opposite off as separate. The predominant meaning of the word, however, is the assertion of the lawful character of something, or, when expressed with the negative particle 'not', the equivalent of *haram* in the sense of 'forbidden'.

Halal is employed on seven occasions as a legal category in a negative expression meaning 'to be unlawful' with reference to women, marriage and divorce; these instances appear to be specific situations in which the general permissibility of an action or circumstance is contravened, perhaps even with the sense that this is temporary, as in Qur'an 2.230: 'If he divorces her finally, she shall not be lawful (*la tuhillu*) to him after that until she marries another husband.' On twelve occasions, *halal* declares things permitted, especially types of food, as in Qur'an 5.5: 'The food of those who were given the Book is permitted to you'; on another eight occasions, *halal* is combined with *tayyibat* (good things) as in Qur'an 2.168: 'Eat of what is in the earth, lawful and good'; and on six occasions it is employed in direct contrast to things forbidden, *haram*, as in Qur'an 16.116: 'And say not concerning that which your tongues falsely describe, "This is lawful, and this is forbidden",' sometimes occurring in situations where the complement of *haram* is seen as being *khaba'ith* (bad things).

Halal is also employed in a sense which is opposite to that of *haram* in its meaning of 'sanctified'. One way to understand the word *halal* in these instances is that it means 'ceasing ritual avoidance behaviour'. *Halal* is used to indicate leaving pilgrim sanctity (i.e. leaving *ihram*) in 5.2 and, in the same verse, pilgrims are ordered 'not to profane God's waymarks or the holy months'. The idea that the sanctified months could be altered comes in for criticism in 9.37, which probably refers to the process of adding a month to the year (*al-nasi'*). This is declared to make a month that is supposed to be sanctified (*haram*) into one that is *halal*, thus making an inviolable month (in the sense that no fighting should take place in it) into one that can be violated. The Qur'an states: 'The month postponed is an increase in unbelief whereby the unbelievers go astray; one year they make it profane (*yuhilluna*) and hallow it another (*yuharrimuna*) to agree with the number God has hallowed (*harrama*) and so profane (*yuhillu*) what God has hallowed (*harrama*).' The sense is of the sacred power conveyed in something which is *haram* then becoming nullified by its being *halal*. The word *mahill*, meaning 'place of sacrifice', which is used three times in the Qur'an, may also partake of the sense of profane space (2.196; 22.33; 48.25).

Halal did not become the preferred term of ethical behaviour, generally (but not always) being restricted to a quality of entities and not reflective of acts themselves. As legal theory evolved, everything was deemed to be *halal* which was not specifically prohibited (and in that sense was the opposite of *haram*), but the ethical system as it developed employed a five-level categorization of acts (*al-ahkam al-khamsa*) and the word *mubah* became most commonly used for 'permissible'. The word *halal* gained a connotation of 'permitted' especially as it applied to dietary restrictions and thus referred to whatever items might be eaten by Muslims, such as ritually slaughtered food (and took on a function parallel to the way *kosher* is used in Jewish parlance).

Further reading

Chelhod, J. (1964) *Les structures du sacré chez les Arabes*, Paris: G.-P. Maisonneuve et Larose.

Gräf, E. (1959) *Jagdbeute und Schlachttier im islamischen Rechte: Eine Untersuchung zur Entwicklung der islamischen Jurisprudenz*, Bonner orientalistische Studien, neue Serie, Bd. 7, Bonn: Selbstverlag des

Orientalischen Seminars der Universität Bonn.

Izutsu, T. (1966) *Ethico-Religious Concepts in the Qur'an*, Montreal: McGill University Press.

al-Qaradawi, Y. (1994) *The Lawful and the Prohibited in Islam*, trans. K. El-Helbawy, M.M. Siddiqui and S. Shukry, Indianapolis: American Trust Publications. Also widely available online.

See also: **calendar; food;** *haram*

ANDREW RIPPIN

HAMKA

Haji Abdul Malik Karim Amrullah, better known by the acronym Hamka, was born in 1327/1908 in the Minangkabau region of West Sumatra. His father was a leading reformist thinker in the region. After attending elementary school, Hamka received no further formal schooling, but was largely self-taught.

Throughout his life Hamka was associated with various reformist bodies, both non-political and political. He rose to senior positions within the Muhammadiya organization. He also became a prominent member of the Masyumi political party, leading to his election to the national parliament in 1955.

International recognition came in the form of an honorary doctorate from al-Azhar University in Cairo in 1959. He travelled widely overseas on invitation as an Islamic scholar in the 1950s and 1960s, but ran foul of the leftist-influenced Sukarno regime at home. In 1964 he was imprisoned for twenty months on accusations of subversion.

The fall of Sukarno in 1966 led to Hamka's rehabilitation. In 1975 he was appointed chairman of the government-sponsored Majelis Ulama Indonesia (Indonesian Council of Religious Scholars). Hamka died in Jakarta in 1401/1981.

Hamka was the most prolific of all modern Indonesian Islamic authors. He composed over 100 books on various subjects: Qur'anic exegesis, mysticism and doctrine; political works; historical studies; works of fiction; and books addressing Minangkabau customary law.

Mystical inclinations coloured much of his approach to Islamic teaching, but his was a reformist Sufi approach that affirmed the legal requirements of the faith. He strongly criticized any syncretistic practice that mixed customary law with Islam. It was during his time in prison that Hamka wrote most of his Qur'anic commentary, entitled *Tafsir al-Azhar*. The materials came initially from a series of lectures delivered in Jakarta at the al-Azhar mosque. This commentary has been published in several editions in Jakarta, Kuala Lumpur and Singapore. It has a lengthy introduction, in which Hamka defines his target audience as, first, young Indonesian Muslims needing a sense of direction in their theological formation and, second, those active in *da'wa* (mission). His commentary shows his reformist inclinations: concerned with a weakening of Islam in the face of contemporary secular intellectual rationalism, Hamka set himself the goal of equipping his readers to cope with modern intellectual challenges by reinforcing basic Islamic principles that were under threat.

Hamka identifies his approach to exegesis as one based on the use of *ra'y* (individual interpretation or opinion). He encourages his readers to develop their own ability to engage critically with the primary texts of Islam. Hamka identifies his sources as the *Tafsir al-manar* (The Lighthouse Commentary) by the reformist Rashid Rida (d. 1353/1935), the commentary by the more Islamist Sayyid Qutb (d. 1385/1966) and diverse classical commentaries in Arabic. He also expresses admiration for the Malay language commentaries by 'Abd al-Ra'uf, Mahmud Yunus and Hashbi Ash-Shiddieqy.

Further reading

Hamka (1992) *Tafsir al-Azhar*, Jakarta: P.T. Pustaka Panjimas.

Nasution, H. *et al.* (eds) (1992) *Ensiklopedi Islam Indonesia*, Jakarta: Djambatan.

Riddell, P.G. (2001) *Islam and the Malay-Indonesian World: Transmission and responses*, London: Hurst & Co., 267–76.

Steenbrink, K.A. (1995) 'Qur'an Interpretations of Hamzah Fansuri and Hamka', *Studia Islamica* 2, 2: 73–96.

Yusuf, M.Y. (1990) *Corak Pemikiran Kalam Tafsir Al-Azhar: Sebuah Telaah tentang Pemikiran Hamka dalam Teologi Islam*, Jakarta: P.T. Pustaka Panjimas.

See also: **tafsir in early Islam**

PETER G. RIDDELL

HANIF

Used twelve times in the Qur'an, *hanif* (pl. *hunafa'*) is a term used to describe Ibrahim/Abraham is the model of the authentic, primordial religion (*al-din al-hanif*), the religion of *fitra*, the religion revealed at the very origins of the human race. In fact, in the light of this Islamic view, all religions have the same origin, since monotheism, particularly as underlined in the Ibrahimic/Abrahamic religions, can be traced back to the first man on earth, the ancestor of humankind – Adam.

Islam regards itself as the 'primordial religion', which is the actual meaning of the Arabic syntagmatic cluster *al-din al-hanif*. As a result, Islamic belief and practice seek to restore humankind to its original, true nature, in harmony with the natural order and belief in the One God. What is more, in the view of today's leading thinkers on the provenance of Islam, the best way to preserve Islam in its integral form is to preserve the *religio perennis* or primordial religion (*al-din al-hanif*) that has its abode in the very heart of Islam, as it does in the heart of all true religious traditional

teachings. Behind the multiplicity and diversity of religions lies this primordial religion, the model of *hanifiyya*, with which everyone is born, only later to become a follower of one or other of these various religious forms. Furthermore, these forms are not evidence of religious falsehood, but of the wisdom of the Divine Providence, taking into account human sensitivities and predilection for one or other of these forms. As a result, the authentic, primordial religion can be only that which is concerned with perfecting the natural human predisposition to perfection and ever-growing awareness of the Presence of God.

Why, though, does the Qur'an lay such emphasis on Ibrahim/Abraham's example of this pristine, unadulterated worship of God? The reason is that Ibrahim/Abraham is the common denominator of the Judaeo-Christian-Islamic tradition, and as such the true model to follow and emulate for all the scions sprung from the Ibrahimic/Abrahamic stock. What is more, according to the Qur'anic *ayas* (2.130–135; 3.65–67, 95–100; 6.79, 161–162; 16.120–124; 22.26–32), the term *hanif* is in direct opposition to the term *mushrik* (polytheist), particularly in the following *ayas* of *sura Yunus* (10.105) and *sura al-Rum* (30.29–30). Also, *sura al-'Imran* (3.67) declares that he was neither Jew nor Christian, whereby the Qur'an seeks to avoid the dispute over Ibrahim/Abraham and set right our consideration of commonality and sameness, instead of merely squabbling over the matter, over the issue of *tahrif*, the transformation of this natural predisposition.

The specific feature of this Ibrahimic/Abrahamic model is that it denotes the fundamental encounter within the horizons of all its sacred traditions and revelations. In the space between these conceptual traditions and/or cultural circles is a range of *tertium comparationis* in the aspiration to overarch all diversity in the very tension of differences in the quest for this decisive place, the crowning outlook from which the universalism of ahistorical structures of thought would finally yield an utterly clear vision, a unification as the renewal of thought, the aspiration to conceptual evolution at the boundaries. And yet the abandonment of absolutism, of an extreme position in the practical and theoretical sense, and of exclusivism certainly does not mean that we are bound to submit to another form of extremism, the kind that derives from relativism. What the *hanifiyya* model in fact denotes is the Ibrahimic/Abrahamic wisdom bestowed on the eternal heritage for the life of the world and permanently entrenched in the foundations of the Judaeo-Christian-Islamic tradition.

In an attempt to understand this universalist view of Islam, many are still struggling with the fact that it is little known, an ignorance exacerbated by unoriginal and often banal newspaper headlines about violence and its consequences. However, these days the general view of Abrahamic religions (Islam belongs to the wider Judaeo-Christian tradition) equates them with a radicalized minority, so that the universalist, inclusive Islamic perspective is sidelined, even by some Muslim communities, who should see in it a salvific model and the *raison d'être* of Islam. For a knowledge of Islam and Muslims, who constitute one fifth of humankind as a whole, has never been so crucial as today, and this is particularly true of its universalist perspective, best reflected in the term *hanif*. In this light, our post-9/11 experience of coexistence, pluralism and tolerance must be built on mutual understanding and respect, not on ignorance, stereotypes, fear and prejudice.

The Prophet of Islam himself brought no new message from some new God, but called on people to return to faith in the one true God of Ibrahim/Abraham and a way of life that they had forgotten or from which they had strayed. Since it is not a new revelation, the Qur'an contains many references to the narratives and figures of the Old and New Testaments, and Islamic belief, in the midst of a polytheistic society, meant in fact the return to a forgotten past, a return to the faith of the true monotheist Ibrahim/Abraham. This is why Muslims see themselves, along with Jews and Christians, as the descendants of Ibrahim/Abraham, descendants belonging to different branches of the same religious family. It is true that there are marked differences between the biblical and the Islamic narratives of Ibrahim/Abraham, even as regards the term *hanif* itself and what it signified in the early days of the Islamic community and in pre-Islamic times. However, what cannot be contested is that the Qur'an and Islam respect Jews and Christians as the children of Ibrahim/Abraham, and have invariably regarded them as 'People of the Book' (*ahl al-kitab*), since all three monotheistic faiths trace their origins back to the same ancestor, Ibrahim/Abraham (3.84). It is evident that Jews, Christians and Muslims, believers who pray to the same God, the God of Ibrahim/Abraham, must become aware of the differences in their modes of worship and their worldviews, and must respect and tolerate those differences. The encounter between them presents a major cultural challenge, but facing that challenge is also the duty of every adherent of these Ibrahimic/Abrahamic traditions. If mutual understanding between the members of these traditions is ever to come about, an essential part of the package must be knowledge of this quintessential concept of primordial religion, *al-din al-hanif*. As a result, the Qur'an invites the members of the Ibrahimic/Abrahamic family to say: 'O People of the Book! Come to common terms as between us and you: that we worship none but Allah; that we associate no partners with Him; that we erect not, from among ourselves, lords and patrons other than Allah' (3.64).

See also: **fitra**

NEVAD KAHTERAN

HANNA

see: **Mary's mother**

HAPPINESS

Happiness in Islam refers to both this world and the hereafter. Happiness in the hereafter is the ultimate goal of the believer, motivating him to strive for true happiness in this world. We will first examine the literal meaning of happiness in the Qur'an, and then discuss the interpretations of it by Islamic philosophers, namely Miskawayh (d. 1030), al-Isfahani (d. 1060) and al-Ghazali (d. 1111).

The Qur'anic view

Man will be accountable on the Day of Judgement: he will experience otherworldly happiness if he has done good, and otherworldly misery if he has done evil. Good people will have their book of good deeds placed in their right hand, and they will be happy:

> As for him who is given his book in his right hand, he shall say, Come! Read my book! I knew I was going to face my accounting. He shall be in a happy life, in an exalted Garden whose fruit-bunches are nigh [to be plucked . . . It shall be said to them:] Eat and drink to your satisfac-

tion in consideration of what you had left in previous days. (69.19–24; see also 56.27–44; 17.71; 74.39)

The happiness of the hereafter is not merely spiritual. The Qur'an does not recognize a hereafter that is peopled by disembodied souls; it does not recognize, it seems, the dualism of body and soul, but speaks of man as a unitary being. The term *nafs*, according to Rahman, was developed later by Islamic philosophers as a substance (*jawhar*) separate from the body, but the Qur'an refers to man himself, his personality, with body and intelligence. The Qur'an does not affirm a mere spiritual heaven and hell as suggested by the Indian philosopher, Muhammad Iqbal. It describes the physical heaven and hell, not as metaphors, but in order to convey their real effects: the vivid portrayal of fire and the garden conveys the psychospiritual effects of these physical conditions, which are more important. Thus the Qur'an states: 'God has promised believing men and women Gardens, underneath which rivers flow, wherein they shall abide, and pleasant abodes in the Gardens of Eden – but the pleasure of God with them is greater and that is the great success' (9.72). Thus the believers and the virtuous will have their greatest reward in the pleasure (*ridwan*) of God. The faces of the believers on that day will be 'fresh with joy and will be looking at their lord' (75.22–23) (Rahman, 1980: 112–13).

The Qur'anic expression *yawm al-qiyama* (Day of Resurrection) was transformed into the philosophical expression *yawm al-sa'ada* (Day of Happiness). The Qur'an indicates that mankind, because of divine predestination, is divided into 'happy' inhabitants of paradise and 'unhappy' dwellers in hell. However, the impact of predestination is mitigated by verses that pertain to free will and responsibility; hence there is the idea of responsibility for our actions, and accountability to God on the Day of Judgement (Daiber, 1994: 657).

Thus the term *sa'ada* (happiness, bliss), which became a central concept in Islamic philosophical literature, connotes man's highest striving for eternal happiness in paradise. Its opposite is *shaqawa* (misery), which denotes man's eternal misery in hell. We earn this supreme happiness by the purification of the soul. Wealth, health and friends help towards this purification, and so we should strive towards these as well, but we should be aware that none of this bounty, physical or spiritual, is possible without the grace of God. Hence we should perpetually pray to God to grant us the good of this world and the hereafter.

Miskawayh's view

Due to the influence of Neoplatonism, this happiness has been described as the 'assimilation to God'. Miskawayh described it as such, but Isfahani replaced it with the Qur'anic concept of *khilafa* (vicegerency) (2.30; 6.165). The true vicegerent conforms to the revealed law and turns to God alone for sustenance, as is suggested in the verse: 'Allah suffices us; Allah will give us of his Bounty, as will his Apostle. We turn humbly to Him' (9.61). This idea of the assimilation to God was also developed by al-Kindi, al-Razi and the Ikhwan al-Safa' (Daiber, 1994: 658).

Aristotle also influenced Muslim philosophers in his assertions that happiness should be pursued for its own sake, and not for the sake of something else, and that the highest happiness is connected to the rational soul. However, Muslim philosophers differ from him in the view that happiness is not confined to this world, but also extends into the hereafter. The quality of worldly happiness determines the quality of otherworldly happiness. There are two levels of worldly happiness: one consists of the right conduct in fulfilling one's basic needs, the other of lessening human wants for the sake of a greater happiness in the hereafter (al-Attas, 1995: 34ff.).

Miskawayh combined both Neoplatonic and Aristotelian elements in his theory of happiness. Man's perfection pertains to two things: the cognitive and the practical faculties. The practical pertains to moral perfection, which lies in the harmony of the faculties of the soul. When he achieves this harmony he becomes a small world, or a microcosm of the universe. Man's happiness lies in becoming a small world (Zurayk, 1968: 35–7). Happiness is the end of all virtues, and is the supreme good, but it cannot be attained without the body and the external virtues of material resources, friends and good fortune. These bodily and external virtues do not provide ultimate happiness, but they aid in its achievement. The happy man is either in the rank of the bodily things, or in the rank of the spiritual things, but whoever is in neither of these two ranks is in the rank of the animals (Zurayk, 1968: 75ff.).

Al-Isfahani's view

Al-Isfahani argues that the path to virtue is the path to happiness. Mere knowledge of the good is not true knowledge, which must correspond to one's state of being. The actual doing of good transforms a person's being. Revelation only guides the intellect as to what the good entails, but the good has to be practised. Thus to do good is to know good, and to do evil is to be ignorant of good. This conclusion follows from al-Isfahani's conviction that the moral person is the happy person. Since people desire their own happiness, they will always desire the good. This emphasis on moral action and the purification of the soul in al-Isfahani transcends Miskawayh's emphasis on cognition as the key to happiness. Al-Isfahani emphasizes the idea of worship, and associates the assimilation to God with the Qur'anic idea of *khilafa*.

Both Miskawayh and al-Isfahani share the view that bodily and external goods are important for the virtues of the soul, but whereas Miskawayh regards them as inevitable burdens of earthly existence from which we need to be liberated, al-Isfahani regards them as forms of happiness, albeit of a lower order.

Both kinds of happiness, bodily and spiritual, worldly and otherworldly, are acknowledged by the Qur'an. Worldly pleasures should, however, be pursued in moderation. Al-Isfahani has a positive view of the body and of the world, which offers a more natural transition in the course of man's ascent to the higher plane of happiness than that suggested by Miskawayh.

Al-Isfahani reminds us that complete virtue and real happiness are in fact the good deeds of the hereafter (*al-khayrat al-ukhrawiyya*). Lower goods that lead to this higher happiness are also virtuous, but we must be guided by our reason to choose them prudently. The four qualities of this otherworldly happiness are: eternity without destruction, ability without weakness, knowledge without ignorance, and wealth without poverty (al-Isfahani, 1987: 129).

Happiness lies in the perfection of our distinctive quality, as suggested in the verse cited by al-Isfahani: 'God has perfected everything, and it is this perfection that all things long for, and He has guided every thing to realise its particular perfection. Our Lord is He who gave everything its nature, then guided it' (20.50).

The Qur'an permits happiness for man (14.34), both otherworldly happiness that will not perish and worldly blessings that will perish. People seek happiness, but they often mistake it for something else. The thirsty imagine a mirage in the desert to be water: 'As to the unbelievers, their works are like a mirage in level ground, which the thirsty supposes to be water, but when he comes close to it, he finds that it is nothing' (24.39) (al-Isfahani, 1988: 128; 1987: 134).

Worldly benefits can lead to happiness if used sparingly, to provide for one's basic needs. The happy ones are those who view happiness as a blessing, and the miserable ones those who do not see it as a blessing. Concerning the latter, the Qur'an states: 'So do not let their wealth and their children win your approval, Allah only wishes to torture them therewith in the present life, so that their souls might depart while they are still unbelievers' (9.55) (al-Isfahani, 1987: 130).

Man cannot attain higher happiness in the hereafter without distancing himself from the temporary world (6.158) and without removing the sickness of his soul (al-Isfahani, 1987: 133). This is what God is referring to when he says: 'And as for the happy, they shall be in Paradise, therein dwelling forever, so long as the heavens and the earth abide, save as thy Lord wills for a gift unbroken' (11.108).

Al-Ghazali's view

In agreement with Miskawayh and al-Isfahani, al-Ghazali holds that if man disciplines his desire (*shahwa*), he will attain the perfection that distinguishes his nature, which is the heart's knowledge of God. This special perfection, and its pleasure, are unique to man, and the pleasures of the senses cannot compare with this higher pleasure.

> Know, the happiness of everything – its pleasure, its serenity – indeed the pleasure of everything accords with the needs of its nature. And the nature of everything accords with what it has been created for. The eye delights in [seeing] pretty pictures and the ear delights in [hearing] harmonious sounds. Every limb can be described like this. The heart's distinctive delight is in the knowledge of God, the Most High, because the heart is created from [divine knowledge. (al-Ghazali, 1987: 139)

Al-Ghazali follows al-Isfahani's positive view of the world. Worldly pleasures are a means to the pleasures of the hereafter. The pleasures of desire and anger, the two lower elements in man, should not be obliterated, but disciplined (Qasem, 1975b: 153–61).

Otherworldly happiness is the highest form of happiness, and the Sufi way, according to al-Ghazali, is the most effective way of attaining it. Neither reason by itself, nor mere external conformity to the revealed law are sufficient to reach ultimate happiness. This goal can only be attained by the purification of the soul, and the Sufis stress the means to it, which is constant meditation and moral action.

References and further reading

al-Attas, Syed Muhammad Naquib (1995) *Prolegomena to the Metaphysics of Islam*, Kuala Lumpur: ISTAC.
al-Ghazali (1964) *Mizan al-ʿAmal*, ed. Sulayman Dunya, Cairo.
—— (1987) ʿ*Kimiya al-saʿada' Majmuʿat rasaʾil al-Imam al-Ghazali*, 5 Beirut: Dar-al-kutub al-ʿilmiyya.
al-Isfahani, R. (1987) *al-Dhariʿa ila Makarim al-Shariʿa*, Cairo: Dar al-wafaʾ.
—— (1988) *Tafsil al-nash'atayn wa tahsil al-saʿda'*, ed. A. Najjar, Beirut: Dar al-gharb al-islami.
Mohamed, Y. (2004) *The Path to Virtue*, Kuala Lumpur: ISTAC.
Qasem, M. Abul (1975a) *The Ethics of al-Ghazzali: A composite ethics in Islam*, Selangor.
—— (1975b) ʿal-Ghazali's Conception of Happiness', *Arabica* 22, 153–61.
Rahman, F. (1980) *Major Themes of the Qur'an*, Minneapolis: Biobliotheca Islamica.
Zurayk, C. (1968) *The Refinement of Character*, Beirut: American University of Beirut.

See also: **caliph; philosophy and the Qur'an**

YASIEN MOHAMED

HAQQ | HAQIQA

One of the beautiful names of God, *haqq* means first of all what is true or real as opposed to subjective opinion or vanity and futility. But the multifarious use of the term helps us to understand how the Qur'an displays the ontological truth of God, on the one hand, and the unquestionability of revelation and its contents, on the other. In Arabic philosophical language, *haqq* means both 'truth' and 'reality', and these senses can be derived straight from the Qur'an. The word *haqiqa* can be used similarly, but while *haqq* is a Qur'anic term, *haqiqa* is not. *Haqq* is repeated more than 200 times in the Holy Book. First of all, several verses testify that God is the truth (*Allah huwa al-haqq*) (for instance, 10.32; 22.6; 24.25), and this means that God is reality in the highest and absolute sense of the term. If God is the whole reality, his being must be himself: the Arabic locution is *Allah huwa huwa* ('God is God' or 'God is himself'). It is the divine identity in philosophical and mystical language, like the biblical 'I am who I am'. After the contention that 'the Truth is One who is the antithesis of the falsehood', the great Shafiʿite theologian al-Ghazali says that God is *haqq* because he is 'the

One truly existing in itself, from which every true thing gets its true reality' (al-Ghazali, 1995: 124). This is the reason why the Qur'an states that 'everything perishes but his face' (28.88) and the verse is one of the main arguments for the theory of *wahdat al-wujud* ('unicity of being'): namely, there is nothing in existence but God, meaning that all creatures are devoid of ontological reality with respect to God. Al-Ghazali argues, however, that things are real and true, not mere appearances, and other Qur'anic verses may be quoted to uphold this view.

The verses 32–36 of *sura* 10 (Yunus) displays at least four meanings of *haqq*:

1. as a divine attribute;
2. as 'good', the alternative to 'evil';
3. as the goal of human life: 'God leads to the Truth';
4. from an epistemological point of view, as the assertion of absolute knowledge by contrast to subjective opinion (*zann*).

Subjective opinion leads the ignorant to believe what it is not true of God (*ghayr al-haqq*; 3.154). To protect us from the danger of going astray, we know that the Qur'an is *haqq*, because God says: 'Those to whom the Book was given know that it is the truth' (2.144). The Qur'an is the straightforward Word of God, so everybody can find in its truth the right path and guidance. Moreover, several verses oppose what is true (*haqq*) to what is vain and false (*batil*). For instance: 'We will hurl truth at falsehood until truth (*haqq*) shall triumph and falsehood (*batil*) be no more' (21.18), or 'God knows very well what you are doing, because God is the Truth (*Allah huwa al-haqq*) and vanity (*batil*) is that which you invoke besides him' (31.30). Another verse stresses the fact that God did not create the world and the cosmos to no purpose: 'We did not create the heavens and the Earth and all that lies between them playing (*la'ibina*) but with Truth (*haqq*)' (44.38). The cosmos is absolutely true and real, and even though God can change it or destroy it whenever he wants, the world is rational and consistent. These utterances can be employed to support a different philosophical view from the *wahdat al-wujud* principle. However, the opposition between *haqq* and *batil* is clear also in al-Ghazali, who argues that the divine essence is necessary because it is true and real ('The Necessary in itself is the pure Truth' – *al-wajib bi-dhatihi huwa al-haqq mutlaqan*), in comparison to the nothingness of the world. In the popular *tafsir* (commentary) of the two Jalals, written in Mamluk Egypt at the end of the fifteenth century, the term *haqq* of 31.30 is rendered by *al-thabit*, namely 'the one who is permanent' or 'enduring and firm'. On the other hand, the world's vanity (*batil*), which unbelievers worship in the place of God, is rendered *al-za'il*, that is 'the ephemeral', 'the transient'. Accordingly, in 34.49, we find: 'Say: Truth has come and falsehood can start nothing and will return no more.' On the one side, there is the whole Being of God, the creator, and the truth of his word nobody can doubt; on the other, there is the reality of creatures – which is only a reflection of God's unity – and the subjectivity of personal opinion. In the theological discussion the opposition between the eternal existence of God and the ephemeral contingency of the world is plainly stressed and grounded in the Holy Book.

From a phenomenological point of view, the Qur'an describes the Truth as something given and certain: God makes the world evident to men who are living and experience it: 'Do you not see that God created the heavens and the Earth with Truth?' (14.19). How can we doubt it? The Qur'an that the believers recite every day is a linguistic space that represents what is clear about our world. Consequently, the prophets are keepers of no 'secret' (*sirr*) and this represents a sharp difference with Christianity. Only God 'has the keys of all that is hidden' (6.59) and the prophets are only enunciating and interpreting the signs of God. So, after having interpreted the dreams of Pharaoh's dignitaries, Joseph adds: 'Did I not tell you that God has made known to me things you do not know at all? ... O my father, this is the meaning (*ta'wil*) of my previous dream; my Lord made it True (*haqq*)' (12.96–100). God is the Truth and he attests the Truth, either in revelation or in the world he created.

Finally, the word *haqq* means the right of men, and especially the poor, to have what is due to them. One example is in 6.141, but the Qur'an is particularly clear at 17.26: 'Give your kin what is due to them, and the poor and the travellers alike, but do not squander your substance wastefully.' So the juridical concept and terminology of human rights are grounded in the Qur'an, with an explicit hint that balance (*'adl*) is necessary in social behaviour.

References and further reading

al-Ghazali (1995) *The Ninety-Nine Beautiful Names of God*, ed. D. Burrell and N. Daher, Cambridge: The Islamic Texts Society.

See also: *'adl*; *al-ghayb*; *zuhd*

MASSIMO CAMPANINI

HARAM | HARRAMA

The dichotomy between forbidden (*haram, harrama*) and permitted (*halal, ahalla*) permeates the Qur'an and provides one element of the foundations of Islamic ethics. The word *haram*, however, has a more complex meaning within the Qur'an than this basic understanding suggests, in that the word mirrors a broader pattern known in many religious worldviews, bringing together a basic sense of 'sanctify' with the meaning of 'forbid'. *Haram* as 'sanctify' implies a direct relation to God, as well as establishing the inviolable and ritually pure nature of that which is designated *haram*. In the sense of 'forbidden', *haram* discloses most strongly the sovereign freedom of God's will. Things alienated from God (*khabith*), actions against the will of God (*fisq*) and the sickness that results from pagan practices (*rijs*) are all suggested as reasons for a thing to be *haram*; however, the power remains with God to change what is *haram*, allowing a conclusion that nothing is *haram* due to its inherent nature alone. The semantic range of the word *haram* is distinct in the Qur'an; while there are other words that suggest a sense of 'sanctify' (*qudus* and *mubarak*, for example, or *baraka*) and other terms are used to mean 'forbidden' (for example, those related to the root *naha*), no other term combines both of these aspects.

The root of the word *haram* is used eighty-three times in the Qur'an. The connotation of 'sanctify' arises especially in relationship to sacred space. God is involved in establishing and maintaining the holy house (*al-bayt al-haram*) in Qur'an 5.97, a secure sanctuary (*haram amin*) in Qur'an 28.57 and 29.67, sacred territory in Qur'an 27.91 and, most of all, the sacred mosque (*al-masjid al-haram*) on fifteen occasions. These last are understood to be references to the *Ka'ba* in Mecca (e.g. 2.144, 149, 150 in the context of the *qibla*; 2.196; 48.27 in the context of the *hajj*; also note *al-bayt al-muharram*, 14.37). The notion of the purity of a sanctified place becomes apparent in reference to *al-masjid al-haram*, as in Qur'an 9.28:

'The idolaters are indeed unclean (*najas*) so let them not come near the sanctified mosque after this year of theirs.' Notions of the security of a sanctified place are also strong in the Qur'an, linked to inviolability in Qur'an 2.191, 28.57, 29.67 and 48.27. Finally, God has in Qur'an 2.198 designated certain places as 'sacred waymarks' (*al-mash'ar al-haram*), places related to the pilgrimage; this may also relate to the *hurumat* (sacred things) in 2.194.

Time is also sanctified in the Qur'an, in the notion of the 'holy month' (*al-shahr al-haram*), which appears in 5.2, 5.97, 9.5 and 9.36–37. The last-mentioned verse is especially noteworthy: 'The month postponed [referring to the practice of calendar intercalculation] is an increase in unbelief whereby the unbelievers go astray; one year they make it profane (*yuhilluna*) and hallow it another (*yuharrimuna*) to agree with the number God has hallowed (*harrama*) and so profane (*yuhillu*) what God has hallowed (*harrama*).' Pilgrims enter a state of sanctity (*hurum*) by the process of *ihram* (5.95), with an emphasis on avoiding hunting.

Haram in all of these passages, then, indicates something directly connected to God and something that God dictates to or appoints for humanity. Obeying these proscriptions is the mark of the believer. Further, things that are *haram* are free from impurity, at least in a physical sense. What is *haram* is secure and inviolable, and violation will bring retribution, either wilfully given on the part of a believer who has committed a violation or extracted by some other means from the guilty unbeliever.

It is clear that passages in which *haram* has the sense of 'sanctity' do not imply that the places or times are in any sense to be avoided; however, in other passages there is a clear indication of matters being forbidden, and thus they are to be avoided when they are designated by the word *haram*. The food laws figure prominently in this regard, as in Qur'an 6.119: 'How is it with you that you do not eat that over which God's name has been mentioned, seeing that he has distinguished for you that which he has forbidden you (*harrama 'alaykum*) unless you are constrained to it?' Meat which has not been properly slaughtered is declared *haram* because it is *fisq* either in itself or *fisq* to consume it, meaning in either instance that it is against God's will (see the use of *fisq* in Qur'an 6.121) to improperly slaughter animals. Flesh of the pig is declared *haram* because it is *rijs* (an abomination), a word used ten times in the Qur'an to speak of things that violate purity; eating of carrion, consuming blood and meat dedicated to other than God are also declared *haram* in Qur'an 2.172–173 and 5.3, as are improper modes of slaughter (also in 5.3) and corrupt things (7.157). Qur'an 8.87 instructs believers not to forbid for themselves the good things, a charge levelled against the Jews in Qur'an 4.160 and 16.118 (with the specific instance of Jacob, cited in Qur'an 3.93, who forbade things for himself, said in Muslim exegesis to be the flesh of the camel).

Haram in the sense of 'forbidden' extends beyond food goods: usury is *haram* (2.275), land can be forbidden to people to enter (the Jews and the Holy Land in 5.26) and the breast of a foster mother can be held back (as in the case of Moses in 28.12). Certain other actions are also forbidden, again in the context of the Jews in 2.85 and the pagans in 6.138, with the ultimate outcome that 'God shall prohibit (*harrama*) him entrance to paradise and his refuge shall be the fire' (5.72).

In sum, that which is *haram* is always declared so by God or, perhaps, by those specially designated by him. Humans, it would seem, cannot on their own declare something legitimately *haram*. Things that are *haram* are simply against the will of God, are things alienated from God or are things connected to the sin of pagan practice.

Finally, one use of *haram* is quite unlike any other instance and is thus highly reminiscent of the biblical use of the word in the sense of 'ban', meaning that something has been 'devoted' to God with resultant ruin and destruction (see Joshua 6: 17–26; Deuteronomy 13: 12–18). This occurs in Qur'an 21.95: 'A ban (*haram*) is on a city which we have destroyed so that they may not return until Gog and Magog are unloosed.'

Some have argued that, with the words *haram* and *halal,* the reader enters the world of taboo, classically described in James Frazer's *The Golden Bough.* In the case of the Qur'an, it has been argued that the presence of this idea reflects a primitiveness of thought which predominated in pre-Islamic Arabia. For the contemporary historian of religion, however, the cross-cultural generalizations that stand behind the word 'taboo' are less easy to accept. A phrase such as 'ritual avoidance behaviour' provides a preferable way to convey a unified sense of what lies behind the word *haram* as it is used in the Qur'an, keeping in mind that it is God's action of separating the item from common use that is key to the concept. This concept would then also enhance the understanding of the opposite term *halal.*

In later Muslim ethical theory, *haram* is understood to be a prohibited act that, if performed, renders one liable to punishment in the hereafter, as opposed to the obligatory act (*wajib*) that produces rewards in the hereafter; 'recommended', 'repugnant' and 'permissible' then constitute further legal categories of action.

Further reading

Chelhod, J. (1964) *Les structures du sacré chez les Arabes*, Paris: G.-P. Maisonneuve et Larose.

Gräf, E. (1959) *Jagdbeute und Schlachttier im islamischen Rechte: Eine Untersuchung zur Entwicklung der islamischen Jurisprudenz,* Bonner orientalistische Studien, neue Serie, Bd. 7, Bonn: Selbstverlag des orientalischen Seminars der Universität Bonn.

Izutsu, T. (1966) *Ethico-Religious Concepts in the Qur'an*, Montreal: McGill-Queens University Press.

Rippin, A. (1979) 'Qur'an 21:95: "A ban is upon any town"', *Journal of Semitic Studies* 24: 43–53.

*See also: **baraka**; **fasaqa**; **food**; **halal***

ANDREW RIPPIN

HARUN

Harun or Aaron, the brother of Moses, is mentioned in the Qur'an twenty times, most commonly in a pair with Moses. Aaron is also included in different lists of prophets along with Jesus, Job, Jonah and Solomon in 4.163 and 6.84. In 26.13, Moses requests that God send for Aaron, and 19.53 states that Aaron was given to Moses as a prophet (see Exodus 7: 1). The Qur'an does not quote any dialogue from Aaron, nor does Aaron appear to play a role in the plagues delivered against Egypt (e.g. 7.127–136). Some verses (e.g. 10.75; 20.49) portray both Moses and Aaron as being sent to Pharaoh, but others (e.g. 43.46; 11.96; 40.23) contain no reference to Aaron. Aaron is also associated with the building of the Golden Calf (20.80–98). Muslim exegesis of 5.26 claims that Aaron died before Moses, before entering the Holy Land, and a tomb identified as being that of Aaron exists on a mountain near Petra in Jordan. The punishment of the Seventy in 7.155 is claimed, by some Muslim exegetes, to be because the leaders of the Israelites accused Moses of killing Aaron.

Further reading

El'ad, A. (1988) 'Some Aspects of the Islamic Traditions Regarding the Site of the Grave of Moses', *Jerusalem Studies in Arabic and Islam* 11: 1–15.

Elder, E.E. (1925) 'Parallel Passages in the Koran: the Story of Moses', *Muslim World* 15: 254–59.

Loewenstamm, S. (1958) 'The Death of Moses', *Tarbiz* 27: 142–57; trans. as *Studies in the Testament of Abraham*, ed. G.W.E. Nickelsburg, Jr, Missoula: Scholars Press, 1976, 185–217.

BRANNON WHEELER

HASAN / HASUNA / AHSANA

Hasan is a noun that means a thing or a person possessing the quality of or being good, goodly, handsome or beautiful. *Hasuna* is a verb, signifying that a thing became good, goodly, beautiful or pleasing. *Hasan* is a popular name among Muslims. It was the name of the oldest son of 'Ali and Fatima, the daughter of the Prophet Muhammad. This term has a vast usage in the Qur'an, as Allah likes those who do good (*al-muhsinin*). *Ahsana* is a verb meaning to do good, to act well or to do pleasing actions or good deeds. In the Qur'an, Yusuf addresses his parents and brothers, expressing his thankfulness and praise to Allah because Allah was kind to him: 'He was indeed good to me, when He took me out of the prison and brought you all here out of the Bedouin life' (12.100).

Husun (beauty) is sometimes considered to have three stages. The first kind is the beauty that appeals to the intellect. This kind of *husun* applies to what is intellectually perceived as reasonable, logical and acceptable. The second kind of *husun* is the pleasantness and attractive-

ness to our *hawa* (passion). The third type of beauty is that which pleases the senses. This last kind is the beauty of nature or the beauty of the fine arts. *Hasana* signifies any thing like wealth, health or other comforts – that could bring pleasure to a person.

The Qur'an states: 'if some good reaches them, they say, this is from Allah' (4.78). It also explicitly and implicitly mentions in numerous places the beauty of Allah's creation: 'Who made everything He has created good' (32.7). The Qur'an has eloquently described the creation of humans and how Allah has formed them with the most beautiful structure: 'And [He] has given you shape and made your shapes good looking and has provided you with good things' (40.64).

The Qur'an encourages good manners, with Allah wanting his servants to be well disciplined and to have excellent manners. In many places in the Qur'an there are golden rules and commandments directed towards helping the servants of God behave and act in good, beautiful and courteous ways. The Qur'an began teaching good manners at the basic unit of society, the family. The good believer is expected to be good to his parents first: 'And We have ordained on man to be good and dutiful to his parents' (29.8). Allah did not only command humans to be good to their parents, but also included this behaviour in a covenant between him and his servants: 'And when we made a covenant with the Children of Israel: worship none but Allah alone and be dutiful and good to parents, and to kindred, and to orphans, and to the poor, and speak good to the people' (2.83). When Maryam (Mary, mother of Jesus) was born, Allah 'accepted her with goodly acceptance. He made her grow in a good manner' (3.37). Allah also instructed his Prophet Muhammad to use well-mannered methods in conveying and delivering the revelation to the world: 'Invite to the way of your Lord with wisdom and fair preaching and argue with them in a way that is better' (16.125).

The Qur'an has encouraged people to do *ihsan* (good deeds), inviting them to be generous and sincere in performing these actions. Good action is open and this suggests that people should naturally act in a goodly and beautiful manner. Righteousness, purity and good deeds are the basic elements of the good Muslim character. They are an integral part of good Muslims, embodied in their deepest consciences. There is always a reward for those who are good. Good deeds and a good reward are inseparable in the Qur'an. The reward is the other side of the coin of good deeds: 'For those of them who did good deeds and feared Allah, there is a great reward' (3.172). The reward that Allah has promised is not equal to the good action of the servant, but is rather much higher: 'Nor do they spend anything small or great nor cross a valley, but is written to their credit that Allah may recompense them with the best of what they used to do' (9.121). This greater reward is mentioned in the *sura Yunus* as *husna* and *ziyada*, meaning 'good reward' and 'more': 'For those who have done good [deeds] is the best reward and even more' (10.26). Muslim scholars described this reward as paradise, with the additional honour of glancing at the countenance of Allah.

The Qur'an also has promised those who do good a good end. They will enter paradise and have an everlasting happy life. For Allah gives an excellent return. Doers of good will receive a good life on earth and an excellent reward in the hereafter: 'So, Allah gave them the reward of this world and the excellent reward of the Hereafter. And Allah loves *al-muhsinin* (the good)' (3.148).

It has been explained by the Prophet that: 'You become a *muhsin* if you pray and worship God in such a way and spirit that you feel you are seeing Him or at least you feel that he is seeing you.' *Ihsan* can happen in two ways: the first way (*ahsan ila*) is to do good to someone, and the second way *ahsan*, lacks the *ila* ('to'). This general term signifies that someone is good by their acquisition of worthwhile knowledge and by their acting in a good manner.

See also: **beauty; parents**

RAFIK BERJAK

HASIBA | HASBUNA ALLAH

Hasiba is the past tense of a term meaning to count, to calculate or to compute. It also means to think, consider and suppose. In the Qur'an, it also signifies the reckoning of people by Allah on the Day of Judgement: 'God is quick in reckoning' (3.19).

Hasbu is a noun that means sufficient. This term is always suffixed with a pronominal *na* ('our' or 'us'), as in *hasbuna Allah*. In the Qur'an the Prophet and his Companions were instructed by Allah to mention this phrase any time they felt distressed: 'Allah alone is sufficient for us, and he the best disposer of affairs' (3.173).

RAFIK BERJAK

HATE

see: qala

HAVA

Hava (Eve), does not appear in the Qur'an as such. She is simply referred to as 'the spouse of Adam' in the fourth *sura*. She was created by God as a companion to Adam, and together they were to live in paradise. Misled by Shaytan (Satan), they both disobeyed God. Repenting, they together sought forgiveness (7.23). In the same *sura*, Allah says: 'O Children of Adam! Let not the Shaytan cause you to fall into affliction as he expelled your parents from the garden, pulling off from both of them their clothing' (7.27). Islamic feminists often point out that she is not regarded in the Book as any more guilty than Adam of disobedience and, by contrast with the Old Testament account, subsequent women are not made to suffer due to the sins of the first woman.

See also: **Adam**

OLIVER LEAMAN

HAYYA | HAYAT | AHYA

Hayya is a verb meaning to live, to be alive or to spend the night awake. It also signifies fertilizing the earth, keeping anyone alive or letting someone live. *Hayya* indicates modesty and shamefulness. *Hayya*, with the stress on the *y*, means come (e.g. to prayer), it also means to be greeted: in the Qur'an, 'when you are greeted with a greeting, greet in return with what is better than it' (4.86). *Yahya* is the present tense of *hayya*, when it means to live or to survive: 'and those who were to live after a clear evidence' (8.42). *Hayy* is the noun meaning alive: it is one of the ninety-nine beautiful names of God (*Allah La Ilaha Illa Huwa*, None has the Right to be Worshipped but Him; *al-Hayy al-Qayyum*, the Ever-living, the Sustainer) (2.255) and is used when Allah creates life (*kulla shayin hay*) from water ('And we have made from water every living thing') (21.30).

Hayat means life. In the Qur'an, life is divided into two kinds. Worldly life is the testing stage of people. Allah gave everyone this life to see how we live it.

Those who live their lives as believers and behave well will pass the great test. Earthly life in the eyes of Allah is 'Only playing and amusement, pomp and mutual boasting among you, and rivalry in respect of wealth and children' (57.20). This earthly life is cheap because it is short and will come to an end soon. However, the second kind of *hayat* is life in the hereafter, everlasting life. Allah encourages mankind to work for life after death: 'And this life of the world is only an amusement and a play! Verily, the home of the Hereafter is life indeed' (29.64). So the hereafter is the life that will never end.

Ahya means to bring to life, to give life or to make alive. In the Qur'an Allah is the *Muhi* (the Giver of Life): 'Is not That Doer of these things able to give life to the dead?' (75.40). According to the Qur'an, the person who has no belief or knowledge is dead and Allah gives him life by guiding him to become a believer in his creator: 'he who was dead and to whom we gave life and light' (6.122). *Ahya* also signifies the revival of land. Allah revives the earth or land by sending rain.

RAFIK BERJAK

HEALTH

A unique, brief and probably authentic statement by the Prophet may be translated as follows: 'There shall be no infliction of harm on oneself or others.' This constitutes a principle that is further emphasized by other statements by the Prophet, such as the *hadith* that says: 'Cursed be everyone who causes harm to a believer or schemes against him.' The Prophet also said: 'God will inflict harm on anyone who harms others.' Another version of this last *hadith* states: 'Anyone who causes harm to a believer shall suffer harm brought against him by God.'

Perhaps the most lucid definition of causing harm was given by Rashid Rida in his commentary on *sura* 5: 'It means that all harm, whether affecting an individual or a group of people, must be removed.' He argues that the Qur'an and *sunna* are the basis of Islam, and the matters of worship (*ahkam al-din*) are permanently fixed. But when it is a matter of deciding about everyday life and its rules (*ahkam al-dunya*), these issues change with changing times.

It is from this principle that we derive the rule that stresses the need to prevent evil and to safeguard personal and general interests. The prohibition on causing sin may be regarded as clearly stated in the Qur'an: 'Say: My Lord has forbidden all shameful activities, whether overt or disguised, and sin (*ithm*)' (7.33). This term is used in its various forms twenty-four times in the text. Another example is: 'Abandon all sin (*ithm*), whether committed openly or in secret' (6.120). In reference to intoxicating drinks and gambling, God says: 'There is great *ithm* (sin) in both, although they have some benefit for people; but their *ithm* (sin) is far greater than their benefit' (2.219). It is clear from this last verse that the term *ithm* is used to emphasize the lack of benefit from these actions. It is forbidden to harm oneself, as God says: 'You shall not kill yourselves' (4.29). He also says: 'Do not expose yourselves to ruin' (2.195). Furthermore, the Prophet said: 'There shall be no inflicting of harm on oneself.' One might conclude from this that it is not permissible for a Muslim to expose himself to the risk of illness or injury in any way or form.

The Prophet said: 'No believer may humiliate himself.' When he was asked how any person would humiliate himself, he said: 'By exposing himself to risks with which he cannot cope.' Islam can be seen as providing advice to steer people away from risks, making it a duty required of every Muslim to do whatever is beneficial to health and safety. They should do this in response to the Prophet's statements: 'Be keen to do what is beneficial to you'; 'Store up enough health to draw on during your illness'; 'Whatever you feed yourself counts as a benefaction.' Similarly, 'Your soul has a [human] right against you; your body has a [human] right against you; your eyes have a [human] right against you.' Muslims also have a duty to take all preventive measures to guard against illness, for prevention leads to health protection, as the Prophet says: 'He who protects himself from evil shall be spared its effects.' That includes keeping away from whatever may cause illness, such as illicit sex, homosexuality and all kinds of immorality. God says: 'Do not approach adultery, for it is a gross indecency and an evil way' (17.32). He also says: 'Do not approach any immorality, open or covert' (6.151). In reference to the people to whom the Prophet Lot was sent, the Qur'an quotes him as saying to them: 'You lust after men instead of women. Truly you are people given to excess' (7.81). In a *hadith* the Prophet is quoted as saying: 'The worst thing I fear for my community is the practice of the people of Lot.'

Ithm may also be seen as including intoxicants and drugs. The Prophet is quoted as saying: 'Every type of intoxicant is forbidden; every narcotic substance is forbidden. Whatever causes intoxication when taken in a large quantity is also forbidden to take in small quantities. Whatever influences the mind is forbidden.' There are several *ahadith* that instruct us to avoid situations replete with danger, such as: 'If you have to sleep while travelling by night, avoid the main road, as it is the track of animals and the refuge of pests' and 'When you go to bed, shake your sheets. You never know what they may have inside.' The Prophet also said: 'Put out lamps when you go to bed, shut the doors, close the waterskins and cover water and food containers.' In another *hadith*, he alerts people to the danger of fire, saying: 'Fire is like an enemy to you: put it out before you sleep.' He also said: 'Whoever sleeps on the roof of a house which has no wall has no claim to make [for social insurance] if he comes to any harm.' The Prophet also discouraged staying alone, urging his followers not to stay at night in a house alone and not to travel alone.

There is no doubt of the importance of taking the appropriate medicine. The Prophet says: 'Seek medical treatment, for God has not created an illness without creating a cure for it.' There is a ban on bringing about harm to one's family. All this is forbidden since it all comes under the prohibition of causing any harm. Islam urges its followers to be kind to their parents. God says: 'We have enjoined on man kindness to one's parents' (29.8). The Prophet prohibited 'holding on greedily to money and asking for it persistently, being unkind to mothers and burying young girls alive, as had been an Arab custom before Islam. The Prophet said: 'Cursed be he who is unkind to his parents.' No one could be more unkind to his parents than one who exposes their health to unnecessary risk. Similarly, Islam instructs parents to take care of their children, and instructs both husband and wife to take good care of each other, laying particular emphasis on a man's duty to look after his wife. The Prophet said: 'Do take good care of women.' He also said: 'My Lord, I place particular importance on the rights of the two weak groups: orphans and women' and 'Your wife has a [human] right against you and your children have a [human] right against you. Give to every one their rightful claims.' In another *hadith*, we read: 'Your household has a right against you.' The Prophet explains the concept of mutual responsibility within the family when he says: 'A man is guardian of his family and he is responsible for them. A woman is guardian of her husband's house and children, and is responsible for them.'

To neglect the rights of parents, wife or children, not to take good care of their health and not to take the necessary measures to prevent their exposition to illness are certainly forbidden, on the basis of the following Qur'anic statements: 'You shall not kill your own children' (6.151); 'You shall not kill anyone, for that is forbidden by God, except through the due process of justice' (6.151); 'Losers are those who in their ignorance stupidly cause the death of their own children' (6.140); and 'No mother shall expose her own child to harm, nor shall any father expose his child to harm' (2.233). It also says in the Qur'an: 'Consult together with all reasonableness' (65.6). In the same context, the Prophet said: 'It is a sufficient harm for any man to allow his dependants to perish.' He also said: 'Whoever does not show compassion to our young ones does not belong to us.' One of the most essential aspects of compassion to young ones is to protect their health and to prevent their illness. Among the most important measures to protect a child's health is breast-feeding for the first two years of its life, because that gives the child the best possible nourishment, enhances its immune system, and helps to provide reasonable birth spacing since breastfeeding often serves as a means of preventing conception. God says in the Qur'an: 'Mothers shall breast-feed their children for two whole years if the parents wish the sucking to take its full course' (2.233). God also says: 'Its weaning comes in two years' (31.14). Similarly, the pledge of loyalty that Muslim women gave to the Prophet contained the vital clause that they shall not cause the death of their own children (60.12).

It might well be thought to be the duty of all Muslims towards the members of their household to: 'Take all necessary measures to prevent illness.' This includes keeping them away from any source of infection, as well as their vaccination, as necessary, in order to immunize them against communicable diseases. When parents are complacent with regard to the vaccination of their children, they expose them to harm, which God has forbidden them to do. Similarly, a foolish or ignorant action by either parent could expose their child to death and make them losers; as we have already seen, God says: 'Losers are those who in their ignorance stupidly cause the death of their own children' (6.140). So one must have done one's best to provide them with the means of healthy living, such as good food, and to teach them the habits of eating moderately and doing exercises which keep them fit.

One of the worst hazards to which children may be exposed is for one of their parents to be a smoker, which means that they are forced to breathe in the smoke of cigarettes and are exposed to all the illnesses that smoking causes. It is no exaggeration to say that this is doubly forbidden as it means, in effect, neglect of the child's right to be protected against illness, and forceful exposure of that child to risk when it is still young and defenceless.

Causing harm to anyone, particularly neighbours, is again forbidden, as the Prophet said: 'There shall be no infliction of harm on oneself or others.' He also said: 'God will inflict harm on anyone who harms others.' Speaking to his Companions, the Prophet once said: 'By God, he is not a believer.' They said, 'Who is this ill-advised loser, Messenger of God?' He said: 'The one whose neighbour does not feel safe against his

designs.' The Prophet said: 'When you restrain yourself from harming others, your action constitutes an act of benefaction that is credited to you.' God says in the Qur'an: 'Those who annoy believers, men or women, without them having deserved it, assume the guilt of slander and commit a clearly sinful action' (33.58). It is not permissible, therefore, for a Muslim to smoke in a confined place, or when he travels in a car, bus or plane. By so doing, he causes harm to his neighbours and exposes them to risk. He must also not smoke, even when he is alone, in order not to expose himself to danger, but the prohibition is much stronger when smoking affects others as well. The same applies to a person who throws rubbish in front of his house. It is annoying to neighbours and passers-by. It equally applies to one who lets the effluent of his plant or factory run into streams or rivers. To all such unsafe practices the ruling that prohibits causing harm or annoyance applies. The Prophet said: 'Whoever offends Muslims in their roads deserves their curses.' The Prophet warned against exposing any individual in society to any annoyance or harm. He also instructed his followers to take all precautionary measures to prevent it. An example is the *hadith*: 'Whoever passes through our mosques or markets carrying arrows should grasp them well with his hand so that he does not accidentally inflict injury on any Muslim.'

The question of disease transmission also comes under this heading. It is not lawful for a Muslim to transmit diseases to his brother, or to be complacent in this connection. Nor is it permissible for him to cause the spread of disease in society. All that is incorporated in the all-embracing rule which forbids all harm. The Prophet ordered that 'no infected person should come close to a healthy one'.

There is an interesting question that was once put to the Prophet: 'When we ask for a cure or take medicine or take some preventive measures, does any of that oppose what God has willed?' He answered: 'They are part of the operation of God's will.' This was the understanding of the second Caliph, 'Umar, when he refused to enter an area into which the plague had spread. His army commander, Abu 'Ubayda, asked him; 'Do you run away from God's will?' He said: 'Yes. We run away from God's will into God's will.' In this 'Umar was in agreement with what the Prophet said: 'If you know that plague is raging in a specific land do not enter it and if it happens in a land where you are, do not seek to leave it.' Illness is part of God's will and combating it is also part of God's will. Disease, medical treatment and preventive measures all work by God's will. The Prophet commented: 'Shall I tell you the definition of a believer? He is one with whom people feel themselves and their property to be safe. A Muslim is someone who does not abuse people by word or deed.'

Further reading

Klein-Franke, F. (1993) 'No Smoking in Paradise', *Le Muséon* 106, 1–2: 155–92.

Rida, Rashid (1956) *Yusr al-islam wa usul al-tashri' al-'amm*, Cairo: Mataba'at nahdat al-misr.

See also: **intoxication; noise; parents**

OLIVER LEAMAN

HEAVEN

The heavenly abode of divinity and the physical sky (*al-sama'*, very often in the plural: *al-samawat*) are in Arabic in general and in the Qur'anic language in particular as inseparable as in many other languages. The mythological concept of the space of the divine in an upper world marks all monotheistic religions and many other religions too. The Qur'anic notion of Islamic revelation as the process of a divine message being sent *down* from God to mankind (*inzal*, *tanzil*) is only one example. The complementary notion to heaven is earth (*al-ardh*). The whole cosmos consists of both spaces 'heaven and earth' (*al-samawat wa-l-ardh*) – although sometimes the Qur'an adds: 'and what is between them' (21.16) – and is God's creation and property. The Arabic word for 'heaven/sky' (*al-sama'*) and its plural *al-samawat* occur more than 300 times in the Qur'an. The conjunction 'heaven and earth' – almost always, since Sumerian mythology, in this order – appears more than a hundred times.

The divine voice in the Qur'an describes the beginning of God's creation of the universe in the following way: 'Have not the unbelievers then beheld that the heavens and the earth were a mass all sewn up, and then We unstitched them and of water fashioned every living thing? Will they not believe?' (21.30). In a different version the Qur'an claims: 'It is He who created for you all that is in the earth, then He lifted Himself to heaven and levelled them seven heavens' (2.29). And yet another cosmogonical verse says: 'Then He lifted Himself to heaven when it was smoke, and said to it and to the earth, "Come willingly, or unwillingly!" They said: "We come willingly"' (41.11).

A miraculous spatial and material aspect of the sky/heaven consists in the fact that it is 'a roof well protected' (21.32), which God raised 'without pillars' (13.2), and that 'He holds back heaven lest it should fall upon the earth' (22.65). The seven heavens evoke the seven climates and the seven spheres of antiquity; in 65.12 God creates seven earths, symmetrical to the seven heavens. Each of the seven heavens was assigned a special function (41.12), heaven carried celestial constellations (*buruj*; 15.16) and the 'lower heaven' was adorned with stars (37.6). One of the most important and most often quoted divine signs in the Qur'an is rain ('water from heaven') (16.65), which alone makes earthly life possible. The verb used for God's 'sending down' rain from the sky is the same as the verb denoting 'to reveal'.

Heaven is the space of God and of different ranks of angels. The seven heavens are also the place of God's throne (*'arsh*) (23.86), a symbol of power and absolute divine rule. The imagery of God's throne, its position in heaven and the role of the angels surrounding it (39.75) was much discussed in exegetical literature, which tried to harmonize the sometimes contradictory Qur'anic details. God punishes by sending down plagues from heaven (2.59). As portentous signs for the approaching Day of Judgement, cosmic catastrophes will shake heaven and earth. God will 'roll up heaven like a scroll' (21.104), 'heaven is split asunder and turns crimson like red leather' (55.37), and so on. Here, heaven seems to be less the place where God resides than the physical firmament.

The dualistic Qur'anic topography of sky/heaven and earth is intertwined with another dualistic topography, the eschatological spaces of paradise and hell. The heaven/earth imagery fulfils the function of showing the beholder the infinite wisdom of the creator and thus leading him to accept the existence and unity of God; the details of the paradise/hell imagery serve as a promise to the believer and a threat to the unbeliever. The two topographies are usually kept apart, but partly overlap in Qur'anic exegesis of the night-journey of the Prophet (17.1), which led him through the wonders of heaven, through paradise and hell, to his encounter with Jibril (53.13–16). Some commentators located 'paradise in heaven'.

Further reading

Jarrar, M. (2002) 'Heaven and Sky', in *EQ*, Vol. 2, 410–12.

See also: **eschatology**

STEFAN WILD

HELL

Hell is the abode of the damned after the Day of Judgement. It is an eschatological place of endless punishment, physical torture, mental anguish and despair. Together with the apocalyptic catastrophes, preceding resurrection and the final judgement, hell provides the most vivid sensual images of Qur'anic rhetorical art.

The topography of hell

There are more than ten different Qur'anic words for hell. The most common designation is 'fire' (*nar*). The second in frequency is a place-name: *jahannam* ('Gehenna'; derived from post-biblical Hebrew *ge hinno/am*, most probably via Ethiopic). Most of the other much less frequent designations are associated with fire and heat (*sa'ir*, 4.10, and *al-jahim*, 2.119, both meaning 'blaze'; *lahab*, 77.31, meaning 'flame'). The eschatological landscapes of the Qur'anic hell and the Qur'anic paradise are symmetrically constructed: hell is a counter-paradise, paradise a counter-hell. These two spaces reflect two aspects of divinity and two interdependent tasks of the prophet. The Prophet Muhammad, like other prophets before him, warns of God's wrath and his punishment (hell) on the one hand, and bears the good tidings of God's grace and mercy (paradise) on the other.

Hell is the opposite of the garden of paradise, a place of shade and well-being, with rivers and trees. Hell is an abode of fire, heat, thirst and pain. There are some words that denote paradise and hell together – like *dar al-akhira* ('the last abode'). But much more frequently these two places are kept strictly apart, even linguistically. The topographies of hell and paradise show a strong symmetry – already remarked upon by classical Muslim exegetes. 9.68 juxtaposes 'God has promised the hypocrites, men and women, and the unbelievers, the fire of Gehenna, therein to dwell forever. That is enough for them; God has cursed them; and there awaits them a lasting chastisement' with 9.72 'God has promised the believers, men and women, gardens underneath which rivers flow, forever therein to dwell, and goodly dwelling places in the Gardens of Eden; and greater, God's good pleasure; that is the mighty triumph.'

The space of hell is an enclosed place (90.20) with seven gates, each for a special class of sinners (15.44); it is located next to paradise and separated from it by a wall 'having a gate in the inward whereof is mercy and against the outward thereof is chastisement' (57.13). It is guarded by 'harsh and terrible angels, who disobey not God in what He commands them' (66.6). The space of hell is marked by extreme and endlessly growing physical suffering, in fact it could be described as a huge chamber of perpetually increasing horrors and torture. As far as the torment of the sinners is concerned, the pain is – like the bliss of the believers – described as affecting all human senses: human skin is burned (4.56), the sinners are tortured with hooked iron rods (22.21), their garments are of fire (22.19), their faces are burnt black (39.60), disgusting food has to be swallowed, pus (44.16) or boiling water is drunk (18.29), there is a suffocating stench, their ears hear the wailing and moaning of other unbelievers (21.100), the snarling of teeth and the crying for

water, and the sinners' eyes see disfigured bodies and maimed limbs. The hellish pendant of the trees of paradise is an infernal tree: 'Lo, the Tree of Ez-Zakkoum is the food of the guilty, like molten copper, bubbling in the belly as boiling water bubbles' (44.43–46). Hell is also a place deprived of sexuality – one of the most interesting instances where the symmetry between the spaces of paradise and hell breaks down. All this imagery is totally physical.

A more psychological aspect is that this pain never ends. The sinner shall 'have hell, he will neither die nor live' (20.74). Sinners who try to escape will be forced back and a voice will tell them 'Taste the chastisement of the Fire!' (32.20). In a striking parallel to the Promethean myth, divine punishment is physical but cannot be relieved by death. In the Qur'an the sinner's skin, burned by hellfire, is restored only to inflict more pain on the restored skin: 'Surely those who disbelieve in Our signs – We shall certainly roast them at a Fire; as often as their skins are wholly burned, We shall give them in exchange other skins, that they may taste the chastisement' (4.56).

Perhaps the most frightening aspect is that the Qur'anic God himself is the direct agent in all this pain. He punishes without mercy, with 'terrible punishment' ('*adhab shaded*) (3.4). One of the strongest Qur'anic statements says: 'It shall be proclaimed to the unbelievers: "Surely God's hatred is greater than your hatred of one another"' (40.10). God in a dramatic dialogue asks hell: 'Upon the day we shall say unto Gehenna: "Art thou filled?" And she [Gehenna] shall say: "Are there any more to come?"' (50.30). In 69.30–33 an unidentified voice commands the angels of hell: 'Take him, and fetter him and then roast him in hell, then in a chain of seventy cubits' length insert him' – this voice commanding the angels in hell sounds like God's voice. The Qur'an emphasizes time and again that God personally prepares Gehenna for mankind (71.18), God supervises the torment and tells the sinners: 'Taste! We will only give you more chastisement' (78.30).

The inhabitants of hell

The fuel of hell include stones and idols (21.98), but consists mainly of men and women (2.24). Part of the *jinn* are in hell (11.119), and the Devil will also be punished by hellfire (17.62). In general, unbelievers (*alladhina kafaru*) (3.10), polytheists (*mushrikun*), idolaters and hypocrites (*munafiqun*) will face eternal damnation. Especially mentioned are: he who slays a believer willfully (4.93); the coward in battle against the unbelievers (8.15–16); whoever mocks God's prophets and his signs (18.102); whoever calls the Qur'an sorcery or human speech (74.24). But there are also lesser sins that deserve the punishment of hell: those who squander the property of orphans (4.10), usurers (2.275), rumour-mongers and slanderers (104.1).

Hell is a possibility for every human being and every *jinn*. For Satan and some humans it is already a certainty: Cain (5.27–32), Noah's wife and Lot's wife (66.10), the Prophet's paternal uncle and arch-enemy Abu Lahab and his wife (*sura* 111). The impression that the inhabitants of hell are more numerous than those of paradise is almost unavoidable. The devil asks God 'if thou deferrest me to the day of resurrection, I shall assuredly master his [Adam's] seed, save a few' (17.62) and it is repeatedly stressed that hell will be full. Equally unavoidable seems the idea that after the advent of Islam only Muslims could hope to achieve salvation. Both concepts began to be challenged by commentators only in the twentieth century.

The chronology of hell

Human fate in the hereafter is decided by God on the Day of Reckoning (*hisab*). God judges each individual according to his or her record (*kitab*): 'Then he whose deeds weigh heavy in the balance shall inherit a pleasing life, but he whose deeds weigh light in the balance shall plunge in the womb of the pit. And what shall teach thee what is the pit? A blazing fire' (101.6–11). The question of whether hell and paradise exist already before the Day of Judgement is not raised in the Qur'an, although it was discussed at length in Islamic theology. In some verses the Qur'an speaks as if hell and paradise already existed. This problem is linked to the question of what happens to the human soul in the time between death and resurrection, a question that is not touched on by the Qur'an either.

About the problem of whether or not damnation is eternal, the Qur'an's words are ambiguous. It is often stressed that the evildoers will dwell in hell forever (*khalidina fiha*) (e.g. 3.87–88). But a verse like 11.107, which states of those in hell that they are 'Therein dwelling forever, so long as heaven and earth abide, save as the Lord will', could be understood as potentially limiting the eternity of damnation. Mu'tazili commentators, as well as many modern ones, interpret this verse thus, running the risk of changing eternal hell into a transient purgatory.

The rhetorical strategy of terror

The function of hell is punishment ('*adhab*). The function of the Qur'anic description of punishment in hell is to frighten the listeners and to win them over to the message of the Prophet. On several occasions the Qur'an threatens with hell those who refuse to believe in hell: 'and We shall say to the evildoers, "Taste the chastisement of fire, which you cried lies to"' (34.42).

In a dialogue between God and some sinners in hell, God justifies himself and explains to the sinners why they are punished: 'As for the unbelievers, theirs shall be the fire of Gehenna; they shall neither be done with and die, nor shall its chastisement be lightened for them. Even so we recompense every ungrateful one. Therein they shall shout: "Our Lord bring us forth, and we will do righteousness, other than that we have done." Whereupon God answers: "What, did We not give you long life, enough to remember for him who would remember? To you the warner came; so taste you now: The evildoers shall have no helper!"' (35.36–37).

The rhetoric of fear is most clearly stated with regard to the imagery of the cursed tree al-Zaqqum (17.60): 'And when we said to thee [Muhammad]: "Surely thy Lord encompasses men" and We made the vision (ru'ya) that We showed thee and the tree cursed in the Qur'an to be only a trial (fitna) for men; and We frighten them (nukhawwifuhum), but it only increases them in great insolence.' The exact meaning of this verse is far from clear. It could refer to the fact that some of the listeners doubted the existence of the Zaqqum-tree in spite of its being mentioned in the Qur'an. But the general purpose of such imagery is according to the Qur'an itself to frighten the listeners – thereby directing them on to the right path. A central aim of Qur'anic revelation is to infuse fear:

God has sent down the fairest discourse as a book, consistent with itself, whereat shiver the skins of those who fear their Lord; then their skins and their hearts soften at the remembrance of God …

Those that were before them cried lies, then the chastisement came upon them from whence they were not aware; so God let them taste degradation in this present life; and the chastisement of the world to come is assuredly greater, did they but know. (39.23–26)

The Qur'an's rhetorical strategy is more one of warning than one of glad tidings. It seems more important to frighten the sinner than to attract the believer. The juxtaposition between God's wrath and God's grace does aesthetically not always work in an exactly identical way: the repetition of pain, especially endless repetition of pain, leads to unlimited pain, whereas it is doubtful whether the endless repetition of joy necessarily increases joy. This is why the aesthetics of hell were always more interesting than the aesthetics of paradise. The proof is that exegetical and especially popular parenetic literature devoted more space to hell than to paradise.

The Qur'anic rhetoric of fear had its most outspoken enemies in mystical circles. In one of the best-known traditions about Rabi'a al-'Adawiyya (d. 185/801), one of the earliest female mystics in Basra, it is related that she walked through the streets with a broom in one hand and a bucket of water in the other. When questioned about her behaviour, Rabi'a answered: 'I want to set fire to paradise and pour water into hell, so that these two veils disappear. Then it will become clear who serves God out of love and not out of fear of hell or hope for paradise.'

For Rabi'a hell was 'a veil'; that was an allusion to exegesis that saw in the Qur'anic imagery of hell metaphors and symbolic language. Were some or even all of these verses not to be taken literally? Some commentators insist today that no verse dealing with the 'unseen' (ghayb) should be taken literally. Others emphasize that, while the punishment of hell is physical, its nature belongs to a reality which is not ours and therefore unfathomable.

Further reading

al-Azmeh, A. (1995) 'Rhetoric for the Senses: A Consideration of Muslim Paradise Narratives', *JAL* 26: 215–31.
Fadel, M.H. (2001) 'Chastisement and Punishment', in *EQ*, Vol. 1, 294–8.
Gwynne, R. (2002) 'Hell and Hellfire', in *EQ*, Vol. 2, 414–20.
Smith, J.I. (2002) 'Eschatology', in *EQ*, Vol. 2, 44–54.

See also: **eschatology; heaven**

STEFAN WILD

HIDAYA

Hidaya means guidance or instruction, and denotes righteousness and the true path, the path of Islam; its opposite is *dalala* (going astray, turning away from the true path). According to a Qur'anic *aya* (*al-Muddattir* 31): 'Thus doth Allah leave to stray whom He pleaseth, and guide whom He pleaseth' (see also 41.46; 50.29; 13.27; 14.4; 16.93; 6.39, 125). However, this may quite legitimately be read and interpreted as meaning that God guides those who wish for guidance and leaves in error those who prefer to be in a state of delusion: the rules of the Arabic language permit the use here of the relative pronoun *man* (*al-'ism al-mawsul*) in the accusative and the nominative ('whom' and 'who'). As a result, the inclination to good or evil is a matter of individual free will, and hence we are personally responsible for our deeds, since they are neither the result of arbitrary predestination nor of divine injustice in the world, for God is just as a matter of definition. Consequently, *al-hidaya wa al-dalal wa al-idlal* (guidance, self-delusion or leading others into fal-

lacy) is a matter of our own initiative and responsibility.

NEVAD KAHTERAN

HILAL

There is debate in Islamic law over the precise timing of Ramadan, and the crescent moon (*hilal*) plays a role in determining when fasting begins and when it finishes. When the birth of the new moon of the month of Ramadan is discovered, the fast begins; it ends with the birth of the *hilal* of the tenth month, Shawwal. If it cannot be seen because of poor meteorological conditions, then a calculation can be made. If after, or on the evening of, the twenty-ninth day of Sha'aban it is impossible to see the *hilal* of Ramadan, it is permissible to complete Sha'aban at thirty days, and the fast begins the next morning. Again, if after the twenty-ninth day of Ramadan it is impossible to see the *hilal* of Shawwal due to weather conditions, Ramadan is assessed as coming to an end after thirty days. The next day becomes the Eid al-Fitr, the Festival of Fast-Breaking. The relevant verse is 'Whoever is present (*shahida*) during the month should spend it in fasting' (2.185). By the term *shahida* may be meant 'to be present', but this leaves out the traveller: he is not then obliged to fast. Nor, by extension, are others who are not able to witness (another aspect of the meaning of *shahida*) the event, like children and the infirm. If no one witnesses the *hilal*, then the fast is not operative. There is a controversy about the need to ascertain the *hilal* to start and end the fast period insofar as whether it is permissible to calculate (*faqdiru*) the dates, given the difficulty of determining it otherwise. Generally the *hadith* agree that one should rely on a reliable (*'adl*) witness if one is not able to be present oneself to see it, and in the absence of such a witness, or where that witness cannot see the sky because of the weather, then calculation plays an acceptable role.

See also: **calendar; fasting**

OLIVER LEAMAN

HILM

The period before the Qur'anic revelation was known in Arabia as the age of ignorance (*jahiliyya*), which connotes the barbarism of the 'reckless temper' of the pagan Arabs (Goldziher, 1967: 202ff.). The opposite of it is *hilm* (forbearance, self-mastery), which connotes the qualities of a civilized person. The expression 'fierceness of paganism' (*hamiyyat al-jahiliyya*) in the Qur'an (48.26) refers to the haughty spirit of the tribal Arab, which the Qur'an contrasts with the calm, tranquil and forbearing way of religion (Izutsu, 1959: 23ff.). The quality of forbearance is a dominant virtue in the Qur'an, and it is manifested in self-control, kindness and abstinence (Isutzu, 1959: 216). Luqman advised his son to be a model of forbearance and humility (31.17–19). Thus *hilm* is a complex and delicate notion, which includes the qualities of justice, moderation and leniency.

The word *hilm* is absent from the Qur'an, but the adjective *halim* is mentioned as a divine attribute and also a quality of Abraham (9.114), Isaac and Shu'ayb; it is generally rendered as 'slow suffering', 'patient' and 'gifted with tolerance'.

This notion of *hilm* is also present in certain verses in the Qur'an, including 'The true servants of the Beneficent are those who walk the earth modestly and who, when addressed by the ignorant one (*jahil*), answer "peace"' (25.63). For al-Ghazali and al-Isfahani, *hilm* emerges

when the irascible faculty is under the control of reason; when anger is tempered by reason, a person becomes forbearing and forgiving. Thus *hilm* is a praiseworthy quality, but not a cardinal virtue of external morality; it is an inward quality of self-restraint and mastery over anger and the desire for revenge.

References and further reading
Fakhry, M. (1991) *Ethical Theories in Islam*, Leiden: E.J. Brill.
Goldziher, I. (1967) *Muslim Studies*, London: George Allen & Unwin, Vol. 1.
Izutsu, T. (1959) *The Structure of the Ethical Terms in the Koran*, Montreal: McGill University Press.
Mohamed, Y. (2004) *The Path to Virtue*, Kuala Lumpur: ISTAC.

See also: **knowledge**

YASIEN MOHAMED

HISTORICAL EVENTS AND THE QUR'AN

In the Qur'an the Muslim understanding of the world is to a degree structured through sacred stories that play a role in the historical consciousness and ritual activities of Muslims.

Qur'anic cosmology formulates images of the world in terms of the struggle between truth and error, between belief and rejection, and between doing good and spreading mischief on the earth: 'the God-conscious who believe in the Unseen, and perform the prayer . . . it is they who follow guidance from their Lord; and it is they who shall attain to a happy state', whereas for unbelievers 'alike it is whether you warn them or not they will not believe . . . in their hearts is a sickness and God has increased their sickness . . . It is they who are spreading corruption but they perceive it not' (2.2–12). This is what underlies much of Qur'anic discourse and sets up the Islamic symbolic mechanism of communication that mediates between the two separate domains. The cosmological problem characterized by the struggle between Truth and Untruth lies at the heart of the exodus story in chapter 2 of the Qur'an, which speaks of conflict in the human condition. In another chapter (28.19) attention is drawn to the sin of tribal prejudice or animosity between Hebrews and Egyptians. The story illustrates the purely human aspects of Moses' life, including his impulses, difficulties and errors, which are seen as part of the human condition. The longest chapter in the Qur'an (chapter 2) also discusses the creation drama as it relates to the primordial man Adam and his spouse, and how, through their act of disobedience (the result of the exercise of free will), they came to lose their innocence and were henceforth removed from the garden. The story of Israel's covenant with God, its rejection/disobedience and the severe punishment that followed are sketched out in terms of a sacred narrative that shifts from past communities to the particular society of Arabia to which Muhammad had brought God's final revealed book.

History and prophecy

The Qur'an makes it clear that God intervenes in human history by sending apostles/messengers (one *hadith* identifies the number as 124,000) to different communities to proclaim the Truth and show the straight path of spiritual success (16.36), as well as warning against disobedience and going astray (by following base instincts symbolized by Satan). The role of these saintly individuals (Messengers) is to teach mankind about God's Word/revelations, with the objective of nurturing righteous living (that is, living a life of service to God), prayer and so on in the faith-based communities. Given this perspective, his-

torical events are alluded to in many Qur'anic verses not with the purpose of relating past stories for their own sake but with the aim of providing moral lessons. This is the reason why Qur'anic cosmology is both primordial and prehistorical, even when historical events are mentioned. Thus the Qur'anic revelation is rooted in an earlier sacred history that is invoked by Muhammad in order to convince his contemporaries to bring their communities within the overall divine plan: 'And remember out of all the accounts relating to the earlier apostles We convey to you in order that We may make firm your heart; for through these accounts comes the truth to you, as well as an admonition and a reminder to all believers' (11.120). This divine plan comprehends both the cosmos and human society (both of which are 'Muslim' insofar as they submit to the will of God, automatically in the case of the former and through the exercise of free will for the latter).

Thus the importance of Abraham lies in the fact that, like Muhammad in his time, he had earlier discerned impiety and the wickedness of idol worship among his people. Muhammad had also rejected idolatry in Arabia, which in Qur'anic cosmology is associated with the *jahiliyya*, the period before the Qur'anic revelation when Arabian society did not orient itself to the divine will. Similarly, the story of Joseph (chapter 12) is narrated in some detail, not so much as an account of the worldly triumph of Joseph over the envious behaviour and machinations of his brothers (chapter 93 also mentions the hardships that Muhammad went through earlier in his life and career), but much more as an illustration of the judgement of God and of Joseph's placing his complete trust in a God who had no associates (12.39).

Myth and history

Sacred history in the Qur'an is grounded in events that have happened in the past and in which the sacred is manifested. In this sense history is mythicized as it involves aspects of redemptive and salvational history. In the story of Moses, with the miraculous escape of his people and the doom of Pharaoh and his forces (chapter 28, *al-Qasas*/History), for instance, the Qur'anic narrative (like the biblical one before it) transforms the migration of Hebrews from Egypt into a divinely guided exodus. The exodus story is told with reference not only to historical occurrences, but also to supernatural ones that are meant to bring out a particular lesson in ethics. Furthermore, the story of Moses and his quest for knowledge (18.60–82) serves as a parable: during his meeting with the mysterious sage (al-Khidr), he gains insights into events whose meaning/understanding goes beyond surface appearance. The Qur'anic purpose here is to communicate by means of metaphor and allegory what pertains to supernatural reality beyond human perception. Similarly, in the Qur'anic story of Dhul-Qarnayn (the Two-Horned One) (18.83–98), the emphasis of which is on faith and ethics, there is a particular focus on the problem of worldly power. Dhul-Qarnayn, who was endowed with both wordly power and spiritual strength, has been identified by some Muslim scholars with Alexander the Great (a rather problematic identification, given that Alexander was not known for adhering to monotheism). The Qur'anic reference to Ya'juj and Ma'juj (Gog and Magog) is considered to be a reference to the Mongols and Tartars, although purely allegorical meaning cannot be ruled out altogether. In the latter case, the terms apply to social catastrophies that would create a lot of destruction before the coming of the Last Hour.

The whole creation drama (in which Adam and Eve figure as part of an exploration of human destiny) refers in the Qur'anic narrative to a primordial past beyond historical time. The story has symbolic meaning intended to express certain truths about human nature or the human condition. For instance, after the fall from grace Adam and Eve became 'conscious of their nakedness' (20.118–119; 7.22), implying that this is an allegory of the state of innocence in which man lived before the fall. In that state of innocence man lived, like all other animals, in the light of his instincts alone; however, with moral and intellectual development and the growth of consciousness – symbolized by the wilful act of disobedience to God's command – he became endowed with the moral free will that distinguishes him from other sentient beings.

The struggle between truth and untruth (crucial, as we have seen, to Islamic symbolism) is played out in the human exercise of free will, which makes humans morally aware of their actions. This transforms history into the realm of freedom, where we are able to save or condemn ourselves. Divine guidance is still there, as God is manifested in word (scripture) and deed (history). Yet humans need to orient themselves to an overall divine plan that comprehends the cosmos as well as human communities. This is precisely why Islamic sacred history begins with God and the creation of the world, followed by the stories (of warners/prophets and their communities) within which historic moments are sanctified by revelation.

Norms of history

From the preceding discussion it is clear that the Qur'an is extremely interested in the knowledge of history (and, by extension, geography) and persistently asks man to 'travel on the earth' to see for himself what happened to previous civilizations and why they rose and fell. Human history consists of this evolutionary development of societies and civilizations from infancy to decay, according to certain norms/patterns, which are essentially ethical. These norms are called 'God's *sunna*' (unalterable practices): 'Such has been God's way with those who passed away aforetime – and never will thou find any change in God's way!' (33.62).

The Qur'anic concept of judgement in history applies to nations and peoples, not to individuals; individuals face their own judgement on the Day of Reckoning. Nations are given respite to change their ways but, when their term is up, if they have not improved on their moral performance they are made to pay for their corruption of the earth by destruction (11.116; 7.34). This corruption of the earth may consist in economic oppression or political and social exploitation of the poor and of subject peoples occupying the lowest rung of social scale (as in the case of Jews versus Pharaoh) (7.137), or it could lie in the vices of idolatry and transgression (as with the people of Noah and Lot). When the weakening of the moral fibre sets in, destruction follows and the 'inheritance of the earth' is given to more deserving people (21.105).

The Qur'an considers it incumbent on succeeding nations to study and learn from the mistakes of the previous ones (hence the Qur'anic exhortation in 3.137 to 'travel on the earth and see the end of those before them'). One should travel through the land and see the remains of past communities/nations so as to learn lessons from them. These were communities that boasted of powerful rulers whose power and fame were the talk of the day, and whose palatial monuments advertised their grandeur ('Thus arrogantly, without the least good sense, did he [Pharaoh] and his hosts behave on earth as if they would never have to appear before Us for judgement') (28.39). Yet neither sky nor earth shed tears for them (44. 29) when their mighty buildings were reduced to ruins after God visited these communities with punishment for their insolence and disobedience. No power in the world could save them from the wrath of God ('For Allah does not love the arrogant, the vainglorious') (4.36). Whenever people lose the capacity to run their affairs, God's judgement in history comes into play and 'the inheritance of the earth is given to good people'. This is an optimistic view about the future if the succeeding nations are willing to bear the responsibility of high moral conduct in the running of their affairs and not to follow the bad example of earlier peoples. This is precisely the reason why God (in his mercy) had sent messengers and revealed books to show humans the right way, if only they would follow it for their own good.

The Qur'an considers norms of history to be universal (33.62). These norms are constant and not subject to change. They represent God's will and guidance. All man has to do is to exercise his choice/freedom and follow these norms; otherwise he ignores them at his own peril ('Verily, God does not change men's condition unless they change what is in their hearts') (13.11). The demise of a people/nation cannot be hastened or postponed, even though its destruction is imminent. As the Qur'an puts it, 'Yet, were God to take men to task for all the evil that they do, He would not leave a single creature on its face, but [He] grants them respite until a term set' (16.61). As for God's punishment, when it does come it affects all (the wandering about in the desert by the Jews after escaping bondage in Egypt affected both the good and bad).

The Qur'an also makes it clear that, for every community to which a warner has been sent, the basis of opposition to the prophetic message has been provided by the wicked people who form the leadership of the community by virtue of their wealth and social position. This is the reason why it is stated in a number of verses that: 'when it is Our will to destroy a community We convey Our command to the wealthy and if they continue in their abominations the sentence passed on the community takes effect, and We break it to smithereens. And how many a generation have We destroyed after the time of Noah!' (17.16–17; also 7.96). Dealing ethically and equitably with people in their socio-economic and political affairs (as the prophets urged pompous leaders to do) is considered to be highly desirable, as it promotes good will and prosperity in society. In fact, the previous verse establishes as a historical norm the direct relationship that exists between the oppression of the rulers (with the pious elements remaining silent and not saying or doing anything) and the destruction that ensues.

Ibn Khaldun was probably the first philosopher of history to be interested in finding an explanation for the rise and fall of states. He looked into the problem of causality and was led to the conclusion that history was not haphazard, but was governed by certain norms that relate to the making and unmaking of societies and civilizations. This fitted well with his Islamic (Qur'anic) world outlook, presented above, which speaks of the existence of norms of history. He believed that there was a constant renewal or replacement of the ruling elite by nomads, whose tribal solidarity, combined with the zeal of faith, is a formidable force.

These nomads conquer the cities and settled lands, as happened in Arabia and North Africa. For Ibn Khaldun civilization and culture arise in the first place due to a desire for dominion, ease and luxury, and, within a few generations of their having been attained, the state is ready to unravel. The drive for affluence eventually exhausts resources and corrupts a regime, which by then has lost group cohesion. Ibn Khaldun, being a sociologist rather a moralist, presents the decline of society in his own terminology and based on his theory.

Our treatment of historical narratives in the Qur'an has not been exhaustive. We have provided a sample of the Qur'anic sacred narratives that form a framework through which the Islamic message has been filtered. It is the perspective that the Qur'an gives to this material that is important for the presentation of its overall message. This means that the sacred narratives (in both their historical and their supernatural/mythical forms, as relating to Muhammad's spiritual experiences) serve the prototypical function of presenting inspiring models. It is from this point of view that we can understand why, in Islamic sacred history, Muhammad's time is considered to be a paradigmatic time. It was a period when people were judged by revelations, whereas after his time (after the closing or completion of the cycle of prophecy, with the foundations of shari'a having been laid down for the guidance of the historic community of Muslims) people were and are now judged by the norms/patterns established by revelation.

Further reading

Asad, M. (trans.) (1980) *The Message of the Qur'an*, Gibraltar: Dar al-andalus.
Geertz, C. (1968) *Islam Observed*, New Haven, CT: Yale University Press.
Paden, W.E. (1988) *Religious Worlds*, Boston, MA: Beacon Press.

Rahman, F. (1989) *Major Themes of the Qur'an*, Minneapolis: Bibliotheca Islamica.

ABDIN CHANDE

HIZB

Hizb is half a *juz'*. In the technical use of the term, the Qur'an is divided into thirty *juz'* (*juz'*, pl. *ajza'*), each of which consists of twenty pages of the Qur'an and is divided into two *hizb*, with each *hizb* further subdivided into four parts. This method of division of the Qur'anic text, which some regard as an innovation (*bid'a*), is intended to facilitate the reading or recitation of the Qur'an over the course of a month, particularly the month of Ramadan. It enables the person reciting the Qur'an (*muqri*) to complete the recitation of one *juz'* each evening during Ramadan when praying *salat al-tarawih*.

Of course, as well as this established meaning of the term *hizb*, it also has the meaning of 'political party', but this sense was introduced only in the twentieth century. In the plural (*ahzab*), the term is also used to designate the people of Nuh (Noah), 'Ad, Faraon, Thamud and Lut (Lot), as well as the *ashab al-ayka* (People of the Wood).

NEVAD KAHTERAN

HOLY

Holy is the usual translation of the Arabic words derived from the root *qaf dal*, represented by the English letters *q/d/s/*. Words derived from this root are *quds*, *al-quddus*, *muqaddas* and *muqaddasa*. These words are used in the Qur'an thus: twice as *al-quddus* meaning the Holy, for God himself, as in 59.23 and 62.1; four times as *ruh al-qudus* meaning the holy spirit, for the angel Jibril, as in 2.87, 253; 5.110 and 16.102; twice as *wadi al-muqaddasi tuwa* for the holy valley of Tuwa, as in 20.12 and 79.16; and once as *al-ardh al-muqaddasa* for *masjid al-aqsa*, the mosque in Jerusalem, and some land surrounding it, as in 5.21.

OLIVER LEAMAN

HONOURABLE
see: **karim**

HOOPOE
see: **hud-hud**

HOURIS

Careful examination of the Qur'anic verses mentioning houris suggests that they are placed in the text in a very specific order, to reveal a transition from a more material form of description to something more spiritual. In the first Meccan period (from the first to the fifth year of the Prophet's Mission, 612–17 CE) we find references to:

... full-breasted [damsels] of the same age ... (78.33)

... wide-eyed houris like treasured pearls as a reward for what they used to do ... (56.22.)

... We have created them by a [special] creation and made them virgins, lovers [or loving] of the same age ... (56.35–7.)

... [damsels] restraining their glances, whom neither men nor *jinn* will have touched before them ... like rubies and coral ... (55.56, 58)

... good and comely [damsels], houris cloistered in pavilions ... whom neither men nor *jinn* will have touched before them ... (55.72., 74)

In the second Meccan Period (the fifth and sixth years of the Prophet's Mission, 617–19 CE), we find:

> ... [damsels] restraining their glances, whose eyes are like hidden eggs ... (37.48)

> ... [damsels] restraining their glances, of the same age ... (38.52)

> ... they and their spouses ... (36.56)

> ... you and your spouses ... (43.70)

In the third Meccan Period (from the seventh year to the Hijra, 619–22 CE), they are described as:

> ... whoever of their fathers, their spouses and offspring have acted honourably ... (40.8; 13.23)

By the time of the Medinan Period (from the Hijra to the end, 622–32 CE), the language has changed even more, and we get references to:

> ... purified spouses ... (2.25; 3.15; 4.47)

One way of understanding this development is by suggesting that it represents a transition from a more material to a more spiritual awareness of the nature of the next world. The pagans of Mecca required the sort of language we find used during that period, while by the time of the Medinan revelations a more abstract form of imagery was appropriate. This is perfectly in line with what the philosophers often said about the way in which religion works, that it is based largely on imaginative language and that imagination is a faculty linked to our lives as material creatures. Images themselves only make sense to such creatures as can visualize things in physical forms. As time goes by, believers can perfect their thinking about religious topics and make that thinking less material and more abstract. One can see this happening in the case of discussions of the houris. At first they were described in ways that would resonate with a public wedded to material images and appetites, but once the public had become more refined in their thinking, and possibly more confident of their religious attitudes, they could have introduced to them a more abstract and sedate notion of what houris actually are.

The verb 'to wed' is used with reference to the houris twice: 'and We shall espouse them (*zawwajnahum*) to wide-eyed houris' (52.20); 'and We shall wed them (*zawwajnahum*) [the God-fearing believers] to fair ones (*bi hurin 'inin*)' (44.54). Both of these verses come from the first Meccan Period, but by the time we get to the Medinan period the language becomes more sedate: 'for them shall be spouses purified (*azwaj-un-mutahhatun*) ...' (2.25); 'For those that are God-fearing, with their Lord are gardens underneath which rivers flow, where they live forever, and spouses purified (*azwaj-un-mutahhatun*), and God's good pleasure' (3.15); 'And those that believe, and do deeds of righteousness, them We shall admit to gardens underneath which rivers flow, therein dwelling forever and ever; there will be for them there purified spouses (*azwaj-un-mutahhatun*) ...' (4.57). This is hardly an erotic image, since the purity of marriage is invoked; on the other hand, there is no doubting the sensuous nature of the Islamic paradise, so relationships between men and women are entirely appropriate even there and then.

There have been alternative interpretations of the nature and role of the houris. The commentator Christoph Luxenberg (2000) takes the term *zawwaj* in 44.54 as a misreading of *zay* for *ra* and *jim* for *ha*: instead of *zawwaj*, the term should be *rawwa*, meaning 'to refresh'. An entirely different reading of the verse is thus provided. Luxenberg deals with the phrase 'to fair ones (*bi hurin 'inin*)' in 44.54 in an interesting way, arguing that the Arabic word *hur* was derived from the Aramaic word for white (*khiv-vawr'*). This may be so, but there also exists an Arabic root that is linked with whiteness and there can be no doubt about the large number of references from the *jahiliyya* to *hur*, where it does mean desirable woman. The term *'inin* is the plural of the singular feminine *'ayna'* and masculine *a'yan*, meaning 'wide-eyed'. Furthermore, if we join Luxenberg in changing the *in* of 44.54 for *'uyun*, then we get the notion of rotundity and the idea that the phrase refers to the grapes! The Qur'anic verse 44.54, 'and We shall wed them (*zawwajnahum*) [the God-fearing believers] to fair ones (*bi hurin 'inin*)' is changed to 'and We will let them [the blessed in Paradise] be refreshed with white jewels'. Not only is the etymology unlikely, but it does not even make sense.

Reference

Luxenberg, C. (2000) *Die syro-aramäische Lesart des Koran: Ein Beitrag zur Entschlüsselung der Koransprache*, Berlin: Das Arabische Buch.

See also: **colours;** *zawj*

OLIVER LEAMAN

HUD

Hud was an Arab prophet, sent to the people of 'Ad (see 7.66–72; 11.50–60; 26.123–140; 41.15–16; 46.21–25). Muslim genealogists claim that Hud is a descendant of Shelah b. Arpachshad b. Shem b. Noah (see Genesis 10: 24) or 'Abdallah b. Rabbah b. 'Ad b. Uz b. Aram b. Shem b. Noah. Hud is said to be the first person to speak Arabic, and the people of 'Ad are listed among the peoples said to be the 'original Arabs' (*al-'arab al-'ariba*). The story of Hud epitomizes the 'prophetic cycle', found also in the accounts of the prophets Noah, Shu'ayb, Salih and Lot, in which the prophet is sent to his people, rejected and the people punished. According to Muslim exegesis, God had endowed the 'Ad with gigantic size and a fantastic city, but they refused to acknowledge God and rejected Hud. God caused a long drought to afflict the 'Ad, during which time they sent a delegation to Mecca to pray for rain. In response to the delegation, God sent a black cloud which contained the storm that destroyed the 'Ad for their disobedience (see 51.41–42; 54.18–21; 69.6–8). Although a number of locations have been identified as the tomb of Hud (e.g. Mecca, Damascus, Jerash), the tomb of Hud in the Hadhramawt, reported to be thirty metres in length, is the destination of a well-established yearly pilgrimage.

Further reading

Breton, J.-F. and Darles, C. (1997) 'Le tombeau de Hud', *Saba* 3–4: 79–81.

Coussonnet, N. and Mermier, F. (1997) 'Le pèlerinage au sanctuaire de Hud, le prophète de Dieu', *Saba* 3–4: 73–7.

De Keroualin, F. and Schwarz, L. (1995) 'Hud, un pèlerinage en Hadramaout', *Quaderni di Studi Arabi* 13: 181–9.

Hamblin, W.J. (1983) 'Pre-Islamic Arabian Prophets', in S.J. Palmer (ed.) *Mormons and Muslims: Spiritual foundations and modern manifestations*, Provo, UT: Brigham Young University Press, 85–104.

Serjeant, R.B. (1954) 'Hud and other Pre-Islamic Prophets of Hadramawt', *Le Muséon* 6: 121–79.

Winnett, F.V. (1970) *The Arabian Genealogies in the Book of Genesis*, Nashville, TN: Abingdon.

BRANNON WHEELER

HUDAYBIYA

A place of historic significance in the history of Islam, Hudaybiyya lies ten miles outside of Mecca to the north. It gave its name to the so-called Truce (or Treaty) of Hudaybiya, which the Prophet concluded with Meccans in 628 CE, six years after the *hijra*.

It is a place where over a thousand Muslims from Medina, led by the Prophet, were stopped by the Quraysh and refused permission to enter the precincts of Mecca; they were on their way to perform the *'umra* (lesser pilgrimage) at the *Ka'ba*. The Muslims were unarmed and decisively dressed in *ihram* for the purpose of making the pilgrimage – which, according to Arab custom, they were fully entitled to do during the sacred months.

This action was based on a vision Prophet Muhammad had concerning his entry into the *haram sharif* (sacred precinct), as mentioned in 48.27. The events at Hudaybiya were deemed to be the fulfillment of that vision and are described in the Qur'an as a 'victory' granted by God.

The peace treaty signed between the Muslims and the Meccans was not seemingly favourable to the Muslims, because (among other things) it included the following stipulations:

1. Muslims would not perform the pilgrimage that year but instead would do so the following year, when the Meccans would vacate the sacred precinct for three days allowing full access to Muslims.
2. Tribal alliances would be freely allowed.
3. Meccans who, without proper authority from their guardians join the Muslims in Medina, would be returned, but not the other way around.

The treaty also confirmed a ten-year peace, which allowed the Muslims to regroup and focus their strength on matters other than defending themselves from Meccan hostilities. 48.10 also mentions the *bay'a ar-ridwan* (oath of God's good pleasure) given to the Prophet by Muslims present at Hudaybiya, which confirmed their loyalty to the Prophet, reflecting Muslim unity as another factor in their ultimate victory.

IRFAN A. OMAR

HUD-HUD

The word for bird is mentioned in the Qur'an five times and birds appear in the Qur'an thirteen times. Among the birds, the hoopoe (*hud-hud* in Arabic) is specifically mentioned in *Sura an-Naml* twice in the following manner:

> And he sought among the birds and said: How is it that I see not the Hoopoe, or is he among the absent? ... But the Hoopoe tarried not far: he compassed [territory] which you have not compassed and I have come to thee from Saba with tidings true. (27.20, 22)

The hoopoe is an elegant bird, related to the hornbill. It gets its unusual name from its call of 'hoop', which rings clear and far, and is repeated two or three times. Often the cry is cut off very short. This may be caused by the bird's bill sharply striking the ground at the end of the note. The hoopoe's call is the basis of its name in many languages, not just English: in Persian and Urdu it is *hud*. It is one of Old World's non-passerine birds. Kingfishers, bee eaters, rollers, hoopoes and hornbills are collectively referred to as roller-like birds. There are about seven species of hoopoe. It is widely distributed across Europe, Asia and northern Africa. It exists in the temperate and tropical regions of the Old World.

This is a small bird, about twelve inches long, the size of a large thrush or mynah, and has short legs with heavy feet and powerful claws. It has a handsome erectile semicircular crest (large crown of feathers tipped with black that constantly opens and closes on the head), which is the hoopoe's most striking feature. It is long and fan-shaped, with feathers that increase in length from front to back. When feeding, the hoopoe's crest is closed; when alarmed or excited, the bird unfurls its crest and opens it out like a fan. Coloured fawn or cinnamon, the hoopoe has black and white stripes on its back, wings and tail: the upper part of the body is a pale brown, with wings of black striped with white, while the underparts are buff, streaked with black; the black tail, which is not very long, is black with one broad, central stripe of white. These bands are clearly seen when the bird is in flight. The short legs it has are well adapted for walking. The hoopoe's beak is long, slender and curves slightly downwards.

When threatened by a bird of prey, the hoopoe flattens itself against the ground and spreads its tail and wings. The head is thrown back and the bill points straight up. Whatever this indicates, it does seem to discourage potential enemies. Hoopoes are found in almost all parts of Asia, even in cities and towns where there are few open spaces left.

Prophet Solomon was a king whose armies consisted of troops made up of men, *jinn* and birds. It is possible that the birds were employed for communicating messages, for hunting and for other services. In the Qur'an (27.20) Solomon, who is described as a prophet, reviewed his birds and found the hoopoe (*hud-hud*) missing. The most mobile arm of his army was the birds, who were light and flew and saw everything. Solomon expressed his anger and his desire to punish the hoopoe if it did not present itself before him with a reasonable excuse. Within a short while, the hoopoe returned and said:

'I have obtained knowledge of things of which you have no knowledge. I have brought sure information about Saba [often identified with a wealthy community of people in southern Arabia, now Yemen]. There I have seen a woman ruling over her people: she has been given all sorts of provisions, and she has a splendid throne. I saw that she and her people prostrate themselves before the sun, instead of Allah!' Solomon said, 'We shall just now see whether what you say is true, or that you are a liar. Take this letter of mine and cast it before them; then get aside and see what reaction they show'. (27.22–28)

That is the last we hear of the bird.

Some have interpreted *hud-hud* as the name of a man and not a bird, since a bird could not possibly be endowed with such powers of observation, discrimination and expression that it should pass over a country and thereby come to know that it is the land of Saba, it has such and such a system of government, it is ruled by a certain woman (Bilqis), its religion is sun-worship and that it should be worshipping one god instead of being idolatrous, then finally, on its return to Solomon, be able so clearly to make a report of all its observations before him. Yet if God, the creator of all animals, tells us that he had taught the speech of the birds to one of his prophets and blessed him with the ability to speak to them, and the prophet's taming and training had enabled a hoopoe to make certain observations in foreign lands and report them to the Prophet, there is every reason to accept this within the logic of the Qur'an itself.

See also: **Bilqis**

OLIVER LEAMAN

HUJJAT

Hijjat signifies an argument, a proof, evidence or testimony. *Hujjat* is also a title given to Muslim scholars, especially Shi'ite religious authorities. There is an expression *Hujjat al-Islam* (Proof of Islam) that is used to describe out-standing thinkers.

In the Qur'an, the perfect *hujjat* belongs to Allah: 'With Allah is the perfect proof and argument, had He so willed, He would indeed have guided you all' (6.149). The Qur'an claims that the oneness of Allah is the perfect argument, and the sending of his messengers and his Holy Books to humanity is the perfect proof or evidence. Allah sent his messengers to the world so that people would have no excuse for not believing in him: 'Messengers as bearers of good news as well as of warning in order that mankind should have no claim against Allah after [their] coming' (4.165). Allah supports his prophets with his *hujjat* to enable them to overcome their opponents: 'And that was our proof which we gave Abraham against his people' (6.83).

The arguments of God are always victorious and his enemies' attempts to dispute them are always a failure: 'And those who dispute concerning Allah [His religion] after it has been accepted, futile is their dispute in the sight of their Lord' (42.16).

See also: **arguments and the Qur'an**

RAFIK BERJAK

HUKM

Hukm means judgement, especially the judgement of God, and in this sense can be connected to divine decree and prophecy. The verses 5.44–48 are important in defining this concept and have been interpreted in contemporary Islam as being highly significant from a political point of view.

The term *hukm* appears approximately thirty times in the Qur'an, but there are also many declensions of the verb *hakama*. The main meaning of the verb and the substantive alike is 'to judge' and 'judgement', and we find in the Holy Book utterances pointing to judgement in legal and political matters. For instance, the famous verse of the powerful (*ayat al-Umara'*) urges the rulers to judge (*hakama*) with justice (*'adl*) in order to lead the state (4.58). Elsewhere, the prophet David is summoned to judge with truth (*haqq*) among his subjects because he is the vicegerent of God (*khalifa*) (38.26). Exceptionally, *hukm* means wisdom, reflection and perception, as in 39.46 (how can the men misunderstand the signs of God?) and in 19.12 (John, probably the Baptist, was given wisdom right from his youth). It is true, however, that *hukm* comes from the same root as the term *hikma*, which means wisdom (but also philosophy in technical language). So God is frequently called *al-hakim*, that is the 'Wise' or the 'all-Knowing' (2.220, 228; 6.83; and many other places).

The function of judge is a special attribute of God. First of all, he is judge because he will judge between men on the Last Day. Many verses develop this concept: 'God will judge their dispute on the Last Day' (2.113; see also 4.131; 7.87; 6.62). Obviously, men must endure the judgement and the decree of God all through their life and on the Day of Resurrection: 'Endure the judgment of your Lord' (52.48; but see also 68.48 and 76.24). Perhaps it is useful to remember that patience (*sabr*) is one of the most important attitudes of the mystics and one of the stations (*maqamat*) on the path to reach God. At least four times the Qur'an says that *hukm* is only from God (*al-hukm illa li'llah*), but on these occasions the term has a wider meaning. In 6.57 *hukm* comes from God because he speaks the truth (*haqq*); in 12.40 and 12.67 because he is the supreme Lord and nobody could withstand his *hukm*; in 28.70 and 28.88 the text is possibly more obscure. For example, in 28.88 we read that God owns the most beautiful names and the *hukm*, but it is difficult to understand whether or not this means the judgement of the Last Day: the term might equally refer to the determination of the laws of nature.

The most interesting instances of the use of the term, however, are those in which the Qur'an points expressly at prophecy. Three times God is said to have given the prophets the Book (*kitab*), judgement (*hukm*) and prophecy (*nubuwwa*) – namely the tools necessary to convey the divine message to people, and the knowledge and wisdom that enable the prophets to act as judge insofar as they are leaders of their communities: Isaac and Jacob, Moses and Jesus, Ishmael and Jonah are those on whom 'We bestowed the Scriptures, the judgement and the prophethood' (6.89; see also 3.79; 45.16). God revealed the Book so that the prophets could judge with it among the people (2.213); the same is said of Muhammad (4.105). But the crucial verses are 5.44–48. The ancient prophets – in particular, the biblical prophets – judge by the Torah (*yahkumu biha al-nabiyyun*). It is they who were committed to keeping the Book on behalf of God himself, so that 'whoever judges not in accordance with

God's revelation (*man lam yahkum bima anzala Allahu*)' is an unbeliever. Also Christians, the followers of the Gospel, 'judge in accordance with what God has revealed therein'. Finally, Muhammad, the Prophet of Islam and the last messenger of God, is commanded: 'Give judgement among men in accordance with God's revelation (*ahkum baynahum bima anzala Allahu*)'. To all appearances, the meaning of *hukm* is here essentially religious, concerning the mission of the prophets to lead humanity and manage its affairs, from a moral and doctrinal point of view, by revelation. Accordingly, the great medieval Qur'anic commentator al-Zamakhshari wrote: 'Whoever judges not according to what God has sent down [in His Book], because they attach little value to it, they are unbelievers' (5.48), as well as transgressors and wicked. They are here characterized as disobedient in their unbelief because they transgressed and were rebellious through their disdain for the signs of God, since they did not judge according to these signs (see Gätje 1971: 136). Here, *hukm* means mainly to profess a world's organization in line with God's directions. To judge and to rule the community by revelation can be understood in a political sense if we believe also that revelation is the constitution of the community and that the prophets are the legislators of their peoples. Was Muhammad the legislator of the Islamic community? The great theoretician of the Muslim Brotherhood Sayyid Qutb thought so and argued that 'Islam must rule (*yahkum*) because it is the only positive doctrine (*'aqida*) ... that is acquainted with its nature and the nature of life. There is no Islam without *hukm* and no Muslim without Islam: And whoever judges not according to what God has sent down, they are unbelievers' (Qutb 1952: 79). Here, *hukm* clearly means political rule, and this is certainly a bold interpretation (*ta'wil*) of the text.

References and further reading

Gätje, H. (1971) *The Qur'an and its Exegesis*, ed. A.T. Welch, London: Routledge & Kegan Paul.

Qutb, S. (1952) *Al-Ma'raka bayna al-Islam wa al-ra'smaliyya* (The Struggle between Islam and Capitalism), Cairo: Dar al-kitab al-'arabi.

See also: **'aqida; hakim; tafsir in early Islam**

MASSIMO CAMPANINI

HULUL

Hulul is a noun meaning staying, stopping, descending and incarnation. The root is the past tense *halla* of a verb that means to untie, unfasten or undo: *Halla al-'uqda* means 'he untied the knot'. In the Qur'an the term is used when Moses asks God to solve his speech problem 'And remove an impediment from my tongue' (20.27). *Halla* also means to solve a problem, to come up with a solution or to solve a puzzle or a riddle. In addition, this term means to reach or, in terms of time, to become, so that *halla shahu ramadhan* means 'it is now the month of Ramadan'. Furthermore, *halla* signifies coming to the end of a period of travelling and settling somewhere. In this sense it is derived from *halla al-ahmal*, meaning to untie the loads of a traveller – indicating the conclusion of a trip. As a result *hulul* means to settle, inhabit or to stay.

Adding the intransitive *hamza* (A) to the beginning of *halla* changes the sense of the word, with *ahalla* meaning to allow, alight or descend, or cause to settle. This is the sense in which the term is used in: 'Have you not seen those who have changed the Blessings of Allah into disbelief, and caused their people to dwell in the house of destruction?' (14.28). *Ahalla* also means having made something permissible, lawful or allowable. In the Qur'an, we find: 'Allah has permitted trading and forbidden usury' (2.275).

Allaha katha wa katha means Allah permitted something: 'Lawful to you [for food], are all the beasts of cattle except that which will be announced to you' (5.1). Allah made lawful to the Prophet Muhammad possession of his wives and slaves: 'O Prophet! Verily, we have made lawful to you your wives' (33.50).

Muslim authors give various interpretations of the concept of *hulul*. For some it is the appropriation of one thing by another or the 'infusion' of one thing into another. In *tasawwuf* (Islamic mysticism) *hulul* expresses 'infusion', the indwelling of God in a creature, and it is often a synonym for *ittihad* (union with God). This refers to the incarnation of God or intermixing with his essence. Al-Hallaj (858–922 CE) used the term *hulul* to describe the mystic path. He claimed to have episodes of falling into trances in the presence of God. He would utter, during those episodes, some unusual comments such as '*Ana-al-Haqq*' meaning 'I am the Truth'. The Truth is one of the ninety-nine beautiful names of God. Muslims refer to Allah as *al-Haqq* (The Truth). Al-Hallaj is reported to have made another controversial claim, it being alleged that he said 'in my turban is wrapped nothing but God', which was taken literally to mean he was claiming to be God.

According to Ibn Taymiyya, *hulul* is connected to another Sufi term, *fana* (death of the self or evanescence), which is used to describe the servant of God terminating his self, desires and passions, and obliterating his ego. It is the avoidance of any other will except for the will of Allah. Therefore the servant worships

Allah alone, and loves only what Allah loves. His passions, will and love are naturally and voluntarily aligned with God's satisfaction. *Hulul* is the extreme form of *fana*. Ibn Taymiyya describes it as a distorted form of *fana*. This form can be illustrated thus: A man fell in the ocean, and his admirer threw himself after him. The first said: 'I fell in the ocean, what made you throw yourself in?' The second replied: 'I was incarnated in you, so I thought you were the same as me.' Ibn Taymiyya criticized this approach, arguing that it misleads people into thinking they are same as God, when precisely the reverse is the case. In his poetry, Rumi tried to explain this mysterious *hulul*. In Rumi's poem 'The Sunrise Ruby', Rumi says: 'There's nothing left of me. I'm like a ruby held up to the sunrise. Is it still a stone, or a world made of redness? It has no resistance to sunlight.' This is the way that al-Hallaj spoke also, with the ruby and the sunrise being one in the same way that humanity and God are one.

Ibn Taymiyya vehemently rejected this mystical interpretation of *hulul* and considered it clearly to be corruption and, in actual fact, heresy. Nothing can become incarnated in God. The Sufis argued that the existence of God is the only true existence and there is no genuine independent existence in his creation. The existence of God's creation is his existence as well, so there is no separation between the two existences. This is a very clear contradiction of the principles of the Islamic faith. In *kalam* (theology) some Muslim *mutakallimun* (theologians) defined *hulul* as the infusion of soul in body. They identified the soul as a mysterious body, but they also rejected *hulul* as the mystics understood it.

RAFIK BERJAK

HUMILITY

In Arabic *tawadu* means modesty and humility. Humility is the quality or state of being humble. The virtue of *tawadu* is the opposite of arrogance, pride and haughtiness. It involves putting pride aside. Prayer is important, since in thanking God we emphasize that we are powerless by contrast with him. All of us are equal to one another, and no one is better than anyone else except in terms of the faith we have, which God sees. In a famous *hadith* the Prophet says that God approves of the humble and disapproves of the haughty. There are many stories of the Companions taking on menial tasks to help them develop their capacity for humility, which of course was always under attack, given their high status and the importance of their roles.

The humble are praised in the Qur'an. We find 'the servants of the All-Merciful are they who walk on the earth in modesty, and if the impudent [rude people] offend them, they continue their way saying "Peace!"' (25.63). The Qur'an praises humility: God loves people who are 'humble toward believers' (5.54) and acclaims them by remarking 'You find them bowing down and falling prostrate' (48.29). It was not only the Companions who were famous for humility, but also the Prophet himself, and the *hadith* are replete with stories to that effect. The important moral basis for humility is the belief that God will decide who is really important or otherwise, and that it is incumbent on Muslims to be patient, an aspect of humility in that patient people do not expect their wants and needs to be satisfied before anyone else's.

The Turkish thinker Said Nursi wrote:

> In social life each man has a window called status through which he looks out to see others and be seen. If the window

is built higher than his real stature, he tries, through vanity and giving himself airs, to stretch himself up to be seen taller than he really is. If the window is set lower than his real stature, he must bow in humility in order to look out, to see and be seen. Humility is the measure of a man's greatness; just as vanity or conceit is the measure of a low character. (*Mektubat* 2: 315)

Why is humility so significant? Humility takes seriously the fact that we live in a world under the control of God. Pride serves to deny the power of God, since it makes us complacent about our achievements, treating them as if they are our achievements and not reflections of what God has brought about and made possible. Perhaps Nursi emphasized humility so much because he found it difficult personally to acquire this disposition. Given the force of his writings and the leadership roles that he took on within his community, he must have frequently felt that he had had imposed on himself ways of living that made humility very difficult to cultivate.

Nursi was rather attracted to asceticism. Yet he emphasized the importance of balancing in life the desire to perfect oneself spiritually and the need to engage in normal social and religious life. There is no point, according to Nursi, in trying to abandon the physical demands of a normal life, since these are aspects of the sort of creature that we are, which God has made us, but it does not follow that we should place more importance on our physical well-being than it deserves. Balance is important, since balance actually reflects our dependence on God. In preserving balance between our spiritual and physical needs we acknowledge and accept the sort of person that God has created, as opposed to trying to create something different. (Islam often sees itself as coming between the sensuality of Judaism and the asceticism of Christianity.)

Nursi severely criticizes the idea that it is acceptable to concentrate on one's personal spiritual welfare at the expense of religious law (*shari'a*). He contrasts the requirements of sainthood and prophecy, and clearly regards the latter as superior. The Prophet is, after all, concerned with the welfare of the community at large, while the saint may only be concerned with his own spiritual welfare. What is important here is balance, since it is balance between the various religious ambitions we might have that makes it possible for us to carry them all out. That is, there are religious obligations that every Muslim must carry out, and then there are also the spiritual aspects of those obligations which some Muslims may seek to cultivate in certain ways, but which by themselves are vacuous. Sometimes people contrast *tariqa* and *shari'a*, suggesting that once one appreciates the spiritual path represented by *tariqa*, there is no longer any need to follow *shari'a*. Indeed, if *tariqa* is the inner meaning of *shari'a*, this seems quite plausible. Yet such an approach would be entirely unbalanced, according to Nursi, and would fail to acknowledge our multifarious nature as a creature that requires both ritual and spiritual rules, both the *zahir* and the *batin*.

The individual who lives a simple life, even perhaps a life that is not outwardly of great value or piety, is highly valued in most religions. That is what ideals are designed to represent, a single simple principle in accordance with which a whole range of problems and issues are resolved. The principle of perfect humility is present in the total submission to the divine will. But this submission is not a world-denying submission, as far as Nursi is concerned. Quite the reverse: individuals should maintain their social obligations and especially their religious obligations, while at the same time maintaining an attitude of humility towards God and other human beings.

Further reading

Nursi, Bediuzzaman Said (1998) *Mektubat* (Letters), in *Risale-i nur*, Istanbul: Sözler Yayınevı.

See also: sabr; zuhd

OLIVER LEAMAN

AL-HUSAYN B. MUHAMMAD AL-NAJJAR

see: **al-Najjar, al-Husayn b. Muhammad**

I

IBN TAYMIYYA, TAQI AL-DIN

Abu'l 'Abbas Taqi al-Din Ahmad b. 'Abd al-Halim was born in Harran on 10 Rabi al-Awwal 661/22 January 1263 and died in Damascus on 20 Dhu'l qada 728/26 September 1328. As a jurist and a theologian he was a leading defender of the Hanbali school of Sunni Islam and has had a lasting effect on Islamic cultural life through his influence on Ibn al-Wahhab.

Ibn Taymiyya came from a well-known family of scholars that had to leave Harran during the invasion of Mongols, and his father got a teaching post at a *hadith* school (*dar al-hadith*) in Damascus. He held a chair at the Umayyad Mosque of Damascus on Fridays. Ibn Taymiyya succeeded his father at the same mosque, where he gave lectures on Qur'anic exegesis (*tafsir*). During his lifetime, because of the Mongol invasions and the onset of the Crusades, the prevailing political and military conditions in the Muslim world worsened.

Ibn Taymiyya started his education at an early age in the Sukkariyya *hadith* school (*dar al-hadith*) of Damascus, where he received his education under the direction of more than 200 prominent scholars of the time. He first memorized the Qur'an in Damascus, then studied Arabic grammar and lexicography under Sulayman b. 'Abd al-Qawi al-Tuft. Ibn Taymiyya studied a number of *hadith* works, namely the six books of *hadith* (*kutub al-sitta*) and, in particular, the *Musnad* of Ahmad b. Hanbal. He also studied secular sciences such as logic and philosophy, and became very interested in theology (*kalam*). By the age of 19 he was already giving juridical opinions (*fatawa*). In 695/1296, Ibn Taymiyya took over the chair of *fiqh* after the death of his teacher Ibn al-Munajja at the Hanbaliyya school (*madrasa*) in Damascus.

Ibn Taymiyya taught a number of students, many of whom became famous Muslim scholars, such as Ibn Qayyim al-Jawziyya, Shams al-Din ibn Muflih, Shams al-Din ibn 'Abdulhadi, Abu'l Fida ibn Kathir and al-Dhahabi. Ibn Qayyim was his closest follower. Ibn Taymiyya roundly attacked Ash'arite thought and what he regarded as deviationist Sufi doctrines, and he and his followers faced considerable political difficulties as a result. His opponents condemned him and charged Ibn Taymiyya with unbelief (kufr) for his legal opinion (fatawa) on prohibiting 'travel to the tombs of the Prophets and Saints', a popular custom of the time which he denounced as bid'a (innovation) and kufr. The Maliki chief judge al-Akhnai and four other chief judges of Cairo issued their decision that he be imprisoned in the citadel of Damascus. Ibn Taymiyya was duly incarcerated in the citadel and died there some two years later. While he was in prison, he wrote a refutation of his opponent al-Akhnai. The latter complained to the ruler, who ordered that Ibn Taymiyya be deprived of the means to write, which seems to have led to his death in the citadel on 728/1328.

Ibn Taymiyya opposed the theological approaches of the Ash'arites, very firmly representing the Hanbali school of law at his time. He declared his opposition to the philosophical theology of the Ash'arites in his popular creed ('aqida), written at the request of the people of Hama in 1299, which is known as al-'Aqida al-Hamawiyya. In this book Ibn Taymiyya discussed the issue of God's being on the throne (al-istiwa), a controversial issue since the question was how an immaterial deity can sit on anything. Another creed was the al-'Aqida al-Wasitiyya, written at the request of Radi al-Din al-Wasiti, who was one of the judges of Wasit (Iraq). Because of

his views on faith in these works, he was charged by his opponents with anthropomorphism (tashbih). In both these works, he relied on the ways of the Companions (of the Prophet) who were inspired by their understanding of the Qur'an and the sunna (prophetic reports). Consequently, his Salafi doctrine can be considered as a revelation-centred theology. As opposed to the theological approach, Ibn Taymiyya argued that the goal of human life is neither to know, nor to speculate about God, nor to love God. The main goal of humanity is to serve God through worship and obedience. Concerning the divine attributes, he adopted the classical traditionalist doctrine, which goes back to al-Shafi'i and to Ahmad b. Hanbal: God should be described as he has described himself in his Book, and as the Prophet has described him in his sunna.

Ibn Taymiyya criticized the philosophers, in particular the logicians, and wrote the al-Rad 'ala al-mantiqiyyin to attack them. In his refutation, he criticized Aristotelian logic. Jalal al-Din al-Suyuti wrote an abridgement of this refutation. Ibn Taymiyya also criticized the monistic position (ittihadiya) attributed to Ibn al-'Arabi and the incarnationist Sufis (hululiya). Ibn al-'Arabi's claims that God's existence is everywhere and that he and his creation are identical are in contradiction to the Qur'an, the sunna and the understanding of the Companions, Ibn Taymiyya argued. For this reason, he declared Ibn 'Arabi to be an unbeliever (kafir). Ibn Taymiyya condemned Sufi practices as heretical innovations. In spite of his severe opposition to Sufism, he was complimentary about some Sufis, among them 'Abd al-Qadir al-Jilani, who was a contemporary. Ibn Taymiyya accepted that such individuals could lead good lives, but rejected their theories.

In the field of theology Ibn Taymiyya criticised Shiʻite doctrines and thoughts. In his *Minhaj al-sunna*, he strongly criticized the theological views of the Shiʻites and the Qadariyya. He also criticized the deterministic approach of the Jahmiyya and the Jabriyya, who deny man's responsibility for his actions. He also opposed the rationalistic approach of the Muʻtazila, who consider human free will to be the basis of human action. On many other issues of theology, he opposed the mainstream views of his time. For him, Islam was a perfect and complete religion at the time of the Companions of the Prophet. The passage of time had led to many subjective interpretations being added to the religion by the Sufis and theologians; he considered these approaches as deviations and innovations in Islam.

Ibn Taymiyya also, however, criticized blind adoption of previous authorities (*taqlid*) and emphasized the importance of investigating the sources of knowledge. Ibn Taymiyya declared war against what he took to be innovation (*bidʻa*) and deviation. In his *al-Jawab al-sahih li-man baddala din al-masih*, which he wrote against the Christian missionaries, he tried to show the contradictions and deviations from God's word in the Bible. His theological and legal views inspired the late eighteenth-century Wahhabi school of thought, whose founder was Muhammad b. ʻAbd al-Wahhab (d. 1792). Ibn Taymiyya's views guided the Wahhabi movement and continue to be a source of inspiration to the Saudi regime and its followers.

A prolific writer, Ibn Taymiyya produced approximately 700 works in various fields of the Islamic sciences. His works deal with theology and the creed, Qurʼanic exegesis, the prophetic traditions (*hadith*), Islamic law, Islamic jurisprudence, and the philosophy, logic and history of religions and sects. In the field of theology there is also *al-Sarim al-maslul ʻala shatimi al-rasul* (The Sharp Sword Drawn Against the Critic of the Messenger). In the field of Qurʼanic exegesis there are the *Muqaddima fi al-usul al-tafsir* (Introduction to the Methodology of Commentary) and *al-Tibyan fi nuzul al-Qurʼan* (The Analysis of the Revelation of the Qurʼan). Ibn Taymiyya's works extend to almost every area of contemporary intellectual life and all tend to be rather bad-tempered. Nearly all of his works are in the style of a refutation or a critique, and the objects of his attacks are treated with considerable hostility. He embodies the theology of the Salafi (Traditionalist) movement and all his works are intense, focused and well-argued.

Further reading

Hallaq, W.B. (1993) *Ibn Taymiyya against the Greek Logicians*, Oxford: Clarendon Press.

Ibn Taymiyya (1984) *al-Jawab al-sahih li-man baddala din al-masih* (The Correct Answer to the One who Changed the Religion of the Messiah), trans. T.F. Michel, *A Muslim Theologian's Response to Christianity*, Delmar: Caravan Books.

—— (1985) *al-ʻAqida al-Wasitiyya* (The Creed of al-Wasitiyya), Muhammed ibn Mani, Mecca: Matbaʻat al-nahda al-hadith.

—— (1988) *Muqaddima fi al-usul al-tafsir* (An Introduction to the Methodology of Commentary), Beirut: Dar al-shams li al-turath.

—— (1991) *Majmuu fatawa: Kitab al-Mantiq*, ed. Abdurrahman b. Muhammad b. Qasim al-Asimi al-Najdi, Riyad: Dar ʻAlam al-Kutub.

—— (1993) *al-Rad ʻala al-mantiqiyyin* (A Refutation to the Logicians), ed. Rafiq al-Ajm, Beirut: Dar al-fikr al-lubnani; trans. W.B. Hallaq, *Ibn Taymiyya against the Greek Logicians*, Oxford: Clarendon Press.

—— (1997) *al-Sarim ʻal-maslul ala shatimi al-rasul* (The Sharp Sword Drawn Against the Critic of the Messenger), ed.

Umar al-Halwani-Muhammad Kabir Ahmad, Beirut.

—— (1998) *al-'Aqida al-Hamawiyya* (The Creed of al-Hamawiyya), ed. Hamed b. Abdulmuhsin, Riyadh.

Islahi, A. (1988) *Economic Concepts of Ibn Taymiyyah*, Lancaster: The Islamic Foundation.

Izutsu T. (1965) *The Concept of Belief in Islamic Theology: A semantic analysis of Iman and Islam*, Yokohama: Yurindo Publishing Company.

Khan, Q. (1973) *The Political Thought of Ibn Taymiyah*, Islamabad: The Islamic Research Institute.

Pavlin, J. (1996) 'Sunni Kalam and Theological Controversies', *HIP*: 105–18.

See also: **Ash'arites and Mu'tazilites; *hulul*; Ibn 'Abd al-Wahhab; *tafsir* – Salafi views; *ta'til***

OLIVER LEAMAN

IBN 'ABD AL-WAHHAB

Muhammad ibn 'Abd al-Wahhab ibn Sulayman ibn 'Ali ibn Muhammad ibn Ahmad ibn Rashid al Tamimi was born in 1115/1703 in 'Ayina to the north of Riyadh in what is today Saudi Arabia. He was known for his religious learning even as a young child, becoming a *hafiz* and leading prayers at an early age. His studies took on a very Hanbali flavour, and he was enthusiastic about the works of Ibn Taymiyya and Ibn al-Qayyim. He went on *hajj* and then to Medina, which at that time was led intellectually by 'Abdulla bin Ibrahim ibn Sayf. Ibn 'Abd al-Wahhab became much respected by Shaykh 'Abdulla and he was allowed to transmit *hadith*, a very significant aspect of the Islamic sciences, especially within the Hanbali tradition.

Ibn 'Abd al-Wahhab then moved on to Nejd, Basra and Syria for the purpose of acquiring further knowledge. He stayed for a long time in Basra, where he pursued his studies under Shaykh Muhammad Majmui in particular. It was at this stage that he started writing his very critical studies of what he regarded as innovations, superstitions and deviations from Islam in the ordinary practices of the inhabitants of those parts of the Arab world with which he was familiar. This did not go down well with the locals, and both he and Majmui were driven out of Basra. Ibn 'Abd al-Wahhab left for the town of Zubayr, almost dying of heat and thirst. He was obliged, due to lack of means, to stay in the area, and went to Ahsa to study with 'Abdulla ibn 'Abd al Latif Shafi'i.

Ibn 'Abd al-Wahhab next went to Harimala to live with his father, who died in 1153. Around this time his campaign to cleanse Islam began to meet with some success, and he gained local adherents, but the local ruling tribes remained hostile to him and his message. He left Harimala for his home town, where he recruited 'Uthman bin Hamd bin Mu'ammar to his cause, and together they destroyed trees that were being worshipped and the dome on a major tomb, as well as supervising the stoning of a woman who had been found guilty of adultery. The ruler in the region managed to bring this cooperation to an end by threatening to withdraw funds from 'Uthman unless he expelled Ibn 'Abd al-Wahhab, and the latter was obliged to leave town on foot and cross the desert. Arriving at Dariya, he found many supporters, in particular the two brothers of Prince 'Abdul 'Aziz bin Muhammad bin Saud. He arranged a meeting with the prince, who became a supporter; in turn, Ibn 'Abd al-Wahhab promised to support the prince as a ruler of the region. A prolonged military campaign got under way, with Ibn 'Abd al-Wahhab its spiritual head. The campaign ended with the conquest of Riyadh in 1187. At this point the Sauds were in a position to rule and Ibn al-Wahhab retired. He continued writing up to his death in Dhu'l Qada 1206.

Al-Wahhab was critical of anything he saw as deviating from Islamic teaching. He classified as *shirk* or polytheism a range of activities then current in Mecca and Medina, such as the excessive glorification of the graves of the Prophet and his Companions. These graves have in many cases been destroyed by the Saudi regime, which came into power very much in sympathy with Ibn 'Abd al-Wahhab's approach. Other practices of which Ibn 'Abd al-Wahhab disapproved were anything connected to Sufism and any practice or belief that involved regarding someone like a *shaykh* as being an intermediary between humanity and God. These customs were regarded as aspects of *taqlid* or conformity to tradition, and Ibn 'Abd al-Wahhab advocated rejecting this entirely since it had come to replace the centrality of the Qur'an and the Traditions in Islam, in his view.

Ibn al-Wahhab defended a number of basic principles. He explained that *'ibada* (worship) is nothing but exclusive obedience to Allah and compliance with his commands. It is a comprehensive term for everything that Allah loves and such words and deeds as he is pleased with. The forms of *'ibada* (worship) that are to be offered to Allah alone are many, including *salat* (prayers), *sawm* (fasting), *zakat* (alms-giving) and *sadaqa* (good actions or charity), slaughtering of sacrificial animals, *tawaf* (walking around the *Ka'ba*) and invocation. He said that anyone who happens to direct any of these acts to anyone other than God becomes a *mushriq* (idolater), as the Qur'an says: 'And whoever invokes [or worships] besides Allah any other *ilah* (god) of whom he has no proof, then his reckoning is only with his Lord. Surely *al-kafirun* [the unbelievers] will not be successful' (23.117).

Ibn 'Abd al-Wahhab distinguished sharply between what is permitted and what is prohibited. The permitted is what is involved in faith and righteous deeds and implied by the glorious names of God and his attributes. The prohibited is to make entreaty or supplication using the name of the Messenger, pious people and saints. The Qur'an says: 'O you who believe! Be mindful of your duty towards Allah and seek the means of approach and strive in His cause as much as you can so that you may be successful' (5.35). Ibn 'Abd al-Wahhab asked people not to undertake any pilgrimages to mosques other than the three mosques supported in an authentic *hadith*:

> Do not undertake a journey but to the three mosques – the Sacred Mosque [in Mecca], my mosque [in Medina] and the distant mosque [in Jerusalem].

Ibn 'Abd al-Wahhab opposed construction over graves, covering and decorating them, a practice which developed over time in the Islamic world and had become popular. He openly declared that to construct buildings over the graves was unlawful. So was shrouding the graves with beautiful coverings and decorating them. It was also prohibited to burn candles over the graves or to set up stone inscriptions. Ibn 'Abd al-Wahhab also declared it illegal to have custodians and caretakers of shrines. Visiting such places was tantamount to idol worship and, he argued, could lead to other prohibited actions, such as kissing them or going round them. He supported his statements with numerous *ahadith* prohibiting such constructions, visiting them and praying in them. The Shaykh quoted the *hadith* of Abu'l-Hayyaj al-Asadi whom 'Ali ibn Abi Talib asked:

> Should I not charge you with a task with which the Messenger of Allah had commissioned me – to leave no statue but to crush it, and no grave raised above the surface of the ground but to level it down?

Ibn 'Abd al-Wahhab defended unity with respect to the special names and attributes of God. On this he held the same views as the *salafi* (traditional predecessors), the four main Sunni law schools and others, namely that the affirmation and recognition of the names and properties of God should neither use *tamthil* (link them with human names and properties) nor explain what was involved in divine action and existence.

Ibn 'Abd al-Wahhab very much disliked and spoke out strongly against innovations (*bid'a*), especially:

1. The celebration and holding of gatherings on the Prophet's birthday.
2. Making *dhikr* (remembrance) and *salawath* before pronouncing the *adhan* (the call to prayer).
3. Verbally pronouncing the *niyya* (intention) on religious ceremonies.
4. Recital of *ahadith* of Abu Hurayra before the *khatib* ascends the *minbar* (pulpit).

He also abhorred and condemned what he took to be the innovative practices of Sufism, such as their *tariqa*s (orders), *tawassuf* itself (mysticism) and other practices they followed that have no authority either from the Messenger or from the Companions, as far as he was concerned.

Ibn 'Abd al-Wahhab, the spiritual source of the recent governments in Saudi Arabia, was as we have seen, one of the most determined enemies of *shirk* or idolatry. He argues from the basis of his interpretation of the Qur'an that there is an intimate connection between *shirk* and *kufr* (unbelief). Al-Wahhab sees the Christians and Jews, although People of the Book, as unbelievers, pointing out that the Prophet did make a clear distinction between them and Muslims; as such, they should not be regarded as just different kinds of believers. In his view, they have very inaccurate views of the nature of God which would not save them from eventually being sent to hell. The Christians really pray to images, he claimed, not through them to God, an entirely disreputable custom. He criticized vehemently those he called modern *mushrikun*, which he takes to be people who call themselves Muslims but really rely on things other than God to help them and to explain how the world turns out to be the way it is. It is easy to see how this line of argument could be developed into an attack on science and modernity, but at the time it served very much as an attempt to cleanse Islam in the Arabian peninsula from a variety of practices it had acquired, including worshipping saints, visiting graves of important people and even giving a special status to things like particular trees. Al-Wahhab argues, and he supports his arguments with considerable textual authority, that idolatry is not just a matter of worshipping statues or rocks, but has a much more subversive meaning. Having a painting on the wall does not mean that we worship it, but it might lead us to think it is important and so to misapply our enthusiasm away from religion. Even a religious painting could implant heretical ideas in us. We might admire the physiology of the people in the painting, or the beauty of the scenery, or the magnificence of the colours. Anything that does not directly link us with God is questionable, and likely to corrupt the individual and consequently the community.

Ibn 'Abd al-Wahhab's attack on idolatry is that it is more dangerous the more subtle it is. Anything that waters down the direct letter of Islam can distract, confuse and lead to the questioning of authority. It is indeed idolatrous in the sense that it may posit for us a set of issues and even images that we then take to be important, and these may have little to do with Islam. They are even more dangerous if they are connected with Islam, since they then suggest that it is appropriate for Muslims to spend time on a variety of indirect activities and so the poison slowly enters the system. That is what *shirk* is: associating God with partners. When Muslims start to interpret their faith through something else, they replace the standard topics on which they should concentrate with other issues, and become distracted from their central task, which is to carry out the main obligations of their faith in the correct manner.

See also: **art and the Qur'an;** *hajj; halal;* **haram; Ibn Taymiyya;** *tafsir* – **Salafi views;** *ta'til*

OLIVER LEAMAN

IBRAHIM

Ibrahim (Abraham) is a prophet mentioned by name some sixty-nine times in the Qur'an. He is described as the founder of the true religion, which was revived by the Prophet Muhammad (e.g. 2.130–140; 3.65–68; 16.120–124). Some verses refer specifically to the 'religion of Abraham' (*milla Ibrahim*) and Muslim exegetes identify this with Islam (e.g. 2.130; 3.95; 4.125). According to 53.36–37 and 87.18–19, Abraham was, like Moses, the recipient of 'scriptures' from God. 4.125 refers to Abraham as a 'friend' (*khalil*) of God (see Isaiah 41: 8; 2 Chronicles 20: 7), and Abraham alone is given the appellation *hanif* in the Qur'an, on ten separate occasions. 6.84–87 provides a long list of prophets associated with Abraham, as does 2.136, and Muslim exegetes state that all prophets after Abraham are his descendants.

Birth and early life

Unlike the biblical account, the Qur'an contains details concerning the birth and early life of Abraham. 6.74 indicates that Abraham's father was named Azar, but later Muslim exegetes say his name was Terah and give him a genealogy similar to that found in Genesis 10. Some Muslim traditions say he was born in Iran or Khuzistan; others say he was born in Babylon, near the city of Kaskar, or in Harran. A number of passages describe Abraham's attempts to turn his father and his people from the worship of idols (e.g. 19.41–50; 21.51–70; 37.83–99), and 21.68–69 makes reference to the furnace into which Nimrod is said to have cast Abraham. Muslim exegetes add that, at Abraham's birth, a star appeared which local astrologers interpreted to herald the birth of a boy who would destroy the kingdom of Babylon. Abraham is also described as maturing quickly and being able to speak from the time of his birth. During his youth, Abraham is said to have induced monotheism from celestial phenomena, as described in 6.74–87.

The Holy Land

21.71–73 mentions Abraham and Lot's move to the Holy Land, the gift of Isaac and Jacob, and the establishment of prayer and almsgiving. According to Muslim exegetes, this refers to Abraham's journeys from Babylon to Egypt, Arabia, Syria and Palestine, where he settled. The birth of Isaac is announced to Abraham and Sarah according to 11.69–74, 15.51–56 and 51.24–30, and Muslim exegetes say that it was the angels Gabriel, Michael and Israfil who gave this annunciation.

In the Qur'an and Muslim exegesis, Abraham is most closely associated with the establishment of the sanctuary at Mecca. 14.35–41 contains Abraham's prayer to establish his offspring in Mecca. Muslim tradition records the story of Ishmael and Hagar being sent to Mecca, where the well of Zamzam was discovered, closely associated with the well of Abraham in Beersheba (see Genesis 21: 31–33). A number of passages refer to Abraham's building of the *Ka'ba* and establishment of the pilgrimage there (e.g. 22.26–27; 3.96–97; 2.125–129). Among the interpretations given to the 'place of Abraham' (*maqam Ibrahim*) mentioned in 2.125 is that this refers to the footprints left by Abraham in a rock while building the *Ka'ba* in Mecca.

Sacrifice

Abraham's sacrifice of his son is also narrated in the Qur'an (37.99–113). The Qur'an does not say which son is to be sacrificed, but 37.112 refers to Isaac by name as being a prophet. Muslim exegetes disagree in their identification of the intended son, some claiming it was Isaac, others saying it was Ishmael. 37.107 mentions a 'great sacrifice' by which the son was redeemed, which Muslim exegetes take to be a special ram that had pastured in the garden of Eden until that time.

Ten words and the resurrection of the birds

2.124 refers to the 'words' by which God tested Abraham. Jewish tradition, perhaps related to the ten 'labours' of Heracles, says that Abraham was tested with ten trials among which was the command to sacrifice his son. Muslim tradition interprets the 'words' to be ten aspects of Muslim practice established by Abraham and related to purification rites.

2.260 narrates the resurrection and return of four birds after Abraham had cut them into pieces and scattered their remains on different mountains (see Genesis 15). According to some exegetes, Abraham held the heads of the birds until the bodies flew towards him and, when he then threw the heads, each attached to its correct body.

Death and burial

According to Muslim exegetes, Abraham was buried, along with his son Isaac and his grandson Jacob, in the city of Hebron, called Khalil after the epithet of Abraham. Some exegetes also mention a special castle, made of pearl, in the garden of Eden, which was prepared especially for Abraham as a place of residence.

Further reading

Bashear, S. (1990) 'Abraham's sacrifice of his son and related issues', *Der Islam* 67: 243–77.

Bijlefeld, W.A. (1982) 'Controversies around the Qur'anic Ibrahim narrative and its "orientalist" interpretations', *Muslim World* 72: 81–94.

Calder, N. (1988) 'From Midrash to Scripture: The sacrifice of Abraham in early Islamic tradition', *Le Muséon* 101: 375–402.

Firestone, R. (1990) *Journey in Holy Lands: The evolution of the Abraham-Ishmael legend in Islamic exegesis*, Albany, NY: SUNY Press.

Mbon, F.M. (1980) 'A Hanif Resigned: Abraham in the Qur'an', *Islam and the Modern Age* 11: 121–48.

Moubarac, Y. (1958) *Abraham dans le Coran*, Paris: J. Vrin.

Troger, K.-W. (1980) 'Mohammed und Abraham: Der Prozess der Ablösung des frühen Islam vom Judentum und seine Vorgeschichte', *Kairos* 22: 188–200.

BRANNON WHEELER

IBRAHIM'S WIFE

Abraham's wife, known as Sara in biblical and exegetical sources, was her husband's first follower. According to commentaries, she sojourned in Egypt with Abraham, where God saved her from the Pharaoh's advances. There, she was given the slave Hajar, who became Abraham's concubine and gave birth to Ishmael. Years later, angelic guests visited Abraham and declared that Sara would bear a child. She first disbelieved the news, laughing and arguing that she was old and barren (11.70–72; 51.29). However, the visitors confirmed that she would deliver a 'knowledgeable son' (51.28). Eventually Sara bore Isaac, through whom Abraham's lineage continued.

KECIA ALI

IDRIS

Idris was a prophet, first mentioned by name in 19.56. 19.57 states that God took Idris up 'to a high place', which is interpreted by Muslim exegetes as a reference to Idris being raised to heaven before he died. Along with Adam, Seth and Noah, Idris is considered to be one of four 'Syrian' prophets according to a saying attributed to the Prophet Muhammad.

Genealogists relate that Idris was the son of Jared, and lived some 600 years after the death of Adam. Most Muslim exegetes identify Idris with the biblical Enoch, but some identify Idris with Elijah, perhaps because both are said to have been immortal. Others conflate him with Adam's son Seth, who is reported to have been sent as a prophet and to have received revelations, but is not mentioned in the Qur'an. Still others claim that Idris was a prophet who lived later, during the time of the Israelites.

A saying attributed to the Prophet Muhammad states that thirty scriptures (suhuf) were revealed to Idris, and some exegetes identify these scriptures with the 'first scriptures' mentioned in 87.8–10.

Idris is credited with the origins of many of the arts of civilization, including writing, and his name is said to have been derived from the Arabic word for studies (dirasa). The association of Idris with Seth and other scriptural traditions also relates to his identification as the Thrice-Great Hermes (Harmas al-Haramisa) associated with the Corpus Hermeticum, and some exegetes say that Idris was the prophet of the philosophers. Later Muslim tradition also links Idris closely to the figure Metatron and other angelic beings associated with Enoch.

According to accounts of the Prophet Muhammad's Night Journey (isra'), Idris is to be found in the fourth heaven. He is described as being tall and white, with a huge stomach, broad chest, little body hair and a lot of hair on his head. Other accounts place Idris in the sixth heaven, including one which states that Idris died after being taken into the sixth heaven by the Angel of Death.

Muslim tradition maintains that four prophets are immortal: two of these immortal prophets, Khidr and Elijah, remain on earth; the other two, Idris and Jesus, reside in heaven.

Further reading

Affifi, A.E. (1950) 'The Influence of Hermetic Literature in Muslim Thought', BSOAS 13: 840–55.

Casanova, P. (1924) 'Idris et 'Ouzair', Journal asiatique 205: 356–60.

Jenkinson, E.J. (1931) 'Did Mohammed Know Slavonic Enoch?', Muslim World 21: 24–8.

Segal, A.F. (1977) Two Powers in Heaven: Early Rabbinic reports about Christianity, Leiden: E.J. Brill.

Walker, J. (1927) 'Who is Idris?', Muslim World 17: 259–60.

BRANNON WHEELER

IGNORANCE

see: knowledge

IHSAN | IHSANI

The term *ihsan* refers to the doing of good deeds or inner purification. The interpretation of this term is in the well-known *hadith* on Jibril's asking the Prophet Muhammad about the three sources of how to behave. These are *islam* (submission), *iman* (belief) and *ihsan* (virtue, doing good deeds), or the outward, the inward and the actualization. Islam is the outward, *iman* the inward and outward, and *ihsan* the actualization of the inward and the outward, which is what is meant by the saying of the Prophet: 'Ihsan is to worship God as if you see Him, and if you see Him not, He sees you despite this,' which the angel Jibril confirmed.

The term *ihsani* (intellectual) of the Tradition of Islam, which has always been haunted by the paradoxes and contradictions of our modern age, means that it is only in fullness that integrated Islam, in which the spiritual and intellectual tradition evolved, gains an awareness of our modern context.

NEVAD KAHTERAN

I'JAZ

see: **inimitability**

ILHAD

Ilhad is a verbal noun, derived from the Arabic verb *lahada*, meaning to deviate, to digress. The word admits of various different translations, including heresy, apostasy and even atheism. The Qur'an's use of the verb and its derivatives favours a definition closer to something you might find in a modern dictionary, for it talks of people who 'deviate in His Names' (7.80), which presumably connotes some kind of wilful misrepresentation by unbelievers of God's nature. Elsewhere we read of those who 'pervert

the truth in Our Signs' (41.40), which, given the dual meaning of *ayat*, may mean either the corruption or misuse of scripture, or the tendency to ignore or misrepresent the signs of God in creation.

COLIN TURNER

ILTIFAT

Iltifat is a noun meaning turning aside, preventing or bending; it also means looking back or averting from. Furthermore, *iltifat* signifies attention, notice or consideration. *Biduni-iltifat* means without consideration. The root verb is *lafat*, which means to draw attention to something. *Iltafata* means to turn towards or to turn back in order to look or see: 'So travel with your family in a part of the night, and let not any of you look back; but your wife' (11.81). *Yulfit* signifies averting or drawing attention away: 'Have you come to us to turn us away from that?' (10.78).

RAFIK BERJAK

ILYAS
see: **Elijah**

IMAM AL-HARAMAYN JUWAYNI
see: **Juwayni, Imam al-Haramayn**

IMAM | IMAMA

The word *imam* is lexically derived from the Arabic verb *amma-ya'ummu*, which, in its several forms, means leading the way, preceding, guiding by one's example or serving as a prototype. The word *imam* is therefore applied to leader, learned man, head or chief. It belongs to the same root as that of the word *umm* (mother) and *umma,* which has been used in the Qur'an variously to mean a religion, community, nation, tribe or distinct individual (as used for Abraham in 16.120: *inna Ibrahim kana ummatan qanitan lillahi*). Here, *umma* is used in the sense of the word *imam*, as a righteous man, one known for his goodness, a cultured man of his age and time, outstanding in his learning, one who has no equal. An *imam* is a remarkably knowledgeable individual, whose example is followed.

In the Qur'an, the term *imam* occurs twelve times, seven times in the singular and five times in the plural form as *a'imma*. It is used to mean leader, exemplar, guide, revelation, archetype, foremost and a pathway. The first occurrence of the word is in *sura al-Baqara* (2.124), with reference to Abraham's appointment as a leader of humanity: 'I am surely making you a leader of the people' (*inni ja'iluka li nas imaman*). It refers to his trials in life as a means of attaining ethical integrity and eventual leadership of humanity. This is reflected again, especially in 21.73, where Abraham and the various prophets are mentioned as being appointed as leaders, inspired to do good, establish worship, give alms and pray to none but Allah. A further example is that of the followers of Moses in 28.5: 'We wanted to be gracious to those who had been weakened in the land making them leaders (*a'imma*) and heirs (*warithin*).' This particular verse was revealed to Muhammad during his move from Mecca to Medina, according to the *Tafsir al-Jalalayn* of al-Suyuti. Muhammad soon did become the leader of the Muslim community in Yathrib, which changed its name to *madinat al-nabi*, the City of the Prophet (abbreviated as Madina), out of respect for him. 32.24 refers to Moses also and to the appointment of leaders among those Banu Israel who were consistently patient believers. Examples such as these, especially those

of Moses, are conveyed to Muhammad again and again during his desperate moments, showing the early struggles and ultimate triumph of Moses.

The word *imam* is additionally used in 25.74 with reference to those who plead to become exemplars for the pious (*wa aj'alna lil muttaqin imaman*). On account of their patience, they are accorded a privileged position in the hereafter, where they would be received with salutations and peace. Al-Tabari includes traditions from Ibn 'Abbas which maintain that these refer to *imams* of piety in the same way as Abraham when informed of his appointment as an *imam*. 'The day when We shall call all humanity with their Imam' (17.71) also refers to the *imams* from Adam's progeny undertaking the task of conveying and upholding God's message. They are witness to the deeds of their communities in relation to their faith. Some commentators explain *imam* in this context as scriptures and others as recorded deeds. This aspect of deeds, according to some exegetes, also occurs in 36.12: 'And we have enumerated everything in *imamim mubin*', although many commentators describe *imamim mubin* as meaning the evident leader. Al-Qummi records a tradition from 'Ali ibn Abi Talib that he was that manifest *imam*.

In 11.17 and 46.12 *imam* refers to the revelations received by Moses and Muhammad, and it is in this sense that the Qur'an is at times referred as *imam al-muslimin* (the guide of Muslims). The plural form (*a'imma*) is used in two other verses: for leaders of unbelief (*al-kufr*) and for leaders inviting people to hellfire (*al-nar*) (9.12; 28.41). The words *imamim mubin* occur again in 15.79, where the reference is to an apparent example of the devastation of cities when they resisted the prophets Lut and Shu'ayb.

There are three distinct categories of Qur'anic usage for the word *imam*: nine times it is used for leaders, seven of which refer to the righteous leaders, initially humiliated and belittled, who become prototypes of proper behaviour; two verses refer to revelations received by Moses and Muhammad; and one verse describes an example. The word *imam* thus refers to leadership, guidance or demonstration, be it in the singular or plural, although it is frequently used today to describe a prayer leader.

Imama is the function of the *imam* – it is what the *imam* does in his responsibility as an *imam*. It is the mode or manner in which the *imam* chooses to function or operate in his position of leadership. Both *imam* and *imama* (*imamat* in Persian) have been interpreted and applied in Muslim history in a variety of ways, and have had a major impact in determining the religio-political dimension of the community. In the non-technical sense, *imam* is often applied to a leader of a community, an authority in a field of scholarship or to the leader of a ritual prayer. In Islamic law and theology, it technically refers to the legitimate supreme leadership of the Muslims after the Prophet, who himself has been described as the exemplar of the community (*imam al-umma*). The *imam* can essentially be described as the mother of the community, the *umm* of the *umma*, all of which terms belong to the same root.

Besides the word *imam* itself, the Imamate is conceptually expressed in the Qur'an in several expressions, including *sultan, amr, mulk, kitab, nur, hikma,* and *huda.* Leadership features predominantly in the narration of the earlier prophets and in the family of the Prophet, with terms such as *al, ahl, qurba, dhuriyya* and *itrat.* In verses 3.33–34 ('God chose Adam and Noah as well as Abraham's family and Imran's family above all mankind') and in 4.54 ('Indeed, We have given the Book, the Wisdom and a

great Kingdom to the Family of Abraham'), the family is clearly unique. 24.55 ('God has promised those of you who believe and do righteous deeds that He will surely make you successors on the earth') alludes to *khilafa* and, in verses 33.72 and 4.58, the *amana* (trust from God) is explained as the Imamate by Shi'i scholars. The *amana,* or the trust that the *imam* undertakes from God, renders him a guarantor (*hujja*) and a link (*sabab*) with the celestial world for those individuals who accept his authority. This authority of the *imam* is part of the universal history, which begins with the pre-creation covenant (*yawm al-mithaq*) and is made manifest through the chain of prophets and their legatees, the *imams.*

All Muslim scholars view the Imamate as a necessity. In his section on appointing an *imam,* the eleventh-century Shafi'i scholar al-Mawardi (d. 450/1058) refers to the *ulu al-amr,* those in authority described in 4.59, as the basis of its necessity from revealed law. For him, the Imamate takes the place of the prophet's caliphate in protecting the faith and governing the world (*al-imama mawdu'a al-khilafa al-nabuwwa fi hirasat al-din wa siyasat al-dunya*). It is therefore obligatory for Muslims to establish the Imamate, although there is a difference of opinion over whether it is prerequisite from reason or from revelation. In al-Mawardi's opinion, appointment of an *imam* is through election, even if it was by a single person, implying the endorsement of designation for a successor, a step away from the Shi'i view of hereditary succession.

Traditional Sunni literature listed in Wensinck (1971) from eight authorities, including al-Bukhari and Muslim, suggests that the pedigree of the *imams* must come from the Quraysh. The *imam* must be obeyed and disobedience punished. Fraudulent leaders were to be penalized and good leaders rewarded. The Imamate is viewed as being similar to the leadership of the Prophet and therefore not to be slighted –'whosoever obeys the Imam, has obeyed Muhammad'. The necessity of the Imamate was never disputed by scholars; the debate revolved around whether or not it was required on rational grounds or only through revealed law. Shi'i scholars such as the early fifth-century Fatimid scholar al-Naysaburi and the Ithna'a-shari scholar al-Mufid (d. 413/1022) argued that the Imamate is indispensable through both reason and revelation. Al-Naysaburi in his *Kitab Ithbat al-Imama* gives rational evidence of leadership in every genera and species, with paradigms of perfect examples in each variety, demonstrating that the *imam* is at the apex of humanity. The Mu'tazili scholar 'Abd al-Jabbar (d. 415/1025) denies that the Imamate is necessary from reason, although he gives arguments that revelation makes it obligatory to have an *imam* in every age.

The Imamate traditionally used to be discussed in works of *usul al-din* (principles of faith) rather than in *furu'* (legal matters), but Sunni scholars following al-Juwayni (d. 478/1085) and al-Ghazali (d. 505/1111) placed the Imamate in works dealing with expositions of law. This was mainly in reaction to the Shi'is, who invariably placed the Imamate in the *usul* as a pivot of the faith. Moreover, scholars found it difficult to apply the classical attributes of the *imam* to the monarchs who held power, irrespective of qualifications. Many later Sunni creeds thus make no references to the Imamate, referring simply to the early *rashidun* caliphs. Shi'is, on the other hand, consider the Imamate to be an essential principle of faith, rather than an institution, with several doctrines ingrained within it including *walaya, nass, ilm, nur, isma* and *shafa'a*.

A second-century illuminary, Muhammad al-Baqir (d. *c*.117/735), views the Imamate as divinely ordained, like the prophethood, basing it firmly in the Qur'an and the Tradition. For him, the *imams* are the guardians and protectors of believers, whose obedience to them is obligatory. The *imams* are the people of the Message, to whom the Book (that is, the Qur'an) is given as an inheritance, and who as such have true knowledge of its interpretation. Knowledge is therefore a central theme in the teachings of the *imams*, according to al-Baqir and his son Ja'far al-Sadiq (d. 148/765), for the role of the *imam* is primarily that of a spiritual guide, initiating followers into inner paths of knowledge and wisdom. Consequently, the *imam*'s task is man's purification, preparing appropriate receptacles for the *haqiqa* (truth), which is the *raison d'être* of 'history' – restoring man to his original home.

In the Sunni view, the *imam*'s function is pre-eminently political. He may perform religious functions, but these do not necessarily lend him any sanctity. He is a protector and executor of the *shari'a*, not divinely appointed, but installed by *ijma'* (consensus). For the Shi'a, the choice of an *imam* is beyond the domain of the community and, being a matter of fundamental belief, *ijma'* cannot be applied, just as it cannot be applied to monotheism, the prophethood of Muhammad or Muhammad's status as God's Messenger. *Imama* is a grace from God; it cannot be acquired.

Historically and conceptually, the various Muslim communities developed the idea of *imama* at different times in history. The reference in the Qur'an to Abraham as an *imam* has been the subject of a number of interpretations for several groups of Muslims, all asserting the Qur'anic legitimacy of their interpretations. The Kharijites, for example, insisting on equality and justice, call for an *imam* to be chosen irrespective of his tribal or racial background. At present, the Ibadiyya of Oman and North Africa are the only surviving Kharijites with a tradition of electing their *imam*. They reject the prerogative of the Quraysh to elect the Imamate. For the Shi'is, the nucleus of the idea on which all agree is that only a descendant of 'Ali b. Abi Talib can be the supreme leader of the world. Unlike the Imamiyya, the Zaydiyya do not recognize a hereditary line of *imams*, but support any descendant of 'Ali's sons, al-Hasan and al-Husayn, who calls for allegiance through *khuruj* or rising. As in Sunni and Mu'tazili theory, their emphasis is on knowledge in religious matters, the ability to pass independent judgement (*ijtihad*) in law, piety, moral integrity and courage. Unlike other Shi'is, they permitted recognition of two simultaneous *imams*, especially during the existence of two separate communities in Yemen and the Caspian Sea. The Caspian Zaydis survived under the Nasiriyya and the Qasimiyya communities, but were converted to Twelver Shi'ism under the Safavid Shah Tahmasp. The two Yemeni communities, the Mutarrifiyya and the Husayniyya had, also disappeared by the fourteenth century. However, the Zaydi community in Yemen survived until the twentieth century, with their last *imam*, Muhammad al-Badr, overthrown in the revolution of 1962.

According to the Imami Shi'a, both Isma'ilis and Ithna'asharis, the Imamate is a divine institution that is hereditary and founded on mankind's need for a supreme leader and authoritative teacher. The world cannot exist without an *imam*, who is endowed with the inner meaning of the Qur'an. There is only one *imam* at any given time, although it is possible to have a silent (*samit*) *imam* as his successor beside him. Since the concealment (*ghayba*) of their twelfth

Imam al-Mahdi in 260/874, the Ithna'asharis, both Usulis and Akhbaris, have referred to the *mujtahids* and *ayatullahs* as religious scholars, who provide direction until his return.

The Isma'ili scholars in Fatimid times, during the fourth century, managed successfully to adapt ancient Greek philosophy to their theology. The *imam* is explained as the quintessence of the cosmos, through whose channel the energy flows to mankind and the world. In esoteric doctrine, the *imam* represents a grade (*hadd*) in religious hierarchy. He assumes the function of the proclaimer (*natiq*) in expounding the exoteric meaning of the revealed law, while his *hujja* unveils its esoteric interpretation (*ta'wil*). The Isma'ilis survived mainly in two branches. The Tayyibi Isma'ilis recognized al-Amir (d. 524/1130) as *imam*, with al-Amir remaining in touch with the community while in hiding. Tayyibi scholars have discussed the cosmological nature and role of the *imam*, making his divine nature (*lahut*) distinct from his human nature (*nasut*). They are guided by the *dai al-mutlaq* as the representative of the community. The Nizari Isma'ilis recognized Nizar as the *imam* after the Fatimid caliph, al-Mustansir (d. 487/1094), and continue to this day to believe in a hereditary living guide (*hadir Imam*) in the person of Karim Aga Khan, their forty-ninth *imam*. In their doctrine of the *qiyama* (resurrection), the *imam* is explained as a revealer of esoteric truths and defined as a manifestation (*mazhar*) of the word or command of God. It is through this recognition of the *imam* that the believer attains spiritual birth or resurrection. The *imam* lights the path of the *murid* in the temporal and spiritual realms through his *ta'lim* (authoritative teaching).

The attitude of Sunni Muslims to the Imamate varies at present. There appears to have been a complete denial of the

Imamate since the abolition of the Ottoman Sultanate in 1922, as endorsed by the Turkish Grand National Assembly. This is also attested by the Egyptian writer 'Ali 'Abd al-Razik in his treatise *al-Islam wa usul al-hukm* (1925). Others, however, have called for restoring the universal Imamate; these include the Syrian Rashid Rida, in his *al-Khilafa aw al-Imama al-uzma*, which was written in 1923. Modern thinkers lay emphasis on the *shura* (consultation) and election as a way of establishing the *imam*: in their view, the *imam* has no special sanctity, although they do make reference to the archetypal prophets Abraham and Muhammad.

Further reading

Amir-Moezzi, M.A. (1994) *The Divine Guide in Early Shi'ism*, trans. David Streight, Albany, NY: SUNY Press.

Arendonk, C. van (1960) *Les débuts de l'Imamat Zaidite au Yemen*, trans. J. Ryckmann, Leiden: E.J. Brill.

Ayoub, M.M. (1988) 'The Speaking Qur'an and the Silent Qur'an: A study of the principles and development of Imami Tafsir', in A. Rippin (ed.) *Approaches to the History of the Interpretation of the Qur'an*, Oxford: Oxford University Press, 177–98.

Crone, P. (2004) *Medieval Islamic Political Thought,* Edinburgh: Edinburgh University Press.

al-Fawaris, A. (1977) *al-Risala fi al-Imama*, ed. and trans. S.N. Makarem, New York: Delmar.

Hajjar, S. and Brzezinski, S. (1977) 'The Nizari Isma'ili Imam and Plato's Philosopher King', *Islamic Studies* 16: 303–16.

Kohlberg, E. (1991) 'The Term *Muhaddath* in Twelver Shi'ism', repr. in his *Belief and Law in Imami Shi'ism*, Aldershot: Gower and Brookfield: Variorum, VT.

al-Kulayni, Abu Ja'far Muhammad b. Ya'qub (1388/1968) *Usul min al-Kafi*, Tehran: Dar al-kutub al-'ilmiyya.

Lalani, A. (1987) 'Ja'far al-Sadiq', in Mircea Eliade (ed.), *Encyclopaedia of Religion*, London and New York: Macmillan, 4760–2.

—— (2000) *Early Shi'i Thought: The teachings of Imam Muhammad al-Baqir*, London: I.B. Tauris.

Linant de Bellefonds, Y. (1968) 'Le Droit Imamite', in *Le Shi'isme Imamite*, Paris: Presses Universitaires de France, 183–99.

MacDermott, M. (1978) *The Theology of al-Shaikh al-Mufid (d. 413/1022)*, Beirut: Dar el-Machreq.

Madelung, W. (1961) 'Das Imamat in der frühen ismailitischen Lehre', *Der Islam* 37: 43–135.

—— (1965) *Der Imam al-Qasim ibn Ibrahim und die Glaubenslehre der Zaiditen*, Berlin: Walter de Gruyter.

Makarem, S. (1967) 'The Philosophical Significance of the Imam in Isma'ilism', *SI* 27: 41–53.

al-Mawardi, 'Ali b. Muhammad (1936/1996) *al-Ahkam al-Sultaniyya wa'l walayat al-diniyya*, Cairo; English trans. Wafaa H. Wahba, *The Ordinances of the Government*, Reading: Garnet Publishing.

Meir, M. (1999) *Scripture and Exegesis in Early Imami Shiism*, Jerusalem: The Magnes Press.

Momen, M. (1985) *An Introduction to Shi'i Islam*, New Haven, CT: Yale University Press.

al-Qadi Abd al-Jabbar al-Asadabadi (1960–) *al-Mughni fi abwab al-tawhid wa-al-'adl*, Vol. 20, Cairo: al-Shirka al-'Arabiya lil-Tiba'a wa-al-Nashr.

al-Qadi al-Nu'man (1951–61) *Da'a'im al-Islam*, Cairo: Dar al-ma'arif; English trans., *The Pillars of Islam*, Vol. 1, trans. Asaf A.A. Fyzee, 2002; rev. I.K. Poonawala, New Delhi: Oxford University Press.

al-Qummi, 'Ali b. Ibrahim (1968) *Tafsir al-Qummi*, ed. Tayyib al-Musawi al-Jaza'iri, Beirut: Matba't al-Najaf.

al-Tabari, Abu Ja'far Muhammad b. Jarir (1954) *Jami' al-bayan 'an ta'wil ay al-Qur'an*, Cairo: Mustafa al-Babi al-Halabi and Sons.

al-Walid, Ali b. Muhammad (1967) *Taj al-'aqa'id wa ma'dan al-fawa'id*, ed. Aref Tamer, Beirut: Dar al-machreq.

Wensinck, A.J. (1971) *A Handbook of Muhammadan Tradition*, Leiden: E.J. Brill.

Wilkinson, J.C. (1987) *The Imamate Tradition of Oman*, Cambridge: Cambridge University Press.

al-Yaman, Ja'far b. Mansur (1984). *Kitab al-Kashf*, Beirut: Dar al-andalus.

*See also: **sunna***

ARZINA R. LALANI

INIMITABILITY

Inimitability (*i'jaz al-Qur'an*) is the central miraculous quality attributed by Muslim dogma to the Qur'an. No human speech and particularly no Arabic speech can match the divine speech, of which the Qur'an consists in form and content.

The term itself does not occur in the Qur'an. But the concept of inimitability finds its Qur'anic basis in a number of verses that challenge and defy the opponents of the Prophet to produce something like the Qur'an, if only a *sura* or verse: 'Say: "If men and *jinn* banded together to produce the like of this Qur'an, they would never produce its like, not though they backed one another"' (17.88). Such verses were called by Muslim exegesis 'Verses of Challenge' (*ayat al-Tahaddi*). In some of these verses, the context is an accusation by enemies of the Prophet that Muhammad had invented a text, which he falsely claimed to be revelation: 'Or do they say, "Why, he has forged it"? Say: "Then produce a *sura* like it, and call on whom you can, apart from God, if you speak truly"' (10.38). Treatises written after the third/ninth century developed a consistent theology of prophetic miracles. All prophets throughout history had to provide miracles as divine proof to their audiences that they were true prophets: Moses, in confrontation with the Pharaoh, changed his staff into a serpent and parted the Red Sea; Jesus raised the dead. Muhammad's proof of his prophethood was the inimitable Qur'an. The inimitability of the Qur'an was not only rooted in its pure eloquence, but also referred to the Qur'an's foretelling of the hidden and the unseen, in other words, to the prophetic (in the narrow sense) parts of the Qur'an. The effect of Qur'anic recitation is described by the Qur'an itself: 'God has sent down the fairest discourse as a book, consimilar in its oft-repeated, whereat shiver the skins of those who fear their Lord; then their skins and their hearts soften to the remembrance of God' (39.23). This shows that the rhetorical effect of the Qur'an was first and foremost due to its recitation: the Qur'an has to be recited and heard to achieve this effect. On the other hand, the rhetorical effect was caused less by the beauty of the text than by its awe-inspiring majesty and its message, which made the listeners 'shiver'. Similar to Jews and Christians, Muslims ascribe to their scripture itself a quality which assures the community that this must indeed be God's word. In other words, the Qur'an authenticates itself. In a hermeneutic circle, the community's experience of the Qur'an bears witness to the authenticity of the Qur'anic message.

The dogmatic discussions of the inimitability of the Qur'an were interwoven with the idea that the Qur'an, as direct divine speech, was uncreated and eternal. The Mu'tazilite position that the Qur'an was created speech suffered a decisive blow when the 'Abbasid caliph al-Ma'mun in 218/815 ruled that everybody who denied the uncreatedness of the Qur'an was guilty of apostasy. Another point of conflict was whether the Qur'an was inimitable because of the intrinsic nature of the text itself, or whether the Arabs could have produced something like the Qur'an if God had not, by a special act of divine intervention (*sarfa*), prevented them from doing so.

Some Muslim scholars devoted much time and energy to finding out exactly why the rhetorical devices, tropes and metaphors in the Qur'an were inimitable. Others, like al-Baqillani (d. 403/1013) and above all 'Abd al-Qahir al-Jurjani (d. 471/1078), found its superiority not so much in single verses but rather in the Book's overall composition and structure. Literary and rhetorical theory encountered Islamic theology in discussions on the inimitability of the Qur'anic text.

In the twentieth century these fierce debates about the nature of the Qur'an as God's speech seem to have subsided. The inimitability of the Qur'an is now mainly invoked by some representatives of literary interpretation (*tafsir adabi*) or rhetorical interpretation (*tafsir bayani*) of the Qur'an, among them the Egyptian 'A'isha 'Abdalrahman (pseudonym: Bint al-Shati', b. 1913). One of her deductions is that there are no synonyms in the Qur'an and that no word in the Qur'an can ever be replaced by any other word. In modern non-Arabic commentaries, inimitability is often accorded little space. The practical importance of the concept of inimitability may also have decreased because the concept presupposes an intimate knowledge of classical Arabic and an appreciation of the aesthetics of Arabic rhetoric. As the proportion of Arabs in the Muslim community is today only around 10 per cent, the concept is difficult to communicate outside of a small circle of scholars. In the strictly Islamist discourse of the late twentieth century, the force of the Qur'an is often seen more in its assumed legal consistency than in its inimitable aesthetic value.

Arabic culture and Islamic culture hold the style of the Qur'an in highest esteem, with listeners to Qur'anic recitation reported to have died under the overwhelming effect of the recitation. In the nineteenth and the early part of the twentieth centuries, the Qur'anic style and, by implication, the dogma of Qur'anic inimitability were often attacked or ridiculed by non-Muslim scholars. In 1910 the German philologist Nöldeke criticized the Qur'anic text as careless, full of mistakes, imperfect and dull; Schwally (1919) spoke of the 'horrible barrenness of the holy text'; and, as late as 1977, Wansbrough called the effect of the text 'tedious in the extreme'. Such statements are usually resented by Muslim scholars and Arab Christians alike.

References and further reading

Kermani, N. (2000) *Gott ist schön: Das ästhetische Erleben des Koran*, Munich: Beck.
Wansbrough, J. (1977) *Qur'anic Studies: Sources and methods of scriptural interpretation*, Oxford: Oxford University Press.

See also: **art and the Qur'an; language and the Qur'an; miraculousness of the Qur'an; style in the Qur'an**

STEFAN WILD

INJIL

The term *Injil*, or Gospel, is ultimately rooted in the Greek word *evangelion*, meaning 'evangel' or 'good news', and is a foreign word within the Qur'an. Although the manner of its introduction into Arabia is uncertain, historians have noted that *Injil* is closely related to the Ethiopian term *wangel* or the Persian *andjil*, speculating that it came with Abyssinian Christians who immigrated into the area sometime around or before the beginning of the sixth century CE; if they are correct, the term was probably widely known in Muhammad's day.

From the twelve references to the *Injil* in the Qur'an, predominantly found in the chronologically later Medinan *suras*, one discovers the notion that Allah revealed a book directly to Jesus ('Isa) (57.27; 3.84), which was communicated to his audience through his teachings. Classical Islamic thought contends that there were many prophetic messengers sent by God to various peoples, some of whom were also given books of divine revelation (4.163). These revelations, such as Jesus' *Injil*, were progressive, confirming previous revelations and being ultimately confirmed by God's final revelation to humanity (3.3). This continuous progression of revelation, parts of what is known as the heavenly 'Mother of the Book' (*umm al-kitab*), were partially given to Moses in the Torah, to Jesus in the *Injil* and finally to Muhammad in the Qur'an (9.111), with the Qur'an believed to represent the fullness of revelation. Revelatory books prior to the Qur'an were culturally specific and superseded or augmented by later revelations.

According to the Qur'an, the revelation of the *Injil* to Jesus was prophesied to Mary when the angel announced the conception of Jesus (3.48). They were later confirmed when the infant Jesus spoke in defence of his mother (19.31) and affirmed when Allah reminded Jesus about the revelation of the *Injil* to the Prophet (5.110). While there is little discussion within the Qur'an about the actual content of the *Injil*, a few points can be noted. First, it is called 'a guidance and an admonition' to those who fear God/evil, and a confirmation of the Torah (3.3; 5.46). As such, one can assume that it contained a number of moral teachings parallel to those found in the Torah and the Qur'an. Second, we are told that Jesus' teachings were to clarify disputed opinions among Jews about the Torah. While the Qur'an is not specific about these clarifications, later Muslim thinkers, such as the historian al-Tabari, stated that some laws forbidden by the Torah were allowed by the *Injil*. Third, the Qur'an speaks of how the *Injil* contained a prophecy regarding Muhammad's birth (7.157). This prophecy, mentioned again in 61.6, had Jesus announcing the coming of another messenger named Ahmad.

While no specific parallel in the New Testament is found, Muslim writers point to Jesus' announcement of the coming 'comforter' as being this prophecy (John 14.16). Fourth, similar to the above prophecy, there are other Qur'anic verses where echoes from the New Testament Gospels can be found. For example, the nativity narratives (3.45–47), teaching parallels between Muhammad and Jesus (e.g. 7.157) and references to Jesus' miracles (e.g. 5.110).

The word *Injil* is also used in reference to the scriptures of people of the Gospel, meaning the Christians (3.65; 5.47; 6.156). According to the Qur'an, their scriptures have given Christians enough light to judge what God has revealed elsewhere; if those Christians remained faithful to all revelations, and many of them have not, they would have experienced happiness (5.47, 66, 68). For, since revelations between the prophets are continuous, the followers of the Torah and Gospel should be like the Muslims (48.29). Christians, however, have rebelled and created institutions, such as monasticism, contrary to what God revealed to them (57.26). This has led to disputes between Christians and between Christians and Jews about many issues, such as the religion of Abraham (19.34).

With Qur'anic references to Jesus and his Gospel, the question of the relationship between Qur'anic and Christian understanding of the Gospel naturally arises. Aside from two *hadith* traditions suggesting that Muhammad's cousin-in-law translated portions of the Gospels before his conversion and a single reference to a Monophysite translation of 640 CE, there is no evidence that the Arabs had a translation of the New Testament Gospels prior to the eighth century CE. Nevertheless, there is some support for the notion that there was some oral Gospel tradition behind these

Qur'anic statements; possibly Muhammad, in his various travels, became familiar with many key teachings and events of Jesus' life.

While the Qur'an makes no particular distinction between the *Injil* and the New Testament Gospels, the singular tense of *Injil* and the accusation that past believers have misunderstood and misinterpreted the Torah and *Injil* (e.g. 19.37; 45.17) have led Muslim theologians to make just such a distinction. With the assumption that the revelatory prophetic books are single and primarily didactic, Muslim theologians perceive the original Gospel of Jesus to be very similar, stylistically, to the Qur'an. Furthermore, bolstered by modern biblical criticism, theologians speak of a 'corruption' (*tahrif*) of the original Gospel. This corruption occurred in order to accommodate later Christian doctrines, such as the Trinity, and transformed the *Injil* into the New Testament Gospels, which may contain fragments of the original prophetic teaching, among action narratives and other fictional accounts. Some Muslim theologians have suggested that the Gospel of Barnabas and the Gospel of Thomas may be the original *Injil* of Jesus, or at least contain more authentic fragments than the New Testament Gospels.

The understanding of 'gospel' differs in Christianity, however, where it possesses multiple meanings. Given that, within the Christian Gospels, *evangelion* is normally the subject of the verb *kerysso* ('to preach'), the first meaning of Gospel is communicating the good news about the Kingdom of God, which includes both Jesus' teachings and actions regarding the coming kingdom. Second is the notion of gospel as a literary genre: that is, it is the literary form of early Christian *keryma* (preaching) about Jesus and the divine kingdom. Although it has parallels in Greco-Roman, Jewish and other Christian writings, the gospel genre forms a unique literary group in ancient literature. Nevertheless, there is still some theological validity to the notion that the New Testament is merely a record of revelation. This gives credence to the notion, among comparative theologians, that Muslim belief regarding the Qur'an parallels Christian belief regarding Jesus, and that *hadith* traditions about Muhammad parallel the New Testament Gospel records.

Further reading

Broyles, C.C. (1992) 'Gospels (Good News)', in J.B. Green and S. McKnight, *Dictionary of Jesus and the Gospels*, Dower's Grove, IL: InterVarsity Press, 283–9.

Cragg, K. (1994) *The Event of the Qur'an*, Oxford: OneWorld.

—— (1999) *Jesus and the Muslim: An exploration*, Oxford: OneWorld.

Esack, F. (2002) *The Qur'an: A short introduction*, Oxford: OneWorld.

Gätje, H. (1997) *The Qur'an and its Exegesis*, Oxford: OneWorld.

The Gospel of Barnabas (1993) ed. M.A. Yusseff, Indianapolis: American Trust Publications.

Hurtado, L.W. (1992) 'Gospel (Genre)', in J.B. Green and S. McKnight (eds), *Dictionary of Jesus and the Gospels*, Dower's Grove, IL: InterVarsity Press, 276–82.

Jeffery, A. (1938) *The Foreign Vocabulary of the Qur'an*, Baroda: Oriental Institute.

Khalidi, T. (2001) *The Muslim Jesus: Sayings and stories in Islamic literature*, Cambridge, MA: Harvard University Press.

McAuliffe, J.D. (1991) *Qur'anic Christians: An analysis of classical and modern exegesis*, Cambridge: Cambridge University Press.

Omar, A. (2003) *The Dictionary of the Holy Qur'an*, Rheinfelden: Noor Foundation.

Parrinder, G. (1996) *Jesus in the Qur'an*, Oxford: OneWorld.

H. CHAD HILLIER

INJURY

Injury (*adha*) signifies physical harm or damage. It is a wrong action or treatment, especially the violation of another's rights, as in, for instance, damage to one's feelings, reputation or welfare. The word *adha* signifies a relatively minor evil.

Adha, in the sense of injury, is applied to two different kinds of injury. The first is physical. In different places in the Qur'an this term is mentioned in this sense, for instance: 'And whosoever of you is ill or has an ailment in his scalp, he must do penance' (2.196). The second kind of *adha* applies to the self. In this regard it means to annoy or to bother someone. It can also signify humiliating or causing someone to suffer emotionally. The Qur'an has in many verses described the *adha* the disbelievers inflict on the Prophet: 'And among them are men who annoy the Prophet' (9.61). In other parts of the Qur'an, this term is used as a deterrent to prevent violators from committing illegal actions: 'And the two persons among you, who commit illegal sexual intercourse, hurt them both' (4.16).

Higher harm than *adha* is *dharar*, which signifies more substantial damage. The Prophet prohibited people from causing this kind of harm. He said: *la dharar wa la dhirar*. This *hadith* means 'harm is prohibited'. Some contemporary Muslim scholars apply this principle to anything that may cause any kind of harm or injury, including the smoking of cigarettes and so on. They consider these actions *haram* (prohibited) under the terms of the above-mentioned *hadith*.

Dharar has also been used in the Qur'an to describe instances of considerable harm, such as the distress caused by serious illness, imprisonment, a sea storm causing a ship to sink, natural disasters like famines, floods, and so on. It is used in reference to the ordeal of Job's long ailment: 'And Job when he cried to his Lord: "Verily, distress has seized me"' (21.83). The Qur'an declares that Allah is the one who causes *dharar* or *dhur*, and that he alone can remove *dharar*.

Jurh signifies injury, cut or wound; the root verb is *jaraha*, meaning to wound, offend or injure someone. The plural of *jurh* is *juruh* or *jirah*. In the Qur'an, the term appears in 'And We ordained therein for them: Life for life, eye for eye, nose for nose, ear for ear, tooth for tooth, and wounds equal for equal' (5.45). *Jawarih* is plural of *jariha* and signifies beasts and birds of prey, as well as the chasing or hunting of animals: 'And those beasts and birds of prey which you have trained as hounds, training and teaching them in the manners as directed to you by Allah; so eat of what they catch for you' (5.4).

Both *jurh* (plural *juruh*) and *ajra* refer to a wound or injury produced on bodies by an iron instrument or the like. *Jarh* signifies the effect produced on objects of the mind by the tongue. *Jiraha* is a synonym for *jurh* and its plural is *jirahat*. The Prophet said: 'whosoever gets injured in the cause of Allah – and Allah only knows who gets injured in his cause – will come on the Day of Judgement with the injury in its original shape; the colour is the colour of blood, but the smell is the fragrance of musk'.

Jarih or *majruh* mean the wounded or the injured person; their plurals are *jaraha*, *majruhin* or *majarih*. The Qur'an has imposed the *qisas*, or the punishment equals the crime, penalty in the cases of intentional assaults that cause bodily harm or injury. Based on the principle that the punishment should fit the crime, this idea is expressed in the *aya*: 'Life for life, eye for eye, nose for nose, ear for ear, tooth for tooth, and wounds equal for equal' (5.45). This law was established in the Torah before Islam, and the Qur'an verified it and mandated it for Muslims. In practical terms, according to this law, if someone assaults another person and intentionally hits him in, for example, the eye, thereby completely destroying it, then the perpetrator should be sentenced to losing his own eye. This is what is known in the Islamic law as *al-qasas*.

It has been reported that, during the Prophet's time, a woman by the name of al-Rubi'a intentionally broke a tooth of another young woman, who then become a *jariah*. The family of al-Rubi'a wanted to escape the *qisas* and offered *arsh* (financial compensation) to settle the case. The family of the injured refused to settle for less than the punishment-equals-the-crime penalty, which meant adhering to the principle of a tooth for a tooth. The Prophet ruled in the victim's favour and al-Rubi'a was sentenced to lose a tooth, just as the victim had done. Eventually, the victim's family softened their position and accepted the *arsh*; thus al-Rubi'a kept her tooth.

When an injury is caused by the intentional amputation of a limb, then the law of equal for equal applies. However, the application of this law is subject to conditions. First, when applying this law, equality must be guaranteed: if the lost arm had been lost, for instance, exactly from the elbow, the victim is permitted to cut the arm of the perpetrator in return only from the same joint. Second, there should be a similarity between the type and the position of the limbs: the right hand will be cut for the right hand and so on. Third, the limbs of both the injured and the perpetrator should be equal: a good healthy hand with five fingers should be cut for an equivalent hand.

See also: ʿ*adl*; **health; noise; punishment**

RAFIK BERJAK

INSAN / NAS

It is difficult to describe human beings. This is because there is much more to a person than meets the eye. We cannot entirely comprehend the nature of human beings unless we can reach into the inner dimensions of humanity, which far exceed the outer parts. As a great world in and of himself, a man is the quintessence (*zubda*) of the universe. The word *insan* means human being and is derived from the Arabic word *ins*. Another view is that *insan* comes from the term *nesy*, which means 'to forget'. Furthermore, *insan* can mean 'pupil of the eye' (*insanu'l-ʿayn*). In the Qur'an, human beings are referred to sixty-five times as *insan*, eighteen times as *ins*, once as *insi,* once as *enasi* and 230 times as *nas* – the plural form of *insan*. The religious view of the nature of man is entirely different from the modern scientific view, both in content and appearance. The Qur'anic description of human beings as 'cruel and ignorant' and yet also 'the most honourable of all creatures' (*ashrafi mahluqat*) is directly tied to man's creation from mud but in the image of God. The Qur'an talks of balancing these two extremities of man's dual nature by practising moderation, and ultimately gives a positive view of humans, portraying them as creatures who have the ability to comprehend the relationship between conflicting tendencies and the ability to control them.

The creation of human beings

The Qur'an is only for human beings, and it addresses not only Muslims but all peoples, including the members of other religions (3.64). The foundation of existence for human beings is their belief in Allah, and this belief is described in great detail in the Qur'an. The Qur'an is not concerned with anything else to as great an extent as it is with human beings. By the order of descent (*nuzul*), the first revealed verse of the Qur'an is about the creation of man, and this verse describes the human being (96.1–2). Furthermore, the name of the seventy-sixth *sura* of the Qur'an is *insan*, and this *sura* emphasizes that point that human beings have been sent into the world to be tested. According to the Qur'anic view, all human beings are of the same origin (*mansha*): 'O mankind! Be careful of your duty to your Lord Who created you from a single soul . . .' (4.1), or later 'Achieving honour and high position in the sight of Allah is through righteousness (*taqwa*), not the superiority of race' (49.13).

The Qur'an raises further interesting issues. The human being should be studied as a whole, together with its conditions of existence, without separating the body and soul into two parts, since there is neither a body separated from the psychic entity nor a stand-alone spirit that exists apart from the body. The origin of man is dust (3.59; 30.20; 35.11) and the first human body was brought to existence by turning that dust into mud, and passing it through various stages (6.2; 7.12; 15.26, 28, 33; 32.7–8, 71; 37.11; 38.71–72; 55.14). The human being is thus a part of nature and all the elements that exist in nature also exist in the human body. The soul of a person comes directly from Allah – the creator of all things – as a bounty (*lutf*): 'So, when I have made him and have breathed into him of My spirit . . .' (15.29; 38.72). Because of this breathing, the transcendent self is the one ultimate certainty that lies at the heart of the very existence of all of us. In addition, the human being holds a distinguished and superior position among all existences in the universe: 'Verily We have honoured the children of Adam' (17.70). According to the Qur'an, the first man was also the first prophet.

The psychological nature of the human

Although what is seen of a human being is his physical existence, what determines the human self is, according to the Qur'an, the unseen inner existence. In other words, the human self does not depend upon physical space and time. The word *nafs* is used 295 times in the Qur'an to represent the self, and it is the site where all human experiences that go beyond psychology are formed. The Qur'anic story of the exile of the first man and his wife from heaven indicates the weaknesses of humans on the one hand, but, on the other, the destiny of a distinguished being who will in the end become the *khalifa* (viceroy) on earth (2.30–31; 4.1; 7.11; 15.26–31; 33.72; 38.71–73). Human psychology is the battleground for conflicting tendencies. Human being is a conflicted form of existence – that is, a human being carries the seeds of both good and evil. At an individual level, a person's character is marked by weakness, lack of perspective, ambition and narrow-mindedness (4.28; 59.9; 64.16; 70.19–21 etc.). The evil tendencies in human nature stem from these traits. These traits are also the roots of personality deficiencies such as feelings of superiority, conceit and hopelessness (17.67, 83). Man is hasty because of his weakness (21.37; 17.11; 75.10–21). The greatest obstacle on the path of maturing and development of *nafs* is the *nafs* itself, for it gets buried in its subjective tendencies (*hawa*): 'Nor do I absolve my own self [of blame]: the [human] soul is certainly prone to evil, unless my Lord do bestow His Mercy . . .' (12.53).

Despite these negative traits, positive attributes are also in human nature. The animalistic side of humans distances us from God, but the spiritual side distances us from the world. In reality, a person should establish a balance between the physical and metaphysical worlds. For human behaviour to be stable and bear beneficial fruit, it is necessary to achieve a balance between conflicting tendencies. The Qur'an makes it possible for people to increase awareness of Allah and purify themselves by changing their inner state. Allah has equipped humans with knowledge, free will (*irada*) and intellect (*'aql*). Furthermore, conversing and reasoning are among the first attributes that make humans really humans; by them, man may acquire many divine attributes, such as knowledge, virtue, will, justice and mercy. In Arabic, *al-insan al-kamil* (the person who has reached perfection) means a wise person, a person who has acquired qualities of high virtue. He, in *tasawwuf* (Islamic mysticism), is the link between the *haqq* (the truth) and the people. *Al-insan al-kamil* is the point where the *haqq* manifests itself. What is meant by *al-insan al-kamil* is the Prophet Muhammad and those who carry on his spiritual heritage. *Al-insan al-kamil* has become, in a real sense, the *khalifa* of Allah on this earth (2.30). In this regard, he is bestowed with the power to rule (*tasarruf*) over the world. He claims ownership (*malik*), passes judgement, takes action and makes alterations – but not in his own name. Owing to his connection to Allah, he has more freedom than a person whose basis of freedom is only himself. This is because the freedom that stems from the divine task is interwoven with a debt of responsibility to the Absolute Being.

The mission of humanity

The basic traits of humanity remain unchanged in all ages. The Qur'an therefore asks us to look back and learn from past events. If the nature of humanity and the problems it faces had changed, this suggestion would be meaningless. Those human beings who are chosen by Allah as the *khalifa* of the world are given the duty of civilizing it and establishing a just social system based on ethics. Even the heavens and mountains abstain from assuming the responsibility that the Qur'an calls *amana* (trust): 'Lo! We offered the trust unto the heavens and the earth and the hills, but they shrank from bearing it and were afraid of it. And man assumed it' (33.72; see also 59.21). This entrusting is indicative of love, free will, responsibility and the power of individuation. In this case, humans should worship God and be conscientious in fulfilling the responsibilities entailed by being *khalifa*. Among all creatures, only humans are given the freedom to choose between obeying the commandments of Allah and not doing so (see 4.15; 53.39–40; 76.3; 90.10–20; 91.7–10). If a man leads a life commensurate with the aim of creation, he can rise to a level above that of the angels – that is, he can claim the highest rank in all of cosmic existence – or he can fall to the lowest levels: 'Surely We created man of the best stature. Then We reduced him to the lowest of the low' (95.4–5). A saying of Hölderlin provides a parallel to this verse: 'Nothing can ascend and/or descend as far as a human can.' For a Muslim, the man of highest state (*al-insan al-kamil*) is Muhammad, who is the messenger of Islam and the point of perfection for all revealed religions. Islam is also regarded as the religion commensurate with the true nature of man (*fitra*) (30.30). Thus being religious is simply a return to the roots of humanity, and being true to real human nature. The moral and spiritual decline of a person, on the other hand, indicates a movement away from this basic human nature (*fitra*).

The universe is created for the benefit of human beings (2.29) and man has added a historical dimension to nature, not only reshaping nature but also giving meaning to it. All events in the universe become meaningful only by the existence of humans. To make the world possible to live in, it is necessary to uphold the concept of high moral character for all. According to the Qur'an, a believer is like a seed that blossoms in a society, and one who finds in himself the love of life and transcendence that are required if one is to be a devoted follower of Allah. A human being carries the responsibility to represent in the community the truths brought by the prophets and to exemplify this truth in the form of a civilization built on foundations of love and peace.

Further reading

al-Bar, M.A. (1989) *Human Development as Revealed in the Holy Qur'an and Hadith*, Jeddah: Saudi Publishing & Distributing House.
Eaton, G. (1999) *King of the Castle*, Lahore: Suhail Academy.
Ibn Manzur, M.M. (1995) *Lisan'ul-'arab*, Beirut: Dar al-ihya' turasi al-'arabiyya.
Iqbal, M. (1996) *The Reconstruction of Religious Thought in Islam*, Lahore: Institute of Islamic Culture.
al-Isfahani, R. (1992) *al-Mufredatu Elfazi'l-Qur'an*, Damascus: Dar al-qalem.
Mir, M. (1987) *Dictionary of Qur'anic Terms and Concepts*, New York and London: Garland Publishing Inc.
Pickthall, M.M. (1981) *The Meaning of the Glorious Qur'an*, Beirut: Dar al-kitab al-lubnani.
Rumi, M.C. (1993) *Masnavi*, Ankara: Publications of the Ministry of Culture (Persian text).
Schimmel, A. (1975) *Mystical Dimensions of Islam*, Chapel Hill, NC: University of North Carolina Press.

See also: **character;** *nafs; ruh; taqwa*
AHMET ALBAYRAK

INTEREST
see: **riba**

INTOXICATION

Islam forbids drinking alcohol, even for the sake of protecting the body from harm (2.19), and it would seem to follow that all intoxicants are thereby ruled out. The Prophet is taken to have said that even a small amount of an intoxicant is forbidden. Indeed, the Qur'an does not explicitly mention 'alcohol', but uses the word *khamar* which means 'intoxicant'. We are told in 2.219:

> They ask you about intoxicants and games of chance. Say: 'In both of them there is a great sin and means of profit for men, and their sin is greater than their profit.' And they ask you as to what they should spend. Say: 'What you can spare?' Thus does Allah make clear to you his signs on which you should ponder.

The Qur'an says that, since the bad effects are greater than the good effects, they are not allowed. This raises the question of whether there could be circumstances in which it would be beneficial to drink alcohol, and so God would allow us to do so. The answer is a clear no: there is a host of *hadith* literature forbidding alcohol and intoxicants, regardless of the potential benefit. In general, most Muslim theologians argue that we can be confident that intoxication is so harmful that anything contributing to it should be avoided.

Of course, anything in this world created by God may in itself be beneficial to us, but we need to observe the divine order to avoid certain things if we are to live in accordance with God's wishes for our ultimate welfare. Alcohol has many deleterious social and health effects, and God took account of these in banning it.

What counts as a relevant intoxicating substance here is an interesting issue, and some have argued that any stimulant, including tea and coffee, should likewise be forbidden. There was a debate in the past over the acceptability of smoking (Klein-Franke, 1993), a debate that may well reappear given contemporary health concerns about the dangers of tobacco use.

Reference

Klein-Franke, F. (1993) 'No Smoking in Paradise', *Le Muséon* 106, 1–2: 155–92.

See also: **haram**; **harm; health; heaven**
OLIVER LEAMAN

INVOCATION OF GOD'S CURSE

see: mubahala

IRADA

In 4.172–173 we read,

> The Messiah will never disdain to be a servant of God, nor will the favoured angels. Whoever disdains His service and is proud, He will gather them all to Himself, then as for those who believe and do good, He will pay them fully their rewards and give them more out of His grace, and as for those who disdain and are proud, He will punish them with a painful doom. And they will not find for themselves besides Allah a guardian or a helper.

It is clear from this that, although the Messiah, Jesus, and the angels do not disobey the commands of God, they are warned of a painful punishment on the Day of Reckoning should they nevertheless commit a wrong. The possibility of neglect of their duties or committing wrong action is necessarily dependent on their being sentient beings with free will and entrusted with the task of transmitting the revelation of God.

The angels and the devils

The refusal of Satan to prostrate himself before Adam and the dialogue between Satan and God occurs several times in the Qur'an. Satan, after having been expelled from intimacy with God, says in 38.82–83: 'I surely will lead every one of them astray except your sincere slaves among them.' And God replies rather grimly: 'I shall fill hell with you and with those who follow you, together' (38.85).

It is clear that punishment can only take place if the punished understand the reason for the punishment. In 34.20 God says, in confirmation of Satan's warning to man, 'And Satan indeed found his calculation true concerning them, for they follow them, all except a group of true believers.' Likewise, we read in chapter 14.22:

> And Satan said when the matter had been decided: 'Indeed! Allah promised you a promise of truth; and I promised you and failed you. And I had no power over you except that I called to you and you obeyed me. So do not blame me but blame yourselves.'

Blame can only be associated with those who possess the power of reason and free will. These verses show that Satan, like the rest of the angels, is a thinking independent. Just as verses occur in the Qur'an concerning the angels and the devils, there also are verses that clearly and vividly describe the *jinn* (spirits or invisible beings, either harmful or helpful). In 46.18 reference is made to those who, invited to believe in Islam, spurn it as just another ancient fable or superstition: 'Such are those in whom the word concerning nations of the *jinn* and mankind which have passed away ....

Indeed they are the losers.' We may understand from this verse that the *jinn*, the invisible entities, live like humanity in different nations, pass a period of time in their different societies and finally die. In the same *sura*, *ayas* 29–32, it seems clear that the *jinn* are in a similar position to human beings in being offered a revelation and having to decide whether to accept it or not. They are free to choose.

Human action

The difference between the natural world and the human is that the former reacts without thought to what confronts it, whereas, even if we are capable of undertaking a certain action, we consider whether we ought to and can think about various alternatives. This enables us to choose freely, and the consequences are that we are responsible for what we do as free people. But how free are we? The implications of many of the remarks in the Qur'an about predestination and necessity suggest that a fatalist attitude is appropriate since God controls everything, including even our decisions (36.8–9). But these frequent remarks could be interpreted as God knowing how we will choose, which does not mean that he forces us to choose in particular ways. He knows that we are fallible and will often err, but that does not mean that we are obliged to err: we could with the help of guidance take the right course, and this option is always available to us. The people of Thamud were guided but rejected it, and so they were punished, except for those who chose the right path and acted virtuously (41.17–18). At the same time as God tries to guide people, the devil does the opposite (22.4; 35.5) and so we are pulled between these two influences.

See also: **Ash'arites and Mu'tazilites; *jinn*; punishment; *qada'*; responsibility**

OLIVER LEAMAN

'ISA

The Qur'an is full of information about Mary, the mother of Jesus ('Isa) and the daugher of 'Imran. Mary receives God's spirit (*ruh*) in her womb, although she was chaste, like her mother (66.12; 19.29), and the child that she bears has no human father. Jesus is like Adam in that he was created by God and was not God's son. The idea that Jesus is the son of God is constantly countered by describing him as the son of Mary. He was only a mortal, sent to the Israelites in order to represent the Day of Judgement, as Jesus himself confirms in the Book. He is only an apostle, his role being to support the law and proclaim the arrival of another messenger to be called Ahmad. This is often taken to be a reference to Muhammad, the final prophet.

The 'death' of Jesus

The apparent death of Jesus and his Second Coming play a particularly interesting role in the Qur'an and in Islam. The text says, referring to the Jewish enemies of Jesus,

> And they made a move, and God made a move. And God is the best of those who make moves. ... When God said: 'O 'Isa, I am to take you in full and raise you towards myself, and cleanse you of those who disbelieve, and place those who follow you above those who disbelieve, up to the Day of Doom. Then you will all return to me, whereupon I shall judge between you on what has been a matter of dispute.' (3.54–55)

In these verses the miraculous event of the Ascension of Jesus Christ are discussed.

'And they made a move' refers to the evil designs of the Jews, who planned to arrest Jesus and to get him crucified. The next sentence ('and God made a move') refers to the plan designed by Allah to save his prophet 'Isa from their ill designs. They sent one of them to Jesus to arrest him and God changed that person's appearance totally, making him resemble Jesus. He raised Jesus to heaven, while the man who had been made to look like Jesus was crucified under the false identity, which was presumably rather unfortunate for him. But then he was an evil person for wishing to harm Jesus, so he was hoist by his own petard, as it were.

Some interpreters have denied that Jesus was saved or that he is alive in heaven and that he will descend to earth at the end of time, but the verses in the Qur'an are quite clear on this point. Let us begin with *wallahu khayrul makirin*, translated as 'and God is the best of those who make moves'. The word *makr* in Arabic denotes a subtle and secret move or plan. The Jews started working on a series of conspiracies and schemes against Jesus, going to the extent of convincing the ruler of the time that Jesus was guilty of some crime. The ruler thus ordered the arrest of Jesus. While this was the scene on one side, the subtle and secret move made by God undid their evil plan.

God said two things to comfort Jesus at the time when the Jews were intent on killing him. He said that his death would come not at their hands but that it would be a natural death. In order to rescue him from the evil designs of those people, God promised to raise Jesus to heaven. This explanation is what was reported by Ibn 'Abbas, as quoted by al-Suyuti in his *al-Durr al-Manthur* (Vol. 2: 36) on the authority of several narrators. The promise means that the saving of Jesus by raising him upwards would not

last forever; it would only be temporary, with Jesus then returning to the mortal world to prevail over the enemies of God at the appropriate time. Later on, death would come to him in a natural sort of way.

The 'divinity' of Jesus

Thus Jesus' return from heaven and his death after having established his victory in the world were not only miracles but also a consummation of the honour and integrity of Jesus. In addition to that, the unfounded Christian belief in the divinity of Jesus was also refuted. Had it not been so, the event of Jesus being raised towards the heavens alive would have further strengthened their false belief that he too was living and eternal like God. The reality is that disbelievers and polytheists have always been vehemently opposed to the prophets, and there are many accounts of this in the Qur'an.

The response of God when people do not believe in a prophet, even after having witnessed the miracles, is that either those people were destroyed through some natural calamity as was done with 'Ad and Thamud and the peoples of Lut and Salih, or Allah would instruct his prophet to leave and go elsewhere. In a new and safer place, somewhere perhaps where they received more support and found a friendlier audience, they were provided with such power and glory that they finally achieved victory against the original people to whom they were sent. For example, Ibrahim (Abraham) migrated from Iraq and sought refuge in Syria. Similarly, Musa (Moses) migrated from Egypt and came to Madyan. Finally, the Last Prophet, Muhammad, migrated from Mecca and came to Medina. It was from there that he finally attacked Mecca and conquered it. This raising of Jesus to the heavens to allow him to escape the threatening designs of the Jews was really an act of emigration in its own way, following which he would return to this world and achieve total victory over the Jews.

How do we know, though, that he was taken up to heaven? One might compare him with an example like that of Adam. Adam's birth differs from the normal birth of the rest of creation, in that he had no parents, and the birth of Jesus took a miraculous form different from the normal birth of human beings. His death is also unusual and will come about after hundreds of years following his return to the world. Why, then, should one be surprised if his emigration too follows a very different pattern from those applicable to everyone else?

A problem with the unusual events surrounding Jesus is that they led many Christians into mistakenly believing and declaring that Jesus was God. Yet if we observe what we are told about him in the Qur'an, we find clear proofs of his role as a human being subservient to God, his obedience to the divine order and his very human traits. It is for this reason that the Qur'an makes pointed reference to the refutation of belief in the divinity of Jesus on all such occasions. Yet it has to be said that the raising of Jesus to heaven would have made the Christian interpretation of Jesus even more plausible.

When God says *mutawaffika* ('I am to take you in full'), he points out his intention to save Jesus entirely from the devices of his enemies, but says nothing about any putative divine status that Jesus may have. Jesus is never called some sort of God who is never to die, with the implication being that a time will come when he too will meet his death. In his *Tafsir*, al-Razi has said that the arrangement of words in sentences in the Qur'an such that an event due later is mentioned first while an event due earlier is placed after that is a very potent form of expression (*al-Tafsir al-Kabir*, Vol. 2: 48).

The raising of Jesus

The second part of the sentence ('I shall raise you towards myself') emphasizes that Jesus has a body. Jesus is not the name of just a spirit, but of a spirit and a body. Interpreting the raising of Jesus in the sense that the act of raising was spiritual only, and not physical, is therefore erroneous. As far as the word, *raf* (raising) is concerned, there are occasions when it is also used to indicate the raising of ranks, as in the following verses of the Qur'an: *Rafa'a ba'dakum fawqa ba'din darajatin* ('and raised some of you in ranks over others') (6.165); *yarfa'illahullazina amanu minkum wallazina utul'ilma* ('and Allah will raise up in rank those of you who believe and those who have been given knowledge') (58.11).

Although it is obvious that the word *raf*, in the sense of the raising of rank or status, has been used figuratively in the context of these verses, there is no reason here to think that the verb can only be used figuratively. Moreover, by using the word *ila* (towards) along with the word *raf* at this particular place, the possibility of such a figurative meaning has been rejected. What is said in this verse is *rafi'uka ilayya* ('I shall raise you towards myself') and there is no reason to think it is not meant literally.

There is also the verse from the *sura al-Nisa* (4.157), which refutes the belief of the Jews; what is said here is *wa ma qataluhu yaqinan barrafa'ahullahu ilayhi*: that is, they certainly did not kill Jesus, rather God raised him towards himself. This later expression is used to mean the raising of the spirit and the body.

God's promises to Jesus

God made five promises to Jesus. The first promise was that his death would not come at the hands of the Jews: it would be a natural death, coming at its appointed time, and that appointed time would come close to the Day of Judgement. Then 'Isa will come down from heaven to earth, as reported in detail in sound *ahadith*, transmitted through unbroken chains. There are many such *ahadith*, and they are a particularly important source of information about Jesus.

The second promise was to raise Jesus to heaven and so save him from violent death at the hands of his enemies. This happened as it was supposed to and his fate is a test for believers (4.159): those who think he died and those who think he died and was raised from the dead are both wrong.

The third promise was *wa mutahhiruka minallazina kafaru* – that is, to have him cleansed of false accusations brought against him by his enemies. That promise was fulfilled when someone of the status of the Prophet Muhammad refuted all the false accusations of the Jews. For instance, the Jews slandered Jesus' parentage because of his having been born without a father. The Qur'an refuted this slander by declaring that he was born without a father because such was the power and will of Allah. We should not be surprised at this: after all, Adam was born with neither father nor mother, and anything that God sets out to do he accomplishes. Indeed, the Qur'an is replete with examples of the extraordinary things God can accomplish. The Jews also accused Jesus of claiming to be God. There are many verses in the Qur'an in which, contrary to this accusation, Jesus is reported to have publicly confessed his being human and a servant and bondsman of God.

The fourth promise appears in 'and placed those who follow you above those who disbelieve', which means that his followers will be made to overcome those who deny and oppose him. This promise was fulfilled in the sense that the belief in and confession of the prophethood of 'Isa are accepted by both Christians and Muslims. This does not necessarily mean that both Christians and Muslims will find salvation, though, since salvation in the hereafter depends on believing in all the teachings of 'Isa. The Christians did not accept that they should believe and have faith in the last of the prophets who would come after Jesus had departed. The Christians did not follow this instruction in matters of faith and belief, therefore they may have deprived themselves of salvation; Muslims, meanwhile, acted in accordance with 'Isa's real words and intentions, and so can confidently expect to be rewarded eventually. An interpretation of the promise that relates to having a dominant position over the Jews is connected to the prophethood of 'Isa. Christians and Muslims have always been in power with respect to the Jews, and always will be, right up to the Day of Judgement.

The fifth promise, that of giving a decision in respect of such conflicts in faith on the Day of Judgement, will certainly be fulfilled at its appointed time. The Jews are the only people in the world who say that 'Isa was crucified, killed and buried, following which he never returned to life. What happened is reported in the *sura al-Nisa* in the Qur'an: God outwitted the enemies of 'Isa by changing a person to look just like him; it was this person that they killed. The words of the verse (4.157) are as follows: 'And they did not kill him and they did not crucify him, but they were taken in by appearance.'

The Christians, by contrast, say that Jesus was killed on the cross but was brought back to life once again and raised to heaven. The same Qur'anic verse refutes this notion as well. It is said here that, like the Jews who rejoiced after their co-religionist was killed, the Christians fell victim to the same mistaken belief in the identity of the crucified individual and believed that it was Jesus who was killed on the cross. The statement *shubbiha lahum* ('they were fooled by appearance') reveals a lack of faith in the Christians just as it does in the Jews, since even the Christians did not acknowledge that God would never allow one of his prophets to suffer death at the hands of his enemies.

The Islamic view of the fate of Jesus

As opposed to the view of these two groups, there is the Islamic belief, clearly stated in this verse and in several others, that God raised Jesus alive to heaven in order to rescue him from the Jews. He was not killed and he was not crucified, which would have been a very inappropriate end for a prophet. Rather, he is alive in heaven today and will return on the Day of Judgement to lead the Muslims to victory over the Jews. That accomplished, Jesus will eventually die a natural death. There is a consensus across the Muslim community on this belief.

This belief stands proved on the authority of several verses of the Qur'an and various reports from *mutawatir ahadith* that have been transmitted along an unbroken chain. In *sura al-'Imran*, there is a reference to past prophets and to the prophets Adam, Nuh, the family of Ibrahim and the family of 'Imran in a single verse (3.33). After that, nearly three sections and twenty-two verses refer to Jesus and his family in meticulous detail – something which does not happen even in respect of the last of the prophets to whom the Qur'an was revealed.

The detail of the Qur'anic account

The Qur'an offers a detailed description of the grandmother of Jesus, her pledge, the birth of his mother, her name, her upbringing, the conceiving of Jesus by his mother then the detailed narrative of his birth, followed by the description of what his mother ate and drank, the birth of the child, her return to the family with the newborn child, their abuse and curses, the miraculous gift of eloquence to the newborn, then his growing up and calling to his people, the opposition he faced and the help given to him by his disciples. We also hear of the hostile attempts by the Jews to trap and kill Jesus, his being raised alive to heaven, and then complete details of his attributes, his appearance, his physique, his clothes and so on. Such detail is not provided by the Qur'an and *hadith* in respect of any other prophet or messenger. This point is an open invitation to everyone to think about why this should be the case and what the meaning behind it might be. It could certainly be argued that the detailed information about Jesus and his background is so stressed because of the need to provide guidance for those who were going to have to cope with directing their lives after the death of the last prophet.

The significance of Jesus and the Day of Judgement

People need guidance right through to the Day of Judgement. Jesus plays a large role in the events leading up to that day, and the *ahadith* go into great detail on how to identity those who would be worthy of the community's following and support when judgement is at issue.

The community must also be careful of those who would like to lead them astray. Among those who were to come after the Prophet the most notorious is the Dajjal, the Antichrist or false Messiah, whose wickedness is so effective and compelling. Therefore, the Prophet related many details of his character, how he will operate and his distinguishing marks, so that there remains no room for the community to doubt about his dangerous nature whenever he appears. Similarly, among the positive figures in religion, Jesus is the most distinguished of those blessed by God with the role of prophecy. God kept him alive in the heavens to come to the rescue of the Muslim community during the wicked period of the Dajjal, having appointed him to kill the Dajjal at a time close to the Day of Judgement. This is why it was deemed necessary that the community should be given very clear indications of his person and qualities as well, so that no human being remains in doubt of the identity of Jesus when he comes on the second occasion: after all, if people cannot identify him, they will not be able to support him. Although Jesus will not come into the world at that time as a prophet, he will come to lead the Muslim community as the *khalifa* (vicegerent) of the Prophet. So the account in the Qur'an, together with the *ahadith*, is taken to provide a blueprint for Jesus' role at the end of the world, and as providing indications for Muslims regarding how they are to recognize him and to prepare for supporting him.

Further reading

Khalidi, T. (2001) *The Muslim Jesus*, Cambridge: Cambridge University Press.

Ridgeon, L. (2000) *Islamic Interpretations of Christianity*, New York: St Martin's Press.

Robinson, N. (1991) *Christ in Islam and Christianity: The representation of Jesus in the Qur'an and the classical Muslim commentaries*, London: Macmillan.

See also: **Dajjal**

OLIVER LEAMAN

ISAAC

Isaac was the second son of Abraham by his wife Sarah, father of Jacob. In Arabic his name is Ishaq, and he is referred to in the Qur'an seventeen times. The root of his name is *sahaqa* (to crush) or *zhaka* (to make fun). The Qur'an does not say which son was the potential victim of the sacrifice ordered by God, but it is generally believed by Muslims not to have been Isaac, but rather Ishmael.

OLIVER LEAMAN

ISHAQ

see: **Isaac**

ISHMAEL

see: **Isma'il**

'ISHQ

'Ishq and the related verb *'ashiqa* are used in Arabic to describe intense and passionate love, an extreme case of *hubb/muhabba* (love). Neither *'ishq* nor *'ashiqa* appear in the Qur'an, but certain descriptions of Jacob (Ya'qub) and the wife of 'Aziz that appear in the twelfth *sura* (12.23–24 and 30–32 regarding the wife of 'Aziz; 12.84–86 and 94–96 regarding Jacob) allow us to qualify them as *'ushshaq* (passionate lovers) of Joseph. Most opinions on the topic are based on esoteric Sufi interpretations, in particular those offered by representatives of the so-called *madhhab 'ishq* (school of love).

Etymology and usage in the *hadith*

An extreme case of *hubb/muhabba*, *'ishq* is generally perceived by the Arabs as something immoderate. It is often regarded as a kind of *junun* (madness) that is greeted by neither approval nor disapproval. Traditional Islamic medicine treats 'ishq as a mental disease caused by seeing something extremely beautiful.

To highlight the etymological connotations and properties of 'ishq, Arab lexicographers related it to 'ashaqa (ivy, formally *Hedera helix*), which is a climbing plant that twines itself round the tree so tightly that it allegedly either makes the latter dry or leaves on it an indelible mark.

Insofar as 'ishq implies immoderation, it is an undesirable characteristic for a Muslim: Allah is known not to like the immoderate (6.141; 7.31). To the extent that the substance of the message of the Qur'an consists of threat and promise, it deals with uncontrollable and overwhelming powers like 'ishq only accidentally.

'Ishq appears in a number of *hadith* (traditions). In one of them, which apparently alludes to the *hubb 'udhri* (chaste love) for which the Banu 'Udhra tribe that inhabited Yemen were famous, a pure secret love for a human being is compared to martyrdom. Some *hadith* talk about a love between God and man that is believed to originate in *dhikr* (remembrance). Certain Meccans – contemporaries of Muhammad – described the Prophet's attitude to his *rabb* (lord) exactly as 'ishq.

Sura Joseph

Sura Joseph is, by and large, the only chapter of the Qur'an in which the issue of 'ishq comes to the surface of the text. The wife of an Egyptian nobleman 'Aziz (known by the later tradition as Zulaykha) and Joseph's father Jacob both passionately love Joseph. However, the character of their love is very different: Jacob's love is deep, wise and unselfish; the love of the wife of 'Aziz is intense and violent, lacking the depth and wisdom

that Jacob has achieved through suffering and self-renunciation.

The exact words used to describe the feeling of the wife of 'Aziz are *shaghafaha hubban* (Joseph 'filled her with love') (12.30). This expression, paradoxically, shows her as the victim of Joseph's beauty; this impression is later supported by the scene of Egyptian ladies cutting their hands at the sight of Joseph. In the case of the wife of 'Aziz, 'ishq appears as an uncontrollable and irresistible force that overwhelms the human being. This force is generated by contemplation of absolute and divine beauty as it appears in a particular created form (another human being).

In a way, the wife of 'Aziz imitates Allah, described in the famous *hadith* as 'beautiful' and 'loving beauty' (see, for example, Muslim 1915: Iman 147). In the Sufi tradition, the wife of 'Aziz is regarded as an epitome of worshippers of beauty, contemplating the divine beauty in its earthly manifestations.

As for Jacob, Joseph is said to be *ahabb* (more loved) (12.8) by him than Jacob loved his other sons. After Joseph's disappearance, Jacob loses his eyesight out of grief over Joseph. Taking Joseph's disappearance as Allah's trial sent to test his god-wariness and patience, Jacob nonetheless never believes his son is dead. In return for his patience, Allah gives him a deep spiritual intuition that can be described as 'irfani (mystical) by its nature: when Jacob's sons leave Egypt, carrying with them Joseph's shirt, Jacob immediately feels the aroma of Joseph, although the caravan is still hundreds of miles away. When the messenger bringing the shirt arrives and casts it over Jacob's face (12.96), the old man regains his eyesight.

Judging by its effects (infallible spiritual intuition and powerful grief), Jacob's love for Joseph is a much deeper feeling than that of the wife of 'Aziz: the sufferings of separation give the lover a spiritual wisdom that cannot be acquired by mere worship of beauty.

Both stories (that of Jacob and that of 'Aziz's wife) contain some of the most mystical passages of the Qur'an. As such, they have been subject to (attempts at) symbolic interpretation almost since the beginning of the exegetic tradition in Islam. However, the first commentaries attempting to read the entire Qur'an as the Scripture of 'Ishq did not appear before the beginning of the twelfth century CE.

Sufi exegesis: the Qur'an as the Scripture of 'Ishq

To read the Qur'an in its entirety as the Scripture of 'Ishq, one needs to adopt a particular methodological approach and master a number of special techniques (such as repeating a phrase aloud many times) that allow the reader to distance himself from the outward and literal meaning of the text and to approach insead its hidden and esoteric sense.

It is known that such early Sufi masters as Dhu'l Nun al-Misri (d. 246/861), Junayd (d. 298/910), Shibli (d. 334/946), Hallaj (d. 309/922) and, in particular, Nuri (d. 295/907), who called himself 'ashiq Allah (the lover of Allah), employed the word 'ishq in their discourses. It is also used by Ibn al-'Arabi (d. 638/1240) and other great Arab Sufis of the later period. However, 'ishq never came to be regarded as the most crucial concept of Sufism in the Arabic milieu, as happened in the Persian environment. The notion of immoderation and exceeding the bounds of courtesy that is implicit in 'ishq seems to have held some special appeal for the Persian mentality, famous for its aesthetic attitude to life and love of beauty.

No doubt these features of Iranian national character put their stamp on Persian Sufism, which explicitly prefers 'ishq to hubb/muhabba or any other related concept. While the word itself may seldom appear in the sayings and writings of the Khorasan school of Sufism before the second half of the eleventh century CE, the notion of 'ishq is unmistakeably present there.

During the twelfth century there appeared a number of treatises in Persian which conceptualized the doctrine of 'ishq, among them Sawanih (Inspirations) by Ahmad Ghazali (d. 520/1126), the Tamhidat (Prolegomena) by 'Ayn al-Qudat Hamadani (d. 525/1131) and Abhar al-'ashiqin (The Yellow Narcissus of Lovers) by Ruzbehan Baqli (522–606/1128–1209). Together with the poetical works of Farid al-Din 'Attar (d. 618/1221) and Jalal al-Din Rumi (d. 672/1273), and perhaps the Flashes (Lama'at) of Fakhr al-Din 'Iraqi (d. 688/1289), they constitute the corpus of key texts of the so-called madhhab 'ishq (the School of Love) – a phenomenon that, regardless of its somewhat elusive properties, is believed to constitute the main current of Persian (and probably Turkish) Sufism.

Among the published and relatively easily available Sufi commentaries, at least three works explicitly represent the approach of the School of Love in treating the Qur'an in its entirety as the Scripture of 'Ishq. These are Kashf al-asrar wa 'uddat al-abrar (Unveiling of the Secrets and Equipment of the Devout) by Rashid al-Din Maybudi (d. after 520/1126), 'Ara'is al-bayan fi haqa'iq al-Qur'an (The Brides of Explication concerning the Hidden Realities of the Qur'an) by Ruzbehan Baqli and, specifically on the sura Joseph, Bahr al-muhabba fi asrar al-mawadda (The Sea of Love concerning the Secrets of Affectionate Friendship) by Ahmad Ghazali. Such treatises as Ruzbehan Baqli's Abhar al-'ashiqin and 'Ayn al-Qudat

Hamadani's *Tamhidat* can themselves be regarded as introductions to symbolic commentary on the Qur'an.

'Ushshaq as Allah's chosen people: the Covenant of 'Ishq

Although the Sufis who represented the School of Love regarded the entire Qur'an as a textbook of 'ishq, they believed that a number of words and phrases in it conveyed the 'ushshaq, specific messages that served as passwords providing access to its most hidden meanings. Among such expressions, the oft-cited phrase *fa sawfa ya'ti Allah bi qawm yuhibbuhum wa yuhibbunahu* ('Allah will bring forth a people whom He loves and who love Him') (5.54) was considered to be of particular importance. (Even though, when read in the context of the relevant verse, *habba* corresponds to a slightly emphasized 'like', falling short of the intensity of love, in this instance the term seems to be close to 'ashiqa.)

The phrase is outwardly part of the warning that Muhammad, on behalf of Allah, gives to some of his unsteady followers, telling them that Allah can easily replace the apostates with people who are worthier. At this moment, the replacement is only a possibility: the would-be substitutes have apparently not yet been brought into existence. (Probably it is hoped that the wavering followers will themselves assume the characteristics of their possible substitutes.)

Sufi writers (Maybudi, for example) typically take the promise of replacement as ready cash, assigning the latter role to themselves. The description 'a people whom He loves and who love Him', in its broader sense, can be attributed to every creature insofar as it perceives itself as an object of Allah's love and, simultaneously, as his lover. However, in a narrower sense, it is commonly applied to accomplished 'urafa (mystics) who have forsaken this world and the hereafter for the sake of the Beloved – that is, Allah – thus realizing fully the principle of *tawhid* (unification, worshipping one god).

It did not escape the notice of Sufi authors that *yuhibbuhum wa yuhibbunahu* implies some sort of *walaya* (guardianship or patron–client relationship) between both sides. The Sufis believe that this *walaya* manifests itself in Allah's beloved as replacement of their bad character traits with good ones (hence the *abdal*, meaning substitutes or replaced ones, is one of several strata in the Sufi hierarchy of sainthood, although the term is sometimes applied to Sufi saints in general), and placing them under Allah's coat, as a result of which they remain unknown to all but Him.

The Sufis claim that the relationship of mutual love between Allah and man was established in pre-eternity, before the material creation of human beings, in the so-called *'ahd alast* ('Am I not' covenant) (7.172). The content of the oft-cited 'covenant' verse, which has been subject to a great number of *batini* (esoteric, but not necessarily Sufi) interpretations, is outwardly limited to an unequivocal affirmation of the eternal and unalterable *rabb–'abd* (lord–servant) relationship between both sides. The followers of the school of love typically read the *rabb* as *ma'shuq/mahbub* (beloved) and the *'abd* as *'ashiq/muhibb* (lover). Thus a solemn testimony to Allah's full authority over his subject was turned into a passionate pronouncement of the lover's *fana* (annihilation) in the beloved. Maybudi, for instance, quotes his teacher 'Abdallah Ansari (d. 481/1088) saying that 'the torrent of lordship was given authority over the dust of servanthood' (Maybudi, 1952, Vol. 3: 795). The *fana*, however, brings the lover to *baqa* (subsistence) in the beloved. In keeping with the terms of the covenant of love, Allah appoints the human being to be the keeper of his *amana* (trust) (33.72). Hence the difference between the general objective of Islam and the goal of Sufism, as it is represented by the School of Love, becomes evident: if the former, in its practical dimension, is supposed to provide means for putting into effect the treaty settled between lord and servant, Sufi practice is aimed precisely at the implementation of the covenant of love that was concluded in pre-eternity between the beloved and the lover.

References and further reading

Ghazali, Ahmad (1986) *Inspirations (Sawanih)*, trans. N. Pourjavady, London: KPI.

Maybudi, R. (1952) *Kashf al-asrar wa 'uddat al-abrar* (Unveiling of the Secrets and Equipment of the Devout), Tehran: Daneshghah.

Muslim (1915) *Al-Sahih*, Cairo: Matba'a Muhammad 'Ali Sabih.

Murata, S. and Chittick, W.C. (1994) *The Wisdom of Islam*, New York: Paragon House, 309–12.

Schimmel, A. (1975) *Mystical Dimensions of Islam*, Chapel Hill, NC: University of North Carolina Press, 107–21.

See also: baqa; **Bilqis; servant;** *shahada*; *tawhid*; **Zulaykha**

YANIS ESHOTS

ISLAM

Islam is an Arabic word meaning submission, in this context to the will of God (Allah), and denotes the name of the religion that was initiated with Adam and finally revived with the last revelation to the Last Prophet, Muhammad (c.570–632 CE), through the Archangel Gabriel in the form of the Qur'an over twenty years. The followers of this religion are called Muslims, not Muhammadans as was in the past sometimes mistakenly assumed in the West (by extrapolation from the naming of Christians after Christ). Islam covers every aspect of life, social, political, economic, ethical and so on.

Lexically, the word *islam* is derived from the verb *salima, yaslamu, salama* or *salam*, probably from the same Semitic origin as the Hebrew term *shalom*. It means:

1. to be safe and sound, unharmed, unimpaired;
2. to be unobjectionable, blameless, faultless;
3. to be certain, established;
4. to preserve, keep from injury;
5. to keep the peace, make one's peace;
6. to forsake, leave;
7. to get, obtain;
8. to become reconciled with one another, make peace with one another; and
9. to surrender, capitulate, submit, abandon.

With its different derivatives, such as *aslama, salam, muslimun* and *muslimin*, the term occurs 138 times in the Qur'an.

Islam itself is repeated eight times in the form of verbal noun. Of the eight, in three places (6.125; 39.22; 61.7) it is used as Islam alone and in two places with a pronoun as *islamakum* (your submission) (49.17) and as *islamihim* (their Islam, surrender) (9.74). The Islams in 6.125 and 39.22 are particularly significant from a theological perspective, for they seem to imply that while Allah opens up some people's hearts and eases their way to Islam, others are led astray. Hence in 6.125 Allah declares that:

> Whomever Allah wants to guide, He opens his heart up to Islam, and whomever He wants to lead astray, He makes his heart extremely constricted, as though he were ascending to heaven. Thus Allah

inflicts His punishment upon those who do not believe.

In 39.22 Allah states that 'He whose heart Allah has opened to Islam shall receive light from his Lord. But woe to those whose hearts are hardened against the remembrance of Allah! Truly, they are in the grossest error.' Nevertheless, considered with other verses, the orthodox view maintains that these verses are not indications of people being predestined to either heaven or hell, but rather human beings have free will to choose whichever path they want to follow.

The connotation of the remaining three appearances (3.19, 85; 5.3) is very important, for they occur concomitantly with the noun religion (din). The classical exegetes almost unanimously take these references to be the definite proofs that the Qur'anic usage of religion always refers to Islam, without which no human being can attain salvation. Sura 3.19 reads 'The [true] religion with Allah is Islam'; 3.85 declares that 'Whoever seeks a religion other than Islam, it will never be accepted of him, and in the Herafter he will be one of the losers'; and, finally, 5.3 concludes the prophetic message in these words: 'Today, I have perfected your religion for you, completed My grace on you and approved Islam as a religion for you.' The majority of Muslims believe that, according to these verses, for anyone to attain salvation they must be a Muslim. This is, one can say, the Muslim equivalent of the Christian doctrine *extra ecclesiam nulla salus* (outside the Church, there is no salvation).

However, there is currently a debate among Islamic scholars who differentiate between the wider, literal meaning of *islam* as submission to the will of God (and its noun form *muslim*, a submitter) and the colloquial use of it in a limited sense as the name of the institutionalized religion Islam (and its noun form, as commonly known, Muslim). In its wider meaning, any of the world religions can be called *islam* and their followers *muslim*, both without capitals, whereas the capitalised Islam and Muslim denote the common understandings and usages.

Basic beliefs

It should be noted that Islam is closely connected with *iman* (faith). The common understanding is that belief in Islam is undertaken first by accepting the basics of *iman* and then by performing the Five Pillars of Islam. However, a contrasting view in 49.14 implies a reverse order:

> The wandering Arabs say: 'We believe.' Say: 'You believe not, but rather say "We submit", for the faith has not yet entered into your hearts.'

Nevertheless, by following the common understanding that faith precedes Islam, these are the universally accepted basics of *iman*: First and foremost is belief in the unity of God (*tawhid*), which is also emphasized as the First Pillar of Islam in the form of *shahada*. God is one and has no associates, and all people should form a united body (*umma*) both in belief and practice. Second is the belief in angels, who are heavenly bodies in the service of God. There are four archangels: Jibril (Gabriel), Mika'il (Michael), Israfil and Azra'il. Shaytan (Satan) or Iblis was known to be an archangel before it was eternally condemned due to its refusal to bow down in front of Adam. Third come the Holy Scriptures, which are believed to have been initiated with the first revelation to Adam and ended with the last revelation to Muhammad. The Qur'an is the last, definitive and true revelation that contains and affirms the eternal reality while amending the falsities that have been insinuated into previous scriptures. Fourth is the prophets, whose exact numbers cannot be known for certain; what is known is that the first was Adam and the last was Muhammad. All have been proclaiming the religion of God, which is generically called Islam. In this sense there has always been only one true religion and that is Islam. Fifth is belief in the Day of Judgement, which will be announced with a horn blast by the angel Israfil, bringing everything to an end and resurrecting the dead. Everybody will be questioned by God and, according to one's deeds, either rewarded with heaven or punished with hell. The last component of faith are the *qada* (Divine Decree) and *qadar* (Predestination). These may seem fatalistic at first sight but tradition holds that they are consistent with free will and human responsibility, for God's divine foreknowledge neither necessitates an event happening nor annuls our ability to act freely.

The Five Pillars

The Five Pillars of Islam are the five basic duties that every devout, sincere Muslim is expected to perform, as explained in an authentic saying of the Prophet. The first requirement for one to come under to the umbrella of Islam is to say *shahada*. This is actually a testimony to the oneness of God and the prophethood of Muhammad, put forward in a traditional format as: 'There is no god but God (Allah) and Muhammad is the messenger of God (Allah)' (*La ilaha illa Allah, Muhammad rasul Allah*). The Second Pillar is *salat*, the prescribed prayers carried out five times a day – at dawn, noon, mid-afternoon, sunset and night, all of which can be performed either in congregation or alone. One must face the Holy *Ka'ba* while praying and be clean ritually. Ritual purity can be obtained either by a minor or a major ablution. There are other prayers for other occasions, such as feasts, funerals and on Friday. Of these, the last is the most important, not only religiously but also politically: involving a sermon, Friday prayers can only be performed congregationally. The Third Pillar, *zakat*, is usually described as the annual taxation of one's excess wealth at certain rates for different valuables. It is considered a form of social welfare programme, by which wealth is redistributed and the accumulation of wealth in the hands of a small elite prevented. It is also seen as a ritual purification of one's wealth. Although the allocation of the *zakat* is prescribed in the Qur'an, the Companions of the Prophet showed that it was open to new interpretations. The Fourth Pillar is *sawm*, that is, fasting during the Holy Month of Ramadan from dawn to dusk by abstaining from eating, drinking, smoking and sexual intercourse. A light meal is recommended just before dawn to provide people with some strength for the day. The Fifth Pillar is *hajj*, which brings both bodily efforts and material sources together, and is the culmination in a Muslim's life, after which it became a custom to add to one's name the title of *hajji*. It is the pilgrimage to the Holy Shrine *Ka'ba* in the city of Mecca, to be performed once in a lifetime, provided one has the means to do so. Regardless of the circumstances, rich or poor, healthy or ill, Muslims usually perform it even if they end up borrowing money to do so. The social and psychological effects of *hajj* on a Muslim are highly significant for, despite the fact that they all come from separate nations, one perhaps for the first time enjoys the feeling of belonging to an *umma*.

Some consider *jihad* to be the Sixth Pillar, but this can hardly be verified. Originally it was taken to mean any holy struggle in the way of God, though, especially after the nineteenth century, *jihad* was portrayed as the holy war against the evil plans of the West towards the Islamic world. But this is a misconception: holy war is an insignificant part of the *jihad* concept, for Muhammad considers holy war to be the lesser *jihad*. The greater *jihad* takes place in a Muslim's inner self and represents the struggle to do good and abstain from evil in all circumstances.

The past and the present

Early on in his life Muhammad used to like seclusion in the cave of Hira, practising with what was known as the *hanif* tradition, which had been handed down from the prophet Abraham. There in Hira he is reported to have started receiving his first call as the Prophet with the first revelations as 'recite' in 610 CE. He was startled and came home shaking. His wife Khadija took him to her uncle Waraqa, who confirmed his true mission as the Prophet but did not live long enough to see it made public. Muhammad conveyed his message to the polytheistic people of Mecca, who vehemently opposed him. When the persecution there became unbearable in 622 CE, he permitted his followers to emigrate to Medina (previously Yathrib), to which city he had been invited by the leaders of the tribes of Aws and Khazraj. This event is called *Hijra* and marks the beginning of the Muslim lunar calendar. In Medina, Muhammad established a brotherhood between the newcomers from Mecca (Muhajirun) and the host people of Medina (Ansar) that transformed the *umma* into a well-organized community out of which came the first Muslim state. They conquered Mecca, without bloodshed, in 628 CE. After Muhammad's passing away in 632 CE, Abu Bakr was chosen as the first *khalifa* (caliph). He was succeeded by 'Umar, 'Uthman and then 'Ali, but the order of succession to Muhammad eventually led to sectarian division within Islam. The Sunnis, who form the majority, hold that Muhammad did not specifically leave any successor and consequently this was the order agreed upon by the *umma*. But the Shi'a, Islam's biggest minority group, believe that Muhammad recommended 'Ali, who was the obvious successor as his son-in-law and the Prophet's closest surviving blood relative, as *khalifa*. In their opinion, 'Ali was robbed of his right to lead the *umma*. The Shi'a have many different subsects, of which the Isma'ilis and the Imami, also known as the Twelvers and the largest Shi'ite community, are the best known. The expansion of Islam was exceptionally fast, considering there were believers everywhere from the Atlantic on one side to China on the other within a century of Muhammad's death.

Today, at the start of the twenty-first century CE, the number of Muslims worldwide is estimated at about a billion. Despite the ending of the caliphate with the collapse of the Ottoman Empire, Islam is still a mighty force to be reckoned with and one of the biggest contenders for world power today. In the face of advancing European expansion through imperialism, there have been several revivalist thinkers and resistance movements. Famous among them are Jamal al-Din al-Afghani, Muhammad 'Abdu, Rashid Rida, Sayyid Ahmad Khan, Muhammad Iqbal, Fazlur Rahman, the Jama'at-i Islami, the Muslim Brotherhood and Tablighi Jama'at. Despite their successful efforts in formulating original versions of orthodox Islam, an authentic Muslim life able to face the encounter with Western modernity without losing its identity remains to be established.

Further reading

Ahmed, A.S. (1988) *Discovering Islam: Making sense of Muslim history and society*, London: Routledge.
—— (1992) *Postmodernism and Islam*, New York: Routledge.
Ahmed, L. (1992) *Women and Gender in Islam*, New Haven, CT: Yale University Press.
Al-Baghadi, 'Abd al-Qahir (1928) *Usul al-din*, Istanbul: Matba'at al-dawla.
Esposito, J.L. (1991) *Islam, The Straight Path*, New York: Oxford University Press.
—— (ed.) (1995) *Oxford Encyclopedia of the Modern Islamic World*, New York: Oxford University Press.
al-Fasi, 'A. (1963) *Maqasid al-shari'a al-Islamiyya wa makarimuha*, Casablanca: Maktabat al-wahada al-'arabiyya.
Hodgson, M.G.S. (1974) *The Venture of Islam*, Chicago, IL: University of Chicago Press.
Hourani, A. (1982) *Arabic Thought in the Liberal Age 1798–1939*, Cambridge: Cambridge University Press.
Hourani, G. (1971) *Islamic Rationalism*, Oxford: Clarendon Press.
Johansen, B. (1999) *Contingency in a Sacred Law*, Leiden: E.J. Brill.
Lapidus, I. (1990) *A History of Islamic Societies*, New York: Cambridge University Press.
Lewis, B. (1993) *Islam and the West*, New York: Oxford University Press.
Makdisi, G. (1965) *Arabic and Islamic Studies in Honor of Hamilton A. R. Gibb*, Leiden: E.J. Brill.
Rahman, F. (1966) *Islam*, London and New York: Oxford University Press.
—— (1982) *Islam and Modernity: Transformation of an intellectual tradition*, Chicago, IL: University of Chicago Press.
Tibi, B. (1988) *Crisis of Modern Islam*, trans. J. von Sivers, Salt Lake City, UT: University Press.
Turabi, H. (1980) *Tajdid usul al-fiqh*, Rabat: Dar al-qarafi li'l nashr wa-tawzi.
Voll, J.O. (1994) *Islam, Continuity, and Change in the Modern World*, 2nd edn, Syracuse, NY: Syracuse University Press.
Wensinck, A. (1979) *The Muslim Creed*, Cambridge: Cambridge University Press.

RIFAT ATAY

ISLAMIC RENAISSANCE
see: Nahda

'ISM / 'ISMA

The theological concept of *'isma* (immunity from sin) is variously defined. It can refer to the *imams*, to prophets in general or only to Muhammad; it can involve full impeccability or merely the inability to persist in error (Ahmed, 1998: 87); it can encompass God-given protection from committing major sins, sins that carry a legal penalty, minor sins or slips; and it can be held to take force only after a call to mission or for the full period of someone's life. As a doctrine, it is espoused, to a greater or lesser extent, by both Shi'a and Sunni.

Although the concept *per se* is not explicitly mentioned in the Qur'an, theologians adduce a number of Qur'anic verses in their elucidation of this phenomenon. Within the Ash'ari tradition, for instance, Fakhr al-Din al-Razi (d. 1209 CE) commences his treatment of *'isma* in *Kitab al-Arba'in fi usul al-din* with a consensual definition of the term as meaning 'immunity from disbelief and innovation (*bid'a*)', a position accepted, he states, by all bar the Khawarij and, on the basis of *taqiyya* (dissimulation), the Rawafid. He also mentions the absolute inability of prophets to misrepresent God's revelations and laws, and disputed infallibility issues related to the delivery of *fatwa* (legal judgement). The bulk of Razi's discussion of the concept is, however, centred on the level of fallibility in a prophet's private life and, in support of the Ash'ari majority position of infallibility from major and minor sins (except through inadvertence) for the period of their mission, Razi cites 33.32 and 33.30, which indicate the special status of the Prophet's wives; 49.6 paired with 2.143, on the basis that Muhammad could not bear witness concerning his community were prophets themselves not trustworthy; 33.57, which would render impossible the mandatory rebuke of prophets for any sin they might commit; 3.31, which would, nonsensically, oblige us to imitate Muhammad in any sinful behaviour; 72.23 and 11.18, which would, again illogically, mean that any fallible prophet could be destined for hell; 61.2, 2.44 and 11.88, all of which suggest that prophets behave in accordance with the dictates they preach; 21.90, another clear indicator of prophetic good behaviour; 38.47, 22.75, 3.33, 2.130, 7.144 and 38.45, which all state that prophets are specially selected and chosen by God, with 35.32 in turn showing how these chosen ones are placed in a class apart, and so on. Razi also briefly concerns himself with the impeccability of the angels, structuring his argument around 16.50, 21.20, the latter part of 21.26 and 21.27, and 35.1 coupled with the middle section of 6.124, before moving on to a more detailed discussion of, for instance, such borderline angelic figures as Iblis, and Harut and Marut.

The rest of Razi's treatment of infallibility deals at length with the specific cases of Adam, Noah, Abraham, Jacob, Joseph, Job, Shu'ayb, Moses, David as an individual, David and Solomon, Solomon as an individual, Jonah, Lot, Zechariah, Jesus, and Muhammad. A complex theological argument is drawn, for instance, around the issue of Joseph's sinlessness (al-Razi, 1303: 45–9). After a brief discussion of Joseph's period of servitude and the matter of why Joseph didn't reveal himself as a prophet at that time, Razi addresses issues related to 12.24. He argues first that those involved bore witness to Joseph's purity and innocence; the husband in 12.28–29, the witness in 12.27, the women in 12.51, Joseph himself in 12.27, 12.33 and 12.52, Zulaykha in 12.32 and 12.51, God in 12.23 and 12.24, and Iblis in 38.82–83, which Razi connects to Joseph via 12.24. He then discusses whether Joseph's desire was an urge to forcibly push Zulaykha away, prevented by God as that might have brought upon Joseph the anger of her people, and whether the grammar of 12.24, on the basis of 28.10, can be taken to suggest that he did not in fact come to feel any such desire. The next topic to be addressed is 12.53, which Razi reads as referring to the nature of temptation rather than any determination on Joseph's part to do wrong, followed by 12.33, concerning which Razi discusses whether this can be interpreted as some sort of rebellion. The placing of the drinking-cup in Benjamin's baggage (12.70) is explained as possibly being God's command; the accusation of thievery in the same verse as maybe not being on Joseph's orders, as perhaps referring to the theft of Joseph from his father, or as being a question rather than an accusation. The final questions discussed by Razi are the matter of why Joseph didn't immediately allay his father's anxiety (maybe he was again acting on God's command) and the issue of his parents' prostration (to God and not in fact to Joseph) in 12.100.

Another perspective on Joseph's infallibility is supplied within the Imami Shi'i tradition, which declares prophets and *imams* to be free of all sin, both before and after their call to mission (cf. al-Sharif al-Murtada, 1988: 2). Al-Sharif al-Murtada (d. 1044) also utilises several Qur'anic passages, along with a number of linguistic arguments, in his discussion of Joseph. Again, he deals first with questions connected with how Joseph could have endured, and how God could have permitted Joseph to undergo, a period of servitude, then with the matter of Potiphar's wife, where he argues, for example, that the second part of 12.24 and the first part of 12.52 belie any suggestion that 12.24 implies Joseph was on the point of succumbing to Zulaykha's advances. Moreover, al-Sharif al-Murtada takes 12.33–34, 51 and 54 as further indications of Joseph's innocence. 12.53 is interpreted as being the words not of Joseph but of Zulaykha; the 'evidence of his Lord' mentioned in 12.24 is interpreted as alluding, inter alia, to a previous gift of infallibility bestowed on the prophet. Al-Sharif al-Murtada then goes on to argue that the wording in 12.33 does not imply a limited preference for the wrongful behaviour Joseph rejects, discusses the infallibility implications of Joseph enlisting someone's help other than God's in removing himself from prison (12.42, the author explains that this may have been done on God's command, or maybe it was Joseph's duty as a prophet to bring about his removal from the loathsome environment of a prison), and deals with the matter of God's role in Joseph preventing Benjamin from returning with his brothers, causing his father anxiety, and related issues (like Razi, al-Sharif al-Murtada states that Joseph was acting throughout in accordance with God's revelation, and that the accusation of thievery was not necessarily on Joseph's command, could refer to the removal of Joseph from his father, or was possibly a question). He then concludes his treatment of Joseph's impeccability with a refutation of those who read 12.100 as sanctioning worship of other than God; deals with the question of Iblis sowing enmity between him and his brothers in the same verse, arguing that this refers to enmity only on the brothers' part; and discusses Joseph's apparent request for worldly power in 12.55, which in fact refers only to his desire to ensure that the nation's money be spent rightfully, and is thus not a cause for blame (al-Sharif al-Murtada, 1988: 50-1, 53-9).

In addition to his treatment of prophets mentioned in the Qur'an, al-Sharif al-Murtada also deals at length with the infallibility of Imams 'Ali, Hasan, Husayn, 'Ali b. Musa and al-Qa'im al-Mahdi, which he sees as a logical deduction; his teacher, al-Shaykh al-Mufid (d. 1022) cites 21.101, 44.32 and 38.47 in his general discussion of the applicability of the state of sinlessness to both prophets and imams (al-Shaykh al-Mufid, 1983: 106).

References and further reading

Abrahamov, B. (1993) 'Ibn Taymiyya and the Doctrine of "Isma"', *The Bulletin of the Martyn Institute of Islamic Studies* 12, 3–4: 21–30.

Ahmed, S. (1998) 'Ibn Taymiyyah and the Satanic Verses', *Studia Islamica* 87: 67–124.

al-Hakim, M. (1994) 'L'infaillibilité et les conditions du maintien de l'ordre universal', *Aux sources de la sagesse* 1, 4: 33–45.

Mohamed, A. (2000) 'A Critique of the Shia's Doctrine of the Infallibility (Ma'sum) of the Imamate', *Islamic Quarterly* 44, 1: 343–57.

Nasr, S.H., Dabashi, H. and Nasr, S.V.R. (1988) *Sh'ism: Doctrines, thought and spirituality*, Albany: SUNY Press, 127–87.

al-Razi, Fakhr al-Din (AH 1303) *Kitab al-Arba''in fi usul al-din*, Hyderabad: Matba'at majlis da'irat al-ma'arif al-'uthmaniyya, 329–68.

Schaefer, U. (1999/2000) 'Infallible Institutions?', *Baha'i Studies Review* 9: 17–45.

al-Sharif al-Murtada (1988) *Tanzih al-anbiya'*, Beirut: Mu'assasat al-'ilmi li'l-matbu'at.

al-Shaykh al-Mufid (1983) *Tashih al-i'tiqad bi-sawab al-intiqad*, Beirut: Dar al-kitab al-islami.

—— (1951) *Awa'il al-maqalat*, Tabriz: np, 42–3.

MARIANNA KLAR

ISMA'IL

The Prophet Ishmael (Isma'il) is mentioned by name twelve times in the Qur'an, most commonly in association with Abraham, Isaac and Jacob. 19.54–55 states that Ishmael was a messenger (*rasul*) and a prophet (*nabi*), and that he instructed his family in prayer and almsgiving. 21.85 mentions Ishmael, along with Idris and Dhu al-Kifl, as being among the steadfast and upright. A number of verses list Ishmael in a line of descent from Abraham that includes Isaac, Jacob and the Tribes (*Asbat*).

Muslim tradition says that Ishmael was the first person to speak clear (*fusha*) Arabic, but that, unlike earlier prophets who spoke Arabic (e.g. Hud, Salih, Shu'ayb), Ishmael learned Arabic as a second language from the Jurhum with whom he had settled in Mecca. Ishmael is also credited, in a saying attributed to the Prophet Muhammad, with being the first person to tame and ride horses.

The Qur'an does not describe the tensions between the mothers of Ishmael and Isaac, but Muslim exegetes narrate how Hagar and Ishmael were sent to Mecca. Muslim tradition also relates that Ishmael married an Amalekite woman whom his father Abraham rejected, and then he later married a woman from the Jurhum who bore him twelve sons. The names of the twelve sons and the tribes to which they gave their names is provided in Muslim tradition. It is from the tribe of Qedar (Qaydhar) that the Prophet Muhammad is said to have originated.

Muslim tradition also recounts how Ishmael helped his father Abraham with the rebuilding of the *Ka'ba* and the establishment of the pilgrimage to Mecca. The Qur'an does not specify which of Abraham's sons he was commanded to sacrifice, and Muslim exegetes disagree as to whether it was Ishmael or Isaac.

According to many exegetes, Ishmael was sent as a prophet to the Jurhum of Mecca, the Amalekites and the people of Yemen. Ishmael is said to have married his daughter Nesmah to his nephew Esau, the son of Isaac, and that their offspring were the Romans. Historians report that Ishmael died when he was 137 years old and he is said to have been buried in Mecca, near one of the Gates of Paradise that will be opened on the Day of Resurrection.

Further reading

Alexander, G. (1938) 'The Story of the Ka'ba', *Muslim World* 28: 43–53.

Bashear, S. (1990) 'Abraham's Sacrifice of His Son and Related Issues', *Der Islam* 67: 243–77.

Bell, R. (1937) 'The Sacrifice of Ishmael', *Transactions of the Glasgow University Oriental Society* 10: 29–31.

Calder, N. (1988) 'From Midrash to Scripture: The sacrifice of Abraham in early Islamic tradition', *Le Muséon* 101: 375–402.

Firestone, R. (1990) *Journey in Holy Lands: The evolution of the Abraham–Ishmael legend in Islamic exegesis*, Albany, NY: SUNY Press.

Schmid, H. (1976) 'Ismael im Alten Testament und im Koran', *Judaica* 32: 76–81, 119–29.

BRANNON WHEELER

ISRAFIL

Although not mentioned by name in the Qur'an, the angel who blows the trumpet marking the end of time is taken to be Israfil (see Ibn Kathir's explanation of 36.51). (Also not mentioned by name is 'Izra'il, the angel of death found in 32.11.) The Qur'an describes this apocalyptic event in two ways. A trumpet (*sur*) will be blown, 'and men will rush to their Lord from their graves' (36.51); likewise, 'The day the trumpet will be blown, you will come forth in crowds' (78.18). But one passage provides for two blowings. The first will cause 'all in the heavens and earth to swoon, excepting those He wills. Then [the trumpet] will be blown again, and they will stand looking on' (39.68). The details and reason for this intermediary period are not clear, an issue that attracts attention in the *hadith* literature and later sources (al-Ghazali, 1995: 173). But a blast or shout (*sayha*) may also mark the end time: 'They await only a single blast, which will take them while they dispute among themselves' (36.49) and 'It will be only a single blast, and they will be brought before us' (36.53). This same blast is used elsewhere in the Qur'an to destroy unbelieving civilizations such as the Thamud (11.67; 36.29).

Further reading

al-Ghazali, A. (1995) *The Remembrance of Death and the Afterlife*, Book 40 of *The Revival of Religious Sciences*, trans. T.J. Winter, Cambridge: The Islamic Texts Society.

Ibn Kathir, I. (n.d.) *Tafsir al-Qur'an al-'Azim* (Interpretation of the Great Qur'an), 4 vols, Cairo: Dar al-taqwa.

RICHARD MCGREGOR

ISRA'IL

Literally 'soldier of God', the name of Jacob, Isra'il is used forty-three times in the Qur'an. The name was extended to describe his descendants, the Israelites.

See also: **Ya'qub**

OLIVER LEAMAN

ISRA'ILIYYAT

Isra'iliyyat is an Arabic term that is applied to traditions from the Qur'an and Muslim exegesis concerning the history of the Israelites. Sometimes the category is also used for transmissions that originate in Israelite sources (such as the Bible) or have been transmitted on the authority of Jews.

Israelites

Accounts relating to the Israelites, especially under the leadership of Moses, are frequent and widespread throughout the Qur'an. In addition to detailed passages referring to Moses and the Israelites in Egypt, the Qur'an contains stories of the time the Israelites spent wandering in the wilderness (manna and quails, the Golden Calf, the Torah, water from rock), their entrance into the Holy Land, the early kings of Israel (Saul, David, Solomon) and later prophets (Jeremiah, Ezekiel, Ezra). 2.67–73 tells the story of the Israelites' refusal to obey God's command to perform a simple sacrifice, and 7.163–166 narrates the story of a city by the sea whose inhabitants transgressed the Sabbath.

Muslim tradition also identifies the bulk of the prophets mentioned by name in the Qur'an as Israelite prophets, beginning with Jacob (also called Israel in 3.93) and culminating with Jesus, who is called the Seal of the Israelite Prophets (see 7.157; 61.6). The Israelites are unique in having been sent numerous prophets and given numerous opportunities to accept the messages revealed by God. Other peoples are only sent one prophet and given one chance before being punished by God with destruction for having rejected his revelation.

Muslim exegetes refer to a number of passages from the Qur'an in which the Torah is said to have been revealed to the Israelites as a punishment for their disobedience. Much of this can be related to the exegesis of 3.93, where the Prophet Muhammad is reported to have challenged the Jews of Medina to deny that God had imposed food prohibitions upon the Israelites before the revelation of the Torah. 6.146 mentions the imposition of food prohibitions and the revelation of the Torah being put upon the Israelites for their disobedience. 4.18 refers to a 'painful chastisement' and 4.160 says that God forbade the Israelites the 'good things' that used to be allowed them.

17.4 refers to the two times Jerusalem was destroyed, which Muslim exegetes take as a reference to its destruction under the Babylonians and the Romans. 2.48 warns that the Israelites will be punished on the Day of Judgement and that no prophet will be able to intercede on their behalf.

Transmitters of Isra'iliyyat

Among the best-known transmitters of Isra'iliyyat traditions is Wahb b. Munabbih (655–732 CE), a companion of the Prophet Muhammad widely cited as a trustworthy source for many oral accounts linked to Jewish and Christian exegetical traditions. Among the works attributed to him is one of the earliest Qur'an commentaries, and a book detailing the folklore of pre-Islamic South Arabia. To Wahb is attributed a no longer extant text entitled *Isra'iliyyat*, which is described as containing many of the traditions later transmitted on his authority.

Another well-known transmitter of Isra'iliyyat is Ka'b al-Akhbar (d. 652 CE), a Yemenite Jew who converted to Islam shortly after the death of the Prophet Muhammad. He is said to have been present when 'Umar b. al-Khattab entered Jerusalem in 636 CE, and eventually settled in Hims. He is credited with many oral and written traditions from the Bible and Jewish sources.

Called the Rabbi of the Arabs (*hibr al-'arab*), Ibn 'Abbas (619–687 CE) was a cousin and young companion of the Prophet Muhammad. He is regarded as one of the greatest authorities on the Qur'an in general and especially the place of Isra'iliyyat traditions in its interpretation. Although he was only thirteen years old at the time of the Prophet Muhammad's death, Ibn 'Abbas is reported to have been responsible for the transmission of large amounts of exegetical traditions to later Qur'an commentaries.

Textual authority of Isra'iliyyat

Muslim scholars disagree concerning the status of Isra'iliyyat traditions in both Qur'an commentary and Islamic law. Many scholars distinguish between the use of Isra'iliyyat to provide narrative detail to stories shared by the Qur'an and Bible, and the relative lack of authority that should be accorded to transmissions given on the authority of Israelite sources or Jewish transmitters when addressing questions of law. Some jurists maintain that the Qur'an abrogates all previous revelations and, as such, the Isra'iliyyat that is still valid would only replicate what is already found in the Qur'an and the sayings of the Prophet Muhammad. Despite the very widespread reliance on Isra'iliyyat traditions in classical Qur'an exegesis, many contemporary Muslim scholars dispute the value of these transmissions and argue that they should be avoided and expunged from popular considerations of the Qur'an.

In contemporary non-Muslim scholarship, the relationship and possible influence of Jewish and Christian sources upon the Qur'an and Muslim exegesis, and vice versa, remain an issue of some contention. Most older studies claim that all parallels between the Qur'an and the Bible prove the reliance of Islam upon Judaism and Christianity. More recently, scholars have taken into account the possibility of a shared common source for the Bible and the Qur'an, and demonstrated the Muslim influence upon Judaism and Christianity.

Further reading

Chapira, B. (1919) 'Lègendes bibliques attribuées à Ka'b el-Ahbar', *Revue des études juives* 69: 86–101.

Cohen, M. (1986) 'Islam and the Jews: Myth, counter-myth, history', *Jerusalem Quarterly* 38: 125–37.

Goitein, S.D. (1936) 'Israiliyat', *Tarbiz* 6: 89–101.

Goldziher, I. (1902) 'Isra'iliyyat', *Revue des études juives* 44: 63–6.

Halperin, D. and Newby, G. (1982) 'Two Castrated Bulls: a study in the Haggadah of Ka'b al-Ahbar', *JAOS* 102: 631–8.

Lassner, J. (1993) 'The "one who had knowledge of the book" and the "mightiest name" of God: Qur'anic exegesis and Jewish cultural artifacts', in R. Nettler (ed.) *Studies in Muslim-Jewish Relations*, Philadelphia, PA: Oxford Centre for Postgraduate Hebrew Studies, 59–74.

Schwarzbaum, H. (1982) *Biblical and Extra-Biblical Legends in Islamic Folk Literature*, Walldorf-Hessen: Verlag für Orientkunde, Dr. H. Vorndran.

Wasserstrom, W.M. (1995) *Between Muslim and Jew: The problem of symbiosis under early Islam*, Princeton, NJ: Princeton University Press.

Wolfensohn, I. (1933) *Ka'b al-Ahbar und seine Stellung im Hadith und in der islamischen Legendenliteratur*, Frankfurt (Doctoral Thesis).

BRANNON WHEELER

ISTIFA

Istifa is a noun meaning to choose or to choose the best. It comes from the root verb *safa*, which means to be clear or pure, or to select the best. In the Qur'an, Allah *istifa* (chose) his messengers and prophets: 'Allah chose Adam, Noah, the family of Abraham and the family of 'Imran above mankind and *jinn*' (3.33). Furthermore, Allah has chosen some women as the best of the world's women, among them the mother of Jesus: 'O Maryam! Verily, Allah has chosen you, purified you, and chosen you above all women' (3.42).

These chosen prophets and holy people, according to Muslim scholars, are selected and differentiated from their contemporaries. In addition, Allah chooses, as with people, some angels over others: 'Allah chooses messengers from angels and from men' (22.75).

RAFIK BERJAK

ITTAQA

Ittaqa is a root verb meaning to fear God, to guard oneself against evil, or to devote oneself to godliness. *Muttaqi* is a subject noun or an adjective that signifies a person who is God-fearing, devout or pious. In Qur'anic language, this term signifies those who guard themselves against sin and harmful things, taking God as shield or shelter. Such people are devout and dutiful believers.

This term has a vast usage in the Qur'an and it is always recommended by Allah that servants (humanity) be *muttaqin*: 'And if they had believed and guarded themselves from evil and kept their duty to Allah ...' (2.103).

See also: **repentance**

RAFIK BERJAK

'IZRA'IL

Not directly mentioned in the Qur'an, 'Izra'il is generally identified with the angel of death.

OLIVER LEAMAN

See also: **Azra'il**

J

AL-JABBAR, QADI ʿABD

ʿAbd al-Jabbar b. Ahmad b. Khalil was born in Asadabad, a town in the south-west of Hamadan, probably around 325/937 and died in Ray in 415/1025. He was one of the last great thinkers of the Muʿtazilite school.

ʿAbd al-Jabbar came from a humble background (his father was a peasant in Asadabad) and he began his education in his hometown where, in the traditional way, he first learned to recite the Qurʾan. He then learned *hadith* from Zubayr b. ʿAbd al-Wahid, a well-known *muhaddith* in Asadabad, and from ʿAli b. Ibrahim al-Qattan in Qazwin. In 339/951 he went to Mecca to perform the *hajj*. On his return, ʿAbd al-Jabbar continued his studies in Hamadan with ʿAbd al-Rahman b. Hamdan al-Jallab and in Isfahan with ʿAbdallah b. Jaʿfar b. Faris. All of these scholars were followers of Ashʿari *kalam* and Shafiʿi *fiqh*. This was probably the reason behind the

report that early in his life ʿAbd al-Jabbar was a follower of Ashʿarite theology. Whatever the truth of this report, it is certain that, unlike most Muʿtazilite scholars who were followers of Hanafi *fiqh*, ʿAbd al-Jabbar was a follower of the Shafiʿi *fiqh*.

In 346/958 he went to Basra to continue his studies there. He first studied *hadith* with Abu Bakr al-Anbari. Then he joined the circle of Ibrahim b. Ayyash, a student of Abu Hashim al-Jubbai, and studied Muʿtazilite *kalam* with him. Later he moved to Baghdad where he joined the circle of Abu ʿAbd Allah Husayn b. ʿAli al-Basri, another student of Abu Hashim. He studied with Abu ʿAbdallah for a long time, and during this time produced his first works. In 360/970 ʿAbd al-Jabbar went to Rama-hurmuz. There he joined the circle of ʿAbdallah b. ʿAbbas Ramahurmuzi, a student of Abu ʿAli al-Jubbaʾi, and had lively discussions with the Muʿtazilite scholars. He also began working on his major work, the *Kitab al-Mughni*, which he completed twenty years later when he was in Ray.

During his stay in Ramahurmuz, 'Abd al-Jabbar's reputation had gradually spread, and with the help of political situation he became a prominent theologian of his time. As a result, he received an invitation from Sahib b. Abbad, an advisor of the Buyid Mu'ayyid al-Dawla. When Ibn Abbad became a vizier of Mu'ayyid al-Dawla in 367/977, he appointed 'Abd al-Jabbar as *qadi al-qudat* (chief judge) of Ray. 'Abd al-Jabbar continued to hold this office until the death of the vizier in 385/995. Then he was dismissed by Fakhr al-Dawla and his property confiscated. Apart from a trip to Mecca in 389/999 and a short stay in Qazwin in 409/1018, 'Abd al-Jabbar lived the rest of his life in Ray.

Although he compiled many works in different branches of the Islamic sciences, 'Abd al-Jabbar is famous for his work in theology, and he is perhaps the last great thinker of the Mu'tazilite school. His works are among the few Mu'tazilite sources that come directly from a member of the school and not from one of their enemies. In accordance with the views of the early thinkers, 'Abd al-Jabbar accepts the five principles of the Mu'tazila, namely, divine unity, divine justice, the promise and the threat, the intermediate position, and commanding the good and prohibiting evil. The first principle expresses the uniqueness of God and includes the discussions of the createdness of the world, its Creator and His attributes. The second defines divine justice as the idea that God is free from all that is morally wrong. God would not impose upon us anything that is unbearable. He does the best for his creatures. His sending a prophet is incumbent upon him, because it is of benefit to humanity. God cannot stand by and do nothing, being just, he has to intervene and send messengers to warn us of the consequences of our behaviour. We need religious law since otherwise we would not know how to behave. Third, God promised reward for the obedient and punishment for the disobedient, and he cannot go against his promise.

Most of 'Abd al-Jabbar's works are not extant. In the *Bayan mutashabih al-Qur'an* (Exposition of the Ambiguous Verses of the Qur'an), he discusses the verses that are difficult to understand literally and explains them using reason and other verses that are clear. In the *Fadl al-i'tizal wa tabaqat al-mu'tazila* (Virtue of Separation and the Generations of the Mu'tazilites), he responds to criticisms that had been directed at the Mu'tazila and gives the biographies of the earlier representatives of the school. In the *al-Mukhtasar fi usul al-din* (Summary of the Principles of Religion), 'Abd al-Jabbar gives a summary of the topics of his huge *al-Mughni fi abwab al-tawhid wa'l 'adl* (Sufficient on the Aspects of Unity and Justice).

Further reading

Heemskerk, M.T. (2000) *Suffering in the Mu'tazilite Theology: 'Abd al-Jabbar's teaching on pain and divine justice*, Leiden: E.J. Brill.

Hourani, G.F. (1971) *Islamic Rationalism: The ethics of 'Abd al-Jabbar*, Oxford: Clarendon Press.

al-Jabbar (1961–72) *al-Mughni fi abwab al-tawhid wa'l 'adl* (Sufficient on the Aspects of Unity and Justice), ed. T. Husayn, Cairo: Dar al-misriyya.

—— (1966) *Tathbit dala'il al-nubuwwa* (Establishing the Evidences of Prophecy), ed. 'A. Uthman, Beirut: Dar al-'arabiyya.

—— (1969) *Bayan mutashabih al-Qur'an* (Analysis of the Ambiguous Verses of the Qur'an), ed. A. Zarzur, Cairo: Dar al-turath.

—— (1986) *Fadl al-i'tizal wa tabaqat al-mu'tazila* (Virtue of Separation and the

Generations of the Mu'tazilites), ed. F. Sayyid, Tunis: Dar al-tunisiyya.

—— (1988) a*l-Mukhtasar fi usul al-din* (A Summary of the Principles of Religion), ed. M. Amara, Cairo: Dar al-shuruq.

Martin, R.C., Woodward, M.R. and Atmaja, Dwi S. (1997) *Defenders of Reason in Islam: Mu'tazilism from Medieval School to modern symbol*, Oxford: OneWorld.

Peters, J.R. (1976) *God's Created Speech: A study in the speculative theology of the Mu'tazili Qadi l-Qudat Abu l-Hasan 'Abd al-Jabbar Ibn Ahmad al-Hamadani*, Leiden: E.J. Brill.

OLIVER LEAMAN

JACOB

see: **Ya'qub**

JAHILIYYA

see: **knowledge**

AL-JAHR BI AL-BASMALA

The *basmala* refers to the invocation 'In the name of God, the Merciful, the Compassionate', which is found at the beginning of each *sura* (chapter) of the Qur'an except *al-Tawba* (Chapter 9) and also forms part of *aya* (verse) 30 of *Naml* (Chapter 27).

The question of reciting the *basmala* relates to recitation of *al-Fatiha* (the opening *sura* of the Qur'an) in each unit (*ruku*) of the Muslim ritual prayer (*salat*), aloud in the first two units during night prayers and silently during daytime prayers. As the *basmala* occurs at the beginning of the *al-Fatiha* and there are conflicting *hadith* as to whether the Prophet Muhammad recited the *basmala* or not in the ritual prayer as part of *al-Fatiha*, the question arose as to whether the *basmala* in fact constituted part of *al-Fatiha*.

According to Abu Hanifa (d. AH 150) and Malik (d. AH 179) the *basmala* at the beginning of a *sura* does not constitute part of the *al-Fatiha* or any other *sura*. Thus Malik opines that it is not to be recited aloud or silently in the obligatory *salat*; Abu Hanifa, on the other hand, argues that it is to be recited, but only silently. According to Shafi'i (d. AH 204), the *basmala* constitutes part of *al-Fatiha* and has to be recited in *salat* and aloud at night. According to Ahmad (d. 243) too, the *basmala* may constitute part of *al-Fatiha* and thus should be recited, silently only in *salat*.

Further reading

Ibn Anas, Malik (1994) *al-Mudawwana al-Kubra* (*Riwayat Sahnun b. Sa'id*), Beirut: Dar al-kutub al-'ilmiyya

Ibn Rushd, Muhammad b. Ahmad (1988) *Bidayat al-mujtahid wa nihayat al-muqtasid*, Beirut: Dar al-ma'rifa.

al-Jaziri, Abd al-Rahman (1993) *al-Fiqh 'ala al-madhahib al-arba'a*, Beirut: Dar al-qalam.

al-Nawawi, Muhyiddin Abu Zakariyya Yahya b. Sharaf (1995) *Sahih Muslim bi sharh al-Nawawi* (*Bab hujjat man qal la yujharu bi al-basmala* and *Bab hujjat man qal al-basmala aya min awwal kull sura siwa bara'a*) Beirut: Dar al-kutub al-'ilmiyya.

—— (1995) *Kitab al-Majmu' sharh al-muhadhdhab li al-shirazi*, Beirut: Dar ihya' al-thurath al-'arabi.

al-Shawkani, Muhammad b. Ali (1997) *Fath al-qadir,* al-Mansura: Dar al-wafa'.

ABDUL GHAFOOR RAHEEM

JALUT

Mentioned by name in 2.249–251, Goliath (Jalut) is associated with an army against which the Israelites fought and were eventually victorious, with the help of David. The name Jalut is related to the Hebrew root of the word (*gly/wt*) and also forms a phonetic pair with the Arabic name, used in the same passage of the Qur'an, for Saul (Talut). Paralleling Jewish and Christian tradition, Muslim exegetes state that Goliath was a giant, an Amalekite and descendant of the giants who inhabited the Holy Land before the arrival of the Israelites under Moses. The battle between David and Goliath is described by Muslim exegetes in terms mirroring the earlier battle between Moses and the giant Og, who was also considered to be an Amalekite. David is said to have knocked Goliath down with pebbles thrown from a simple sling, and then decapitated the giant with his own sword. Some exegetes relate that three different stones called out to David and were transformed into a single stone before striking Goliath in the forehead. Muslim tradition reports that David kept the sword of Goliath and that it was passed down through the prophets until it was inherited by the Prophet Muhammad from the Jews of Medina.

Further reading

Barthélemy, D. *et al.* (1986) *The Story of David and Goliath*, Orbis Biblicus et Orientalis, 73.

Jason, H. (1979) 'The Story of David and Goliath: A folk epic?', *Biblica* 60: 36–70.

Jensen, P. (1922) 'Das Leben Muhammeds und die David-Sage', *Der Islam* 12: 84–97.

BRANNON WHEELER

JAZA

Jaza is a past-tense root verb meaning to have rewarded, recompensed, availed or given. The term signifies that something has been paid or given in return for a service.

Jaza could mean to satisfy, suffice or make content. *Jaza'* is a noun meaning repayment, compensation or what satisfies another. In the Qur'an we are told: 'And fear a Day when a person shall not avail another, nor will intercession be accepted from him nor will compensation be taken nor will they be helped' (2.48).

For believers, the *jaza'* (reward) is paradise; for transgressors of the boundaries set by God, hellfire is their *jaza'* (recompense). The Qur'an emphasizes the significance of reward, so it is no surprise to find this and linked terms used 118 times in the text.

RAFIK BERJAK

JERUSALEM

The status of Jerusalem in the Qur'an needs to be linked with the status of a number of important figures that appear in the Jewish bible and the Gospels. Abraham, Moses, David, Solomon, Zechariah, John the Baptist and Jesus are, according to Islam, among the prophets and messengers of God. Jews and Christians recognize David and Solomon as great kings and patriarchs of ancient Israel, but not as prophets. However, in Islam they are regarded as prophets, and the Qur'an not only recounts their stories and also endeavours to restore their status by removing some of the charges and allegations made against their characters by earlier, deceitful authors.

David was accused in the Bible of committing adultery (2 Samuel 11–12) and Solomon was accused of idolatry (1 Kings 11). The Qur'an absolves them of these charges (28.21–25; 38.30). This shows, Muslims say, that David and Solomon are more revered and respected in Islam than in the Jewish and Christian traditions, and the city associated with them, Jerusalem, is also given high status in Islam. Jerusalem is historically associated with these prophets, so naturally it is a city sacred to Muslims, since Islam considers itself a continuation of the spiritual and ethical movement that began with the earlier prophets. Historically and theologically, Islam believes itself to be the true inheritor of the earlier traditions of the prophets and messengers of Allah. It is for this reason that the Qur'an called Palestine – the land associated with the lives of many of God's prophets – *al-ardh al-muqaddasa* (the Sacred Land) (5.21) and its surroundings *barakna hawlaha* (God's Blessed Precincts) (17.1).

The sacredness of the city of Jerusalem, according to Islam, lies in its religious history. This is the city that witnessed the life and works of the greatest prophets and messengers of God. Here divine grace had been at work for a long time, with Allah's great prophets and messengers living and moving in its streets and surrounding countryside. Mecca and Medina are blessed cities in Islam because of their association with the prophets Abraham, Ishmael and Muhammad; in a similar way Jerusalem is blessed and important in Islam because of its association with other prophets of Allah, namely David, Solomon and Jesus. Jews and Christians do not recognize Ishmael and Mohammad as God's prophets and messengers, so they do not consider Mecca and Medina to be sacred cities; by contrast, Muslims believe that Moses, David, Solomon and Jesus are all prophets, so Islam recognizes the sacredness and importance of Jerusalem.

Jerusalem in the life of Prophet Mohammad

Due to its theological and religious status, Jerusalem had a very important place in the life of the Prophet Muhammad. In the year 620 CE, almost 18 months before his *hijra* (migration) from Mecca to Medina, the famous *isra'* and *mi'raj* (Night Journey and Ascension) occurred. One night, in a miraculous way, the Prophet was taken on a journey from Mecca to Jerusalem, then from there to heaven. The Night Journey was a great miracle that Muslims believe was

performed for Prophet Muhammad as an honour and as confirmation of Mecca's spiritual link with Jerusalem.

Both of these events took place on the same night. The angel Gabriel took the Prophet from Mecca to Jerusalem. There it is reported that the Prophet stood at the Sacred Rock (*al-sakhra al-musharrafa*), went to the heavens, returned to Jerusalem where he met with many prophets and messengers who had gathered to meet him and led them in prayers. After these experiences the Prophet was taken back to Mecca. The story of *isra'* and *mi'raj* is full of wonderful signs and symbols. Muslim thinkers, mystics and poets have interpreted it in various ways. There is, however, one essential point, which is that this event examplifies every Muslim's deep devotion and spiritual connection with Jerusalem.

During the *mi'raj*, the Prophet is reported to have received from God the command about the five daily prayers (*salah*) that all Muslims must perform. Upon his return to Mecca, the Prophet instituted these prayers. It is significant to note that Jerusalem was made the direction (*al-qibla*) that Muslims must face while saying their prayers. Jerusalem is thus called *ula al-qiblatayn* (the first *qibla*). The Prophet and the early community of Islam, during their stay in Mecca, worshipped in the direction of Jerusalem. After the *Hijra*, Muslims in Medina also continued to pray facing Jerusalem for almost seventeen months. Then came God's command to change the direction of prayer from Jerusalem to Mecca (2.142–150). Muslim historians and commentators on the Qur'an have explained the meaning and purpose of this change, which in no way diminished the status of Jerusalem in Islam. The *Ka'ba* in Mecca was meant to be the *qibla* from the beginning, because the Qur'an said that it was the First House (*awwal bayt*) (3.96) established for mankind to worship the One God. The *Ka'ba*, however, was full of idols when the Prophet Mohammad began preaching his message of *tawhid* (the unity and transcendence of Allah). A separation had to be made between the people and the pagan worship that they used to perform at the *Ka'ba*. Jerusalem served that purpose very well. Once monotheism was fully established in the minds and hearts of the believers and the *Ka'ba*'s position with regard to Abraham and monotheism made clear, the way was open to restore the *Ka'ba* as the direction of prayers.

There are many instances of this type of change or abrogation (*naskh*) in Islamic legislation. As one example, visiting graves was forbidden at the beginning of Mohammad's messengership. Later it was permitted, because Muslims had learned the difference between visiting a grave and ancestor worship. At first, the Prophet forbade his people to write down his words except when he explicitly told them that what he was saying was revelation – the Qur'an, the Word of God. Later, when people had learned the difference between the Qur'an and *hadith* (sayings and deeds of the Prophet), Muhammad gave them permission to write down *hadith* as well. It is widely held by Muslims that the *Ka'ba* in Mecca was the original direction of prayers for all the prophets, so that the cleansing of the structure of idols re-established the status quo, rather than putting in place a new practice. According to one *hadith*, the Black Stone (*al-hajar al-aswad*) had been in Mecca at the *Ka'ba* since the time of Adam. It was the prophets Abraham and Ishmael who built the *Ka'ba*, under Allah's command and direction (2.125–127).

If we examine the wording of the Qur'an we find no explicit references to Jerusalem by name or by any of its alternative names, such as al-Quds, Bayt al-Muqaddas or Ursalim. There is one reference to the *masjid al-aqsa* ('most distant mosque') in the account of Muhammad's miraculous Night Journey, mentioning the holiness of what is taken to be a site in Jerusalem. The passage is 'Praise be He who at night bore aloft His servant from the Sacred Mosque to the most remote mosque, whose surroundings we blessed, so that We might show him some of Our signs' (17.1). It is sometimes claimed that it was only after the Islamic conquest of Jerusalem in 637 CE that the view became established that the mosque called 'the most remote' was the Temple of Jerusalem, and that Muhammad had experienced a transmigration (*mi'raj*) to heaven while standing on the rock around which the Dome of the Rock was erected. There was, in fact, quite a controversy about whether Jerusalem was the site of the *masjid al-aqsa*, particularly as the reference in the Qur'an that may well be to Palestine. It describes the site as near *ghulibati l-rumu fi adna'l-ardhi* ('the Greeks [i.e. the Byzantines] have been vanquished in the nearby land') (30.2–3), which suggests that the distant mosque could not be the one in Jerusalem. It could also be claimed that Jerusalem was not even the first direction of prayer for Muslims. The Qur'an (2.142) does mention a normal direction of prayer (*qiblatihimi 'llati kanu 'alayha*) prior to Muslims being commanded to face the (Meccan) 'Sacred Mosque' (*al-masjid al-haram*) but, although this is often taken to be Jerusalem, there is no explicit claim that the former or first direction of prayer was in fact Jerusalem.

Further reading

Sahas, D. (1972) *John of Damascus on Islam*, Leiden: Brill.

Grabar, I. (1996) *The Shape of the Holy: Early Islamic Jerusalem*, Princeton, NJ: Princeton University Press.

Hasson, I. (1996) 'The Muslim View of Jerusalem, the Qur'an and Hadith', in J. Prawer and H. Ben-Shammai (eds) *The History of Jerusalem: The Early Muslim Period*, New York: New York University Press, 349–85.

See also: **abrogation; Dawud;** *qibla*

OLIVER LEAMAN

JIBRIL/JIBRA'IL

The angel Gabriel (Jibril or Jibra'il) is mentioned three times by name in the Qur'an, but is also understood as having been referred to in other instances. One confusing passage runs:

> Say, 'Whoever is an enemy of Gabriel – who by Allah's will has brought revelation down to your heart, which confirms what came before it, and is a guidance and good tiding for the believers – Whoever is an enemy of Allah, his angels, his messengers, Gabriel and Michael, surely Allah is an enemy to the unbelievers'. (2.97–98)

This revelation is understood to be the Prophet's retort to the Jews, who had claimed his message was not a continuation of their revelation since Gabriel was their enemy (al-Nisaburi, n.d.: 15). Gabriel is also mentioned as taking the Prophet's side in a household dispute (66.4). Although not named, the 'mighty one' who transmits revelation to the Prophet from a distance of 'two bow's length or closer' (53.5–9) is understood to be Gabriel. Because it performs much the same function, the spirit that bears revelation has become identified with Gabriel: 'This has been sent down by the Lord of the worlds. Sent down with the faithful spirit' (26.192–193). However, in some places the Qur'an distinguishes explicitly between the angels and the spirit (70.4; 97.4). In the *hadith* and *sira*, Gabriel plays an important role: he acts as the Prophet's guide during his heavenly ascension (*mi'raj*), after having cut him open and cleansed his heart with water from the well of Zamzam (Ibn Hisham, n.d., Vol.1: 166).

Reference and further reading

Ibn Hisham (n.d.) *al-Sira al-nabawiyya* (The Life of the Prophet), 4 vols, Beirut: al-Maktaba al-'ilmiyya.

al-Nisaburi, A. (n.d.) *Asbab al-nuzul* (The Occasions of Revelation), Beirut: al-Maktaba al-thaqafiyya.

RICHARD MCGREGOR

JIHAD / JAHADA

Jihad or *jahada* means, in Arabic, struggle or effort. In the Qur'an the longer phrase *al-jihad fi sabil Allah*, meaning striving or exerting oneself in the path of God, is frequently used. The Qur'an also describes the believers as those 'who strive with their wealth and themselves' (*jahadu bi-amwalihim wa-anfusihim*) (8.72). These fuller Qur'anic locutions admit of many semantic and interpretative possibilities: the giving of charity; the manumission of slaves; quietist and activist approaches, including armed resistance to social and other forms of injustice. It appears that, by the late eighth century CE, the concept of *jihad* as armed struggle had become predominant in most quarters and the word thereafter continued to be used primarily, but not exclusively, in this sense.

Further reading

Afsaruddin, A. (2005) 'Obedience to political authority: An evolutionary concept', in M. Khan (ed.) *Islamic Democratic Discourse: Theory, debates, and directions*, Lanham, MD: Lexington Books.

See also: **qital; war and violence**

ASMA AFSARUDDIN

JINN

The term *jinn* occurs more than twenty-nine times in the Qur'an. There is a whole *sura* called *surat al-jinn*, which speaks clearly and explicitly about the *jinn*. The *jinn* live in a world we cannot see. They eat, drink and procreate. Similar to humans, some are righteous while others are not. The *jinn* were created before the creation of mankind, and their origin is from fire (15.26–27). They are a part of divine creation separate from humanity and the angels, but they share certain qualities with us, like intellect, discrimination and the capacity for freedom. They have the power to choose between true and false, right and wrong. *Ayas* indicate the existence of the *jinn*: 'I only created the *jinn* and man to worship me' (51.56).

See also: **irada**

OLIVER LEAMAN

JOB

see: **Ayyub**

JOHN OF DAMASCUS

John of Damascus, from the house of Mansur, is one of the most respected theologians in the Eastern tradition, one of only three people to share the official title 'the Theologian'. John's influence is hard to establish directly, but Harry Wolfson calls him 'the connecting link between the Church Fathers and early Islam' (Wolfson 1972, 119). His work *The Orthodox Faith* is the first 'Summa' developed in the Christian tradition, the first truly systematic theology. The principal literary products that draw on John's Muslim context are his description of Islam in *De Haeresibus* and his doctrine of images. A third work, *The Discussion of a Christian and a Saracen*, is of disputed authorship but belongs firmly in the Damascene tradition (probably Abu Qurra).

John appropriates almost all of *De Haeresibus* from other authors, most notably the Anakephaleoses of Epiphanius' *Panarion* (Sahas, 1972: 80–81). Only three of its 103 chapters are thought to be original. One is chapter 101, dealing with the religion of the 'Ishmaelites', its origin, Muhammad, the Qur'an, doctrine, and practice. Sometimes it takes the form of a dialogue between Christians and Muslims, but its rhetoric is descriptive rather than polemical. Of course, at this time Muslims and Christians were debating with each other widely, and needed to be able to identify strong and weak points for disputation. For example, John asks the Muslims why there are no witnesses like Moses and the prophets to Muhammad's own prophethood when the Qur'an demands witnesses for so many other reasons. One of the impressive aspects of John's approach is his accurate portrayal of Islam and its conception of God. John accepts the unity of God and interprets the Trinity not as a diversity in God but as a reference to the way that God can be known. He argues against Islam that the stress on the unity of God does not work well with the distinction between God and his book, the Qur'an, leading to a bifurcation in Islam between God and his spirit, something resolved much more neatly, he suggests, in Christianity.

What is interesting about John's approach is his familiarity with Islam and his determination to argue that Christianity does not associate partners with God (*shirk*), despite what the Qur'an sometimes suggests. He quite rightly points out that the precise nature of the link between God and the Qur'an is itself not a simple issue, and the createdness or otherwise of the Qur'an did indeed become a highly controversial topic in the Islamic world. Since he was based in Damascus, John presumably had a better grip on what Muslims were actually arguing. He used his defence of the Trinity as not interfering with the nature of *tawhid* or divine unity to defend another doctrine antagonistic to many interpretations of Islam, the acceptability of images of the divine. In just the same way, he argued, God participates in the person of Jesus Christ and in the Bible, so he can be thought of as being incarnate in icons and images.

Reference

Sahas, D. (1972) *John of Damascus on Islam*, Leiden: Brill.
Wolfson, H. (1972) *The Philosophy of the Church Fathers*, Cambridge, MA: Harvard University Press.

See also: **Christianity**

OLIVER LEAMAN

JOHN THE BAPTIST
see: **Yahya**

JONAH
see: **Yunus**

JUDAISM

The Qur'an accepts the Jews (Banu Isra'il) as having a covenant with God, and classifies them as People of the Book, but describes them as having repeatedly broken their covenant, changed (*tahrif*) the Torah from what God gave them to what is convenient for them, and tended to oppose God's prophets. This opposition has even gone to the extremes of the Jews killing, or trying to kill, their prophets.

It is clear that some of the positive and negative comments have a background in Muhammad's experiences of living in an environment with significant Jewish tribes in the political framework. Initially he may have thought that they would be interested in his message, and early favourable comments perhaps reflect this optimism. He was soon disillusioned, though, and the tribes in the Medina area often allied themselves with the opponents of the new religion, so the Qur'an reflects this with many bitter attacks on the Jews and their treachery. The final defeat of the Jews of Khaybar in 628 CE and the massacre of the male population with the enslavement of the women and children brought to an end active opposition from the local Jews. As the Islamic empire expanded, it incorporated significant Jewish minorities and a *dhimmi* system was initiated, under the terms of which the Jews became a protected minority if they paid a specific tax for non-Muslims.

The Qur'an sometimes treats the Jews as equivalent to Christians as People of the Book, but often as worse than the Christians. God is described as having punished them for their disobedience by giving them burdensome laws governing what was acceptable food, what is *haram* or forbidden for them (6.146). One source of their punishment was their *zulm* or wrongdoing (4.160–161), which was usury, something they were strictly forbidden to do. Many of the Jews compete with each other as sinners (5.62) and, in the *sura al-Baqara*, they are roundly criticized for arguing ceaselessly about the precise way in which they are supposed to carry out a sacrifice, because they wished to avoid the sacrifice altogether. The behaviour of the Jews leads the Qur'an frequently to link them more with the polytheists than with the other People of the Book, since the claim is that they are not really believers and have a propensity to lead believers astray if left to act freely. Finally, Muslims are warned against being friends with the Jews and trusting them.

OLIVER LEAMAN

JUWAYNI, IMAM AL-HARAMAYN

Abu'l Ma'ali Rukn al-Din 'Abd al-Malik b. 'Abd Allah was born in Bushtanikan near Nishapur on Muharram 18, 419/17 February 1028 and died in the same village on Rabi' al-Akhir 25, 478/20 August 1085. He was a defining figure in the Ash'arite tradition of Sunni Islam. Juwayni received his early education from his father, who was a famous teacher in Nishapur, and from his uncle, 'Ali b. Yusuf. When his father died in 438/1047, Juwayni took over his father's teaching post, despite his youth. He became a leading defender of the Ash'arite tradition, which was then gaining strength in the region. These were not favourable times for Ash'arites: the Seljuk sultan Tughrul Beg's vizier 'Amid al-Mulk, who was a Shi'ite–Mu'tazilite supporter, banned the Ash'arites and other groups critical of the Mu'tazilites from teaching and disseminating their views in other ways. As a result, Juwayni left, going first to Baghdad and then, in 450/1058, reaching the Hijaz. He lived in Mecca and Medina for four years. There he continued teaching, and his status led to his honorary title of Imam al-Haramayn (Imam of the Two Holy Cities). After the death of Tughrul Beg, the new sultan Alp Arslan replaced the vizier 'Amid al-Mulk with the famous vizier Nizam al-Mulk. The new vizier favoured the Ash'arites and invited them to return home. He also founded a number of

madrasas called Nizamiyya in different cities, including Baghdad and Nishapur, so as to spread the Ash'arite version of Islam. As a result of this invitation, Juwayni returned to Nishapur and was appointed to the Nizamiyya where he taught until the end of his life. Among his students was al-Ghazali, who in turn taught at the Nizamiyya.

Juwayni was particularly interested in jurisprudence (usul al-fiqh) and theology (kalam). In jurisprudence, though he followed the Shafi'ite tradition, he tried to develop his own methodology. This can be seen in his Kitab al-Burhan fi usul al-fiqh (Book of Demonstration on Jurisprudence). Juwayni contributed more to the development of kalam than to any other branches of the Islamic sciences. Juwayni generally followed the Ash'arite tradition; however, on a number of issues he gave the tradition a new orientation. He used philosophical methods more than any of his predecessors. Hence he considered rational enquiry about God's existence to be a religious duty. To solve the problem of God's attributes, Juwayni inclined towards the Mu'tazili Abu Hashim's theory of modes (ahwal). Although he used the arguments from the createdness of atoms and accidents and from the finitude of time to prove the createdness of the world, he considers the argument from particularization (takhsis), which is the combination of the argument from createdness and from contingency, as the strongest for the purpose.

Juwayni wrote a number of works on fiqh, usul al-fiqh and kalam. On Shafi'ite fiqh, he wrote Nihayat al-madlab fi dirayat al-madhhab (End of the Quest in the Knowledge of the School). On jurisprudence, he wrote a number of works among which Kitab al-Burhan fi usul al-fiqh (Book of Demonstration on Jurisprudence) is worth mentioning here.

Juwayni also wrote a number of works on theology and the creed. His *al-Shamil fi usul al-din* (Summa on the Principles of Religion) and *al-Irshad* (Guidance) give systematic discussions of *kalam* issues. In *al-ʿAqida al-nizamiyya* (Nizamian Creed) and *Lumaʿ al-adilla fi qawaydi ahl al-sunna* (Radiance of Proofs on the Creed of the People of the Sunna) he briefly gives the creed of Sunni Islam.

Further reading

Allard, M. (1965) *Le problème des attributs divins dans la doctrine d'al-Ashʾari et de ses premiers grands disciples* (The Problem of Divine Attributes in the Doctrine of al-Ashʾari and his First Major Disciples), Beirut: Recherches publiées sous la direction de l'Institut de Lettres Orientales de Beyrouth.

Gardet, L. and Anawati, G. (1948) *Introduction à la théologie musulmane* (Introduction to Muslim Theology), Paris: Études de philosophie médiévale.

Hourani, G. (1985) 'Juwayni's criticisms of Muʾtazilite ethics', in G. Hourani (ed.) *Reason and Tradition in Islamic Ethics*, Cambridge: Cambridge University Press, 124–34.

al-Juwayni (1950) *Kitab al-irshad ila qawati ʿal-adilla fi usul al-iʾtiqad* (The Guide to the Cogent Proofs of the Principles of Faith), ed. M. Musa and A. ʿAbd al-Hamid, Cairo, n.p.

—— (1965) *Lumaʿ al-adilla fi qawaidi ahl al-sunna* (Radiance of Proofs on the Creed of the People of the Sunna), ed. F.H. Mahmud, Cairo.

—— (1969) *al-Shamil fi usul al-din* (Summa on the Principles of Religion), ed. A. S. Nashshar et al., Alexandria.

—— (1979) *Kitab al-Burhan fi usul al-fiqh* (Book of Demonstration on Jurisprudence), ed. A. al-Dib, Devha.

—— (1979) *Nihayat al-madlab fi dirayat al-madhhab* (End of the Quest in the Knowledge of the School), ed. A. al-Dib, Devha.

—— (1979) *al-ʿAqida al-nizamiyya* (Nizamian Creed), ed. A.H. al-Sakka, Cairo.

Saflo, Mohammad Moslem Adel (2000) *al-Juwayni's thought and Methodology: With a translation and commentary on Lumaʿ al-adillah*, Berlin: Klaus Schwarz Verlag.

OLIVER LEAMAN

K

KA'BA / AL-BAYT AL-'ATIQ

The word *ka'ba* in Arabic is derived from the root meaning 'cube'. In the Qur'an, the *Ka'ba* is God's house of worship and prayers. The Lord twice refers to it as 'My House' (*bayti*) (2.125; 22.26) and Abraham, when addressing God, calls it 'Your Sacred House' (*baytika al-haram*) (14.37). In all, this house of worship is referred to eighteen times in the Qur'an, using four basic epithets: *al-ka'ba*, *al-bayt* (the House), *al-bayt al-haram* (the Sacred House) and *al-bayt al-'atiq* (the Ancient House). The word *Ka'ba* itself occurs only twice, in the *sura* entitled *al-ma'ida* (the Table) (5.95, 96), where it is made clear that the *Ka'ba* and the Sacred House are synonymous: 'God has made the *Ka'ba*, the Sacred House, an establishment for people'. The significance of these two instances of the word *Ka'ba* occurring in a chapter that is devoted to the Christian theme of the Last Supper should

not be ignored. Both the *Ka'ba* and the Table sent down by God are meant to be perceived as signs or miraculous events in the history of religion and are thus appropriately both housed in a single *sura*. Other epithets for the *Ka'ba* can be found in another eight chapters, namely 2, 3, 8, 11, 14, 22, 33 and 106, with four repetitions each in chapters 2 (*al-baqara*) and 22 (*al-hajj*). It is thrice referred to as *al-bayt al-haram* (5.97; 14.37), and twice as *al-bayt al-'atiq* (22.29, 33), with all other instances using the shortened form *al-bayt* or *Bayt*. The specific location of the *Ka'ba* is also given, at Becca (3.96), in a valley with no cultivation (*ghayri dhi zar'*) (14.37). The main purpose of this sacred shrine was to erect a sanctuary for worshippers in which to establish prayers (*salat*) and the circumambulation of the *Ka'ba*:

And remember when we made the House a place of visitation for people and a sanctuary. And so take you Abraham's station (*maqam Ibrahim*) as a place of prayers and We made a covenant with Abraham and Ismaʿil that they should purify My House for the circumambulators (*taʾifin*), the ones in religious seclusion (*ʿakifin*), the bowers (*al-rukaʿ*) and the prostraters (*al-sujud*). (2.125)

The *Kaʿba* is also described as the 'first House (of worship) appointed for man' (3.96). This refers to the fact that it was first built by Adam under the instructions of the angel Gabriel as place for worshipping God. (It is perhaps significant to note that Eve (Hava or Hawwaʾ) is said to have died in the city of Jeddah; her graveyard is well known to local inhabitants and, appropriately, named Hawwa's Graveyard.) According to Tradition, the *Kaʿba* was an earthly replica of a divine prototype in heaven called *al-bayt al-maʾmur* (literally, the Ever-inhabited House), around which the angels circumambulated and which was located exactly above the sacred site of the *Kaʿba*. This heavenly prototype was shown to the Prophet Muhammad during his ascension to the seven heavens when the five ritual prayers were legislated. Tradition has it that 70,000 angels sing praises, perform prayers and circumambulate the House daily in solemn procession. It is important to note that *al-bayt al-maʾmur* is referred to once in the Qurʾan in the form of an oath (52.4). During the time of Adam and Eve, the *Kaʿba* was said to have been a radiant and lustrous structure whose stones were from the very floors of paradise. The sacred Black Stone, now located in the south-east corner of the *Kaʿba*, is said to be a remnant of these heavenly stones. Thus in the dense darkness of that prehistoric time, it also provided Adam and Eve with the necessary light. However, after Noah's deluge, the structure of the *Kaʿba* was obscured. Eventually, the angel Gabriel revealed

its site to Abraham and Ismaʿil, and they were directed to rebuild it on its former foundation. The *maqam Ibrahim* (the Place of Abraham) (2.125) is still indicated there today, together with the footprints of the Patriarch. The area for one mile around the *Kaʿba* was sacred and no warfare was to take place there nor any blood be spilled. Abraham and Ismaʿil were also instructed in the ceremonies of the pilgrimage (the *Hajj*), which now included not only circumambulation of the *Kaʿba* but also the ritual of the *saʾ*, the movement back and forth seven times between *al-marwa* and *al-safa* in a re-enactment of Hajar's movement as she searched for water in the valley of Becca. When pilgrims today drink from the spring of Zamzam, which is located in the Sacred House, they are celebrating the miraculous appearance of the angel Gabriel who brought forth water for the thirsty Hajar and her son Ismaʿil.

The *Kaʿba* is most often associated with Mecca or Becca. Although most people believe these two words to be interchangeable, in fact there is major distinction between them. According to Muslim scholars, Becca is the sacred site immediately surrounding the *Kaʿba*, and Mecca the Peaceful City (*al-balad al-amin*) (95.3) that houses them both. These two terms thus have a part–whole relationship. Both sacred site and peaceful city are inextricable. Thus, when Abraham prays for his family, resettled near the *Kaʿba*, he also prays for the city of Mecca long before it was ever established:

And [remember] when Abraham said: 'My Lord, make this [the Sacred House] a city of security (*baladan aminan*) and provide its people with fruits and produce, those of them who believe in God and the Last Day'. (2.126)

He also prays to God to send the people of this city a prophet: 'Our Lord! Send them a messenger from amongst them who shall recite to them your verses and teach them the Book and the Wisdom, and purify them; for You are the Almighty, the All-Wise' (2.129).

The *Ka'ba* is also intricately connected with the ritual of the *Hajj* (Pilgrimage). It is said that the call for the *Hajj*, initiated by Abraham after he had built the *Ka'ba*, was itself a kind of miracle. According to Tradition, Abraham asked the angel Gabriel how people from all the regions of Arabia could possibly hear his proclamation. God's answer is documented in 22.27: 'And proclaim to people the *Hajj*. They will come to you on foot and on every lean beast; they shall come from every deep and distant ravine.' The formulaic words *labayk allahuma labayk* ('I hear your calls Our God'), which have been repeated by pilgrims since the time of Abraham, attest to this miraculous proclamation.

Since Abraham's time, the tribe responsible for administrating the *Ka'ba* and the Holy City of Mecca has played an important role in the life of the Arabs. It was really only in Mecca that the feuding tribes of Arabia could peacefully meet for worship and trade. During the Prophet Muhammad's time, the tribe of Quraysh were the acknowledged keepers of the sacred site. Today, the keys to the *Ka'ba* remain in the possession of the Shaybi tribe, who were entrusted as keepers of the *Ka'ba* long before the advent of the Prophet Muhammad. According to Tradition, after the conquest of Mecca the elders of the Shaybi tribe were told by the Prophet himself that only a tyrant would deprive them of their ancient heritage.

Further reading

Dirks, J. (2001) *The Cross and the Crescent: An interfaith dialogue between Christianity and Islam*, Baltimore, MD: Amana Corporation.

Ibn Kathir, Alhafiz (1977) *al-Bidaya wa al-nihaya*, Vol. 1, Beirut: Maktabat al-ma'arif.
Khalil, S. (2003) *Atlas al-Qur'an: Amakin, Aqwam, A'lam*, Beirut: Dar al-fikr al-mu'asir.
Milhas, R. (ed.) (2001) *al-Zarqani: Akhbar Makka*, Vol. 1, Mecca: Dar al-thaqafa li l-tiba'a.
al-Sha'rawi, M. (2001) *Qisas al-anbiya wa al-mursalin*, Cairo: Islamic Turath Books.
al-Tabari, M.H. (1989) *The History of al-Tabari*, Vol. 1, Albany, NY: SUNY Press.

See also: **Arab; Becca;** *hajj*

AFNAN H. FATANI

KALAM / KALIMA / KALLAMA

Kalam, in the sense of *kalam Allah* (the Word of God), must be distinguished from *'ilm al-kalam*, the science of discourse on God, and it is also different from *kalimat Allah*, a single divine utterance (Gardet: 468–71). *Kalam Allah* is found at least three times in the Qur'an (2.75; 9.6; 48.15). The verb *kallama* (to speak) is used in the following contexts: when God speaks to the Prophets (2.253); when God speaks clearly to Moses (4.164; 7.143; 2.254), who is chosen to transmit his word (7.144); when explaining that God only speaks to men by revelation or by a sign (2.118), and that God never speaks to the ungodly (2.174; 33.77).

The Qur'an makes no mention of *kalam* or *mutakallim*, but, in theological discourse, God is described as *muta-kallim* (speaking) since he possesses the attribute of speech (*kalam*). And what relationship does it have to the divine essence? The Mu'tazilites held that the Word of God is created, and does not subsist within the essence of God; the philosophers viewed it as an eternal idea that had emanated from the Prime Being; the Hanbalites affirmed the absolute eternity of the Word subsisting in God; finally, the Asha'rites also affirm that it is uncreated (*qadim*) and without beginning, but they regard the sounds and letters as expressions that are not part of the divine essence. Thus al-Juwayni argues that the word is eternal, and when it applies to things within time, it does not mean it began in time (Gardet: 469). Ibn Taymiyya held that the word is the Word of God, but not its sound. In modern times, Muhammad 'Abdu stressed the Asha'rite distinction between the Qur'an as the Word of God without intermediaries, and its sounds and letters as belonging to the world of creation.

The communicative relationship between God and man in the Qur'an takes place from God to man and from man to God. In this entry we will deal with the communication that takes place from God to man, in the form of revelation (*wahy*), inspiration (*ilham*) and signs (*ayat*). Revelation is mysterious because it is not a normal form of communication, but one that involves descending (*tanzil*), which is a vertical form of communication, from God to man, not a horizontal one, from man to man. In spite of its mystery, the revelation is couched in human language so as to be understood by humans. The Qur'an itself refers to God's speech as 'a word' (*kalima*) in 'And God will wipe out the falsehood, and establish the truth as truth with His words' (40.23–24). In another verse, God addresses Muhammad and refers to revelation as a speech (*qawl*): 'Verily, we are going to cast upon thee a weighty word' (72.5). Revelation defies human comparison and analysis, but since it is written in human language we can analyse its linguistic meanings.

Revelation is abnormal because the speaker is God, not man, and because there is no ontological equality between

God and man: there has to be a Prophet as a recipient. Prophet Muhammad was the recipient of the Qur'an, and the Arabic language was chosen to be its medium. This is not incidental: the Arabic language that Muhammad spoke was *chosen* as the medium. God's message is eternal, but there is debate about whether the sounds and letters are also eternal. Many theologians do not regard them as eternal, but as part of language (*lisan*). Revelation (*wahy*) is therefore equivalent to God's speech (*kalam Allah*), as suggested in the verse: 'If anyone of the polytheists come to you [O Muhammad] seeking their protection as a client, make him thy client so that he may have the chance of hearing God's speech (*kalam Allah*)' (9.6). It is clear from the context of this verse that God's speech refers to what has been spoken and what has been revealed to Prophet Muhammad (Izutsu, 1987: 151–153).

That the Qur'an, or the previous scriptures, are the speech of God is suggested in the following verses:

> Can you, then, hope that they will believe in what you are preaching – seeing that a good many of them were wont to listen to the Word of God and then, after having understood it, to pervert it knowingly? (2.75)

> As soon as you [O believers] are about to set forth on a war that promises booty, those who stayed behind [aforetime] will surely say, 'Allow us to go forth with you' – [thus showing that] they would like to alter the Word of God. (48.15)

There is context to this latter verse. It is an allusion to 8.1, 'All spoils of war belong to God and His Apostle', meaning that no warrior can claim the booty and that, if he fights for it, he violates the Qur'anic principle that war be fought in God's cause only (Asad, 1980: 786).

The 'Word of God' here refers to the Qur'an. It addresses Muslims who had high expectations that the Jews would accept its message, but were disappointed to find that they regarded their own religion as a kind of national heritage reserved to the children of Israel alone. It also refers to the Israelites who did not preserve their own scriptures, and who corrupted the Bible for their own personal ends. The Qur'an repeatedly charges them with having altered the words of scripture (Asad, 1980: 17).

God uses the verb *kallama* (a transitive verbal form of *kalam*) with reference to his speaking to Moses. It appears that Moses was accorded an unusually special privilege in this respect, and therefore God speaks to him exclusively in Mount Sinai: 'And unto Moses God spoke directly' (*kallama takliman*) (4.162–164). This would suggest that Moses was granted a exceptional divine favour, as suggested in the verse: 'Those Apostles, some of them We have caused to excel others. Among them there is one to whom God Himself spoke (*man kallama Allahu*), and some there are whom He has raised in rank' (2.253–254). It is in this sense that theologians called Moses *kalim Allah*, meaning that God had bestowed on him a special favour by speaking to him directly.

God's communication is tied up with man's purification, as suggested in the following verse:

> Those who suppress any part of the Scriptures which God has revealed, and barter it away with a paltry price, shall swallow nothing but fire into their bellies. On the Day of Resurrection God will neither speak with them nor purify them. A woeful punishment awaits them. (2.174)

Thus the ungodly will not receive divine inspiration (*ilham*), and thus will always remain ignorant, in darkness. The verse comes in the context of the believers who are exhorted to partake of the lawful bounties as stated in the scriptures, but the unbelievers suppress this truth of the scriptures and are ungrateful to God. God will never speak to them, neither in this world, nor in the hereafter: 'They shall be totally ignored' (Qutb, 1999: 170).

Communication is also connected to a sign, and not necessarily to scripture as suggested in the verse:

> The ignorant ask: 'Why does God not speak to us, or give us a sign?' The same was asked by people before them: their hearts are all alike. We have made the signs very clear for those with firm conviction. (2.118)

Those with this kind of conviction are pure at heart, and will be receptive to the signs, and understand their meanings and purpose (Qutb, 1999: 113).

According to al-Ghazali, God only speaks to the godly, to the knowers (*'arifin*) and saints (*awliya'*), and he speaks to them via a light of certainty (*al-yaqin*). Only purified souls can become recipients of this divine light, which makes them capable of spiritual perception (*basira*). 2.174 refers to this kind of inspiration (*ilham*) and this kind of perception.

According to al-Raghib al-Isfahani, *kalam* (speech) is apprehended by hearing, and *kalima* (a written word) is apprehended by sight. These two usages appear in thirty-two verses of the Qur'an (al-Raghib al-Isfahani, n.d.: 457–8). Note, for example: 'And had not a word gone forth from thy Lord for an appointed term, the matter would surely have been judged between them' (42.14).

References and further reading

Abdel Haleem, M. (1976) 'Early kalam', *HIP*: 71–88.

Asad, M. (1980) *The Message of the Qur'an*, Gibralter: Dar al-andalus.

Izutsu, T. (1964) *God and Man in the Koran*, Tokyo: The Keio Institute of Cultural and Linguistic Studies.

Leaman, O. (2003) *An Introduction to Classical Islamic Philosophy*, Cambridge: Cambridge University Press.

Mohamed, Y. (2004) *The Path to Virtue*, Kuala Lumpur: ISTAC.

Qutb, S. (1999) *In the Shade of the Qur'an*, I, trans. and ed. M.A Salahi and A.A. Shamis, Leicester: The Islamic Foundation.

al-Raghib al-Isfahani (n.d.) *Mu'jam mufradat al-Qur'an*, Beirut: Dar al-fikr.

See also: **Ash'arites and Mu'tazilites;** *daraja*; **Judaism**

YASIEN MOHAMED

KARIM

Karim is a noun meaning noble, distinguished, generous or bountiful. The root verb *karuma* signifies to be noble, high-minded or generous. A stress on the *r*, or adding the transitive hamza *a* at the beginning, transforms the verb into the transitive form: thus *karrama* and *akrama* indicate honouring someone.

In the Qur'an, this term has been used to describe God: 'certainly my Lord, Rich, Bountiful' (27.40). His face is *zu-al-jalal-wa'l-ikram* ('And the face of your Lord, full of majesty and honour, will remain for ever') (55.27). Adding the attribute of generosity and nobility to God signifies his *ihsan* (beneficence) and his *in'am* (blessings and grace).

Human beings are also described in the Qur'an as noble and respected. The person who possesses good manners and excellent standards of conduct qualifies to earn the title *karim*. The best quality of a person is to be *muttqi* (pious): 'Verily, the most honourable of you with Allah is the most pious' (49.13). In another verse, human beings as a whole are honoured by Allah: 'And indeed We

have honoured the Children of Adam, and We have carried them on the land and sea' (17.70).

Anything highly revered is *karim*. The Holy Qur'an is itself given this adjective: 'That is indeed an honourable recitation' (56.77).

The angels are honoured in the Qur'an as well: 'Has the story reached you, of the honoured guests of Abraham?' (51.24) and 'In the hands of scribes. Honourable and obedient' (80.15, 16).

Allah describes his prophets and messengers as honoured slaves: 'And they say: The Most Gracious has begot a son. Glory to Him! They are but honoured slaves' (21.26).

RAFIK BERJAK

KHAYBAR

Traditionally populated by Jewish farmers, Khaybar was a fertile, well-irrigated tract of volcanic land, 90 miles north of Medina, which became a centre of dissent and focus of unrest, particularly after the Siege of Medina. Gradually developing into an almost wholly Jewish colony, complete with citadels and fortresses, it became the headquarters of the Jewish garrison and the last and most formidable Jewish stronghold in the Arabian peninsula. Most of the expelled members of the Banu Nadhir were domiciled in Khaybar, where they made tactical alliances with other Jewish tribes as part of a larger Jewish conspiracy to attack Medina. It was during their preparations for this that the Prophet marched against Khaybar, assisted by 1,400 men, including 200 cavalry. Those who had 'lagged behind' on the Hudaybiyya mission were famously barred from taking part, while two dozen women accompanied the troops to help tend to the injured. The citadels of

Khaybar were besieged for three weeks. A fierce battle finally ensued, with 'Ali b. Abi Talib displaying legendary strength and heroism. Following the Muslim victory, Muhammad forged a tactical alliance with the conquered Khaybarites by marrying Safiyya, daughter of the chief of the Banu Nadhir. The Jews were allowed to remain in Khaybar on the proviso that they give the Muslims in Medina half of all the grain and fruit produced on their farms each season. Prophetic Tradition has it that the Jews were more than content with the arrangement, lauding Muhammad's sense of justice as something upon which 'the heavens and earth stand'.

COLIN TURNER

KHAYR

Khayr means good, excellent. *Rajul khayr* means a man possessed of the good. *Khayr* also signifies a better or best in the Qur'an: Allah is *khayr* (best). The term appears in many positions, particularly when there is an argument between the Prophet and his adversaries. On the issue of the crucifixion of Jesus, the Qur'an maintains that Jesus was not crucified: 'And they plotted [to kill Jesus] and Allah planned too. And Allah is the best of those who plot' (3.54). Many verses in the Qur'an end with an established fact: Allah is always the best. For instance, 'Nay, Allah is your protector and he is the best of help' (3.150). In some examples involving Allah, *khayr* (the best) is multiplied: 'He is the best of *raziqin* (sustainers), the best of judges and the best of those who forgive'.

Khayr min means better than. This expression is used to compare two things in order to determine the better: 'Kind words and forgiving of faults are better than charity followed by injury'

(2.263). When Allah created Adam and told the angels to prostrate themselves to him, they all did so except Iblis (Satan), who said 'I am better than him [Adam], you created me from fire and him from clay.'

Khayr also signifies goodness in general, the opposite of *shar* (evil). Allah is *khayr* (better) *wa abqa* (and everlasting). *Khayr* can refer to Allah's blessings, the good he gives to whosoever he wishes: 'And if he intends any good for you, there is none who can repel His favour' (10.107).

True believers in Islamic monotheism and real followers of Prophet Muhammad are *khayr umman* (the best nation): 'You are the best of peoples ever raised up for mankind'.

'And whatever good they do, nothing will be rejected of them' (3.115).

RAFIK BERJAK

AL-KHAZIN

'Ala al-Din Abu al-Hasan 'Ali b. Muhammad Ibrahim 'Umar b. Khalil al-Shihi al-Baghdadi al-Shafi'i al-Sufi was born in Baghdad in 678/1279, but spent most of his life in Syria. He is best known by the nickname al-Khazin (the Collector), because he was a book collector in Damascus. Later Arab writers describe him variously as learned, gregarious, cheerful and a mystic of striking appearance. He died at Aleppo in 741/1340.

Al-Khazin's literary legacy rest principally in his writings on Tradition and Qur'anic exegesis. He wrote *Maqbul al-manqul* (The Acceptability of What is Transmitted), a study of the Traditions in ten volumes, in which he principally drew Tradition material from works by al-Shafi'i, Ahmad ibn Hanbal, Imam Malik and the six canonical collections of Sunni *hadith*.

In the introduction to his Qur'anic commentary, *Lubab al-ta'wil fi ma'ani al-tanzil* (The Core of Interpretation in the Meanings of Revelation), al-Khazin identifies al-Baghawi's *Ma'alim al-tanzil* as the primary source, describing it as a collection of the most reliable of the Prophet's sayings, free from error of any form. The degree of dependence is indicated by the alternative title for al-Khazin's commentary: *al-Ta'wil li-ma'alim al-tanzil* (The Interpretation of the Signposts of the Revelation).

Al-Khazin also draws on the Tradition collections of Bukhari, Muslim, Abu Da'ud, al-Tirmidhi, al-Kisa'i and others for his commentary. His exegetical style is narrative-based. His stories are very readable, and are couched in a style and at a linguistic level that makes them accessible to non-specialist readers with a knowledge of Arabic.

The reputation of al-Khazin's commentary has been somewhat compromised in the Arab world. Al-Suyuti (d. 911/1505) did not bother to mention it in his *Tabaqat al-mufassirin* (Exegesis and the Commentators). Suyuti's student, al-Dawudi (d. 944/1538), expanded Suyuti's study in his own *Tabaqat al-Mufassirin*, adding extra commentators, including Khazin, but the entry is purely descriptive, not evaluative. The modern scholar al-Dhahabi is particularly critical of *Lubab al-ta'wil fi ma'ani al-tanzil* for drawing on superstitious stories; denigrating the good name of prophets; being unnecessarily verbose; and presenting detailed stories without commenting on their accuracy or reliability.

Al-Khazin stands accused of citing from the Isra'iliyyat without the eye of a discerning critic. The centuries-old Jewish–Muslim controversy seems to have played a significant role in circumscribing the circulation of al-Khazin's commentary in the Arab world. In contrast, in Muslim Southeast Asia, where the absence of Jewish communities means this controversy has less immediate relevance, al-Khazin's commentary has attracted widespread Muslim scholarly interest since the earliest Islamic period in the region. It continues to be widely referred to by Southeast Asian Muslims in the twenty-first century.

Further reading

al-Dawudi, Shams al-Din Muhammad b. Ahmad. (n.d.) *Tabaqat al-mufassirin* (The Generations of Commentators), 2 vols, Beirut: Dar al-kutub al-'ilmiyya.

al-Dhahabi, Muhammad Husayn (1405/ 1985) *al-Tafsir wa al-mufassirun* (Exegesis and the Commentators), 3rd edn, 3 vols, Cairo: Wahba.

al-Khazin, 'Ala al-Din Abu al-Hasan 'Ali (n.d.) *Lubab al-ta'wil fi ma'ani al-tanzil* (The Core of Interpretation in the Meanings of Revelation), Beirut: Dar al-thaqafah.

Riddell, P.G. (1993) 'Controversy in Qur'anic Exegesis and its Relevance to the Malayo-Indonesian World', in A. Reid (ed.), *The Making of an Islamic Political Discourse in Southeast Asia*, Melbourne, Monash University, 59–81.

—— (2001) *Islam and the Malay-Indonesian World: Transmission and responses*, London: Hurst & Co.

See also: **tafsir in early Islam**

PETER G. RIDDELL

AL-KHIDR

The personal name al-Khidr (or al-Khadir, 'the green one') is not mentioned in the Qur'an, but it does appear in Muslim exegesis, where it is generally identified with one of 'Our [God's] servants' (18.65). This servant of God is, together with Moses and an anonymous young man who accompanies Moses, one of the central characters of the Qur'anic parenetical story (18.60–82).

The short but complicated and enigmatic parable portrays this servant of god as guiding Moses and his young man through a journey to the right path. The servant of god stipulates that Moses promise never to question his – the servant of god's – actions. In three episodes, Moses and his young companion are scandalized by the seemingly inexplicable, immoral and unjustifiable conduct of their guide: he drills a hole into a ship, in order to make it sink; he kills an innocent young man; and he sets up a wall which was tumbling down without asking for reward. Moses loses patience and asks for an explanation of all three instances. At the end of their journey the servant of god puts Moses to shame by disclosing the hidden motives of his actions. He alone is guided by the right interpretation of the world (ta'wil) (18.82). Divine omniscient justice prevails against the limitations of human understanding, and divine knowledge transcends all human knowledge. Most commentators have seen and continue to see in this servant of god, inspired by superior wisdom, the pre-Islamic figure of al-Khidr.

Sura 18 contains two more parables: the story of the people of the cave (*ashab al-kahf*) (18.9–26) and a short version of the journey of the 'Two-Horned' (*Dhu l-qarnayn*) (18.83–98), often identified with Alexander the Great, who reaches the end of the world in order to build a dam against the evil forces of Gog and Magog (*Ya'juj wa Ma'juj*). The sources of the Khidr-story go back to mythological motifs appearing in the Akkadian Epic of Gilgamesh, in the Alexander romance and in Jewish legends centred around the mythical figure of Elijah. The story as it is told by the Qur'an interweaves several narrative motifs: the figure of the travelling companion, the test of patience, the quest for the spring of life, and so on.

The identification of the servant of god with al-Khidr is attested to in traditions from the Prophet, which may be the reason why it is rarely contested by Muslim commentators. There is less exegetical unanimity about whether the Moses mentioned here is the Egyptian Moses or not. The historicity of stories such as the Khidr narrative is normally not challenged by Muslim exegesis. For the father of modern radical Islam, Abu l-A'la Mawdudi (1903–79), in his commentary *Tafhim al-Qur'an* (Making the Qur'an Understood), the Khidr story is history. Some conservative commentators today suggest that, in view of the parabolic character of this passage, it is unnecessary to identify the location to which Moses and his companion set out ('the junction of the two seas', *majma' al-bahrayn*) (18.60) with a geographical place on our maps. Mawdudi still wanted to locate it in the area of Khartoum, where the Blue Nile and the White Nile meet. But when the Egyptian Muhammad Ahmad Khalafallah (d. 1997) attempted in his book *The Art of Narrative in the Noble Qur'an* (1953) to dehistoricize together with the al-Khidr passage the whole Qur'anic genre of stories (*qasas*) and parables (*amthal*), and thereby consider them in some way as divine fiction, he was forced out of his job. His ideas, however, survive in the 'literary interpretation' of the Qur'an (*tafsir adabi*).

Outside of the Qur'an, but influenced by the prevailing exegetical identification of the central figure of 18.60–82 with al-Khidr, al-Khidr has been and is ubiquitous and one of the most complex legendary figures of the Muslim religious *imaginaire* throughout the ages. He embodies eternal youth and the eternal pilgrim, he appears in initiatory dreams to Sufis, works miracles and has for centuries been the centre of a learned intra-Muslim debate. Is he an angel, a prophet or only a friend of god?

Further reading

Franke, P. (2000) *Begegnung mit Khidr: Quellenstudien zum Imaginären im traditionellen Islam*, Stuttgart: Franz Steiner.
Khalafallah, Muhammad Ahmad (1953) *The Art of Narrative in the Noble Qur'an*, Cairo, n.p.

STEFAN WILD

AL-KHO'I, AYATULLAH AL-UZMA SAYYID ABUL-QASIM

Al-Kho'i was born on Rajab 15, 1317/ 19 November 1899 at Kho'i in Iranian Azerbayjan, and died of heart failure at his Kufa home on Safar 8, 1413/8 August 1992. Ayatullah al-Uzma (Grand or Supreme Ayatullah, the highest theological degree in Shi'a Islam) Abu'l-Qasim al-Kho'i was well versed in religious Persian and Arabic poetry and languages, and in the Turkish language as well. In 1330/1912, then only thirteen years old, he moved to al-Najaf, known to the Shi'a as al-Najaf al-Ashraf, in Iraq to further his eduction, and this was to be a very significant move both for him and for subsequent Shi'i scholarship.

He was to stay there for seventy years, making this higher education centre into the leading centre for Shi'i studies in the world, and in particular graduate studies, where he took on the legacy of Shaykh al-Ansari (1799–1864) and continued his tradition of teaching the principles of law and religion. The topics his writings have covered include Islamic law, religious biographies, philosophy and commentary on the Qur'an. Particularly significant are his smaller and more popular works, which have been transmitted throughout the Shi'i world and serve as a source of inspiration to that community.

Al-Kho'i was obviously a skilled administrator. From 1970 he presided over Najaf's theological school, known as *al-hawza al-'ilmiyya* (the school of knowledge and scholarship), after having been elected successor to the late Ayatullah al-'Uzma Sayyid Muhsin al-Tabataba'i al-Hakim. Al-Kho'i attained the title of 'Ayatullah' when he was still in his early thirties. The *hawza* at al-Najaf al-Ashraf has for the past ten centuries attracted students from all over the world. The main topics taught at the *hawza* are philosophy, theology and jurisprudence, and the number of students and teachers has reached many thousands. It is famous for its libraries and also for the concentration of scholars in the city, but sadly many depredations took place at the hands of the Ba'athist government and during the fighting and various invasions of Iraq.

Al-Kho'i himself was imprisoned by Saddam Hussein, albeit briefly, and spent the last ten years of his life under house arrest. When he died the government tried to prevent large public displays of grief and cut off the cities of Najaf and Kufa, but prayers were conducted by Ayatullah 'Ali al-Sistani, and there was a considerable degree of public grief evident at his demise. The institutions he established, both in Najaf and overseas, continued to pursue their educational and charitable aims, and his works remain classics in modern Shi'i philosophy.

Further reading

Khu'i, Abu al-Qasim ibn 'Ali Akbar (1998) *Prolegomena to the Qur'an*, New York: Oxford University Press.

OLIVER LEAMAN

KITAB

Kitab (normally given, with the definite article, as *al-kitab*) means book or scripture. It is a central, elusive and highly controversial keyword in the Qur'an.

Apart from its ordinary meanings – (act of) writing, book, letter (in the sense of written communication), and legal document or contract' – which sometimes occur in the Qur'an, two main strands of religious meaning of *kitab* provide the bulk of the more than 200 times that the term occurs.

First, it is used to mean a book containing the sum total of divine revelation and guidance, transmitted by messengers and prophets at different times and places to mankind in the form of divine laws, decrees, prescriptions and obligations. In this sense, *al-kitab* includes, in addition to the Qur'an, Jewish, Christian and Sabean scriptures. This meaning seems close to *umm al-kitab* (Mother of the Book), the divine matrix of all scripture, in the contexts of 3.7 and 43.2–4. The single message or revealed book of a prophet may also be called *kitab*. This is especially true of the message received by the Prophet Muhammad, which was later collected as the Qur'an; this could be called *kitab*, but only as far as the Prophet had transmitted it. The present usage of *al-kitab* as a synonym for the canonical form of the Qur'anic text in its content, form and scope, which is widespread within and outside Muslim religious discourse, is foreign to the Qur'anic text itself: as the canonically closed text did not exist at the time of revelation, this meaning of the word cannot have been intended.

Second, the term is used for the book in which God preserves his knowledge of everything existing, including the records of the words and deeds of human beings, the events and length of their lives, their afflictions and visitations, punishments and rewards. This seems to be close to the idea of *umm al-kitab* (Mother of the Book) in 13.39, which exegesis often identifies with the 'Preserved Tablet' (*al-lawh al-mahfuz*) (85.21 and four other occasions) – that is, the

heavenly slate of destiny, in which all human deeds are recorded. A *kitab* will be brought forward on the Day of Judgement to serve as a basis for God's reckoning and judgement. Each person may then have a separate *kitab*.

The variety of meanings poses the problem that, in many instances, we cannot be sure in which sense the word *kitab* is meant when it occurs in the Qur'an. We even do not know exactly what is meant when the Qur'an calls itself *kitab*, although the term *kitab* is, together with *Qur'an*, the most important and frequent Qur'anic word of self-classification.

Traditional Muslim exegesis was, of course, aware of the fact that *kitab* had more than one meaning in the canonical text. The Qur'anic expression 'People of the Book' (*ahl al-kitab*) (e.g. 2.105) meant Jews, Christians and other groups to whom a scripture had been revealed, but not Muslims. In such a case, *kitab* could not mean the Qur'anic text. But, by and large, Muslim exegesis considered the terms 'the book' or 'book' and *Qur'an* as synonyms whenever the context seemed to allow it. This concept has been challenged in one publication, which is centred around a revisionist interpretation of the relation between the terms *al-Qur'an* and *al-kitab* (Shahrour, 1992). But even much earlier we find important traces of different exegetical traditions reflecting the opaqueness of the term 'book'. The beginning of *sura* 2, which can be taken after the prayer of *sura* 1 as in some way the heading of codified Muslim revelation, is: *Alif Lam Mim*. That is the book (*kitab*), about which there is no doubt, a guidance to the God-fearing'. Muslim exegesis reflects the ambiguity of the term *kitab* by proposing, with different emphasis, that the 'the book' mentioned in this verse may be:

1. the whole Qur'anic text,
2. the mysterious letters *Alif Lam Mim*,

3. the *suras* of the Qur'an, as hitherto revealed, or
4. the Gospel or the Torah.

Some non-Muslim scholars propose that by *Qur'an* and *kitab* the text meant originally two different collections or sources, possibly with different grades of canonicity, which were later amalgamated to shape the present canonical text. Others deny that *kitab* indicates primarily that Qur'anic revelation was or ever was meant to be a written codified corpus. Rather, the term *kitab* is taken to indicate that the origin of the words of the Prophet Muhammad uttered as revelation have divine authority: they are *kitab* because they come from God (Madigan, 2001a, 2001b).

On the other hand, the very ambiguity of the term may indicate that the Qur'anic text is both *kitab* and *Qur'an*, in the sense that it is written scripture and at the same time oral recitation. The dialectic between scripture and recitation are another feature pervading the Qur'anic text. The divine voice asserts and swears 'it is surely a noble recitation (*Qur'an*) in a hidden book (*kitab*), none but the purified shall touch, a sending down from the Lord of all Being' (56.77–80). What is this 'it': this verse, this ensemble of verses, this *sura*, the whole text revealed so far? What is meant here by 'book'? What is meant here by 'a *Qur'an*'? How is this Qur'an *in* a book? Where and how is the book hidden? How can anybody touch it? Traditional Muslim exegesis had different and mutually exclusive answers to some of these questions, but these answers usually did not allow for a historical textual development. The term *Qur'an* is more frequent in the Meccan *suras*, to be gradually replaced by the term *kitab* in the Medinan *suras*. Muslim tradition reports that the Prophet used scribes in Medina to whom he dictated passages of revelation, the best known being Zayd Ibn Thabit (d. between 42/662 and 56/675). This may reflect a growing interest in having a written aid to memory for recitation.

Often the pre-existing divine book, which nevertheless could be touched, was almost inevitably associated somehow with leaves, letters and ink, and sometimes assumed an almost physical reality. Pious tradition had it that each Arabic letter on the slate of *al-lawh al-mahfuz* (Preserved Tablet) was as big as the mythical mountain Qaf. Such reification of the *kitab* is abhorrent to many modern commentators, among them Abu Zayd.

We may never be sure what the term 'book' means in a given verse. But we can assume that not only the term was fluid but that the self-view of the Qur'anic text and therefore also the meaning of the term changed radically in the course of its reception and/or in the course of its canonization.

References and further reading

Madigan, D.A. (2001a) 'Book', in *EQ*, Vol. 1, 242–51.
—— (2001b) *The Qur'an's Self-Image. Writing and Authority in Islam's Scripture*, Princeton, NJ: Princeton University Press.
Shahrour, M. (1992) *Al-Qur'an wa-l-kitab. Qira'a mu'asira li-l-Qur'an al-karim*, Cairo and Damascus.

See also: **canon; Preserved Tablet; self-referentiality**

STEFAN WILD

KNOWLEDGE

The concepts of knowledge and ignorance are much used in the Qur'an and there are two modes of acquiring knowledge of God. One mode is by observation and reason, and the other is by the soul. The philosophers and theologians have given more emphasis to knowledge acquired by reason, while the Sufis have stressed the knowledge of God via the human soul.

The Arabic root verb 'to know' (*'alima*) and its derived forms occur in the Qur'an about 750 times. The Qur'an is meant to provide truths, which have made an impression on Muhammad's contemporaries. However, these truths can have an effect on any listener, if only they are repeated constantly and single-mindedly. The repetitive use of the same words drives its message home to the listener, especially if it has great religious significance.

Man's knowledge and God's knowledge

The Qur'an repeatedly states that God's knowledge is superior in quantity and quality to man's knowledge, and that he knows secrets unknown to man (6.59; 11.31). Man's knowledge is, in any case, derived from God's, so man cannot know more than God. The angels also can only know what God has taught them. It is only by the will of God that man can know anything from the divine knowledge (2.140, 32, 255).

True human knowledge is connected with religious insight, and so it is the prophets who possess knowledge that comes to them from God. This is not ordinary human knowledge (7.62). Revelation contains knowledge, so the Holy Qur'an describes itself as a book that God has sent according to knowledge (7.52). Many passages in the Qur'an equate religious faith (*iman*) with knowledge (*'ilm*) (30.56). Even one's state of being is connected to knowledge; hence God elevates by degrees those who have knowledge and who believe. Faith and knowledge are connected, so those who believe will come to know (58.11; 2.26) and they will

have certain knowledge (*yaqinun*) of the other world (2.4). Here we are not talking of some vague religious knowledge, but about the knowledge arrived at by believers who ponder and reflect upon the signs of God. The Qur'an refers to mundane knowledge which is derived by the senses, making the eye and ear responsible for such knowledge (32.9; 67.23; 17.36). There are various shades of knowledge and human perception, and the Qur'an makes use of Arabic roots that connote these variations in human perception, including *'/r/f*, *'/q/l*, *f/k/r*, *f/h/m*, *dh/k/r*, *y/k/n*, *basr* and *basir*. These levels of knowledge and perception are interdependent: the one does not exclude the other (Rosenthal, 1970: 28–32).

Knowledge may be acquired by human action, but God also bestows knowledge directly. When we speak of human knowledge we have to bear in mind, at all times, its distinctiveness from divine knowledge, albeit that even the human knowledge ultimately derives from a divine source. It is the Qur'anic attitude to knowledge which became the driving force for all scholars of the classical legacy to produce works pertaining to every branch of knowledge, be it theology, jurisprudence, mysticism or science. And all these branches of knowledge, whether religious or secular, have been integrated into the metaphysical system of *tawhid*.

Ignorance (*jahal*)

Ignorance (*jahal*) is the opposite of knowledge, but it is also wrong conduct. Ignorance could either mean the absence of knowledge, or the disparity between a particular belief and reality.

The term *jahiliyya* appears four times in the Qur'an and, according to Goldziher (1967), it should be understood as the opposite of *hilm* (forbearance), not the opposite of knowledge. Rosenthal disagrees, arguing that the term signifies ignorance, not barbarity. It refers to the ignorance of the pagan Arabs who rejected God (Rosenthal, 1970: 32ff.). Both scholars are partially correct, as the Qur'an refers to both meanings of ignorance. The Qur'an refers to immorality, particularly the uncontrollably violent temperament of pre-Islamic Arabs, and also to ignorance by contrast with knowledge. The meaning of knowledge here should be qualified. We do not mean scientific knowledge, but knowledge as it relates to belief. The pagan Arabs who worshipped idols were ignorant, not merely because they worshipped, but also because they held beliefs about the sacred power of these stones which do not correspond with reality.

The views of Goldziher and Rosenthal could be located within the three meanings of *jahal* given by al-Raghib al-Isfahani, who states:

> First, it is the mind's emptiness of knowledge, and some theologians hold that this pertains to immoral actions; second, it is believing in something contrary to what it is; third, it is to do something contrary to what ought to be done, such as deliberately avoiding obligatory prayer. (al-Isfahani, n.d.: 100)

Goldziher's view corresponds with the first meaning, and Rosenthal's with the third. Thus the meaning of ignorance refers to both the absence of the true knowledge of reality and the immoral conduct of the Arabs.

In his ethical treatise, al-Isfahani deals with ignorance under four categories. The third refers to one who is fanatical in believing to be true a false opinion. Such people will never change. The fourth level refers to those who know the truth, yet hold on to what is false. They are like Satan, full of pride, as God states: 'Your God is the One God; but because of their false pride, the hearts of those who do not believe in the life to come refuse to admit this [truth]' (16.22) (see also al-Isfahani, 1987: 222).

The second meaning of ignorance is evident in the following verse: 'O you who believe, if an iniquitous person comes to you with a slanderous tale, then verify [the truth of it], lest you hurt a people out of ignorance, and afterwards be filled with remorse for what you have done' (49.6). The tale-bearer is characterised as iniquitous because the very act of spreading unsubstantiated rumours will affect the reputation of other people, which constitutes a spiritual offence. It is imperative that the honour and reputation of every person of the community be respected and protected, and one should either not listen to false rumours or substantiate the truth of such statements, lest one should hurt other people out of ignorance.

Knowledge (*'ilm*) and faith (*iman*)

As we have seen, knowledge is associated with faith in one god, so, according to al-Maturidi (d. 333/944), *iman*, *ma'rifa* and *tawhid* are all aspects of knowledge. The majority of Muslims defined faith (*iman*) as affirmation by a combination of the heart and the tongue (Rosenthal, 1970: 97–108).

For al-Ghazali, there are three levels of knowledge that correspond to the three levels of faith. The faith of the ordinary masses (*'awamm*), which is based on imitation (*taqlid*); the faith of the theologians (*mutakallimun*), which is based on reason; and the faith of the knowers (*'arifin*) and saints (*awliya'*), which is based on the light of certainty (*nur al-yaqin*). Gnostics and saints possess spiritual insight (*arbab al-basa'ir*).

There are basically two broad approaches to the knowledge of God:

one is by reflecting on God's signs in the universe, and the other is by knowledge of man's soul. The first approach is rational in nature, and the second approach requires a supra-rational process that implies direct experience of the soul. A pure soul is capable of this direct, intuitive experience, and thus of knowledge of God.

Four Means to Knowledge

The Four Means to Knowledge, according to Isfahani, are as follows. First is the knowledge that comes from the self-evident intellect (*badihatu al-'aql*). This can also be translated as 'innate intelligence', as it corresponds to knowledge arrived at without deduction and analysis. It also corresponds to al-Isfahani's view of self-evident knowledge (*ma'rifa badihiyya*). It is present in all normal people, even if there is a disparity between their mental and sensory capacities. Second is the knowledge from perception (*nazar*), either prior to thought or prior to the senses. 'Perception' refers to both physical sight and spiritual insight. It is the 'close inspection of physical sight and spiritual insight (*basira*) to apprehend and have a vision of something'. Physical perception is the ability of the masses (*zamma*), but the elite (*khawwas*) are capable of both perceptions. The word 'looking' in the verse: 'On that day, faces shall be radiant, looking upon their Lord' (75.23) comes from reason or the senses. These perceptions are acquired. Third, is the knowledge from hearsay; this knowledge is from blind imitation, and cannot be true knowledge. Fourth, is the knowledge from divine inspiration (*wahy*), either from seeing an angel (26.193), from hearing the Divine Word without the interference of the senses (as in the case of Musa?) or from it being cast into the mind while awake. This knowledge, of Prophets, sages and witnesses, comes from a Divine Light. It is the highest knowledge, and is referred to as '*aql al-mustafad, ma'rifa* or *basira* (al-Isfahani, 1987: 230).

This fourth means of knowledge is rooted in the soul. It is acquired through devotional acts, but the illumination of the soul comes from God, not man. Man is not the source of it, only its recipient. Although the illumination is an act of divine grace, man is still required to make an effort to purify his soul. Only then will God illuminate his soul, and only then is man able to apprehend God intuitively.

Thus neither reason nor the senses can provide direct knowledge of God. Instead, this must come from an aspect of human nature that is akin to God. That aspect is the human soul. As mentioned, the soul is not the source of illumination, only God is. In Islamic epistemology, however, all knowledge ultimately refers to knowledge of God, even if it is knowledge about 'other than God', for no knowledge of God can be gained without an intermediary. The senses are an indirect intermediary, and the soul is a direct intermediary.

The innate knowledge of God

The innate knowledge of God is a natural knowledge that does not require any effort or investigation. It is a general knowledge of God that resides in the human soul and innate nature (*fitra*). We know instinctively that we are created and that there must be a Creator: 'Since this knowledge is in the soul, the unmindful will know it if they are told about it, and they will know that they are equal to everyone else, as anyone else is equal to them' (al-Isfahani, 1987: 200). This innate knowledge corresponds with the innate intellect, and because of it even the unmindful can come to know God, as implied in the following verses:

> And if you ask them: 'Who created the heavens and the earth?' they will certainly say 'Allah'. (31.25)

> So, set your face towards religion uprightly. It is the original nature according to which Allah fashioned mankind. There is no altering of Allah's creation. That is the true religion; but most men do not know. (30.30)

Thus knowledge of God's existence is self-evident. It requires no education, reflection or evidence. It is contained in the innate nature of man (*fitra*), which is universal and unchanging. However, misleading education can temporarily take away this natural belief in God.

The soul's knowledge of God

As noted above, the soul is a medium of higher knowledge. If it is illuminated, it will enable its possessor to gain intuitive knowledge of God. The illumination comes from God in the form of a Divine Light. The soul's knowledge is the key to knowledge of God, and the soul's ignorance is the key to ignorance or forgetfulness of God (al-Isfahani, 1987: 76). To support this idea, al-Isfahani cites the following verse: 'Be not like those who forgot Allah, and so He made them forget themselves' (59.19). Furthermore, he states:

> Knowledge of God is only possible with the knowledge of your soul; when you know it, you will know the world, and when you know the world, you will recognize that it is distinct from God. This is the aim of the knowledge of God. (al-Isfahani, 1988: 66)

Thus the soul is the key to an understanding of the world, and through the world, we understand God as the Creator. As a microcosm of the world, man is a mirror that reflects the realities of the world, which in turn are indications of the realities of God. This is knowledge of God through the cosmos. The other means of knowing God is through the soul, from which one arrives at an intuitive knowledge of God. These two methods are not mutually exclusive; they both lead to knowledge; one is direct, via the soul; the other is indirect, via the senses.

Al-Ghazali's view

For al-Ghazali, the discipline of the soul is the key to intuitive knowledge of God. This discipline includes moral action and Sufi meditation. Al-Ghazali said: 'The knowledge of God (*ma'rifa*) is the end of every cognition and the fruit of every science (*'ilm*) according to all schools of thought' (Rosenthal, 1970: 142). But to know God, you have to know your soul. 'The soul is the heart which you identify with the inner eye (*'ayn al-batin*) and is your internal reality.... Knowledge of its reality and its qualities is the key to the knowledge of God' (Field, 1991: 124–6). This knowledge of the soul leads to the direct apprehension of God. This is the highest knowledge, known as *mukashafa* (literally 'disclosing'). Prophets and saints possess this knowledge, and it is the knowledge of the illuminated soul, coming to man only through divine inspiration (Bin Ismail, 2002: 33–45).

The Verse of Light

For both al-Ghazali and al-Isfahani, knowledge is associated with light, and they base their views on certain Qur'anic verses. The Qur'an states that people dispute about God without knowledge, guidance or an illuminating book. The latter is the Qur'an, which provides the light of religious insight (31.20). Elsewhere in the Qur'an is the statement that God guides to his light (*nurihi*) whomsoever he wills (24.35) (Rosenthal, 1970: 157). The Verse of Light itself reads as follows:

> Allah is the light of the heavens and the earth. His light is like a niche in which there is a lamp, the lamp is in a glass, and the glass is like a glittering star. It is kindled from a blessed olive tree, neither of the East nor the West. Its oil will always shine, even if no fire has touched it. Light upon light, Allah guides to His light whomsoever He pleases and gives the examples to mankind. Allah has knowledge of everything. (24.35)

The Verse of Light refers to the light of religious knowledge that God transmits to prophets and believers. It also refers to the Sufi doctrine of God as the prime Light and Source of all being, life and knowledge.

Al-Isfahani states:

> God bestowed upon us by virtue of the intellect (*al-ʿaql*) which He has placed within us, and His book, which He has sent down to us, a guiding light (*nuran hadiyan*). Furthermore, the oil is a metaphor for the Qur'an, which sustains the intellect as the oil sustains the lamp. Because the Qur'an is so clear, it suffices, even without the intellect's support. Then He says 'light upon light', which refers to the light of the Qur'an and the light of the intellect. (*ʿaql*) (al-Isfahani, 1987: 170)

The expression 'light upon light' refers to the effect of the light of the Qur'an upon the light of the intellect. These two lights illuminate each other, and are mutually related. This mutual illumination corresponds to al-Isfahani's view about the mutual relation between reason and revelation. In support of his perspective

of light as a source of knowledge, al-Isfahani cites the verse 'Indeed, a light and a clear book has come to you from Allah' (5.15), and other verses that concur (5.15; 6.122; 42.52; 39.22; 24.35).

Al-Isfahani and al-Ghazali agree that the illumination of the soul comes from the divine source of light. The light is cast into such believers as have a sound heart and are possessed of spiritual insight (*basira*), enabling them to directly apprehend the realities of all things, including God. Such people can acquire knowledge either by observation or by spiritual insight. The spiritual insight of God is immediate and direct. It is intuitive, not mediated by the senses but through the soul, which is illuminated by the Divine Light.

A fundamental difference between al-Isfahani and al-Ghazali is that, for al-Ghazali, the Divine Light is the only real light, from which all lights and illuminated beings emerge. All the other lights are metaphorical lights and manifestations of the Divine Light. For al-Isfahani, however, the Divine Light illuminates all realities, including the intellect and the Qur'an. They are all created by God, through his light, but not through a process of Neoplatonic emanation.

References and further reading

Bin Ismail, M.Z. (2002) *The Sources of Knowledge in Ghazali's Thought*, ed. A. Razak, Kuala Lumpur: ISTAC.

Faris, N.A. (trans.) (1962) *The Book of Knowledge*, Lahore: Muhammad Ashraf.

Field, C. (1991) *The Alchemy of Happiness*, Lahore: Muhammad Ashraf.

Goldziher (1967) *Muslim Studies*, Vol. 1, London: George Allen & Unwin.

al-Isfahani, R. (1987) *al-Dhariʿa ila mkarim al-shariʿa*, Cairo: Dar al-wafa'.

—— (1988) *Tafsil al-nashʾatayn wa tahsil al-saʿdatayn*, ed. A. Najjar, Beirut.

—— (n.d.) *Mu'jam mufradat alfaz al-Qur'an*, ed. Nadim Mar'ashli, Beirut: Dar al-fikr.

Mohamed, Y. (1996) *Fitrah: The Islamic concept of human nature*, London: Taha Publishers.

—— (2004) *The Path to Virtue*, Kuala Lumpur: ISTAC.

Rosenthal, F. (1970) *Knowledge Triumphant. The concept of knowledge in medieval Islam*, Leiden: E.J. Brill.

*See also: **fitra**; **hilm**; **nafs**; **nur**; **revelation***

YASIEN MOHAMED

L

LA

La is a negation. It means 'no' as the opposite of 'yes', and usually negates the meaning of what follows it. It can be used before a verb 'and my tongue expresses not well' (26.13) or before a noun 'There is no harm in it' (37.47). Preceding a verb in the present tense, *la* expresses the negative imperative: 'And do not throw yourselves into destruction' (2.195). In the indefinite accusative form, it expresses general negation: *La Ilaha illa Allah*, for example, means there is not God (there is no God) but Allah. When *la* precedes a verb in the past tense, it is often repeated: *la wa la*. This is the case in 75.31: 'So he neither believed nor prayed'.

RAFIK BERJAK

LAGHW AND *LAHW*

The notion of some activities being *laghw* and *lahw* (idle and distracting) (23.3; 31.6) is clearly intended to distinguish between activities worth pursuing and those that ought not to be taken up. Is music *halal* (permissible) or is it *makruh* (despicable) and therefore *haram* (forbidden)? It depends on which arguments one regards as stronger. It is difficult to call for a complete ban on music because of a very well-attested *hadith* in which the Prophet enquired of 'A'isha his wife whether a woman who was married to an Ansari had any entertainment, since the Ansar are fond of entertainment. Muhammad did not seem to disapprove of this Ansari tradition. Ibn 'Abbas also reported that when 'A'isha gave one of her female relatives in marriage to an Ansari, the Prophet asked whether a singer had been sent for. When he heard that this had not been done, he suggested that it should have been done, and even quoted a popular song of the time. Also, Abu Bakr wanted to silence two girls from playing the hand drum and singing, and the Prophet stopped him, since it was Eid, a time of celebration.

This apparent acceptance of at least some forms of music was not followed by many of the major legal schools, and even Malik ibn Anas of Medina came down hard against most singing. However, it is reported that he approved of simple singing, if it had a beneficial purpose (e.g. placating camels or helping women in childbirth) and if the sole accompaniment was the *duf* (a simple drum). In this restrictive attitude, he is followed by many other commentators. Modern Islamic musical performers such as Yusuf Islam (Cat Stevens) argue that only a limited amount of instrumentation is acceptable. This point is taken up nicely by Ibn al-Jawzi the Hanbali who, in his *Talbis Iblis* (The Deception of the Devil), says that *ghina'* (singing) was originally the simple rhythmical chanting of poems, with the aim of leading people to a religious life. However, once this developed into a throbbing and more complex melody it became *bid'a*, an innovation designed to distract the listener, and something that should be banned. Such complexity is undesirable (*al-taghyir* is *bid'a*), since it breaks the rules of simplicity. It results in music becoming the end of the process of attention, rather than it having a further and deeper end which is something religious, such as contemplation on a verse from the Qur'an.

Ibn Khaldun argues that as civilizations develop, their artistic forms become more complex. Qur'anic recitation was originally part of the simplicity of Arab tribal life, but later on became much more complex, involving degrees of musicality that would have been thought very extravagant at earlier times. He then reports that, while Malik is said to be opposed to the use of melodies in *tajwid*, al-Shafi'i allowed them (II, 400). He criticizes the use of music in recitation, arguing that it distracts from the clarity of presentation of

the text itself, which is after all the primary point of the activity. Pleasure distracts also from the text, since the point of the text is not to give pleasure: it is not a performance. He then claims that, provided the recitation is melodious and 'simple', it is acceptable. But at the stage when luxury and extravagance are all the rage, this desire for simplicity is hardly likely to have much resonance with society. It is then too late to go back to the old way of doing things, since people are obsessed with the pursuit of the *laghw* and *lahw* (things that are idle and distracting).

Is music *laghw* and *lahw* (idle and distracting)? According to Ibn Taymiyya, one should distinguish between the *sama'* (listening) of the Companions of the Prophet and those who are only after amusement (Ibn Taymiyya, 1966: 295). He argues that there are reasons to be worried about the use of *sama'*. It manipulates our emotions, it overexcites and it is too subjective. He goes on to argue that those *ahadith* on this topic which seem to approve of music are not clear. He suggests that the *hadith* in which the Prophet heard the singing of the servant girls did not imply that he listened to the singing, and so approved of it. He may have heard it, but this could have been inadvertent, and when he made references to singing and music this might have meant that he was wondering whether what would normally take place was taking place. It does not mean that he thought it ought to take place, that he approved of it. According to Ibn Taymiyya, if we look at the consequences of *ghina'* (singing), we can see what is distracting about it. It overstimulates us by affecting our passions and can distract us from the Word of God.

Shihab al-Din al-Suhrawardi would allow dance if it is carried out for the right motives, since as he says *inna' l-*

a'mala bi' l-niyyat (acts are [assessed] by their intentions). Al-Ghazali also argues that, just because an action resembles an impious action, one should not necessarily condemn it if it is carried out in the right sort of way. There is no condemnation in the Qur'an of *lahw* and *batil* (the distracting and the vain), provided that the latter is there for gentle amusement that does not distract us from more important things for too long. On the other hand, the sort of *lahwa al-hadith* which is mentioned in *sura Luqman* does suggest that if it is equivalent to 'idle talk' then it will be difficult to justify. The Qur'an does not want to take an overwhelmingly serious attitude to everything, since this would be to interfere with the principle of moderation.

From a legal point of view, we need to distinguish between two categories of what is *batil* or empty. One objectionable kind is where one becomes so enchanted with what should not be an object of our attention that it takes our attention away from what we should be considering. There may be nothing wrong with the frivolous object in itself, but its evil derives from its role as a distraction. Music can easily fall into this category. On the other hand, the relaxation afforded by entertainments like music may make us better able to concentrate on what is really important, our religious duties. It may even form a part of those duties if skilfully blended with aspects of religious practice.

Further reading

Ibn al-Jawzi (AH 1340) *Naqd al-'ilm wa'l-'ulama' aw Talbis Iblis*, ed. M. Dimashqi, Cairo. Idaret al-tiba'a al-muniriya.

Ibn Khaldun (1993) *Muqaddima*, Beirut: Dar al-kutub al-'ilmiyya.

Ibn Taymiyya (1966) *Kitab al-sama' wa' l-raqs, Majmu'at al-rasa'il al-kubra*, Vol. 2, Cairo, n.p.

Leaman, O. (2004) *Islamic Aesthetics: an introduction*, Edinburgh: Edinburgh University Press: 76, 119.

al-Qaradawi, Y. (1994) *The Lawful and the Prohibited in Islam*, trans. K. El-Helbawy, M.M. Siddiqui and S. Shukry, Indianapolis: American Trust Publications. Also widely available online.

See also: **art and the Qur'an; *halal*; *haram*; music**

OLIVER LEAMAN

LA'NA

La'na is a verbal noun derived from the Arabic *la'ana*, 'to curse, damn or execrate'. The curse of God (*la'nat Allah*), which is seen to fall upon various groups and communities in the Qur'an, may be understood in the sense of withdrawal of divine mercy or grace from those who either reject God's truth themselves or in some way hinder others from receiving it. Thus we read that God has cursed the unbelievers (33.64), the hypocrites (9.68), and those who believe in sorcery and evil (4.52). Violation of God's laws may also invite damnation: some of the Jews, for example, were cursed not only on account of their unbelief (4.46) but also for breaking the Sabbath (4.47). The recipient *par excellence* of the divine curse is, of course, Satan himself (4.118).

See also: **mubahala; oaths**

COLIN TURNER

LANGUAGE AND THE QUR'AN

The Qur'an is the oldest book in the Arabic language-system and even today is regarded as the final authority regarding diction, morphology, syntax, grammar and rhetoric in Arabic. The Qur'an is revered by Muslims not only as a book of religious guidance and knowledge but also as a divine miracle of language, the very speech of God, which no man can rival or surpass. The doctrine of inimitability (*i'jaz al-Qur'an*), the notion that the Qur'an is miraculous in both form and content, is the logical consequence of this view.

In the Qur'an, the language of the text is explicitly described as a 'pure Arabic tongue' (*lisanun 'arabiyyun mubin*) (16.103), clearly intelligible to the Prophet Muhammad's Arabian audience since it was their native language: 'We have sent it down as an Arabic Qur'an so that you may understand' (*inna anzalnahu Qur'anan 'arabiyyan la'alakum ta'qilun*) (12.2). The word 'Arabic' is mentioned ten times in the Qur'an, with three instances of collocation with the word 'tongue' (*lisanun*) and seven of collocation with the word 'Qur'an'. The perfected state of this Arabic text, in both form and content, is also referred to: 'An Arabic Qur'an that is free of defects' (*Qur'anan 'arabiyyan ghayra dhi 'iwajin*) (39.28). In terms of style, the Qur'an is said to be revealed in the 'best of discourse' (*ahsana al-hadith*) (39.23), with the power to 'make shiver' (*taqsha'ir*) and 'soften' (*talin*) the hardest of skins and heart. No language other than Arabic is ever mentioned. However, all foreign or non-Arabic 'tongues' and nations are referred to by the generic term *a'jamiyyan* (16.103; 41.44; 26.198). It is made explicit that every nation had been sent a messenger who, by necessity, speaks in the native tongue of his people: 'And we have not sent a messenger except in the tongue [language] of his people (*bi-lisani qawmihi*) to make clear to them [the message]' (*wa ma arsalna min rasulin illa bi-lisani qawmihi li-yubayyina lahum*) (14.4). Hence all scriptures – the Torah, the Gospels and the Qur'an – are equally revered as divine revelations from God, notwithstanding the fact they were transmitted in different languages. The Word of God is said to exist in a heavenly archetypal book called the 'Preserved Tablet' (*al-lawh al-mahfuz*) (85.22), which is presumably written in an ideal Proto-language out of which came all scriptures of the world.

Nowhere is the gap between Muslim and Western scholarship as wide as it is in the area of language. Three of the thorniest linguistic issues concern vocabulary, declensional system and syntax. Muslim scholars have devoted their attention to listing and defining the superior properties of the Qur'an, citing such aspects as its extensive vocabulary, symmetrical morphology, complex syntactical patterns (fronting, deletion, parallelism), numerous figurative devices (scholars have listed over a hundred different kinds of device, including metaphor, simile, synecdoche, allegory, metonymy, repetition, antithesis and hyperbole), and innovative use of conventional literary forms (parables, oaths, narratives, dialogues and so on). In contrast, Western scholars ever since Theodore Nöldeke, the so-called 'Dean of Qur'anic Studies', have deemed it necessary to attack the notion of the Qur'an's divine origin by demeaning the language and critically searching for so called 'linguistic defects'. For example, in his detailed discussion of the 'stylistic and syntactic peculiarities of the language of the Koran', Nöldeke (1910: 5–23) describes the syntax as 'clumsy', 'ugly', 'inappropriate', 'very unusual', 'very hard', 'rough' and so forth. He sums up his discussion as follows: 'Muhammad may have meditated long over the contents of his revelation before he gave it to the world, but he paid scant attention to its form.' Obviously, this sort of criticism cannot be reconciled with the doctrine of *i'jaz*, commonly held throughout Islam, according to which the Qur'an is a true miracle not only in subject matter but also as a work of art (Paret, 1983: 204).

Although it is customary for discussions of the language of the Qur'an to include references to figurative devices and literary forms, the discussion here will concentrate mainly on three linguistic issues: vocabulary, declensional endings and syntax, basically because of the centrality of these features and their far-reaching implications for Qur'anic Studies. In essence, it is not possible to understand the developments in the field without some knowledge of these three controversial issues, which have dominated the interest of Western commentators for the past century.

Doctrine of inimitability (of form)

The doctrine of inimitability is derived from passages in the Qur'an where God explicitly states the text's divine origin ('This Qur'an is not such as can be produced by other than God; it is a confirmation of what came before it, and a fuller explanation of the Book wherein there is no doubt, from the Lord of the worlds') (10.37) and passages where God challenges the pagans of Mecca to produce ten *suras* or even a single *sura* as powerful as those that make up the Qur'an ('Or do they say he [Muhammad] has forged it? Say: Bring you then a *sura* like unto it, and call upon [to aid you] whomever you can besides God, if you are truthful') (10.38). According to Muslim scholars, this challenge (*tahaddi*) was not a rhetorical device; the Prophet's opponents could not take up the challenge simply because they could never match the power and beauty of God's words. It is important to note that the Prophet Mohammad was explicit about not confusing his words with those of the Qur'an, hence the emergence of the science of *hadith* (in literal terms, 'new developments' or 'news' of the Prophet), which documents his own sayings, his own actions and his own

exegeses of the Qur'an. In the West, the divine origin of the Qur'an is often contradicted, with many scholars describing it as 'Muhammad's book', following the lead of the first English translation of the Qur'an, by Alexander Ross, which was entitled *The Alcoran of Mahomet*. To date, whole books are still devoted to speculating on the possible informants that were providing the Prophet with such accurate details of sacred history and inspiring him with such powerful diction and imagery. A quote from Paret (1983: 208) illustrates how adamant Western scholars are in denying even the slightest possibility of the Qur'an's divine origin: 'Whoever Muhammad's authorities may have been, one thing is certain: the material was translated into Arabic from another language. This translation was in all probability carried out in an oral form and during Muhammad's lifetime, perhaps especially for him.'

There are basically two broad divisions in the doctrine of inimitability: inimitability of content and inimitability of form. The first includes such categories as scientific accuracy, accuracy of predictions and prophecies, and innovation in legislative and civic laws. The latter division is devoted to rhetoric and style (*balagha*), comprising such features as figurative expressions, context (*wujuh*), cohesion, syntactic patterns (among them fronting, *taqdim*; postponement, *ta'khir*; and deletion, *admar*) and declensional endings (*i'rab*). It is significant to note that the Meccans never questioned the Qur'an's linguistic excellence. What they rejected was the novelty of its ideas, especially the notion of resurrection and monotheism: 'Has he made the Gods all into One God. Verily this is a curious thing ... We have not heard of this in the previous religion. This is nothing but an invention!' (38.5–7). The language, on the other hand, was deemed so superior, indeed so 'beautiful', that even in the eyes of the Prophet Muhammad's bitterest opponents it transcended the merely human. This dilemma is documented in a telling passage in the Qur'an (74.18–25), where al-Walid b. al-Maghira, the most prominent elder of Quraysh and the Prophet's most committed opponent, is forced to state in public his own evaluation of the Qur'an, in particular whether he believed it to be 'mortal' speech or 'divine':

Lo! He thought and schemed. Death seize him, how he schemed. Again, death seize him, how he schemed. Then he reflected. Then he frowned, and scowled. Then he retreated and was proud. Then he said: 'This is naught but the magic of old. This is naught but the speech of mortals.'

This passage makes it clear that the pagans of Mecca realized instinctively that the Qur'an could not have been the words of Muhammad, hence their accusation of sorcery and their insistence that the verses he was reciting must have been fabricated or forged:

And those who disbelieve say: 'This is nothing but a lie that he has fabricated, and other people have helped him with it.' In fact, what they say is an injustice and a distortion. And they say: 'Tales of the ancients which he has had written down; and they are dictated to him mornings and afternoons.' (25.4–5)

Because the language of the Qur'an was so captivating, the Quraysh had to literally ban their people from listening to Muhammad's recitations. It is significant to note that many of the elders and nobles of the Quraysh, though hardened at first against the new ideas preached by the Qur'an, finally succumbed to the beauty of its language. We know, for example, that 'Umar b. al-Khatab, the second caliph, proclaimed his conversion immediately upon hearing the verses of *sura Taha* (20).

From the ninth century onwards, the theme of inimitability had been extensively discussed by Muslim theologians who believed that the Prophet had not performed any miracle except one: namely, the miracle that, although he could neither read nor write, he had received a revelation that was far superior to anything that the Arab poets and orators had ever written or heard. The most famous works on the doctrine of inimitability are two medieval treatises by al-Jurjani (d. 1078), *Dala'il al-i'jaz* (the Arguments of Inimitability) and *Asrar al-balagha* (the Secrets of Eloquence). To comprehend fully the centrality of this doctrine for Muslim scholars, one must first keep in mind the fact that the tribes of the Arabian peninsula had a thriving poetic tradition, and that poetry, composed and recited by skilled poets, was an integral and important element of their tribal life. Furthermore, the language in which these poems were composed showed a high degree of literary sophistication, richness in diction and complexity of derivational morphology and syntactic patterning. One must also remember that the mode of poetic transmission was not just oral but also written, since many of the more famous poems (such as those by Umru'u l-Qays) were written down and even hung on the walls of the *Ka'ba* (called *al-mu'alaqat* or the Suspended Odes). Although many Western scholars have claimed that the 'suspension' of the Odes was a mere fable invented in order to explain the name *al-mu'alaqat*, the fact is that it was an ancient Arabic tradition to hang important documents and treatises on the *Ka'ba*. We know, for example, that when the Quraysh cut off relations with the Prophet Muhammad and his clan, a declaration or quittance was written on a sheet and hung up inside the *Ka'ba*. There is thus no reason to believe that the Arabs would not have hung their most famous poems there, given the seriousness of attention and high esteem given to poetry and poets.

Vocabulary

From a linguistic point of view, the Qur'an was the most important event in the history of the Arabic language. It not only codified the grammar and lexicon of the language, it also presented the Arabs with linguistic possibilities never before imagined by poets and orators. It enriched the lexicon by using words in entirely new contexts, by reviving ancient and rare words, and by the symmetrical use of synonyms, antonyms, hyponyms, homonyms, polysemy and other semantic and phonological relationships between words.

The main controversy concerning the vocabulary of the Qur'an centres on the question of whether or not the Qur'an contains foreign loanwords. The consensus among Muslim grammarians and lexicographers is that the Qur'an is written in a 'pure Arabic tongue' and hence cannot contain any foreign words whatsoever. Although some words were found to be in other languages or used in similar religious contexts, these were viewed as cognates that existed in all Semitic languages, i.e. they all derived from the same common stock of Semitic words. Certainly much of the vocabulary of the Qur'an was difficult and tradition has it that some words, such as the word *abban* in 80.31 (*wa hadaiq ghulban/wa fakihatan wa abban*, 'And gardens dense with trees and fruits and *abban*') were at first left unresolved by the Prophet's companions. These difficult and rare words later became known as *ghara'ib* or *gharib* and were the subject of much

discussion by medieval exegetes. The first Arabic dictionary, the famous *Kitab al-'Ayn* written by al-Khalil, documents all words of Arabic origin, citing copious examples to prove that many of the rare and archaic words were indeed used by the Bedouins and could in fact be found in pre-Islamic poetry. Interestingly enough, many of the archaic terms of the Qur'an have now become familiar everyday words. These include *hanan* (compassion) (19.13), *alim* (painful) (11.26), *athathan* (belongings) (19.74) and *nadiyan* (place of gathering) (19.73), now commonly used to refer to a club (*nadi*). The commentary by Muqatil b. Sulayman (d. 150/767), one of the earliest commentators on the Qur'an, contains a large number of familiar words that he felt were in need of explanation, e.g. *mubin* (clear), which he replaced by *bayyin*; *naba'un* (news), replaced by *hadith*; *nasib* (share), replaced by *haz*. Some words were also revealed to have dialectical variation, e.g. *yay'as* (13.31) meant 'to know' in the dialect of Bani Malik and not 'to despair', while *al-ara'ik* (18.31) meant 'beds' in the dialect of Yemen.

The basic problem in Western scholarship arises when Arabic is looked upon not as a sister or equal language of Hebrew, Aramaic and other Semitic languages, but as being derived from these languages, i.e. when it is treated as an offspring that presented the original language in a degenerated form. It is this view that compels some Western scholars to constantly look for the etymology of Qur'anic terms in other Semitic languages, convinced that Arabic must by necessity have borrowed its lexicon from these older and more sophisticated languages. In fact, the resemblances between the three main Semitic languages (Hebrew, Aramaic and Arabic), especially in terms of the lexicon, is so striking that at a very early date some Western scholars had begun to remark on this relationship. They collectively called them 'Oriental languages', a name that included not only Akkadian, Hebrew, Aramaic and Arabic but also Ethiopic and even Armenian and Persian; the term 'Semitic languages' was used for the first time only in 1781, by A.L. Schozer. Some scholars of the sixteenth century, Erpenius, for example, even used Arabic to assist them in the study of Hebrew and to explain obscure expressions in Hebrew that could no longer be understood. For example, the Hebrew word *oz*, which occurs no fewer than 164 times in the Old Testament, has traditionally been rendered as 'strength' or 'might' (e.g. Exodus 15: 2, 'The Lord is my strength'), but it can be further elucidated by reference to the cognate Arabic word *'izz*, meaning not only 'strength' but also 'honour', 'glory' and 'self-esteem' (Seale, 1978: 59–60). Its opposite, as it occurs in the Qur'an, is not weakness but servility or humiliation (*dhul*).

Western scholars who adhere to the extreme view that Arabic is a degenerate offshoot have come up with hundreds of words that they claim are derived from a variety of languages: Hebrew, Aramaic, Syriac, Persian, Ethiopic, Turkish and Greek. Jeffrey (1938), for example, in his *Foreign Vocabulary of the Qur'an*, classifies more than 270 words other than proper names that have been regarded as foreign and summarizes the views of European scholars as to their origin. These are divided into three basic types:

1. entirely non-Arabic words, such as *istabrak* (silk, brocade), *zanjabil* (ginger), *firdaws* (paradise);
2. Semitic roots found in Arabic, but used in a new sense, e.g. *fatir* (creator), *darasa* (studied), *sawami'* (cloisters); and

3. words that are genuinely Arabic and commonly used, but used in technical senses or with religious meanings influenced by other languages, e.g. *nur* (light – used in the sense of religion) and *kalima* (word – when used of Jesus).

Other oft-quoted examples of foreign vocabulary include *al-qistas* (scale) (17.35), derived from Greek; *al-sijjil* (15.74), derived from Persian; *al-tur* (mount) (2.63), derived from Syriac; and *kifl* (measure) (57.28), derived from Ethiopic.

Muslim scholars view such etymological claims as attempts to undermine the true antiquity of the Arabic language. For one thing, it does seem ludicrous for the Qur'an to be using foreign words from Greek and Turkish to appeal to the Bedouins of Arabia. In addition, there is certainly no way that the Prophet would have been familiar with the use of such Greek words as, for example, *dikastes* (to judge), from which the Qur'anic word *qistas* meaning 'scale' or 'balance' (17.35; 26.182) is said to have been derived. Indeed, Jeffrey's study is loaded with some highly far-fetched foreign etymologies that are simply untenable as far as modern linguistic theories are concerned. The most obvious example is the word *sijjil* ('And we sent upon them birds in flights, hurling them with stones of *sijjil*') (105.4), which according to Jeffrey (1938: 164–5) is a compound of the two Persian words *säng* (stone) and *gil* (clay, mud). He argues that its meaning is 'lumps of baked clay' and that the two words entered Arabic via Middle Persian. What makes this analysis untenable is the fact that neither of these two Persian words that the Arabic language allegedly compounded are ever lexicalized in the Persian vocabulary. For the lexicon to synthesize two non-existent words is just not linguistically feasible. As Fred

Leemhuis (2001: 118) explains, the trouble with this derivation is that it reeks of having been constructed after the conclusion was reached that *sijjil* must mean the same thing as 'mud', a construction based on the juxtaposition of the parallel Qur'anic phrase 'stones of mud' (51.33). In more recent times, Western scholars (Leemhuis 2001: 124) have come up with a new and much more elaborate etymology for the word. This time the Arabs are said to have borrowed an Aramaic word, *sgyl* – meaning altar stone or sacrarium. This word is itself a direct or indirect loan from the Akkadian *sikillu*, denoting a smooth, shiny stone, which in turn is a non-Semitic Sumerian loanword denoting a kind of plant. The Qur'anic expression *hijaratin min sijjin* would thus quite ambiguously read 'stones of flint'. All this etymological speculation is surprising, given the fact that the word *sijjil* is an ancient Arabic word, already well known before Islam, and derived from the consonantal root *sjjl* meaning 'to mark' or 'to inscribe' – hence the use of the derivative *sijjin* in 83.8, which is quite explicitly defined as 'an inscribed book' (*kitabun marqum*). Hence modern Muslim commentators with a scientific orientation have suggested that *sijjin* might possibly refer to DNA inscriptions, since it is a historical fact that the hurling of these stones against Abraha, the Abyssinian viceroy of Yemen during his campaign against Mecca and the Ka'ba, coincides with the outbreak of smallpox in the region.

A new approach to the language of the Qur'an might shed more light on its vocabulary. According to Robert Brunschvig (2002: 285–95), applying a *negative* approach, i.e. stating not what words are in the Qur'an but rather what words are not included, reveals that the Qur'an is remarkably selective in its terminology. For example, summer (*sayf*) and winter (*shita'*) are used, but never spring (*rabi'*) or autumn (*kharif*). Obviously, these results are significant and demand that closer scrutiny be given to the lexicon of the Qur'an in an attempt to isolate and define the various semantic fields operative in the text. In the case of *sayf* and *shita'*, it appears that there is an attempt to reclassify the seasons into a three-way semantic system of oppositions rather than the conventional four-way system. In addition to the two extreme points of summer and winter, the Qur'an (2.189) posits a third season or time period (*mawaqit*) that falls in between these two poles. This interim season is termed *al-ahilla* and is closely aligned to the pilgrimage months (the tenth and eleventh months, and the first ten days of the twelfth month of the lunar year): 'They ask you about the new moons (*al-ahillati*), say: "These are periods of time (*mawaqitu*) for mankind and for the pilgrimage".' Hence we can say that the omission of autumn and spring is a functional strategy in the Qur'an geared to redefining the lexical field of seasons into a more religiously oriented three-member system of time; between them, *sayf*, *shita'* and *al-ahilla* constitute the Arabic system of seasons. All three members are mutually incompatible, but together they cover all the relevant area of seasons since there are no other seasonal terms mentioned in the Qur'an. A more detailed study using the negative approach will, undoubtedly, reveal more significant classifications.

System of declensions

The role of inflections in Qur'anic Arabic has been a matter of considerable controversy. To understand the centrality of declensional endings in the Arabic language-system, it is best to first look briefly at the language of pre-Islamic poetry.

As scholars have pointed out, the linguistic structure of the large body of pre-Islamic Arabic poetry that has come down to us reveals a high degree of elaboration in the inflectional system of the language, a richness in derivational morphology and a markedly 'synthetic' character. For example, a single word like *aktatabaha* ('he caused it to be written, continuously') (25.5) conveys the idea of person, number and tense, along with the root meaning of 'write' and the added semantic content of repetitiveness that is signalled by the duplicative form of the middle consonant /t/; this would require three or four words in English. The three key synthetic Proto-Semitic features are:

1. a set of short vowel case inflections suffixed to the nouns, adjectives and pronouns, e.g. *al-maliku* (nominative), *al-malika* (accusative) and *al-maliki* (genitive);
2. the suffixation of *-n* (so-called 'nunnation') in Arabic *tanwin* to designate indefiniteness, i.e. *-un* (nominative), *-an* (accusative) and *-in* (genitive); and
3. a set of short vowels suffixed to imperfect verbs to indicate mood.

In the other Semitic languages contemporaneous with sixth- and seventh-century classical Arabic these features have all been lost. Hence, compared with the other Semitic languages living at the same time – Aramaic, for example – Arabic appears more archaic in origin, i.e. its conservatism should be taken as evidence of its antiquity.

In the nineteenth century, when it became possible to attempt a reconstruction of the Proto-Semitic language analogous to the reconstruction of Proto-Indo-European, Arabic was found to be one of the most archaic Semitic languages and in many respects became the model for the description of the Semitic language type. (The results of these studies in Semitic comparative linguistics were collected and summarized in Brockelmann, 1908–13.) This was basically because of its apparent conservatism, in particular its retention of a complex declensional system. These declensions were a part of the very grammar of the language, without which it would be difficult or impossible to understand the semantic relations of words in a sentence. It thus seems surprising that some Western scholars should advocate the untenable hypothesis that classical Arabic did not contain the inflectional endings and that they were simply fabrications of later philologists. One can only assume that this hypothesis was posited mainly to support the preconceived notion that Arabic was a degenerate offshoot of Hebrew and Aramaic, since acknowledging the presence of these declensions would inadvertently attest to the antiquity of Arabic. From a modern linguistic perspective, negating the Arabic declensional system would entail a total restructuring of all synthetic languages. One would have to to assume that Latin, for example, did not indicate distinctions of number, gender or case, that there was basically no distinction between *domini* and *dominum*; or that Old English did not retain the genitive suffix *–um*, which is found in the familiar word *heofonum* in the Old English version of The Lord's Prayer.

To strengthen the notion that the language of the Qur'an did not contain declensions, a further hypothesis was maintained by Western scholars, namely that diglossia had already existed in pre-Islamic Arabia, i.e. that there existed two forms of the language, a written and more elevated form that used declensional endings, and a vernacular form that was free of all such case endings. The former variety is usually called Qur'anic *koine*, while the latter is referred to as collectively as Pre-Islamic dialects. According to Zwettler (1978: 109), the Arab poets were specialists in an archaic form of the language and they were the only ones who were still able to handle the complicated declensional endings. In his view, the case system was beyond the ordinary speaker and could only be acquired by professional poets and their transmitters after a long period of training. The problem with this claim is that it assumes that the case endings were absent in everyday Bedouin speech, and this is certainly not the case. For one thing, even today the Bedouins use declensional endings in their colloquial speech. In addition, if we assume that diglossia had already existed in pre-Islamic Arabia, how can we account for the fact that inflectional endings are present in ancient South Arabian and Nabataean inscriptions? In these inscriptions compound names (noun plus noun constructions) like *'abdu 'l-ilahi* (the servant of God) are fully inflected, i.e. the first noun is in the nominative case (*–u*) and the second noun is in the genitive (*–i*). Tradition also provides us with numerous instances of wrong declensional usage by newly converted Muslims at the time of conquest. These distortions of case endings were the subject of much debate among the Prophet's Companions, who feared not only that the pure classical language of the Qur'an would be corrupted, but that the very meaning of the verses would be distorted. Evidently, this supports the view that the language still contained declensional endings and that these could not be omitted without the risk of at least ambiguity or at worst the sentence losing its meaning altogether. Equally noteworthy is the fact that in the old commentaries on the Qur'an no distinction

was made between declensional vowels and other vowels embedded between consonants, i.e. the end *–u* of *yaktubu* was the same as the medial *–u*, although the latter is the declensional ending. This is basically due to the fact that the vowels were not viewed as distinct phonemes but as features of the consonants. Each of the twenty-eight consonants of the alphabet had three different realizations or allophones, e.g. the consonant /*b*/ could be realized as *ba*, *bi* or *bu*, and likewise /*k*/ was produced as *ka*, *ki* or *ku*. One cannot, therefore, separate the declensional vowels, basically because they are part and parcel of the phonological and morphological structure of the language.

Certainly in the Qur'an, where the free word order, syntactic deletions, fronting of objects and postponement of main verbs are prevalent, these declensional endings become indispensable markers of meaning. For example, in the *idafa* construction, or possessive noun$_1$ plus noun$_2$ pattern, such as is found in 7.50 (*wa nada ashabu al-nari ashaba al-janati*, 'and the dwellers of the fire will call the dwellers of paradise'), the genitive *–i* case endings in *ashabu al-nari* ('the dwellers of the fire') and *ashabu al-janati* ('the dwellers of paradise') are crucial, since there is no other device to carry the possessive relationship between noun$_1$ and noun$_2$. The free word order in 9.3 also necessitates the use of declensions: *inna allaha bari'un min al-mushrikina wa rasuluhu*, 'God is absolved from the idolaters (*al-mushrikina*) and His messenger (*rasuluhu*)'. In this example, any slight change in the declensional endings would lead to a blasphemous statement: a change of *rasuluhu* to *rasulihi*, from nominative *–u* to genitive *–i*, for example, would imply that God is absolved from both the idolaters and the Prophet, and not that both God and the Prophet are absolved of the idolaters. Another classic example is 35.28: *inama yakhsha allaha min 'ibadihi al-'ulama'u*, 'But fearing God (*allaha*) from among His servants are the scholars (*al-'ulama'u*)'. Here again, any slight change in declensional endings would suggest that it was God who was fearful of the scholars and not vice versa.

Other Western scholars went a step further in the theory of diglossia, postulating their own highly subjective hypotheses regarding the relationship between the text of the Qur'an and the vernacular speech of Mecca. Karl Vollers (1906) argues that the revelation must have originally taken place in the colloquial language of the Prophet and the Meccan tribes, which was basically without case endings (*i'rab*). He bases his claim on what he perceives to be orthographical resemblances, i.e. the omission of the glottal stop (*hamza*), between the text of the Qur'an and the local pronunciation of the Hijaz. According to Vollers, the text was transformed during the period of the conquests into a language that was identical with the poetic language of the Najd area. The reason behind this transformation, he asserts, was the wish to raise the language of the Qur'an to the level of that of the poems. Those who were responsible for the alleged translation were particularly strict in the matter of the *hamza* and case endings. Although quite popular among Western commentators when it first appeared, Vollers' theory has now been abandoned, having been called into question by a number of Western scholars. The presupposition of a large-scale conspiracy in early Islam concerning the linguistic transformation of the text is also no longer held by anyone. Certainly, the delivery of the text in a vulgar variety of the Arabic language is not only unacceptable but also untenable.

As Versteegh (1997) explains, because the existence of a poetic register of the language is undisputed, it is highly unlikely that the revelation could have been written in anything but this prestigious variety of the language. In the late 1940s a number of European writers, most notably Blachère and Gaudefroy-Demombynes (1956) and Rabin (1951), reached the conclusion that the language of the Qur'an was essentially identical, in vocabulary, verbal forms, syntax and pronunciation, with the elevated language of the ancient Arabic poets. It was this language that was subsequently to live on through the centuries as the language of classical Arabic literature. For Rabin, the language of the Qur'an 'stands somewhere between the poetical standard *koine* and the Hijazi dialect'. This view has now been accepted by most Western scholars.

There are three basic kinds of evidence for the presence of declensions in the Qur'an. These can be listed as follows:

1. The rhyming patterns of many of the *suras* are based on case endings. Consider, for example, *sura* 4 (*An-nisa'*, the Women) where 171 verses out of a total of 176 end in the accusative (*–an*) case endings – pronounced as *–a* with deletion of the /n/ in 'pausal form' (end position). The *sura* succeeds in mobilizing a number of word classes that can syntactically function as accusatives; these are:
   (a) accusative nouns functioning as direct objects, such as *sa'iran*, *sabilan*;
   (b) accusative adjectives, such as *raqiban* and *kabiran*, which function as complements of the modal verb *kana* ('was');
   (c) accusative adjectives, such as *ma'rufan*, *sadidan* and *aliman*, which function as post-modifiers of nouns that themselves function

as direct objects in the accusative case; and

(d) accusative adjectives of state or condition (termed *hal* in Arabic grammar and equivalent to subject/object complements in English), such as *da'ifan* and *khalilan*.

What is most interesting is the fact that all five exceptions to these accusative rhyme-words end in the nominative case with *–un/-u* (*halimun*, *'azimu*, *muhinun*, *rahimun* and *hakimun*), suggesting that these stylistic variations are meant to front the highly symmetrical morphological and declensional system operative in the text. (For a comprehensive quantitative survey of the rhyming patterns in the Qur'an, see Stewart, 2001.)

2. Declensions are present in the early first-/seventh-century Qur'anic manuscripts, written in the so-called Hijazi script (*Masahif San'a*), that were discovered in Yemen. Although the text is consonantal, i.e. it is not vowelled, nevertheless all three declensional endings (nominative, accusative and genitive) are clearly embedded in the morphological structure of plural words. For example, in 7.42 (*Masahif San'a* 60–61) the added *alif* attached to the ends of the words *'adhab* and *di'f* in the noun plus adjective combination *'adhaban di'fan* clearly indicates the accusative ending *–an* ('So give them double torments (*'adhaban di'fan*) of Hell'). In addition, the nominative case (*–un*) is present in the declensional ending of the plural adjective *khalidun* (also at 7.42: 'These are the dwellers of paradise. They will therein be eternal (*khalidun*)'). The genitive declension is embedded in the two plural nouns *al-mujrimin* and *al-zalimin* (7.40 and 7.41 respectively: 'Thus do We recompense the criminals (*al-mujrimin*)' and 'Thus do We recompense the

oppressors (*al-zalimin*)'. (Pages 60 and 61 of *Masahif San'a* can be found in Gruendler, 2001: 135–44, Template VI.)

3. For medieval Arab grammarians, the Qur'an put a fixed corpus of language at their disposal. They perceived their task as being simply to account for every single linguistic phenomenon and, in particular, the case endings in the sentence. These were referred to as *i'rab*, a term that originally meant the correct use of Arabic according to the language of the Bedouin but came to mean declension. The presence of declensions can be deduced from various medieval references, among them the first Arabic dictionary, *Kitab al-'Ayn*, compiled by al-Khalil b. Ahmad (d. 175/791), and the first grammar, the famous *Kitab* by Sibawayhi (d 177/793). In both these ancient sources, data are obtained not only from the Qur'an and verses of poetry, but also from contemporary Bedouins. It is clear from these sources that Arab lexicographers and grammarians regarded the Bedouin as the true speakers of Arabic and they were praised for the purity of their language. Many grammarians of the ninth and later centuries also resorted to unlettered Bedouin informants to settle disputed points of Arabic grammar, claiming that they alone still spoke the language with full case endings and mood markers. We can thus infer that the Arabs of Muhammad's time also spoke a similar, if not even more conservative, type of fully inflected synthetic language. We can equally infer that the classical Arabic of the Qur'an, with all its declensional endings, was in fact a living language among the Bedouins at the time, and that classical Arabic (the poetic register) and the so-called vernacular, essentially represented one and the same language.

Declensions were a consistent feature in both registers simply because Arabic was a synthetic language and this was the way all speakers of synthetic languages made themselves understood.

The relationship between the language of everyday life and the elevated style of the Qur'an and poetic corpus in seventh-century Arabia is still much disputed. The consensus of Muslim scholars has always been that the language of the Qur'an was the language of the Prophet and his Companions, in other words that their everyday speech was identical in terms of morphology, syntax and lexicon with the language of the Qur'an; they agree too that it was the same language as that of pre-Islamic poetry. The majority of Muslims also hold that the Qur'an was revealed in the language of the Prophet's tribe, Quraysh, and that this in itself was an eclectic synthesis of 'all that was best' in the various tribal dialects. Tradition has it that the Qur'an was revealed in seven different dialects or 'readings' (sab' huruf) that are but manifestations of the Arabic language-system: i.e. they all belong to the general vocabulary of the 'arabiyya from which native speakers freely selected items. From this, one should not conclude that the various Bedouin dialects were strikingly different or that they represented different languages. In fact, the language of the pre-Islamic poems, which represented many different Bedouin tribes (al-a'rab), is basically one and the same, since the dialectical variations between poems are too trivial to be taken into account. This is a phenomenon called by Arab grammarians tadakhul al-lughat (the intermingling of dialects). As an example, we may quote the case of the tribe of Bani Tamim who, in their production of words with the back vowel /a/, shifted or inclined their tongue towards the front of the mouth, producing a long front vowel /i/; this dialect was later classified by grammarians as imala (inclination). Thus, instead of the expected yahsabu, the Bani Tamim would say yahsibu. Since all Bedouins were regarded as native speakers, these pre-Islamic variants were accepted by the Arab tribes as part of the genius of the Arabic language which, just like any other Semitic language, contained in its lexicon a large number of synonyms and homonyms. One must assume that the 'Arabic tongue' (lisanun 'arabiyyun) mentioned in the Qur'an refers to all the dialects of the tribes living in the Arabian peninsula, and not just the western dialect of Quraysh or Mecca. Although the Qur'an was revealed in the Hijaz, and was first written down in an orthography reflecting western pronunciation, to regard the Qur'an as being in a particular dialect is to utterly reverse the facts of the case. In the final analysis, all readings were understood by the Bedouins and hence there can be no room for doubt that in the Qur'an we have the Arabic language as it was spoken throughout the length and breadth of Arabia.

The syntax

When Sibawayhi wrote the grammatical description of the Arabic language in his famous Kitab in the eighth century (barely 150 years after the death of the Prophet), what was revealed was a remarkably symmetrical and complex system of morphology and syntax. It is this remarkable symmetry, which sprang as if from nowhere, that perplexed Western scholars and led many of them to try to link the grammar of the Qur'an to foreign linguistic traditions, or else to accuse the Arab grammarians of inventing the grammar, even though it was obvious that the writings of these medieval grammarians were no more than a detailed description of the syntax of the Qur'an.

Perhaps the thorniest issue concerning the language of the Qur'an is that of the form and syntax of the Qur'an. Even a so-called 'fair-minded' and sympathetic scholar like R.A. Nicholson (1930: 161) has these vicious remarks to offer in his *Literary History of the Arabs*:

> The preposterous arrangement of the Koran is mainly responsible for the opinion unanimously held by European readers that it is obscure, tiresome, uninteresting: a farrago of long-winded narratives and prosaic exhortations, quite unworthy to be named in the same breath with the Prophetic Books of the Old Testament.

Unfortunately, Nicholson's textbook has been the standard English-language history of Arabic literature ever since its publication in 1907; one can only imagine how imbedded these negative views of the Qur'anic style have become. Here is what Bell (2001: 16) has to say about *sura* 66 (the Prohibition):

> This *surah* is very disjointed, and seems to consist of a collection of discarded passages of various dates. Verses 1 and 2 go together, but as they are addressed to the Prophet personally, they possibly were not publicly recited. It is very unlikely that verses 3 and 4 were published. If recited at all, they were probably recited to the two wives.

The popular notion among Western scholars that the form of the Qur'an was 'disjointed' or 'chaotic' has been asserted only since its fragmentary and piecemeal process of revelation, over a period of twenty-three years, had been firmly established and documented. By continually hammering away at this alleged disjointedness, Western scholars could make the claim that the form of the Qur'an was as fragmented and disjointed as its manner of revelation.

The divergent views of Muslim and Western scholars regarding the form and syntax of the Qur'an are obviously irreconcilable. What Muslim scholars see as an instance of beautiful wording is immediately perceived by Western scholars as a linguistic defect. Where Muslim scholars hail the cohesiveness of the text, Western scholars speak about the difficulty of comprehending it or even finding logical connections between subordinate and main clauses. According to Paret (1983: 204), for example, the syntax is so disjointed that the reader is compelled to perform some 'mental acrobatics' to understand the connection between the various constituents of a sentence. As he sees it, the reader is constantly forced to supply missing information in order to understand the text. However, a closer look at Paret's parenthetical insertions reveals that these are not only redundant but in many instances inaccurate. Part of the problem, of course, is the sloppy language that Paret uses to translate the text, and the strange punctuation and parentheses that he employs combine to impart a false impression of disjointedness. Here, for example, is his rendition of 77.1–5: 'By those who are sent one after the other [in bands?] surge onwards, breach[?] and scatter[?] [everything] and exhort [men] to forgiveness or as a warning!' In contrast to the incoherence of this English translation, the Arabic original is highly symmetrical and cohesive on both the syntactic and semantic levels. This is how the text should read:

> By the dispatchers (*al-mursalat*) that are dispatched successively (*'urfan*). By the violent winds (*al-'asifati*) that blow violently (*'asfan*). By the scatterers (*al-nashirati*) that scatter (*nashran*). By the separators (*al-fariqati*) that separate (*farqan*).

By the deliverers (*al-mulqiyati*) of the revelation (*dhikran*).

The difficulty of this passage stems from the fact that all the nouns are synecdoches of angels and winds, both of which are sent by God to specific locations and for specific purposes. The noun *mursalati*, an agentive noun derived from the root verb *r/s/l/* ('to send'), refers to these entities not only metaphorically but also syntactically. Anyone familiar with the Qur'an will immediately recognize and retrieve the referents of *mursalati*, since angels and winds are always in the Qur'an syntactically collocated with the tri-consonantal root verb *r/s/l/*. The same is true for all the other nouns: *'asifat* are the violent winds of destruction, *nashirat* are the regenerative winds that 'scatter' (*tanshur*) clouds and rain, *fariqati* are the angels that 'fragment' (*tufariq*) the verses of the Qur'an, and *muliqiyat* are the angels that 'deliver' (*tulqi*) God's revelations. Semantically, all these nouns are part of one lexical field that has been signalled by the initial *mursalati*, i.e. all refer to the successive dispatchers sent by God to warn people of the coming Day of Judgement, be they angels, prophets or winds. The semantic affinities between these five nouns are further accentuated by the successive use of the cognate sequences: *'asifati–'asfan, nashirati–nashran, fariqati–farqan*.

Perhaps part of the inability of Western writers to perceive the cohesiveness of the text – what Paret refers to as the 'logical connection between the subordinate and main clause' – stems from the basic opposition between Western and Eastern standards of rhetorical eloquence. In the Arabic language-system, eloquence is synonymous with brevity and compactness; hammering home an idea in as few words as possible is a sign of linguistic competence. Indeed, the pre-Islamic poets were renowned for their brevity and their ability to pack rich meanings into condensed structures; hence their recourse to the syntactic device of deletion or ellipsis. In the Qur'an syntactic deletions are similarly prevalent, but they are most often stylistically mobilized to mirror or re-enact the theme of the passage. Hence Qur'anic ellipsis is extensively studied by linguists and literary critics alike, and regarded as a basic feature of the text's miraculousness or inimitability. In contrast, Western critics see such stylistic deletions as an indication of 'confusion' or 'disruption'. It might be significant to note that, according to some Arab scholars, when the Qur'an addresses Arabs and Bedouins, the discourse is full of syntactic deletions. But then when it addresses non-Arabs, the discourse becomes immediately more simple and prosaic, with numerous explanations and repetitions. One of the more prominent instances of deletion can be found in 30.51: 'And if We send a wind and they see it [the crop] turn yellow, they would after that [their initial gladness] become disbelievers'. Here the crucial word that is omitted is *zar'an* ('the crop'), referred to by the preposition *hu* in *ra'a-hu* ('see it'). To retrieve the missing word, one has to be familiar with the Qur'an and be able to recognize other parallel passages in which the word *zar'an* is provided. This passage has puzzled Western commentators, basically because of the strangeness of the image of ?'yellow winds'. Some, like Rippin (2001: 363), have suggested that it refers to a 'sandstorm'. Obviously, once we retrieve the deletion, it becomes clear that the colour yellow refers to the familiar withering of vegetation frequently alluded to in the Qur'an. On a more stylistic level, the deletion of *zar'an* is highly iconic. Since the winds referred to here are winds of destruction, not of regeneration, it would appear that the syntactic deletion is iconically meant to re-enact the destruction of crops in external reality.

Let us take another example to illustrate the divergent views of Muslim and Western scholarship. Interestingly enough, this example is also concerned with the twin themes of winds and resurrection. Here is one of the so-called 'sign' passages which, according to Bell, is a classic illustration of the 'maundering style' of the Qur'an:

> He it is who sends the winds as heralds in front of his mercy [i.e. the rain], until when they have lightened heavy clouds, We [note the change of pronoun] drive it to dead soil, and send down water thereby, and bring forth therein all kinds of fruits; thus do We bring forth the dead, maybe ye will be reminded. The vegetation of good land comes forth by the permission of its Lord, but of that which is bad it comes forth only scantily; thus do we turn the signs about for a people who show thankfulness. (7.55–56)

Bell describes this passage as wandering from clouds and rain to the resurrection and then without apparent reason bringing in vegetation a second time. He therefore suggests that the reference to the resurrection has been worked into a passage that originally had nothing to do with it. In order to correct the text and rectify the sudden change of pronouns, he proposes to leave out the latter half of the last verse altogether, creating the following passage:

> He it is who sends the winds as heralds in front of his mercy until, when they have lightened heavy clouds, the vegetation of good land comes forth by the permission of the Lord, but of that which is bad it comes forth only scantily.

By deleting the reference to the resurrection, Bell believes he has made the passage not only into a 'perfectly intelligible statement', but, in fact, 'a very good sermon-illustration implying that lack of response to God's bounty is due to poverty of soul'. What are we to make of Bell's elaborate reworking of the original text? First of all, it is necessary to correct a few non-equivalent English translations: the verb 'lightened', (aqallat) should be rendered as 'to carry' or 'to collect'; the verbs 'send down' and 'bring forth' should be rendered in the causative tense, i.e. as 'cause to send down' and 'cause to bring forth'; and, finally, 'scantily' should be rendered as 'with difficulty' (nakidan). These corrections should highlight the following temporal progression: first the winds are sent by God (yarsil), but when they (of their own volition) collect (aqallat) enough rain-laden clouds, God drives them (suqnahu) to a dead land and they become vehicles by which water is poured (anzalna bihi al-ma'), and in turn vehicles by which fruits and produce are brought forth (akhrajna bihi). This progression should explain the sudden change of pronouns from 'He' to 'We', from speaking of God in the third person to God himself speaking in the first person plural 'We'. In other words, the initial use of the third person singular 'He' is meant to correlate to the regular and consistent movement in the universe, e.g. the blowing of winds. The shift to 'We' occurs when there is a basic variation in the pattern, i.e. when these rain-carrying winds are suddenly diverted from their path to a new location (a dead land), made to empty their load and thus bring about the fruition of what was once dead soil. The sudden shift to the first-person 'We' is made to syntactically mirror this sudden rerouting of the winds. What seems to augment this iconic correspondence between syntax and meaning is the fact that the He/We alternation is consistently employed throughout the Qur'an whenever there is a reference to the winds of resurrection. All references to the regular blowing of winds use a consistent third-person pronoun throughout the verse in question. For example, in 30.48 we find:

> God is He who sends the winds so that they stir the clouds, and so He spreads them (*yabsutuhu*) along the sky as He wills (*kayf yashaa*), and then He fragments them (*yaj'alahu kisfan*) so that you see the raindrops come forth from their midst. Then when He makes them fall upon (*asaba bihi*) whomever he chooses (*man yashaa*) from among His servants ('*ibadihi*), lo, they are glad.

Although this passage resembles our previous passage, the basic difference between them is that here there is no reference to resurrection whatsoever, nor is there a reference to the redirecting of the winds (*suqnahu*). The verb used here, *yabsutuhu*, which is rendered as 'to spread' or 'to distribute', is not a verb that requires a sudden shift to the first person 'We'.

In many ways, Bell's deletion disjoints the original text, rather than making it more intelligible. This is basically because the semantic gap between the collecting of rain-laden clouds and the sprouting of the good land is too wide. The necessary and logical progression between these two poles is missing, i.e. the act of diverting the winds to a barren land, causing the rain to fall and then the soil to sprout. The reference to the 'good land' and the 'bad land', and the comparison between them in terms of ease/difficulty of sprouting, are 'intelligible' only after this reference to the generic act of sprouting and fruition is made. Notice also that the 'good land' here does not refer to rain falling on an already fertile land, but rather to rain falling on a barren land that is in the process of being revived or resurrected. In contrast, the 'bad land' is one that remains 'barren' even after the fall of God's 'mercy'. It is thus hard to perceive in these verses Bell's so-called 'sermon-illustration' that 'lack of response to God's bounty is due to poverty of soul'. The only sermon that this passage illustrates is that, for God, bringing forth the dead is just as easy as rerouting the winds, causing barren lands to sprout or, indeed, the syntactic shift in pronouns. The reference to the 'good' and 'bad' land is, therefore, not a sudden intrusion as Bell suggests, but a logical progression from resurrection to the Day of Judgement, when the distinction between 'good' and 'bad' will be made apparent. There is a subtle suggestion that the resurrection will be an easy event for the righteous but a 'difficult' ordeal (*nakadan*) for the 'bad'.

References and further reading

Bell, R. (2001) 'The Beginnings of Muhammad's Religious Activity', in A. Rippen (ed.) *The Qur'an: Style and contents*, Aldershot: Ashgate, Vol. 24, 259–84.

Blachère, R. and Gaudefroy-Demombynes, M. (1952) *Grammaire de l'arabe classique (Morphologie et syntaxe)*, 3rd edn, Paris: G.-P. Maisonneuve et Larose.

Brockelmann, C. (1908–13) *Grundriß der vergleichenden Grammatik der semitischen Sprachen*, 2 vols, Berlin; repr. Hildescheim: G. Olms, 1966.

Brunschvig, R. (2001) 'Simple Negative Remarks on the Vocabulary of the Qur'an', in A. Rippen (ed.) *The Qur'an: Style and contents*, Aldershot: Ashgate, Vol. 24, 285–96.

Corriente, F. (1971) 'On the Functional Yield of Some Synthetic Devices in Arabic and Semitic Morphology', *Jewish Quarterly Review* 62: 20–50.

Denffer, A.V. (1983) '*Ulum al-Qur'an*: An introduction to the sciences of the Qur'an, London: The Islamic Foundation.

Gruendler, B. (2001) 'Arabic Script', in *EQ*, Vol. 1, 135–44.

Jeffrey, A. (1938) *Foreign Vocabulary of the Qurʾan*, Baroda Oriental Institute.

Jenssen, H. (2001) 'Arabic Language', in *EQ*, Vol. 1, 127–35.

al-Jurjani (1954) *Asrar al-balagha*, ed. H. Ritter, Istanbul Government Press.

—— al-Jurjani (1960) *Dala'il al-iʾjaz*, ed. M. Rida, 6th edn, Cairo, n.p.

al-Khalil b. Ahmad (1988) *Kitab al-ʿayn*, ed. M. al-Mukhzumi and I. al-Samarraʾi, 8 vols, Beirut, n.p.

Leemhuis, F. (2001) 'Qurʾanic Siggil and Aramaic sgyl', in A. Rippen (ed.) *The Qurʾan: Style and contents*, Aldershot: Ashgate, Vol. 24, 117–26.

Muqatil b. Sulayman (1980–87) *al-Tafsir*, ed. A.M. Shihata, 5 vols, Cairo, n.p.

Nicholson, R.A. (1930) *Literary History of the Arabs*, Cambridge: Cambridge University Press.

Nöldeke, T. (1910) *Neue Beiträge zur semitischen Sprachwissenschaft*, Strasburg: K.J. Trübner.

Paret, R. (1983) 'The Qurʾan', in A.F.L. Beeston *et al.* (eds) *The Cambridge History of Arabic Literature: Arabic literature to the end of the Umayyad Period*, Cambridge: Cambridge University Press, 186–217.

Rabin, C. (1951) *Ancient West Arabian*, London: Taylor's Foreign Press.

Rippin, A. (2001) 'Colours', in *EQ*, Vol. 1, 361–5.

Seale, M.S. (1978) *Qurʾan and Bible: Studies in interpretation and dialogue*, London: Croom Helm.

Sibawayhi (AH 1316). *Kitab*, 2 vols, Baghdad: Bulaq.

Stewart, D. (2001) 'Saj' in the Qurʾan: Prosody and structure', in A. Rippen (ed.) *The Qurʾan: Style and contents*, Aldershot: Ashgate, Vol. 24, 213–52.

al-Suyuti, Jalal al-din (2003) a*l-Itqan fi ʿulum al-Qurʾan*, ed. F. Zamarli, Beirut: Dar al-kitab al-ʿarabi.

Versteegh, K. (1997) *The Arabic Language*, Edinburgh: Edinburgh University Press.

Vollers, K. (1906) *Volkssprache und Schriftsprache im alten Arabien*, Strasburg: K.J. Trübner; repr. 1981.

Welsh, A.T. (1986) 'Al-kuran', in *EI*.

Zwettler, M. (1978) *The Oral Tradition of Classical Arabic Poetry: Its character and implications*, Columbus: Ohio State University Press.

See also: **arguments and the Qurʾan;** *aya*; **inimitability**

AFNAN H. FATANI

AL-LAWH AL-MAHFUZ
see: **Preserved Tablet**

LAYLAT AL-QADR

The Prophet Muhammad said, 'Whoever prays on *Laylat al-Qadr* out of faith and sincerity, shall have all their past sins forgiven.' The Prophet also said, 'Seek it in the last ten days, on the odd nights.' It is considered the best of nights, because of the words,

> Lo! We revealed it on the Night of Power. Ah, what will reveal to you what the Night of Power is! The Night of Power is better than a thousand months. The angels and the Spirit [Jibril] descend then, by the permission of their Lord, on their missions. [That night is] Peace until the rising of the dawn. (97.1–5)

Imam Nawawi and others explain that 'The Night of Power is better than a thousand months' means that it is better than spending a 1,000 months without it. Given the significance of this night, it is a good idea to select this night especially for the worship of God, supplication (*duʿa*), remembrance (*dhikr*) and other appropriate religious activities.

There is a lot of argument about when the Night actually occurs, since it is not clearly revealed. In general, it is agreed that it is most likely to be in the last ten nights of Ramadan, with the odd nights being more likely. Of the odd nights, the night of the 27th (which is the night before the 27th of Ramadan, for the Islamic day starts with nightfall) is most probable. Al-Shafiʿi said that it is most likely to be the 21st, then the 23rd, then the 27th. Al-Nawawi followed the position that it moves around within the last ten nights. However, it could be outside the last ten nights, but still within Ramadan. It may even be outside Ramadan, according to some early and late scholars. This has been transmitted from many of the Companions of the Prophet, including Ibn Mas'ud. It is one of the reported positions of Imam Abu Hanifa, and also of 'Ibn Arabi (whose position is quoted by Ibn 'Abidin with support), Abu'l Hasan al-Shadhili, Sha'rani and many others generally aligned with Sufism. However, most are of the opinion that the likeliest night is that of the 27th of Ramadan.

See also: **calendar;** *malak*; *tafsir* – Salafi views

OLIVER LEAMAN

LETTERS

The Arabic word for letter, in the sense of alphabetical letter, is *harf* (plural *huruf*). Surprisingly enough, there is not one single occurrence of this word in the whole of Qur'an. At first glance, this omission seems remarkable in light of the fact that, according to Tradition, the recitation of a single letter of the Qur'an is itself a form of prayer and worship. What are we to make of this seemingly deliberate omission? Those familiar with the Qur'an will immediately recall the presence of a huge number of alphabetical letters or graphemes emphatically placed at the beginning of certain chapters and recited as letters of the alphabet. In a sense, then, this omission is functional in that it is meant to front or highlight the value of these letters, called in Arabic *muqatti'at* (the disconnected), *fawatih al-suwar* (the beginning of the *suras*) or *awa'il al-suwar* (the beginning of *suras*), and commonly referred to as 'abbreviated letters' or 'mysterious letters' by Western scholars. Ultimately, this omission

fronts the Arabic *abjad* alphabetical system of twenty-nine letters, derived from the ancient Phoenician writing script (1500 BCE) of twenty-two graphemes, which Arabic shares with all Semitic languages, including Aramaic and Hebrew. It should not be forgotten that each letter in this system also has a numerical value, ranging from 1 to 1,000. It is also significant to note that these abbreviated letters caused much controversy when they were first revealed and even today continue to baffle and intrigue. Muslim scholars often classify them as part of the controversial *mutashabihat* (or verses of 'resemblances') mentioned in 3.7.

The abbreviated letters: *al-muqatta'at*

A number of conjectures have been made as to the meaning of the abbreviated letters found in the opening verses of twenty-nine chapters of the Qur'an. Medieval Muslim scholars saw them as abbreviations, e.g. *alif-lam-ra* for *al-rahman*, *alif-lam-mim* for *al-rahim*, *sad* for *sadiq ya Mohammad*, *ya-seen* for *ya sayyid al-mursalin,* etc. These symbolic interpretations, however, are no longer seen as adequate. A variety of other interpretations were also offered by medieval scholars, the most popular being that they are alphabetical letters whose meaning is based on their numerical value in the *abjad* alphabetical system; that they introduce the rhyme or assonance of their respective *suras*; that they are intended to represent the Arabic alphabet; and that they provide proof that the Qur'an was written in the familiar language of the Arabs. Arab scholarship is divided as to the exact meaning of each letter or combination of letters, but it is unanimously agreed that only God knows their exact meanings.

Western scholars have provided us with a number of highly controversial interpretations. The most famous is Nöldeke's highly biased and radical theory that the abbreviated letters are the initials or monograms of the owners of the manuscripts used by Zayd when he first compiled the Qur'an (Nöldeke, 1860: 215). Nöldeke later reversed his position in response to refutations by Loth (1881: 603) and due to the fact that the letters occur only in late Meccan and early Medinan *suras*. A number of arbitrary and far-fetched theories by Schwally (1919: 68–78) and Watt (1970: 206–12) have likewise been rejected. In general, Western scholars now accept the view that the letters are part of the revelation, having no specific meanings other than as allusions to the Qur'an or the Heavenly Book.

There are a total of fourteen letters arranged in various combinations in the Qur'an. These, arranged in alphabetical order, are *alif, ha, ra, sin, sad, ta, 'ayn, qaf, kaf, lam, mim, nun, ha* and *ya*. A striking fact that cannot be seen as coincidental is that collectively they represent all the consonantal sounds or phonemes in Arabic, based on classifications of manner and place of articulation. Equally striking is the numerical correspondence between the twenty-nine letters of the Arabic alphabet (counting the glottal *hamza*) and the twenty-nine *suras* which contain abbreviated letters. One must also note that the abbreviated letters are always followed by formulaic statements referring to the Qur'an, or the Book; these state that it is a 'clear Book' (*kitab mubin*) or that it is in the Arabic tongue (*lisanin 'arabin mubin*). Al-Suyuti's *Itqan* makes an exception in the case of *suras* 29, 30 and 68. Yet a close reading (Ali, 1977: 120) shows that these *suras* are no exception: in 68 (the Pen), for example, the very first verse begins with the word 'pen' (*qalam*) and a

reference to the writing down of records (*wa ma yasturun*), and ends with the statement that the Qur'an is a message for all the world. One *sura*, 42, has two sets of abbreviated letters *ha-mim* and *'ayn-sin-qaf*, perhaps suggesting a shift from monosyllabic words to more elaborate grammatical constructions such as noun phrases (e.g. determiner plus noun) or sentence-patterns such as nominal clauses. The following list gives the *sura* number, the combination of letters and the opening formulaic verses. Note that there are three *suras* containing only one letter, nine *suras* with two-letter combinations, thirteen *suras* with three-letter combinations, two *suras* with four-letter combinations and two *suras* with five-letter combinations.

Sura	Letter/letters	Formulaic verse
38.	*sad*	By the Qur'an full of reminders
50.	*qaf*	By the glorious (*al-majid*) Qur'an
68.	*nun*	By the pen and what they write
20.	*ta-ha*	We have not sent down the Qur'an upon you to cause you distress
27.	*ta-sin*	These are the verses of the Qur'an and the clear Book
36.	*ya-sin*	By the wise Qur'an
40.	*ha-mim*	A revelation of the Book from God, the Almighty, the All-knowing
41.	*ha-mim*	A revelation from *Al-rahman, Al-rahim*
43.	*ha-mim*	By the clear Book
44.	*ha-mim*	By the clear Book
45.	*ha-mim*	

		A revelation of the Book from God, the Almighty, All-wise
46.	*ha-mim*	A revelation of the Book from God, the Almighty, All-wise
2.	*alif-lam-mim*	That is the Book whereof there is no doubt
3.	*alif-lam-mim*	He has sent down the Book upon you in truth
29.	*alif-lam-mim*	Do people think they will be left alone and not tested because they say: We believe
30.	*alif-lam-mim*	The Romans have been defeated
31.	*alif-lam-mim*	These are the verses of the wise Book
32.	*alif-lam-mim*	A revelation of the Book wherein there is no doubt from the Lord of the Worlds
10.	*alif-lam-ra*	These are the verses of the wise Book
11.	*alif-lam-ra*	A Book whose verses have been made decisive and then explained in detail
12.	*alif-lam-ra*	These are the verses of the clear Book
14.	*alif-lam-ra*	A Book we have sent down upon you to lead people from darkness into light
15.	*alif-lam-ra*	These are the verses of the Book and the clear Qur'an
26.	*ta-sin-mim*	These are the verses of the clear Book
27.	*ta-sin-mim*	These are the verses of the Qur'an and the clear Book
7.	*alif-lam-mim-sad*	A Book sent down upon you so let there be no impedi-

		ment in your heart, to warn thereby and a reminder to believers
13.	*alif-lam-mim-ra*	These are the verses of the Book which have been sent down upon you from your Lord in truth
19.	*kaf-ha-ya-'ayn-sad*	A reminder of your Lord's mercy upon his servant Zachariah
42.	*ha-mim 'ayn-sin-qaf*	Thus does God, the Almighty, the All-wise, reveal to you and to those before you

In recent years, Muslim scholars have attempted to find numerical signification in the above combinations. Certainly, there does seem to be some symmetry and the repetition of identical combinations in consecutive *suras* is noticeable. However, no adequate theory has yet been offered. One interesting observation that deserves mention is that every *sura* that has an abbreviated *ta*, which stands for snake in the *abjad* alphabet, also contains the story of Moses and the snake. Perhaps the most adequate explanation that one can posit is the linguistic one that classifies these letters into their respective sound types: stops, fricatives, nasals and approximants (namely, glides and liquids). The stops are represented by four sounds: glottal *alif*, $/q/$ the voiced velar, $/k/$ the voiceless velar and $/t/$ an emphatic alveolar. Fricatives are represented by five letters: $/h/$ and $/'/$ are voiceless/voiced pharyngeal sounds respectively, the $/s/$ and its emphatic counterpart $/s/$ are both alveo-dentals, and the $/h/$ is glottal. The nasals are represented by the $/m/$, a bilabial, and $/n/$, an alveolar. The glides are represented by the /y/. The liquids are represented by /l/, an alveolar, and /r/, a retroflex. We thus find that, collectively, these letters represent all the places of articulation and manner of articulation that are used in the Arabic language. On a more universal level, they could be identified with a kind of universal phonetic alphabet that defines the possible set of symbols from which all languages are drawn.

References and further reading

Ali, A.Y. (1977) *The Holy Qur'an: Translation and commentary*, Chicago: American Trust Publications.

The Holy Qur'an: English translation of the meaning and commentary (1990), rev. and ed. The Presidency of Islamic Researches, al-Madina al-Munwara: King Fahad Holy Qur'an Printing Complex.

Loth, O. (1881) 'Tabari's Korancommentar', *ZDMG*, xxxv: 603ff.

Nöldeke, T. and Schwally, F. (1909) *Geschichte des Qorans: Über den Ursprung des Qorans*, Leipzig: Dietrich'sche Verlagsbuchhandlung, Vol. 1, 215.

—— (1919) *Geschichte des Qorans: Die Sammlung des Qorans*, Leipzig: Dietrich'sche Verlagsbuchhandlung, Vol. 2, 68–78.

al-Suyuti, J.A. (2003) *Al-itqab fi 'ulum al-Qur'an*, ed. F. Zamarli, Beirut: Dar al-kitab al-'arabi.

Watt, M.W. (ed.) (1970) *Bell's Introduction to the Qur'an*, completely revised and enlarged, Edinburgh: Edinburgh University Press.

See also: **kitab**; **self-referentiality; style in the Qur'an**

AFNAN H. FATANI

LIGHT VERSE

See: **Knowledge**

LOT

see: **Lut**

LOT'S WIFE

see: **Lut's wife**

LOVE

see: **'ishq**

LUT

The prophet Lut (Lot) is mentioned by name in the Qur'an twenty-seven times. Several long passages tell the story of Lot and the people of Sodom to whom he is sent (e.g. 7.80–84; 11.74–83; 15.61–77; 26.160–175; 27.54–58; 29.28–35; 37.133–138; 51.31–37; 54.33–40), a number of which (e.g. 11.74–76; 29.31–32; 51.31) relate Lot to Abraham. Muslim exegetes explain that Lot was the son of Abraham's brother Haran, and that he travelled with Abraham from Babylon and settled in the city of Sodom in the land of Gomorrah.

The people of Sodom are, in Muslim tradition, taken to epitomize sinful people. In 29.28–29, Lot accuses his people of having indecent sex, having sex with men, practising highway robbery and having 'wicked sex' in their meeting hall. In 7.80–81, Lot says that his people commit obscenities never before practised, and prefer sex with men over sex with women. Muslim exegetes add that the people of Lot would rape people who passed on the road, and that they were notorious for farting in public places.

Several verses in the Qur'an refer to the people of Lot who were saved when the city was destroyed (e.g. 7.83; 26.170–171; 29.32–33; 37.134–135). Muslim exegesis has different traditions regarding the number of believers who were saved. In one tradition, Abraham bargains with Gabriel, getting him to agree not to destroy the city if there were in it fourteen believers: Abraham thought he had saved the city, but included in the number of people he counted Lot's wife who, according to the Qur'an, was not a true believer (e.g. 7.83; 27.57; 29.32–33) and lingered behind. 26.171 and 37.135 mention an 'old woman' from the family of Lot who was not saved, and Muslim exegetes take this to be a reference to Lot's wife.

Muslim exegetes also narrate in detail how the angels sent to Abraham went to Sodom in human form to warn Lot and were threatened with rape by the people there. In some of these accounts, it is Lot's wife who betrays the angels to the people.

53.53 mentions the overturned (*mu'tafika*) cities that were destroyed by God. Muslim exegetes identify this with the cities of Sodom, Zeboiyim (Sab'a), Zoar (Sa'ra), Gomorrah (Amara) and Adma (Duma). The angels are said to have taken the cities up into the heavens, turned them over, and cast them upside down into the earth. The Qur'an mentions stones (e.g. 11.82; 15.74), a 'rain' (e.g. 7.83; 26.173; 27.58) and a 'thunder' (e.g. 29.34) sent by God to destroy the people of Sodom. 51.33–34 specifies stones of clay, marked by God, and Muslim exegetes say that the rocks were marked with the name of the people they killed.

Further reading

Blenkinsopp, J. (1982) 'Abraham and the Righteous of Sodom', *Journal of Jewish Studies* 33: 119–32.

Firestone, R. (1990) *Journey in Holy Lands: The evolution of the Abraham–Ishmael legend in Islamic exegesis*, Albany, NY: SUNY Press.

BRANNON WHEELER

LUTF

From the Shi'ite point of view, the Imamate (God-directed leadership) is God's bounty (*lutf*) upon humanity through which the religion is refined. God said: 'Today I have perfected your religion and completed my bounty upon you, and I have chosen Islam to be your religion' (5.3). According to the Shi'a, the Imamate is the grace (*lutf*) of God which attracts humanity towards him and keeps them away from disobedience, yet without compelling them in any way. Grace (*lutf*) is one of God's attributes, and he is exalted in not lacking such an attribute.

In fact, the Qur'an states that: 'Allah is gracious to His servants' (42.19) and this description of God as embodying grace is not uncommon in the Book. The messengers of God were entrusted with the responsibility of bringing new commandments from God to the community. However, some of the messengers were also *imams*. From a Shi'i point of view, the successors of the last Messenger of God were not messengers or prophets and, as such, they did not bring any new message nor did they cancel any of the regulations set by the Prophet. Their mission is to explain, elaborate *shari'a* (divine law) for the people and confirm what the people already know. They are the only individuals who have full knowledge of the Qur'an and the *sunna* of the Prophet Muhammad in his absence, and thus they are the only people qualified to properly interpret the verses of the Holy Qur'an and explain its meaning, as mentioned in Qur'an itself (see 3.7 and 21.7).

An *imam* is a gracious addition to humanity, since when people have a righteous leader who guides them, they can get closer to righteousness and give up corruption and deviations in the matter of religion. A divinely appointed *imam* is also the most appropriate person to rule as the head of the community, someone who can maintain justice and remove oppression and confusion. If a divinely appointed leader is not infallible (*ma'sum*), he would be liable to errors and also to deceiving others. In such a case, no implicit confidence may be placed in his sayings, commands or actions.

A divinely appointed *imam* is the most appropriate person to rule as the head of the community, and people are supposed to follow him in every matter. If he commits a sin, people would be bound to follow him in that sin as well, because of their ignorance of whether that action was a sin or not. After all, he is the most knowledgeable person in the community. Such a situation is not possible, as a result of divine grace, since obedience in sin is evil, unlawful and forbidden. Moreover, it would mean that leader should be obeyed and disobeyed at the same time: obedience to him is obligatory, yet forbidden, which is clearly a contradiction and not commendable.

Besides, if it were possible for an *imam* to commit sin, it would be the duty of other people to prevent him from doing so, as every Muslim is obliged to forbid other people from unlawful acts. In such a case, the *imam* would be held in contempt and, instead of being the leader of community, he would become their follower and his leadership of no use as far as religion was concerned. The *imam* is the defender of divine law and this work cannot be entrusted to fallible hands, nor could any fallible person perform this task properly. Thus infallibility is an indispensable condition for a divinely appointed *imam* or caliph who is the protector and interpreter of the religious law.

We read in the Qur'an that: 'O you who believe! Obey Allah and obey the messenger and those vested with authority (*ulu'l-amr*) from among you' (4.59). This verse obliges Muslims to obey two things: first, they must obey God; second, they must obey the Messenger and those vested with authority (*ulu'l-amr*). The arrangement of the words shows that the obedience of *ulu'l-amr* might be regarded as having the same status and being as much obligatory as is the obedience to the Messenger, because the Qur'an uses just one verb for both of them without repeating that verb. There is also the suggestion that *ulu'l-amr* is of the same importance as the Messenger, otherwise God would not have joined them together in this verse under one verb. God employs a separate verb for himself before mentioning the Messenger and *ulu'l-amr*, which shows that God has higher authority than that of the Messenger and *ulu'l-amr*.

It is also clear from the above verse that *ulu'l-amr* are not restricted to messengers, otherwise Allah would only have said: 'Obey Allah, and obey the Messenger'. But He added *ulu'l-amr* (those who are given authority by God). This is one of the sources of the concept of *imams* and the necessity of obedience to them. The authority of the Messenger of God over the believers was unlimited and comprehensive. Any order given by him, under any conditions, in any place, at any time, was to be obeyed unconditionally. Supreme authority was given to him because he was sinless (*ma'sum*) and free from all types of error and sin. Otherwise, God would not have ordered us to obey him with no question or doubt.

There is a tradition in *Sahih al-Bukhari* which proves that both prophets and divinely appointed caliphs are infallible. Also, from *aya* 4.59, it looks as though the *ulu'l-amr* have been given exactly the same authority over Muslims as the Messenger, and that obedience to *ulu'l-amr* has the same standing as obedience to the Messenger. It naturally follows that *ulu'l-amr* must also be sinless and free from any type of error; otherwise, obedience to them would not have been linked with obedience to the Prophet and would not be required without any condition.

The Sunni tend to interpret *ulu'l-amr minkum* as 'the rulers from among yourselves', i.e. Muslim rulers. Yet it would be reasonable to suggest that this is a difficult reading to reconcile with history. Rulers in the Islamic world have often been cruel and despotic in the past, and some still are, and yet we are told that they are the *ulu'l-amr* mentioned in this verse. If God were to order us to obey such kings and rulers, an impossible situation would be created for Muslims. The ordinary people would be condemned to incurring the displeasure of God, no matter what they did. If they obey these rulers, they have disobeyed God: 'Do not obey a sinner' (76. 24). And yet if they disobey such rulers, they have also disobeyed God in his command to obey Muslim rulers.

Fakhr al-Razi concluded in his *al-Tafsir al-kabir* that this verse proves that *ulu'l-amr* must be infallible. He argues that God has commanded people to obey *ulu'l-amr* unconditionally. It is therefore essential for the *ulu'l-amr* to be infallible, since, if there is any possibility of their committing sin, it would mean that one has to obey them and also disobey them (because they are sinners) in the same action, which is impossible. However, in order to dissuade his readers from the Shi'a, Fakhr al-Razi (n.d., Vol. 10: 144) developed the clever theory that the Muslim community as a whole is infallible. Since the verse contains the word *minkum* (from among you) this shows that *ulu'l-amr* should be interpreted as only part of the Muslim community, since they come from among the whole community, and so could not be the whole *umma*.

Ja'far al-Sadiq (the sixth Imam) said that this verse about the *ulu'l-amr* was revealed about 'Ali and his sons al-Hasan and al-Husayn. Upon hearing this, someone asked the Imam: 'People say, "Why did Allah not mention the name of 'Ali and his family in his Book?"' The Imam answered:

> Tell them that there came the command for *salat* (prayer), but God did not mention whether three or four units ought to be performed; it was the Messenger of Allah who explained all the details. And [the command of] *zakat* (religious tax) was revealed, but God did not say that it is one in every forty dirhams; it was the Messenger of Allah who explained it. And *hajj* (pilgrimage to Mecca) was ordered, but Allah did not say that we should perform *tawaf* (turning around Ka'ba) seven times; it was the Messenger of Allah who explained it. Likewise, the verse was revealed: 'Obey Allah, and obey the Messenger and those vested with authority from among you', and it was revealed about 'Ali and al-Hasan and al-Husayn [who were the only living Imams at the time of the Prophet].

If God had ever mentioned the name of 'Ali in the Qur'an explicitly, those who felt rancour against him would have attempted to alter the Qur'an, or so it is suggested in the Shi'i interpretation of grace. Thus this was the grace of Allah, that he codified all the branches of knowledge of religion in the Qur'an to be understood only by those who are really able to grasp it, and in this way God kept the Qur'an intact.

Further reading

al-Razi, Fakhr al-din (n.d.) *al-Tafsir al-kabir*, Tehran: Dar al-kutub al-'ilmiyya (no publisher: this is an offset of the edition of Muhammad Muhyi'l-Din, Cairo 1352/1933).

See also: **al-Razi; Shi'a; *ulu'l-amr***

OLIVER LEAMAN

LUT'S WIFE

The wife of Lut (Lot), referred to as Waliha in extra-Qur'anic sources, appears along with Noah's wife (Waligha or Wa'ila) in 66.10 as 'an example for those who disbelieve'. Though these women 'were under two of our righteous servants', they were not faithful to their husbands. The Qur'an does not elaborate on the specifics of their misdeeds, but in the classical exegetical literature their sins often include wifely disobedience.

Some commentators suggest that Lot's wife was in league with the sinners of his town, and provided them with information and support. She is repeatedly referred to as 'among those who lag behind' when Lot's household flees the destruction visited on the inhabitants of the city (11.81; 15.60; 27.57; 29.33; 37.135).

The earthly fate of Noah's wife is not explicitly described in the Qur'an. Most interpreters state that she was among those members of Noah's family 'against whom the pronouncement has already gone forth' (23.27; 11.40); thus she was drowned in the flood. A few exegetes, though, hold that she was saved from the flood only to betray Noah later.

Modern exegeses stress that both of these women are held responsible for their own sins, as all disbelievers will be. This point is strengthened by the Qur'anic juxtaposition of their stories with that of Asiya (66.11), wife of the sinful Pharaoh, who achieves reward on her own merits and is not tarnished by his evil deeds.

Further reading

Stowasser, Barbara (1996) *Women in the Qur'an, Traditions, and Interpretation*, Oxford: Oxford University Press, 39–43.

See also: **hell; Nuh; ulu'l-amr**

KECIA ALI

M

MALAK / MALA'IKA

Derived from the Arabic roots *m/l/k/* and *l/'/k/*, the term *malak* (angel) is used fifteen times, and its plural (*mala'ika*) seventy-five times. Angels appear often in the Qur'an, performing a variety of tasks, including playing a role in the drama of Adam's creation. Usually in the heavens, they are at times to be found on earth or even in the netherworld.

Few details are given as to their appearance. They may have two, three or four pairs of wings (35.1); they do not need to eat (25.7; 25.20); and, according to the Egyptian women of the story of Joseph, are exceedingly beautiful. Angels may act as soldiers, fighting alongside the righteous (3.124). As watchers, they record humanity's actions (50.18). They take the souls of the dead and guard over hell (32.11; 43.77); these guards are understood to be nineteen in number (74.30). On the Day of Judgement Allah's throne will be borne by the angels (69.17). The Ark of the Covenant,

holding the *sakina* (inspired peace), will also be borne by the angels (2.248). The *mala a'la* (37.8; 38.69) are taken to be the Lofty Council of angels, who repel eavesdropping demons with bolts of fire. The description of the 'two angels at Babylon', Harut and Marut, who teach people some kind of benign magic, seems out of place in the usual presentation of angels (2.102). Other angels known by name are Gabriel (Jibril) and Michael (Mika'il) (2.98). The former is associated with the bringing down of revelation (26.193 calls him the Faithful Spirit), and in *hadith* literature he accompanies Muhammad on his heavenly ascension or *mi'raj*. Later sources identify 'Izra'il as the angel of death, and Israfil as the angel whose trumpet blast will mark the end time (69.13). The two angels Munkar and Nakir, although not mentioned in the Qur'an, come to be widely identified as the examiners of the dead in their tombs (al-Ghazali, 1995: 135).

The possibility of sending an angel with the Prophet Muhammad is taken seriously. In 6.8–9 the question of why none was indeed sent in this capacity is settled. It seems angels sent in this way would have taken away a sceptical audience's opportunity to eventually accept the message. Less clear is the subsequent point that any such angel would have had to have been in human form, thus increasing the audience's confusion.

Belief in angels, mentioned alongside belief in God, the Last Judgement, the Book and the Messengers is incumbent upon Muslims (2.177). Allah is the enemy of those who oppose his angels (2.98).

More importantly, the angels function as intermediaries between the divine and creation. They announce the glad tidings of John the Baptist to Zakariyya and Jesus to Mary. John the Baptist is declared truthful to a Word from God, subsequently identified as Jesus (3.39; 3.45). Angels may also serve as messengers. However, the vast majority of messengers mentioned in the Qur'an are human. The mission of angels should be understood in a general sense, and not confused with the doctrines of prophecy. The spirit (*ruh*) at times appears alongside the angels in this intermediate function. Passages describe the coming down of the angels and the spirit during the Night of Power (*Laylat al-Qadr*), and the descent of the angels alongside the spirit of God's command, to humanity (97.4; 16.2). Completing this is the move upwards, which both the spirit and the angels undertake; in 70.4 this ascent is described as taking them one day, a distance which would otherwise require 50,000 years – presumably for a human – to cover. Exegetes differ as to the identity of this spirit.

The drama of the creation of Adam is mentioned in at least seven separate places in the Qur'an. In the most complete narrative (2.30–34), God announces, 'I will create a vicegerent on earth', to which the angels reply, 'Will You place therein one who will make mischief and shed blood? While we celebrate Your praises?' This exchange echoes the angels' principal occupation, praising their lord. (Some exegetes claim the angels objected because of their special knowledge of human nature.) The narrative continues with Allah teaching Adam 'the names of all things', and then challenging the angels to recite these names. Their inability to comply betrays their simple nature: 'We have no knowledge beyond that which You have taught us.' Adam then tells the angels their own names, and they are commanded to prostrate themselves to him, yet one named Iblis (Satan) refuses, saying: 'I am better than he is. You created me from fire and him from clay' (7.12). Iblis is cast out of heaven, and destined to oppose humanity until the end of days. The Qur'an is unclear, however, regarding his nature: he is clearly one of the angels in 7.11, yet he is made from fire, as the *jinn* are (55.15). In the *hadith* literature, angels are understood to be made from light.

Islamic philosophers and mystics have elaborated upon the angelic theme. Ibn Sina (d. 428/1037) identified the various spheres of the Neoplatonic universe (living and rational) as angels. The founder of the Illluminationist school, Shihab al-Din Suhrawardi (d. 587/ 1191), elaborated a cosmology of light in which angels would play an archetypal role, similar to the Platonic forms (Corbin, 1986: 294). Thinkers of the Akbarian school, established by Ibn 'Arabi (d. 638/1240), distinguished the angels of the incorporeal world from those of the corporeal. The four archangels Gabriel, Michael, 'Izra'il and Israfil could represent the four divine attributes: life, knowledge, will and power. These angels could also correspond to various human sensory organs (Murata, 1991: 330).

References and further reading

Corbin, H. (1986) *Histoire de la philosophie islamique*, Paris: Gallimard.

al-Ghazali, A. (1995) *The Remembrance of Death and the Afterlife (Book 40 of The Revival of Religious Sciences)*, trans. T.J. Winter, Cambridge: The Islamic Texts Society.

Ibn Kathir, I. (n.d.) *Tafsir al-Qur'an al-'Azim* (Interpretation of the Great Qur'an), 4 vols, Cairo: Dar al-taqwa.

Ibn Sina (1938) *Lexique de la langue philosophique d'Ibn Sina*, trans. and ed. A.M. Goichon, Paris: Desclée de Brouwer.

Murata, S. (1991) 'The Angels', in S.H. Nasr (ed.) *Islamic Spirituality: Foundations*, New York: Crossroad Publishing, 324–44.

RICHARD MCGREGOR

MANSLAUGHTER

Qatl signifies the killing of a human being. It also means homicide, murder, assassination, indirect killing, involuntary manslaughter and unintentional homicide.

In legal language, manslaughter is the unlawful killing of a human being without malice aforethought. According to *fiqh* (Islamic jurisprudence), manslaughter or killing without malice aforethought comprises two types: *shibeh al-amad* (semi-intentional murder) and *al-khata'* (involuntary manslaughter).

When someone causes the death of another person with no intention of killing them, that is considered involuntary manslaughter or unintentional homicide. The killer is doing something legal, which happens to cause the death of someone. For instance, a hunter may intend to shoot an animal but the shot kills a passer-by instead, or a person digs a well and someone falls in it and dies. In addition, if a juvenile or a madman

commits an intentional murder, it is considered manslaughter. The consequences of unintentional killing involve two things. First, there is the payment of a light penalty of blood money, which is delayed and due over three years. The Prophet said: 'The blood money for accidental killing or unintentional murder which resembles intentional – such as is done with a whip and a stick – is a hundred camels, forty of which are pregnant'. Second, there is the *kuffara* or atonement, and that involves freeing a believing slave. If the killer is unable to do so, then he should fast two consecutive months. 'For those who find this beyond their means, a fast for two months running: by way of repentance to Allah' (4.92).

Semi-intentional murder is the killing of a person by means of an action that would not normally threaten a life. Killing someone by hitting them with a light tool, like a light stick or a small rock, or by punching them with the fist, or by striking them with a whip are some examples of what is considered semi-intentional murder. However, if the blow was aimed at a vital part of the body, or if the victim was very young or sick and might have been expected to die from the blow, then the killing is considered intentional murder. Similarly, if the victim was strong but the killer continued the beating until he killed him, this is also a case of intentional murder. Semi-intentional murder is where the killing has occurred in a manner somewhere between intentional murder and unintentional homicide: it is neither entirely intentional nor unintentional, since the beating, for example, is intentional but the killing is not.

Nonetheless, the murderer will carry the *ithm* (sin of the murder), because, although he only intended the beating, he still had caused the death of his victim. Furthermore, the killer is charged to pay the *kuffara*. Since the killing was unintentional, the *kuffara* is again based on the Qur'anic rule 'And whoever kills a believer by mistake it is ordained that he should free a believing slave. And pay blood money to the deceased's family' (4.92).

RAFIK BERJAK

MANUSCRIPTS AND THE QUR'AN

The Qur'an, by virtue of its sacred nature in Islam, was the most copied Arabic text in the manuscript age. It was believed that copying the Qur'an would bring blessings on the scribe and the owner. For this reason it was often not copied to be read, but to be cherished as an object of reverence or to be used in instruction. Except for the first Muslim century or so, manuscript Qur'ans were richly decorated with vegetal and geometric motifs, and were characterized by their polychrome nature. The use of gold and silver, although originally frowned upon, had by the early 'Abbasid period become a widespread phenomenon.

Chrysography (writing in gold) and the use of coloured inks (especially rubrication, writing in red ink) flourished throughout the subsequent centuries. Rubrication was used in particular for chapter headings, for vocalization, for the superscript *alif* of prolongation, and for abbreviations of pause marks and the names of established reciters.

In the early period under the Umayyads (44/661–132/750), the Qur'an was copied not only by Muslims (often converts) but also by Christian scribes. In subsequent periods, practically every Muslim calligrapher of note tried his hand at its execution. Calligraphers were also sometimes illuminators, even bookbinders. Some individuals made very many copies of the Qur'an: Yaqut al-

Musta'simi (d. 698/1298) is said to have made up to 1,001 copies. Exquisite calligraphy, illumination and book-cover designs accompanied the production of many medieval and post-medieval Qur'ans, and Qur'anic production had a profound influence on the making of non-Qur'anic manuscripts.

From the point of view of the history of the Qur'anic text, the most important manuscripts of the Qur'an are those that can be dated from the earliest period until the introduction (in the East) of the new, so-called 'proportioned scripts' that are associated with the 'Abbasid vizier Ibn Muqla (d. 328/940). The period in question extends from the second quarter of the first/mid-seventh centuries to the last quarter of the fourth/tenth centuries; it embraces the reign of the Caliph 'Uthman (23/644–35/656), who was responsible for the first canonical edition of the Qur'an, as well as the Umayyad and early 'Abbasid rulers.

Towards the end of this formative period, the fully pointed and vocalized text (*scriptio plena*) of the Qur'anic text was finally established. Most of the fundamental reform took place under 'Abd al-Malik, the fifth Umayyad caliph (65/685–86/705), who is credited with, among other things, the re-editing of the 'Uthmanic text of the Qur'an with vowel-punctuation (a measure generally attributed to his governor al-Hajjaj ibn Yusuf) and the construction of the Dome of the Rock in Jerusalem in 72/691–92, complete with Qur'anic inscriptions. The inscriptions in the Dome of the Rock in fact represent the earliest known dated passages from the Qur'an. In these inscriptions, many letters are already provided with diacritical points.

As far as we know, there are no surviving manuscripts of the pre-'Uthmanic versions of the Qur'an. Manuscripts attributed to the rightly guided (orthodox) caliphs and other early personalities are not authentic, but rather they are 'pious' forgeries. All the so-called 'Uthmanic Qur'ans that have been examined were made after the reign of the caliph and it has been established on palaeographical grounds that most of them originated at least a century after his death.

There are no specific dates associated with the Umayyad and early 'Abbasid group of manuscripts. Only some thirteen codices are datable to the third/ninth century. Most of the codices and fragments of this period have no colophons, and even bequest statements (*waqf*), which act as *termini ante quem*, are rare. In most cases, their dating is based therefore on palaeographical and art-historical grounds. The majority of the manuscripts are single leaves and bifolia, and only a small number constitute substantial fragments. Among the better-known published fragments are the ones preserved in the British Library (BL Or 2165), the Bibliothèque nationale de France (arabe 328a), and the Institute of Oriental Studies, St Petersburg (E-20).

With the exception of perhaps one manuscript on papyrus, all the early known fragments are written on parchment. The exclusive use of parchment as a writing surface for the Qur'anic text may have its roots in the Jewish tradition. The Talmud, for instance, required that a copy of the Torah scroll (Sefer Torah) be written on kosher parchment. Parchment remained the preferred writing surface for Qur'anic codices for a number of centuries, so much so that Ibn Khaldun (d. 808/1406) commented that its use 'was an expression of respect for what was to be written down, and of desire that it should be correct and accurate'. The first Qur'ans on paper appear only in the fourth/tenth century, and they are associated with a group of scripts known as the New Abbasid Style (see below).

Although early Qur'ans were mostly written in codex form, there are surviving early fragments in parchment rolls of the type known as *rotulus*, which are unrolled vertically (as opposed to a *volumen* – such as the Jewish Torah – which is unrolled horizontally). The earliest codices of the Qur'an associated with the Umayyad period were most likely made in single volumes. This can be judged from the large fragments that have survived (London, Paris, St Petersburg). By contrast, many of the early 'Abbasid manuscripts were copied in a number of volumes. This is evident from the large scripts employed and the smaller number of lines per page. The making of these codices must have necessitated the slaughter of a large number of animals: for instance, during the second/eighth century, a complete manuscript of the Qur'an required between 500 and 700 parchment skins.

Originally the format of the codex was vertical, but it changed to horizontal at the beginning of the second/eighth century. The preference for horizontal formats and thick/heavy-looking scripts may have been dictated by, on the one hand, the desire to show the superiority of the Qur'anic revelation and, on the other, to distinguish the Islamic from the Jewish and Christian traditions of using rolls and vertical formats for their scriptures. The change in script and format (from vertical to horizontal) coincides with the Christian–Muslim polemic of the first 'Abbasid century. It is, therefore, possible that the early 'Abbasid Qur'ans had an apologetic dimension, effectively proclaiming the superiority of the Qur'anic revelation over Jewish and Christian scriptures.

Until fairly recently, most scholars referred to the Qur'ans of this early period as Kufi or Kufic Qur'ans, sometimes distinguishing between Kufi and Hijazi. The Kufi/Kufic appellation is, however, misleading, as it embraces under one name a great variety of scripts and styles that were in use in those days. Recent research groups the scripts used predominantly for the copying of Qur'ans during the first three to four centuries into three main categories: Hijazi scripts, Early Abbasid scripts, and New Abbasid Style or, more briefly, New Style (NS).

The earliest known manuscripts of the Qur'an, copied in scripts used in Mecca and Medina, are called collectively by their regional name of Hijazi, and most of them are associated with the Umayyad period. They appear to follow no particular rules for the script and even within a single volume one may encounter a diversity of styles. Nevertheless, these scripts are characterized by their distinct ductus with the elongated shafts of the free-standing *alif* and other ascenders slanting to the right, and by the right-sided tail (foot) of the isolated *alif*. The right-sided foot on the isolated *alif* can be either very pronounced or barely perceptible (e.g. BL Or 2165, the so-called *ma'il Qur'an*). A good example of a Hijazi codex is the Paris manuscript (arabe 328a), which was written by two different scribes and is believed to have originated in the second half of the first/seventh century.

Although it is likely that by the end of the first Muslim century a fully developed system of letter-pointing and vocalization was already in place, it was not necessarily used systematically, especially the vocalization. Indeed, the scripts of these manuscripts exhibit sporadic use of diacritics (in order to distinguish homographs), the absence of the *alif* of prolongation, as well as a total lack of vocalization. Vocalization and orthoepic signs (such as *hamza* and *shadda*) in the form of multicoloured dots, a hallmark of many manuscripts of the early 'Abbasid period, were

often added by later scribes and/or scholars. Likewise, the *alif* of prolongation was often added or inscribed (even in the late Middle Ages) superscript in red ink.

In the earliest manuscripts, headings of chapters (*suras*) were not indicated. Instead, a blank space was left at the end of one *sura* and the beginning of another. This blank space (originally one line) was subsequently filled in by very primitive (crude) panels, with geometrical or vegetal designs, most likely borrowed from architectural and textile forms and patterns. These panels often had, at one or both ends, devices that resemble the shape of the Roman writing tablet (*tabula ansata*). Verses were originally separated by means of slanted (oblique) strokes, and dots arranged in various forms, either clustered or in groups of three, four, six and the like.

With the coming of the 'Abbasids, a completely new set of scripts gradually emerged, currently known as Early 'Abbasid scripts. The old scripts – originally inelegant and irregular – were, in the space of a few decades, transformed completely. The best example of this transformation may be the inscriptions of the Dome of the Rock. During the third/ninth century these large scripts reached a high degree of perfection and complexity, although at the cost of separation from current practice. It was this separation that led to their being almost completely abandoned after the fourth/tenth century. The main characteristic of these scripts was again their ductus. This time, however, it was the heavy-looking, relatively short and horizontally elongated strokes that found favour. The slanted isolated form of the *alif* completely disappeared and was replaced by a straight shaft, with a pronounced right-sided foot, set at a considerable distance from the following letter.

The manuscripts written in Early 'Abbasid scripts, unlike their Hijazi predecessors, are often richly illuminated in gold and colours. *Sura* headings are often clearly marked and enclosed in rectangular panels with marginal vignettes or palmettes protruding into outer margins. Elegant discs and rosettes separate individual verses, as well as groups of five and ten verses. Here we encounter the use of the alpha-numerical system (*abjad*) placed within discs to indicate verse-counts (e.g. *ya'* – 10; *kaf* – 20; *lam* – 30). A typical device to mark the end of a group of five verses was the letter *ha'* (representing 5), and its stylized versions in the form of teardrops or pear-shaped devices, as well as an *alif* executed in two or more colours. On the other hand, groups of ten verses were indicated by means of elegant roundels or medallions.

During the early 'Abbasid period, in the third/ninth century, there began to appear manuscripts written in a different style, which in earlier Western literature is variously referred to as 'semi-Kufic', 'bent Kufic', 'Eastern Kufic', 'Persian Kufic' and the like. These New Style (NS) scripts represent a dressed-up version of the 'Abbasid bookhand, i.e. the scripts used for the copying of non-Qur'anic texts. The NS was used for copying the Qur'an until the sixth/twelfth centuries, even as late as the seventh/thirteenth century. Unlike manuscripts copied in Early 'Abbasid scripts, NS manuscripts had vertical formats. By the seventh/thirteenth century, however, the NS had been relegated to book titles, *sura*-headings and other ornamental purposes. Quite a number of extant codices and fragments written in the New Style are on paper, as opposed to parchment.

At the same time as the NS began to be used in the production of Qur'anic manuscripts in the East, Maghribi scribes developed their own style of handwriting based on the 'Abbasid bookhand. This development was already clearly visible at the beginning of the fourth/tenth century. Medieval Maghribi Qur'ans, with their characteristic square-like formats, followed the old 'Abbasid tradition of using multi-coloured vowel and orthoepic signs, and a path of development unaffected by the 'proportioned scripts' of the East. A fine example of a late fourth/tenth century Maghribi copy is the Sultan Muley Zaydan Qur'an, which is preserved in the Escorial Library, Madrid (ár. 1340) and has been recently published in facsimile.

It appears, from surviving evidence, that single volume Qur'ans had no 'title pages' and that the recto of the first folio was usually left blank. It was only when the Qur'an began to be copied in a number of volumes that we begin to see the introduction of statements relating to the volume number, albeit still without specifying the nature of the work. The reference to the nature of the work (i.e. that it is the Qur'an) is sometimes found later on double-page illuminated frontispieces, the most common inscription being the quote from 56.77–80: 'It is surely a noble Qur'an, in a preserved Book, none shall touch it but the ritually pure, sent from the Lord of all beings.'

Qur'ans of the early 'Abbasid period were bound in wooden boards, structured like a box enclosed on all sides, and having a movable upper cover that was fastened to the rest of the structure with leather thongs. There are very few surviving examples of these so-called 'boxed books', and even these examples have only partially survived. The best known are those of Qayrawan and San'a. Clasps (*qufl*) made of gold for closing the volume appear to have been a later development, as was the introduction of the characteristic fore-edge and pentagonal flaps, as an extension of the lower cover.

Around the middle of the fourth/tenth century, a completely new set of formal scripts appeared. These new scripts, known from later Arabic literature as 'proportioned scripts', are associated in Arabic tradition with Ibn Muqla's reform of writing. Their use for the copying of the Qur'an is attested already by the end of the century. The best surviving example is a medium-sized copy of the Qur'an executed in Baghdad in 391/ 1000–01 by the celebrated calligrapher 'Ali ibn Hilal, known as Ibn al-Bawwab. This codex (Ms 1431), preserved in Chester Beatty Library (Dublin), was reproduced in facsimile in Graz (Austria) in 1983.

Although referred to as *naskh* or *naskhi* in earlier Western writings, the main text of the Qur'an of Ibn al-Bawwab was copied in a script that is either a type of old *naskh* or most probably a script mentioned in later Arabic sources as *masahif*, that is a script from the *muhaqqaq* family used for medium-sized Qur'ans. The text is fully vocalized and the unpointed (*muhmal*) letters are distinguished from their pointed counterparts by a superscript 'v' and a miniature version of the relevant letter (e.g. *ha'* and *'ayn*). The codex opens with six preliminary pages of illumination, four of which contain inscriptions relating to the computation of *suras*, verses, words, letters and diacritical points, given on the authority of the caliph 'Ali ibn Abi Talib (d. 40/661). Other full-page illuminations include a tailpiece and two double-page finispieces. The last two pages give an alphabetical listing of individual letter-counts in the text. Following an earlier tradition, Ibn al-Bawwab uses a stylized Kufic *ha'* for groups of five verses and

the alpha-numerical system (*abjad*) for verse-counts.

The principal formal scripts that established themselves in the East from the fifth/eleventh century onwards were, on the one hand, *muhaqqaq*, *rayhan* and *naskh*, and, on the other, *thuluth*, *tawqi'* and *riqa'*. These scripts, with some later modifications, survived in manuscript production until the end of the manuscript age. The first three are associated with book production and the other three with state administration. The old scripts, however, were not entirely abandoned. The New Style or stylized Kufic, for instance, were often used as incidentals such as *sura* headings. Indeed, the Qur'ans of this period often display two or more scripts, not just within a chapter but also on the same page.

The Qur'anic production in the period after Ibn al-Bawwab is associated with famous names of calligraphers and patrons, the most celebrated of whom is the aforementioned Yaqut al-Musta'simi, whose extant Qur'ans are, unfortunately, notoriously difficult to authenticate. A number of lavish Qur'ans from this period are now (fully or partially) available in facsimile or on CD-ROM. They include the British Library's large, seven-volume Sultan Baybars Qur'an (Add 22406–13), calligraphed by Ibn al-Wahid in 705/1305–6; a small but exquisite copy executed by Shaykh Hamd Allah al-Amasi (Şeyh Hamdullah) (d. 926/1520), preserved in the Ankara Etnografya Müzesi; and the largest Ottoman Qur'an, which was made for Sulayman the Magnificent in the tenth/sixteenth century by Ahmad Qarahisari (Ahmed Karahisari) and is preserved in the Topkapi Palace Library, Istanbul (H.S. 158). The text of this last-mentioned Qur'an is executed in four scripts: *muhaqqaq*, *rayhan*, *naskh* and *thuluth*.

Like the early 'Abbasid Qur'ans, these Qur'ans continued to be richly decorated in gold and colours. The letter shapes in such scripts as *muhaqqaq*, *thuluth* and *tawqi'* were outlined and the text was vocalized. The outlining and vocalization were often done in a colour different from the colour of the main letter shape (often in blue or black if the main script was in gold). In many extant copies, we encounter the writing of the superscript *alif* of prolongation in red, as well as verse-counts and prostrations indicated in exquisite marginal roundels and medallions.

In contrast to the often large and deluxe copies, Qur'ans were also made as amulets in the form of rolls and small octagon-shaped books. Miniature octagon Qur'ans are usually between 3.5 and 7.5cm in diameter. A number of these Qur'ans have survived from between the tenth/sixteenth and thirteenth/nineteenth centuries. Both roll and octagon Qur'ans are written in micrography, in miniature versions of either a *naskh* or *ghubar* script.

Further reading

Bayani, Manijeh, Contadini, Anna and Stanley, Tim (1999) *The Decorated Word: Qur'ans of the 17th to 19th centuries*, London: Nour Foundation in association with Azimuth Editions and Oxford University Press.

Déroche, François (1992) *The Abbasid Tradition: Qur'ans of the 8th to 10th centuries AD*, London: Nour Foundation in association with Azimuth Editions and Oxford University Press.

Gacek, Adam (1991) 'A collection of Qur'anic codices', *Fontanus: From the collections of McGill University* 4: 35–53.

James, David (1988) *Qur'ans of the Mamluks*, London: Thames & Hudson.

see also: **calligraphy and the Qur'an; language and the Qur'an**

ADAM GACEK

MARRIAGE

The Qur'anic discussion of marriage is extensive and varied, including both general statements and detailed regulations. Considered together, the verses exhibit an unresolved tension between mutuality and hierarchy. Marriage is for purposes of love and intimacy, and is characterized by mercy. It furthers the divine creative plan through procreation and establishes the kin relationships that are the basis of social organization. Marriage bestows rights and obligations on spouses. However, the reciprocity of claims does not imply sameness of husbands and wives. Husbands have greater rights in certain areas, including divorce, polygamy and the settlement of marital conflicts.

Creation and pairing

God created the first human being and its mate (*zawj*) out of a single soul (*nafs*) (4.1; 7.189; 39.6). Drawing on biblical and *hadith* accounts, traditional exegesis assumes that the first human being was male, and that its mate was female, but this is not explicitly indicated in the Qur'an. The term *zawj* is grammatically masculine, but can apply equally to a specifically male or female spouse; likewise, its plural, *azwaj*, is used for both wives and husbands (2.232; 21.90; 33.28). Amina Wadud (1992), among others, has convincingly argued that most scriptural usages of these terms should be read as gender-neutral.

The pairing of man and woman in marriage has both individual and social aims, including the safeguarding of chastity and the protection of lineage. God created spouses from the same nature (16.72), and placed 'love and mercy' between them, in order for them to dwell together in tranquillity (7.189; 30.21). Spouses are garments for one another (2.187). Marriage facilitates chastity, which is an important virtue for Muslim men and women alike (33.35). Those who can marry are exhorted to do so, but those who cannot fulfil its obligations should wait until they have the resources, which God will provide (24.32–33).

Beyond the channelling of sexual desires, there is a larger purpose to the joining of male and female in pairs: procreation of the human species (7.189; 16.72; 25.54; 35.11; 49.13). God created the first human being (and its mate) directly, but populates the earth through human reproduction (25.54). As 4.1 states of the first pair, '[God] brought forth from them many men and women'. The kin relationships established by marriage lead to the formation of tribes and nations, and thus serve as the basis for all of human society.

Impediments to marriage

A number of Qur'anic verses address the question of who can marry whom. Impediments to marriage can be based on of kinship, number or religion. Those a man cannot marry because they are too closely related by blood include his mother (understood to include grand-mothers, and so on up); daughters (including granddaughters, and so on down); sisters; maternal and paternal aunts; and maternal and paternal nieces. Foster relationships created by wet nur-sing give rise to the same prohibitions that blood kinship does (4.23).

Ties of affinity create other barriers to marriage. Two sisters cannot be com-bined in marriage to the same man (4.23); a *hadith*, on the Prophet's authority, extends this prohibition to the combining of aunt and niece. In both cases the prohibition only pertains to concurrent marriage, disappearing once the first marriage is dissolved.

However, marriage with ascendants or descendants of a potential spouse can create permanent impediments. A man cannot marry a woman who was mar-ried to his father or his son, nor can he marry the mother of a woman he has married. However, with the daughter of a previous wife, the prohibition only exists if the first marriage was con-summated (4.22–23).

Religion is another a factor in deter-mining who can marry. Muslims, of course, may marry one another and Muslim men are permitted to marry women from among the People of the Book (*ahl al-kitab*) (5.5). The Qur'anic text makes no explicit mention of Mus-lim women marrying Christian or Jew-ish men, but juristic consensus has held it forbidden. Muslims may not marry polytheists (*mushrikun*) (2.221); mar-riage ties between believers and unbelie-vers (*kuffar*) are not lawful and should be dissolved (60.10–11).

Sexual immorality creates another barrier to marriage. Committing *zina*, fornication or adultery, renders a Muslim an inappropriate marriage partner for a Muslim who has not done so; pure women and men are suited for each other, just as impure women and men are suited for each other (24.26). A Muslim guilty of *zina* should only marry another Muslim who is similarly guilty, or a polytheist (24.3). However, most interpreters have held that sincere repentance on the part of the offender (24.5) removes this impediment to marriage.

Because women must be mono-gamous, married Muslim women fall into that category of women whom it is not permissible for anyone to marry (4.24). Being married does not automatically constitute an impediment to marriage for a Muslim man, since he is allowed to practise polygyny. However, if he already has four wives, the maximum number he is permitted by 4.3, any additional marriage he contracts cannot be valid.

The Qur'an permits slaves, with the permission of their owners, to marry other slaves or free persons (2.221; 4.25; 24.32). This sanction of full legal marriage by slaves in Islamic scripture and law is unusual in comparison to other slave-holding systems. Most discussions of marriage between slaves and free people assume that a free man is marrying an enslaved woman. Such a marriage is permissible when the man cannot afford to marry a free woman and fears committing sexual sin (4.25). While some Muslim jurists interpreted these conditions strictly, holding that marriage to a female slave was only acceptable when both conditions were satisfied, others saw the verse as providing guidance, not binding legal direction.

Contracting a marriage

Marriage is established by mutual agreement. Qur'anic discussions of marriage usually assume the involvement of kin, particularly that of the wife, in making arrangements. Some verses presume that a female will be married off by male relatives (2.221) or that her relatives will have a role in deciding whether or not she can marry a particular man (2.232). Legal arguments over whether women may contract their own marriages, as one doctrine holds they can, have sometimes hinged on the use of active and passive verbs in these verses. Most jurists have held that women require a male agnate or a judge to conclude marriage on their behalf.

In addition to consent, marriage requires payment of dowry in the form of monetary consideration from the husband to the wife. Payment of dowry correlates with the husband seeking chastity, not lewdness, from his partner (4.24, 5.5). Dowry is given freely on

marriage (4.4); it becomes the wife's property and none of it should be taken back, even in case of divorce, unless the wife is guilty of 'clear lewdness' (4.19–20). If she is not thus guilty, she need only give back part of the dowry if she is divorced before consummation (2.236), or if she wants to ransom herself from her husband (2.229).

The Qur'an does not explicitly discuss temporary marriage (*mut'a*), a form of contractual union where the spouses part, without divorce, after a stipulated time period, though some have held that 4.24 alludes to this type of union. Permitted at various times during the life of the Prophet, Sunni Muslims have held that Muhammad permanently forbade *mut'a* before his death. Shi'i Muslims, on the other hand, continue to regard it as legal.

Spousal rights and obligations

Marriage establishes rights and obligations between spouses. Inheritance is a mutual right, though the husband receives twice the share of his wife's assets that she does of his (4.12). For the most part, though, claims established by marriage are gender-differentiated. A wife has rights to receive dowry and support (4.34) and to be treated with fairness (4.19; 4.129) or released with kindness (2.231). Correspondingly, a husband has the right to approach his wife sexually as he wishes (2.223), to have a greater say than her in matters of divorce (2.228), and – according to most interpreters – to expect obedience from her and to correct disobedience (4.34).

Two of these verses enumerating male marital privileges have become central in recent attempts to reinterpret and explain Qur'anic views of marriage. The first, which discusses male divorce prerogatives, states that women 'have [rights] due to them like [the duties] they owe [to men] according to what is equitable (*al-ma'ruf*), and men have a degree over them' (2.228). Those Muslims who argue for female rights in marriage tend to focus on the clause establishing that men and women have similar rights and duties. Those who argue for male superiority in marriage highlight the degree that men are given over women, as do some non-Muslim polemicists. What, though, is this degree that husbands have over their wives? Most classical exegetes, and many contemporary ones, have understood it to imply both authority and responsibility.

The husband's role is further elaborated in 4.34, where men are declared to be 'in charge of' or 'responsible for' women, in part due to their financial expenditures. Righteous women, according to this verse, are *qanitat*, which most commentators understand simply as 'obedient' to their husbands. However, the term is used elsewhere in the Qur'an only for obedience to God, and *qanit(a)* is used for both men and women alike (33.35). Therefore, some argue, there is no reason for considering a woman's righteousness to be defined by obedience to her husband rather than to God. In fact, all commentators and jurists, classical and contemporary, agree that a husband's authority over his wife does not translate into absolute control. A Muslim woman's first loyalty and obligation are always to God. Where traditional interpretations and reformist or feminist ones diverge is over whether the husband is owed obedience in anything that does not contravene his wife's religious obligations.

The most controversial portion of 4.34 addresses the measures to be taken by men who fear women's *nushuz*. While *nushuz* is not specifically defined in the Qur'anic text, women's *nushuz* has generally been understood as disobedience, rebelliousness or sexual refusal toward their husbands. (In contrast, male *nushuz* is viewed as antipathy or rejection: 4.128 permits a woman who fears her husband's *nushuz* to arrive at a settlement with him by abandoning some of her rights.) Men who fear women's *nushuz* may 'admonish them, and abandon them in bed, and strike them'. The verb translated here as 'strike' (*daraba*) appears numerous times in the Qur'an with other meanings, leading a number of contemporary thinkers to question why it must be understood as hitting or beating in this context. They have argued that the Qur'anic depiction of women in other verses as full human beings and partners in the relationship of marriage cannot be reconciled with scriptural permission for physical chastisement. Most Muslim scholars, though, accept a husband's right to discipline a disobedient wife, if admonition and abandonment in bed have had no effect. However, they place strict limits on the number, severity and location of any disciplinary blows.

A Muslim wife is not without recourse in marital disputes. Where spouses cannot come to an agreement between themselves, arbiters from both families should attempt to repair the breach (4.35). However, efforts at reconciliation or settlement may fail. Because marriage is intended for purposes of intimacy and companionship, it can be dissolved when it no longer fulfils those purposes.

References and further reading

Ali, K. (2003) 'Gender, Ta'a (Obedience), and *Nushuz* (Disobedience) in Islamic Discourses', in Suad Joseph (ed.), *Encyclopedia of Women and Islamic Cultures*, Leiden: E.J. Brill.

Barlas, A. (2002) *'Believing Women' in Islam: Unreading patriarchal interpretations of the Qur'an*, Austin, TX: University of Texas Press.

Farah, M. (1984) *Marriage and Sexuality in Islam: A translation of al-Ghazali's book on the etiquette of marriage from the Ihya*,

Salt Lake City, UT: University of Utah Press.

Wadud, A. (1992) *Qur'an and Woman*, Kuala Lumpur: Penerbit Fajar Bakti.

See also: ***daraja***; **divorce**; ***zina***

KECIA ALI

MARTYRDOM
see: ***shahada***

MARY

Mary (Maryam, meaning 'pious') is the most prominent woman in the Qur'an. Highly regarded because of her virtue and devotion to God (66.12), she is considered the best woman of her day (3.42) and a 'sign to the nations' (21.91). The only woman mentioned by her proper name, Mary is found over thirty times within the scripture. Traditional sayings of the Prophet Muhammad state that she is one of the four most praiseworthy women of history and is the only woman to be protected from the touch of Satan at birth, a protection shared by her son Jesus ('Isa).

As in the New Testament, the Qur'anic story of Mary is intimately linked with that of her son. This is made evident, aside from the number of times the name 'Jesus, son of Mary' appears, from the placement of Mary's life story within the larger nativity narrative of Jesus. The story of Mary begins with the prayer of her mother, the 'wife of 'Imran', who, being childless, desired to become pregnant. Mary's mother, not named in the Qur'an but known as Hanna by Muslim historians and commentators, dedicated her future child to God's service (3.35). In discovering that she had given birth to a girl, perhaps previously assuming that it would be a boy, Hanna invoked divine protection on Mary and her offspring (3.36). As such, the Lord accepted Mary, raised her in 'purity and beauty', and assigned her to the guardianship of Zachariah, the father of John the Baptist. Residing in a chamber of the Jerusalem Temple, Zachariah is repeatedly surprised to find her divinely provided for, whereby Mary reminds him that God provides for whomever he wills without limit (3.37).

Some time later, Mary withdraws to a 'place in the east' (19.16), possibly referring to an eastern chamber within the Temple, a cave or an eastern city such as Bethlehem. There she receives an announcement from an angelic messenger: 'O Mary! God gives you glad tidings through a word from him; his name will be Christ Jesus, the son of Mary' (3.45). Mary, astonished at the message, asks how this can be so, since she is chaste. The reply, rejecting pagan concepts of divine–human sexual relations, is that God does what he wills and he merely needs to say the word and it will occur. (3.47; 19.20–21)

Muslim commentators and historians have elaborated these narratives. For instance, there are different accounts of Mary's encounter with Gabriel. Commonly, historians such as al-Tabari recount that, when Mary and Joseph lived in the Temple, she, for one reason or another, made a temporary sojourn out of the Temple. While away, perhaps travelling eastward, Mary encounters Gabriel, who, appearing as a man, announces that he is sent by God to give her a son. Fearful of the man, Mary cries out to God for protection, upon which Gabriel assures her that it was God giving her the child, not he, then blowing the divine breath into her chest through her sleeve she becomes pregnant. Upon her return, her husband Joseph, who is not mentioned in the Qur'an, is the first to notice and, eventually, acknowledge the miraculous event.

On the occasion of her labour, the Qur'an portrays Mary, wishing she were dead, driven to a palm tree in anguish. At that point, a voice from beneath her, perhaps Jesus, comforts her by saying that God has provided a small brook for drinking and ripe dates from the tree to eat, but she must refrain from talking to any person (19.24–26). Subsequently, the Qur'an moves forward to a later time, when Mary returns to her people with her infant son. There they ask why she has brought this 'strange thing' to them, since her mother and father were neither immoral nor unchaste people. In response, Mary points to the infant in her arms, expecting some response from the child. Her critics snort: 'How should we speak to one who is a child in the cradle?' (19.29). At which point, the infant Jesus speaks and asserts his prophetic mission in defence of his mother's chastity.

Modern textual critics have underlined particular aspects that need further examination. First, there are parallels between this story and certain Christian apocryphal writings, such as the *Protoevangelium of James* and the *Gospel of Ps. Matthew*. Such parallels do not necessarily indicate a textual dependence, but may indicate a historical oral or folk connection. Second, the idea that certain people, most commonly Christians, regarded Mary as divine (4.171: 5.116) has led some to contend that the Qur'an presents a Christian trinity of Allah, Jesus and Mary. Recent textual criticism has attempted, though it is still inconclusive, to find historical connections for this, suggesting that perhaps popular veneration of Mary or a certain sect (e.g. Mariamites) were specifically being criticized here. Third is the reference to Mary as the 'sister of Aaron' (19.28), which has led some critics to argue that there is confusion between Mary and Miriam, the sister of Moses and Aaron. Muslim tradition and commentary,

however, clearly distinguished the two women from each other, and noted that, in Arabic, the phrase could indicate a more general or metaphorical relationship such as kinship or spiritual affinity, even though such practice was not recognized by the Arab Christians of Muhammad's day.

Further reading

Cragg, K. (1999) *Jesus and the Muslim*, Oxford: OneWorld.

McAuliffe, J.D. (1981) 'Chosen of All Women: Mary and Fatima in Qur'anic exegesis', *Islamochristana* 7: 19–28.

Parrinder, G. (1997) *Jesus in the Qur'an*, Oxford: OneWorld.

Perlmann, M. (trans.) (1987) *History of al-Tabari*, New York: SUNY Press, Vol. 4.

Sahih al-Bukhari (2000) trans. M.M. Khan, Vols 1–9, Riyadh: Darussalam.

Sahih Muslim, trans. al-Mundhiri, vols 1–2, Riyadh: Darussalam.

Shoemaker, S. (2003) 'Christmas in the Qur'an: The Qur'anic account of Jesus' nativity and Palestinian local tradition', *Jerusalem Studies in Arabic and Islam* 28: 11–39.

Tottoli, R. (2002) *Biblical Prophets in the Qur'an and Muslim Literature*, Richmond, Surrey: Curzon.

Wheeler, B.M. (2002) *Prophets in the Qur'an*, New York: Continuum.

H. CHAD HILLIER

MARYAM

see: **Mary**

MARY'S MOTHER

Mary's mother, referred to in the Qur'an as 'a woman [or wife] of 'Imran' (3.35), is known in biblical and Muslim exegetical sources as Anne or Hanna. While pregnant, presumably anticipating the birth of a son, she dedicates the child in her womb to God's service (3.35–37). She is surprised when she delivers a girl, but 'God knew best what she brought forth'. Hanna names her daughter Mary and seeks God's protection for the child from the devil. Islamic tradition holds that this supplication is the reason why both Mary and her son Jesus escape being touched by the devil at birth.

Hanna is mentioned again only in 19.28, when the unmarried Mary has returned with the infant Jesus to her people. They express their astonishment at Mary's apparently sinful behaviour, when 'your father was not an evil man nor was your mother a whore'. Jesus miraculously speaks, however, defending his mother's character, implicitly showing that she has not strayed from her own mother's righteous precedent.

KECIA ALI

MATA

Mata is an interrogative particle meaning when or at what time: 'When Allah's help [will come]' (2.214). It is also a conditional term carrying the adverb of time: for example, 'When you visit us we shall honour you'. *Ila mata* means until when or how long.

Mata appears as many as nine times in the Qur'an. The disbelievers kept asking in a sceptical manner about the Day of Judgement: 'And they say "When will this promise be fulfilled, if you are truthful?"' (36.48). They were not seriously asking about that day, of course, but rather expressing their doubt about it.

RAFIK BERJAK

MATHAL | MITHL | TAMATHIL

Mathala is a root verb that means to resemble, imitate, compare anyone with or to someone else or to bear a likeness. *Mithl* means likeness, like, similar or resemblance. *Mathal* is a noun meaning

parable, likeness, similitude, like, reason or proverb. An example of the use of *mathal* to mean parable, simile or example is: 'And indeed we have set forth for mankind in the Qur'an every kind of parable' (30.58). *Mathal* is used to make the meaning clearer and the idea easily conceived: 'And these similitudes were put forward for mankind' (29.43). *Laysa kamithlihi sha'yun* (42.11) is translated 'There is nothing like a likeness of him', with *ka* (like) and *mithl* (like) used in combination for emphasis; God is not only above all material limitation, but even above imitation by metaphor.

Mathala also means to stand humbly before a ruler. The Prophet said: 'The arrogant who likes to make people stand up for him in exaggerated praise shall be seated in Hell.' *Tamath-thala* means to present yourself in a different form: 'We sent to her our angel, and he appeared before her as a man in all respects' (19.17).

Dharaba al-amthal means to present proverbs, to speak in parables, to impart words of wisdom or to refer to the moral of a story. *Amthal* is the plural, meaning similes, similitudes or parables and is a main method of the Qur'anic style. Simile is the literary term that describes a figure of speech involving the explicit comparison of two different things, often using the words *like* or *as*. Similes are used as a means of articulation in the Qur'an for many purposes, among them clarification of meaning and the conversion of mental images into a more tangible state. In debate and argument, the use of simile helps to defeat opponents.

There are two major kinds of simile in the Qur'an. First is *al-zahir* or the apparent: 'Their likeness is as the likeness of one who kindled a fire; then, when it lighted all around him, Allah took away their light and left them in darkness' (2.17). This example concerns hypocrites. The light in this simile represents Islam, by whose rules the hypocrites pretend to abide. The darkness, however, insinuates the reality of their interior disbelief. The second kind is the *kamin* (hidden) simile. In the Qur'an hidden similes are those that can be related to popular human-created proverbs. For example, there is a saying that the best of things is the intermediate between extremes. This proverb is echoed in the Qur'an on four occasions, one of which is: 'And those who, when they spend, are neither extravagant nor niggardly, but hold the medium way between those extremes' (25.67).

Tamathil is a plural term meaning images or statues. This term is used twice in the Qur'an. It is mentioned once during the argument between Abraham and his people, in which Abraham criticizes their way of worshipping idols: 'what are these images, to which you are devoted?' (21.52). It is also mentioned in reference to the services rendered for Solomon by the *jinn* (34.13).

See also: **parables;** *zahir*

RAFIK BERJAK

MAWDUDI, SAYYID ABUL A'LA

Mawdudi was one of the twentieth century's leading radical interpreters of Islam. His turbulent life, lived in the context of the emerging nation of Pakistan, included four periods of imprisonment, and in 1953 he was actually condemned to death. His writings were in Urdu, subsequently translated into Arabic, and he is a leading example of the growing influence on Islamic theology of writers from beyond the Arab world.

Mawdudi was born in Aurangabad, India, in 1903, and quickly demonstrated remarkable scholarship: when only fourteen, he translated Qasim Amin's *Al-mar'a al-jadida* from Arabic into Urdu. It seems to have been his research and writing on the subject of *jihad*, prompted by the assassination of a prominent Hindu by a Muslim, that launched him on a writing career that ultimately totalled more than a hundred books, the first of them significantly entitled *Jihad in Islam*. In 1926 Mawdudi received his *ijaza* (certificate in religious training), thereby gaining recognition as an *'alim* (a Muslim scholar). His radical views owed much to Hasan al-Banna of the Muslim Brotherhood, and he in turn influenced Sayyid Qutb, executed in 1966 by the Egyptian authorities.

Mawdudi's ideas were promoted through the monthly journal *Tarjuman al-Qur'an* and his major work was *Towards Understanding the Qur'an* (*Tafhim al-Qur'an*), the writing of which occupied Mawdudi for thirty years. This massive work is based on the premise that Allah alone is sovereign, and that the Muslim community should be governed by *shari'a* law. Islam was announced (*da'wa*) to bring the world under Islam, and within any Muslim majority state the non-Muslim minority are to be designated *dhimmis*, surrendering certain political rights in exchange for Muslim protection.

The *Tafhim*, perhaps significantly not represented as mere *tafsir*, combines an explanation of the meaning of the original text of each *sura* with what amounts to a political and ideological interpretation of its significance for the present time. Thus, towards the end of his comments on *sura al-Baqara* (*sura* 2), Mawdudi sets out from the Muslim perspective a comprehensive theology of the poor, and an extended consideration of the ethical issues raised by the Qur'an's stance on usury. In his comments on the following *sura* (*sura al-'Imran*), he offers an explanation of how the Jewish Bible and Christian texts had become corrupt, and a detailed reconstruction of the Battle of Uhud. His comments on *sura* 4 (*al-Nisa'*), by contrast, are largely concerned with theological issues: Mawdudi explores the practical problems raised by the statutory prayer times, and the various possible interpretations of the verses which relate to the death of Jesus.

Mawdudi was an idealist operating within the limitations of Muslim theology and rejecting the influence of Western philosophy, economics and political theory. He was equally opposed to the influence of Hinduism on Islam and the consequences of more general inter-faith practices. In 1941 he established *Jama'at-i-Islami*, which became a vehicle for his demand for the establishment of an independent Islamic state once India had gained independence from British rule. He remained at the head of *Jama'at-i-Islami* for more than thirty years and the organisation continues to provide the ideological base for the *jihad* groups that are involved in the struggle to remove Kashmir, with its Muslim majority, from Indian control.

Mawdudi offered a detailed plan for the projected Muslim state. There would be a President and a *Shura* Council, elected only by Muslims. The affairs of state would be directed by a Prime Minister, assisted by an appointed Cabinet. There would also be an independent judiciary, administering *shari'a* law. Non-Muslims living in the new state and therefore under Muslim protection (*dhimmis*) would have the right to vote in municipal elections and to serve on municipal councils but not on any higher level administrative bodies. In other words Mawdudi rejected the idea of a state from which non-Muslims were excluded, but embraced the more radical concept of the state as subsuming all other religious systems. In this

sense, at least, he was of the Salafiyya, those reformists who looked back to the first three generations of Muslims (*al-Salaf wa'l-khalaf*, 'the predecessors and their successors') as the only true guides to Islamic praxis: the subjection of non-Muslims to Muslim authority rather than the establishment of exclusivist Muslim enclaves.

Mawdudi's political activities in Pakistan led to his imprisonment on four occasions, and in 1953 he was sentenced to death by a court established under martial law, for writing what was termed a seditious article. The sentence was later commuted to life imprisonment. He was in the forefront of the attacks on the Ahmadiyya movement in Pakistan in 1953.

In some ways Mawdudi was a pragmatist. For example, in 1965 he supported the presidential candidacy of Fatima Jinnah, despite his belief that women should not hold high office. When he was taken ill, it was to the United States that he turned for treatment, despite his long-standing condemnation of Western influence on Islam. He died in Buffalo in 1979.

Mawdudi was a radical revolutionary, disillusioned with the compromises being made by Islam's political leadership and their attempts to come to some kind of rapprochement with the non-Muslim world. For him, Islam was a revolutionary movement, aimed ultimately at the overthrow of any other social order. He had little sympathy with the pretensions of the *'ulama,* nor with Sufi notions of *jihad* as struggle with the self. Rather, it is the means of bringing about a universal, all-embracing revolution, employing every available means.

Mawdudi was and continues to be a controversial figure in the Muslim world, subject both to reasoned criticism and to attacks on his integrity. Some of

those who opposed him were even prepared to label him an agent of the
American Central Intelligence Agency,
and cast doubt on his scholarship on the
grounds that he never received a formal
Islamic education. His writings were
frequently dismissed as being mutually
contradictory, and his opinions were
characterized as immoral, as constitut-
ing innovation (bid'a) and even as
heresy. In 1951, in Delhi, an assembly of
the 'ulama, the Jamiyyat al-'ulama, passed a fatwa against him, and in 1976 a
further fatwa was published, designating
him a heretic. Despite such opposition,
Mawdudi continues to be a major influence on the thinking of the Muslim
world, and his writings provide at least
one blueprint for radical Islamists.

Further reading

Ahmad, A. (1967) *Islamic Modernism in
India and Pakistan 1857–1964*, London:
Oxford University Press.
Aijaz, Zakir (trans.) (n.d.) *Selected Speeches
and Writings of Maulana Maududi*, Kar-
achi: International Islamic Publishers.
Ali, Rahnemer (ed.) (1994) *Pioneers of Isla-
mic Revival*, London: Zed Books.
Haddad, Yvonne (1995) *Islamicists and the
Challenge of Pluralism*, Washington, DC:
Center for Contemporary Arab Studies at
Georgetown University.
Kepel, Gilles (2002) *Jihad, the Trail of Poli-
tical Islam*, London and New York: I.B.
Tauris.
McDonough, Sheila (1984) *Muslim Ethics
and Modernity: a comparative study of the
ethical thought of Sayyid Ahmad Khan and
Mawlana Mawdudi*, Waterloo, ON:
Wilfred Laurier University Press.

See also: **Sayyid Qutb;** *tafsir* – **Salafi
views**

PETER COTTERELL

MECCA
see: **Arab; Becca**

MECCAN AND MEDINAN
SURAS AND THE QUR'AN

The style and emphasis of the
Meccan *suras*

One of the difficulties for a reader of the
Qur'an is the general lack of chronology
in the sequence of its chapters. Many of
the *suras* are mixtures of passages from
Muhammad's years of preaching in
Mecca and his years as leader of the
Muslim community in Medina. The
shorter *suras* generally come from the
Meccan period and the longer passages
of the later *suras* from the Medinan
period. Many Western critics prefer the
former to the latter, finding them more
spiritual and less legalistic, more concise
and less verbose.

The early Meccan *suras* concentrate
on issues that must have made a striking
impression on Muhammad, such as the
lack of faith his audience showed in his
message, the judgement to come, and
the destiny of all humanity to end up in
either heaven or hell. In these early passages, Muhammad communicates messages in his role as someone sent to call
his people to the right path and to warn
them about the punishments awaiting
evil-doers. '*Innama anta munthir* (Verily
you are but a warner)' (79.45) is the
address found in various forms in these
passages (see also *suras* 74.2; 87.9). As
Cragg points out, Muhammad is several
times reminded in the Meccan period
that his only task is *al-balagh*,
communication (Cragg, 1971: 146). The
contrast and indeed conflict between
pagan Arab religion and the absolute
unity of God, between *jahaliyya* and
Islam, between *shirk* and *tawhid*, only
come out explicitly in the later Meccan
suras. Allah, the name for God, only
begins to appear with regularity in these
later Meccan *suras* as well, with the

rather impersonal *ar-Rabb* (the Lord) being generally used in the very earliest *suras*. In Muhammad's earliest preaching, the warning about the Day of Judgement is much more frequently mentioned than the issue of the unity of God, and it was these revelations about the afterlife that his opponents bitterly criticized during the first twelve years.

A contrast is often made between the mainly prophetic character of the Meccan *suras* and the legalistic style of most of the Medinan *suras*, and the earlier *suras* are sometimes regarded as more moving and personal than those that come later. Of course, the Prophet was in a different position earlier on, surrounded by enemies and with few supporters, and with little scope to turn the message into actuality, whereas in Medina he could establish a political authority and organize the city along the lines specified by God.

One of the contrasts between the two periods is the style of address, which is much more personal earlier on and impersonal later. The Meccan passages usually speak to Muhammad himself or to people generally, the Medinan passages are often addressed to Muhammad's followers with the introduction '*Ya ayyuhallathina a'manuu* (O you who believe!)'. What follows is often about law, which is of its nature impersonal, and the laws of Islam are found mainly in the passages dating from Muhammad's period in Medina. We find details on campaigns, confiscations, customs, contracts (2.282) and behaviour, the abolition of usury (2.278), the laws of inheritance (4.11–12), the prohibited degrees of relationship (4.23), the property of orphans (4.6–10), the prohibitions on wine and gambling (5.93–94), comments on public events, statements of policy, criticism of those who did not see eye to eye with the Prophet (mainly the Jews), and some detail about his

domestic problems, how he resolved them, and so on. Muhammad is given special permission to exceed the limit placed on Muslims not to take more than four wives at a time (33.50–52), and believers are commanded to salute him (33.56) and even given strict details regarding etiquette to be observed when approaching his apartments:

> O you who believe! Enter not the Prophet's houses, until leave is given you, for a meal, [and then] not [so early as] to wait for its preparation: but when you are invited, enter; and when you have taken your meal, leave, without seeking familiar talk. Such [behaviour] annoys the Prophet: he is ashamed to dismiss you, but God is not ashamed [to tell you] the truth. (33.53)

This is in marked contrast with 80.1–12, where he may have been criticized for lack of humility on a particular occasion.

In fact, the style of the Medinan period has sometimes been criticized by contrast with the earlier *suras*, as by Bell: 'The slovenliness, the trailing sentences, the mechanical rhymes of the later portions of the Qur'an, have often been remarked on' (Bell, 1926: 96). During the later *suras*, the Prophet comes to great prominence, and revelations about the biblical prophets take a pattern rather similar to his own prophetic history and experience. This consists of dialogues between a prophet and his relations, in which the former preaches monotheism and right living to the latter, who have strayed from the monotheistic path (Noah, 21.76–77; Abraham, 37.83–99; and so on). Hud, the prophet of the 'Ad people, is said to have discoursed with his countrymen in this manner:

> 'O my people! Worship God! Ye have no other god but Him.' ... the leaders of the unbelievers among his people said 'Ah! We see that you are an imbecile.' ... He

said, 'O my people! I am no imbecile, but [I am] an apostle from the Lord ... Do you wonder that there has come to you a message from your Lord through a man of your own people, to warn you?' ... They said, 'Do you come to us so that we may worship God alone, and give up the cult of our fathers? Bring us what you are threatening us with if you are telling the truth!' He said, ... 'Are you arguing with me over names which you have made up, you and your fathers, without authority from God?' (7.65–71)

This passage deals with Muhammad's own struggle with the pagan Meccans. He too concentrated on proclaiming the unity of God, was rejected as one possessed, and likewise defended his claims. (Hud, as in all the stories of the prophets the Qur'an records, is made to describe Allah in typically Qur'anic terms: e.g. *rabbil-'alamin*, 'The Lord of the Worlds'.)

Again there is the emphasis on the prophet being called from his own people who, however, prefer the cult worship of their ancestors. Muhammad likewise threatened his people with destruction and was challenged to bring it about (8.32) and, like the supposed prophet Hud, reviled their idols as *'asma' summaytumu ha antum wa aba 'ukum* (names which you have devised, you and your fathers) (7.71; 53.23).

Muslim and non-Muslim commentators take different lines on the contrast between the Meccan and Medinan passages. Believing that the Qur'an is eternal and that it was simply dictated to Muhammad, Muslim writers are generally disinclined to admit the existence of any contrast. They are not inclined to accept any idea of a development in the Qur'anic text as this seems to imply that the text had much to do with Muhammad's career and might even suggest that he was its author. On the other hand, verses are often explained by Muslim commentators in terms of the events that were pertinent to some as opposed to other verses. Indeed, this is often used as a guide to when abrogation is and is not appropriate. A rather radical Muslim commentator, Fazlur Rahman, has no problem in perceiving a contrast between the two periods of versification:

A voice is crying from the very depths of life and impinging forcefully on the Prophet's mind in order to make itself explicit at the level of consciousness. This tone gradually gives way, especially in the Medina period, to a more fluent and easy style as the legal content increases for the detailed organization and direction of the nascent community-state. (Rahman, 1966: 30)

He goes on to say:

It is interesting that all these descriptions of experiences and visions belong to the Meccan period; in the Medina era we have a progressive unfolding of the religio-moral ideal, and the foundation for the social order for the newly instituted community but hardly any allusions to inner experiences. (Rahman, 1966: 128)

Muhammad Taha argued that the Meccan verses are much more universal than the Medinan verses, and the latter only reflect the exigencies of the time when the Prophet was trying to keep the community together in exile. Once he returned to Mecca, the Medinan verses could be accepted as only having applied in an earlier period and could be rejected. This in an unusual interpretation and resulted in its author's execution. Those hostile to Islam find the later Medinan verses representative of an increasingly autocratic and unsympathetic Muhammad, someone who was enjoying the use of power and getting back at his enemies. The earlier verses are seen as concise and to the point, often moving in their style and content, while the later are ponderous and unwieldy, representing the desire to establish a religion and law when the significance of persuasion was no longer current. It has to be said that law is not the most gripping subject matter for anyone, and so it is hardly surprising that the revelations that are replete with legal distinctions and information do not exactly inspire the reader or hearer.

On the other hand, the distinction between the style of the two periods should not be overdone. After all, we are told:

> God! There is no god but He, the Living, the self-subsisting, the eternal. No slumber can seize him nor sleep. His are all things in the heavens and on earth. Who is there can intercede in His presence except as He allow? He knows what [comes to His creatures as] before or after or behind them. They will grasp only as much of his knowledge as he allows. His Throne cloth extends over the heavens and the earth, and He feels no fatigue in guarding and preserving them. For He is the Most High, the Supreme [in glory]. (2.255)

This is the *ayat al-Kursi*, the Verse of the Throne, named after the throne of God described in it. The other striking passage from the Medinan period is a rare verse of obvious beauty, which tends to move into the mystical realm in its description of God's glory and has accordingly been highly esteemed by the Sufis:

> God is the Light of the heavens and the earth. The parable of His Light is as if there were a niche and within it a lamp: the lamp enclosed in a glass: the glass as it were a brilliant star lit from a blessed tree, an olive neither of the East nor of the West, whose oil is almost luminous, though fire hardly touched it: Light upon Light! God guides whom He will to His light: God provides parables for men: and God knows all things. (24.35)

These two passages are rightly highly esteemed by Muslims and are typical of the constant endeavour in the Qur'an to glorify God in suitable terms. Nevertheless, they do appear to be more easily related to the earlier *suras* of the Meccan period than the otherwise legislative spirit of most of the Medinan passages. It is in the Meccan *suras* that we find 'quite a number of verses expounding this theme of God's goodness and power. Indeed, quantitatively this is by far the most prominent aspect of the message of the early passages' (Watt, 1953: 63).

Time of revelation

When *suras* were revealed is an important aspect of Qur'anic hermeneutics. For example, it is sometimes said that the early revelation was written when Muhammad was weak and the later when he was stronger. So the later revelation is filled with injunctions that call the believers to be harsh with the unbelievers and kill them wherever they find them. It sometimes seems that the believers needed to be encouraged to fight when they were initially disinclined to do so: 'Fighting is prescribed for you, and you dislike it. But it is possible that you dislike a thing which is good for you' (2.216). Is it really the case that fighting is good for people? But when this did not work, Muhammad apparently coerced them with: 'Unless you go forth, He [God] will punish you with a grievous penalty, and put others in your place' (9.39).

If the later revelations abrogate the earlier, then 9.29 suggests constant hostility even against the People of the Book. At first fighting was forbidden, then it was permitted, and after that it was made obligatory. The Meccan part, however, although mostly abrogated, is often used by defenders of Islam to show it in a positive light. As against the milder Meccan *suras*, we find later on:

> Take not the Jews and the Christians for your friends and protectors: They are but friends and protectors to each other. And he among you that turns to them [for friendship] is of them. Verily Allah does not guide a people. (5.51)

There is also: 'Then, when the sacred months have passed, slay the idolaters wherever you find them, and capture them and besiege them, and prepare for them each ambush' (9.5). Plus: 'And fight them until persecution is no more, and religion is for Allah' (2.193). There are several bellicose verses of this nature: 'When you meet the unbelievers, strike their necks; finally, when you have thoroughly subdued them, restrain them firmly' (47.4; see also 8.12).

These verses are very much part of the second part of the revelation, and those suspicious or hostile to Islam regard them as the 'real' viewpoint of the religion which it adopted when it was strong enough to enact its wishes. The much gentler verses from the earlier period do not, in this view, represent what Islam is really about. Yet although this contrast between earlier and later verses is interesting and important, it has to be acknowledged that such a strategy for attacking Islam is misguided. First, Muslims themselves are interested in the timing of the revelation when they consider its interpretation, and they certainly do not think that the earlier verses become irrelevant just because later ones may be contrary to them. Second, verses in the Qur'an are not the only source used by Muslims to discover God's will. There are also the Traditions (*ahadith*) and the *sunna* of the Prophet, and of course the mass of legal and theological reflection on the text of the Qur'an and these other significant sources of meaning.

References and further reading

Bell, R. (1926) *The Origin of Islam in its Christian Environment*, London: Macmillan.

Cragg, K. (1971) *The Event of the Qur'an: Islam in its scripture*, London: George Allen & Unwin.

—— (1975) *The Mind of the Qur'an: Chapters in reflection*, London: George Allen & Unwin.

Rahman, F. (1958) *Prophecy in Islam: Philosophy and orthodoxy*, London: George Allen & Unwin.

—— (1966) *Islam*, New York: Rinehart & Winston.

Watt, W.M. (1953) *Muhammad at Mecca*, Oxford: Clarendon Press,

—— (1973) *The Formative Period of Islamic Thought*, Edinburgh: Edinburgh University Press.

See also: **abrogation; Arab; *asbab al-nuzul*; Qur'anic Studies**

OLIVER LEAMAN

MICHAEL / MIKHA'IL

Michael/Mikha'il is a name of one of the chief angels or archangels. It can be pronounced Mika'il or Mikal, and is referred to at 2.98. The name is a compound from two components: *Mik*, meaning who is like, and *il* meaning God. His role is to provide nourishment for bodies and knowledge for souls. He stands above the Swarming Sea (52.6) in the seventh heaven, and if he were to open his mouth, the heavens would fit within it like a mustard seed in the ocean.

According to a *hadith*, 'Every prophet has two viziers from those in heaven and two from the earth; my two from heaven are Gabriel and Michael.' When Israfil blows the trumpet, Gabriel will stand at his right hand and Michael at his left.

OLIVER LEAMAN

MIRACULOUSNESS OF THE QUR'AN

It is often claimed that there is an extraordinary eloquence and purity of style in the word order or composition of the Qur'an. Each word and each sentence, indeed the whole Qur'an, complete and complement the rest. For example, in order to indicate the severity of God's punishment, the clause 'If but a breath from the torment of your Lord touches them' (21.46) points to the smallest amount of that torment. That is, the clause emphasizes this slightness, so the whole phrase establishes that meaning.

The words 'if but' (*layn*) suggest uncertainty and therefore imply lightness, here of the punishment. The verb *massa* means 'to touch slightly', and also signifies lightness. *Nafhatun* (a breath) is merely a puff of air, the very epitome of what is slight and inconsequential; grammatically, it comes from the word used to represent 'singularity', which again brings out its apparent lack of significance. The *tanwin* (double *n*) at the end of *nafhatun* indicates indefiniteness and suggests that it is so tiny and insignificant that it can hardly be known at all. The partitive *min* implies a part or a piece, so not even something of an ordinary size. The word *adhab* (torment or punishment) is less severe compared to *nakal* (exemplary chastisement) and *iqab* (heavy penalty), and thus suggests a lesser punishment. Even the use of *Rabb* (Lord, Provider, Sustainer), which tends to be a warmer word, whereas some of the other names of God emphasize his overwhelming power, authority and sternness, also gives the phrase a gentler tone. The clause suggests that if so slight a breath of torment or punishment has such a result, one should reflect on the severity of divine chastisement by contrast. The parts of this short clause are related to each other and expand the meaning in a highly impressive manner. Every word and phrase has been selected with extreme care and skill.

Here is another example. The sentence 'They spend out of what we have given them [as livelihood]' (2.3) is so rich in meaning that it indicates five of the conditions that make charity acceptable to God. In order for his charity to be acceptable to God, someone must give out of his means an amount that means he will not be the necessary recipient of charity himself: 'out of' in 'out of what' brings this sense to the fore. He must not be charitable from someone else's possessions, but he must give out of his own property: the phrase 'what we have given them' shows this, with the meaning being 'Give out of what we have given you'. An important aspect of this is that the recipient of charity should not feel that a special favour has been done to him, since what he is given is only what the giver was himself given by God in the first place. 'We' in 'We have given' indicates this, for it means: 'It is I who have given you the means out of which you give to the poor. Therefore, by giving to a servant of mine out of my property, he is under no sort of obligation to you.'

But it is not just the giving that is important, it must be given to someone who will make good use of the gift. The implied reference to livelihood is relevant here, suggesting that the gift must play a part, and perhaps a continuing role, in the ability of the recipient to make a living. The giving is for God's sake and in God's name, and it represents essentially a transfer of property from God to someone who will make good use of it. Together with those conditions, the word 'what' in 'out of what' suggests that whatever God grants humanity is part of our 'sustenance' or 'livelihood'. Therefore, one must give not only material things, but more widely from what one has, so doing a good deed, offering a piece of advice, general assistance and teaching are all included in the meaning of *rizq* (sustenance) and *sadaqa* (charity).

This short sentence, then, brings out a much wider meaning, one that is intended to make the reader and listener think about the wide scope of what is meant by being charitable and receiving God's benevolence, yet which is at the same time encapsulated within a small number of words.

It is often claimed by commentators that there is a wonderful eloquence in the meanings of the Qur'an. Consider the following example: 'All that is in the heavens and the earth glorifies God; and he is honoured and mighty, the all-wise' (59.24). Verses such as 'All that is in the heavens and the earth glorifies God' or 'The seven heavens and the earth and those in them glorify him' (17.44) are very stirring indications of God's power and authority, and his ability to hold the whole world in his hand. It is not possible to think of finer ways of expressing these points, and the effect that they have had on their hearers is not difficult to imagine. The verses of the Qur'an represent its uniqueness and beauty, not to mention its novelty and originality. That is why it has succeeded in convincing so many people of its truth. It imitates nothing and no one, nor can it be imitated. Its style does not pall, even after long periods of study, and the text does not lose its freshness over time. Of course, since the content is very important for its readers, the style can be seen as an aspect of divine grace. God wishes to warn us of the consequences of behaving wrongly and so makes comprehensible what a life of virtue will be, and what our eventual reward for it is. The language is an intimate part of this: it persuades at the same time as it delights.

For example: 'And the sun runs its course to a set resting place' (36.38). The expression 'runs its course' brings out the systematic nature of the seasons and their ultimate source in the free will of their creator. It also implies the design and intelligence that lie behind nature. This comes out even more in the use of the word 'lamp': 'he has made the sun a lamp' (71.16), where we have the idea that the world is like the interior of a building, constructed by God just as our houses are constructed by us, with a plan and in order to benefit the inhabitants. The sun is like the light that one puts in a house so that what is inside can be made visible. This is an idea that emphasizes God's power but also his care for his creatures, since even the sun, that distant and vital aspect of the natural environment, is under his control and was designed for our benefit.

There is a famous story that a Bedouin heard the phrase 'Proclaim openly what you are commanded' (15.94) and did, in fact, prostrate himself. When asked if he was a Muslim, he replied in the negative. It was the language itself that had caused him to bow.

When it comes to deterrence and threat, the Qur'an is particularly effective in its use of language. In its attack on slander, the Book asks: 'Would any of you like to eat the flesh of his dead brother?' (49.12). The idea that backbiting is like eating the flesh of a dead brother makes it especially horrible. The *hamza* at the beginning is interrogative and, in the interrogative mode, this is a characteristic Qur'anic idiom, asking the reader to reflect on what he reads. Through the second word in the Arabic, which means 'like', the phrase emphasizes the possibility of liking something so repugnant. The phrase 'any of you' asks how a group of people could so abandon civility to act in such a way, and directs itself at a group of people including the reader or hearer. The fourth word, through the phrase 'to eat the flesh', asks whether one wants to behave like a wild animal in dealing with others. The fifth, through the phrase 'of his brother', relates the example not only to someone close to one but even to oneself, since attacking a close relative is an attempt to destroy someone who forms a part of one's own identity. It refers to someone who is so close that the idea of even offending him is blame-worthy. The word 'dead' emphasizes the lack of respect that is involved in the action: here is a body that one ought to treat very differently. Slander is, then, very concisely but comprehensively shown to be unacceptable.

One of the aims of the Qur'an was to persuade materialists that this world is not all there is to existence: 'Look, therefore, at the marks of God's mercy: how he revives the earth after its death. Indeed, it is He who is the reviver of the dead in the same way, and he has power over all things' (30.50). This verse is effective in its presentation of God's role in both reviving the dead and organizing the natural world. In raising to life again every spring hundreds of thousands of plants and supporting the general cycle of life and death, God provides a lot of examples of resurrection. In particular, the point is made that there are no diffi-culties for the creator of everything in reviving the dead. By the adverb 'how', the Qur'an refers to the manner or way of the resurrection; it is described in detail in many other *suras*.

In *sura 50* the Qur'an proves the res-urrection in what is often taken to be such a brilliant, beautiful and elevated manner of expression that it convinces as certainly as the coming of spring, an image in the verse itself. In reply to the unbelievers' denial of the return to life of the bones and flesh that has rotted away, it declares in a manner like the flowing of water (another image used in the verse):

> Have they not then observed the sky above them, how we have constructed it and beautified it, and how there are no rifts therein? And the earth We have spread out, and have flung firm hills therein, and have caused every lively kind to grow therein, a sight and a reminder for every penitent servant. And We send down from the sky blessed water whereby We give growth to gar-dens and the grain of crops, and lofty date-palms with ranged clusters, provi-sion for men; and therewith we quicken a dead land. Even so will be the resurrec-tion of the dead. (50.6–11)

The style of its exposition flows like water, glitters like stars and, like food for the body, it gives to the heart plea-sure, delight and nourishment.

Another example, among the most perfect examples from the category of proof and demonstration, says: 'Ya Sin. By the Wise Qur'an. Certainly you are among those sent [as Messengers of God]' (36.1–3). The oath in the verse points out that the proof of Muham-mad's messengership is validated by the Qur'an itself, which he presents to the community. This seems circular reason-ing, since the proof of his messengership is the Qur'an, but the latter is hardly such a significant text unless he is a messenger. So there is a fine agreement in both the text of the book, the role of the messenger and the Book itself, which is designed to convince the listener of the remarkable nature of what here exists. The wisdom of the Qur'an calls on us to examine its arguments and, if we find them compelling, we are then also compelled to accept the role of the Prophet as a prophet; we might then go on to examine aspects of his mission that are not directly validated by a text in the Qur'an.

Another concise and clear example of the category of proof and demonstration: '[Man] said: "Who will revive these bones when they have rotted away?" Say: "He will revive them who created them in the first place; He has absolute knowledge of every creation"' (36.78–79). The precise order of nature gives evidence of its divine origins, since it is so well designed that it could not have come about in any other way.

> Then your hearts became hardened thereafter and were like stones, or even harder; for there are stones from which rivers come gushing, and others split, so that water issues from them, and others crash down in the fear of God. God is not heedless of the things you do. (2.74)

This verse, addressed to the Children of Israel, means that while the hard rock poured tears like a spring from its twelve 'eyes' in the face of a miracle of the Prophet Moses, and in particular his staff, but what has happened to you that you become indifferent in the face of all the miracles of that prophet with your eyes dry and hearts hardened and unfeeling?

For the category of silencing and overcoming, consider the following example: 'If you are in doubt concerning what We have sent down with Our servant, then bring a *sura* like it, and call your helpers and witnesses, other than God, if you are truthful' (2.23). So the suggestion is that if there are doubts concerning the divine authorship of the Qur'an, with the implication that it is merely the product of a human mind, come forward and produce something like it. The Prophet is not a poet: 'We have not taught him poetry; it is not seemly for him' (36.69). To the claim that there could be more than one deity, the Qur'an responds: 'Were there gods in earth and heaven other than God, this would lead to confusion' (21.22).

Actually, the idea is that were there two headmen or elders in a village, two governors in a town, two sovereigns in a country, there would remain no order and everything would be chaos. Whereas, from the wings of a small insect to what are referred to as the lamps of the heavens, there is such a delicate order and harmony in the universe that there is no room for associating partners with God. Everything is too perfect and unified for that to be feasible. 'The Most Merciful One has settled Himself on the Supreme Divine Throne' (20.5) shows that divine rule over the world is like the rule in a kingdom, and God administers the universe as though he were a king seated on his throne and exercising his will.

In a familiar discussion of the theological language, we have to acknowledge that for most of the Islamic thinkers the Divine Throne ('arsh) and Chair (kursi) are unknown to us, although the fact that they exist cannot be doubted by Muslims. However, since God speaks according to our level of understanding, he usually speaks in parables and metaphors. In a nice phrase, Nursi says that earth is the throne of life ('arsh al-hayat) and water the throne of mercy ('arsh al-rahma). This means that in the world God creates most things from earth and water, and rain is the embodiment of his mercy. What might be meant by 'arsh may be all the physical things that God uses in directing and carrying out his commands, or it may be an immaterial entity running through all of creation, from which God controls and administers the universe. While 'arsh may be linked with the divine world, an interpretation of kursi may be concerned with other unseen worlds of immaterial forms.

See also: **backbiting; language and the Qur'an;** *tafsir* **in early Islam;** *ta'til*

OLIVER LEAMAN

MI'RAJ

In *Sahih Muslim* Anas ibn Malik reports in detail on the Prophet's description of his night journey. He reports that he was presented with al-Buraq, a white animal larger than a donkey but smaller than a mule, and the animal was able to place its hoof at a distance equal to the range of vision. The Prophet got on and came to *Bayt-al muqdis*, assumed to be Jerusalem. He tethered the animal to the ring that had been used by previous prophets. The Muhammad entered the mosque and prayed, and was met by Gabriel who brought him a vessel of wine and a vessel of milk. He chose the milk, and Gabriel said: 'You have chosen *al-fitra* (the natural way).'

They both ascended into the lower heavens and requested that they be opened. It was said: 'Who are you?' The archangel responded: 'Gabriel.' It was then said: 'Who is with you?' He responded: 'Muhammad.' It was then said: 'Has revelation been sent to him?' Gabriel responded: 'Revelation has been sent to him.' The lower heavens were then opened and they met Adam. He welcomed the Prophet and prayed for his well-being.

Gabriel and Muhammad then ascended to the second heaven and Gabriel requested that it be opened. It was said: 'Who are you?' He responded: 'Gabriel.' It was then said: 'Who is with you?' He responded: 'Muhammad.' It was then said: 'Has revelation been sent to him?' He responded: 'Revelation has been sent to him.' The second heaven was then opened. There they met Jesus and John, who also welcomed them and prayed for Muhammad's well-being. They then went to the third heaven and requested that it be opened. It was said: 'Who are you?' He responded: 'Gabriel.' It was then said: 'Who is with you?' He responded: 'Muhammad.' It was then said: 'Has revelation been sent to him?' He responded: 'Revelation has been sent to him.' The third heaven was then opened and they saw Joseph, who was famous for his beauty. He welcomed and prayed for Muhammad.

The account continues with visits to the fourth heaven to meet Enoch, the fifth for Aaron, the sixth for Moses and the seventh for Abraham. On each visit Gabriel assures the resident that Muhammad had received revelation and so the reception was friendly. Muhammad saw all manner of wonders and was told by God to institute fifty daily prayers. On his way down, he meets Moses again, who asks him how many prayers had been ordered. When Moses hears it was fifty, he suggests that Muhammad return to God to ask for a reduced number. As a result of repeated visits, God reduces the prayers to five a day, and with that welcome information Muhammad ends his miraculous journey.

The significance of the account is huge in the literature that followed the Qur'an. First of all, it links Muhammad with the earlier prophets, all of whom validate his message and status as a prophet. Second, the idea of secrets being made available to him as the doors open and of his taking those secrets back to earth is a popular topic in the literature of *tasawwuf* or mysticism. Finally, it establishes on a sound footing the number at least of the daily prayers, which are seen to have this dynamic account as its source.

OLIVER LEAMAN

MISHKAT

The word *mishkat* has been the subject of much discussion. It is generally translated as 'niche' and occurs only once in the Qur'an, in the famous and oft-quoted 'Light Verse' or *ayat a-Nur* (24.35), where the light of God is compared to a niche (*mishkat*) within which is a lamp enclosed in brilliant glass. According to Muslim scholars, the word is Arabic and was in common use during the Prophet Muhammad's time. It is described as the little shallow recess in the wall of an Eastern house, fairly high from the ground, in which a light or lamp was usually placed. Its height enabled light to diffuse throughout the room and minimized shadow. The background of the wall and the sides of the niche helped to throw the light effectively into the room. If the wall was whitewashed, it also acted as a reflector. The rhetorical use of this word was seen to be a perfect and yet familiar way of describing God's infinite Glory.

Controversy centres around the origin of the word *mishkat*. Western scholars like Nöldeke believed the term to be an Abyssinian (Ethiopic) word for window. Hence they concluded, although no one could supply a source, that the Prophet Muhammad must have heard of such a parable of light elsewhere. Some scholars even suggested a Christian source, since the light, they claimed, was reminiscent of the theme of the light of the monk's cell which guides travellers across the desert in some pre-Islamic poetry. In essence, the controversy over the origin of this word is representative of the huge gap between Muslim and Western views concerning the vocabulary of the Qur'an. To Muslim scholars all the words of the Qur'an are Arabic in origin. Their argument is based on statements in the Qur'an that it was revealed in a clear Arabic tongue (*lisanun 'arabiyun mubin*), but also on the more pragmatic fact that a messenger to the Arabs, a people well versed in the art of poetry and oration, must of necessity speak Arabic. Furthermore, Arabic was an ancient Semitic language that shared a common stock of vocabulary and imagery with other Semitic languages like Aramaic, Hebrew and Ethiopic. As such, it would be impossible to decide which language was more ancient or which was the Proto-Semitic. As for Western scholars, some still claim that hundreds of common Arabic words, among them *qalam* (pen), *kitab* (book), *rahma* (mercy), *bayt* (house), *warda* (rose), *aya* (sign), *jahannam* (hell), *salat* (prayers) and the famous *mishkat*, ultimately come from Hebrew and Aramaic. The general implication, of course, is that Arabic is a primitive language that is basically incapable of conveying simple ideas like book and pen, or even more complex notions like mercy and compassion. Something of the confusion in their arguments can be seen in the following quote from Bell (1968: 116) concerning the word *al-rahman* (the Merciful), used as an epithet for God in the Qur'an:

> The word does not seem, however, to be directly derived from Aramaic. It is found in South Arabian inscriptions, and may have come through that channel. Or it may be a native Arabian formation from the root *rhm*. In any case, like the kindred word *rahma* in the sense of 'mercy', it comes ultimately from Hebrew and Aramaic.

References and further reading

Bell, R. (1968) *The Origin of Islam in the Christian Environment*, Edinburgh: Frank Cass & Co.
The Holy Qur'an: English Translation of the Meaning and Commentary (1990) rev. and ed. The Presidency of Islamic Researches, al-Madina al-Munwara: King Fahad Holy Qur'an Printing Complex.

AFNAN H. FATANI

MITHAQ

Mithaq is a noun that signifies covenant, agreement, treaty or alliance. *Mithaq* can be used to describe an agreement between two parties. It is a confirmed contract, guaranteed by an oath. In the Qur'an the covenant between God and his servants is mentioned as many as twenty-six times. Allah took the covenant from the prophets: 'And remember when We took from the Prophets their covenant' (33.7). There are many Prophets and Messengers of Allah, but only five are of *alu-al-'azm* (with strong will). They are Muhammad, Noah, Abraham, Moses and Jesus. The above verse specifies them as the strong upholders of the covenant with Allah: 'And from you [Muhammad] and from Noah, Abraham, Moses and Jesus, son of Mary, we made with them a strong covenant' (33.7).

The Qur'an mentions the covenant of God with the Children of Israel very often, for example: 'And We made with them a firm covenant' (4.154). Allah reminds the Jews in the Qur'an of his covenant on different occasions, including: 'And when we made a covenant with the Children of Israel' (2.83). That covenant stipulates, among other things, that they shall worship Allah alone and that they shall be dutiful and good to their parents and their relations, to orphans and to the poor. They were to speak well to people, and to perform prayers and give charity.

The covenant of God was also made with the Muslims during the time of the Qur'an's revelation: 'And remember Allah's covenant with which he bound you and you said "We hear and obey"' (5.70).

The marriage contract is a strong covenant between man and woman. If a Muslim is tempted to replace one wife with another, he is not allowed to take back the least bit of what he had paid her as a dowry: 'And how could you take it back; while you have gone unto each other, and they have taken from you a firm and strong covenant?' (4.21).

Those who honour their covenant with God are the blessed, are men of understanding. To 'those who fulfil the covenant of Allah and break not the covenant' (13.20) is promised entry to the everlasting gardens in paradise. However, those who dishonour God's covenant are damned: 'Because of their breach of their covenant, we cursed them and made their hearts grow hard' (5.13).

Muthiq means compact, bond, solemn pledge or the undertaking of an oath. Jacob's sons asked him to allow their brother, Yusuf, to go and play with them. He said: 'I will not send him with you until you swear a solemn oath to me in Allah's name' (12.66). *Wathaqa* means to place one's confidence or faith in something, or to trust. *Wathaq* is a bond, fetter or shackle. 'Then bind a bond firmly' (47.4). *Wathiqa* means to rely on, while *awthaqa* means to tie up or chain, and also to make firm, solid, or to be sure or certain.

See also: **'ahd; covenant; divorce**

RAFIK BERJAK

MODESTY

Modesty is promoted in the Qur'an for both men and women, but the controversial area of discussion has tended to concentrate on the latter. What, as far as women are concerned, is modesty in Islam?

Often it is taken to be covering the whole body, except eyes, ankles and toes. According to a *hadith* of Abu Da'ud, the Prophet had said that when a woman became adult, no part of her body should be seen except her face and ankles. Those who are in favour of including the face in *satr/sitr* (veiling) limits think that a woman's *satr* for a non-*mahram* (close male relation) includes her face, while the *satr* limits defined in the *hadith* are a woman's *satr* for a *mahram*. (The normal understanding of *maharim*, the plural form of *mahram*, are a woman's close male relations, including father, brother, nephew, husband, possibly some of the husband's close male kin, and any male breastfed by her mother.) It should be noted that the above instructions were given by the Prophet to Asma', the Prophet's sister-in-law, and 'A'isha's elder sister when she came before the Prophet wearing a very thin dress. It should also be remembered that a woman's brother-in-law is not normally regarded as a *mahram*.

The following verse of Qur'an is important in laying down the guidelines for the limits of exposable parts of a woman and the people from whom she must conceal her *satr*:

> Say to the believing women that they should lower their gaze and to guard their chastity; that they should not display their adornments except what [ordinarily] appears; that they should draw their veils over their bosoms and not display their adornments except to their husbands, their fathers, their husbands' fathers, their sons, their stepsons, their brothers, their brother's sons, their sister's sons, their women, or those whom they possess [as war captives], or their male attendants lacking in sexual vigour, or small children who have no carnal knowledge of women; and that they should not stamp their feet in walking so as to reveal their hidden trinkets. Believers, turn to Allah together in repentance that you may be successful. (24.31)

What does 'lower their gaze' mean? The Arabic words for gaze in this context are *basar* and *'ayn*, which means eyes. Also, 'lower' is not the exact translation of the Arabic word derived from the root *ghadh*. Its actual sense is to check the intensity of what takes place (see 31.19 and 49.2). It means that the prohibition is not about gazing

itself, but its nature, so that an intense or lusty gaze is prohibited. This prohibition is not limited to women only: in the immediately preceding verse (24.30), men are instructed to check their gazes and guard their chastity in the same words. Women are told they should not display their adornments: hence there has arisen an actual order for the concealment of *satr*. Women are required to draw their veils over their bosoms and, in addition, they are required to conceal their adornments. There are two exceptions to this and therefore the words are used twice to describe the two exceptions each time. The first exception limits adornments to 'Except what [ordinarily] appears'. There are a number of different interpretations of this, attributed to different authorities. The second issue is in relation to the people before whom these adornments may be exposed. These two exceptions – how much may be exposed and before whom the adornments may be exposed – are linked. The two exceptions described in the same verse and followed by the same phrase could be taken to complement each other.

As we have seen, the upper limit of concealment has been relaxed with respect to the people listed in the verse. It means that if it is not permitted to expose the face, it is not permitted to be exposed before all except the people described in the verse. Now the list includes 'their women'; in other words, women would not be permitted to reveal their faces before any woman other than 'their women'. Who are 'their women'? The word can be taken to mean the women of their acquaintance who are of sound character, or their servants, or frequent companions. But this would make life difficult for women. They would not be permitted to show their faces before any woman other than the women they know. The face is not included in a woman's *satr* for non-*mahram*s. The verses like 33.53, which are quoted to prove the order of concealment of face, are surely special instructions for the wives of the Prophet. The *satr* of a woman is a discussion of a principle that Islam has not necessarily ordered a woman to cover her face before a non-*mahram*. If she takes care to cover her face as the Prophet's wives were ordered, then it is appropriate. But whether this is ordered by the text is a moot point. Muhammad Ashmawi has challenged the necessity for Muslim women to be veiled at all, something defended by Sayyid Tantawi, the mufti of Egypt at the time. Ashmawi argues that veiling is a pre-Islamic custom that has been mistakenly taken up by legal thinkers in Islam. There is, then, a lively debate on what precisely is involved in the Qur'anic injunction for the preservation of modesty.

Further reading

Ashmawi, S. (1994) 'Fatwa al-hijab ghayr shar'iyya', *Ruz al-yusuf*, 8 August: 28.
—— (1994) 'al-Hijab laysa farida', *Ruz al-yusuf*, 13 June: 22.
al-Ghazali, Z. (1995) *Ayyam min hayati*, Cairo: Dar al-shuruq.
al-Qaradawi (1996) *Al-niqab li'l mara'a: Bayna al-qawl bi bid'iyyatihi wa'l-qawl bi wujubihi*, Cairo: Maktabat wahba.
Tantawi, M. (1994) 'Bal al-hijab farida islamiyya', *Ruz al-yusuf*, 27 June: 68.

See also: **veil**

OLIVER LEAMAN

MOHAMMED ARKOUN
see: **Arkoun, Mohammed**

MONEY

God refers to the inequalites of the world of work in 43.32: 'We have apportioned among them their livelihood in the life of the world, and raised some of them above others in rank so that some of them take labour from others.' This verse refers to the reality of the social situation in which each individual has a different capacity and different talents. The Qur'an takes a realistic view of the economic conditions that prevail and suggests ways of ensuring that commercial transactions are regulated in an effective and ethical manner. A number of topics are mentioned and rulings are given on them.

Interest

'Allah will deprive usury of all blessing, but will give increase for deeds of charity' (2.276). Jabir ibn 'Abdullah reported that the Prophet cursed the accepter of interest and its payer, the one who records it, and the two witnesses; and he said: 'They are all equal' (Muslim). Abu Hurayra related that the Prophet said: 'On the night of the Mi'raj I came upon a group of people whose bellies were like houses. They were full of snakes which could be seen from outside their bellies. I asked Gabriel who they were, and he told me that they were the people who had practiced *riba* (interest)' (*Ahmad, Ibn Maja*). 'Abdullah ibn Hanjala related that the Prophet said: 'A dirham of *riba* (interest) knowingly taken by a man is a sin thirty-six times worse than committing *zina* (fornication)' (*Ahmad, Daraqutni*).

Charity

'And they are commanded to do nothing else than to serve Allah, be sincerely devoted to him, behave well in religion, and establish regular worship and regular charity (*zakah*). That is true religion' (98.5). The reference to charity here signifies its high status in the Qur'an. 'Abbas related that a man asked the Prophet: 'Tell me what should I do to be admitted to Paradise?', and the Prophet answered: 'Worship Allah, associating nothing with Him, observe *salat* (prayers), pay *zakat* (alms) and strengthen the ties of kinship' (*Bukhari, Muslim*).

Charity and punishment

It is narrated by Anas bin Malik that the Prophet said: 'Verily charity appeases the wrath of Allah and eases the sufferings of death' (*Tirmidhi*).

Inheritance and wills

'And for everyone We have appointed heirs for what parents and near relations leave; and as for those with whom your right hands have made a covenant, give them their due. Lo! Allah is ever witness over all things' (4.33). Ibn 'Umar related that the Prophet said: 'It is the duty of a Muslim man who has something which is to be given as a bequest not to have it for two nights without having his will written regarding it' (*Bukhari, Muslim*). Anas related that the Prophet said: 'If anyone deprives an heir of his inheritance, Allah will deprive him of his inheritance in Paradise on the Day of Resurrection' (*Ibn Maja*). It is reported by Jabir that the Prophet said: 'The flesh and body that is raised on unlawful sustenance shall not enter Paradise. Hell is more deserving to the flesh that grows on one's body out of unlawful sustenance' (*Ahmad*). Abu Sa'id related that the Prophet said: 'The truthful and trustworthy businessman will be in the company of prophets, saints and martyrs on the Day of Judgement' (*Darimi, Tirmidhi*). This last saying in particular does support the idea that there is nothing problematic in religious terms about the commercial sector of the economy.

Debts

It is narrated by Abu Musa Ash'ari that the Prophet said: 'After the major sins which must be avoided, the greatest sin is that someone dies in a state of debt and leaves behind no asset to pay it off' (*Darimi*).

Loans

Abu Qatada related that the Prophet said: 'If anyone would like Allah to save him from the hardships of the Day of Resurrection, he should give more time to his debtor who is short of money, or remit his debt altogether' (*Muslim*).

Using wealth

'Believers are merely those whose hearts feel wary whenever God is mentioned and whose faith increases when His verses are recited to them. On their Lord do they rely. Those who keep up prayer and spend some of what We have provided them with are truly believers' (8.2–4). Asma' related that the Prophet said: 'Spend, and do not count, lest Allah counts against you. Do not withhold your money, lest Allah withholds from you. Spend what you can' (*Bukhari, Muslim*). Abu Hurayra related that the Prophet said: 'The Lord's commandment for every one of His slaves is "Spend on others, and I will spend on you"' (*Bukhari, Muslim*).

The poor

'Have you observed him who denies religion? That is he who repels the orphan, and urges not the feeding of the needy' (107.1–3). Safwan ibn Salim related that the Prophet said: 'Anyone who looks after and works for a widow and a poor person is like a warrior fighting for Allah's cause, or like a person who fasts during the day and prays all night' (*Bukhari*).

Hoarding

'O you who believe! Lo! many of the priests and the monks who devour the wealth of mankind and only want to prevent [humanity] from the way of Allah. They who hoard up gold and silver and spend it not in the way of God, unto them give tidings [O Muhammad] of a painful doom' (9.34).

Extravagance

'Give the kinsman his due, and the needy, and the wayfarer, and squander not [your wealth] wantonly. Lo! the squanderers were ever brothers of the devils, and the devil was ever ungrateful to his Lord' (17.26–27). Amr ibn Shuayb, on his father's authority, said his grandfather related that the Prophet had said: 'When you eat, drink, give charity and wear clothes, let no extravagance or pride be mixed up with what you do' (*Ibn Maja, Nasai*).

Miserliness

Abu Hurayra narrated that the Prophet said: 'Every day two angels come down from Heaven and one of them says, "O Allah! Compensate every person who spends in your cause," and the other says, "O Allah! Destroy every miser"' (*Bukhari*). Abu Sa'id Khudri related that the Prophet said: 'There are two habits which are never present together in a believer: miserliness and bad manners' (*Tirmidhi*). Jabir reported that the Prophet said: 'Avoid doing injustice to others, for on the Day of Judgement, it will turn into manifold darkness, and safeguard yourself against miserliness, for it ruined those who were before you.

It incited them to murder and treating the unlawful as lawful' (*Muslim*).

Moderation in giving

'And let not your hand be chained to your neck nor open it with a complete opening, in case you sit down rebuked, denuded' (17.29). So one should be moderate in charity, indeed, moderate in all things. The Qur'an approves those 'who, when they spend, are neither prodigal nor grudging; and there is always a clear line between the two' (25.67).

Bribery

'And eat not up your property among yourselves in vanity, nor seek by it to gain the hearing of the judges that you may knowingly devour a portion of the property of others wrongfully' (2.188).

Contentment

Abu Hurayra narrated that the Prophet said: 'Wealth lies not in having vast riches, it is in contentment' (*Bukhari, Muslim*).

Envy

Ibn Mas'ud said:

> I heard the Prophet saying: 'There is no [acceptable] envy except in two cases: for a person to whom Allah has given wealth and he spends it in the right way, and for a person to whom Allah has given wisdom [religious knowledge] and he gives his decisions accordingly and teaches it to others.' (*Bukhari*)

The best charity

Abu Hurayra narrated that the Prophet said: 'The best charity is that which is practised by a wealthy person. And start

413

giving first to your dependants' (*Bukhari*).

On begging

Hakim bin Hizam narrated that the Prophet said:

> The upper hand is better than the lower hand [i.e. he who gives charity is better than he who takes it]. One should start giving first to one's dependants. And the best type of charity is that which is given by a wealthy person [from the money which is left after his necessities]. And whoever abstains from asking others for some financial help, Allah will give him and save him from asking others, Allah will make him self-sufficient. (*Bukhari*)

Abu Hurayra related that the Prophet said: 'He who makes a habit of asking from others reaches out for a brand of fire, so let him refrain or continue, as he wishes' (*Muslim*). Presumably people who ask for help from others fall foul of the virtue of patience (*sabr*).

Business conduct

Jabir related that the Prophet said: 'May Allah show mercy to a man who is kind when he sells, when he buys, and when he makes a claim' (*Bukhari*).

Further reading

Ahmad, M. (2002) *Man and Money*, Karachi: Oxford University Press.

Mallat, C. (ed.) (1988) *Islamic Law and Finance*, London: Graham & Trotman.

Mills, P..S. and Presley, J.R. (1999) *Islamic Finance: Theory and practice*, Basingstoke and New York: Palgrave.

al-Omar, F. and Haq, A. (1996) *Islamic Banking*, Karachi: Oxford University Press.

Rodinson, M. (1977) *Islam and Capitalism*, Harmondsworth: Penguin.

Zineldin, M. (1990) *The Economics of Money and Banking*, Stockholm: Almqvist & Winksell.

See also: **wealth**

OLIVER LEAMAN

MORALITY

Early Islamic ethical trends modified the old Arabian ideal of *muru'a* (manliness) into a new ideal of virtuous happiness in this world and the hereafter. Morality refers to the degree of conformity to the moral principles acquired by a society. Good manners and morality provide are building bricks of a noble character. Sins that are committed under the impulse of man's lust conflict with Islamic morality and human nature, especially the element of shame (*haya*), which prevents people from doing wrong. Through a process of Islamic education, this shame can be nurtured in such a way that it acts as a deterrent.

Early Arab virtues

A good starting point for understanding the morality of the Qur'an is to learn about the morality of pre-Islamic Arabia. Many of the moral qualities of the pagan Arabs were transformed with their conversion to Islam, with the period before the Qur'anic revelation known in Arabia as the age of 'ignorance' (*jahiliyya*).

However, Goldziher argues that the term should be translated as 'barbarism', because Muhammad intended to contrast Islam with barbarism rather than ignorance. The word 'ignorance' also connotes the 'reckless temper' of the pagan Arabs, which is the antithesis of Islamic *hilm* (forbearance, self-mastery). The pagan Arabs were torn between ignorance and forbearance: they lost their temper easily and were prone to violence, yet they admired the quality of forbearance and self-control (Goldziher, 1967: 202ff.).

Concerning impetuousness, the Qur'an states:

> When the unbelievers instilled in their hearts fierceness, the fierceness of paganism, Allah then sent down His serenity upon His apostle and upon the believers, and imposed on them the word of piety, they being more deserving and worthier. Allah has knowledge of everything. (48.26)

The expression 'fierceness of paganism' (*hamiyyat al-jahiliyya*) in the Qur'an refers to the haughty spirit of the tribal Arab, which inspired many blood feuds in pre-Islamic Arabia. The Qur'anic verse above contrasts this to the calm, tranquil and forbearing way of religion. Connected to this, blind anger is the pagan 'manliness', which also subsumes under it the qualities of generosity (*jud*) and honour (*karam*) (Izutsu, 1959: 23ff.).

The meaning of *muru'a* changed with Muhammad, who taught the pagan Arabs that forgiveness is not a vice, but the highest virtue of *muru'a* (Levy, 1969: 193ff.). Thus, the term covers both the physical and spiritual qualities of man: the physical aspect started with the pagans and the spiritual aspect with Islam.

Pre-Islamic morality was tied up with tribal loyalty, but the Qur'an transformed it into a personal morality. 'No burdened soul shall bear the burden of another, and every person will be accountable on the Day of Judgement for himself' (29.13; 16.25). Islam favoured a universal brotherhood in which kindness and equity should count for more than custom and law. The morality of the Qur'an may be summed up as: 'Believe and do right' (18.105). Belief in one God is fundamental to Muslim ethics: it is the foundation of man's accountability to God and of his happiness in this world and the next.

Of all the human virtues, the Qur'an insists most frequently and most urgently on benevolence to the poor, the needy, the stranger, the slave and the prisoner. This is expressed in the form of compulsory alms-giving (*zakat*) and, more importantly, in the form of voluntary charity (*sadaqa*).

Morality in the Qur'an

Any kind of Islamic ethics, whether religious or philosophical, is ultimately based on the Qur'an. The term should be understood in this broad sense. Islamic philosophers gave Greek ethical concepts a new meaning based on the Qur'an. Therefore, to appreciate the later development of Islamic ethics, one should first understand the nature of ethics in the Qur'an.

The ethical dimensions of the Qur'an are integral to the social context in which it was revealed. That is, both the context of the pagan Arabs and the early Companions of the Prophet. The various religious, legal and moral obligations are interconnected as they are subsumed under God's will. However, there is also a teleological dimension, in terms of which people obey God because he is good, and seek, by means of their innate character (*fitra*), to progress towards happiness and to become the best community among humankind.

As mentioned, through the impact of the Qur'an, the vengeful spirit of the Arabs was transformed into a positive quality of *hilm*, which became the dominant virtue in the Qur'an. In a certain sense the spirit of *hilm* dominates the ethos of the Qur'an as a whole. The constant exhortation to kindness (*ihsan*), the emphasis laid on justice (*'adl*), the forbidding of wrongful violence (*zulm*), the adherence to abstinence and the control of passions, the criticism of groundless pride and arrogance – all are concrete manifestations of this spirit of *hilm* (Izutsu, 1959: 216).

The following Qur'anic verse refers to *hilm*: 'The servants of the Merciful are those who walk humbly upon the earth, and when the ignorant address them, say "Peace"' (25.63). Socially, *hilm* is the great ethical quality, but forbearance does not only come from noble character, but also from man's relationship with God (Denny, 1985: 115).

There are many ethical virtues in the Qur'an that are also formulated in the spirit of *hilm*, but suffice it to mention Luqman's advice to his son:

> O my son, perform the prayer, command the honourable and forbid the dishonourable and bear patiently what has befallen you … Do not turn your face away from people and do not walk in the land haughtily. Allah does not love any arrogant or boastful person. Be modest in your stride and lower your voice; for the most hideous voice is that of asses. (31.17–19)

Goodness (*khayr*) and Righteousness (*birr*)

The term *khayr* (goodness) is used comprehensively, covering the material and religious field. It also connotes wealth, as when a rich man asked the Prophet:

> They ask you what they should spend. Say: 'Whatever bounty (*khayr*) you give is for the parents, the near of kin, the orphans, the needy and the wayfarer. And whatever good (*khayr*) you do, Allah is fully cognizant of it.' (2.215)

The term also connotes pious work: 'Perform the prayer and give the alms-tax. Whatever good (*khayr*) you do for your own sake, you will find it with

Allah, surely Allah is cognizant of what you do' (58.13).

The word *birr* (righteousness) is inseparable from social justice and love for others:

> Righteousness is not to turn your faces towards the East and the West; the righteous is he who believes in Allah, the Last Day, the angels, the Book and the Prophets; who gives of his money, in spite of loving it, to the near of kin, the orphans, the needy, the wayfarers and the beggars, and for the freeing of slaves; who performs the prayers and pays the alms-tax. Such are those who keep their pledges once they have made them, and endure patiently privation, adversity and times of fighting. (2.177)

Justice and responsibility

Justice is a supreme virtue in Islam to the extent that it stands in order of priority after belief in the Oneness of God and the truth of the Prophet. There are many verses in the Qur'an that command believers to adopt it as a moral ideal: 'God commands you to deliver trusts to their owners, and if you judge between people, to judge justly' (4.58); 'O believers, be upholders of justice, witnesses for Allah, even if it be against yourselves, your parents or kinsmen. Whether rich or poor, Allah takes better care of both. Do not follow your desire to refrain from justice' (4.135). The Qur'an not only calls to faith, but also to moral action. Believers are required to obey God and his Prophet, who is the standard of moral conduct and piety.

On marriage and eating

Islamic law prescribes marriage, and commends the one who marries to have children. Procreation outside marriage is unlawful and marriage is described as essential for the survival of the human race. The fornicator is like one who wastes water for fun, not for the cultivation of land. The worst fornication is sodomy. Fornication or adultery (*zina*) is like planting a seed on someone else's land, sodomy is like wasting the seed (al-Isfahani, 1987: 313–317).

Sodomy leads to the breakdown of the family and to sexually transmitted diseases. So whatever excites the passions, and leads to illicit sexual relations, is prohibited. The Qur'an states: 'And approach not adultery, for it is a shameful deed and an evil, opening the road to other evils' (17.32).

There are two kinds of food. One is essential for the health of the body, but should be taken moderately. Eating more than what is required is medically and legally detestable. The Prophet said: 'The most contemptible container is a glutted stomach of lawful food and drink.' A full stomach fortifies passion, Satan's sturdy stalwart. The other kind of food is inessential for the body, and the lack of it will cause no harm. Alcohol is an example of this kind of food, and it incites the lower senses. A believer eats enough for the day, and fills a third of his stomach with food (al-Isfahani, 1987: 313).

The work ethic

Islam is a world-affirming religion. The Prophet was himself a merchant and used to pasture sheep, and encouraged others to do likewise to earn a living. The Qur'an has a strong work ethic, stating that 'Man will get nothing but what he strives for' (53.39) and 'For men is the benefit of what they earn. And for women is the benefit of what they earn' (4.32).

Lawful work is a religious obligation, and even religious duties should not interfere with it. The Qur'an urges Muslims to return to work after the Friday congregational worship (62.10). We work for wealth, but wealth should not be pursued as an end in itself. Wealth should be spent frugally, and a portion should go for charity so no poverty can creep into the midst of plenty. On frugality, the Qur'an states: 'And squander not [your wealth] wastefully. Surely the squanderers are the devils' brethren. And the devil is ever ungrateful to his Lord' (17.26–27). Thus, the Qur'an promotes spending without wasting, and being moderate: 'And those who, when they spend, are neither extravagant nor niggardly, but hold a just [balance] between those [extremes]' (25.67). Thus, Islam affirms this world, requires one to do lawful work, and to be moderate in spending one's wealth.

References and further reading

Denny, F.D. (1985) 'Ethics and the Qur'an Community and World View', in R.G. Hovannisian (ed.) *Ethics in Islam*, Malibu: Undena Publications, 103–21.

Donaldson, M.D. (1953) *Studies in Muslim Ethics*, London: SPCK.

Fakhry, M. (1991) *Ethical Theories in Islam*, Leiden: E.J. Brill.

Goldziher, I. (1967) *Muslim Studies*, London: George Allen & Unwin, Vol. 1.

al-Isfahani, R. (1987) *al-Dhari'a ila makarim al-shari'a*, Cairo: Dar al-wafa'.

Izutsu, T. (1959) *The Structure of the Ethical Terms in the Koran*, Tokyo: Keio Institute of Philological Studies.

Levy, R. (1969) *The Social Structure of Islam*, Cambridge: Cambridge University Press.

Mohamed, Y. (2004) *The Path to Virtue*, Kuala Lumpur: ISTAC.

See also: **'adl; character; *fitra*; *khayr*; knowledge**

YASIEN MOHAMED

MOSES

see: **Musa**

MOTHER OF THE BOOK

The expression *umm al-kitab* (literally, 'the Mother of the Book') occurs three times in the Qur'an. It has always been an opaque and controversial term, causing much exegetical speculation. In 3.7, we find:

> It is He who sent down upon thee the Book, wherein are verses clear that are the *umm al-kitab*, and others ambiguous. As for those in whose heart is swerving, they follow the ambiguous part, desiring dissension, and desiring its interpretation, and none knows its interpretation save only God.

The Qur'an distinguishes verses that are *mutashabih* (probably meaning 'ambiguous') from those that are *muhkam* (most likely meaning 'clear'). The latter are said to constitute the *umm al-kitab*. 43.2–4 says: 'By the clear book, behold, We have made it an Arabic Qur'an; haply you [pl.] will understand; and behold, it is in the *umm al-kitab*, with Us; sublime indeed, wise'; 13.39 states: 'God blots out, and He establishes whatsoever He will; and with Him is the *umm al-kitab*.' The preceding verse says that it is God's privilege to entrust his messengers with signs (*ayat*, which may also mean 'verses' in this context). If these verses are taken together, *umm al-kitab* seems to signify a heavenly proto-type, the substance, essence or 'matrix' of all holy books, including not only the Qur'an but also Jewish and Christian scripture. The Qur'an, as the Muslim community preserves and knows it, is neither identical with *umm al-kitab*, nor independent of it.

Yet, although such a meaning seems warranted by the contexts of 3.7 and 43.2–4, it is possible that in 13.39 the meaning of *umm al-kitab* is different. Muslim scholars often identify it here with the 'Preserved Tablet' (*al-lawh al-mahfuz*) (85.21 and on four other occasions), i.e. the heavenly slate of destiny on which all human deeds, together with the Qur'an itself, are recorded. The expressions *umm al-kitab* and *al-lawh al-mahfuz* apparently share with the more general term *kitab*, as used in the Qur'an, a high degree of ambiguity. It cannot be determined with certainty where in the Qur'an something like the prototype of scripture or the slate of destiny or both meanings is meant by these terms. The metaphorical expression *umm al-kitab* as self-classification of the Qur'anic text seems, however, primarily concerned with the relationship between the Qur'an, on the one hand, and Jewish and Christian scripture on the other. Its opaqueness may reflect the Qur'an's changing view of its own textuality.

Muslim commentaries developed what Madigan (2001) called a 'topography of revelation', beginning with the 'well-guarded tablet' and involving the 'noble scribes' (80.15–16) who transmitted the text to Gabriel (Jibril), before Gabriel in turn gave it to the Prophet. Later speculative exegesis saw many things in *umm al-kitab*, e.g. a designation of the first *sura* (al-Fatiha), which was felt to encompass all scripture or the principle of all writing. More philosophical and mystical-esoteric explanations identified it with the Neoplatonic first intellect or with pre-existing divine knowledge. According to the Syrian commentator M. Shahrour's (b. 1928) no less speculative modernist interpretation, *umm al-kitab* means not so much a part of revelation but rather a specific modality of revelation that contains the *muhkam*-verses, the 'Seven Oft-Repeated' (*sab' al-mathani,* an enigmatic name for that part of scripture that occurs at 15.87) and another group of verses, which Shahrour calls 'verses of elucidation' (*ayat al-tafsil*).

Reference

Madigan, D.A. (2001) *The Qur'an's Self-image: Writing and authority in Islam's scripture*, Princeton, NJ: Princeton University Press.

See also: **aya; Preserved Tablet**

STEFAN WILD

MOTHERS OF THE BELIEVERS

see: **ummuhat al-mu'minin**

MUBAHALA

Bahala is a root verb meaning to curse. *Al-bahl* (the curse) also means a scarcity of water. In the Qur'an, *al-mubahala* (invocation of God's curse) was mentioned as a decisive solution to the dispute over Jesus between the Christians of Najran and the Prophet Muhammad. Allah ordered the Prophet to call on them to invoke God's curse (*mubahala*) in order to determine who was telling the truth: 'Say, let us call our sons and your sons, our women and your women, ourselves and yourselves – then we pray and invoke the curse of Allah upon those who lie' (3.61).

See also: **fig; oaths**

RAFIK BERJAK

MUHAMMAD

It is now commonplace to suggest that Muhammad is one of the great founders of a world religion. What this assertion belies is the enormous controversy surrounding the Prophet of Islam, both past and present, during his own lifetime and ever since. While other major religious figures are as revered, no other spiritual leader has been as vilified as Muhammad. Beyond the extraordinary contradictory images of him, contemporary analysis is further complicated by diverse ideological pressures in society, especially in the context of global Islamic terrorism and a resurgent phobia against Islam.

Interpreting Muhammad involves primary awareness of the canonical version of Muhammad's life as accepted by most Muslims. This orthodox Islamic reading can then be analysed with more focus on the explicit Qur'anic data on the Prophet. This must be related to the broader Islamic sources used in constructing a biography of Muhammad. Here, the epistemic value of these sources must be analysed and scrutiny given to the intellectual and moral credibility of some of the material. Finally, there are underlying ideological and theological paradigms that influence the interpretation of the Prophet.

These various paradigms work in complex symbiotic ways with the data about Muhammad, data that both shapes and is shaped by opposing verdicts that have dominated Islamic and Western culture.

The life of the Prophet

It is impossible to be precise about the birth date of Muhammad. It is generally accepted that he was born about 570 CE. According to Islamic tradition, his father died before Muhammad was born and his mother died shortly after his birth. Muslims believe that this is the context for the rhetorical question of 93.6: 'Did He not find thee an orphan and give thee shelter [and care]?' Again, tradition states that Muhammad was raised by his grandfather and then by an uncle (Abu Talib) who watched over him until he reached his teenage years.

The standard Muslim histories of the Prophet mention that he went twice to Syria on trading missions with his uncle.

These reports provided an apologetic motif not only for evidence of Muhammad's acumen in business but for early witness to his future greatness. It is said that Muhammad's prophetic status was foretold by Christian monks, on the first trip by Bahira (in some accounts an unnamed head of the convent gives the prophecy) and on the second journey by a monk named Nastur.

Muhammad was married in about 595 to a woman merchant named Khadija. The Muslim histories state she was either 28 or 40 at the time and had been married twice before. It is claimed that she married Muhammad after he had completed successful trade for her in Syria. She bore him four daughters and probably two sons (the boys died early). Khadija also affirmed Muhammad's divine revelation, assuring him that he was not being influenced by demonic spirits.

Muslims believe that Allah's call to Muhammad occurred on the seventeenth night of the Arabic month Ramadan in 610. According to both the *sira* and the traditional commentaries on the Qur'an, the archangel Gabriel (Jibril) is said to have visited him on Mount Hira, near Mecca. 2.97 says of Gabriel that 'he brings down the [revelation] to thy heart by Allah's will'. *Sura* 96 is viewed by most Muslims as the first revelation from Allah.

It is customary for Muslims to argue that Muhammad was illiterate (*ummi*), a position used to advance the argument for the divine inspiration of the Qur'an. This is also a convenient way to rebut charges that Muhammad copied ideas from Jewish and Christian scriptures. Most Muslims use 29.48 to support the notion that the Prophet was illiterate. 'And thou wast not [able] to recite a Book before this [Book came], nor art thou [able] to transcribe it with thy right hand: In that case, indeed, would the talkers of vanities have doubted.' A minority of Muslims, however, note that 25.4–6 seems to imply that the Prophet could write.

There has been much speculation about the episode of 'the Satanic verses', which forms the basis for the title of Salman Rushdie's controversial novel. It is reported in a rather disputed tradition (one accepted by Watt, 1964, and Guillaume, 1955) that Muhammad at one time included a positive reference in *sura* 53 to three pagan goddesses (al-Lat, al-'Uzza and Manat). Gabriel is said to have excised the false teaching about these deities in a later revelation to the Prophet.

Most traditional biographers claim that there was a pause (*fatra*) of three years before Muhammad began to preach to his fellow Meccans in 613 CE. His message was largely ignored at first, though there were some converts (notably Abu Bakr). Muhammad's early focus on social reform appealed most to the poorer clans. His preaching also allowed focus on the *Ka'ba* and accommodated certain pagan elements in pre-Islamic pilgrimage rituals. 2.158 gave permission for Muslims to trace a spiritual route between Safa and Marwa, two hills that once had stone idols on them. Muslims to this day follow the same pilgrimage during the *hajj*.

As Muhammad turned his prophetic voice against idolatry and polytheism, he incurred the anger of and insults from powerful tribal leaders. Abu Lahab, one of his uncles, also resisted Muhammad, earning the uncle and his wife eternal damnation, according to the *tafsir* on *sura* 111. Part of the reason for Meccan support for polytheism had to do with vested commercial interests in supporting traditional Arab religious views and customs. Various *suras* attempt to allay fears of financial loss for those who follow the path of Allah.

Nevertheless, Muhammad was derided as a magician (*sahir*) and soothsayer (*kahin*), and said to be possessed by *jinn* (ghost-like beings often viewed as evil in both traditional Islamic theology and Muslim folklore). These accusations suggest something about the manner in which Muhammad received the alleged revelations from Gabriel. He must have exhibited some behaviour that led to such interpretations, right or wrong, conduct that would later provide the rationale for a sceptical European audience to dismiss his so-called inspiration as epileptic seizures.

Muslims believe that in 620, one year after the death of Khadija, the angel Gabriel brought Muhammad by night to Jerusalem on the back of a heavenly winged creature named Buruq. Traditional biographers claim that 17.1 refers to this supernatural journey. 'Glory to [Allah] Who did take His servant for a Journey by night from the Sacred Mosque to the farthest Mosque, whose precincts We did bless.' In Jerusalem the Prophet was offered a choice of wine or milk. He chose the latter, earning commendation from Gabriel. Muhammad and his angel companion then ascended to the seventh heaven, conversing with various saints (Jesus, Moses, Abraham, and so on) at each level. Muslims believe that the Dome of the Rock in Jerusalem is built on the spot where the ascension (*mir'aj*) took place.

Two years later, in 622, Muhammad was forced to flee to Medina (formerly Yathrib), about 250 miles north of Mecca. His diplomatic skills were exhibited in initial peaceful coexistence with various Jewish tribes, Christians and pagan Arabs who lived there. The Constitution of Medina (possibly referred to at 8.56) captures something of this serenity, although the Prophet clearly has the upper hand: 'Whenever you differ about a matter it must be referred to God and to Muhammad.'

Unfortunately, the relative calm behind the Constitution gave way to increasing tensions, especially with the Jews, who failed to accept Muhammad as the Prophet. The early attempt in Medina to harmonize Muslim rituals with Jewish tradition was abandoned, most notably in the facing of Mecca rather than Jerusalem for prayer. Muhammad's claim to unity with the People of the Book was overshadowed by strident assertions that both Jews and Christians deliberately distorted their scriptures.

For eight years the Prophet engaged in repeated military battles with his Meccan enemies. The early victory in the famous battle at Badr on 15 March 624 was used as proof that Allah gave His blessing to the strategy of *jihad*. 3.123 states: 'Allah had helped you at Badr, when ye were a contemptible little force; then fear Allah; thus may ye show your gratitude.' A major setback at Uhud in 625 (the Prophet was wounded) raised some doubts among some Muslims and the Jews of Medina but, overall, Muhammad proved a capable warrior.

The Prophet's military focus has always been used against him by non-Muslim critics. Objections have been made particularly to the death penalty he imposed on the Kurayza, the last major Jewish clan left in Medina. He accused these Jews of complicity in the last Meccan attack in 626–627, known as the 'War of the Trench'. According to one account by Ibn Hisham, the Prophet ordered the beheading of over 600 Jewish men. 33.6 is said to refer to this episode: 'And those of the People of the Book who aided them – Allah did take them down from their strongholds and cast terror into their hearts. [So that] some ye slew, and some ye made prisoners.'

Muhammad also organized many raids to the north of Medina, participating in two of them. One expedition against the Mustalik clan received most attention because of allegations of immorality against 'A'isha, one of Muhammad's wives. She had been accidentally left behind on the return trip to Medina. Rumours circulated about her and the lone Muslim soldier who brought her back to the camp. The stir in the Muslim community was quieted when Muhammad received revelation exonerating 'A'isha. 24.12 is said to address the gossip: 'Why did not the believers – men and women – when ye heard of the affair, put the best construction on it in their own minds and say: "This [charge] is an obvious lie"?'

In 628 Muhammad led a group of his followers to Mecca and negotiated a treaty at al-Hudaybiyya with his most powerful Meccan adversaries. Muhammad also captured other regions of Arabia (including the oasis of Khaybar). It is claimed that the Prophet wrote letters sometime in 628 or 629 demanding that the political leaders in Alexandria, Persia, Abyssinia and Byzantine convert to Islam. These letters are most likely the product of later Muslims' hands, although Muhammad did carry on some correspondence with leaders in close proximity, including Mukawkis of Egypt.

In 629 Muhammad made a pilgrimage to Mecca and was reconciled with his own clan. In January of the next year he took control of Mecca and destroyed the idols in the Ka'ba, but Medina continued to be his home base. He led further military campaigns in northern Arabia. By this time Muhammad's power was widely recognized, although his own followers tried to resist his plans for a raid to Tabuk (near Jordan's southern boundary). Many tribes near Medina and in other parts of Arabia submitted to his leadership, although the scope of this early Muslim empire has been overstated by Islamic historians.

Muhammad returned to Mecca for a final pilgrimage in early 632. He was in poor health at the time and soon travelled back to Medina. He died, according to tradition, on 8 June of that year, in the embrace of 'A'isha. His burial place remains the second most important pilgrimage site in the Islamic world.

Muhammad in the Qur'an

The preceding account represents, more or less, the canonical version of Muhammad's life accepted by orthodox Muslims. As well, this biographical outline serves as the starting point for the scholarly study of Muhammad, even though both early and contemporary Islamicists reach different conclusions about the extent of its historical authenticity. Scepticism about this standard biography was first raised because of scholarly attacks on the integrity of the *hadith* and the *sura*. A few academics (Lammens, 1929; Wansbrough, 1977; Crone and Cook, 1977; Cook, 1983) are virtually totally agnostic about constructing a biography of Muhammad. Against this, other historians (Welch, 1996, and Peters, 1994, for example) have argued for the priority of the Qur'an as the witness to Muhammad.

What is ironic in this focus on the Qur'an is the way in which the sacred text seems to contradict some major facets of Islamic orthodoxy. For example, the traditional picture of Muhammad as a miracle worker hardly rises from explicit teachings in the Qur'an. The Islamic scripture restricts the miraculous element in Muhammad's life to his supernatural reception of divine revelation. 29.50 implies that Muhammad's task is to be a warner, not a miracle worker. Thus, the true miracle in Islam is the Qur'an, a dogma which has led some Muslim apologists to construct even mathematical arguments for its divine origins.

The famous accounts of the Prophet's miracles have little support in actual Qur'anic material. For example, the description of the famous Night Journey and subsequent *mir'aj* could never be drawn from the actual words in *sura* 17. The story of the Prophet splitting the moon in two has strong support in the *hadith* but it is not necessarily the meaning of 54.1, which says 'The Hour (of Judgement) is nigh, and the moon is cleft asunder'. Likewise, the *hadith* about the opening of the child Muhammad's chest by two angels has no textual basis in the Qur'an.

According to the *hadith*, Muhammad is said to have provided both food and water supernaturally on several occasions. He brought divine comfort to a palm tree that was upset when the Prophet no longer needed to lean against it during his sermons. On another occasion two trees moved at the command of the Prophet. His food is said to have exclaimed praise to him. One *hadith* even notes the Prophet's affirmation that both a cow and a wolf spoke. The fact that the Qur'an knows nothing of these miracles suggests a later apologetic necessity for miracles in response to Christian critics.

The Qur'an also provides little basis for the Islamic tradition that Muhammad was sinless. This notion is nowhere asserted and several passages about forgiveness seem to be directed at the Prophet. 40.55 states 'Patiently, then, persevere: for the Promise of Allah is true: and ask forgiveness for thy fault, and celebrate the Praises of thy Lord in the evening and in the morning', and 47.19 expresses something similar. At face value, Muhammad is rebuked in *sura* 80 because of his indifference to a blind man who had interrupted him.

Regardless of these points, Muhammad remains at the centre of the Qur'an. Though his name is mentioned only four times, he is the subject of many passages. He is, most famously, 'the Seal of the Prophets' (33.40) and a judge to his followers (4.65), and he is to be respected by them (2.104; 4.46). Allah himself is a witness to Muhammad's mission (13.43; 46.8), one that was predicted by both Moses (46.10) and Jesus: 'And remember, Jesus, the son of Mary, said: "O Children of Israel! I am the apostle of God [sent] to you, confirming the Law [which came] before me, and giving Glad Tidings of an Apostle to come after me"' (61.6).

Muhammad is the universal messenger from God (34.28) and the symbol of Allah's mercy to the world (9.61; 28.46–47; 76.24–26). In 53.10–12 it is written: 'So did [God] convey the inspiration to His Servant – [conveyed] what He [meant] to convey. The [Prophet's] [mind and] heart in no way falsified that which he saw. Will ye then dispute with him concerning what he saw?' The Qur'an describes Muhammad as gentle (3.159), very concerned about his followers (9.128) and in deep distress for unbelievers (12.97; 25.30). It also says that he was a man of prayer (74.3) and had an 'exalted standard of character' (68.4). Muhammad is told to adore Allah (96.19), remain faithful to the revealed message (46.9), follow Allah's duty for him (30.30) and work hard (66.9). According to *sura* 33, Muhammad's abrogation of traditional Arabic marriage norms is allowed by Allah. He can marry his cousins and any woman he wants 'who dedicates her soul to the Prophet'. The Qur'anic material probably reflects Muslim consternation over the fact that the Prophet married his own stepson's wife.

Sura 33 also illustrates some tension surrounding other social customs. Muhammad's followers are told to visit the Prophet's home only when they have permission, to arrive right at meal-time (not before), to leave quickly after the meal and to avoid 'familiar talk' with the Prophet. It is said that 'such [behaviour] annoys the Prophet: he is ashamed to dismiss you, but God is not ashamed [to tell you] the truth'. Some of Muhammad's followers, including 'A'isha, sometimes found such 'divine' interventions more convenient than genuine.

What Muslims have never doubted are the large theological themes in Muhammad's teaching. The ultimate dogma here is the greatness and oneness of Allah, the word for God used over 2,500 times in the Qur'an. Likewise, Muhammad's revelations about the Trinity, biblical material, Jesus, morality, creation and the Day of Judgement are accepted without reservation in Islamic tradition. For example, Muslim denial that Jesus died on a cross is based on the singular declaration against it at 4.157. As the Qur'an notes repeatedly, Jews and Christians were not impressed with the Prophet's reshaping and understanding of their scriptures and traditions.

Even with the scope of the above material, Islamicists who insist on the priority of the Qur'an also recognize its limitations as a historical document. F.E. Peters writes: 'it is a text without context ... isolated like an immense composite rock jutting forth from a desolate sea' (Peters, 1994: 259). 'By far the most trustworthy source, but at the same time the most difficult to utilize as a historical source, is the Qur'an' (Buhl and Welch, 1965). The Meccan *suras* provide no historical information about the birth and early life of Muhammad, nothing about his marriage to Khadija,

and very little historical detail about his calling and early ministry.

There is some improvement in the historical sense of the material after the migration to Medina in 622. These *suras* provide more specifics about time, place and persons, though still in a rather imprecise manner. It is no wonder that every biographer has had to turn to the traditional Islamic sources to construct a full-blown narrative. Until major documents are discovered from the time of Muhammad, where else can historians turn? Even most secular Islamicists are not inclined to restrict the search for the historical Muhammad to the Qur'an alone.

Muhammad and other Islamic sources

The search for the historical Muhammad beyond the Qur'an remains problematic for two equally serious reasons. First, as Ignaz Goldziher and Joseph Schacht showed, the *hadith* (with its corresponding Muslim jurisprudence) are anchored to the *Sitz im Leben* of the eighth and ninth centuries CE. Kenneth Cragg notes:

> When virtually no issues could be argued, still less settled, except by connection with cited acts and opinions of Muhammad, the temptation to require or to imagine or to allege such traditions became irresistible. Supply approximated to demand, and the growth of both made more ingenious and pretentious the science of supporting attribution. (Cragg, 2004)

The collections of al-Bukhari (810–70 CE) and Muslim (817–75 CE) have attained chief canonical status for Sunni Muslims. Non-Muslim scholars have always applauded their energy, but have grown increasingly sceptical of their enterprise, especially since Shi'a Islam has its own collection of *hadith*. There were and are no historically objective grounds to separate the spurious from the authentic in the hundreds of thousands of traditions examined by Sunni or Shi'ite scholars. In spite of this, a few non-Muslim biographers (notably Armstrong, 1992) show an uncritical and selective dependence on the *hadith*.

Recourse to non-Qur'anic sources also leads to a further complication. If the *sira*, *tafsir*, *hadith* and *maghazi* material becomes primary in a biography, non-Muslim scholars are faced with difficult and sometimes embarrassing data about the Prophet, unless looking through the lens of devout Islamic faith. Of course, scrutiny along critical lines also runs counter to dominant eirenic approaches to Islam (Watt, 1964; Smith, 1977), ones linked to the concerns about orientalism expressed most famously by Edward Said. Nevertheless, Islamicists can make appropriate use of Said without capitulating to the kind of naïvety that sometimes appears in pluralist visions of Islam.

Scholars should note, therefore, the distinction between the non-legalistic spirit of the Qur'an and the Talmudic-like nature of Islamic jurisprudence. The Sufi tradition is based, in part, on some dismay over the increasingly juridical nature of Islam. Further, there is surely intellectual space to confront what seem to be superstitious, anti-feminist and rather undiplomatic elements in the *hadith*. Do angels really have wings? Did the Prophet teach that females make up the majority in hell? What did Muhammad believe about the *jinn*? Did Muhammad teach that Allah turned Jews into pigs and apes? What was his attitude regarding the beating of wives?

Raising epistemic and ideological concerns does not negate the need to study non-Qur'anic sources. This material has

formed the dominant portrait of Muhammad since the ninth century. It will be intriguing to see whether future investigation provides scholars with a sophisticated hermeneutic that reaches back to the historical Muhammad. Further, thinking about the Prophet's alleged deeds and words leads to a recognition of the powerful paradigms that shape debate about him.

Whose Muhammad? Which Islam?

There has never been one monolithic, univocal view of Muhammad, neither while he was alive nor at any point since. Intense debates about him occupied Meccans in the seventh century CE, fomented Christian missions a few centuries later, and now form part of worldwide political and social discourse. Islam itself has its own internal divisions that lead to different perspectives on the Prophet. This applies most significantly to epochal strife between Sunni and Shi'a, but also to ongoing tensions with the Sufi tradition and the more sectarian responses to Islam (Bahai, Druze, Ahmadiyya, Black Muslim).

Overall, three distinct views cover the range of perspectives about Muhammad. The most significant emerges from the world of Islam, wherein he becomes the embodiment of all that is good and true. This highest estimate by Muslims parallels the Christian adoration of Jesus, the Hindu love for Krishna, the Sikh reverence for Guru Nanak and the Buddhist focus on Gautama, although Islam refrains from giving any hint that Muhammad was divine.

In all forms of Islam Muhammad is the exemplar. The great philosophers of Islam cut their beards in accordance with the custom of the Prophet. Some Muslims refuse to eat watermelon because there was no evidence that Muhammad ever ate one. There is a tradition in

Sunni Islam about how to brush one's teeth based on the Prophet's habits of hygiene. Female circumcision has been stopped in some African countries by convincing tribal Muslim leaders that this ritual was never advocated by Muhammad. Millions of Muslims take the *hajj* because the Prophet performed a similar pilgrimage before his death.

No vision of Islam can proceed without appeal to Muhammad. Thus Muhammad is the inspiration for feminism (Mernissi, 1991; Hasan, 2004), gay rights, democracy (Sachedina, 2001) and an Islamic renaissance (Schwartz, 2003). Even the most heinous acts of Islamic terrorism are rooted in belief that it is the express will of Allah and his prophet. Osama bin Laden invoked the Prophet in statements about the Muslim pilots of 9/11. Muslim apostates have been killed even in the United States and Europe because Muhammad is said to have ordered defectors put to death. Professed allegiance to Muhammad allowed the former Taliban regime to destroy famous Buddhist statues in Bamiyam, but not the poppy fields yielding opium near Kandahar.

The praise of Muhammad is reflected in folk Islam through the worship of relics of the Prophet. Maxime Rodinson (1976) mentions that two hairs from Muhammad's head were found in Constantinople and were stowed in forty bags sewn one inside the other. The power of the 'evil eye' is known especially since it even had a negative influence on God's prophet. Sufi masters write glowingly of their mystical encounters with Allah and Muhammad.

There is also the widespread insistence in Islam that the Prophet is not to be questioned. Muslims often have more tolerance for unbelief about Allah than for ridicule of the Prophet. Many Muslim apologists are completely mystified by Christian attacks on him, pointing out that Muslims have never railed against Jesus. Islamic outrage over Salman Rushdie and the *fatwa* invoked against him by the Shi'ite cleric Ayatollah Khomeini had to do with the novelist's perceived insults against Muhammad and his favourite wives.

This high view of Muhammad has been met through history by its polar opposite. For over 1200 years Muhammad has also been viewed as the embodiment of evil. This disdain began in the early Middle Ages (John of Damascus and Eulogius of Cordova) as Christian and Muslim armies fought for control of lands stretching from North Africa, across the Middle East, and into Europe. The wars were viewed by many Christians as the necessary struggle against the Antichrist himself – Muhammad. Dante's *Inferno* puts the Islamic leader in the lower realms of hell. Diatribes against Muhammad continued after Dante and were repeated in the Reformation (especially by Martin Luther) and through to the present day.

Across these centuries Muhammad has been pictured as barbaric and immoral. He is either a hypocrite or delusional, and his revelations the product of epileptic seizures. There is no hint that Muhammad might have been sincere; he founded his religion by the sword, for material gain and sexual reward. His policies on polygamy and his marriage to a youthful 'A'isha remain central in polemics against him. Several American fundamentalist leaders have recently accused Muhammad of being a paedophile. It is a longstanding complaint that he is really a Christian heretic, since he denied the Trinity and misrepresented the Bible. He was influenced by magic, but could do no miracles. His love for *jihad* has been used to explain Islamic expansionism, just as his dictatorship has been used to elucidate Islamic authoritarianism.

There are a few inklings of a more nuanced view of him in the sixteenth through to the eighteenth century (Jean Bodin, Bayle, Leibniz, George Sale). In the nineteenth century, Thomas Carlyle presented a positive assessment in his *The Hero as Prophet* (1840). Alexander Webb, a former Presbyterian, was the ambassador for Islam at the 1893 Parliament of the World's Religions in Chicago. In the twentieth century key Christian scholars argued for a high estimate of Muhammad. This new approach was advanced chiefly by W. Montgomery Watt, Kenneth Cragg, Wilfred Cantwell Smith and Hans Küng, the controversial and famous Catholic scholar.

Küng took up the question of Muhammad's status in his *Christianity and the World Religions*. He presents seven parallels between Muhammad and the prophets of Israel, outlines the immense contribution of Muhammad, and concludes by citing Vatican II. One of its documents states that the Catholic Church 'also looks upon the Muslims with great respect: They worship the one true God who has spoken to man.' Küng then offers this assessment:

> In my opinion, that Church – and all the Christian Churches – must also 'look with great respect' upon the man whose name is omitted from the declaration out of embarrassment, although he alone led the Muslims to the worship of the one God, who spoke through him: Muhammad the Prophet. (Küng, 1986)

These disparate views of Muhammad continue to dominate academic, religious and popular discourse. That a division remains about him is probably no surprise, since his emergence in the seventh century CE as a professed prophet of Allah immediately created conflicting views of him. While Muhammad could never have imagined how the future would treat him, he would surely have thought that his message would always demand a decisive response. History has at least witnessed him being correct on that salient point.

References and further reading

Andrae, T. (1960) *Mohammed: The man and his faith*, trans. T. Menzel, New York: Harper & Brothers.

Armstrong, K. (1992) *Muhammad*, San Francisco: Harper.

Bennett, C. (1998) *In Search of Muhammad*, London: Continuum.

Cook, M. (1983) *Muhammad*, New York: Oxford University Press.

Cragg, K. (2004) 'Hadith', *Encyclopedia Britannica*, 688–91.

Crone, P. and Cook, M. (1977) *Hagarism*, Cambridge: Cambridge University Press.

Guillaume, A. (1955) *The Life of Muhammad*, translation of Ibn Ishaq, *Sirat Rasul Allah*, London: Oxford University Press.

Hasan, A. (2004) *Why I Am a Muslim*, Shaftesbury, Dorset: Element Books.

Küng, H. (1986) *Christianity and the World Religions*, Garden City, NY: Doubleday.

Lammens, H. (1929) *Islam: Beliefs and Institutions*, London: Methuen.

Lings, M. (1983) *Muhammad*, Rochester, NY: Inner Traditions.

Mernissi, F. (1991) *The Veil and the Male Elite*, trans. Mary Jo Lakeland, New York: Perseus.

Motzki, H. (ed.) (2000) *The Biography of Muhammad*, Leiden: E.J. Brill.

Peters, F.E. (1994) *Muhammad and the Origins of Islam*, Albany, NY: SUNY Press.

Rodinson, M. (1976) *Muhammad*, trans. Anne Carter, Harmondsworth: Penguin.

Sachedina, A. (2001) *The Islamic Roots of Democratic Pluralism*, Oxford: Oxford University Press.

Schimmel, A. (1985) *And Muhammad is His Messenger*, Chapel Hill, NY: University of North Carolina Press.

Schwartz, S. (2003) *The Two Faces of Islam*, New York: Doubleday.

Smith, W.C. (1977) *Islam in Modern History*, Princeton, NJ: Princeton University Press.

Wansbrough, J. (1977) *Qur'anic Studies*, Oxford: Oxford University Press.

Warraq, Ibn (2000) *The Quest for the Historical Muhammad*, Buffalo, NY: Prometheus.

Watt, W. Montgomery (1964) *Muhammad: Prophet and statesman*, London: Oxford University Press.

Welch, A. (1996) *Kur'an, Encyclopedia of Islam*, Vol. VI, 360–76.

JAMES A. BEVERLEY

MUHAMMAD 'ABDU
see: 'Abdu, Muhammad

MUHAMMED B. IDRIS AL-SHAFI'I
see: al-Shafi'i, Muhammed b. Idris

MUHKAM
see: aya; ta'til

MUQATIL B. SULAYMAN

Muqatil b. Sulayman was born in the late 600s CE in Balkh. Little is known of his early life, not even his exact date of birth, but he lived and taught in Marv, Baghdad, Mecca and Madina, and died in Basra in 767 CE. Although also a traditionalist, he is best known as an exegete, and to him is attributed the first full exegesis of the Qur'an, *Tafsir Muqatil b. Sulayman* (Shahata, 1979–88). His two other major works, also on *tafsir*, are *Kitab tafsir al-khams mi'at aya min al-Qur'an al-karim* (Goldfeld, 1980) and *al-Ashbah wa'l-naza'ir fi'l-Qur'an al-karim* (Shahata, 1975). Nwyia (1970) has shown how Muqatil's work laid the foundations of a hermeneutic that lent itself to the development of a vocabulary in which a mystical reading of the Qur'an could be expressed. However, recognition of his importance in the development of exegesis across a wide academic public stems from Wansbrough's *Qur'anic Studies* (1977).

Muqatil's *tafsir* is lucid, intellectually penetrating and displays significant pedagogic sensitivity. At the time he wrote, many of the established procedures of classical *tafsir* were not yet developed. Muqatil records *asbab al-nuzul* (occasions of revelation), identifies individuals in situations, complements Qur'anic narratives with information drawn from the *haggada* (to use Wansbrough's terminology) and draws out eschatological lessons implicit in events, pointing out, for example, that the threats against unbelievers such as Abu Jahl at Mecca were realised when they were slain at the Battle of Badr. However, Muqatil includes no *isnad* (chain of transmission) for authorities cited, no *shawahid* to establish the meaning of words and no grammatical analyses, and allows for no variety of views. His work *Kitab tafsir al-khams mi'at aya*, again in Wansbrough's terminology, is *halakhic* in character. It is a study of verses imposing legal obligations, such as almsgiving, the pilgrimage, divorce and *jihad*. The third book, *al-Ashbah wa'l-naza'ir*, is perhaps the most interesting. Muqatil takes a number of words that appear in the Qur'an and illustrates the various aspects of meaning they reveal in the different contexts in which they occur. Thus, for example, he uncovers ten aspects of meaning in the word *nur* (Nwyia, 1970: 112).

Muqatil's work, despite its importance, has encountered hostility. Indeed, it is banned from circulation in present-day Egypt. He is accused of anthropomorphism and of disrespect for the prophets in his use of *Isra'iliyyat* – for example, in his treatment of 12.22–23, he gives a graphic account of how Joseph almost succumbed to Zulaykha's temptation. Gilliot (1991) has given an account of these charges, and set them in the context of the period in which Muqatil wrote. Rippin (*EI*) notes that his work is rarely cited, and points out that al-Tabari makes no use of him. Against this it should be remarked that Fakhr al-Din al-Razi cites him frequently in *al-Tafsir al-kabir*. In any case, Muqatil's work requires further sympathetic study. At the very least, it is important both in its own right as contributing to the history of Islamic theology, and as having played a central role in the early development of *tafsir*.

References and further reading

Gilliot, C. (1991) 'Muqatil, grand exégète, traditionniste et théologien maudit', *Journal asiatique* CCLXXIX, 1–2: 39–91.

Goldfeld, I. (ed.) (1980) *Kitab tafsir al-khams mi'at aya min al-Qur'an al-karim*, Shfaram.

Nwyia, P. (1970) *Exégèse coranique et langage mystique: Nouvel essai sur le lexique technique des mystiques musulmans*, Beirut: Dar al-mashriq.

Shahata, Abd Allah Mahmud (ed.) (1975) *al-Ashbah wa'l-naza'ir fi'l-Qur'an al-karim*, Cairo.

—— (ed.) (1979–88) (ed.) *Tafsir Muqatil b. Sulayman*, Cairo: al-hay'at al-misriyya al-'amma li'l-kitab, 5 vols.

Wansbrough, J. (1977) *Qur'anic Studies*, Oxford: Oxford University Press.

A.H. JOHNS

MURDER

Murder is the unlawful, premeditated killing of a human being by another. Informally, murder is an unpleasant, troublesome or dangerous state of affairs; in legal terms, murder is the killing of a human being with malice and a premeditated motive. God has honoured mankind. He created man with his own hand and blew in him from his own soul. God ordered the angels to prostrate themselves before Adam, i.e. the representative of all humanity. And God put everything on earth and in space at our disposal. The expectation was that the man be God's caliph or representative on earth. Allah gave man powers and talents to enable him to rule the earth and reach his ultimate potential for both material development and spiritual progress.

Islam guarantees many rights for humans, including the right to life. The Prophet in his farewell pilgrimage said: 'O people, verily your blood and your money are sacred.' The right to life is a sacred one and must not be violated. 'And do not kill anyone whose killing Allah has forbidden, except for a just cause', says the Qur'an (17.33). Three kinds of people can be killed legally: a married person who has committed adultery; a murderer; and an apostate, someone who has defected from Islam and returned to *kufr* or paganism.

Islam prohibits the killing of children by their parents. In the pre-Islamic *jahiliyya* period, some pagan Arabs used to kill their own children, particularly females, thereby evading the responsibility of raising them and providing for them. The Qur'an comes down hard on these murderers: 'And when the female infant buried alive is questioned, for what sin was she killed?' (81.8–9). The Qur'an also warns parents about killing their children from fear of want, with Allah promising to provide for them and for their parents: 'And kill not your children for fear of poverty. We shall provide for them as well as for you. Surely, the killing of them is a great sin' (17.31).

Islam holds Qabil, the son of Adam who murdered his brother Habil, responsible for every unjustly murdered soul until the Day of Judgement. This is based on the Islamic principle that whoever first does an evil deed carries its sin and the sins of anyone who follows him and commits the same offence. According to the Qur'an, Qabil was the first man to commit a murder, consequently he carries the sin of every killer in the human race:

The selfish soul of the other led him to the murder of his brother: he murdered him, and became among the losers ... On that account; we ordained for the children of Israel that if anyone slew a person, it would be as if he slew the whole people. (5.30, 32)

The killing of a person in Islamic jurisprudential terms is the destruction of a structure God has created and given life to. It also deprives the victim of the right to life and is an act of aggression against the victim's family. The murder of a Muslim, a *dhimmi* (a non-Muslim citizen in a Muslim state) or suicide, which is regarded as self-murder, are all equally prohibited crimes in Islam. Regarding suicide, God said: 'And kill not your selves; surely, Allah is most merciful to you' (4.29). In another verse, God cautions people against endangering their lives: 'And do not throw yourselves into destruction' (2.195). The Prophet reinforced this ban, drawing a graphic picture for those who commit suicide. He said:

Whoever throws himself from a mountain and kills himself will throw himself in hellfire forever. And whoever poisons himself and dies would carry his poison with his hand and takes it in hell forever. And whoever stabs himself with a piece of metal and kills himself would carry his weapon and stab himself with it in hellfire forever.

It has been reported in an authentic *hadith:* 'That who kills himself with a weapon, will be punished with the same weapon on the Day of Judgement.' This is based on the principle that the punishment should fit the crime.

Islam considers the killer of one soul as the killer of the whole human race. Due to the seriousness of murder and the vehement abhorrence with which it is viewed, murders will be the first cases to be opened on the Day of Judgement. In Qur'anic terms, murder is a grave sin and murder of a believer an offence that will not be forgiven. The Book threatens the killer with suffering an everlasting torment in hell: 'He that kills a believer by design shall burn in hell forever. He shall incur the wrath of God, who will lay his curse on him and prepare for him a mighty scourge' (4.93). The Prophet himself described the killing of a believer as a serious crime in the eyes of God, saying 'The demolition and disappearance of the world is easier on God than the killing of a believing soul unjustly.' Elsewhere, the Qur'an says: 'Never should a believer kill a believer' (4.92). The murder of non-Muslim citizens is also prohibited in many sayings (*ahadith*) of the Prophet Muhammad. He promised hellfire to anyone who kills a *mu'ahid* (someone protected by a peace treaty): 'That who kills someone with whom there is a treaty will never smell the scent of paradise which can be smelled from a forty-year distance.'

Intentional killing, according to *fiqh* (Islamic law), is 'the killing of a person whose blood is sacred with a weapon that might be fatal'. The conditions of intentional killing are that the killer is an adult, is in his/her right mind and has intended to kill the victim; that the victim is a human being whose blood is sacred; and that the tool of the crime is a weapon which is usually used for killing. If any one of these conditions is not met, then the killing may be considered unintentional.

The Qur'an declares *al-qisas* (the law of equality in punishment) as a legal deterrent to protect lives. 'And there is [a saving] of life for you in *al-qisas*, O men of understanding' (2.179). This old biblical law, an eye for an eye, was ratified and re-established in Islam. The Qur'an mentions that law in the *sura al-Ma'ida*: 'And we ordained therein for them [the children of Israel]: life for life, eye for eye, nose for nose, ear for ear, tooth for tooth, and wounds equal for equal' (5.45). Islam does not discriminate between victims, whether they are old or young, male or female. Every soul has the right to live and no one is allowed to deprive another human being of life.

See also: **manslaughter; punishment**

RAFIK BERJAK

MUSA

The Prophet Musa (Moses) is mentioned by name more often than any other person in the Qur'an (137 times). The accounts of Moses and the Israelites are by far the most numerous of the stories of the prophets in the Qur'an, and very influential on Muslim exegesis. 19.51 states that Moses was a messenger (*rusul*) and a prophet (*nabi*), and Muslim exegetes accord to him roughly the same genealogy as is given in biblical accounts, making him the son of 'Imran, a Levite.

Birth of Moses

The story of the enslavement of the Israelites, including the killing of the first-born males by Pharaoh, is recorded in the Qur'an (e.g. 7.137; 26.57–59; 28.1–6). The Qur'an does not explicitly specify that the people enslaved by Pharaoh were the Israelites, but Muslim exegetes explain that Pharaoh's failed attempt to lower the chosen status of the Israelites is one of the main themes of the Moses story.

20.38–41 and 28.7–13 describe Moses being cast into the sea, picked up by the family of Pharaoh, and raised in Pharaoh's house. Muslim tradition relates that in order to hide Moses from the Egyptians, his mother used to put him in an ark tied to a rope and float him down the Nile, but one day she forgot to fasten the end of the rope to the bank and this was the cause of his being found by Pharaoh's wife. The mother of Moses is one of only two women (along with Mary, the mother of Jesus) to receive revelations from God in the Qur'an. Some exegetes claim that 'Asiyya, the wife of Pharaoh, was really an Israelite who worshipped God in secret.

Midian

28.14–28 narrates Moses' killing of an Egyptian and his flight to Midian. According to some exegetes, the Israelite whom Moses helped was Samiri (i.e. 'the Samaritan'), who is also said to be responsible later for the animation of the Golden Calf that was worshipped by the Israelites. Other exegetes add that the man who informed Moses that Pharaoh was seeking to kill him was named Hizqil, and was the same Egyptian who is said to have believed in Moses (see 40.28).

The account of the sojourn of Moses in Midian is conflated by Muslim exegesis with the story of Jacob and Laban (see Genesis 28–32). Moses lifts a rock off the well of Midian, he works for a number of years in order to marry Zipporah, Zipporah's sister is named Leah, and Moses strikes his flocks with his rod by the watering trough causing them to produce speckled young in the year before he returns to Egypt. Muslim exegetes report that Moses' father-in-law was named Jethro, but also consistently identify him with the Arab prophet Shuayb, who is said to have been sent to the people of Midian.

The first revelation received by Moses is related in the Qur'an (e.g. 20.9–24; 27.7–12; 28.29–35; 79.15–19). Moses is sent by God to Pharaoh, is given his brother Aaron as his spokesperson, and is given signs in the form of his hand becoming leprous and his rod becoming a serpent.

Moses and Pharaoh

The many encounters between Moses and Pharaoh are described in detail by the Qur'an (e.g. 7.103–126; 10.75–83; 17.101–103; 20.49–69; 26.10–51; 79.20–26). 28.36–42 refers to Pharaoh's command to his lieutenant Haman that he build a tower like the Tower of Babel in order to demonstrate that Moses was lying about the existence of his God. Pharaoh is said to have ruled for over 400 years and not been subject to sleep, hunger or sickness, thus encouraging his belief that he alone was God (see 10.88; 79.24). 10.84–89 describes the conditions of the Israelites in Egypt, and 40.23–46 narrates a scene in which an Egyptian comes to believe in Moses after the contest between Moses and Pharaoh's magicians.

The plagues (flood, locusts, pestilence, frogs and blood) against the Egyptians are described in 7.127–136. 26.52–68 and 44.17–33 narrate the exodus of the Israelites from Egypt, the parting of the sea, and the drowning of Pharaoh and his armies. Other passages emphasize the punishment of Pharaoh and his people (e.g. 10.90–92; 11.96–99; 43.46–56), and many exegetes interpret the reference to Pharaoh's body in 10.92 as meaning his body was saved by God so that the Israelites would know that he had died.

Revelation of the Torah

The Israelites' experience of wandering in the wilderness is described in numerous passages (e.g. 2.47–61), which also include the revelation of the Torah; the Golden Calf; the sending of the cloud, manna and quails; the water from the rock; and the grumbling of the Israelites about their food and living conditions. Moses' experience on the mountain is narrated in 7.142–147, and numerous passages in the Qur'an refer to the revelation and content of the Torah, especially as it compares to other revealed books like the Psalms, the Gospels and the Qur'an.

The Golden Calf episode is detailed in 7.148–158 and 20.80–98. These passages and Muslim tradition make both Aaron and Samiri responsible for the Golden Calf and the Israelites' worship of it. As punishment for this worship, the Israelites are made to kill one another until more than 70,000 of their number have been obliterated, and Muslim exegetes explain how Moses filed down the Golden Calf and flung its remains into the sea.

Muslim tradition also describes the Tent of Meeting or Tabernacle that was built by the Israelites in the wilderness. It is said that this Tabernacle was the *Ka'ba* of the Israelites, and that they prayed in its direction until the building of the Temple in Jerusalem. 7.160 refers to the water drawn from the rock by the rod of Moses, and Muslim tradition describes this rock as an enormous piece of Mount Sinai which the Israelites transported around with them in the wilderness.

Holy Land

5.20–26 refers to the Israelites' refusal to enter the Holy Land because of their fear of the giants that inhabited that land. Muslim tradition relates the encounter between the twelve Israelite spies and the giants, and the combat between Moses and the giant Og, who is said to have survived from before the Flood in the time of Noah. 7.159 mentions the People of Moses, which is interpreted by Muslim exegetes to be a reference to a special group of righteous Israelites who were taken by God to the ends of the earth, where they continued to live until they were visited by the Prophet Muhammad during his Night Journey.

Other passages in the Qur'an refer to specific episodes in the life of the Israelites after they settled in the Holy Land. 2.67–73 relates how the Israelites disobeyed God's command to sacrifice a red (or yellow) cow, and 7.163–166 tells of a city by the sea that is inhabited by a people who transgressed the Sabbath and were turned into apes (see 2.65; 5.78).

Death of Moses

Both Moses and Aaron are said to have died before entering the Holy Land, although some traditions report that Moses was present at the conquest of Jerusalem. The tomb of Moses is said to be in the *kathib ahmar* (red mound), which is variously considered to be located near the River Jordan, near Jerusalem and in Damascus.

Further reading

Elder, E.E. (1925) 'Parallel Passages in the Koran – the Story of Moses', *Muslim World* 15: 254–9.

Moreen, V.B. (1994) 'Moses in Muhammad's Light: Muslim Topoi and Anti-Muslim Polemics in Judaeo-Persian Panegyrics', *Journal of Turkish Studies* 18:185–200.

Moubarac, Y. (1954) *Moïse dans le Coran*, Paris: J. Vrin.

Wheeler, B. (2001) *Moses in the Qur'an and Islamic Exegesis*, Richmond, Surrey: Curzon.

BRANNON WHEELER

MUSA'S / MOSES' MOTHER AND SISTER

In the Qur'anic narratives concerning the infancy of the Prophet Moses, his mother and sister appear, along with Pharaoh's wife 'Asiyya, and they are all instrumental in saving his life. In order to keep him from the threat posed by Pharaoh to male Israelite children, Moses' mother must hide him. God inspires her to cast Moses into the river in a chest (20.38–39; 28.7). (This inspiration, *wahy*, is understood by some medieval Muslim scholars as evidence that she was herself a prophet.) Moses' sister, at their mother's direction, follows the chest, and witnesses her brother being taken into Pharaoh's household (28.11). When, as part of a divinely ordained plan, Moses refuses to nurse, his sister cleverly manages to get their mother employed as his wet nurse. Thus, her grief at separation from her son ends; God has reunited them, 'that her eye might be cooled and she not be sad' (20.40; 28.12–13).

KECIA ALI

MUSIC

References to music in the Qur'an are so oblique as to be ambiguous. One verse commonly used to present the Qur'anic viewpoint on music is 34.10. The commentator Yusuf Ali interprets this verse as signalling that even the hills and birds sing and echo in praise of God, reflecting the musical gifts of David evident in the Psalms.

Another verse, which lends itself to a negative view of music, is 31.6. Some commentators interpret the phrase *lahwa al-hadith* ('idle tales') as referring here to music. Al-Tabari (d. 310/923) attributes conflicting interpretations of singing and of playing a drum to different Companions of the Prophet. Ibn Kathir suggests the term can refer to both singing and musical instruments.

The ambiguity concerning the Qur'anic view of music is reinforced by reference to the prophetic traditions. The authoritative collection by al-Bukhari (d. 256/870) includes several reports suggesting that Muhammad disapproved of music. One account has the Prophet saying 'from among my followers there will be some people who will permit fornication, the wearing of silk, the drinking of alcoholic drinks and the use of musical instruments', leading to God destroying such people. Other *hadith* reports have Muhammad taking a particular dislike to bells, associating this instrument with Christianity. Furthermore, other reports associate music and musical instruments with Satan, debauchery and licentiousness.

Such perspectives from the sacred scripture of Islam have resulted in an ongoing and unresolved debate among Islamic scholars down the centuries. Nevertheless, rich musical traditions have developed in different parts of the Islamic world. Significant names in this regard are al-Isbahani (d. 356/967) of Medina, who wrote *Kitab al-aghani al-kabir* (The Great Book of Songs) in twenty volumes, and Ziryab (d. 243/857) of al-Andalus, a leading pioneer of Andalusian Arab musical styles.

The Andalusian scholar Ibn Hazm (d. 456/1064), adopting a pro-music position, subjected *hadith* accounts condemning musical instruments to scrutiny, and concluded that they were weak. Further support for such a position was found among Sufis. Al-Ghazali (d. 505/1111) argued that music could, if properly used, bring the believer closer to God. Similarly favourable views were expressed by al-Hujwiri (d. 469/1077) and Jalal al-Din Rumi (d. 672/1273).

Some of the most critical, anti-music attitudes have been found in the statements of Islamic individuals and groups in the twentieth century. After the Islamic revolution in Iran in 1979, Ayatollah Khomeini (d. 1410/1989) accused music of corrupting youth and banned all music from radio and television. Similarly, when the Taliban seized power in Afghanistan in 1996, all recreational music was banned.

Further reading

Jenkins, J. and Olsen, P.R. (1976) *Music and Musical Instruments in the World of Islam*, London: World of Islam Festival Publishing Co. Ltd.

Michon, J. (1991) 'Sacred Music and Dance in Islam', in S.H. Nasr (ed.) *Islamic Spirituality: Manifestations*, New York: SCM Press, 469–505.

Racy, A.J. (1995) 'Music', *The Oxford Encyclopedia of the Modern Islamic World*, Oxford: Oxford University Press, Vol. 3, 180–3.

Shiloah, A. (1995) *Music in the World of Islam: A socio-cultural history*, Aldershot: Scholar Press.

Touma, H.H. (2003) *The Music of the Arabs*, new edn, Cambridge: Amadeus Press.

See also: **art and the Qur'an;** *laghw* **and** *lahw*; *sama'*; *tajwid*

PETER G. RIDDELL

MYRMIDONS
see: Zubaniyya

N

NADHIR / NUDHUR / ANDHARA

Nadhir is a noun and it means warner, the one who informs and cautions or puts one on guard. The Qur'an reveals that Allah sends his messengers to warn mankind. They inform people about the Day of Judgement and warn them about the everlasting torments of hell. *Nadhir* often follows *bashir* (the bearer of good news): 'Verily, We have sent You with the truth, a bearer of glad tidings and a warner. And there never was a nation but a warner had passed among them' (35.24). *Mundhir* is a synonym of *nadhir*: 'You are only a warner, and to every people there is a guide' (13.7). *Nudhur* is the plural form, meaning warnings: 'Then taste you my torment and my warnings' (54.39). In the same *sura*, we also find: 'And indeed. Warnings came to the people of Pharaoh' (54.41).

Nadhr is a singular term meaning vow or dedication to God. The plural is again *nudhur*, but in this context it usually represents voluntary promises, self-imposed obligations or religious orders. The root verb is *nadhara*. The verb *andhara*, however, with the initial *a*, signifies to warn.

In the Qur'an, this term has, in its different forms, been used as many as 130 times. This abundant use of the term points to its importance in the Qur'an, making it obvious that revelation was sent to mankind to warn them about the Day of Judgement, the unseen hereafter and whatever is waiting for them. Hence every messenger is a *nadhir* (warner).

RAFIK BERJAK

NAFS

Nafs, in the literature of the *jahiliyya* (pre-Islamic period), meant the self or person, while *ruh* meant breath and wind. In the Qur'an, however, *nafs* is made more specific and refers to the soul, while *ruh* means a special angel messenger and a divine quality.

Nafs and *ruh*

Nafs and its plurals *anfus* and *nufus* have five uses. In most cases they mean the human self or person. Sometimes *nafs* refers to God. In 6.130 the plural is used twice to refer to the company of men and *jinn*: 'We have witnessed against ourselves' (*anfusina*). It can mean the human soul: 'While the angels stretch forth their hands [saying]: "Send forth your souls (*anfus*)"' (6.93). This soul has three characteristics. First, it is *ammara bi'l su'*, commanding to evil (12.53). This concept represents human physicality. It is associated with *al-hawa*, which, in the sense of 'desire', is always evil. It must be restrained and made patient, and its greed must be feared. Second, the *nafs* is *lawwama*, i.e. it upbraids (75.2); the souls (*anfus*) of deserters are straitened. Third, the soul is addressed as *mut-ma'inna*, tranquil (89.27). These three terms form the basis of much of later Muslim ethics and psychology. It is interesting that *nafs* is not used in connection with the angels.

Ruh sometimes is used differently. Allah blew (*nafakhta*) of his *ruh* into Adam, giving life to Adam's body (15.29; 38.72; 32.9), and into Maryam, for the conception of 'Isa (21.91; 66.12). Here *ruh* equates with *rih* and means the 'breath of life' (see Genesis 2: 7), the creation of which belongs to Allah. Four verses connect *ruh* with the *amr* (command) of God, and the meanings of *ruh* and *amr* are connected. In 17.85, it is stated: 'They ask thee [O Muhammad] about *al-ruh*; say: *al-ruh min amri rabbi* (the spirit is from the divine command), and you are provided with only a little knowledge.' In 16.2 God sends down the angels with *al-ruh min amrihi* upon whomsoever he wills of his creatures to say: 'Warn that the fact is, "There is no God but Me, so fear"'.' In 40.15 God 'casts *al-ruh min amrihi* upon whomsoever He wills of His creatures to give warning'. At 42.52 the Qur'an gives:

> We revealed (*awhayna*) to you [Muhammad] *ruhan min amrina* (inspiration by command); you did not know what the book was, nor the faith, but We made it to be a light by which we guide whomsoever we will of our creatures.

The suggestion is that this *ruh* from Allah is for prophecy. In the Qur'an *ruh* is often used to refer to particular people and angels, and describes a particularly close relationship with the deity.

Nafas (breath and wind), cognate to *nafs* in root and to *ruh* in some of its meanings, does not occur in the Qur'an, but is used in the early poetry. Any attribution to God of *nafs* as 'soul' or 'spirit' is avoided. In man, *nafs* and *ruh* are identified, and sometimes *nafs* applies to the mind and *ruh* to life, or man has *nafsani* (two souls). The influences that affected the post-Qur'anic uses of both *nafs* and *ruh* were the Christian and Neoplatonic ideas of *ruh* with human, angelic and divine applications, and the more specifically Aristotelian psychological analysis of *nafs*. These influences are clearly shown in the records of the religious controversies. Finally, there is a type of *ruh* that serves as the name for the simple substance that is the seat of the intellectual processes. It differs from the animal *ruh*, a refined but mortal body in which reside the senses. Instead the incorporeal *ruh* is identified with *al-nafs al-mutma'inna* and *al-ruh al-amin* of the Qur'an.

Nafs and *qalb*

Sin may come about through ignorance. Knowledge can be either acquired (*kasbi*) or innate (*fitri*). Every soul has innate knowledge of good and evil. Much of Islamic spirituality is geared to the awakening of that innate sense of good and evil. But this innate understanding of good and evil is sometimes not strong enough to ensure correct behaviour: circumstance and upbringing can blind the *fitra*. The Prophet said: 'Seeking knowledge is an obligation on every Muslim male and female' (*Bukhari*). In this *hadith* we have one of the rare occasions where the Prophet specifically uses the Arabic term *farida* or 'obligation' to emphasize the importance of knowledge.

Ibn Qudama compares the heart to a fortress, a fortress that is constantly under siege by the devil. He says:

> Know that the heart is like a fortress. The Shaytan is the enemy who wants to invade the fortress, own, and control it. And there is no way to protect the fortress except by guarding the entrances. The doors cannot be guarded if we are ignorant of them and the Shaytan cannot be repelled except through knowledge of his routes of penetration. The doors and pathways of Shaytan are the qualities of the slave and they are many. (Ibn Qudama, n.d.: 193–4)

The word heart (*qalb*) has a number of different applications, often quite different from modern applications. Here it refers to the entire non-physical part of us. The heart is able both to listen to instruction from God and others, and to reject such instruction. *Al-Shaytan* is able to influence us, since we do not know enough about ourselves and take as important what we think we know only through imagination. We may become, for example, envious of the general good fortune of another individual, or we become greedy for more possessions. We have free will and so can go awry. The natural light (*nur*) of the heart becomes occluded in these cases. Nonetheless, we are equipped (*bi'l-fitra*) to understand the strategy of

the devil. Once we become unaware of what is really happening around us, the devil can have influence over us, since he uses our already confused thinking to sow even more confusion. We adopt a life of sin, while at the same time possibly thinking we are living as we should.

The *nafs* as self

The Prophet said, according to al-Bayhaqi, that: 'Your worst enemy is your *nafs* within you'. In another tradition he is reported to have said: 'We now return from the lesser *jihad* to the greater *jihad*, the *jihad* against the *nafs*' and also 'He who knows himself knows his Lord'. The idea is that, if one is aware of one's own lack of importance and powerlessness as compared with God, then one is in an excellent position to take control of one's emotions. The individual who is ignorant of himself (his *nafs*) will be ignorant of God. In the Qur'an, Allah says: 'O righteous soul (*al-nafs al-mutma'inna*) return to your Lord, rested (*al-nafs al-radiya*) and satisfied (*al-nafs al-mardiyya*). Enter into my *janna*, enter together with my slaves' (89.27–30). In another verse Allah revealed that Zulaykha said: 'Surely it is the *nafs* (*al-nafs al-ammara bi al-su'*) that commands with evil.'

In *sura al-Qiyama* Allah, the Most High, says 'Verily I swear by the Day of Judgement and verily I swear by the reproaching self (*al-nafs al-lawwama*).' He also says, in the *sura al-Shams*, 'By the *nafs* and its creation, He then inspired (*al-nafs al-mulhama*) it with its knowledge of evil and good.' Taken together, these verses shows the structure of the *nafs*. At the first level it is powerful, passionate and moves us to action. It tempts us to exceed the boundaries of the good. Once it is restrained, the self calms down to becomes the reproaching *nafs*. We know that God in some instances swears by certain things to underline their importance. In *sura al-Qiyama*, for instance, he swears by the Day of Judgement and the reproaching self, both of which play key roles in the process of moral change and development. While improving itself, the self comes into contact with forces higher than it and becomes the inspired self. After that, it reaches a stage of complete peace (*al-nafs al-mutma'inna*) and stops resisting the word and instructions of God. It then quickly progresses to the stages of the peaceful self and the satisfied self.

The self is perfected (*al-nafs al-kamila*) by divine grace. Everyone has basically two sides. On the one hand is the physical body and on the other is the spiritual. The latter self we know as our emotions, our thoughts and feelings, our passions and desires, even our complexes. These non-physical elements we collectively refer to as our 'self'. The earlier and later scholars of *tasawwuf* used the term *al-nafs al-insani* (human soul) to refer to our emotional and rational nature, and the term *al-nafs al-hayawani* (vital or animal soul) to refer to the element that animates the body and gives it perception. The vital soul is also the source, according to them, of our passions and of physical drives like hunger, anger and sex. The *nafs* is also called the *ruh* or spirit when it is still in its pure state prior to creation. Once the *ruh* enters the body and gives it life, it acquires a new character. It aquires an outer dimension called the vital soul (*al-nafs al-hayawani*) and an inner dimension called human soul (*al-nafs al-insani*). We start off with a *ruh* and end up with a *nafs*. When we are dominated by our passions, we are at the level of the *al-nafs al-ammara bi al-su'* or the evil self.

Nafs and passion

In this condition our passions determine the way we think and feel, and consequently the way we act. The vices of pride, arrogance, envy, slothfulness, hate and greed then predominate. This is the veil that imprisons us and prevents the *nur* of the Divine Presence from penetrating our hearts and minds. As we are subjected to the discipline of knowledge, *salah*, fasting and other *'ibadat* (aspects of worship), we gain mastery and greater control over our selves. As a result, our thoughts and feelings are increasingly purified, deeper levels of the *ruh* or *nafs* are uncovered or, if you will, deeper functions of the mind are realized and awakened. Once the passions quieten down and the inherent tendencies of the *ruh* start to emerge and awaken, we have progressed to the level of *al-nafs al-mutma'inna* or the peaceful self.

Nafs and *jalis*

It says in 18.28 'And tie yourself to those who call on their Lord in the mornings and at night seeking only His face' and, towards the end of the same *aya*, 'do not follow those whom we closed off their hearts from our remembrance and who follow their own whims and desires'. It is clear from this verse that God instructs his Prophet and consequently the entire *umma* to associate with others on the basis of certain criteria. On the one hand we are instructed to associate with the spiritually enlightened and on the other to break ties with the spiritually dead. The word used in the verse to connote spiritual blindness is *ghafla*. The meanings of this term include the shortcomings of negligence, forgetfulness and intellectual blindness. It is also worth noting that these traits form the basis of the unrepentant sinful life. So we are obliged to be discriminatory in the choice of our associations, and for a very important reason. According to a tradition, the Prophet said:

> The example of a good companion (*jalis*) and a bad one is like a perfume vendor and a blacksmith. The perfume vendor either gives you something or you purchase an item from him or you receive a pleasant fragrance from him. The blacksmith, however, either burns your clothes or you acquire a bad smelling odour from him.

In another tradition, narrated by Abu Dawud and Tirmidhi, the Prophet said: 'A man adopts the *din* (religion) of his close friends, so look carefully at the person you befriend.' Abu Hurayra narrates that the Prophet said: 'Women are married for their wealth, pedigree, beauty and *din*, go and marry them for their *din* and you will succeed.' It is human nature to absorb to a degree the qualities of people we respect, admire and regularly associate with. This process of absorption is effectively compared by the Prophet to the way perfume and the stench of the blacksmith's shop or even the smoke and smell of burning wood cling to one's clothes. The central focus of a Muslim ought to be his *din*, for the simple reason that *din* is ultimately his vehicle of nearness to Allah, the Most High.

This principle is given an interesting context in the *hadith* quoted earlier about *din*. After indicating the common and largely materialistic motives of the choice of partners, the Prophet says 'Go marry them for their *din*'. The reason for this, Imam Nawawi indicates in his *Gardens of the Pious*, is precisely because our wives are our closest companions. And when a woman is strongly orientated towards the religious life, we should actively seek her companionship to improve our own. Passive friendships, refusal to exercise our intellects in the choice of friendships and lack of discrimination in the choice of marital partners can open up all the woes of a sinful and spiritually alienated life. Al-Ghazali, however, reminds us in his *Beginning of Guidance*:

> Know that your Companion that never leaves you whether you are travelling or staying at home, asleep or awake, indeed in life as in death, is your Lord, Master, Owner and Creator, and whenever you perform remembrance of Him, He is your company. And He, the Most High, has said so [al-Ghazali is referring to a *hadith qudsi* here], 'I am the *jalis* of [someone who regularly sits with] the person who remembers Me.' He said: 'I know what you know not.' (2.30)

Nafs, ruh and psychology

As an illustration of this point, it is relevant to think of the objections that the angels made to the order that they bow down before Adam. The angels were afraid not of an unintelligent being, as such beings had roamed the earth in various shapes and forms for a long time. It was, however, their fear that if such a being were given vice-gerency on earth, i.e. the power to represent God on earth, it would be physically capable of causing the destruction of all that surrounded it and eventually itself. If such a being were unrefined like the animals and influenced by the whims of its desires, it would swallow the earth like the giant whale that opens its mouth and engulfs all that is before it. God, however, in his supreme wisdom, knew what the angels did not know: he was to create a being that would far exceed any beast, though it would be of this world just as the beast was. He instilled in it a special secret that was unique and irresistible. This was the *ruh*. After all, we are told: 'Then

He fashioned him in due proportion, and breathed into him from His spirit (*ruh*). And He made for you hearing, seeing and feeling (*al-afida*); little thanks do you give!' (32.9).

It is this *ruh* or spirit that defines a human being. Without it, the human being is no longer human, since this is what connects him with God. Without connecting his self (*nafs*) with the divine *ruh*, the human being is lost to civilization and only intent on self-preservation. A well-known story has someone narrate:

> We had made a pilgrimage to Mecca along with Imam Sajjad ['Ali ibn al-Husayn] and when we looked down at the Desert of Arafat it was full of Hajjis (pilgrims). There were many of them that year. The Imam said: 'There is a lot of noise, but few are true pilgrims.' The man said: 'I do not know how the Imam gave me the insight, but when he asked me to look down again, I saw a desert full of animals, like being in a zoo, among whom a few human beings were moving about.'

When one does not have a connection to this *ruh*, which, in its essence, is beyond the understanding of man, one fails to be among those who are upright. As Shaykh Fadhlalla Haeri has explained: 'The *ruh* gives the *nafs* energy.' With respect to the soul, it is the *nafs* that is apparent to the outside world, and its power is the *ruh*. Without this *ruh*, the human being is inclined towards evil. The two are in a marriage, and the *nafs* must remain obedient to the *ruh* in order to be considered alive. The window to this essence is the *qalb* (heart). By heart, we do not mean that physical organ which the human being has in common with other mammals. Rather we mean the essence of humanity. Al-Ghazali explains this relationship by stating that the *qalb* is a subtle, divine and spiritual faculty, which has a relation to the corporeal *qalb*. That subtle thing is the essence (or true nature) of a man. In man, it is what perceives, knows, is aware, is spoken to, punished, blamed and responsible. It is, then, conclusive that the heart can either be pure and establish the connection between the *nafs* and the *ruh*, or it can become defiled, containing a sickness. We are told: 'In their hearts is a disease and Allah has increased their disease; and grievous is the chastisement because they are false' (2.10). Al-Ghazali further argues that, just as the body can contain sickness and receive remedies for its sicknesses, so too can the *qalb* (our essence) also receive remedies. Indeed, ignorance of God represents poison for the heart, disobedience to God its incapacitating sickness, knowledge of God the antidote, and obedience to Him by resisting passion its healing remedy. The only way to treat the heart, by removing the malady and regaining health, lies in the use of remedies, just as that is the only way to treat the body.

Thus, the *qalb*, which in this case can be translated as both 'heart' and 'intellect', interacts with the body's senses and internalizes that which is around it. The brain, in turn, is a sensory organ that must be regulated and interpreted by the *qalb*, which is beyond the scope of physical harm or benefit. This is referred to as *'aql*. Al-Ghazali refers to *'aql* as the knowledge of the true nature of things – it represents the kind of knowledge that resides in the *qalb*.

If the heart contains a disease or poison from the corruption of the world around the human being, its owner cannot be said to have true knowledge. He may have intelligence, but if such information serves to his detriment and possibly the detriment of the world around him, it is not *'aql*. It is for this reason that there exists in the world those who possess the knowledge of good and evil, right and wrong, and yet persist in their evil, using their intelligence for domination over other human beings. These people are no better, and even worse, than the animals. Therefore, the window to the self (*nafs*) is the intellect (*qalb*), and the light (*nur*) that keeps the self illuminated is the *ruh* (spirit). The cleanliness and illumination of our house depend on what is allowed through the window; we require a screen to filter out harmful diseases rather than an open window through which anything can come and go as it pleases. Success (*fawz*), then, depends on the cleanliness of one's window (*qalb*); God has described the Day of Judgement as: 'a day when wealth and children shall not benefit in any way; but only those who come to God with a sound heart (*qalbin salim*) will be saved' (26.88–89). We must open our rational minds to knowledge (*'ilm*), thus empowering the *'aql* (intelligence), which is part of the intellect and heart (*qalb*), serves as the window to the self (*nafs*) and is linked with the spirit (*ruh*). The key to this opening (*fatiha*) is the Qur'an, its tool is remembrance of Allah (*dhikr*) and its explication is the life of the Prophet Muhammad. We are told: 'The spirit is of the command of my Lord: of knowledge only a little that is communicated to you' (17.85). This spirit is breathed into Adam (15.29), it is the life in every conscious being, and 'Isa is a spirit coming from God (4.171). The Qur'an is identified as a spirit in 42.52, a spirit that stands with the angels on the Day of Resurrection (78.38) and is sent to Maryam, appearing before her as a man (19.17). Clearly it is a concept of great significance in the Qur'anic moral psychology.

It is important to note that the Qur'an was revealed 'to the heart' of the Prophet Muhammad by Gabriel (2.97). At 26.193–194 we read that it was transmitted by the faithful spirit (*ruh*) 'upon your heart', thus cementing the links between the heart (*qalb*) of humanity and the spirit (*ruh*) or Gabriel. The psychology of the Qur'an takes seriously the idea that we are in between the material and the spiritual.

Further reading

Ibn Qudama (1961) *Mukhtasar minhaj al-qasidin* (Abridgement of the Path of the Seekers), Damascus: Maktab al-Shabab al-Muslim.

See also: **character; death; knowledge**

OLIVER LEAMAN

NAHAR

Nahara is a root verb signifying to flow, repulse or chide. *La Tanhar* 'Do not repulse. And repulse not the beggar' (93.10).

As a noun, *nahar* means river or stream: 'and We caused a river to gush forth in the midst of them' (18.33). The plural *anhar* (rivers or streams) is used in the Qur'an many times, particularly in portraying paradise. One example is 'Their reward with their Lord is Eden [paradise] underneath which rivers flow' (98.8). *Nahar*, with an elongation of the second vowel, means the daytime, from dawn to sunset: 'We have made the sign of the day to enlighten you' (17.12).

RAFIK BERJAK

NAHDA

One of the most important events in modern times in the Islamic intellectual world was the creation of the *Nahda* (rebirth, renaissance). This really started in Syria, but gained its full momentum in Egypt, which was then as it has been subsequently the engine room of Islamic intellectual life. The *Nahda* movement represented an attempt to do two things. One was to introduce some of the main achievements of Western culture into the Islamic world. The other was to defend and protect the major positive features of Arab culture, and revive them in the face of assaults from Western imperialism. The most important aspect of the movement is its attempt to combine these policies, to react to the apparent decadence of the Arab world not by rejecting Arab culture but by purifying it and introducing to the Arab world aspects of modernity from without, at least those aspects that were seen as acceptable from an Islamic point of view.

The main *Nahda* thinkers were al-Tahtawi, al-Afghani and 'Abdu, who in their different ways, sought to confront modernity not by rejecting it, nor by rejecting Islam, but by effecting some kind of synthesis. Islamic culture has often sought to revitalize itself in response to criticism from other systems of thought that appear capable of presenting a more attractive or modern view of the world. Some areas of the Islamic world have, on occasion, totally rejected the importation of foreign ideas or, conversely, sometimes completely given themselves up to such ideas. The *Nahda* movement suggested that this was a false choice: one could accept some ideas and reject others, thus preserving tradition while at the same time adopting modernity.

The *Nahda* movement argued that Islam is itself a profoundly rational system of thought, and has no problem in accepting science and technology, and combining them with respect for the teachings of the Qur'an. So there is no reason for Muslims to abandon their faith if they want to acquire the material benefits of Western forms of modernity. On the other hand, the significance of reviving Islam or Arabism played a considerable part in the political rhetoric of the time. Some thinkers sought to reject the carving up of the Middle East into nation-states by Western imperialism, and argued for the Islamic world to be formed into an international *umma* or community as it had been originally, or at least as it had been ideally perceived. On the other hand, the Ottoman Empire, which had represented one way of doing this, was a generally unsatisfactory alternative to the nation-state, since that Empire was characterized by the very decadence so criticized by many of the *Nahda* thinkers.

The most important intellectual figure in this movement was undoubtedly Sayyid Jamal al-Din Afghani (1838–97 CE), who as his name suggested, had close connections with Afghanistan, where part of his early education took place. He seems to have been deliberately unclear in public about his precise ethnic origins, in order to prevent that from being a divisive factor in his attempts to address the whole Islamic community. A similar question hangs in the air as to whether he was a Sunni or Shi'i Muslim, doubtless for the same motive of trying to transcend deep divisions in the Islamic world. At the age of around 18, al-Afghani moved to India, where he came across the thoroughly modernist ideas of Sayyid Ahmad Khan (1817–98), ideas that he was later to attack in his *Refutation of the Materialists*. Ahmad Khan bent over backwards in his writings to show the British rulers of India that Islam was a religion capable of accepting rationality, and it was against this apologetic tone that al-Afghani directed his barbs. In 1870 he visited Egypt and Turkey, where he was welcomed: the Ottoman authorities and thinkers were involved in the *Tanzimat* changes, designed to modernize the Empire, and regarded al-Afghani as having a like mind. In 1883 he spent some time in London and Paris, summoning to the latter city Muhammad 'Abdu from Lebanon to work with him on a journal. While in Paris, al-Afghani's refutation of the views of the famous orientalist Ernest Renan was important in establishing a view of Islamic culture independent of that current in the West. In 1886 the Shah of Iran invited al-Afghani to advise him, but political differences caused him to leave for Russia. He ended up in Istanbul, where he spent his last six years, sometimes supported by the Sultan 'Abd al-Hamid II and often under suspicion of involvement in subversive activities.

The internationalist nature of al-Afghani's career is significant, representing nicely his belief that the Islamic world should be united. But his arguments were not based on Islam alone, they also borrowed a great deal from what he regarded as the valuable insights of science and philosophy. Islamic philosophy is perfectly compatible with modern science and technology, he argued, and Muslims should be encouraged to acquire the necessary skills in order to resist the impact of Western imperialism. Part of the Islamic renaissance ideology is that there should be a rebirth and rediscovery of the main intellectual and political achievements of the Islamic world during its heyday, and so the movement was to a degree a traditional revival (*ihya'*) campaign. During the high points of Islamic culture, as the supporters of the movement suggest, there was an openness to new ideas, wherever they came from, which came to an end with the imposition of an orthodoxy that discouraged *ijtihad* (independent judgement).

Al-Afghani wrote very little, but what he did write had considerable impact. His *Refutation of the Materialists* suggests that the source of evil is materialism, the philosophical doctrine that argues that the world has developed out of a set of material preconditions. This actually became a theme of the *Nahda*: materialism is wrong and the West is mistaken in pursuing it. Al-Afghani also criticizes the theory of evolution, which he sees as denying God's role in designing the world. His critique has a social aspect also, in that materialism is held to reject attempts to found society on any common moral values and to be critical of religion as such, and of Islam in particular. This sort of critique of what is seen as Western culture has, since the nineteenth century, become quite common in the Islamic world.

In his response to Renan, al-Afghani tries to show that the Arabs and Islamic civilization are capable of producing philosophy and science. Al-Afghani argues that Muslims had, in the past, been in the forefront of science and philosophy, and there is no reason to think this would not be repeated in the future. On the other hand, he accepts that religion and philosophy are in constant conflict, suggesting that Muslims could catch up with those Christians who rejected aspects of their religion after the Enlightenment. It is not clear from his response how much of traditional Islam is expected to survive such a transformation of intellectual life, and al-Afghani set up the issue in such a way as to dominate the continuing discussions of this topic in the Islamic world through the nineteenth and subsequent centuries.

The influence of his ideas was amplified by the efforts of Rashid Rida (1865–1935), who founded in 1898 the journal *al-Manar* (The Lighthouse) in Cairo. The central theme of the journal was that there is no incompatibility between Islam, on the one hand, and modernity, science, reason and civilization on the other. (It might be added that Rida tended to emphasize religion and was a firm opponent of secularism, the latter doctrine always being a tempting prospect for the thoroughgoing modernist.) His general compatibility thesis was supported in various forms by a variety of Arab intellectuals, and it was instituted in the framework of Arab society in various ways. For example, Rifaʿa Rafiʿ al-Tahtawi (1801–73) was sent to Paris in 1826 to find out what Western culture was all about. He was at that time a teacher at al-Azhar, the ancient Islamic university in Cairo, but had also started reading Western books and learning French, a language of which he became an able translator. One of the most important things he brought back to Egypt from his experience of Europe was the desire to establish a European-style university in Egypt, a university that would base itself on general knowledge, not just the traditional Islamic sciences, and would seriously study the intellectual contributions of the West. It is worth pointing out how far his efforts here were supported by the state: the ruler of Egypt, Muhammad ʿAli, encouraged al-Tahtawi's efforts and promoted him within the state structure. Although changes of regime did lead to occasional pauses in the modernization campaign, al-Tahtawi did manage to place that campaign firmly within the bureaucratic structure of the state, going so far as to initiate the education of girls. The *Nahda* reformers often managed to stay close to the machinery of the state and were thus able to make practical changes in line with their beliefs and theological approach.

One of the links al-Tahtawi managed to make, in addition to that between modernity and Islam, was the link between nationalism and Islam. For a period he took control of Egyptian antiquities and opposed their transfer abroad, arguing that there is no incompatibility between the universal message of Islam and the desire of an Egyptian to celebrate his country's heritage. Of course, within the context of the Ottoman Empire, nationalism turned out to be a much more dangerous doctrine than modernity. Modern Arab commentators on al-Tahtawi often criticize him for being too close to the West, but they fail to recognize his situation as an Egyptian intellectual within a distinct imperialist environment, that of the Ottoman Empire, for whom what the West had to offer was in part an escape from that Empire and the invigoration of what some saw as a stale form of Islam. Although al-Tahtawi was definitely not a thinker of the stature of al-Afghani and his followers, he was more effective in that he spent his life within the administrative structure of Egypt and helped bring about material changes in that structure, especially in its educational institutions. A similarly placed bureaucrat, Khayr al-Din al-Tunisi (1810–89), also initiated secular education in his country, Tunisia, based on the same ideas that progress meant science and was not incompatible with Islam. This spirit of reform was widespread throughout the Middle East, and small groups of intellectuals campaigned in favour of both science and liberalism, seen to be part and parcel of the same ideological movement. They sought to combine the study of the Qurʾan with the study of secular sciences, not to replace the former with the latter but to reconcile Islam and modernity.

Muhammad ʿAbdu (1849–1905) used his position as head of al-Azhar, the leading theological university in the Sunni Islamic world, to propound the message of the *Nahda* that the Islamic world should accept modernity while at the same time not rejecting Islam. The period of stagnation that he identified with the tenth to fifteenth centuries CE was a time when the early scientific and philosophical progress of the Islamic cultural world came to an end, and the political and religious authorities had a mutual interest in maintaining control by restricting the intellectual curiosity of those over whom they ruled so effectively. What was now needed, he argued in the nineteenth century, was reform of all the institutions of the Islamic world, while preserving the timeless truths of Islam and the Qur'an itself. He suggests that the connection between religion and modernity, in particular between Christianity and modernity, is entirely misplaced. After all, as he argues, Christianity also advocates belief in the transience of everyday life, not the concern for possessions and comfort so characteristic of modern industrial societies, yet it finds no inconsistency in combining its core beliefs with modern ways of operating. Thus this need not be a worry for Muslims either. The effective broadcasting of his views throughout the Islamic world through the media and the liberal *futuwa* (legal rulings) from al-Azhar played a leading role in defining a relevant role for Islam within the framework of the modern state. It also represented a new approach to the Qur'an, where the Book was reinterpreted to present a modernist programme. The idea that there were parts of the Qur'an that could be adapted to changing circumstances had an impact, as did 'Abdu's other suggestion that the basic principles of the Book were true for all time and could never change. A good deal of debate started over which rules fall into which category.

Wider responses to colonialism and modernity

These ideas that were enlivening cultural life in the Arab world also found adherents further away. Improved communications brought reformist ideas from Egypt to the Dutch East Indies, today Indonesia, and the Muhammadiyya movement was set up by Ahmad Dahlan (1868–1923), who had lived in Egypt and met 'Abdu. On the other hand, it was not difficult for the ideas of the *Nahda* to be taken in other directions, as they were by 'Abd al-Rahman al-Kawakibi (1854–1902). He had lived for most of his life in Syria and, while he advocated modernity, liberalism and pan-Islamism, he did so within the context of leadership by the Arabs, not the Ottomans, criticizing the latter for what he called their love of despotism and conservatism. In addition, the southward expansion of Russia and wars with Iran created many new Muslim subjects for the Czar, and also much discussion among Muslim intellectuals as to how to respond effectively to the onslaught from the north.

One set of ideas that had a good deal of currency in the nineteenth century was known as Mahdism. A *mahdi* is someone who is divinely chosen to deliver the community from danger, and increasing pressure from the industrial West on the Islamic world led to many *mahdi*s appearing, especially in Africa. In times of crisis and rapid change, messianic hopes often take a material form. Commerce had traditionally been concentrated on the cross-continental routes, but the influence of colonialism meant that power shifted to increasingly competitive coastal ports. In an area between Guinea and Senegal, 'Umar ibn Sa'id ruled between 1852–64, trying to avoid the French, although he would fight them when absolutely necessary. In Libya, the Sanusi clan (in particular Sayyid al-Mahdi al-Sanusi) established their rule, while Muhammad Ahmad ibn 'Abdullah drove the Turks and Egyptians out of the Sudan, killed General Gordon in Khartoum and, for a short time, ruled that huge country. At the end of the nineteenth century, the Somalis discovered a *mahdi* in Muhammad 'Abdallah Hasan, who went on to resist the British and later the Italians. The crisis, as traditional Islamic cultures were increasingly overwhelmed both physically and culturally by colonialism, led to the rapid growth of such millennial movements, which offered a potent message of resistance, religion and salvation, as well as an interpretation of the Qur'an that fostered their claims to authority.

But the search for a *mahdi* was not limited to Africa. It occurred also in Persia and India, leading to the construction of highly heterodox sects, such as the Bahai and the Ahmadiyya movements. The former originated with Sayyid 'Ali Muhammad, who came from Shiraz and was declared by some to be the Bab or door through which humanity would be united with the concealed *imam*, who himself is the link between this world and the divine realm. The movement was fiercely resisted by the Persian regime and the Bab himself was shot, along with many of his supporters, but it took a strong hold in the form of followers of Mirza Husayn 'Ali or Baha' Ullah (Glory of God), and turned into a complex religious movement. Over time, this movement has become more and more distinct from orthodox Islam, even of the Shi'i variety.

In India, in 1891 Mirza Ghulam Ahmad declared himself to be the *mahdi* and Christ combined, and acquired a large number of followers. Some of the latter regarded him merely as a reviver of Islam, but others saw him as a prophet, which goes against the basic Islamic principle that the Prophet Muhammad was the last prophet. As one might imagine, these groups have often not been treated well by the Muslim communities in which they live, but early and continuing persecution does not seem to have pre-vented them from growing into relatively large and successful movements. They are active today, proselytising and determinedly asserting themselves as members of the Islamic *umma* (community).

Islam and the Islamic world saw itself as definitely in retreat once it came under the domination of Christian powers. The expansion of the Christian colonialist powers continued to dominate the world, economically and militarily. The Ottoman Empire, whose ruler was the caliph, formally the head of the Sunni Islamic world, was in retreat and widely regarded as a crumbling and corrupt edifice. Modernity, in the form of science and technology, appeared to be the creation and possession of the Christian countries, and its slow acceptance in the Islamic world caused much questioning about how far Muslims could adopt such apparently alien ideas. How far could the Qur'an become relevant in the new technological and scientific world? This was very much the question raised by the *Nahda* and it is still being asked today. How the question is answered is important in defining the direction that the interpretation of the Qur'an will take in the future.

Further reading

Hourani, A. (1982) *Arabic Thought in the Liberal Age 1798–1939*, Cambridge: Cambridge University Press.

Keddie, N. (ed.) (1972) *Scholars, Saints and Sufis*, Berkeley, CA: University of California Press.

—— (1983) *An Islamic Response to Imperialism: Political and religious writings of Sayyid Jamal al-Din 'al-Afghani'*, Berkeley, CA: University of California Press.

Kedourie, E. (1966) *Afghani and Abduh: An essay on religious unbelief and political activism in modern Islam*, London: Frank Cass & Co.

Kurzman, C. (2002) *Modernist Islam: A source book*, New York: Oxford University Press.

Mardin, S. (2000) *The Genesis of Young Ottoman Thought: A study in the modernization of Turkish political ideas*, Syracuse, NY: Syracuse University Press.
al-Tahtawi (2003) *An Imam in Paris: al-Tahtawi's visit to France (1826–31)*, trans. D. Newman, London: al-Saqi.

See also: **Arabic language; education and the Qur'an**

OLIVER LEAMAN

AL-NAJJAR, AL-HUSAYN B. MUHAMMAD

Al-Husayn b. Muhammad al-Najjar was born in the city of Bam, where he lived throughout his life. Said to have been a weaver at *dar al-tiraz* (the embroidery house), he was a follower of the Murji'i theologian Bishr al-Marisi in theology and of Abu Hanifa in *fiqh* (jurisprudence). His date of birth is unknown, but he died in 220/835.

Al-Najjar's doctrine became well known towards the end of the reign of al-Ma'mun (198–218/813–33) in the region of Rayy. Al-Ash'ari classifies him among the Murji'a, while al-Shahrastani places him among the Jabriyya (determinists) and stresses that most of the Mu'tazila around the Rayy region were faithful to his doctrine. On the other hand, several reports link him with the Mu'tazila, while others classify him and his followers as belonging to the *ahl al-ithbat* (the affirmationists, i.e. those who affirm God's *qadar*). The lack of unanimity is due to the fact that his opinions on the theological questions that interested the *ahl al-kalam* (scholars of theology) were not all alike. On some issues his opinions were like those of the *ahl al-sunna* (Sunni thinkers), while on others they were more like the views of the Mu'tazila.

Al-Najjar followed the main Murji'i position in the definition of *iman* (belief). Like the other Murji'a, al-Najjar did not consider *'amal* (act or deed) as part of *iman*. This was a huge controversy in early Islam, which dealt with how far someone could disqualify himself as a Muslim through action that contravened the rules of Islam. Could the behaviour of someone who believed apparently condemn him as an unbeliever? The Murji'a argued that this was the case: only God could tell who was a believer and who was not, so the decision had to be delayed (*irja'*) until God decided. Al-Najjar defined belief as knowledge of God, his Messenger and his rules; reverence for God; and verbal confession. Anyone who neglects one of these tenets of belief becomes an unbeliever. Al-Najjar nonetheless suggests that someone who neglects one of these principles of religion should not be called an infidel because of his negligence, arguing for the possibility of a difference between believers in terms of their respective merits. It should be assumed that a Muslim retains enough belief to remain a Muslim, unless there is evidence of a direct denial of the principles of Islam.

Again, al-Najjar thinks that the works of men are created by God; men are the agents of them. There is nothing in God's realm except what he wills. The power (*istita'a*) may not precede the act. God has imposed on unbelievers duties which they are unable to fulfil. The man who dies, dies at his term (*ajal*), and the man who is killed, is killed at his term.

The Mu'tazilites al-Murdar and al-Iskafi wrote books against al-Najjar. It is reported that his death followed defeat in a debate with the Mu'tazilite al-Nazzam, but one always has to be suspicious of reports of thinkers provided by those antagonistic to them.

Al-Najjar had followers in Jurjan and Rayy. His followers were called Najjariyya or Husayniyya, and were divided into three groups: the Burghuthiyya,

Zaghfaraniyya and Mustadrika. None of his books is extant.

Further reading

al-Ash'ari, Abu'l-Hasan 'Ali b. Isma'il (1969) *Maqalat al-islamiyyin* (The Ideas of the Muslims), ed. M. 'Abd al-Hamid, Beirut: Maktabat an-nahda.

al-Baghdadi, 'Abd al-Qahir (1910) *al-Farq bayn al-firaq* (The Difference between Erroneous Groups), ed. M. Badr, Cairo: Matba'a al-ma'arif.

al-Sam'ani, 'Abd al-Karim b. Muhammad al-Tamimi (1988) *al-Ansab* (Lineages), ed. M. Al-Hulv, Beirut: Dar al-jinan.

OLIVER LEAMAN

NAJWA

Najwa is the root of a verb that means to whisper, converse in secret or confide in someone. God says that secret conversations are not hidden from him: he hears the private and confidential consultations between people. 'There is no *najwa* (secret counsel) of three but He is the fourth' (58.7). *Najwa* was not a praiseworthy practice during the Prophet's time. The Qur'an forbids people from private conversations, particularly in the presence of the Prophet. Engaging in such conversations was considered at best inappropriate, at worst a sin. Indeed, some people who held secret counsel were conspiring against the Prophet or encouraging others to disobey him.

RAFIK BERJAK

NASKH

see: **abrogation**

NASS

The word *nass* (pl. *nusus*) is derived from the Arabic verb *nassa*, meaning to appoint, specify, fix, determine, raise, set up, designate or define. *Nass* therefore refers to a text, wording, citation, stipulation or a passage, especially one from the Qur'an. According to the *Lisan al-'Arab* and Lane's *Arabic English Lexicon*, the *nass* in terms of the Qur'an and *ahadith* is an expression that makes specific reference to a statute or ordinance in the actual words of the Qur'an and the Sunna without having to resort to interpretation. In *usul al-fiqh*, therefore, the term is technically used for text in the Qur'an or *hadith* used to justify a ruling. This is, for example, how al-Shafi'i uses the term in his *Risala*. He also uses it to specify an explicit statement in the Qur'an as opposed to a general one made specific by a *hadith*. Thus Muslim jurists use *nass* as evidence or proof, particularly if text from the Qur'an or Sunna is being used to justify an assertion. The other usage for *nass* is that of the *nass* used for the *matn* – the text of the Qur'an as opposed to the *isnad* – the chain of transmission in *hadith*, thereby justifying the hadith's authority.

The plural *nusus* is used in a similar manner, as well as for the actual words of an author, book, passage or piece of writing. Al-Ghazali uses one authoritative statement (*nass*) as a prescription from the Prophet, i.e. 'the Imams are of Quraysh'. Unlike al-Juwayni, al-Baghdadi and al-Mawardi, al-Ghazali considered this descent incontrovertible. As far as general usage is concerned, the words *nassan wa ruhan*, for instance, signify 'in letter and spirit' and the expression *mansus alayhi* is used for being appointed, specified, determined or laid down in writing. The term occurs in this form in al-Nu'mani's *Tafsir* in relation to the Imam's appointment, with *imam mansus alayhi min Allah* meaning 'the Imam is appointed by Allah'.

The word *nass* does not occur as such in the Qur'an, but many verses provide the underlying concept, such as 43.28 ('And He made it a Word to remain in his [Abraham's] progeny') and 3.34 ('God chose Adam and Noah, the family of Abraham ... above other people, as descendants, one from the other'). In Shi'i Islam, *nass* has a specific meaning: it refers to an extremely important principle in relation to the institution of Imama, a principle that concerns how the Imam is appointed. This appointment (*ta'yin*), through *nass* (a statement of designation) by his predecessor, can be verbal or written. An example can be found in al-Ash'ari's *Maqalat*, where Shi'a (or *Rawafid*, as he prefers to call them) agree that the Prophet proclaimed 'Ali b. Abi Talib his heir, and publicized the fact (*wa hum mujmi'una 'ala anna l-nabiyya nassa 'ala 'Ali b. Abi Talib bi ismihi wa azhara dhalika wa a'lanahu*). Al-Kulayni gives a detailed description of the *ishara* (authoritative signal) and *nass* (designation) by which Imama is bequeathed to the Imams. Qadi al-Nu'man also has a section on the *tawqif* (indication) of the Imams, which relates to the manner in which the Imamate is established and gives the intellectual positions adopted by various groups before offering his own Fatimid position, namely that the Imamate is instituted by *nass wa tawqif*.

However, this is systematically undermined by Qadi 'Abd al-Jabbar, who discards all the *nusus* given by the Shi'a, either showing their linguistic and theological interpretations to be invalid or claiming that these traditions were *ahad* – that is, transmitted by isolated authorities and therefore not sound. Al-Mufid, however, is of the view that since the Imams take the place of the prophets as teachers of mankind, and are God's proof on earth, the community has no power to elect or appoint them. For him, the Imamate is established either through miracles, or by a formal appointment by *nass* or, less formally, *tawqif*.

Historical sources suggest that among many of the early Shi'a, support for 'Ali's family did not yet translate itself into upholding the rights of a specific individual; nor did it necessarily indicate a preference for the descendants of al-Husayn. It could well be that it was these circumstances that made the doctrine of *nass* (designation) a significant determinant in the selection of the Imam. This doctrine involved the idea of a pre-ordinance, given public reality by the formal act of the Imam designating his successor. The doctrine is compatible with hereditary succession, but does not preclude the possibility of the *nass* moving outside the hereditary chain.

It seems quite obvious from the number of groups within the Shi'a that, for most of the early Shi'i sympathisers, it did not matter who the leader was, provided he was a Hashimid. The doctrine of the *nass* was used by al-Husayn to ensure the passage of the Imamate to his son 'Ali Zayn al-'Abidin, to the exclusion of al-Hasan's sons or any other descendants of 'Ali. However, since the concept of the Imamate had not been clearly articulated at that time, the doctrine of *nass* could also work in favour of others who claimed it. It seems that such a claim to *nass* was put forward on behalf of Ibn al-Hanafiyya by the various groups who supported him after al-Husayn's tragic death. The fact that these groups used the idea of *nass* shows that some conception of succession by designation existed at a very early stage. Until then, the various claimants were restricted to the 'Alids, but the claim that Abu Hashim had passed his heritage to the 'Abbasids, as well as the assertions of Bayan and Abu Mansur, claiming *nass* from al-Baqir, shows that the doctrine was widely used.

According to al-Shahrastani, the Jar-udiyya branch of the Zaydiyya (fol-lowers of Zayd b. 'Ali, half-brother of al-Baqir) upheld the belief that the Pro-phet nominated 'Ali 'by a description [of his qualities] without the mention of his name (*bi al-wasf duna al-tasmiya*)'. In Zaydi literature, his nomination was made in a manner that the believers could understand, not directly and of necessity, but merely by inference. Later this thesis of 'obscure nomination' (*nass khafi, ghayr jali*) was universally advo-cated by the Zaydiyya.

Unlike the Zaydiyya, al-Baqir's school offered a stronger argument in its conviction that the Prophet had, before his death, expressly designated and appointed 'Ali as his successor by *nass* – that is, by means of explicit designation (*nass al-jali*). Insisting on the *nass* meant that the Imam had his authority by divine appointment and not from any human electors or from the *bay'a* (pledge of allegiance) of ordinary peo-ple. Furthermore, since the Imam's authority was from above, 'true knowl-edge was confined only to the *imams* in the Prophet's family; not to every mem-ber of the Prophet's family and certainly not to the whole community'. It was thus, he held, that the whole tradition of the community was invalid as a proper source for law. This also meant that al-Baqir did not allow the practice of *ijti-had* and *ikhtiyar*, nor did he advocate individual opinions (*ara'*) of the kind advocated by the Batriyya branch of the Zaydiyya. The Imam's followers should be able to seek his judgement on each new question that arose, because he was the only authority able to guarantee the true tradition of law. For the inspired Imam was the recipient of that special sum of knowledge (*'ilm*) handed down by *nass* to him, and this was hereditary and the exclusive right of each succeed-ing *imam*.

The hereditary character of the *nass* was the crucial point in the principle of the Imamate that al-Baqir advanced. The hereditary *nass* was placed as a restriction on all those who could otherwise claim the *nass* and thereby acquire licence for leadership. It was in this manner – by *nass al-jali* – that al-Baqir appointed his son, Ja'far al-Sadiq. This *nass* embodied for its recipient exclusive authoritative knowledge (*'ilm*), which was traced direct to 'Ali, of whom the Prophet had said 'I am the city of knowledge and 'Ali its gate.' This knowledge included the interpretation of the Qur'an and its legal judgements, as well as authority to judge in changing times and under new adversities. The bestowal of *'ilm* through *nass* involved the transmission of *nur* (light), which is a symbol of that eternal knowledge (*'ilm*) which forms part of the Prophet Muhammad's testament (*wasiyya*) to 'Ali, and thereafter to the *imams* who were to follow him.

The *nur* and *'ilm*, which the Imam is meant to possess by virtue of *nass*, ren-der him *mas'um*, or protected from error and sin. Al-Baqir based this concept on his interpretation of 33.33. The legal and political implications of this doc-trine are clear: the Imam has absolute power over the community and, since he is appointed by God and infallible, the community can be responsible neither for appointing nor electing him. Thus, there is no room for *ijma'* (consensus) in al-Baqir's theory of the Imamate.

Further reading

Abu al-Fawaris (1977) *al-Risala fi al-Imama*, ed. and trans. S.N. Makarem, New York: Delmar.

Amir-Moezzi, M.A. (1994) *The Divine Guide in Early Shi'ism*, trans. David Streight, Albany, NY: SUNY.

Arendonk, C. van (1960) *Les débuts de l'Imamat Zaidite au Yemen*, trans. J. Ryckmann, Leiden: E.J. Brill.

Bar-Asher, M. (1999) *Scripture and Exegesis in Early Imami Shiism*, Jerusalem: The Magnes Press.

Corbin, H. (1964) 'Divine Epiphany and Spiritual Birth in Ismailian Gnosis', in *Man and Transformation*, Princeton, NJ: Princeton University Press, 69–160.

Donaldson, D. (1933) *The Shi'ite Religion*, London: Luzac & Company.

Hodgson, M. (1955) 'How Did the Early Shi'a become Sectarian?', *JAOS*, 75: 1–13.

Jafri, S. (1979) *Origins and Early Development of Shi'a Islam*, London & New York: Longman.

al-Kulayni, Abu Ja'far Muhammad b. Ya'qub (1388/1968) *Usul min al-Kafi*, Tehran: Dar al-kutub al-'ilmiyya.

Lalani, Arzina R. (2000) *Early Shi'i Thought: The teachings of Imam Muhammad al-Baqir*, London: I.B. Tauris in association with The Institute of Ismaili Studies.

MacDermott, Martin J. (1978) *The Theology of al-Shaikh al-Mufid*, Beirut: Dar el-Machreq.

Madelung, Wilfred (1997) *The Succession to Muhammad: A study of the early caliphate*, Cambridge: Cambridge University Press.

Momen, Moojan (1985) *An Introduction to Shi'i Islam*, New Haven, CT: Yale University Press.

al-Qadi Abd al-Jabbar al-Asadabadi (1960) *al-Mughni fi abwab al-tawhid wa-al-'adl*, Vol. 20, ed. A. Ahwani, Cairo: al-Mu'assa al-Misriga.

al-Qadi al-Nu'man (1951–61) *Da'a'im al-Islam*, Cairo: Dar al-ma'arif; English trans. *The Pillars of Islam*, Vol. 1, trans. Asaf A.A. Fyzee, rev. I.K. Poonawala, New Delhi: Oxford University Press, 2002.

al-Qummi, 'Ali b. Ibrahim (1968) *Tafsir al-Qummi*, ed. Tayyib al-Musawi al-Jaza'iri, Beirut: Matba't al-Najaf.

al-Walid, Ali b. Muhammad (1967) *Taj al-'aqa'id wa ma'dan al-fawa'id*, ed. Aref Tamer, Beirut: Dar al-machreq.

al-Yaman, Ja'far b. Mansur (1984) *Kitab al-Kashf*, Beirut: Dar al-andalus.

See also: **Shaykh Mufid; Shi'a**

ARZINA R. LALANI

NATIQ

The verb root *nataqa*, from which the term *natiq* is derived, means to speak, utter, articulate or pronounce, as in 23.62: 'And with Us is a Record which speaks the truth'. In another instance, it is used to underline the certainty of the revelation: 'Just as the truth that you can speak' (51.23).

Antaqa is the transitive form, meaning to cause something to speak. On the Day of Judgement, disbelievers' ears, eyes and skin will testify against them saying: 'Allah has caused us to speak – He causes all things to speak' (41.21).

Mantiq signifies the faculty of speech or diction. It is used when Solomon says: 'O mankind, we have been taught the language of birds' (27.16). The phrase *'ilm al-mantiq* refers to the science of logic.

RAFIK BERJAK

NATURAL WORLD AND THE QUR'AN

In the creation of the heavens and the earth, the Qur'an states that there are signs for people of understanding. 'Our Lord, You did not create all this in vain ... Save us from the retribution of Hell' (3.190–191). There is not taken to be a problem in reconciling the divine creation of the world with a scientific understanding of its structure. In fact, the Qur'an brings out many of the features of the world and why they are as they are, since it is 'A Book, whose verses are explained in detail – a Qur'an in Arabic, for people who have knowledge (*ya'alamuna*)' (41.3). We are also told: 'Say: "Travel through the earth and see how God initiated creation; in the same way will God produce a later creation: for God has power over all things"' (29.19–20). This emphasis on observing the world and deriving appropriate conclusions is frequently there:

> Say, 'Look at all the signs in the heavens and the earth.' All the proofs and all the warnings can never help people who decided to disbelieve. (10.101)

God's signs in his creations can be attained by human perception:

> It is He [God] who sends down rain from the sky: from it you drink, and out of it [grows] the vegetation on which you feed your cattle. With it He produces for you corn, olives, date-palms, grapes and every kind of fruit: verily in this is a sign for those who contemplate (yatafakkaruna). He has made subject to you the night and the day, the sun and the moon, and the stars are subject to his command: verily in this are signs for men who use their reason. (ya'qiluna). (16.10–12)

The words tafakkur (to think), tafaqquh (to understand), tadabbur (to contemplate), 'aql (using reason), suduri (chest), qalb (heart), 'ilm (knowledge), 'ulama (those who have knowledge), ulu'l 'ilm (those with knowledge – 3.18), ulu'l absar (those who have vision – 24.44), ulu'l al-bab (those who have understanding – 3.7; 38.29), ulu'l yadi wa'l absar (possessors of power and vision – 38.45) and ulu'l 'azmi (those with firmness of heart – 46.35) are all used in the Qur'an. We are told: 'Without doubt, the worst of beasts in God's sight are the deaf, the dumb, who do not use their 'aql (reason/sense)' (8.22).

Natural phenomena can be understood, as everything is in the order and balance of God's law:

> We have made the night and the day as two signs: the sign of the night we have obscured, while the sign of the day we have made to enlighten you; that you may seek bounty from your Lord, and that

you may know the number and count (hisab) the years: all things have we explained in detail. (17.12)

Everything has been made precisely: 'The sun and the moon are perfectly calculated. The stars and the trees prostrate themselves. He constructed the sky and established the law. You shall not transgress the law' (55.7–8). The Qur'an also refers to the 'perfect balance of everything' (15.19) in nature and to 'God's knowledge of everything' (33.40). The Almighty 'teaches man that which he knew not' (96.5). The more we understand God's creation, the more we know the greatness of God,

> who has created seven heavens in harmony. You can see no fault in the Beneficent One's creation; then look again. Can you see any gaps? Then look again and yet again, your sight will return to you weakened and made dim. (67.3–4)

But we also have to realize our limitations: 'Glory to God, who created in pairs all things that the earth produces, as well as their own kind and [other] things of which they have no knowledge' (36.36).

Understanding how the world works from a Qur'anic perspective can be a tool to raise people's standard of living. By understanding science we are able to utilize what God has provided for us, and we are expected to be thankful for his blessing: 'It is he who has made the earth manageable for you, so travel through its tracts and enjoy what he has provided' (67.15). For example,

> It is God who has made the sea of service to you that the ships may run on it by his command, and that you may seek his bounty, and you should be grateful. He has made useful for you what is in the heaven and the earth, it is all from him.

Here are portents for people who reflect. (45.12–13)

One of our aims should be to create a society that balances the material and the spiritual:

And seek by means of what God has given you the future abode, and do not neglect your portion of this world, and do good as God has done good to you, and do not seek to make mischief in the land, surely God does not love the mischief-makers. (28.77)

Caring for the environment is important: 'The servants of the Most Gracious are those who treat the earth gently, and when the ignorant speak to them, they only utter peace' (25.63).

The Qur'an is the guide and provides solutions and answers to every aspect of life, and it is unaffected by any condition, time, circumstances, frame or paradigm. 'We [God] have revealed to you this book [Qur'an] to provide exposition for everything, and guidance, and mercy, and good news for the submitters to God [Muslims]' (16.89). We read: 'Say, "If the ocean were ink for the words of my Lord [in the Qur'an], the ocean would run out, before the words of my Lord run out, even if we double the ink supply"' (18.109). There are many verses that show us natural phenomena that remind us of and attract our attention towards God, the creator and source of the universe. For example,

Your Lord is the one God, who created the heavens and the earth in six days (yawm), then assumed all authority. The night overtakes the day, as it pursues it persistently, and the sun, the moon and the stars are committed to serve by His command. He entirely controls all creation and everything is under his command. Most Exalted is God, Lord of the universe. (7.54)

We also read: 'Do not the unbelievers see that the heaven and earth were one unit then We ripped them apart' (21.30). Originally the sky was smoke (dukhan) (41.11), 'and the heavens we created with might and we are expanding it' (51.47) 'as if it were a brilliant star … whose oil is well lit, even no fire touches it' (24.35). A good example of divine planning ccurs in: 'He has ordained the sun and the moon, each one runs for an appointed time' (13.2). The sun, moon and earth are all designed to follow a regular path, a path that is ultimately in our interests (36.39; 79.30).

There are a number of verses that describe God's making of living things: 'and We made, from water, every living thing' (21.30); 'We have created man from clay' (23.12); 'Then We placed him [man] as [a drop of] sperm in a place of rest, firmly fixed. Then We made the sperm into a clot of congealed blood; then of that clot We made a lump; then we made out of that lump bones and clothed the bones with flesh; then we developed out of it another creature. So blessed be God, the best to create!' (75.4); 'And He [God] created you in stages [or phases]' (71.14).

All this design is not blind but directed by an intelligent being who has in mind the final resolution of our lives on the Day of Judgement and Resurrection:

And the Day that the trumpet will be sounded – then will be smitten with terror those who are in the heavens, and those who are on earth, except such as God will please [to exempt]: and all shall come to His [presence] as beings conscious of their lowliness. When you look at the mountains, you think that they are standing still. But they are moving, like the clouds. Such is the manufacture of God, who perfected everything. He is fully cognizant of everything you do. (27.87–88)

There are references to what could be the end of the world: 'And when the heaven splits asunder and becomes red like a rose' (55.37); 'When stars lose their lustre' (77.8); 'when the stars have collapsed, when the oceans boil over in a swell' (81.6); 'Lo! the day of decision is a fixed time, a day when the trumpet is blown and you come in multitudes, And heaven is opened and becomes like gates' (78.17–19). Study of the natural world is supposed to put us in mind of the next world:

> O people, if you have any doubt about resurrection, [remember that] We [God] created you from dust, and subsequently from a tiny drop, which turns into a hanging [embryo], then it becomes a foetus that is given life or deemed lifeless. We thus clarify things for you ... you look at a land that is dead, then as soon as we shower it with water, it vibrates with life and grows all kinds of beautiful plants. (22.5)

There is even a reference to God as being in charge of evolution: 'He is Allah, the creator, the evolver, the giver of forms' (59.24). Everything is controlled by God (3.109) and 'He created you in stages' (71.14). Many Muslims reject the theory of evolution, since it seems to operate entirely independently of God, but there are resources in the Qur'an sufficient to identify evolution with the divine plan and thus to introduce God into the picture.

The example of water and light

There are many references in the Qur'an to water, reflecting the Book's revelation in a hot and dry region of Arabia. One of the most impressive references is:

> Do you not see that Allah sends down from the clouds water, then brings forth with it fruits of different colours. And in the mountains there are streaks, white and red, of different colours, and some intensely black. And of people and animals and cattle there are different colours likewise. Only those of His servants fear Allah who possess knowledge. (35.27–28)

In the Qur'an, 'ulama are likened to mountains (jibal) from which rivers and streams of knowledge flow, and among which springs and fountains of illumination arise. The aya runs:

> And there are some rocks out of which streams burst forth, and there are some of them which split asunder so water flows from them, and there are some of them which fall down for the fear of Allah. (2.74)

These streams and rivers may be of water that is 'white, delicious to those who drink' (37.46) – that is, good and refreshing to the soul. But they may be red, like blood, which turns a peaceful world into one of violence. Likewise, black also refers to 'ulama who give rise to fitna and gloom, and from whom come forth false beliefs that lead to vice and immorality. The point to be noted here is that colours come down from the sky in the form of light, as we are told at 35.27–28.

This reference to colours raining down from the sky could be seen as alluding to white light coming down from above, bearing the colours, just as rain descends from the clouds. This represents a truth about colour that we know today but was not understood at the time of the revelation. Hence the remark about the importance of people gaining knowledge, since here we have religious and scientific information being provided together.

Light from the sun is so powerful that, if it directly reached the earth, it would harm it. Fortunately, and by what might be seen as divine design, the heat evaporates water from the surface of the earth to form clouds. The word *judud* ('streaks') means fast-moving rays. Just as rainfall causes the earth to produce plants and fruits of different types and colours, light from above, by falling on things on earth, creates different colours.

The different types of plant are produced according to the types of soil, even though the rain that falls on them is the same. Likewise, the light falling everywhere is the same, but a particular thing on earth will absorb certain colours from white light and reflect others, and these reflected rays strike the retina of the human eye to produce in us the colour of that object.

The colours that are absorbed by a substance react by creating chemical changes, and this may well produce something very useful to us. In the *aya*, an analogy is drawn between rain in the form of water and rain in the form of light, which brings with it colours. Both rain and colour come from God, they both fall on something and the end result is something generally useful and productive. Both kinds of phenomena are linked to divine revelation, and this is compared to the bounty falling to earth from heaven.

Colours are part of our natural perception, while the message of God pertains to our inner perception. No reasonable person can deny the need for rain and for light in the natural world, nor can anyone believe that only some places need rain and light, yet others do not. Some consider that while the benefit of rain and light is not limited to one nation, yet spiritual rain and light were confined to just one people and land. They err, and the Qur'an makes clear the generality of its message. After all, rain falls to the benefit of all.

In the eleventh verse of *surat az-zukhruf*, rain is defined as water sent down in due measure. The verse is as follows: 'And He who sends down [from time to time] water from the sky in due measure, and We raise to life through it a land that is dead. Even so will you be raised [from the dead]' (*surat az-zukhruf*, 43.11).

'We send down pure water from the sky. That with it We may give life to a dead land, and slake the thirst of things We have created – cattle and men in great numbers' (25.48–49). This observation of the organization of the natural world is supposed to make us think of who the organizer is, and what our role towards him should be.

Trees

Trees are usually mentioned together with rain and water. Verses mentioning wood and wood products are plentiful, in paradise and hell, but also illustrating many of the events described in the Qur'an. Submission of the earth and the heavens for the purpose of humanity is a theme of the Book. While there is a priority for humanity, the dominance of humanity over the earth demands from us responsible behaviour, to keep and maintain the established order. There is the idea of diversity leading to balance and to a certain equality between the different forces on the earth:

> And the earth we have stretched out and have thrown on it firm mountains, and have caused to grow upon it of everything a measured quantity. And we have made for your means of livelihood therein, and for those for whom you do not have to provide. (15.19–20)

Also we read at 16.13: 'And what he has produced for you in the earth varying in hue, verily, in that it is a sign for a people who are mindful.' This is a point that the text emphasizes again and again: the importance of human beings thinking about creation, how it came about, who created it, and what their duties are to it and to its creator.

At 55.2–13 we read:

> The merciful taught the Qur'an; he created man, taught him plain speech. The sun and the moon have their appointed time; the herbs and the trees adore him; and the heavens, he raised them and set the balance, that you should not fail to respect. But weigh correctly, and stint not the balance. And as for the earth, he has arranged it for living creatures; in it are fruits and palms, with sheaths; and grain with chaff and many shoots; then which of your Lord's bounties will you deny?

There is variety, created by God, and many *hadith* suggest that it has to be preserved actively by humanity. A most impressive *hadith* has been reported by al-Bayhaqi: 'When doomsday comes, if someone has a palm shoot in his hand he should plant it.' It is remarkable that in this situation, the end of the world, someone is asked to care for plants!

But this reference to a tree does bring out the importance of the natural world in the Qur'an, both as evidence of divine care for his creatures and as a realm in which we have to behave responsibly. The references to nature are not generally linked to the moral, though, but rather to the epistemological, so we get the idea that the world is an arena for our contemplation, and the results of that contemplation should be the acknowledgement of the divine role in nature. Commentators often suggest that there are scientfic truths in the Qur'an that are only now being properly understood, since at the time science was not developed enough to grasp them as scientific hypotheses. Whatever we think of that, the role of water, trees, plants and animals in our natural world is something anyone may think about, and the Qur'an encourages us to do so, and to draw the further implications that these must have a creator behind them with a plan. We are expected to wonder what that plan might be and to seek guidance in the Qur'an as to how to help realize it.

It is perhaps worth adding a word of caution about the linking of the Book with science, a common practice in much of the literature. It is not difficult to find passages in the Qur'an which could be descriptions of scientific theories, but we should remember that theories are just theories. They may seem to be usable now and to describe nature, but in the future they could be overtaken by more accurate and more general theories, so we should not seek to find too much congruity between the Qur'an and natural science. Of course, it could be claimed that there never will be a theory that is not covered by the Qur'an, and the implications of that are that the Qur'an speaks in such general terms that it would cover absolutely any theory whatsoever. That makes it harder to link usefully with any particular theory. What we could take from the Book is not so much a set of accurate descriptions of how the world works from a scientific point of view, but an often beautiful and perceptive description of how the world may appear to be to us. From that we may derive ideas about how we should relate to that world, and indeed to each other, and we may go on to form ideas about what is behind the world as a whole. The frequent references in the Qur'an to plants, animals, natural events, the weather, water and so on reveal an attitude of respect for the natural world, an attitude based not on a particular scientific theory but on an aesthetic and ethical understanding of the natural order.

Further reading

Bakar, O. (1996) 'Science', *HIP*: 926–46.

al-Bayhaqi, Ahmad ibn (n.d.) *Sunan al-Bay-hayi al-Kubra*, Hyderabad, n.p.

Hill, D. (1993) *Islamic Science and Engineering*, Edinburgh: Edinburgh University Press.

Hourani, G. (1975) *Essays on Islamic Philosophy and Science*, Albany, NY: SUNY Press.

Nasr, S.H. (1993) *The Need for a Sacred Science*, Albany, NY: SUNY Press

See also: **camel; colours; education and the Qur'an; fig; noise; science and the Qur'an**

OLIVER LEAMAN

NICHE OF LIGHT

see: **mishkat**

NIGHT JOURNEY

see: **Jerusalem;** *mi'raj*

NIGHT OF POWER

see: **laylat al-qadr**

NI'MA

Ni'ma is a noun meaning blessing, favour, benefit, grace or kindness. 'And remember Allah's favour towards you' (3.103). God reminds the Muslims that, before the revelation, they were enemies to one another. However, he joined their hearts together, so that by his grace they became brethren in Islam. *Ni'ma* and its forms appear often in the Qur'an: the root verb, *na'im* (to receive the blessing) and its other forms appear 144 times. The frequent usage of this term reinforces the key Islamic idea that all blessings are from God and that he is the only one that bestows them, on whomsoever he wills.

See also: **lutf**

RAFIK BERJAK

NINETY-NINE NAMES OF GOD

It is traditionally held that God has ninety-nine beautiful names and there is general agreement on some of them. Others, however, come into some lists but not others. They are often recited by Muslims, since 'The most beautiful names belong to God: so call on Him by them' (7.180). After all, 'He is Allah, the Creator, the Originator, the Fashioner, to Him belong the most beautiful names: whatever is in the heavens and on earth, do declare His praises and glory. And He is the exalted in might, the wise' (59.24).

A fairly standard rendering of the names follows. It should be borne in mind that there are plenty of formulations that leave out some of these names and include others instead.

Allah Allah, he who has the Godhood, which is the power to create the entities.

Ar-Rahman The Compassionate, the Beneficent, he who has plenty of mercy for the believers and the blasphemers in this world and especially for the believers in the hereafter.

Ar-Rahim The Merciful, he who has mercy for believers.

Al-Malik The King, the sovereign lord, he who is with complete dominion, he whose dominion is clear from imperfection.

Al-Quddus The Holy, he who is pure from any imperfection and has no children or adversaries.

Al-Salam The Source of Peace, he who is free from every imperfection.

Al-Mu'min Guardian of Faith, he who witnessed for himself that no one is God but him. And he witnessed for his believers that they are truthful in their belief that no one is God but him.

Al-Muhaymin The Protector, he who witnesses the sayings and deeds of his creatures.

Al-'Aziz The Mighty, the strong, the defeater who is not defeated.

Al-Jabbar The Compeller, he for whom nothing happens in his dominion except that which he willed.

Al-Mutakabbir The Majestic, he who is clear from the attributes of the creatures and from resembling them.

Al-Khaliq The Creator, he who brings everything from non-existence to existence.

Al-Bari' The Evolver, the Maker, the Creator who has the Power to turn matter into things.

Al-Musawwir The Fashioner, he who forms his creatures in different ways.

Al-Ghaffar The Great Forgiver, the Forgiver, he who forgives the sins of his slaves time and time again.

Al-Qahhar The Subduer, the Dominant, he who has perfect power and is not restricted in his actions.

Al-Wahhab The Bestower, he who is generous in giving plenty without any return.

Al-Razzaq The Sustainer, the Provider.

Al-Fattah The Opener, the Reliever, the Judge, he who opens for his slaves the secular and religious world.

Al-'Alim The All-Knowing, the Knowledgeable; nothing is absent from his knowledge.

Al-Qabid The Constricter, the Retainer, the Withholder, he who constricts his provision by his wisdom and expands and widens it with his generosity and mercy.

Al-Basit The Expander, the Enlarger, he who constricts his provision by his wisdom and expands and widens it with his generosity and mercy.

Al-Khafid The Abaser, he who lowers whoever he wishes by his destruction and raises whoever he wishes by his endowment.

Al-Rafi' The Abaser, he who lowers whoever he wishes by his destruction and raises whoever he wishes by his endowment.

Al-Mu'iz The Honourer, he who gives esteem to whoever he wishes, hence there is no one to degrade him.

Al-Muthil The Dishonourer, the Humiliator, he gives esteem to whoever he wishes, there is no one who could degrade him.

Al-Sami' The All-Hearing, the Hearer, he who hears all things that are heard by his eternal hearing without any ear, instrument or organ.

Al-Basir The All-Seeing, he who sees all things that are seen by his eternal seeing without an eye or any other instrument.

Al-Hakam The Judge, he is the ruler and his judgement is his word.

Al-'Adl The Just, he who is entitled to do what he does.

Al-Latif The Subtle One, the Gracious, he who is kind to his slaves and grants favours to them.

Al-Khabir The Aware, he who knows the truth of things.

Al-Halim The Forbearing, the Clement, he who delays punishment for those who deserve it and contemplates forgiving them.

Al-'Azim The Great One, the Mighty, he who deserves to be exalted, and is removed from all imperfection.

Al-Ghafur The All-Forgiving, the Forgiving, he who forgives a lot.

Ash-Shakur The Grateful, the Appreciative, he who gives a lot of reward for a little obedience.

Al-'Aliyy The Most High, the Sublime, he who is removed from the attributes of his creatures.

Al-Kabir The Most Great, the Great, he who is greater in status than everything else.

Al-Hafiz The Preserver, the Protector, the one who protects whatever and whoever he wishes to protect.

Al-Muqit The Maintainer, the Guardian, the Nourisher, the Sustainer, he who has power.

Al-Hasib The Reckoner, he who gives satisfaction.

Al-Jalil The Sublime One, the Beneficent, he who is attributed with great power and glory.

Al-Karim The Generous One, the Bountiful, the Gracious, he who is attributed with great power and glory.

Al-Raqib The Watcher, the Watchful, he that is removed from nothing.

Al-Mujib The Responsive, the Hearkener, he who answers whoever is in need if he asks him and rescues the needy if they call upon him.

Al-Wasi' The Vast, the All-Embracing, the Knowledgeable.

Al-Hakim The Wise, the Judge of Judges, he who is correct in his behaviour.

Al-Wadud The Loving, he who loves his believing slaves and his believing slaves love him.

Al-Majid The Most Glorious One, the Glorious, he who has perfect power, high status, compassion, generosity and kindness.

Al-Ba'ith The Resurrector, the Raiser (from death), he who resurrects his slaves after death for reward or punishment.

Ash-Shahid The Witness, he who is present to everything that happens.

Al-Haqq The Truth, the True, he who truly exists.

Al-Wakil The Trustee, he who gives satisfaction and is relied upon.

Al-Qawi The Most Strong, the Strong, he who has complete power.

Al-Matin The Firm, the holder of extreme power which is constant and does not waver.

Al-Jame' The Gatherer, the Collector, he who brings things together however he wants.

Al-Hamid The Praiseworthy, the praised one who deserves to be praised.

Al-Muhsi The Counter, the Reckoner, he who is acquainted with the number of things.

Al-Mubdi' The Originator, he who created the human being.

Al-Mu'id The Reproducer, he who brings back creatures after death.

Al-Muhyi The Restorer, the Giver of Life, he who constructed a living human from matter that does not have consciousness. He gives life by giving souls back to bodies on the Day of Judgement and makes hearts alive by the light of knowledge.

Al-Mumit The Creator of Death, the Destroyer, he who renders the living dead.

Al-Hayy The Alive, he who is attributed with a life that is unlike our life and is not that of a combination of soul and matter.

Al-Qayyum The Self-Subsisting, he who remains and does not end.

Al-Wajid The Perceiver, the Finder, the rich who is never poor.

Al-Wahid The Unique, the One, he who is without a partner.

Al-Ahad The One.

Al-Samad The Eternal, the Independent, the master who is relied upon in supplying our needs.

Al-Qadir The Able, the Capable, he who is characterized with power.

Al-Muqtadir The Powerful, the Dominant, he who has perfect power so that nothing is withheld from him.

Al-Muqaddim The Expediter, the Promoter, he who puts things in their right places. He promotes what he wishes and delays what he wishes.

Al-Mu'akhkhir The Delayer, the Retarder, he who puts things in their right places. He ensures that everything happens at the appropriate time.

Al-Awwal The First, he whose existence is without a beginning.

Al-Akhir The Last, he whose existence has no end.

Az-Zahir The Manifest, he who has nothing above him and nothing beneath him, since he exists without having a place. He is not to be associated with physical bodies.

Al-Batin The Hidden, he that has nothing above him nor beneath him, since he is not linked to place.

Al-Wali The Guardian, he who owns things and manages them.

Al-Muta'ali The Most Exalted, he who is removed totally from the attributes of creation.

Al-Barr The Source of All Goodness, the Righteous, he who is kind to his creatures, who provides them with sustenance and supports whoever he wishes.

At-Tawwab The Accepter of Repentance, the Relenting, he who grants repentance to whoever he wishes among his creatures and accepts that repentance.

Al-Muntaqim The Avenger, he who victoriously prevails over his enemies and punishes them for their sins. He who destroys them.

Al-'Afuww The Pardoner, the Forgiver, he who has the power to provide forgiveness.

Ar-Ra'uf The Compassionate, he who has great mercy. His mercy is his will to endow benefits upon whoever he wishes among his creatures.

Malik Al-Mulk The Eternal Possessor of Sovereignty, he who controls and gives dominion to whoever he wishes.

Dhul-Jalali wal-Ikram The Lord of Majesty and Bounty, he who deserves to be exalted and not denied.

Al-Muqsit The Equitable, he who is just in his judgement.

Aj-Jami' The Gatherer, he who gathers creatures on a day that there is no doubt about, that is the Day of Judgement.

Al-Ghani The Self-Sufficient, he who does not need the creation.

Al-Mughni The Enricher, he who satisfies the necessities of creatures.

Al-Mani' The Preventer, the Withholder.

Ad-Darr The Distresser, he who makes harm reach whoever he wishes and visits benefits upon whoever he wishes.

An-Nafi' The Propitious, he who makes harm reach whoever he wishes and visits benefits upon whoever he wishes.

An-Nur The Light, he who guides.

Al-Hadi The Guide, he who with his guidance leads the guided to what is beneficial for them and protects them from what is harmful.

Al-Badi' The Incomparable, he who created creation and formed it without any preceding example.

Al-Baqi The Everlasting, he who cannot not exist.

Al-Warith The Supreme Inheritor, the Heir, he whose existence persists.

Ar-Rashid The Guide to the Right Path, he who guides.

As-Sabur The Patient, he who does not quickly punish the sinners.

OLIVER LEAMAN

NISA

The term *nisa* literally means women. It is the title of the fourth chapter of the Qur'an and one of the longest, consisting of 176 verses. The chapter deals with women's rights and was revealed shortly after the Battle of Uhud between the third and fifth year of the *Hijra*.

In this *sura* there are references to the care of orphans and the conditional allowance of polygamy, as well as conditions and regulations about marriage and divorce. The word *nisa* (sing. *niswa*) and its other formulations (*nisa'ukum*, your women; *nisa'uhum*, their women; etc.) are repeated fifty-seven times throughout the Qur'an. While it is too simplistic to assume that mere numbers are any indication of gender equality, it is interesting to note that the word *rijal* (sing. *rajul*), meaning men, and its other formulations (*rijalukum*, your men; *rijalahum*, their men; etc.) is also repeated fifty-seven times.

Based on the Qur'an, there has been a variety of interpretations of women's rights and responsibilities that ranges from traditional to modernist and from conservative and fundamentalist to Islamist and progressive. Most interpretations insist that the rights given to women in the Qur'an are far greater than those that they had at the time of *jahiliyya*, the pre-Islamic period. Many also argue that these rights were greater than those of their European counterparts until the eighteenth century. The assumption is that, before the rise of Islam, women were considered chattels and part of men's property. They received no inheritance, but were inherited themselves. They did not have the right to choose their spouses and were subjected to polygamy and infanticide. While the Qur'an gives evidence of this and the patriarchal context in which it was revealed, it refutes many of its precepts. Yet studies have confirmed that nomadic matriarchal cultures were also present in Arabia. Within these matriarchal societies, there is evidence of polyandry and of women divorcing their husbands simply by changing the direction of the entrance to their tents. Veiling and seclusion were not practised and there were women poets, warriors and traders. Accordingly, while the Qur'an denounces the then-common practice of

female infanticide, gives women right to property, and commands men to treat women kindly and to give them their rights, some of its principles can and have been interpreted in a way that has placed limitations on women's liberties. Restrictions on women's right to divorce, child custody, and mandatory forms of veiling and seclusion are a few of these cases. There are not many interpretations, however, that argue from Qur'anic precepts for the spiritual inferiority of women. Women and men are often addressed together concerning how their duties pertain to matters of belief and religious practice. According to the Qur'an, it is the gender-undifferentiated human that is destined to seek deliverance and has the potential to attain it.

Further reading

Ahmed, L. (1992) *Women and Gender in Islam*, New Haven, CT, and London: Yale University Press.

Barlas, A. (2002) 'Believing Women', in *Islam: Unreading patriarchal interpretations of the Qur'an*, Austin, TX: University of Texas Press.

Wadud, A. (1999) *Qur'an and Women: Rereading the sacred text from a woman's perspective*, Oxford: Oxford University Press.

See also: **modesty; veil; women**

BAHAR DAVARY

NO
see: la

NOAH
see: **Nuh**

NOISE

The Qur'an is critical of those who might be said to corrupt the earth:

There is the type of man whose speech about this world's life may dazzle you, and he calls God to witness about what is in his heart: yet he is the most contentious of enemies. When he turns his back, his aim everywhere is to spread mischief through the earth and destroy crops and cattle. But Allah loves not mischief. (2.204–205)

These verses were apparently revealed after a man named al-Akhnas ibn Shuriq came to the Prophet Muhammad to embrace Islam, but as he left he happened to pass by a pasture filled with grazing animals. He set it alight and killed the cattle. The verses were sent down as a sign of divine disapproval.

The point is that God disapproves when the resources that have been provided for the benefit of mankind are spoiled in any way. Selfishness and violence lead humanity to become corrupters of the earth.

Mischief has appeared on the land and sea, because of [the need] that the hands of man have earned, that [Allah] may give them a taste of some of their deeds: in order that they may turn back [from evil]. (30.41)

Mischief on the land and sea is inflicted by our interference with the natural laws and environmental balance. Environmental pollution, the disruption of the natural balance of things in order to make profit, can easily be identified as corruption on earth. 'Seek not mischief in the land, for Allah loves not those who do mischief' (28.77).

Islam and its *umma* are directed to seek the mean. While Islam's followers do not consider the various elements of nature to be deities, at the same time they do not tamper with or spoil them. The relationship between the Muslim and the universe is one of harmonious benefit and use. When God makes an oath on things, he draws attention to the fact that man should recognize their value and take care of them: 'By the sun and its splendour. By the moon as it follows it. By the day as it shows up [the sun's] glory. By the night as it conceals it. By the firmament and its structure. By the earth and its expanse' (91.1–6); 'By the night as it conceals [the light]. By the day as it appears in glory. By the creation of male and female' (92.1–3); 'I call to witness the siting of the stars. And that is indeed a mighty adjuration if you only knew, that this is indeed a Qur'an most honourable' (56.75–77).

With such oaths, God calls on us to revere other creatures and aspects of his creation. In the Qur'an, there are verses that call on us to avoid noise, such as: 'Neither speak thy prayer aloud, nor speak it in a low tone, but seek a middle course between' (17.110); 'O you who believe, raise not your voices above the voice of the Prophet. Nor speak aloud to him in talk, as you may speak aloud to one another, lest your deeds become void and you perceive not. Those that lower their voices in the presence of the apostle of Allah – their hearts has Allah tested for piety: for them is forgiveness and a great reward' (49.2–3); and 'And be moderate in your pace, and lower your voice, for the harshest of sounds without doubt is the braying of the ass' (31.19). The Qur'an and the *sunna* advocate quiet and self-control, as well as caring for the feelings of others and avoiding anything that can hurt them: even a loud voice. The first verse orders Muslims not to voice their prayers too loud, nor in an inaudible voice. They should seek a middle course in the *jah-riya* (articulated so as to be heard) in prayer and not the *sirriya* (sub-vocalized). In the second verse, the Muslims are asked to lower their voices in the presence of Prophet Muhammad. The injunction is both particular and general. Noise must be avoided generally and particularly in solemn gatherings. The last verse carries Luqman's exhortations to his son, and approves of them. The exhortations of previous prophets and apostles that are mentioned in the Qur'an are meant to be a source of advice for Muslims. In Luqman's exhortation, the son is advised to lower his voice and avoid speaking unnecessarily loud. To instil this message in his son, Luqman uses the metaphor of the braying ass, which implies that any pollutant of the environment or anything that is conducive to public discomfort is just as unpleasant and hateful.

At the time of Prophet, his Companions were considering how to call for the five daily prayers at their appointed time. Suggestions included blowing a horn, drumming or ringing bells, but all were turned down by Prophet Muhammad. The suggestion is that he favoured a moderate and seemly amount of noise for prayer, enough to satisfy the purpose of prayer, but not so much as to disturb people or to show off the apparent piety and enthusiasm of the community. Some of the devotional guides to *salat* or prayer, such as Maharib (1991), try to steer a moderate course between encouraging enthusiasm in prayer, even to the extent of leading the supplicant to tears, while avoiding loud and demonstrative performances.

Reference

Maharib, R. (1991) *Kayfa takhsha'ina fi al-salat?*, Cairo: Dar al-'ulum al-islamiyya.

See also: **salat**

OLIVER LEAMAN

NUH

The Prophet Nuh (Noah) is mentioned forty-three times by name in the Qur'an. Noah's importance in the Qur'an and in Muslim exegesis, exemplifying a certain prophetic type, is much greater than the minor role he plays in the biblical account.

The story of Noah and the Flood is contained in several long passages in the Qur'an (e.g. 7.59–64; 10.71–73; 11.25–49; 21.76–77; 23.23–30; 26.105–122; 29.14–15; 37.75–82; 54.9–17; 71.1–28). Noah's basic message is that his people must acknowledge the existence of God and obey him. 71.23 mentions the names of five gods worshipped by the people of Noah: Wadd, Suwa, Yaghuth, Ya'uq and Nasr. These false gods are described by Muslim exegetes as having been introduced to the people of Noah by Satan.

29.14 states that Noah was sent to his people for 950 years, and Muslim exegesis claims that he was anywhere from 50 to 480 years old at the time he was sent. It is said that Noah lived for another 350 years after his prophetic mission. A saying of the Prophet Muhammad tells us that there were ten generations between Adam and Noah, but other Companions of the Prophet Muhammad report that Noah came as a prophet before Idris.

The Ark is described in detail by Muslim exegetes. It is said that Noah worked on the boat for 400 years, using wood from a special tree that had grown for 40 years until it reached a height of 300 cubits. The size of the boat is described variously, usually as a long rectangle but also as a great round bowl. Ibn 'Abbas relates that Jesus ('Isa) resurrected Ham, the son of Noah, and had him describe the Ark to his disciples.

11.43 refers to one of Noah's sons, said by Muslim exegetes to have been called Yam, which means 'sea' in Arabic, who refused to get on the Ark and was drowned. Noah's other sons (Shem, Ham, Japheth), along with their wives and various other people, are reported to have sailed in the Ark with Noah and his wife and all of the animals. Some exegetes claim that a giant named Og, the son of a daughter of Adam out of wedlock, survived the Flood because of his incredible stature.

The Ark is said to have come to rest in a city called the Eighty (*thamanin*) because there were supposed to have been eighty people on the Ark. Before the waters receded, the Ark is reported to have circumambulated the *Ka'ba* in Mecca, and Muslim tradition claims that the grave of Noah is in the mosque of Mecca.

Further reading

Bailey, L.R. (1989) *Noah: The person and the story in history and tradition*, Columbia SC: University of South Carolina Press.

McClain, E.G. (1978) 'The Kaba as Archetypal Ark', *Sophia Perennis* 4, 1: 59–75.

BRANNON WHEELER

NUMAN B. SABIT ABU HANIFA

see: **Abu Hanifa, Numan b. Sabit**

AL-QADI AL-NU'MAN

The founder of Isma'ili jurisprudence, Abu Hanifa al-Nu'man b. Muhammad al-Tamimi, al-Qadi al-Nu'man, was born around 290/903 in Qayrawan, North Africa, then a centre of Isma'ili cultural life.

Al-Nu'man entered the service of 'Abdullah al-Mahdi (d. 322/934), the Isma'ili ruler and *imam* who established the Fatimid regime in Ifriqiya in 297/909. He served the first four Fatimid caliphs in a variety of roles, such as keeper of the palace library and judge at Tripoli and Mansuriyya (the new capital from 337/948, under the Fatimid caliph-imam al-Mansur), ending up with an appointment in 337/948 by al-Mansur to the position of chief judge (*qadi al-qudat*) of the whole Fatimid state. Al-

Nu'man stayed in a high judicial position in the state for a long time, and even ran the meetings of wisdom (*majalis al-hikma*) every Friday in the palace to instruct audiences of Isma'ilis in the esoteric teaching, known as *hikma*, together with the *ta'wil* or esoteric interpretation of the Qur'an, in accordance with the Isma'ili approach. Al-Qadi al-Nu'man died in Cairo, the new Fatimid capital, on the last day of Jumada II 363/27 March 974 and the ruler al-Mu'izz himself led the funeral prayer.

Al-Nu'man produced a great deal of written material. He is best known as the founder of a legal system for a Shi'i state, based on the universalist principles of the Fatimid state but acknowledging the minority status of the Isma'ilis within Muslim society in North Africa. He codified Isma'ili law by incorporating a disparate supply of sources, including Imami, Zaydi as well as Sunni sources; the result was the *Da'a'im al-Islam*, in two volumes. Dealing with acts of devotion (*'ibadat*) and secular matters (*mu'amalat*), this work was approved by al-Mu'izz and became the civil legal code of the Fatimid state. Isma'ili law gave significance to the central Shi'i doctrine of the Imamate, providing Islamic legitimation for a state ruled by the family of the Prophet Muhammad or the *ahl al-bayt,* a familiar Shi'i theme particularly emphasized by the Isma'ilis. The *Da'a'im* has continued to serve as the principal legal authority for the Tayyibi Musta'li branch of Isma'ilism, and especially for the Isma'ili Bohras of South Asia.

Further reading

al-Nu'man (1960) *Asas al-ta'wil*, ed. 'Arif Tamir, Beirut: Dar al-thaqafa.
—— (1967–72) *Ta'wil al-da'a'im*, ed. M.H. al-A'zami, Cairo: Dar al-ma'arif.
—— (1970) *Iftitah al-da'wa*, ed. W. al-Qadi, Beirut: Dar al-thaqafa.

Poonawala, I.K. (1977) *Bibliography of Isma'ili Literature*, Malibu, CA: Undena Publications, 48–68.
—— (1996) 'Al-Qadi al-Nu'man and Isma'ili Jurisprudence', in F. Daftary (ed.) *Mediæval Isma'ili History and Thought*, Cambridge: Cambridge University Press, 117–43.

See also: **imam; ulu'l-amr**

OLIVER LEAMAN

NUMBERS

Numbers are important in the Qur'an, basically because they are also perceived to be miracles or signs (*ayat*) of God's infinite will. One must keep in mind that the Qur'an is viewed by Muslims as a numerical miracle, not only because many of the numbers mentioned in the verses are still scientifically accurate today, but also because there seems to be a remarkable symmetry in the very distribution of phonemes, words and verses among its 114 *suras*. Many recent studies have used computational methods and statistical measurement to accurately quantify and decode this perceived symmetry. One such study attempts to prove that the number nineteen (cf. 74.30) is the common denominator throughout the Qur'an's mathematical system, i.e. that it is part of a mathematical code in the text (Khalifa, 1992: 375–6). The theory goes that when all the numbers mentioned in the Qur'an are added together, the total comes to 162,146; this number is said to be significant because it can be divided by nineteen: $19 \times 6,534 = 162,146$. Other instances of the nineteen code include the 114 (19×6) *suras*; the famous first revelation (96.1–5) consisting of 19 words and 76 (19×4) letters; *sura* 96, the first in the chronological sequence, consists of 19 verses. Quantitative studies of the vocabulary of the Qur'an have also produced a number of interesting

numerical values. For example, a study by Al-Suwaidan (available at www.islamicweb.com/begin/numbers.htm) reveals that major opposing terms occur exactly the same number of times: for example, *al-hayat* (life) and *almawt* (death) occur 145 times each; the same is true for *al-dunya* (the world) and *al-akhira* (the hereafter), which occur 115 times each. More interesting, perhaps, is the observation that the word *shahr* (month) occurs 12 times, and the word *al-yawm* (day) on 365 occasions.

As it is often remarked, the Arab genius is expressed as a gift for calculation and the Qur'an provided early Arabs with further proof in all its symmetry and precision that it was indeed a miracle from God. According to Tradition, the most manifest miracle that the Prophet Muhammad had been given was the Night Journey to Jerusalem and the subsequent ascension (*mi'raj*) to the seventh heaven that houses God's heavenly throne and the magnificent Lote-tree. It is to the *sura* that recounts this miraculous journey that one must turn to find the most vivid expression of the significance of numbers in the Qur'an:

> And we have appointed the night and the day as two signs (*ayatayni*). Then We obliterated the sign of night while we made the sign of day illuminating, that you may seek bounty from your Lord, and that you may know the number of the years and the Reckoning. (17.12)

It is indeed the notion of time, and such numbers as are intricately connected with the passage of time, that is repetitively referred to in the Qur'an. When the notion of ascension towards God is coupled with the concept of time, the impact is striking. Consider, for example, *sura* 70, which is entitled *sura al-Ma'arij* (The Ascensions). Here is the number arrived at when the Qur'an calculates for man the time needed to ascend to God, who is here quite significantly referred to as 'The God of Ascensions' (*allahi dhi l-maʿarij*): 'The angels and the Spirit [Gabriel] ascend to Him in a Day the measure whereof is fifty thousand years'. This is the second largest number mentioned in the Qur'an. The highest is the exact double of that amount (i.e. 100,000), mentioned in 37.147 in reference to the number of people that the Prophet Jonah was sent to lead: 'And We sent him to a hundred thousand or more. And they believed; so we indulged them for a time.'

There are basically two common words for number in Arabic: *raqam* (pl. *arqam*) and *ʿadad* (pl. *aʾdad*); the Qur'an uses only the latter. The noun *ʿadad* and the derivatives of the root verb *ʿ/d* (to count) occur more than twenty-five times in the Qur'an. In most cases the word is followed by a specific number. In all, the Qur'an mentions thirty different numbers: the numbers from 1 to 12, 19, 20 to 80 (in tens), 99, 100, 200, 300, 1,000, 2,000, 3,000, 5,000, 50,000 and 100,000. As we can see, these numbers can be classified into ones, tens, hundreds and thousands. Also important is the fact that all the primary and odd numbers from one to ten are mentioned. There are no millions involved. The most common contexts in which numbers occur are years, months, nights, days, ears of corn, people, angels, good deeds, *suras*, wells, clans and planets. One of the most frequently occurring numbers is seven, which is mentioned a total of twenty-eight times. This is obviously due to the repetition of familiar subjects such as the seven heavens, the seven seas, the seven Companions of the Cave, the seven heifers in Pharaoh's dream and the seven days of destructive winds (69.7). In addition, there are more distinctive Qur'anic concepts such as the seven *mathani* (or duplicate verses), the

seven gates of hell (15.44), the seventeen angels carrying the Throne of God (69.17), the seventy arm's-length chain of hell, and the asking for forgiveness seventy times (9.80). The second most familiar number is perhaps twelve, which includes the twelve months of the year, the twelve planets in Joseph's dream, and the twelve tribes of Israel. One of the most discussed numbers, though, is the number nineteen, which occurs only once in a very short verse of the Qur'an (three words long) and refers to the nineteen angels guarding *saqr* (hell): 'Over it are nineteen' (74.30). What is more important than the number itself is the lengthy and elaborate explanation offered in the adjacent *aya*. Indeed, this disproportion in length calls attention to the number nineteen itself, and also gives us an important clue as to how numbers are functionally mobilized in the Qur'an for theological purposes:

> And We have not made the guardians of the Fire other than angels, and We have not made their number (*ʿiddatahum*) but as a trial for those who disbelieve, in order that the People of the Book may be certain, and those who believe may increase in faith, and those who have been given the Book and the believers may not doubt, and those with diseased hearts and the disbelievers may say: 'What did God intend by this example?' Thus God leads astray whom He wills and guides whom he wills, and none knows the hosts of your Lord but He; and this is naught but a reminder to mankind. (74.31)

To understand the above verse, a historical reference must be made to the fact that, according to the Qur'an, both the Torah (*Tawrat*) and the Gospels agree regarding the nineteen angels guarding hell, since that number was 'fixed' by God – and hence the remark that the People of the Book 'may be certain'. In the final analysis, numbers are like the Furies, the avenging angels of Greek mythology: they are tormenters in the eyes of wrong-doers, but angels of mercy in the eyes of the law-abiding. To use a parallel image from the Qur'an, they are like the gate separating heaven from hell, 'from the inside a mercy, and from the outside a torment' (57.13).

Reference

Khalifa, R. (trans.) (1992) *The Qur'an: The final testament*, Tucson: Islamic Productions.

*See also: **ahl al-kitab***

AFNAN H. FATANI

NUR

The significance of the word *nur* (light) in the Qur'an can be inferred from the fact that there is a whole *sura* entitled *al-Nur* (The Light), which contains what is perhaps the best known and most often quoted verse of the Qur'an. This so-called Light Verse or Parable of Light (24.35) was singled out by Prophet Muhammad as being especially blessed. The phrase 'light upon light' (*nurun 'ala nur*), which occurs in the final lines, has become a proverbial statement in the Islamic world and is most often used to denote God's infinite beauty, guidance and light. Muslim scholars believe that the reference to God's light in the Qur'an is not meant to express his reality, which is inexpressible in any human language, but only to allude to the illumination he bestows upon the mind and the feelings of all who are willing to be guided. Tabari and Ibn Kathir quote Ibn 'Abbas as saying, in reference to the Parable of Light, 'It is the parable of His light in the heart of a believer' (cf. Asad, 1980: 541). Interestingly enough, Western scholars have perceived a Christian atmosphere in the Light Verse, espe-

cially the specific reference in verse 36 to 'men whom neither merchandise nor traffic beguile from the remembrance of God'. Bell (1968: 113), for example, is certain that these men refer to Christian priests or monks. For Muslims, of course, the 'houses' of God wherein men pray 'mornings' and 'evenings' is undeniably an allusion to the mosques wherein all Muslims perform their obligatory ritual prayers.

The word *nur* occurs a total of forty-nine times in the Qur'an, in a number of derivatives: *al-nur* (the light), *nuran* (a light), *nurikum* (your light), *nurana* (our light), *nurihi* (his light), *nurihum* (their light), *al-munir* (the illuminated) and *muniran* (illuminating). The participal form *al-munir* occurs only four times and always as a postmodification of the word *kitab* (book) or *al-kitab*, which refers to the Qur'an as well as to the Torah (*Tawrat*). In addition to referring to God, the word is ascribed to the Prophet Muhammad, the Qur'an, the Book, the Torah, the moon, and the faithful men and women (*al-mu'minin*). The participal *muniran* occurs twice in the text: once as a modifier of the word 'moon' (*qamaran*) in 25.61, and once as an attribute of the Prophet (33.47) in the expression *sirajan muniran* (an illuminating lamp), which coordinates with four other epithets (witness – *shahidan*; bearer of glad tidings – *mubashiran*; warner – *nadhiran*; and summoner or caller to God): 'O Prophet, We have sent you as a witness, and a bearer of glad tidings, and a warner, and a summoner to God by His leave and an illuminating lamp' (*sirajan muniran*). *Nur* occurs twenty-four times in the definite form (with the article *al-*), where it is most often collocated with the word darkness (*zulumat*) and the verb *yukhriju* (to lead out), suggesting a movement outwards from darkness into light, and from ignorance into faith. It is also used in eight basic senses (*wujuh*; pl. *awjuh*) or referential meanings. These can be summarized as follows:

1. *Nur* as a reference to the religion of Islam: 'They [the disbelievers] want to extinguish God's light (*nura allahi*) with their mouths, but God refuses but to perfect His Light, though the disbelievers be averse' (9.32).

2. *Nur* as a reference to faith: 'God is the Protector of those who believe. He leads them out from darkness into light (*nur*). But as for those who disbelieve, their protectors are false idols; they lead them out from light (*nuri*) into darkness' (2.257).

3. *Nur* as a reference to God's commandments and moral laws in the Torah and Gospels: 'Verily We did send down the Torah, therein was guidance and light (*nurun*) by which the Prophets judged' (5.44); 'And in their footsteps, We sent Jesus, the son of Mary, confirming the Torah that had come before him, and We gave them the Gospels (*injil*) in which was guidance and light (*nurun*)' (5.46).

4. *Nur* as a reference to the light of day: 'Praise be to God who created the heavens and the earth, and originated the darkness and the light (*al-nur*); yet those who disbelieve hold others as equals with their Lord' (6.1).

5. *Nur* as a reference to the guiding light that God gives the faithful on the Day of Resurrection: 'On the Day when the hypocrites, men and women, will say to those who have believed: "Wait for us, so that we may borrow your light (*nurikum*)!" It shall be said to them: "Turn back behind you, and seek for a light (*nuran*)"' (57.13). The expression 'turn back behind' here refers

to the previous life on earth, with the meaning that the hypocrites should have sought a light while they lived on earth. *Nur* is thus not an abstract notion but a physical commodity one can attain both on earth and on the Day of Resurrection.

6. *Nur* as a reference to the commandments and injunctions of the Qur'an: 'Therefore believe in God and His messenger and in the light (*al-nuri*) which We have sent down. And God is All-aware of your deeds' (64.8).

7. *Nur* as a reference to justice: 'And the earth shall shine with the light of its Lord (*bi-nuri rabaha*), and the Book shall be placed [open], and the Prophets and the witnesses shall be brought forward, and it shall be judged between them with truth, and they shall not be wronged' (39.69).

8. *Nur* as a reference to the light of the moon: 'See you not how God has created the seven heavens one above the other, and how He has made the moon a light (*nuran*) therein and made the sun a lamp?' (71.15–16); 'It is he who has made the sun radiance (*diya'an*) and the moon a light (*nuran*)' (10.5).

(al-Damaghani, 1985: 466)

References and further reading

Asad, M. (1980) *The Message of the Qur'an*, Gibraltar: Dar al-andalus.
Bell, R. (1968) *The Origin of Islam in the Christian Environment*, Edinburgh: Frank Cass & Co.
al-Damaghani, A. (1985) *Qamus al-Qur'an*, ed. A. Al-ahal, Beirut: Dar al-'ilm.

See also: Injil; **knowledge**; *mishkat*; **philosophy and the Qur'an**

AFNAN H. FATANI

NURSI, SAID

Said Nursi was born in the village of Nurs in Bitlis, a Kurdish area of the Ottoman Empire, in 1294/1877. He died in Urfa on 25 Ramadan 1379/23 March 1960. Of modest origins, he quickly impressed with his skill in debate and intellectual ability, which led to his being given the name *Bediuzzaman* (Wonder of the Time). In Van, Nursi founded his own *medrese* in order to put into practice his ideas on education and how to defend Islam. He was in favour of a form of education that fostered both the natural and religious sciences. At the end of 1325/1907, Nursi arrived in the Ottoman capital, Istanbul, to seek official support for his plans to establish a university, as well as ideas regarding the development of the Eastern Provinces. On the proclamation of the Second Constitution on 24 Jamazalakhir 1326/23 July 1908, Nursi made public speeches supporting freedom, the constitution and their conformity with Islam. He was active in the Society for Muslim Unity and spent a short time in prison for political activities.

Between 1328/1910 and 1329/1911, Nursi travelled from Istanbul to Van via the Black Sea and Tiflis, Georgia, then to the Arab world and Damascus. In his travels, Nursi promoted the benefits of constitutionalism and how it could be made the basis for progress and unity across the Islamic world. In Damascus, in the Umayyad Mosque, he delivered his celebrated Damascus Sermon, a trenchant summary of his views at that time. Nursi remained in Istanbul for some time during 1911, before returning to Van in 1912 in order to build his university on the shores of Lake Van – but the construction work never started. During World War I, he was appointed the local commander-in-chief and, with his students, fought against the Russians. Finally Nursi was captured and sent as a prisoner of war to a camp at Kosturma on the Volga. He escaped and in 1918 he returned to Istanbul.

Nursi started to write books and got involved in social activities. During 1920 and 1921, Nursi withdrew into solitude and underwent a profound mental and spiritual transformation, although he continued to write during this time. In autumn 1922, Nursi was invited to Ankara. There he was given an official ceremony in the National Assembly and invited to make a speech to congratulate the war veterans and offer prayers. He declined Mustafa Kemal's offers of various posts and left Ankara for Van. Between 1923 and 1925 political changes in Turkey forced Nursi to retire from politics and social affairs into a life of seclusion. Keeping with him only a small number of his students, he immersed himself in worship and contemplation. In 1925 Nursi was sent into exile first to the West Anatolian town of Burdur and then to Isparta and eventually to the remote village of Barla. Nonetheless, his writings had evoked a powerful popular response and they began to spread secretly through the region. The authorities exerted pressure on Nursi and he was finally sent back to Isparta, where he was kept under strict surveillance. In 1935 Nursi and 120 of his students were arrested and sent to prison. They were charged with opposing the new republic's reforms and belonging to a secret political organization. Nursi was sentenced to eleven months in prison. During this time, despite appalling conditions, he kept writing, producing works that were called *Risale-i Nur* (Treatises of Light). In 1943 Nursi was arrested and imprisoned for another nine months. On his release he spent his time under virtual house arrest. In 1948 he was once again arrested and only released the next year.

In the last ten years of his life he was allowed more freedom, travelling widely through Turkey to visit his students and disciples.

Said Nursi was constantly involved in Qur'anic exegesis. He developed an original way of approaching the Qur'an and Islam. For Nursi, since one of the major causes of unbelief was the natural sciences, it was necessary to put great effort into understanding and discussing them. He was quite confident that, by the spiritual as well as intellectual power of his works, he would not only revive Islamic intellectual tradition, but also construct a new community. His search for truth led him to concentrate on the meaning of the Qur'anic verses; his contemplation on the Qur'anic verses led him to a kind of meditation on the universe. According to Nursi, the universe displays divine power and beauty, whereas the Qur'an deciphers the secrets of the universe. For him natural sciences can only be instruments for expounding the Qur'anic truths. He wanted to read the natural sciences as a kind of knowledge about God. Through this kind of approach to the natural sciences, he tried to protect religious faith from attacks from positivistic scientific ideas, but also make them to serve religious ends. He was conscious of what he took to be materialism's spiritual deconstruction of individuals and society. Therefore he tried to defend both personal religious faith and the integrity of the community. Nursi values knowledge in accordance with its subject matter. Philosophy, in a profane sense, was useless, since it could not properly convey the knowledge of the Creator. Instead, philosophy surrenders to reason and to non-religious forces. By severing it from its divine source, reason has been given the status of *shirk* (idolatry) by modern European philosophy. Nursi insists that reason, if it were properly employed, arrives naturally at the glorious Names of God. Whatever reason discovers from the secrets of nature displays the divine power and will. For him, everything is a mirror of the All-Glorious Maker's Names. Reason is a means of reinforcing and even coming to more appropriate understanding of what was revealed in the Qur'an. Reason is a creation of God. Like other creations of God, it should lead to a better understanding of God himself. Reason is given to humanity both to improve the conditions of life and to reach a better understanding of God. But, according to Nursi, a proper use of reason will always seek guidance from the knowledge that has been already revealed in the Qur'an.

Nursi's writings

Nursi emerged from the tradition of Islamic sciences, but he presented the essence of what the Islamic sciences contained in a different form. In this respect, Nursi and his works are revolutionary. Nursi's *Risale-i Nur* collection was gradually written in order to give a proper response to the problems of the age. It is composed of many treatises, mainly *Sözler* (Words), *Mektubât* (Letters), *Lem'alar* (Flashes), *Şualar* (Rays), *Muhakemat* (Reasonings), *Münazarât* (Debates), *Isharat al-'ijaz, al-Mathnawi al-'arabi al-nuri, al-Hutba al-shamiyya* (the Damascus Sermon) and other small treatises. The main corpus of the *Risale* is written in classical Ottoman Turkish; those parts written in Arabic were translated into Turkish. It incorporates both a rational style and its own intimate existential and very personal style. The *Risale* did not attempt to offer solutions to the problems of age through the traditional Islamic sciences, such as *fiqh* and *kalam*. Instead, Nursi addressed problems directly and offered solutions to them depending on his own reactions to the Qur'an. Therefore, the *Risale* cannot be assimilated to any of the traditional Islamic sciences.

In 1911, in his Damascus Sermon, Nursi offers six remedies from the Qur'an for the illnesses of the Muslim world. The Arabic text of the sermon was printed twice soon afterwards and published in the following year in Istanbul. *Münazarât* was published in 1331/ 1913 and contains Nursi's political ideas about the benefits of constitutionalism, about progress and about the unity of the Islamic world. In these works, he also speaks about his project of educational reform and his plan for establishing a university. *Muhakemat*, published in 1913, deals with a number of issues causing confusion in the minds of scholars. It is written in the form of an introduction to the Islamic sciences, just like ordinary *Tafsir* (Qur'anic exegesis) and *Akaid* (Islamic tenets). Nursi started to write *Isharat al-'ijaz* as a Qur'anic commentary in 1331/1913 and continued work on it during World War I, even on the front. *Isharat* deals with the rules of rhetoric, logic, the principles of religion and other sciences. It aims to supply proofs and explanations of the Qur'an's miraculousness, and speaks of belief, unbelief and worship.

Nursi wrote *al-Mathnawi al-'arabi al-nuri* between 1922 and 1923. *Al-Mathnawi* is a metaphysical work that explains divine unity by means of the universe and its beings. It is also an account of his own spiritual journey, in which he describes how he battled with two idols: ego in man and nature in the outer world. Nursi wrote *Sözler* between 1926 and 1929. It represents Nursi's mature thought and can be described as a commentary on Qur'anic meanings. In it, Nursi displays his own original style.

He felt that all works were written through the inspiration of the Qur'an. In *Sözler*, various theological and religious issues are explained through allegorical comparison. By employing a persuasive style and convincing arguments, Nursi aims to develop a spiritual consciousness that detects the signs of the Creator not only in the human soul but also in nature. It touches on various theological subjects, speaking of the issue of the hereafter, resurrection, the miraculousness of the Qur'an, predestination, the ascension of the Prophet, miracles, and the oneness of God with regard to the created world.

Nursi wrote *Mektubât* between 1929 and 1932. It was written in response to various theological questions and is therefore more intimate and informal. It speaks of various issues, such as rituals, Islamic brotherhood, miracles of the Prophet, the spiritual status of the Prophet's Companions, Nursi's own spiritual development, his attitude towards politics and other worldly things, justice, predestination and interpretations of dreams. Nursi wrote most of *Lem'alar* between 1932 and 1934. It deals with various religious issues and is based on his own spiritual experience. It aims to create an intimate relationship between his followers and God, which was considered a sign of reaching perfection in belief. *Şualar*, which was generally written between 1936 and 1940, marks the final form of reflective thought on the universe. It is the most important part of the *Risale*, representing the mature metaphysical thought of Nursi. Its aim is to purify the human spirit by leading it to meditate on nature, to reach a consciousness of divine unity. It speaks of a spiritual journey, and also contains a defence of his writings against charges made by Turkish government officials, who throughout his life made things difficult for him.

Further reading

Cobb, Kelton (1993) 'Revelation, the Discipline of Reason, and Truth in the Works of Said Nursi and Paul Tillich', in Ibrahim M. Abu-Rabi' (ed.) *Islam at the Crossroads: On the life and thought of Bediuzzaman Said Nursi*, Albany, NY: SUNY Press, 129–50.

Vahide, Şükran (1993) 'A Chronology of Said Nursi's Life', in Ibrahim M. Abu-Rabi' (ed.) *Islam at the Crossroads: On the life and thought of Bediuzzaman Said Nursi*, Albany, NY: SUNY Press, xii–xiv.

—— (1993) 'Toward an intellectual biography of Said Nursi', in Ibrahim M. Abu-Rabi' (ed.) *Islam at the Crossroads: On the life and thought of Bediuzzaman Said Nursi*, Albany, NY: SUNY Press, 1–32.

OLIVER LEAMAN

O

OATHS

An oath intensifies a promise to do something or to abstain from doing it by invoking the name of God. Another type of oath is sworn in order to assert the truth of a statement. Both kinds of oaths usually invite divine punishment if the promise is not kept or if the statement turns out to be untrue. In the Qur'an, the divine voice frequently confirms the truth of its words by different kinds of oaths. These Qur'anic oaths pose a number of dogmatic and literary problems.

First, in pre-Islamic society, oaths served ritual functions but were also a common part of everyday discourse. The Qur'an condemns the irreverent use of oaths by Muslims: 'Take not your oaths as mere mutual deceit' (16.94). The believers say about their enemies: 'What, are these the ones, who swore by God most earnest oaths that they were with you [Muhammad]?' (5.53). Already Satan had announced to God in an oath: 'by Thy glory I shall pervert them

[mankind] all together' (38.82). Oaths were apparently so frequently used that the Qur'an seems lenient towards people who use oaths thoughtlessly in casual speech:

> God will not take you to task for a slip in your oaths; but He will take you to task for such bonds as you have made by oaths, whereof the expiation is to feed ten poor persons with the average of the food you serve to your families. (5.89)

Thus a broken oath could be expiated by a meritorious act. There were also pre-Islamic divorce practices, which involved an oath of male sexual abstention (*ila'*), that were modified and regulated by the Qur'an (2.226ff.). Another divorce practice using oaths was called *li'an*: the husband accuses his wife five times of adultery, without having to provide legal proof and without having to face the punishment prescribed for making unprovable allegations of this kind; when the wife, for her part, swears five times that she is innocent, there is no judgement but divorce takes place (24.6–10).

Second, the assertive oath by which the divine voice seems to confirm its own words is one of the most characteristic rhetorical devices of the Qur'an. These oaths form the beginning of a number of *suras*, but also occur within the body of the *suras*. Historically, such oaths seem already to have been part of the oracular language of pre-Islamic soothsayers. In the Bible, God uses oaths to strengthen his words (Numbers 14: 21; Psalms 95: 11). Qur'anic oaths of the type 'By the star when it plunges, your [2nd pers. pl.] comrade [Muhammad] is not astray, neither errs' (53.1) are more frequent in Meccan than in Medinan *suras*. The Qur'anic text swears not only by celestial bodies, but also by sacred places or by times of day and night. These oaths are usually introduced by the particle *wa-*. Sometimes the divine speaker introduces the oath with the words 'No! I swear by ...' (*la uqsimu bi-*), with a notable change to the first-person singular from the first-person plural usually used by the divine speaker when referring to himself. A particularly strong oath is 'By the wise Qur'an, thou [Muhammad] art truly among the Envoys on a straight path' (36.1), in which the divine speaker swears by his own revelation in order to assure Muhammad and the listeners of the truth of Muhammad's prophethood. In some cases, the divine speaker swears 'by Allah' (*tallahi*) (16.63), blurring the line between divine and human speech.

In many instances, however, the assertive character of these oaths seems to fade and to change into a rhetorical means of foreshadowing a later scene in the composition of a *sura*. Such an oath then serves as a literary 'matrix' and gives an associative grounding to the imagery

that follows. This imagery usually draws eschatological scenarios regarding the Day of Judgement and the terrors that will precede it. Examples include oaths invoking awe-inspiring but enigmatic feminine entities, depicted in *sura* 100 as most probably galloping horses during a raid; in other cases (*suras* 37, 51, 77 and 79), the exact meaning was already unclear to Muslim exegesis and there is no agreement about them among European translators and commentators. The enigmatic character of such oaths was most probably intentional and served as a feature of oracular speech.

A dogmatic problem for post-Qur'anic theology is the question of why the divine voice in the Qur'an would use an oath at all, when its word could by definition be nothing but true. The answer given by Ibn Qayyim al-Jawziyya (d. 751/1350) was that the Qur'an was revealed in Arabic, and as Arabs used oaths in their discourse the divine speaker did as the Arabs do.

Further reading

Arberry, A. (1964): *The Koran Interpreted*, trans. with intro., Oxford: Oxford University Press.

Kandil, L. (1996) 'Untersuchungen zu den Schwüren im Koran unter besonderer Berücksichtigung ihrer literarischen Relevanz für die Surenkomposition', in Wild, S. (ed.) *The Qur'an as text*, Leiden: Brill, 41–58.

See also: **fig;** *mubahala*

STEFAN WILD

OPPRESS
see: *zalama*

ORIGINS, ORGANIZATION AND INFLUENCES ON THE QUR'AN

The special focus on the origin of the Qur'an that characterized Western writings on the Qur'an in the early twentieth century was not accidental. The intellectual atmosphere of the time, in which the obsession with origin prevailed, inclined Western scholars to do so. Furthermore, the assumption that Islam is a derivative religion and, accordingly, that the Qur'an is itself a derivative book was a widespread and deeply rooted assumption in Christian Western literature.

Two distinct features of Islam feature in these discussions. First, as Muslims see it, the main elements of Islam and the Qur'an are completely based on *wahy*, that is inspiration, revelation by God to the Prophet. These elements include such teachings of Islam as the monotheistic understanding of divinity and belief in prophecy, angels, the afterlife and so on. Muslims believe that all these derive from God and are not borrowed from any other source. The second feature concerns those elements that are not of Islamic religion but rather of Islamic civilization, established on the main elements of religion but also drawing on elements of surrounding cultures. These include, then, intercultural borrowings. In conversions from one religion to another, converts are sometimes found to carry with them elements of their former practice and understandings; in effect, then, they have imported such elements to the new civilization that Islam, as a religion, established in various parts of the world. It is accepted that Islamic civilization has incorporated and absorbed such elements of other civilizations, and Muslims freely acknowledge influences from other cultures.

The classical Western attitude towards the origin of Islam

The Christian scholastic approach explained the origins of other religions in five different ways as:

1. a creation of evil forces;
2. explicable through historical diffusion from an original monotheism;
3. containing symbolic Christian truths;
4. demonstrably inferior in their practices and beliefs; and
5. expressing the innate, independent spiritual capacity of all humans to come to some understanding of the divine.

(Paden, 1988: 17–25)

Southern, on the other hand, sees three historical stages in the Western Christian approach to Islam. The Christian view of Islam in the first stage (the Age of Ignorance) is a total denial of its validity. In the second stage (the Age of Reason and Hope), the Qur'an is regarded as containing some truth, which is believed to derive from Judaeo-Christian religions and hence the Qur'an is not thought to be original. The third stage is what Southern called 'the moment of vision' (Southern, 1962: 31).

Watt's analysis of the medieval European perception of Islam is not so different from Paden's. Watt sees these elements as the main beliefs of medieval Christianity regarding the nature of Islam:

1. It is a falsehood and a deliberate perversion of the truth.
2. It is a religion of violence and the sword.
3. It is a religion of self-indulgence.
4. Muhammad is the Antichrist.

(Watt, 1972: 73)

In the medieval Christian European perspective, as Swiss theologian Hans Küng expresses it, Islam was 'heretical, a deliberate falsification, a blend of violence and sensuality'. The Prophet, on the other hand, was to medieval Christians 'an impostor, possessed by the devil, the anti-Christ'. The intention, as it seems, is 'to slander the competition' or 'to immunise Christians against competing belief' because 'over and against this caricature of Islam, it was easy to set an idealised picture of Christianity as a religion of truth, peace, love and abstinence' (Küng, 1986: 20).

Western orientalist discourse

In his *Orientalism* (1978), Said states that, in Western discourse, the whole of the Orient is secondary. The Orient and oriental were 'always *like* some aspect of the West' and, similarly, 'Arab, Islamic, Indian, Chinese, or whatever, become repetitious pseudo-incarnations of some great original (Christ, Europe, the West) they were supposed to have been imitating'. In Said's view, this attitude had shown no change: 'Only the source of these rather narcissistic Western ideas about the Orient changed in time not their character'. He observes:

> Thus we will find it commonly believed in the twelfth and thirteenth centuries that Arabia was 'on the fringe of the Christian world, a natural asylum for heretical outlaws' [quoted from Norman Daniel (1960), *Islam and the West*: 246, 96] and that Muhammad was a cunning apostate, whereas in the twentieth century an Orientalist scholar, an erudite specialist [Said refers here to D.B. Macdonald (1933), 'Whither Islam?', *Muslim World* 23], will be the one to point out how Islam is really no more than second-order Arian heresy.

According to Said, this is a process of 'converting the Orient from something into something else' and the orientalist is, as Said sees it, persuaded that he must persist in this time-honoured fashion 'for himself, for the sake of his culture, in some cases for what he believes is the sake of the Oriental'. With particular reference to Islam, Said notes that in orientalist discourse, Islam is judged to be 'a fraudulent new version of Christianity'. According to some orientalist arguments, on the other hand, Islam is seen not as an original religion but 'as a sort of failed Oriental attempt to employ Greek philosophy' (Said, 1978: 62–3).

Modern period

Rationalism, positivism, evolutionism and historicism were in fashion in the nineteenth century. It was the practice in every field of study to understand history as charting progress from the primitive to a developed and more civilized stage. The literature of the time abounded with origin studies concerning this or that social, political, religious or linguistic phenomenon. Titles of treatises of the time characteristically included words such as 'origin', 'development' or 'growth'. Above all, it was Charles Darwin's *Origin of Species* (1859) that gave rise to this trend.

The prevailing evolutionary atmosphere inclined scholars towards genetic questions. It became the fashion, in discussing any phenomenon, to talk about origins. From art to music, from architecture to philosophy, in almost every discipline, scholars developed an interest in origin. As a branch of evolutionary science, anthropology was growing apace, a discipline that was not concerned with the truth or falsehood of religions. Religion began to be regarded as a matter that was subject to evolution. Later, this is all described as 'the obsession with origins'.

Observing the historical development of Western thought, we find that methodological and theoretical developments in social sciences are paralleled within the field of religious studies, in particular in Semitic and biblical studies. In turn, such developments influenced Western Islamic studies. The typical historicist approach to the rise of Islam came from the Jewish scholar Abraham Geiger with his *Was hat Mohammed aus dem Judentum aufgenommen?* (1833). Here Geiger employs historicism, with an emphasis on the dependence of the Prophet on Jewish tradition. Arent Jan Wensinck, in his *Mohammeden de Joden te Medina* (1908), and Ch. C. Torrey, in his *The Jewish Foundation of Islam* (1933), also contributed to the theory of Jewish influence in the establishment of Islam. On the other hand, J. Wellhausen (*Reste Arabischen Heidentums*, 1897), Tor Andrae (*Der Ursprung des Islams and das Christentum*, 1926), Richard Bell (*The Origin of Islam in its Christian Environment*, 1926) and Karl Ahrens (*Muhammad als Religionsstifter*, 1935) promoted the dependence of Islam on Christianity.

An important stage in the study of the origins of the Qur'an was John Wansbrough's publication of two works: *Qur'anic Studies: Sources and Methods of Scriptural Interpretation* (1977) and *The Sectarian Milieu: Content and Composition of Islamic Salvation History* (1978). Abandoning the historical-philological approach, Wansbrough applies literary theory to the study of Islamic sources. Wansbrough questions the traditional Muslim chronological framework that Western scholarship also adopted. To Wansbrough, the Qur'an was a composition that came out of Jewish-Muslim sectarian polemics during the second century of Islam. It is not the product of the Prophet but of the early Muslim community somewhere in Northern Arabia. Although Wansbrough's own student John Burton believes that the Qur'an took its shape and form at the time of the Prophet himself, many other students of Wansbrough, such as Andrew Rippin, Norman Calder and Gerald Hawting,

followed in their teacher's footsteps. Crone and Cook followed the same line in their suspicions about Muslim historiography and their attempt to reconstruct early Muslim history in *Hagarism: The Making of the Islamic World* (1977).

Two books published in English at the end of the twentieth century not only indicate that the topic still survives in Western discourse, but also show how important the subject has been for Western Christian polemics against Islam. The first, published by 'Ibn Warraq' (a pseudonym), deals with *The Origins of the Koran* (1998); the second, also by 'Ibn Warraq', tackles *The Historical Muhammad* (2000).

These scholars almost all come from a theological background, have church and missionary connections, and almost all, alongside their scholarly interest, had missionary and theological motives in studying the origin of the Qur'an. Having claimed that Islam is a combination of various religions and cultures, they seek to prove that Islam and the Qur'an are mainly dependent on Judaeo-Christian sources, as this enhances the prestige of those influencing elements. As some of these scholars were ordained priests and some were missionaries, their aim and their common project in seeking to identify the origin of the Qur'an are inescapably polemical and apologetic.

Generally speaking, in such discussions of the origin of the Qur'an, the Prophet is kept at the centre of the discussion and it is to the Prophet himself that authorship of the Qur'an is typically attributed. These scholars all share the view that, as the author of the Qur'an, the Prophet Muhammad came under the influence of both Judaism and Christianity. In this context, they believe that both Jewish and Christian sources served as the inspiration of the Prophet, but it was mainly Judaism that, as Muir puts it, 'has given its colour' to Islam. The Jewish influence is regarded as being so intense that Islam, for Tisdall, 'might almost be described as a heretical form of later Judaism'. Although, for Torrey, Islam is definitely an eclectic religion and different elements played their role in establishing it, he argues strongly for Jewish influence on the Qur'an and Islam, and just as decisively rejects Christian influence. Even the Christian elements in the Qur'an came through either Jewish instruction or the existing culture of Arabia. Muhammad, he claims, anyway did not distinguish the two religions and at first considered Christianity to be a 'Jewish sect'.

Contrary to Islamic understanding, Western scholarship portrays the Prophet as a person who could read and write. Conferring on the Prophet the authorship of the Qur'an allows these scholars to argue that to understand the Qur'an one must understand the Prophet. To understand the Prophet, however, one is bound to consult the Qur'an, as well as tradition (*hadith*).

These are very important indications of a typical Christian and, in particular, Protestant understanding of Islam. In their view, for example, although the Prophet could read and write, he did not use written sources, but rather received the information orally. In addition, they feel that it was secondary sources – rabbinical and apocryphal traditions – that mainly influenced the Prophet. The authentic Gospel and Old Testament were beyond the Prophet's reach, since 'Gospel Christianity' and 'Old Testament Judaism' did not exist in the Arabian peninsula, but rabbinical and Judaeo-Christian traditions were in circulation. So the Prophet did not come across the Bible directly, nor did he have formal knowledge of Judaism and Christianity. From all this, it is evident that the Western view of the Qur'an and Islam is a view refracted through the conditioning lens of Christian tradition.

Critique of the study of origin

Watt, as one of the Western scholars who aimed to understand Islam from within, takes a slightly different position. Although he does not agree with the orthodox Muslim view that the Qur'an is entirely supernatural in origin, Watt does not seem to be happy to talk of 'sources' of the Qur'an. Therefore, Watt is both sympathetic in approaching Islam and critical of Western scholarship.

In Watt's view, the influence of Judaeo-Christian sources was on the Arabian peninsula; it was not directly but indirectly instrumental in the existence of the Qur'an and Islam. That is to say, the Bible or Judaeo-Christian sources are not the direct sources of the Qur'an, but helped to create the environment in which the Qur'an came into existence. In this context, as a source of Islam and the Qur'an, Watt invokes Jung's theory of the collective unconscious, asserting that the Qur'an is also a product of the collective unconscious. This theory takes away Muhammad's active role in producing the Qur'an and ascribes it instead to the collective unconscious of the community.

As regards Judaeo-Christian influence, Watt underlines the close literary and historical relation between Islam and the Judaeo-Christian religions, declaring that the Qur'an (as it admits itself) stands within the tradition of Judaeo-Christian monotheism. Watt seems to support what he considers to be the view of some Christians, namely that the Qur'an is the work of divine activity. Muhammad, as Watt frequently declares, is a sincere and genuine prophet, and the Qur'an is 'in some sense the product of divine initiative and therefore revelation'.

Western scholarship at the beginning of the twentieth century, Watt acknowledges, was 'excessively concerned with the attempt to discover the "sources" of Qur'anic statements'. The influence of Darwin's evolutionary theories was considerable when it came to a discussion of the origin of the Qur'an for, in view of early Islam's Judaeo-Christian geographical neighbourhood, and taking account of the religious and intellectual ties between Islam and the Judaeo-Christian religions and between the Qur'an and the Bible as texts, Darwin's legacy encouraged Western scholars to find the origin of Islam and the Qur'an in a Judaeo-Christian context.

It is one thing to discover the origins of the Qur'an in the Judaeo-Christian environment, but it is quite another to characterize the Qur'an as 'a poor selection of ideas from the Bible'. There is unmistakably an element of religious partisanship involved here. It clearly owes little to any genuinely 'evolutionary' approach to considering and configuring the origins of Islam. Western scholarship 'presents the Qur'an as a selection of ideas from Judaism and Christianity with little distinctive merit and no novelty or originality'. This negative Western attitude towards Islam and the Qur'an persisted, in Watt's view, as 'a belated survival from the war propaganda of the crusading period'.

Watt charges Western scholars with abusing scholarship to confirm their own prejudice. The Western mentality of the time worked under the assumption that, as Watt put it, showing 'what a thing originally was' or 'what it was derived from' provided the most important lead towards an understanding of 'what it really was'. Watt, however, points out that 'the study of sources does not explain away the ideas whose sources are found, nor does it detract from their truth and validity'. These studies of origins do no more than satisfy intellectual curiosity. Watt illustrates the 'fallacy of this view' with the test-case example of Shakespeare's *Hamlet*. In Watt's opinion, to know which story materials Shakespeare had read as the 'sources' of *Hamlet* is unlikely to affect our appreciation of the play itself. So the Qur'an is, in Watt's view, arguably an entity that might similarly and legitimately be treated, in the last analysis, as independent of its sources – sources whose influence may nonetheless be acknowledged.

Regarding the origins of the Qur'an or of Islam in general, it has been underlined by Muslim scholars that 'the surviving idea, in the West, of copying by Muhammad, cannot be conclusively proved'. The Western argument is mainly based on parallels, but parallels are very deceptive: both versions may, for example, be derived from a third common source. Furthermore, Muslim scholars have asked Christian Western scholars the following question: If the source of revelation is one and the same (that is God), what prevents God revealing to Muhammad concepts similar to those which exist in earlier scriptures?

Although, Rodinson believes, studies of the origins of Islam are crucial, as 'Islam was not born in a sealed container in an environment sterilized against the germs of the other ideologies', there are dangers arising from excess in this kind of investigation: one danger is neglecting the originality of Islam; a second is that a study of influence cannot fully explain origin.

Essentially, earlier arguments about Islam and the Qur'an were based on parallels between them and other religions and scriptures. 'When scholars investigate the apparent transmission of material from one monotheistic scripture to another,' Waldman notes, 'they

479

tend to assume that earlier materials are normative and later ones derivative' (Waldman, 1985: 1). Waldman, in her analysis of *sura Yusuf*, emphatically expresses the literary differences between the Bible and the Qur'an, and shows her preference for treating biblical and Qur'anic accounts of the story as independent rather than dependent one on the other. Brannon M. Wheeler, too, challenges this earlier/later dichotomy in his evaluation of the story of Moses and the 'servant of God' (18.65–82). Wheeler is convinced that the story does not depend, as assumed by Wensinck in his article, on Jewish sources ('al-Khadir', *EI*: 902–3), but vice versa: the Jewish texts adapted the story from Islamic sources (Wheeler, 1998). In recent works, we observe that scholars have started to underline the mutual influences, rather arguing for one-way traffic, between Islam and Judaeo-Christian, biblical religions (Lazarus-Yafeh, 1981).

References and further reading

Ahrens, K. (1935) *Muhammad als Religionsstifter*, Berlin: Deutsche Morgenländischen Gesellschaft.

Bell, R. (1968) *The origin of Islam in its Christian environment*, London: Frank Cass.

Bennett, Clinton (1992) *Victorian Images of Islam*, London: Grey Seal.

Buaben, Jabal M. (1996) *Image of the Prophet Muhammad in the West*, Leicester: The Islamic Foundation.

Crone, P. and Cook, M. (1977) *Hagarism: the Making of the Islamic world*, Cambridge: Cambridge University Press.

Geiger, A. (1833) *Was hat Mohammed aus dem Judentum aufgenommen?*, Bonn: Prize Essay.

Hourani, Albert (1991) *Islam in European Thought*, Cambridge: Cambridge University Press.

Ibn Warraq (1990) *The Origins of the Koran*, Amherst: Prometheus.

—— (2000) *The Quest for the Historical Mohammad*, Amherst: Prometheus.

Küng, Hans (1986) *Christianity and the World Religions*, Garden City, NY: Doubleday.

Lazarus-Yafeh, Hava (1981) 'Judaism and Islam, Some Aspects of Mutual Cultural Influences', in *Some Religious Aspects of Islam*, Leiden: E.J. Brill.

Paden, W.E. (1988) *Religious Worlds*, Boston: Beacon Press.

Rodinson, M. (1977) *Islam and Capitlaism*, Hammondsworth: Penguin.

Said, E. (1978) *Orientalism*, New York: Pantheon.

Southern, R.W. (1962) *Western Views of Islam in the Middle Ages*, Cambridge, MA: Harvard University Press.

Torrey, C. (1933) *The Jewish Foundation of Islam*, New York: Jewish Institute of Religion.

Waldman, Marilyn R (1985) 'New Approaches to "Biblical" Materials in the Qur'an': *Muslim World* 75: 1–16.

Wansbrough, J. (1977) *Qur'anic Studies: Sources and Methods of Scriptural Interpretation*, Oxford: Oxford University Press.

—— (1978) *The Sectarian Milieu: Content and Composition of Islamic Salvation History*, Oxford: Oxford University Press.

Watt, W (1972) *The Influence of Islam on Medieval Europe*, Edinburgh: Edinburgh University Press.

Wellhausen, J. (1897) *Reste Arabischen Heidentums*, Berlin: thesis.

Wensinck, J. (1908) *Mohammed de Joden te medina*, Leiden: thesis.

Wheeler, Brannon M. (1998) 'The Jewish Origins of Qur'an', *Journal of American Oriental Society* 118, 2: 153–71.

BILAL GÖKKIR

P

PARABLES

In many ways, it can be said that the language of all scriptures is a language of parables. Many of these parables are closely interlinked, creating the impression of religious intertextuality or a sort of universal Book of Faith. Because of their complexity, perhaps certain truths can be conveyed to man only by means of parables or allegories (Asad, 1980: 541). The Qur'an explicitly refers to this universality of parables: 'And for each of them [the prophets], we struck parables' (25.39). As scholars have noted, many of the parables in the Qur'an are reminiscent of the Bible, especially Psalms. For example, in 14.24, the comparison between a 'good word' (*kalimatan tayyibatan*) and a 'good tree' (*shajaratin tayyibatin*) is said to be reminiscent of the comparison of a good man to a tree in Psalm 1. The famous Throne Verse or *ayat al-Kursi* bears echoes of Isaac 66: 1: 'Heaven is my throne and the earth is my footstool'

(Frieling, 1978: 128). Indeed, in 48.29, two parables from the Torah (*Tawrat*) and the Gospels are cited as examples of good or righteous people of all religions. Although parables have often been defined as 'didactic' stories that answer a question or point out a moral, it is not the didacticism that makes them so important to the language of religion, but rather the cognitive role that they play in illustrating abstract religious concepts. Like charts and diagrams, parables set out to make the unfamiliar appear familiar, the abstract concrete. A 'true' parable parallels, detail for detail, the situation that calls forth that parable for illustration (Holman and Harmon, 1986: 357).

In the Qur'an, parables (*mathal*, pl. *amthal*) are used extensively, in a variety of forms and covering many themes: 'And indeed We have explained for people in this Qur'an every kind of parable (*mathalin*), but most people [accept nothing] but disbelief' (17.89). In various other places, parables are highlighted as instruments of cognition and as a means of providing a 'better' explanation of all things: 'And every time they come to you with a parable (*mathalin*), we bring you the truth and a better explanation' (25.33). From this, it should not be concluded that it is easy to understand some of the more elaborate comparisons presented in the parables. In fact, many of the Prophet Muhammad's opponents were perplexed by them. They seemed to be taunting them, daring them to understand the gist of the comparison. A number of verses in the Qur'an contain the potent question: 'What does God intend with such a parable?' (2.26; 74.31). Indeed, one often has to think about the grounds of the comparisons. Take, for example, 3.59: 'Verily the likeness of Jesus before God is like the likeness of Adam. He created him from dust then said to him, "Be", and he was.' The likeness here between Jesus and Adam cannot be deduced simply from reading the parable; one has to work to understand it. This is what Muslim scholars call *zahir lafz al-jumla*. The pivotal word is 'created', and the connection conveyed by this parable is not that God created both Jesus and Adam from dust, since all men are created thus, but the deeper fact that they are alike in their origin – neither were born of two parents.

It is important to note at the outset that the word *mathal* is not only used to denote parables in the Qur'an; in fact, it introduces a variety of rhetorical devices, such as examples, similes, metaphors, proverbs and stories. In essence, the word is derived from the preposition *mithl*, meaning 'like', and it is most often collocated with the particle *ka*, which is equivalent to 'as if' or 'as it were'. When prefixed to a noun, this particle is called *kaf al-tashbih* (the letter *kaf* of resemblances or metaphors), such as in the schematic construction

'*mathalu ka*-[word] [word] *ka*-[word]' (e.g. 14.26). The word *mithl* and all its derivatives occur more than 200 times in the Qur'an; obviously not all of these are instances of parables. Many of the longer and more elaborate parables start with the formulaic construction: *mathalahum ka-mathali* ('their example is like the example of'). Other formulaic constructions include 'Strike for them a parable (*mathalan*)' (*wa adrib lahum mathalan*) (36.13); 'And God strikes parables (*alamthala*) for men in the hope that they may take heed' (*wa yadribu allahu alamthala lil-nasi la-'alahum yatadhakkarun*) (14.25); and 'Dost thou not see how thy Lord has struck a parable (*mathalan*)' (*alam tara kayfa daraba allahu mathalan*) (14.24).

The material of Qur'anic parables is drawn from a huge variety of spheres. However, familiar entities in the natural world are the ones most often used to explicate religious concepts. These entities include rocks, animals, plants, rain, lightning, thunder, winds, tempests, mountains, fire, stars, the earth, the sky and the seas. In 18.45, for example, worldly life is compared to the fall of rain and the cycle of vegetation:

> And strike for them a *mathal* of the worldly life: it is like the water which we send down from the sky, and then the plants of the earth mingle with it. But then they become dry and broken and are scattered by the winds. And God is capable of all things.

To illustrate the idea that a disbeliever's good deeds are always in vain, a parable is set up comparing his deeds to 'ashes on which the winds blow furiously as in a tempestuous day' (14.18). Another short parable criticizes those who worship idols by comparing their action to that of a spider building its web (29.41). We are also told that God is not ashamed to strike

parables ranging from the most insignificant of creatures, the gnat (ba'uda), to the
very highest (2.26). Of course, this is
reminiscent of the biblical imagery used
by Jesus: 'Woe unto you, scribes and
Pharisees, hypocrites! ... which strain at
a gnat, and swallow a camel' (Matthew
23: 23, 24).

One major difficulty facing the reader
is trying to distinguish between parables
and extended similes, examples and
narratives, since (as noted above) the
word mathal seems equally to be applied
to all of them. As Paret (1983: 201)
explains, the Qur'an is rich in images. In
general, these images are used only for
purposes of comparison and are not to
be identified with the object or event in
question. When an image denotes
directly the object or event that it originally served to paraphrase and elucidate,
it becomes a metaphor. Examples of
short similes can be found in 22.2, for
example, where the horrors of doomsday
are presented in a series of very brief but
vivid images:

> On the Day you behold it, every nursing
> mother shall neglect what she has nursed,
> and every pregnant woman shall deliver
> her load, and you shall see people drunk,
> and yet they are not drunk, but severe
> will be the torment of God.

But how can we distinguish between a
metaphor and the more elaborate and
didactic parable? The distinction, Paret
maintains, is not always easy to make.
Perhaps the basic difference between
parables and other forms of comparison
in the Qur'an is one of length: an extended simile presents a very brief story, a
parable can extend for many verses.

The longest parable in the Qur'an is
the parable of the Two Gardens (18.32–
44), which extends for twelve verses:

> And strike for them a mathal of two men.
> To one of them, We gave two gardens of
> grapes and We surrounded them with
> date-palms; and We set out between
> them sown fields. Each of these gardens
> yielded its produce, and failed naught in
> any wise.

The real climax of the story occurs
when, in a moment of arrogant pride,
the man says to his friend: 'I do not
think this will ever perish. Nor do I
think the Hour will ever come and if
indeed I am returned to my Lord, surely
I shall find better than this when I
return to Him.' What we are witnessing
here is the actual moment when a man
of faith falls into disbelief – there seems
to be, in fact, only a thin line separating
joy and arrogance, righteousness and
sin. The protagonist in this parable does
not seem to be doing anything sinful in
terms of evil conduct; his error was one
of speech, as his friend tells him: 'It were
better for you to say, when you entered
your garden: As God wills. There is no
power except in God, when you saw me
less than you in wealth and children.'
The moral of the parable is finally ham-
mered home in verse 46, when we are
told that 'Wealth and children are the
adornments of worldly life – but the
abiding things, the deeds of righteousness, are better with your lord in
reward and better in hope.'

It is important to note that, when seen
together, the parables in the Qur'an
form a network of related ideas and
syntactic constructions which, when
juxtaposed, can decode the meanings of
difficult passages. Take, for example,
6.7–8, where the basic attempt is to
illustrate how disbelievers are bent on
denying the manifest truth of the
Qur'an. This theme can be found in many
places in the text, but the key to understanding it lies within the elaborate and
intertextual parable, which involves the

opening of the gate of the heavens and ascending/descending upon a ladder:

> Had we sent down upon you a book on a parchment, so that they could feel it with their hands, those who disbelieve would have said: 'This is naught but manifest sorcery.' They say: 'Why has an angel not been sent down unto him?'

In 52.44, the notion of concrete pieces of the heavens falling from the sky is introduced: 'And if they were to see a piece of the heaven (*kisfan*) falling down, they would say: "Stacked up clouds".' This complete denial of palpable truths is echoed in another parable in 15.14–15: 'And if we opened to them a gate in heaven and they were to keep on ascending thereto, yet they would say: "Our eyes have been dazzled, nay, we are a people bewitched".' The same storyline is present, with the same protagonists (the disbelievers and God) and the same heaven out of which God sends his messages, but the main difference is that the gate (*bab*) of heaven is now clearly present and, instead of a book on parchment, we now infer the presence of an actual ladder (*sullaman*) upon which they are asked to ascend. In 6.35, this ladder is provided:

> And if their aversion is hard on you, then, if you can, seek a tunnel in the earth or a ladder (*sullaman*) to the sky, so that you may bring them a sign. But had God willed, he would have gathered them to the guidance.

Seen in totality, these repetitive images form an interconnected parable running through the pages of the Qur'an.

The most famous parable in the Qur'an is the Parable of Light (24.35), which begins: 'God is the Light of the heavens and the earth; the likeness of his light is as a niche, wherein is a lamp. The lamp in a glass, the glass as it were a glittering star.' This verse has been the subject of much speculation, but what is most striking about the parable is the complex effect that it creates. What we find is a series of embedded structures, one within the other, 'light upon light', almost *ad infinitum*. Commentators usually perceive the parable to have ended at 24.35. However, it in fact extends for five more verses. At 24.40 we are presented with the opposing theme of 'darkness' (*zulumatin*) and the imagery is not one of recursiveness, but of a stacked or multi-decked darkness in an abysmal ocean of 'waves upon waves'. Separating these two diametrically opposed parables, we have the parable of the mirage in an open desert (*qi'in*), which offers a new form, a form that speaks of endless linearity.

Many of the more complex parables are concerned with illustrating God's attitude towards polytheists and hypocrites. A good example is 22.31, where disbelief is compared to falling or plummeting from the sky: 'And whoever assigns partners to God it is as if he had fallen from the sky, and the birds of prey had snatched him or the wind had thrown him to a far and desolate place.' What are we to make of this parable? Basically the comparison sets out to illustrate the physical torments awaiting people who associate other partners with God. Three basic stages can be deduced: a tumultuous fall from grace, horrific torture, and lingering death and despair. The first stage is compared to a literal plummeting from the sky. The second introduces a bird of prey (perhaps a vulture or eagle) snatching at the flesh of the idolater in mid-air. The third stage sees the idolater being finally taken away to a far-off nest to be feasted on. This highly elaborate parable is often explained by a tradition which reports that when the angels carry a disbeliever's body after his death and they ascend to the sky, the gates of heaven refuse to open and his soul is thus hurled from on high. The use of the 'or' (*aw*) conjunction seems to suggest two options for the idolater: either a horrific mid-air death or a lingering one of torture.

Something of the complexity of Qur'anic parables can be illustrated by the parable of the fire-kindler (2.17), one of the most quoted parables and one that has been discussed extensively by many scholars. It sets out to illustrate the actions of hypocrites who confess their faith in front of the faithful, but when they are alone with their 'own devils' they renounce, insisting that they had only believed in mockery. The point being made is that they have elected to purchase darkness and loss rather than light and guidance. It starts with the formulaic *mathalahum kamathal*:

> Their parable is that of one who kindled a fire but when it illuminated all around him, God took away their light and left them in utter darkness, where they cannot see. Deaf, dumb, blind; they cannot turn back. Or [like the parable] of a cloud-burst from the sky within which is darkness and thunder and lightning, they place their fingers into their ears to ward off the peals of thunder in fear of death and God encompasses all who deny the truth. The lightning well-nigh snatches their vision; whenever it lights their path they walk therein and whenever it darkens upon them they stand still. And if God willed he would indeed have taken away their hearing and their sight. For verily God is capable of all things.

Controversy about this parable centres on the difficulty of comparing a whole group of hypocrites to just one fire-kindler. This has led some commentators to discuss at length why there is a sudden shift from the third-person singular pronoun (one/him) to third-person plural (their/them/they). This controversy is partially cleared up when we realize that most commentators erroneously associate the fire-kindler with the hypocrites, while in fact he is not from among them, but rather someone who is meant to resemble the Prophet, a person with a message of light that should have brightened the darkness encircling these people. In fact, the fire he kindles does succeed in illuminating the surroundings. What is then taken is not that original light that he had provided but the inner light of the hypocrites. We never see the fire-kindler again in the parable and we must assume that he has accomplished his role as fire-kindler. Presumably, the place is still lit, but the hypocrites are unaware of the light and have to eagerly await whatever small glimpses of guidance are offered by the lightning.

One of the first problems thus appears to be determining what the basis of comparison is in this parable. What specific action of the hypocrites is the parable illustrating? Is it their inability to distinguish darkness from light, the erroneous path from the path of guidance? Or is it their extreme fear of death? Or perhaps it is their constant shifting between right and wrong? Or is it really all of these simultaneously, hence the elaborateness and length of the parable?

References and further reading
Asad, M. (trans.) (1980) *The Message of the Qur'an*, Gibraltar: Dar al-andalus.
Frieling, R. (1978) *Christianity and Islam*, Edinburgh: Floris Books.
Holman, C.H. and Harman, W. (1986) *A Handbook to Literature*, New York: Macmillan.
Paret, R. (1983) 'The Qur'an: Language and style', in A.F.L. Beeston *et al.* (eds) *The Cambridge History of Arabic Literature: Arabic literature to the end of the Umayyad period*, Cambridge: Cambridge University Press, 196–205.

See also: *aya*; **language and the Qur'an**; *mathal*; **style in the Qur'an**

AFNAN H. FATANI

PARADISE

Paradise (*al-janna*; literally, 'garden') has two aspects. First, it is the garden that was created for Adam and his wife, and from which they were evicted after falling prey to Satan's temptation. Second, it is the abode of righteous believers after the Day of Judgement at the end of time, given to them in compensation for their good deeds. The first is a paradise lost at the beginning of human history, the second a projected eschatological place of utopian and perpetual bliss at the end of human history. The rhetorical strategy of describing eternal bliss in the Qur'an aims at winning the hearts of those who do not yet believe and fortifying in their convictions those who already believe. Eschatological paradise is, in contradistinction to Adam's paradise, depicted with a vivid wealth of sensual details, and each space is usually clearly identified.

Adam's paradise

The Qur'an tells us little about the paradise of Adam and his (in the Qur'an) nameless wife. This paradise is the space of sinless humanity and the setting for two main events, on which the text concentrates. God announces to the angels his intention to create Adam as a vicegerent (*khalifa*) on earth (2.30ff.; 38.71ff.). God creates Adam from clay and teaches Adam 'all the names' (2.31). Then one of the angels (Iblis) rebels against God's command to bow before Adam (2.34). The Qur'an does not specify when in this order of events Adam's wife is created. Some commentators believe that Adam's wife was created before he entered paradise, which could mean that Adam's creation and the rebellion of Iblis did not take place there. The different versions of the Qur'anic story of Adam's fall concur in that the temptation of Adam and his wife takes place in paradise. (The main elements of this story are shared by Jewish scripture (Genesis 2: 8–3: 24), but there are many important differences in the details.) When Adam and his wife are evicted from paradise and 'go down' to earth (2.36; 7.24–25; 20.123), human history begins – outside paradise. We learn little about the garden except that there were trees with fruit in it, among them 'the tree of eternity' (20.120). The exact relationship between Adam's garden on the one hand and paradise in the hereafter on the other is not dealt with in the Qur'an. Post-Qur'anic theology tends to teach that paradise has eternally existed or that it had an existence outside of time.

Eschatological paradise

The topography of paradise

In contrast to the paucity of descriptive detail concerning Adam's pre-historic 'garden', we find a wealth of Qur'anic information about paradise after the Day of Judgement. *Al-janna* is the most frequent name of this abode of the elect, who are called 'the dwellers of the garden' (*ashab al-janna*) (46.14). This paradise is a utopian counter-world to normal human life on the Arabian peninsula, where garden stands against desert, abundance of water against drought, shade against insufferable heat, a life of luxury and peace against hardship and fear. The gates of paradise are guarded by angels (39.73), its breadth 'is as heaven and earth' (3.133). In many respects this paradise is also a counter-space to hell. The spaces of paradise and hell lie next to each other (57.13). The topographies of hell and paradise are, to a large extent, symmetrically constructed.

The expression 'the gardens of Eden' (*jannat 'Adn*) corresponds to the biblical *gan Eden* (Genesis 2: 15). But the Qur'an never uses this expression for Adam's garden (13.23 etc.). Another, much rarer Qur'anic word for 'paradise' is *firdaws* (18.107; 23.11) – ultimately a loan from an Iranian language, which, via the Greek *paradeisos*, was taken over into most European languages.

The pleasures of paradise

Paradise has an eternally moderate climate (76.13), shade is everlasting, grapes and pomegranates abound, rivers of wine, milk, honey and fresh water flow through it (47.15), recalling the four rivers of paradise in Genesis 2.10–14. The believers can call for every kind of fruit (44.55), they receive 'what their souls desire' (43.71), they are clad in silk and brocade, they wear golden bracelets and recline upon 'close-wrought couches' (56.15). Immortal youths offer flesh and fowl, they serve wine out of 'goblets, ewers and a cup from the spring' (56.18).

The virgins of paradise (houris)

The word *huri* is derived from the Arabic adjective *hur* or *hur 'in*, both plurals meaning 'women, who have wide eyes with a marked contrast of intense white and deep black'. This is a mark of beauty. Believers, in reward for their righteousness, will be wed to houris: 'We [God] shall espouse them [pl. masc.] to wide-eyed houris' (44.54); 'Perfectly We formed them [pl. fem.], perfect, and We made them spotless virgins, chastely amorous, like of age for the Companions of the Right' (56.35–38). They are 'like hidden pearls' (56.23), 'maidens restraining their glances, untouched before them by any man or *jinn*' (55.56).

Sexuality, therefore, is like eating and drinking an essential and integral part of the anthropocentric imagery of paradise. Sexuality is always consummated, never postponed. The sensuality of the Qur'anic paradise and especially the houris were a classical topos of Christian anti-Islamic polemics. Muslim theology and piety developed the Qur'anic ideas further. Al-Ghazali (d. 1111) taught that sexuality in this world was but a faint prefiguration of the bliss of paradise. Speculations about the number of houris assigned to the Prophets and about the physical aspects of their eternal virginity coalesced with the idea that the Muslim martyr should be inspired in Holy War by the image of the houris. This kind of exegesis has been rekindled by militant Muslim groups in the 1980s and 1990s, especially in connection with suicide attacks. On the other hand, there is an old exegetical tradition that regards the houris and other parts of the Qur'anic description of paradise as metaphors or allegories. According to this tradition, the descriptions of paradise were – like those of hell – not to be taken literally. Some modern and feminist exegetes, bothered by the predominantly male character of the bliss of paradise, have proposed that pious women can expect male houris.

The origin of the idea of the virgins of paradise has been widely debated in non-Muslim scholarship. Zoroastrian ideas, a misunderstanding of Syriac patristic texts, and Christian devotional paintings of women have been suggested as possible sources. Luxenberg (2000) again took up the Syriac hypothesis, arguing that the Qur'anic houris owe their existence to a misunderstanding of an Aramaic word for grapes.

Interaction between God and man in paradise

God greets the elect in paradise with the word 'peace' (36.58). There they are 'in the presence of a king, omnipotent' (54.55); they live in God's good pleasure, which is greater than gardens and rivers (9.72). The verses 'Upon that day faces shall be radiant, gazing upon their Lord' (75.22–23) have, by some commentators, been interpreted as confirmation that the elect would see God in paradise. Other exegetes countered by referring to the verse: 'The eyes attain Him not' (6.103). This was a famous point of dispute between Mu'tazili and orthodox thinkers. In general, the description of God's interaction with the believers in paradise pales in comparison to the vivid anthropocentric images of sensual delight mentioned above.

References and further reading

Afsaruddin, A. (2002) 'Garden', *EQ*, Vol. 2, 282–7.
al-Azmeh, A. (1995) 'Rhetoric for the Senses: A consideration of Muslim paradise narratives', *JAL* 26: 215–31.
El-Saleh, S. (1971) *La vie future selon le Coran*, Paris: Vrin.
Jarrar, M. (2002) 'Houris', *EQ*, Vol. 2, 456–7.
Luxenberg, C. (2000) *Die syro-aramäische Lesart des Koran: Ein Beitrag zur Entschlüsselung der Koransprache*, Berlin: Das Arabische Buch, 221ff.

See also: **heaven; houris**

STEFAN WILD

PARENTS

The Qur'an, which assumes that the family is the basic unit of society, lays out specific duties for parents. It commands them to maintain, protect and guide their children, showing tenderness and mercy. The responsibility for maintenance of their wives that is incumbent upon husbands also applies to children: 'And the man to whom the child belongs shall be responsible for their [the mother's] food and clothing equitably' (2.233). Maintenance consists of food, clothing and shelter, in accordance with the level of the man's wealth. But mothers are also required to care for their children. The Qur'an stipulates that they must nurse for two years, if possible (2.233). If nursing becomes burdensome, and the parents agree on it, a substitute may be found.

Parental responsibility for the support of children continues after death, through bequests of accumulated wealth. The Qur'an specifies inheritance shares:

> For men there is a share of what parents and near relatives leave, and for women there is a share of what parents and near relatives leave, whether it is a little or a lot, a fixed share. And when relatives and orphans and the poor are present at the division, give them from it and speak to them judicious words. And let those who fear, if they leave behind them their own weak children, for them, fear God and say the appropriate word ... God commands you concerning your children: A male shall have as much as the share of two females, but if there are females [only], more than two, then they get two-thirds of what is left, and if there is one, she shall have the half. (4.8–12)

The disproportion between female and male shares is a reflection of the historical context in which the Qur'an was revealed: daughters were expected to marry and be supported by their husbands; sons, on the other hand, were expected to marry and support not only their nuclear families but their extended families as well.

The Qur'an pays particular attention to parental responsibility for daughters, criticizing disrespect for them as unjust:

When one of them is given the good news of [the birth of] a girl, his face darkens as he suppresses his unhappiness. He hides from people because of the evil the good news meant to him [and wonders] whether to keep her in disgrace or push her into the earth. Indeed, evil is what they judge. (16.58–59; see also 43.18)

It forbids female infanticide, a common practice in pre-Islamic Arabia. The Qur'an warns of a time 'when the girl buried alive will be asked for what sin she was killed?' (81.9–10).

The Qur'an also calls for respect and kindness on the part of children toward parents. When recounting the failures of earlier generations to submit to the will of God, it highlights the failure to behave with 'kindness to parents and to relatives and orphans and the poor' (2.83). The Qur'an tells believers to 'worship God and do not associate anything with him, and be kind to parents and relatives and orphans and the needy and neighbours who are relatives and neighbours who are strangers and companions and travellers and slaves' (4.36; also 17.23). Children are to show both respect and gratitude toward parents: 'And we have required people concerning parents – mothers bear you in great weakness and nurse you for two years – "Give thanks to me and to your parents. To me you will return"' (31.14; also 46.15). People who respond this way are described as the righteous, those who will dwell in paradise.

Children are also required to bequeath property to surviving parents, and the Qur'an again specifies exact shares:

And parents shall each have a sixth of the inheritance if [the deceased] has a child, but if he has no child and his parents are his heirs, then his mother gets a third, and if he has brothers and sisters, then his mother gets one sixth [of what is left] after any bequests he may have made and debts [have been paid]. You do not know which of your fathers and your children is nearer to you in benefit [so this] fixing [of shares] is from God. Indeed, God is all-knowing, wise. (4.11)

Nevertheless, the Qur'an cautions children not to obey wayward parents: 'We have certainly admonished people to be good to parents, but should they exert pressure upon you to associate others with Me [in things] of which you have no knowledge, then do not obey them' (29.8; see also 4.135). But even when children cannot obey parents because they are unrighteous, they must be respectful and kind towards them. The story of Abraham is recounted to make this point:

'O my father, why do you worship what does not hear, see or help you? O my father, knowledge has come to me that has not come to you, so follow me and I will guide you to an even path. O my father, do not serve Satan, the rebel against the merciful one. O my father, I am afraid that a punishment from the merciful one will take hold of you, as a friend of Satan.' And he answered, 'Do you turn away from my gods, Abraham? If you do not stop, I will punish you, so leave me alone.' And [Abraham] said, 'Peace to you. I will ask forgiveness of my Lord for you. He is merciful to me. And I will stay away from you and from what you call upon that is not God, and I will pray to my Lord; let my prayers to my Lord not be disappointed.' (19.43–48; also 9.114; 60.4)

See also: **suffering**

TAMARA SONN

PEACE

Salam (peace) comes from the same root as *islam* (peaceful submission to God) and *muslim* (the one who peacefully submits). The root letters *s/l/m/* are the

489

basis of Islam's conception of itself, referring to its objective as peace, internal as well as external, temporal as well as eternal, existential as well as philosophical. *Al-salam*, referring to God as the source of all peace, is one of the ninety-nine names of God mentioned in the Qur'an (59.23). In the Qur'an, peace means not just the absence of war, but also the eradication of the grounds for conflict and corruption. Peace is the true purpose of God's creation. Although peace is the objective, war is not entirely avoidable. Islam is not a pacifist religion, thus peace in the Qur'an does not mean extreme pacifism. Ultimate peace is attainable by human beings only at the level of complete 'surrender' (*aslama*, *islam*) to God's purpose and will.

The Qur'an speaks of peace as being two-fold: it has both ultimate and worldly dimensions. There is a natural connection between the two, as one who strives to establish peace in the world is righteous and promised paradise in the hereafter, when the greeting will be 'Peace' (14.23). The Qur'an seeks to establish peace between communities, recognizing and acknowledging social, cultural and religious differences. It places high importance on maintaining good relations between adherents of different religions because, according to the Qur'an, religious freedom is a basis for sustainable peace. Thus the Qur'an calls on all believers to 'enter into complete peace and follow not the footsteps of the devil' (2.208). Thus the Qur'an emphasizes tolerance as a beginning point in the journey towards peace.

Peace in the worldly sense is synonymous with security: that is, individuals and communities must feel secure from each other. This can also be translated in a spiritual sense, where the contemplative journey of one's soul is not threatened by the temptations of this material existence. Once this level of peace is achieved, it is synonymous with life in the garden into which the righteous will enter 'in peace and security' for eternity (50.34). Within this life, peace from God descends into the hearts of believers as 'tranquillity', which adds to their faith (48.4). This peace of the heart (*sakina*) is known to have comforted the Prophet and other Muslims in their times of trial. One such moment was at Hudaybiyya, where the patience of Muslims was tested and from which they emerged victorious (48.26).

The Qur'an seeks to eradicate violence and injustice, and thus has decisive things to say concerning aggression. For example, 5.32 says: 'whosoever kills a person ... it is as though he killed all humanity, and whosoever saves a life, as though he saved all humanity'. Thus the Qur'an emphasizes *al-'afw* (forgiveness) as the path of those who are closer to God. True believers are those who 'when angered are willing to forgive' (42.37). Similarly *al-sabr* (patience) is described in the Qur'an as one of the greatest virtues. It appears many times in connection with those who have faith: 39.10 says: 'those who patiently persevere will truly receive a reward without measure'; 13.24 speaks of the greeting to those entering paradise because they 'persevered in patience'. Peace is prescribed by the Qur'an, even in the face of hostility and injustice. 41.34 suggests that believers 'repel evil with goodness' – as a result, even a hateful person will become a friend. A common Muslim practice is to greet one other using the words *al-salam 'alaykum* (peace be unto you), to which the reply is *wa 'alaykum al-salam* (and unto you be peace as well).

Peace is the true purpose of God's creation, therefore the Qur'an sends greetings of peace on many prophets of the past who strove (*jahada*) to establish justice and peace in the world. Thus, for example, 27.59, 37.79, 37.108, 37.119,

37.129 and 37.181 are all verses describing the sending of 'Peace and salutations' by God to Noah, Abraham, Moses and Aaron, Elijah and to all the unnamed messengers. Again, 36.58 says: '"Peace" – a word [of salutation] from a Lord most Merciful.'

Although peace is the objective, war is not completely avoidable. It is assumed that there will be times when the rights of the weak are usurped and injustice takes place. In order to defend the weak and the righteous, the Qur'an permits defensive war. However, the Qur'an instructs Muslims to always 'incline' towards peace (8.61), because God does not love the aggressors (2.190). Islam regulates and limits the use of violence. If all else fails, one must take up arms to defend one's rights to a livelihood and to freedom of religion. Thus armed resistance is permitted. However, there are strict conditions that must be met before one is able to fight a war of defence and such a war cannot be called a Holy War, since there is nothing 'holy' as such in Islam except God. In history some such wars of defence have been called *jihad*, which primarily means 'to strive in the way of God', but its meaning also includes a war of defence. In certain circumstances such a war is enjoined by the Qur'an, in which it is referred to as *qital* (22.39; 2.190). In the Qur'an the term *jihad* and other derivatives of the root letters */h/d/* are meant to signify inner spiritual struggle. Hence, in the Prophetic tradition (*hadith*), a clear distinction is made between the 'lesser *jihad*' (armed struggle, wars of necessity/defence) and the 'greater *jihad*' (personal struggle with and striving against the lower self).

The Qur'an contains numerous references to peace. Most importantly, peace is referred to as 'the greeting of the righteous' who will be the inhabitants of the 'garden' or paradise (7.46; 10.10;

14.23). The identification of heavenly reward after death (*al-akhira*) with being at 'peace' is unmistakable, because for the Qur'an the ultimate peace is achieved on one's return to the Source of all Peace (*al-salam*). And God calls all to the 'Home of Peace' (*dar al-salam*) (10.25).

Further reading

Abu-Nimer, M. (2003) *Nonviolence and Peace Building in Islam: Theory and practice*, Gainsville, FL: University Press of Florida.

Yusuf Ali, A. (1992) *The Meaning of the Holy Qur'an*, Baltimore, MD: Amana Corporation.

See also: akhar; **forgiveness**; *jihad*; **war and violence**

IRFAN A. OMAR

PEN
see: qalam

PERSECUTION

According to the Qur'an, our present life, with all its joys and sufferings, is merely transitory and illusory. The passage of human life continues after crossing the valley of death. While our present life is but temporary and fleeting, the life after life is permanent and perpetual. Death may be the ultimate human suffering in this world, but it is certainly not the end of life. Death is just like a door through which we have to pass to enter into a new dimension of life. In Islam, the next life is a reality beyond any doubt. Both the dimensions of human life – the life in this world and life yet to come – are aspects of life itself. The only difference is that the second phase of human life is a result of how we conduct ourselves in the first part of life.

The pleasures as well as the pains will continue in the life hereafter.

Therefore many who have lived a life full of sufferings in this world may enjoy blissful and everlasting life in heaven, and many who have enjoyed the sinful pleasures of this material world may go through a lot of torment in hell in the life yet to come. Islam accepts that suffering starts as early as the very process of human conception in a mother's womb and during the process of childbirth. 'And we have enjoined man to be good to his parents – his mother bears him in suffering after suffering of weakness' (31.14). Again we read:

> Certainly there was a long period of time when man was almost insubstantial. We created him from a sticking sperm-drop that We caused him to pass through a trial of precarious stages; then, turned him into a being capable of hearing and seeing. Verily, We have shown him the way whether he be grateful or ungrateful. (76.2–3)

Another example is: 'We have enjoined on every human being to be good to his parents. His mother bears him with pain, and brings him forth with severe pangs [of childbirth]' (46.15).

Not only do both the mother and the new-born baby have to go through a difficult period in the process of childbirth, but the Qur'an also acknowledges the existence of human suffering in various forms throughout human experience. First, there are natural disasters and climatic tragedies like earthquakes, floods, lightning, storms and famine. We can also include in such calamities the outbreak of contagious, epidemic and endemic diseases, plagues and pestilence. Moreover, there are innumerable illnesses and bodily sufferings. These calamities and diseases occur as a result of natural laws that exist in the universe, in which human life is an important but very small part. The laws of nature that sometimes cause these sufferings are put in place by God the Merciful (al-rahman) actually to support life on the earth as a whole. This point was made many times by Muslim theologians in response to the 2005 Indian Ocean tsunami that killed so many, particularly Muslims.

Then there are the human actions that cause other humans to suffer physical pain and mental anguish, sometimes even death, such as false accusation, wrongful imprisonment, kidnap, rape, theft, physical and emotional abuse, economic exploitation, slavery, wrongful occupation of other's property or land, war, and murder. We may also add to this list environmental destruction and pollution caused by human greed. These dubious actions are a result of human free will and, although we often know that we should not commit such acts, we are keen on achieving some end and ignore the illegitimate nature of the means we employ. To control the suffering caused by human beings, God has commanded us not to harm others and those who do so must face the consequences. Those who may escape punishment in this world, for them God's punishment shall be waiting in the life to come.

Third, there are acts where suffering is self-inflicted. These could be either accidental or intentional. The Qur'an prohibits inflicting self-injury and especially committing suicide, and it is very clear on the point that even the most minute action committed in this life by any human being will be recognized by God for what it is: 'Then whosoever has done so much as an atom's weight of good will see its good result, and whoso has done an atom's weight of evil will also see its evil result' (99.7–8).

Again, the Qur'an says:

Every soul shall taste death. And you shall be paid in full your rewards only on the Day of Resurrection. So whosoever is removed away from the Fire [of Hell] and is made to enter Heaven, [that person] had indeed attained his goal. And life of this world is nothing but an illusionary enjoyment. You shall surely be tried in your possessions and in your persons. (3.185–186)

Therefore, according to a normal interpretation of the Qur'an, it does not matter how much a person suffers in this world, as long as he or she is engaged, as far as they can be, in avoiding evil and furthering good. The joys and comforts of the life yet to come are greater, unparalleled and everlasting in comparison with the human sufferings of this life. The human sufferings of this present life are termed 'a trial' – a test, an evaluation and a validation to measure the success and strength of each human soul, its capacity to do good deeds. So, according to the Qur'an, all the negative events that we may have to go through in this life are actually tests and trials from God. If we pass the test by holding on to our faith and remaining patient, showing complete trust in God during the period of suffering, and we continue to do good deeds and avoid evil thoughts and actions, then the end result is that God grants us boundless rewards in the next life.

The Qur'an says:

Do you think that you will enter Heaven, while you have not yet suffered similar adversity which befell those who have passed away before you? Distress and affliction befell them, and they were made to suffer violent shaking, so that the Messenger and those who believed along with him cried out: 'When will come the help of God?' Then they were told: 'Behold! Surely the help of God is always nearby.' (2.214–15)

Thus, by understanding the continuous nature of life in its totality, human suffering does not remain an issue to be settled by challenging the existence or goodness of our Lord God the Creator. Once we are able to conceive and believe that every soul has to enter another dimension of life by passing through the door of death, only then can we fully appreciate the existence of God, who touches the depth of our souls to enhance our spiritual strength through our endurance of suffering, thereby making us the eventual winners. The Qur'an further elaborates this point by narrating to us how all the men and women of God, the Prophets, the Messengers and the righteous people – both male and female – have gone through all sorts of human suffering, but none of them ever lost their hope, their trust in God's help, and they endured all the pain, anguish and fear with utmost patience, sincerity and perseverance. In the end, they all benefited through their faithfulness.

For example, Adam and Eve had to encounter the devil, who tempted them and made them suffer so that they forgot a clear commandment from God. As a consequence, they lost paradise and entered a life of labour and pain. But still they retained dominion over all other creatures on the earth and received the forgiveness of God. Abraham was put to the terrible trial of having to offer his first-born child in sacrifice, but he ended up being the father of nations – his progeny becoming countless like the stars in the heavens. The sufferings of Job (Ayyub) are proverbial, but he retained his confidence in divine justice, and his suffering becomes a means of refining his righteousness. Under the threats of Pharaoh, Moses had to run to save his life and led his people for forty years, suffering many pains and disappointments at the hands of his enemies and his own people, but he never lost his faith in God. Jesus and his mother Mary are particularly renowned for their patience at the hands of their enemies. Mary had to suffer the insult of becoming pregnant prior to getting married. Jesus suffered physical torments and was put on the cross to be killed, and in a most unpleasant and public manner. God did not forsake him, and God honoured his mother, and now billions revere them both as innocent and sinless. The descendants of those who made them suffer have since then been unable to expand from being a very small group, generally at the mercy of those who honour the Virgin Mary and Jesus.

Muhammad was very successful in both religious and worldly matters. His role was to inspire humanity to faith in the One God and also to establish a state that would embody the correct social and religious principles. At the start of his mission, he suffered the most bitter persecution and oppression at the hands of his own people, precisely those people that he wanted to help and guide. Even when he and his followers were forced to leave their hometown Mecca and had resettled in Medina – a town more than 200 miles away from Mecca – their enemy did not allow them to live in peace, and constantly attacked them.

Muhammad also suffered many personal tragedies. He lost some his children while they were young, and some died in his lifetime as grown-ups. He had four sons, but none of them survived to adulthood. But despite all the enormous human suffering throughout his life, Muhammad was said always to be cheerful as a result of his firm faith in the existence of God. As we read: 'The truly righteous are those who endure with fortitude misfortune, hardship and peril. That is, who are patient in poverty and affliction, and in time of war' (2.177). We read:

O you who believe! Seek [God's] help with perfect patience and prayer; for surely God is with the patiently persevering (sabirin). And do not count as dead those who are killed in the cause of God. Rather they are living; only you perceive not [their life]. And We will certainly reward you after trying you with something of fear and hunger and some loss of substance and of lives, and fruits [of your toil]. Give glad tidings to the patiently persevering; who, when a calamity befalls them, say: 'Surely to God we belong and to Him shall we return.' It is they on whom descend the blessings and mercy (rahma) from their Lord God; and it is they who are rightly guided.' (2.153–57; see also 47.31)

Muslims should seek redress against persecution by holding fast to the Qur'an and the sunna of the Prophet: 'Then, whoever follows my guidance shall neither go astray, nor fall into distress and misery' (20.123). Supplicating God (du'a) and the performance of good deeds are two ways to go. Yusuf (Joseph) was saved because of his sincerity, and the People of the Cave were saved because of their truthfulness, both good examples of how taqwa (piety) leads to an escape from the perils of persecution. Iman (faith) and dhikr (remembrance of God) are said to serve as protection and defence in times of trouble.

An excellent example is that of the Prophet and his followers, who were subjected to persecution and insult. The Quraysh prevented the Prophet from offering his prayers at the Ka'ba; they pursued him wherever he went; they attacked him and his disciples, and insulted them. The Prophet and the Muslims remained patient and prayed to God for help. Whatever happened, the Prophet did not swerve in his mission. He continued preaching to the Arabs in a most gentle and reasonable manner. He used inspiring words which excited the hearts of his listeners. He warned them of the punishment that Allah had inflicted upon the ancient tribes of 'Ad and Thamud who had stubbornly rejected the teachings of Allah's messengers to them. He spoke to them of the Day of Reckoning, when their deeds in this world shall be weighed before the perfect judge, when the children who had been buried alive shall be asked for what crime they were put to death.

The Quraysh were alarmed, as the number of believers had been increased by the conversion of many important members of the tribe. Their status was at risk, too, since they were custodians of the idols that the Prophet had threatened to destroy and replace with nothing. They were in charge of the worship that Muhammad opposed. They earned their living through running the Mecca idol business, and the Prophet was seeking to change all that, so it is hardly surprising that they were not delighted at his message. The Quraysh are said to have organized a system of persecution in order to destroy the new movement before it became firmly established. With the exceptions of the Prophet, who was protected by Abu Talib and his kinsmen, and Abu Bakr, all other converts were subjected to different sorts of torture. Some of them were thrown into prison, starved and then flogged. The Prophet was even approached and offered a pay-off to abandon his mission. In response, the Prophet is reputed to have recited the first thirteen verses of *sura* 41, which deals with *tawhid*, *akhira*, the creation of the universe and the fate of the people of 'Ad and Thamud – not what his enemies were hoping to hear.

Persecution by the Quraysh intensified, but Muhammad had heard of the hospitality of the neighbouring Christian king of Abyssinia, al-Najashi (Negus). He recommended that those of his Companions who were without protec-

tion should seek refuge in the kingdom of that pious king. Some fifteen of the unprotected adherents of Islam promptly availed themselves of his advice and sailed to Abyssinia. Here they were welcomed with a gracious reception from Negus. This is called the first *hijra* (migration) in the history of Islam; it occurred in the fifth year of the Prophet Muhammad's mission (i.e. 615 CE). These emigrants were soon followed by many of their fellow sufferers, until the number reached eighty-three men and eighteen women.

The Quraysh, annoyed at the escape of their victims, sent deputies to the king of Abyssinia to request that he deliver up the refugees, so that they might be put to death for rejecting their old religion and embracing a new one. The king asked them what religion they had adopted in preference to their old faith. Ja'far ibn Abu Talib, the brother of 'Ali, acted as spokesman for the exiles. He is reported as having said:

> O king, we were plunged in the depth of ignorance and barbarism, we adored idols, we lived promiscuously, we ate dead bodies, and we spoke abomination, we disregarded every feeling of humanity and sense of duty towards our neighbours, and we knew no law but that of the strong, when Allah raised among us a man, of whose birth, truthfulness, honesty, and purity we acknowledged. He called us to profess the unity of God and taught us to associate nothing with him; he forbade us to worship idols and required us to speak the truth, to be faithful to our agreements, to be merciful, and to regard the rights of others ... We have believed in him, we have accepted his teachings and his injunctions ... Hence our people have persecuted us, trying to make us stop worshipping God and return to the worship of idols of wood and stone and other. They have tortured us and injured us. Finding no safety among them, we have come to

your kingdom, trusting you will give us protection against their persecution.

This speech was effective in saving the emigrants from being sent back to the judgement of the Quraysh. It gives an interesting picture of the sort of persecution that they perceived themselves as having had to endure.

While the followers of the Prophet sought safety in foreign lands against the persecution of their people, the Prophet himself continued to present the revelation. Mecca and its surroundings were frequented by many travellers and they are said to have taken the message back to their own communities, where it had a considerable impact. The Meccans were not pleased at having their livelihood interfered with in this way, and no doubt they did not believe that the Prophet's mission was genuine, so they warned his uncle Abu Talib that, if Muhammad continued, it would lead to war not only against Muhammad but against Abu Talib also. But the Quraysh again failed to force Abu Talib to abandon his nephew. The chief declared his intention to protect his nephew against any danger or violence. He appealed to the sense of honour of the two families of Bani Hashim and Bani Muttalib, both families being related to the Prophet, to protect their family member from falling victim to the hatred of rival parties. All the members of the two families responded appropriately to the appeal of Abu Talib except Abu Lahab, one of the Prophet's uncles, who sided with the persecutors. This unnatural behaviour on Abu Lahab's part earned him a *sura* of the Qur'an in which he is roundly denounced.

During this period, 'Umar al-Khattab adopted Islam. In him, the new faith gained a valuable adherent, and he was to be an important factor in the future development and propagation of Islam. Up to this point, he had been an aggressive opponent of the Prophet and a bitter enemy of Islam. His conversion is credited to the miraculous effect on his mind of *sura* 20 (*Ta Ha*), which his sister was reading in her house when he went there with the intention of killing her for embracing Islam. The party of the Prophet had been strengthened also by the conversions of his uncle Hamza and of Abu Bakr and 'Umar, all of them important men. This history is used to demonstrate that persecution is only to be expected and should not throw the believer into confusion. As it says at 2.214:

Do you think that you will enter paradise without undergoing such trials as were experienced by the believers before you? They met with adversity and affliction and were so shaken by trials that the Prophet of the time and his followers cried out: 'When will Allah's help come?' Then they were comforted with the good tidings that 'Yes, Allah's help is near.'

Persecution and suffering are not events to make believers question their beliefs, but rather spurs to intensify those beliefs and encourage virtuous action.

See also: sabr; **suffering**

OLIVER LEAMAN

PHILOSOPHY AND THE QUR'AN

The Qur'an is often the subject matter in Islamic philosophy or, as Seyyed Hossein Nasr has usefully put it, the source of philosophical meditation. He argues very plausibly that many non-Muslim commentators have failed to appreciate the centrality of the Qur'an in Islamic philosophy, assuming that the references to the Book are merely rhetorical flourishes to illustrate but not to deepen the argument itself. Whether we should accept Nasr's thesis that most Islamic philosophy is part of the perennial tradition in philosophy, where we move from the open to the hidden, and where certain general principles are involved in all abstract thought is quite another issue. Nasr is certainly correct in thinking that mysticism is highly significant in Islamic philosophy. Almost every Islamic philosopher in the classical period was committed to some form of mysticism. Often the approach they followed was to criticize Peripatetic (*mashsha'i*) or Aristotelian philosophy for being far too limited in scope, since it only dealt with the world of nature (*zahir*) and avoids strenuously the world of the hidden (*batin*). Mystical philosophy is required to investigate the more basic issues, in particular those that lie behind the world we experience and indeed also the exoteric understanding of the Qur'an.

The varieties of Islamic philosophy

Some critics of Peripatetic thought, like ibn Sab'in (614/1217–669/1270), argued that Aristotelian philosophy and logic were of limited usefulness, but had no function in helping us to understand the way things really are. Logical thought divides a concept into its parts, and analytical philosophy separates arguments into smaller constituents. This manner of reasoning fails to represent accurately the basic unity that exists in reality; as a result of God's *tawhid* (unity), any accurate philosophy is going to be based on unity, not division. In a dramatic description of burying Peripatetic thought, Ibn al-'Arabi (1165–1240) transported the bones of Ibn Rushd (Averroes) back to al-Andalus. This represented the new mystical philosophy replacing the older form of thought, limited as the latter was to an analytical understanding of concepts.

Many philosophers linked mysticism with Peripatetic philosophy, arguing that they were just different ways of working theoretically, and that mysticism went deeper into the nature of reality. It is important to distinguish the sort of mysticism, which the philosophers were keen to defend from charges of subjectivity. It was argued that there is a science of mysticism, and Sufism presented itself in a rigorous and organized manner, with the aim being to realize spiritual growth and to gain in knowledge of how things really are.

Illuminationist (*ishraqi*) thought comes from the term *ishraq* (east) and sets out to replace Peripatetic thought by abandoning the notion of definition and substituting for it immediate or intuitive knowledge. The Peripatetic view is that reasoning starts with definition, in terms of genus and differentia, a process of explaining something by breaking it down into its smaller parts, very much what we mean by analysis. Illuminationist thinkers, such as al-Suhrawardi (1154–91), argue that this is to explain the unknown in terms of something even less known than itself, which is vacuous. They also replace deductive knowledge, the sort of knowledge we get from using the principles of Aristotelian reasoning, with knowledge by presence, which they describe as knowledge that is so immediate it cannot be doubted. It is here that the notion of light comes in, as part of the term *ishraq*, since such knowledge is lit up in a way that makes it impossible to doubt, and this is a result of the way in which light flows through the universe and brings to existence and awareness different levels of being. God is often identified with the Light of Lights, the light that is the source of all other light and does not itself require illumination. As one might imagine, the Light Verse is popular with *ishraqi* thinkers, and they frequently write about it.

The Islamic sciences

The Islamic sciences are traditional techniques that have been developed for answering theoretical questions that are relevant to the religion of Islam, and these sciences comprise law, theology, language and the study of the religious texts themselves. There has always been a lively debate about how the texts should be interpreted, what scope there is for the use of independent reason, and how far analogy may be used. There was also a long discussion about the objectivity or subjectivity of ethical rules, over the issue of whether an action can be considered just if and only if God says that it is just, or whether it is just in itself. Here, as so often, philosophy impinged on a long and heated debate in *kalam*, on this occasion between the Mu'tazilites and the Ash'arites over the objectivity of moral categories. Both sides used the Qur'an to provide passages in support of their positions. According to the Mu'tazilites, if 'good' means 'what God orders', then all those passages in the Book that refer to things as good and ordered by God need to be understood as tautologies, since they really mean that God orders what he orders. But the Ash'arites countered that this merely shows that there is some linguistic artificiality in analysing sentences, not that they should not be analysed in those ways. In any case, if ethical rules are regarded as objective, the Ash'arites suggest, this leaves God with very little if anything to do to establish how we should live. This is really the main point of disagreement between the philosophers, whatever their particular doctrinal standpoint, and theologians. The latter think that a proper reading of the Qur'an establishes it as all one needs in order to understand the nature of reality. For the philosophers, though, one also needs other theoretical guides, guides that will interpret the Qur'an correctly and show what it really means. For some Sufis, one also needs particular spiritual guides.

Another debate was over the reconciliation of the social virtues that arise through living in a community, as specified by the Qur'an, and intellectual virtues that tend to involve a more solitary lifestyle. What need is there for the advanced philosophical or mystical thinker, who can approach the truth directly through the use of reason, to be a part of the social and religious activities of the community as a whole? The philosophers tended to argue that social activity is required for intellectual or spiritual activity, but sometimes it seems that the only link here is prudential, and that the philosophers' commitment to formal religion is weak.

Political philosophy

Political philosophy looked to Greek thinkers for ways of explaining the nature of the state, yet also combined Platonic ideas with Qur'anic notions, ending up with the position that the state ought to embody both the material and the spiritual interests of the individual. The philosopher is the best ruler because he can understand where the general interest lies, and religion is the means by which each individual can be taught how to behave and how to fit in with others. The role of the ruler is linked with that of the *imam*, making the ruler responsible for all aspects of the welfare of the community.

The soul

A particular source of controversy was the debate over the nature of the soul, the thinking part of human beings. Many Peripatetic thinkers followed Aristotle in regarding the soul as the form of a person, which implies that once the body or matter dies, its soul or form disappears also. Yet the Qur'an has a well-developed notion of an afterlife, and the soul together with the body would then seem to be eternal. Some philosophers suggested that this religious notion should be taken as allegorical, and means that our actions in this life have consequences which are not limited to only this life, and a good way of illustrating that is by talking about us as having eternal souls. Other thinkers tended to develop a Platonic account of the soul as something eternal and immaterial, which also seems to offend against the Qur'anic account of the afterlife as a very physical sort of place. They tended to argue that the religious account places emphasis on the physical because for most people that is what is important. Given the importance of imagination in our lives, we need to form a material idea of things if they are to make real sense to us, and imagination involves our sensory equipment, i.e. our bodies. It is a way of making vivid to us why it is important for us to behave well, since the more spiritual understanding of the links between this world and the afterlife is available only to a limited number of intellectuals and should not be forced on to those who prefer to see the future in more material terms.

Logic

Logic became a very important part of Islamic philosophy, especially the idea that logic consists of a set of techniques that lies behind what we think and what we do, but is actually independent of philosophy itself. It is often seen as a tool of philosophy, not a part of it. Even poetry was taken to have a logical structure, albeit of low demonstrative power, but the rules of poetry are taken to be formed in terms of logical rules. There exists a variety of logical approaches that are available to different people for different purposes, and on some occasions when one wants to evoke an emotional response, poetry is appropriate. For the theologian and the lawyer, though, dialectic is the right logical technique, since this works logically from generally accepted propositions (the religious or legal text) to conclusions that are shown to be valid, but only within the constraints set by the premises. Within the context of Islam, then, if we accept the premises of the Qur'an, certain conclusions quite logically follow, but their validity is limited by the fact that they depend on premises which not everyone accepts. Philosophers work at the highest level of reasoning; according to them, they are the only people who use completely certain and general premises, and so their conclusions are universally valid. That means that absolutely everyone has to accept them if they are operating appropriately at the rational level. The same goes for knowledge. Ordinary people are limited in their knowledge to what they can find out through their experience and through their understanding of what they are told. This basically means they are limited to their senses and the images and stories of religion. By contrast, philosophers can reach much higher levels of knowledge through their use of logic and their ability to perfect their understanding of the very general abstract principles that underlie the whole of reality and represent the highest level of awareness that we human beings can acquire.

Philosophy's relationship with the Qur'an

Philosophy came into conflict and harmony with the Qur'an in a variety of ways. Conflict is easier to notice. Some of the theories that the philosophers developed did not fit nicely within the structure of doctrines like those in the Qur'an. Some seemed to go against Islam. For example, few philosophers believed literally in resurrection of the body and soul, yet that does seem to be asserted by the Qur'an. Few philosophers could take literally the idea that God knows everything, given his lack of sensory equipment. Not only could he not know everything, they often argued that the only things he could know are abstract and eternal things, and that means he is essentially disengaged from the daily life of the world of our everyday experience. Perhaps the most damaging claim that philosophers made was to their special take on religion: they could understand what religion is really about, while professional religious people like theologians are actually floundering in the intellectual darkness. Since religious language was seen as logically inferior to philosophical language, it is clear who has the upper hand when issues of controversy arise, and it is the philosophers. Ibn Rushd, in his *Fasl al-maqal* (Decisive Treatise), emphasizes this point when he claims that in cases of difficulty of interpretation only the philosophers can be called upon to resolve the difficulty. The theologians, whom one might think are the right people for the job, are lost in dialectical language and cannot come up with a certain conclusion.

Quite apart from any doctrinal dispute on a particular issue, this last claim is very damaging to the universal aspirations of religion. It might well seem that the last word on a religious topic should be a religious word, not something from some other theory, and the idea that a higher level of theory needs to be introduced to resolve religious issues is potentially threatening to the confidence of the ordinary believer in the religious sciences. It is worth making clear that this is not just an issue for Peripatetic philosophy, but for all the varieties of philosophy in the Islamic world, including Sufi and *ishraqi*. In attempting to carve out a role for themselves in the Islamic cultural environment, they each claim that they are an essential part of any proper understanding of the nature of reality, and thus of the Qur'an which serves as the blueprint for the structure of that reality.

The role of the Qur'an in Islamic philosophy

This is not to say that the Qur'an is used in the same way in the different schools and by the whole range of philosophers. It certainly was not. On many occasions a *sura* or *aya* is thrown into an argument but plays no real part in it. The point is perhaps to establish the Islamic credentials of the argument itself, or the thinker, and on occasions one might even say that the point of the quotation is merely decorative. For example, Ibn Rushd refers to 3.7 when he is criticizing al-Ghazali for discussing allegorical interpretations of scripture in works that are accessible to ordinary believers. The *aya* goes: 'And no-one knows their interpretation except God'. One should not discuss such difficult verses with people who are not qualified to understand them: they should be described as ambiguous and left alone. What the *aya* seems to be saying, though, is that only God should tackle such topics; it does not say that only those qualified to do so should, thereby bringing in the philosophers. In fact, what Ibn Rushd does in his book is explain or seek to explain such difficult verses, albeit in a way he says is limited only to an appropriate audience. But if God is the only person who can tackle them, then Ibn Rushd is directly contravening the *aya*. Yet he uses the *aya* to criticize someone else's attempt at interpretation! It has to be said that the *aya* is being used merely as decoration: it does nothing for the argument and, in fact, if it was taken seriously, works against the argument. It plays the same role as the traditional flourish at the start and end of books during this period, where there is a reference to God as the only one who knows (in which case why write the book?) or to the divine attributes.

Other philosophers use the Qur'an more centrally in their work. For example, al-Ghazali spends a lot of time in his *Ihya' 'ulum al-din* (Revival of the Sciences of Religion) series of books discussing the various stages of changing our character in order to bring us closer to God. The Aristotelian notion of a personality trait was adapted in Islamic thought by the term *malaka*, which Ibn Khaldun defines as 'a firmly rooted quality acquired by doing a certain action and repeating it time after time, until the form of that action is firmly fixed' (Ibn Khaldun, 1958: 346).

There was a discussion by al-Ghazali of Miskawayh's view that our dispositions were adapted by God when he settled on rituals in the Qur'an. According to Miskawayh, many of the rules in the Book are based on our natural dispositions, so they work on the basis of things we already enjoy doing. We like associating with other people, so communal prayer is emphasized; we enjoy going on trips, hence the *hajj*; we appreciate, in general, having rules that regulate our behaviour, so the Qur'an and Islam specify various restrictions on human behaviour. God, then, uses our natural likes and dislikes to embed religion more firmly in our hearts. Quite the reverse is the case, according to al-Ghazali. These religious practices make such

an impact on us because they represent what we would not naturally want to do. By subduing our will to the word of God, al-Ghazali suggested, we put ourselves in the right frame of mind for approaching our Creator, and the various passages in the Qur'an that instruct us in the moral qualities we need to acquire are a spiritual guide to how we should change our characters. This is a good example of the Qur'an becoming part of the philosophical discussion itself, not merely as an illustration of independent arguments, but part and parcel of the text itself. The Qur'an plays a real role in the argument, since the various moral prescriptions are seen as stages in what it is to refine our characters in the appropriate way. The notion of a character and what it involves certainly comes in its sophisticated form from Aristotle and his followers, but when al-Ghazali came to discuss it he really did justify it with examples from the Qur'an, and those examples show how useful that concept is in explaining what it is for us to change who and how we are.

It might seem an unfair comparison, since the al-Ghazali text is so directly centred on religion and the Ibn Rushd text is not. But that is not at all true. Both have religion as their topic, so you would expect the use of the Qur'an to be important in both. Yet it is much more important for the al-Ghazali discussion than for Ibn Rushd. Whether this is generally true of works in Sufism and in Peripatetic thought is not here under discussion. It could be argued that *ishraqi* philosophy does use the Qur'an more centrally than even Sufi thought. Again, such a general claim cannot be defended here, but it could be argued that Mulla Sadra, the outstanding *ishraqi* thinker, does take the Qur'an very directly to be the object of his work. The Qur'an, like reality, has a syntax and a semantics, a language and a system of meaning, and the Qur'an is the blueprint behind the creation of the world. Philosophy is also a way of understanding the world that uses reason, but not only reason. It also accesses very general and abstract ideas, which it regards as basic to the structure of the world, and those ideas are very much based on the Qur'an. This is not the place to comment on the virtues of any particular type of philosophy with respect to any other, but it is relevant to comment on how close *ishraqi* thought is to the Qur'an. Mulla Sadra's thought, in general, can easily be considered a profound meditation on particular aspects of the Qur'an, and it has as its basis a theory of how the understanding of reality is mirrored in the Qur'an itself. Again, it should not be thought that the use of the Qur'an is central because of the topic: it is central because the Qur'an is involved in any and every aspect of *ishraqi* metaphysics, regardless of the direct topic. One can distinguish here, for instance, *ishraqi* thought from the *Qistas al-mustaqim* (Correct Balance) by al-Ghazali, which attempts to show that Islam calls for the use of logic, and indeed that logic can be derived from Islam. Although this work is replete with references to the Book, they really do very little work, peppering the text without contributing to it except by way of providing vaguely connected assertions.

The relevant question to ask when considering the links between philosophy and the Qur'an is what difference the Qur'an makes to philosophy, and vice versa. It has been argued that the Qur'an makes very little difference to the *Fasl al-maqal* of Ibn Rushd and the *Qistas al-mustaqim* of al-Ghazali. The Qur'an plays an important part in the *Ihya' 'ulum al-din* of al-Ghazali, since without it the whole discussion would

not make much sense. It would still make some sense, though, since we could talk about the development of personality traits without having a conception of how those traits work to help us come closer to God. By contrast, much of the thought of Mulla Sadra makes no sense at all without the Qur'an. This is because its leading principles and presuppositions are thoroughly Qur'anic, and one would have no reason to accept them without accepting the Qur'an.

The effect of philosophy on the Qur'an

How about the implications for the Qur'an that result from the application of philosophy? Here again it will depend on what type of philosopher one is. It is a fairly generally accepted argument by many types of Islamic philosophy that the Qur'an and philosophy both come to the same conclusions, albeit differently expressed and for different audiences. The Qur'an is accessible to everyone, the conclusions of philosophy only to an intellectual and/or spiritual elite. Could philosophy ever challenge the Qur'an? It certainly could if it came to conclusions that went in the contrary direction from the Book, and if those conclusions appeared to be rigorously established. Much of the opposition to different kinds of philosophy came from Muslims who believed that philosophy is *bid'a*, (innovation) and produces ideas that do not cohere with those of Islam.

Perhaps an even greater threat to the Qur'an is the use of philosophy at all to produce an alternative way of analysing and understanding reality. Could it come to replace the Qur'an as a route to knowledge? It could if its conclusions and principles are contrary to Islam, but otherwise there is no reason to think that it is any more opposed to Islam than any other form of knowledge, perhaps mathematics or medicine. Of course, it will be said that the conclusions of philosophy often are opposed to religion, and these arguments have to be dealt with by any religion that wishes to rest on secure intellectual foundations. But there is no general reason to think that, in the encounter of faith and philosophy, Islam is any worse or better off than any other religion.

References and further reading

al-Ghazali (1980) *Qistas al-mustaqim*, trans. R. McCarthy, 'The Correct Balance', in *Freedom and Fulfillment*, Boston, MA: Twayne: 287–332.
—— (1985) *Ihya' 'ulum al-din*, ed. A. al-Sirwan, Beirut: Dar al-qalam.
Ibn Khaldun (1958) *The Muqaddimah: An introduction to history*, New York: Pantheon.
Ibn Rushd (1976) *Fasl al-maqal*, trans. G. Hourani, *Averroes on the Harmony of Religion and Philosophy*, London: Luzac.
Leaman, O. (1999) *Brief Introduction to Islamic Philosophy*, Oxford: Polity.
—— (2002) *Introduction to Classical Islamic Philosophy*, Cambridge: Cambridge University Press.
Nasr, S.H. (1996a) 'The Meaning and Concept of Philosophy in Islam', *HIP*: 21–6.
—— (1996b) 'Mulla Sadra: his teachings', *HIP*: 643–62.
—— (1996c) 'The Qur'an and *hadith* as Source and Inspiration of Islamic Philosophy', *HIP*: 27–39.

See also: **arguments and the Qur'an; Ash'arites and Mu'tazilites; character; morality**

OLIVER LEAMAN

POLYGAMY

Contemporary Muslim debates over polygamy (or, more properly, polygyny) focus on two crucial Qur'anic verses. The first states:

> If you fear you will not deal justly with the orphans, marry such as seem good to you from the women, two or three or four; but if you are afraid you will not be fair, then only one or what your right hands own. (4.3)

Said to have been revealed after the death of numerous Muslims in the Battle of Uhud, this verse refers directly to the situation of fatherless children. There is a difference of opinion as to whether it suggests marriage to the orphaned females themselves or to widows with children to support. However, it was generally understood in the premodern period to apply to polygamy in general. Its most important provision was the imposition of an upper limit of four wives; pre-Islamic Arab custom did not impose any such maximum.

Qur'an 4.3 is the only verse to explicitly declare the permissibility of polygyny, but 4.23 assumes its acceptability when it stipulates that two sisters cannot be married to the same man simultaneously. Other questions associated with plural marriages are treated in verses addressed to the Prophet Muhammad and his wives, the Mothers of the Believers. While the rulings are specific to the Prophet's household, the verses assume that polygamy is practised more widely.

The other verse that directly addresses polygamy declares that 'You are never able to be just between women, even if you ardently desire to be, but do not incline completely away from one, leaving her suspended' (4.129). There is a tension between this verse and 4.3 on the issue of justice and fairness between wives. Egyptian author Qasim Amin noted the conflict, opining that 'the Qur'an both legitimizes polygamy and warns against it' (Amin, 2000: 85). The notion that polygamy could be a perilous endeavour is not a recent one. The Prophet is reported to have cautioned against neglecting a wife, stating that a man who has two wives and favours one over the other will be resurrected at the final judgement with one side of his body drooping. For most of Muslim history, however, the concern for just treatment of multiple wives was seen as a matter to be left to the conscience of the individual Muslim husband.

Pre-modern Muslim scholars took it for granted that polygamy was permissible. Indeed, no discussion of polygamy *per se* is found in early legal works treating questions of marriage and divorce. Rather, jurists assumed that polygamy was legal and set about treating more specific questions having to do with matters such as the establishment of separate quarters for wives and the allocation of time between them. While historically unusual except for the wealthy few, the practice of polygamy was widely accepted as normal by classical and medieval *'ulama.*

Beginning in the nineteenth century, however, polygamy became the subject of widespread debate among Muslim intellectuals. A number of Muslim reformists and, more recently, Muslim feminists have challenged traditional views on polygamy. Modern authors who disapprove of polygamy take a range of positions on whether it should be simply discouraged, legally restricted or prohibited, and what type of role, if any, the state should play in setting limits on polygamous marriages. In all of these debates, Qur'an 4.3 and 4.129 hold centre stage.

A few thinkers have directly challenged polygamy, arguing that doing justice is set forth in 4.3 as a requirement for the permissibility, not merely advisability, of marrying more than one wife; since the Qur'an declares justice between wives an impossibility in 4.129, logically polygamy is forbidden. Most, however, have rejected this view, arguing that it fails to take into account the acceptance of polygamy by the Prophet and his community.

Others have taken a more historical approach. Pakistani scholar Fazlur Rahman argued that polygamy, like slavery, was an entrenched practice when Islam arrived, and could not have been immediately eradicated. However, according to him, the ultimate intent of the divine revelation was to abolish these institutions and polygamy should therefore be prohibited today. Muhammad 'Abdu took the view that, while polygamy had been a salutary practice overall in early Muslim history (though not always without personal cost to the individual women who had to share their husbands), in modern Egypt polygamy led to discord and even violence within the family. He argued, in keeping with long-standing legal principle, that something otherwise lawful could be forbidden if it led to social ills; this was the case for polygamy.

'Abdu's disciple Rashid Rida was less categorical. While noting that monogamy was the norm, and indeed the ideal (a crucial point made by feminist exegetes generations later), he thought that there were situations in which personal and societal need overcame the normative weight attached to monogamy. This influential line of argument has been a staple of twentieth- and twenty-first-century apologetics for polygamy. These texts invoke demographic imbalances due to war, or infertility or illness of the first wife; in these cases, polygamy is extolled as a means of support and protection for vulnerable women, as in 4.3. On other occasions, authors make reference to the 'naturally' greater sexual appetites of men, based on biological imperatives. Apologists for polygamy often contrast the honest nature of concurrent marriages to wives with equal legal privileges and guarantees to the *de facto* polygamy of affairs, girlfriends or even serial monogamy, as practised in the West.

Some Muslim feminist authors have suggested that this type of argument is cultural bias masquerading as authoritative religious doctrine (though they also do not shy away from noting the hypocrisy in some Western polemics against Muslim polygamy). Adopting some arguments from the modernists, exegetes such as Riffat Hassan, Asma Barlas and Amina Wadud have stressed the importance of the one man–one woman pairing in Qur'anic portrayals of creation, marriage, family and society. Though disagreeing on certain points, they stress the exceptional and limited nature of Qur'anic polygamy. Indeed, the question of polygamy is important not only for its intrinsic interest for those concerned with Islamic family law in the contemporary world, but also for broader debates over whether Qur'anic rules must always be literally applied or whether their specific provisions are context-specific, and thus liable to change with changes in social conditions.

Reference

Amin, Q. (2000) *The Liberation of Women and the New Woman: Two documents in the history of Egyptian feminism*, trans. S. Sidhom Peterson, Cairo: American University of Cairo Press.

See also: **marriage; polygyny**

KECIA ALI

POLYGYNY

Polygyny is the marriage of one man to multiple women. Polygamy, the term usually used to describe this type of marriage, encompasses both polygyny and polyandry (the marriage of one woman to more than one man). Compared to other forms of marriage, polyandry is rare. Muslim accounts of pre-Islamic Arab practice describe several types of marital regimes under which women maintained sexual relationships with more than one mate, including one that resembles simple prostitution. However, the extent to which these are accurate descriptions of actual practice has been debated.

Polygyny, by contrast, has been widely practised historically, including among the Arabs before the coming of Islam. It is sanctioned by the Qur'an, the practice of the Prophet Muhammad and his community, and Islamic law. Marriage to more than one woman at a time is explicitly allowed by 4.3, and implicitly accepted by other verses (e.g. 4.129) that assume polygyny and attempt to regulate its practice.

Though not precisely marriage, the sexual access Qur'anically granted (4.3; 23.6; 70.30 etc.) to male owners of female war captives or slaves also allows men to maintain lawful relationships with multiple women.

See also: **marriage; polygamy**

KECIA ALI

PRESERVED TABLET

The term 'tablet' appears in the Qur'an five times: three times in reference to the tablets revealed to Moses, once in reference to a celestial Preserved Tablet (*al-lawh al-mahfuz*), and once in reference to Noah's Ark (54.13).

The story of Moses and his tablets on the mountain mentions a revelation, which is much more than the Ten Commandments of the account given in the Hebrew Bible. 7.145 runs: 'We wrote for him [Moses], upon the tablets, from all matters, exhorting and explaining all things.' The Qur'an commentator Ibn Kathir (d. 774/1372) relates the traditional interpretation that these tablets are made of emerald and contain the laws on *halal* and *haram* in addition to the entire Hebrew Bible (*Tawrat*). He adds to this explanation a reference to the *hadith* 'God was before all else; His throne was upon the water, and He wrote of all things upon the tablet.' This last sense of a celestial eternal tablet seems to fit better the Preserved Tablet mentioned 85.22, which we shall return to. The Moses story also mentions him throwing down the tablets in anger (7.150), and picking them back up once his anger had subsided (7.154). To the latter passage the Qur'an adds the following: 'Written upon them was guidance and mercy for those who fear their Lord.' Ibn Kathir fills out the picture, saying: 'It is understood that they were broken and then put back together. Some say the fragments were stored away in vaults of the kings of Isra'il until the advent of Islam.'

The Preserved Tablet is mentioned only once, and is linked explicitly to the Qur'an: 'But this is a glorious Qur'an, upon a Preserved Tablet' (85.21, 22). The *hadith* provides more detail: 'God created the preserved tablet from a white pearl with a ruby surface; its pen and its writing being of light – upon which all worldly affairs are laid out.' Thus it functions as a book of fate, or the medium through which God's will is executed in creation. At the same time, the specific identification of the Qur'anic revelation with the Preserved Tablet is given priority. Regarding the revelation to Muhammad, 'We sent it down to him on the Night of Power' (97.1); Ibn Kathir again elaborates with a *hadith* from Ibn 'Abbas to the effect that 'God sent down the Qur'an all at once from the Preserved Tablet to the place of glory in the lowest heaven. Then He sent it down according to the various occasions, over thirteen years, to the prophet.' Elsewhere in the Qur'an, this Preserved Tablet is referred to as the Mother of the Book. The passage runs: 'We have made it an Arabic Qur'an, that you may understand. Truly it is the Mother of the Book, in Our presence, lofty and full of wisdom' (43.3–4). The third-/ninth-century Sufi Sahl al-Tustari calls the Preserved Tablet the heart of the mystic believer, while al-Qushayri (d. 465/1074), evoking a Neoplatonic cosmology, describes the Tablet as extending from God's Throne down to the realm of the angels.

Further reading

Ibn Hanbal (1998) *Musnad* (Islamic Traditions), 11 vols, Beirut: 'Alam al-kutub.

Ibn Kathir, I. (n.d.) *Tafsir al-Qur'an al-'azim* (Interpretation of the Great Qur'an), 4 vols, Cairo: Dar al-taqwa.

al-Qushayri, A. (2000) *Lata'if al-isharat* (The Subtleties of the Signs), 3 vols, Cairo: al-Hay'a al-misriyya.

al-Tustari, S. (2002) *Tafsir al-Qur'an al-'azim* (Interpretation of the Great Qur'an), ed. M. Geratallah, 3 vols, Cairo: Dar al-thaqafiyya.

See also: **qada'; revelation**

RICHARD MCGREGOR

PROPHECY

The general belief of Muslims concerning the revelation, based on the Qur'an, is that the text of the Qur'an is the actual speech of God transmitted to the Prophet by one of his chosen angels. The name of this angel, or heavenly being, is Gabriel (Jibril) or the Faithful Spirit. He transmitted the word of God over a period of twenty-three years to the Prophet. He would bring the divine instructions to the Prophet, who would relate them faithfully to the people using the same words in the form of a verse. The Prophet thus used the meaning of the verses to call the people to an understanding of faith, of belief, of social laws and of individual duties. These instructions from God to his Messenger represent the prophecy, or the message; the Prophet transmitted this message without making any addition to or detraction from it in any way.

The Qur'an, however, strongly denies that it is the speech or the ideas of the Prophet or, indeed, any other man. In 10.38 and 11.13 the Qur'an declares that, if it is the word of man, then detractors of Islam should be able produce similar words about every subject treated in the Qur'an: belief in the afterlife, morals, laws, stories of past generations and other prophets, wisdom, and advice. The Qur'an urges them to seek help anywhere if they do not realize that it is the word of God and not of man, but adds that even if *jinn* and man joined forces together, they would not be able to produce a Qur'an like it.

In 2.23 the Qur'an challenges those who consider it merely the speech of Muhammad to produce a book similar to it or even just one chapter like it. The force of this challenge becomes clear when we realize that it is issued for someone whose life should resemble that of Muhammad: namely, the life of an orphan, uneducated in any formal sense, not able to read or write, who grew up in the unenlightened age of the *jahiliyya* (the age of ignorance) that preceded Islam. In 4.82 the Qur'an asks why no inconsistencies or changes appeared in the verses, with neither the wording nor the meaning of the verses having altered despite being revealed over a period of twenty-three years. If it was the word of man and not the word of God, then it would have certainly been affected by change, like all other things in the temporal world of nature and matter.

The angel Gabriel

We read in 2.97: 'Say [O Muhammad, to mankind]: Who is an enemy to Gabriel! for it is he who has revealed [the Qur'an] to your heart by God's permission.' This verse refers to Jews who wanted to know who had revealed the Qur'an to the Prophet. He replied that it was Gabriel and they said: 'We are enemies of Gabriel as he it was who gave us the laws and legal punishments and as we are enemies to him, we do not believe in the book which he has brought.' Thus God replies to them in the verse that Gabriel revealed the Qur'an to the Prophet by God's permission. God further says that the Qur'an is to be believed, and that it is not the speech of Gabriel. It is important to note that the Qur'an, in the words of the above verse, was revealed 'to the heart' of the Prophet Muhammad by Gabriel. At 26.193–194 we read that it was transmitted by the 'faithful spirit' 'upon your heart'. By comparison of these two verses it becomes evident that it is the angel Gabriel who is meant here by 'faithful spirit'.

In 81.19–23 God describes the transmittance of revelation:

> That this is in truth the word of an honoured messenger [Gabriel], mighty, established in the presence of the Lord of the Throne, one to be obeyed and trustworthy and your comrade [the Prophet] is not mad. Surely he saw him on the clear horizon.

Thus God says, in 6.124, 'And when a sign comes to them, they say: "We do not believe until we are given that which God's messengers are given. God knows best with whom to place His message".' Thus we read, in 20.50, 'Our Lord is He who gave everything its nature, then guided it correctly' and again, in 87.2–3, 'Who creates, then disposes, who measures then guides'. We also know that man is not excluded from this general law – that is, he has a direction and an aim towards which he develops, having been endowed with faculties that allow him to fulfil this aim. All his happiness lies in achieving this aim; his sorrow, grief and misfortune are the result of his failure to achieve this aim. He is guided to this special purpose by the Creator.

As we read in 76.3: 'Indeed, we have shown him the way whether he be grateful or disbelieving.' In 80.19–20 we find: 'From a drop of seed, He creates him and proportions him. Then makes the way easy for him.' The way we ought to live, which fits perfectly the requirements of humanity, is the way taught by the Prophets and Messengers of God. It is the way brought to them by God, through revelation, and established as undeniably true and valid by the example of their own lives and their intimate knowledge and contact with God.

The revelation of the Qur'an

In 2.213, we are told: 'Mankind was one community and God sent [to them] prophets as bearers of good news and as warners and revealed to them the book with the truth that it may judge between mankind concerning that in which they differed.' Here we understand 'one community' to mean a society at peace, its members living without dispute or difference. After a period of time, men differed with one another and as a result God sent the Prophets. Again he says, in 4.163–165: 'Indeed We have inspired you as we have inspired Noah ... Messengers of good news and a warning in order that mankind might have no argument against God after the Messenger.' Intellect alone does not make man accountable to God and this is why he must be awakened to the reality of his inner condition by other and often more dramatic means. These *ayat* suggest that the way of revelation and prophecy is the only way of removing differences between men. Revelation and prophecy are supposed to be the com-

plete and absolute proof to humanity of the truth of God's message.

The acceptance of the way of the revelation, however, always brings with it a reference to the law. By accepting the code of behaviour revealed by the Prophets, one entrusts one's judgement to God who, with his boundless power and knowledge, constantly watches over us; only he can reward good deeds or punish bad ones in an absolutely just way. God says, at 12.40, 'The decision rests with God only' and, at 99.7–8, 'And whoever does an atom's weight of good will see it then and whoever does an atom's weight of bad will see it then'. The theme continues in 22.17 ('Indeed God will decide between them on the day of resurrection, God is certainly witness over everything') and in 2.77 ('Are they unaware that God knows what they keep hidden and what they make public?'). In 33.52 we read: 'And God is watcher over all things.'

The Path of Revelation is protected against mistakes

The Path of Revelation is part of the Creator's programme. He never makes mistakes, neither in creation nor in the system of belief and the laws of the Qur'an, which come to us through revelation. God points out in 72.26–28 that he is the Knower of the Unseen and that he reveals his secret to no one except to every Messenger he has chosen, and he makes a guard go before the Messenger and a guard behind him, that he may know that they have indeed conveyed the message of the Lord. It is important that the Prophets and Messengers of God must be infallible, both in receiving the revelation and in preserving it against alteration and attack. They are instruments at the disposal of the Creator's wisdom. Were they to make an error in receiving or teaching the message of the revelation or to be led astray by the whispering of evil people, were they themselves to commit wrong or deliberately change the message they had to deliver, then the wisdom of God would be unable to perfect its programme of guidance.

God confirms in 16.9 that he is in total control of human guidance by means of his Messenger: 'And God's is the direction of the way, and some do not go straight.' The Prophets and Messengers mentioned in the Qur'an are men of precisely these qualities. The Qur'an does not mention their number; it only names a few, namely Adam, Nuh (Noah), Hud, Salih (Methusaleh), Ibrahim (Abraham), Lut (Lot), Isma'il (Ismael/Ishmael), al-Yasa' (Elisha), Dhu al-Kifl (Ezekiel), Ilyas (Elias/Elijah), Yunus (Jonah), Idris (Enoch), Ishaq (Isaac), Ya'qub (Jacob), Yusuf (Joseph), Shu'ayb, Musa (Moses), Harun (Aaron), Da'ud (David), Sulayman (Solomon), Ayyub (Job), Zakariya' (Zacharias), Yahya (John), Isma'il Sadiq al-Wa'd, 'Isa (Jesus) and Muhammad.

How the Qur'an was revealed

Qur'anic revelation, according to the Qur'an itself, is an utterance on behalf of God to his Prophet; the Prophet received the speech of God with all his being, not just by way of learning. In 42.51–52 we read:

> And it was not to be for any man that God should speak to him unless [it be] by revelation or from behind a veil or [that] we send a messenger to reveal what He will by His leave. Truly He is exalted, wise. And thus We have inspired in you [Muhammad] a spirit of Our command. You did not know what the Book, nor what the Faith was. But We have made it a light whereby We guide whom We will of our slaves. And truly you surely guide to a right path.

On comparison of these two verses we discover three different forms of prophetic communication. First, God speaks without there being any veil between him and man. Second, God speaks from behind a veil: like the tree on the Tur mountain from behind which Moses heard God speaking. Third, God's speech is brought to man by an angel who had previously heard the revelation from God.

The second of the two verses above shows that the Qur'an has reached us by means of the third of three possible ways. Again, God says, in 26.192–195, '[A revelation] which the Faithful Spirit [Gabriel] has brought down upon your heart, that you may be [one] of the warners, in plain Arabic Speech' and, in 2.97, 'Who is an enemy to Gabriel! For it is he who has revealed [this book] to your heart.' From these verses we understand that the Qur'an was transmitted by way of an angel named Gabriel, or the Faithful Spirit, and that the Prophet received the revelation from him with all his being, all his perception, and not merely by listening. The verse says 'on your heart', which in Qur'anic terms means perception or awareness. In 53.10–11 we read: 'And He revealed to His slave that which He revealed. The heart did not lie [in seeing] what it saw'; and in 98.2 reception of the revelation is indicated as a reading of 'pure pages' by God's Messenger.

Prophecy in Islamic philosophy

There was a long discussion of this issue in Islamic philosophy, and it generally took the line that God would only pick the appropriate person for the task. Since God knows everything about everything, he is not in the position of a football manager picking a team. For one thing, the manager does not know how a particular player will do in the competition, whether he will become injured, or even if he can afford him. These are not problems for God, who can pick the dream team and no obstacles can arise. But this brings us to a difficulty: if God would only pick the best, does this mean that God has to pick the best? If he has to pick the best, then it looks as though he is not free to pick whomever he wishes, hardly a tempting proposition for an omnipotent deity. It looks as though the right person to prophesy can force God to pick him, in just the same way that '2 + 2' can oblige God to draw the conclusion '4'.

What are the best features of prophecy? They are the ability to communicate with the widest possible public. That is what prophets do and this gives them an ability that philosophers do not necessarily have, since philosophers are skilled at communicating with a more limited and intellectually restricted audience. Prophets range in degree, as does everyone, and some have this ability in higher proportions than do others. It very much looks, on the account of prophecy current in Islamic philosophy, that the very best communicators can demand that God chooses them, in just the same way that the very fastest runners and most skilled gymnasts can demand to be included in a particular team. As with the sports team, issues of personality come in to it, so that a particular sportsperson may be wrong for the team despite his or her skills, since they may not be able to get on with other people in the team and so would be more of a liability than a help. This could not be used as an objection to the perfect communicator being a prophet who must be picked, since presumably he would always know how to express himself to others to obviate any personal problems that might otherwise arise.

It is perhaps worth pointing to a contrast between prophets in the Jewish Bible and prophets in the Qur'an. The former are often rather disreputable in their behaviour, and are not always treated well by the Jews. This leads the Qur'an to contrast the treatment of prophets by Muslims and by Jews, with the former being far better behaved in this respect. The Qur'an is also a lot more polite about the Prophets, who appear throughout as paradigms of virtuous behaviour, very different from the account found in the Bible. Of course, this might be because that account is a result of falsification of the original text by the Jews, something that the Qur'an puts right – or so it is sometimes said. Whatever we say on this issue, it is surely relevant that the prophets in Islam are ethically of a very high order, especially from the point of view of arguing with God and in exemplifying patience. On the account of prophecy provided by al-Farabi, it does very much look as though a morally upright individual who at the same time is an excellent communicator and skilled in abstract thought has perfect credentials for being a prophet. If at a particular time a prophet is needed, then God has no choice but to accept him and use him.

This brings us to another difficulty from a theological point of view. If God does not choose the messenger, does he at least choose the message? Or will the prophet, through his grasp of the situation and use of his intelligence, added to his desire to help people, be able to work it out by himself? This runs against the biblical account that has God communicating to the community through the prophet, but does this mean that God actually tells the prophet what to say? Since the prophet has the right sort of mind and communicative ability to express the truth and to know the truth, what need is there for God to do anything at all? This inevitably reminds us of the criticism that al-Ghazali brought against the Islamic philosophers: they talk about God but give him nothing to do. The implication is that God really is superfluous and so it is intellectually dishonest to talk about him as though he played a part in what takes place.

How would a prophet know what the future was going to be, unless God told him? The answer is that he would be able to perfect his thinking and so connect his particular mind to the active intellect, or come close to this, and that active intellect represents the ideal of abstract thought itself, insofar as human beings can, while material, come into contact with it. This enables the prophet to link particular events in the world of generation and corruption to other such events, since he understands how everything is connected to everything else. Ibn Sina uses the notion of quick-wittedness, clearly based on Aristotelian *agkhinoia*, which allows someone to apply major premises, i.e. univeral truths, to the minor premises of experience and so derive accurate predictions of what is going to happen in the future. This naturalistic account of prophecy seems to undermine many of the features of the Qur'anic account, and for that and other reasons was often strenuously opposed in the Islamic intellectual world.

Further reading

Black, D. (1996) 'Al-Farabi', *HIP*: 178–99.
Leaman, O. (2002) *An Introduction to Classical Islamic Philosophy*, Cambridge: Cambridge University Press.
Nasr, S.H., Hamid, D. and Nasr, V. (eds) (1988) *Shi'ism: Doctrines, thought, and spirituality*, Albany, NY: SUNY Press.

*See also: **nafs**; revelation; **ruh***

OLIVER LEAMAN

PROVERB
*see: **mathal***

PUNISHMENT

The Qur'anic concepts of punishment, affliction, suffering and torment are interconnected and most often expressed (around 400 times) by the word '*adhab*. The origin of '*adhab* may be a human ruler, but most often it is God who punishes. God allots chastisement to individuals and communities in this world, as well as to individuals in the hereafter (the chastisement of fire in hell). Expressions like 'a painful chastisement' (3.177) are often synonymous with 'hell'. Occasionally, the word '*adhab* may also mean 'legal punishment' (4.25).

Punishment stories are an important type of Qur'anic narrative, especially in the Meccan period. Throughout history, unbelief and rebellion against God and his Messengers are punished by divine intervention. The people of Thamud, for example, rejected the Divine Messengers sent to them and 'the chastisement seized them' (26.158) as a sign for humanity. In 5.112 Jesus ('Isa) is asked by his disciples to ask God to send down a table with food from heaven. Jesus' request is granted, but the divine voice says 'Verily, I do send it [the table] down to you. Whoso of you hereafter disbelieves, verily I shall chastise him with a chastisement wherewith I chastise no other being' (5.115).

A post-Qur'anic concept is 'the punishment in the tomb' ('*adhab al-qabr*). It was extensively developed in Tradition and depicts how angels question and test man between death and the Day of Judgement. This idea led to the concept of two judgements, one immediately after an individual's death and another at the Day of Judgement. In support of this doctrine, Qur'anic verses like 6.93 are quoted:

If thou couldst only see when the evil-doers are in the agonies of death, and the angels are stretching out their hands. Give up your souls! Today you shall be recompensed with the chastisement of humiliation for what you said untruly about God, waxing proud against His signs.

See also: **suffering**

STEFAN WILD

PUNISHMENT AND ORIGINAL SIN

One of the fundamental issues that Islam and Christianity disagree about is the original sin of Adam. The Qur'an describes the creation of Adam, his sin and its implications in various places in the text. Adam's sin and its outcome are depicted in the following verses of the Qur'an:

O Adam dwell with your wife in the Garden and enjoy as you wish but approach not this tree or you run into harm and transgression. Then Satan whispered to them in order to reveal to them their shame that was hidden from them and he said: 'Your Lord only forbade you this tree lest you become angels or such beings as live forever.' And he swore to them both that he was their sincere adviser. So by deceit he brought them to their fall: when they tasted the tree their shame became manifest to them and they began to sew together the leaves of the garden over their bodies. And their Lord called unto them: 'Did I not forbid you that tree and tell you that Satan was your avowed enemy?' (7.19–22)

When Adam and Eve realize that they disobeyed God by eating the fruit, 'They said: "Our Lord, we have wronged ourselves. If You do not forgive us or give us mercy, we shall certainly lose"' (7.23). God accepts their plea: 'Thus did Adam disobey his Lord, so he went

astray. Then his Lord chose him, and turned to him with forgiveness, and gave him guidance' (20.121–122).

Adam and Eve were instructed not to eat from a certain tree. Satan characteristically tricked them into disobeying and, as a result,

[God] said: 'Get down [from the Garden], one of you an enemy to the other [i.e. Adam, Eve and Satan]. On earth will be a dwelling-place for you and an enjoyment – for a short time.' He [God] said: 'Therein you shall live, and therein you shall die, and from it you shall be brought out [resurrected].' (7.24–25)

Adam and Eve were ordered to leave the Garden and descend to earth, where they and their children will live and die, and where Satan will also be present to try to continue to deceive them. In the text, Adam does not lay the responsibility for their joint disobedience on Eve. God doesn't curse Eve for her mistake, nor does he curse Adam for committing a sin, and Adam's sin is not passed on to future generations. It seems unfair to behave otherwise, since why should someone be punished due to the faults of someone else? The Qur'an states:

That no burdened person [with sins] shall bear the burden [of sins] of another. And that man can have nothing but what he does [of good and bad]. And that his deeds will be seen, then he will be recompensed with a full and the best recompense. (53.38–41)

The sin of Adam has no consequences for his descendants. Similarly, the virtue of Ibrahim (Abraham) did not benefit his descendants: 'And when his Lord tried Abraham with certain words, he fulfilled them. He said, "Surely I will make you a leader (*imam*) of men." Abraham said, "And of my offspring?" "My covenant does not include the unjust," said He' (2.124). These passages are often used by Sunni opponents of the doctrine that the family of the Prophet, or other prophets and their companions, are specially suited for authority because of their familial links with such outstanding people.

See also: **ahl al-bayt**; devil; sin

OLIVER LEAMAN

PURIFY

Tahara or *tahura* means to be pure, clean, chaste or righteous. The term *taharat* signifies that a woman is free of her menstrual cycle. *Tah-har* is to purify or cleanse. *Tat-hir* or *taharh* is a verbal noun meaning purification.

Purification is the topic with which all the *fiqh* (jurisprudence) books begin. It is a requirement that has to be met prior to many worship practices, include touching or reciting the Qur'an: 'none can touch it, but the purified' (56.79); it is also a prerequisite for performing one of the obligatory or voluntary prayers, for the *tawaf* (circumambulation) of the Ka'ba and so on. The Qur'an states that Allah is in favour of those who cleanse themselves by taking a bath and washing thoroughly their bodies, including their private parts, prior to their prayers. 'Truly, Allah loves those who purify themselves' (2.222).

The Prophet thought purification was an important issue: he said *al-tahara nisf al-iman,* meaning 'purification establishes half of faith'. Furthermore, he said that no prayer shall be accepted from anyone who does not make *wudu* (ablution).

There are two kinds of purification in Islam: physical ritual purity and spiritual self-purification. Ablution or ritual body washing is the major physical ritual purification. It was mandated in the Qur'an as a precondition to any

prayers: 'O you who believe! When you intend to offer the prayer, wash your faces and your hands up to the elbows, rub your heads [with wet hands] and [wash] your feet up to the ankles' (5.6). Purification is also mandatory after sexual activity. The Muslims are instructed by the Qur'an to bathe if they have had sexual intercourse. The state after having had sex or a wet dream is called *janaba*, meaning major ritual impurity. 'If you are in a state of *janaba* (ritual impurity) purify yourselves [bathe your whole body]' (5.6).

In addition, Muslims are obligated to bathe on different occasions following the *sunna*, the tradition of the Prophet. Bathing is obligatory before attending the Friday prayer, which is the main weekly Muslim ceremony. The Prophet said: 'The purification for Friday is a must for every adult and so is *al-siwak* (a small stick used as a toothbrush). And he is also to wear perfume if he can afford it.' Virtual ablution is required prior to attending the two Eids (feasts) and their prayers. During the *hajj* (pilgrimage) ritual bathing is also necessary at various points. These include bathing before putting on the sheets of *ihram* (the traditional garments of the Mecca pilgrim); before entering Mecca; and to stand on Mount Arafat. Furthermore, the prophetic tradition insists on bathing after washing a corpse.

In addition to bathing after sexual activity, women are required to undertake major ablution (ritual bathing) after the conclusion of menstruation and at the end of *nifas* (the period of recovery in bed, usually lasting around six weeks, that follows childbirth). Until she has bathed, a woman is not permitted to perform prayers or to circumambulate the Ka'ba. Nor is she to fast or to touch or recite from the Qur'an.

Physical purity and cleanliness also apply to the places where prayer is

513

offered. The Prophet insisted that prayer would not be accepted by God unless it was performed in a clean place. Similarly, Ibrahim was ordered by Allah to purify the Meccan sanctuary, the *Ka'ba*, which is referred to in the Qur'an as the House of Allah. The purity of the House of Allah pertains to the removal of any impure bodies from the Mosque, including idols: 'And sanctify My House for those who go around it, and those who stand up [for prayer], and those who bow and make prostration [in prayer]' (22.26). Not only the place, but also the clothing of those praying there should be clean: 'And purify your garments' (74.4). In short, physical purity is a necessary precondition for any prayer to be accepted, hence Muslims must apply physical purity rituals to body, place of worship and clothes.

Self-purity is another major subject in the Islam. The Prophet has said: 'Allah is pure and He shall not accept anything but purity.' Allah wants Muslims to be purified. Starting with the Prophet Muhammad and his family, Allah removes impurity from his righteous servants and purifies them. 'Allah wishes only to remove *ar-rijs* (evil deeds and sins) from you, O members of the family of the Prophet, and to purify you with a thorough purification' (33.33).

The Qur'an declares that Allah similarly purified Mary (Maryam), the mother of Jesus: 'O Maryam! Verily, Allah has chosen you, purified you, and chosen you above all the women' (3.42).

The Qur'an placed man at the junction of two paths, the first leading to goodness and the second to evil, and gave him the freedom to choose. Consequently, the victor is he who chooses the first route, which can be achieved by the purification of the self. 'Indeed he succeeds who purifies his own self. And indeed he fails who corrupts his own self' (91.9–10). The purification of the self can be achieved by obeying and performing all that Allah ordered, and by following the Tradition of Prophet Muhammad, in addition to embracing the true Islamic faith of monotheism and by doing good deeds.

Islam imposes strict obligations on Muslims; however, it also provides some exceptions. A sick person, for instance, is exempt from certain duties, as are the weak, the poor and so on. The Qur'an declares that Allah does not want to place Muslims in difficulty, but only 'wants to purify you, and to complete His favour to you that you may be thankful' (5.6).

See also: **ablution**

RAFIK BERJAK

Q

QADA' / QADAR

Both *qada'* and *qadar* are used particularly to refer to the omnipotence of God, who gave the world its shape and reigns supreme over all creatures. *Qada'*, however, also conveys the concept of judgement. Both terms are of great importance in theological terminology, especially in relation to issues of divine decree and predestination.

The term *qada'* does not appear in this precise form in the Qur'an, but we find many declensions (approximately sixty) of the verb *qada*, from which the substantive *qada'* is derived. Having at first the meaning 'to settle' and 'to finish', *qada* is used in the Holy Book especially to indicate the decisions and decrees of God. Accordingly, the word refers to divine omnipotence and is often coupled by the theologians with *qadar* (this time, a Qur'anic term), meaning the power and the capability to do something: *Qada' wa'l-qadar* is a familiar locution in theological language. Al-Ash'ari argued

that orthodox Muslims (*ahl al-sunna*) 'believe that good and evil happen by decree and predestination from God ... and by no means can men help or harm themselves' (al-Ash'ari, 1969, Vol. 1: 346). Louis Gardet and Georges Anawati (Gardet and Anawati, 1981: 151) translate *qada'* as *prédétermination* and *qadar* as *décret*, but Robert Caspar is more accurate in rendering *qadar* as *prédestination* (Caspar, 1987: 130). The word *qadar* is closely connected with the issue of free will in the history of Islamic theology. Indeed, theologians who claim that man has the ability to act and to choose freely are called Qadarites; they are sometimes identified with the Mu'tazila. Al-Ghazali was really keen to interpret the locution *qada' wa'l-qadar* in light of Qur'anic aims:

> The Decree of God (*qada'*) is explicit in four intentions: pious deeds, sins, benefits and misfortunes ... The decree (*qada'*) is the existence of all existents on the Preserved Tablet (*al-lawh al-mahfuz*) as a

515

whole and in detail; predestination (*qadar*) is the particularization of the previous decree bringing into being [the things] in the material world one after another. *Qada'* is the eternal will and the divine providence (*'inaya*) required for the arrangment of existents in a specific order; *qadar* suspends that will with regard to things on particular occasions. (al-Ghazali, 1970: 21–2)

Actually, *qada'* acquires particular philosophic nuances in relation to God's capability and power to bestow rational order and arrangement on the world. First of all, he decided to create the world and the world was brought into being at once by the creative power of the Word. On four occasions, we read: 'When He decided (*qada*) a thing, He needs only say "Be" and it is (*kun fa-yakunu*)' (2.117; 3.47; 19.35; 40.68). The creation by the Word is a commonplace in Semitic religious tradition: we find it in the Bible, but also the Babylonian myth of Marduk tells us how the god produced his weapons by the creative word. Moreover, the verb *qada* is used in the Qur'an to point out the creative act's perfection: 'He formed seven heavens (*qadahunna sab' samawat*) in two days' – that is, God settled the universe and gave it the laws necessary for it to function perfectly. God's decision reveals his provident far-sightedness: 'God decided to accomplish what He had ordained (*yaqdiya Allah(u) amran kana maf'ulan*) so that he who was destined to perish might perish indisputably' (8.42). The decision of God shows at the same time his justice (*'adl*) and his truth (*haqq*), mainly in the Day of Judgement. God 'will judge upon them with right balance (*qada baynahum bi'l-qist*) and nobody will be wronged' (10.54). In the Qur'an, however, *qada* is used to mean also human judgement and decision. For instance, in a single verse (20.72) we find

three declensions of the verb: 'Decree [against us] as much as you judge, but you can decree [only] upon the life of this world' (*fa-aqyi ma anta qadi innama taqdi hadhihi'l-hayata al-dunya*). (The magicians of Pharaoh are speaking here to the king, in front of Moses.)

Like *qada'*, the word *qadar* and the terms derived from it refer to the omnipotence of God in the first place. More than thirty times in the Qur'an God is defined as 'He who is powerful over all things' (*Allah 'ala kulli shayy' qadir*). This power is sometimes connected with knowledge and science: God is powerful as a knower (*'alim qadir*) (16.70; 20.45; 42.50). Philosophers and theologians alike say that God is creator because he possesses knowledge, and power and science are two sides of the same coin. Al-Ghazali maintained that God is the only real agent because he wills and know, and Averroes argued that God created by his knowledge. In the Qur'an, creation is performed 'giving measure', 'decreeing' and 'settling'. God decreed destiny and measure (*qaddara taqdiran*) for all things when he created them (25.2). He created, settled and imposed his decree on the earth and the heavens (87.3). For all men and the entire universe are subject to God's pleasure: 'God gives abundantly to whom He will and spares (*yaqdiru*) whom He will' (13.26). Up to this point, we have only met verbal nouns and adjectives. But *qadar* appears in exactly in this form eleven times, with four substantial nuances of meaning:

1. *Qadar* means the 'appropriate measure' in, for instance, 15.21: 'We hold the store of all wealth and send it down in appropriate measure'. By analogy, God lets the soil live by sending water 'with measure' (23.18; 43.11).

2. At least twice the term clearly means the divine decree: the destiny of Moses is decreed by God (20.40); God's command is a determined decree (*kana amr Allah qadaran maqduran*) (33.38).
3. *Qadar* stands for the rationality of God's creation at 54.49: 'Indeed, We created everything according to a fixed decree.'
4. Finally, *qadar* hints at the appointed time decreed by God for the life and development of human beings (6.2; 77.22).

Although *qada' wa'l-qadar* are not specifically coupled in the Qur'an, theologians are right to connect them, because the meanings they have in the Holy Book are very close.

References and further reading

al-Ash'ari (1969) *Maqalat al-islamiyyun* (The Sayings of Muslims), Cairo: Maktaba al-Nahya al-Misriyya.
Caspar, R. (1987) *Traité de Théologie Musulmane* (Treatise of Islamic Theology), Rome: PISAI.
Gardet, L. and Anawati, G. (1981) *Introduction à la théologie musulmane* (Introduction to Islamic Theology), Paris: Vrin.
al-Ghazali (1970) *Kitab al-arba'in fi usul al-din* (Book of the Forty Principles of Religion), Cairo: Maktaba al-Jindi.

See also: **Ash'arites and Mu'tazilites;** *irada*; **Preserved Tablet**

MASSIMO CAMPANINI

QALA

Qala is a root verb that means to hate or detest. The term is used in the Qur'an twice. It is used at one point to assure the Prophet Muhammad that his Lord never left him. At the early stage of the revelation Gabriel delays his coming to the Prophet and the Prophet grieves. The people say Muhammad's God *qalaha* (has abandoned him), but then

Muhammad receives the revelation 'Your Lord has neither forsaken you nor hates you' (93.3). The second example is the Prophet Lot's hatred for his people's practice of sodomy. He says: 'I am indeed of those who disapprove with severe anger and fury of your actions' (26.168).

RAFIK BERJAK

QALAM

Qalam signifies pen, reed pen or pencil. It is derived from the root verb *qalama*, which means to cut, clip, pare or trim; the *qalam* (pen) was so-called because it gets cut, clipped or trimmed. According to al-Qurtubi, Allah created four things by his own hand: the pen, the Throne, the Garden of Eden and Adam. Adam was taught by Allah how to write with a pen. Abu Hurayra recorded that the Prophet had said: 'When Allah created His Creation He wrote in His Book which is placed above the Throne: "Verily, My Mercy overcomes My Anger".' Moreover, the Prophet said: 'the first thing Allah created was the pen. And He said to it "Write". It wrote everything that shall happen until the Day of Judgement. It is with Him ... above His Throne.'

The early Muslim scholars identified three kinds of pen: the first is the one Allah created by his own hand and ordered to write; the second type covers the pens of angels, with which they write *al-maqadir* (the measurements or quantities and events) and *al-a'mal* (the deeds); the third kind represents the pens of people. Allah enabled people to use pens to write down their thoughts and so that they could address various needs. Many virtues of writing are recognized in Islam, among them the fact that writing is a major method of developing *al-bayan* (the faculty of eloquent speech), a gift given to man: 'He taught him [man] eloquent speech.'

The pen is seen by some commentators as a great favour bestowed on humanity by God. Without the gift of writing, there would be no preserved religion, nor would life have been established on earth. The pen also indicates the Mercy and Generosity of Allah towards his servants. He allowed them to learn what they have ignored and he took them out of the darkness of ignorance into the light of knowledge. 'Read! And your Lord is the Most Generous. Who has taught the [writing] with the pen?' (96.3–4). The Qur'an expresses the importance of knowledge in many places. 'Alima (knew), the root verb of 'ilm (knowledge), and its many different forms are used in the Qur'an 854 times.

The pen is also a symbol for the 'ulama (scholars). They use the pen to record their knowledge and convey their teachings to the world. The Qur'an has special regard for those scholars who have both knowledge and belief. They are the ones who fear Allah the most: 'It is only those who have knowledge among His slaves that fear Allah' (35.28).

In the Qur'an, the term aqlam (pens) signifies the casting of lots, a method of deciding something by chance, especially by choosing from among several pieces of paper. 'You [Muhammad] were not with them, when they cast lots with their pens as to which of them should be charged with the care of Mary' (3.44).

See also: bayyana

RAFIK BERJAK

QARUN

Qarun (Korah) was a rich man and a member of the tribe of Moses, who is said to have become arrogant due to his wealth, to have rebelled against the truth because of his pride (uluvv), to have created chaos in the world and to have duly been punished by God. His name is mentioned four times in three different chapters of the Qur'an.

In the version of the story that is narrated in surat al-Qasas (28.76–83), Qarun was so rich that the keys to his treasure could not be carried by a single man. Despite this enormous wealth, he is said to have been mean. He stopped doing good deeds for society and exalted himself above his people, causing envy and jealousy.

According to the Qur'an, one of the most important criteria for identifying a religious man is whether or not he gives to others from what God gave him. Despite warnings from some of his fellow tribesman, Qarun continued to claim that he had earned his wealth by himself. Eventually, he forgot God altogether, thus becoming infidel. As punishment, God sank him and his dwelling-place underground.

In two other versions of the story (29.39–40; 40.23–25), Qarun is mentioned together with Pharaoh and Haman. It is said that Moses was sent to Qarun, just as to Pharaoh and Haman, with clear signs. But all three of them insisted that Moses was a sorcerer and a liar, rejecting him in their arrogance and ordering the sons of those who believed in Moses and joined him to be killed. In the end, each of the three men were punished for their sins in different ways, such as a storm blast, sinking and drowning.

In Islam, Qarun is considered an archetypical infidel (kafir), led astray by his wealth and fighting against God's religion.

Further reading

Asad, M. (1980) The Message of the Qur'an, Gibraltar: Dar al-andalus.

Yusuf Ali, A. (1999) *The Meaning of the Holy Qur'an,* Baltimore, MD: Amana Publications.

See also: **money; wealth**

IBRAHIM SUMER

QASAS

Qasas is the title of *sura* 28. It is taken from *aya* 25, where the phrase *wa qassa alayhi al-qasas* occurs. *Qasas,* a noun meaning narrative, story or tale, comes from the root *q/s/s/* and occurs in the Qur'an five times (3.55; 7.175; 12.3, 111; 17.25). It specifically refers to miraculous events, particularly in reference to the lives of prophets. As a Qur'anic term, *qasas* is used for both popular and edifying religious stories, as well as, much more widely, history.

NECMETTIN GÖKKIR

QIBLA

In the *sura al-Baqara* we read:

> It is not righteousness that you turn your faces towards the East and the West, but righteous is the one who believes in Allah, and the Last Day, and the angels and the Book and the prophets; and gives away wealth out of love for Him to the near of kin and the orphans and the needy and the wayfarer and to those who ask and to set slaves free; and keeps up prayer and pays the poor-rate; and the performers of their promise when they make a promise; and the patient in distress and difficulty and in the time of conflict. These are they who are truthful; and these are they who keep their duty. (2.177)

This passage refers to the change in the direction in which Muslims are to offer their prayer. This took place when the Muslims moved to Medina, about sixteen months after the *Hijra*. Prior to this, Muslims prayed facing towards Jerusalem.

They were then commanded by divine revelation to face towards the sacred house at *Ka'ba* in Mecca. Is this change of direction important in itself, or only important because it was commanded by God?

The importance of what direction to face during prayer is such that the Prophet individually, and the Muslims in general, are addressed on the topic five times in the Qur'an. They are told to face towards the *Ka'ba* wherever they are, and whenever they get ready to pray. The importance of facing this direction (*qibla*) is suggested by a *hadith* in which the Prophet calls the Muslims the *ahl al-qibla,* and forbids labelling anyone a *kafir* who prays in the right direction. This was revealed at Medina. But Jerusalem, the first direction (*qibla awwal*), is north of Medina, and the mosque in Mecca, the final direction (*qibla akhir*), lies south. Why then the reference to turning to the east and west? This is probably an expression meaning people anywhere, surely a most appropriate expression given the way in which Muslims soon became spread all over the world. The change of direction symbolized the ending of God's special relationship with the Jews, for whom Jerusalem is so important, and the establishment of support for those coming from the Mecca area. Had the Jews embraced Islam, perhaps Jerusalem would have stayed as the direction of prayer, but given their stubbornness and treachery, according to the Qur'an, a new direction became desirable. The change also symbolizes God's absolute power to choose anywhere as the *qibla*: nothing constrained him to decide one way or another. The *Ka'ba* in Mecca could be seen, too, as representing a purer monotheism, one that God wanted to establish at the heart of Islam.

See also: **Jerusalem;** *salat*

OLIVER LEAMAN

QIRA'AT

see: ***hafiz***; **inimitability**

QITAL

The word *qital* means, in general, fighting or physical combat. It occurs several times in the Qur'an and is, under specific circumstances, one of multiple ways of striving in the path of God (*al-jihad fi sabil Allah*). This usage is exemplified in 2.190 and 244, 3.13, 4.74–76, 9.111, and so on. In the Qur'an, *jihad* is a broad term encompassing many different ways of enjoining what is good and forbidding what is evil, a key moral imperative in the Qur'an. But after the first/eighth century, the notion of *jihad* was reduced in juristic and administrative literature increasingly often to just physical combat, thus becoming practically synonymous with *qital*.

ASMA AFSARUDDIN

QUR'AN, THE

For Muslims, the Qur'an is the word of God, preserved on a well-guarded tablet (85.22) and revealed, through the angel Gabriel (Jibril), to the Prophet Muhammad in 611 CE. The miraculous event first occurred when Muhammad, aged 40, was meditating in a cave on Mount Hira', three miles from Mecca, on the night of al-Qadr (the Night of Power), which is 23 Ramadan. The revelation was intermittent and lasted between twenty and twenty-five years. The Qur'an consists of 114 *suras* (chapters), which vary in length from just three *ayas* (*suras* 108 and 110) to 286 (*sura* 2), not including the first *sura*, which is the opening of the Qur'an and consists of seven *ayas*. The Qur'an is divided into Meccan *suras*, so called because they were revealed in or around Mecca, and Medinan *suras*, revealed in or around Medina. Muslim scholars differ on the matter of whether these *suras* were arranged by the Prophet Muhammad himself or by his Companions after the Prophet died in 11/632. For non-Muslim scholars, such as Richard Bell (1953: 41), the arrangement of the *suras* was done after the Prophet's death.

The constituents of each *sura* are called *ayas*, which are believed by Muslim scholars to have been arranged by the Prophet himself (al-Zarkashi, 1988, Vol. 1: 64; al-Suyuti, 1996, Vol. 1: 175; al-'Asqalani, 1997, Vol. 9: 50). The Qur'an claims (3.3; 6.38; 16.64, 89) it is a reaffirmation of and complementary to previous scriptures (5.44; 41.43), and describes itself as 'enlightenment for the people, guidance and mercy' (28.43), 'a healer' (10.57). It emphasizes the fact that it includes all that has been mentioned in the previous two scriptures (i.e. the Old Testament and the Bible), but insists that it has perfected these scriptures and, most importantly, abrogated their legal rulings (5.43–44; 6.91; 7.157; 41.43). For this reason, Bell (1953: 172) claims that Judaism and Christianity have indirectly influenced the Qur'an. Pedersen (1984: 13) is also of the view that the Old and New Testaments have the same basic ideas as the Qur'an about what happens in heaven and on earth, the fate of men, and the consequences of their good and evil deeds. While Muslim scholars claim that the Qur'an is free from editorial intervention and stands exactly as it was revealed to the Prophet Muhammad, non-Muslim scholars (again Bell, 1953) are of the opinion that the Qur'an received some additions from the Companions after the Prophet's death. Cragg (2001: 10) is of the opinion that Muhammad was consciously involved in the composition of the Qur'an. Yet, for Muslim scholars, the Qur'an is Muhammad's eternal miracle and it is beyond human faculties to imitate it; this is referred to as *i'jaz al-Qur'an* (the inimitability of the Qur'an).

The word *qur'an* means recitation or reading, and the first word of the first *sura* revealed to the Prophet was *iqra'* (read). *Qur'an* can also be morphologically derived from the verb *qarana* (to put something together) or the plural noun *qara'in*, whose singular form is *qarina* (linguistic consonance, conceptual connectivity), meaning that the Qur'an's constituent *ayas* are coherently connected and logically sequenced. Al-Qurtubi claims that *qur'an* is derived from the verb *qara'a* (to read, recite), but al-Shafi'i is of the view that the word is not derived from this verb and is rather one of the names of the Book of God. This view is supported by Ibn Kathir, who also used to recite the word *qur'an* without the *hamza* (glottal stop) as *quran*. From an intertextual point of view, the derivation of the word *qur'an* from *qara'in* is more appropriate. Etymologically, the term is linked to the Syriac word *qeryana* (scripture reading, lection) and to the Hebrew *miqra'* (recitation, scripture). The word *qur'an* occurs sixty-eight times in the Qur'an and has been given over thirty attributes. The Qur'an is divided into four parts: the first part includes *suras* 1–6, the second comprises *suras* 7–18, part three is *suras* 19–35, and part four is made up of *suras* 36–114. It is interesting to note that the first *sura* of the Qur'an refers to lordship, while the last refers to divinity.

The Qur'anic message

The Qur'an repeatedly highlights four major tenets of faith (*usul al-iman*). These are:

1. Monotheism (*tawhid*): referring to the oneness or unity of God, this is the antonym of polytheism (*al-shirk*), which means the association of others with God (2.22, 255; 3.2; 25.2; 59.23; etc.).
2. Prophethood (*al-nubuwwa*): confirmation of the prophethood of Muhammad and that the Qur'an is the word of God (25.1; 3.31–32; 16.64; 28.85–87; 36.2–3; etc.).
3. Eschatology (*al-ma'ad*): referring to Resurrection and the Day of Judgement (7.187; 20.124; 36.51; 42.9; 50.42–43; etc.).
4. Reward and punishment (*al-thawab wal-'iqab*): usually presented in the form of an antithesis, where believers are rewarded with the garden (*al-janna*) but unbelievers are punished with the fire (*al-nar*) in the hereafter (2.81–82; 30.15–16; 56.88–94; 64.9–10; etc.).

The themes of the Qur'an

The Qur'an refers to various recurrent themes: believers (2.227; 98.7); the People of the Book, i.e. the Scripturists (2.105; 3.64); polytheists (2.105; 3.151); hypocrites (8.49; 9.67); the Prophets (4.163; 13.27; 20.13); parables of various Prophets (2.40–93) and previous nations (36.31; 40.82–83); Islamic legal rulings (2.226–237; 4.19–25); justice (5.42; 7.29; 49.9); fighting in the cause of God (2.190; 9.38); spending on charity (2.254; 64.16); looking after orphans and the needy (9.60; 22.28); patience (3.200; 103.3); righteousness (6.153; 7.26); admonition and morality (4.112; 6.151–152); respect for parents (2.83; 31.14); enjoining what is right and forbidding what is wrong (3.114; 9.112); and God's omnipotence (23.12–22; 36.36–42).

References and further reading
Abdul-Raof, H. (2001) *The Qur'an Outlined: Theme and text*, London: Taha Publishers.

—— (2003) *Exploring the Qur'an*, Dundee: Al-Maktoum Institute Academic Press.

al-'Asqalani b. Hajar (1997) *Fathu al-Bari Sharhu Sahih al-Bukhari*, Riyadh: Maktabat dar al-salam, Vols 1–13.

al-Baqillani, Abu Bakr Muhammad (1994) *I'jaz al-Qur'an*, Beirut: Dar Ihya' al-'Ulum.

Bell, R. (1953) *Introduction to the Qur'an*, Edinburgh: Edinburgh University Press.

—— (1991) *A Commentary on the Qur'an*, Manchester: The Victoria University of Manchester, Vols 1–2.

Cornell, V.J. (1995) 'The Qur'an as Scripture', *The Oxford Encyclopedia of the Modern Islamic World*, 387–94.

Cragg, K. (2001) *Muhammad in the Qur'an: The task and the text*, London: Melisende.

Pedersen, J. (1984) *The Arabic Book*, Princeton, NJ: Princeton University Press.

al-Qurtubi, Abu 'Abd Allah Muhammad (1997) *al-Jami' li Ahkam al-Qur'an*, Beirut: Dar al-kitab al-'arabi, Vols 1–20.

al-Razi, Fakhr al-Din (1990) *Mafatih al-ghayb*, Beirut: Dar al-kutub al-'ilmiyya, Vols 1–32.

Robinson, N. (1996) *Dicovering the Qur'an: A contemporary approach to a veiled text*, London: SCM Press.

al-Suyuti, Jalal al-Din (1996) *al-Itqan fi 'Ulum al-Qur'an*, Beirut: Dar ihya' al-'ulum, Vols 1–2.

al-Zarkashi, Badr al-Din (1988) *al-Burhan fi 'Ulum al-Qur'an*, Beirut: Dar al-kutub al-'ilmiyya, Vols 1–4.

HUSSEIN ABDUL-RAOF

QUR'ANIC STUDIES

Qur'anic Studies (*'ulum al-Qur'an*) is a discipline that developed after the death of the Prophet and is concerned with the investigation of various Qur'anic topics, such as the compilation of the Qur'an, reasons for revelation, abrogating and abrogated *ayas*. The historical journey of Qur'anic Studies began when the attention of Muslim scholars was attracted to Qur'anic calligraphy dating to the period during and after the Caliphate of 'Uthman b. 'Affan (d. 656), a style that later became known as Uthmani calligraphy. In the middle of the seventh century CE, during the Caliphate of 'Ali b. Abi Talib (d. 661), Muslim scholars were concerned with a grammatical analysis of Qur'anic discourse whose objective was to preserve the linguistic accuracy of the Qur'an and thus facilitate its exegesis. During the second half of the first century of the Hijra, the focus in Qur'anic Studies was shifted to other topics, such as abrogation, semantic ambiguities in the Qur'an, exegesis, and Meccan and Medinan revelations. Muslim scholars were more interested in exegesis than anything else during the second century of the Hijra: their research effort culminated in the emergence of comprehensive exegesis on the whole Qur'an by a distinguished scholar known as Ibn Jarir al-Tabari (d. 924). Qur'anic Studies in the period from the third to the seventh century of the Hijra was characterized by thorough research of specific topics and the appearance of thesauruses of many volumes. The eighth century of the Hijra was marked by the thesaurus of Badr al-Din al-Zarkashi (1344–91) and the ninth century by work from Jalal al-Din al-Suyuti (d. 1505). Research continued in Qur'anic Studies, but the focus was mainly on exegesis, as it still remains.

Among the major topics of Qur'anic Studies, nine command particular attention.

Meccan and Medinan revelations

Qur'anic *suras* and *ayas* are classified as Meccan and Medinan. The leitmotifs of these two categories of revelation are different. As priority in Mecca was the establishment of a sound faith, the pivotal themes of the Meccan revelations were belief in God, monotheism, eschatology, and reward and punishment. The Meccan revelations lasted for thirteen years until the Prophet migrated to Medina in 622 CE. The main focus of the Meccan revelations was to set the scene for a cohesive bond between the created and the Creator, and for the substitution of people's heedlessness towards their Lord for gratitude to him for his infinite favours through total submission to his will. The Meccan revelations included all the *ayas* and *suras* that were revealed in or around Mecca. The first revelation in Mecca was *sura* 96 and the last revelation either 23 or 29. There are eighty-five Meccan *suras*. However, it is interesting to note that within a Meccan *sura*, we may encounter some Medinan *ayas* and vice versa. Meccan revelations are characterized by a number of theological and linguistic features, such as monotheism, prophethood, eschatology, reward and punishment, arguments with and refutation of unbelievers' theses, exhortation through reference to parables about previous Prophets and unbelieving nations, God's wrath, reference to Adam and Iblis (except for 2), onomatopoeic sounds, *sura*-initial cryptic letters (except for 2 and 3), concise sentence structure, and the occurrence of expressions such as 'prostration' and 'O mankind' (except for the last part of 22.77).

The Medinan revelations, however, included all the *suras* and *ayas* that were revealed after the *hijra* in 622, in or around Medina; for this reason, they included revelations received in Mecca or 'Arafa (only thirteen miles from Mecca) but only after the *hijra*. The Medinan revelations lasted for about ten years. There are twenty-nine Medinan *suras*, whose leitmotifs include the Scripturists (*ahl al-kitab*), Islamic legal rulings, social constitution, economic and family affairs, struggle for the sake of God (*jihad*), martyrdom, and the hypocrites. The Medinan revelations also focus on the regulation of religious duties including daily prayers, fasting, charity and inheritance.

Inimitability of the Qur'an

Modern and traditional Muslim scholars alike have held the view that the Qur'an is inimitable, a view that is established on the authority of 2.23–24, 11.13–14 and 17.88, in which the Arabs and the rest of mankind are challenged to produce a book like the Qur'an. The inimitability of the Qur'an (*i'jaz al-Qur'an*) was developed as a discipline by Abu Bakr al-Baqillani (d. 611), who argued that the Qur'an was the Prophet's eternal miracle and as such was beyond imitation by humans. Some of the aspects of inimitability are:

1. Qur'an-specific linguistic and aesthetic features, such as the propositions, linguistic coherence, stylistic shifts, presentational techniques, semantically oriented phonetic features, and simple and complex modification;
2. ethical values relevant to past, present and future generations;
3. historical facts that were given by the Qur'an before they actually took place;
4. scientific facts that have since been approved by various modern sciences; and
5. legislative information that includes details designed to regulate socio-economic affairs relevant to present and future generations.

Consonance in the Qur'an

This linguistic discipline emerged as a category of exegesis developed by such exegetes as al-Razi (d. 1209) and al-Biqa'i (d. 1480). It investigates the cohesive semantic links between consecutive *ayas* and *suras*. According to this field of Qur'anic Studies, there is thematic connectivity and textual progression between the beginning, the end, the beginning and the end, or the end and the end of *suras*. Cohesive semantic bonds and sequentiality also apply to the constituent *ayas* of a given *sura*. Although Muslim scholars unanimously agree on the arrangement of the *ayas*, they differ over the sequential order of the *suras* and whether or not the *suras* were divinely ordained.

Argumentation in the Qur'an

This is a discipline that is concerned with the presentation of a Qur'anic argument that aims to refute the theses presented by its opponents. For instance, an opponent's view of monotheism is given first, then the proper antithesis is presented, followed by substantiation through detailed reference to God's omnipotence, and then the conclusion of the argument, which provides further back-up to the antithesis, as in 30.16–31.

Reasons for revelation

This field is directly related to exegesis, as it provides the scenario for each revelation. Reasons for revelation reflect the daily life of the Prophet and provide guidelines for unmasking the underlying message of a given revelation, as at 4.105, which highlights the point that justice is paramount, regardless of the faith, race or colour of the accused.

Abrogating and abrogated

This is to do with the replacement of one *aya* with another, as is confirmed by 2.106. Since the revelation of the Qur'an was gradual and at different stages, there are some Islamic legal rulings that were enforced at first but later abolished in the face of other revelations. Furthermore, Islamic law was implemented in stages, in order not to alienate people,

taking into consideration man's weakness and people's pre-Islamic habits and customs. For instance, the abolition of alcohol and gambling was phased in through *ayas* 2.219, 4.43 and, finally, 5.90–91. However, non-Muslim scholars take this as showing that, within the Prophet's lifetime, the contradictions, corrections and qualifications that occur in the Qur'an had already began to attract attention and arouse discussion.

Clear and ambiguous

Although Qur'anic *ayas* have accessible meanings (as we are told in 11.1), some *ayas* are ambiguous either theologically or linguistically (as we are informed by 39.23). The clear *ayas* refer to what is allowed and what is prohibited, the legislative limits, and compulsory actions. Ambiguous *ayas*, however, refer to theological matters such as God's attributes; in addition, the meaning of the cryptic letters is not yet known. Other *ayas* that are linguistically similar but stylistically different are also ambiguous, as at 6.32, 7.169 and 12.109.

Parables and similitudes

These are employed in the Qur'an to boost morale and strengthen faith, as we are told at 2.26. They are narrated in a simple manner, without the use of flowery description. Qur'anic parables illustrate the life and experience of previous Prophets, such as Noah, Hud, Salih, Abraham, Lot, Moses and Jesus, as in *suras* 2 and 3; previous nations, such as 'Ad and Thamud, as in 7.65–79; righteous people, such as Luqman, as in 31; the suffering of righteous people, such as the Sleepers of the Cave, as in 18 and 85; and the life of evil-doers, including Pharaoh in 20 and 26, and Gog and Magog in 18.94. A parable may occur at length in one *sura*, but it can also occur in various other *suras* in brief, complementing the same theme. For instance, the parable of the creation of Adam occurs in ten different *suras*, among them 2.30–39, 3.59, 4.1, 7.25–31 and 38.67–88. Although these parables are repeated elsewhere, they are presented in completely different styles and use markedly different narrative techniques. The only isolated parable is that of Joseph, which occurs only in *sura* 12. Qur'anic similitudes, however, are used as a short, sharp shock that helps the reader to contemplate their underlying morality (as we are told by 59.21). Similitudes also occur in different *suras*, as exemplified by 2.261 and 264, 24.35, and 48.29.

The seven modes

This field of Qur'anic Studies is concerned with the study of the various dialects spoken by the Arab tribes who inhabited the Arab peninsula before and after the revelation of the Qur'an. A mode is, therefore, a prestigious form of Arabic and the dialect of Quraysh is the standard one. For Muslim scholars, the Qur'an was revealed in the seven different forms of language spoken by the major Arab tribes. These seven modes represent different interpretations that include differences in grammatical categories (2.37); changes in grammatical category that lead to a change in meaning (12.31); differences in letters with or without dots, as with two different renderings of *al-sirat* that both have the same meaning (straight path) (1.6); singular or plural forms (23.8); differences in the morphological form (34.19); and differences in the employment of synonyms (101.5).

Further reading

Abdul-Raof, H. (2003) *Exploring the Qur'an*, Dundee: Al-Maktoum Institute Academic Press.

'Atar, Hasan Diya' al-Din (1988) *al-Ahruf al-Sab'a wa Manzilat al-Qira'at Minha*, Beirut: Dar al-basha'ir al-islamiyya.

al-Baqillani, Abu Bakr Muhammad (1994) *I'jaz al-Qur'an*, Beirut: Dar ihya' al-turath.

Donaldson, D.M. (1953) *Studies in Muslim Ethics*, London: SPCK.

al-Salih, Subhi (1997) *Mabahith fi 'Ulum al-Qur'an*, Beirut: Dar al-'ilm li al-malayin.

al-Suyuti, Jalal al-Din (1996) *al-Itqan fi 'Ulum al-Qur'an*, Beirut: Dar ihya' al-'ulum, Vols 1–2.

al-Wahidi, Abu al-Hasan 'Ali (1984) *Asbab Nuzul al-Qur'an*, Riyadh: Dar al-qibla li al-thaqafa al-islamiyya.

al-Zarqani, Muhammad 'Abd al-'Azim (1988) *Manahil al-'Irfan fi 'Ulum al-Qur'an*, Beirut: Dar al-kutub al-'ilmiyya, Vols 1–2.

See also: **mathal; parables; style in the Qur'an**

HUSSEIN ABDUL-RAOF

QURAYSH

see: **Abu Lahab; Arabia; language and the Qur'an; persecution; *tafsir* in early Islam**

QURBAN

Qurban signifies sacrifice. It indicates whatever the servant offers to try to achieve Allah's satisfaction. In the story of the two sons of Adam, 'When each offered a sacrifice, it was accepted from the one but not from the other'.

For the *qurban* to be accepted, it should come from a pious person: 'Allah accepts only from those who are pious' (5.27). It is explained in *sura al-Hajj* (The Pilgrimage) that 'It is neither their meat nor their blood that reaches Allah, but it is piety from you that reaches Him' (22.37). Therefore humility is required with any sacrifice.

RAFIK BERJAK

R

RADD / IRTIDAD AND THE JUSTIFICATION OF THE CRIMINALIZATION OF APOSTASY

The words *ridda* and *irtidad* (apostasy) mean to turn away from something and to turn into something else. In the Qur'an, the phrase *irtidad* is used to indicate the rejection of Islam by a Muslim or the embracing by a Muslim of another faith (conversion). A Muslim who rejects the Islamic faith and turns to another faith is called *murtadd*. From the viewpoint of the psychology of religion, apostasy is at the opposite end of embracing faith, and it follows the same psychological path as conversion. At both extremities it is possible to find common psychological traits. The apostates are warned harshly in the Qur'an, and are informed that their good deeds will be nullified and they will end up in hell: 'And if any of you turn back from their faith and die in unbelief, their works will bear no fruit in this life and in the Hereafter; they will be companions of the Fire and will abide therein' (2.217); 'Those who turn back as apostates after Guidance was clearly shown to them – the Satan/Evil One has instigated them and busied them up with false hopes' (47.25) (see also 3.86–91, 106; 5.5, 54; 4.115, 137; 16.106; 39.65). The Qur'an prescribes no guidance as to the proper form of punishment for apostasy. Capital punishment or banishment for apostasy in Islamic law (according to the Hanafites it is not applicable to women) is based on some Prophetic *hadith* (*Bukhari*, al-Jihad, 149, al-I'tisam, 28, Diyat, 66; *Abu Dawud*, al-Hudud, 1; *Muslim*, Qasame, 25, 26).

Regarding *irtidad* as wrongdoing is not a sign of intolerance of other religions, and is not aimed at one's freedom to choose a religion or to leave Islam and embrace another faith. On the contrary, it is more correct to say that the punishment is enforced as a safety precaution when warranted if apostasy becomes a mechanism of public disobedience and disorder (*fitna*). At this point, what is punished is the action of ridiculing the high moral flavour of Islam and posing a threat to public order. Otherwise, Islam prohibits spying on people and investigating their private lives, beliefs and personal opinions. Some contemporary religious thinkers are of the opinion that there should be no capital punishment in Islam for apostates since the narrated *ahadith* on this subject suffer from serious weaknesses with respect to both attribution (*isnad*) and text (*metn*), and that they cannot serve as a basis for judgement because they are solitary (*ahad*) and they lack certainty. Furthermore, no one can be forced to convert to Islam: 'There is no compulsion in religion' (2.256). On the basis of this verse of the Qur'an, it can be said that an apostate cannot be punished for abandoning Islam unless he or she disturbs the peace and order in the community. Also, this world is the arena for testing people, and for this to be a fair test, people must have the freedom to choose their own faith without fear of oppression. It should be pointed out that apostasy has turned into a political issue with the spread of Western colonialism and the consequent intensification of Christian missionary activities in Muslim lands. With the new tide of resurgent Islam as a reaction to the secular tide that had dominated the Muslim world since the middle of the nineteenth century, as well as the contemporary political conflicts between the Middle East and the West, apostasy has become a thorny issue for both Western missionaries and secular humanists and for many Western-educated Muslim intellectuals also.

Further reading

Ayoub, M. (1994) 'Religious Freedom and the Law of Apostasy in Islam', *Islamo-Christiana* 20: 75–91.

Juynboll, W. (1980) 'Apostasy (Muhammadan)', in J. Hastings (ed.) *Encyclopaedia of Religion and Ethics*, Vol. I, 625–6, Edinburgh: T. & T. Clark.

AHMET ALBAYRAK

See also: **Ridda**

AL-RAHMAN

The first *aya* of *al-Fatiha*, the opening of the Qur'an, establishes that the two words *al-rahman* and *al-rahim* refer to God, and specifically to God. They are used extensively, both together and separately, throughout the Qur'an to describe or refer to God. They have the same root: *rahm*, which could mean 'womb' or 'place of origin', the latter of which is more applicable here. Derivatives of this word are *rahim* (merciful) and *rahma* (mercy). However, the name *al-Rahman* has a different meaning from *rahim* but is related to *al-rahim*. *Al-rahman* is often translated into English as 'the Almighty', or some variant of 'merciful'.

The name *al-Rahman* is used as equivalent to the name Allah, and the two names can be used interchangeably, as described in 17.110. When the two terms, *al-rahman* and *al-rahim*, are used together (in that order) in the Qur'an, their usage clearly declares the ultimate authority and power of God (2.163; 41.2; 59.22), while *sura* 19 is the *sura* in which the name *al-Rahman* is mentioned most frequently (sixteen times). In *aya* 18 of this *sura*, Maryam asks for protection from *al-Rahman* against one whom she perceives as a man entering her private chambers, but who in fact is the Archangel Jibril (Gabriel). She is asking for protection from the most powerful, the Almighty. Also in 19.45, Ibrahim says to his father, an unbeliever and idol-worshipper: 'I fear you could be struck with the wrath (*azab*) of *al-Rahman*, and [in retribution] Satan would be your guide.' Again, the direct reference is to the power of God but there is also an implication that a merciful God would not wish Satan to be the guide of anyone.

In 19.85–96, one of the most powerful and definitive uses of the meaning of the name, and used here repeatedly, forcefully condemns the idol-worship of 'Isa (Jesus) by Christians and any allegation that the Almighty shares power with any other being, or procreates. God is the only creator, and there is none like him, and everything else is his creation. These *ayas* mention that the mountains, the heavens and the earth all prostrate in awe and worship of *al-Rahman*. The emphasis here is obviously on God's power and ultimate authority, but there is also the subtle reference to the mercy with which he applies that authority. The name *al-Rahim* (the All-Merciful) is mentioned in the Qur'an (in reference to God) exactly twice as many times (114 times) as the name *al-Rahman* (the Almighty) (57 times), thus his power, being the stricter element, is balanced with twice as much mercy, so that his mercy extends over all that exists (7.156).

In every instance of the usage of the name *al-Rahman* in the Qur'an, the only appropriate interpretation is expressed in the name 'The Almighty'. In another clear example (20.1–5) we have the description culminating when *al-Rahman* 'ascends' to his throne (more accurately 'assumes power on', for *istawa* has no sense of 'going up' in the way that the term 'ascend' does and God is higher than his throne). This is the perfect image of power and authority, the assumption of full authority over everything. The concept of mercy is irrelevant here and so it is not mentioned. In the beginning of the *sura* 20, which in a sense completes the description of *al-Rahman* in *sura* 19, even the approach to the name *al-Rahman* is preceded by

fear (see *aya* 3). The proper attitude of *mu'minin* (faithful people) to the Almighty is indeed fear. Then the source of the Qur'an is clearly declared (*aya* 4): the creator of the earth and the high heaven. *Aya* 5 declares God's authority (not his mercy or beneficence) as *al-Rahman*. *Aya* 6 declares his ownership of the heavens, the earth and all that is between them, and what is within the earth; *aya* 7 asserts his complete omniscience. This sequence culminates in *aya* 8, wherein the 'Power Claim' or *la illaha ila Allah* (There is no god but Allah) is given. This specific statement is of great power and significance – its declaration, a practice called the *shahada*, is considered equivalent to the declaration of one's Islamic faith. Its use in the Qur'an is always with power and emphasis. Here it completes the image of divine authority as total and complete.

The cumulative effect of these words and their relationship to the name *al-Rahman* emphasize and demonstrate powerfully to us the fact that this name refers to none other than the Almighty. This portion of *surat taha* (20.1–8) suggests that 'His are the best names' or *al-'asma' al-husna*. Although *al-husna* is often translated as 'beautiful' it actually means 'good' both in the aesthetic sense (beautiful) and in the general sense. In the general sense, one of the attributes of 'goodness' in a name is how it fits the context. In the Qur'an many *ayas* end with a pair of names, emphasizing appropriate attributes to the issue or story revealed in that *aya*. It is after all important for us to know how his particular attribute is illustrated by a particular revelation. The fact that God's names are the developing theme revealed by these eight *ayas* would indicate that these *ayas* are telling us something directly about the meaning of the name *al-Rahman*, which was also referred to in 17.110 as one of the *'asma' al-husna* (beautiful names). Specifically, they show the appropriateness of this name to the most graphic description of God's power and authority, the power and authority which belongs solely to him. In the *surat taha*, following a powerful account of the Day of Judgement and God's power on that day, *ayas* 108 and 109 give an awesome description of his authority and power on that same day, when all will be totally submitted to him and no intercession will be allowed.

These two *ayas* are followed by *aya* 110, a vivid description of divine omniscience, and by *aya* 111, which states that all faces will be submitted to the living, the eternal (*al-hayy al-khayyum*), and that those who carry the burden of even a single act of oppression will be doomed (apparently without God's forgiveness, since we have to look elsewhere for references to 'mercy' and 'beneficence'). The *sura* continues by mentioning that he (*al-Rahman*) teaches (us) the Qur'an, and that he created humanity and taught us to distinguish between things (including right from wrong). His creation of the sun and moon and the heavens, and the prostration of the stars and the trees, all are mentioned and all demonstrate his great and ultimate power over all things as the Almighty. He also includes a warning in the first set of *ayas* in this *sura* to people not to be unfair in weighing (i.e. not to cheat others for one's own personal gain). The refrain in this *sura* challenges humans and *jinn* to deny any of his marvels, and does not offer mercy for those who do so. Is the appropriate description for this set of acts 'merciful' – or is it more appropriately understood to be the description of the Almighty? While he is also the 'All-Merciful', it might be argued that we must first fear his power and authority before we can be eligible for considera-

tion for his mercy. Hence the cumulative language found here that emphasizes divine power and authority.

See also: **ninety-nine names of God**

OLIVER LEAMAN

RAMADAN

The Qur'an is confident in promoting the idea that fasting is appropriate for eschatological reasons, and that it is a well-established practice: 'O you who believe, fasting is decreed for you, as it was decreed for those before you, that you may attain salvation' (2.183). We read: 'Specific days [are designated for fasting]; if one is ill or traveling, an equal number of other days may be substituted. Those who can fast, but with great difficulty, may substitute feeding one poor person for each day of breaking the fast. If one volunteers [more righteous works], it is better. But fasting is the best for you, if you only knew' (2.184). Restrictions are not total: 'Permitted for you is sexual intercourse with your wives during the nights of fasting. They are the keepers of your secrets, and you are the keepers of their secrets. God knew that you used to betray your souls, and He has redeemed you, and has pardoned you. Henceforth, you may have intercourse with them, seeking what God has permitted for you. You may eat and drink until the white thread of light becomes distinguishable from the dark thread of night at dawn. Then, you shall fast until sunset. Sexual intercourse is prohibited if you decide to retreat to the *masjid* [during the last ten days of Ramadan]. These are God's laws; you shall not transgress them. God thus clarifies His revelations for the people, that they may attain salvation' (2.187).

The point is made that fasting is not an innovation that arose with the Qur'an but is a basic practice of monotheists which the Qur'an confirms and also moderates, so that it forms a useful role in changing the character of the individual and cementing his or her relationship with both God and the community as a whole. The month of Ramadan, when the Qur'an was said to have been sent down, has come to be known as the name of the major Islamic fast. Here, as in many other matters, the Qur'an portrays itself as continuing long-practiced customs, albeit generally returning to their original purity and purpose.

See also: **character; fasting;** *salat*

OLIVER LEAMAN

AL-RAZI, FAKHR AL-DIN

Fakhr al-Din al-Razi is one of the greatest intellects in the history of Islam. He was born at Rayy (Iran) in 1149, and died at Herat in 1210. The son of a renowned religious teacher, he studied the traditional Islamic disciplines in Rayy and was a convinced Ash'arite. He was a theologian and jurist, and wrote numerous treatises on a wide range of disciplines, including metaphysics, logic and dogmatics. As an Ash'arite, he showed himself an accomplished dialectician, notably in his controversies with the Mu'tazilites. He travelled widely, as far afield as Samarkand and India, and was renowned for his piety.

In the later years of his life, he turned himself increasingly to the Qur'an, finding within it a locus for the testing and justification of all his ideas, ideals and values, and the wellspring of an extraordinary spirituality. His commentary on the Holy Book is the most important of his works. In his 'Testament' he wrote: 'I have had experience of all the methods of kalam and of all the paths of philosophy, but have not found in them either satisfaction or comfort equal to

that which I found in reading the Qur'an.' The fruit of his encounter with the Qur'an is *al-tafsir al-kabir* (The great commentary), or more properly, *Mafatih al-ghayb. Mafatih al-ghayb* is a Qur'anic phrase meaning 'The Keys to the Unseen World' (6.59), i.e. the world beyond human sight and reason, the Qur'an being the source of cognition of things known only to God. The most readily available printing – we are far from a critical edition – is a Tehran offset of a Cairo edition.

Razi experiences the Qur'an, despite the atomic character of its revelation, as a unitary event, a single discourse. Formally he treats it seriatim, the structure of the work being a word-by-word exegesis. He uses with great skill the basic techniques of word definition, *qira'at*, etymologies, glosses, *shawahid, hadith* and *asbab al-nuzul*. In so doing, he offers a panorama of the views of his predecessors, from Muqatil al-Sulayman onwards, although indicating the opinions preferred by he himself and his school. In addition, he takes up diverse topics prompted by a word or a phrase relevant to an issue that concerns him, or suggests a new and unexpected objection to his faith that may require an answer. These become excursuses which may be lengthy. To situate them in his *tafsir*, he devises a complex structure of *mas'ala, su'al, bahth, qawl* and *maqam* in which he provides a place for discussion of the narrations, the moral and legal imperatives and the spiritual dimensions of the Qur'an. This he does in the light of his theological, philosophical insights, revealing an extraordinary intellectual range, an inspiring spirituality and a profound sense of human values.

Attention may be drawn to some of the concerns that he elaborates. He argues consistently and at length throughout the work against the teaching of the

Mu'tazilites, in particular as expressed by Zamakhshari, whose *tafsir al-Kashshaf* he quotes at length. He opposes relentlessly the doctrines that man is the creator of his own acts, and that God can be obliged to bestow his graces (*lutf*; pl. *altaf*) on his creatures.

He has first-hand knowledge of at least some of the Judaic and Christian scriptures. In commenting on the divine favours given to the people of Israel (2.40), he presents accurate Arabic renderings of passages from Genesis, Deuteronomy, Isaiah, Habakkuk and the gospel of John to argue the role of the Arabs in the divine dispensation and the primacy of Mecca over Jerusalem.

To him is attributed in its fullest form the doctrine of the impeccability of the prophets: the idea that a prophet cannot be guilty of any sin, inclination to sin or be liable to any imperfection in the communication of his message. To do so he at times goes to the length of subverting the normal rules of Arabic grammar, for example at 12.24 when he asserts that there is an adiposis preceding a protosis in an effort to avoid the suggestion that Zulaykha was almost successful in her attempt to seduce Joseph.

As a Sunni, in *surat al-Nur* (24.22), he devotes a lengthy excursus to demonstrating that Abu Bakr is greater than 'Ali. The ultimate proof of Abu Bakr's greatness is his readiness to forgive his nephew Mistah for the part he played in spreading the slander against his daughter (and wife of the Prophet) 'A'isha. Such an act of forgiveness Razi regards as more difficult than warfare against the unbeliever.

He justifies the use of *ta'wil*, when an acceptance of a literal sense of the Qur'anic words would be contrary to reason. Thus at 38.75 he uses biting sarcasm leavened with humour to dismiss the claims of those who insist on accepting literally the image of God that would result from a composite picture constructed from the anthropomorphic statements of him given in the Qur'an. If such a misshapen being were offered as a slave, Razi asserts, no one would buy him.

But more important than this is Razi's capacity to enter into the psychology and emotions of the characters presented in narratives of the prophets. In discussing them he reveals a remarkable sensitivity to the complexities and tensions in human motivation. So, for example, at 11.71 he gives an account of nine reasons given for Sarah's laughter when Abraham's visitors announce that in old age she is to bear a child.

Strikingly, at times he uses poetry, not simply to establish the meaning of a word but to create an empathy with an individual in a situation that the Qur'an presents. Thus when he explains why the detention of Benjamin in Egypt intensifies Jacob's grief for the loss of Joseph (12.84), he quotes a line of poetry telling how when a new grief falls upon an old one, it is as though the scar is torn off an old wound and it bleeds afresh.

Finally, when he takes a reader into his confidence and invites him to share his pain, he speaks across the centuries. As for example at the conclusion of his exegesis of *sura* Yusuf, he asks that anyone who has gained something from his book recite *al-Fatiha* for his son Salih Muhammad who had recently died while on a journey, and for all who die away from home, far from brethren, mother and father. As a work of exegesis it is unique, and speaks to many of the concerns of the modern world.

Further reading

Fakhr al-Din al-Razi (n.d.) *al-tafsir al-kabir*, Tehran: Dar al-kutub al-'ilmiyya; an offset of the edition of Muhammad Muhyi'l-Din, Cairo 1352/1933.

Johns, A.H. (1986) 'Razi's Treatment of the Qur'anic Episodes Telling of Abraham and his Guests: Qur'anic exegesis with a human face', *MIDEO* 17: 81–114.

Kholeif, F. (1966) *A Study on Fakhr al-Din al-Razi and his Controversies in Transoxania*, Beirut: Dar el-Machreq.

Street, A. (1997) 'Concerning the Life and Works of Fakhr al-Din al-Razi', in Peter G. Riddell and Tony Street (eds) *Islam: Essays on scripture. thought and society*, Leiden: E.J. Brill, 135–46.

A.H. JOHNS

READING

The Arabic word *qira'a* 'reading, recitation' has three meanings: the recitation of parts or the whole of the Qur'an; a variant reading of one Qur'anic word or passage; and a particular reading of the whole Qur'an following a single tradition.

1. *Recitation.* The Qur'an is primarily a revealed recitation. The Arabic word *qur'an* literally means 'recitation', and in one of the earliest *suras* the Prophet is admonished '... and chant the Qur'an very distinctly' (73.4). We do not know exactly what the word *tartil*, here translated as 'chanting distinctly', meant at the time, but it clearly denoted a special oratory and liturgical style which differed from normal speech. The Muslim tradition of how the Qur'an should be recited covered three main areas: (a) the proper and clear pronunciation of consonants and vowels; (b) the rules of pause in recitation and of resumption of recitation; and (c) the musical and melodious features of Qur'anic recitation.

(a) *Articulation.* The proper and conscious articulation of the Arabic sounds was the most basic precondition for the public recitation of the Qur'an. In many cases the transmission of the correct ways of recitation was oral, as can be deduced from the high percentage of blind readers. The manuals were often based on the highly developed field of early Arabic phonetics of the second/eighth century and later. In modern times, when more and more non-Arabs recite the Qur'an, a correct articulation may present problems. Therefore, most non-Arab reciters of the Qur'an try to follow a training in countries such as Egypt or Saudi Arabia. Certain consonants in special positions had more than one mode of articulation: the phoneme $/r/$, for example, should sometimes be trilled; some consonants should be nasalized (*ghunna*); lengthened vowels should be markedly longer before a glottal stop, etc. But possibly more important than all this was a complicated system of partial and complete assimilation (*idgham*) between the end of one word and the beginning of the next. The graphic unities *min ba'd* (2.27) were to be pronounced in recitation as *mimba'd* (partial assimilation); *ujibat da'watukuma* (10.89) should be rendered as *ujibadda' watukuma* (total assimilation). The influential standard Qur'an of Cairo (1924 and later) uses an elaborate system of modified vowel-signs and a set of additional ortho-epic symbols for minute details. The system is explained in an appendix to this edition. These rules are based on older manuals, the most important one being the *Tiraz 'ala dabt al-Kharraz* by al-Tanasi (d. 899/1493). But the set of signs and symbols used in the Cairo edition is not identical to any older system.

Many classical handbooks cover these matters in even greater detail. Such texts do not always allow the non-initiated to understand the description of the phonemic or phonetic reality of the prescribed recitation without the guidance of a reader trained in the art of recitation (*tajwid*). None of these ortho-epic signs, however, is considered to be part of the revealed, canonical text.

(b) *Pausal forms*. Classical Arabic distinguishes between the form of a word within a sentence or within a smaller unit of speech on the one hand and the form of the same word at the end of a sentence or in an isolated position on the other, i.e. a distinction is made between a contextual form and a pausal form. In Qur'an recitation the end of the verse (*fasila*) normally requires a pausal form, but there are many instances when a pause for breath can be required or admitted within a verse. Then a pause (*waqf*) and the pausal form of the word preceding the pause are indicated. There were some cases in which a pause made a difference in meaning. In 3.7 the Qur'an says within a long verse about a certain kind of Qur'anic verses: '... and nobody knows its interpretation save only God. And those firmly rooted in knowledge say:...'. Where the English rendering shows the full stop, the Arabic text shows a special *waqf*-sign indicating that at this point the pause is preferable or obligatory. Without such a sign the following reading would be possible: '... and nobody knows its interpretation save only God and those firmly rooted in knowledge. They

say:...'. This reading without *waqf* conveys the opposite of what the verse with *waqf* means. However, these *waqf*-signs are not considered part of the canonical text, although the recitational praxis behind these signs might well be part of a canonical tradition.

(c) *Styles of recitation, musical and melodious features*. An important point is the pace of recitation, a slow and measured style usually being identified with the *tartil*-style, which was recommended by God to the Prophet (73.4). The pace also depended on the size of the auditory – in the pre-microphone age this was of great importance. The most contested feature of Qur'anic recitation was the liturgical melody, which was apparently always inseparable from public recitation. While music and singing were in a Qur'anic context frowned upon by scholars, there was always a melodious tone in recitation, which was similar to the tone of the call to prayer (*adhan*). This tone set recitation apart from all other kinds of official and formal speech. The chant-like quality of modern recitation has been adequately studied, but we know nothing about earlier stages, and we are not sure how much modern melodies reflect earlier traditions. In any case, traditional Muslim scholarship never tried to develop a musical notation for Qur'anic recitation, but depended in this respect wholly on oral tradition. Whatever the style of recitation, it was, and is, indispensable that it be introduced by the formula 'I seek refuge with God from the accursed Satan' (16.98) and by the *basmala*, even when the recitation does not coincide with the beginning of a *sura*. It also must end with the formula 'God has spoken truly' (taking up 33.23).

2   *Variant reading-traditions.* Reading written Arabic before the fourth/tenth century required a fair amount of interpretation, therefore every written text was polyvalent. This was especially true for the codices of the Qur'an. Disagreement about the precise way the Qur'an should be recited was inseparable from the question of how the codices should be read. These problems began most probably soon after the death of the Prophet, because parts of the Qur'an were from the start transmitted by oral tradition in different versions. Muslim reports inform us that in the time preceding the collection of the 'Uthmanic codex, there were differences of opinion even about the number of *suras* and their arrangement, and even more differences on the wording which sometimes radically altered the sense. After the 'Uthmanic codex became canonical seven different readings of this codex were declared equally authoritative, legitimate and divinely inspired. These canonical readings were ascribed to seven 'readers' who broadly represented the most important local traditions: Abu 'Amr ibn al-'Ala' (Basra, d. c.154/770); 'Asim Ibn Bahdala (Kufa, d. 128/745); Hamza Ibn Habib (Kufa, d. 156/772); Ibn 'Amir (Damascus, d. 118/736); Ibn Kathir (Mecca, d. 120/738); al-Kisa'i (Kufa, d. 189/805); and Nafi' Ibn 'Abdalrahman (Medina, d. c.169/785). A generation later, seven more 'readings' were recognized as canonical, making a total of fourteen. Further readings were preserved by learned tradition, but were considered by Muslim tradition as 'deviant' (*shadhdh*), i.e. non-canonical.

Many of these thousands of post-'Uthmanic readings touched on minute details of pronunciation and vowelization, few of any importance, and even fewer with any serious bearing on the religious sense of the text. For the general sense important examples include the beginning of *sura* 30.2–3 'The Byzantines have been vanquished in the nearer part of the land' – where a canonical variant read an active verbal form instead of the passive one – 'The Byzantines have vanquished ...'. Of a certain dogmatic importance was perhaps 85.21–22 – 'It is a glorious Qur'an on a preserved tablet' – where there is a canonical variant meaning: 'It is a glorious Qur'an preserved on a tablet'.

In general the different canonical readings were and are of little consequence. In the Muslim tradition these variants are normally gleaned neither from early Qur'anic manuscripts nor directly from oral tradition, but from Arabic writings on the variant readings. Whereas the very early manuscripts and fragments of the Qur'an found in Sana'a (Yemen) have not yet been systematically studied, it is clear that they show at least remarkable orthographic peculiarities. We find the word 'Allah' written with a ya' between the penultimate /l/ and the final consonant /h/, an orthography which is not attested to anywhere else. Whether deeper differences between the form of the Sana'a codices and the 'Uthmanic tradition exist remains to be seen.

Further reading

Brocket, A. (1988) 'The Value of the Hafs and Warsh Transmissions for the Textual History of the Qur'an', in A. Rippin (ed.)

Approaches to the History of the Interpretation of the Qur'an, Oxford: Oxford University Press, 31–45.

al-Sa'id, L. (1975) *The Recited Koran*, Princeton, NJ: Princeton University Press.

Versteegh. C.H.M. (1993) *Arabic Grammar and Qur'anic Exegesis in Early Islam*, Leiden: E.J. Brill.

See also: **basmala; canon; language and the Qur'an; manuscripts and the Qur'an**

STEFAN WILD

RECITATION
see: **tajwid**

RECITING ALOUD THE *BASMALA*
see: **al-jahr bi al-basmala**

REPENTANCE

Repentance plays a vital role in the Islamic orientation towards God. The Arabic word for repentance is *tawba*, literally meaning 'turning toward'. The act of repenting means turning ourselves towards God and asking him to forgive our failures and help us to overcome them. It is important to react in a practical way as well as to adopt the right mental attitude to the undesirable action. As the Qur'an says: 'Allah is the Most Merciful of those who have mercy.' Since God is always described as merciful, one can be confident that he will reward genuine attempts at repentance. But for sins we have carried out against human beings action is vital if they are to forgive us; it cannot be assumed that they are merciful by nature.

The concept of *tawba* is at first unilateral and then reciprocal. In Arabic there is a saying that 'if a human being makes *tawba* toward God, God makes *tawba* toward him'. As soon as the creature turns towards God in repen-

tance, God turns towards him and is ready to forgive him. One of the interesting aspects of the Islamic discussion of repentance is that it is not only important when one has done something wrong, but also when one has done something right. This is because it may well be that one could have done it even better, done even more, and perhaps one may intercede on behalf of others who are having difficulties in acting. Forgiveness is discussed by Noah thus:

> He said, 'My Lord, I have called my people night and day, but my calling them has only made them flee from me all the more; and every time I called them that you might forgive them, they put their fingers into their ears, and drew close their garments, and persisted in their iniquities and were disdainfully proud. Then I called them to righteousness openly, then preached to them in public, and appealed to them in private and I said, Seek forgiveness of your Lord; for He is the great forgiver; He will send down rain for you in abundance, and He will grant you increase of wealth and children, and will cause gardens to grow for you and will cause rivers to flow for you. What is the matter with you that you do not hope for greatness and wisdom from Allah? And He has created you in different forms and different conditions. Don't you see how Allah has created seven heavens in perfect harmony, and has placed the moon in it as a light, and made the sun a lamp? And Allah has caused you to grow out of the earth as a good growth.' (71.5–17)

This constant repetition of the balance with which the universe is constructed is relevant to the issue of repentance, since the implication is that God will balance our negative actions with positive reward if we only repent of them.

Forgiveness may be invoked on behalf of our enemies, and those who oppose us. For example, Abraham's denial of polytheism was attacked by his father, who was after all in the idol business, and his son prayed for his repentance, which probably made his father even angrier:

> And mention in the Book the story of Abraham. He was a truthful man and a Prophet. Behold, he said to his father, 'Why do you worship what cannot hear or see, and can do nothing for you? O my father, there has indeed come to me knowledge that has not come to you; so follow me, I will guide you to a straight path. O my father, worship not Satan; surely, Satan is a rebel against the Merciful. O my father, indeed I fear that a punishment from the Merciful will be applied to you and you will become a friend of Satan.' He replied, 'Do you turn away from my gods, O Abraham? If you don't stop, I will surely stone you. Now leave me alone for a long while.' Abraham said, 'Peace be upon thee. I will ask forgiveness of my Lord for thee. He is indeed gracious to me.' (19.41–47)

Along similar lines we have the story of Joseph and his brothers who, when they came before Joseph again, said, 'noble chief, poverty has smitten us and our family, and we have brought a paltry sum of money, but nonetheless give us full measure, and be charitable to us. Surely, Allah does reward the charitable.' Joseph answered: 'Do you know what you did to Joseph and his brother out of ignorance?' And they replied: 'Are you Joseph?' Joseph then said: 'Yes, I am Joseph and this is my brother [Benjamin]. Allah has indeed been gracious to us. Whoever really fears Allah and is steadfast – Allah never suffers the reward of the good to be lost.' His brothers replied, 'By Allah; surely Allah has preferred you above us and we have indeed been sinners', to which Joseph's response was: 'No blame shall lie on you this day; may Allah forgive you! And

He the most merciful of those who show mercy' (12.88–92). The significance of repentance arises within the context of testing: 'Do men think that they will be left alone on saying, "We believe", and that they will not be tested? We did test those before them, and Allah will certainly know those who are true from those who are false' (29.2–3).

One might ask why God tests us, if he knows how we are going to behave, a given in that he knows everything. Tests are important ways for us to discover who we are and how we are going to respond to the trials of the world. So when Abraham is tested he is put in the position of having to choose between faithfulness to the One God and staying within his local community, and even obedience to his father, a very important moral obligation in Islam as well as in other ethical systems.

'The human soul is certainly prone to evil, unless my Lord do bestow His mercy to it' (12.53). Sin is prevalent in human life, not only the obvious sins that others will point out to us and that we can easily observe when we examine our behaviour, but also the more subtle forms of sin that are involved in arrogance, lust, greed and so on that are so deeply imbedded in our characters that they are difficult to root out. The point of always calling for forgiveness, even when not conscious of any particular sin, is to direct our minds to these more serious (because more tenuous) flaws in ourselves: 'you who believe! be careful of [your duty to] Allah with the proper care which is due to Him, and do not die unless you have accepted Islam' (3.102).

Al-Qurtubi suggests that when 3.102 was revealed, the Prophet was asked whether it was not too extreme a demand – who can really carry out his entire duty to his creator? As a consequence we find the revelation of 64.16, which states: 'Be careful of your duty to

God as much as you can'; the verse prior to this was abrogated. It could also be said that the second verse is a clarification of the first. Ibn 'Abbas says that 'proper care' (*haqqa tuqatihi*) has not been abrogated: it means that 'one should strive with proper exertion (*haqqa jihadihi*) in the path of God', a phrase that we find in another verse: 'And strive in God['s cause] as you ought to strive (*jahidu fi-llah haqqa jihadihi*)' (22.78). The verb *ittaqa* and its derivatives occur hundreds of times in the Qur'an; and while most contexts will not allow it to be equated with *jihad*, a considerable number offer at least that possibility. 'O people! Be careful of [your duty to] your Lord, Who created you from a single being and created its mate of the same [kind] and spread from these two, many men and women; and be careful of [your duty to] Allah, by whom you demand of each other [your rights], and [be careful] about the ties of kinship; surely Allah always watches over you' (4.1). This is very much a theme of the Qur'an – the necessity of the believer to repent and see it as a defining feature of his or her relationship with God.

Repentance and the missing *basmala*

We read: 'Allah loves those who turn [to Him] in repentance, and He loves those who keep themselves pure' (2.222). Speaking of himself, God says: 'He is always forgiving to those who turn back [to Him] (*fa-inna-hu kana li'l-awwabina ghafura*)' (17.25). Thus one expects the constant possibility of forgiveness to be available to those who genuinely repent. Yet in front of the *sura* specifically labelled 'on Repentance', there is no *basmala*, unlike every other *sura* in the Holy Book. The chapter is called *surat at-Tawba* and also sometimes *al-Fadiha* (the Disgracer) because it disclosed the secrets of the hypocrites. Written copies of the Qur'an and reciters omit the *basmala* at the beginning of this *sura*, but there is disagreement about the reason for that. Ibn Kathir follows a report in *Bukhari* which suggests that this is one of the last *suras* to be transmitted to the Prophet, and that the absence of the *basmala* in the *mushaf* (compilation) collected by the Companions reflects the Prophet's grim mood at the thought of the polytheists performing *tawaf* (walking around) around the *Ka'ba* in Mecca naked. It was the *hajj* season and Muhammad had just returned from the battle of Tabuk, and sent Abu Bakr to lead the *hajj* in his stead. The absence of the *basmala* reflects this grimness of mood.

'Uthman ibn 'Affan said that the meaning of *sura* 9 is similar to the preceding *sura*. That is why they are put together and included in the 'Seven Long Ones'. The Companions disagreed about whether they consisted of two *suras* or one *sura*, and that is why the *basmala* between them is omitted. 'Ali ibn Abi Talib said that the *basmala* conveys security while this *sura* was sent down with the sword. That is why it does not begin with security. This comment is reported in the book by the two Jalals (*Jalalayn*), and the general view seems to be that the ninth *sura* is such an ominous message that it would be inappropriate to head it with a phrase that takes away from its threatening nature.

Further reading

al-Suyuti, Jalal al-din (1403/1983) *Tafsir al-Jalalayn*, Beirut: Dar al-qalam.

See also: **basmala; forgiveness;** *ittaqa*
OLIVER LEAMAN

REPULSE
see: nahar

RESPONSIBILITY

Responsibility implies voluntary action. If an action is based on compulsion, ignorance or insanity, then the agent cannot be held responsible. Aristotle agreed that the principle of voluntary action must be internal to the agent. Muslim philosophers, however, were not only concerned with the dialectical relation between human freedom and responsibility, but also with the bearing of divine power upon human action. The standard argument is that if man's fate is determined by God, how could he be responsible for his actions?

The following verses confirm man's freedom of choice:

> The truth is from your Lord. Whoever wishes, let him believe; and whoever wishes, let him disbelieve. (18.29)

> O Children of Adam, when apostles from your own people come to you reciting to you My revelations – then those who fear God and mend their ways have nothing to fear, and they will not grieve. But those who deny Our revelations and reject them arrogantly – those are the people of the Fire; therein they shall abide forever. (7.35)

So man is free to accept or reject the truth from God; but whatever the choice, that person will face the consequences on the Day of Judgement.

The Qur'an speaks of God sealing people's hearts. This is not an arbitrary act of God, however, but is based on the actions of men themselves, as suggested in the following verses:

> God will not guide those who reject His signs. (16.104)

> God will only lead astray those who are wicked. (2.26)

> God will only seal up those hearts that are arrogant. (40.35)

The Qur'an repeatedly states that every man is responsible alone for what he does – a doctrine that underlies the Qur'anic rejection of redemption.

Man has no power over nature, which is God's domain, and no one can tamper with it: 'There is no change in the creation of God'. Man has power only over his own will, and can direct it towards goodness or wickedness. However, man cannot control his will without the power of God. This also applies to a will to evil; God grants him the power, but does not compel him, to commit the evil.

Man should strive for his success and happiness in this world and in the hereafter: 'Man gets nothing but what he strives for' (53.39); 'God does not change the condition of the people unless they change themselves' (13.11). The latter verse either means that God will not withdraw his blessings from man as long as man remains good, or that God will not bless man unless man changes his inner state to become recipients of God's grace (Asad, 1980: 360). The first meaning corresponds with the views of Ibn Kathir, al-Tabari, al-Jawzi and al-Qurtubi (Idris, 1983: 3–5).

Sin and repentance

The Qur'an does not accept original sin, but states that Adam and Eve were forgiven their sin after Adam had received his Lord's words (2.37). Thus, man is responsible for his sin, and could repent for it. The Qur'an states: 'I am, indeed, All-forgiving unto him who repents, does the righteous deed and is well guided' (20.82).

In the Bible, Adam and Eve ate the forbidden fruit, and the whole of mankind was born with this original sin. St Augustine, who developed the concept of original sin, held that man's nature is corrupted, and therefore, he cannot save himself by himself but must turn to a saviour and depend on divine grace to be redeemed of his original sin. In the Qur'an, Adam and Eve did go astray, but they sought sincere repentance and were therefore forgiven. Their progeny fell from bliss because of their error, but their children do not inherit the blame from their parents. It is inconceivable to the Muslim mind that someone must be responsible for sins committed by someone else (Mohamed, 1996: 29–30). Man is responsible for his sins, but he is not cursed because of it. The Qur'an itself states that God forgives those who have sinned: 'Then Adam received words [of guidance] from his Lord, and God accepted his repentance: truly, He is the Acceptor of Repentance, the Compassionate' (2.37).

Islam holds that man is born in a state of original goodness (*fitra*). The Prophetic Tradition states: 'Every newborn child is born in a state of *fitra*.' This is confirmed by the verse: 'Set your face to the religion in sincerity, which is Allah's *fitra*, upon which he created mankind. There is no changing in the religion of Allah. That is the right religion, but most people know not' (30.30). This is a more optimistic view of human nature. This does not mean that man does not have an inclination to evil; the evil inclination emerges after birth, due to his lower, commanding self (*al-nafs al-ammara*) and the negative socialization that impinges upon it. Thus, man can deviate from his original purity, but it is never obliterated, and he can always return to it by following God's guidance. Man is free to choose or to reject God's guidance. He is responsible for his choice.

Legal responsibility

The Qur'anic principle of freedom and responsibility is applied to Islamic law. A person is responsible to the law if he or she acted consciously and freely.

Islamic legal theory recognizes two main phases in the life of a human being, and each phase implies certain responsibilities. The first phase is from a foetus up to the age of seven, and the second from the age of seven until death. The foetus or the child is not responsible for his actions, but society is responsible for him or her (Mohamed, 1996: 125–7). Responsibility begins in the second phase. There are two stages in the second phase. The first is from seven to the age of *bulugh* (sexual maturity), which is at about fourteen years. At this stage the child is responsible to his or her parents, not to God and the parents are responsible to God for the child's religious education and practice. In the next stage, from sexual maturity until death, the individual is fully responsible for practicing the laws of Islam and it is they who will be accountable on the Day of Judgement for any omission.

A person may be sexually mature, but not intellectually mature. Such a person cannot manage his or her own financial affairs, and society takes responsibility for handling such affairs until mental maturity is achieved. Sanity is essential for responsibility; thus the insane are not responsible for performing religious obligations (Mohamed, 1996: 127–30).

References and further reading

Asad, M. (1980) *The Message of the Qur'an*, Gibraltar: Dar al-andalus.

Fakhry, M. (1991) *Ethical Theories in Islam*, Leiden: E.J. Brill.

Idris, G.S. (1983) *The Process of Islamization*, Plainfield: IA: The Muslim Students Association of America and Canada.

Mohamed, Y. (1996) *Fitrah: The Islamic concept of human nature*, London: Taha Publishers.

Rahman, F. (1980) *Major Themes of the Qur'an*, Minneapolis: Bibliotheca Islamica.

See also: **Adam; Ash'arites and Mu'tazilites; character; *irada*; *nafs*; punishment**

YASIEN MOHAMED

REVELATION

The Arabic term *wahy* means revelation or inspiration. In its more technical sense, *wahy* is understood as the Word of God which is communicated to his prophets and messengers. It can also mean the scripture as revealed to particular prophets: the Torah to Moses, the Gospel to Jesus and the Qur'an to Muhammad (in whose case the revelation began in 610 CE and continued until his death in 632). Here we examine the pre-Islamic cultural context for the understanding of revelation and how the Qur'an deals with the concept.

Although the Qur'an refers to the Meccan community as one that had received no scripture, the pre-Islamic Arabs in Hijaz (known to Muslims as polytheists or *mushrikun*), had some understanding of concepts such as divine 'inspiration' or 'revelation' and 'scripture'.

Pre-Islamic Arabs in settled communities such as Mecca and Medina (Yathrib) knew of and had contact with the Jewish and Christian religions and their scriptures. There is evidence that there were Christians in Mecca, Waraqah b. Nawfal, the relative of the Prophet Muhammad's wife, being one. In the town of Medina, to which the Prophet migrated in 622, three of the major tribes were Jewish, and there was considerable interaction between the Medinan Jews and the non-Jewish Arab tribes of Aws and Khazraj.

The Meccans of the time of Prophet Muhammad judged the Qur'anic revelation based on their understanding of 'inspiration'. Two types of text with which they were familiar had, in their view, similarity to the new text: Arabic poetry and *saj' al-kuhhan* (see below). First, in the view of the Meccans, poetry was closely connected to inspiration from a higher spiritual source, called *jinn*. In fact, the Meccans often attributed the creative aspects of poetry to *jinn*: poetry was not merely a talent but something bestowed by *jinn*. For the Meccans, the Qur'an was like poetry, and it shared some of its characteristics. Both were expressed in Arabic. Both had spontaneous creative qualities to which ordinary people could not aspire without the support of a 'higher source'. Both had unique stylistic and structural features that were not part of the language of ordinary people. This might explain why, when Prophet Muhammad began preaching and reciting the Qur'an, his opponents accused him of being a poet (21.5) or a 'poet possessed' (37.36). The Qur'an denies that it is poetry and rejects any link between the Qur'an and *jinn*, and affirms that it was God alone who communicated the Qur'an to the Prophet (69.41; 36.69).

Second, the Meccans associated the Qur'an with alliterative texts recited by soothsayers, which again linked the Qur'an in their eyes to inspiration from a higher spiritual source. The soothsayers were influential figures believed to have access to *jinn* and the ability to seek their assistance in matters such as predicting future events. In their view, soothsayers relayed matters to the *jinn*, and conveyed the *jinn*'s responses to humans in a language familiar to them that came to be called *saj' al-kuhhan*. The initial Meccan reaction to the Qur'an – the accusation that the Prophet was a soothsayer – indicates that the Meccans judged the Qur'an on the basis of its linguistic character, thus relating it to the genre *saj' al-kuhhan*. This was probably because many early verses of the Qur'an were highly alliterative, abrupt and in short sentences and phrases, which resembled *saj' al-kuhhan*. This link was also rejected by the Qur'an (Saeed, 1999; Abu Zayd, 1998: 33–9).

A considerable number of verses in the Qur'an have a direct bearing on the concept of revelation (*wahy*), be it the revelation received by Prophet Muhammad or those by other prophets. The Qur'an uses the word *wahy* and its variants on a number of occasions spanning both the Meccan and Medinan periods. The terms are used often in the sense of transmitting a message from God to human beings or non-human beings. These usages indicate that *wahy* is not limited to a relationship between God and his prophets. In fact, there are several forms of *wahy* mentioned in the Qur'an: inspiration to inanimate objects (99.4–5; 41.12); to animals (16.68–9); to human beings in general, such as the mother of Moses (28.7); to prophets in particular, such as Jesus (5.111; 4.163); and to angels (8.12).

The Qur'an provides some detail as to the way in which revelation comes from God to human beings: 'It is not fitting for a human being that God should speak to him except by inspiration, or from behind a veil, or by the sending of a messenger to reveal, with God's permission, what God wills' (42.51). The most immediate mode of communication comes directly from God to the person intended, without voice or messenger. The person who receives it 'understands' the message and that it is from God. The second method, from behind a veil, means that God speaks to a person through another medium such as a vision or a dream. The best example is that of God's speaking to Moses 'from behind' the burning bush. The third method, through a messenger (an angel), is considered to be the surest and clearest form of revelation, albeit the least direct. Many Muslim theologians believed that this was the most common form of the revelation of the Qur'an to the Prophet. From their point of view, the angel brought the word of God to the Prophet *verbatim*, without any alteration or change, in a language that the Prophet could understand, namely Arabic (26.195). It should be noted, however, that there are differences among Muslim scholars as to the exact nature of the 'code' used between God and the angel on the one hand, and the code between the angel and the Prophet. Similarly, there are differences on the issue of whether there exists a text of the Qur'an written in Arabic on the 'Preserved Tablet' (*al-lawh al-mahfuz*) (Abu Zayd, 1998: 40–55).

As to any human element in the revelation of the Qur'an, the Qur'an stresses that the Prophet was required only to receive the sacred text and that he had no authority to change it (10.15). The Qur'an strongly denies that it is the speech or the ideas of the Prophet or, indeed, of any other man (Tabataba'i, 1984: 65). It also asserts that the revelation came directly from God and in Arabic, so that it could be without human-induced errors or inaccuracies. Again, in 2.23 the Qur'an challenges those who consider it merely the speech of Muhammad to produce a book similar to it or even one chapter like it. The Qur'an argues that if it were from a source other than God, there would be many inconsistencies and inaccuracies in the text. It comes from God alone so that people can learn from its purity: 'Do they not consider the Qur'an [with care]? Had it been from any source other than God, they would surely have found therein much discrepancy' (4.82). The angel was entrusted with a direct message in Arabic, not simply with meanings and ideas. It was intended to be immediately comprehensible to ordinary people: 'Verily this is a revelation from the Lord of the World: with it came down the Spirit of Faith and Truth to thy heart and mind, that you mayest admonish in the perspicuous Arabic tongue' (26.192–5).

Revelation, according to the Qur'an, is an initiative of God, who reveals his will to the human prophet. The Prophet Muhammad, however, was not reduced to a passive bystander; although a recipient, he was active. This is not to say that he composed the content of the revelation, but that he received it in full consciousness, witnessing in his heart the grandeur of the presence of the voice of God. Muslim theologians were less concerned with the experience of revelation than with what was said or communicated in the experience. Nor did God make himself known through revelation; it was his will that was revealed, and in an understandable human language. There is nothing in the Qur'an to suggest that the Prophet 'saw' God in the experience of 'revelation'.

For the Prophet, the revelation was real, even though the modality of both the revelation and the experience could only be described in metaphorical terms; for example, as the Prophet explained in a *hadith*, as the 'ringing of a bell'. Despite being unable to give a precise description of the experience, the Prophet was firm in his view that the context of revelation was objective, not subjective. His experiences of seeing the intermediary, of hearing the voice at times and of comprehending what was said (as reported in *hadith*) all indicate the objective reality of the content of the revelation (Rahman, 1966: 31–2).

The mainstream view of revelation in Islam considers the language an essential aspect of the content of the revelation. The words of the Qur'an are thus equivalent to the verbal revelation given to the Prophet. When the Qur'an states that God says, speaks or commands, these terms are taken literally. Via the intermediary, the Prophet receives this Arabic communication and transmits it verbatim to his followers, who in turn do the same for the generations succeeding them. It is thus considered to be a faithful transmission of a verbally revealed message in the same format as it was revealed. Thus, the Muslim conception of revelation is equivalent to a dictation theory of revelation.

The Qur'an considers itself to be God's speech, a concept that was not foreign to the Qur'anic view of revelation. Nor is it difficult to demonstrate that, in the Qur'an, it is taken for granted that God speaks, and has spoken from the beginning of creation, in any number of language contexts.

Muslim theologians had some difficulty in coming to terms with the idea of God's speech, particularly as it related to the Qur'an. The question was whether the speech of God, as represented in the Qur'an, was 'created' (like any other being) or 'uncreated' (an attribute of God). Some theologians, particularly the Mu'tazilites, found it difficult to accept the view that the speech of God in the Qur'an was uncreated, and they argued that the Qur'an, although the speech of God, was nonetheless created. Their opponents, the Ash'arite theologians, argued that the Qur'an as speech of God should not be considered 'created'. However, even to the Ash'arites, the 'uncreatedness' of the Qur'an was not to be accepted without qualification. From their point of view, there were three levels of speech in relation to the Qur'an: language and utterance (*lugha wa nutq*); letters and writing (*huruf wa kitaba*); and spirit and meaning (*ruh wa ma'na*). It was only in the last sense that the Qur'an, as the speech of God, could be said to be 'uncreated' or co-eternal with God. Both Mu'tazilites and Ash'arites agreed that the Qur'an was the word of God, that the Prophet did not compose the Qur'an, and that the

Qur'an, in words, ideas and composition, were attributable to God alone.

Several verses indicate that, even during the lifetime of the Prophet, the Qur'an came to be conceived of as scripture or a book (*kitab*) like earlier scriptures given to prophets before Muhammad (98.1–3). This is the case even though the Qur'an came to be compiled as a 'book' only after the death of the Prophet. Clearly, the Qur'an considered itself to be scripture: 'And recite what has been revealed to thee of the Book of thy Lord: none can change His words' (18.27); 'We have revealed for you a Book in which is a message for you' (21.10).

In the modern period, a number of Muslim scholars have attempted to rethink the dictation theory of revelation as accepted in Islamic theology. In this context, the Pakistani-American scholar Fazlur Rahman (d. 1988) believed that early Muslim theologians did not have the intellectual capacity to confront the issue of the close relationship between Prophet Muhammad and the Qur'an (Rahman, 1966: 31). For Rahman it was important to emphasize the role of the Prophet in the genesis of the revelation; that is, the close connection between the Qur'an as the Word of God, the Prophet, and his mission and the socio-historical context in which the Qur'an was revealed. However, Rahman did not argue that the Qur'an was the word of the Prophet; his concern was the lack of emphasis, in the widely accepted view of revelation, on the close relationship between the Qur'an and the socio-historical context of the revelation (Rahman, 1982: 5). This relationship, if emphasized, would allow Muslim scholars to reinterpret some sections of the Qur'an in light of contemporary realities and challenges. This interest in rethinking the dictation theory of revelation is expected to continue as increasing emphasis is placed on the socio-historical context of the Qur'an in understanding its message.

References and further reading

Abu Zayd, N. (1998) *Mafhum al-nass: Dirasa fi 'ulum qur'an*, Beirut: al-Markaz al-thaqafi al-'arabi.

Ali, M. (1992) *Introduction to the Study of the Holy Qur'an*, Columbus, OH: Ahmadiyya Anjuman Isha'at Islam Lahore Inc.

Esack, F. (1998) *Qur'an, Liberation and Pluralism*, Oxford: OneWorld.

Izutsu, T. (1964) *God and Man in the Koran*, Tokyo: The Keio Institute of Cultural and Linguistic Studies.

Rahman, F. (1966) *Islam*, Chicago: University of Chicago Press.

—— (1982) *Islam and Modernity*, Chicago: University of Chicago Press.

Saeed, A. (1999) 'Rethinking "Revelation" as a Precondition for Reinterpreting the Qur'an: A Qur'anic perspective', *Journal of Qur'anic Studies* 1, 1: 93–114.

Tabataba'i, S. (1984) *The Qur'an in Islam*, trans. Alaeddin-Pazargadi Tehran: Sepehr.

ABDULLAH SAEED

REVENGE

The Arabic term for revenge is *intiqam*. The root verb is *naqama*, meaning to take revenge or vengeance: 'And you take vengeance on us only because we believed' (7.126). Allah is always able to exact revenge on his enemies: 'And Allah is All-Mighty, always capable of retribution' (3.4). The revenge of God is his punishment: 'So we took retribution from them' (6.136). *Muntaqim* is an avenger. God warns those who are reminded of the verses of their Lord then turn aside from them: 'We shall exact retribution from the criminals' (32.22).

RAFIK BERJAK

RIBA

The root *r/b/w/*, from which *riba* is derived, is used in the Qur'an twenty times. Of these, the term *riba* itself is used eight times (see, for example, 2.275–278; 3.130; 4.161; 30.39). In the Qur'an the root *r/b/w/* has the meanings of growing, increasing, rising, swelling, raising and being big and great. These usages appear to have one meaning in common: 'increase' in a qualitative or quantitative sense. The concept of *riba* here is dealt with as it is addressed in the Qur'an but this entry also touches upon the issue as it appears in the *hadith* literature and upon the debate in the modern period.

Several verses in the Qur'an refer to *riba*. Some are from very early in the Prophet Muhammad's mission, others from later. The first verse containing the term *riba* can be dated to early in the Prophet's mission in Mecca, probably in the fourth or fifth year (614 or 615 CE), possibly even earlier. The verse reads: 'And whatever you may give out in *riba* so that it may increase through other people's wealth does not increase in the sight of God; but whatever you give by way of charity, seeking God's pleasure, will receive manifold increase' (30.39). The Qur'an here would appear to be condemning the practice of *riba* and the resulting exploitation of the disadvantaged in the Meccan community. The early appearance of these references indicates the importance accorded this issue throughout the Prophet's mission.

The second *riba*-related verse appears to have been revealed in Medina, immediately after the battle of Uhud (3/625), nearly eleven years after the first condemnation of *riba* in Mecca: 'O Believers! Do not consume *riba*, doubling and redoubling, and fear God so that you may prosper' (3.130).

The last *riba*-related verses were revealed towards the end of the Prophet's mission, most probably around 8/630, or later, and clearly prohibit the practice. There is general agreement among exegetes that verses 2.275–278 were the last verses revealed in relation to the prohibition (Ibn Kathir, 1987, Vol. I: 335). The Qur'an points out that *riba* is not the same as trade (*bayʿ*), which is lawful, and it warns those who profit from *riba* that they will be punished by God (2.275–280).

The contexts of these verses affirm the moral emphasis placed by the Qur'an upon the prohibition of *riba*. Several verses immediately preceding the final *riba*-related verses extol the giving of money (*infaq*) for the sake of God (2.261–262, 272), to relieve the suffering of the poor, the needy and the disadvantaged. Having contrasted *riba* with *sadaqa* (charity), the Qur'an commands Muslims to waive *riba* and take only the principal lent to the borrower (2.278). Finally, the Qur'an exhorts Muslims to be sympathetic towards debtors who are finding it difficult to repay on time. For several early exegetical authorities, it was poor debtors who ought to be helped if they were unable to pay their debts. In such cases, the Qur'an adds that overlooking the principal would be preferable, and that forcing further debt on an already burdened debtor is unethical, immoral and against its humanitarian objectives.

Two important statements in the final *riba*-related verses shed light upon the nature of *riba* as prohibited in the Qur'an. The first is '*lakum ruʾusu amwalikum* (You are only entitled to your principal')', and this is immediately followed by '*la tazlimuna wa-la tuzlamun* (Do not commit injustice and no injustice will be committed against you)' (2.279). While these two statements appear to be interdependent, the exegetical literature (*tafsir*) emphasizes the first but almost completely ignores the second. Based on this reading, Muslim scholars, both in the pre-modern and modern periods, have condemned any form of increase over and above the principal in a debt or a loan as *riba*, however small and inconsequential the amount might be.

The Qur'an addressed itself to a society based upon a subsistence economy, where meeting even day-to-day basic needs was difficult. There was no legal system to protect debtors from exploitation by powerful and affluent money-lenders. The debtor was at a disadvantage on two fronts: poverty and the debilitating effect of seemingly unrepayable debt. The Prophet's association of poverty with debt and his constant prayers seeking refuge from both illustrate the situation most vividly.

The condemnation of *riba* and its ultimate prohibition in the Qur'an were preceded by the proscription of several other morally objectionable forms of behaviour towards the socially and economically disadvantaged of the Meccan community. In a number of other verses the Qur'an states that beggars and the destitute have a right to a share of the wealth of the affluent (70.24–25). It reiterates the importance of outlaying money to relieve the suffering of the poor. There are many instances of the rich being commanded to provide financial support for relatives (8.41), orphans (2.177, 220; 8.41; 76.8–9), debtors (9.60), beggars, wayfarers (2.177; 8.41; 9.60), migrants (24.22), prisoners of war (76.8–9), the divorced (2.236), the deprived (51.19; 70.19–25), the destitute (8.41; 76.8–9), the poor (2.271; 9.60) and slaves (2.177; 9.60; 58.3). Wealth is both a trust and a test (2.155; 3.186; 8:28). Amassing wealth without consideration for the socially and economically disadvantaged will not lead to salvation either in this world or the hereafter; it has no intrinsic value in the eyes of God (34.37).

The Qur'an makes giving obligatory by means of *zakat* (alms) and also maintains that Muslims should give voluntarily and generously in any situation that demands intervention in order to reduce suffering. Spending can be in the form of a donation. Where a donation is not possible, however, a loan can be made but must not impose another burden on the recipient. Such a loan is referred to in the Qur'an as *qard hasan* (a benevolent loan). If on maturity of the *qard hasan* the debtor is experiencing hardship and is unable to pay, no extra charges or any form of interest should be imposed. On the contrary, the debtor should be given time to repay.

While the Qur'an appears to deal with *riba* primarily as being loan- or debt-related, most of the *hadith* referring to *riba* are related to certain types of sale (*bay'*). Among the most prominent *hadith* related to *riba* is the 'six commodities *hadith*'. While there are many versions of this in *hadith* literature, the best-known version reads: 'The Prophet said: "Gold for gold, silver for silver, wheat for wheat, barley for barley, dates for dates, and salt for salt should be exchanged like for like, equal for equal and hand-to-hand [on the spot]"' (Muslim, *Sahih*). According to this *hadith*, Muslims may sell these six commodities only if they follow the guidelines outlined in the *hadith*. For example, if gold is sold for gold, both counter-values must be exchanged on the spot and in equal measure; any increase in one counter-value or a deferment of delivery of one counter-value will be considered *riba*, and is therefore prohibited. The reason for the prohibition of *riba* in sales appears to be potential injustice to the economically weaker party in a barter transaction.

The six commodities *hadith*, and other similar *hadith*, became the basis of the doctrine of *riba* discussed in Islamic law. Juristic discussion tended, first, to probe into the '*illa* (efficient cause) of the prohibition of each commodity in the six commodities *hadith*. Identification of the *'illa* was intended to extend the prohibition to similar commodities by means of the jurisprudential method of 'analogy' (*qiyas*). Based on the *hadith*, the jurists divided *riba* into *riba al-fadl* and *riba al-nasi'a*, which are, respectively, an excess in a counter-value and the deferment of a counter-value in a transaction involving the sale of the commodities mentioned in the *hadith*.

During the modern period, debate about *riba* continued to follow premodern conceptions and arguments developed in *fiqh*. Following the introduction into Muslim societies of interest-based banking, debate on the permissibility, or otherwise, of interest intensified from the 1940s onwards in the context of the emergence of the global Islamic neo-revivalist movements. These movements (examples include the Muslim Brotherhood of Egypt and Jama'at Islami of Pakistan and those influenced by their ideological frameworks) called for the transformation of the existing political, legal, social and economic institutions of Muslim societies to ones more in line with Islamic norms and principles. One of the key institutions they focused upon was banking and financial institutions based on interest, which they argued should be transformed into Islamic ones free from interest.

During the modern period, on the question of whether interest is permissible or not, Muhammad 'Abdu (d. 1905) and Rashid Rida (d. 1935) were among the first to address the question of interest on deposits. They seem to have believed that at least some forms of interest (such as interest on deposits) could be considered permissible if a *mudaraba* (commendam) scheme could be devised to legitimize the interest (Mallat, 1988: 74). The Egyptian

authority on Islamic law, 'Abd al-Razzaq Sanhuri (d. 1971), saw compound interest as the main intent of the Qur'an's prohibition of *riba*. Interest on capital, in his view, could be justified on the basis of 'need' (*haja*), but to prevent misuse and exploitation the state should limit interest rates and control methods of payment (Sanhuri, *Masadir al-Haqq*, Vol. III: 241–4). The contemporary Syrian thinker Doualibi argued that the Qur'an prohibited interest on 'consumption loans' specifically, presumably because of its concern for people who might borrow just to meet their basic needs. Following this line of thinking, some have argued that there is no *riba* attached to interest paid or received by corporate bodies such as companies and governments, and others that Islam prohibits 'usury' not 'interest'. There is also the argument that *riba* should be equated with real interest, not nominal interest.

Several scholars of the mid- to late twentieth century also interpreted *riba* from a 'moral' perspective, distancing themselves from the literalism that dominated much of the thinking of the neo-revivalists on this issue. Muhammad Asad (d. 1992), a modernist commentator on the Qur'an, maintained that *riba* involved 'an exploitation of the economically weak by the strong and resourceful' (Asad, 1984: 633). Fazlur Rahman (d. 1988), the Pakistani-American academic, argued that the *raison d'être* of the prohibition of *riba* was injustice (*zulm*), as stated in the Qur'an at 2.279, and that 'well-meaning Muslims with very virtuous consciences sincerely believe that the Qur'an has banned all bank interest for all times in woeful disregard of what *riba* was historically, why the Qur'an denounced it as a gross and cruel form of exploitation and banned it' (Rahman, 1964: 26).

Despite the appeal of these views, the neo-revivalists and their sympathizers, who increasingly seem to represent mainstream Muslim opinion today on the issue of *riba* and interest, have continued to reject any reinterpretation of *riba* to accommodate bank interest. The Council of Islamic Ideology of Pakistan, which in the 1980s developed a blueprint for the transformation of the Pakistani financial system into an Islamic one, claimed that there was 'complete unanimity among all schools of thought in Islam that the term *riba* stands for interest in all its types and forms' (1983: 7).

With the dawning of the twenty-first century, the role of Islamic (i.e. interest-free) financial institutions in Muslim communities has become even more significant, and the change is noticeable. Institutions affected include village banks, major international development banks, insurance (*takaful*) companies and investment funds, all of which are in competition with conventional interest-based institutions, but all of which are also in cooperation with them. To try and solve this contradiction, several Muslim majority states – for example, Malaysia, Kuwait and Egypt – now run dual banking and finance systems, one based on interest, the other on Islamic or interest-free principles. Even interest-based banks (including major international banks) now offer Islamic products or Islamic windows to their Muslim clientele and to interested non-Muslims.

References and further reading

Ahmad, K. (1994) 'Elimination of *riba*; Concept and problems', in *Elimination of Riba from the Economy*, Islamabad: Institute of Policy Studies.

Asad, M. (1984) *The Message of the Qur'an*, Gibraltar: Dar al-andalus.

Chapra, M. (1985) *Towards a Just Monetary System*, Leicester: Islamic Foundation.

Council of Islamic Ideology (1983) *Consolidated Recommendations on the Islamic Economic System*, Islamabad: Council of Islamic Ideology.

Ibn Kathir (1987) *Tafsir al-Qur'an al-'azim*, Beirut: Dar al-Ma'rifa.

Mallat, Chibli (1988) 'The Debate on *riba* and Interest in Twentieth Century Jurisprudence', in C. Mallat (ed.) *Islamic Law and Finance*, London: Graham & Trotman.

Rahman, F. (1964) '*Riba* and Interest', *Islamic Studies*, March. 3: 1–43.

—— (1979) 'Islam: Challenges and opportunities', in A.T. Welch and P. Cachia (eds) *Islam: Past influence and present challenge*, Albany, NY: SUNY Press, Vol. 3, 1–43.

Saeed, A. (1999) *Islamic Banking and Interest*, Leiden: E.J. Brill.

Saleh, N. (1986) *Unlawful Gain and Legitimate Profit in Islamic Law*, Cambridge: Cambridge University Press.

Sanhuri, 'Abd al-Razzaq (1967) *Masadir al-haqq fi al-fiqh al-islami*, Beirut: al-Majma' al-'Arabi al-Islami.

Uzair, M. (1978) *Interest-free Banking*, Karachi: Royal Book Company.

Vogel, F. and Hayes, S. (1998) *Islamic Law and Finance*, The Hague: Kluwer Law International.

See also: **money**

ABDULLAH SAEED

RIDA

Radiya is a root verb meaning to be satisfied, content or to agree or approve. According to the Qur'an the *rida* of the slave with Allah is to be content with his ruling and the *rida* of Allah with his slave is when he sees him following his commands: 'Allah will be pleased with them, and they with Him' (98.8). *Radiya* also signifies to choose or to approve: 'And have chosen for you Islam as your religion' (5.3). *Al-ridwan* is pleasure of a high degree. The Prophet Muhammad and his companions were 'Seeking bounty from Allah and (His) great pleasure' (48.29).

RAFIK BERJAK

RIDDA AND THE CASE FOR DECRIMINALIZATION OF APOSTASY

Ridda, usually translated as apostasy, literally means 'turning back', as in *murtadd*, the active participle from the verb *irtadda*, it refers to the 'one who turns back'. In Islamic law, the *murtadd* (apostate) is defined as the person who had earlier witnessed to the unity of God and to the veracity of Muhammad's prophethood, but chose later to renege on Islam to revert back to the paths of eternal perdition while under no duress or coercion to do so (al-Jaziri, n.d.: 42). In many instances the actual conceptual structure of *ridda* is quite a complicated issue to grapple with: Muslim jurists of the early period of Islam tend to discuss apostasy alongside other concepts such as heresy, political deceit or dissembling (*zandaqa*), blasphemy (*istihza'* or *sabb al-rasul*), hypocrisy (*nifaq*) and unbelief (*kufr*), as if these concepts were synonymous (al-Jaziri, n.d: 422–7). Thus, *ridda* may not only arise following a Muslim's change of religious conviction (*i'tiqad*), but may follow from acts performed, utterances proclaimed, or religious duties abnegated by him or her (al-Jaziri, n.d: 422–7).

Although the term *ridda* itself does not figure in the Qur'an, a number of its derivatives do occur. Those who abandon the Islamic faith appear, according to the Qur'an, to be in fact committing an act as abhorrent in nature as that of unbelief. Their ultimate fate in the hereafter is no different from that awaiting the disbelievers, the polytheists and the hypocrites to a certain extent. The following passages of the Qur'an are those relating most directly to the issue of apostasy:

> O you who have attained to faith! If you ever abandon your faith (*man yartadda*

> *minkum 'an dinihi*), God will in time bring forth [in your stead] people whom He loves and who love Him – humble towards the believers, proud towards all who deny the truth. (5.54)

> [Your enemies] will not cease to fight against you till they have turned you away from your faith, if they can. But if any of you should turn away from his faith (*wa man yartadid minkum 'an dinihi*) and die as a denier of the truth – these it is whose works will go for naught in this world and in the life to come; and these it is who are destined for the fire, therein to abide. (2.217)

> Truly, those who turn their backs [on this message] (*irtaddu 'ala adbarihim*) after guidance has been vouchsafed to them, [do it because] Satan has embellished their fancies and filled them with false hopes. (47.25)

> If, then, he [Muhammad] dies or is slain, will you turn about on your heels (*inkalabtum 'ala a'qabikum*)? But he that turns about on his heels can in no ways harm God – whereas God will requite all who are grateful [to Him]. (3.144)

The final verse quoted does not contain a derivative of *ridda*, but the use of the figurative expression '*inkalabtum 'ala a'qabikum*' here brings up the idea of 'turning back'. Asad (1984: 89), quoting al-Tabari, explains that this verse was revealed in the context of the battle of Uhud, when rumours about the Prophet's death 'caused many Muslims to abandon the fight and even brought some of them close to apostasy'.

On conversion

From the earliest days of Islam to this day, apostasy continues to be considered in Islamic societies one of the most grievous acts that a Muslim person could ever commit. Islamic law insists that is impermissible for a Muslim to follow the path of irreligion or to convert to a religion other than Islam, and that no effort should be spared to prevent a member of the community from doing so (al-Jaziri, n.d: 422–7; al-Jaza'iri, 1979: 535). Understanding how conversion to a religion such as Christianity came to be seen as 'unacceptable', even as inconceivable, may prove quite intriguing, particularly since the Qur'an does not seem to preclude the possibility that adherents of other monotheistic faiths are also among the saved and 'need have no fear, and neither shall they grieve'. This inconceivability, Watt (1974: 250) observes, stems from the general tendency in the Muslim world to assume that a person in their right mind would never 'turn down the better in favour of the inferior'. Muslims cannot, according to this view, understand the motive for renunciation or conversion because they believe that 'anyone who penetrates beneath the surface of the inner essence of Islam is bound to recognise its superiority over the other religions'. This issue, however, is not always seen or argued through the 'principle' of superiority of one religion over another (Nursi, 1998: 505). For Nursi (d. 1960), people of other monotheistic faiths can indeed be on a path compatible with Islam; they may even be within it, and are saved, without them necessarily knowing or intending to be on that path. But while he regards the non-acceptance of Islam by people of other faiths as perfectly excusable to a degree, he deplores the Muslim's acceptance of a faith other than Islam, after he or she had earlier heard of the Prophet Muhammad and was familiar with his message. The Prophet Muhammad is the 'seal of all prophets', meaning not that he is simply the last of them, nor that he annuls whatever message they brought, but that he embodies the cul-

minating point of all that was revealed, affirming, thus, all that had preceded him. It is for this reason, Nursi argues, 'a person who denies Muhammad, who with his miracles and works was the pride of the universe and glory of mankind, certainly can in no respect receive any light and will not recognize God'. The Muslim person who converts to another religion or does not accept Muhammad's prophethood has 'owing to his denial, accepted annihilation and nihility'. Hence for someone such as Nursi the issue is not so much about 'turning down the better in favour of the inferior' but precisely over 'what religion, if any at all, does the apostate in effect turn to after he or she renounces the "seal" of prophecy that affirms and embraces all the other revelations?' It is following this line of argument that many scholars have upheld that for a Muslim to gain salvation, 'all the ways are closed except the way of Muhammad'.

Apostasy in Islamic law

Despite differences of opinion as to whether the punishment for apostasy ought to be regarded as a prescribed *hadd*, for which there should be evidence in the Qur'an or the *sunna*, or as discretionary punishment (*ta'zir*) whose terms the judge alone decides, jurists of the various schools of Islamic law are broadly in agreement that apostasy is a grave offence, and they overwhelmingly prescribe the death penalty as a punishment for it. Among those who differed with this ruling were Companions such as Sufiyan b. Sa'id al-Thawri (d. 161/778), who held the view that an apostate ought never to be killed but constantly invited back to Islam, and scholars such as Ibn Taymiyya, who was generally in favour of a discretionary punishment. Today, while the majority of the Muslim states do not prescribe the death penalty for apostasy, Yemen, Sudan and Saudi Arabia continue to do so.

Although it is not hard to glean from the Qur'an that it views apostasy as a serious moral aberration, understanding or explaining how the punishment for it became a 'temporal' one instead of a chastisement in the hereafter, as the *ridda* verses seem to clearly suggest, is far from a straightforward matter. Again the question of the death penalty for apostasy is quite a difficult issue to grapple with, particularly if we come to espouse the view that the general ethos of the Qur'an is repugnant to the idea of compulsion in religion.

While there are number of scholars who maintain that there exists textual evidence for the death penalty, their views have been challenged often on the basis that all those verses which deal directly with apostasy warn only of a chastisement in the hereafter, never of any temporal punishment or *hadd* as in the case of theft or fornication.

Those who argue for the death penalty among the jurists generally advance the *hadith* found in the *Sahih* of Bukhari according to which the Prophet is reported to have said, 'Whoever changes his religion kill him' as evidence for their case. In another *hadith* the Prophet is reported to have said: 'The blood of a Muslim who confesses that there is no God but Allah and that I am the messenger of Allah, cannot be shed except in three cases: a life for a life; a married person who commits illegal sexual intercourse; and the one who leaves the fold of Islam, breaking thus his commitment with the community of Muslims (*al-tarik al-islam al-mufariq li al-jama'a*).'

There are historical reports that the Prophet himself ordered the execution of a number of Muslims turned apostates upon his return to Mecca as further proof that the *sunna* contains ample evidence for temporal punishment for

this offence. In addition, it is not uncommon that the wars (*hurub al-ridda*) waged by the first Caliph Abu Bakr against the tribes that abnegated their religious duty to pay their taxes (*zakat*) to the central authority in Medina after the Prophet's death serve as support for the proponents of temporal punishment, and this despite the fact that Umar b. Khattab did not readily agree with Abu Bakr on the decision to go ahead with that war.

Against the commonly held view among Muslim jurists that there is evidence for the death penalty in the *sunna*, some Muslim scholars – Mohammad Hashim Kamali, Abdullah Saeed, and even leading Islamists such as Rashid al-Ghannushi and Hasan al-Turabi – have all recently questioned the law of apostasy and found much of its basis wanting. They argue that the death penalty and other laws surrounding the issue of apostasy are not only post-Qur'anic, but are, at best, based only on some isolated traditions (*ahad*) of the Prophet. The message of the Qur'an and the living practice of the Prophet, they affirmed, could not possibly allow for compulsion or coercion in religion, and maintained that the death penalty ruling and much of the laws related to apostasy are revokable. Kamali (2000) argues that just as there is clearly no evidence that the Qur'an prescribes temporal punishment for apostasy, there is equally no evidence that the Prophet sentenced anyone to death for apostasy once the motive behind the reports are scrutinized.

Saeed notes that of all those who were facing the death penalty upon the Prophet's return to Mecca only a few were actually executed, and that even an earlier scribe of the Prophet, 'Abd Allah b. Sa'd b. Abi al-Sarh, who had repeatedly claimed he had corrupted the text of the Qur'an dictated to him by Muhammad, was let off. Those scholars who are calling for re-examination or a rethinking of apostasy laws are mainly of the view that these laws should be looked at in light of the 'particular' and precarious socio-political environment in which the Muslim community was born, when the unity of the nascent community was of paramount importance.

Following this, it is argued, the Prophet's actions could suggest that the death penalty for apostasy was upheld less for a mere religious conversion and more as a result of a political act or allegiance akin to treason of the highest order. 'A'isha's version of one of the *ahadith* that may be advanced by the proponents of the death penalty serves this time as evidence for the pressing need to make a difference between seditious and non-seditious apostasy. Instead of *al-tarik al-islam al-mufariq li al-jama'a* 'A'isha narrates: '... [And] a man who leaves Islam and engages in fighting against Allah and His Prophet shall be executed, crucified or exiled.' Indeed, a number of pre-modern jurists, it is observed, have discussed the case of the apostates alongside the case of enemy combatants. *Sahih Muslim*, a major *hadith* collection, which has a chapter entitled 'Rulings on the subject of the *muharibun* and the apostates' is seen as a good example of the connection between the laws of apostasy and 'political treason'. The Hanafi school's position on the female apostate is also quite interesting in this regard. It maintains that a woman who commits apostasy ought not to be killed, not only because the killing of women was forbidden by the Prophet, but rather on the basis that a woman was unlikely to take up arms and pose a threat to the community. It is mainly from the pool of Hanafi rulings that the opponents of the early laws on apostasy manage to contrive their argument for a need to develop a new conceptual tool to deal

with this legal issue. While maintaining that apostasy was a grave offence, the prominent jurist Sarakhsi (d. 490/1096) had already called for the necessity to make a difference between rulings pertaining to 'religious, non-seditious apostasy' and those pertaining to a 'politically subversive apostasy' or high treason. The former he considered a matter entirely between 'the servant worshipper and His Lord', and the latter he described as a legitimate public policy aiming at protecting the well-being of the community (*siyasatun mashru'a li masalih ta'ud ila al-'ibad*).

References and further reading

Asad, M. (1984) *The Message of the Qur'an*, Gibraltar: Dar al-andalus.

al-Jaza'iri, Abu Bakr (1979) *Minhaj al-muslim*, Cairo: Maktabat al-kulliyat al-azhariyya.

al-Jaziri, Abd l-Rahman (n.d.) *Min kitab al-fiqh lsquo;ala al-madahib al-arba'a*, Beirut: Dar al-fikr, Vol. 5.

Kamali, M. (2000) *Islamic Law in Malaysia: Issues and developments*, Kuala Lumpur: Ilmiyya Publishers.

Nursi, Bediuzzaman Said (1998) *Mektubat*, Istanbul: Sözler Yayınevı.

Saeed, A. and Saeed, S. (2003) *Freedom of Religion, Apostasy and Islam*, Burlington, VT: Ashgate.

al-Sarkhasi, Muhammad Ahmad (n.d.) *Kitab al-Mabsut*, Beirut: Dar al-ma'rifa, Vol. 10.

Watt, M. (1974) *The Majesty that Was Islam: The Islamic world 661–1100*, New York: Praeger.

Yohanan, F. (2003) *Tolerance and Coercion in Islam*, Cambridge: Cambridge University Press.

ABDULLAH SAEED

RIGHTEOUS (TO BE)

see: salaha

RIZQ

Derived from the Arabic verb *razaqa* (to provide with the means of subsistence), the verbal noun *rizq* in its Qur'anic usage denotes anything given by God to man as a means of nourishment and sustenance, be it material or spiritual; it is thus often translated as 'bounty'. One of God's innumerable names is '*al-Razzaq*' (the All-Provider), and every instance of the provision of bounties mentioned in the Qur'an has God as its subject. Provision of all things necessary to life on earth is from God alone: creatures themselves do not 'carry their own sustenance' (29.60–63). Some *rizq* is 'sent down from the sky' (40.13), while all *rizq* is given 'in due measure, in accordance with wisdom' (42.27).

COLIN TURNER

ROPE OF ALLAH, THE
see: **Habl Allah**

RUH
see: **Jibril;** *nafs*

RUMOUR

Rumour in Arabic is *isha'a* or *shay'a*. *Isha'a* is spreading or circulation of news. Rumour spreading is a sin and is an action forbidden in Islam. The Qur'an warns those who spread rumours that they shall suffer painful torment because of their devastating effects on the Muslim society: 'Verily, those who like [to see] adultery spread among those who believe, they will have a painful torment' (24.19). Rumour is perceived by Islam as a destructive action that threatens healthy societies. Those who spread rumours, particularly rumours about women, including their own wives, that accuse them of adultery without any proof, are to be flogged with eighty stripes and their testimony will be rejected forever after.

See also: **'A'isha; backbiting**

RAFIK BERJAK

S

SABEANS

An enigmatic religious community, the Sabeans are mentioned three times in the Qur'an, appearing each time alongside the Jews and the Christians as 'People of the Book'. Their identity has been the subject of much debate by Muslim exegetes and Western scholars, yet it remains unknown. Some have identified the Sabeans as the gnostic Mandeans of southern Iraq, although it is highly unlikely that such a community would have been known to Muhammad and the Medinan community, while de Blois argues that they might possibly have been Manicheans and Yusuf Ali posits a possible connection with the Queen of Sheba.

COLIN TURNER

SABIQA

The term *sabiqa* (or *sabq*) meaning 'precedence' in general and, more specifically, 'precedence in submission and service to Islam', was a key concept in the early socio-political history of Islam, and was invoked to 'rank' the faithful according to their excellences. In addition to early conversion, precedence in emigrating for the sake of Islam (both to Abyssinia and to Medina) and to participate in the early battles of Islam also conferred great merit. The two concepts of 'precedence' and 'moral excellences' (*fadl/fadila*) became conjoined to create a paradigm of the most excellent leadership. Such a paradigm finds scriptural sanction in Qur'anic verses such as 'Those who precede[d] are the ones who precede (*al-sabiqu al-sabiqun*); they are those who will be brought near [to God] in the gardens of bliss' (*surat al-Waqi'a*, 56.10–12); and 'Those among you who spent and fought before the victory are not of the same rank [as others] but greater in rank than those who spent and fought afterwards' (*surat al-Hadid*, 57.10).

The above verses are quoted in both Sunni and Shi'i sources in support of a divinely mandated hierarchy of moral excellence in Islam. Sunni sources uniformly assign the greatest excellence to the Prophet's Companions from among the Muhajirun (the Emigrants from Mecca) and the Ansar (the 'Helpers' in Medina), but even among these they recognize a certain order of precedence based on their time of conversion and record of service to the early Muslim community. In the debates regarding succession to Muhammad after his death, the sources state that the *sabiqa* of Abu Bakr and 'Ali, the two principal contenders, became a source of contention between the two opposing factions and generated a prolific apologetic literature on both sides.

Further reading

Afsaruddin, A. (2002) *Excellence and Precedence: Medieval Islamic discourse on legitimate leadership*, Leiden: E.J. Brill.

ASMA AFSARUDDIN

SABR

Sabr means patience; its root is *sabara*. It appears in the Qur'an, in its many different forms, 103 times. We read in the Qur'an, 'Surely the patient will be paid their wages in full without measure' (39.10), and this is representative of the important role that *sabr* plays in Islam, thus 'And whatever misfortune befalls you it is because of what your hands have earned. And He pardons much' (42.30). We also read, 'And we tested them with good and evil in order that they might turn back' (7.168), and this brings out nicely the significance of patience in the face of the tests that God sets us. Even believers – and it might be said especially believers – are tested: 'Alif Laam Mim. Do people think that they will be left alone because they say, "We believe", and will not be tested?

Indeed We tested those before them' (29.1–3).

It is interesting that we are told to 'Guard strictly the [five obligatory] prayers, especially the middle prayer and stand before Allah in obedience' (2.238). The verses prior to this deal with divorce. The verses after it also deal with divorce. Why was this verse placed in the middle? It seems out of place – what is its relevance to divorce? It might be suggested that in the difficult times a person goes through when issues of divorce arise they should not forget to remember God, that is they should not forget to pray. It could well be prayer (*salat*) together with *sabr* that will pull them through: 'O you who believe! Seek help in patience and prayer. Truly, God is with those that are patient' (2.153).

Further reading

al-Qaradawi, Y. (1989) *Al-sabr fi al-Qur'an*, Cairo: Maktabat wahba.

See also: **character; divorce;** *hukm;* **imam;** *salat*

OLIVER LEAMAN

SACRIFICE

Sacrifice is a religious rite in which an object is offered to a divinity in order to establish, maintain or restore the relationship of a human being to the sacred order. In its original usage sacrifice denoted only a religious practice, however, over time, the meaning of the word has expanded. In Arabic *qurban* signifies sacrifice defined as an offering to God.

The root verb is *qariba* or *qaruba*, meaning to be near to, approach or offer. Sacrifice in Islamic terms is whatever a slave offers to approach Allah's satisfaction and to express gratitude and appreciation for His bounties and favours. The Qur'an promises those who offer thanks to Him to increase his gifts to them: 'If you give thanks, I will give you more' (14.7).

The first sacrifice was offered to Allah by the two sons of Adam, Qabil (Cain) and Habil (Abel). Habil had offered the sacrifice of the best ram of his flock, while Qabil unwillingly offered a cheap share of worthless corn. The sacrifice of Habil was burnt up by a fire from heaven, signifying the acceptance of his sacrifice; Qabil's offering was not touched by the fire, implying that it was rejected. The Qur'an states: 'And recite to them the story of the two sons of Adam in truth; when each offered a sacrifice, it was accepted from one but not from the other' (5.27).

The most generous sacrifice is the offer of the self for the cause of God. Allah promises paradise to those who sacrifice their selves and their wealth for God. The Qur'an states that this promise was also given in the Torah and the Gospel: 'Verily, Allah has purchased of the believers their lives and their properties and their return shall be the paradise' (9.111). The Holy Book also describes the story of Prophet Ibrahim and his son Isma'il as an example of self-sacrifice:

> When Isma'il became a young man his father, Ibrahim said to him one day, 'My son, I saw in a dream that I am sacrificing you, what do you say in this regard?' Isma'il replied, 'Father, carry out what you have been commanded. If Allah wills, you will find me patient and steadfast.' When both had submitted to Allah's will and Isma'il was cast down upon his face, a voice from Heaven called out, 'O Ibrahim, you have indeed fulfilled your dream, thus do We reward the righteous. This was indeed a manifest trial. And we ransomed the boy by means of a great sacrifice, and left a tradition of Ibrahim forever for the coming generations. Peace be upon Ibrahim for he was one of our believing servants.' (37.102–111)

Animal sacrifice is a tradition offered by Muslims every year on the Eid al-Adhha, the Feast of the Sacrifice in commemoration of the sacrifice made by the prophet Ibrahim and his son Isma'il. When the Prophet was asked: 'What is sacrifice?' He replied, 'It is the *sunna* of your father Ibrahim.' He also said that 'The person who sacrifices with a willing heart and with the *niyyat* (intention) of reward, on the Day of Judgement that sacrifice will shield him from the fires of hell.' Additionally, we are told that to Allah alone the Muslim should offer, among other things, his sacrifice – 'My prayer, sacrifice, life, and death are for Allah the Lord of the peoples' (6.162) – and that this is a condition of its acceptance – 'For you Lord pray and offer sacrifice' (108.2). Further, the purpose of the sacrifice is to express one's gratitude to Allah for his many blessings – 'Thus we subjected these animals to you so that you may express your gratitude' (22.36) – thus the person who is offering should be pious and humble – 'Verily Allah accepts from those who are *al-muttaqun* (pious)' (5.27). Animals to be sacrificed should all be *halal* (permissible, domesticated animals). Generally, goats, sheep, rams, cows and camels are offered, and the sacrifice should be chosen from the best kind of animal. It has been reported in *Bukhari* and *Muslim* that the Prophet sacrificed two rams of beautiful dark eyes and large horns. He slaughtered them himself, putting his foot on the side of the neck and saying '*B'ismillah, wa-Allah Akbar* (In the Name of Allah and God is Great)'.

According to the Qur'an, the offering of animal sacrifice is part of the regular practice of the system of obedience of all divine laws, although the way and procedure may differ for different nations: 'We have appointed for every community a way of offering the sacrifice so that the people may mention the name of Allah over the cattle He has given them' (22.34).

Animal sacrifice offered for Eid al-Adhha is a *sunna*; it is not an obligation for those who are not on pilgrimage. For pilgrims, sacrifice depends on the type of pilgrimage – it could be *wajib*, a necessary duty, or simply have been recommended. The purpose of the sacrifice is not merely to kill an animal, but to please family and friends as well as the poor. The recommendations are to retain one part of the meat, about a third, for one's family; to send another third to friends and relatives; and to donate the last third to the poor. From this perspective, a sacrifice is an act of charity, which includes one's family, friends and the community.

The Qur'an explains that God does not benefit by the sacrifice, but what pleases him is the fact that people are conscious of him and follow his commands: 'Their flesh will never reach God, nor their blood. What reaches Him is your piety' (22.37). When the Prophet was asked what benefit do we get from the sacrifice he answered: 'A reward for every hair or a strand of wool of the sacrificed animal.'

See also: **qurban**

RAFIK BERJAK

SAHARA

Sahara is a verb meaning to bewitch, charm or enchant. A *sahir* is a wizard or sorcerer, a person who practices sorcery or turns a thing from its natural state into something else. The story of the Pharoah's sorcerers and their interaction with Moses plays a significant role in the Qur'an: 'However, when Moses cast his miraculous staff it ate up their magic. ..., And all the sorcerers fell down prostrate' (7.117, 120).

RAFIK BERJAK

SAHIB

Sahib is a noun meaning companion, associate or fellow. *Sahiba* is the verb, meaning to accompany, associate or befriend someone: 'If I ask you anything after this, keep me not in your company' (18.76).

According to its normal usage, *al-sahib* is someone who keeps company with a person, animal, place or time: 'He said to his companion: "Be not sad, surely Allah is with us"' (9.40). The Qur'an refers to the Prophet Muhammad as the People's Companion in many verses, although the people of Mecca at first did not believe the Prophet about his putative revelation and accused him of being a sorcerer, priest, soothsayer or madman. The Qur'an continues to remind them of the fact that Muhammad is their companion, their fellow, someone who has lived among them for years and whom they trust, and should continue to trust – 'Your companion has neither gone astray nor has erred' (53.2); 'And your companion is not a madman' (81.22).

Ashab, referring to the dwellers of paradise and hellfire, means 'people of ...': 'Not equal are the companions of the fire and the companions of paradise. It is the companions of paradise that will be successful' (59.20). *Sahiba* is the feminine form, and in the Qur'an signifies a wife. It is used in reference to the oneness of Allah: 'He has taken neither a wife nor a son' (72.3): 'In the Day of Judgement, disbelievers would wish to ransom himself from the punishment by his children (and his wife)' (70.11–12).

RAFIK BERJAK

SAHIBA

see: **sunna; tafsir in early Islam**

SAJADA | MASJID

The Arabic verb *sajada* denotes the act of prostration, which in the pre-Islamic Near East was common both as an act of submission before a superior and as an expression of humility before an object of worship. The Queen of Sheba and her people, for example, were found to be 'worshipping (*yasjudun*) the sun besides Allah' (27.24). With the establishment of the canonical prayer (*salat*), prostration became an integral component of Muslim devotion, presumably reflecting the adoration which, according to the Qur'an, the cosmos displays with regard to its creator: 'Do they not look at Allah's creation [even] among [inanimate] things – how their very shadows turn round, from the right and the left, prostrating themselves to Allah, and that in the humblest manner?' (16:48). In the Meccan verses of the Qur'an, the word *masjid* should not be understood in the technical sense of a mosque as we understand it today, but rather as any zplace in which the worship of, or prostration before, God takes place. The Qur'an identifies two mosques as possessing particular significance for Muslims: the *masjid al-haram* and the *masjid al-aqsa*. The *masjid al-haram* almost invariably denotes the *Ka'ba* and its precincts. The *masjid al-aqsa*, or 'furthest place of worship', is traditionally understood to be Jerusalem, the first *qibla* of the Muslims in Medina. Some exegetes have posited a more esoteric reading, claiming that the term refers to the ultimate point of submission reached by the Prophet during his legendary 'Night Journey' (*isra'*).

COLIN TURNER

SALAM

see: **peace**

SALIH

A prophet mentioned by name in the Qur'an ten times. A saying attributed to Muhammad states that Salih was one of four 'Arab' prophets including Hud, Shuayb and Muhammad himself. According to the Qur'an (e.g. 7.73; 11.61; 26.141; 27.45), Salih was sent to the people of Thamud. 15.80 refers to the people of al-Hijr, which is interpreted to mean the city of Mada'in Salih (Greek city of Hegra). Several other passages in the Qur'an refer to the people of Thamud but do not mention Salih by name (e.g. 17.59; 41.17; 54.23; 91.11).

The Qur'an refers to the 'she-camel' as a sign to the people of Thamud (e.g. 7.73; 11.64; 17.59; 26.155; 54.27; 91.13). Muslim exegetes explain that this was a camel which Salih caused to appear out of a rock, and that the people of Thamud were tested by allowing the camel to drink all it wanted of their water on different days of the week. The Qur'an refers to the people of Thamud hamstringing the camel (e.g. 7.78; 11.65; 26.157; 54.29; 91.14) and Muslim exegesis identifies the person who did this deed, and describes in detail the plotting that led up to its occurrence.

The account of Salih is used by Muslim exegetes to exemplify the prophetic cycle in which the prophet is rejected by his people who are then destroyed. According to Muslim exegesis, God's punishment left all the people of Thamud lying dead in their elaborate homes that they had carved out of the sides of mountains. The punishment includes the people being crushed and flattened (91.14), an earthquake (7.78) and a scream (11.67; 15.83; 54.31). During a campaign to Tabuk, the Prophet Muhammad stops by Mada'in Salih and warns his followers not to enter the city or drink the water from it. A tomb ascribed to Salih is visited by Muslim pilgrims in the

Hadhramawt near the tomb of the prophet Hud.

Further reading

Halèvy, J. (1905) 'Le prophète Salih', *Journal asiatique* 5: 146–50.

Hamblin, W.J. (1983) 'Pre-Islamic Arabian Prophets', in S.J. Palmer (ed.) *Mormons and Muslims: Spiritual foundations and modern manifestations*, Provo, UT: Brigham Young University Press, 85–104.

Kawar, I. (1958) 'The Last Days of Salih', *Arabica* 5: 145–58.

Stetkevych, J. (1996) *Muhammad and the Golden Bough: Reconstructing Arabian myth*, Bloomington, IN: Indiana University Press.

See also: **punishment**

BRANNON WHEELER

SALAHA

Salaha is a verb meaning to be righteous. Islam encourages piety: 'Eden Paradise which they shall enter and also those who acted righteously from among their fathers' (13.23). *Salih* means goodly, right, virtuous or pious: 'To Him ascend the goodly words, and the righteous deeds exalt it' (35.10). *Aslaha* is to amend, reconcile; this term appears often following *taba* (repented), and the result is forgiveness from Allah: 'So that if any of you does evil in ignorance, and thereafter repents and does righteous deeds' (6.54). The term in its variations appears in the Qur'an 179 times. The numerous instances of this term indicate its importance: that revelation was sent down to set things right and correct life on earth, to improve humanity's relation with the Creator.

RAFIK BERJAK

SALAT

There are many references in the Qur'an to *salat* or prayer and to the importance of prayer, but not a great deal on the specifics of how to carry out these religious obligations. A familiar way of working out what to do for prayer consists of looking at the Qur'an, the *hadith* and *sunna*, the practice of the Prophet's Companions, the opinions of legal scholars who use *qiyas* (analysis) and judgement (*ijtihad*) in their studies, their consensus (*ijma*'), the comments and opinions of early '*ulama* (scholars) and the comments and opinions of later '*ulama* together with the *fatwa*s of living '*ulama*.

In Shi'ite versions of this process, in addition to these authorities there are the infallible *imams* (all relatives and descendants of the Prophet Muhammad, starting with 'Ali) to which is added the living substitute *imam*. This seems to imply that the Qur'an is not a particularly easy book to understand; however, this is very different from how it presents itself. Islam, an Arabic word meaning submission, represents the state of mind of people who submit to God alone. All of God's Messengers – Noah, Abraham, Moses, Solomon, Jesus and all previous monotheists – were Submitters (2.131; 5.111; 7.126; 10.72, 84; 22.78; 27.31, 42, 91; 28.53; 72.14). Thus, the only religion approved by God is submission to God's will (3.19). It is God who uses this attribute to describe those who submit to his law (22.78).

Prayer and the religion of Abraham

Islam is referred to as the 'religion of Abraham': 'And Muhammad was a follower of Abraham' (16.123). It appears in many verses to provide a contrast to the behaviour and beliefs of Meccan idol worshippers who claimed that they were following Abraham themselves

(2.130, 135; 3.95; 4.125; 6.161; 12.37–38; 16.123; 21.73; 22.78).

It is worth pointing out that Abraham performed prayers (21.73), and so there should be no mystery about what is involved in prayer. The Qur'an also talks with approval of the Jews obeying rituals such as the Sabbath. God claimed the Qur'an is complete (6.11–116), and that might be taken to mean the main principles of belief and practice were established before the Qur'anic revelation (8.35; 9.54; 16.123; 21.73; 22.27; 28.27). Messengers after Abraham practiced *salat* (prayers), charity and fasting (2.43; 3.43; 11.87; 19.31, 59; 20.14; 28.27; 31.17).

The Meccan *mushrikun* (idolaters) also thought they were following Abraham in their religious practices. Although they are often regarded as worshipping 'statues' or 'icons', it is possible that they were instead praying for *shafat* (intercession) from some deity, such as al-Lat, al-'Uzza or al-Manat (53.19–23). They may claim to be monotheists (6.23), but they were really *mushrikun* since they associated partners with God (39.3). This is an important distinction, because the more sophisticated appeal to intercession (6.145–150; 39.3) represents a form of *shirk* that is much more subtle, and indeed dangerous, for Muslims than the mere worship of idols. Even respecting the *masjid* built by Abraham (9.19) can be *shirk* if it involves not praying to God but rather asking for intermediaries to intercede on one's behalf. Although they carried out prayers, fasting and pilgrimage (2.183, 199; 8.35; 9.54; 107.4–6), this could often be in an inappropriate manner and with the wrong intentions. It was precisely this point that led radicals such as Ibn al-Wahhab to attack a whole range of practices carried out by Muslims that seemed to him to be in opposition to the purity of the Islamic view of God's unity.

Even *zakat* (alms-giving) could be an action that does not fulfil the obligation of prayer (53.34) if it is not carried out for the right reasons. These religious terms were well known at the time of the revelation to the Prophet, and God provided additional details about what he wanted to happen (16.103; 26.195). Further, when God wanted to add a new meaning to a known word, he informed us, often through a later revelation; thus, 16.123 suggests that the religious practices in Islam were in place when Muhammad was born and so he was instructed to 'follow the religion of Abraham', implying such practices must have been well known.

Details of prayer

The various books of *ahadith* give plenty of detail on the topic of prayer. But how does a believer decide between conflicting suggestions? Does he just pick the word of his favourite *imam*? How does he know that that *imam* is acting in accordance with the practice of the Prophet? There are many different stories in the different traditions, and these often point in conflicting directions. In one of the longest *hadith* in the *Bukhari* collection, Muhammad took the advice of Moses and negotiated with God to reduce the number of prayers from fifty times a day (one prayer for every 28 minutes) to five times a day. This *hadith* portrays Muhammad as a compassionate intermediary, saving his followers from tough demands.

Observing *salat* is frequently mentioned alongside charity, emphasizing the social context and responsibility of those who observe the prayer (2.43, 83, 110; 4.77; 22.78; 107.1–7). It is observed to commemorate and remember God alone (6.162; 20.14) and protects Submitters (Muslims) from sin and doing harm to others (29.45). It should be observed continuously until death (19.31; 70.23, 34).

Ablution

To observe prayer one must make ablution (4.43; 5.6). Ablution is nullified only by sexual intercourse, the passing of urine or defecation. Ablution remains valid even if one has passed gas, or shaken hands with someone of the opposite sex or a menstruating woman. (A menstruating woman may observe contact prayers, whatever the local customs may suggest (5.6; 2.222; 6.114–115)). There is no particular dress code for prayer. The covering of our bodies is a social and cultural necessity aimed at protecting ourselves from harassment, misunderstanding and undesired consequences (7.26; 24.31; 33.59).

Prayer times

The Qur'an mentions three periods of time in conjunction with salat. In effect, the Qur'an breaks up salat into Dawn Prayer, Night Prayer and Middle (Noon) Prayer. The prayers are mentioned together (24.58) and the Middle Prayer by itself (2.238). For prayer one must face the masjid built by Abraham, the Ka'ba (2.125, 143–150; 22.26). During an emergency prayer may be reduced to one of the daily prayers, but usually all should be performed, thus reducing our ordinary contact with the external world (4.101–103). Unlike fasting, prayers cannot be performed after they are missed; they must be observed on time (4.103).

Believers, both men and women, are invited to a particular location to pray together once a week on every Juma (congregational) day, and Friday – a day named after its purpose – has been designated as the day of congregational prayer by the Qur'an (62.9). Afterwards they return to their work and normal daily schedule (62.9–11). Those who go to masjids should dress well as masjids are for public worship and meetings (7.31). The mosques themselves should be dedicated to God alone; no other name should be inscribed on the walls and no one other than God should be addressed there (72.18–20).

One should start the salat in the standing position (2.238; 3.39; 4.102) and should not change place except during unusual circumstances, for example, while driving (2.239). Submission to God should be declared physically and symbolically by first bowing down and prostrating (4.102; 22.26; 38.24; 48.29). The congregation must comprehend the meaning of their prayers, as these are the moments in which we communicate directly with God (4.43). They must be reverent (23.2).

Along with understanding the salat, we can recall one of God's attributes, and this will be linked with a particular need we may have at the time of our prayer (17.111). Prayer is to commemorate God, and only God (6.162; 20.14; 29.45). Prayer is to praise, exalt and remember his greatness, his mercy and, ultimately, our dependence upon each of his attributes (1.1–7; 20.14; 17.111; 2.45). We should not even mention other names besides that of God, since this interferes with our devotion and acknowledgement of our dependence on him (72.18; 29.45).

Prayer style

Prayers should be recited in a moderate tone, and we should neither try to hide what we are saying nor try to pray loudly in public (17.110). If we pray with a congregation, we should listen to the recitation of the men or women who lead the prayer (7.204; 17.11). Even after prayer we should endeavour to continue to think about God (4.103).

Funeral prayers are observed to remember those who died as monotheists and to provide support for their relatives, but they are not obligatory (see below). This is a particularly controversial issue for those seeking to rid Islam of local customs or popular beliefs that may get in the way of monotheism. There are many sectarian innovations that differ from sect to sect. Some of the innovations are: combining the times of prayers; shortening prayers; adding extra prayers; addressing the Prophet Muhammad as if he is alive and present; adding Muhammad's name to the *shahada*; reciting extra chapters after *al-Fatiha*; washing the mouth and nose as parts of making ablution; brushing the teeth with a *misvak* (a dry branch of a tree beaten into fibres at one end as a toothbrush) just before starting the prayers; and so on.

As we have seen, only three prayers are mentioned by name in the Qur'an. In other words, the word *salat* is qualified with descriptive words in three instances. These are:

Salat al-fajr Dawn Prayer

(24.58; 11.114).

Salat al-'isha Evening Prayer

(24.58; 17.78; 11.114)

Salat al-wusta Middle Prayer

(2.238; 17.78)

All of the verses that define the times of the prayers are attributable to one of these three prayers: 'This is be to be done in three instances: before the dawn prayer, at noon when you change your clothes to rest, and after the evening prayer' (24.58). The times of the Dawn and Evening Prayers are defined: 'You shall observe the contact prayers at both ends of the daylight, that is, during the adjacent hours of the night' (11.114). Traditional translators and commentators consider the last clause – *zulfan min al-layl* – of this verse as a separate night

prayer. However, it could be interpreted not as an addition but as an explanation of the previous phrase, because it explains the temporal direction of the ends of the day. The limits of *nahar* (daylight) is marked by two distinct points: sunrise and sunset. In other words, two prayers should be observed not only after sunrise and before sunset, but before sunrise and after sunset.

Furthermore, the traditional understanding runs into the problem of contradicting the practice of the very tradition it intends to promote. Traditionally, both morning and evening prayers are observed in a time period that is considered in the Qur'an to be *layl* (night), with *layl* starting from sunset and ending at sunrise. However, if the expression *tarafayin nahar* (both ends of the day) refers to Dawn and Evening Prayer, and these are part of *layl* (night), then the last clause cannot be describing another time of prayer. We are told: 'You shall observe the contact prayer when the sun goes down until the darkness of the night. You shall also observe the Qur'an at dawn. Reading the Qur'an at dawn is witnessed' (17.78–9). The going down of the sun can be understood either as its decline from its height at the start of the noon prayer or its decline behind the horizon marking the start of the evening prayer. However we interpret the passage, the idea of praying three times a day is not in any way controversial.

Does the Middle Prayer take place at noon?

'You shall consistently observe the contact prayers, especially the middle prayer, and devote yourselves totally to God' (2.238). 38.32 implies that the time of the Middle Prayer ends with sunset. We can easily understand the Middle Prayer as a prayer occurring between the two other prayers mentioned by name (Dawn and Evening). The Old Testament has at least three verses referring to prayers (*salat*) and they confirm this understanding. Although Muslims may not trust the biblical translations verbatim, they need not consider them as errors since the consistency of such passages is striking: 'As for me, I will call upon God; and the Lord shall save me. Evening, and morning, and at noon, will I pray, and cry aloud: and he shall hear my voice' (Psalms 55: 16–17) (see also 1 Samuel 20: 41). Also: 'Now when Daniel knew that the writing was signed, he went into his house; and his windows being open in his chamber toward Jerusalem, he kneeled upon his knees three times a day, and prayed, and gave thanks before his God, as he did aforetime' (Daniel 6: 10).

Nursi offers a charming comparison of the times of prayer with the stages of our lives. The time of *Zuhr*, just past midday: This resembles and points to midsummer, and the prime of youth, and the period of man's creation in the lifetime of the world, and calls to mind the manifestations of mercy and the abundant bounties they contain (*Ninth Word, Fifth Point*) *Fajr* is childhood, *Zuhr* is youth, *'Asr* is like autumn and old age, *Maghrib* is linked with death and *'Isha* nightfall and the final judgement. Nursi is outlining the symbolic meanings of the different prayer times. *Zuhr* comes at the time of the day when quite a bit of the day is over, but there is still most of it to come, and so is accurately compared with youth. The pattern for the day is becoming established, yet some of its freshness may still remain, and the precise nature of what is to follow remains undetermined. Nursi's work relates particularly well to young people because he ideally addresses an audience with some experience, but with much experience still to come, an audience

which still has the capacity to change, yet which has had enough experience already to understand the necessity for change.

Prayers for the Dead

In the Qur'an, God prohibits all believers from offering prayers for disbelievers or idol worshippers regardless of whether they are dead or alive: 'Neither the prophet, nor those who believe shall ask forgiveness for the idol worshippers, even if they were their nearest of kin, once they realize that they are destined for Hell' (9.113). For those who die as disbelievers or idol worshippers, nothing and no prayer can change their fate: 'With regard to those who have deserved the retribution, can you save those who are already in Hell?' (39.19).

Is it legal to offer prayers for believers?

We should distinguish between prayers for believers who are still alive and prayers for believers who have died. When we pray for a living parent, a relative or friend we usually implore God to cure them of an illness or assist them in adversity, etc. This kind of prayer asks for God's mercy on them while they still live. This prayer is encouraged in the Qur'an and is heard by God: 'And lower for them the wings of humility, and kindness, and say: "My Lord, have mercy on them, for they have raised me from infancy"' (17.24). Some have interpreted this verse so as to make it permissible to offer prayers for our loved ones whether they are dead or still alive. However, if we examine this verse and the one just before it we find good reason for thinking that God is inviting us to pray for our parents while they are still alive.

The previous *aya* reads: 'you shall never use a word of contempt to them [the slightest gesture of annoyance], nor shall you shout at them; you shall treat them amicably' (17.23). The words 'you shall treat them amicably' can only mean while they are still alive; it is not possible to treat a dead person amicably. After they are dead, they will receive a judgement in accordance with their work on earth and in accordance with God's mercy; nothing we can do will change that. We also read that the angels offer prayers for those (living?) on earth: 'The heavens above them almost shatter, out of reverence for Him, and the angels praise and glorify their Lord, and they ask forgiveness for those on earth. God is totally the forgiver, most merciful' (42.5) It must be emphasised here that prayers for living believers is encouraged by God for a number of reasons. Prayers for living believers is not related to the judgement they will receive from God on Judgement Day. This judgement is exclusively reserved for the Almighty, and we are told in the Qur'an that it is based primarily on each one's deeds and work on earth.

Consequently, and since we are not imploring God to alter or change the judgement they receive on the Day of Judgement, thus this kind of prayer cannot be classed as a form of intercession. Prayers for living believers (which is not intercession), and imploring God in general, are a genuine expression of our worship of God. To implore God is to trust and accept his absolute authority to answer our prayers. The link between imploring God and worshipping him is made evident in the following Qur'anic words: 'Your Lord says, "Implore me and I will respond to you. Surely those who are too arrogant to worship me will enter Hell forcibly"' (40.60)

The words 'Implore me' and 'Worship me' in this verse confirm that calling on God is an essential expression of worship: 'Should My servants ask you about Me, I am always near. I answer their prayers when they implore Me. Thus they should respond to Me and believe in me, so that they may be guided' (2.186).

Is there any point in offering prayers for believers after their death?

Prayer for the dead is a form of intercession. When we pray for a living relative or friend we usually implore God to cure them of an illness or assist them in adversity. This kind of prayer calls for God's mercy on them while they still live. We have seen how this prayer is encouraged in the Qur'an and is heard by God. Prayer for a loved one, who we believe to have died as a believer, is categorically different, for here we are not imploring God to cure them of their illness or assist them in adversity, but we are actually imploring God to alter or amend his judgement and to forgive their sins on the Day of Judgement. Any plea imploring God to amend, alter or improve the judgement he decrees on a person on the Day of Judgement is defined as an attempt to intercede for them. What this means in reality is that we are interceding with God to issue them a more favourable judgement! Ultimately, this raises the question of whether we can call on God to exercise more mercy when he is already Allah the Most Merciful and when he has decreed that mercy is his attribute? 'Say, "To whom belongs everything in the heavens and the earth?" Say, "To God. He has decreed that mercy is his attribute"' (6.12).

The concept of intercession seems to be rejected in the Qur'an: 'O you who believe, you shall give to charity from the provisions we have given to you, before a day comes where there is no trade, no nepotism, and no intercession. The disbelievers are the unjust' (2.254). On Judgement Day any intercession is useless unless it coincides with God's will: 'Intercession with Him will be in vain, unless it coincides with His will' (34.23); 'It is not up to you; He may redeem them, or He may punish them for their transgressions' (3.128). Moreover, many verses in the Qur'an make it very clear that on Judgement Day, and in accordance with God's absolute justice, no person shall be credited for anything other than their own acts, and no soul should carry the burden of another: 'No soul benefits except from its own works, and none bears the burden of another' (6.164). 'Every human being is credited only with what he or she did' (53.39) What this means is that on Judgement Day no soul will benefit except from what it has achieved personally; all our prayers to someone will not benefit them in their judgement. It is utterly useless to make *hajj* on behalf of our dead parent because they will receive credit only for things they have done themselves. The same applies to fasting on behalf of someone dead or giving *zakat* on their behalf. All this is useless. *Hajj*, fasting, *zakat*, all have to come from the individual as acts of worship and God does not allow us to worship him on behalf of others: 'What a day; the Day of Judgment! That is the day when no soul can help another soul, and all decisions, on that day, will belong to God' (82.18–19). The moment a human being dies, his or her record is sealed and nothing can change it one way or another.

When we analyse this issue we have to understand that many Islamic scholars think that to pray for a dead person, even if they were good sincere believers, is indirectly in rejection of Qur'anic truth. Let us look at the following verses: 'Proclaim: "O My servants who

exceeded the limits, never despair of God's mercy. For God forgives all sins, he is the perfect forgiver, most merciful"' (39.53); 'God does not forgive idolatry, but He forgives lesser offences for whomever He wills' (4.48). By virtue of these two verses and other Qur'anic verses, we are given a glimpse of God's infinite mercy. God would actually forgive all the sins of believers as long as they avoid idol worship.

If we pray for God to forgive the sins of dead believers, are we not guilty of questioning the promise of God made in 39.53? 14.41 might indicate that we are invited in the Qur'an to pray for our parents and implore God to have mercy on them on Judgement Day. The verse is as follows: 'Our Lord! Forgive me and my parents and believers on the day when the account is cast' (14.41). Immediately, we note a very important difference between 17.24 and 14.41. In 17.24 the prayer for the parents in their lifetime is provided by God. However, in 14.4 1 the prayer we read is not given by God; it is a prayer spoken by Abraham. Perhaps if this prayer was spoken by Abraham, then it is something that should be generally followed. But this is a personal prayer spoken by Abraham and thus it might not be appropriate as a law which everyone should follow. In fact we are told later that Abraham was not to pray for his father, who was an idol worshipper. This indicates that the prayer offered by Abraham (for his parents) could not have been authorized by God, and 9.114 confirms that it was invalid. Later, in 11.74–76 we are told how Abraham also attempted to offer a prayer for the people of Lot, and that this too was rejected by God. Similarly, the prayers of Noah for his son (11.46) and of Muhammad for his uncle (111.1–3) were also rejected by God.

If we examine 14.41 one more time, we would be able to see how it is out of line with: '34.23: 'Intercession with Him will be in vain, unless it coincides with His will' (34.23). This suggests that come the Day of Judgement, nothing will have any effect except the will of God. God's judgement is based purely on our deeds and our belief and not on how devoutly others have prayed for us.

Funerals

Before we analyse this verse, a word has to be mentioned about one of the rituals practiced in Islamic countries today when a Muslim dies. Shortly before the burial proceedings, the dead person is taken in the coffin inside a *masjid* and a *salat* is observed in prayer for that person. Some have interpreted the words in 9.84 to be related to this ritual, which is known as *salat al-janaza* (Funeral Prayer). But we should consider the legality of such a ritual. To start with, we are told in 72.18 that the *masjid* is for one purpose alone, and that is to worship God. The *masjid* is not for taking coffins of dead people inside and offering *salat* for them. Moreover, we are told in 6.162 that the *salat* (as all other rituals) should be observed for the name of God and nothing else. To set up a *salat* in response to the death of a human being is in violation of this. Proponents of this non-Qur'anic *salat* will argue that it is not a *salat* in the traditional sense since it has no bowing nor prostration and is much shorter. However, this excuse is not acceptable because it is not the form that validates or invalidates a ritual, it is the point of the ritual. Since this *salat* is done purely in dedication to the dead person then it is unlawful whatever form it may take.

9.84 quite clearly states 'Do not support any of them when they die, nor shall you stand at their grave. They have disbelieved in God and His messenger, and died in a state of wickedness.' The key words in this verse are used in the Qur'an in a number of verses. They do not mean 'do not pray for them' (as some have interpreted). Nor do they refer to (as others have interpreted) the widely practiced 'funeral *salat*'. By cross-referring with a number of verses where these same words are used (33.43; 9.103; 33.56) we realize that these words simply mean 'do not support them', for 'He [God] is the One who "*yussalli alaykum* (supports you)", together with His angels, to lead you out of darkness into the light. He is most merciful towards the believers' (33.43).

Does God pray for believers?

'Take from their money [O messenger] a charity to purify them and sanctify them. And support them, for your support reassures them. God is all-hearing, omniscient' (9.103). Here again it can hardly be meant that the Prophet should pray for these people: 'God and His angels *yussallun ala al-nabi* (support the prophet). O you who believe, you shall *sallu alayhi* (support him), and recognise and accept him [as God's messenger]' (33.56) Once again it is clear that neither God nor the angels conduct a *salat* for the Prophet, nor are the believers required to do so. Consequently, it can be established that the prohibition in 9.84, discussed above, which is related to the words '*la tussalli ala ahadan minhum*', is a prohibition from supporting any dead disbeliever. This begs the question: how exactly could we support a dead person? Support can be expressed only by taking part in the funeral, taking part in the burial, contributing to the cost of the funeral or later memorials and so on. Thus the idea of supporting anyone who is dead is beside the point.

Can we trust in God's mercy?

Various verses outline details of God's mercy: 'None despairs of his Lord's Mercy, except the strayers' (15.56); Can we [by praying] prompt God to exercise more mercy on our beloved ones when God's mercy is infinite? We read: 'Say, "To whom belongs everything in the heavens and the earth?" Say, "To God". He has decreed that mercy is his attribute' (6.12). Since God forgives all sins for the believers (39.53), what exactly would we be praying for if we prayed for a dead believer? Do we not believe 39.53, which declares 'Proclaim: "O My servants who exceeded the limits, never despair of God's mercy. For God forgives all sins. He is the forgiver, most merciful"'. Can we ignore the truth of 53.19 and 6.164 and insist that our loved one's will benefit from our prayers? 'Every human being is credited only to what he or she personally has done' (53.39). After all: 'No soul benefits except from its own works, and none bears the burden of another' (6.164).

Interceding for the dead

Is it acceptable to intercede on behalf of our loved ones who died and are awaiting Judgement when the Qur'an states that there will be no intercession on this day?: 'O you who believe, you shall give to charity from the provisions we have given to you, before a day comes where there is no trade, no nepotism, and no intercession. The disbelievers are the unjust' (2.254). The answer is no, because a strong belief in the Qur'an and its teachings leads all believers to accept without any doubt that all believers will be eventually pardoned – not because someone prayed for them, but because of God's infinite mercy.

See also: **death; Ibrahim; noise; parents; shafaᶜa; sunna**

OLIVER LEAMAN

*SAMA*ᶜ

God is often referred to in the Qur'an as having the ability to hear, and in terms of hierarchy this is often placed above the ability to see, perhaps signalling the especial significance of what is heard and the whole process of hearing. This has led to an interesting discussion of the importance, and acceptability of music, an art form that is of course accessed through hearing. Within the Sufi tradition music is generally highly regarded. *Sama*ᶜ literally means 'audition', and in the Sufi tradition it refers to listening with the heart, as it were, in the sense of a kind of meditation. It constitutes a sort of focusing on the melody in order to get to what the melody conceals.

There is in the Islamic world a long tradition of valuing *sama*ᶜ*,* and a long tradition of opposition to music in any form. For the Sufis, music can only be effective if it is carried out in the right place, at the right time and in the right company, and this fits closely with the Tarab culture that envelops traditional Arabic music. The right time is when the hearts of the audience are open and ready to appreciate what they hear. This could be at any time; what is vitally important is that the music is not just to entertain but has some deeper spiritual benefit. The right place is similarly not necessarily a specific spot, but a place in which one can achieve the right frame of mind. Finally, the right company is very important – one needs to be with the right people, and sometimes this is interpreted as being with people who are on a similarly high spiritual plane as oneself, or higher, so that one can be drawn up to their level.

Some have argued that this sort of careful stage-setting is not at all essential, and that sama' is helpful to anyone, however unsophisticated or unprepared they may be (Lewissohn, 1997: 10–11). The state (*hal*) that results from the music is a spiritual state of aesthetic awareness that ends up achieving a metaphysical depth, and the notes represent the divine harmony. Similar points are made by the Sufis about dance and poetry, both of which are also often rejected by many in the Islamic community.

Nonetheless, these art forms may be effective in developing the spiritual awareness of the believer, and as such should be pursued and encouraged and made part of the believer's practice. Not just any dance or music or poetry fits into this category, however, and it is important to acknowledge that what makes these sorts of activities permissible is nothing about the activities themselves, but what they indicate about the nature of the inner or hidden world, or what they do for us in helping us connect with that inner world. Simply enjoying music is in itself of no ultimate value; it only becomes a worthwhile practice if it has a deeper meaning.

Sama' is often referred to in the Qur'an in relation to God, and his ability to hear everything is an aspect of his omniscience. Often hearing is ranked before sight, and is held to be a superior faculty. This is perfectly understandable given the importance of listening to the Qur'an and the idea that simply hearing the Holy Book is enough to win new adherents.

References and further reading

Kermani, N. (1999) *Gott ist schön: Das ästhetische Erleben des Koran*, Munich: C.H. Beck.

Leaman, O. (2004) *Islamic Aesthetics: An introduction*, Edinburgh: Edinburgh University Press.

Lewissohn, L. (1997) 'The Sacred Music of Islam: Sama' in the Persian Sufi tradition', *British Journal of Ethnomusicology* 6: 1–32.

See also: **art and the Qur'an; music; reading**

OLIVER LEAMAN

SANAM | ASNAM

The pre-Islamic *sanam* (pl. *asnam*) was an idol – usually made of stone, sometimes of wood and other materials – that resembled a living form, constructed as an object of veneration. The *Ka'ba* was said to house some 360 such idols and images (*awthan*). The few references to *asnam* in the Qur'an refer mostly to Abraham's community and their devotion to idols and images (6.74; 26.72) and to Abraham's destruction of his community's pantheon (21.57). When fleeing from Egypt the Children of Israel are also said to have come across a people 'devoted entirely to some idols they had' (7.138).

COLIN TURNER

SANDHILLS
see: ahqaf

SATAN
see: **devil**

SATISFACTION
see: rida

SAUL
see: **Talut**

SAYYID QUTB

Sayyid Qutb (1906–66) is the author of *Fi zilal al-Qur'an* (In the Shade of the Qur'an), perhaps the most influential Qur'an commentary written in the fourteenth/twentieth century. Particularly in its later edition it presents a very radical form of Islamism, but its influence is not limited to radical Islamist circles. Among other things, its distinctive approach to the literary aspect of the Qur'an is of potential interest to all of its readers, whether Muslim on non-Muslim.

Qutb's life and career

Qutb was born in 1906 in a village in Asyut Province, Upper Egypt. He received his elementary education at the newly founded state school but also memorized the Qur'an and even organized Qur'an recitation competitions between his colleagues and the students of the *kuttab* (traditional Qur'an school). Like many others he was caught up in the nationalist demonstrations of 1919. Soon thereafter was sent to Cairo for his secondary education and then attended Dar al-'Ulum (a teacher training institution reflecting both traditional and modern approaches), graduating in 1933. He joined the Ministry of Education and worked there, first as a teacher and then as an official, until 1952. During this period he became part of the secular literary elite, publishing poetry and literary criticism, as well as social and political commentary, two novelettes and an account of his childhood village. After the end of World War II censorship he articulated a strong and even angry concern for social justice and anti-imperialism. Through 1947 his ideological position can be described as secular nationalist, but from 1948 he began to write Islamist articles and also produced an important

Islamist book, *Social Justice in Islam* (*al-'adala al-ijtima'iyya fi al-Islam*), first published in 1949. From 1948 to 1950 he was on an educational mission in the USA, an experience which convinced him that the USA was morally bankrupt, in spite of its technological achievements, and undoubtedly strengthened his Islamist views.

Upon his return he joined the Muslim Brothers (the leading Islamist organization of the time), either in 1951 or 1953, and quickly became its chief ideologue. He initially supported the 1952 Free Officers revolution and briefly was close to its leadership, however, the Brothers soon fell out with the regime. Qutb and others were imprisoned from January to March 1954 and then in November, after an assassination attempt against Abdel Nasser, he and others were given long prison sentences and four of the Brothers were executed. Although suffering torture and ill health, he was allowed to continue writing and publishing, subject to a government-appointed censor. The prison experience in general, and in particular an episode in 1957 in which more than twenty Brothers were killed, appears to have radicalized his thinking.

Qutb was released in May 1964 but rearrested in August 1965 and charged with plotting to overthrow the government. He was executed on 29 August 1966. One of the main evidences against him was his extremely radical book, *Milestones* (*Ma'alim fi al-tariq*), published during his brief period of freedom and generally understood to call for an Islamic revolution. His execution led to his being viewed as a martyr, a status that lends considerable moral authority to his writings.

The writing of *Fi zilal*

During his secular period Qutb made significant contributions to the literary study of the Qur'an in several articles and in two books – *Al-Taswir al-fanni fi al-Qur'an* (Artistic Portrayal in the Qur'an) (1945) and *Mashahid al-qiyama fi al-Qur'an* (Scenes of the Resurrection in the Qur'an) (1947 or 1948). Particularly notable is his idea of artistic *taswir* (lit.: picture-making), the creation of emotionally forceful pictures, scenes and images in the mind of the reader as the key to the Qur'an's power. He also deals with matters such as the musical rhythms and 'atmosphere' of the text. In these writings the Qur'an is treated from a literary rather than a religious point of view, but there is no indication that the author rejects or questions the Qur'anic doctrines. Much of this material reappears in his Qur'anic commentary, which contains frequent footnote references to these works.

The writing of the commentary itself began with a series of seven articles entitled '*Fi zilal al-Qur'an*' that appeared in the Cairo periodical *Al-Muslimun* in 1952. Qutb then decided to produce his commentary as a book, issuing fascicles at regular intervals, each covering one of the thirty parts of the Qur'an (following the standard division of the Holy Book for means of recitation). The first sixteen parts were published between October 1952 and his first imprisonment in January 1954, while two more parts were produced during that imprisonment. Circumstances then prevented him from continuing to work on it until after he was sentenced in July 1955. He completed the remaining parts in 1959, but in the last three parts he adopted a new, more radical and activist approach. He then began to revise and expand the earlier parts in line with this new approach, completing the 'new' first ten parts before his release from prison in 1964, followed by three more parts during his period of freedom. He also incorporated long excerpts from *Fi zilal* into *Milestones* and the last edition of *Social Justice* (which appeared in 1964).

Fi zilal was published – without authorization – by several publishers before Dar al-shuruq was given sole publication rights. Its version (1973 and later reprints) is the standard version; it includes the revised thirteen parts and also a revision of the first *sura* (*al-Hijr*) of part fourteen, not included in other editions. *Fi zilal* has been translated wholly or in part into a number of languages, including English, French, Turkish, Farsi, Urdu and Indonesian.

Characteristics of *Fi zilal*

Undoubtedly the most striking characteristic of the commentary is its author's close personal involvement with the text of the Qur'an and his effort to apply it to contemporary life. The commentary appears to have begun with Qutb's desire to record and share the scattered thoughts that came to him during the periods of his life lived 'in the shadow of the Qur'an', but it came to be a major presentation of his views on basic doctrinal and social issues, as well the literary issues mentioned above. The work follows the order of the Qur'an. Each *sura* has an introduction (except for the first three in the earlier edition) and the verses are grouped together for comment into units, often called 'lessons', that are seen to be unified by theme and literary characteristics. Frequently there is a verse-by-verse commentary within these units. While Westerners, in particular, tend to see the Qur'an as rather disjointed, Qutb strongly insists on the literary and topical unity and coherence of the Qur'an as a whole and of the individual *suras*, an insistence that increases in the later parts of the commentary.

As far as is possible Qutb relies on the Qur'an itself for interpretation, but he also considers the *sunna* of the Prophet Muhammad authoritative and refers with some frequency to the *sira* of Ibn Ishaq (transmitted by Ibn Hisham) and the *hadith* collections, especially those of Ahmad ibn Hanbal and Malik ibn Anas. He largely avoids the detailed grammatical, linguistic, theological and *fiqh* discussions of the classical commentaries, since he considers that they veil the Qur'an from its readers. He does not, however, entirely ignore these commentaries or these issues, but makes frequent reference to Ibn Kathir, al-Tabari and Zamakhshari, and less frequent reference to several others. Among modern commentaries he refers most often to the *Manar* commentary, written by Rashid Rida under the influence of Muhammad 'Abdu, sometimes agreeing with it and sometimes criticizing its rationalist and modernist tendencies. He also refers to other modern writers such as Abul Hasan Nadwi, Abu'l-A'la' Maududi (although apparently he was not acquainted with his commentary, *Tafhim al-Qur'an*), Muhammad Asad and his own brother, Muhammad Qutb.

He strongly objects to explaining away Qur'anic miracles in rationalist terms and argues that miracles and aspects of the unseen world (*ghaybiyyat*) mentioned but not explained in the Qur'an should be accepted but not analysed, because we do not need to know them to carry out the will of God. He criticizes efforts made to trace the origins of modern science in the Qur'an (the so-called *tafsir 'ilmi*, or scientific interpretation, as espoused in *Jawahir al-Qur'an* by al-Tantawi) as this is to subject the Qur'an to changing human

ideas. No firmly established scientific fact contradicts the Qur'an in his view, but for the most part the Qur'an does not go into scientific details. For similar reasons Qutb rejects the reinterpretion of Qur'anic social teachings in terms of modern (i.e. Western) thought, as for example the modernist claim that *jihad* is always defensive. Sometimes he does in fact reinterpret passages, at least from the critic's point of view, but usually without openly admitting this. One such example is his claim that slavery is permitted only because of conditions obtaining at that time that no longer obtain. In general, the Qur'an should be interpreted in terms of the plain meanings of its words, with due attention to the historical circumstances and the prophetic *sunna*. This interpretation is to be applied in the contemporary situation, which may require some flexibility but no violation of the basic intent (see below). In *Fi zilal* Qutb undertakes to point the way to such application.

The teachings of *Fi zilal*

The doctrine presented in *Fi zilal* is uncompromisingly theocentric and based explicitly on the proposition that there is no god but God. This means the liberation of humanity from servitude to anything but God. All activities of life, including social and political life, are to be carried out in accordance with God's commands as found in the Qur'an because all activity is worship (*'ibada*), either of God or of *taghut* (idol/despot). These ideas become increasingly uncompromising and action-oriented in the revised parts of the commentary. In commenting on the Qur'anic passages about creation Qutb writes almost poetically of the harmony and unity of the universe. Humans are part of this if they follow God's commands (*shari'a*) and thus fulfil their role as God's *khalifa* (caliph, deputy) in the world, a high honour and a role stressed by Qutb. Scientific discovery and technological progress are part of this role, as is the ordering of society by the *shari'a*. Societies that are not so ordered violate the harmony of the universe and in the later parts are increasingly described as *jahili* (ignorance). In the final parts he insists that all contemporary societies, including those that claim to be Muslim, are in a state of *jahiliyya*. The response of true Muslims, sooner or later, must be *jihad*, as it was for Muhammad, and *jihad* is here understood as a kind of revolutionary struggle. The contrast between this and the modernist idea of *jihad* as defensive illustrates the difference in Qutb's view between illegitimate reinterpretation of the Qur'an and its legitimate application. These are the ideas that led to his arrest and martyrdom and the ideas that have drawn attention to Qutb's writings. Still, while *Fi zilal* provides inspiration for the radical and extremist wings of Islamism, not all who read it attend to its most radical teachings. Attractively written and broad in its coverage, it can provide something for almost everyone.

Further reading

Boullata, Isa J. (2000) 'Sayyid Qutb's Literary Appreciation of the Qur'an', in *Literary Structures of Religious Meaning in the Qur'an*, Richmond, Surrey: Curzon Press, 354–71.

Carré, Olivier (2003) *Mysticism and Politics: A critical reading of 'Fi Zilal al-Qur'an by Sayyid Qutb (1906–1966)*, trans. Carol Artigues, Leiden and Boston: E.J. Brill.

Sayyid Qutb (1979) *In the Shade of the Qur'an*, Vol. 30 (*suras 78–114*), trans. M.A. Salahi and A.A. Shamis, London: MHW Publishers; (1999–2003) Vols 1–8 (*suras 1–9*), trans. M.A. Salahi and A.A. Shamis, Leicester: Islamic Foundation.

See also: **Nahda**

WILLIAM E. SHEPARD

SCIENCE AND THE QUR'AN

Science is based on queries. The religion of Islam, which has its primary root in the Qur'an, is based on faith. Before discussing the connection between science and the Qur'an, it would be appropriate to ask: 'Is enquiry forbidden in Qur'an?' This is indeed the million-dollar question, and once this question has been settled, it would be easier to shed light on the meeting point of the Qur'an and science. But the answer to the question exists in the Qur'an itself. Many tend to think that enquiries do not have a place in Islam but this is an erroneous view: the first support for making enquiries in the Qur'an in order to arrive at the truth appears as early as verse 2.260:

> And when Abraham said: 'My Lord! Show me how Thou givest life to the dead', He said: 'Dost thou not believe?' Abraham said: 'Yes, but (I ask) in order that my heart may be at ease.' (His Lord) said: 'Take four of the birds And cause them to incline unto thee, then place a part of them on each hill, then call them, they will come to thee in haste. And know that Allah is Mighty, Wise.'

It is interesting to know that Abraham had complete faith in his Creator and raised his query only to know the ways in which Allah performs the task that he does. In the above verse, Abraham was advised to take four of the birds and cause them to 'incline unto' him. This word 'incline' is very important: if a bird is inclined to someone, then that someone is likely to know all the information concerning the nature and habitat of the bird. According to the verse, such a bird, when torn to pieces, will respond to the call of the person to whom the bird is inclined and to whom none of the secrets of its life is unknown. Similarly, man, whom Allah created from inert matter, will respond after death to the call of Allah, who knows all the secrets of man's existence. But all of this is a matter of detail; the essential question is 'Did Allah discourage the query of Abraham or did He entertain it?' From the verse shown above it is evident that Allah entertained the query.

Thus, the stand of the Qur'an in respect of query is very clear. If someone wants to understand what is permitted and what is forbidden in the Qur'an, then he or she is encouraged to do so, namely to enquire. The answers obtained through such means may resolve many misunderstandings and embolden the faith of the questioner. In fact, mankind has been asked repeatedly in the Qur'an to ponder over the working of nature and find out the truths (i.e. the natural order of the universe). In verse 10.101 Allah asked the Prophet Muhammad to say to the people: 'Behold all that is in the heavens and on earth'. This beholding of things is the work of scientists. Obviously, scientific work has been encouraged in the Qur'an at the very highest level by Allah himself.

The investigation of truth (which is the basic task of scientists) forms one of the strongest points of the Qur'an. One of the names of the Qur'an is *al-Furqan*, the root word being *'faraq'*, to distinguish or tell one thing from another. The Qur'an distinguishes between injustice and justice, right and wrong, truth and falsehood. The insistence in the Qur'an upon truth is marked, and even the preaching of Islam through compulsion is strongly discouraged: 'Let there be no compulsion in religion: Truth stands out clear from error ...' (2.256).

The Qur'an emphasized the importance of truth before modern scientists engaged themselves with investigating it. It is truth, and truth alone, that creates a concordance and symphony between the Qur'an and science, although this is not necessarily something universally recognized. The reason for this may be that many of those who have studied science have not also studied the Qur'an, and vice versa. The modern education system existing in many countries tends to present science and the Qur'an as two disparate things, whereas anyone who has studied both science and the Qur'an is likely to come to the conclusion that the more one investigates nature, the more one understands the verses of the Qur'an that point to the Creation, and also that there is congruence, not conflict, between science and the Qur'an.

There are almost 750 verses in the Qur'an which have a bearing on science. Books on this topic – *The Bible, the Qur'an and Science* and *Scientific Indications in the Holy Qur'an* – state that there is not a single verse in the Qur'an which is assailable from a scientific point of view.

No Muslim student should ever feel uncomfortable with the investigation of truth in nature, especially when the text the student follows asserts in an unambiguous way that Allah has sent down the Holy Book (the Qur'an) in truth (see 2.213, 252; 3.3, 60, 108; 4.10, 170) and that what has been revealed through Muhammad is the truth (13.1). These verses pose a challenge to scientists – the seekers of truth. For example, there is a scientific indication in the Qur'an that all things (not only living ones) have been created in pairs (36.36). This indication should challenge a scientist to investigate the truth of it, with all the powers of reasoning and experimentation. It is interesting to mention in this connection that the investigation of truth requires knowledge. And it is emphasized clearly, in verses 22.54 and 34.6, that 'those who have been given knowledge may know that it is the truth from your Lord'.

In verse 45.6, Allah refers to his signs as truth. Again, it has been mentioned in the Qur'an itself that these signs can be comprehended by knowledgeable people. At this point let us summarize the Qur'anic assertions about truth: what has been revealed in the Qur'an has been revealed in truth; signs of Allah are truths; the creation of the heavens and the earth and all that is between them has occurred except with truth (44.39). These Qur'anic assertions should convince the truth-seeking scientists that there is no conflict between the Qur'an and science. The Qur'an points to truths of creation and science investigates them.

The Qur'an is not a book of science. It is a Book of Guidance to mankind for all its useful activities. Since science and technology is regarded as an integral part of human culture, it is only natural to expect that the Qur'an would highlight man's investigation into nature. In fact, the Qur'an does so most beautifully – its first word of revelation is 'read'. The work encourages learning and places the highest emphasis upon the acquisition of knowledge. It gives importance to knowledgeable people. It also points to facts of science but does so most wisely by indicating some Grand Principles of science. Mention may be made in this connection to *sura* 3.190–191:

> Behold! In the creation of the heavens and the earth and the alternation of night and day – there are indeed Signs for men of understanding. Those who celebrate the praises of Allah, standing, sitting, and lying down on their sides, and contemplate the creation of the heavens and the earth and say: 'Our Lord! You have

> not created this in vain! Glory be to You, and save us from the penalty of Fire.'

It is worthwhile mentioning in connection to this that there are 30 million life forms in the world and scientists have studied only about 5 million of these. The remaining life forms need to be preserved and studied in detail as the loss of any of these may have far-reaching consequences for the ecological balance of the world, and hence for our own existence. No wonder the modern ecologists who are advocating the preservation of biodiversity have adopted the cardinal principle that 'nothing has been created for nothing'. This principle, which gives rise to the entire discipline of ecology and acts as a Grand Principle of science, is an echo of a statement found in 3.191. Another Grand Principle is indicated in *sura* 25.2: 'it is He who created all things, and ordered them in due proportions'.

The existence of proportion or measure has been discussed by mathematicians who note that the florets of a sunflower which appear to be so beautiful are arranged in increasing distances from the centre in the ratios of 0, 1, 1, 2, 3, 5, 8, 13, 21, a method known as Fibonacci numbers. When mathematically modelling a sunflower, one now notices a certain measure in its formation. Thus, although the Qur'an is not a book of science, it points to many scientific facts through some wisely worded Grand Principles which can encompass many laws of nature. It is the responsibility of the truth-seeking scientists to study these laws.

What is it that scientists do? No scientist makes any law: he or she only discovers it. Laws governing the behaviour of inert and living matter already exist in the natural order and scientists through queries and experimentation discover these laws. What would happen to nature if scientists did not discover these laws? Would nature behave differently than at present? Certainly not. Nature would run its course according to the laws ordained for it. It is simply that one would not know these laws if they had not been revealed by scientists. For example, if Tycho Brahe, Johannes Kepler, Nicolaus Copernicus, Galileo Galilei, Isaac Newton and Albert Einstein had not been born, would planets revolve around the sun in a different manner than at present? No; the planets would continue to move around the sun according to an inverse square law of gravitation, and this law can be deduced from the combination of the law of motion of matter discovered by Newton and the planetary laws discovered by Kepler. The Qur'an itself states, in *sura Yasin* (36.40), '*Wa kullun fi falakin – yasbahunn*', that is, 'each [just] swims along in [its own] orbit [according to law]'. It is interesting to note that before the time of Copernicus no one had any concept of the 'orbit of heavenly bodies', even though this orbit is mentioned in the Qur'an more than 1400 years previously. More fascinating is the fact that the Qur'an states that the motion of the heavenly bodies is governed by laws, those very laws which have only since been discovered by scientists.

It is also noteworthy that Allah asks men and women to believe in him not by considering the tortures of hell or the pleasures of heaven but by looking at his creation from the scientific point of view. Thus, in 21.30 Allah asks: 'Do not the unbelievers see that the heavens and the earth were joined together [as one unit of creation] before we clove them asunder; we have made every living thing from water. Will they not then believe?' This would seem to point to the Big Bang theory of creation (which is currently the accepted theory of creation of the universe). The verse also refers to the creation of life. Thus, two of humankind's big questions – namely, 'How was the universe created?', and 'How did life begin?' – are included here, and unbelievers are asked to have faith in the Creator by understanding the creation of the universe and the creation of life from a scientific point of view. Thus, scientific truth is being regarded as the basis of faith rather than in opposition to it.

Insofar as the Qur'anic emphasis on scientific truth is considered, mention may be made of the word *ayat* (meaning, among other things, sign). The word appears many times in the Qur'an and in various contexts. Upon examination one finds that although traditionally every verse of the Qur'an is called an *aya*, the fact is that the things which have been mentioned as *ayat* (Signs of Allah) are matters of scientific significance. For example: 2.164 says:

> Behold! In the creation of the heavens and the earth; in the alternation of the Night and the Day; in the sailing of the ships through the ocean for the profit or mankind; in the rain which Allah sends down from the skies, and the life which He gives herewith to an earth that is dead; in the beasts of all kinds that He scatters through the earth; in the change of the winds, and the clouds which they trail like their slaves between the sky and the earth – [Here] indeed are Signs for a people that are wise.

The creation of the heavens and the earth which is mentioned in this verse falls under the domain of astrophysics and astronomy; the alternation of night and day is the subject matter of geography and meteorology; the sailing of the ship in oceans reminds one of Archimedes' Principle and is dealt with in the subject of fluid dynamics; the revival of the earth through rainfall is the subject of science dealing with the weather, botany and agriculture; the scattering of the beasts of all kinds is a matter of zoology and genetics; and the change of the winds and the clouds which trail between the sky and the earth are the subject matters of the science of meteorology. It is these scientific matters that have been mentioned as *ayat* (signs).

The word *ayat* has been mentioned at other places in the Qur'an and in other senses also but the things which have been mentioned as *ayat* are mostly of a scientific nature. The Creator is not seen but his creation is. And the aim of science is to study this creation in all its details. Thus, as a study of the signs of the Creator, it is in science that we find the means of understanding the truths of creation. There was a time when the early Muslims spent almost 800 years to arrive at scientific truths. Although we have talked of scientific truths here, there are other kinds of truth in the realm of human and social values, love and beauty, fellow feeling, etc. In the religion of Islam, these truths are also to be felt at heart and practised in everyday life.

One must add some words of caution here. First, the Qur'an, being a divine revelation, is based on absolute truth, as is indicated in the Qur'an itself. Anybody having faith in this absolute truth is welcome to use the Qur'an as a test for scientific truth, but not vice versa. Second, in connection with finding the meeting ground of the Qur'an and science through the seeking of truth, one must consider only those scientific truths which have been thoroughly investigated and have stood the tests of time. A question which may be posed in this connection is: 'What if we come across a verse which cannot be explained from the point of view of science?' The answer to this question lies in the fact that science, for purposes of the investigation of truth, is based on a certain methodology. This methodology is, however, not without its limitations. The possibility exists that there could be a part of reality which transcends our biological limitations and evades the scientific methodology employed. Thus, all truths may not be subject to science. While scientists cannot leave things open-ended and need a starting point and a set of methods if they are to carry out their investigations, they must also bear in mind that if at the present stage of our scientific knowledge a Qur'anic verse cannot be scientifically comprehended, there remains the possibility that advances in the field will shed further light on the verse. In this connection, mention may be made of the following verse:

> Glory be to Him Who created all the pairs of that which the earth grows and of themselves and of that which they know not. (36.36)

When this verse was revealed more than 1400 years ago man knew about the creation, in pairs, of flora and fauna. However the verse refers not only to this particular instance of creation but also to things of which people were unaware at that time. Much later, in the 1920s, P.A.M. Dirac discovered the theory of particles and anti-particles through his investigation of the equation of motion of a free electron. As a result of this, today we know that all fundamental particles of nature have their anti-particles, namely electrons and positrons, protons and anti-protons, neutrons and anti-neutrons, etc. More, with the advancement of high-energy particle physics, we also understand that creation of pairs can happen both in the world of the living and that of the inert. Consequently, one now appreciates the meaning of the above verse a little better than one did in the past. The point being made here is that the Qur'an contains absolute truths, and as one investigates the truths of the created world, one's comprehension of the Qur'anic verses becomes more and more complete.

We are in a new millennium, with many scientific challenges. If we are to face these challenges, then not only should we prepare ourselves for technological advancement but we should also learn to preserve the values of life. Truth and truth only should be the basis of all our actions and of all our thoughts. The Qur'an is proclaimed in Islam to be the source of truths. It is not only to be read but also to be understood. The understanding of the Qur'an can increase only with the advancement of scientific knowledge.

Further reading

Bucaille, M. (1979) *The Bible, the Qur'an and Science*, trans. Alastair D. Pannell, Indianapolis: American Trust Publications.
Maulana Abdullah Yusuf Ali (1967) *The Meaning of the Holy Qur'an, Text, Translation and Commentary*, Lahore: Ashraf.
Islamic Foundation Bangladesh (1995) *Scientific Indications in the Holy Qur'an*, Bangladesh: Islamic Foundation, 2nd edn.

See also: **natural world and the Qur'an; numbers and the Qur'an**

M. Shamsher Ali

SEAL
see: tabʿa

SECRET CONVERSATION
see: *najwa*

SELF-REFERENTIALITY

A text is self-referential when it speaks about itself and thus reflects on its own textuality. The Qur'an demonstrates this feature, which can also be called 'self-reflexivity' or 'meta-textuality', to a notably higher degree than Jewish or Christian scripture. It may well be the most self-referential text among the great Holy Books known to humankind. This self-referentiality of the Qur'anic text has been recognized as such only recently and has not yet been investigated systematically. Some of the most obvious instances of this self-referentiality are discussed below.

Self-predication and classification

The Qur'an abounds in classifying self-predication. The text impresses on the listener/reader that it combines a variety of textual genres. It calls itself a number of different names, very often assigning a specific function of the text to a given name: *tanzil* (revelation), *kitab* (book), *dhikr* (remembrance, commemoration), *qasas* (stories), *mathal* (similitude, parable), *naba'* (news), etc. The most important among these self-classifications may be *qur'an*. This latter term, literally 'recitation', is used in numerous and often contradictory ways, which leads to the impression that the Qur'an understands itself 'not so much as a completed book, but as an ongoing process of divine "writing" and "re-writing"' (Madigan, 2001). However, it never denotes the Qur'anic text in the sense of the closed canonical corpus which Muslims and non-Muslims today call the Qur'an. Often, the precise meanings of these terms are obscure, although the Arabic commentaries have tried to and continue to try hard to explain their specificity. A frequent, mysterious name which the Qur'an calls itself is *furqan*, which in two of the best English translations has been rendered as variously as 'criterion' (Yusuf Ali) and 'salvation'

(Arberry). This difference mirrors the perplexity found in the Muslim commentaries. As *furqan* may be the Arabic rendering of the name of a pre-Islamic form or part of scripture (Jewish or Christian), the use of this term could be explained as an attempt to identify terms of pre-Islamic canons as parts of Muslim scripture.

Negative statements of the text on the text

Negative self-predications in the Qur'anic text can be seen at least in part as emerging features of either theological controversy within the Muslim community before the canonization of the text or as features of transreligious polemics between the developing Muslim community and their non-Muslim contemporaries. When the Qur'an says that 'it' (meaning a part of Qur'anic revelation) 'is the speech of a noble Messenger, not the speech of a poet' (69.40–41), the function of this verse is evidently to correct or to refute contemporaries of the Prophet, who claimed exactly that. The Qur'an stresses time and again that it is not or does not contain 'falsehood' (*batil*; 41.42), 'doubt' (*rayb*; 2.2) or 'fairy-tales of the ancient ones' (*asatir al-awwalin*; 6.25). The most important negative statement may well be, 'Not by the Satans has it [i.e. the Qur'an] been brought down ...' (26.210), which also reflects a contemporary reproach which the text had to refute. Some of the features, which the Qur'anic text expressly and repeatedly disclaims, are the same as those that, according to the Qur'an, earlier prophets such as Nuh (Noah) or Musa (Moses) had to disavow on divine authority with regard to the revelations given to them.

The first traces of interpretation (*ta'wil*)

Verse 3.7 has been rightly claimed as the historical cornerstone of Muslim exegesis, as exegesis within the canonical text:

> It is He who sent down upon thee the Book, wherein are verses clear that are the Mother of the Book (*umm al-kitab*) and others ambiguous. As for those in whose heart is swerving, they follow the ambiguous part, desiring dissension, and desiring its interpretation, and none knows its interpretation save only God.

Distinguishing between Qur'anic verses that are 'clear' (*muhkam*) and those that are 'ambiguous' (*mutashabih*) urges believers to beware of those who follow the ambiguous part, i.e. those 'desiring dissension'. The final words of 3.7 – 'none knows its interpretation save only God' – also has an alternative reading, that of 'none knows its interpretation save only God and those firmly rooted in knowledge'. The variant readings of this verse points to a pre-canonical dissension of the community, touching the core of what Muslim exegesis could or should do.

Special linguistic indicators marking truth and authenticity

A frequent marker of direct divine speech in the Qur'an is the imperative 'Say' (*qul*), which occurs hundreds of times scattered throughout the text and marks the divine voice addressing the Prophet and commanding him to speak. It conveys – in parallel with the Hebrew formula 'The Lord God sayth' (Isaiah: 56.8) in the Bible – that the following text is, verbatim, God's word, and that the Prophet merely transmits it. Indicators of God's confirmation of his words are also the frequent Qur'anic oaths at the beginnings of certain *suras*, in which God attests the truth and authenticity of his revelation. God attests the truth of his word by swearing upon celestial bodies 'by the plunging star' (53.1); by holy places and their symbols –'by the fig-tree and the olive tree and the Mount Sinai' (95.1–2); and also by God's Holy Book itself – 'by the glorious Qur'an' (50.1); and so on. Many of these oaths also serve a literary function as matrices of an imagery developed in the following passages of the *sura*, but their primary function seems to be assertive and to mark oracular, i.e. superhuman, speech.

Asserting scriptural authority over Jewish and Christian scripture

The Qur'an readily acknowledges the existence of pre-Islamic revelation – in at least one case such a revelation is called 'Qur'an' (34.31). In cases of what seem to be conflicting revelations, the Qur'an asserts its competence to judge between the competing revelations and to correct them. In other words, the Qur'an authenticates itself by referring the readers/listeners to preceding scriptural traditions. At the same time it reserves the right to declare certain parts of non-Islamic scripture incorrect, or at least their interpretation as wrong. Thus, the Christian teaching of Christ's death at the cross is rejected in 4.157 as a vainglorious statement of the Jews. Implicitly, the Qur'an took the side of Christian groups who taught that Christ had not died on the cross.

In line with Muslim dogma, the speaker in the Qur'an is God, and this Qur'anic God is constantly occupied by watching, classifying, interpreting and justifying, but also by adjusting, modifying and even cancelling the words to be transmitted by the Prophet. Seen from outside, the canonical text and the

process of canonization seem to be intimately linked in a defence of the text's authority.

The basic assumption of this project is that the meta-textual self-referentiality of the Qur'anic text stems primarily from its rivalry with the practice of polytheist animism on the one hand and its competition with previous prophetic revelations (Judaism and Christianity) on the other. The different stages of the canonization of what became the Qur'anic text is linked to changing Qur'anic attitudes towards competing religious cults and ideas, and mirrors the changing attitudes, under the leadership of Muhammad, of the Muslim community towards Jews and Christians. To these, another group must be added: those who were in some way close to monotheism (the 'sectarian milieu' with its 'monotheist syndrome' as Wansbrough has put it), but who did not necessarily identify with Judaism or Christianity. The Christian and Jewish contemporaries of the Prophet were sometimes closer to, and sometimes more distant from, the Muslim community – their distance or proximity being vital parameters for the meta-textual passages of the Qur'anic text.

The project in which the author has been involved consists mainly in a close and systematic reading of the complete Qur'anic text according to the criteria, of which the most important are mentioned above. About a quarter of the text has been already screened. While the project takes into consideration a variety of approaches to the Qur'anic text that have been shown as promising (see the work of Angelika Neuwirth, Harald Motzki, John Wansbrough, Jane Dammen McAuliffe, Andrew Rippin, Fred Leemhuis, Uri Rubin, Navid Kermani and others), it is methodologically mainly indebted to Jan Assmann's studies on 'cultural memory', the meaning of canonicity and the link between canon and exegesis on the one hand and recitation and exegesis on the other hand. Of special interest will be the so-called pre- or non-'Uthmanic variant readings of the Qur'an.

A close reading of the Qur'an in this project is always conducted on two levels, on the level of Muslim mainstream dogma and exegesis (the inside view), and on the historical-critical or reception-oriented level of different hermeneutical approaches (the outside view). It will furthermore take into account a selection of early Muslim Arabic commentaries which may in some cases retain traditions shedding light on the emergence of the Qur'anic text. The problem of assessing the historical value of the *asbab al-nuzul* ('occasions of revelation') literature will also be discussed. As a last step, different views of modern Muslim commentaries on the phenomenon of self-referentiality will be analysed (see work by Muhammad Shahrur, Nasr Hamid Abu Zaid, Farid Esack). The final aim is a study which will be called 'The Qur'an as Metatext'.

Further reading

Madigan, D.A. (2001) *The Qur'an's Self-image: Writing and authority in Islam's scripture*, Princeton, NJ: Princeton University Press.

See also: ***asbab al-nuzul***; ***aya***; **canon; kitab; language and the Qur'an; oaths**

STEFAN WILD

SERVANT

A servant is a person hired to carry out the orders of an individual or corporate employer, in particular a person employed in a house, for domestic duties or as a personal attendant. Another definition of a servant is a devoted follower, a person willing to serve another.

Khadim (pl. *khadam* or *kuddam*) denotes the first kind of servant and can be used to refer to both males and females. In modern Arabic *kadima* refers to a female servant; however, its use was rare in classical Arabic. In the *hadith* of 'Abd al-Rahman he divorced his wife and gave her on that occasion a young black woman as a *khadim*. In another *hadith* 'Ali said to his wife Fatima (the daughter of the Prophet): 'ask your father for a *khadim* (servant) so she will protect you from the heat that you have been suffering'.

The Arabic verb *'abada* signifies to serve, worship, adore, venerate, obey, submit, devote. The noun *'abda* means a servant, a human being or a slave. The plural is *'ibad* or *'abid*.

Servant or slave are exchangeable terms in the Qur'an and signify a worshipper of God. Because of its religious connotation, *'abd* is used in the Qur'an rather than *khadim*, which is not mentioned in the Qur'an. 'Abdullah is a compound name from *'Abd* and *Allah*, meaning servant of God. The noun, *'abd*, implies that the person carrying it as a title accepts the authority of one God. The Qur'an refers to the Prophet Muhammad as 'Abdullah and *'abduna*, the servant of Allah or Our servant, or *aydihi*, God's servant: 'And when the servant of Allah (Muhammad) stood invoking Him they were crowded around him' (72.19). And in the *surat al-Isra'* (The Journey by Night), the first verse says, 'Glorified be He who took His servant (Muhammad) for a journey by night from Al-Masjid Al-Haram, the sanctified Mosque [in Mecca] to the Masjid Al-Aqsa the remote mosque [in Jerusalem]' (17.1).

The Qur'an was revealed by God to his servant in order for it to be disseminated to the whole world: 'Blessed be He who sent down the criterion of right and wrong [i.e. this Qur'an] to his

579

servant that he may be a warner to the 'alamin (mankind and jinn)' (25.1). Allah reveals to his servant clear signs: 'it is He who sends down manifest proofs or signs to His servant that He may bring you out from darkness into light. And, He revealed to His servant whatever He revealed' (53.10). Allah ordered his messenger to worship him alone and to spread his message and he guarantees his safety: 'Is not Allah sufficient for His servant?' (39.36). The Qur'an also refers to all the prophets and messengers of Allah as servants or slaves of God. When Noah invited his people to believe in Allah 'They rejected Our servant and said, "A madman!"' (54.9). Allah tells Prophet Muhammad many stories about his previous prophets to support him and to connect his message to theirs: 'Be patient of what they say, and remember our slave Dawud (David), endowed with power' (38.17).

'Abdayn is the dual form of servant and means two servants: 'Allah sets forth an example for those we disbelieve: wife of Noah and the wife of Lot. They were under two of our righteous servants, but they both betrayed them' (66.10).

'Ubudiya, signifying humble veneration, slavery or worship, is the verbal noun of 'abada and means demonstrating humbleness. 'Ibada means worship, devotional service, divine service or, according to Islamic law, the collective acts of devotion and religious observances. According to al-Raghib, 'ibada is of a higher level than 'ubudiya because it is the ultimate degree of demonstrating humbleness. Allah is the only being who deserves this, for as is stated in the Qur'an, 'He has commanded that you worship none but Him, that is the straight religion, but most men know not' (12.40). Therefore, 'ibada is the core of monotheism.

'Ibada can be of two kinds, one is by taskhir, which is the verbal noun of sakh-khara and means to bring something into service, to compel something to be of service to something else or to make something subservient. This kind of 'ibada applies to those of God's creations that are inanimate. In the Qur'an taskhir refers to Allah's compelling the heavens and the earth to be of service to humanity: 'Allah is He who has created the heavens and the earth, and caused water to descend from the sky, thereby producing fruits as food for you, and made the ships to be of service unto you, that may run upon the sea at His command, and has made of service unto you the rivers, and made the sun and the moon constant in their courses to be of service unto you, and has made of service the night and the day' (14.32). Further, in the sura of al-Ra'd 'Allah is He who has risen up the heavens without visible supports, then mounted the Throne, and compelled the sun and moon to be of service' (13.2). All the elements of nature are governed by Allah in a manner to serve human beings; they act only according to the laws specified for each of them by him. According to Fahkr al-Razi, in following this perfect scientific order these elements are actually performing their own form of worship. By carrying out Allah's orders, through this process of taskhir or by providing services to the human being as assigned by God, they are acting as servants of Allah.

The second kind of 'ibada is worship by choice, and it applies to animate beings with a free will. Man and jinn alike are invited by God to worship him, and in this case the invitee is called 'abd or servant of God: 'O mankind! Worship your Lord, who created you and those who were before you so that you may become the pious' (2.21). This invitation by God is repeated many times in the Qur'an in many contexts. In the *sura* of al-Nisa'a for example, we read 'Worship Allah and join none with him' (3.36).

'Abd has four meanings in the Qur'an. First is as a slave, the human being that can be bought and sold in the slavery market: 'And Allah puts forward an example of a slave under the possession of another; he has no power of any sort' (16.75). When Islam was established, slavery was normal business among the ancient societies. Although Islam did not totally abolish slavery, it dealt with it as a status quo and introduced some regulations to control the relationship between master and slave. The Prophet encouraged the Muslims to be kind to their slaves. Addressing his companions he said: 'They are your brothers, so feed them from whatever you eat and provide clothes for them from whatever you wear.' Yet Islam tried to emancipate slaves on many occasions. *Tahriru raqaba*, meaning the freeing of a slave, was an act of piety. In certain situations it was mandatory; violations of some Islamic laws were met with a fine of the freeing a slave as reparation to God. For example, the unintentional killer of another Muslim should free a slave: 'And whosoever kills a believer by mistake; he must set free a believing slave' (4.92).

The second kind of *'abd* is a servant by creation. Anything Allah creates belongs to him, and is his servant: 'There is none in the heavens and the earth but comes unto the Most Gracious [Allah] as a slave' (19.93). From an Islamic perspective there are three types of existence. The first is Allah as *wajib al-wujub*, meaning that his existence is necessary. Second, is that which he creates, *ja'iz al-wujud*, the existence of which depends purely on the will of Allah and each of which is his servant. Finally is existence which is impossible, and this is the existence of any partner with God.

The latter is a false existence and so is discarded; the remaining two types – the existence of the Creator and of what has been created through his will – are left as the real existences.

The third kind of servant is the servant who performs a system of worship. This type is the servant of God who worships Allah sincerely. The Qur'an gives many examples of this type, normally referring to the righteous prophets and devoted worshippers: 'And remember our slave Ayyub (Job) when he invoked his Lord' (38.41). Elsewhere, Noah is mentioned as a thankful slave or *'abd*: 'O offspring of those whom We carried with Noah! Verily, he was a grateful servant' (17.3). The Qur'an describes such devoted and God-fearing believers as the servants of God. These servants are protected by the divine powers and blessings. When Iblis (Satan) was cursed by God because of his disobedience and for refusing to bow to Adam, he plotted to deceive humanity by popularizing the path of error upon earth, saying 'I shall mislead them all'. Allah's response was, 'Certainly, you should have no authority over My slaves' (15.42). *Surat al-Furqan* (The Criterion) lists the attributes and characteristics of the ideal servants of God, called there 'Ibadu al-Rahman or the slaves of the Most Gracious. Such people walk on the earth in humility. If provoked by insulting comments from the foolish they reply with mild words of gentleness. They spend the night in worship of their Lord. They ask their Lord to avert from them the torment of Hell. When they spend money, they are neither extravagant nor niggardly but they follow the middle course between the two extremes. They invoke no other God other than Allah, nor kill such persons as Allah has forbidden. They do not commit illegal sexual relations. The servants of Allah were also described in sura al-Mu'minin (The Believers) as successful believers who offer their prayers with full submissiveness. They turn away from evil talk and pay the *zakat* (alms) and guard their chastity. Finally, the people of Moses were described as the servants of Allah. When Moses was ordered by Allah to leave with his people by night he was told: 'Depart you with My servants by night. Surely you will be pursued' (44.23).

The fourth kind of servant is the servant of the earthly life. Someone who devotes themselves to such a life and who sees everything in existence from a materialistic point of view is known in Islamic tradition as the servant of *dunya* (worldly life). The Prophet was not in favour of this type of servant. He says: 'May the slave of *dirham* and the slave of *dinar* (two types of money) be wretched and unfortunate.' Thus, not every person is a servant of God.

The real servant of God is *'abed*, and the term *'abd* is on this occasion more general in its meaning. While *'abd* covers the four kinds of servants listed above, *'abed* applies particularly to the righteous servant of God: 'Say, O disbelievers I worship not that which you worship. Nor will you worship that which I worship. And I shall not worship that which you are worshipping' (109.1–4). Pagan Arabs meanwhile used the names of 'Abd al-Shams (the Servant of the Sun) and 'Abd al-Latt (the Servant of al-Latt), the latter an Arabian goddess that used to be worshipped among others before Islam.

The plural of *'abd* is *'abid* and the plural of *'abed* is *'ibad*. The Qur'an uses the terms in both their singular and plural forms. It states that God is just to his servants in general – 'And I am not unjust to the slaves' (50.29) – and points out that God does not do people injustice regardless of whether they worship Him or worship others.

Finally, the verb *'ab-bada*, with a stress on the *b*, signifies to humiliate and enslave someone. The Qur'an records its use in the argument between Moses and Pharaoh after the return of Moses to liberate the enslaved Children of Israel from Egypt, when Moses exclaimed in protest: 'And this is the past favour with which you reproach me, that you have enslaved the children of Israel' (26.22).

RAFIK BERJAK

SHAFA'A

The Arabic term *shafa'a* means 'intercession'. In the Qur'an, intercession is described as the prerogative of God alone, as in 39.44, which reads 'Say! Intercession belongs to God', and 6.51, which states that 'there is no patron nor intercessor beside Him'. Two other verses assert that no intercession will be accepted on the Day of Judgement (2.48, 254). Yet the categorical nature of these pronouncements is ameliorated somewhat by other verses that leave open the possibility that some may be allowed to intercede at God's discretion. For example, 43.86 reads: 'Those whom they call on besides God shall not be able to intercede except for those who bear witness to the truth.' Another verse asks: 'Who may intercede with Him without His permission?' (2.255). The Qur'anic attitude, therefore, may be described as being mainly against human intercession, while allowing for divine concession in this area as God sees fit.

Many of the statements attributed to the Prophet Muhammad on the issue of intercession as recorded in authoritative Sunni *hadith* compilations, however, are remarkable in departing from this Qur'anic view. These statements convey the image of Muhammad as being an active intercessor on behalf of his community come the Day of Judgement.

According to one *hadith* recorded by the famous *hadith* compiler al-Bukhari (d. 256/870), the validity of intercession is extended to all those who do not ascribe partners to God.

In Shi'i thought, belief in the intercession of the *imams* on Judgement Day, in addition to that by the Prophet, is axiomatic. In Sufism the *awliya'* ('friends of God'; 'saints' in popular parlance), who are possessed of great charisma, are believed to be able to intercede on behalf of lesser humans in this world. Such a belief has pervaded popular or 'folk' Islam to a considerable degree, so that people often flock to the shrines of particularly well-known 'saints' to petition them for special favours on earth. More conventional or 'orthodox' Muslims tend to look askance at such practices however, considering them to smack of idolatry. The strict Wahhabi school of thought predominant in Saudi Arabia today denies the possibility of human intercession and regards the practice of shrine visitation very unfavourably.

ASMA AFSARUDDIN

See also: **Ibn 'Abd al-Wahhab**

AL-SHAFI'I, MUHAMMED B. IDRIS

Abu 'Abdullah Muhammed b. Idris al-Qurashi was born in Gaza or Asqalan in 150/767 and died in Cairo in 204/819. He was the founder of the Shafi'ite legal school in Islam. His family belonged to the Quraysh tribe. His father died when Shafi'i was two years old and he moved to Mecca where he grew up with his mother. There he had a traditional education in grammar and law, memorizing the Qur'an and the *Muwatta* of Malik at a very early age. When he was 13 he went to see Malik who was said to have been deeply impressed by his memory

and intelligence. Shafi'i learned classical Arabic and traditional Arabic poetry during his residence with the tribe of Hudhayl in Mecca. Then around 170, he moved to Medina and studied Islamic law with Malik b. Anas. After Malik's death, he continued his studies in Baghdad under Hanafite teachers. He continued his education with one of the main contemporary Hanafite scholars Muhammad b. Hasan Shaybani, and with Ahmad b. Hanbal. He went on to start to devise his own legal system in Baghdad and in 200/814 he went to Egypt where he changed his whole theoretical direction and formulated an entirely new legal approach. These two systems are known as 'the old' (*al-qadim*) and 'the new' (*al-jadid*), corresponding to his views in Iraq and Egypt. Some of Shafi'i's pupils, like al-Buwayti, al-Muzani and al-Bulqini, transmitted 'the new legal system' in the *Kitab al-Umm*, while the most prominent transmitters of 'the old legal system' were Ibn Hanbal, al-Zafarani and Abu Thawr, in the *Kitab al-Hujja*.

In his legal theory, Shafi'i tried to restore the sources of Islamic law to some sort of balance with each other. He accepted as the four main sources the Qur'an, Tradition (*hadith*), analogical reasoning (*qiyas*) and the consensus of the community (*ijma'*). Analogical reasoning and independent legal reasoning (*ijtihad*) are two terms used for the same idea, and are equally acceptable. Shafi'i argued for analogical reasoning as a fourth authoritative source of religious decisions and beliefs by contrast with Ibn Hanbal and others who rejected it as going beyond the meaning of the text. Shafi'i also severely criticized the methods of juristic preference (*istihsan*), the practice of interpreting the law in accordance with one's own beliefs on what would be in the general interest. He condemned *istihsan* as too subjective because it leaves it up to the judge to decide what he thinks the law ought to be. One area in which Shafi'i refused to get involved was the interpretation of verses about the attributes of God. His writings and teaching provide evidence that he exercised a good deal of caution with respect to these texts, which he felt should be accepted as they are and not examined too closely.

Shafi'i's most influential work is the *al-Risala fi al-usul* (A Treatise on Legal Principles), probably the first work on the foundations of jurisprudence or *fiqh*. It was written at the request of 'Abd al-Rahman b. Mahdi, who was a traditionist in Basra. His *Kitab al-Umm* (The Motherbook) consists of his legal opinions (*fatawa*) delivered in Egypt. His *Kitab al-Hujja* (Book of Evidence) is a compilation of his legal opinions given in Baghdad. Other books include the *Kitab al-Ihtilaf al-hadith* (Book of the Conflicts of the Traditions) and *Isbat al-nubuwwa wa raddi 'ala barahima* (The Establishment of Prophecy and Refutation of the Brahmans).

Further reading

Burton, J. (1990) *The Sources of Islamic Law,* Edinburgh: Edinburgh University Press.

Khadduri, M. (trans and int.) (1987) *Al-Shafi'i's Risala: Treatise on the foundation of Islamic jurisprudence*, Cambridge: The Islamic Texts Society.

Macdonald, D. Black (1985) *Development of Muslim Theology Jurisprudence and Constitutional Theory*, London: Darf Publishers Ltd.

Schacht, J. (1975) *The Origins of Muhammadan Jurisprudence*, Oxford: Clarendon Press.

al-Shafi'i (1979) *al-Risala fi al-usul* (A Treatise on Legal Principles), ed. A. Shakir, Cairo: Dar al-turath; trans. M. Khadduri, Cambridge: The Islamic Texts Society, 1987.

—— (1984) *Jama' al-'ilm* (The Compendium of Knowledge), ed. M. Abdulaziz, Beirut: Dar al-kutub al-'ilmiyya.

—— (1993) *Kitab al-Umm* (The Motherbook), ed. Mahmud Mataraji, Beirut: Dar al-kutub al-'ilmiyya.

OLIVER LEAMAN

SHAHADA

The Arabic word *shahada* is customarily understood to mean 'martyrdom', and the participal form *shahid* to refer to 'a martyr'. Yet the word *shahid* and its derivatives do not occur in this sense in the Qur'an; although it appears over fifty times, it signifies rather a 'legal' or 'eye-witness'. The *locus classicus* for the concept (rather than the term) of martyrdom is 3.169, which states: 'Those who are slain in the way of God are not to be reckoned as dead; rather they are alive with their Lord, sustained.' Exegetical glosses on the critical phrase 'in the way of God' explain it as referring to a wide array of activities: embarking on the pursuit of knowledge, giving birth to a child, being afflicted with a fatal disease and engaging in military defence of Islam.

It is in the *hadith* literature that we come across the full-blown concepts of martyr and martyrdom, with an emphasis on dying for the sake of the faith on the battlefield. The authoritative *hadith* collections contain chapters entitled such things as 'Merits of Jihad'. Jihad here is used primarily in the sense of armed combat against the foes of Islam, and many of these reports detail the posthumous rewards reserved in paradise for the martyr. All the sins of the martyr are said to be forgiven, except for debt. The martyr will be buried in bloodstained clothes without the ritual bath and is assured of admittance into heaven without any reckoning

The broader definition of a martyr as one 'who strives in the way of God with his hand, his tongue, and his heart', as occurs in the standard *hadith* works, persisted and allowed for different kinds of self-sacrifice in the cause of God to continue to be recognized as exceptionally meritorious activity. Early *hadith* works, such as the *Musannaf* of 'Abd al-Razzaq (d. 211/827), contain a number of reports which relate competing definitions of *shahid*. One such report states that the *shahid* is one who dies in his bed and is without sin; such a person would enter heaven. Another early report in the same work relates that there are four types of *shahada* or martyrdom for Muslims: the plague, parturition or delivery of a child, drowning, and a stomach ailment, with no mention of military activity. Other reports challenge the excessive rewards promised to the military martyr and posit other virtues or activities as deserving of more merit; one such virtue is patient forbearance: see, for example, the third-/ninth-century work by Ibn Abi al-Dunya (d. 894) which relates:

> The Messenger of God, peace and blessings be upon him, wept and we asked him, 'What has caused you to weep, O Messenger of God?' He replied, 'I reflected on the last of my community and the tribulations they will face. But the patient from among them who arrives will be given the reward of two [military] martyrs.'

This example clearly contests those reports which assign the highest merit to military martyrs.

These early and competing meanings were superseded by the importance of military activity some time during the eighth century, coinciding with the increasing militarization of the Islamic state. The non-militant meanings enjoyed a resurrection particularly among the Sufis, the mystics of Islam, who emphasized the spiritual struggle of the believer against his or her carnal self as the true and greater *jihad*.

Further reading

al-An'ani, A. (1971) *al-Musannaf*, ed. H. al-A'zami, Beirut: al-Maktabi al-islami.

Ayoub, Mahmoud (1987) 'Martyrdom in Christianity and Islam', in *Religious Resurgence: Contemporary cases in Islam, Christianity, and Judaism*, Syracuse, NY: Syracuse University Press, 67–76.

al-Dunya, ibn Abi (1997) *al-Sabr wa'l thawab 'alayhi*, Beirut: Dar ibn Hazm.

Lewinstein, K. (2002) 'The Reevaluation of Martyrdom in Early Islam', in *Sacrificing the Self: Perspectives on martyrdom and religion*, Oxford: Oxford University Press.

Wensinck, A.J. (1941) 'The Oriental Doctrine of the Martyrs', *Semietische Studien uit de nalatenschap*, Leiden: A.W. Sijthoff

See also: **sabr**

ASMA AFSARUDDIN

SHAYKH MUFID

Abu 'Abd Allah Muhammad b. Muhammad b. Nu'man al-Harithi al-Baghadi al-'Ukbari (338/949– 413/1022), commonly known as Shaykh Mufid, was born and lived in a village until his father took him to Baghdad to further his education. There he worked largely with Shi'i and Mu'tazili scholars. He showed such promise that one of his teachers recommended that he study under one of the leading scholars of the period, 'Ali b. 'Isa al-Ramani. He also studied under the leading Shi'i traditionist of the time, al-Shaykh al-Saduq.

The Buyids, who were in power during this period, were much more tolerant of Shi'ism than some previous and subsequent rulers, so this was a good time for someone with Shi'i affiliations to work in Baghdad. He acquired the name of Shaykh Mufid ('he who provides benefit') due to his skill in argument, in particular for the subtle distinctions he managed to draw in theological debate. He had three pupils who were to go on to positions of significance in Shi'i thought. These were al-Sharif al-Radi, al-Sharif al-Murtada and the future Shaykh al-Ta'ifa, Muhammad b. al-Hasan al-Tusi.

Shaykh Mufid wrote a large number of books on a wide variety of topics and died in the month of Ramadan in the year AH 413/1022. Al-Sharif al-Murtada led the funeral prayers and gave a eulogy. After being buried in his own house, Mufid's body was later removed and buried near to the shrine of two of the Imams (*al-Kazimayn*) in Baghdad.

Shaykh Mufid's work was restricted largely to the field of theology but was of great import as it took Shi'i thought to a new conceptual level: as a result of his efforts the movement became highly systematic and logically organized. Of particular significance is his book *al-Irshad*, which deals with the twelve Shi'i Imams. This describes the circumstances of the Imamate of each Imam, the miracles that each performed by which he gave evidence of his Imamate, the virtues of each, and the circumstances of the death of all the Imams as well as the disappearance of the last Imam. It also outlines the *nass*, or nomination, of each Imam. Mufid concentrates, as one would expect, on 'Ali b. Abi Talib (d. 40/661) and in particular on his career during the Prophet's lifetime. 'Ali is described as the person of outstanding virtue, the most appropriate successor to the Prophet. The traditions in which the Prophet is said to declare this are emphasized, especially the tradition of Ghadir Khumm. Mufid outlines some of 'Ali's writings, his reticence during the rule of the first three caliphs and the political events of the time. The circumstances of 'Ali's murder by lbn Muljam are discussed at length. What is interesting and influential about the text is the clear organization of the evidence for each Imam's miraculous acts and how these provide evidence for the Imamate itself, clearly a vital aspect of Imami Islam. In this way Mufid's work set the agenda for a great deal of continuing debate on this topic in the Shi'i intellectual world.

Further reading

Mufid, Muhammad ibn Muhammad (AH 1377) *Kitab al-Irshad*, al-Mayamawi edn, Teheran.
—— (1981) *Kitab al-Irshad*, trans. I. Howard, *Book of Guidance into the Lives of the Twelve Imams*, Elmhurst, NY: Tahrike Tarsile Qur'an.
Muhajerani, A. (1996) 'Twelve-Imam Shi'ite Theological and Philosophical Thought', *HIP*: 119–43.

OLIVER LEAMAN

SHAYTAN

see: **devil**

SHI'A

Lexically, the word *shi'a* is derived from the Arabic verb *sha'a/yashi'u*, which in its various forms can mean to spread, disseminate, divulge or publicize as well as adhere to, conform with or take sides. The feminine noun *shi'a* thus, represents a distinct group of people who agree with one another in following a cause; hence adherents, disciples or followers. In the Qur'an, the expression *shi'a* and its two plural forms, *shiya'* and *ashya'* occur eleven times, with the first use occurring in *sura al-An'am* and the last in *sura al-Qamar*. The primary meaning that comes across in these verses is that of factions, ancient communities of faith, people with similar views, followers and supporters as conveyed for instance in 37:83: 'Verily Abraham was certainly among Noah's followers (*wa inna min shi'atihi la-Ibrahim*).' The verb form occurs once, at 24.19: 'Those who love to spread (*an tashi'a*) scandal among the believers.'

The first occurrence of *shi'a* in 6.65 is in the plural form, *shiya'an* factions, referring to God's power to send calamities and reduce mankind to factions (*aw yalbisakum shiya'an*). Obviously a negative connotation, this is a warning to mankind for having failed to pay heed to God's message. Exegetes offer varying opinions, assessing whether *shiya'an* referred to the Jews and Christians or whether it meant Muslim groups divided by arbitrary opinions. The early fourth-/tenth-century Qur'an commentary by Abu Ja'far b. Jarir al-Tabari (d. 310/923) talks of diverse groups with varying inclinations in which people had become enmeshed. 'Ali b. Ibrahim al-Qummi, a Shi'i Ithna'ashari scholar, who flourished in fourth/tenth century, citing a tradition on the authority of al-Baqir (d. *c.*117/735) refers to religious differences in groups denigrating each other. Another Shi'i author of Tayyibi-Isma'ili persuasion, 'Ali b. al-Walid, in his work *Taj al-'aqa'id*, refers specifically to disputes in the community after the Prophet's death. He states that Muslims have behaved in exactly the same way as communities before them and that instead of following the dictates of religion, they have followed their personal desires, opposing the legatee (*wasi*) and rejecting the legacy (*wasiya*) of the Prophet.

This plural form, *shiya'an*, occurs again in 6.159, the *sura* warning believers not to associate themselves with those who divide their religion and become disparate groups (*kanu shiya'an*). In *sura al-Rum* 30.32, God exhorts believers not to join hands with those who divide their religion by forming parties (*min al-ladhina farraqu dinahum wa kanu shiya'an*). Meanwhile 28.4 addresses the Pharaoh, who had arrogantly raised himself to an overbearing position thus creating divisions amongst his people (*wa ja'ala ahlaha shiya'an*).

Yet another plural form, *ashya'*, in 34.54 refers to those who had fiercely questioned the truth in the past and how a transformation had occurred in their hearts and desires. Al-Tabari calls these individuals the unbelievers from the ancient communities, noting that *al-ashya'* is the plural of *shiya'* and *shiya'* the plural of *shi'a*, and therefore that *ashya'* thus becomes the plural of plurals. This same term in 54.51 addresses the polytheists among the Quraysh, warning them of how communities in the past had been destroyed (*kama fu'ila bi- ashya'ihim*) for this crime.

The verses examined so far convey negative meanings of the word *shi'a*. There are, however, an equal number of verses which demonstrate positive support. One such example is 15.10, which employs the term to describe the ancient communities among whom messengers had been sent: 'Indeed, We sent [messengers] before you among communities of the past (*wa laqad arsalna min qablika fi shiya' al-awwalin*).' God had certainly sent many messengers among the ancient communities before Muhammad, observes al-Tabari (d. 310/923), who also states that the friends of a person are his *shi'a*. The Mu'tazili scholar, al-Zamakhshari (d. 538/1144) explains them as groups and parties, stating that the *shi'a* is a party that agrees upon a path and *madhhab* and among whom God sent messengers, whose role was to warn. He also mentions the *sunna al-Awwalin* in the Qur'an. Al-Baydawi (d. *c.*685/1286) considers the *shiya'* as meaning 'among their sects', i.e. plural of *shi'a*, a party agreeing upon a path and *madhhab* spreading as people follow it, but adds that its origin is *shiya'*, communities in which men were raised and made God's messengers.

In 28.15 the word *shi'a* (Shi'a) is used twice for the followers of Moses, all exegetes agreeing that *hadha min shi'atihi* refers to the religion of Moses. Commentators agree that *min shi'atihi* in 37.83 refers to Abraham, who followed Noah's religion: 'Verily among those who followed Noah was certainly Abraham (*wa inna min shi'atihi la Ibrahim*).' The Fatimid scholar, Ja'far b. Mansur al-Yaman explains that as a follower of Noah, Abraham was a true believer of God and was therefore chosen by God to promulgate his *shari'a* (law or path) as a proclaimer (*natiq*) after Noah.

Exegetes are thus unanimous in explaining the phrase *min shi'atihi* as referring to Abraham being a devotee of Noah's religion in his method and his community. Al-Zamakhshari cautiously notes that certain laws had changed although there was a commonality among most. Al-Qummi quotes al-Baqir as congratulating the Shi'a on their name. When people complained about insults being hurled at them on account of the name, he reminded them 'haven't you heard God's words – *wa inna min shi'atihi la Ibrahim*. Indeed, Abraham was among those who certainly followed Noah?' In the *Taj al-aqa'id* of 'Ali b. al-Walid, these verses are given intertextually to reflect religion as devotion to 'Ali alongside the Prophet's tradition on Noah's Ark, which states that true believers are henceforth called Shi'a.

Thus, in four instances (6.65, 159; 28.4; 30.32), the term '*shiya'an*' has been used to convey the meaning of factions while on four other occasions (15.10; 28.15 twice, and 37.83) *shi'a* is applied to ancient communities of faith when referring to their prophets. When the Qur'an speaks of *shiya' al-awwalin* and *shi'atihi*, it essentially means the previous rightly guided communities, but *kanu shiya'an* is used in the divisive sense, while the plural *ashya'* is applied to former erring people and *min kulli shi'atin* (19.69) refers to communities in general.

The word 'shi'a' in early sources

The word *shi'a* can be used either with or without the article. When used without the article, it always accompanies a qualifier – *shi'at 'Uthman, shi'at Mu'awiya* and *shi'at 'Ali* to mean followers as used in early sources. Nasr bin Muzahim al-Minqari (d. 212/827), uses the term *shi'a* and *ashab* as supporters or followers when referring to those who supported 'Ali and Mu'awiya. Al-Ya'qubi (d. 284/897) uses the expression *ashab 'Ali* and *ashab Mu'awiya* but the use of the term *shi'a* is quite distinctly shown in a communication to al-Husayn b. 'Ali from Sulayman bin Surad where he mentions the Shi'a and the Shi'a of his father ('Ali b. Abi Talib). The communiqué further states how the community in general, Husayn himself and the Shi'a-following in particular, had been struck by this great calamity.

When specified (*al-Shi'a*), that is when used with the definite article (*al*), it invariably meant 'Ali's followers described in the *Kitab al-zina* by Abu Hatim al-Razi (d. 322/933) an early Ismaili scholar, as those who were devoted to 'Ali or close to 'Ali in the lifetime of the Prophet. Among those that he describes as *Shi'at 'Ali* and *Ashab 'Ali* were Salman al-Farisi, Abu Dharr al-Ghifari, Miqdad al-Aswad and Ammar bin Yasir. The author further states these men were anxiously awaited in paradise and that this epithet, *al-shi'a*, was thereafter applied to all those who upheld the excellence of 'Ali.

The *Maqalat al-islamiyyin* of al-Ash'ari (d. 324/935–36) describes the Shi'a as those who follow 'Ali and those who place him before other companions of the Prophet. Al-Baghdadi (d. 429/ 1037) in his *al-Farq bayn al-firaq*, opts to use *rafida* or *rawafid* but uses *shi'a* in his *Usul*. A more comprehensive definition is given by al-Shahrastani (d. 548/1153) who defines the Shi'a as those who follow (*shaya'u*) 'Ali in particular, asserting his imamate and caliphate by appointment and delegation made either openly or secretly, and who believe that the imamate does not depart from his descendants. Ibn Qutayba (d. 276/889) usually speaks of the Shi'a and the Rafida, the latter apparently ranking 'Ali above 'Uthman. There is a definite unwillingness to speak of the heretics as Shi'a since the term has usually been in a positive light. Ahmad b. Hanbal for instance asserts that the *ahl al-sunna wa'l hadith* were the true *shi'a* of 'Ali as they had due affection for the family of Muhammad and recognised the rights of 'Ali.

It is therefore quite evident that the word *shi'a* was a term used mainly for those groups who were close to 'Ali. According to the *Fihrist* of Ibn Nadim (d. 385/995), 'Ali himself habitually called certain of his associates *shi'ai* – my followers or supporters. The word *shi'a* thus, unlike other such names, did not originate as a nickname or pejorative term given by opponents, but was usually used by men of themselves.

The early Shi'a

Today the Shi'a is a major branch of Islam with several subdivisions – the Zaydiyya, the Isma'iliyya and the Ithna'ashariyya amongst others – all of whom uphold the rights of the Prophet's family (*ahl al-bayt*). This section will give a brief survey of how the personal following of 'Ali developed historically into the early Shi'a.

Usually the Shi'a are envisaged as those who had either political or social misgivings concerning the ruling authorities. This is not how Shi'i consciousness identifies itself, however. Although Shi'i Islam did eventually become the focus of many social, political as well as some spiritual and religious inclinations that had become displaced with the rise of Islam, for the Shi'a themselves their version of Islam refers to the inexplicable spiritual phenomenon experienced by Muhammad and the role of 'Ali and the *imams* in helping them to understand the meaning of this unique occurrence. (Ironically, many scholars ignore this aspect of Shi'i thought whereby the *imams*, as the *qayyim al-Qur'an* (Keepers of the Book), not only transmit but also explain the true essence of the revelation.) This aspect, as well as that of love, devotion and commitment (*walaya*) to 'Ali and the *imams*, is usually forsaken in analyses of the early period of Islam. Thus, for the Shi'a, the foundation of their interpretation of Islam lies in the various Qur'anic verses, the several prophetic traditions and in the many historical events that culminated in 'Ali's appointment as Muhammad's successor at Ghadir Khumm. Their worldview constitutes the esoteric aspect of Islam

It was this same commitment that led some, as early as the *saqifa* assembly, to object to giving allegiance to Abu Bakr on the basis that they would not pledge *bay'a* to anyone but 'Ali. The sources do not mention why 'Ali was chosen. They also fail to explain why the Ansar (Helpers) were willing to give up their own candidate, Sa'd b. 'Ubada, for a compromise in favour of 'Ali who was a *muhajir* (emigrant) from the Quraysh. From a historical point of view, what is important is that reports which put forward such sentiments about 'Ali and his family are contained in the earliest preserved sources.

These sentiments survived in varying degrees for the twelve years of leadership by Abu Bakr then 'Umar. When 'Uthman was offered the caliphate on the ground of 'Ali's apparent evasiveness, sentiments for 'Ali became even more vocal. These included views from supporters (shi'a) such as 'Ammar b. Yasir and Miqdad, who pleaded and persuaded people to honour and distinguish him whom the Prophet had honoured and asked why they would turn away from the Prophet's family (ahl al-bayt).

It was also during this time that a popular movement in favour of 'Ali first appeared in Kufa calling for the removal of 'Uthman. This was a result of the discontent with 'Uthman's kinsmen occupying governorships, other leading posts and accumulating enormous wealth in the process. Now, in addition to his initial supporters, many others now began to show support for 'Ali. Malik al-Ashtar became the leader of the movement, and although he and the Kufans played no role in the siege of the caliph's palace carried out by the Egyptians, he played a major role in securing 'Ali's succession.

Amidst the chaos that ensued in Medina, 'Uthman was assassinated and 'Ali was elected as the fourth caliph in the year 35/656. 'Ali's followers, the Shi'at 'Ali as opposed to the Shi'at 'Uthman, heralded him as the most excellent of Muslims (afdal al-muslimin) acclaiming him as the wasi, or legatee of Muhammad. But immediately he had to face a rebellion from two of the Prophet's companions, Talha and al-Zubayr, who were joined by 'A'isha, a widow of the Prophet and daughter of Abu Bakr. The three were defeated by 'Ali at the battle of the Camel with particular help from Malik al-Ashtar, who managed to rouse Kufan support. 'Ali also encountered major opposition from Mu'awiya, a

relative of 'Uthman and the governor of Syria, who not only refused to obey decrees but also incited people against him. This led to the prolonged and inconclusive battle of Siffin in 36/657, which in turn ended in the secession of the Khawarij (Kharijiyya/Kharijites) or 'separatists' from 'Ali's army. In the midst all this, already at Siffin, 'Ali was addressed by Abu'l Aswad al-Du'ali in distinct devout devotion. Al-Du'ali perceived in 'Ali's face the full moon, an image that filled the audience with deferential wonder, and declared that the Quraysh had now realized that 'Ali was the noblest of them all in merit and religion. Thus begins the Shi'i tradition.

'Ali's speeches and letters reveal that he considered the Prophet's family as being entitled to the leadership of the Muslim community. However, he also believed, on the basis of his close kinship and association with Muhammad and his endeavours in the cause of Islam, that he personally had the greater right to the succession. The tradition of Ghadir Khumm was first given publicity by 'Ali himself after Siffin, when he invited those companions who had heard the Prophet's statements there to testify to this in front of the mosque of Kufa. With this event, the most basic beliefs of the Shi'a can be traced back to 'Ali himself.

When 'Ali was assassinated in 40/661, by the Kharijites, Ibn Muljam, his son al-Hasan was immediately recognized as caliph. Following bribes and threats to al-Hasan's commanders, Mu'awiya signed a peace treaty with him on the basis of which full amnesty was given to the Shi'at 'Ali and Mu'awiya was denied the right to appoint a successor. The Shi'a were deeply disappointed and there were protests; many gathered in the house of Sulayman b. Surad and wrote to al-Husayn urging him to rise against Mu'awiya, who declined, honouring the validity of his brother's agreement. Mu'awiya, however, breached the treaty, ordering the cursing of 'Ali from the pulpit in the Friday prayers and insisting on the presence of several Shi'i leaders. Among those present was Hujr b. 'Adi al-Kindi and some of his associates who were rounded up after protesting. While some were freed through family intervention, Hujr and others were asked to publicly curse and denounce 'Ali. When they refused to comply, they were executed. Rather than crushing the opposition, this merely intensified the resentment of the Shi'a, demonstrating the strong feeling felt towards 'Ali by such individuals.

When Mu'awiya died and his son Yazid came to power in 60/680, al-Husayn and 'Abd Allah b. al-Zubayr refused to pledge allegiance. The Shi'a of Kufa and Basra wrote letters to al-Husayn declaring that they had no *imam* other than him (al-Husayn's own letters reveal very clearly his role as an *imam*). His cousin Muslim b. 'Aqil was sent to investigate and report the situation. However, after taking up the challenge the promised support crumbled and al-Husayn met his tragic death at the hands of Umayyad forces at Karbala in 61/680. This tragedy evoked powerful emotions among the Shi'is and became the focus of profound themes of guilt and betrayal.

Until al-Husayn's time, there seems to have been no dispute about leadership among the Shi'a. But after his death, differences arose. Many acknowledged not only the descendants of al-Hasan and al-Husayn, the sons of 'Ali by Fatima, but also Muhammad b. al-Hanafiyya, his son by Khawla of the Banu Hanifa tribe. The identity of the Shi'i *imams*, that is, which of 'Ali's descendants inherited his authority, as well as the discussion about the nature and extent of such authority, have always

been one of the main reasons for the existence of several tendencies and inclinations among the Shi'a who, after al-Husayn, were never again a monolithic group.

Within a year of Karbala, a penitent movement known as the Tawwabun rose up to fight the Umayyads but were overwhelmed by the Umayyad forces and most lost their lives. Those who survived joined al-Mukhtar al-Thaqafi, who had been exiled for his part in the Kufan revolt under Muslim b. 'Aqil. Mukhtar now organized his own movement calling to avenge al-Husayn's death and it is believed that he initially approached al-Husayn's son, Zayn al-'Abidin. When he refused, Muhammad b. al-Hanafiyya was named the figurehead of Mukhtar's movement. Mukhtar managed to mobilize the *mawali* (the non-Arab Muslims) who were marginalized under the Umayyads. In 66/685 he led a successful revolution in Kufa, proclaiming Muhammad b. al-Hanafiyya as the Mahdi, the divinely guided saviour who would establish justice upon earth and deliver the oppressed from tyranny (*zulm*). This notion proved appealing to the *mawali* and Mukhtar enjoyed some success but this was short-lived. His movement survived, however, under the name of Kaysaniyya, while the active Shi'a went underground until such time as they rose up in support of the 'Abbasid cause.

A small group of the Shi'a, did support al-Husayn's only surviving son, 'Ali b. al-Husayn, known as Zayn al-'Abidin ('the Ornament of the Pious'). And. although for a generation the descendants of Fatima were generally eclipsed in the leadership of the Shi'a, including Zayn al-'Abidin, his son, Muhammad al-Baqir, did actively engage in systematic teaching. And although he refused to be drawn into politics, he nonetheless managed to carve out a significant role for himself. These were crucial times during which the foundation of Qurʾanic Studies was laid. This necessarily involved the interpretation of the Qurʾan, which in turn relied upon the actions and teachings of the Prophet Muhammad. Based in Medina, the centre of religious learning and where much of the discussion took place, al-Baqir was at the centre of this.

Only a few decades prior to al-Baqir, his grandfather al-Husayn and his entourage were afflicted by the tragedy of Karbala and the reduction of the Shiʿa to a handful of people. Yet by the end of his lifetime, al-Baqir had given the movement not only a distinct identity with a coherent theory of Imamate, but also a separate legal school, the *madhhab ahl al-bayt*, with well-defined views on several aspects of *fiqh* or jurisprudence. The Shiʿa under al-Baqir did not shy away from the current issues and discussions, but proposed their own solutions; they entered the arena with confidence and had their solutions accepted by others in the fields of law, theology and religious practice.

Further reading

Amir-Moezzi, M.A (1994) *The Divine Guide in Early Shiʿism*, trans. David Streight, Albany, NY: SUNY Press.

al-Ashʿari (1980) *Maqalat al-Islamiyyin*, ed. H. Ritter, Wiesbaden: Franz Steiner.

al-ʿAyyashi, Muhammad b. Masʿud al-Samarqandi (1960) *Tafsir*, ed. Bashim al-Mahallati, Qum, Chapkhanah-i ʿIlmiyah.

al-Baghdadi, Abu Mansur (1970) *al-Farq bayn al-firaq*, ed. al-Kawthari, Beirut: Dar al-maʿarif.

al-Baydawi, ʿAbd Allah b. ʿUmar (1968) *Anwar al-tanzil wa asrar al-taʾwil*, Cairo: Mustafa al-Babi al-Halabi & sons.

Daftary, F. (1990) *The Ismaʿilis: Their history and doctrines*, Cambridge: Cambridge University Press

Halm, Heinz (1991) *Shiism*, trans. Janet Watson, Edinburgh: Edinburgh University Press.

Hodgson, Marshall (1955) 'How Did the Early Shiʿa become Sectarian?' *JAOS*, 75: 1–13.

Jafri, S. and Husain, M. (1979) *Origins and Early Development of Shiʿa Islam*, London: Longman.

Lalani, Arzina R. (2000) *Early Shiʿi Thought: The teachings of Imam Muhammad al-Baqir*, London: I.B. Tauris

Madelung, W(1987) 'Shiism: An overview', in Mircea Eliade (ed.), *Encyclopaedia of Religion*, London and New York: Macmillan, Vol. 13, 242–7.

—— (1997) *The Succession to Muhammad: A study of the early caliphate*, Cambridge: Cambridge University Press

Meir Bar-Asher (1999) *Scripture and Exegesis in Early Imami Shiism*, Leiden: E.J. Brill.

al-Minqari, Nasr bin Muzahim (1962) *Waqʿat al-Siffin*, ed. A.M. Harun, Cairo: Matbaʿt al-Madani.

Momen, Moojan (1985) *An Introduction to Shiʿi Islam*, New Haven, CT: Yale University Press.

al–Nasafi, ʿAbd Allah b. Ahmad (1900) *Tafsir al-Nasafi*, Dar al-kitab al-arabi, Vol. 3.

al-Qummi, ʿAli b. Ibrahim (1968) *Tafsir al-Qummi*, ed. Tayyib al-Musawi al-Jazaʾiri, Beirut: Matbaʿt al-Najaf.

al-Razi, Abu Hatim (1972) *Kitab al-zina* [excerpts], ed. ʿAbd Allah al-Samarraʾi's *al-Ghuluww wa al-firaq al-ghaliyya fi al-hadarat al-Islamiyya*, Baghdad: Dar al-hurriyah.

al-Shahrastani (AH 1314) *Kitab al-milal waʾl nihal* Bombay: Matbaʿt al-Haydari.

Sharon, M. (1983) *Black Banners from the East*, Jerusalem: E.J. Brill.

al-Tabari, Abu Jaʿfar Muhammad b. Jarir (1954) *Jamiʿal-bayan ʿan taʾwil ay al-Qurʾan*, Cairo: Mustafa al-Babi al-Halabi & Sons.

al-Walid, Ali b. Muhammad (1967) *Taj al-ʿaqaʾid wa maʿdan al-fawaʾid*, ed. Aref Tamer, Beirut: Dar al-machreq.

Watt, W.M (1973) *The Formative Period of Islamic Thought*, Edinburgh: Edinburgh University Press.

—— (1960) 'Shiʿism under the Umayyads', *Journal of the Royal Asiatic Society*: 158–172

Wellhausen, Julius (1975) *Die religiös-politischen Oppositionsparteien im alten Islam*, trans. R. C. Ostle and S. M. Walker as *The Religio-Political Factions in Early*

Islam, Amsterdam: North-Holland Pub. Co. .

al-Yaman, Ja'far b. Mansur (1984) *Kitab al-Kashf*, Beirut: Dar al-andalus.

al-Ya'qubi (1960) *Ta'rikh*, Beirut: Dar Sadir, Vols 1 and 2.

al-Zamakhshari (1970) *al-Kashshaf*, Beirut: Dar al-ma'rifa.

ARZINA R. LALANI

SHIELD (TO)

see: *taqa*

SHU'AYB

One of several indigenous Arab prophets mentioned by the Qur'an. A middle Meccan narrative (26.176–191) has Shu'ayb sent to the 'Companions of the Wood' (*ashab al-ayka*), a community mentioned four times in the Qur'an but whose identity remains unknown. On the basis of this and other narratives, Shu'ayb was understood to have come after Hud, Salih and Lut. He is also portrayed as having been sent to Madyan, and it is possible that the Companions of the Wood were either Madyanites or a group or clan living among them. While Shu'ayb's appearance in the Madyan led some classical exegetes to identify him as Jethro, father of Moses, there is nothing in the sources to substantiate this.

COLIN TURNER

SIHR

A term derived from the Arabic verb *sahara*, to bewitch; to charm; to fascinate. Usually translated as 'magic' or 'sorcery', *sihr* is the dubious art of deception through the creation of illusion, and can be traced back to the occult practices of Harut and Marut in ancient Babylon (2.102). The Qur'an paints a vivid portrait of Pharaoh's Egypt as a malevolent dictatorship propped up by the trickery and treachery of an elite corpus of sorcerers (*sahirun*), who dismissed Moses as a minor magician and challenged him to a contest to see whose magic was the most powerful. The sorcerers finally admitted that their work was based on pure illusion and that Moses was indeed inspired by God.

Jesus was also accused of sorcery by his detractors (5.110). During the time of Muhammad, one of the most popular forms of sorcery was to tie knots in a rope and then recite incantations over them to place 'knots' in the heart of the victim, hence the Qur'anic invocation in which refuge is sought from 'the evil of those who whisper over knots' (113.15).

See also: sahara

COLIN TURNER

SIN

It is often said that Islam believes that humankind is basically good and so there is no need for God to redeem us. At 30.30 there is a reference to humanity having been constructed as pure *fitra*, while at 20.115 the reason for Adam leaving the Garden of Eden is given as his forgetfulness, nothing else. His banishment is not described as permanent, and we are not told of any necessity for him to repent.

However, the angels suggest that if humans were given their head, they would succumb to corruption and shed blood (2.30). The devil anticipates that he will pervert and subjugate most of mankind (15.39; 17.62). And Adam is sometimes described as not having forgotten God's prohibition, but as being reminded of it by Satan (7.20); thus, by eating the fruit he rebelled against God and strayed (20.121).

Adam is not that enthusiastic about the type of creaturehood that God assigns to him in the Qur'an, or so we may assume when we observe his attempts to circumvent the divine plan and become as an angel or immortal (7.20; 20.120–121). Finally, Adam and Eve both know they have done wrong (7.23) and feel shame (7.22; 20.121). The Qur'an notes that Satan tempts 'the children of Adam' (7.26–27), and describes us as feeble (4.28), despairing (11.9), unjust (14.34), quarrelsome (16.4), tyrannical (96.6) and lost (105.2). It is worth remembering also that each community is sent an apostle (16.36), but one after another they reject him (e.g., 15.10–11; 50.12–14).

The rather pessimistic conclusion to all this is that 'Most men are not believers' (12.103). Joseph, after successfully rejecting the advances of Potiphar's wife, notes that 'The soul is certainly an inciter to evil' (12.53) and comments 'If God were to punish humans for their wrongdoing, He would not leave a single creature' (16.61).

Further reading

al-Sharawi, M. (1989) *The Miracles of the Qur'an*, trans. M. Alserougii, London: Dar al-taqwa

See also: **nafs**

OLIVER LEAMAN

AL-SINGKILI, 'ABD AL-RA'UF

'Abd al-Ra'uf b. 'Ali al-Fansuri al-Singkili (c.1615–1693) was one of the most prominent Islamic reformers of the Malay world in the seventeenth century. Born in the West Sumatran coastal town of Singkel, a vassal state of the Sultanate of Aceh, 'Abd al-Ra'uf's childhood coincided with the years of Aceh's greatest imperial grandeur.

In 1642 'Abd al-Ra'uf travelled to Arabia where he studied Islamic law, dogma, the Prophetic Traditions, history, Qur'anic recitation, Sufism and other subjects. Key teachers were Ahmad al-Qushashi (991–1071/1583–1661) of Medina and his successor Ibrahim al-Kurani (1023–1101/1615–1690). The latter authorized 'Abd al-Ra'uf to establish a school of the Shattariyya Sufi order in Aceh, which was to trigger the spread of the Order throughout the archipelago.

Between his return to Aceh in 1661 and his death around 1693, 'Abd al-Ra'uf wrote prolifically under the patronage of successive sultans. His writings, mostly in Malay with a few in Arabic, reflect his own neo-Sufi leanings. He sought to overcome the legacy of a doctrinal polemic between the followers of the reforming Nur al-Din al-Raniri (d. 1068/1658) and those of the earlier monistic Sufi scholars Hamzah Fansuri (d. *c*.998/1590) and Shams al-Din al-Samatrani (d. 1039/1630). Successive Acehnese sultans commissioned 'Abd al-Ra'uf to write *Mir'at al-tullab*, a work on jurisprudence, as well as a commentary upon the famous *Arba'ina hadith* (Forty Hadith Accounts) by al-Nawawi (d. 1277).

Arguably 'Abd al-Ra'uf's most important work is his commentary on the Qur'an, *Tarjuman al-mustafid* (The Interpreter of that which gives Benefit). This was compiled around 1675 and represents the first commentary on the whole Qur'an to be written in Malay. Both its sources and authorship are composite, with the core of the commentary drawn from *Tafsir al-Jalalayn*, supplemented by excerpts from the commentaries of al-Baydawi and al-Khazin. His student Da'ud Rumi then added information on the variant readings and selections drawn from other commentaries, probably after Abd al-Ra'uf's death.

Tarjuman al-mustafid remained the only substantial commentary on the whole Qur'an in Malay for almost 300 years. It was first published in Istanbul in 1302/1884, and even today it continues to be printed and widely used throughout Malaysia, Sumatra and Java. It has thus survived the appearance of a significant number of more recent commentaries in Malay/Indonesian.

'Abd al-Ra'uf was venerated as a saint after his death. His tomb in north Sumatra continues to attract pilgrims each year, many of whom accept the view popular in Aceh that 'Abd al-Ra'uf was the one who first brought Islam to the region.

Further reading

'Abd al-Ra'uf (1951) *Tarjuman al-mustafid*, Singapore: Sulayman Maraghi.

Johns, A.H. (1998) 'The Qur'an in the Malay World: Reflections on 'Abd al-Ra'uf of Singkel (1615–1693)', *Journal of Islamic Studies* 9, 2: 120–45.

—— (1999) '"She desired him and he desired her" (Qur'an 12:24: 'Abd al-Ra'uf's treatment of an episode of the Joseph story in *Tarjuman al-mustafid*', *Archipel* 57: 109–34.

Riddell, P.G. (1984) 'The Sources of 'Abd al-Ra'uf's Tarjuman al-mustafid', *Journal of the Malaysian Branch of the Royal Asiatic Society* LVII, 2: 113–18.

—— (1990) *Transferring a Tradition: 'Abd al-Ra'uf al-Singkili's Rendering into Malay of the Jalalayn Commentary*, Berkeley, CA: Centers for South and Southeast Asian Studies, University of California.

—— (2001) *Islam and the Malay-Indonesian World: Transmission and responses*, London: Hurst & Co., 125–32, 161–5

Rinkes, D.A. (1909) *Abdoerraoef Van Singkel*, Heerenveen: Hepkema.

See also: hafiz; **al-Suyuti**; *tafsir* **in early Islam**

PETER G. RIDDELL

SOLOMON
see: **Sulayman**

SORCERER
see: **sahara**

SPEAKER
see: **natiq**

SPOUSE
see: **zawj**

STYLE IN THE QUR'AN

Rafael Talmon (2002: 220) draws our attention to the linguistic mechanism of Qur'anic Arabic and informs us that linguistic studies specific to the Qur'an are few but not detailed enough. Our present work, however, attempts to provide an insight into the stylistic and linguistic peculiarities of Qur'anic discourse. Western scholars who have been intrigued by these peculiarities include Fleischer, Reckendorf, Brockelmann, Ewald, and Nöldeke (Talmon, 2002: 348).

The Qur'an is characterized by Qur'an-bound stylistic features such as stylistic shift and presentation technique. Stylistic shift is a major linguistic property of Qur'anic discourse and is interrelated to exegesis. It takes different forms and is conditioned by various factors. The variation in Qur'anic style occurs at different levels of language such as word level or sentence level. The Qur'an also adopts the stylistic mechanism of presentation of leitmotifs and tenets of faith which are referred to as *mabadi' al-iman*. Let us first investigate some of the major stylistic features of the Qur'an.

Word order

In Qur'anic discourse, we encounter two *ayas* whose linguistic structure is different due to the different word order in each of them, as in:

qul la amliku linafsi naf'an wala dharran
(Say, 'I do not possess for myself any benefit or harm'). (7.188)

qul la amliku linafsi darran wala naf'an
(Say, 'I do not possess for myself any harm or benefit'). (10.49)

The stylistic variation is represented by the occurrence of the word (*naf'an* – benefit), first in 7.188 and its occurrence at the end in 10.49. This change in word order is attributed to the surrounding lexical environment of each *aya*. The word (*naf'an*) signifies a positive meaning; it has occurred first because other positive meaning words have also occurred first as in 7.178 and 7.188 where positive meaning words also occur before negative meaning words – *yahdi* (to guide) comes before *yadhlil* (to misguide), and *khayr* (welfare, wealth) occurs before *su'* (harm). Similarly, the word *darran* (harm) occurs first in 10.49 because of the lexical influence of other *ayas* such as 10.18 and 10.107 in which (*darran*) has occurred four times before the word *naf'an*.

Word form

This refers to the grammatical function of the word and has a direct impact upon the underlying meaning of the *aya*. For instance, some words occur in the verb form while others occur in the active participle form as in 53.59–61. The stylistic change lies in the occurrence of the verbs *'ajaba* (to wonder), *dahika* (to laugh) and *baka* (to cry) in *ayas* 59–60, while the active participle *samid* (heedless, lost in vain amusements) is used in *aya* 61; the active participle is referred to in Arabic as *ismu al-fa'il*. In order to highlight the continuity of the action of heedlessness and that this group of people are repeatedly wasting their time in vanities, the active parti-

ciple is employed to echo this meaning. However, this same group of people occasionally do other things such as wondering curiously with a strange feeling against something, laughing at times and not crying, i.e. not feeling sorry for their negative curiosity. These occasional actions are stylistically best represented by a verb rather than by any other linguistic form.

Shift

Shift is referred to in Arabic as *iltifat*, which is a recurrent linguistic property of Qur'anic discourse used as rhetorical ornamentation. The most common form is pronoun shift, as in:

alam tara ila rabbika kayfa madda al-arda...thumma ja'alna al-shamsa ... thumma qabadnahu ilayna ... wahuwa alladhi ja'ala lakum ... linuhyi bihi ... wahuwa alladhi maraja al-bahrayn ...
(Have you not considered your Lord how He extends the shadow ... Then We made the sun ... Then We held it in hand ... It is He who has made for you ... that We may bring to life thereby ... It is He who has released the two seas ...). (25.45–53)

where a stylistic shift in pronoun has taken place from the second person pronoun in *rabbuka* (your Lord) to first person plural in *ja'alna* (We made), and in *qabadna* (We held) to third person singular pronoun in *huwa* (He), to first person plural in *nuhyi* (We bring to life), to third person singular pronoun in *huwa* (He).

Selection of words

Some *ayas* are structurally identical but stylistically different due to the employment of different words, as in:

tilka hududu Allahi fla taqrabuha (These are the limits set by Allah, so do not approach them. (2.187)

tilka hududu Allahi fla ta'taduha (These are the limits of Allah, so do not transgress them. (2.229)

where the stylistic variation is attributed to the selection of the verb *taqrabu* (to approach) in 2.187 and the employment of a different verb – *ta'tadu* (to transgress) – in 2.229. This stylistic change is conditioned by the context of each *aya*. In *aya* 187, the context refers to a serious prohibition stated by the Islamic legal ruling *wala tubashiruhunna wa 'antum 'akifuna fi al-masajid* (Do not cohabit with your wives as long as you are staying for worship in the mosques (2.187)), which does not allow a husband to cohabit with his wife in the mosque. This serious warning is introduced by the verb *taqrabu*. However, the context of *aya* 229 also refers to a warning but of a less serious nature. *Aya* 229 highlights the command that urges the divorced couple to be fair with each other regarding the presents given by the husband to his wife and that they both should not transgress beyond the allowed bounds; therefore, the verb *ta'tadu* is stylistically more appropriate.

The context of situation also has an impact upon the selection of words that occur at the end of the *aya*, as in:

dhalikum wassakum bihi la'allakum ta'qilun; (6.151)

dhalikum wassakum bihi la'allakum tadhakkarun; (6.152)

dhalikum wassakum bihi la'allakum tattaqun; (6.153)

(This has He instructed you that you may use reason/remember/become righteous.)

These three *ayas* undergo stylistic shift where three different words – *ta'qilun* (to use reason), *tadhakkarun* (to remember), *tattaqun* (to become righteous) – occur at the end of the *aya* due to their different contexts of situation and their relevant moral lesson. The word *ta'qilun* is employed in 6.151 and urges the reader to use his/her intellect pertaining the five commandments (to observe monotheism, to respect one's own parents, not to kill one's own children, to avoid shameful deeds and not to commit murder), i.e. these can be observed by people with sound reasoning. The context of 6.152 refers to four different commandments (not to take away the orphan's property, to be just, to give just witness and to fulfill the covenant of God), i.e. things which must be remembered. Finally 6.153, by contrast, highlights the leitmotif of righteousness and urges the reader to observe it and avoid what goes against it; therefore, the word (*tattaqun*) is stylistically and semantically most appropriate for this *aya*.

Rhyme

Stylistic shift also occurs in the Qur'an due to the different phonetic co-text (the surrounding textual environment) of the *ayas*. Let us consider the following examples:

rabbi musa wa harun (7.122)

rabbi harun wa musa (20.70)

Although the two *ayas* have the same meaning, each *aya* ends with a different name: 7.122 ends with *harun*, which is the same as for 26.48, while 20.70 ends with *musa*. This is attributed to the phonetic co-text where in *sura* 7 the assonance, i.e. the rhyme of the *ayas*, is the /un/, while the rhyme of *sura* 20 is the long vowel /a/.

Phonetic co-text also applies to the following examples:

Wa 'indahum qasiratu al-tarfi 'in (With them will be women limiting their glances, with large, beautiful eyes) (37.48)

Wa 'indahum qasiratu al-tarfi atrab (With them will be women limiting their glances and of equal age) (38.52)

where the macro phonetic environment surrounding each of the two *ayas* has influenced the lexical variation from *'in* (large, beautiful eyes) to *atrab* (of equal age) in order to achieve symmetrical rhyme and phonetic compatibility at *aya*-final level that can match the previous rhyme of each *aya*.

Wording

Stylistic variation can also result from the different wording of different *ayas* which have an identical meaning, as in:

man dha alladhi yashfa'u 'indahu illa b'idhnih (Who is that can intercede with Him except by His permission). (2.255)

ma min shafi'in illa min ba'di idhnih (There is no intercessor except after His permission). (10.3)

wala tanfa'u al-shafa'atu 'indahu illa liman adhina lahu (Intercession does not benefit with Him except for one whom He permits). (34.23)

These stylistically different *ayas* signify the same leitmotif of intercession that cannot be accepted without God's leave. Although each *aya* is expressed in a different style they all have the same signification. here are some more examples:

thumma tuwaffa kullu nafsin ma kasabat (Then every soul will be compensated for what it earned). (2.281)

watuwaffa kullu nafsin ma 'amilat (And every soul will be fully compensated for what it did). (16.111)

wawuffiyat kullu nafsin ma 'amilat (And every soul will be fully compensated for what it did). (39.70)

walitujza kullu nafsin bima kasabat (So that every soul may be recompensed for what it has earned). (45.22)

The above four *ayas* are stylistically distinct but semantically identical. They all signify the same leitmotif of divine justice on the Day of Judgement and that every individual will only reap the fruit of his or her deeds.

Grammaticality

The rules of grammaticality as followed in the Qur'an are at times broken. This means that the grammatical form of some *ayas* does not conform to the grammatical norms of Arabic, as in:

wa akhadha alladhina zalamu al-sayhatu (The shriek seized those who had wronged). (11.67)

According to Arabic grammar, this *aya* is grammatically inaccurate because the subject noun *al-sayhatu* (the shriek, the mighty blast) is in the feminine form while its verb *akhadha* (to seize) occurs in the masculine form. According to Arabic grammar, there has to be a gender agreement between the subject and its verb, i.e. when the subject is masculine, its verb should occur in the masculine form, and when it is feminine its verb needs to take the feminine form. In Qur'anic discourse, however, some *ayas* violate Arabic grammar because they employ false feminine nouns which are referred to in Arabic as *mu'annath ghayr haqiqi*. Therefore, the feminine subject noun *al-sayhatu* has an underlying meaning of the masculine noun *al-sawtu* (the mighty blast).

Another example of ungrammaticality is found in the following *aya*:

wa'in ta'ifatani min al-mu'minina iqtatalu (If two factions among the believers should fight each other) (49.9)

where the subject noun *ta'ifatani* (two factions) is employed in *al-muthanna* (the dual form) while its verb *iqtatalu* (to fight each other) occurs in the plural form; this is counter to the grammatical norms of Arabic and the verb should, therefore, be in the dual form also, i.e. *iqtatalata*. However, 49.9 is stylistically acceptable because the underlying meaning of the plural verb *iqtatalu* designates an implicit pronoun *hum* (they) which can be grammatically used to refer to either plural or dual.

Presentation

The Qur'an has an interesting presentation style of the four major tenets of faith, namely monotheism, prophethood, eschatology, and reward and punishment. These tenets of faith can occur in any one of the following forms:

1. a single tenet of faith is presented within an individual *aya*, such as 35.23;
2. more than one tenet of faith is presented within an individual *aya*, such as 40.3 where reward and punishment, monotheism and eschatology are presented;
3. more than one tenet of faith is presented in a series of interrelated *ayas*, such as 2.21–25, where monotheism is presented by *ayas* 21–22, prophethood by *aya* 23, and reward and punishment by *ayas* 24–25;
4. some tenets of faith are followed by specific leitmotifs, such as God's omnipotence and creative power, or reference to evocation, i.e. reference to previous disbelieving nations and God's wrath, as in 54.17 which refers to prophethood which is followed by evocative *ayas* 18–21 that refer to the people of 'Ad, and as in 57.1–3 that highlight monotheism and which is followed by *ayas* 4–6 that refer to the leitmotif of God's omnipotence and is followed by *ayas* 7–9 that highlight prophethood;
5. asseverative *ayas* are followed by a given tenet of faith, as in *sura* 53 which starts off with an asseverative *aya* 53.1 followed by *ayas* 2–4 that highlight prophethood;
6. tenets of faith that can be found in a single short *sura*, as in 101 where eschatology is presented by *ayas* 1–5, and reward and punishment are introduced by *ayas* 6–11; and
7. one tenet of faith dominates a single *sura*, as in 112 where monotheism is the only tenet of faith listed.

Further reading

Abdul-Raof, H. (2000) 'The Linguistic Architecture of the Qur'an', *Journal of Qur'anic Studies* 2, 2: 37–51.

al-Qurtubi, Abu 'Abd Allah Muhammad (1997) *'al-Jami' li Ahkam al-Qur'an'*, Beirut: Dar al-kitab al-'arabi, Vols 1–20.

Talmon, R. (2002) 'Grammar and the Qur'an', in *EQ*, 345–67.

al-Zamakhshari, Abu al-Qasim Jar Allah (1995) *al-Kashshaf*, Beirut: Dar al-kutub al-'ilmiyya, Vols 1–4.

See also: **art and the Qur'an; inimitability; language and the Qur'an**

HUSSEIN ABDUL-RAOF

SUBHAN

This word is used only for Allah (God), and characterizes him. It consists of the Arabic letters *sin/be/ha*, and its origin is the word *subha'tu*, which means glorifying, praying and non-obligatory worship. The word *subhan* expresses the overwhelming might of God who is beyond all imperfections and attributes associated with human and non-human beings, and the sovereignty of God in granting bounty to whomsoever he wishes for as long as he wants.

The phrase is usually used with the possessive suffix *i*. *Subhani* means that which belongs to God and which is associated with God – just like the phrases *ilahi* and *rabbani*. In *tasawwuf*, it takes the meaning *ana'l-Haqq* (I am the creative truth). *Subhanallah* (Glory be to God) is used to reject a heresy that is incommensurate with greatness of Allah. Therefore, this refers more to God himself, and distinguishes the Creator from the created, thus 'So glorify the name of your Lord Most High' (69.52). *Subhanallah* is used to indicate that 'You are the way You are; I believe in You as You are and all praise be to You.' The phrase *subhanallah* that contains the holy attribute *jalal* (Divine Majesty) is indicative of the how far the servants and creatures are from Allah: 'Glorified is He, Who is high above all that they say! – Exalted and Great' (17.43). This is *tasbih* (glorification) and *dhikr* (invocation) of Allah; 'The seven heavens and the earth, and all that is therein, declare His glory: there is not a thing but celebrates His praise; And yet you understand not how they declare His glory! Verily He is Oft-Forbearing, Most Forgiving!' (17.44; also 16.48; 24.41; 57.1; 59.1; etc.). However, everything praises Allah in its own particular way, and we may not be quite aware of it (Rumi, 1993: lines 1495–1500). *Subhanallah* rectifies faith since invocation of a divine name brings about the remembrance of God and an awakening from the state of forgetfulness.

References and further reading

Mir, M. (1987) *Dictionary of Qur'anic Terms and Concepts*, New York and London: Garland Publishing Inc.

Nasr, S.H. (1999) *Ideals and Realities of Islam*, Lahore: Suhail Academy.

Rumi, M.C. (1993) *Masnawi*, Ankara: Publications of the Ministry of Culture.

Schimmel, A. (1975) *Mystical Dimensions of Islam*, Chapel Hill, NC: University of North Carolina Press.

Schuon, F. (1999) *Understanding Islam*, trans. D.M. Matheson, Lahore: Suhail Academy.

AHMET ALBAYRAK

SUFFERING

The question as to why there is evil or suffering in the world (why it occurs within God's creation) is of central importance to all religions. In the case of Islam its scripture makes it clear that this life is short and that the life of the hereafter is more enduring and everlasting. For those who fail to realize this and instead cultivate or develop strong attractions exclusively for things of this world, they do nothing but set themselves up for disappointment and suffering. The Qur'an puts it more dramatically by declaring that those who care for the life of this world and its bounties will be repaid in full for all that they did in this life and shall not be deprived of their just due– but their repayment in the hereafter will be nothing but torment, for everything they have done is in vain and worthless (11.15–16).

The latter verse refers to a major reason for the existence of suffering – the attachment to worldly things. This, however, does not explain why a kind, merciful God allows for all manner of suffering to exist in the first place. It fails to explain undeserved suffering, as in the case of torture, intractable diseases, natural disasters and climatic tragedies. Does God permit these instances of suffering to take place, despite being a God of love and compassion/mercy, or do they happen against his will? The latter makes no sense if God is all-powerful and in control of the universe. Which leads to: is suffering part of the purpose of God?

Types of suffering

Suffering comes in many forms:

1. suffering of those who are close to God;
2. suffering designed to spare one from more severe suffering;
3. suffering of those who stray from the straight and narrow (Islam, 1987: 127–8).

The first type of suffering is meant to deepen the faith of believers by testing their patience and steadfastness in the face of life's challenges. The Qur'an makes it clear that those who are dear to God suffer severe trials as a test of their faith and as a way of sparing them from the torments of the hereafter. According to the teachings of the Qur'an all the tragedy, affliction, grief, loss of wordly goods and fear that we may go through in this life are meant to test our patience in adversity (2.155; 21.35). For those who succeed in the test and continue doing good deeds in their life God promises them boundless joy, happiness and his everlasting pleasure (2.112).

The Qur'an sees suffering as purposeful (as contained within God's omnipotence); it fosters a religious disposition, forms character and helps to distinguish between the true and the false (Bowker, 1970: 111). The ungrateful or thankless ones despair whenever misfortune befalls them and forget their previous good fortune, whereas the sincere ones remain steadfast irrespective of whatever life's challenges come their way (11.9–11).

The second type of suffering seeks to jolt some people from their complacency by calling their faith into question. This could be a warning sign for them to mend their ways and thus save themselves from the more severe punishment that would otherwise await them in the next life. The test in this case is for the good of the type of believer who expects only good fortune, who doesn't know how to handle misfortune and who seeks to blame others for it. The Qur'an considers such a believer to be one whose faith wavers between belief and disbelief, especially in the event of a setback (22.11).

The Qur'anic example of the reverse suffered by the early Muslims at Uhud after the success at Badr serves to illustrate this point in more general terms. Some of those involved in the Uhud campaign did not realize that the setback they suffered was possibly an outcome of their own actions or their own wrong choices (4.78–79).

The question remains though as to why the defeat at Uhud resulted in even the innocent (who had not disobeyed the Prophet's orders) suffering injury and even death. The Qur'an is very clear in its response: for the innocent the Uhud episode was a trial or a test of their faith; it was not some form of punishment. As for those believers who died during this and other military campaigns, they were considered to have attained the lofty status of martyrdom, to have achieved the death of the truly virtuous (3.193).

The final type of suffering aims at dispensing justice by punishing evildoers or making an example of them as a warning to others. The Qur'an provides many examples of the consequences of sin through the instrumentality of natural disasters (Noah, Lot, Hud, Moses). It also elaborates as a general rule that, to every community to which a prophet had been sent, its people were visited with misfortune and hardship so that they might humble themselves. Yet, if after the misfortune was lifted and prosperity followed, the wicked ones returned to their evil ways, by doing so they doomed their communities to destruction (7.94–96).

Even when it seems that the wicked do prosper, and the believers do not, this is only in the short term, with the balance restored in the afterlife. As the Qur'an states: 'There are men who say: "Our Lord: give us [the bounties] in this world"': But they will have no portion in the Hereafter' (2.200). This makes it clear that while the wicked may seem to prosper, in the end they will be overtaken by suffering: 'the life of this world is alluring to those who reject Faith, and they scoff at those who believe. But the righteous will be above them on the Day of Resurrection: God bestows His abundance without measure on whom He will' (2.212).

From the Qur'anic point of view the fact of suffering does not negate belief in God's mercy and omnipotence; rather, it illustrates the instrumental function of suffering.

> And thus it is: if We let man taste some of Our grace, and then take it away from him – behold, he abandons all hope, forgetting all gratitude [for Our past favours]. And thus it is: if We let him taste ease and plenty after hardship has visited him, he is sure to say, 'Gone is all evil from me!' – for, behold, he is given to vain exultation, and glories only in himself. [And thus it is with most men –] save those who are patient in adversity and do righteous deeds: it is they whom forgive-

ness [of sins] awaits, and a great reward. (11.9–11)

This attitude of acceptance or patient endurance of life's trials is recommended as nothing is to be gained by despair (or, worse, giving up and committing suicide, something which is prohibited). One should place one's trust in the overriding control and mercy of God. This can be achieved through cultivating an attitude of complete submission to God: 'Say: truly my prayer, my sacrifice, my living, my dying belong to God, the Lord of the Universe' (6.162).

Other types of suffering: voluntary and involuntary

Does this mean then that in the face of life's trials one should resign oneslf to one's misfortunes and seek no change in their situation? This can hardly be the case given that there are particular instances of suffering and injustices that can be removed. This is the whole purpose behind the Qur'anic call for the establishment of a just society based on righteousness. According to the Qur'an, the need to alleviate other people's suffering (including that of the kin, orphans, the needy, the wayfarer, the begger, the slave, etc.) is what constitutes piety whereas, for instance, miserliness is a perversion of human nature (2.177).

Whatever injustice or evil one may see in the world, this should not lead one to think that this is an indication that God is not in control or that Satan had the upper hand in creation. The Qur'an provides a mythological content to the experience of temptation symbolized by Satan's fall (followed by respite given to him to continue to tempt and to provoke humans to evil). Yet, despite all this, God is still in control and the

Satanic principle serves only a purpose or function accorded to it by God. Ultimately therefore final victory belongs to God alone, who is the supreme judge and arbiter of our affairs, as the following verse indicates: 'Those who wish for the [things of] the Hereafter, and strive therefore with all due striving, and have Faith, they are the ones whose striving is acceptable [to Allah]. Of the bounties of thy Lord We bestow freely on all – these as well as those: the bounties of thy Lord are not closed' (17.19–20). This is what is promised to righteous people, that is, those who do not crave the transitory things of this life (by making them the sole object of life) but who instead strive and devote their lives to attaining the more enduring things of the hereafter. In this context, we may mention that some Muslims (the mystics of Islam) have taken this striving a step further in their contemplative love of God by seeking voluntary privation. This is a form of suffering which seeks to purify the heart and empty it of all wordly concerns by distancing oneself from worldly things.

Another question of import is whether humans can atone for sins by having others suffer on their behalf. According to the Qur'an no person (irrespective of how saintly or godly they may be) can bear the burdens/sins of others (53.38–40). This eliminates the need for a saviour figure (crucial to Christianity), the crucifixion or sacrifice of whom serves the purpose of atonement for the sins of humanity (as with Jesus Christ or Mithras in ancient Persia). In fact, the Qur'an rejects the whole doctrine of vicarious atonement. There are a number of reasons for this: (1) humans are not born with original sin (the merciful God had forgiven Adam and Eve for their specific sin); (2) God had tested Abraham by requiring him to sacrifice his son (and having passed this test by

being ready to do what God had commanded him to do Abraham was then asked to sacrifice a ram instead); and (3) the Qur'an emphasizes the doctrine of personal responsibility by which each person will be judged according to what they have earned on this earth. The latter point denies the possibility of any 'mediation' between the sinner and God.

In light of the above, the theological debates in the post-Qur'anic period between those who emphasized the omnipotence of God and those who emphasized humankind's free will, seem to miss the point. The issues of intercession (only hinted at in the Qur'an; see, for instance, 2.255, the Throne verse) and predetermination receive far more coverage (than is warranted by a careful reading of the Qur'an) in the prophetic traditions which (at least on the question of human responsibility) reflect the political mood of the Umayyad period. Despite al-Ash'ari's attempts to reconcile God's omnipotence with human responsibility, ultimately the problem of suffering remained more a fact of life than a matter to be settled by academic debate.

There still remains the question of undeserved suffering as in instances of torture, the mistreatment of children, miscarriages of justice, economic exploitation, intractable/congenital diseases, mass killings, death through natural disaster, plague, childbirth, drowning, as well as cruelty to animals. How should these be explained? One first has to separate suffering caused by human action (for instance, physical and mental abuse, mistreatment of children, cruelty to animals, and so on), from suffering as a consquence of 'natural' disaster (plague, childbirth or drowning). In the case of the former, every effort should be made to alleviate or, better, prevent such suffering. In the latter cases the *hadith* literature makes it clear that such people die as martyrs (Muslim, *Mishkat*, 18). Further, some forms of suffering, such as sickness (which calls for patience), offer a means to atone for previous sins. And some natural disasters – while they could be used as a demonstration of God's wrath – are a consequence of the operation of natural laws.

There is one more dimension to suffering (unique to Shi'ism) which needs to be mentioned and which focuses on the martyrdoms of 'Ali, al-Hasan and al-Husayn. The whole complex of ideas about the deaths of these infallible Imams brings Shi'ism close to Christianity in terms of their shared belief in redemptive suffering, that is, in the saving effects of martyrdom (for Shi'ism) and crucifixion (for Christianity). Jesus for the Christians and Husayn for the Shi'is emerged victorious despite suffering cruel and humiliating defeats or deaths at the hands of their enemies. The benefits of such innocent suffering created in both faiths a messianic belief in the restoration of peace, goodwill and justice which is associated with the Second Coming.

The Qur'anic view of suffering remains focused on the power of God and the responsibility of human beings. This means that suffering is caused by ourselves (motivated by our attraction to worldly things, power and disobedience to God). Ultimately, however, suffering is a fact of life, a reality of creation, which is of necessity situated outside God. The Qur'an tells us that the present life – with all its joys and hardships (90.4) – is merely transitory and illusionary, in contrast to the next life which is blissful and everlasting. Realizing this, a discerning believer therefore seeks the good in this world *and* the good in the next life, which is characterized by the absence of suffering of any kind.

Further reading

Asad, M. (trans.) (1980) *The Message of the Qur'an*, Gibraltar: Dar al-andalus.

Bowker, J. (1970) *Problems of Suffering in Religions of the World*, Cambridge: Cambridge University Press.

Islam, A. (1987) *The Nature of Self, Suffering and Salvation*, Allahabad, India: Vohra Publishers & Distributors.

Robson, J. (trans.) (1975) *Mishkat al-Masabih*, Kashmir Bazar, Lahore: Sh. Muhammad Ashraf, Vols I and II.

See also: **persecution;** *sabr*

ABDIN CHANDE

SULAYMAN

Prophet and third king of the Israelites, mentioned by name seventeen times in the Qur'an. 27.16 says that Sulayman (Solomon) was the heir of David, and Muslim exegetes relate that although David had other sons, Solomon was the only one who inherited his prophetic mantle. Solomon is described by Muslim historians and exegetes as one of only four kings who ruled over the entire earth.

Solomon and the animals

The Qur'an attributes to Solomon the ability to speak with animals: 27.16 refers to Solomon's ability to speak the language of birds, and Muslim exegetes relate his translation of conversations between birds. The Hoopoe (*hud-hud*), in particular, is singled out as the messenger of Solomon: 27.20–28 narrates Solomon's conversation with a hoopoe whom he had sent to spy on the Queen of Sheba. The bird is also said to have scouted out water ahead of the armies of Solomon when they were travelling.

Verses 27.18–19 refer to an encounter between Solomon's armies and a valley of ants, and implies that Solomon is able to understand the speech of an ant that comments on his armies. Some exegetes detail that the ant's name was Jiris, and that on another occasion Solomon observed and overheard the ant praying to God for rain.

Solomon and the Queen of Sheba

Verses 27.29–44 narrate the encounter between Solomon and Bilqis, the Queen of Sheba. Although the name Bilqis does not appear in the Qur'an, she is said to have been the daughter of a South Arabian king and a female *jinn* named Rihana bt. al-Sakan. Exegetes report that Solomon sent a letter with the hoopoe to the queen asking her to acknowledge God and the kingship of Solomon. Before the queen arrived in Jerusalem, Solomon sent one of his magical servants to fetch the queen's throne so that she could be asked about it upon her arrival. The throne is said to have been encrusted with all types of gems, gold and jewels, and, according to Muslim pilgrimage accounts, was later used to make one of the pillars of the Umayyad mosque in Damascus.

27.44 describes the fantastic tower built by Solomon, made of glass under which water flowed so that the queen thought she was walking on water when she entered. Some exegetes claim that when she uncovered her legs (see 27.44) Solomon saw that they were hairy and was repulsed. In some accounts, Solomon marries Bilqis, but in others he does not. Solomon is said to have ordered the *jinn* under his control to construct three castles – Ghamdan, Salihin and Baytun in the Yemen – for the queen.

Solomon's control of the wind, demons and *jinn*

Muslim traditions attributes to Solomon control over the wind, demons and the *jinn* (21.81–82; 34.12–13; 38.34–40). The wind is said to have carried Solomon across the face of the earth so that he could go from Damascus to Istakhar to Marw to Balkh in a single day. Consistent with contemporaneous Jewish and Christian tradition, Muslim exegetes also explain that Solomon used the demons and *jinn* under his control to build Jerusalem and the special temple there. Other cities, such as Palmyra and Istakhar, are also said to have been built by the demons and *jinn* under Solomon's control.

It is said that Solomon had a special ring with which he controlled the demons and the *jinn*. Muslim exegesis on the 'test' mentioned in 38.34 relate that this ring was once stolen and a special demon ruled in Solomon's place for a period of time until Solomon was able to retrieve the ring after it was swallowed by a fish.

Judgement and the wives of Solomon

21.78–79 refers to the judgement of both David and Solomon, and Muslim exegesis relates cases in which Solomon's judgement is supposed to have bested that of David.

Solomon is reported to have had 1,000 women including both wives and concubines. According to the Prophet Muhammad, the king is reputed to have claimed that he could sleep with and impregnate seventy women in one night.

The death of Solomon

34.14 relates that the death of Solomon was indicated by an earthworm which ate at his staff. Muslim exegetes explain that Solomon died while leaning against the staff, and that the *jinn* only became aware of his death and their freedom from his control when a worm finally ate through the staff causing Solomon to fall over. It is also reported that his death took place while the demons and *jinn* were still in the process of building Jerusalem, and that they continued to build the city until they discovered that Solomon had died.

Further reading

Chastel, P. (1916–17) 'La légende de la reine de Saba', *Revue de l'Histoire des Réligions* 119: 204–25; 120: 27–44; 160–74.

Clapp, N. (2001) *Sheba: Through the desert in search of the legendary queen,* New York: Ballantine.

Duling, D.C. (1984) 'The Legend of Solomon the Magician in Antiquity: Problems and perspectives', *Proceedings of the Eastern Great Lakes Biblical Society* 4: 1–22.

Lassner, J. (1993) *Demonizing the Queen of Sheba: Boundaries of gender and culture in postbiblical Judaism and medieval Islam,* Chicago: University of Chicago Press.

Pritchard, J. (ed.) (1974) *Solomon and Sheba,* London: Phaidon.

Rösch, A. (1880) *Die Königin von Saba als Königin Bilqis,* Leipzig.

Salzberger, G. (1907) *Die Salomo-Sage in der semitischen Literatur,* Berlin.

See also: **Bilqis; *hud-hud***

BRANNON WHEELER

SUNNA

Sunna (pl. *sunan*) is derived from the root s/n/n/(*sanna–yasunnu–sannan*). The verb has various meanings: to sharpen, whet, hone, grind (something); to mould, shape, form; to prescribe, introduce, enact, establish (a law, a custom); to indent, jag, notch (something); to grow teeth or cut one's teeth, to grow old, to age; to take, follow (a course or way). The noun *sunna* means habitual practice, customary procedure or action, norm, or usage sanctioned by tradition.

During the times when the Qur'an was revealed, *sunna* was used, besides other meanings, to describe the original, continuous and standard way of behaving (both good or bad) in the sight of the Arabs (Özsoy, 1994: 53). Even though the word was used to denote both good and bad deeds during the early stages of Islam, after its specific application to the actions of the Prophet, describing negative actions such as *bidʿa* (innovation) came to be employed in opposition to *sunna*. In the first centuries, in addition to the Prophet's actions, *sunna* also included the actions of the Companions and what was done to oppose *bidʿa*. The theologians also defined *sunna* as that which is opposed to *bidʿa*. As time passed, in Islamic terminology, *sunna* came to mean the *sunna* of the Prophet, which contained his actions.

During the early centuries, different meanings were ascribed to *sunna* and *hadith*; *sunna* was used to describe the actions of the Prophet whereas *hadith* was employed for his verbal utterances only. Nevertheless, during this period the scope of *sunna* was wider than *hadith*, including not only the actions of the Prophet but also what society approved of. The scope of the meanings of *sunna* and *hadith* had gradually changed as the *ahl al-hadith* (People of Tradition) turned into a movement. As a result, the view that both were in fact the same gained precedence, but still *sunna* was accepted as a particular concept covering, specifically, the actions of the Prophet.

In its singular form, *sunna* is repeated in the Qur'an in fourteen different places, while the plural *sunan* occurs only twice. Of the fourteen occurrences, in eight it appears with the phrase *sunnat Allah* (the law, custom of Allah) (33.38, 62; 35.43; 40.85; 48.23). Although both concepts – *sunna* and Allah – were known by the *jahiliyya* Arabs (pre-Islamic Arabs), the phrase *sunnat Allah* was most likely introduced in the Qur'an. We can see that the word also occurs in other forms, such as *sunnatuna* (our way, law), *sunnat man qad arsalna qablak* ([This was Our] way with the messengers We sent before you) (17.77), *sunnat al-awwalin* (the way of those who went before them) (8.38; 15.13; 18.55; 35.43) and as the plural *sunan* (3.137; 4.26). None of these usages carries the conceptual meanings the word later acquired.

The Qur'an utilized *sunnat Allah* to describe Allah's way of dealing with previous societies. It is clear that other occurrences of the word, apart from one (4.26), have a similar meaning to *sunnat Allah*. In 4.26 the word occurs in the plural form, *sunan* (*sunan alladhina min qablikum*), which is similar to *sunnat al-awwalin* and can be translated as 'the way of those who went before them'. The verse in which the phrase occurs (4.26) comes after the verses dealing with family law. In this case, the most fitting meaning would be 'the ways prescribed for those before you' or 'the life styles of those before you' (Özsoy, 1994: 59–60).

If *sunna* is taken to mean 'law', the words in *sunnat al-awwalin* and *sunnat man qad arsalna qablak* should be taken as 'the law' and 'the law that is related to those before', and as 'Allah's law', referring to the law-giver, in *sunnatuna* and *sunnat Allah*. *Sunan*, however, refers directly to the 'laws' (Özsoy, 1994: 61).

Although the concept of *sunnat Allah* contains the meaning of law, the Qur'anic phrase does not describe the laws that govern the physical realm. However, by naming the physical laws as *ayat Allah*, the tradition aimed at placing them under the secure umbrella of the Qur'anic *sunnat Allah* to which the Qur'an refers as unchanging. Later, towards the end of the nineteenth century and as a result of the influence of positivism, the phrase *sunnat Allah* made a comeback as 'physical laws'. The purpose then was to establish the relationship between the fact that the universe operates according to certain physical laws and the principles of the Qur'an. But during the twentieth century, fresh intellectual developments led to the assertion that *sunnat Allah* defines the social laws in operation within society (Özsoy, 1994: 69–70).

In *ahadith*, *sunna* was used with a variety of meanings such as 'to be a pioneer in a good or bad deed, to open up an era, to show exemplary behaviour, way, custom, life style, way of behaving'. In a well-known narration, the Prophet is reported to have said: 'Whoever innovates a good deed in Islam, he will be rewarded for that action and share the reward of those who followed him in that forever' (Muslim, *Zakat* 69; see also, Muslim, '*Ilm* 15; Nasai, *Zakat* 64; Ahmad b. Hanbal, IV: 357, 361). In another *hadith*, the Prophet said: 'It [Ramadan] is such a month in which God commanded you to fast and I made it a *sunna* for you to pray during its nights (*Shahrun katab Allah alaykum siyama wa sanantu lakum qiyama*)' (Ibn Maja, *Iqama* 173; Nasai, *Siyam* 40; Ahmad b. Hanbal, I: 191). One *hadith* urges Muslims to stick to the practices of the Prophet and of the Rightly-Guided Caliphs: 'I strongly recommend you to hold on firmly to my *Sunna* and of the Rightly Guided Caliphs, who will lead you to the right path (*Fa alaykum bi sunnati wa sunna al-khulafa al-rashidin al-mahdiyyin*)' (Abu Dawud, *Sunna* 5; Tirmidhi, '*Ilm* 16; Ibn Maja, *Muqaddima* 6; Darimi, *Muqaddima* 16; Ahmad b. Hanbal, IV: 126–7). Another *hadith* also warns those who turn away from *sunna*: 'He who wearies of my *sunna* does not belong to me (*fa man raghiba 'an sunnati fa laysa minni*)' (Bukhari, *Nika* 1).

Some reports indicate that *sunna* is the second source of Islamic practice next to the Qur'an: 'I left you two things to which if you hold onto firmly, you will not go astray: The Book of Allah [the Qur'an] and the *sunna* of His Prophet! (*taraktu fikum amrayn lan tadillu ma masaktum bihima: Kitab Allah and sunna nabiyyih*)' (Malik, *Qadar* 3). It is interesting to note that in some similar variations of the report, *sunna* is replaced with '*ahl al-bayt*' (the Prophet's family and their descendants) (Tirmidhi, *Manaqib* 31; Ahmad b. Hanbal, III: 59), while in others only the Qur'an (Muslim, *Hajj* 147) is mentioned. One can interpret this differentiation in the narrations as the multifaceted effects of political arguments in the development of *sunna*. Another commonly used example in showing the importance of *sunna* as the second referential source in Islam is the story of Mu'adh b. Jabal. Before sending him as governor to Yemen, the Prophet questioned him as to how he would solve a problem he might encounter there. He replied that first he would consult the Book of Allah, then the *sunna* of the Prophet. Upon further questioning, if neither was of any help, he said he would judge in the matter depending on his own reasoning. Hearing this response, the Prophet praised Allah by saying 'Praise be to Allah who granted success to the envoy of His Prophet' (Tirmidhi, *Ahkam* 3; Abu Dawud, *'Aqdiya* 11; Darimi, *Muqaddima* 20; Ahmad b. Hanbal, V: 236, 242).

As the conveyor of the revelation, there is nothing unusual about the Muslim acceptance of the Prophet as the religious authority right from the early stages of Islam. Even during his lifetime Muhammad's practices were regarded in parallel with the Qur'an. The practices of the Prophet were vital, particularly in the performance of prayers (*salat*). Besides, for a Muslim, the pre-Islamic usages and customs of Arabs, having either been approved directly or tolerated with partial rearrangement by the Prophet, were now Islamic principles. Thus, it would not be wrong to say that Arabic customs, with some prohibitions and corrections, have continued within the framework of *sunna* during the time of Islam too.

Depending on their fields of interest, Muslim scholars have defined *sunna* in varying ways. According to the *muhaddithun* (the Traditionists), it contains the information related to us as verbal utterances of the Prophet, actions he performed or approved of, and stories describing his bodily appearance and ethical behaviours. This understanding of *sunna* even includes the Prophet's good deeds and characteristics prior to his receiving *nubuwwa* (mission of prophecy).

In the eyes of the jurisprudents, the sayings and actions of the Prophet, which have evidential value, can be called the *sunna*. Because for them *sunna* is one of the foundational sources of Islam, bodily features and ethical characteristics cannot be considered part of *sunna*. As an illustration of this understanding, al-Amidi (631/1233) cites two different definitions. According to one, *sunna* is the extra prayers ascribed to the Prophet. According to the other, *sunna* includes the unrecited (*ghayr matluww*), ordinary, legal evidence reported of the Prophet. This second definition covers the sayings and actions of the Prophet and details of those things of which he approved (al-Amidi, I: 169).

According to the jurists (*fuqaha*), *sunna* is what the Prophet had established with his words and actions excepting *fard* (obligations) and *wajib* (necessities). In this regard, *sunna* as the sayings, actions and approvals of the Prophet is accepted as the elucidation of the Qur'an and is in parallel with it. For instance, al-Shafi'i considers the Qur'an and *sunna* as equally binding sources (al-Shafi'i, n.d.:104–5, 471).

There are various views as to when '*sunna*' or 'the *sunna* of the Prophet' started to be used within a legal context. 'The *sunna* of the Prophet' is mentioned in a couple of places in *al-Muwatta* of Malik b. Anas (179/795) (Malik, *Faraid* 4; *Qadar* 3; *Bay'a* 3). Schacht maintains that at the beginning of the second/eighth century, the Iraqis conceptualized the political and theological meaning of the term 'the *sunna* of the Prophet' into a legal concept. They identified this legal understanding of *sunna* with the local, narrow understanding of '*sunna*' which represents the idealized practice of a local group and of the doctrine of the scholars who belong to this group (Schacht, 1986: 43). But Schacht's views of *sunna* have been criticized. Fazlur Rahman also developed the concept of the 'living *sunna*' which includes both the Prophetic Tradition and the common values Muslims agree upon (*ijma'*) (Rahman, 1995: 44–5). Rahman believes that the specific content of the *sunna* of the early Islamic period was largely the product of Muslims. According to his reasoning, the creative power behind this reshaping was personal judgement (*ijtihad*), which took shape in the form of *ijma* under the general guidance of the Prophetic Tradition. He asserts then that the content of *sunna* and *ijma'* are the same (Rahman, 1995: 32). On his view, 'living *sunna*' is not a matter of forgery, but a process of interpretation and renewed expression of the Prophetic Tradition (Rahman, 1995: 90).

During the first two centuries of Islam, in the field of law (*fiqh*), within the general principles of a jurist (*faqih*), *sunna* was used with such a broad meaning as to include the sayings or doings of the Prophet, the Companions and of the first generations of Muslims.

Nevertheless, al-Shafi'i (204/820) scaled down such a wide-ranging understanding by limiting *hadith* to the sayings, deeds and attitudes of the Prophet and *sunna* with the Tradition of the Prophet (Özafşar, 1998: 81). Even then, there are some differences among the legal schools (*madhahib*) as regards the definition of *sunna*. For the Hanafis, it is the practices of the Prophet and the Companions, whereas for the Shafi'is, it contains only the practices of the Prophet (al-Sarakhsi, 1953: 113–14).

Whether *sunna* was the result of revelation or not has been the subject of enquiry. The common view is that the origin of *sunna* was revelation; *sunna*, with all its varieties, was either the product of a revelation God sent to Muhammad or at least was elevated to the level of revelation once it was recognized for what it was. Thus, and according to one classification, revelation is divided into two categories: one which is recited (the Qur'an) and one which is not recited (*sunna*), one oral and one not. In another classification, the Qur'an is considered as 'open/clear revelation (*wahy jali*)' while the *hadith* are considered to be 'hidden revelation (*wahy khafi*)'. These classifications are part of the efforts to guarantee divine support for *sunna*. However, opinions are sharply divided. Because, while some scholars maintain that all of the *sunna* was the product of revelation, others believe that some parts of it were revealed and others were the personal judgement (*ijtihad*) of the Prophet. At the farthest extreme, some hold that *sunna* had nothing whatsoever to do with revelation. The view that the *sunna* was the result of revelation goes back as early as to the second/eighth century. Hassan b. 'Atiyya (130/748?), who was one of the teachers of al-Awza'i (157/774), says: 'Gabriel/Jibril revealed the whole of *sunna* to the Prophet just like he did the

Qur'an' (Darimi, *Muqaddima* 49). In some narrations, there are reports that the information about how worship should be conducted was revealed by Gabriel. For instance, the teaching of the times of the five daily prayers was one such revelation (Abu Dawud, *Sala* 2; Tirmidhi, *Mawaqit* 1).

The proponents of the view that *sunna* was revealed tried to base their opinions on some verses (6.50; 10.15; 16.44; 53.3). The fact that the Prophet had resolved these problems by relying on his personal judgement (*ijtihad*) in cases where there was no revelation does not contradict the view that *sunna* also originated with revelation. After all, it is generally accepted that the Prophet was always under divine guidance. Thus, when he made a mistake in his opinions, he was corrected by revelation.

The links between Qur'an and *sunna* with respect to abrogation is another problematic issue with which the scholars had to grapple. Muslims commonly accept that the Qur'an abrogated *sunna* but whether *sunna* can actually abrogate the Qur'an was a hotly debated issue. According to the Hanafis, a *mutawatir* (reported by numerous authorities) or *mashhur hadith* (vouched for by more than two Companions) can abrogate the Qur'an owing to the fact that a widely known *hadith* is almost as strong as an authentic one. The *ahad hadith* (reported by one transmitter), according to the reliable opinion of the scholars, cannot abrogate any of the verses, for it has a lower degree of authenticity/reliability. Even then, the examples cited for the abrogation of the Qur'an by *sunna* are usually related to specifying, limiting/ restricting, bringing in exceptions, not in the direct sense of the term. On the other hand, some scholars opposed the idea of *sunna* abrogating the Qur'an even in the case of an authentic or well-known *hadith*. Al-Shafi'i, for instance, is

one of the supporters of this view (al-Shafi'i, n.d.: 106; al-Amidi, III, 153). For al-Shafi'i, the Qur'an can only be abrogated by the Qur'an itself. His evidence is at 2.106: 'None of Our revelations do We abrogate or cause to be forgotten, but We substitute something better or similar' (al-Shafi'i, n.d.: 108).

The verses commanding people to obey the Prophet (5.92; 3.31, 32; 4.13–14, 59, 64–65, 80; 59, 7; 24.63; 33.36) are considered as the most important basis for the law-giving power of *sunna*. However, it should be noted that these verses refer directly to obedience to the Prophet; they include no clear reference to the legitimate power of the *sunna* collected in later times. The primary concern of the Muslims of later times must have been the authenticity of the *sunna*, not obedience to the Prophet.

Sunna was classified into several categories relying both on its structure and on the way it was transmitted. Structurally, it is divided into verbal, actual and approval categories. According to the Hanafis, depending on the number of transmitters in a chain, *sunna* is divided into three categories: *mutawatir*, *mashhur* and *ahad*. The rest of the scholars divide it into two: *mutawatir* and *ahad*. To them, *mashhur* is not a category on its own, it is rather regarded as *ahad*; this is because in *mashhur*, the number of transmitters from the first generation in the chain of transmission did not reach the level of *tawatur* (reported by many). They also categorise *sunna* as *al-gharib* (authentic, but resting on the authority of only one Companion), *al-'aziz* (an authentic tradition coming from two Companions) and *al-mustafid* (reported by more than two Companions).

The jurisprudents generally divide *sunna* into three categories, relying on its content and role: *sunna* as affirmative of the Qur'an; *sunna* as elaborative of the Qur'an; and *sunna* as the bearer of new judgements and rules (Ibn Qayyim, 1973, II, 307). According to another classification of the Hanafis, *sunna* is divided into two types. One is that to follow it is guidance while to disobey is erroneous since it involves rejecting the *sunna al-Huda* (the guiding *sunna*). Religious festival prayers, the call for prayer (*adhan*), and performing prayers with a congregation are considered to be covered by *sunna* and thus are required acts. There are also actions that are good to perform but which are not a sin to ignore (*sunna al-Zawaid*: the ordinary *sunna*). Many of the habitual actions of the Prophet, such as his way of sitting, getting up, dressing and riding, count among this group (al-Sarakhsi, I, 114).

As in the Sunni schools, for the Imami Shi'i also *sunna* is the second source of Islamic practice after the Qur'an. But their distinction between *hadith* and *sunna* is slightly different. The reports of either the Prophet or of any of the Twelve Imams are called *hadith*. The flawless people (those who are *ma'sum* – i.e. the Prophet or any of the Twelve Imams) and their sayings and actions are called *sunna*. They represent religious authority as the heirs of the Prophet.

From the early periods onwards, the notion of *sunna* represented the middle way and the Muslim consensus. Thus, some members of certain sects that defended the middle way against the extremists called themselves as *ahl al-'adl wa al-sunna* (People of Justice and *sunna*). Opinion varies as to when the phrase *ahl al-sunna* came into circulation. Even though it started to be used at a rather late period as a *madhhab* (sect) name, it is very likely that the phrase could have emerged towards the end of the first/seventh century. Hence, its appearance in a report by Muhammad b. Sirin (110/729) (Muslim, *Muqaddima* 7; Tirmidhi, *'Ilal* [*hadith* no. 47, V: 740]) indicates that it began to be used at an early period. During earlier times, although the term *ashab al-sunna* (The Partisans of *Sunna*) was also used, it did not refer to a particular sect. To define the majority of Muslims, *ahl al-sunna* (The People of *Sunna*) and similar names may have been used from the third/ninth century onwards (Fiğlali, 1986: 55).

Although there is no mention of the phrase *ahl al-sunna* in the Qur'an, to try to find some support for it there have been some vague interpretations of 3.106–107 by relying on a commentary from Ibn 'Abbas. The verses state that: 'On the Day when some faces will be [lit up with] white, and some faces will be [in the gloom of] black: To those whose faces will be black [will be said]: "Did ye reject Faith after accepting it? Taste then the penalty for rejecting Faith." But those whose faces will be [lit with] white, – they will be in [the light of] Allah's mercy: therein to dwell [for ever].' According to the report by Ibn 'Abbas, 'those whose faces will be black' are the *ahl al-bid'a* (People of Innovation) and 'those whose faces will be [lit with] white' are the *ahl al-sunna* (Ibn Taymiyya, 1986: V, 133–4). However, it is very unlikely that the verses have any implication whatsoever for any group or sect. The stories of reports from the Prophet about *ahl al-sunna* in some recent books are most probably forgeries (see for instance, Shahrastani, 1992: I, 5).

Today, the name of the largest Muslim sect is commonly known as *ahl al-sunna wa al-jama'a* (the People of the *Sunna* and the Community) or *ahl al-sunna* for short. The name connotes allegiance both to the practices of the Prophet and to the majority of Muslims. Although the term emerged out of political necessity, it manifested itself, in time, in the fields of theology and jurisprudence, due to the fact that the political parties had to establish bases for themselves in theological and moral/ legal fields. *Ahl al-sunna* established a common creed accepted by the majority of Muslims in rejection of the more fanatical paths offered by groups that emerged early in the history of Islam and refused to compromise in any way; the Kharijites are one such example. The most important feature of *ahl al-sunna* was to protect the *umma* against possible dangers by persuading the extremists to follow a more moderate path. The main theological school (*madhhab*), through the efforts of al-Ash'ari (324/935–36), al-Maturidi (333/ 944) and their followers, was able to unite and hold the *umma* to a commonly agreed middle ground by restraining the radical movements.

The schools of *ahl al-sunna*, although they differ on some issues, agree on many of the essentials of Islam, and this what separates them from other sects and allows them to be grouped together. Some of what they agree upon is as follows. They accept the first four caliphs as legitimate rulers, the Qur'an as God's uncreated word, that everything happens according to the divine decree, the reality of the attributes of God and their eternity, and that God will be seen in the hereafter with our eyes (Yavuz, 1994: 528).

There are various views about how wide the scope of the *ahl al-sunna* umbrella is. If one takes into consideration the fact that 90 per cent of Muslims follow the Salafiyya, the Ash'ariya and the Maturidiya, all of which are accepted as Sunni sects, it wuld seem to include the majority of Muslims.

References and further reading

Abbott, N (1957–67) *Studies in Arabic Literary Papyri*, 2 vols, Chicago: University of Chicago Press.

Ahmad b. Hanbal, Abu 'Abdullah b. Muhammad b. Hanbal al-Shaybani (1993) *al-Musnad*, Istanbul: Çağrı Yayınları.

Ahmad Hasan (1968) 'The *Sunna* – Its Early Concept and Development', *Islamic Studies* 7, 1: 47–69.

al-Amidi, 'Ali b. Muhammad (1402) *Al-Ihkam fi Usul al-Ahkam* (The judgement on the methodology of judgement), ed. 'Abd al-Razzaq 'Afifi, 2nd edn, Damascus and Beirut: al-Maktab al-Islami.

al-A'zami, M.M. (1996) *İslam Fıkhı ve Sünnet: Oryantalist J. Schacht'a Eleştiri* (Islamic Law and Sunna: A critique of the orientalist J. Schacht), trans. M Ertürk, Istanbul: İz Yayıncılık.

Abu Dawud, Sulayman b. Ash'as al-Sijistani (1992) *Sunan,* Istanbul: Çağrı Yayınları.

Abu Zaid, N.H. (2003) İmam Şafii ve Ortayol İdeolojisinin Tesisi' (Imam al-Shafi'i and the construction of the Middle Way Ideology), trans. S. Özer, in *Sünni Paradigmanın Oluşumunda Şafiinin Rolü* (The Role of al-Shafi'i in the formation of the Sunni Paradigm), ed. M.H. Kırbaşoğlu, Ankara: Kitabiyat.

al-Bukhari, Abu 'Abdullah Muhammad b. Ismail (1992), *al-Sahih*, Istanbul: Çağrı Yayınları.

al-Darimi, Abu Muhammad 'Abdullah b. Abdurrahman (1992) *Sunan*, Istanbul: Çağrı Yayınları.

Erdoğan, M. (1995) *Akıl-Vahiy Dengesi Açısından Sünnet* (Sunna from the Perspective of the Reason–Revelation Equilibrium), Istanbul: Marmara Üniversitesi İlahiyat Fakültesi Yayınları.

Erul, B. (1999) *Sahabenin Sünnet Anlayışı* (The Companions' Notion of Sunna), Ankara: Türkiye Diyanet Vakfı Yayınları.

Fığlalı, E.R. (1986) *Çağımızda İtikadi İslam Mezhepleri* (Doctrinal Islamic Sects in Our Age), 3rd edn, Istanbul: Selçuk Yayınları.

Görmez, M. (1997) *Sünnet ve Hadisin Anlaşılması ve Yorumlanmasında Metodoloji Sorunu* (The Question of Methodology in Understanding and Interpretation of Sunna and Hadith), Ankara: Türkiye Diyanet Vakfı Yayınları.

Graham, W (1975) *Divine Word and Prophetic Word in Early Islam*, The Hague: Mouton.

Guillaume, A. (1924) *The Traditions of Islam: An Introduction to the study of the hadith literature*, Oxford: Clarendon Press.

Ibn Maja, Abu 'Abdullah Muhammad b. Yazid al-Kazwini (1992) *Sunan*, Istanbul: Çağrı Yayınları.

Ibn Manzur, Abu al-Fadl Jamal al-Din Muhammad b. Mukarram b. 'Ali (1994) *Lisan al-'Arab* (The Language of the 'Arab), 3rd edn, Beirut: Dar al-fikr.

Ibn Qayyim al-Jawziyya, Abu 'Abdullah Shams al-Din Muhammad b. Abu Bakr (1973) *I'lam al-Muwaqqi'in an Rabb al-'Alamin*, ed. T. 'Abd al-Ra'uf Sa'd, Beirut: Dar al-jil.

Ibn Taymiyya, Abu al-'Abbas Taqiyy al-Din Ahmad b. 'Abd al-Halim al-Harrani (1986) *Minhaj al-sunna al-Nabawiyya* (The Method of the Prophetic Sunna), ed. M.R. Salim, Riyad: Jami'a al-Imam Muhammad.

Juynboll, G.H.A. (1983) *Muslim Tradition*, Cambridge: Cambridge University Press.

Kırbaşoğlu, M.H. (1993) *İslam Düşüncesinde Sünnet: Yeni bir yaklaşim* (Sunna in Islamic Thought: A new perspective), Ankara: Fecr Yayınevi.

Koçkuzu, A.O. (1985) *Hadislerde Nasih Mensuh* (The Abrogating and the Abrogated in Hadiths), Istanbul: Marmara Üniversitesi İlahiyat Fakültesi Yayınları.

Koçyiğit, T. (1985) *Hadis Istılahları* (Hadith Terminologies), 2nd edn, Ankara: Ankara Üniversitesi İlahiyat Fakültesi Yayınları.

Macit, N. (1995) *Ehl-i Sünnet Ekolünün Doğuşu: İlk öncüleri ve görüşleri* (The Emergence of Ahl al-Sunna School: First pioneers and their thoughts), Erzurum: İhtar Yayıncılık.

Malik b. Anas, Abu 'Abdullah (1992) *al-Muwatta'*, Istanbul: Çağrı Yayınları.

Muslim, Abu al-Husayn b. al-Hajjaj (1992) *Sahih*, ed. M.F. 'Abd al-Baqi, Istanbul: Çağrı Yayınları.

Nasr, S.H. (1989) 'Sunna and Hadith', in *Islamic Spirituality, Foundations*, London: SCM Press. Vol. I.

Özafşar, M.E. (1998) *Hadisi Yeniden Düşünmek: Fıkhi hadisler bağlamında bir inceleme* (Rethinking Hadith: An enquiry within the context of legal hadith), Ankara: Ankara Okulu Yayınları.

Özsoy, Ö. (1994) *Sünnetullah: Bir Kur'an ifadesinin kavramlaşmasi* (Sunnat Allah: Conceptualization of a Qur'anic expression), Ankara: Fecr Yayınları.

Rahman, F. (1995) *Tarih Boyunca İslami Metodoloji Sorunu* (Islamic Methodology in History), trans. S. Akdemir, Ankara: Ankara Okulu Yayınları.

Robson, J. (1951) 'Tradition, the Second Foundation of Islam', *Muslim World* 41: 22–33.

al-Salih, S. (1981) *Hadis İlimleri ve Hadis Istılahları* (Hadith Sciences and Hadith Terminologies), trans. M.Y. Kandemir, 3rd edn, Ankara: Diyanet İşleri Başkanlığı Yayınları.

al-Sarakhsi, Abu Bakr Muhammad b. Ahmad b. Abu Sahl (1372/1953) *Usul al-Sarakhsi* (The Methodology of al-Sarakhsi), ed. Abu al-Wafa al-Afgani, Cairo: Dar al-kutub al-'arabi.

Schacht, J. (1986) *İslam Hukukuna Giriş* (An Introduction to Islamic Law), trans. M. Dağ and A. Şener, Ankara: Ankara Üniversitesi İlahiyat Fakültesi Yayınları.

al-Shafi'i, Muhammad b. Idris (n.d.) *al-Risala* (The Treatise), ed. A.M. Shakir, Beirut: Dar al-Kutub al-'Ilmiyya.

al-Shahrastani, Abu al-Fath Muhammad b. 'Abd al-Karim (1992) *al-Milal wa al-Nihal* (Book of Religious and Philosophical Sects), ed. A.F. Muhammad, 2nd edn, Beirut: Dar al-kutub al-'ilmiyya.

Siba'i, M. (1989) *İslam Hukukunda Sünnet* (Sunna in Islamic Law), trans. K. Tunç, Istanbul: Girişim Yayınları.

al-Suyuti, Jalal al-Din Abdurrahman (1978) *al-Itqan fi Ulum al-Qur'an* (Perfection in the Qur'anic Sciences), 4th edn, Istanbul: Kahraman Yayınları.

al-Tirmidhi, Abu 'Isa Muhammad b. 'Isa (1992), *Sunan*, Istanbul: Çağrı Yayınları.

Yavuz, Y.Ş. (1994) 'Ehl-i Sünnet' (Ahl al-Sunna)', in *Türkiye Diyanet Vakfı İslam Ansiklopedisi* (Turkey Religious [Affairs] Foundation Encyclopaedia of Islam), Istanbul, Vol. X, 525–30.

Yusuf, S.M. (1966) *An Essay on the Sunna*, Karachi: Institute of Islamic Culture.

See also: **abrogation; Abu Hanifa; Ash'arites and Mu'tazilites;** *hadith*

ADNAN DEMIRCAN AND RIFAT ATAY

SUNNA AND ITS ROLE IN INTERPRETATION

What is the role of the *sunna* with respect to the Qur'an? The *sunna*, as well as detailing the way shown by God's Messenger to practice Islam perfectly, has two main functions. Like the Qur'an, the *sunna* is a source of legislation; it enjoins and prohibits, it sets down principles to establish religious obligations and necessities, and to determine what is lawful or unlawful. In addition to this function, the *sunna* interprets the Qur'an, Thus the phrase in the daily prescribed prayers: 'Guide us to the straight path, to the path of those you have blessed, not of those who incurred [Your] wrath, nor of the misguided' (*al-Fatiha*, 1.5–7). The verses mention two groups of people but do not say precisely who they are. The Prophet interpreted those who incurred God's wrath as the Jews and the misguided as the Christians.

The Jews, we are told, killed many of their prophets and through their character and materialistic tendencies have contributed much to moral corruption, social upheaval and sedition in the world. Although in the times of the prophets Moses, David and Solomon they too once played a guiding role, they were readily misled and incurred both God's wrath and public ignominy. Those who are of the same character, who follow their way whether they are Jews or not, are also included in the meaning of the phrase 'those who incurred [Your] wrath'.

As for the Christians, they at first obeyed Jesus and followed his way despite persecutions of the severest kind. They resisted both Jewish hypocrisy and Roman oppression. However, over time they succumbed to the influence of those who had already deviated from the chosen path. By the time Christianity came to be accepted as the official religion of the Roman Empire, many Christians had long gone astray and been deprived of their original scripture. Except for a few who remained devoted to the original creed of Jesus, the Christians had for a long time imported foreign elements into their religion. By interpreting the phrases 'not of those who incurred [Your] wrath, nor of the misguided', the Prophet identified them and clarified in what way and by what beliefs and deeds a man incurs God's wrath and goes astray. This is a warning for the Muslims not to follow in the footsteps of the Jews and Christians.

Out of many examples showing how the *sunna* interprets the Qur'an, we can also cite the following two. When the verse, 'Those who believed and did not mix their belief with wrongdoing: for them is security and they are those who are truly guided' (6.82) was revealed, the Companions, well aware of the meaning of wrongdoing, came to the Prophet in fear and said: 'Is there anybody among us who has never done wrong?' The Prophet explained: 'It is not as you think. It is as Luqman said to his son: "Do not associate any partners with God; surely, associating partners with God is a grave wrongdoing"' (31.13) (Bukhari, *Tafsir*: 31.1). 'A'isha (often called the Mother of the Believers) and Ibn Mas'ud are of the opinion that the noon prayer in the verse 'Attend the prayers without any omission and the middle prayer' (2.238) is in fact the afternoon prayer. Once 'A'isha ordered her servant to write a copy of the Qur'an for herself and reminded her: 'When you come to the verse, "Attend the prayers without any omission, and the middle prayer", inform me.' When this verse was to be copied out, 'A'isha dictated to her servant: 'Attend the prayers without any omission, and the mid-time prayer, the afternoon prayer.' She explained, 'This is what I heard from God's Messenger, upon him be peace and blessings' (*Tirmidhi*). Although there are some other interpretations of the mid-time prayer, 'A'isha and Ibn Mas'ud were certain that it is the afternoon prayer.

In addition to interpreting the ambiguities of the Qur'an, the *sunna* also expands on what is only briefly outlined in it. To cite a few examples. The Qur'an frequently orders: 'Perform the prayer accurately'. However, it does not mention how and when to perform it. Although some leading interpreters deduce the times of the prayer from some verses such as 'Perform the prayer correctly at the two ends of the day and nigh of the night; surely the good deeds remove the evil deeds' (11.114), the exact time of each prayer was established by the Prophet. He explains:

> On two occasions, the Archangel Gabriel led me in the five daily prayers at the Ka'ba. On the first, he performed the noon prayer at noon when the shadow of a thing was only as long as the base of it. When the shadow was as long as the thing itself, he performed the afternoon prayer. He performed the evening prayer at the time a fasting person breaks his fast, the late evening or night prayer when the dusk disappeared and the dawn prayer when it is no longer permissible for a fasting person to eat and drink. On the second occasion, he performed the noon prayer when the shadow was long and the afternoon prayer when it was twice as long. He performed the evening prayer at the time he had performed it on the first occasion, the night prayer when it was one third of the night, and the dawn prayer when it was lighter but before sunrise. Then he turned to me and said: 'O Muhammad, each of the five daily prayers should be performed between these two ends of its times as the Prophets before you did it.' (*Abu Dawud, Tirmidhi*)

In addition to the times of the daily prayers Muhammad taught his *umma* also the conditions of the prayer and the obligatory, necessary and commendable acts validating and ennobling it, as well as the acts invalidating and damaging it. Whether in words or through actions, he passed on to his *umma* all the details of the acts of worship – prayer, fasting,

alms-giving, pilgrimage and so on and, as he told them, 'Perform the prayer the way you see me praying.' He also said to them, 'Learn from me the rites and ceremonies of pilgrimage' after he actually performed it in the company of his Companions. If the Qur'an had elaborated the whole of the religious rites or the acts of worship down to their smallest details, the Book would have been many times its present size.

The *sunna* restricts general laws and commands in the Qur'an. For example, the Qur'an lays down the general principles of inheritance, without excluding anyone from it. But, when Fatima, the daughter of the Prophet, went to Abu Bakr, the first caliph, to transfer to her the heritage of her father, the latter replied: 'I heard God's Messenger say: "We, the community of the Prophets, do not leave anything to be inherited. What we leave is for charity."' This *hadith* excludes the prophets and their children from the law of inheritance. Likewise Muhammad decreed that a killer who is left a legacy should be disinherited (*Tirmidhi*). That is, if a man kills his parents, he cannot inherit from them; or if he kills his brother or uncle, he cannot inherit from them.

The *sunna* also specifies or particularizes what is general in the Qur'an. The Holy Book tells us: 'And the thief, male and female, cut off the hands of both, as a recompense for what they have earned, and a punishment exemplary from God; God is All-Mighty, All-Wise' (5.38). It is not clear in the command, however, for what value of stolen goods the hand of a thief should be cut off. Also, in the verse 'O believers, when you stand up to pray, wash your faces, and your hands up to elbows' (5.6), the part of the arm up to the elbows is included in the meaning of the hand. So, the Qur'an does not mention specifically what part of the 'hand' of a thief should be cut off. In addition, it does not specify under what circumstances this punishment should be applied. For example, 'Umar, the second caliph, did not apply it in time of famine.

It is the *sunna* that provides us with the details we need in order to apply Islamic law. The Qur'an decreed: 'O you who believe! Consume not your goods among yourselves in vanity [through theft, usury, bribery, hoarding and so on], except it be trade by mutual agreement between you' (4.29). Islam encourages trade as a way of making one's living, as long as it is carried out in accordance within the law. One condition is, as stated in the verse, 'mutual agreement'. However, Muhammad ordered: 'Do not sell fruits until their amount is definite on the tree [to determine what amount of them will be given as alms]' (*Bukhari, Muslim*). He also decreed: 'Do not go to meet peasants outside the market to buy the goods they will sell [Let them earn the market prices of their goods]' (*Muslim*).

God established general principles in the Qur'an and left their exposition and application in various circumstances to God's Messenger. He also authorized him to issue rulings as necessary and ordered the believers: 'Whatever the Messenger brings you, adopt it, and whatever he forbids you, refrain from it' (59.7). Hence the great significance of the *sunna* of the Prophet for Islam. It serves to help interpret the text of the Qur'an and also to provide living examples for the Islamic community to follow.

Further reading

Ali, K. (2004) 'A Beautiful Example: The Prophet Muhammad as a model for Muslim husbands', *Islamic Studies* 43, 2: 273–92.

See also: **money; *salat*; wealth**

OLIVER LEAMAN

SURA

Aya (pl. *ayat*) actually means 'sign' and is the shortest division of the Qur'anic text, i.e. a phrase or sentence. A *sura* (pl. *suwar*) means literally 'row' or 'fence'. It represents the main divisions of the Qur'anic text, i.e. a chapter or part, set apart from the preceding and following text. The Qur'an has 114 *suras* of unequal length, the shortest consisting of four and the longest of 286 *ayas*. All *suras* (with the exception of the ninth) begin with the *basmala* (*b'ismillah ir-rahman ir-rahim*) and there is evidence that this is not a late addition to the text but was there from the start of the reception of the revelations and their organization (27.30).

All the *suras* in the Qur'an have names, which serve as a heading. The names are often derived from an important or distinguishing word in the text itself or it is one of the first few words with which the *sura* begins. Both the order of the *ayas* within each *sura* and the arrangement of the *suras* themselves are said to have been determined by the Prophet under guidance from Gabriel in the year of his death, when Gabriel is supposed to have twice come to revise the text with him.

There are four kinds of *sura*:

al-tiwal (long ones): 2–10;

al-mi'un: *suras* with approximately 100 *ayat*: 10–35;

al-mathani: *suras* with less than 100 *ayat*: 36–49;

al-mufassal: the last section of the Qur'an beginning with *sura Qaf*: 50–114.

No.	Arabic name of *sura*	Arberry's translation
1	*al-Fatiha*	The Opening
2	*al-Baqara*	The Cow
3	*al 'Imran*	The House of Imran
4	*al-Nisa'*	Women

5	*al-Ma'ida*	The Table
6	*al-An'am*	Cattle
7	*al-A'raf*	The Battlements
8	*al-Anfal*	The Spoils
9	*al-Bara'a/*	Repentance
	al-Tawba	
10	*Yunus*	Jonah
11	*Hud*	Hood
12	*Yusuf*	Joseph
13	*al-Ra'd*	Thunder
14	*Ibrahim*	Abraham
15	*al-Hijr*	El-Hijr
16	*al-Nahl*	The Bee
17	*Bani Isra'il/*	The Night
	al-Isra'	Journey
18	*al-Kahf*	The Cave
19	*Maryam*	Mary
20	*Ta Ha*	Ta Ha
21	*al-Anbiya'*	The Prophets
22	*al-Hajj*	The Pilgrimage
23	*al-Mu'minin*	The Believers
24	*al-Nur*	Light
25	*al-Furqan*	Salvation
26	*al-Shu'ara'*	The Poets
27	*al-Naml*	The Ant
28	*al-Qasas*	The Story
29	*al-'Ankabut*	The Spider
30	*al-Rum*	The Greeks
31	*Luqman*	Lokman ALM
32	*al-Sajda*	Prostration ALM
33	*al-Ahzab*	The Confederates
34	*al-Saba'*	Sheba
35	*Fatir/*	The Angels
	al-Mala'ika	
36	*Ya Sin*	Ya Sin
37	*al-Saffat*	The Rangers
38	*al-Sad*	Sad S
39	*al-Zumar*	The Companies
40	*al-Mu'min*	The Believer
41	*Ha Mim/*	Distinguished
	Fussilat	
42	*al-Shura*	Counsel
43	*al-Zukhruf*	Ornaments
44	*al-Dukhan*	Smoke
45	*al-Jathiya*	Hobbling HM

46	*al-Ahqaf*	The Sand-Dunes HM
47	*Muhammad*	Muhammad
48	*al-Fath*	Victory
49	*al-Hujurat*	Apartments
50	*Qaf*	Qaf Q
51	*al-Dhariyat*	The Scatterers
52	*al-Tur*	The Mount
53	*al-Najm*	The Star
54	*al-Qamar*	The Moon
55	*al-Rahman*	The All-Merciful
56	*al-Waqi'a*	The Terror
57	*al-Hadid*	Iron
58	*al-Mujadala*	The Disputer
59	*al-Hashr*	The Mustering
60	*al-Mumtahana*	The Woman Tested
61	*al-Saff*	The Ranks
62	*al-Jumu'a*	Congregation
63	*al-Munafiqun*	Hypocrites
64	*al-Taghabun*	Mutual Fraud
65	*al-Talaq*	Divorce
66	*al-Tahrim*	The Forbidding
67	*al-Mulk*	The Kingdom
68	*al-Qalam*	The Pen N
69	*al-Haqqa*	The Indubitable
70	*al-Ma'arij*	The Stairways
71	*Nuh*	Noah
72	*al-Jinn*	The Jinn
73	*al-Muzammil*	Enwrapped
74	*al-Mudaththir*	Shrouded
75	*al-Qiyama*	The Resurrection
76	*al-Dahr/*	Man
	al-Insan	
77	*al-Mursalat*	The Loosed Ones
78	*al-Naba'*	The Tiding
79	*al-Nazi'at*	The Pluckers
80	*'Abasa*	He Frowned
81	*al-Takwir*	The Darkening
82	*al-Infitar*	The Splitting
83	*al-Mutaffifin*	The Stinters
84	*al-Inshiqaq*	The Rending
85	*al-Buruj*	The Constellations
86	*al-Tariq*	The Night-Star
87	*al-A'la*	The Most High

88	*al-Ghashiya*	The Enveloper
89	*al-Fajr*	The Dawn
90	*al-Balad*	The Land
91	*al-Shams*	The Sun
92	*al-Layl*	The Night
93	*al-Duha*	The Forenoon
94	*al-Inshira*	The Expanding
95	*al-Tin*	The Fig
96	*al-ʿAlaq*	The Blood-Clot
97	*al-Qadr*	Power
98	*al-Bayyina*	The Clear Sign
99	*al-Zilzal/*	The Earthquake
	al-Zalzala	
100	*al-ʿAdiyat*	The Chargers
101	*al-Qariʿa*	The Clatterer
102	*al-Takathur*	Rivalry
103	*al-ʿAsr*	Afternoon
104	*al-Humaza*	The Backbiter
105	*al-Fil*	The Elephant
106	*Quraysh*	Koraish
107	*al-Maʿun*	Charity
108	*al-Kawthar*	Abundance
109	*al-Kafirun*	The Unbelievers
110	*al-Nasr*	Help
111	*Lahab/Tabbat*	Perish
112	*al-Ikhlas*	Sincere Religion
113	*al-Falaq*	Daybreak
114	*al-Nas*	Men

OLIVER LEAMAN

AL-SUYUTI

The writings of Abu al-Fadl ʿAbd al-Rahman ibn Abi Bakr ibn Muhammad Jalal al-Din al-Misri al-Suyuti al-Shafiʿi covered almost the entire gamut of the Islamic sciences. He was the most productive of all Islamic authors. One of his most famous works is a commentary on the Qurʾan which he wrote jointly with one of his teachers.

Al-Suyuti was born of mixed Circassian and Persian parentage in Cairo in 849/1445. His family settled in Asyut in upper Egypt. His father, a teacher of Shafiʿi law at the Shaykhu mosque and school in Cairo, died when al-Suyuti was aged six.

Al-Suyuti studied with some of the foremost scholars in Cairo from both the Shafiʿi and Hanafi schools of law. He reportedly learnt from over 100 teachers. One of these was Jalal al-Din Muhammad b. Ahmad b. Muhammad b. Ibrahim al-Mahalli al-Shafiʿi (791/1389–863/1459), who had risen to prominence as a specialist in diverse Islamic disciplines, especially principles of Islamic law.

The young al-Suyuti studied wide-ranging subjects: Tradition, exegesis, jurisprudence, scholastic theology, history, philosophy, philology and rhetoric. He also had a certain interest in Sufism and was involved in the Shadhili Sufi order. This accounts in part for the frugal lifestyle which characterizes most of his life.

At the age of 18 he became a teacher of Shafiʿi law at the mosque of Shaykhu in Cairo. He later also taught *hadith* at the same institution. His travels increased as his reputation developed, taking him throughout Egypt, to Damascus, the Hijaz, Yemen, Morocco and beyond. After an active career of teaching and writing, al-Suyuti gave up the former in 1501 to devote his final years to writing. He died in 911/1505 at the age of 62 in Cairo.

Al-Suyuti's literary output was both prolific and diverse. According to the *Dalil makhtutat al-suyuti* (Directory of al-Suyuti's manuscripts), over 700 works bear his name. However, some of these titles are brief legal opinions (*fatawa*) of a few pages in length. He wrote extensively on Tradition, exegesis, history, Sufism and jurisprudence. Because of his own wide-ranging education, his approach to specific topics often reflected multi-disciplinary perspectives, although his writing was always anchored in Tradition.

Al-Suyuti's legacy in the field of Qurʾanic exegesis is considerable. He wrote a ground-breaking study of the Qur'anic and exegetical sciences entitled *al-Itqan fi 'ulum al-Qur'an* (The Perfection of the Science of the Qur'an). In addition to writing about exegesis, he also produced his own exegesis of the Qur'an in two principal works. First was his commentary *al-Durr al-manthur fi al-tafsir bi al-ma'thur* (The Scattered Pearls: A commentary of the Qur'an based on transmitted reports), a multi-volume work which has appeared in several published editions. It presents an essentially tradition-based approach to exegesis of the Qur'an.

Al-Suyuti's greater impact in the field of exegesis has been through the more popular commentary entitled *Tafsir al-Jalalayn* (The Commentary of the Two Jalals). This work contains the combined efforts of his teacher Jalal al-Din al-Mahalli as well as those of al-Suyuti himself. Al-Mahalli produced commentary on Qur'anic verses from the beginning of *sura* 18 (*al-Kahf*) until the final verse of the Qur'an, *sura* 114.6. He also wrote a commentary on the first *sura*, *al-Fatiha*, but died without being able to complete the commentary. Al-Suyuti later brought the work to fruition with commentary on verses from 2.1 to 17.111, reportedly completing this task in just forty days.

Tafsir al-Jalalayn includes an ongoing paraphrase of the Qur'anic text. It draws material from the authoritative *hadith* collection, as well as narrative elements from earlier exegetical sources. It also presents linguistic explanations, including information on the variant readings (*qira'at*). The authors generally avoid identifying sources within the text. The exegetical comment provided elucidates the Qur'anic text without drowning the scriptural core in extensive detail. This commentary is relevant for a broad-based audience, one which is far less specialized than is the case with more sophis-

ticated commentaries such as those by al-Tabari, al-Zamakhshari and al-Razi. It serves as a very clearly arranged compendium, providing its readers with a taste of wide-ranging Islamic sciences.

Al-Suyuti's reputation during his lifetime was marked by controversy. His prolific output brought him both acclaim and criticism. His chief adversary was Muhammad al-Shakhawi (d. 902/1497) who resented al-Suyuti's increasing acclaim. Some critics also commented that his unusually high literary output resulted in inaccuracy and untidy scholarship. Furthermore, his extensive numbers of *fatawa* points to his combative method of engagement with his scholarly peers. Such was the opposition to him in some quarters that in 1501 he was pushed out of teaching through the combined opposition of religious scholars whom he had alienated. This problem was exacerbated by his self-image; just before the centennial year of 900/1494, al-Suyuti announced himself as the *mujaddid* (renewer of Islam) of the ninth century, a claim seen as deluded and lacking in humility by his adversaries.

Nevertheless, such controversy has not had a negative impact on *Tafsir al-Jalalayn*. Although it has sometimes been regarded with a degree of disdain by specialists because of the lightweight nature of the commentary included, this has not prevented it from achieving a significant level of popularity throughout the Islamic world from the time of its composition to the present day. In its defence, it was never designed to challenge the larger commentaries in terms of exegetical sophistication. Rather, it was intended to make the science of Qur'anic exegesis accessible to the literate Muslim public at large, and in this it has clearly succeeded. The *Tafsir al-Jalalayn* has been translated into many non-Arabic Muslim languages. Its popularity in Southeast Asia is particularly considerable. 'Abd al-Ra'uf al-Singkili drew on it for the core of *Tarjuman al-Mustafid* (The Interpreter of that which gives Benefit), the first commentary in Malay upon the whole Qur'an, completed around 1085/1675. Furthermore, *Marah Labid* (Rich Pasture), the first commentary on the whole Qur'an written in Arabic by a Malay scholar, Muhammad Nawawial-Jawi, drew on *Tafsir al-Jalalayn* as one of its sources. Copies of the work are to be found in collections throughout the Malay/Indonesian region, as well as in the Indian sub-continent.

Further reading

al-Dhahabi, Muhammad Husayn (1405/1985) *al-Tafsir wa al-Mufassirun* (Exegesis and the Commentators), 3rd edn, 3 vols., Cairo: Wahba.

Riddell, P.G. (1984) 'The Sources of 'Abd al-Ra'uf's Tarjuman al-Mustafid', *Journal of the Malaysian Branch of the Royal Asiatic Society* LVII, 2: 113–18.

—— (1990) *Transferring a Tradition: 'Abd al-Ra'uf al-Singkili's rendering into Malay of the Jalalayn Commentary*, Berkeley, CA: Centers for South and Southeast Asian Studies, University of California.

Sartain, E.M. (1971) 'Jalal al-din al-Suyuti's relations with the people of Takrur', *Journal of Semitic Studies* XVI: 193–8.

—— (1975) *Jalal al-Din al-Suyuti*, 2 vols, Cambridge: Cambridge University Press.

al-Suyuti, Jalal al-din. (1403/1983) *Tafsir al-Jalalayn*, Beirut: Dar al-qalam.

See also: **Arkoun, Mohammed;** *tafsir* in **early Islam**

PETER G. RIDDELL

T

TA'A

Ta'a is a root verb meaning to obey or
to comply: 'And whosoever obeys Allah
and His Messenger will be admitted to
Paradise' (4.13). The Muslims are commanded to obey Allah, his messenger
and their leaders: 'Obey Allah and obey
the Messenger and those of you who are
in authority' (4.59). *Taw'an* (voluntarily
or willingly) means to act of one's own
free will. Its opposite is *karhan* (compulsory or unwillingly): 'Come both of
you willingly or unwillingly. They both
said: "We come willingly"' (41.11).
Muta' means obeyed, and the Qur'an
describes archangel Gabriel as 'obedient
and trustworthy' (81.21).

RAFIK BERJAK

TAB'A

Tab'a is a root verb meaning to seal,
imprint, print and rusted. In the Qur'an
it is used eleven times. It signifies that
Allah seals up the hearts of those who

choose to disobey him: 'Nay, Allah has
set a seal upon their hearts because of
their disbelief' (4.155). Allah also sealed
the hearts of those who were rich and
disobeyed the Prophet: 'Allah hath
sealed their hearts: So they know not'
(9.93). Hence *tab'a* is a punishment
from God resulting in the sinner's confusion and their inability to follow the
right path. This punishment causes the
loss of the benefits and fruits of belief:
when the heart is hardened the person
loses the sweet taste of *iman* (faith).
Thus, 'Therefore were your hearts hardened; they became like a rock' (2.74).
The heart is the perceptive centre of
faith, and when the heart is corrupted
the person will no longer respond to any
guidance.

The Qur'an clarifies that Allah seals
up the hearts of those who had believed
but who did not honour their belief:
'That is because they believed, and then
disbelieved; therefore their hearts are
sealed, so they understand not' (63.3).
Thus danger awaits those who know but

621

pretend that they do not, and their sin is worse than that of the ignorant. Those who know hold a bigger responsibility. Their knowledge of the truth obliges them to announce it and not hide it. 'Such are men whose hearts Allah has sealed, and they followed their lusts [evil desires]' (47.16).

RAFIK BERJAK

AL-TABARI

Abu Ja'far Muhammad ibn Jarir ibn Yazid al-Tabari wrote a commentary on the Qur'an which served as a major landmark in the history of Islamic scholarship. In addition, he was a prolific writer across a wide range of Islamic disciplines.

Al-Tabari was born in Persia in 224–225/838–839, in the mountainous region of Tabaristan near the Caspian Sea. He was born into a period when the 'Abbasid Empire, centred on Baghdad, the scientific, commercial and artistic centre of the Mediterranean world.

Al-Tabari's thirst for knowledge manifested itself from an early age. By age seven he had learned the full text of the Qur'an by heart. His education took him throughout the 'Abbasid domains, from Rayy in Persia to Baghdad and thence to Cairo, where he interacted with the Shafi'i law school.

In 256/870 al-Tabari settled in Baghdad, where he was to remain for the rest of his life. He achieved great prominence as a scholar, so much so that a separate *madhhab* (law school), the Jaririyya, was named after him. However, this school was not to survive him by more than two generations.

Fame brought controversy and al-Tabari became embroiled in various debates. First he aroused opposition from followers of Ahmad ibn Hanbal (d. 241/855), the founder of the Hanbali law school, for making no reference to him in his work *Ikhtilaf al-fuqaha'* (The Differences among the Jurists) and later commenting that Ibn Hanbal was a scholar of Tradition, not a jurist. This opposition was no doubt reinforced by the fact that the Jaririyya school represented competition for the Hanbalis. Moreover, Baghdad had witnessed intense ideological conflict during the first half of the third/eighth century between the rationalist theological school of the Mu'tazila and the more literalist Tradition-focused *ahl al-hadith* (*hadith* school). Ahmad ibn Hanbal's efforts in favour of the latter contributed greatly to the demise of the Mu'tazila. Al-Tabari's arrival in Baghdad coincided with the decline of the Mu'tazila, and he was to take a decidedly anti-Mu'tazila line in his famous Qur'an commentary.

By the time of his death in Baghdad in 310/923, al-Tabari had written a vast collection of works, many of which have not survived. These engaged with diverse fields of knowledge: exegesis, history, jurisprudence, recitation of the Qur'an, grammar, lexicography as well as various other disciplines. The *Kitab al-fihrist* (Catalogue) by Ibn al-Nadim (d. 995), which lists all books written in Arabic either by Arabs or non-Arabs, serves as an invaluable record of the breadth of al-Tabari's writing.

Two works stand out among the collection. First, his *Ta'rikh al-rusul wa al-muluk* (The History of Messengers and Kings) contains a history of the world from its creation until 302/915. It has been translated into English in thirty-nine volumes. Second, and arguably his greatest work, is the monumental Qur'an commentary entitled *Jami' al-bayan 'an tafsir al-Qur'an* (Collection of Explanations for the Interpretation of the Qur'an). Its existence had been known for centuries, but a surviving example in manuscript form eluded scholars until

Otto Loth located one and published a study of it in 1881. The first published edition of the entire commentary appeared in 1903 and ran to thirty volumes. It is reported in classical Arabic sources that al-Tabari restricted his commentary to thirty volumes out of compassion for his students; he had originally intended to write 300 volumes.

The commentary carries great weight within the classical Arabic literary corpus. Surviving examples of Qur'an commentary writing which pre-date it are few in number, and are often subsumed within other written works but the content of al-Tabari's work goes a long way towards filling in the exegetical gaps from earlier periods. In it he sets out in lucid form the opinions and preferences of earlier commentators, including those with whom he disagreed. However, he does not present diverse opinions for the sake of it, making his own views clear where disagreement between his predecessors is recorded. The commentary itself begins with a generous introduction that engages with wide-ranging exegetical concerns and demonstrates al-Tabari's sophisticated understanding of hermeneutical concepts and processes.

The work includes a vast number of exegetical traditions drawn from the canonical *hadith* collections. However, al-Tabari was no mere copyist, and his selection of traditions shows his own exegetical inclinations. The extent to which al-Tabari depends on traditions for his exegetical content places his work firmly in the *ahl al-hadith* camp. He firmly rejects the allegorical approach to interpretation of the Mu'tazila, insisting that the immediately visible surface meaning of a Qur'anic verse is crucial for correct interpretation. He also meticulously reproduces the *isnad* (chain of authorities) for each tradition cited. This results in his commentary being somewhat cumbersome and turgid in parts, but it is essential in terms of his claim to authority. This dependence on traditions for the interpretative process has also resulted in controversy, with some scholars accusing him of having drawn on weak traditions with defective chains. However, this has not had a major impact upon the overwhelmingly positive reputation of the *Jami' al-bayan 'an tafsir al-Qur'an*.

The commentary contains copious amounts of information on grammatical issues, including records of *qira'at* (variant readings) of various Qur'anic passages. It thus serves as a key resource for later scholarship on the *qira'at*.

Al-Tabari's commentary has served as a model for many later commentators. Among the more prominent writers to have been influenced by al-Tabari's style are al-Samarqandi (d. *c.* 375/985), al-Tha'labi (427/1035), al-Baghawi (d. between 1117 and 1122), Ibn 'Atiyya (d. 1147), Ibn al-Jawzi (d. 1200), Ibn Kathir (d. 1373) and al-Suyuti (d. 1505). Many studies of the work have been carried out, with the study (in French) by Claude Gilliot of particularly note.

Further reading

Cooper, J. (ed.) (1987) *The Commentary on the Qur'an by Abu Ja'far Muhammad b. Jarir al-Tabari*, Oxford: Oxford University Press.

Gilliot, C. (1990) *Exégèse, langue et théologie en Islam: L'exégèse coranique de Tabari (m. 311/923)*, Paris: J. Vrin.

McAuliffe, J.D. (1991) *Qur'anic Christians: An analysis of classical and modern exegesis*, Cambridge: Cambridge University Press.

See also: **tafsir** **in early Islam**

PETER G. RIDDELL

TABUT

Arabic term commonly used to denote a 'casket' but used specifically in the Qur'an to refer to the 'Ark' of Noah and the 'Ark' of the Covenant.

The Ark of Noah is described by Muslim tradition as being of very large size. Exegetes relate that Noah worked on the boat for 400 years, building it from the wood of a special teak tree which had grown for forty years until it was 300 cubits tall. The Ark is said to have been anywhere from 300 by 50 cubits to 1200 by 600 cubits in length and width. Ibn 'Abbas relates that Jesus resurrected Ham, the son of Noah, to describe to his disciples the size and structure of the Ark.

The Ark of the Covenant is mentioned in 2.248 as containing the 'Sakina' and the remains left behind by the family of Moses and the family of Aaron. The Sakina is defined variously as the 'presence' of God (Heb. Shechinah), a blowing wind with a face like the face of a man or two heads, or a spirit with the head of a cat, two wings and a tail. Ibn 'Abbas reports that the Sakina was the basin of gold from paradise in which the hearts of the prophets were washed. The remains of Moses and Aaron in the Ark of the Covenant are reported to have included the rod of Moses and pieces of the Tablets, the rod of Aaron, some manna, the clothes of Aaron and the shoes of Moses and Aaron. Others report that the term 'remains' refers to what was left of the knowledge of the Torah.

Further reading

Goldziher, I. (1893) 'La notion de la sakina chez les Mohametans', *Revue de l'histoire des réligions* 27: 296–308.
McClain, E.G. (1978) 'The Kaba as Archetypal Ark', *Sophia Perennis* 4, 1: 59–75.

BRANNON WHEELER

TAFSIR IN EARLY ISLAM

The word *tafsir* (pl. *tafasir*) is a noun derived from the verb *fassara/yufassiru/tafsir*, meaning explanation, exposition, elucidation, explication, interpretation and commentary. It also means 'to elucidate what is meant from a difficult word' (Ibn Manzur, 1994, V: 55; al-Zabidi, n.d., III: 470). Technically, *tafsir* is the term encompassing both scholarly efforts to explain the Qur'an and make it more understandable and also the branch of Islamic science that deals with it. The word *tafsir* occurs in the Qur'an just once, at 25.33: 'They never bring you any simile but We bring you the truth and a better exposition (*tafsiran*).'

Ta'wil is word that has a similar meaning to *tafsir*. *Ta'wil* is derived from the verb *awwala/yuawwilu/ta'wil*, meaning to interpret dreams, explain, explicate, *tafsir*, *kashf* (discover), elucidate and result. Some scholars think that *tafsir* and *ta'wil* had different meanings from early on, while others believe that at least up until the end of third/ninth century there was no differentiation in meaning. The word *ta'wil* appears in the Qur'an in seventeen different places across fifteen verses, and has various meanings such as 'the end or intended result of something', 'interpretation of a dream' and 'exposition of a saying'. Once conceptualized, it was used to denote a person using his other rational and intellectual abilities to interpret a word or a text.

The need for commentary on the Qur'an has existed from its conception and stems both from the nature of the text and of the process of the development of Islamic society. In essence, the Qur'an was revealed in the dialect of the Quraysh tribe, who lived in Mecca, home of the Prophet. However, once Islam spread to other Arab tribes, it was possible that some words were either not understood correctly or taken out of context. Also, the Qur'an employs some strange words that not everybody can easily grasp at first glance.

The demand for resolution of apparent contradictions in some verses was another reason driving interpretation of the Qur'an in the early period of Islam. The fact that some verses in the Qur'an were *muhkam* (clear in meaning), while others were *mutashabih* (ambiguous) forced Muslims to expend extra effort in making the *mutashabih* verses better understood. The Qur'an emphasized this problem more concretely in 3.7 by pointing to 'those in whose hearts there is vacillation, they follow what is ambiguous in it, seeking sedition and intending to interpret it'.

Another important issue in need of explication was the stories the Qur'an narrated. Unlike the biblical narratives, the Qur'anic stories were scattered throughout the text and included repetitions. They generally did not give much detail and were mostly utilized to support the message of the Prophet. Lack of detail in stories made their interpretation necessary to satisfy enthusiastic Muslims eager to know more about them.

The social, political, economic and cultural change that Islamic society underwent after Muhammad's time was another reason behind the need for commentary. Expansion into the lands of Persia and Byzantium under the political successors of the Prophet brought new problems, and to solve these Muslims turned to the Qur'an as a source of advice and knowledge. Moreover, it was not long before the political struggles were carried to the religious sphere, where, in addition to the *ahadith*, some used the Qur'an to defend their position, even at the price of taking the verses out of context.

Although the Qur'an has been interpreted from its very inception, there are reports calling for caution or even asking readers to abstain from comments about the verses. Some *hadith* suggest that those who give their own opinions about the Qur'an have been warned it is wrong: 'Whoever talks about the Qur'an relying on one's self-knowledge is wrong, even if he is right' (al-Tirmidhi, *Tafsir*: 1; Abu Dawud, *'Ilm*: 5). Another *hadith* has such people destined for hell.

It is very likely that the utilization of the Qur'an through *tafsir* during the intense political struggles and intellectual differences of the early periods resulted in a tentative approach towards the *tafsir* movement and the narrations that followed. Thus Ahmad b. Hanbal (d. 241/855) says: 'Three things have no reality: *tafsir,* fierce battles (*malahim*) and military expeditions (*maghazi*)' (al-Suyuti, *Itqan*, II: 227).

As far as *tafsir* methods are concerned, several approaches can be observed. First, the Qur'an comments on itself; this is considered the best *tafsir*. The *tafsir* of the Qur'an by the Qur'an occurs in several ways, such as limiting an absolute statement, restricting the general meaning, explaining ambiguous positions, vague expressions and unfamiliar words, defining the best possible meaning among several alternatives and explicating short and terse expressions in detail. Sometimes the explanation may come after a verse in the same *sura*. For instance, in 5.1, 'Lawful unto you [for food] are all beasts, with the exceptions named', is followed almost immediately by 'Forbidden to you [for food] are: dead meat, blood, the flesh of swine, and that on which has been invoked the name of other than Allah; that which has been killed by strangling, or by a violent blow, or by a headlong fall, or by being gored to death; that which has been [partly] eaten by a wild animal; unless ye are able to slaughter it [in due form]; that which is sacrificed on stone [altars]' (5.3). Sometimes the commentary is offered in another *sura*. For example, the *tafsir* of the 'Master of the Day of Judgement' (*malik yawm al-din*, 1.4) can be found in 82.17–19: 'And what will explain to thee what the Day of Judgement is? Again, what will explain to thee what the Day of Judgement is? [It will be] the Day when no soul shall have power [to do] aught for another: For the Command that Day will be [wholly] with Allah.'

Traditionally, it is held that the *tafsir* of the Qur'an begins with the Prophet. No doubt the Prophet would have had to encounter some questions about the revelation he had received and conveyed to his people. Thus, some verses begin with the expression 'They ask thee (*yas'alunaka*)'. It was quite natural that some of the questions asked of the Prophet were answered by the Qur'an, while others were answered by him, for it is possible that, from time to time he was asked questions – mostly by people who were not members of his tribe – about the descriptions or the language used in the Holy Book. Therefore, even if it was not systematic, he certainly commented on some parts of the Qur'an. Nevertheless, the Qur'anic parts that the Prophet commented upon must have been very small, for there was no need for wide-ranging explanations– the Qur'an was able to be understood by most of its contemporaries due to the fact that the contexts of most verses were known already.

The *tafsir* of the Prophet was mostly to elaborate upon those questions directed to him about the verses, to give more detail about the concise expressions, to explain strange words or to make the statements required of his mission. Hence, his *tafsir* was not of a systematic type compared to the *tafsir* movement observed in later periods. One cannot talk of the Prophet's *tafsir* as though he were making long, comprehensive interpretations of the verses and words, only of a commentary explaining what might be meant. The *sunna* of the Prophet is particularly important here as it explicates the succinct expressions of the Qur'an.

Also of use was the commentary as an aid to performing the rituals of the religion. Muslims needed the Prophet's guidance to learn the times of the daily prayers and how they are performed, the quantity of alms-giving (*zakat*) and of its payment time, and to instruct them how to carry out such practices as performing *hajj* (pilgrimage).

During the lifetime of Muhammad, and in a situation in which he was *the* authority, the *tafsir* of the Companions could only have served to transmit the Prophet's *tafsir*. Upon encountering a problem in understanding the Qur'an, Muslims solved it by referring it to the Prophet. Muslims consider the *sunna* of the Prophet in general as related to the Qur'an and they accept its explanation. In fact, some verses declare that the Prophet was also commissioned to elaborate upon the Qur'an. One such verse states: 'We have sent down unto thee [also] the Message; that thou mayest explain clearly (*li tubayyina*) to men what is sent for them, and that they may give thought' (16.44). Another states: 'We sent not a messenger except [to teach] in the language of his [own] people, in order to make [things] clear to them (*li yubayyina*)' (14.4).

The *tafsir* of the Prophet can be found in different sources. One is as expected, namely the *tafsir* books; another is the *tafsir* sections of *hadith* collections. Other reports can be found in sources such as history books. There are several instances of this: the Prophet explained that 'the Middle Prayer' (*al-salat al-wusta*) (2.238) was the 'late afternoon ('*asr*) prayer' (Tirmidhi, *Tafsir* 2); and the Prophet's exaplanation of the phrases 'the white thread' (*al-khayt al-abyadh*) and 'black thread' (*al-khayt al-aswad*) (2.187) as 'daylight' and 'nighttime darkness' respectively (Bukhari,

Tafsir 28; Tirmidhi, *Tafsir* 2). Finally, the Prophet's explanation of the term 'wasat' in 2.143: 'Thus, have We made of you an *umma* justly balanced (*umma wasat*)', is supposed to mean 'just' (Tirmidhi, *Tafsir* 2).

It was natural that there were different approaches towards the *tafsir* of the Qur'an among the Companions of the Prophet and their followers (*tabi'un*). Some abstained from *tafsir*, either when they witnessed its use – or rather misuse – in political quarrels or due to the fear of moral responsibility. 'Umar, the Second Caliph, is reported to have punished Sabigh b. 'Isl with a beating due to his comments on *mutashabih* verses (Darimi, *Muqaddima* 19; Malik, *Jihad* 19). However, this seemingly stern position does not reflect 'Umar's general attitude towards *tafsir*. He not only permitted *tafsir* of other verses but also reported the *tafsir* of the Prophet (Abbott, 1967: 455). When a question about the Qur'an was put to Sa'id b. al-Musayyab (d. 94/712), he used to say, 'I do not say anything about the Qur'an.' Some of the Followers and the Companions thought it very important to explore and explain the parts of the Qur'an they felt were unexplained or closed in meaning, but their numbers were few. Like that of the Prophet, the *tafsir* method of the Companions was also about the ambiguous parts, not about the text as a whole. The Companions both reported the *tafsir* of the Prophet and also commented on the Qur'an, relying on their view and understanding. By reporting the occasion for the revelation of some *suras* or verses (*asbab al-nuzul*), they made significant contributions to the *tafsir* movements even after their time. The examples of the *tafsir* of the Companions found in the sources are generally concerned with either linguistic clarification or elucidations about a pronouncement that cannot be fully understood.

The important elements in the *tafsir* of the Companions are the reports of those who had associated with the Prophet long enough and had knowledge of the occasion of the revelation of the verses (*asbab al-nuzul*). In later times, the scholars considered the *tafsir* of the Companions an important source after that of the Prophet. Certainly, there were differences among the Companions with respect to knowledge as well as ability. It can also be said that they quite obviously had varying opinions on the understanding of certain verses. After the death of Muhammad, Muslims put forward their own opinions (*ijtihad* and *ra'y*) to solve problems arising from different understandings. Additionally, during the times of the Companions, among the sources consulted for the *tafsir* of the Qur'an were the cultures of other religions and nations, or Muslims associated with the neighbourhood, with Jewish culture heading the list.

'Ubayy b. Ka'b (d. 19/640), 'Abdullah b. Mas'ud (d. 32/652), 'Ali b. Abu Talib (d. 40/661), Abu Musa al-Ash'ari (d. 42/662–63), Zayd b. Thabit (d. 45/665), 'Abdullah b. al-'Abbas (d. 68/687–88) and 'Abdullah b. al-Zubayr (d. 73/692) were some of the well-known Companions associated with the *tafsir* movement. The most renowned of them all was 'Abdullah b. al-'Abbas, the son of the Prophet's paternal uncle, although he did not have the opportunity to be with the Prophet for long. Ibn 'Abbas was considered to be an authority in the fields of *tafsir*, *hadith*, *fiqh*, military expeditions (*maghazi*), the accounts of the Arabs (*ayyam al-'Arab*) and Arabic literature. It is reported that the Prophet prayed for him by saying 'Oh, my Lord! Teach him wisdom and the *ta'wil* of the Book' (Ibn Sa'ad, 1985, II: 365; Ahmad b. Hanbal, 1993, I: 269). Ibn 'Abbas also benefited from the Jewish converts to Islam, namely, 'Abdullah b. Salam

(43/663–64) and Kaʿb al-Akhbar (32/652–53). It is also possible that his authority was broadened by the erroneous ascription to him of some narrations because of his position as the father of the ʿAbbasids: – it is certain that some of the *tafasir* credited to Ibn ʿAbbas do not belong to him.

The period of the Followers (*tabiʾin*) is an era that witnessed significant developments in the field of *tafsir*. Initially, the science of *tafsir* began as part of *hadith* studies, but during this time it developed into an independent science in its own right. Even then the method of the chain of transmission (*isnad*) was used to relate *tafsir* remarks. The increase in differences of opinion around the meaning of some verses during this period is one of the important indicators of discussions in this era. Students gathered around some of the Companions mentioned above not only narrated what they heard from their teachers but they themselves also commented upon the Qurʾan.

Of this period, some of the important teachers and their students are as follows. Among the students of Ibn ʿAbbas were Saʿid b. Jubayr (d. 95/713), Mujahid b. Jabr (d. 103/721), Ikrima al-Barbari (d. 105/723), Tawus b. Kaysan (d. 106/724), ʿAta b. Abu Rabah (d. 114/732), Saʿid b. al-Musayyab (d. 94/712), ʿUbaydullah b. ʿUtba (d. 98/716) and al-Qasim b. Muhammad b. Abu Bakr (d. 107/725?); of ʿUbayy ibn Kaʿb were Abu al-ʿAliya al-Riyahi (d. 90/709), Muhammad b. Kaʿb al-Qurazi (d. 108/726), Zayd b. Aslam (d. 136/753); and of the well-known commentator of Iraq, ʿAbdullah b. Masʿud, were ʿAlqama b. Qays (d. 62/682), Masruq (d. 63/683), al-Aswad b. Yazid (d. 75/694), al-Hasan al-Basri (d. 110/728) and Qatada b. Diʾama (d. 117/735).

Most of the names just listed, as well as others such as Wahb b. Munabbih (d. 114/732), Nafʿi (d. 117/735), ʿAmr b. Dinar (d. 126/744) and Wasil b. ʿAta (d. 132/749), comprise some of the most renowned *mawali* scholars. And during this era, the importance of the *mawali tafsir* scholars and the role that the *they* played in the development of the *tafsir* schools can easily be recognized. Although there were differences of opinion among the Arabs before the *mawali* accepted Islam, these differences were not so opposed or sufficiently strong as to constitute a separate school. The interest of the *mawali* in *tafsir* catalysed things. One trigger was the need to explain the Qurʾan because of the fact that Arabic was not the mother tongue of the *mawali*. Another was the comparative lack of Arab involvement in *tafsir* and other Islamic sciences, the result of their previous nomadic lifestyle and accompanying lack of any solid grounding in intellectual research. Also of influence was the Arab preoccupation with the day-to-day running of things – as the ruling power and political elite, Arabs held most of the administrative offices.

Jewish and Christian cultures also have an important role to play in the development of *tafsir*. The term Israʾiliyyat usually denotes that which was borrowed from Jewish culture, especially in *tafsir* literature, but its scope is wide enough to include news and reports imported from Christianity and other cultures. For example, to complete the missing parts of succinctly told stories in the Qurʾan, Muslim scholars generally referred to the Bible, which told them about those incidents in more detail. There was a dramatic increase in the number of Israʾiliyyat borrowings during the times of the Followers, this information mostly deriving from Jewish Muslim converts.

The traditional sources have various positions as to whether to include reports from foreign sources. In one *hadith* the Prophet is reported to have said: 'Even if it is one verse, convey my message, tell it again from the sons of Israel (Banu Isra'il), and there is no problem in doing that. [But] If anybody forges lies about me, let him prepare his place in hell' (Bukhari, *Anbiya*: 50). Nevertheless, there are also reports of the Prophet criticizing consultation of the Torah. It is narrated that he became angry when he saw a piece or page from the Torah in 'Umar's hand (Ahmad b. Hanbal, 1993, III: 470–1; IV: 265–6). Apart from these, there are also reports suggesting taking a middle way. In one *hadith*, the Prophet enjoins: 'Neither accept nor deny the [reports of the] People of the Book. Say to them "We believe in God and what was revealed to us"' (Bukhari, *Tafsir:* 11).

Although there are reports indicating that some scholars in the first century had written *tafsir* books, this does not mean that they commented on the Qur'an in its totality. They can be thought of as short treatises containing either explanations on the meaning of some verses that caused disagreement among Muslims or narrations they received from the Prophet or from the Companions about the *tafsir* of some verses. One such *tafsir* is ascribed to Sa'id b. Jubayr, who wrote a *tafsir* book at the request of 'Abd al-Malik b. Marwan and sent it to him. Later, 'Ata b. Dinar found this *tafsir* in the Caliphate Library (*diwan*) and narrated from it (Ibn Abu Khatim, 1952, VI, 332). Unfortunately it is no longer extant. There are reports also claiming that scholars such as Mujahid b. Jabr, 'Ikrima, al-Hasan al-Basri, 'Ata b. Abu Raba and Sufiyan b. Sa'id al-Thawri (d. 161/778) had produced examples of the *tafsir* genre. However, it is Muqatil b. Sulayman who is recognized as the first person to comment on the whole Qur'an. Many of the early *tafsirs* did not survive long enough to

come down to us and many of them are included in the *tafsir* of al-Tabari (d. 150/923). We can also find linguistic *tafsirs*, that is *tafsirs* focusing on linguistic analysis, right from early times: Zayd b. 'Ali's (d. 121/738) *Tafsir gharib al-Qur'an al-majid* (The *tafsir* of the foreign words of the noble Qur'an) and *Ma'ani al-Qur'an* (The meanings of the Qur'an) by Wasil b. 'Ata (d. 131/748) are examples of this type.

All early religious and political movements that emerged in the Islamic world put great effort into defending their views by relying on the Qur'an. In order to do so they interpreted certain verses in such a way that they supported their cause. This was one of the elements that motivated the *tafsir* of the Qur'an. Some reports in the traditional sources indicate that certain people attempted to explain the political events during the time of the Companions by relying on the Qur'an. The son of Sa'id b. Abu Waqqas, Mus'ab, related: 'I asked my father who was meant in "Shall we tell you of those who lose most in respect of their deeds?"' (18.103) I asked whether it was it the *Haruriyya* (Kharijites). His father replied 'No, they are the Jews and the Christians … whereas *Haruriyya* were those who were mentioned in "But those who break the Covenant of Allah, after having plighted their word thereto"' (13.25). Sa'id used to describe them as *fasiq* (rebellious and wicked) (Bukhari, *Tafsir:* 18).

The Kharijites, one of the influential sects in the first century of Islamic history, based their existence on unwavering allegiance to the Qur'an. Reports pointing to the name of the sect as being inspired by verse 4.100 – 'And whosoever leaves his home as an emigrant unto Allah and His Messenger (*wa man yakhruj min baytih muhajiran ila Allah wa rasulih*)' – are part of Kharijite efforts to defend their position in the light of the

Divine Word. The famous Kharijite slogan, 'Judgement only belongs to Allah (*La hukm illa li Allah*)' is inspired by the verse 'Command is for none but Allah (*In al-hukm illa li Allah*)' (12.40, 67).

Their strict reliance on the Holy Book meant they tried to find in it answers to all the questions they encountered in their daily life. Among the first Kharijites, there was no one who spent long enough with the Prophet to make him knowledgeable about the contexts in which the verses were revealed. Thus, it is highly likely that they took the verses out of context when trying to understand them. It has been said that the Kharijites' understanding of the Qur'an was rather narrow-minded and superficial owing to the fact that they were mostly from the Bedouin tribes and had limited experience in dealing with the subtleties of life in large urban communities.

Examples of how the Kharijites understood and commented on certain Qur'anic verses are related in the sources of their opponents. What we do not have is satisfactory information regarding which of the first Kharijites commented on the work, although reports exist that confirm the conversion of 'Ikrima, one of the well-known scholars in the Followers' period and the *mawla* of 'Abdullah b. al-'Abbas, to the sect. Naturally, the *tafsir* of the Qur'an was used to defend the views of the Kharijites as well as to criticize them.

As a political phenomenon of the first century, the Shi'at 'Ali (supporters of 'Ali) also placed special emphasis upon the *tafsir* of the Qur'an to defend their views. While the work by Jabir al-Ju'fi (d. 128/746), which is generally acknowledged as the first Shi'i *tafsir*, is not extant, there is mention of another *tafsir* by Muhammad al-Baqir (d. 114/733). Depending on the *tafsir* examples ascribed to some Shi'i groups, we can reasonably argue that they commented upon the verses without taking into account their context. For instance, it is said that Bayan b. Sem'an (d. 119/737), leader of one of the early Shi'a movements, claimed that his name was mentioned in the verse: 'Here is a *plain statement* (*bayan*) to men, a guidance and instruction to those who fear Allah' (3.138) (Ibn Qutayba, 1972: 72).

The reign of the Umayyads was the period during which theological discussions of the Qur'an created the need for *tafsir*. It was the time when terms such as *jabr*, *tashbih* and *irja'*, from which originated many of the sects, were introduced. We can trace the beginnings of those discussions in some reports. Mujahid is reported to have said: 'The best worship is a good opinion (*afdal al-'ibada al-ra'y al-hasan*)' (Ibn Qutayba, 1972: 57). With these words, he was possibly replying to criticisms levelled against the tendency to favour the *tafsir* of those verses relying upon personal opinion. He explained the verse 'Looking towards their Lord (*ila rabbiha nazira*)' (75.23) as meaning 'They expect reward from their Lord'. He further elaborated his views on the subject by adding 'Nobody from His creation can see Him' (al-Tabari, 1985, XXIX: 192). However, Muhammad b. Sirin (d. 110/729) is reported as saying, by way of comment on the verse, 'See you not those that dispute concerning the signs of Allah? How are they turned away [from reality]?' (40.69); 'If it was not revealed about the Qadriyya, I do not know who it was revealed about' (al-Tabari, 1985, XXIV: 83).

References and further reading

Abbott, N. (1967) 'The Early Development of Tafsir', in *Studies in Arabic Literary Papyri II: Qur'anic commentary and tradition*, Chicago: University of Chicago Press, 106–13.

Abu Dawud, Sulayman b. Ash'as al-Sijistani (1992) *Sunan,* Istanbul: Çağrı Yayınları.

Abu Zaid, N.H. (2001) *İlahi Hitabın Tabiatı* (The Nature of the Divine Message), trans. M.E. Maşalı, Ankara: Kitabiyat.

Ahmad b. Hanbal, Abu 'Abdullah b. Muhammad b. Hanbal al-Shaybani (1993) *al-Musnad,* Istanbul: Çağrı Yayınları.

Albayrak, H. (1993) *Kur'an'ın Bütünlüğü Üzerine: Kur'an'ın Kur'an'la tefsiri* (On the Wholeness of the Qur'an: The tafsir of the Qur'an by the Qur'an), 2nd edn, Istanbul: Şule Yayınları.

Aydemir, A. (1979) *Tefsirde İsrailiyyat* (Israiliyyat in Tafsir), Ankara: Diyanet İşleri Başkanlığı Yayınları.

al-Bukhari, Abu 'Abdullah Muhammad b. Ismail (1992) *al-Sahih,* Istanbul: Çağrı Yayınları.

Cerrahoğlu, I. (1968) *Kur'an Tefsirinin Doğuşu ve Buna Hız Veren Amiller* (The Birth of the *Tafsir* of the Qur'an and the Hastening Causes for It), Ankara: Ankara Üniversitesi Ilahiyat Fakultesi Yayınevi.

—— (1988) *Tefsir Tarihi* (The History of *Tafsir*), 2 vols, Ankara: Diyanet İşleri Başkanlığı Yayınları.

al-Darimi, Abu Muhammad 'Abdullah b. Abdurrahman (1992) *Sunan,* Istanbul: Çağrı Yayınları.

al-Dhahabi, Muhammad Husayn (1976) *al-Tafsir wa al-Mufassirun* (Commentaries and Commentators), 2nd edn, al-Medina: Dar al-kutub al-haditha.

Ibn Abu Khatim, Abu Muhammad Abdurrahman b. Abu Khatim Muhammad b. Idris al-Razi (1952) *Kitab al-Jarh wa al-Ta'dil* (The Book of Criticism and Decency), Beirut: Dar al-kutub al-'ilmiyya.

Ibn Manzur, Abu al-Fadl Jamal al-Din Muhammad b. Mukarram b. 'Ali (1994) *Lisan al-'arab* (The Language of the Arab), 3rd edn, Beirut: Dar al-fikr.

Ibn Qutayba, Abu Muhammad 'Abdullah b. Muslim (1972) *Ta'wil Mukhtalif al-Hadith* (The Solution to the Contradicting *Hadiths*), ed. Muhammad Zuhri al-Najjar, Beirut: Dar al-jil.

Ibn Sa'd, Muhammad (1985) *al-Tabaqat al-Kubra* (The Biggest Biography), Beirut: Dar al-sadr.

Leemhuis, F. (1988) 'Origins and Early Development of the *Tafsir* Tradition', in A. Rippin (ed.) *Approaches to the History of the Interpretation of the Qur'an,* Oxford: Clarendon Press, 13–30.

Malik b. Anas, Abu 'Abdullah (1992) *al-Muwatta',* Istanbul: Çağrı Yayınları.

Ozturk, M. (2001) 'Tefsir-Te'vil Karşıtlığının Tarihsel ve Epistemolojik Kökeni' (The Historical and Epistemological Roots of the Opposition between *tafsir* and *ta'wil*)', *Islami Araştırmalar* 14, 1: 77–89.

—— (2003) *Kur'an ve Aşırı Yorum: Tefsirde batinilik ve batini te'vil geleneği* (The Qur'an and its Extreme Interpretation: Esotericism in *tafsir* and the esoteric *ta'wil* tradition), Ankara: Kitabiyat.

al-Raghib al-Isfahani, al-Husayn b. Muhammad (1986) *al-Mufradat fi gharib al-Qur'an* (The Strange Terms of the Qur'an), Istanbul: Kahraman Yayınları.

al-Suyuti, Jalal al-Din Abdurrahman (1978) *al-Itqan fi 'Ulum al-Qur'an* (Perfection in the Qur'anic Sciences), 4th edn, Istanbul: Kahraman Yayınları.

al-Tabari, Abu Ja'far Muhammad b. Jarir (1985) *al-Jami' al-Bayan an ta'wil ay al-Qur'an* (The Completion of Commentaries on the Verses of the Qur'an), Beirut: Dar al-fikr.

al-Tirmidhi, Abu 'Isa Muhammad b. 'Isa (1992) *Sunan,* Istanbul: Çağrı Yayınları.

Versteegh, C.H.M. (1983) *Arabic Grammar and Qur'anic Exegesis in Early Islam,* Leiden: E.J. Brill.

Yıldırım, S. (1983) *Peygamberimizin Kur'an'ı Tefsiri* (Our Prophet's Exegesis of the Qur'an), Istanbul: Kayıhan Yayınları.

al-Zabidi, Muhib al-Din Abu al-Fayd Muhammad Murtada al-Husayni (n.d.) *Taj al-'Arus min Jawahir al-Qamus* (The Crown of the Bridegroom for the Jewels of Lexicon), Dar al-fikr.

al-Zarkashi, Badr al-Din Muhammad b. 'Abdullah (1957–59) *al-Burhan fi 'Ulum al-Qur'an* (The Guide for the Qur'anic Sciences), ed. Muhammad Abu al-Fadl Abraham, Dar Ihya' kutub al-'arabiyya.

See also: **ahl al-kitab**; **aya**; **Isra'iliyat; language and the Qur'an; Muqatil b. Sulayman;** *sunna*

ADNAN DEMIRCAN
AND RIFAT ATAY

TAFSIR – SALAFI VIEWS

Tafsir (exegesis, commentary) of/on the Qur'an, it might be argued, is the most important Islamic science because the right application of Islam is based on a proper understanding of the guidance given by God. The word *tafsir* is derived from the root *fassara*, which means to explain, to interpret. *Tafsir* is used for explanation, interpretation and commentary on the Qur'an, comprising all ways of obtaining knowledge in order to acquire a proper understanding of the text, explain its meanings and outline its legal implications. The word *mufassir* (pl. *mufassirun*) is used for the person doing the *tafsir*, the commentator. The word *ta'wil*, which is also used to describe commentary, is derived from the root *awwala*, and also means explanation or interpretation.

A distinction is often made between *tafsir* that explains the 'outer' (*zahir*) meanings of the Qur'an and *ta'wil* which is considered by some to mean the explanation of the inner and concealed (*batin*) meanings of the Qur'an, in so far as a knowledgeable person can have access to them. *Tafsir* is of great importance because God has sent the Qur'an as a book of guidance to humanity. It sees the purpose of our lives to worship him, i.e. to seek his pleasure by living the way of life God has invited us to adopt. We can do so within the framework of the guidance that God has revealed concerning this, but we can do so only if we properly understand its meanings and implications of the Book.

Some Muslim scholars have warned against *tafsir*. Ahmad b. Hanbal said: 'Three matters have no basis: *Tafsir*, *malahim* (tales of eschatological nature) and *maghazi* (tales of the battles)' (Ibn Taymiyya, *Muqaddima* 1971: 59.). By this is meant that there is much exaggeration and unsound material in these areas, but it does not mean that neither of them ought to be considered. Ibn Hanbal himself based his position on his interpretation of the Qur'an. Any *tafsir* which is acceptable to those sceptical of

the enterprise like Ibn Hanbal needs to adhere to certain conditions. The *mufassir* (commentator) should be sound in belief (*'aqida*), well grounded in the knowledge of Arabic and its rules as a language, well grounded in other sciences that are connected with the study of the Qur'an (the relevant history and Tradition, for example), and should possess the ability for precise comprehension. The important thing is to reject the use of mere opinion, and one can do this by basing the *tafsir* of the Qur'an on the Qur'an itself. This comes first and then there is a hierarchy of authorities, ranging from seeking guidance from the words and explanations of the Prophet, the reports from the *sahaba* (Companions), the reports of the *tabi'un* (Followers) and finally the opinions of eminent scholars.

As Ibn Kathir explains, the best *tafsir* is the explanation of the Qur'an by the Qur'an. The next best is the explanation of the Qur'an by the Prophet Muhammad, who, as Shafi'i explained, acted according to what he understood from the Qur'an. If nothing can be found in the Qur'an nor in the *sunna* of the Prophet, one turns to the reports from the *sahaba* (Ibn Taymiyya 1971: 95). If nothing can be found in the Qur'an, the *sunna* and the reports of the *sahaba*, one turns to the reports from the *tabi'un* (Ibn Taymiyya 1971: 102). However, nothing can match the explanation of the Qur'an by the Qur'an and the explanation of the Qur'an by the Prophet.

Tafsir bi'l-riwaya (by transmission) also known as *tafsir bi'l-ra'y* (by sound opinion; also known as *tafsir bi'l-diraya*, by knowledge) is the sort of commentary which comes highest in status for the Salafi or traditionalist thinkers. This is based on all explanations of the Qur'an which can be traced back through a chain of transmission to a sound source, such as the soundest source of all, the Qur'an itself. Then there is the explanation of the Prophet, the explanation by Companions of the Prophet. They were witnesses to the revelations, were educated and trained by the Prophet himself and were closest to the period of the first Muslim *umma*(community). Of course all reports of explanations by the Prophet or by a *sahabi* must be sound according to the science of *riwaya* as in *'ulum al-hadith*. This is why so much trouble is taken to ensure that the transmission of *hadith* are sound.

The interpretation of the Qur'an by the Qur'an is the highest source of *tafsir* and many of the questions which may arise out of a certain passage in the Qur'an have their explanation in other parts of the very same book, and often there is no need to turn to any sources other than the word of God, which in itself contains *tafsir*. To seek to explain an *aya* from the Qur'an by referring to another *aya* from the Qur'an is the first and foremost duty of the *mufassir*. In many cases this suffices to resolve the matter. Only if this does not suffice, need he refer to other sources of *tafsir*.

A case in point often mentioned is the detailed explanation of 5.3 by 5.4, concerning permissible and prohibited meat. Another example of explanation of one *aya* in the Qur'an by another concerns a question which might arise from *sura* 44. 3. It is explained in *sura* 97.1: 'We sent it down during a blessed night', we read in *sura* 44.3. Which night is this blessed night, in which the Qur'an was sent down? 'We have indeed revealed this in the *laylat al-qadr'* (97.1). So it was the Night of Power. A third example is the explanation of *sura* 2.37 by *sura* 7.23: 'Then learnt Adam from his Lord words of inspiration, and his Lord turned towards him, for He is always present and most merciful' (2.37). These 'words of inspiration' are explained by the

Qur'an as follows: 'Our Lord! We have wronged our own souls. If you forgive us not, and bestow not upon us your mercy, we shall certainly be lost' (7.23).

There are numerous examples of explanation of the Qur'an by the Prophet, who either himself asked the Angel Gabriel for explanation of matters not clear to him, or who was asked by the Companions about the Qur'an. Al-Suyuti has given a long list of explanations of the Qur'an by the Prophet *sura* by *sura*: 'And eat and drink until the white thread of dawn appears to you distinct from its black thread' (2.187). In a report we read that 'Adi b. Hatim said: 'O Allah's Apostle! What is the meaning of the white thread distinct from the black thread? Are these two threads?' He said: 'You are not intelligent, if you watch the two threads.' He then added, 'No, it is the darkness of the night and the whiteness of the day' (Itqan II: 191–205).

Next in value after explanation of the Qur'an by the Qur'an itself and of the Qur'an by the Prophet himself ranks the explanation of the Qur'an by the *sahaba*. Among them, the following best known for their knowledge of and contribution to the field of *tafsir* are Abu Bakr, 'Umar, 'Uthman, 'Ali, Ibn Mas'ud, Ibn 'Abbas, 'Ubay b. Ka'b, Zaid b. Thabit, Abu Musa al-Ash'ari and 'Abdullah b. Zubayr. 'Abdullah b. 'Abbas (d. 68/687) is often considered to be the most knowledgeable of the Companions in *tafsir*. Since he was related to the Prophet, being his cousin, and his maternal aunt Maymuna was one of the Prophet's wives, he was very close to the Prophet and learnt much about the revelation. It is said that he saw the Angel Gabriel twice. Apart from his detailed knowledge of everything concerning *tafsir*, he is also given the credit for having emphasised one of the basic principles of *'ilm al-tafsir* (science of *tafsir*) which has remained important to this day, namely, that the meaning of words, especially of unusual words in the Qur'an ought to be traced back to their usage in the language of pre-Islamic poetry.

There is a long list of such explanations quoted by Suyuti. The following is an example of *tafsir* from a *sahabi*, in fact, Ibn 'Abbas, confirmed by 'Umar:

'So celebrate the praises of your Lord, and ask for His forgiveness. Verily! He is the one who accepts repentance and forgives' (110.3). Ibn 'Abbas reported: 'Umar used to make me sit with the elderly men who had fought in the battle of Badr. Some of them did not like that and said to 'Umar: 'Why do you bring in this boy to sit with us, while we have sons like him?' 'Umar replied 'Because of what you know of his position' [i.e. his religious knowledge]. One day 'Umar called me and made me sit in the gathering of those people, and I think that he called me just to show them [my religious knowledge]. 'Umar then asked them in my presence: 'What do you say about the interpretation of the statement of Allah?': 'When comes help from God, and the conquest?' (110.1). Some of them said: 'We are ordered to praise Allah and ask for His forgiveness, when Allah's help and the conquest [of Mecca] comes to us'. Some others kept quiet and did not say anything. On that 'Umar asked me: 'Do you say the same, O Ibn 'Abbas?' I replied: 'No'. He said: 'What do you say then?' I replied: 'That is the sign of the death of Allah's Messenger which Allah informed him of. God said: '[O Muhammad] when comes the help of Allah [to you against your enemies] and the conquest [of Mecca] [which is the sign of your death], – you should celebrate the praises of your Lord and ask for His forgiveness, and He is the one who accepts repentance and forgives' (110.1–3). On that 'Umar said: 'I do not know anything about it

other than what you have said' (*Bukhari*, Vl: 494). Another example is the *hadith* where 'Ata' said: 'When Ibn 'Abbas heard: 'Have you not seen those who have changed the favour of Allah into disbelief?' (14.28), he said: 'Those were the disbelieving pagans of Mecca' (Bukhari Vl:222).

There are many more from among the *tabi'un* known for their interest in *tafsir*, because many more people had embraced Islam and the need for knowledge about the Qur'an had increased. Also, the Prophet himself and many of his Companions were no longer available to give this guidance, and therefore greater efforts had to be made to satisfy this need for proper understanding of the book of God. Of the *mufassirun* from among the *tabi'un* one distinguishes three groups, according to their origin and area of activity, those from Mecca, Medina and Iraq.

According to many, the Meccan *mufassirun* from among the *tabi'un* are the most knowledgeable in *tafsir*, because they learnt about it from 'Abdullah b. 'Abbas. They are many in number, and among the best known out of many others are Mujahid (d. 104/722), 'Ata' (d. 114/732) and 'Ikrima (d. 107H). Mujahid, the best known among them, is reported to have gone through the Qur'an three times with Ibn 'Abbas and to have asked him about the 'when' and 'how' of each verse that had been revealed (Ibn Taymiyya 1971: 102.)

For example, Humayd b. Qays Makki reported: 'I was with Mujahid and we were circumambulating the *Ka'ba*. A man came and asked whether the fasts of penalty with respect to an oath should be observed continuously or severally. Humayd replied that if he liked he could observe them severally too! But Mujahid said: 'Not severally, for the reading of 'Ubayy b. Ka'b is to fast three days continuously' (*Muwatta Malik*: 617).

Sound reports must be distinguished from unsound ones, for many views have been falsely attributed to some *sahaba* and *tabi'un* (especially to Ibn 'Abbas and Mujahid, the most renowned ones among them), which cannot be traced back to them when the *isnad* or source is investigated. Those reports must of course be rejected. Material from the *ahl-al-kitab* (the People of the Book), in particular the Jewish traditions (*isra'iliyyat*) must be sorted out and evaluated. Material which crept in due to theological, philosophical, political and other considerations, must be excluded unless it is based on a solid source.

The second kind of *tafsir*, after *tafsir bi'l-riwaya*, is the so-called *tafsir bi'l-ra'y*. It is not based directly on transmission of knowledge by the predecessors, but on the use of reason and *ijtihad* (independent judgement). *Tafsir bi'l-ra'y* does not mean 'interpretation by mere opinion', but rather involves deriving an opinion through *ijtihad* based on sound sources. While the former has been condemned in the *hadith*, the latter is acceptable when used in its proper place as sound *ijtihad*, and was also approved by the Prophet, e.g. when he sent Mu'adh bin Jabal to Yemen. *Tafsir bi'l-ra'y* as a whole has been declared *haram* or forbidden on the basis of the following *hadith*: 'From Ibn 'Abbas: 'Allah's messenger said: 'He who says [something] concerning the Qur'an without knowledge, he has taken his seat of fire'' (Ibn Taymiyya 1971: 105, from Tirmidhi, who says it is a sound report). However, this *hadith* can be explained in two ways. It might mean that no one should say of the Qur'an what is not from the *sahaba* or *tabi'un*. Or that no one should say of the Qur'an what he knows to be otherwise. The obvious meaning of the *hadith* is that one should not say something about the Qur'an without having the proper knowledge i.e.

without having gone through the proper search for the sources of the interpretation via the Qur'an itself, the Companions, etc. This clearly brings out the difficulties in drawing a tight line around what counts as proper commentary on the Qur'an, a debate that continues in all religions to dominate the definition of the faith itself.

References and further reading

Ibn Taymiyya (1971) *Muqaddima fi usul al-tafsir*, Kuwait, n.p.
al-Suyuti, J.A. (2003) *Al-itqan fi 'ulum al-Qur'an*, in F. Zamarli (ed.), Beirut: Dar al-kitab al-'arabi.

OLIVER LEAMAN

TAFWID

The root verb *fawwad* means to entrust, return or to authorize. This term has been used only once in the Qur'an. It is mentioned in the *sura* of Ghafir (*sura al-Mu'min* (the Forgiver or the Believer). A believer of the people of the Pharaoh, he advised his people to follow the right path, to pursue monotheism as sent with Moses. He explained that believing in Allah is the only way to attain salvation. After he received a hostile response from them he said: 'Soon you will remember what I say to you and my affairs I return to Allah' (40.44).

RAFIK BERJAK

TAHARA
see: **purify**

TAJWID

The proper recitation of the Qur'an is the subject of a separate discipline ('*ilm al-tajwid*) which determines down to the most minute detail how the Qur'an should be recited, how each individual syllable is to be pronounced, the need to pay due attention to the places where there should be a pause, to elisions, where the pronunciation should be long or short, where letters should be sounded together (*harf* to *harf*) and where they should be kept separate, and so on. Numerous works in Arabic have been written on this discipline, and there are also later works in other languages. According to Islamic teaching, one of the finest and most highly regarded deeds is Qur'anic recitation. What is more, the utterance of the words of the Qur'an (*tilawat al-Qur'an*) is a good deed (*thawab*), regardless of whether their exoteric and esoteric meaning is understood or not, while the significance and value of the act derive from the conviction, knowledge and recognition that the Qur'an is a revelation from the Lord of the Worlds. Recitation is an ability, skill and art of a phonetic nature, and is based on precisely defined laws and criteria, the practical realization of which depends upon skill in diction. The scientific discipline that specifies, draws up and explains the principles of the proper recitation of the Qur'an and the methodology for putting it into practice is thus called *'ilm al-tajwid*, or *fann al-tajwid*, or *ahkam al-tajwid*, or *tajwid al-Qur'ani*, all of which designate knowledge of the rules and laws of exact Qur'anic recitation.

Tajwid also means embellishment, beautification, adornment and a striving for perfection (deriving from the verb *jawwada*). A person who studies this discipline is known as a *mujawwid* (specialist in *tajwid*), and the person who works with a beginner on practical exercises is called a *muqri'* (mentor for Qur'anic recitation), while a person who is well versed in these rules and how to put them into practice is called a *qari* (reciter). However, the word *tajwid* does not occur in the Qur'an, instead the term *tartil* is used: 'And recite the Qur'an in slow, measured rhythmic tones (*tartilan*)' (*al-Muzzammil*, 73.4), which in the context of this topic has the same meaning. Furthermore, as regards the terminological meaning of the word, it is closely associated with the meaning of and gives greater exactitude to the original acoustic base (*makharij*) in which phonemes are created in a natural way, with their own permanent and transient acoustic features (*sifat*).

There are several definitions of *tajwid* as a scientific discipline, each of which emphasizes accurate diction, something to which particular care must be given when reciting the Qur'an, and the rules of which are usually derived from classical sources. In his work *al-Itqan fi 'ulum al-Qur'an* (Introduction to the Qur'anic Sciences,; Cairo), Jalal al-Din al-Suyuti gives this definition:

> *Tajwid* is the scientific discipline that studies the original acoustic base and its centres in which phonemes arise, and the inter-relations of which produce many acoustic variants and nuances, such as nasalisation, assimilation, stress or non-stress of the vocal features, length and prolongation of vowels, allophones (variants of pronunciation) of vocals, and all the other details relating to the recitation of the Qur'an. (n.d.: 132)

However, in an attempt to bring together classic and modern definitions of this science, one may say that *tajwid* is Qur'anic orthoepy (correctness of diction), which studies all refinements and nuances of articulation of consonants and vowels, relevant and irrelevant, as well as their inter-relations and the way they reflect, directly or indirectly, on the meaning, sense, moral and message of the Qur'anic *ayas*. Practical performance is effectively also reflected at the specific melodic level (*tanghim*), in which both the primary and the secondary rules and criteria must be known and applied, which again depends on innate ability, extensive practice and the responsibility of each individual.

Then again, when considering the subject, terminology and methodology of this scientific discipline, and analysing its definitions, historical emergence and evolution, it could be said that *tajwid* is the revealed Qur'anic phonetics, which deals with three features of the Qur'an itself:

1. the articulation of the Qur'anic phonemes;
2. pausal (*waqf*) and initial (*ibtida'*) form;
3. the phonetic modifications that occur as a result of the mutual influence of phonemes, whether within a single word or as part of a syntagmatic cluster.

In the case of the first and the second points, the proper articulation of the phonemes and the use of the rules of pausal and initial form are a strict requirement (*wajib*), since failure to do so would alter the actual meaning of the Qur'anic *ayas*. The application of the rules of the third element (*madd, ikhfa', idgham, iqlab, izhar*, etc.) is *sunna*, and failure to apply them is reprehensible (*makruh*). This is because in the Qur'an (*al-Muzzammil*, 4) God commands: 'And recite the Qur'an in slow, measured rhythmic tones', which means proper, precise, careful, responsible, calm and humble recitation accompanied by reflection on the messages of the Qur'an. The commandment in this *aya* falls into the category of obligation (*wajib*), because *tartil* (precision, perfection) is the very attribute of the Qur'an, and as the Qur'an itself says: 'Thereby, and We have rehearsed it to thee in slow, well-arranged stages, gradually (*tartilan*)' (*al-Furqan*, 25.32).

What is more, the most worthy recitation of the Qur'an is when language, reason and the heart are engaged together. Language preserves the proper diction of the phonemes, reason interprets their meaning and the heart fosters their instructions, advice and warnings. Language utters, reason recognizes, and the heart receives the message.

Another area to be studied is tempo. Recitation of the Qur'an may be fast or slow, but it must be adapted to one's own abilities in pronunciation and diction. In this sense, *tajwid* is divided into:

1. *tartil* (slow and measured recitation);
2. *hadr* (rapid recitation);
3. *tadwir* (recitation at a moderate speed).

Keeping in mind all the above, it may be said in conclusion that *tajwid* studies the laws and methods of the proper recitation of the Qur'an. *Qira'at* is ability and skill in the practical realization of these norms, and the quality of their application depends on the responsibility and the skill in diction and pronunciation of each individual. During recitation and training, the auditive-visual method is the most effective. Beginners in recitation, particularly in the earliest stages, must have a mentor who will help them with practical exercises in the application of these rules. It is a well-known fact, as the author of this entry is aware, that the proper recitation of the Qur'an is best learned through listening to 'live' Qur'anic recitation according to the rules of *tajwid*, because this enables one both to learn it according to the rules and to enjoy its harmonic melodics, constructed on a firm, aesthetically refined rhythm which induces a sense of wellbeing and has an ennobling effect.

Finally, since the Qur'an is the main source of all Islamic teaching and doctrine, this was the reason for the evolution of this discipline and the fact that many works were written, including works on the recitation of the Qur'an in seven or ten ways (*qira'at sab'a* and *qira'at 'ashara*). The *qira'at* are the different linguistic, lexical, phonetic, morphological and syntactical forms that are permitted in reciting the Qur'an, and are not in any sense 'variants'. The source of these diverse refinements is the fact that the Qur'an incorporates into its linguistic system the most familiar Arabic dialects and vernacular forms in use at the time that the Qur'an was revealed.

Further reading

http://cmcu.georgetown.edu/Islamic resources/Issues Concerning the Qur'an/, and *Multilingual Links for Learning the Rules of Tajweed* on web page: http://www.dallal.com/Tajweed_com.htm, and *Rules of Tajwid* on web page: http://ccat.sas.upen.edu/bvon/pages/tajwid.htm

See also: **reading**

NEVAD KAHTERAN

TALAQ
see: **divorce**

TALUT

The first king of the Israelites, the story of Talut (Saul) can be found at 2.246–251. According to Muslim exegetes, the name Talut means 'tall' (*tawil*), and refers to the extraordinary stature of Saul. In consonance with biblical accounts, Muslim exegetes explain that Saul's only remarkable feature was his stature, that he was from a common profession and that he was of the tribe of Benjamin rather than the tribe of Judah from which kingship was supposed to descend. In 2.249 Saul is described as leading into battle an army whose ranks have been reduced by a test at a river (Gideon in Judges 7); this

army is compared to the small number of warriors who fought with Muhammad at the battle of Badr. Muslim exegetes also relate the conflict between Saul and David, including Saul's summoning of Joshua from the dead to ask for advice before dying with thirteen of his sons. Other exegetes report that it was the prophet Samuel who is summoned from the dead by Saul.

Further reading

Lindsay, J.E. (1994) "Ali ibn 'Asakir as a Preserver of Qisas al-Anbiya': The case of David b. Jesse', in H. Busse (ed.) *The Tower of David/Mihrab Dawud: Remarks on the history of a sanctuary in Jerusalem in Christian and Islamic times*, Jerusalem: Hebrew University Press.

BRANNON WHEELER

TAQA

Taqa or *waqa* means to keep one protected: 'So, Allah saved them from the evil of that Day' (76.11). *Itiqa* or *tuqa* means to take safety measures in order to prevent harm: 'Except by way of precaution, that ye may guard yourselves from them' (3.28). It also applies to fearing evil: 'And fear the Fire' (3.131). Fearing prosecution, *taqiya* was often pursued by the Shi'ites. Their religious beliefs were kept secret and revealed only to those who shared their interpretation of Islam.

RAFIK BERJAK

TAQI AL-DIN IBN TAYMIYYA
see: **Ibn Taymiyya, Taqi al-Din**

TAQLID

A term used in Islamic jurisprudence to refer to the practice of following precedent. It is not derived from the Qur'an but from a word meaning designation for public acceptance of an animal for sacrifice or a person for a leadership position, by the hanging of a necklace or emblem around the neck.

The Qur'an is recognized as the primary source of legislation in Islam. Its specific legal rulings are relatively few; the majority of the Qur'an comprises moral exhortation and reiteration of prophetic history for didactic purposes. However, when the Qur'an does offer specific legislation, it is incorporated into Islamic law. In cases for which the Qur'an does not offer specific legislation, legal scholars are expected to follow the practice of Muhammad (the *sunna* of the Prophet). This is generally accepted to have been preserved in reports (called 'traditions' or *ahadith*; singular: *hadith*) from reliable witnesses, transmitted orally at first and then recorded and codified by the ninth century CE). When issues arise for which there is no specific norm established in the Qur'an or *sunna*, the interpretations agreed upon by consensus (*ijma'*) of the religious authorities in the first few generations of Muslims are considered authoritative.

A fourth source of Islamic legislation is *ijtihad*, or intellectual effort (from the root *jahada*, to strive) to derive appropriate legislation from the Qur'an and *sunna* for novel cases. By the tenth century, the Muslim community recognized five major schools of Islamic legal thought (*madhahib*; sing: *madhhab*). Each was named for a major scholar who was believed capable of deriving fresh legal rulings from the first three sources. These were Ja'far al-Sadiq (d. 765), Abu Hanifa (d. 767), Malik ibn Anas (d. 795), al-Shafi'i (d. 820), and Abu ibn Hanbal (d. 855). Each was known as a *mujtahid*, or one who could practice *ijtihad*. By that time many scholars were in agreement that the science of jurisprudence (*fiqh*) had been perfected, and that sufficient legislation

had been generated from the sources to serve the needs of the Muslim community. As it is traditionally expressed, the 'door of *ijtihad*', therefore, was 'closed'. Each *madhhab* developed handbooks of legislation that were to guide legal scholars from then on. Following these precedents is what is generally meant by *taqlid*. Scholars after the generations of *mujtahidun* were denoted *muqallidun* (those who follow precedent).

In traditional practice, therefore, *ijtihad* was considered rarely necessary; efforts at *ijtihad* were rejected as irreligious innovation (*bid'a*). The products of legal reasoning already agreed upon became known as *shari'a*, divinely revealed law. Allowing a precedent to guide legal decisions – *taqlid* – was equated with piety. Reformers, however, distinguish between divine law (*shari'a*) and the products of human reasoning (*fiqh*). They believe the former is revealed in the Qur'an and *sunna*, and is perfect and changeless. But it must be interpreted by human beings for application in daily life, and such interpretations are fallible. They must therefore be revisited regularly, and evaluated for their effectiveness in achieving divinely revealed goals of justice and social well being.

Many reformers also reject the limitation of the *sunna*, the normative practice of Prophet Muhammad, to the contents of authenticated *hadith* reports. Rather than imitating specific actions of the Prophet, these reformers claim, believers should seek to emulate the moral ideals and motivation of those actions. Ideals and goals remain constant, but specific actions may no longer be effective in achieving the intended goals, given the passage of time and changing social circumstances. In such cases, *ijtihad* must be exercised to determine effective ways to achieve the original goals. Reformers therefore decry *taqlid* as a source of stagnation in Islamic law and identify it as responsible for the loss of relevance of Islamic law in the modern world. *Taqlid* is often seen as the reason that Islamic law has been marginalized in the modern world, relegated to the limited areas of traditional family law and religious practice, while foreign legal systems have been imposed by many governments to deal with modern commercial, economic and social issues.

Some progressive reformers extrapolate from the critique of *taqlid* in the field of jurisprudence to the area of Qur'anic hermeneutics. Pakistani scholar Fazlur Rahman (d. 1988), for example, criticizes the literal application of Qur'anic precedents and those found in some *hadiths* as *taqlid*. In his analyses, which have influenced many contemporary reformers, Rahman focuses on the historicity of revelation. In order to comprehend the normative teachings of the Qur'an and practice of Prophet Muhammad, the role of the circumstances of revelation (*asbab al-nuzul*) must be examined. This type of analysis is predicated upon the perception that the mission of Prophet Muhammad was twofold: to effect social change in the specific context of seventh-century Arabia, and to establish a model for all humanity for all time. Both goals are believed to have been achieved, their record preserved and transmitted in the Qur'an and the *sunna*. The Qur'an and the *sunna*, therefore, must be recognized as historically contextualized examples of universal goals and ideals.

The challenge for believers is to distinguish between the specific examples and the overall ideals. In order to do this, they must take into consideration the circumstances of revelation as well as the overall moral ethos of the Qur'an and *sunna*. Rahman's critique is based on the claim that traditional interpreters have failed to do that. Among the examples he cites is that of women's share of inheritance, described in the Qur'an as one half that of men (4.11). Failing to distinguish between text and context, traditional interpreters assumed that the principle involved in the verses was the superior claim of males over females. Rahman claims that this assumption violates the overall teaching of the Qur'an and the sprit of the *sunna*, which he proposes is the full personhood of females and their equality with males. In the circumstances in which the verses in question were revealed, females were economically and socially marginalized. Including them in inheritance shares would have been a significant step in correcting those circumstances. Given the Qur'an's insistence on human equality, it is highly unlikely that it would advocate that half the human race always be kept economically inferior. Rahman therefore proposes that the universal teaching of the inheritance verses is that women must be included in inheritance as a reflection of their full personhood. This is the value that must be applied in all circumstances; the disproportional amount of their share is a variable dependent upon circumstances and those circumstances should change. For Rahman and other progressive reformers, therefore, those who fail to distinguish between the universal teachings of the Qur'an and *sunna*, and who advocate specific measures suitable during the time of revelation to further Islam's overall reform goals but which are not necessarily conducive to those goals in today's circumstances, are engaging in inappropriate *taqlid*.

See also: **asbab al-nuzul; Nahda; nisa**

TAMARA SONN

TAQLID – SHI'I VIEWS

Taqlid literally means to follow (someone), to imitate. In Islamic legal terminology it means to follow a *mujtahid* in religious laws and commandment as he has derived them. A *mujtahid* is a person who is an expert in the field of Islamic jurisprudence (*fiqh*); he may also be called a *faqih*. In order to see where and why the practice of *taqlid* gained acceptance in the Shi'i world, it is necessary first to explain how it is seen in that community.

Human nature dictates that we can function properly only within society, and society requires laws and regulations. Islam teaches that God has sent a series of messengers and prophets with divine laws for our guidance from the very beginning of humanity on earth. The final Messenger and Prophet was Muhammad, who brought the last and most perfect of God's religious messages, Islam, to serve as a guide for humanity.

God is the creator of man and the universe, and so only he can make laws for us. The prophets and messengers are merely the teachers and announcers of divine laws and regulations; they cannot make laws themselves. In Shi'i Islam the Imam is the successor of the Prophet and acts as the preserver and interpreter of Islam and its divine law, the *shari'a*. In the earliest period of Islamic history, the Prophet guided the Muslim community (*umma*) in every step it made, and was there to solve all its difficulties. After the Prophet the Shi'a received guidance directly from *imams,* beginning with Imam 'Ali, and extending until the death of the Eleventh Imam, Hasan al-'Askari. Then, during the period of the Lesser Occultation (*al-ghaybatu al-sughra*) of the Twelfth Imam, he himself successively appointed four representatives who acted as the link between the Imam and his followers.

However, when the present Imam went into his Greater Occultation (*al-ghaybatu al-kubra*) in 329/941 the Shi'a had no alternative but to observe *taqlid*. The idea of blindly following tradition is criticized in the Qur'an: 'they say, "Enough for us is what we found our fathers doing". What, even if their fathers had knowledge of naught and were not rightly-guided?' (5.104) This strong condemnation of the idol-worshippers is repeated elsewhere: 'And when it is said to them, "Follow what Allah has sent down", they say, "No, but we will follow such things as we found our fathers doing"' (2.170 and 31.20). It is clear then that *taqlid* is only acceptable if one has a correct person or model to follow.

The following passage of the Qur'an, according to the Shi'ite scholars, directed Muslims to a form of *taqlid* that involves following the rulings of those who have gained sound knowledge in religion:

> Of every group of them, a party only should go forth [for *jihad*] so that [among those who are left behind there should be some] who should [undertake to] gain knowledge in religion, in order for them to warn their people when they consult them, so that they take heed to themselves. (9.122)

On the basis of the above passage a person 'who undertakes to gain knowledge in religion' is made responsible for putting Muslims on their guard by warning them about their obligations, whether religious or moral. Accordingly, whether the Muslims commit themselves to follow his legal decisions or not, the Qur'an requires this knowledgeable person to fulfil this role. When there is such a learned person in the community, then it is obligatory to refer to him in matters related to the religious practice. Consequently, in Islamic jurisprudence *taqlid* denotes a commitment to accept and act in accordance with the rulings of the *shari'a* as deduced by a well-qualified, righteous jurist (*mujtahid*).

It also suggests adopting his rulings with confidence, without investigating the reason that led the jurist to make his decisions. In other words, it is important for believers to feel confident in their religious observances, and that confidence can be attained either through *ijtihad* (i.e. personally investigating all the proofs that led to a particular legal decision), *ihtiyat* (taking the safe, prudent line by adopting a precautionary stance in those matters of which one is unsure) or *taqlid* (passing the responsibility for one's religious acts to a qualified jurist-scholar). However, the obligation to follow a *mujtahid* in one's religious practice does not mean accepting his opinions in other fields of religious knowledge, such as theology or mysticism, history or philosophy; nor does it imply that such a scholar is to be regarded as infallible (*ma'sum*) at any point.

The question of the *marja' al-taqlid* or highest religious authority is actually the rational decision dictated by the necessity to consult those who are specialists in matters of the *shari'a*. This rational necessity for *taqlid* has also led to the necessity of following the most learned (*al-a'lam*) among the scholars, someone who is the point of reference – *al-marja'* – for all the Shi'a. However, the question of 'the most learned' in *taqlid* is inherently subjective. How can one determine who is the most learned when every scholar can claim to be the most learned? There is no doubt that those *mujtahids* who ruled it obligatory for believers to follow the decisions of the 'most learned' jurist wanted to centralize the leadership of the jurist in the community and establish a common pattern for religious practice of the faithful.

By declaring one's *taqlid* of the most learned *mujtahid*, a believer establishes a direct link between his religious acts and the rulings of the *marja'*. This sense of linkage also generates a sense of loyalty to the *marja'*, which is formalized through a juridical pronouncement (*fatwa*) requiring the ordinary person to declare his intention to follow the most qualified member of the community through *taqlid*. *Taqlid*, then, is the rational counterpart of a *mujtahid's* knowledgeable position in matters related to religious practice.

See also: **Shi'a**

OLIVER LEAMAN

TAQWA

Taqwa is one of the many words in the vocabulary of Islam whose exact equivalent cannot be found in English. It has been translated variously as 'fear of God', 'piety', 'righteousness', 'dutifulness' and 'God-awareness'. It is a virtue whose importance must not be underestimated, for it is emphasized in numerous passages of the Qur'an, among which is the following: 'And make provision for yourselves; the best provision is *taqwa*' (2.197). The *aya* (verse) from which this passage is taken pertains to the pilgrimage to Mecca. Interpreters of the Qur'an have explained that some people used to start for a pilgrimage to Mecca without sufficient means, that they trusted God would provide for them. In this *aya* it is forbidden for one to become a burden on society in this way. Trust in God should not be used as an excuse to throw off our responsibility.

Commentators observe that the meaning of the passage referring to the spiritual journey of life is *taqwa*. And we must adequately prepare ourselves for this journey, for it is a false piety that prompts one to neglect preparation and rely on God alone. The best way of doing this is *taqwa*.

The word *taqwa* is derived from the Arabic root (*waqa*), from which verbs are formed which signify protecting, preserving, guarding and other related ideas. *Taqwa* has the sense of protecting oneself from moral peril, preserving one's virtue and guarding oneself against the displeasure of God. *Taqwa* is thus a kind of awareness or consciousness by means of which one protects oneself from sliding into evil. In what is possibly the first occurrence of the word to have been revealed in the Qur'an, in *sura al-Shams* (91.8), *taqwa* is contrasted with wrongdoing, which is described as a kind of gushing forth. Here the impression is of *taqwa* taking the role of a restraint, a means to channel one's impulses so that they do not get out of control. This, however, might give the erroneous impression that *taqwa* is an external constraint governing natural tendencies. On the contrary, the Qur'an teaches that both the sinful tendency and *taqwa* come from God. What this means is that God has provided us with a knowledge of wrong and right. We can understand the verse as indicating that humanity naturally has a kind of power which God has created in us in such a way that, if we neglect it, we will veer from the straight path. But God has also inspired us with a kind of self-discipline or conscience by which we may keep ourselves moving in the right direction. When we look at it in this way, it is obvious why *taqwa* should be described as the best provision for the journey of life. It is the best provision because by means of *taqwa* we may have the conscience and the consciousness, the moral and spiritual presence of mind, necessary to keep us from straying.

Some of those with a sense of *taqwa* are cautious about associating others with God, careful about the difference between sin and evil and cautious of anything that might be damaging to him or her. The Qur'an often reports on the fact that the outward observance of ritual is not sufficient for *taqwa*. After the *aya* mentioning the change in the direction of prayer (*qibla*) from Jerusalem to Mecca, we are told:

> It is not righteousness that you turn your faces towards the East and the West, righteousness is rather one who believes in Allah, the Last Day, the angels, the Book, the apostles, and gives his wealth out of love for Him to the near kin and the orphans, the poor, the wayfarer, the needy and for those in bondage; and establishes prayer, pays the poor tax (*zakat*); and those who fulfil their promise when they make a promise, the patient ones in distress and affliction and in the time of war, these are the people who are truthful and these are the people who have *taqwa*. (2.177)

Here we learn that *taqwa* cannot be reduced to the performance of religious rites, but that it requires faith (*iman*) and practice performed out of love for God. With respect to animal sacrifice, it is written that neither their flesh nor their blood reaches Allah, but *taqwa* reaches him (22.37). This awareness which is *taqwa* is to be found in the heart, and by means of it the signs, symbols and rites ordained by God may be properly respected: 'And that whoever respects the symbols of Allah, it is from the *taqwa* of the hearts' (22.35). Without *taqwa* there is transgression. When one is motivated by hatred of one's enemies instead of love for God, self-control and awareness slip away: 'O you who believe! Always be upright for Allah, bearing witness with justice, and do not let hatred of a people incite you to be unfair to them. Be fair! That is the nearest to *taqwa*. Fear Allah! Indeed, Allah is aware of what you do.'

Taqwa certainly can be seen to have political implications. It is not a meditative state which takes one away from the world, but is a way of finding one's route through the world, which in its social and political dimensions requires justice and fairness. In the above *aya* a cognate of *taqwa* as a transitive verb in the command form also appears: *itta-qallah*. This is usually translated as 'fear of God'. This is not fear in the sense of being frightened that something terrible is about to happen, but rather awareness of the significance of the Creator and of our responsibility to him. The command directed at the believers of *ittaqallah* is a command to be vigilant over oneself by being aware of the presence of God. Thus we read: 'Verily, we have enjoined those who have been given the book before you, and you [O Muslims] to *ittaqallah*' (4.131).

If this awareness is a gift from God, how can he command it? *Taqwa* is a gift placed within the hearts of humanity by God and yet he commands us to have *taqwa*. Another *aya* resolves the issue: 'And those who follow guidance, He increases them in guidance and grants them their *taqwa*' (47.17). God has provided humanity with an innate awareness of him and with morality, but it must be taken up and made active by our own efforts and the direction of our attention towards God. This effort and orientation is not something we are expected to do by ourselves, only with guidance, yet we also have to make a contribution towards acquiring the correct attitude. Someone who follows guidance is rewarded with further awareness and understanding of what he or she ought to do. Further understanding leads to a deeper appreciation of the guidance God has given us through his prophets, and the acceptance of and submission to this deeper understanding and insight are rewarded by God by increasing awareness, and so it goes on. There is a cohesion between the spiritual activity of the believer, his conscience and consciousness, and the granting of mercy and blessings from God in the form of guidance that leads to increased awareness of him. This cumulative process describes how the process of *taqwa* increases in the individual as he or she grows in their spiritual lives as they respond increasingly to what God has to offer.

See also: ittaqa

OLIVER LEAMAN

TA'TIL

Muslims who read the Qur'an and believe in its divine source have the problem of explaining what they understand by expressions which confer upon God attributes such as knowing, hearing, acting, creating, speaking, seeing and so on. Some would say that since God is completely different from anything we know, his real attributes cannot be expressed in human language because human languages are necessarily confined to things which fall within our sense experience. But since human language is the only one we understand, God is using it to give us a glimpse of something which is really beyond our comprehension, and so we should not be surprised if we frequently fall into difficulties when discussing the deity. If our language does not apply to God in any real sense, then it cannot convey to us anything about him and so we should be very careful about using it to think that we gain any knowledge. On the other hand, if they do convey to us even a glimpse of the nature of the deity, there must be a link between them and the real attributes of God.

Other commentators would acknowledge the existence of such a relation, but would say that the words are used in their metaphorical and not in their real sense. For example, when in the Qur'an it is said of God that he sees or hears, what is meant is that he 'knows' because seeing and hearing in their real senses apply to mortal creatures only. There are at least three objections to this view. It might be argued that 'to see' is distinct from 'to hear', and both are different from, although related to, knowing. Then if it is claimed that all the words of our language are used in the metaphorical sense when they apply to God, we need to link this sense with a normal use. However, it is not that easy to define a normal use for many words that is distinct from their divine use. Finally, if the claim is that this applies to some and not all words and expressions describing God, then a valid argument must be given to explain the difference between the two types.

No such argument exists unfortunately. The truth is that, as Ibn Taymiyya clearly demonstrated in many of his works, whatever is said of some divine attributes can be said of other and more ordinary uses of the attribute. A less ambitious theory would attribute to God features such as existence, knowledge, life, power, will, seeing and hearing in their real sense, but would take as metaphorical attributes love, pleasure, anger and hate. The reply to a person who makes such a distinction between these two classes of attributes – affirming the former and denying the latter – is to say there is no difference between what is affirmed and what is denied. What applies to one of them does indeed apply to the other. If you say that God's will is like the will of human beings, so also would be his love and pleasure. This looks very much like anthropomorphism. But if it is said that God has a will that applies to him just as a human being has a will that applies to him, it will be said he also has a love that fits him, and an anger that fits him; and the human being has an anger that fits him.

If one interprets things such as love, hate and anger in an anthropomorphic way, the same can be said about will, knowledge and power. This was the approach of Ibn Taymiyya in trying to fight the idea that language when applied to God can only be used in a negative sense or in a metaphorical sense. Al-Ghazali also wanted to insist that when we make claims about God we are using the language in the same sort of way as we would normally use it, since otherwise our language about God is without any significant meaning. To use the word 'God' but deny that God shares any of our properties, or that when we make claims about his possession of such properties we are speaking in a very special sense, is to deny the word any real meaning. Or so al-Ghazali claimed in his attack on the philosophers in his *Tahafut al-falasifa*, where he argued plausibly that although philosophers talk about God a lot, he is clearly a very different figure than in traditional religion since his traditional attributes are understood in a very different way.

Is this not the same as likening God to human beings, leaving us with the problem of anthropomorphism? Ibn Taymiyya rejects the view that language is used in a real sense only when it applies to created things. He thinks that some descriptive words have general meanings that as an abstract concept do not apply to anything in particular, human or divine. But when these words are used to describe a particular, then they describe something which is peculiar to the particular in question. For example, if we describe two people as 'clever', the meaning of 'clever' when it applies to one is not the same as its meaning when it applies to the other. They may each be clever in different ways.

Does this mean that all words are equivocal? Ibn Taymiyya thinks that although the referents are different, the word has an abstract meaning that is common to both referents. This, he thinks, applies even in the case of God. When we describe him as exercising a will, for example, we are not likening him to human beings, we are not saying that he wills in the same way as we will. It is wrong, he insists, to think that the real meanings of such words are their meanings as they apply to human beings. Descriptive words, as such, are neutral. They take their specific forms according to the particulars that they describe. And just as there are differences between particular created things, there are differences between God and the world of created things. How do we know about the attributes of God? According to the school of the *ahl al-sunna*, some of the divine attributes can be known by reason alone, although most are known by revelation also. Other attributes of God are not known except through the divine revelation to God's chosen prophets or messengers. Those that can be known by reason alone may be divided into three categories: God's attributes as existent; his attributes as a living being; and his attributes as a creator and someone deserving of worship.

It is of paramount importance to understand the difference between the attributes of something as an existent and its attributes under other descriptions or headings. Failure to grasp this has led both believers and unbelievers into confusion about their conceptions of God. The mistake starts when either the theist or the atheist assumes that all the attributes of the physical are limited to its attributes under this physical description. Once this mistake is committed, it is easy to argue from it that, because God is not physical, nothing which is said of physical things can be said of him in any real sense. In their attempt to exalt God above all material things, they ended up depriving him of the very necessary attributes of the existent, thus making him a mere word that designates nothing. The *ahl al-sunna* were very much against this trend, and they dubbed the people who followed it *mu'attila*, meaning negators. By contrast, the *ahl as-sunna* called themselves the people of *ithbat*, of affirmation. The negators talk of God only in negative terms: all they say about him is that he does not have the attributes possessed by material things. The affirmers, on the other hand, believe that the basic attributes of God are positive ones.

The negative attributes which God is said not to have are only the negations of these positive attributes and what is logically implied by these negations. They think that as a creator, God must exist and exist objectively. To exist objectively God must have all the attributes of objective existents. God must therefore be somewhere and cannot thus be everywhere. Why not? Because to be everywhere is to fail to be distinguished from other existents and thus not to have a special identity. To believe that he is everywhere leads, moreover, to yet other absurdities. If God was everywhere before he created some things, then where did he create them? To say that he created them inside himself is absurd. To say that he created them outside himself contradicts the statement that he is everywhere. To say that God shrank to leave some space for them is absurd. More, it contradicts the assumption that he is infinite. It also leads to the absurdity that whenever anything passes out of existence God extends himself to fill the empty space.

Where is God then? The *ahl al-sunna* do not hesitate to answer that he is above his throne in heaven. Does this mean that he is limited? If by this is meant his person, then the answer is yes.

But although his person is confined to a particular 'region', his power, knowledge and other attributes are not thus limited. God is in heaven, but his power and knowledge are everywhere. He cannot in this sense, therefore, be said to be limited. The negators believed that God cannot be known at all by the five senses because they thought that to be thus known is to be physical. The affirmers agreed that he cannot be observed by us while we are in this world. But this is not because it is in his nature not to be observed; it is rather because of our own present nature as human beings.

There are verses in the Qur'an and authentic sayings of the Prophet Muhammad which affirm that believers shall behold God in the next world. In fact, beholding him would be their greatest joy. They would be able to behold him because their nature would be different from what it is now. The affirmers do not depend on this religious argument alone. They also believe that it is a contradiction in terms to say that something exists objectively and yet cannot in principle be observed. It is only non-existents which cannot in principle be observed, or as some suggest, a thing which cannot be observed by any of the senses is equivalent to nothing. As an existent, then, God must exist outside our minds, i.e. he cannot be a mere idea or an abstract concept. Second, he must have some defining qualities. Third, he must exist in a 'place', that is distinct from those places occupied by other existents. Otherwise, he would be one with them and hence could not be anything in his own right. Fourth, he must, in principle, be observable.

As a living existent God must have the attributes of willing, knowing, seeing, hearing, etc. In short, God must have all the attributes which living things necessarily have as living things, and not because of their materiality or animal-ity. But God is the creator of everything. As such, he must be eternal and hence self-sufficient, unique and perfect. All the other attributes that he has must be seen in the light of these basic attributes. Thus if we say that he knows, his knowledge must be different from that of any of his creatures in that it must be knowledge which is not preceded by ignorance and thus acquired through the senses or any other means. The same must be said of all the other attributes. That is why it is one of the pillars of Islam in at least one of its formulations to believe that God is unique in his person as well as in his attributes. Just as none of his creation resembles him, so none of their attributes resemble his attributes.

While we know the meanings of the divine attributes, we do not know their modality or the form they take when they apply to his unique person. Some of the attributes of God we cannot know except through his own words as revealed to chosen prophets. In Islam these words are confined to the Qur'an and the *sunna*. These sources attribute to God things like his being above the throne, having hands, smiling, etc. The negators take all these attributes to be metaphorical. The position of the *ahl al-sunna*, however, is to affirm about God whatever he affirms about himself in the Qur'an or through his Prophet, but without *tashbih*, that is without likening him to created things, or without *ta'til*, that is without explaining away his attributes as metaphorical. We understand them, affirmers say, in the light of the principle stated in *aya* 42.11: 'There is nothing whatever like him, and he is the one that hears and sees all things (*laysa kamithlihi shay'un wa huwa as-sami' ul-basir*).'

A particularly strong critic of the so-called anthropomorphists is Ibn al-Jawzi, who says in his analysis of this *aya* that since Allah knows that human beings cannot comprehend him, he described himself using words which they understand. Then, after establishing his existence by using such words, he negated any resemblance between those words and what we normally understand by them through this *aya*, which pulls up the drawbridge of meaning behind him, as it were. Ibn al-Jawzi also points out that the Messenger did not produce the allegorical *ahadith* all at once. Rather, he mentioned a word from time to time. Thus, whoever collects these *ahadith* together in a way that suggests they should be taken together has committed a grave blunder.

We should bear in mind also that the *ahadith* are very few in number, and authentic reports among them are still fewer, and then they are Arabic, which allows the use of idiom and metaphor.

As Ibn al-Jawzi says in *Talbis Iblis* (1340: 111ff.), those who transmit *ahadith* have taken literally the material language of the reports when they refer to God because they did not often have much to do with the jurists who specialize in the science of how to interpret the allegorical (*mutashabih*) sayings in line with the decisive and clear ones (*muhkam*). Even the Hanbalis speak about the fundamentals of religion in an inappropriate manner, having taken the attributes of God in a very physical sense. Thus, they heard that Allah created Adam in his image, and so attributed to God a face in addition to his essence, as well as a mouth, lips, teeth and so on. They admitted that there was no mention of a head, but other parts of the body they are happy to ascribe to the deity. Abu Isma'il 'Abdullah ibn Muhammad al-Ansari al-Harawi compiled a collection of forty *hadith*, in which he drew upon what Ibn al-Jawzi considered to be weak, weird and fabricated *hadith* to attribute various bodily organs to Allah. Al-Subki relates, in *Tabaqat al-shafi'iyya al-kubra*, that Abu Isma'il al-Harawi said:

> I asked Yahya ibn 'Ammar about Ibn Hibban, saying 'Did you see him?' He said, 'How could I not have seen him, considering that we expelled him from Sijistan? He had a lot of knowledge, but not much religious feeling. He came to us and denied that Allah has limits, and so we drove him out of Sijistan.' (Subki says) 'Look at how ignorant this critic is! I wish I knew who is more deserving of criticism! One who affirms limits for his Lord, or one who denies them?'

> [Ibn al-Jawzi continues] 'And I have advised the followers as well as the followed, and told them, "O our companions! ... Your great Imam, Ahmad ibn Hanbal used to say, while he was under the whips, 'How can I say that which has not been said?' So, beware of innovating into his *madhhab* (school) what is not a part of it. Then, you have said regarding the *hadith*, 'They should be taken according to their literal [meaning]', but the literal [meaning] of 'foot' is a [bodily] limb, and whoever says, 'He *istawa* (sits, ascends) upon the Throne with His Holy Self', has considered Him as being in the realm of sense-perception'."

Istiwa is an allegorical attribute and is mentioned in a number of verses of the Qur'an. The position of the *salaf* (the original Muslims) is therefore that we affirm it as an attribute of God, but precisely how we must leave to him to define. Anas b. Malik was once asked, 'How did He *istawa* upon the Throne?', at which Malik became furious, and replied, 'The *istiwa* is known, its specification is inapplicable, to believe in it is obligatory, and raising questions about it is an innovation. And, I see you as nothing but an innovator.' Afterwards he turned to his companions and said: 'So, expel him [from this gathering].'

The interpretation of *istawa* given by some of the Ash'arites means that Allah conquered (i.e. established his authority over) his throne. It is worth noting that the approach of the *salaf* is not anthropomorphic (*tashbih*), and the approach of the latter Ash'aris is not a negation or denial (*ta'til*) of the attributes. Ibn al-Jawzi complained at the end of his book that many readers did not like such an interpretation because they were caught up in the interpretations of their corporealist *shaykh*s. They concluded that what Ibn al-Jawzi takes to be the Salafi interpretation is not their *madhhab*, nor the *madhhab* of those *shaykh*s whom they blindly follow. Ibn Hanbal, according to Ibn al-Jawzi, does not take an extreme position concerning the issue of how God has his attributes.

References and further reading

Ibn al-Jawzi (1340) *Naqd al-'ilm wa'l-'ulama' aw Talbis Iblis*, ed. M. Dimashqi, Cairo.
Pavlin, J. (1996) 'Sunni *kalam* and theological controversies', *HIP*: 105–18.

See also: **al-Ash'ari; Ibn Taymiyya;** *kalam***; language and the Qur'an**

OLIVER LEAMAN

TAWADU

see: **humility**

TAWAKKUL

The verbal noun *tawakkul* does not appear in the Qur'an, but various forms of its root *w/k/l/* do. The noun of the first form, *wakil*, means guardian, who in every case in God. All other instances of the verbal form mean to trust in God. Four distinct uses may be found. One is the term in phrases that both enjoin trust and assure divine reciprocation. A second is the function of trusting in God as a deterrent against evil. Third, is when a creedal element is apparent.

Fourth, a theological assertion is made in a number of cases which point to God as the sole agency in all affairs.

Several passages entreat the listener to have trust in God and follow this with an assertion that he is the trustworthiest. Muhammad is told: 'Put your trust in Allah, for He suffices as Guardian' (33.3). The Prophet is also told to wash his hands of the unbelievers: 'so keep clear of them, and put your trust in God, for He suffices as Guardian' (4.81). The injunction also applies more generally: 'If anyone puts his trust in Allah, sufficient for him (is Allah)' (65.3). Beyond the fact that God is the most trustworthy, a related advantage is that trust in God shields one from the devil's influence: '[Satan] has no authority over those with faith, and who put their trust in their Lord' (16.99). Likewise for satanic gossip, which will have no effect on believers who have put their trust in God (58.10).

This trusting also appears alongside several creedal statements asserting some of the basic tenets of the faith. Readers are told: 'Put your trust in Him, the Living, who never dies, and celebrate His praises' (25.58). Elsewhere other divine attributes are asserted: 'Put your trust in the Powerful and the Merciful' (26.217). The assertion of God's oneness, that constitutes the first part of the Muslim *shahada* or witness of faith, is made along with *tawakkul*. The Prophet is told: 'Say, "He is my Lord. There is no god but He. In Him I trust, and to Him I turn"' (13.30). Readers more generally are told to 'obey Allah and his messenger ... By God, there is no god but He. Let the believers put their trust in Allah' (64.12–13).

Beyond these creedal statements, a more subtle use of *tawakkul* is presented in passages that make a theological claim regarding God's omnipotence. The prophets recognize that although they bring an authoritative word, like all other humans, they are without true power. Thus trust must be had only in God: 'We are only human like you; but God grants [what He wills] to him He pleases from among His servants. We bring you no authority except as God allows, for the faithful put their trust in Allah' (14.11). Abraham echoes this recognition of divine omnipotence when he says to his father: 'I will pray for your forgiveness, though I have no sway over God in any matter. [He prayed]: Our Lord, in You do we put our trust, and to you do we turn in repentance' (60.4). In the life of the early community, the Muhammad is told to evoke God's omnipotence, tying it to *tawakkul*. To those who were half-hearted in their support of the Prophet's mission, and would not commit themselves and their resources fully, the Prophet is commanded to say: 'All that will happen to us is decreed by God. He is our protector; and the faithful put their trust in Him' (9.51). It is no surprise that *tawakkul* should go hand in hand with divine omnipotence, since the human choice to trust in God mediates the totalizing attribute of omnipotence. Room is thereby left for each to participate in a situation that would otherwise exclude all but the divine.

The *hadith* literature makes occasional mention of *tawakkul*, but does not develop it into an important theme. Typically, the use is consistent with that found in the Qur'an: humanity must not encroach upon divine omnipotence. Muhammad declares that 'Seventy thousand of my community will enter Paradise, without a reckoning of their sins. They are those who do not resort to charms or foretelling omens, rather they trust in their Lord.'

Another concept associated with *tawakkul* is that of the Oneness of God (*tawhid*), yet this association is not as much Qur'anic as it is the product of mystical speculation. The great Sufi thinker Sahl al-Tustari (d. 283/896) identifies divine Oneness as the inner core of *tawakkul*. In his commentary he responds to the question, What is *tawakkul*? by saying, 'The essential reality of *tawakkul* is the declaration of [God's] oneness' (al-Tustari, 2002: 104–5). On the one hand, for al-Tustari *tawakkul* is a mystical state, 'limitless and indescribable', second in importance only to dwelling with the truth; on the other hand, he continues to understand it in terms of one's relationship to God and the world. He writes: '*Tawakkul* is the rejection of the body by [bending it to] servitude, the devotion of the heart to [God's] lordship, and ridding oneself of [worldly] power.' The theologian-mystic al-Ghazali (d. 505/1111) also devoted a chapter of his *Revival of the Religious Sciences* to the themes of *tawhid* and *tawakkul*. The idea of abandoning worldly concerns, as evidence of one's trust in God, can be found among early Sufis of the eighth century. Shaqiq al-Balkhi (d. 194/810) is credited with formalizing *tawakkul* as part of the mystical discipline. His doctrine was an extreme one which even discouraged working for a living, as this would show undue concern for one's well being, and exhibit a lack of trust in the divine decree. However, this harshness was tempered in the later Sufi tradition. *Tawakkul* became more of an attitude than a rigorous world-negating practice, with conceptions such as those of al-Tustari expressed above becoming the norm (Knysh, 2000: 34).

References and further reading

al-Bukhari, A. (1994) *Sahih al-Bukhari* (The Sound Traditions of Bukhari), Cairo: Dar al-fikr.
al-Ghazali, A. (2000) *Ihya' 'ulum al-din* (The Revival of Religious Sciences), 4 vols, Cairo: Dar al-fikr.

Knysh, A. (2000) *Islamic Mysticism: A short history*, Leiden: E.J. Brill.

al-Tustari, S.(2002) *Tafsir al-Qur'an al-'Azim* (Interpretation of the Great Qur'an), ed. M. Geratallah (ed.), 3 vols, Cairo: Dar al-thaqafiyya.

RICHARD McGREGOR

TAWBA

see: repentance

TAWHID

Tawhid (monotheism) is the cornerstone of Islam. As it is their fundamental doctrine, the Muslims are described as 'the nation of *tawhid* (*ahl al-tawhid*)'. The doctrine of *tawhid* signifies total obedience and submission to God in worship and in deed. *Tawhid* designates the oneness of God (divine unicity), his absolute existence, and that he has no equal. It is embodied in the first profession of faith in Islam: 'there is no god but Allah' (*la ilaha illa Allah*)'. Although the word *tawhid* does not occur in the Qur'an, this tenet of faith has occurred recurrently throughout the work. *Tawhid* occurs as substantiation to God's omnipotence, the prophethood of Muhammad and eschatology. *Tawhid*, therefore, occurs in refutation to the argument of the literalists (2.116, 255; 3.3, 62–64, 171; 73.31), the dualists (5.116; 16.51; 23.91), the Trinitarians (5.73), and the polytheists (22.5–6; 72.2).

Features of *tawhid*

The notion of *tawhid* is characterized by three main features:

1. oneness of lordship (*tawhid al-rubu-biyya*), which refers to the belief in one God who is the creator and sustainer of every thing, and that he is one and without a partner in his dominion and actions.

2. oneness of worshipping God (*tawhid al-iluhiyya*), which signifies that only God is worthy of worship and that he has no rival in his divinity.

3. oneness of God's names and attributes (*tawhid al-'asma' wa'l-sifat*), which refers to God's names and attributes that none of us can be named by or be equal to.

Historical overview

Tawhid has been examined by Muslim scholars in terms of divine unicity, divine immutability and divine essence. Although Muslim scholars stress the absolute unicity of God and that the divine essence is beyond human comprehension, they understood *tawhid* from different perspectives. For traditional Muslim scholars, rational theology (*'ilm al-kalam*) was synonymous with divine unicity (*'ilm al-tawhid*). While the traditionalist Muslim scholars adopted the same early Islamic community non-rationalist approach to God's attributes, the Mu'tazila, during the seventh century, adopted a rationalist approach to the same theological issue. The Mu'tazila was a school of thought which began during al-Hasan al-Basri's lifetime (d. 728). They claimed that the Qur'an was created, was not part of the divine essence since the Qur'an can be comprehended by humans while God's essence is inaccessible to human reason, and that God's attributes and names in the Qur'an were allegorical. For them, the essence of God was unitary, eternal and unchanging. Their opponents, however, believed that the Qur'an was uncreated, part of the essence of God, and that God's attributes and names are not allegorical. In other words, they adopted a literal exegesis to references to God in the Qur'an.

During the middle of the ninth century, Ash'arite Muslim scholars also claimed that the Qur'an was uncreated and believed in the literal meanings of God's attributes and names. For them, God's attributes are befitting to him alone; we are told in 42.11 that 'there is nothing like unto Him'. In Qur'anic Studies, God's attributes are referred to as ambiguous (*mutashabihat*). Imam Malik (d. 790) held the view that all anthropomorphic expressions of the Qur'an, i.e. references to God, must be believed *without questioning how* (*bila kayf*). He stressed that the notion of rising above the throne as it occurs in 20.5 is not known, the how of it is not intelligible, asking about it is an innovation (*bid'a*) and to believe in it is a duty. Al-Tabari (d. 923) was particularly careful in refuting the Mu'tazila's rationalist interpretation of God's attributes. Other orthodox Muslim scholars such as al-Zarkashi (1344–91) and al-Suyuti (d. 1505) also emphasized that God's attributes had subtle definitions and sensitive theological semantic significations that were inaccessible to human comprehension. However, at the end of the ninth century, the Mu'tazila were accused of innovation.

In the middle of the thirteenth century, Ibn Taymiyya rejected both the Mu'tazilas' allegorical interpretation and the traditionalists' literal understanding of God's attributes. He highlighted the absolute unity of God and noted that God was reflected in his creation. Ibn Taymiyya argued for accepting the attributes of God without worrying about their underlying meanings.

During the middle of the nineteenth century, the notion of God's omnipotence and omniscience was stressed by Muhammad 'Abdu (1849–1905), who himself was influenced by Ibn Taymiyya. 'Abdu later stressed *tawhid* from a socio-political perspective, directing *tawhid* towards religious pluralism, i.e. the unity of religion regardless of diversity.

Similarly, Sayyid Qutb in the middle of the twentieth century also linked *tawhid* to politics and urged Arab and Muslim governments to adopt Islamic law.

The message of *tawhid*

As the central message of the Qur'an, *tawhid* reiterates several underlying meanings:

1. the need to abandon the worship of any god except Allah (1.5; 2.22; 17.23);
2. putting one's trust in only Allah, a true monotheist firmly believes that his/her success or failure can be given only by Allah and that his/her supplication and personal request should be made only to Allah (2.45, 165; 5.35; 27.62; 40.60; 65.3);
3. intercession (*al-shafa'a*) on our behalf to God for a personal request is forbidden (6.51, 94; 17.56–57; 82.19).
4. intercession between Allah and human beings can be achieved only with God's permission (2.255; 20.109; 21.28; 53.26).

In a socio-political/economic context, the ultimate Qur'anic message of *tawhid* is to emancipate people, to eliminate inferiority and to establish a positive bond with the Creator. The notion of emancipation and the direct link between the created and the Creator is referred to in 49.13, which highlights the monotheistic message that the most noble of us, in the sight of God, is the most righteous, and in 65.3, which highlights the message that God is sufficient for anyone who puts his or her total trust in him.

Polytheism

The reverse side of *tawhid* in the Qur'an is polytheism (*shirk*), which is the association of partners with God or the worship of others in addition to God. While *tawhid* stresses total reliance on God, polytheism refers to the belief that other human or non-human creatures can influence our life, have the power to make us prosperous or poor, have the power to make us live or die and can do good or bad to us; these polytheistic beliefs are referred to in 39.38. There are three categories of polytheism.

1. Major polytheism (*al-shirk al-akbar*), which is related to any act of worship that is directed to other than God, e,g, idolatry. This represents a gross rebellion against the Lord and is a major sin. There are four aspects of major polytheism:

   (a) polytheism of supplication (*shirk al-du'a*), which is to invoke, supplicate or pray to other deities besides Allah;

   (b) polytheism of intention (*shirk al-niyya*), which is the intention to worship not for the sake of Allah but for the sake of other deities;

   (c) polytheism of obedience (*shirk al-ta'a*), which is to be obedient to the authority of others other than Allah; and

   (d) polytheism of love (*shirk al-mahabba*), which is to show your love to those other than Allah.

2. Minor polytheism (*al-shirk al-asghar*), which refers to acts of worship or religious deeds performed only to garner praise, fame or wordly gains.

3. Covert polytheism (*al-shirk al-khafiyy*), which refers to dissatisfaction with what one has been given by the Lord. It also applies to anyone who assumes that had one only done this or that, one would have got what one aspired to.

Further reading

Abdul-Raof, H. (2003) *Exploring the Qur'an*, Dundee: Al-Maktoum Institute Academic Press.

al-Maqdisi, Abu 'Abd Allah Muhammad (1995) *Manaqib al-A'imma al-'Arab*. Beirut: Dar al-mu'ayyad.

al-Shaykh, 'Abd al-Rahman b. Hasan (1992) *Fath al-Majid*, Riyadh: Maktabat Dar al-Salam.

Sonn, T. (1995) 'Tawhid', *The Oxford Encyclopedia of the Modern Islamic World*, Oxford: Oxford University Press: 190–8.

See also: **Ash'arites and Mu'tazilites; Ibn Taymiyya;** *shafa'a*; *al-Tabari*

HUSSEIN ABDUL-RAOF

TA'WIL
see: tafsir

TAYAMMUM

The practice, when water is absent, or when there is not enough time to access a water source, of using fine earth to purify oneself prior to the performance of the canonical prayers. Conditions which may necessitate *tayammum* appear briefly in 4:43, although inevitably it is to the books of jurisprudence that one must turn for more detailed instructions. Health reasons – skin problems, for example – may also dictate recourse to *tayammum*, while the jurists also mention a number of materials, such as sand, stone or even snow, as legitimate alternatives to fine earth. The practice of *tayammum* is substituted for both the minor and the major ablutions, according to circumstance.

COLIN TURNER

AL-THA'LABI, ABU ISHAQ AHMAD

Abu Ishaq Ahmad b. Ibrahim al-Tha'labi al-Nisaburi was one of the earliest of the commentators to follow al-Tabari; he died in 427/1035. Few details are available about his life. He is variously referred to in classical Arab sources as al-Tha'labi or al-Tha'alabi. He was versatile, achieving fame as a reader, exegete, and preacher.

He is particularly famous for composing two works. His Qur'an commentary is entitled *al-Kashf wa al-bayan 'an tafsir al-Qur'an* (Unveiling and clarifying the interpretation of the Qur'an). He also wrote a famous collection of stories of the prophets. Al-Tha'labi's commentary includes a lengthy introduction, in which he presents his methodology and sources. He categorizes the commentators of his era into several groups:

1. those who followed heresy;
2. those who were excellent authors but still mixed heretical details with reliable materials;
3. those who simply reported and copied without comment or criticism;
4. those who shortened the chains of transmission, copied from journals and scripts, wrote on a whim, mentioned the meagre and abundant, weak and strong;
5. those of great skill and ability in the science of interpretation, basing their discussion on rigorous use of sources;
6. those whose exegesis was devoid of authoritative statements and who did not clearly distinguish between what was allowed and what was forbidden.

The approach to exegesis taken by al-Tha'labi was narrative-based, and belongs within the general stream of exegesis modelled by al-Tabari. He presented a considerable number of Traditions from the canonical collections, as well as apocryphal stories in support of theological issues or lessons presented. His own collection of Stories of the Prophets grew out of his commentary. This points to the extent of narrative in *al-Kashf wa al-bayan*.

His commentary received mixed reviews from scholars of succeeding generations. The biographer Ibn Khallikan (d. 681/1282) described al-Tha'labi as unique in his era in the field of exegesis. The geographer Yaqut (574–626/ 1179–1229) wrote admiringly of al-Tha'labi's commentary being an important source for information on grammar, the variant readings of the Qur'an and insights into interpreting the sacred text. However, Abu al-Ghafar b. Isma'il al-Farisi reported that controversy surrounded al-Tha'labi's use of traditions, some of which carried weak chains of transmission.

The fact that *al-Kashf wa al-bayan* has never been published is probably due to its ambiguous reputation. Nevertheless, manuscripts of this work are held in libraries around the world. Detailed studies of this commentary are few in number. The principal ones are Goldfeld's detailed examination of the preface to the commentary and Saleh's critical engagement with the entire commentary.

References and further reading

al-Dawudi, Shams al-Din Muhammad b. Ahmad. (n.d.) *Tabaqat al-Mufassirin* (The Generations of Commentators), 2 vols, Beirut: Dar al-kutub al-'ilmiyya.

al-Dhahabi, Muhammad Husayn (1405/ 1985) *al-Tafsir wa al-Mufassirun* (Exegesis and the Commentators), 3rd edn, 3 vols, Cairo: Wahba.

Goldfeld, I. (1984) *Qur'anic Commentary in the Eastern Islamic Tradition of the First Four Centuries of the Hijra: An annotated edition of the preface of al-Tha'labi's 'Kitab al-Kashf wa l-Bayan 'an Tafsir al-Qur'an'*, Acre: Maktabat wa-Matba'at al-Suruji lil-Tiba'ah wa-al-Nashr.

Saleh, Walid A. (2004) *The Formation of the Classical Tafsir Tradition: The Qur'an* commentary of al-Tha'labi (*d. 427/1035*), Leiden: E.J. Brill.

al-Suyuti, Jalal al-Din (1976) *Tabaqat al-Mufassirin* (The Generations of Commentators), Cairo: Wahba.

See also: **tafsir in early Islam**

PETER G. RIDDELL

THAWAB

A term meaning the result of one's deeds. Its root is *thawaba* (*thaba*) meaning to return to the original state.

In the Qur'an there is a reference to 'A reward from Allah, and from Allah is the best of rewards' (3.195). *Thawab* is generally used to express positive rewards: 'And Allah gave them a reward in this world, and the excellent reward of the Hereafter' (3.148). However, this term may also express negative consequences: 'Something much worse than that regarding the recompense from Allah' (5.60).

Athaba is the transitive verb meaning to reward: 'Allah rewarded them with Gardens under which rivers flow' (5.85).

RAFIK BERJAK

TOLERANCE

In the Qur'an tolerance is viewed a necessary prerequisite for coexistence. It assumes social, cultural and religious differences that require toleration even if these differences do not meet with the approval of the parties involved. Tolerance without greater acceptance indicates a sense of conditioned approval. However, the Qur'an views tolerance as an important starting point in establishing greater peace. The Qur'an seeks to establish peace between various religious communities and acknowledges differences of belief and cultures. It places great emphasis on maintaining good relations between adherents of various religions because, according to the Qur'an, religious freedom is an important basis for sustainable peace. The Qur'an calls all believers to 'enter into complete peace and follow not the footsteps of the devil' (2.208). This aspect is highlighted in the Qur'anic discourse on tolerance.

Diversity is recognized and highly praised in the Qur'an. Thus 30.22 asserts that in diversity and 'variations' are the signs of God for those with vision and those who are wise. This implies that differences must not only be expected but be tolerated. They are viewed as a cause for celebration, hence 49.13: 'O humankind, We created you from single [pair] of male and female ... so you may know each other.' The Qur'an recognizes diversity and difference in terms of gender, skin, colour, language and belief, as well as that of rank, and it asserts that differences are not only inherent and will always be there but they are a blessing from God. Again, the Qur'an asserts in 11.118: 'If God had willed He could have made humankind one people ...'. And again: 'We have ordained a law and assigned a path to each of you. Had God pleased, he could have made you one nation, but it is His wish to prove you by that which He has bestowed upon you. Vie, then, with each other in good works, for to God you shall all be returned, and He shall declare to you what you have disagreed about' (5.48).

From acknowledging differences to promoting a pluralist ethos the Qur'an outlines a firm standard for all, Muslims and non-Muslims alike, based on the universal values of justice and equality. For the Qur'an, peace is the ultimate goal, and if there is to be peace, there must first be tolerance. Diversity not only extends to physical features and social and cultural phenomena but also to the extent of choosing one's religion. The Qur'an recognizes various religious communities and a strong foundation for Qur'anic tolerance can be seen in the following verses. 17.70 speaks of human beings as being given an honourable position among all of creation. This is followed by the responsibility to care for all creation in mankind's role as *khalifa* (vicegerent) of God on earth. Similarly, 5.32 and 6.98 speak about the common origins of humanity which makes all human beings 'related' to each other. Thus, despite the differences, various ethnic and religious groups are urged to see the bigger picture and rise above the 'tribal' loyalties that divide them. The Qur'an also notes blessings of diversity; in verses 2.136 and 42.13 it specifically acknowledges other religions, such as that of Noah, Abraham, Moses and Jesus.

Tolerance is linked with justice and equality. The Prophet Muhammad was commanded by the Qur'an to be just among people and his example is upheld and is to be imitated and followed faithfully by Muslims. Thus 4.135; 5.8 and 60.8 emphasize that justice and equality are a must for Muslims. However no single human being is capable of and is in a position to judge others. 16.124, 31.23, 42.48 and 88.25ff. address the fact that judgement belongs to God alone and each person will receive their reward from the Lord based on their works. The emphasis on justice does not place limits on tolerance of others, even those who are in violation of others' rights. Tolerance can be seen in the life of the Prophet Muhammad, who is referred to in the Qur'an as a model example for humanity. His many policies reflect the Qur'anic view of tolerance of others. An example of this may be the crafting and implementation of the so-called 'Constitution of Medina', which regarded Muslim, Jewish and pagan groups as 'one community' sharing in the task of protecting one another

from outside aggression, while each group retains their right to freedom of religion. Another story of Prophet Muhammad is told about his years in Medina. One day he was sitting with some of his companions and a funeral passed by. The Prophet stood up as a sign of respect. When one companion remarked, 'O Prophet of God, this was a Jewish person's funeral!,' the prophet replied, 'Was he not a human being?'

Tolerance in the Qur'an is viewed as only the beginning in a realization of a sustained peace between communities. Thus the Qur'an asks Muslims to engage in dialogue with others, especially the *ah al-kitab* ('People of the Book'). 3.64 instructs Muslims to: 'Say, "O People of the Book! Come to common terms as between us and you: That we worship none but God; that we associate no partners with Him; that we erect not, from among ourselves, Lords and patrons other than God."'

Tolerance of others who are different in culture, language and/or belief is greatly emphasized in the Qur'an. In its early years Islam's popularity and survival depended on the 'flexibility' it displayed to the peoples of various regions that came under Muslim rule. Historians point to one example of such an approach in the eighth and ninth centuries when the vast majority of non-Muslim peoples came under Islamic political rule. These non-Muslims retained their religious, cultural as well as ethnic privileges for centuries without feeling the need to convert to the religion of their rulers. However, through the centuries, many Muslim rulers acted in accordance with their own political and economic ambitions, which often violated the Qur'anic dictates of tolerance. For example, the imposition of *jizya* (head tax) on non-Muslim male members in some Muslim states was often made to symbolize their humiliation. Similarly, restrictions placed upon non-Muslims in terms of building new places of worship were unjust, even according to many Muslim jurists. Contrary to Qur'anic teachings on tolerance, some Muslim rulers continue to apply unfair regulations even now, and their intolerance of non-Muslims as well as different Muslim groups is a matter of prime concern in many Muslim societies. Even though the Qur'anic prescriptions for, and teachings on, tolerance are clear and are agreed upon by most Muslims, today these must be reinterpreted to suit the demands of a peculiar nature of interaction between Muslims and non-Muslims. Such a reinterpretation should be mindful of those secular, democratic as well as pluralist values that are universally recognized.

Further reading

Abu-Nimer, M. (2003) *Nonviolence and Peace Building in Islam: Theory and practice*, Gainsville, FL: University Press of Florida.
Ali, Y. (1992) *The Meaning of the Holy Qur'an*, Baltimore, MD: Amana Corporation.

IRFAN A. OMAR

TRANSLATION AND THE QUR'AN

Translation (*tarjama*) of the Qur'an has always been a problematic and controversial issue for Muslims. The reasons for this controversy are diverse, but first and foremost among them is the fact that to Muslims the Qur'an represents the verbatim words of God as revealed to the Prophet Muhammad through the angel Gabriel. Whether one accepts this premise or not is a matter of religious preference, but the fact remains that the Qur'an is a self-referential text within which God refers to his verses (*ayat*) as striking linguistic miracles

revealed in a 'pure Arabic tongue' (*lisa-nun 'arabiyyun mubin*; 16.103). How could one possibly translate a linguistic miracle, an arrangement of divine words and sounds that has the potential not only to 'shiver skins' and 'soften hearts' (39.23) but also to 'shatter stones' (13.31) and to 'humble mountains' (59.21)? Wouldn't that necessitate a distortion of God's words, perhaps even a negation of the miracle itself?

Muslim scholars also base their argument on the idea of the inimitability of the Qur'an. Since God himself challenged the polytheists of Mecca to produce one *sura* as miraculous as those of the Qur'an, it was inferred that the language of the text could not be reproduced or imitated in any form or manner. Equally important is the fact that reciting the Qur'an in Arabic is itself a form of worship or prayer, where every sound produced is counted as a glorification and praise of God; hence, reciting it in any other language was not considered proper worship. According to the majority of scholars, obligatory prayers (*salat*) could only be performed in Arabic since reciting the opening prayer (*al-Fatiha*) in any language other than Arabic would render the prayer invalid. And thus it was that early Muslim theologians refused to sanction the translation of the Qur'an, the whole enterprise being deemed a sacrilegious act of the highest order.

Although, as a rule, this attitude of the Muslims towards the Qur'an perplexes Westerners, it should not be regarded as something unique or specific to Muslims. As Crystal points out in his analysis of the language of religion, not all religions favour the translation of their sacred book because of the sacredness of the language itself. This premise is perhaps especially true of the Qur'an since its language is revered as miraculous and 'inimitable' (*i'jaz al-Qur'an*).

Indeed, among orthodox Muslims, Arabic is 'the language of the angels (*lughat al-mala'ika*)' and the language of the first prophet that God created on earth, Adam. In many ways these objections to the translation of the Qur'an are parallel to the objections of early Church officials to Jerome's project of translating the Old Testament directly from the Hebrew on the grounds that it might displace the Septuagint, the Greek version of the Old Testament, and hence threaten the very ideology and stability of the Church. In a letter to Jerome written in 403, Augustine, bishop of Hippo, explained the reasons for his concerns: 'many problems would arise if your translation began to be read regularly in many churches, because the Latin churches would be out of step with the Greek ones' (cf. White, 1990: 92). He goes on to explain how a 'word' in Jerome's version of the prophet Jonah that had been rendered 'very differently from the translation with which they were familiar and which was ingrained in their memories', caused a great uproar among the congregation who criticized the text and 'passionately denounced it as wrong'. It is essentially these same fears that prompted early Muslim scholars to passionately reject all translations of the Holy Book since they believed it their duty to preserve the Qur'an in its uncorrupted and original pure Arabic.

Although modern Muslim theologians now acknowledge the importance and necessity of translating the Qur'an, not all types of translations are deemed acceptable. A so-called literal translation that follows closely the syntactic patterns of the original regardless of meaning is unanimously rejected. This is not only because it distorts the text but also because a literal reproduction might be perceived to be as verbatim and as divine as the Arabic original, and

might thus be liable to supersede it. This fear is understandable when we consider, for example, how the Septuagint prepared by Hellenistic Jews in the third century BC displaced the original Hebrew text and became the source of all the Latin translations that were widely used by Christian congregations. The only acceptable type of translation is the interpretive or exegetical type in which one renders not the actual words but an interpretation or a paraphrase. One translates, therefore, 'the meanings' of the Qur'an and not the Qur'an itself. In fact, most Muslim translations are labelled 'translations of the meanings of the Qur'an', and they are never given by themselves but always printed beside the Arabic text. What is being rendered in these bilingual translations is not the various connotations or so-called secondary senses of words but rather their primary or core sense. The idea is that one cannot capture all the possible connotations of the words of the Qur'an since that is part of its miraculousness. One particular verse in the Qur'an concerning the question as to why the Qur'an was revealed in Arabic and not in any other language, might perhaps indirectly resolve the whole issue of permissibility: 'And if We had made this Qur'an in a foreign tongue, they would have said if only its verses were explained. What! Not in Arabic and [its messenger] an Arab? Say, it is for those who believe a guide and a healing. And for those who disbelieve there is deafness in their ears and it [the Qur'an] is blindness unto them' (41.44). From this we can infer that although it is the meaning of the Qur'an that is all important, this meaning cannot be accessed or explained except through knowledge of the Arabic language. The problem with most Western translations is that they were undertaken by Christian missionaries and Orientalists who have hardly any active knowledge of the Arabic language.

Translation and ethics

Because of the above theological objections and the revered religious status of the Qur'an as the verbatim words of God, Muslim scholars up until the 1930s deemed it safer not to enter the field of Qur'an translation or even to question the adequacy of early Western translations. Thus for centuries the discipline was left entirely in the hands of hostile Christian missionaries and some very biased Western scholars. Since it is *a priori* that translations have far-reaching social effects, it seems important not only to evaluate the linguistic accuracy of these Western translations, but also to ask whether they are ethical. As Pickthall states in the introduction to his translation, no Holy Scripture can be fairly presented by one who disbelieves its inspiration and its message. One extreme example of such liberties with the Qur'anic text is the translation offered by Richard Bell, subtitled 'With a critical re-arrangement of the Surahs'. In essence, Bell is not a translator but an author. He not only rearranges the order of the chapters (*suras*) but actually restructures the order of the verses or *ayas*, translating them not in accordance with their actual order of occurrence but according to what he believes to be the thematically correct order of the text. To explain what he perceived to be 'confusion' in the material, Bell put forward the hypothesis that many of the verses were 'discarded material' written by scribes on the backs of sheets. He pictured the prophet as setting down his messages on small pieces of writing material as occasion permitted, and from time to time, revising, correcting and making additions between the lines, on the margins and on the backs of the

sheets (cf. Finegan, 1952: 489). He thus went about the text diligently looking for possible breaks and designating passages as 'scraps' that allegedly got into the Qur'an by mistake. In many instances he offers extremely hostile captions to his translations. For example, next to his rendering of the oath at the beginning of *sura* 89, he writes the following: 'An absurd oath (?) Meccan'. Unfortunately, even today, despite the subjectivity and the arbitrariness of his methodology, Bell is hailed by Western scholars as a 'pioneer in the field', and his translation is still cited and adhered to. It seems surprising that even though most Western scholars are now confident that the text of the verses has been generally transmitted exactly as it was found in the Prophet's legacy, the general tendency among scholars is not to discredit Bell's work or to question the reasons behind his hostile and unscholarly attempts at damaging a sacred text not only revered by millions of Muslims but also renowned for its literary and linguistic excellence. Although the review article by W.M. Watt expresses reservations about Bell's hypothesis on the disjointedness of the Qur'an, this is merely an introduction or summary of his work, certainly not a critical evaluation of it. The fact that Bell took a coherent Arabic text, readily understood by any native-speaker of the language, and cut and pasted it into something incoherent and disjointed clearly raises ethical questions that have yet to be addressed. One must also remember that apart from Bell's imaginative restructuring, there were numerous linguistic deviations from the original which emerge clearly when his translation of any passage is juxtaposed with any literal or standard Western translation of the text. On the lexical level, some very common and familiar words in Arabic are mistranslated so as to make the text appear ludicrous. Undoubtedly, it is because of such unethical practices that Muslims are so deeply suspicious of all Western translations of the Qur'an. Only when such bias is removed and openly discredited will Western commentators eventually be able to discover that many Western translations and editions are not only deficient but ethically questionable. It will be useful here to refer to Antoine Berman's concept of translation ethics which is based on the idea that 'bad' translations engender towards a foreign culture a domestic attitude that is ethnocentric: 'generally under the guise of transmissibility [it] carries out a systematic negation of the strangeness of the foreign work' (Berman 1992: 5). Good translations, on the other hand, aim to limit this ethnocentric negation: they stage an 'opening, a dialogue, a cross-breeding, a decentering', thereby forcing the domestic language and culture to register the foreignness of the foreign text. In essence, what is needed for the development of Translation Studies is a translator who, in the words of Kamesar (1993: 48), 'is capable of appreciating the aesthetic merits of works in a language not his own'.

Methods of translation

It seems clear from a survey of existing English versions of the Qur'an that most offer what is generally known as a 'semantic translation', where the contextual meaning of the original is more important than the primary senses of the lexical words and where the translator is inevitably selective and therefore interpretive and evaluative. To date, Qur'an translations have never sought to reproduce the form and content of the original in a literary manner. In fact, the most that a translator aims at is a 'functional equivalence', where the emphasis is on communication of message at the expense of lexical equivalence. Translators have constantly resorted to interpretation, even elaborately explaining a difficult non-core word, convinced that the relevant background knowledge is inaccessible to the reader and that a literal one-to-one translation is impossible. A survey of a number of English translations, including those by Pickthall and by 'Ali, reveals a recurring discrepancy between the original text and the translation which stems from a controlled selective procedure whereby, to get around the problem of difficult Arabic terms, translators simply transferred the terms according to their referent in the real world rather according to the core sense they possess within the language system of the original. In linguistic terms, they transferred their referential/contextual meaning rather than their denotative or dictionary meaning.

Most difficult words undergo a process of semantic reduction, from general to particular, during the process of lexical transfer from Arabic into English. For example, the word *al-falaq* (113.1), a generic term referring to the process of 'splitting', has been restricted in most translations to one particular type of splitting, namely 'daybreak' or 'dawn'. Although the notion of 'splitting' is still encapsulated in the English equivalent 'daybreak' and in the idiom 'the crack of dawn', the generic sense of the word *al-falaq* is lost in translation. The same process of semantic reduction is evident in the word *ghasiqin* (113.3), a generic term which refers to all entities that fall or plunge, but which is commonly translated as 'darkness' or 'night'. As with *al-falaq*, a specific referent is selected from a list of potential referents that include 'tears', 'rain' and 'floods', as well as 'sun' and 'moon' and all other entities that descend by necessity. To suggest that this dynamic word denotes 'night' is as inaccurate as equating 'fall' with common collocational partners such as 'night' or 'rain'. This selective strategy, although inadequate, continues to be viewed as standard and has been applied to and accepted by all formal translations. As a result, translations of the Qur'an into English over the past six decades have obscured much of the semantic complexity and referential versatility of the text by capturing too small a part of the Arabic lexicon. Although it is often unclear why the translator ignores the generic reference of a complex word and prefers to choose a particular referent, the extensive generality of these errors suggests that this is not simply a matter of wrong deductions about the semantic structure of these words, but that it can be attributed to more conscious and controlled errors of vocabulary.

If we compare Pickthall's 1930 translation and that by 'Ali in 1934, we will find that both – surprisingly enough – commit the same errors of translation, a fact which strongly implies that they were influenced by a common commentary (tafsir) of the Qur'an. In other words, they both resorted to interpreting the text rather than trying to access the denotative meaning of difficult words or trying to find a one-to-one English equivalent for them. The majority of these semantic errors of transfer tend to be inextricably linked with external influences upon a translator. These influences can be classified into three basic types: First, the influence of the long tradition of written commentary (tafsir) which itself has taken on special religious significance. This acquired secondary reverence has led to an over-emphasis upon the importance of traditional interpretations of a difficult word and a corresponding neglect of its dictionary or denotational meaning. Second is the influence of the most common

referent in the language-system. And finally there is the influence of older translations, especially monumental works such as those by Pickthall and 'Ali. These influences seem to force or dictate certain lexical errors, controlling to a very large extent the structure of the English translation. It is perhaps important to mention here that these influences are indeed acknowledged by most translators. 'Ali, for example, states in his preface that he was following the definitions of 'received commentators' and that where they differed with respect to the meaning of a certain word, he chose what appeared to him to be the 'most reasonable opinion from all points of view'.

The referential versatility of Qur'anic words

No doubt the translation of a highly complex and intricate book such as the Qur'an requires extensive research. It is, in many ways, analogous to the compilation of a dictionary, which as lexicographers have pointed out, involves several stages, the most important being isolating the difficult or non-core words and pinpointing their primary and secondary senses. This is essentially a semantic task involving the comparison of a sequence of words, i.e. synonyms, near synonyms, hyponyms and antonyms, all of which fall under the same lexical field. As stated above, the basic problem with the majority of translations today is that translators tend to simplify the enormous problems involved in defining the exact referential and denotational meanings of complex words by restricting their range of selection to a narrow domain and by selecting the variant most often used by well-known translators. A quote from Crystal (1997) on the linguistic difficulties of translating the 'Word' provides us with an important starting point for the whole topic:

> The linguistic issues involved may relate to major conflicts of cultural or historical interpretations, or be localized problems of style. A phrase such as 'Give us this day our daily bread' is not easy to translate into a language such as Eskimo, where the stable food is not bread; nor is it easy to handle the biblical parable of the fig-tree, which refers to seasonal change, in a language where there are no words for seasons, such as Yucatec.

Part of the difficulty in translating the Qur'an is the presence of a huge number of difficult and archaic words with a wide range of contextual meanings. To highlight the problem this versatility poses to translators, it is best to offer an illustrative example. Consider the words *al-waswas* and *yuwaswisu*, derived from the root verb *wsws*, and translated respectively as 'the whisperer' and 'whispereth' in Pickthall's and most other English versions of the Qur'an: 'And from the evil of the sneaking whisperer/who whispereth in the hearts of mankind' (114.4–5). The definition of the root verb *wsws* provided by the monolingual dictionary *al-Muhit* is as follows:

1. of the devil – to talk evil words to someone;
2. of the self (*nafs*) – to talk evil to oneself;
3. of a man – to talk repetitively in secret.

The noun *al-waswas* and the gerund *waswasa* are also listed under the same entry:

1. *al-waswas* – name of the devil
2. *waswasa* –
   (a) whispering sounds of hunting-dogs;
   (b) the clank of jewellery or light metal;
   (c) every evil thought that comes to the heart.

As the above definition reveals, the verb *waswasa* is etymologically a mimetic term associated with the clank of jewellery or light metal. Like tick-tick and choo-choo in English, the duplicative syllabic structure of *waswasa* comes close to being a direct transcription of the repetitive voice of its common referent, Satan. The fact that *waswas* is derived from Form II verbs, formed by the duplication of the middle consonant and which have semantic values of repetitiveness and intensification, adds to the basic iconicity of the word. The synonyms offered in most bilingual dictionaries include to whisper, to suggest, to prompt evil thoughts. Although *waswasa* is a strong collocator of Satan and the inner self (*nafs*) wherein the devil is assumed to reside, the meaning of the verb is usually extended to include any secretive incitement to evil or sin. A closer analysis of this verb reveals that its most essential sense-components in decreasing order of importance are as follows:

1. +SATAN
2. +NEGATIVE
3. +VERBAL SPEECH
4. –SOUND
5. + /s/
6. +ICONIC
7. +REPETITIVE

The above components reveal that the English verb 'to whisper' lacks three essential components that are integral to the Arabic verb, namely [+SATAN], + [NEGATIVE] and [–SOUND]. It is important to realize that the process of *waswas*-ing is selectively restricted to Satan in the Arabic language system. Even when the grammatical subjects are human agents, they are meant to be assuming the role of the devil. Thus, the Arabic noun *shaytan* ('devil') and the verb *waswasa* mutually attract each other like the sequence dog–bark or cat–purrs. The English verb 'whisper', on the other hand, has a positive sense-component derived from its association with the rustle of leaves, wind and soft agreeable sounds. It is also significant to note that the verb 'whisper' fails the so-called back-translation test because the common one-to-one word for 'whisper' in Arabic is *washwasha* and not *waswasa*. In addition, one must keep in mind that whispering denotes some measure of soft or low-frequency sounds, i.e. it has a [+SOUND] component that is incompatible with the mute internal speech of *waswas*. Sensing this componential non-equivalence and in an attempt to compensate for the loss of the crucial [+SATAN] encapsulated in *waswas,* Pickthall inserted the word 'sneaking', thus hoping to convey some of the negativeness of the Arabic original while 'Ali chose to insert the adjective 'evil' in brackets after the verb. There are probably a number of reasons for Pickthall's and 'Ali's translation of *waswas* as 'whisperer'. Foremost among them is undoubtedly the fact that *washwasha* and *waswasa* are very similar semantically and phonologically; both are speech words that are low in frequency and high in susurration. They are also both intrinsically iconic. However, although they are clearly related, these two verbs are not interchangeable in Arabic. Unfortunately, ever since Pickthall's translation of *waswas* as 'whisperer', this noun has readily been accepted as the standard and most accurate translation basically because there appears to be no exact one-to-one equivalent in the English lexicon. Some translations have attempted to correct this translation error by their use of the more abstract English noun 'prompter', which reproduces the repetitive and internal activity of inciting that is characteristic of the devil. However, it does so at a great semantic loss since it sacrifices the iconic quality of the Arabic word which renders explicit the actual susurrating voice of Satan. In addition, it is not intrinsically evil and hence also fails to capture the crucial [+SATAN] component inscribed in the original. Furthermore, the theatrical connotations attached to the word 'prompter' automatically distance it from the cultural sphere of *waswas*.

Since there appears to be no immediate English verb with the exact corresponding sense-components, the best strategy is to follow the common translation procedure of distributing the semantic components of *waswasa* over a larger semantic area. A quick survey of the lexical field of negative speech retrieves the following alternatives of 'tempt', and 'hiss'. The first verb 'tempt' appears to embrace a large number of sense-components, in particular the first four essential components of the Arabic verb. It thus seems to be a near-perfect equivalent, especially since 'The Tempter' is a conventional English epithet for the devil. However, the basic drawback which has apparently hindered the widespread use of this verb is its syntactic limitation; it cannot be used in conjunction with the prepositional phrase of direction ('in the hearts of men'). On a more minor scale, it also lacks the /s/ and iconic components (items 5 and 6). Hence, it loses a basic functional and aesthetic factor since the strident /s/ embedded within the word *waswas* is actually an icon of the externally mute but internally ringing and reverberating incitements of the devil. Our second option, the intransitive verb 'hiss' (to make a 'sharp sibilant /s/ sound'), appears to embrace the maximum amount of sense-components because of its strong [+ /s/] and [+ ICONIC] components, in addition to its strong collocation with 'snakes' and 'serpents', which in turn are figuratively collocated with Satan. This English verb can thus more readily substitute for *al-waswas*. With this term we come close to the primary meaning of the Arabic word without sacrificing aesthetic value.

It is this prevalent versatility of Arabic lexemes that has led to the popular Western notion that Arabic words lack a stable or core meaning, and that the vocabulary of the Qur'an is basically 'contradictory'. Take, for example, the statements of a notable linguist such as John Lyons, who argues that Arabic has no single lexeme meaning 'camel' but rather 'a variety of words for different kinds of camels'. This statement is obviously part of a general misconception on the part of Western scholars. Although Arabic does indeed have a variety of names for camels, designating broad or universal categories such as age and gender, they are in fact no different to the English sequence 'calf', 'cow', 'bull' and 'stud'. There is indeed a single core word for camel in Arabic – *jamal* – a common and familiar term as ancient as the letter *jim* (gamma in Greek), the third letter of the Arabic *abjd* alphabet, of which the word *jamal* was originally an icon. The precise definition of the word given by the medieval scholar al-Farra' is 'the male of a female camel or *naqa*' (*zawj al-naqa*). In the Qur'an the word *jamal* is used in a metaphorical and proverbial context in 7.40, where it is stated that for those who belie the signs of God, the gates of Heaven will not be opened nor will they be able to enter Paradise – 'Until the camel passes through the eye of a needle (*hata yalija al-jamalu fi sammi al-khiyat*)'. Surprisingly enough this metaphor has become the subject of much debate with some commentators trying to attach far-fetched alternate meaning to this common Arabic word. One of the most ludicrous suggestions is the one offered by Watt (originally found in Ibn 'Abbas) – 'polyglot nautical slang of the Eastern Mediterranean', with the added implication that the word must have been of foreign origin. Although the triconsonantal root *j/m/l* is also used in the Bible in more or less the same metaphorical context (Mark 10: 25), this is generally ignored or offered as a passing remark. Obviously, this similarity is not surprising given the fact that such metaphors or images appear to be part of a common stock shared by all Semitic languages, i.e. Hebrew, Aramaic and Arabic.

Qur'anic dictionaries and translation aids

No doubt the main drawback for Qur'an translation has been the absence of comprehensive bilingual dictionaries that accurately document and explicate the various senses of Arabic words, both common and rare, and elucidate the range of contexts in which they occur. It must be stressed at this point that this versatility should not be treated as unique or specific to the Arabic language system but rather as similar to cases of English polysemy where a lexeme has more than one related meaning: for example, as linguists explain, people see no problem in saying that the word 'chip' has several different meanings in English, i.e. a piece of wood, food or an electronic circuit. The basic problem in Arabic is that polysemy has not been thoroughly investigated by Arab and Western lexicographers. To date there is no user-friendly Arabic thesaurus accessible to translators in which the vocabulary of the language is divided into semantic areas and each area given a detailed sub-classification. One must assume that the translator does not possess specialized knowledge of the Qur'an, that he or she is coming 'cold' to the text and therefore must be equipped with research aids, such as guides to interpretation (*tafsir*), a concordance and good monolingual/bilingual dictionaries. However, apart from Lane's 1863 *Arabic–English Lexicon* and Penrice's 1873 brief *Dictionary and Glossary of the Koran*, there are no 'contextual dictionaries' to aid translators by providing citational evidence and accurate information about usage, derivates and etymology. In short, any translator of the Qur'an is immediately hampered by the basic lack of reference books that are readable and companionable and that provide the most frequently sought meanings as well as the more archaic, rare or idiomatic. A distinction must be made here between the classical definition of a word and a more modern one. In general, when translating the Qur'an, one must avoid using the definitions of modern Arabic dictionaries upon which contemporary translators frequently depend because these are often at variance with the language of the original, reflecting the degree of change that has crept into the meaning of certain concepts. The basic need is for a bilingual dictionary of classical usages, which in the final analysis is also a dictionary of the Qur'an. Indeed, the use of textual material from the Qur'an for citation purposes has been standard practice in Arabic lexicography for a very long time. Even today the Qur'an continues to provide a rich source of vocabulary which can be, and is, exploited for the compilation of monolingual dictionaries. However, this procedure of amassing enormous numbers of instances from the Qur'an is quite often unsystematic and cannot be relied upon to resolve definitively the problem of multiple word meanings for distinguishing between polysemous words or for elucidating idiomatic expressions. Consider, for example, the following idiomatic expression – 'And let not your hand be tied to your neck [like a miser] nor stretch it forth to its utmost reach [like a spendthrift] so that you become blameworthy and deprived [poor]' (17.29). Obviously, these idiomatic metaphors can only be explained by the addition of the above parenthetical material which is often supplied by so-called explanatory translations of the Qur'an, such as the comprehensive 1997 edition by M. al-Hilali and M. Khan. However, it is imperative for the enhancement of the field of Qur'an translation to have all such idiomatic usages documented and codified in dictionary format rather than scattered within the various commentaries and translations. One must not assume that a comprehensive listing of such expressions is available in monolingual dictionaries of the Qur'an; even if they are, they are of little use to translators since these compilations have not been translated into English or into any other language. As Cragg so aptly remarked in 1998, it is as if the Qur'an were a 'holy text of a newly discovered exotic tribe living in one of the obscure folds of Mother Earth'. (The contextualized Arabic–English dictionary of Qur'anic usages, compiled by the University of London's Centre of Islamic Studies, and estimated to consist of some 6000 entries, will certainly fill a huge gap in the field – see 'Bibliographical Resources'.)

A brief history of Qur'anic translations

The Qur'an has been translated into most of the languages of Asia and Europe as well as some of the African languages, for example Swahili; basically into all languages spoken by Muslims. Hamidullah's 1936, *Qur'an in Every Language*, contains examples of translations in 102 languages. Victor Chauvin's 1913 monumental bibliography contains a listing of every edition of every Western and Oriental translation, whether complete or selective, for the period from 1810 to 1885. As for the earliest translated version of the Qur'an, there is no doubt that translations of some verses and chapters had already been made at the time of the Prophet Muhammad as an aid for those who did not understand the language. According to a report by Abu Sufyan, the Prophet Muhammad's letter to Heraclius, the Byzantine emperor, which included a passage from the Qur'an (3:64), had to be translated. Similarly, verses from the chapter on *Maryam* (the Virgin Mary) which were recited by the Muslims in front of the Emperor Negus of Abyssinia were also translated. The oldest translation of the full text of the Qur'an is the Persian translation (now extinct) said to have been made during the time of the Orthodox caliphs by Salman al-Farsi, a companion of the Prophet. One of the oldest surviving works in Persian is the translation of the monumental Arabic commentary by al-Tabari which was made for the ruler of Transoxiana and Kurasan, Abu Salih Mansur bin Nuh (961–976). The precise date is not recorded but the preface explains how the commentary came to be made after Muslim scholars (*'ulama*) had signed an edict (*fatwa*) permitting Qur'anic translations. It is believed that this edict and this Persian word-for-word translation opened up a new horizon in the development not only of Qur'an translations but Qur'anic sciences in general. It also became the basis for the first Turkish version of the Holy Book.

European translations

When we look at the list of translations into European languages, beginning with the first Italian version by Andrea Arrivabene in 1547 and continuing up until the eighteenth century we find that many of the authors did not speak Arabic themselves but were merely translating or paraphrasing translations derived from the first Latin version produced in 1143 by Robertus Ketenensis. In addition, many modern translators, such as Sale, who professed to have translated the Qur'an direct from the Arabic, did not themselves have active or first-hand knowledge of the language. That is to say, they acquired only an academic understanding of Arabic from books; none had ever been familiar with Arabic in its spoken form and in all probability would not have been able to communicate with native speakers of the language. Obviously this deficiency made their rendering of the Arabic text erroneous and distorted. As Arab scholars explain, the same state holds true today with regard to many orientalists and professors of Arabic language in the West, whose poor knowledge of the Arabic language is usually kept secret.

Although many recent translations of the Qur'an into European languages are the work of honest scholars genuinely endeavouring to render the meaning of the Arabic original as closely as possible, there is no doubt that the first translations were carried out by Christian clergymen whose main and stated concern was to discredit the book rather than to translate it. As Asad states in the foreword to his translation: 'it cannot be denied that among the existing translations in almost all the major European languages there is many a one that has been inspired by malicious prejudice and – especially in earlier times – by misguided missionary zeal'.

The oldest Latin translation, made by Robert Ketenensis at the behest of Peter the Venerable, abbot of Cluny, was completed in 1143 and now exists in the autograph of the translator in the Bibliothèque de l'Arsenal in Paris. This Latin text formed the basis for several medieval versions of the Qur'an. According to some scholars, such as Daniel (1960), Ketenensis is said to have been 'always liable to heighten or exaggerate a harmless text to give it a nasty or licentious sting, or to prefer an improbable but unpleasant interpretation of the meaning to a likely but normal and decent one'. His work was recopied in the seventeenth century by Dominicus Germanus, whose work resides at Montpellier. In 1543 it was published in three editions at Basel by Theodor Bibliander (Buchmann) in a volume comprising the Clunic corpus together with various other works of Christian propaganda. All editions contained a preface by Martin Luther.

A second Latin translation, professed to be derived directly from the Arabic text, was first issued in 1698 by Ludovico Marracci, a confessor to Pope Innocent XI. He introduced his work, dedicated to the Holy Roman Emperor Leopold I, with an introductory volume which contained a 'Refutation of the Qur'an'. This version included not only the Arabic text but also quotations from various Arabic commentaries carefully selected and designed to give the most negative possible impression of Islam to Europe. Marracci's main motivation, as he himself states, was to discredit Islam by inserting elaborate quotations from Muslim authorities themselves. Many European translations were based on Maracci's work, the best known being those by Savory (1751, in French) and Nerreter (in German). To give a sense of authenticity, the title page of one edition of Savory's translation even stated that it was published in Mecca in AH 1165.

The first translation in a modern European language was the Italian version made by Andrea Arrivabene, published in 1547. Although its author claims that it was derived directly from the Arabic, Western scholars now believe that it is clearly a paraphrase of Ketenensis' text as published by Bibliander. Arrivabene's version was used for the first German translation by the Nuremberg preacher Solomon Schweigger in 1616, which in turn formed the basis of the first Dutch translation, made anonymously and issued in 1641. The first French version, by André du Ryer, came out in a great many editions in 1647 and again in 1775. All editions of this version contained 'a summary of the religion of the Turks'. In turn, it fathered a number of well-known translations, most notably the English version by Alexander Ross which formed the basis for the Dutch (by Glazemaker), German (by Lange) and Russian (by Postnikov and Veryovkin) versions. During the eighteenth century a number of translations appeared, the most famous being those by Sale (English, 1734), by Savory (French, 1751) and Boysen (German, 1773). Throughout the nineteenth century most translations were normally derived from these three and all three are still available today. The twentieth century and up to the present day has also seen the appearance of monumental translations made by the most prominent Arabists and Islamic scholars.

English translations

André du Ryer's 1647 French translation gave rise in 1649 to the first Qur'an translation into English, a work by Alexander Ross, chaplain of King Charles I. This English version, called *The Alcoran of Mahomet*, was Anglicised' with one stated purpose – 'for the satisfaction of all that desire to look into the Turkish vanities'. To see the extent of Ross's prejudices, one need only look at his introductory letter, 'From the Translator to the Christian Reader', in which he warns Christians of 'their enemies', describes the Qur'an as 'the heresy of Mahomet' and tries to justify why he published this 'dangerous book'. As for the translation itself, it is full of instances of omissions and distortions. Another edition was issued in 1688 to which is prefixed 'The life of Mahomet, the Prophet of the Turks, and Author of the Alcoran. With a needful Caveat, or Admonition, for them who desire to know what use may be made of, or if there be danger in Reading the Alcoran.'

The most popular English translation of the eighteenth century was George Sale's *The Koran, commonly called The Alcoran of Mohammad*, professed to have been derived 'immediately' from the original Arabic and containing explanatory notes taken from the most approved commentators. His well-known 'Preliminary Discourse', based, according to Nallino, on the Latin translation by Marracci, became so popular that it was translated into several European languages and published either as an accompaniment to the Qur'an or separately. Ironically enough, it was even back-translated into Arabic by Protestant missionaries based in Egypt. A new edition appeared in 1844 which contained a memoir of the translator and various readings and illustrative notes from Savory's French translation. Not only were many reprints made of this edition, but it was also appeared as No. 22 of Sir John Lubbock's 'Hundred Books' (1892). Several American editions also appeared in Philadelphia and New York in 1975 and it was used by E.M. Wherry as a basis for his comprehensive commentary on the Qur'an. Considering that Sale's famous preliminary was based on work by Marracci, whose aim was to discredit Islam in the eyes of Europe, it is remarkable that Sale's translation should be looked upon even today as the standard English translation.

During the nineteenth century two well-known English translations were published: the first by Rev. J.M. Rodwell appeared in 1861 and that by E.H. Palmer in 1880. Although quite popular in the English-speaking world, these two translations contain much hostility and bias. For example, the preface to Rodwell's *Koran* stated that the work was translated directly from the Arabic, and is replete with allegations against the Prophet and the Qur'an. It is also the first to have invented the so-called chronological order of the chapters (*suras*), an untenable notion which was later developed into an elaborately far-fetched theory by Bell. The version by Palmer, a Cambridge scholar, is severely marred by his view that the style of the Qur'an is 'rude and rugged' and that it therefore ought to be translated into colloquial language. Quite striking also is the carelessness of Palmer's work and the conscious attempt to demean the lofty eloquence of the Arabic original. Suffice it to note that sixty-five instances of omissions and mistranslations in Palmer's work have since been pointed out by scholars (cf. Nykl, 1936).

Among the more popular and well-known English translations of the twentieth century are those by Pickthall (1930), 'Ali (1934), Bell (1937), Arberry (1955) and Asad (1980). What is surprising is the fact that no substantial work has so far been done to critically examine the mass of existing English translations of the Qur'an; i.e. to analyse the quality of the major translations and to highlight their hallmarks and shortcomings. More, it is only in this century that the first English versions made by Muslims appear. The first Western Muslim to undertake an English translation was the Arabic scholar Marmaduke Pickthall in 1930. His work, entitled *The Meaning of the Glorious Koran*, was an almost literal rendering of the Arabic original, with every effort being made to choose language befitting the Arabic Qur'an which he describes as 'that inimitable symphony the very sounds of which move men to tears and ecstasy'. Pickthall's translation has become something of a standard for English-speaking Muslims since it was approved by the authorities of the al-Azhar university in Cairo. His basic aim, as stated in the introduction, was to present to English readers what Muslims the world over hold to be the meaning of the words of the Qur'an, and 'peradventure something of the charm'. Unfortunately, however, it provides very few explanatory notes and background information, a fact that restricts its usefulness for an uninitiated reader of the Qur'an. A number of translations by Indian scholars also appeared within a few years of Pickthall's work, the better known and more scholarly being that by Yusef 'Ali's, entitled *The Holy Qur'an: Text, translation and commentary*, in 1934. Like Pickthall's earlier attempt, this was a faithful rendering, albeit more of a paraphrase than a literal translation. Nonetheless the work has come to dominate the field of Qur'an-translation by Muslim scholars. Ever since its appearance, the text, with its copious notes and elaborate commentary, has been welcomed by Muslim scholars as the best and most accurate English translation available and has usually been adopted as the standard or basis for all future translations. Finally, there is Asad's 1980 translation, *The Message of the Qur'an*, which is perhaps the most impressive and represents a formidable addition to the field. Unfortunately, it includes a number of interpretations that are not in line with Orthodox views, most notably his theory of the *mutashabihat*, and his strange rendition of some *sura* titles – *sura* 53 (*al-Najm*), commonly rendered as 'The Star', is translated as 'The Unfolding'. Many times he also refuses to take some Qur'anic statements literally, thus denying the occurrence of such miraculous events as the casting of Abraham into the fire, and Jesus speaking in the cradle. Although his explanatory notes are exhaustive and highly useful, they sometimes provide unreliable background information about the *suras*.

References and further reading

Bibliographical material on the subject of Qur'an translation was scant before the relatively recent appearance of *World Bibliography of the Translations of the Meanings of the Qur'an* (Istanbul, OIC Research Center, 1986), which provides authoritative publication details of the translations of the Qur'an in fifty-six languages.

Abdel Haleem, M. (2001) *Understanding The Qur'an: Themes and styles*, London and New York: I.B. Tauris.

al-Alalam'i, Z. (2002) *Dirasat fi 'ulum al-Qur'an al-Karim*, Riyadh

'Ali, A.Y. (1991) *The Meaning of the Holy Qur'an*, Baltimore, MD: Amana Corporation.

Arberry, A. (1964) *The Koran Interpreted*, Oxford: Oxford University Press.

Asad, M (1980) *The Message of the Qur'an*, Gibraltar: Dar al-andalus.

Badawi, S. (2002) 'Arabic-English Dictionary of Qur'anic Usage', *Journal of Qur'anic Studies* IV, 2: 113–17.

Bell, R. (1960) *The Qur'an: Translated with a critical rearrangement of the surahs*, 2 vols, Edinburgh: T. & T. Clark.

Berman, A. (1992) *The Experience of the Foreign: Culture and translation in Romantic Germany*, trans. S. Heyvaert, Albany, NY: SUNY Press.

Cragg, B. (1998) *Readings in the Qur'an*, Sussex: Sussex Academic Press.

Crystal, D. (1997) *The Cambridge Encyclopedia of Language*, Cambridge: Cambridge University Press.

Daniel, N. (1960) *Islam in the West: The making of an image*. Edinburgh: Edinburgh University Press.

Denffer, A. (1983) *'Ulum al-Qur'an: An introduction to the sciences of the Qur'an*, London: The Islamic Foundation.

Draz, M.A. (2000) *Introduction to the Qur'an*, London and New York: I.B. Tauris.

Finegan, J. (1952) *The Archaeology of World Religions*, Princeton, NJ: Princeton University Press, Vol. III.

Gruendler, B. (2001) 'Arabic Script', in *EQ*, Vol. 1, 135–44.

al-Hilali, M.T. and Khan, M. (1993) *Interpretations of the Meanings of the Noble Qur'an in the English Language*, Riyadh: Maktaba Dar-as-salam.

Kamesar, A. (1993) *Jerome, Greek Scholarship, and the Hebrew Bible: A study of the quaestiones hebraicae in genesim*, Oxford: Clarendon Press.

Kidwai, A.R. (1987) 'Translating the Untranslatable: A survey of English translations of the Qur'an', *The Muslim World Book Review* 7, 4. Available online at http://soundvision.com/Qur'an/english.html.

Lane, E.W. (1955–56) *Arabic English Lexicon*, New York: Frederick Ungar Publishing Co.

Lyons, J. (1997) *Semantics*, Cambridge: Cambridge University Press, Vol. I.

Mayer, T. (2002) 'Review Article: The Qur'an and its interpretive tradition by Andrew Rippin', *Journal of Qur'anic Studies* IV, 2: 91–104.

Nykl, A.R. (1936) 'Notes on E.H. Palmer's The Qur'an', *JAOS*: 56, 77–84.

Palmer, E.H. (1880) *The Koran*, Oxford: Clarendon Press.

Paret, R. (1965) 'Al-Kur'an', in *EI*, Vol. 5, 400–17.

Pearson, J.D. (1983) 'Bibliography of Translations of the Qur'an into European Languages', in A.F.L. Beeston *et al.* (eds) *The Cambridge History of Arabic Literature: Arabic literature to the end of the Umayyad period*, Cambridge: Cambridge University Press, 502–20.

Penrice, J. (1991) *A Dictionary and Glossary of the Koran*, India: Adam Publishers & Distributors.

Pickthall, Marmaduke M. (1930) *The Meaning of the Glorious Koran: An Explanatory Translation*, London, George Allen & Unwin, 1952.

al-Qatan, M. (1998) *Mabahith fi 'ulum Al-Qur'an*, Beirut: al-Resalah Publishers.

Rippin, A. (2001) 'Reading the Qur'an with Richard Bell', in *The Qur'an and its Interpretive Tradition*, Burlington, VT: Ashgate, Vol. IV, 639–47.

Rodwell, J.N. (1861) *Koran: Translated from the Arabic, the surahs arranged in chronological order*, London: Williams & Norgate.

Sale, G. (1900) *The Koran*, London and New York: Frederick Warne & Co. Ltd.

Venuti, L. (1998) *The Scandals of Translation*, London and New York: Routledge.

Wansbrough, J. (1977) *Qur'anic Studies: Sources and methods of scriptural interpretation*, Oxford: Oxford University Press.

Watt, W.M. (1967) *Companion to the Qur'an*, London: George Allen & Unwin.

Wherry, E.M. (1921) *A Comprehensive Commentary of the Qur'an: Comprising Sale's translation and preliminary discourse*, London: Kegan Paul.

White, C. (ed. and trans.) (1990) *The Correspondence between Jerome and Augustine of Hippo*, Lewiston, NY: Edwin Mellen Press.

See also: **aya; language and the Qur'an; self-referentiality**

AFNAN H. FATANI

TRUST IN GOD

see: **tawakkul**

TUBBA

44.37 mentions the people of Tubba and Muslim exegesis explains that this refers to the people of Sheba in South Arabia. The term 'Tubba' is said to be the title used by the Himyarite kings of South Arabia, and that the people are called by this name after the Pharaoh of Egypt and Khusrow of Iran. Exegetes relate that one of the kings of Tubba passed by Medina and Mecca upon his return from a trip to Samarkand, when the city was in the hands of the Jurhum. The king was prevented from attacking Mecca by two Jews who advised him that the *Ka'ba* was built by Abraham and that a prophet would rise up in the city at the end of time. Thus the king circumnavigated the *Ka'ba*, sacrificed 6,000 animals there and was the first person to dress the *Ka'ba* with a *kiswa*.

Further reading

Chelhod, J. (ed.) (1984–85) *L'Arabie du Sud, Histoire et civilisations: Le peuple yéménite et ses racines*, Paris: G.-P. Maisonneuve et Larose.

Eph'al, I. (1984) *The Ancient Arabs: Nomads on the borders of the Fertile Crescent, 9th–5th Centuries B.C.*, Jerusalem: Magnes Press.

Gibb, H.A.R. (1962) 'Pre-Islamic Monotheism in Arabia', *Harvard Theological Review* 55: 269–280.

BRANNON WHEELER

TUFAN

The name of a flood mentioned at 7.136. The allusion may be to Noah's flood, since the drowning in the Red Sea occurred after the plagues. But the story of Noah, given in this *sura*, suggests that Noah's flood is not being talked about here. We must therefore regard this statement as either an addition to the Jewish story or as referring to the drowning in the Red Sea. Baydawi thinks that this refers to an event in Egypt, unusual rains, which lasted for eight days, and the overflowing of the Nile which caused great suffering among the Egyptians but not among the Israelites.

OLIVER LEAMAN

TURN AWAY FROM

see: iltifat

U

ULU'L-AMR

This phrase (in the genitive form) occurs in Qur'an at 4.59, which states, 'O those who believe, obey God and the Messenger and those in possession of authority (*uli 'l-amr*) among you'; it means 'authority'. It has given rise to various exegetical understandings in different historical contexts. Mujahid b. Jabr (d. 720) in his early *tafsir* work states that, according to the Companion 'Abd al-Rahman b. Awf, *uli 'l-amr* refers to 'those possessing critical insight into religion and knowledge', while a second variant report relates that the phrase refers to 'those possessing critical insight, knowlege, [sound] opinion and virtue'. Another early exegete, Muqatil b. Sulayman al-Balkhi (d. 767), records in his exegetical work that the key phrase '*uli 'l-amr minkum*' was revealed specifically in reference to the military commander Khalid b. al-Walid in a particular historical context, and, more broadly, that it refers to the commanders of military contingents (*saraya*).

The tenth-century exegete al-Tabari (d. 923) records a broader range of meanings attributed to this phrase and gives us a sense of the evolution in its interpretation. He cites several Companion reports which link this verse primarily to two groups of people: to specific military commanders appointed by the Prophet and to the people of knowledge and insightful understanding. Other variants of this latter report, such as '[the *uli 'l-amr*] are the possessors of insightful understanding in religion and intellect'; 'people of insightful understanding and religion', 'people of knowledge' and 'the possessors of knowledge and insightful understanding' are recorded on the authority of various sources. Other exegetes were inclined to understand *ulu'l-amr* as referring to all the companions of Muhammad (*ashab Muhammad*). Another significant report recorded by al-Tabari is attributed to the Companion Ubayy b. Ka'b who relates that *ulu'l-amr* was a reference to the political

672

rulers (*al-salatin*), an interesting ana-chronistic usage of this word here since sultans did not rise in the Islamic world until at least two centuries after the age of the Companions.

It is this politicized meaning, how-ever, that becomes privileged in the later political treatises and exegetical works. For example, the political the-orist al-Mawardi (d. 1058) in his *al-Ahkam al-Sultaniyya* refers to 4.59 and explicates it as ordaining virtually unquestioning obedience on the part of Muslims to their appointed leaders, as does Ibn Taymiyya (d. 1328). This later line of interpretation has fostered the widespread and unjustified assumption that Qur'an 4.59 mandates obedience to political rulers, and the verse has been used as a proof-text to promote both political quietism and authoritarianism.

Further reading

Ibn Jabr, Mujahid (n.d.) *Tafsir*, Islamabad.
Ibn Taymiyya (1951) *al-Siyasa al-shariyya*, ed. 'A. al-Nashshar and A. Zaki, Cairo: Dar al-kutub al-'arabi.
Muqatil b. Sulayman (1969) *Tafsir*, in 'A. Shihata (ed.) Cairo: Mu'assasat ak-halabi.

ASMA AFSARUDDIN

UMM AL-KITAB

see: **Mother of the Book**

UMMUHAT AL-MU'MININ

'Mothers of the Believers' is an honorific title granted by a late Medinan verse (33.6) to the wives of the Prophet Muhammad who, at the time of its revelation, numbered around nine. For most of his adult life Muhammad was monogamously married to Khadija bint al-Khuwaylid, who was the mother of all of his surviving children. (His Coptic concubine Mariya bore him a son, Ibrahim, who died in infancy.) After Khadija's death, Muhammad remarried numerous times. 'A'isha, the young daughter of his friend and early convert Abu Bakr, was his only virgin wife; the others were widows, as Khadija had been, or divorcees. Sawda bint Abi Zam'a was the first to join his house-hold, which expanded to include, among others, Hafsa, the daughter of close companion 'Umar b. al-Khattab; Mec-can aristocrat Umm Salama; and Zay-nab bint Jahsh, former wife of his adopted son Zayd. Muhammad also concluded a number of marriage con-tracts that were never consummated, and these women were not considered to be among the 'Mothers of the Believers'.

A variety of reasons have been sug-gested for the Prophet's multiple mar-riages. One clear purpose was the strengthening of alliances in a tribal society where ties of blood and affinity were essential; it is not coincidental that the Prophet was son-in-law to two of the four Rightly-Guided caliphs who suc-ceeded him, and father-in-law to the other two. Some have also ascribed charitable motives to his acts; marriage to the Prophet served to bring dignity and comfort to female converts left without a husband and protector. And while modern Muslim scholars usually reject the notion, sexual appetite played a significant role in medieval discussions of Muhammad's marriages. What Eur-opean polemicists portrayed as rank sensualism appeared in classical Muslim texts as masculine prowess, further proof of Muhammad's sound human nature and prophetic status.

Muhammad, of course, was not an ordinary man. A series of revelations in *sura* 33 spelled out specific rights and duties for the members of the Prophet's household; other verses addressed inci-dents of domestic conflict and turmoil

(24.11–26; 66.1–5). Unlike other Muslim men, the Prophet could have more than four wives, marry 'a believing woman who gave herself' to him without a dowry, and choose how and when to allocate his time among his wives (33.50). However, he was subject to restrictions not imposed on other Muslim husbands: he could not take additional wives or exchange his current wives for others (33.52), and he was required to give each wife a choice as to whether to remain married to him, forgoing earthly luxuries, or to separate from him and enjoy 'the life of this world' (33.28–29). All of his wives, beginning with 'A'isha, were reported to have chosen Islam and its Prophet with no hesitation.

Because the Prophet was not an ordinary man, his wives were 'not like any [other] women' (33.32). Their unique status meant they would be subject to doubled punishment for 'clear lewdness' (33.30; compare with 4.19); they were also entitled to doubled reward for doing good works and fulfilling their obligation of devout obedience to God and God's Messenger (33.31). The most significant restriction on the Prophet's wives was the prohibition against other Muslim men marrying them after his death (33.53). Many commentators linked this prohibition to their status as 'Mothers of the Believers'; marriage was forbidden as it was with one's own mother (4.23). However, while actual kinship permitted relaxation of the rules of covering and sex-segregation, the fictive motherhood ascribed to the Prophet's wives did nothing of the sort.

In fact, most of the revelations concerning the Prophet's wives as a group sought to ensure proper social distance between them and unrelated males by imposing visual segregation and, to a lesser extent, physical seclusion (e.g., 33.32–33). The Prophet's wives did not observe strict confinement in their mosque apartments, and it has been argued that these verses sought to provide them with a sphere of privacy, to give them an elite status, and to protect them from attacks upon their honour which, in turn, could damage the standing of the Prophet. The crucial verse prescribing a curtain or barrier (*hijab*) between any (male) petitioner and a wife of the Prophet (33.53) is said to have been revealed following some overfamiliarity or inappropriate lingering at a mixed gathering. *Hijab*, originally a practice of Muhammad's wives, was eventually generalized by jurists to all free Muslim women, although in practice it was strictly observed only by the elite.

Further reading

Ibn Kathir (2000) *The Life of the Prophet Muhammad*, trans. T. Le Gassick, Reading: Garnet, 415–35.
Stowasser, Barbara F. (1996) *Women in the Qur'an, Traditions, and Interpretation*, Oxford: Oxford University Press, 85–134.

*See also: **fitra; nisa***

KECIA ALI

'UZAYR

According to 9.30, the Jews claim that Ezra is the son of God while Christians call Christ the son of God. Muslim exegetes explain that the 'Jews' of this verse refers to only a small handful, or only one of the Jews from Medina in the time of the Prophet Muhammad. It is also said that what is meant by 'son of God' is that Ezra was responsible for memorizing and preserving all of the Torah after it had been lost during the Babylonian Exile of the Israelites under Nebuchadnezzar. Some Muslim sources do not consider Ezra to have been a prophet, and sometimes he is identified as the person (along with Jeremiah) who is killed and resurrected by God after passing by a city in ruins (see 2.259).

Further reading

Ayoub, M. (1986) 'Uzayr in the Qur'an and Muslim Tradition', in W.M. Brinner and S.D. Ricks (eds) *Studies in Islamic and Judaic Traditions: Papers presented at the Institute for Islamic-Judaic Studies*, Atlanta, GA: Scholars Press, 3–18.
Casanova, P. (1924) 'Idris et 'Ouzair', *Journal asiatique* 205: 356–60.

BRANNON WHEELER

V

VEIL

The terms *sitr, hijab* and *purdah,* translated as 'veil', 'cover' or 'curtain', are often used interchangeably to connote the notion of Muslim women's modest dress. Throughout the Qur'an, the word *hijab* is used seven times, and most frequently does not refer to a physical veil. In five of those instances it simply refers to a kind of barrier, not corporal but spiritual: a barrier between believers and unbelievers (17.45); a hindrance between unbelievers and the Prophet (41.5); a separation between *ashab-al-jannat* (dwellers of paradise) and *ashab-u-narr* (dwellers of the inferno) (7.46); God revealing from behind a veil (42.51); and David's repentance as a result of the veiling of beautiful worldly things (38.32). The other two references involve women but do not refer to women's clothing. One is the story of Mary, mother of Jesus, and her choice of seclusion, *fattakhadat min dunnehem hijaban*: 'she chose to withdraw from them' (19.17). The other is a specific recommendation to men in their communication with the wives of the Prophet: 'and when you ask of them anything – ask it from behind a curtain; that is purer for your hearts and for their hearts' (38.32). While the Qur'an uses the word *hijab* only when it speaks of the wives of the Prophet and their distinctive position, the injunction to veil has been interpreted more broadly to include all Muslim women.

The Qur'anic word *khumur,* is also translated as 'the veil'. Muslim men and women are instructed to 'lower their gaze and [to] be modest'. Women are further advised not to 'display their adornments except for that which is apparent and to draw their *khumur* over their bosoms' (24.30–31). Moreover, verses 59–60 of chapter 33 speak of an outer garment or a loose flowing dress; a *jilbab,* that women are recommended to 'draw close to them' for their safety and protection; 'so that they may be recognized and not annoyed' (33.59–60).

Making reference to these verses, the *'ulama* have constituted an injunction for women to cover their body and their hair in their associations with men to whom they are not related. According to proponents of the veil, the social function, namely assuring women's safety, is one among the many benefits of the sanction of the veil. The main purpose, however, is the perpetuation of sexual attractions within the framework of the family. Thus, it is interpreted as a barrier that renders sexual modesty rather than a restraint on active participation of women in the society. While many Muslim women have embraced the notion and practice of veiling (to various degrees) as an essential element of virtue and religiosity, there are those who believe that seclusion and veiling are ancient Near Eastern customs and as much a Christian or Jewish precept as an Islamic one.

Further reading

Ahmed, L. (1992) *Women and Gender in Islam*, New Haven, CT: Yale University Press.

Mernissi, F. (1991) *The Veil and the Male Elite: A feminist interpretation of women's rights in Islam*, New York: Addison-Wesley

Stowasser, B.F. (1994) *Women in the Qur'an: Traditions, and Interpretation*, New York: Oxford University Press.

See also: **modesty**

BAHAR DAVARY

WAHY

see: **revelation**

WALI – ISSUES OF IDENTIFICATION

The concept of *wali* in the Qur'an has given rise to a number of interesting controversies. Who are the friends of God? Are particular spiritually elevated individuals closer to God than everyone else, and so deserving of special respect? Can Muslims take as friends people who are not Muslims?

Who are the friends of God?

The Jews, as reported in the Qur'an, claimed they were the beloved (*awliya'*) of Allah. They were told: 'If you claim that you [alone] are the *awliya' Allah* to the exclusion of all other people, then you should be longing for death – if what you say is true' (62.6). From the point of view of the Qur'an, 'longing for death'

signifies fighting in the way that Allah struggled for the cause of Islam and defending the faith by confronting the enemy: 'They fight in the cause of Allah, and slay and are slain' (9.111). Sitting in monasteries (*khanqas*) in order to conduct a *jihad al-akhbar* against one's self (*nafs*) is not *qital fi sabil Allah*. It is people who have faith and who fight in the way of God who are called the *Hizbullah* by the Qur'an (58.22) as opposed to the non-Muslims who are *Hizbush Shaytan* (Party of Satan) (58.19).

It could be argued that the category of *awliya' Allah* is the whole community of Islam. To be the *wali* of Allah is what is involved in being a Muslim. In this community there is no special group whose behaviour and features differ from the majority. It is widely believed that they have the power to cause harm or grant benefits. This is why people turn to them to pray for help, and are afraid of their displeasure. From the Qur'anic viewpoint, this type of belief could easily be regarded as a result of fanciful imagination and superstition, and thus as weak and feeble. The Qur'an says: 'The parable of those who take other than Allah for their *awliya'*, is that of the spider that makes for itself a house: for, behold, the frailest of all houses is the spider's house. Could they but understand this!' (29.41).

Do the friends of God have special power?

As for causing harm or helping others, the Qur'an says that the *awliya'* 'Tell them [O Prophet] that do you accept besides Allah as *awliya'* those who do not have the power to benefit or harm themselves?' (13.16). We also read: 'Say [O Prophet]: "It is not within my power to avert harm or bring benefit to myself, except as Allah may please"' (10.49). We are told: 'he whom Allah guides, is on the right path; and he whom he leaves in error, you will not find for him a *wali* or *murshid*' (18.17).

Wali means one who may be obeyed, and *murshid* is one who shows mankind the correct path to follow: 'O you who believe! Remain conscious of Allah and seek to come close to Him (*wasilata*), and strive hard in his cause, so that you may be successful' (5.35). The word *wasila* (close) in this verse is sometimes taken as a proof that the veneration of people who are described as friends of God is permissible.

In Arabic, the word *wasila* means medium and instrumentality, but also status, nearness, dignity, station, rank, honour. 5.35 means that we must always be conscious of the laws of Allah, and try to achieve high status, rank, station, dignity, in the eyes of Allah. The way to do this is to work hard and stay on the straight and narrow. In doing so, we should attain the closeness to God for which we are striving. The idea that

through *taqwa* (awareness of God), nearness to God is achieved, is to be found in many verses of the Qur'an, one of which is: 'Verily, the noblest among you in the sight of Allah, is the one who is most deeply conscious of Him' (49.13). If the word *wasila* is linked with instrumentality, means, medium, then the implication is that through *taqwa* (sincerity or piety) we should strive to become a channel for God: 'And if My servants ask you [O Prophet] about Me – behold, I am near; I respond to the call of him who calls, whenever he calls unto Me: let them, then, respond to Me, and believe in Me, so that they might follow the right way' (2.186). 'This account of things unseen We reveal to you' (3.44) was how God addressed the Prophet and this implies that anyone who claims knowledge of the unseen is a prophet receiving revelation. Yet Muhammad was the last prophet. These verses are thus interpreted to argue against thinking of particular people or places as intermediaries between this world and the next.

Can Jews and Christians be friends of Muslims?

The first verse addressing this issue appears in 5.51 of the Qur'an and states: 'O, you who believe [in the message of Muhammad], do not take Jews and Christians as *awliya'* to one another, and the one among you who turns to them is of them. Truly, God does not guide wrongdoing people' (5.51). The word *awliya'* (sing. *wali*), is commonly translated into English as 'friends'. Given this translation, the verse appears to be a very clear statement opposing friendly relations between Muslims, on the one hand, and Jews and Christians on the other. But within its proper historical context, the word *awliya'* here does not mean 'friends' at all. While it is true that one of the meanings of *awliya'* is friends, it also has additional meanings such as 'guardians' and 'protectors'. Interestingly enough, we find that when we consult the traditional commentaries on the Qur'an we are told that this verse was revealed at a particularly delicate moment in the life of the early Muslim community, and here it is necessary to explain, to a certain extent, the existential situation of the Muslims at this time in Arabia, thus situating verse 5.51 within the right context.

Before 5.51 was revealed, the Prophet of Islam and the Muslims had only recently migrated as a community from Mecca to Medina, some 400 km to the north. They had done so, according to Islamic histories, to escape the persecution to which they were subjected at the hands of their fellow tribesmen and relatives in Mecca. Most Meccans worshipped various idols as gods and feared the increase of interest in the message of Muhammad within the city, even though Muhammad was himself from Mecca. The Meccans feared the growing presence of the Muslims because the Muslims claimed that there was only one true God, who had no physical image, and who required of men virtue, generosity and fair and kind treatment of the weaker members of society. This simple message threatened to overturn the social order of Mecca, based as it was upon the worship of multiple gods and the privilege of the strong and the wealthy. It also threatened to disrupt the economic benefits derived from this worship of multiple gods, namely, the annual pilgrimage season when people from all over the Arabian peninsula would come to worship at the *Ka'ba* – a cubical structure which the Qur'an claims was originally built by Abraham and his son, Ishmael, as a temple to the One God, before polytheism took over.

The message of Islam threatened to replace the social and economic system of Meccan polytheism with the worship of the One God, who would not allow that others be worshipped alongside him. Although the Prophet of Islam preached his message of monotheism and virtue peacefully, he and his small band of followers were eventually driven from the city by torture, threats of assassination and various other forms of humiliation and abuse. The Muslims then migrated to the city of Medina where the Prophet had been invited to come and live in safety with his followers and where the main Arab tribes of the city willingly accepted his message.

According to the commentary tradition in Islam, it was not long after this migration to Medina that verse 5.51 was revealed. Specifically, we are told that this verse came down around the time of the battle of Badr (3.123) or perhaps after the battle of Uhud (3.152). In these early days, even though the Muslim community constituted no more than perhaps a few hundred people and had already left the city of Mecca, the Meccans continued to confront them militarily, and these two early battles, as well as others, were crucial events in the history of the early Islamic community.

Militarily, the Meccans were a far more powerful force than the Muslims, and in addition the Meccans had allies throughout Arabia. Given the small numbers of Muslims, the Prophet and his fledgling community faced the real possibility of utter annihilation should they lose any of these early conflicts. Within this highly charged environment some members of the Muslim community wanted to make individual alliances with other non-Muslim tribes in the region. Within the city of Medina there were Jewish tribes who constituted a powerful presence in the town and who were on good terms with the Meccans, and to the north of the city there were also numerous Christian Arab tribes. Some Muslims saw the possibility of making alliances with one or more of these groups as a way of guaranteeing their own survival should the Meccan armies ultimately triumph. This was the stark reality of Arabia at that time – that it was only through the protection of one's tribe or one's alliances with other tribes or clans that one's own individual security could be ensured.

From the perspective of Islam, however, the Prophet realized that a young community, when faced with great peril, could not allow such dissension in the ranks of the faithful as would be created by various individuals taking bonds of loyalty with other groups not committed to the Islamic message. Indeed, from the Islamic point of view, such actions, had they been allowed, would constitute a disaster that would seriously undermine Muslim unity, break the morale of the community and perhaps cause the many individuals making such alliances to lack fortitude in the face of the clear and present danger of the Meccan armies and their allies.

Keeping all these historical issues in mind, it becomes obvious that the translation of *awliya'* as 'friends' is misleading, and that it should be rendered perhaps as 'protectors' or 'guardians' in the strict military sense of these terms. Verse 5.51 thus should be read as: 'Do not take Christians and Jews as your protectors. They are protectors to one another...'. This is the message of the verse, and the appropriateness of this understanding is supported not only by the historical context for its revelation but also by the fact that nowhere does the Qur'an oppose simple kindness between peoples, as is clear from other Qur'anic verses such as, 'God does not forbid that you should deal kindly and justly with those who do not fight you

for the sake of [your] religion or drive you out of your homes. Truly, God loves those who are just' (60.8), and 'The good deed and the evil deed are not equal. Repel [the evil deed] with one that is better. Then truly the one between whom there is enmity, shall become a firm friend' (41.34).

Another verse that has caused much confusion is 9.5. This is a Qur'anic verse often mentioned in the attacks by Islamic groups hostile to the West when arguing that Muslims should not ally themselves with non-Muslims. It is also a verse that has been referred to by those critical of Islam's credentials as a peaceful and civilized faith. It says: 'But when the forbidden months are past, then fight and slay the polytheists (*mushrikun*) wherever you find them, seize them, beleaguer them, and lie in wait for them in every stratagem [of war].' Contrary to what may be thought from a literal reading of this translation, this verse is does not constitute a blanket order to attack any and all non-Muslim people.

Here again the issue of historical context is crucial to our understanding. Verse 9.5 was revealed specifically in relation to the Muslims fighting the idolaters of Mecca. The Meccan idolaters are referred to in the Qur'an by the technical term *mushrikun* (sing. *mushrik*). This term comes from a three-letter Arabic root *sh/r/k/* which means 'to associate' or 'take a partner with something', so that the word *mushrikun* literally means 'those who take a partner [to God]', that is to say, 'polytheists' or 'idolaters'. It should be noted, therefore, that the injunction in this verse to fight against the 'polytheists' does not pertain to either Jews or Christians from the point of view of Islamic law. Interestingly, Jews and Christians are never referred to within the Qur'an by the term *mushrikun*. In fact these two groups have a very different role according to the Qur'an which, when not addressing them as individual communities, often refers to the two together using the technical term *ahl al-kitab* (People of the Book), meaning people other than the Muslims who have been given a book or scripture by God.

Given these facts, it is interesting that this verse should be cited as a declaration calling upon Muslims to fight Jews and Christians – the verse says nothing about Jews, Christians or the People of the Book in general. On the other hand, the verse does give Muslims the right to defend themselves against those who would not let them worship God, and thus could be extended to include the People of the Book, whose behaviour, it could be claimed, gave rise to the suggestion that they should be reclassified as *mushrikun*.

*See also: **ahl al-kitab**; **fitna**; **al-ghayb**; **taqwa***

OLIVER LEAMAN

WALI / WALAYA / WILAYA

The term *wali* (pl. *awliya'*) is derived from the Arabic root *w/l/y/* and means being near, close, adjacent or following someone or something. Thus, *wali* is one who is near or intimate as a friend, helper, companion, partner, relation, beloved, heir, benefactor, saint, protector or guardian. In the Qur'an the words *wali* and its plural *awliya'* occur eighty-six times, with the first occurrence in *sura al-Baqara* and the last in *sura al-Jumu'a*. Other derivations also occur in words such as *yali, walaya, wāli, awla, mawla, walla, yuwalli, walli, muwalli* and *tawalla* and thus, together with *wali* and *awliya'*, there are more than 200 citations. Besides being used as a term for God as a Protector and Guardian in the sense of a divine attribute, in the Qur'an the term *wali* also

means a friend, ally, patron, next-of-kin, protector or a guardian.

God's exclusive status as the most influential friend and helper (*wali nasir*) is one of the major themes of Qur'anic teaching. He is the Protector of those who believe (2.257), sufficing for them not only as an aide and a companion, but also as the best intercessor, who forgives compassionately (*anta waliyyuna fa'ghfir lana wa'rhamna wa anta khayru al-ghafirin* (7.155)). As one who has sent down the Book and also as 'wali of the believers', God befriends the righteous (7.196) in this world and the next (12.101), leading them from darkness to light. *Wali* and *mawla* are used in the Qur'an synonymously to mean a close social relationship, such as affiliation and alliance. A *wali* or *mawla* can claim certain rights of inheritance and has responsibilities to assist allies against enemies, in cases such as retaliation against the unjust killing of kinsmen (*wilayat al-dam*; 17.33). A *wali* can be legally responsible as a guardian to give the bride in marriage by contractual agreement and also to administer the property of orphans, minors and those who are legally incompetent.

Inheritance and support expected of a *wali* may also be of a spiritual kind, as in the Qur'anic version of the birth of John the Baptist, where Zacharias, having no (natural) son, asks God to give him a 'wali from thee, who will be my heir and will inherit from the family of Jacob' (19.5–6). Likewise, the weak and oppressed Muslims left alone in Mecca, after Muhammad's migration to Medina, ask God to give them 'a wali from thee and a helper from thee' (4.75), obviously as a protector rather than an heir. In 41.34 God asks believers to return bad deeds with something better so that the animosity among them is transformed, and the individual becomes the intimate friend (*wali hamim*).

Believers, too, are guardians of each other (*ba'duhum awliya' ba'd*), enjoining good and forbidding evil, observing prayers and alms-giving, all the while obeying God and his Messenger (9.71). *Awliya'* is also used for unbelievers, hypocrites and wrongdoers and for Jews and Christians, all of whom help each other in pursuing their own desires rather than following the (right) way (*shari'a*). The new Muslim *umma* was patterned after the model of Abraham's community, Abraham being neither Jew nor Christian. The Jews especially are frequently asked in the Qur'an to prove their assertion of being 'the exclusive friends of God (*awliya' Allah min dun al-nas*)' (62.6–8; 2.94–95).

Several Qur'anic verses elucidate that those who sneer and arrogantly 'turn away' will have no *wali* or *mawla*, that is, no one to turn to for help or guidance. The enemies of God are doomed to dwell forever in hellfire (41.28–31), whereas angels will descend upon the righteous who as 'friends of God shall have no fear'. The unbelievers, those who follow *al-Taghut* – the idols – as their *awliya'*, will be led from light into darkness (2.257) (see also 5.56; 4.119). The verbal forms *walla* and *tawalla* are used – actually or metaphorically – in the sense of either turning one's back or face towards a sacred place, a prophetic message or a hostile army; God also turns to and takes care of the pious (see 7.196; 45.19).

Walaya

The verbal noun *walaya* occurs twice in the Qur'an, at 8.72 and 18.44, and means the function and position of the *wali*. When read with *fatha, walaya* conveys the meanings of guardianship, friendship and protection. This is in contrast to *wilaya* as read with *kasra*, which usually signifies power and author-

ity. It must be noted, however, that vocalization is not indicated in the texts and lexicographers are not unanimous regarding this. Yet, both terms have become primary notions in the socio-political and spiritual lives of Muslims: in Persian the reference is to *valayat/vilayat*, and in Turkish to *vilayet*.

In the Qur'an, *walaya* is expressed in the fable of the rich but immoral owner of the two gardens and his poor but pious companion. In the story the rich man ends up a loser despite his prosperity and power because 'ultimately, the *walaya* belongs to God, the Truth!' (18.44). Verse 8.72 reflects the new community in Medina in which three groups are identified in terms of *walaya*: those who emigrated and struggled on the path of God; those who gave them refuge in Medina and helped them; and those who did not emigrate. The first two, known in history as the *muhajirun* (emigrants) and the *ansar* (helpers), are allies or friends of each other (*awliya'*), while the Prophet is advised to disregard the *walaya* of those who believed, but did not emigrate, until such time as they emigrate.

The Qur'anic verse 5.55, which was revealed in Medina, extends the divine *walaya*, stating: 'Your *wali* is only God, his Messenger, and those believers who perform the prayer and give alms, whilst bowing in prayers.' Thus, the person of the Prophet plays a central role, stressed in later parts of the Qur'an also and culminating in the pledge of allegiance made to him at Hudaybiya (48.9–10). This pledge (*bay'a*) is symbolically extended in Islam to the successors – caliphs, in Shi'i tradition, to the *imams*, and also later to the Sufi *shaykhs*. In some ways, the *wali* acquires the good qualities of his friend, that is, God, and thereby possesses authority, capacity and ability as well as charisma of a certain kind.

Among the Shi'a, 5.55 refers to 'Ali b. Abi Talib's *walaya*. It carries two corresponding meanings. First, it signifies the ontological status of the *imams*, referring to the role of initiating believers in inner wisdom. The *wali-imam* is the friend and the closest helper of God and God's prophet; as such, he immediately follows the latter in his mission; he is the chief, the master of believers, *par excellence*. *Wali* is thus identical with *wasi* as recipient of the sanctity or purity of the prophets or the *mawla* (master, guide, protector and patron). It is in this respect that Imamate is the inner aspect of prophethood, according to Ahmad al-Naysaburi, the Fatimid scholar flourishing in the early fifth/eleventh century. 'Ali thus combines in his person the role of the *imam* and *wali*, embodying the esoteric aspect of Muhammad. This is reiterated in other Shi'i literature of the period, the Islamic Imamate incorporating the Imamate (*al-batin*) of all previously revealed religions. 'Ali therefore represents the principle of esoteric religion as a whole. As such, he existed before all mankind; he was sent secretly with each prophet, and openly with Muhammad. He is the seal of the absolute *walaya*.

When applied to the followers, *walaya* represents the unfailing love, faith and submission to their guide; true Shi'a are thus called the *mutawalli* (faithful friend or protégé) of the *imams*. *Walaya* remains the key to salvation, without which no worship is valid. It is for this reason that in classical Shi'i traditions such as those of al-Kulayni and al-Qadi al-Nu'man, *walaya* appears as the principal pillar of Islam.

Wilaya

Wilaya as noted above, when read with *kasra*, usually refers to authority or power. It has a range of meanings in the legal, political and religious realms. In legal usage, the right of the *wali* to avenge the victim – *wilayat al-dam* (*wilayat* of blood) – is among the many forms through which requital can be exercised. Al-Jurjani (1339–1413) distinguishes between *walaya* as legal kinship of a patron (*mawla*) with a manumitted slave or with the clients of non-Arab Muslims (*mawali*), and *wilaya* as the legal power to make a decision affecting another, whether the latter likes the decision or not. This has become more evident in family law and political thought. In family law a *wali* could inherit the guardianship of a bride for marriage (*wilayat al-nika*) and legal responsibility for the orphans, minors and others who are legally incompetent.

Wilaya in the political sense relates to sovereign power and authority as reflected in the leader (*imam al-muslimin*) of the Muslim community after Muhammad and commander of the faithful (*amir al-mu'minin*). Although there is an important distinction between Sunni and Shi'i views on the nature and the scope of this authority, in advocating their beliefs, both communities refer to the same Qur'anic verse: 'obey God and the Messenger and those in command – *uli al-amr*', thus *wilayat al-amr*. In contrast to the Sunni view of *wilaya* with reference to state-building, in Shi'i belief the transfer of *wilaya* from Muhammad to 'Ali is understood as the universal process of revelation to be completed by the *imams* as inheritors of the hidden substance and traditional wisdom of the previous prophets. It is only this transfer of knowledge that perfects the religion of Islam (5.35).

As well as the numerous usages of *wilaya* in early and medieval texts, there is also the modern term *wilayat al-faqih* (the government of a learned scholar), a new principle laid down in the constitution of Iran after the Islamic revolution.

This is known as relative *wilaya* as opposed to the absolute *wilaya* of the *imams*.

Walaya/wilaya is also central to Sufism. At an early stage, the amazing deeds of God's friends are recorded and transmitted by Ibn Abi'l Dunya (d. 281/894) among others. Abu Nuʿaym al-Isfahani (d. 430/1038) used this work in his comprehensive text *Hilyat al-awliya'*. A number of issues concerning *awliya'/ wilaya* are discussed by Abu Saʿid al-Kharraz (d. *c.* 286/899) specifically, whether or not the *wali* receives inspiration (*ilham*) as well as the distinction between the miracles (*ayat*) of the prophets and those of the *awliya'* (*karamat*). The subject is dealt with in greater detail by al-Hakim al-Tirmidhi (d. *c.* 295–300/907–912) in his famous treatise, *Sirat al-awliya'* also known as *Khatm al-awliya'* or *Khatm al-wilaya*. He makes a distinction between the *wali haqq Allah* and the *wali Allah*. The former draws near to God through observance of duties and thereby achieves God's proximity, while the *wali Allah* attains God through divine grace, attracted to God by God. After understanding God in his names completely, the *wali Allah* loses himself in God's essence. His soul/ego is eliminated and he is in God's hands so that when he acts, it is God who acts through him.

For both al-Kharraz and al-Tirmidhi, prophecy is an additional benefit of *walaya*, al-Tirmidhi elevating Muhammad's position to that of the law-giving prophet. Thus, the *awliya'* and the ordinary prophets rank lower than the law-giving ones (*natiq* in Ismaʿili philosophy), of whom Muhammad is without question the greatest. All aspects of prophecy are combined in Muhammad, who is perfect. This is the meaning of *khatm al-anbiya'* (the seal of the prophets) – perfection in prophecy, not in being the final prophet, or at least as

argued by al-Tirmidhi, who insists that there will be a seal of the *awliya'* sent by God at the end of time. This doctrine was omitted by al-Hujwiri from his summary of al-Tirmidhi's teaching, the former apparently fearful of confusion with Ismaʿili philosophy. It was, however, discussed by Ibn ʿArabi (d. 638/1240), who talks of two seals (*walaya*): that of Jesus as the seal of general *walaya*; and that of himself as the particular Muhammadan *walaya*. Both follow the seal of prophecy and are under the primordial reality of Muhammad, known also as the reality of realities or the *logos*.

For more than a millennium the *wali* (or *sayyid*) has played a major role in the social and religious life of people in many countries including the Maghreb, West Africa, Chad, Sudan, India, Pakistan, Indonesia, Turkey, the Balkans, the Caucasus, Azarbaijan, Malaysia, China, Iran and Central Asia.

Further reading

Abu Nuʿaym al-Isfahani (1932) *Hilyat al-Awliya'*, Cairo.

Amir-Moezzi, M.A. (1994) *The Divine Guide in Early Shiʿism*, trans. David Streight, Albany, NY: SUNY Press.

—— (2002) 'Notes à propos de la *Walaya* imamite', *JAOS* 122, 4, Oct.–Dec.: 722–41.

Böwering, G. (1980) *The Mystical Vision of Existence in Classical Islam: The Qur'anic hermeneutics of the Sufi Sahl al-Tustari*, Berlin and New York: Walter de Gruyter.

Chittick, W. (1989) *The Sufi Path of Knowledge*, Albany, NY: SUNY Press.

Corbin, H. (1971–72) *En Islam iranien, aspects spirituals et philosophiques*, 4 vols, Paris: Gallimard.

—— (1993) *History of Islamic Philosophy*, trans. L. Sherrard with the assistance of Philip Sherrard, London: KPI.

Geertz, C. (1968) *Islam Observed: Religious development in Morocco and Indonesia*, Chicago: University of Chicago Press .

al-Hujwiri (1936) *Kashf al-mahjub*, trans. R.A. Nicholson, *Kashf al-mahjub: The oldest Persian treatise on Sufism*, 2nd edn, 1976; repr. Lahore.

al-Kulayni, Abu Ja'far Muhammad b. Ya'qub (1968) *Usul min al-Kafi*, Tehran: Dar al-Kutub al-Islamiyya.

Lalani, A. (2000) *Early Shi'i Thought: The teachings of Imam Muhammad al-Baqir*, London: I.B. Tauris.

Meir, M. (1999) *Scripture and Exegesis in Early Imami Shiism*, Leiden: E.J. Brill.

Momen, M. (1985) *An Introduction to Shi'i Islam*. New Haven, CT: Yale University Press.

Nanji, A. (1976), 'An Isma'ili Theory of Walayah in the Da'a'im al-Islam of Qadi al-Nu'man', in *Essays on Islamic Civilization Presented to Niyazi Berkes*, ed. D.P. Little, Leiden: E.J. Brill, 260–73.

al-Naysaburi, Ahmad b. Ibrahim, *Kitab Ithbat al-Imama*, ed. and trans. A. Lalani, *Degrees of Excellence: A Fatimid treatise on leadership in Islam*, London (forthcoming).

al-Nu'man (1951–61) *Da'a'im al-Islam*, Cairo: Dar al-ma'arif; English trans., *The Pillars of Islam*, trans. Asaf A. A. Fyzee, rev. I.K. Poonawala, New Delhi: Oxford University Press, 2002, Vol. 1.

al-Qummi, 'Ali b. Ibrahim (1968) *Tafsir al-Qummi*, ed. Tayyib al-Musawi al-Jaza'iri, Beirut.

Radtke, B. and O'Kane, J. (1996) *The Concept of Sainthood in Early Islamic Mysticism*, Surrey: Curzon.

Rubin, U. (1979) 'Prophets and Progenitors in Early Shi'a Tradition', *Jerusalem Studies in Arabic and Islam* I: 41–66.

Schacht, J. (1979) *The Origins of Muhammadan Jurisprudence*, Oxford: Oxford University Press.

Smith, G. and Ernst, W. (eds) (1993) *Manifestations of Sainthood in Islam*, Istanbul: Isis Press.

al-Tabari, Abu Ja'far Muhammad b. Jarir (1954) *Jami' al-bayan 'an ta'wil ay al-Qur'an*, Cairo: Dar al-Ma'arif.

al-Walid, Ali b. Muhammad (1967) *Taj al-'aqa'id wa ma'dan al-fawa'id*, ed. Aref Tamer, Beirut: Dar al-Mashriq.

van Ess, J. (1991–97) *Theologie und Gesellschaft im 2. und 3. Jahrhundert Hidschra: Eine Geschichte des religiösen Denkens im frühen Islam*, Berlin and New York: Walter de Gruyter, Vols i–vi.

ARZINA R. LALANI

WAR AND VIOLENCE

The Qur'an contains verses that address specifically the concepts of war, fighting and violence (and their opposite corollaries, peace and the eschewal of violence). A distinctive Qur'anic view exists as to what constitutes legitimate and illegitimate war, the conditions for launching a legitimate war and its limits. The different legal and ethical articulations of war and peace that have emerged in Islamic thought testify to the different – and conflicting – ways of reading and interpreting some of the key Qur'anic verses dealing with this topic. Some of these variant ways of understanding the text will form a part of the discussion below.

The specific Qur'anic terms that have a bearing on this topic are *jihad*, *qital* and *harb*. *Jihad* is a very broad term and its basic Qur'anic signification means 'struggle', 'striving', 'exertion'. The lexeme *jihad* is frequently conjoined to the phrase '*fi sabil Allah*' (lit. 'in the path of God'). The full locution in Arabic – *al-jihad fi sabil Allah* – consequently means 'struggling/striving for the sake of God'. This translation points to the polyvalency of the term and the potentially different meanings that may be ascribed to it in different contexts, since the phrase 'in the path of/for the sake of God' allows for human striving to be accomplished in multiple ways. *Qital* is the term that refers specifically to 'fighting' or 'armed combat' and is a component of *jihad* in specific situations. *Harb* is the Arabic word for war in general. The Qur'an employs this last term to refer to illegitimate wars fought by those who wish to spread corruption on earth (5.64); to the thick of battle between believers and non-believers (8.57; 47.4); and, in one instance, to the possibility of war waged by God and his Prophet against those who would continue to practice usury (2.279). This term is never conjoined to the phrase 'in the path of God'.

At the semantic level, the simplistic translation of *jihad* into English as 'holy war', as is common in some scholarly and non-scholarly discourses, constitutes a severe misrepresentation and misunderstanding of its Qur'anic usage. According to the Qur'anic worldview, human beings should be engaged constantly in the basic endeavour of enjoining what is right and forbidding what is wrong. The struggle implicit in the application of this precept is *jihad*, properly and plainly speaking, and the endeavour refers both to an individual and a collective effort. The means for carrying out this struggle may vary, depending upon individual and collective circumstances, and the Qur'an often refers to those who 'strive with their wealth and their selves (*jahadu bi-amwalihim wa-anfusihim*)' (8.72).

Many of the Qur'anic strictures pertaining to both non-violent and armed struggles against evil and the upholding of good cannot be understood properly without relating them to specific events in the life of the Prophet. A significant number of Qur'anic verses are understood traditionally to have been revealed in connection with certain episodes in Muhammad's life. Knowledge of the 'occasions of revelation (*asbab al-nuzul*)', as obtained from the biography of the Prophet and the exegetical literature, is indispensable for contextualizing key verses that may at first sight appear to be at odds with one another. A specific chronology of events needs to be mapped out so that the progression in the Qur'anic ethics of warfare and the taking of human life may be understood against its historical backdrop, to which we proceed next.

The Meccan period

According to our sources, from the onset of the revelations to Muhammad in *c.*610 CE until his emigration to Medina from Mecca in 622 during what is known as the Meccan period, the Muslims were denied the right of physical retaliation against their persecutors, the pagan Meccans, by the Qur'an. Verses of this period instead counsel the Muslims steadfastly to endure any hostility. While recognizing the right to self-defence for those who are wronged, the Qur'an maintained that to bear patiently the wrongdoing of others and to forgive those who cause them harm is the superior course of action. Three significant verses (42: 40–43) reveal a highly important dimension of *jihad* in this early phase of Muhammad's career:

> The requital of evil is an evil similar to it: hence, whoever pardons and makes peace, his reward rests with God – for indeed, He does not love evil-doers. Yet surely, as for those who defend themselves after having been wronged – no blame whatever attaches to them: blame attaches but to those who oppress people and behave outrageously on earth, violating all right; for them is grievous suffering in store!

> But if one is patient in adversity and forgives, this is indeed the best resolution of affairs. Further, pardon and forgive them until God gives His command. (2.109; see also 29.59; 16.42)

Sabr ('patience', 'forbearance') is thus an important component of *jihad*. The verses quoted above underline the non-violent dimension of *jihad* during the Meccan period, which lasted thirteen years compared to the Medinan period of ten years. The Qur'anic verses which were revealed during this period and which dictated the conduct of the Prophet and his Companions are thus extremely important in any discussion on the permissibility of engaging in armed combat within the Islamic context. As these early verses show, in the early period the Muslims were allowed to engage in self-defence but without resort to fighting. For the most part, this meant resisting the Meccan establishment by first secret and then active public propagation of the faith, through manumission of slaves who had converted to Islam, and, for some, by emigration to Abyssinia (Ethiopia), where the Christian king was sympathetic to the early Muslims, and later to Medina.

Both Muslim and non-Muslim scholars, medieval and modern, have tended to downplay the Meccan phase in the development of the Qur'anic doctrine of *jihad*. It is, however, practically impossible to contextualize the Qur'anic discourse on the various meanings of *jihad* without taking this phase into consideration. Only by so doing can the introduction of the military aspect of *jihad* in the Medinan period be appropriately and better understood as a 'last resort' option, as something to try when attempts at negotiations and peaceful proselytization among the Meccans had failed.

The Medinan period

In 622 CE, which corresponds to the first year of the Islamic calendar, Muhammad received divine permission to emigrate to Medina, along with his loyal followers. There he set up the first Muslim polity, combining the functions of prophecy and temporal rule in one office. The Medinan verses, accordingly, increasingly have more to do with the organization of the polity, communitarian issues and ethics, and the defence of the Muslims against Meccan hostilities. A specific Qur'anic verse permitting fighting was revealed in Medina, although its precise date cannot be determined. The verse states:

Permission [to fight] is given to those against whom war is being wrongfully

waged, and indeed, God has the power to help them: those who have been driven from their homes against all right for no other reason than their saying, 'Our Provider is God!' For, if God had not enabled people to defend themselves against one another, monasteries, churches, synagogues, and mosques – in all of which God's name is abundantly glorified – would surely have been destroyed. (22.39–40)

Within a year of his emigration to Medina, the Prophet had organized small raids directed particularly against Meccan caravans travelling along the trade route to Syria. These small-scale skirmishes were apparently designed to harass the Meccans as they carried out their normal commercial activities and to signal thereby the new political power of the Muslims in Medina. Some have seen in these raids a continuation of the pre-Islamic custom of the *ghazwa*, or minor expeditions carried out by one tribe against another, often in an effort to exact revenge for harm inflicted upon an individual member of the tribe, in accord with the prevailing code in the pre-Islamic era of *lex talionis*. As we have seen above (42.40–43), the Qur'an admits the legitimacy of *lex talionis*, but at the same time asserts that to forgive is better. The third raid under Muhammad's directive was led by a man named 'Abd Allah b. Jahsh during the month of Rajab in the second year, a month in which fighting was traditionally forbidden according to pre-Islamic Arab custom. Ibn Jahsh was specifically instructed by the Prophet not to attack any Meccan caravans but simply to survey the various positions of the tribe of Quraysh outside Mecca. He disobeyed these instructions, however, and attacked a caravan he and his band came upon, killing one person in the process; he then returned to Medina with two captives and the booty. This incurred Muhammad's severe displeasure, and as a consequence the Prophet refused to accept the captured rewards and reprimanded Ibn Jahsh for his recalcitrance. It was concerning this event that the Prophet then received the following revelation:

> They ask you concerning fighting in the prohibited months. Answer them: 'To fight therein is a serious offence. But to restrain men from following the cause of God, to deny God, to violate the sanctity of the sacred mosque, to expel its people from its environs is with God a greater wrong than fighting in the forbidden month. [For] disorder and oppression are worse than killing. (2.217)

Until the outbreak of a fully fledged war a little later in the same year, the Qur'an, here and in the verses previously cited, refers to the reasons – *jus ad bellum* – that justify recourse to fighting. In verses 42.40–43, where self-defence is allowed but not through violent means, the reasons comprise the wrongful conduct of the enemy and their oppressive and immoral behaviour upon earth. In verses 22.39–40, also quoted above, a more explicit reason is given: the wrongful expulsion of the Muslims from their homes for no other reason than their avowal of belief in the One God. The Qur'an goes on to assert that if people are not allowed to defend themselves against aggressive wrongdoers, all the houses of worship – it is worthy of note that Islam is not the only religion indicated here – would be destroyed and thus the Word of God would be extinguished. In the final verse cited (2.194), the Qur'an acknowledges the enormity of fighting during the prohibited months but at the same time asserts the higher moral imperative of maintaining order and challenging

wrongdoing. Therefore, when both just cause and righteous intention exist, war as self-defence becomes obligatory.

'Fighting is prescribed for you, while you dislike it. But it is possible that you dislike a thing which is good for you, and that you love a thing which is bad for you. But God knows and you know not' (2.216). The Qur'an further asserts that it is the duty of Muslims to defend those who are oppressed and to cry out to them for help (4.75), except against a people with whom the Muslims have concluded a treaty (8.72).

With regard to the initiation of hostilities and conduct during war (*jus in bello*), the Qur'an has specific injunctions. 2.190 reads, 'Fight in the cause of God those who fight you, but do not commit aggression, for God loves not aggressors', thus forbidding Muslims from initiating hostilities. Recourse to armed combat must only be in response to a prior act of aggression by the opposite side.

In the month of Ramadan in the third year of the Islamic calendar (624), fully fledged hostilities broke out between the Muslims and the pagan Meccans in what became known as the battle of Badr. In this battle, the small army of Muslims decisively defeated a much larger, and more experienced, Meccan army. Two years later came the battle of Uhud, during which the Muslims suffered severe reverses. This was followed by the battle of Khandaq in 627. Apart from these three major battles, a number of other minor campaigns were fought before the Prophet's death in 632. Some of the most trenchant verses exhorting the Muslims to fight were revealed on the occasions of these military campaigns. One such verse is 9.5, termed the 'Sword verse' (*ayat al-sayf*), which states: 'And when the sacred months are over, slay the polytheists wherever you find them, and take them captive, and besiege them, and lie in wait for them at every conceivable place.'

Another verse (9.29) is often conjoined to the above, and runs: 'Fight against those who – despite having been given revelation before – do not believe in God nor in the Last Day, and do not consider forbidden that which God and His messenger have forbidden, and do not follow the religion of the truth, until they pay the *jizya* (head tax) with willing hand, having been subdued.'

The first of the 'Sword verses' (9.5), with its internal reference to the polytheists who may be fought after the end of the sacred months, would circumscribe its applicability to the pagan Arabs of Muhammad's time; this is in fact how many medieval jurists such as al-Shafi'i understood the verse. The second of the 'Sword verses' is seemingly directed at the People of the Book, that is, Jews and Christians, but again a careful reading of the verse indicates clearly that it does not mean all People of the Book, only those who, in contravention of their own laws, do not believe in God and the Last Day and who, in a hostile manner, impede the propagation of Islam.

In 2.193 the Qur'an makes clear that, should hostile behaviour on the part of the foes of Islam cease, then the reason for engaging them in war also lapses. This verse states: 'And fight them on until there is no chaos (*fitna*) and religion is only for God, but if they cease, let there be no hostility except to those who practice oppression.' The harshness of the two 'Sword verses' is thus considerably mitigated and their general applicability significantly restricted by juxtaposing with them conciliatory verses. Among such verses is that characterized as the 'Peace verse' (8.61): 'If they incline toward peace, incline you toward it, and trust in God. Indeed, He alone is all-hearing, all-knowing.' And

'Slay them wherever you catch them, and turn them out from where they have turned you out; for persecution is worse than slaughter. But if they cease, God is Oft-forgiving, Most Merciful' (2.191–192). Also: 'God does not forbid you from being kind and equitable to those who have neither made war on you on account of your religion nor driven you from your homes. God loves those who are equitable' (60.8).

These verses make warring against those who oppose the propagation of the message of Islam and consequently resort to persecution of Muslims contingent upon their continuing hostility. Should they desist from such hostile persecution and sue for peace instead, the Muslims are commanded to accede to their request. 60.8 further makes clear that non-Muslims of goodwill and a peaceful nature cannot be the targets of war simply on account of their different religious background. However, a number of medieval jurists came to privilege the 'Sword verses' over the conciliatory verses in specific historical circumstances, thus departing in significant ways from the Qur'anic view of justified war and violence.

Medieval and modern conceptions of *jihad*

'There is no compulsion in religion; the truth stands out clearly from error' affirms the Qur'an (2.256). Another verse (10.99) states: 'If your Lord had so willed, all those who are on earth would have believed; will you then compel mankind to believe against their will?' The Qur'an, according to these two verses, clearly does not advocate the forcible conversion of non-Muslims to Islam since the diversity of humankind is part of the divine design. 'And of His signs', the Qur'an says, 'is the creation of the heavens and the earth and the diversity of your tongues and colours. Surely there are signs in this for the learned!' (30.22).

A majority of the medieval jurists agreed that the purpose of *jihad* in the sense of armed combat was not to compel non-Muslims to convert to Islam. However, the political and historical circumstances in which the Muslims found themselves from roughly 661 onwards, after the era of the four Rightly-Guided caliphs (632–661), led the jurists in particular to fashion a code of religiously mandated war that was based in part on a particularistic reading of specific Qur'anic verses and in part on *realpolitik*. In a process that may be described as *hineinterprieren* (lit. 'back-interpretation'), medieval legal scholars attempted to read back into certain Qur'anic verses justification for offensive military action against non-Muslims. *Jihad*, for a number of these scholars, came to mean exclusively 'armed combat'; the polyvalence of the term *jihad* in Qur'anic usage was progressively sacrificed by them.

The historical context for this development was the rapid conquest of non-Islamic realms in the decades immediately following the Prophet's death, an event regarded by many as attesting to the superiority of Islam. Offensive military action designed to expand the political domain of Islam and thus help spread the message of Islam (but not necessarily to forcibly convert the conquered populations) was now sanctioned by some of the medieval jurists. By no means was there consensus on this changed perception of *jihad* as, primarily, military activity that could be invoked in the offensive rather than the strictly defensive sense. During the Umayyad period (661–750), some of the jurists who resided in Damascus and who thus were close to the imperial seat of power were anxious to justify the continuing border skirmishes of the Umayyad

rulers with the Byzantines. The Syrian jurist al-Awza'i (d. 773), for example, was inclined to the view that aggressive war may be considered obligatory in certain circumstances, whereas jurists from Hijazi (the province of western Arabia that includes Mecca and Medina), for example, Sufiyan b. Sa'id al-Thawri (d. 161/778), tended to think of *jihad* as primarily defensive, and that only this defensive war may be considered obligatory for the individual. Other early Hijazi jurists tended to place greater emphasis upon religious practices such as prayer and mosque attendance and did not consider *jihad* obligatory under any conditions. These few examples illustrate that *jihad* was by no means a static and unitary concept in the early history of Islam; the invocation of this term and its interpretations were undoubtedly shaped by specific historical and political contingencies.

It was not until the 'Abbasid period that the classical conception of *jihad* was formulated. In many ways, the principal architect of this formulation was the famous ninth-century jurist Muhammad al-Shafi'i (d. 820), who regarded the world as being divided into the 'Abode of Islam' (*dar al-Islam*) and the 'Abode of War' (*dar al-harb*). He also recognized an intermediary realm, 'the Abode of Truce/Treaty' (*dar al-'ahd*), which included all non-Muslim polities that had entered into agreements with the Muslim ruler. A permanent state of hostility was assumed to exist between the 'Abode of Islam' and the 'Abode of War', until the latter took the necessary steps to become part of the 'Abode of Truce/Treaty'. There is no precedent in the Qur'an or the *hadith* literature for these terms or conceptualizations. For al-Shafi'i and those jurists who concurred with him, this was a satisfactory explanation of the existing political realities of their time, which could be made to appear consonant with the Qur'anic view of *jihad*. One powerful way of effecting the latter was by means of the principle of *naskh* (abrogation). Some medieval jurists of a more 'hawkish' persuasion claimed that the so-called Sword verses of the Qur'an, by virtue of having been revealed later, effectively abrogated the earlier, conciliatory verses; thus maintaining that *jihad* must be continually waged against unbelievers. Other jurists continued to affirm that the 'Sword verses' of the Qur'an had to be read in conjunction with the conciliatory verses and that it was at the discretion of the Muslim ruler whether to launch *jihad*.

Over time the terms *dar al-Islam* and *dar al-Harb* also underwent significant changes, so that by the twelfth century some jurists were of the opinion that non-Muslim territory in which Muslims were free to practice their religion could be subsumed under the rubric *dar al-Islam*. Furthermore, some medieval Muslim thinkers have paid little or no attention to the supposedly obligatory nature of military *jihad*. It is significant that the celebrated scholar, Abu Hamid al-Ghazali (d. 1111) makes no mention of the lesser, physical *jihad* in his magnum opus, *Ihya' 'ulum al-din* ('The revival of the religious disciplines'), but refers only to the greater spiritual struggle as religiously incumbent upon the believer. The implications of this are significant: al-Ghazali was the man who was acknowledged by the general consensus of the Muslim community to have been the 'Renewer of the Faith' in his time. That the project of renewal as conceived by al-Ghazali did not grant recognition to military combat as a religiously mandated activity is telling evidence that this was by no means the universally agreed-upon position in the medieval period. By the nineteenth and twentieth centuries, reform-minded scholars such as Muhammad 'Abdu (d. 1905) and later his student, Rashid Rida (d. 1935), would recognize that the bipolar division of the world had been defunct for a while and explicitly affirm that peaceful coexistence was the normal state of affairs between the Islamic and non-Islamic worlds. Mahmud Shaltut (d. 1963), who, like 'Abdu, became the rector of al-Azhar University in Cairo, expressed a similar conviction He further stated that Muslims and non-Muslims were equal with regard to rights and duties, and that only defensive wars are permissible in response to external aggression.

In recent times, and in their bid to establish the hegemony of political Islam, militant Muslim groups have resurrected the medieval bipolar view of the world and emphasized the 'Sword verses' to advocate armed opposition to non-Muslims and those whom they perceive to be nominal Muslims. Western (and non-Western) polemical literature tends to report this discourse as symptomatic of an inherently violent and essentialist Islam. Both groups do great violence to the Qur'anic discourse on *jihad* and the multiple semantic and interpretive possibilities inherent within it.

Further reading

Hashmi, S. (1999) 'Interpreting the Islamic Ethics of War and Peace', in T. Nardin (ed.) *The Ethics of War and Peace: Religious and secular perspectives*, Princeton, NJ: Princeton University Press, 146–66.

Mottahedeh, R and al-Sayyid, R. (2001) 'The Idea of the Jihad in Islam Before the Crusades', in A. Laiou and R. Mottahedeh (eds) *The Crusades from the Perspective of Byzantium and the Muslim World*, Washington, DC: Dumbarton Oaks.

Peters, R. (1996) *Jihad in Classical and Modern Islam*, Princeton, NJ: Markus Winter Publishers.

See also: **jihad**; **qital**; **tolerance**

ASMA AFSARUDDIN

WARNER

see: **nadhir**

WASWAS

Meaning 'whispering', *waswas,* is used four times in the Qur'an as a verb and once as a noun, where it functions as an attribute of Satan. In Qur'an 7.20 and 20.120, Satan whispers to Adam and Eve in the Garden of Eden; in Qur'an 50.16, the mythic context of creation continues although it is the 'self' about which it is said that God knows that it whispers to itself. In Qur'an 114.4–5, Satan is portrayed as the evil whisperer who insinuates himself into the hearts of men. This alliterative, onomatopoeic word, based on a repetitive feature found in the structuring of a few Arabic verbs, suggests an intensive quality in Satan's actions. In general, onomatopoeia, as a clustering and modulation of groups of sounds which are reinforced, developed and elaborated by alliteration, rhythm and rhyme, provides an extra dimension to the significance of a word through its sound and seems particularly appropriate as a way of conveying the insistence of evil as it is experienced in human life.

Satan is seen as responsible for a number of specific and more general sins in the Qur'an related to actions that draw people away from God. The force of evil, presented as the personified entity of Satan or as a collection of 'devils', does this in ways in which vocal attributes figure highly, thus Satan calls (31.21), speaks (14.22; 59.16), uses words (81.25) and makes promises (2.268). Devils are credited with reciting (2.102) and having speech (6.112). 'Whispering' is to be seen as a part of Satan's overall verbal approach to humans. The powerlessness of the individual before Satan is conveyed through the word; the subtlety of the evil influence of Satan is suggested by *waswas* in its very repetition and thus in its insistence that Satan does not just call or speak once but over and over again.

Further reading

Calasso, G. (1973) 'Note su *waswasa* "sussurrare"', nel Corano e nei *hadit'*, *Annali Istituto Orientale di Napoli*, NS 23: 233–46.

Izutsu, T. (1964) *God and Man in the Koran: Semantics of the Koranic Weltanschauung*, Tokyo: Keio Institute of Cultural and Linguistic Studies, 164–5.

See also: **devil; translation and the Qur'an**
ANDREW RIPPIN

WATER

see: **natural world and the Qur'an**

WEALTH

Qur'anic attitudes to wealth

Wealth may be defined as an abundance of money or material possessions. A man who makes ends meet is not regarded as wealthy, but a wealthy man is one who has a surplus of wealth and possessions, over and above his salary or means for his basic needs. So wealth does not refer to money only, but also material possessions. God's bounties are not only material possessions, however; they also include health, status, good friends and relatives. There are about sixty-nine verses in the Qur'an that refer to God's bounties; the following examples remind us that God is the source of all bounties:

> For Allah is He who gives all sustenance. (51.58)

> There is no moving creature on earth but its sustenance depends on Allah. (11.6)

693

We have honoured the sons of Adam: provided them with transport on land and sea; given them for sustenance things good and pure. (17.70)

If you are grateful, I will add [more favours] unto you. (14.7)

These verses also affirm that God did not intend man to live merely from hand to mouth, but that he should enjoy the fruits of the world. Furthermore, those who show gratitude to God for their bounties, God will grant them even more of his sustenance.

Wealth should be striven for

The striving for wealth (*kasb*), and theoretical reflections upon it, were more prevalent from the third/ninth century onwards; it was at this time that it was positively affirmed – as long as it was the fruit of honest toil.

Wealth is one of the bounties of God that should be striven for. The Qur'an praises industry, and urges man to earn his livelihood: 'Man will get nothing but what he strives for' (53.39); also: 'For men is the benefit of what they earn. And for women is the benefit of what they earn' (4.32). Prophet Muhammad himself exemplified industry in his role as shepherd and merchant, stating: 'If one of you should take a rope and bring a bundle of firewood on his back and sell it [to earn a living], it would be better for him than begging from others' (*Bukhari*). He also stated that honest work is a religious obligation, and formal religious duties ought not to interfere with it. Thus, when Muslims go to the mosque for Friday congregational prayer, they must return to work after prayer to seek their livelihood (62.10). Work generates wealth, and this wealth should also benefit the less fortunate; if the rich are frugal, there should be no poverty.

The Qur'anic approach is to enjoy the lawful pleasures of life moderately and to follow the mean between the excessive expense of satisfying desires and abstention from what is lawful: 'O you who believe, forbid not the good things which God has made lawful for you and exceed not the limits' (5.90). Thus, the Qur'an teaches frugality, both in consuming and spending. Frugality is a principle of the work ethic. It means that one could spend of one's wealth, but should not be extravagant: 'And squander not [your wealth] wastefully. Surely the squanderers are the devil's brethren. And the devil is ever ungrateful to his Lord' (17.26–27). The rule is to be moderate without wasting and to be economical without stinginess. Furthermore: 'And those who, when they spend, are neither extravagant nor niggardly, but hold a just [balance] between those [extremes]' (25.67).

Wealth as an external virtue

According to Isfahani (1987), wealth is one of the external virtues or bounties of God, in addition to health, friends and social status. All these bounties or virtues assist one in acquiring higher virtues, namely, the four cardinal virtues of justice, temperance, courage and wisdom. These are the virtues of the soul, and they are essential to happiness in both this world and the next. Of all the external virtues, wealth ranks lowest in the scale of value. Yet it plays an important role in the performance of two main pillars of Islam, that is, *zakat* and *hajj*.

For our worldly life, wealth is of great significance, but compared to the other virtues it is the least important. The virtues of the soul are of greater value as they provide for happiness in this world and the next. For Isfahani, 'Money serves, but is not to be served (1987: 30).

Only when money serves the higher virtues can it become a virtue. Reason should always prevail in the matter of wealth, otherwise one can become a slave to it (Isfahani, 1987: 389).

Isfahani cites the following Qur'anic verses to demonstrate the value of wealth: 4.5; 63.9; 23.55–56; 74.11 (Isfahani, 1987: 389). He also provides ethical guidelines for its use. One should spend money according to need, like a traveller who stops at a shop to buy what is necessary but who keeps the remainder of the money for the rest of the journey. We should not lie, fret, be depressed or sin for the sake of money. We should not serve money, rather, money should serve us. Nor should we revere it, otherwise we will be enslaved by it (Isfahani, 1987: 390).

Abraham asked God to free his family from idol-worship, saying that they had become attached to 'worldly accidents', that they had diverted from God, the Creator of all things. The Qur'an describes those who have become engrossed with material possessions as 'My wealth has not availed me, and my authority has vanished from me' (69.28) (Isfahani, 1987: 390).

References and further reading

Bin Nik Yusoff (2001) *Islam and Wealth*, Selangor: Pelanduk Publications.
al-Ghazali (1964) *Mizan al-'Amal*, ed. Sulayman Dunya, Cairo.
Isfahani, R. (1987) *al-Dhari'a ila Makarim al-Shari'a*, Cairo: Dar al-wafa'.
Mohamed, Y. (2004) *The Path to Virtue*, Kuala Lumpur: ISTAC.

See also: **money;** *riba*

YASIEN MOHAMED

WOMEN

The identity of women, throughout the history of Islam, has often been determined by androcentric interpretations of the Qur'an. Some presume that Islam is intrinsically a patriarchal religion. Although it proclaims that both men and women have the potential to attain spiritual deliverance, in the course of history, men were the primary mediators between religious truth and women. The *shari'a*, the divine law (derived from the Qur'an and *sunna*, the tradition of the Prophet) by (almost all) male jurists defines the parameters of women's rights and obligations. Thus, jurisprudence plays an undeniable role in representing the Qur'anic image of woman. Not all jurists agree on all issues, however: there are differences within the four Sunni schools and the Ja'ari and Isma'ili schools of law. Imam Abu Hanifa, for example, was of the opinion that a woman can become a *qadi* (Judge) based on the grounds that women as well as men are charged in the Qur'an with the responsibility of enforcing good and fighting evil. Within some of the other schools, women were excluded from this position often on a non-Qur'anic charge of being too emotional.

Notions of *hijab*, segregation, seclusion, *nika*, marriage and *talaq*, and the accompanying conditions (including polygamous or child marriages), inheritance and the position of women in the public domain are some issues around which differences exist within the different schools of law. Many Muslims, based on the very statements of the Qur'an, believe that Islam adheres to equality among men and women and that it inspires its followers to struggle against oppression and injustice. This does not contradict the fact that many of them also infer that Islamic law has been selectively applied, emphasized, ignored or circumvented in accordance with individual or group interests at times and in different areas of the Muslim world. The influences of various customs and the cultural baggage of Muslims from different ethnic backgrounds have been at a disadvantage in promoting the cause of women. In many cases, it was only the cultural influence that determined the patriarchal interpretation of the Qur'an, which in turn required women to be housebound and to look after the family – this is nowhere mentioned in the Qur'an as being part of a woman's duty. Nonetheless, the duty of a woman to look after her husband and children became part of the *shari'a* law, and thereby sacrosanct.

Most non-Muslim scholars of Islam also believe that the Qur'an and its guidelines improved the status of women in Arabia compared to during the *jahiliyya*, or pre-Islamic era. They concur that Muslim women were given more liberties than their counterparts throughout the rest of the world, including Europe, up until the eighteenth century. Among these liberties was the right to property and to contract and trade. The message of the Qur'an regarding gender justice was revolutionary for its time, yet like most revolutions it has been robbed of its most esteemed values, and within certain communities has been turned into a system of female subordination and male authority. This shift, coupled with a kind of self-congratulation for the progressive initiatives of the Qur'an, has made for an unhealthy social amalgamation, wherein women are highly honoured and yet simultaneously restricted. And both the liberties, and the restrictions and limitations, are drawn from the precepts of the Qur'an. Thus it is the Qur'an that is at the base of this multiplicity of views and which continues to define the role of women today. Any discussion of women in Islam starts with the references of the Qur'an and is interpreted by the *sunna* and *hadith*. Some contemporary Muslim scholars have reservations about the use of the *hadith* literature due to uncertainties about its reliability. Nonetheless, it remains a primary source for Qur'anic exegesis, with some commentators including a note on the degree of the reliability of certain *ahadith* in order to maintain credibility.

Interpretations of the Qur'an vary from traditional, moderate conservative, modern, to progressive, yet all agree that the Qur'an presents an equitable account of women and men and of the relations between the two. However, these various interpretations differ in their definition of equity and its application. Their views regarding equality are more distinct. The traditional and conservative positions often oppose equality among men and women as resulting in homogenization of the masculine and feminine roles, something they view as a disturbance to the social order. In the Qur'an some verses address women and men, some are injunctions about women and men, and others are exclusively man-to-man discourse about women. While some view the patriarchal tone of some of the verses as socially and historically situated, others criticize and interrogate certain verses on issues of gender justice. In other words, they do not exclude the Qur'an from the charges of exclusion of women's voices. Yet others differentiate between the ideals of Islam and its realities. They claim that while the ideals as presented in the Qur'an *do* render justice to women, the realities of certain Islamic cultures *do not*. As 'Ali the cousin and son-in-law of the Prophet proclaimed: 'the Qur'an is a book ... and does not speak. Therefore, it should have an interpreter and people alone can be its interpreters.' The varieties of interpretations of the status of women in the Qur'an can be summarized as follows.

The conservative interpretation often propagates a lower status for women in the social and legal domain, and suggests inferiority in physiology and psychology as well. The conservatives uphold such views in light of the verses that give only half-credit to the testimony of a woman when compared to that of a man and the ruling that women should not pray or fast (or recite the Qur'an) while menstruating. Moderate conservatism subscribes not to inequality of male and female but suggests a mutual complementarity of the two. In their system of family order women are trusted with the emotional task of childrearing and men with rationality. At times the traditional roles of woman as mother and wife are so highlighted that a woman's performance of the domestic duties of her household is considered *jihad*.

The modernists' precept that Islam is compatible with modernity suggests changes within Muslim family law, changes that have had a direct effect upon the status of women both within the family and within society. The justification for these changes in what is often perceived as the immutable divine law is based on a distinction between *'ibadat* (laws concerning worship) and *mu'amelat* (social transactions). This distinction provides a ground for the modernist to conclude that, while the *'ibadat* are not subject to interpretative change, the *mu'amelat* can be reconsidered and reinterpreted by each generation. Thus, changes within Muslim family law which fall under the category of *mu'amelat* are not only permissible but necessary, if the law harms or is no longer of benefit to the community. They should be revisited and reformulated in the context of our time, not merely to benefit women but for the common good and the moral rebirth of the Islamic community (*umma*).

The common good of the *umma* is the concern of contemporary Islamic revivalists also. Their primary notion is that Islam stands for equality of men and women and that it inspires its followers to struggle against all kinds of oppression and injustice against women. The active social role of women in the community and their political participation are not only permitted but encouraged. Based on the notion that there is no conflict between family and state, revivalists maintain that the role of women in the family is not trivialized and abandoned but respected and acknowledged, and that neither of these roles should be sacrificed for the sake of the other.

Contemporary feminist readings of the Qur'an take offence at the androcentric quality of Muslim society and condemn the segregation of women throughout Islamic history. Pro-feminist readings of the Qur'an attribute patriarchy and androcentrism not to the sacred text and the essence of Islam but to the later hierarchization of the message of the Qur'an. They often differentiate between the Qur'an's early Meccan message – which was tolerant and egalitarian – and its Medinan message – which revealed adaptation to the social and political status of the new Islamic community. It was the institutionalization of Medinan authoritarianism, they claim, that led to segregation of women. With references to the Qur'an and *hadith* pro-feminists maintain that the women of the household of the Prophet were not only dynamic and influential but were also fully involved in the public affairs of the early Islamic community. There was no segregation at times of worship; men and women occupied the same space in the mosque; and women as well as men could interpret the law.

Throughout the Muslim world those who endeavour to maintain gender justice refer to egalitarian verses of the Qur'an such as 'whosoever does good deeds whether male or female, they shall enter the garden and shall not be dealt with unjustly' (4.124) or 'they [women] have rights similar to those against them' (2.228). While there are many such verses that can be used as an authoritative means to seek justice, others are not so helpful: 'men are *qawwamun*, the protectors and maintainers of women, because God has preferred some of them over others and because they support them from their means' (4.34). This verse and what follows, which permits wife-beating, and the verse regarding polygamy, together with centuries of male interpretation, do not render justice as far as gender is concerned.

A hermeneutic approach to the Qur'an criticizes the traditionalists' exclusion of women's voices from the realm of interpretation. While some Muslims may have no objection to criticizing the Qur'an for this exclusion, others view it as a misapprehension to think that this silence is rooted in the Qur'an itself. The argument is that there is a distinction between the text and its interpretations. The text and its principles do not change, yet the capacity within a community of people for understanding and reflection on such principles can, and does, change. The principles of the Qur'an are eternal and can be applied in various social contexts. This separation of principles and their applicability offers an infinite realm of interpretation. In this sense the stated purpose of the Qur'an, which is universality and timelessness, would be limited if a time-restrained, culturally biased interpretation becomes a meta-narrative and is taken to be the final word on the matter. The Qur'an is a book, and its interpreters are people whose understanding is bound not only by their intellectual rank but also by their cultural, social, economic and political status as well as their gender.

Further reading

Ahmed, L. (1992) *Women and Gender in Islam*, London: Yale University Press.

Bodman, H.L. and Nayereh Tohidi (1998) *Women in Muslim Societies: Diversity within unity*, Boulder, CO: Lynne Rienner Publishers.

Esposito, J.L. (1988) *Women in Muslim Family Law*, Syracuse, NY: Syracuse University Press.

Kausar, Z. (1996) 'Oikos/Polis Conflict: Perspectives of gender feminists and Islamic revivalists', *The American Journal of Islamic Social Sciences* 13, 4.

Mernissi, F. (1991) *The Veil and the Male Elite: A feminist interpretation of women's rights in Islam*, New York: Addison-Wesley.

Mir Hosseini, Z. (1999) *Islam and Gender: The religious debate in contemporary Iran*, Princeton, NJ: Princeton University Press.

Moghadam, V.M. (1993) *Modernizing Women: Gender and social change in the Middle East*, Boulder, CO: Lynne Rienner Publishers.

Stowasser, B.F. (1987) 'Liberated Equal or Protected Dependent: Contemporary religious paradigms on women's status in Islam', *Arab Studies Quarterly* 9, 3: 260–83.

—— (1994) *Women in the Qur'an: Traditions, and Interpretation*, New York: Oxford University Press.

Wadud, A. (1999) *Qur'an and Woman: Rereading the sacred text from a woman's perspective*, New York: Oxford University Press.

See also: **modesty;** *nisa*; **veil**

BAHAR DAVARY

WUDU

see: **ablution**

Y

YA SIN

Ya sin is the title of s*ura* 36 in the Qur'an. It was revealed in Mecca and consists of eighty-three *ayas* (verses). *Ya sin* consists of *ya* and *sin,* and these are letters. The early Muslim commentators gave different interpretations to the abbreviated letters with which many of the *suras* begin. Some suggested that they are among the names of God. Others said that they are merely the titles of the *suras* they start.

Al-Zamakhshari, followed by others, suggested that the abbreviated letters were mentioned at the beginnings of the *suras* as challenging signs indicating the miracle of the Qur'an (*al-i'jaz*). The Qur'an presents to the Arabs, the people of poetry and literary rhetoric, their own letters challenging them to construct a Qur'an like it or at least a *sura*. *Ya sin* is a special *sura* in the Qur'an. The Prophet was reported to have said: 'Everything has a heart, or a core and the heart of the Qur'an is *Ya sin*.' He encouraged Muslims to recite it and he recommended that every Muslim memorize it by heart. He also encouraged them to recite it for the sake of the souls of dying people. Some Muslim scholars explained that reciting *Ya sin* eases difficult matters. Reading *Ya sin* to the dying helps them to pass away easily and peacefully.

Many commentators think that *Ya sin* signifyies 'O man', addressing Prophet Muhammad. Quoting Ibn 'Abbas, they said it derives from a non-Arabic language, a *habasha* or Abyssinian term. Sibawayh, the master of Arabic grammar supported this idea. He grammatically analysed the term as *maf'ul* or an accusative object of a verbal clause, and he confirmed that *Ya sin* is an *'ajami* (non-Arabic) noun, and also the title of the *sura*. Others have said that *Ya sin* is one of the names of Prophet Muhammad, and they connected it to two verses. Thus they would read: 'O *Ya sin* [Muhammad], by the Qur'an, full of wisdom, truly, you are one of the Messengers'. Al-Warraq has said it means: 'O you, the master of the mankind'. The Prophet said that Allah gave him in the Qur'an seven names and *Ya sin* is one of them.

Ya sin could also signify one of the names of God. Malik did not permit people to use *Ya sin* to name their children. His opinion was that people should not use it as their name because God says '*Ya sin* is my name, by the Holy Qur'an'. Ibn 'Arabi, agreeing with Malik, said: 'the slave can be called by the names of the Lord if the human possesses the qualities of those names: such as knower, able, speaker'. But Malik banned the use of *Ya sin* because its meaning as a name of God is unknown, and God probably wants to have it only for himself, therefore its use is not permissible. God uses his name in this *sura* as an oath to assure the Prophet and to confirm to the world that the Prophet is a genuine messenger with an authentic book, the Qur'an, full of wisdom and guidance for mankind.

RAFIK BERJAK

See also: **letters and the Qur'an**

YAHYA

Most probably based on the Christian Arabic or Syriac name 'Yohanna', the Qur'anic Yahya, also known as John the Baptist, is derived from the word *hayya*, meaning 'to make alive' or 'to quicken'. This definition, commentators have suggested, speaks of his miraculous birth and his mission to renew faith. As such, one can see how he can figure prominently as a bridge between Islam and Christianity. Both traditions consider him to be 'rightly-guided' and among the company of 'the righteous', including Abraham, Moses and Elijah (6.83–88). John was called to revive the passion for God among his people, coming in the tradition of the biblical prophets. More importantly, the scriptures of both traditions understand his mission as intrinsically linked with the life of Jesus.

Although appearing five times in the Qur'an, the bulk of John's story occurs within two nativity *suras* (3 and 13) which parallel the nativity narrative in the gospel of Luke. John's birth, according to the Qur'an, was surrounded by the miraculous: he was born to an elderly father and barren mother, announced by an angel and the sign of his birth was that Zachariah remained mute for three days.

The Qur'anic narrative begins with John's father, the elderly priest Zachariah, who, concerned with the morality of his kin and being childless, prayed that God would present him with a 'pure' child who would inherit the divine blessings promised to the 'children of Jacob' (3.38; 21.89–90). Zachariah's prayer was answered when an angel appeared to him, within the Temple, and proclaimed: 'Allah bears you the glad tiding of John, who shall confirm the word of God and who shall be noble, utterly chaste, a prophet from among the righteous' (3.39). *Sura* 19 adds '*lam naj' al lahu min qablu samiyaa*' (19.7) to this announcement, which can be translated as either 'we have made none like him before among your family' (cf. Luke 1: 60) or 'we have never given that name to a prophet before him'.

The Qur'an speaks of John's life as blessed, in that he was given wisdom as a child, was compassionate, pious and was a dutiful son. As a prophet, God commissioned John to 'hold onto the Book with strength' (19.12), which Muslim commentators have suggested was his commission to proclaim the Torah, for he did not come with his own revealed scripture. With such high reverence given, the Qur'an eulogizes John through a benediction shared only with Jesus: 'And peace upon him on the day he was born, and the day he dies, and on the day he is raised to life' (19.15).

Resulting from the limited material about John within the Qur'an, Muslim commentators have elaborated aspects of his life, and particularly his death. These include: stating that Zachariah was around 100 years of age when John was born; that he was born six months before Jesus; that he was included in the company of Jesus' disciples as a teacher; and that his tomb can be found in Damascus, where he was buried after his execution for condemning the king's planned marriage to his niece. Problems occurred, however, when some of the commentators placed his execution during the reign of Nebuchadnezzar (sixth century BCE). Likely born of a confusion between the numerous biblical characters named Zachariah, notably the book of Zechariah b. Berechiah, commentators portray Nebuchadnezzar as receiving a divine commission to avenge John's execution, as a pretext for his conquest of Jerusalem. Muslim historian al-Tabari acknowledges this confusion and notes that John was born shortly before Jesus, who was born 300 years after Alexander the Great's conquests and who died before the ascension of Jesus.

Further reading

Parrinder, G. (1995) *Jesus in the Qur'an*, Oxford: OneWorld.
Perlmann, M. (trans.) (1987) *History of al-Tabari*, New York: SUNY Press, Vol. 4.
Tottoli, R. (2002) *Biblical Prophets in the Qur'an and Muslim Literature*, Richmond, Surrey: Curzon Press.
Wheeler, B.M. (2002) *Prophets in the Qur'an*, New York: Continuum.

H. CHAD HILLIER

YA'JUJ WA MA'JUJ

Ya'juj wa Ma'juj (Gog and Magog) are a pair of peoples mentioned by name in the Qur'an at 18.94. The following verses 18.95 and 18.96 describes Dhu al-Qarnayn's building of a barrier between two mountains to hold back the hordes of Gog and Magog, while verses 18.97–99 state that only at the end of time will God allow Gog and Magog to come forth through the barrier created by Dhu al-Qarnayn. Muslim exegetes add to this passage that Gog and Magog were among the nations that inhabit the middle part of the earth along with the humans and the *jinn*. The two mountains between which Dhu al-Qarnayn builds the barrier against Gog and Magog are identified as being in Armenia and Azerbaijan. The people who ask Dhu al-Qarnayn to build the barrier against Gog and Magog are described by Muslim exegetes as being a nation of upright people who lived in an area bordering the region of the Turks.

The Qur'an and Muslim exegesis also describes the barrier built by Dhu al-Qarnayn in some detail. Stretching 100 parsangs in length and 50 parsangs wide, the barrier is piled with rock and coated with two layers of molten brass, a layer of molten iron and erected with brass supports. The people of Gog and Magog are said to resemble beasts, living like wild animals and eating everything upon the earth including all plants and animals. Other traditions relate that the people are nourished by the rain, and it is after the rain that the women flow with milk and attract the men who have frequent intercourse like wild dogs. Instead of nails, the people of Gog and Magog have claws, and instead of teeth they have fangs. Their palates are hard like the palates of camels and when they eat the movement can be heard. They are said to multiply and grow more quickly than any other thing upon the earth, and that, in time, their size and number will increase and overcome the earth. It is further reported that each of the males and females among the Gog and Magog do not die until they have given birth to 1,000 offspring, and that they eat a giant serpent which is thrown up out of the sea each year.

Many Muslim exegetes identify the Gog and Magog in the Qur'an with the Gog and Magog described in the Bible (see Ezekiel 38: 2, 14–22; 39: 6). Jewish and Christian sources refer to Alexander the Great's building of the barrier against Gog and Magog, and assign Gog and Magog a primary role in the eschatological battle at the end of time. A saying of the Prophet Muhammad asserts that Gog and Magog will pour forth and cover the earth at the end of time. Muslims will hide in their cities while Gog and Magog eat and drink everything upon the earth until God destroys them all by sending worms to bore into their necks.

Further reading

Anderson, A.R. (1932) *Alexander's Gate, Gog and Magog and Enclosed Nations,* Medieval Academy of American Publications 12, Cambridge, MA: Harvard University Press.
Wheeler, B. (2002) *Moses in the Qur'an and Islamic Exegesis,* Richmond, Surrey: Curzon Press.
Yamauchi, E.M. (1982) *Foes from the Northern Frontier,* Grand Rapids, MI: Baker Book House.

BRANNON WHEELER

YA'QUB (JACOB)

Prophet and eponymous ancestor of the Israelites, Jacob is mentioned by name sixteen times in the Qur'an, mostly commonly in conjunction with his father Isaac and grandfather Abraham.

Most of these references are found in statements addressed to or about Abraham and the offspring with which he was blessed by God.

The Joseph story

Jacob features prominently in the Joseph story (*sura* 12). 12.13 indicates Jacob knew in advance that his sons would claim that a wolf ate their brother Joseph, and in 12.18 Jacob appears to reject his sons' claim that Joseph had been eaten. Muslim exegetes add that Jacob remarked that although Joseph's shirt was stained with blood it was not torn nor ripped from a struggle with the animal. In 12.83 Jacob again rejects his sons' claim that their brother Benjamin was stolen from them while in Egypt, and in 12.87 Jacob tells his sons to return to Egypt and ask about both Joseph and Benjamin, indicating that he took them to be still alive.

12.93 narrates how Joseph gave his shirt to his brothers so that they could take it back to Jacob. Muslim exegetes explain that Jacob had become blind because he had cried for so long over the loss of Joseph. In 12.94 Jacob claims that he can smell Joseph from a distance which Muslim exegesis says was a distance of eight days' travel. 12.96 states that Jacob's sight returned when the shirt of Joseph was thrown over his face. 12.100 describes how Joseph lifted up his parents onto the throne and they prostrated themselves before Joseph as he had foreseen in his dream. Muslim exegetes mention that in the biblical account the mother of Joseph had already died by this time, and relate that either God resurrected her from the dead or that it was Joseph's aunt and Jacob's other wife, Leah, who came with Jacob and prostrated herself on the throne. Muslim exegetes also mention that the king of Egypt and his armies rode out to greet Jacob upon his arrival in Egypt because of his greatness.

Some exegetes explain that Joseph was taken away from Jacob because he had slaughtered a sheep while he was supposed to be fasting. According to another tradition, Jacob had agreed to tithe his sons to God, Joseph being the first-born of his wife Rachel, and when he failed to honour the agreement he was attacked by God (see Genesis 32: 22–33 and Exodus 4: 24–26).

The prohibition of food

3.93 states that no food was prohibited to the Israelites before the revelation of the Torah except that which Israel (i.e. Jacob) himself prohibited. Some exegetes claim that the food prohibited by Jacob was the meat and milk of the camel. This is because Jacob was afflicted with sciatica, and he had vowed that if God cured him he would no longer eat his favorite food of camel meat and milk; alternatively it was camel meat and milk that would help to alleviate his affliction. Other exegetes assert that Jacob prohibited the eating of sinews because he was afflicted by sciatica. It is also said that his affliction was caused by the injury Jacob received at the hands of the angel with whom he wrestled after failing to tithe his property to God.

Moses and Jacob

28.21–28 relates the sojourn of Moses in Midian. Muslim exegetes conflate the entire episode with the story of Jacob and Laban found in Genesis 28–31. Moses lifts a rock off the well of Midian, works in Midian for a period of time in order to marry one of two daughters (named Zipporah and Leah), then leaves only after causing the sheep of his father-in-law to produce only speckled offspring. The close association of Moses with the Israelites is suggested in the identification of Moses, with Jacob the father of the Israelite tribes.

Jacob's death and burial

Muslim tradition states that Jacob settled in Egypt and lived there for seventeen years before he died. He bequeathed to Joseph that he should be buried with Isaac and Abraham. Joseph is reported to have taken Jacob's body and buried it in a cave in Hebron which Abraham had purchased from Ephron b. Sakhr; he then performed a funeral ceremony lasting for seven days. It is also said that when Jacob died the people of Egypt cried for seventy days, and that Joseph had the physicians of Egypt prepare his body for forty days. Muslim exegetes report that Joseph was also embalmed, placed in a special coffin and transported with Moses and the Israelites back to Palestine where he was buried with Jacob, Isaac and Abraham.

Further reading

Bashear, S. (1990) 'Abraham's Sacrifice of His Son and Related Issues', *Der Islam* 67: 243–77.

Durand, X. (1977) 'Le combat de Jacob: Gn 32, 23–33', in A. Vanel (ed.) *L'Ancien Testament: approches et lectures*, Paris, 99–115.

Lemaire, A. (1978) 'Les Bene Jacob: Essai d'interprétation historique d'une tradition patriarchale', *Revue biblique* 85: 321–7.

Morrison, M.A. (1983) 'The Jacob and Laban Narrative in Light of Near Eastern Sources', *Biblical Archaeologist* 46: 155–64.

Wheeler, B. (2001) *Moses in the Qur'an and Islamic Exegesis*, Richmond, Surrey: Curzon Press.

See also: **fasting; food**

BRANNON WHEELER

YAWM

Yawm is the time of day from the sunrise to sunset, i.e. the daytime. It also signifies the regular 24-hour day. Its plural is *ayyam*: 'And remind them of the Days (*ayyam*) of Allah' (45.14). That is, remind them of the good days which Allah bestowed on them. By contrast, this could mean warn them of the torment that had befallen the people of Noah, 'Ad and Thamud and remind them of the forgiveness that was granted to others. That is, rule them with lenience and firmness.

Yuman is the dual form meaning two days. An Arabic legend tells that the life of al-Nu'man, one of the ancient kings of al-Hira in Iraq, was divided into two days: one a day of intrepidity; the other a day of happiness. *Yawm* here signifies lifetime.

While *al-yawm* literally means the day, according to Sibawayah it signifies the present time or today: 'Today I have completed for you your religion' (5.3). Some scholars, such as Ibn Mandhur, have interpreted this verse as a declaration by Allah that he has ordained what is needed in terms of religion, and they agree that this interpretation is fine and permissible on the ground that the religion of Allah is never incomplete.

According to al-Raghib, the day signifies the daytime from sunrise to sunset. However, it can also denote a period of time, any period. For example: 'Those of you who turned back on the day when the two hosts met' (3.155). The Arabs, when expressing exaggeration, say '*Al-yawm yawmak*', meaning 'Today is your big day'. Likewise, the *hadith* of 'Umar: charity has its day (the Day of Judgement). 'Umar meant that charity's reward would come on the Day of Judgement. *Yawm* also signifies time in general: 'Those are the days of *harj* (excitement)', signifying the time of excitement.

When the pagans asked the Prophet in defiance to hasten their torment, the Qur'an responded that Allah will not fail in his promise. However, a day in God's account is as a thousand years on earth: 'And verily, a day with you Lord is a thousand years of what you reckon' (22.47). Al-Farra suggested that one day of torment will pass so slowly that they will they feel it to be long. Al-Tabari provided in his commentary diverse interpretations by different commentators concerning the meaning of that long day. Some said it is one of those days in which Allah created the heavens and earth. Others argue that Judgement Day lasts for 1,000 years. Abu Hurayra reported the Prophet stating that poor Muslims enter paradise before rich ones by half a day. When Abu Hurayra asked him what a half day was, Muhammad replied: 'Do you not read the Qur'an?' Answering 'Yes', he was told that 'one day for your Lord is as a thousand years of what you reckon. Mujahid said those long days are the days of the Hereafter.' Al-Tabari agrees with the last view and concludes that the day is experienced as too long because it is very heavy, full of fear and horror. Allah has mentioned the length of that day to assure the disbelievers that even if that day seems very long to you it is only a day in his eyes. Therefore it is coming and the torment will reach you sooner or later.

Another lengthy day is mentioned in the Qur'an at 70.4: 'The angels and *ruh* (Gabriel) ascend to Him in a day the measure whereof is fifty thousand years.' Some commentators took this to mean that this day of God is in our measurement equivalent to 50,000 years; others that it is the Day of Judgement. It is been reported that a man exclaimed (about a day whose space is 50,000 years), 'What a long day!' The Prophet replied: 'by God who owns my soul, it will be imposed on the believer until it becomes lighter for him than praying an obligatory prayer in this earthly life'. Some scholars also stated that Allah alone knows about the day of 50,000 years. When he was asked about that day, Ibn 'Abbas said: 'Allah has mentioned two days: a day that measures thousand years and one that measures fifty thousand years, and He is the most knowledgeable about them and I do not like to speculate in the Book of Allah about something that I am ignorant of.'

Al-yawm al-qiyama signifies the Day of Judgement, the Day of Resurrection or the Day of Reckoning. In the Qur'an this day has other names such as *al-yawm al-fasal* (the Day of Separation or Sorting Out) and *al-yawm al-din* (the Day of Religion or Resonance). The Day of Judgement is an essential issue in the Islamic faith. Allah is 'The only Owner of the Day of Recompense [Judgement]' (1.4). To believe in that day or otherwise is what distinguishes the winners from the losers: 'On the Day [of Resurrection] some faces will become bright, and some faces will become dark' (3.106).

Islamic revelation made clear that this earthly life is nothing more than a short passing-through stage. It is a testing time for every human being: 'And only on the Day of Resurrection shall you be paid your wages in full' (3.185).

Believing in the Day of Judgement, from an Islamic viewpoint, necessitates preparing and working hard to pass the 'exam' successfully. All human beings from Adam until the last person who lives and dies on earth will be resurrected by Allah and stand up before God face to face and be questioned about their lives on earth: 'On the Day, every person will be confronted with all the good he has done and all the evil he has committed' (3.30). Those who receive their books in their right hands will go to paradise and those who receive them in their left hands will go to hell: 'Our Lord verily You who will

gather mankind together on the Day about which there is not doubt' (3.9).

See also: **malak**

RAFIK BERJAK

YUNUS

A prophet mentioned by name four times in the Qur'an. Muslim exegetes also identify the title 'Dhu al-Nun' (i.e. 'He of the Fish') in 21.87 and 'Sahib al-Hut' (i.e., 'Person of the Fish') in 68.48 with Jonah. 37.139 states that Jonah was a messenger (*rusul*).

Nineveh and the fish

37.139–148 narrates the story of Jonah boarding a ship, casting lots, being swallowed by a fish, being cast up naked and sick, and having a tree grow over him. Muslim exegetes say that God sent Jonah to the people of Nineveh. Some exegetes say that after the people rejected him they were not punished by God, so Jonah became angry and fled by boat, was thrown overboard and swallowed by a fish. Other exegetes relate that it was because he did not want to go to Nineveh that Jonah fled by boat and was then swallowed by the fish. 10.98 indicates that the people of Nineveh did repent and God removed from them the punishment Jonah had promised. Muslim exegetes say that the people of Nineveh put on sackcloth and removed the female animals from their young. All of the people, including their sheep, riding animals and pack animals prayed that God would remove the punishment from them. 21.87 and 37.143 refer to Jonah's calling out to God from the belly of the fish. Muslim tradition says that Jonah spent anywhere from one to forty days inside the fish. It is said that the first fish was swallowed by another fish so that Jonah was in the darkness of two fish and the sea (see 21.87). In a saying attributed to the Muhammad, it is related that God ordered the fish not to chew Jonah or eat him as food.

37.145 and 68.49 mention Jonah being spat out naked. Muslim exegesis says he was like a chicken without feathers or a child when it is born and has nothing. The 'tree' mentioned in 37.146 is said to have been a gourd that grew up over Jonah on the beach. It provided Jonah with shade and he could eat from its fruit all day long, whether cooked or not, including the seeds and their shells. Other exegetes report that an animal would come to Jonah in the morning and evening and Jonah would drink of its milk.

The virtues of Jonah

Muslim exegetes state that Jonah was saved by God because he continued to praise God while still in the belly of the fish. The angels heard Jonah praising God and interceded on his behalf and thus God ordered the fish to spit him up on the beach.

There are a number of sayings of the Prophet Muhammad in which the virtue of Jonah is extolled. For example, the Prophet is reported to have said that one should claim to be better than Jonah as a worshipper, and that no prophet was more virtuous than Jonah. It is also reported that a Muslim hit a Jew who said that Moses rather than Jonah was chosen above all others.

Further reading

Cohn, G.H. (1969) *Das Buch Jona im Lichte der biblischen Erzählkunst*, Assen: Van Gorcum.

BRANNON WHEELER

Z

ZABUR

Zabur (pl. *zubur*) literally means book or letter. *Zabur* is the name of the Holy Book of Psalms in the Hebrew Bible revealed to Dawud, Biblical King David, who in the Qur'an and Islamic belief, by contrast with the Bible, is regarded as a prophet. There are two clear Qur'anic references to the fact that *Zabur* was revealed to the prophet Dawud: 4.163 and 17.55. Both verses contain the same wording – *wa atayna Dawuda zabura* (and we gave *Zabur* to Dawud) – indicating that *Zabur* was revealed to Dawud. In *sura* Anbiya 21.105, however, there is a reference to actual content, namely that in *Zabur* it was written that 'good people will inherit the earth' (cf. Psalms 37: 29, 'the righteous will inherit the land and dwell in it forever').

BILAL GÖKKIR

ZAHIR

Two terms need to be linked here: *nusus* (sing. *nass*) and *zawahir* (sing. *zahir*). By *nusus* is meant those Qur'anic texts which are absolutely clear, which have a single meaning and about which there is no ambiguity whatsoever. *Zawahir* refers to those meanings which are the most open and obvious, although the text may have another meaning besides its evident sense.

This distinction might seem strange since the Qur'an does emphasize that it is not difficult to understand it if one is fair: 'What, do they not contemplate over the Qur'an? Or is it that there are locks upon their hearts?' (47.24). Also: 'Indeed we have struck for the people in this Qur'an every manner of parable; hopefully they will remember' (39.27). After all: 'Truly it is the revelation of the Lord of all Being, brought down, by the trustworthy spirit upon your heart in a clear Arabic language, that you may be one of the warners' (26.192–195). And: 'This is an exposition for mankind, and a guidance and admonition for the God-fearing' (3.138). The Book is not difficult: 'Thus have we made it easy on your tongue, so that let's hope they may remember' (44.58) since 'And We have made the Qur'an easy to understand' (54.17)

There are many similar verses. Had the text been mysterious and replete with hidden meanings, how could it have been so successful in winning adherents? The Qur'an refers to itself constantly as easy to understand and open to all. The meaning of adhering to the Qur'an is to grasp its message and to act in accordance with it, and there is no other meaning apart from this. There are traditions narrated by so many different chains of transmission as to establish their authenticity beyond doubt and they order that traditions must be checked against the Qur'an. Any that contradict it should be rejected as invalid or false, and their acceptance be prohibited, because they are not the words of the Prophet or for the Shi'i of the *imams*. These traditions prove categorically the canonical authority of the literal meanings of the Qur'an, i.e. the meanings as understood by the ordinary speakers of the language familiar with the literary (*fasih*) Arabic. To this category also belong those traditions that order the correlation of contractual conditions with the Qur'an and reject those opposing it. For example, the Qur'an says, 'If an ungodly (*fasiq*) person comes to you with a tiding, verify it' (49.6), and this is taken to show that a potential slanderer should always be treated with suspicion unless he or she can back up their claims.

There are some who have rejected the authority of the literal meanings of the Qur'an, arguing that understanding of the Qur'an is limited to a few people. They argue that the ability to understand the Holy Book is limited to those who have been addressed by it. The protagonists of this view rely on a number of traditions which require that comprehension of the Qur'an implies total comprehension, knowing both its literal and hidden meanings, along with its *nasikh* and *mansukh*, and this is limited to those who have been addressed by it: 'Then We bequeathed the Book on those of Our servants We chose' (35.32).

Another reason for doubting the doctrine of *zawahir* is the prohibition of *tafsir bi al-ra'y*, interpretation using subjective or personal opinion. Only a qualified interpreter can produce an objective and accurate reading of the text, it might be suggested. *Tafsir* implies unveiling, and this does not include taking of literal meanings of the verses, because such a meaning is not something hidden that has to be uncovered. A *tafsir* in accordance with the ordinary use of words is thought by the Shi'a to be dangerous since we can easily mislead ourselves in thinking we know what something means when in reality we ought to adhere to those who really know how to interpret it.

Therefore, if a person acts in accordance with his interpretation of the Qur'an without following the views of those qualified to determine and limit (*taqyid* and *takhsis*) the role of these statements, it will be *tafsir bi al-ra'y*. On the whole, the adoption of literal meanings after a due search for internal and external indications (*qara'in*) present in the Qur'an and the traditions, or for a rational proof, not only cannot be considered *tafsir bi al-ra'y*, it cannot be considered *tafsir* at all. *Tafsir bi al-ra'y* can be understood as implying something other than acting in accordance with the literal meanings.

It is said that the Qur'an contains sublime and mysterious meanings and this quality of it is a hurdle in comprehending its meanings and fully grasping its import. After all, there are many books whose meanings cannot be comprehended except by knowledgeable experts; accordingly, how could the Qur'an, which contains all knowledge regarding both past, present and future, be understood? The reply to this point is that the Qur'an has literal meanings which can be grasped by anyone acquainted with the Arabic language and its rules, and it recommends behaviour which one may act upon once one understands what is required. Experts can certainly explain the text well and resolve difficulties, but the main points of the text are often entirely perspicuous.

Sometimes the literal meaning is not intended. It may be said that we know in a *mujmal* way (without knowing all the specific details) that there exist restrictive proofs (*mukhassisat* and *muqayyidat*) which limit the application of the general statements (*'umumat* and *itlaqat*) of the Qur'an. This means that some of its literal meanings are certainly not what are intended, for such general statements have been restricted in their scope. All the literal meanings of the Qur'an and all its general statements may be regarded as indistinct (*mujmal*) incidentally, although they are not in fact such essentially. Consequently, it is not valid to act according to such meanings as this will prevent one acting in violation of the genuine instructions of God.

Mujmal knowledge (that there are some general statements whose literal meaning is not the intended one) can act as a hindrance to accepting all the literal meanings when one resolves to act in accordance with them without due investigation regarding their real import. After the *mukallaf* (a person responsible for religious duties) has investigated and discovered such instances to the extent of gaining a *mujmal* knowledge of their presence in the Qur'an, the hindrance posed by the prior

mujmal knowledge is removed and it fails to have any effect.

Given this, it could well be argued that there remains no problem in acting upon the literal meanings. The same thing is true of the *sunna* (traditions), where it is also the case that there are proofs which limit the jurisdiction of its general statements. Hence, had the *mujmal* knowledge (regarding the *zawahir* of the Qur'an) been a hindrance in the way of accepting its literal meanings even after such knowledge is rendered ineffective, it would also be a hindrance in accepting the literal meanings of *sunna*.

The opponents of acting on the *zawahir* point out that the Qur'anic verses forbid the following of the *mutashabihat*. God says: 'In it are *muhkam* (clear) verses which are the foundation of the Book, and other verses which are *mutashabih*. As for those in whose hearts is deviation, they follow its *mutashabih* (ambiguous) verses' (3.7) The term *mutashabih* also includes literal meanings or, at least, the possibility of its including literal meanings makes it incapable of being accepted as authority.

The word *mutashabih* has a perspicuous meaning, and there is no ambiguity or vagueness in it. It means a word having two or more meanings, both of which can be regarded as the meaning of that word. Thus, when such a word is used in a verse, the possibility arises that any one of these meanings may in fact be intended. For this reason, it is necessary to observe restraint in giving a judgement in favour of any of the meanings unless there is an indication to specify it. Accordingly, a word having a single literal meaning is not considered *mutashabih*. If we accept that the word *mutashabih* is itself ambiguous, and that there exists a possibility of its including literal meanings, our doing so does not prevent us from acting in accordance with the literal meanings. This is after the practice of intellectuals (*sirat al-ʿuqalaʾ*), which sanctions the acceptance of the literal meaning of a speech or writing.

Therefore, a sole possibility is incapable of preventing this practice from being acted upon, for it requires a categorical proof in order to do so. Otherwise this practice will undoubtedly be followed. For this reason a master is able to prove his servant's fault if the latter acts against the literal meanings of the former's speech, and it is valid for the master to punish him for the violation. Similarly, the servant may justify himself *vis-à-vis* his master if he has acted in accordance with the literal meaning of his master's words where it is opposed to his real intent. On the whole this practice is followed in accepting the literal meanings, unless there exists a categorical proof against the particular meaning.

The occurrence of *tahrif* (textual corruption) in the Qurʾan prevents us from accepting the literal meanings because of the possibility of there having been, alongside the literal meanings, indications determining their real intent, indications that might have been lost due to *tahrif*. However, the traditions commanding us to refer to the Qurʾan are by themselves an argument against *tahrif*. Even if we presume the occurrence of *tahrif*, we are obliged by these traditions to act in accordance with the Qurʾan. The conclusion that follows for many theologians is that it is necessary to act on the literal meanings of the Qurʾan; that the Qurʾan is the basis of the *shariʿa*; and that the *sunna* should not be acted upon when it opposes the Qurʾan.

Tafsir means the elucidation of the intent of God in the Qurʾan. Therefore, it is neither permissible in this regard to rely on conjectures (*zunun*) or on one's preferences (*istihsan*), nor on anything whose validity has not been established by reason or the *shariʿa*. This is because following conjectures and attributing anything to God without his permission is forbidden. We read: 'Say: "Has God permitted you, or do you forge a lie against God?"' (10.59); 'And follow not that of which you have no knowledge' (17.36). There are other such verses and traditions that forbid acting without knowledge, and there are a sufficiently large (*mustafida*) number of traditions from both Sunni and Shiʿa sources forbidding *tafsir bi al-raʾy*.

This makes it clear that it is not valid to follow the *tafsir* of any exegete, irrespective of his being rightful in his creed or otherwise. Such a practice would amount to following conjecture, and conjecture is not a substitute for knowledge. It is necessary for an exegete to follow the literal meanings as understood by a linguistically competent Arab and we have already seen that literal meanings are authoritative, or follow the dictates of sound reason, for reason is an inward authority in the same way that the Prophet is an outward authority (*hujja*). Literal meanings may also follow the traditions established which have been narrated from the Prophet and whoever else one defers to in religion, because they are the authorities to be referred to within the religion (*al-maraji' fi al-din*). The Prophet declared the duty of making recourse to them when he said, in a tradition popular with the Shiʿi: 'Verily, I am leaving behind two weighty things amongst you: the Book of God and my family, my Ahl al-Bayt. If you hold on to them, you will never go astray after me.' The dangers of looking for hidden meanings in the Qurʾan is then emphasized by many commentators. Of course, Sufi and Ismaʿili commentators would tend to take a different line on this. The issue as always with scriptural commentary is how plausible or necessary the search for secrets and mysteries in the text really is.

See also: **sunna**; **tafsir in early Islam**
OLIVER LEAMAN

ZAKI | ZAKA'

Zaki is a root verb meaning to grow, to thrive or to be pure in heart. *Zaka'* is growth, moral purity or righteousness: 'And had it not been for the Grace of Allah and His Mercy on you, not one of you would have been pure from sins' (24.21). *Zaki* applies to anything that is pure and from a *halal* (lawful) source: 'And let him find out which is the pure lawful food' (18.19).

The Muslims are commanded to purify their selves: 'Indeed he succeeds who purifies his own self' (91.9). Allah purifies whomever he chooses: 'Allah sanctifies whom He wills'. And the Prophet was sent to purify the Muslims: 'We have sent among you a Messenger of your own, reciting to you Our Verses and purifying you' (2.151).

RAFIK BERJAK

ZALAMA

Zalama signifies to oppress, suppress or tyrannize. It also signifies to do wrong or evil, to treat unjustly or to deprive anyone of a right. *Zalam* is the root verb and it has twenty-five different forms. It and they appear have been used in the Qur'an as many as 289 times. This vast number of occurrences signifies the importance of this issue for Islam.

Islam opposes *zulm* (injustice). In a *hadith* God says: 'O, my slaves. I prohibited injustice on Myself so do not do injustice on each other.' The Prophet also said, 'Injustice is darkness on the Day of Judgement'. *Zulm* signifies putting a thing in the wrong place. The Arabic proverb, 'Whoever assigned the wolf to guard the sheep has done wrong', demon-

strates this meaning. Pertaining to man's actions, there are three kinds of *zulm*. The first is between man and God: anyone who rejects faith in God and his revelation is *zalim* (aggressor), thus 'Those who reject faith and do wrong – Allah will not forgive them' (4.167). The second is between man and man: the Prophet said that this is the worst kind of *zulm* for Allah does not forgive those who do injustice to other people – 'Those who unjustly eat up the property of orphans, eat up a Fire into their own bodies' (4.10). The victim is the only one who has the right to forgive his oppressors. The third is between man and himself: 'They harmed Us not but they used to do injustice on themselves' (7.160).

RAFIK BERJAK

ZAMZAM

According to tradition, the Prophet reported that Hajar searched desperately for water in the hills of Safa and Marwa to give to her newly-born son Isma'il. As she ran from one place to another in search of water, her child rubbed his feet against the sand. A pool of water surfaced, and by the grace of God, shaped itself into a well which came to be called Zamzam. This image has been repeated in many other traditions, which use the symbol of cool water and relief provided by God in emergencies to telling effect.

Today, located a few metres east of the *Ka'ba*, is the well of Zamzam, which is 35 metres deep and topped by a dome. In her desperate search for water, Hajar ran seven times back and forth in the merciless heat between the two hills and today this same act is a rite incumbent on all those performing the *hajj*. Zamzam water is also said to possess healing properties, and is a popular gift given to loved ones by pilgrims returning from Mecca.

COLIN TURNER

ZAWJ / AZWAJ

Zawj signifies to couple, to marry any-one to or to pair off. *Azwaj* is plural and it means companions, mates or spouses. The verb *zawaja* means to join together, to give in marriage or to unite as a fel-low. This term is used in the Qur'an eighteen times. It signifies the natural order by which Allah creates the world: 'And of everything we have created pairs' (51.49). Since Allah created Adam and Eve, people have been created as couples: 'O Adam! Dwell you and your wife in paradise' (7.19).

The wedding of male and female is a sign of God's divinity: 'He created for you wives from among yourselves' (30.21). He created people as husband and wife to maintain the life of the human race. This marriage is not only physical but it also generates love rela-tionships between the two genders: 'And He has put between you affection and mercy' (30.21).

Even plants are created in pairs: 'And of every kind of fruits, He made in pairs' (13.3). To maintain this natural order; when the massive flood obscured the earth, Noah was ordered to carry on his ship of 'each kind a couple; male and female' (11.40). In the hereafter the dwellers of paradise enjoy everlasting pleasures with their spouses: 'They and their wives will be in pleasant shade, reclining on thrones'. On the other hand, the angels of hell are ordered to 'Assemble those who did wrong with their companions' (37.22) and lead them on to hell.

RAFIK BERJAK

ZINA

There are many forms of *zina*, and the worst are a category of actions such as adultery and fornication, which have in common having sexual intercourse without being married to the person:

And those who invoke not any other god along with Allah, nor kill such life as Allah has forbidden, except for just cause, nor commit illegal sexual intercourse (*zina*) and whoever does this shall receive the punishment. The torment will be doubled to him on the Day of Resurrec-tion, and he will abide therein in dis-grace; except those who repent and believe and do righteous deeds, for those Allah will change their sins into good deeds, and Allah is Oft Forgiving, Most Merciful. (25.68–70)

And come not near to unlawful sexual intercourse. Verily, it is a *fahisha* (a great sin) and an evil way. (17.32)

It is often pointed out that God does not forbid *zina*, he forbids even coming close to it, and this emphasizes the ser-iousness of the offence: 'Do not come near to adultery for it is shameful and an evil, opening the road [to other evils]' (17.32).

The second reference appears in 24.2, and it speaks of the regulation of sexual behaviour and reprobation of false slander against women: 'The woman and the man guilty of fornication, flog each of them with a hundred stripes and let a party of believers witness their punishment.'

On the face of it this calls for the same punishment for men as for women; nor is there any mention of stoning. Some have argued that the type of *zina* at issue here is fornication not adultery, and that the former deserves a hundred stripes. The latter according to the *sunna*, the practice of the Prophet, does involves stoning. It is worth pointing out that for such a charge to stick there have to be, in the case of women, four witnesses. And the penalties for being wrong are severe: 'And those who launch a charge against chaste women and produce not four witnesses [to sup-port their allegations] flog them with eighty stripes, and reject their evidence ever after, for such men are wicked transgressors' (24.4). In the case of men two witnesses are sufficient, and the implication here is that the honour of women is so important that only a large number of witnesses can justly bring that honour into question.

OLIVER LEAMAN

ZUBANIYYA

Zubaniyya is a plural word meaning Myrmidons, the angels that thrust the damned ones into hellfire: 'We will call on the angels of punishment' (96.18). The singular form has never been used and *Zubaniyya* itself is used once only in the Qur'an. The root of the word is *zabana*, meaning to push, to thrust or to push away. In Classical Arabic the she-camel (*tazbun halibaha*) pushes away her milker. Thus the angels of torment are called *Zubaniyya* because they push the sinners into Hell: 'Over which are angels stern and severe who disobey not the commands of Allah' (66.6).

RAFIK BERJAK

ZUHD

Zuhd is failing to be concerned about the *dunya* (the life of this world). Ibn Taymiyya is supposed to have defined it as abandoning in this life what is of no significance in the next life, and there is a nice discussion of how *zuhd* can be fostered by being grateful not only for what God has permitted but also for what he has forbidden. This does not mean practising asceticism. On the contrary, we should enjoy the things that God has provided for us to enjoy.

It is sometimes said that we should practise *zuhd* in our heart and *dunya* in our hand: 'Know that the life of this world is only play and amusement, pomp and mutual boasting among you, and rivalry in respect of wealth and children, as the likeness of vegetation after rain, thereof the growth is pleasing to the tiller; afterwards it dries up and you see it turning yellow; then it becomes straw. But in the Hereafter [there is] a severe torment, and forgiveness of God and enjoyment, whereas the life of this world is only a deceiving enjoyment' (57.20). Being a *zahid* (someone who rightly views the matters of the everyday world with some detachment) helps one put the present world in its appropriate context. It is balance that is important here, since the Qur'an constantly emphasizes the importance of being moderate and seeing aspects of life in their appropriate context. The *zahid* is someone who knows that everyday issues are not what is really important. On the other hand, he does not detach himself entirely from the everyday world, since he is a physical being whom God has placed there both to enjoy its benefits and to be tested.

OLIVER LEAMAN

ZULAYKHA

Zulaykha, also known as Potiphar's wife or Ra'il, is one of the most complex female characters in the Qur'an. Her association with the prophet Joseph has a long and varied treatment in extra-Qur'anic materials as well, from *tafsir* to Persian poetry to romantic folktales. She appears both as a seductress exemplifying the debased and treacherous female nature and as proof that love and repentance can transform hearts and lives.

In the Qur'anic narrative Zulaykha is the unnamed wife of the 'Aziz, the Egyptian notable who takes Joseph into his household as a servant. When Joseph has 'reached full manhood', Zulaykha attempts to seduce him. He rebuffs her advances, so she tries to

713

make it appear as though he has attacked her. Her ruse uncovered, the 'Aziz declares that it reflects 'the guile of you women; indeed, your guile is great'. When rumours of her passion for her servant circulate among the women of the town, Zulaykha invites them to a banquet where the women are overcome by Joseph's beauty. In order to avoid the guile of all of these women, Joseph ends up imprisoned (12.21–35). Eventually Zulaykha repents and declares his innocence and her own guilt (12.50–53).

For Sufi exegete al-Qushayri (d. 465/ 1072), Zulaykha personifies the human struggle against one's base instincts. When faced with temptation, Joseph exemplifies the highest standards of control over himself, while Zulaykha's failure to resist her own powerful desires is more typical. Persian poets Rumi and Jami' highlight her repentance as a powerful example for others, of either sex. Most interpreters, however, see the story as demonstrating a male closeness to the divine and a female affinity with the devil; Zulaykha exemplifies women's trickery. In these texts the refrain 'Your guile is great', directed to an individual woman but implicating all females, echoes frequently. Even if Zulaykha herself subsequently repents, other women remain controlled by their base desires. One scholar has even suggested that 'The misogynist view in Islam ... has its literary roots in the Joseph story in the *Qur'an*' (Malti-Douglas, 1991: 50). Part of the reason the story is so firmly entrenched in Muslim consciousness is the Prophet's reported allusion to it in reprimanding his own wife or wives for some misconduct – he refers to women's guile, and declares that 'You are the companions of Joseph.'

In later poetry and stories, Zulaykha appears as a changed woman, in multiple senses. She has repented to God of her attempted seduction and has remained faithful to the memory of Joseph, whom she ultimately marries. On their wedding night God restores her youth and beauty. In some versions, the 'Aziz turns out to have been a eunuch; thus, she has always remained a virgin. In others, God restores her virginity along with her allure.

References and further reading

Goldman, S. (1995) *The Wiles of Women / the Wiles of Men: Joseph and Potiphar's wife in Ancient Near Eastern Jewish, and Islamic folklore*, Albany, NY: SUNY Press.

Malti-Douglas, F. (1991) *Woman's Body, Woman's Word: Gender and discourse in Arabo-Islamic writing*, Princeton, NJ: Princeton University Press.

Stowasser, B.F. (1996) *Women in the Qur'an: Traditions, and Interpretation*, Oxford: Oxford University Press.

Uddin, S. (2001) 'Mystical Journey or Misogynist Assault? Al-Qushayri's interpretation of Zulaikha's attempted seduction of Yusuf', *Journal for Islamic Studies* 21: 113–35.

See also: **Bilqis**

KECIA ALI

Bibliographical Resources

Bibliographical resources on the Qur'an are extensive and rich. There are two highly useful encyclopedias available, the *Encyclopedia of the Qur'an*, edited by Jane McAuliffe and just being completed as this is written in 2005, as a multi-volume collection of entries. The authors are impressive and the size of the entries is large, so a great deal of detail is presented in this series of volumes. Each entry has up-to-date references so the reader is directed to relevant material existing elsewhere. The *Encyclopedia of Islam* in its second edition is also coming to an end and has a lot of material on the Qur'an. This is less user-friendly than the *Encyclopedia of the Qur'an*; it is a very scholarly work and rather forbidding in style, but is particularly valuable for the large amount of bibliographical material presented under each entry. Other encyclopedias include the *Encyclopedia of Religion*, the *Encyclopedia Iranica* and the various modern publications, for example, *The Oxford Encyclopedia of the Modern Islamic World* and the *Oxford History of Islam* (ed. J.L. Esposito, New York: Oxford University Press, 1999). *The Oxford Dictionary of Islam*, edited by John Esposito (New York: Oxford University Press, 2003) and the *Popular Dictionary of Islam* written by Ian Netton (London: Curzon, 1992) are reliable and well written. These are widely available and useful sources of reference material on modern theological issues. The *Index Islamicus* (Cambridge: Islamic Bibliography Unit, Cambridge University Library) is, as its name suggests, an index of material related to Islam, and among that is of course plenty of discussion of the Qur'an. On style, the *Encyclopedia of Arabic Literature* (ed. J. Meisami and P. Starkey, London: Routledge, 1988), is well organized and comprehensive.

Two excellent sources of scholarly references are Sezgin's *Geschichte des arabischen Schrifttums* (9 vols, Leiden: E.J. Brill, 1967–), especially the first volume in the series, and Brockelmann.

Journals are a particularly useful source of reference material. Here the *Journal of Qur'anic Studies* is important, particularly in bringing together authors from both the Islamic and the academic world as a whole. A range of journals that deal with religion and the Middle East have entries on the Qur'an, of course, and *Der Islam* and *Studia Semitica* are among the better ones here for Qur'an commentary. For issues that relate to inter-religious dialogue, *Muslim World* is very important. It has to be said that it is rare to find an article in a journal that deals with an issue in the Qur'an in a self-contained way. Often the article will link the discussion to a similar and related discussion in another religious tradition, or to a political or historical issue, and this might be seen as an aspect of a generally orientalist approach to Qur'anic studies that has often seen it as important not in itself but for what it tells us about something else. This is a good example of how articles on the Qur'an in Western languages often differ from those in Arabic or Persian.

The more traditional material discussing the Qur'an is like theological discussion in any religion, relatively self-contained and based on an accumulated background of documents and issues that have built up over many centuries. It exhibits fine distinctions and close argument and attempts to bring out the complexity of the Qur'an as a text. It participates in a long and interconnected debate that has been gradually constructed ever since the Qur'an was revealed, and proceeds in a rather different way from the scholarly debate as it exists mainly in the European language journals. This is not in any way to praise or disparage either tradition, but is simply a reminder to the reader that there are these differences of approach and one should be aware of them when examining the material that is readily available in European languages.

There is a specific entry on cyberspace in this volume, so that should be consulted for relevant information on this topic. However, readers will no doubt be aware that anyone can say anything on cyberspace, and so accuracy often falls prey to passion.

On the topic of gender, the forthcoming *Encyclopedia of Women and Islamic Cultures*, edited by Suad Joseph and published by E.J. Brill, will no doubt be very helpful. The list of references contain extensive bibliographical information.

There are some useful glossaries of terms that appear in the Qur'an. Kassis (1982) is particularly useful. There are two books by Mustansir Mir and even the

rather ancient book by Penrice is usable by the reader of Arabic. Dictionaries are important, but what is needed is a scholarly dictionary of Qur'anic Arabic, and so far that does not exist. This gap will be rectified in 2005 when Muhammad Abdel Haleem of the School of Oriental and African Studies and Elsaid Badawi of the University of Cairo are due to complete the first comprehensive and contextualized *Arabic-English Dictionary of Qur'anic Usage*, which will be a welcome contribution to the literature. *Al-qamus al-islami* published by Harf is a useful electronic source of information.

Commentaries in English are not extensively available, by contrast with their existence in Arabic and other Islamic languages. No doubt this has a good deal to do with their size; translators blanch at working on commentaries that are enormous, and most of the really important ones are huge. A number of Tabari's books have been translated very well, and these give a good idea of the classical Sunni tradition of commentary. For modern Sunni commentary, there is Mawdudi and Sayyid Qutb, while for modern Shi'i commentary al-Kho'i is clear and incisive. There is a range of Sufi materials available that reflect some of the areas of work on the Qur'an from this tradition, and the chapter by Alan Godlas in *Encyclopedia Iranica* is by far the best guide to this material.

Translations are always a controversial issue, and especially of the Qur'an. I include a variety of translations here, all of which are interesting and which include relevant bibliographical material. The entry in this volume on 'Translation and the Qur'an' should be consulted by interested readers.

Philosophy is covered in the *History of Islamic Philosophy*, and there is a chapter on bibliography in the volume. The volume as a whole is a useful source of reference material. Smaller entries but with up-to-date references can be found in the *Encyclopedia of Philosophy* (London: Routledge) and in the forthcoming *Encyclopedia of Philosophy* (New York: Macmillan). Other philosophical encyclopedias do not have any significant material on Islamic topics.

The other sections here have reference material that will indicate to the reader where to go for further information. The books have been selected for their bibliographical content and broken down into specific areas that will help the reader to follow up in more detail many of the entries that are to be found in this volume.

Note: dates are those of publication of the edition cited in the reference.

Primary reference material

Kassis, H. (1982) *A Concordance of the Qur'an*, Berkeley, CA: University of California Press

McAuliffe, J. (ed.) (2001–) *Encyclopaedia of the Qur'an*, Leiden: E.J. Brill

Mir, M. (1987) *Dictionary of Qur'anic Terms and Concepts*, New York: Garland.

Penrice, J. (1996) *A Dictionary and Glossary of the Qur'an*, East Hanover, NJ: Laurier Books

Sezgin, F. (1967–) *Geschichte des arabischen Schrifttums*, 9 vols, Leiden: E.J. Brill

Watt, W.M. (1970) *Bell's Introduction to the Qur'an*, Columbia: Columbia University Press

—— (1989) *Verbal Idioms in the Qur'an*, Michigan Series on the Middle East No. 1, Michigan: University of Michigan Press

Wheeler, B. (2002) *Prophets in the Quran*, London and New York: Continuum

Dictionaries

'Abd al-Baqi, M.F. (1982) *Al-Mu'jam al-mufahras li-alfaz al-Qur'an* (Indexed dictionary of the words of the Qur'an), Istanbul: al-Maktaba al-islamiya

al-Hilali. M. and Khan, M.M. (trans.) (1999) *Interpretation of the Meanings of the Noble Qur'an in the English Language,* Riyadh: Darussalam

Ibn Hajar (1993) *Bulugh al-maram min adilat al-ahkam*, trans. al-Muhieddin, Beirut: Dar al-fikr

Ibn Manzour (1999) *Lisan al-'arab*, Beirut: Dar ihya al-tawrat al-'arabi

Lane, E.W. (1955–56) *Arabic English Lexicon*, New York: Frederick Ungar Publishing Co.; repr., Beirut: Librairie du Liban; 1968

Omar, A.M. (2003) *The Dictionary of the Holy Quran*, Hockessin, DE: Noor Foundation

Zadah, 'A. (1991) *al-Mu'jam al-mufaras li al-fadh al-Qur'an* (Indexed dictionary of the words of the Qur'an), Damascus: Dar al-Fajr

Commentaries and exegetical material in European languages

Abdel Haleem, M. (1976) 'Sunni kalam', *HIP*: 71–88

—— (1990) 'The Story of Joseph in the Qur'an and the Old Testament', *Islam and Christian–Muslim Relations* 1: 171–91

—— (1992) 'Grammatical Shift for Rhetorical Purposes: Iltifat and related features in the Qur'an, *BSOAS* LV 3: 407–31

Abdul, M. (1977) *The Qur'an: Shaykh Tabarsi's commentary*, Lahore: Sh. Muhammad Ashraf

Ali, S. (1964) *The Holy Qur'an*, Karachi

Arkoun, M. (1982) *Lectures du Coran*, Paris: G.-P. Maisonneuve et Larose

Arnaldez, R. (1983) *Le Coran: guide de lecture*, Paris: Desclée

Ayoub, M. (1982)*The Qur'an and Its Interpreters*, Vol. 1, Albany, NY: SUNY Press; Vol. 2, 1992

—— (1983) *The Great Tidings*, Tripoli

Azad, A. (1990) *Tarjuman al-Qur'an*, trans. Syed Abdul Latif, Bombay, 1962–67; repr. New Delhi

Baljon, Jon M.S. (1880–1960) *Modern Muslim Koran Interpretation*, Leiden: E.J. Brill

Banna, H. (1978) *Five Tracts of Hasan al-Banna': A selection from the Majumu'at Rasa'il al-Imam al-Shahid Hasan al-Banna'*, trans. C. Wendell, Berkeley, CA: University of California Press

Barlas, A. (2002) 'Believing Women', in *Islam: Unreading patriarchal interpretations of the Qur'an*, Austin, TX: University of Texas Press

Beeston, A. (1963) *Baidawi's Commentary on Surah 12 of the Qur'an: Text, accompanied by an interpretive rendering and notes*, Oxford: Oxford University Press

Behbudi, Muhammad Baqir (1997) *The Quran: A new interpretation*, trans. Colin Turner, Richmond, Surrey: Curzon

Bell, Richard (1953) *Introduction to the Qur'an*, Edinburgh: Edinburgh University Press

—— (1960) *The Qur'an Translated: With a critical rearrangement of the Surahs*, trans. Richard Bell, Edinburgh: T.&T. Clark

—— (1991) *A Commentary on the Qur'an*, ed. C. Edmund Bosworth and M.E.J. Richardson

Berque, J. (1990) *Le Coran*, Paris: Sindbad

—— (1993) *Relire le Coran*, Paris: Albin Michel

Blachère, R. (1977) *Introduction au Coran*, Paris: G.-P. Maisonneuve et Larose

Burrell, D. and Daher, N. (trans.) (1992) *Al-Ghazali: The ninety-nine beautiful names of God*, Cambridge: The Islamic Texts Society

Burton, J. (1979) *The Collection of the Quran*, Cambridge: Cambridge University Press

—— (1985) 'The Interpretation of Q87, 6–7 and the Theories of Naskh', *Der Islam* 62: 5–19

Cook, M. (2000) *The Qur'an: A very short introduction*, New York: Oxford University Press

Cragg, K. (1971) *The Event of the Quran: Islam in its scripture*, London: George Allen & Unwin

—— (1973) *The Mind of the Quran: Chapters in reflection*, London: George Allen & Unwin

Crone, P. (1994) 'Two Legal Problems Bearing on the Early History of the Qur'an', *Jerusalem Studies in Arabic and Islam* 18: 1–37

Endress, G. (1983) *An Introduction to Islam*, trans. C. Hillenbrand, New York: Columbia University Press

Firestone, R. (1990) *Journeys in Holy Lands: The evolution of the AbrahamIshmael legends in Islamic exegesis*, Albany, NY: SUNY Press

Haeri, F. (1993) *Keys to the Qur'an*, Reading: Garnet

Hawting, G.R. *et al.* (eds) (1993) *Approaches to the Quran*, London: Routledge

Izutsu, T. (1980) *God and Man in the Koran*, Salem: Ayer Co.

—— (2002) *Ethico-Religious Concepts in the Quran*, Montreal: McGill-Queens University Press

Jansen, J.J.G. (1974) *The Interpretation of the Koran in Modern Egypt*, Leiden: E.J. Brill

Jeffrey, A. (1958) *Islam*, New York: The Liberal Arts Press

Johns, A. (1981) 'Joseph in the Qur'an: Dramatic dialogue, human emotion and prophetic wisdom' *Islamochristiana*: 37–70

Khalidi, T. (2002) *The Muslim Jesus*, Cambridge, MA: Harvard University Press

Khalifa, R. (2000) *Quran, Hadith, and Islam*, Fremont, CA: Universal Unity

Khu'i, Abu al-Qasim ibn 'Ali Akbar (1998) *Prolegomena to the Qur'an*, New York: Oxford University Press

Kinberg, N. (1996) *A Lexicon of al-Farra's Terminology in his Qur'an Commentary*, Leiden: E.J. Brill

Madigan, D. (1995) 'Reflections on Some Current Directions in Qur'anic Studies', *The Muslim World* 85: 345–62

Margoliouth, D.S. (1894) *Chrestomathia Baidawiana: The Commentary of el-Baidawi on Sura III translated and explained for the use of students of Arabic*, London: Luzac

Mawdudi, M. Abu al-A'la (1973) *The Meaning of the Qur'an (Tafhim al-Qur'an)*, Delhi 1973: Board of Islamic Publications

Mir, M. (1986a) *Coherence in the Qur'an*, Indianapolis: American Trust Publications

—— (1986b) 'The Qur'anic Story of Joseph: Plot, themes and characters', *The Muslim World* LXXVI: 1–15

Momen, M. (1985) *An Introduction to Shi'i Islam*, New Haven, CT: Yale University Press

Paret, R. (1977) *Kommentar und Konkordanz*, Stuttgart: Kohlhammer

Qutb, Sayyid (1979) *In the Shade of the Qur'an*, trans. M.A. Salahi and A.A. Shamis, London: MWH Publishers

Rahman, Fazlur (1980) *Major Themes of the Qur'an*, Minneapolis, MN: Bibliotheca Islamica

Rippin, A. (1985) 'Literary Analysis of Qur'an, Tafsir and Sîra', in R.C. Martin (ed.) *Approaches to Islam in Religious Studies*, Tucson, AZ: University of Arizona Press, 151–63.

Rippin, A. (ed.) (1988) *Approaches to the History of the Interpretation of the Qur'an*, Oxford: Clarendon Press

—— (ed.) (2000) *The Qur'an: Formative interpretation*, Aldershot: Ashgate/Variorum

—— (ed.) (2001) *The Qur'an: Style and contents*, Aldershot: Ashgate

—— (2002) *The Qur'an and Its Interpretive Tradition*, Aldershot: Ashgate

Robinson, N. (1991) *Christ in Islam and Christianity: The representation of Jesus in the Qur'an and the classical Muslim commentaries*, London: Macmillan

—— (1996) *Discovering the Qur'an: A contemporary approach to a veiled text*, London: SCM Press

Sale, G. (1896) *A Comprehensive Commentary on the Qur'an*, London: K. Paul, Trench, Trübner and Co., Limited

Sells, M. (1999) *Approaching the Qur'an: The early revelations*, Ashland: White Cloud Press

Stowasser, B.F. (1994) *Women in the Qur'an: Traditions and interpretations*, New York: Oxford University Press

al-Tabari, Abu Ja'far Muhammad b. Jarir (1987) *The Commentary on the Qur'an*; an abridged translation of *Jami' al-bayan 'an ta'wil ay al-Qur'an*, int. and notes J. Cooper, general eds, W.F. Madelung and A. Jones. London and New York: Oxford University Press

Wadud-Muhsin, A. (1999) *Qur'an and Woman: Reading the sacred text from a woman's perspective*, New York: Oxford University Press

Wansbrough, J. (1977) *Qur'anic Studies: Sources and methods of scriptural interpretation*, Oxford: Oxford University Press

Watt, W.M. (1994) *Companion to the Qur'an*, Oxford: OneWorld

Watt, W.M and Bell, R. (1970) *Introduction to the Qur'an*, Edinburgh: Edinburgh University Press

Wild, S. (ed.) (1997) *The Qur'an as Text: Islamic philosophy, theology, and science*, Leiden: E.J. Brill

Commentaries in Arabic

Alusi, Mahmud ibn 'Abd Allah (1983) *Ruh al-ma'ani fi tafsir al-Qur'an al-'azim wa-al-sab' al-mathani*, Beirut: Dar al-Fikr

'Askari, al-Hasan ibn 'Ali (2001) *Tafsir al-Imam Abi Muhammad al-Hasan ibn 'Ali al-'Askari*, Beirut: Mu'assasat al-tarikh al-'arabi

Baghawi, al-Husayn ibn Mas'ud (1987) *Tafsir al-Baghawi al-musamma maalim al-tanzil*, Beirut, Lubnan: Dar al-Ma'rifa, 1977–1982

Bint al-Shati' (1997) *al-Tafsir al-bayani lil-Qur'an al-karim*, Misr: Dar al-Ma'arif

Fayd al-Kashi, Muhammad ibn Murtada (1979–) *Tafsir al-safi*, Beirut, Lubnan: Mu'assasat al-a'lami lil-matbu'at

Firuzabadi, Muhammad ibn Ya'qub (1976) *Tanwir al-miqbas min tafsir ibn 'Abbas*, Multan: Faruqi kutub khanu

al-Ghazali, Zeynab (1996) *Ila ibnati: al-juz' al-awwal*, Dar al-tawzi' wa'l-nashr al-islamiyya

Ibn al-'Arabi (1978) *Tafsir al-Qur'an al-karim*, Beirut: Dar al-andalus

Ibn Kathir, Isma'il ibn 'Umar (1983) *Tafsir ibn Kathir*. Riyad: Dar tiba.

'Jalalayn' al-Qur'an al-karim: bi-al-rasm al-'Uthmani. Wa-bi-hamishihi tafsir al-Jalalayn lil-Imamayn al-jalilayn Jalal al-Din Muhammad ibn Ahmad al-Mahalli [wa-]Jalal al-Din 'Abd al-Rahman ibn Abi Bakr al-Suyuti. Mudhayyalan bi-kitab lubab al-nuqul fi asbab al-nuzul lil-Suyuti, ed. Muhammad Rajih, Beirut, Lubnan: Dar al-qalam

al-Qurtubi, Muhammad bn Ahmad al-Ansari (1993) *al-Jami' l'Ahkam al-Qur'an* (The al-Qurtubi Commentary on The Holy Qur'an) ed. al-Bukhari, Beirut: Dar ihya' al-turath al-'arabi

Qutb, Sayyid (1966) *Fi zilal al-Qur'an*, Beirut: Dar al-shuruq

Razi, Fakhr al-Din Muhammad ibn 'Umar (1990) *al-Tafsir al-kabir, aw, mafatih al-ghayb*, Beirut: Dar al-kutub al-'Ilmiya

Rida, R. (1970) *Tafsir al-Qur'an al-hakim al-shahir bi-tafsir al-manar*, Beirut: Dar al-ma'arifa li'l tab'a wa'l-nashr

al-Tabari (1997) *Tafsir al-Tabari: al-musamma Jami' al-bayan fi tawil al-Qur'an*, Beirut, Lubnan: Dar al-Kutub al-'Ilmiya

Tabarsi, al-Fadl ibn al-Hasan (1983) *Majma' al-bayan fi tafsir al-Qur'an*, Qum: Maktabat ayat Allah al-'uzma al-mar'ashi al-najafi

Wali Allah al-Dihlawi (1963) *al-Fawz al-kabir fi usul al-tafsir*, Delhi

al-Zamakhshari, Abu al-Qasim (n.d.) *al-Kashshaf 'an haqa'iq al-tanzil*, Beirut: Dar al-fikra

Translations of the Qur'an

Abdel Haleem, M. (2004) *The Qur'an*, Oxford: Oxford University Press

Ali, Abdullah Yusuf (1989) *The Holy Qur'an: Text, translation and commentary*, Washington, DC: Amana Books

Ali, Ahmed (1988) *Al-Qur'an: A contemporary translation*, Princeton, NJ: Princeton University Press

Ali, Maulvi Muhammad (1935) *The Holy Quran*, Lahore: Ahmadiyya Anjuman-iishaat-i-Islam

Arberry, A. (1955) *The Koran Interpreted*, 2 vols, London: George Allen & Unwin

Asad, Muhammad (1980) *The Message of the Qur'an*, Gibraltar: Dar al-Andalus

Cleary, T. (1994) *The Essential Koran*, New York: HarperCollins

—— (2004) *The Qur'an*, Louisville, KT: Fons Vitae

Dawood, N.J. (1956) *The Koran, Harmondsworth: Penguin*

The Koran (1909) trans. J.M. Rodwell, London: J.M. Dent & Sons, 1909; repr., 1974

Pickthall, Marmaduke M. (1952) *The Meaning of the Glorious Koran: An Explanatory Translation*, London, George Allen & Unwin

The Qur'an (1997) trans., with Arabic text, Muhammad Zafrulla Khan, Northampton: Olive Branch Press

The Qur'an: The first American version (1985) trans. and commentary T.B. Irving (Al-Hajj Ta'lim 'Ali), Brattleboro, VT: Amana Bks

The Qur'an Translated: With a critical rearrangement of the Surahs, (1960) trans. Richard Bell, Edinburgh: T. & T. Clark

Gender

Abu-Lughod, L. (2002) 'Do Muslim Women Really Need Saving? Anthropological reflections on cultural relativism and its others', *American Anthropologist* 104, 3: 783–90

Afshar, H. (1998) *Islam and Feminisms: An Iranian case study*, New York: St Martin's Press

Ahmed, L. (ed.) (1992) *Women and Gender in Islam: Historical roots of a modern debate*, New Haven, CT: Yale University Press

Awde, N. (trans. and ed.) (2000) *Women in Islam: An anthology from the Qur'an and Hadiths*, New York: St Martin's Press

Bewley, A. (1995) *The Women of Madina*, London: Ta Ha Publishers

El Guindi, F. (1999) *Veil: Modesty, Privacy, and Resistance*, New York: Oxford University Press

Esposito, J. (1982) *Women in Muslim Family Law*, Syracuse, NY: Syracuse University Press

Haddad, Y. and Esposito, J. (eds) (1988) *Islam, Gender and Social Change*, Oxford: Oxford University Press

Lewis, R. (1996) *Gendering Orientalism: Race, femininity, and representation*, London: Routledge

Mernissi, F. (1987) *Beyond the Veil*, Bloomington, IN: Indiana University Press

—— (1991) *The Veil and the Male Elite: A feminist interpretation of women's rights in Islam*, Reading, MA: Addison-Wesley

—— (1992) *Islam and Democracy*, Reading, MA: Addison-Wesley

—— (1993) *The Forgotten Queens of Islam*, trans. Mary Jo Lakeland, Minneapolis: University of Minnesota Press

Roded, R. (1994) *Women in Islamic Bibliographical Collections; From Ibn Sa'd to Who's Who*, Boulder, CO and London: Lynne Rienner Publishers

Ruggles, D. (ed.) (2000) *Women, Patronage, and Self-Representation in Islamic Societies*, Albany, NY: SUNY Press

Shatzmiller, M. (1988) 'Aspects of Women's Participation in the Economic Life of Later Medieval Islam: Occupation and mentalities', *Arabica* 35, 1: 36–58

Spellberg, D.A. (1994) *Politics, Gender, and the Islamic Past: The legacy of 'A'isha Bint Abi Bakr*, New York: Columbia University Press

Wadud, A. (1999) *Qur'an and Women*, Kuala Lumpur: Penerbit Fajar Bhakti Snd

Yamani, M. (ed.) (1996) *Feminism and Islam: Legal and literary perspectives*, New York: New York University Press

Pre-Islamic Arabia

Abbott, N. (1957) *Historical Texts*, Vol. 1, Studies in Arabic Literary Papyri, Chicago: University of Chicago Press

Bravmann, M. (1972) *The Spiritual Background of Early Islam*, Leiden: E.J. Brill

Bulliet, R. (1990) *The Camel and the Wheel*, New York: Columbia University Press

Crone, P. (1987) *Meccan Trade and the Rise of Islam*, Princeton, NJ: Princeton University Press

Crone, P. and Hinds, M. (1986) *God's Caliph: Religious authority in the first centuries of Islam*, Cambridge: Cambridge University Press

Groom, N. (1981) *Frankincense and Myrrh: A study of the Arabian incense trade*, London: Longman

Kister, M.J. (1980) *Studies in Jahiliyya and Early Islam*, London: Variorum Reprints

—— (1990) *Society and Religion from Jahiliyya to Islam*, London: Variorum Reprints

Lecker, M. (1986) 'On the Markets of Medina (Yathrib) in Pre-Islamic and Early Islamic Times', *Jerusalem Studies in Arabic and Islam* 8: 133–45

Shahid, I. (1970) 'Pre-Islamic Arabia', in P.M. Holt, A.K.S. Lambton and B. Lewis (eds), *The Cambridge History of Islam*, Cambridge: University of Cambridge Press, Vol. 1, 3–29

—— (1984a) *Byzantium and the Arabs in the Fourth Century*, Washington, DC: Dumbarton Oaks Research Library and Collection

—— (1984b) *Rome and the Arabs: A prolegomenon to the study of Byzantium and the Arabs*, Washington, DC: Dumbarton Oaks Research Library and Collection

—— (1989) *Byzantium and the Arabs in the Fifth Century*, Washington, DC: Dumbarton Oaks Research Library and Collection

—— (1995) *Byzantium and the Arabs in the Sixth Century*, Washington, DC: Dumbarton Oaks Research Library and Collection

Smith, S. (1954) 'Events in Arabia in the 6th Century A.D.', *Bulletin of the School of Oriental and African Studies* 16: 425–68.

Muhammad: life and work

Andrae, T. (1936) *Muhammed: The man and his faith*, trans. T. Menzel, London: George Allen & Unwin

Armstrong, K. (1992) *Muhammad: A biography of the prophet*, San Francisco: HarperSanFrancisco

Cook, M. (1983) *Muhammad*, New York: Oxford University Press

Donner, F. (1979) 'Muhammad's Political Consolidation in Arabia up to the Conquest of Mecca', *Muslim World* 69: 229–47

Forward, M. (1997) *Muhammad: A short biography*, Oxford: OneWorld

Hawting, G.R. (1986) 'Al-Hudaybiyya and the Conquest of Mecca: A reconsideration of the tradition about the Muslim takeover of the sanctuary', *Jerusalem Studies in Arabic and Islam* 8: 1–23.

Ibn Ishaq, Muhammad (1955) *The Life of Muhammad*, ed., trans. and int. A. Guillaume. Karachi and Oxford: Oxford University Press

Ibn Kathir (2000) *The Life of the Prophet Muhammad*, trans. T. Le Gassick, Reading: Garnet Publishing

Ibn al-Nadim (1970) *The Fihrist*, ed. and trans. Bayard Dodge, 2 vols, New York: Columbia University Press

Kennedy, H. (1986) *The Prophet and the Age of the Caliphates*, London: Longman

Kister, M.J. (1963) 'Notes on the Papyrus Account of the 'Aqaba Meeting', *Le Muséon* 76: 403–17

—— (1964) 'Notes on the Papyrus Text about Muhammad's Campaign against the Banu al-Nadir', *Archiv Orientalni* 32: 233–6.

—— (1965a) 'The Expedition of Bi'r Ma'una', in George Makdisi (ed.) *Arabic and Islamic Studies in Honour of Hamilton A. R. Gibb*, Leiden: E.J. Brill, 337–57

—— (1965b) 'The Market of the Prophet', *Journal of the Economic and Social History of the Orient* 8: 272–6

—— (1974) 'On the Papyrus of Wahb b. Munabbih', *Bulletin of the School of Oriental and African Studies* 37: 545–71

—— (1994) 'And He was Born Circumcised ... Some Notes on Circumcision in Hadith', *Oriens* 34: 10–29

—— (1995) 'The Sons of Khadija', *Jerusalem Studies in Arabic and Islam*: 1659–95

Lecker, M. (1984) 'The Hudaybiyya Treaty and the Expedition against Khaybar', *Jerusalem Studies in Arabic and Islam* 5: 1–11

—— (1985) 'Muhammad at Medina: A geographical approach', *Jerusalem Studies in Arabic and Islam* 6: 29–62

—— (1995) 'The Death of the Prophet Muhammad's Father: Did Waqidi invent some of the evidence?', *Zeitschrift der deutschen morgènländischen Gesellschaft* 145, 1: 9–27

Le Gassick, T. (2000) *The Life of the Prophet Muhammad*, Reading: Garnet

Newby, G. (1989) *The Making of the Last Prophet: A reconstruction of the earliest biography of Muhammad*, Columbia, SC: University of South Carolina Press

Peters, F.E. (1991) 'The Quest for the Historical Muhammad', *International Journal of Middle Eastern Studies* 23: 291–315

Rodinson, M. (1980) *Muhammad*, New York: Pantheon Books

Rosenthal, F. (1968a) *A History of Muslim Historiography*, Leiden: E.J. Brill

—— (1968b) 'The Influence of Biblical Tradition on Muslim Historiography', in

Bernard Lewis and P.M. Holt (eds) *Historians of the Middle East*, London: Oxford University Press, 35–45

Rubin, U. (1985) 'The Constitution of Medina: Some Notes', *Studia Islamica* 42: 5–20

Schimmel, A. (1985) *And Muhammad Is His Messenger: The veneration of the Prophet in Islamic piety*, Studies in Religion, Chapel Hill, NC: University of North Carolina Press

Serjeant, R. (1983) 'Early Arabic Prose', in A.F.L. Beeston, T.M. Johnstone, R.B. Serjeant and G.R. Smith (eds) *Arabic Literature to the End of the Umayyad Period*, Cambridge: Cambridge University Press

al-Tabari, Abu Ja'far Muhammad b. Jarir (1879–1901) *Ta'rikh al-rusul wa'l-muluk* (*Annales*), ed. M.J. de Goeje, 15 vols, Leiden: E.J. Brill

—— (1988) *Muhammad at Mecca*, ed. and trans. W.M. Watt and M.V. McDonald, Vol. 6, *The History of al-Tabari*, Albany, NY: SUNY Press

—— (1989a) *General Introduction and From the Creation to the Flood*, ed. and trans. Franz Rosenthal, Vol. 1, *The History of al-Tabari*, Albany, NY: SUNY Press

—— (1989b) *The Foundation of the Community*, ed. and trans. W.M. Watt and M.V. McDonald, Vol. 7, *The History of al-Tabari*, Albany, NY: SUNY Press

—— (1990) *The Last Years of the Prophet*, ed and trans. Ismail K. Poonawala, Vol. 9, *The History of al-Tabari*, Albany, NY: SUNY Press

Tibi, B. (1994) *Im Schatten des Allahs*, Munich: Piper

Watt, W.M. (1953) *Muhammad at Mecca*, Oxford: Clarendon Press,

—— (1956) *Muhammad at Medina*, Oxford: Clarendon Press

—— (1961) *Muhammad, Prophet and Statesman*, New York: Oxford University Press

—— (1988) *Muhammad's Mecca: History in the Quran*, Edinburgh: Edinburgh University Press

—— (1990) 'The Reliability of Ibn Ishaq's Sources', in *Early Islam: Collected Articles*, Edinburgh: Edinburgh University Press, 13–23.

Wolf, K. (1990) *Conversion and Continuity*, Toronto: Pontifical Institute of Medieval Studies

Methodological approaches and controversies

Berg, H. (1997) 'The Implications of, and Opposition to, the Methods and Theories of John Wansbrough', *Method and Theory in the Study of Religion* 9.1, 3–22.

Chodkiewicz, M. (1986) *Le sceau des saints: prophétie et sainteté dans la doctrine d'Ibn Arabî* (The Seal of the Saints: Prophethood and Sainthood in the Doctrine of Ibn 'Arabi), Paris: Gallimard

Cook, M. (2000) *Commanding Right and Forbidding Wrong in Islamic Thought*, Cambridge: Cambridge University Press

Crone, P. and Cook, M. (1977) *Hagarism: The Making of the Islamic World*, Cambridge: Cambridge University Press

Denny F. (1988) '"God's Friends": The sanctity of persons in Islam', in Richard Kieckhefer (ed.) *Sainthood: Its manifestations in world religions*, Berkeley, CA: University of California Press, 69–97.

—— (1994) *An Introduction to Islam*, New York: Macmillan

Donner, F. (1998) *Narratives of Islamic Origins: The beginnings of Islamic historical writing*, Princeton, NJ: Darwin Press

Elmore, G. (ed.) (1999) *Islamic Sainthood in the Fullness of Time*, Leiden: E.J. Brill

Iqbal, M. (1965) *The Reconstruction of Religious Thought in Islam*, Lahore: Ashraf

Peters, F. (1994) *The Hajj: The Muslim pilgrimage to Mecca and the Holy Places*, Princeton, NJ: Princeton University Press

Renard, J. (1996) *Seven Doors to Islam: Spirituality and the religious life of Muslims*, Berkeley, CA: University of California Press

Schimmel, A. (1963) *Gabriel's Wing*, Leiden: E.J. Brill

—— (1975) *Mystical Dimensions of Islam*, Chapel Hill, NC: University of North Carolina Press

—— (1985) *And Muhammad Is His Messenger: The veneration of the Prophet in Islamic piety*, Studies in Religion, Chapel Hill, NC: University of North Carolina Press

Schimmel, A. and Ray, S. (1997) *My Soul is a Woman: The feminine in Islam*, London: Continuum

Taylor, C. (1998) *In the Vicinity of the Righteous: Ziyara and the veneration of Muslim saints in late medieval Egypt*, Leiden: E.J. Brill

Wansbrough, J. (1977) *Qur'anic Studies: Sources and methods of scriptural interpretation*, Oxford: Oxford University Press

—— (1978) *The Sectarian Milieu: Content and composition of Islamic salvation history*, New York: Oxford University Press

Hadith

Burton, J. (1994) *An Introduction to the Hadith*, Edinburgh: Edinburgh University Press

Cook, M. (1997) 'The Opponents of the Writing of Tradition in Early Islam', *Arabica* 44: 43–53

—— (1981) *Early Muslim Dogma,* New York: Cambridge University Press

Ibn 'Abidin (1272/1855) *Radd al-mukhtar 'ala al-durr al-mukhtar*, 5 vols; Bulaq repr., Beirut: Dar ihya' al-turath al-'arabi, 1407/1987

Ibn Hajar al-'Asqalani (1390/1970) *Fath al-Bari bi sharh Sahih al-Bukhari*, 14 vols, Cairo: al-Maktaba al-salafiyyaal-Nawawi, Abu Zakariyya Yahya (1990) *Sharh matn al-arba'un al-nawawiyya*, Cairo: Dar al-tawzi' wa'l nashr al-islamiyya

Musnad al-Imam Ahmad (1313/1895) 6 vols, Cairo; repr, Beirut: Dar sadir, n.d.

Rippin, A. (1990) *Muslims: Their religious beliefs and practices*, Vol. 1, *The Formative Period,* London: Routledge

Robinson, N. (1991) *The Sayings of Muhammad*, London: Duckworth

Sahih al-Bukhari (1376/1956) 9 vols, Cairo, 1313/1895; repr., 9 vols in 3, 1403/1983; Beirut: Dar al-jil (n.d.)

Sahih Muslim (n.d.) 5 vols, Cairo; repr., Beirut: Dar al-fikr

Sahih Muslim bi Sharh al-Nawawi (1349/1930) 18 vols, Cairo; repr., 18 vols in 9, Beirut: Dar al-fikr, 1401/1981

Siddiqi, M. (1993) *Hadith Literature: Its origin, development and special features*, ed. Abdal Hakim Murad, Cambridge: The Islamic Texts Society

Sunan Abi Dawud (n.d.) 4 vols, Cairo; repr. 4 vols in 2, Istanbul: al-Maktaba al-islamiyya, n.d.

Sunan al-Tirmidhi (n.d.) 5 vols, Cairo; repr, Beirut: Dar ihya' al-turath al-'Arabi, n.d.Wensinck, A. (1927) *A Handbook of Early Muhammadan Tradition*, Leiden: E.J. Brill

Islamic political thought

Abou El Fadl, K. (2001) *Rebellion and Violence in Islamic Law*, New York: Cambridge University Press

Eickelman, D. and Piscatori, J. (1996) *Muslim Politics*, Princeton, NJ: Princeton University Press

Esposito, J. (1999) *The Islamic Threat: Myth or reality?* 3rd edn, New York: Oxford University Press

Hefner, R. (2000) *Civil Islam: Muslims and democratization in Indonesia*, Princeton, NJ: Princeton University Press

Kelsay, J. (1993) *Islam and War*, Louisville, KT: John Knox Press

Lewis, B. (1990) *Race and Slavery in the Middle East: An historical enquiry*, New York: Oxford University Press

—— (1996) *Cultures in Conflict: Christians, Muslims, and Jews in the age of discovery*, Oxford: Oxford University Press

Peters, R. (1996) *Jihad in Classical and Modern Islam*, Princeton, NJ: Markus Winter

Rosenthal, E. (1962) *Political Thought in Medieval Islam: An introductory outline*, Cambridge: Cambridge University Press

Rosenthal, F. (1960) *The Muslim Concept of Freedom Prior to the Nineteenth Century*, Leiden: E.J. Brill

Philosophy

Fakhry, M. (1998) *A Short Introduction to Islamic Philosophy, Theology and Mysticism*, Oxford: OneWorld

—— (2004) *A History of Islamic philosophy*, 3rd edn, New York: Columbia University Press

Hourani, G. (1985) *Reason and Tradition in Islamic Ethics*, Cambridge: Cambridge University Press

Leaman, O. (1996) 'A Guide to Bibliographical Resources', *HIP*: 1173–9

Nasr, S. and Leaman, O. (eds) (1996) *History of Islamic Philosophy*, 2 vols, New York: Routledge

Modernism

Abedi, M. and Fischer, M. (1990) *Debating Muslims: Cultural dialogues in postmodernity and tradition*, Madison, WI: University of Wisconsin Press

Abu-Rabi', Ibrahim (1996) *Intellectual Origins of Islamic Resurgence in the Modern Arab World*, Albany, NY: SUNY Press

Ahmed, A. (1992) *Postmodernism and Islam*, London: Routledge

Brown, D. (1996) *Rethinking Tradition in Modern Islamic Thought*, Cambridge: Cambridge University Press

Esposito, J. and Voll, J. (eds) (1996) *Islam and Democracy*, New York: Oxford University Press

—— (2001) *Makers of Contemporary Islam*, New York: Oxford University Press

Hourani, A. (1962) *Arabic Thought in the Liberal Age 1798–1939,* London and New York: Oxford University Press

Kurzman, C. (ed.) (2002) *Modernist Islam: A source book*, New York: Oxford University Press

Rahman, F. (1965) *Islamic Methodology in History*, Karachi: Central Institute of Islamic Research

—— (1982) *Islam and Modernity: Transformation of an intellectual tradition,* Chicago: University of Chicago Press

—— (ed.) (1998) *Liberal Islam*, New York: Oxford University Press

Sachedina, A. (2001) *The Islamic Roots of Democratic Pluralism*, New York: Oxford University Press

Sivan, E. (1985) *Radical Islam: Medieval theology and modern politics*, New Haven, CT: Yale University Press

Soroush, A. (2000) *Reason, Freedom and Democracy: Essential writings of Abdolkarim Soroush*, trans. and ed. M. Sadri and A. Sadri, New York: Oxford University Press

Tibi, B. (1988) *Crisis of Modern Islam*, trans. J. von Sivers, Salt Lake City, UT: University Press

—— (1992) *Islamischer Fundamentalismus, moderne Wissenschaft und Technologie*, Frankfurt am Main: Suhrkamp

Law

Abu el Fadl, K. (2002) *Speaking in God's Name: Islamic law, authority and women*, Oxford: OneWorld

Anderson, J. (1959) *Islamic Law in the Modern World*, New York; New York University Press

al-Baghawi (1400/1980) *Sharh al-sunna*, 16 vols, Damascus: al-Maktab al-islami

Coulson, N. (1964) *A History of Islamic Law*, Edinburgh: Edinburgh University Press

Hallaq, W. (1997) *A History of Islamic Legal Theories*, Cambridge: Cambridge University Press

—— (2001) *Authority, Continuity and Change in Islamic Law*, Cambridge: Cambridge University Press

Hodgson, M. (1974) *Ventures of Islam*, Chicago: University of Chicago Press

Johansen, B. (1999) *Contingency in a Sacred Law*, Leiden: E.J. Brill

Lambton, A. (1981) *State and Government in Islam*, Oxford: Oxford University Press

Masud, M., Messick, B. and Powers, D. (1996) (eds) *Islamic Legal Interpretation: Muftis and their fatwas*, Cambridge, MA: Harvard University Press

Mayer, A. (1995) *Islam and Human Rights*, London: Westview Press

Motzki, H. (2002) *The Origins of Islamic Jurisprudence: Meccan fiqh before the classical schools*, trans. M. Katz, Leiden: E.J. Brill

Schacht, J. (1986) *An Introduction to Islamic Law*, Oxford: Clarendon Press

Muhammad and the Jews

Ahmad, B. (1979) *Muhammad and the Jews*, New Delhi: Vikas Publishing House

Arafat, W. (1976) 'New Light on the Story of Banu Qurayza and the Jews of Medina', *Journal of the Royal Asiatic Society* 100–67

Faizer, R. (1996) 'Muhammad and the Medinan Jews: A comparison of the texts of Ibn Ishaq's Kitab Sirat Rasul Allah with Al-Waqidi's Kitab al-Maghazi', *International Journal of Middle East Studies* 28: 463–89

Geiger, A. (1970) *Judaism and Islam*, ed. M. Perlmann, New York: Ktav Publishing House

Gil, M. (1974) 'The Constitution of Medina: A reconsideration', *Israel Oriental Studies* 4: 44–66

—— (1984) 'The Origin of the Jews of Yathrib', *Jerusalem Studies in Arabic and Islam* 4: 203–24

—— (1987) 'The Medinan Opposition to the Prophet', *Jerusalem Studies in Arabic and Islam* 10: 65–96

Goitein, S. (1958) 'Muhammad's Inspiration by Judaism', *Journal of Jewish Studies* 9: 149–62

Newby, G. (1988) *A History of the Jews of Arabia from Ancient Times to their Eclipse Under Islam*, Columbia, SC: University of South Carolina Press

Stillman, N. (1979) *The Jews of Arab Lands: A history and source book*, Philadelphia: Jewish Publication Society of America.

Books highly critical of Islam

Conservative Booknotes is an excellent source of hostile material. There is also:
Ibn Warraq (1995) *Why I Am Not a Muslim*, New York: Prometheus Books
—— (ed.) (1998) *The Origins of the Koran: Classic Essays on Islam's Holy Book*, Amherst, MA: Prometheus Books
Manji, I. (2003) *The Trouble with Islam*, New York: Random House

Islam and the non-Islamic world

Braude, B. and Lewis, B. (eds) (1982) *Christians and Jews in the Ottoman Empire*, 2 vols, New York: Holmes & Meier.

Daniel, N. (1962) *Islam and the West: The making of an image*, Edinburgh: Edinburgh University Press
Hourani. A. (1991) *Islam in European thought*, Cambridge: Cambridge University Press
Lewis, B. (1993) *Islam and the West*, New York: Oxford University Press
Reeves, M. (2001) *Muhammad in Europe: A thousand years of Western myth-making*, New York: New York University Press
Ridgeon, L. (2000) *Islamic Interpretations of Christianity*, New York: St Martin's Press
Southern, R. (1962) *Western Views of Islam in the Middle Ages*, Cambridge, MA: Harvard University Press
Turner, J. (1997) *The Holy War Idea in Western and Islamic Traditions*, University Park, PA: Pennsylvania State University Press

Qur'anic Passages Index

Name Index

743

NAME INDEX

Adam 11–12, 15, 58, 59, 62, 88, 91, 92, 95, 102, 115, 158, 168, 179, 202, 208, 215, 242, 253, 265, 266, 291, 305, 309, 314, 315, 319, 337, 382, 429, 436, 441, 482, 486, 493, 512, 523, 525, 538, 539, 593–4, 603, 633, 648, 658, 693
'Adi b. Hatim 633
Adud al-Din al-'Iji 35
al-Afghani, Jamal al-Din 1, 317, 442–3
Afsaruddin, A. 6–7, 200–1, 331–2, 520, 553–4, 582–3, 584–5, 672–3, 686–92
Ahab, King of Israel 193
Ahmad 176, 297, 327
Ahmed, S. 318
Ahrens, K. 477
'A'isha 7, 21–6, 22, 25–6, 113, 171–2, 174, 175, 354, 410, 422, 424, 426, 531, 551, 614, 673
'A'isha 'Abdalrahman 296
al-Akhnai 281
al-Akhnas ibn Shuriq 462
Albayrak, A. 152–5, 202, 300–3, 526–7, 600
Alexander the Great 143, 182, 266, 344, 701, 702
'Ali, A.Y. 98, 150, 374, 660, 661, 663, 668; see also Ali, Yusuf
Ali, K. 85, 287–8, 380, 389–93, 394–5, 433, 503–5, 673–4, 714
Ali, M.S. 571–6
Ali, Yusuf 553
'Ali Abd al-Razik 294
'Ali b. Abi Talib 17, 28–32, 68, 111, 138, 216, 218, 290, 293, 317, 388, 449, 495, 522, 531, 537, 554, 558, 579, 586, 588, 590, 604, 627
'Ali b. al-Walid 587, 588
'Ali Ibn Mas'ud 633
'Ali Zayn al-'Abidin 449
al-'Allaf, Abu'l Hudayl 32–3
Allah 33–41; see God
'Alqama b. Qays 628
al-Amasi, Shaykh Hamd Allah 388
Ameur, Redha 220–2
al-Amidi, 'Ali b. Muhammad 608
Amin, Qasim 396
al-Amir 293
Amir-Moezzi, M. A. 31
Ammar bin Yasir 588
'Amr b. Dinar 628
Amr ibn Shuayb 413
Anakephaleoses of Epiphanius 332
Anas bin Malik 174, 175, 177, 407, 412, 648
Anawati, Georges 515
Andrae, T. 477
Angel of Death 171, 288, 321–2, 324
Anne: see Mary's mother
Antichrist 164–6, 426: see Dajjal

Arberry, A. 97, 150, 577, 668
Aristotle 34, 52, 61, 139, 157, 245, 498, 511, 538
Arkoun, Mohammed 66–71
Armstrong, K. 425
Arrivabene, Andrea 667
Asad, M. 98, 148, 339, 340, 467, 481, 538, 546, 548, 668, 669
al-Asadi, Ma'rur bin Suway 111–12
Ash-Shiddieqy, Hashbi 241
al-Ash'ari, Abu al-Hasan 8, 82–3, 84, 205, 447, 449, 515, 588–9, 603, 612
al-Ash'ari, Abu Musa 82, 83, 412, 627, 633
Ashmawi, Muhammad 411
'Asim ibn Bahdala 8, 138, 534
'Asiyya 85, 380, 431, 433
Asma' 22, 113, 410
al-'Asqalani 520
Assmann, Jan 578
al-Aswad, Miqdad 588
al-Aswad b. Yazid 628
'Ata 634
'Ata b. Abu Rabah 628, 629
'Ata b. Dinar 629
Atay, R. 318, 606–13, 624–31
al-Atrash, Farid 81
'Attar, Farid al-Din 312
al-Attas, S.M.N. 245
Augustine of Hippo 658
Averroes: see Ibn Rushd
al-Awza'i 609, 691
Ayatullah al-Uzma Sayyid Abul-Qasim al-Kho'i see: see al-Kho'i, Ayatullah al-Uzma Sayyid Abul-Qasim
'Ayn al-Qudat Hamadani 312
Ayyash, Ibrahim b. 325
al-'Ayyashi 31
Ayyub 104, 581
al-A'zam, Imam: see Abu Hanifa
Azar 286
al-Azhar 445
'Aziz, wife of 311–12, 713–14
Azra'il 105, 315

Baal 193
al-Badr, Muhammad 293
al-Baghawi (al-Farra') 108–9, 117, 343, 623, 704
al-Baghdadi, Abu 'Ubayd al-Qasim b. Sallam 200, 589
al-Baladhuri 30
al-Banna, Hasan 396
al-Baqi, 'Abd 167
al-Baqillani 295
al-Baqir, Muhammad 31, 292, 449, 450, 587, 588, 591, 630
Baqli, Ruzbehan 312

Subject index